THE BOWL WITH ONE SPOON

Volume One

The American Empire and the Fourth World

MCGILL-QUEEN'S NATIVE AND NORTHERN SERIES
BRUCE G. TRIGGER, EDITOR

1 When the Whalers Were Up North:
Inuit Memories from the
Eastern Arctic
Dorothy Harley Eber

2 The Challenge of
Arctic Shipping: Science,
Environmental Assessment,
and Human Values
*David L. VanderZwaag and
Cynthia Lamson, Editors*

3 Lost Harvests:
Prairie Indian Reserve Farmers
and Government Policy
Sarah Carter

4 Native Liberty, Crown Sovereignty:
The Existing Aboriginal Right
of Self-Government in Canada
Bruce Clark

5 Unravelling the Franklin Mystery:
Inuit Testimony
David C. Woodman

6 Otter Skins, Boston Ships,
and China Goods:
The Maritime Fur Trade
of the Northwest Coast, 1785–1841
James R. Gibson

7 From Wooden Ploughs to Welfare:
The Story of the Western Reserves
Helen Buckley

8 In Business for Ourselves:
Northern Entrepreneurs
Wanda A. Wuttunee

9 For an Amerindian Autohistory:
An Essay on the Foundations
of a Social Ethic
Georges E. Sioui

10 Strangers Among Us
David Woodman

11 When the North Was Red:
Aboriginal Education
in Soviet Siberia
*Dennis A. Bartels and
Alice L. Bartels*

12 From Talking Chiefs to a
Native Corporate Elite:
The Birth of Class and Nationalism
among Canadian Inuit
Marybelle Mitchell

13 Cold Comfort:
My Love Affair with the Arctic
Graham W. Rowley

14 The True Spirit and
Original Intent of Treaty 7
*Treaty 7 Elders and Tribal Council
with Walter Hildebrandt, Dorothy First
Rider, and Sarah Carter*

15 This Distant and
Unsurveyed Country:
A Woman's Winter at
Baffin Island, 1857–1858
W. Gillies Ross

16 Images of Justice
Dorothy Harley Eber

17 Capturing Women:
The Manipulation of Cultural
Imagery in Canada's Prairie West
Sarah A. Carter

18 Social and Environmental
Impacts of the James Bay
Hydroelectric Project
Edited by James F. Hornig

19 Saqiyuq
Stories from the Lives
of Three Inuit Women
Nancy Wachowich in collaboration
with Apphia Agalakti Awa,
Rhoda Kaukjak Katsak, and
Sandra Pikujak Katsak

20 Justice in Paradise
Bruce Clark

21 Aboriginal Rights and
Self-Government
The Canadian and Mexican
Experience in North American
Perspective
Edited by Curtis Cook and
Juan D. Lindau

22 Harvest of Souls
The Jesuit Missions and Colonial-
ism in North America, 1632-1650
Carole Blackburn

23 Bounty and Benevolence
A History of Saskatchewan Treaties
Arthur J. Ray, Jim Miller,
and Frank Tough

24 The People of Denendeh
Ethnohistory of the Indians of
Canada's Northwest Territories
June Helm

25 The *Marshall* Decision and
Native Rights
Ken Coates

26 The Flying Tiger
Women Shamans and
Storytellers of the Amur
Kira Van Deusen

27 Alone in Silence
European Women in the
Canadian North before 1940
Barbara E. Kelcey

28 The Arctic Voyages of
Martin Frobisher
An Elizabethan Adventure
Robert McGhee

29 Northern Experience and the
Myths of Canadian Culture
Renée Hulan

30 The White Man's Gonna Getcha
The Colonial Challenge to the
Crees in Quebec
Toby Morantz

31 The Heavens Are Changing
Nineteenth-Century Protestant
Missions and Tsimshian
Christianity
Susan Neylan

32 Arctic Migrants/Arctic Villagers
The Transformation of Inuit
Settlement in the Central Arctic
David Damas

33 Arctic Justice
On Trial for Murder -
Pond Inlet, 1923
Shelagh D. Grant

34 Eighteenth-Century Naturalists of
Hudson Bay
Stuart Houston, Tim Ball, and Mary
Houston

35 The American Empire and
the Fourth World
Anthony J. Hall

36 Uqalurait
An Oral History of Nunavut
John Bennett and Susan Rowley

The American Empire and the Fourth World

The Bowl with One Spoon
Volume One

ANTHONY J. HALL

McGill-Queen's University Press
Montreal & Kingston • London • Ithaca

© McGill-Queen's University Press 2003
ISBN 0-7735-2332-4

Legal deposit fourth quarter 2003
Bibliothèque nationale du Québec

Printed in Canada on acid-free paper.
Reprinted 2004

This book has been published with the help of a grant
from the University of Lethbridge.

McGill-Queen's University Press acknowledges the
financial support of the Government of Canada
through the Book Publishing Industry Development
Program (BPIDP) for its publishing activities. It also
acknowledges the support of the Canada Council for
the Arts for its publishing program.

National Library of Canada Cataloguing in Publication

Hall, Tony, 1951–
    The bowl with one spoon / by Anthony J. Hall.

    (McGill-Queen's native and northern series 34)
    Includes index.
    Contents: pt. 1. The American empire and the fourth
    world.
    ISBN 0-7735-2332-4 (v. 1)
        1. Indians of North America – Government relations.
    2. America – Civilization – European influences.
    3. Property – North America.   4. Social justice – Canada.
    I. Title.   II. Series.   III. Title: The American empire
    and the fourth world.

    E91.H34 2003   970'.00497   C2002-905551-2

This book was typeset by True to Type in 10/12 Baskerville

Original maps by Robin Poitras, cartographer, University
of Calgary

I dedicate this book to my father, JAMES JAMISON HALL, *and to my friend and mentor the late* ERNEST DEBASSIGE *of West Bay, Ontario. Both men fought for their country in the Second World War, my father as a subject of the crown and Ernie as an ally of the crown in the tradition of Tecumseh.*

Contents

Preface   xi

Acknowledgments   xxxi

Illustrations and maps   xxxiii

Introduction: Globalization since 1492   3

PART ONE   SURVEYING THE BASE LINES

1   Charting Territory, Giving Names   59

2   Imagining Civilization on the Frontiers of Aboriginality   137

3   Globalization, Decolonization, and the Fourth World   209

PART TWO   PATENTING THE LAND

4   Revolution and Empire   295

5   The Bowl with One Spoon   371

6   Expansion or Immigration into Indian Country?   427

7   Two Legal Countries   469

Notes   535

Index   619

Preface

> The Spanish War then created opportunities for acquiring such stations, far out in the Pacific as well as in the Caribbean. It placed in America's grasp territories which, if not seized, could go to potential rivals. And it offered a chance for Protestant Christianity (also a species, by Social Darwinist canons) to score a gain in its struggle for survival against Catholicism and heathenism.
>
> Ernest R. May, *American Imperialism: A Speculative Essay*, 1967

As columns of US tanks rolled into the centre of Baghdad in April 2003, the resurgent military mastery of the American empire was on global display. In seizing control of Iraq from the regime of Saddam Hussein, the US government injected its unique brand of high-tech martial power into the heartland of ancient Mesopotomia. This legendary domain between the Tigris and Euphrates waterways, a site of some of humanity's earliest break-throughs in agriculture, irrigation, literacy, and civic formation, has long been viewed as one of Western civilization's primary seedbeds. There were many rich ironies, therefore, in the extension of the so-called War on Terrorism into Iraq, a country situated near the cultural headwaters of the civilizational stream now surging through the United States in its current role as the "the West's" chief agency of global domination.

The extension of the US government's War on Terrorism to the goal of "regime change" in Iraq placed a new light on the old myth that the West's destiny in global history is synonymous with the destiny of civilization itself. As presently structured, the West's most tangible instruments of global pre-eminence lie in the power of the US government and in the closely related operations of the world's largest commercial corporations. In 1960 retiring US president Dwight D. Eisenhower identified the most instrumental agency at the hub of this mix of institutions as the military-industrial complex. The production of ever-more-lethal and sophisticated weapons of mass destruction constitutes this technopoly's most advanced frontiers of innovation and control, linking the destiny of all living beings on our shared planet. Among its many global functions, this military-industrial technopoly has become one of capitalism's most high-octane stimulants as well as its primary police force.[1]

The intertwined complex of US public institutions and corporate leviathans that currently dominates global capitalism was spawned most prolifically in the process which saw the United States emerge from West-

ern Europe's imperial colonization of the Western Hemisphere. It was
spawned with particular fecundity in the expansion of the United States to
continental proportions. This expansion was characterized by the conquest of many Indigenous peoples and their lands. Before their ingestion
by the United States, these North American lands and their Aboriginal
inhabitants had been colonized by the Netherlands, Sweden, France,
Spain, Russia, and, of course, Great Britain. Central to this process of
annexation through conquest was the transformation of huge expanses of
the earth's most diversified, bounteous, and hospitable territory into titled
private property whose ownership was vested not only in human persons
but also in those corporate polities that first acquired their legal personality as "natural persons" in the United States. To understand the most
aggressive motifs of globalization at the present time, there is no more
telling history to explore, ponder, narrate, and debate than the process
which saw the world's sole remaining superpower emerge from European
imperialism generally and from British imperialism more specifically.

The surge of US territorial acquisition and transformation in North
America gave rise to one of the West's most heavily dramatized and romanticized sagas of frontier conquest. A few common themes emerged from
the rationales used to justify the seizure by the United States not only of its
western frontiers but of the global fate of the West itself. These justifications for conquest and domination have been remarkably consistent with
the rationales once dispensed in explaining the imperial annexations and
impositions of European empires. Such rationales have been permeated
by a view of human history as a linear progression marking the ascent of
civilization over the alleged savagery of those peoples who have slowed or
impeded Western dominance. Only rarely has the story of the West's rise
to global pre-eminence been presented in more complex and nuanced
narratives, describing all manner of mergers, clashes, and accommodations *among* civilizations.

As the architects of the American empire have increasingly gazed
towards the Arab-speaking and Muslim worlds as the next frontiers of their
social, military, political, and commercial re-engineering, it has become
essential to understand the persistent power of the West's master parable.
The key to that parable is the concept of all human interaction as a struggle to advance civilization's conquest of savagery and barbarism. In mounting its War on Terrorism in the wake of the September 11, 2001, tragedies,
the regime of George W. Bush drew heavily on the evangelical impulse of
the West's old civilizing mission. The US president and his advisers
renewed the justification once popularized to explain both European
imperialism and Manifest Destiny.

Where the United States emerged in its early years as both opponent
and agent of European imperialism, Manifest Destiny seemed to invest the
American nation's expansionist energies with a sense of providential mission and sanction. Manifest Destiny was initially directed at extinguishing

[handwritten margin notes:] incl. the barbarism of nature "Red in tooth and claw." - Need to control the restless, unwashed masses - "The crisis of democracy"

the Old World titles of Indigenous peoples as well as the Old World claims
of the European powers that had previously colonized the Western Hemisphere. In the Cold War era the Red menace driving the build-up of the
American war machine was no longer perceived to be Indians and British
Red Coats. Instead, the perceived enemy had been globalized to encompass the real and imagined threats of international communism. Then, in
the post–September 11 world, the imagery of terrorism replaced that of
savagery and communism as the main explanatory catch-all to describe the
real, illusory, or manufactured enemies of the American way of life.

In framing the underlying assumptions of the War on Terrorism, there
was virtually no recognition by the government of the United States of the
ironies entailed in mounting such a campaign in a society born of violent
revolt by a heavily armed citizenry against the sovereign authority of a duly
constituted government. There was virtually no public recognition that the
very shape and workings of Western civilization are inextricably bound up
with the violent overthrow of old orders in the course of the American Revolution, the French Revolution, and the Russian Revolution. Indeed, without the violence of the American Civil War, who can say how much longer
the institution of slavery would have been tolerated and accommodated
within the structures of American federalism? In making these observations I am not implying that there is no need to mobilize against genuine
zealots who constitute very real menaces to the integrity of public order
and the physical safety of civilian populations. What I am alleging, however, is that, without some substantial public reckoning with how to negotiate the complex of connections linking power and coercion, both outside
and inside the institutions of sovereign governments and their corporate
progeny, the War on Terrorism is in danger of becoming little more than
a self-serving cover for the worst sorts of oligarchies. Already this unorthodox "war" has enabled many opportunists lodged in corrupt and discredited regimes to demonize their critics, repress their foes, and entrench
their own power as though its monopoly under their own control was some
final, utopian outcome of history fulfilled.

The War on Terrorism has deep roots in American history that cut far
beneath the events of September 11. While the labels of the demonized
other may have changed over time, the imagined attributes of the stigmatized foes of the American Dream have remained remarkably consistent
since the era of the founding of the United States. In their very first act of
self-justification, the founders carved out in 1776 a special category to
encompass a class of humanity deemed bereft of inalienable rights, a class
of people thought to embody such potential for unpredictable violence
and anarchy that they were placed outside the assertions of equal rights
proclaimed as the *raison d'être* of the revolutionary republic. In an internal
contradiction too long neglected by scholars and teachers of American
history, this class of humanity was characterized as predators to be excluded and extinguished in building the edifice of universal liberty. The War

on Terrorism gave renewed force and legitimacy to prejudices similar to those that once induced the authors of the Declaration of Independence to refer to the Indigenous peoples of North America as "merciless Indian savages." Their "known rule of warfare," the founders proclaimed in the most famous and consequential political manifesto ever penned, "is an undistinguished destruction of all ages, sexes, and conditions."

This identification of Aboriginal Americans with savagery and with the indiscriminate destruction of people and property would cut a bloody swath through American history in the rise of the United States to continental, hemispheric and, ultimately, global pre-eminence. From the beginning of this ascent, those distinct peoples who stood in the way of the United States's territorial ambitions were dehumanized and criminalized in the text of the Declaration of Independence. They were collectively set up as the target of what, in today's terms, might be characterized as a campaign of territorial, commercial, and political aggrandizement disguised behind the cover of a self-righteous war on terrorism. They were collectively subjected to a regime of racial and moral profiling that has seen the lawless violence once directed at "merciless Indian savages" extended, to name only a few, to Aboriginal Hawaiians, indigenous Philippinos, nationalist Vietnamese, socialist Central and South Americans, revolutionary Cubans, and displaced Palestinians. Who knows how many other groups on the next frontiers of American power in both the Arab-speaking and Muslim worlds will find themselves demonized because of the arbitrary judgments made by those in charge of an endless War on Terrorism? Who knows who will be the next to be stripped of their inherent right of self-defence, let alone of their rights of life, liberty, and the pursuit of happiness? Who knows what government, what people, what nationality will next be denied all access to anything approaching due process in the international community, all in the name of the superpower's self-declared imperative of pre-emptive attack? Who knows how many groups or individuals within the imperial heartland of the informal American empire will be denied all civil and political rights because it is claimed they represent a danger of "an undistinguished destruction of all ages, sexes and conditions?"

In the spring of 2003 the world watched, fixated, as the governments of the United States and its British imperial parent defied the international authority of the United Nations. Without the approval of the UN's Security Council, the sole agency on the planet with the international authority to sanction lawful warfare, the former and current superpowers joined forces to install an Iraqi government more in keeping with their interests. The decision of the governments of the United States and Britain to defy the jurisdiction of the United Nations brought to the surface a range of new schisms dividing the West and, indeed, the entire global community. The resulting controversy revealed a profound difference of opinion among governments, politicians, and organized bodies of citizens within most countries. At the core of this disagreement was the question: Will the

planet henceforth be governed through the exercise of some sort of democratic rule of law, centred, however imperfectly and precariously, at the
United Nations? Or does the military and commercial power of the United States render the government of that superpower as the highest authority, as the ultimate court of final resort in the making of world order?

When that question seemed to be answered, for the time being at least,
by the raw assertion of political and military will entailed in the US-led
invasion of Iraq, the unwritten, unregulated, and informal nature of the
American empire came under increasingly close scrutiny throughout the
global community. How much longer, it was asked, could the United States
claim the power and privileges of its dominant role in global finance, global geopolitics, and global control of weapons of mass destruction without
bearing the costs that have traditionally accompanied the possession of formal empire? How much longer would the rest of the world tolerate the
overt and covert interventions in their own domestic affairs by a multifac-
eted superpower apparently unconstrained by any rules other than those
attending its own internal calculations of self-interest? At what point might
it become no longer feasible for the United States to claim all the rights
and privileges of a global empire without assuming in more predictable,
codified, consistent, and verifiable ways the large responsibilities that go
along with an imperial role in planetary governance?

In the course of the American military intervention in Iraq, a reminder
of earlier resistance struggles on former frontiers of American power
appeared in the skies above ancient Mesopotamia. The names given these
airborne devices of war served as a reminder of the historical background
of contemporary controversies over the place and function of international law. They provided a symbol that most of the great issues to be addressed
in the formulation and enforcement of international law are closely connected to the unbroken cycles of colonization that continue to relegate
most of the world's people and peoples to subordinate status. Along the
extended supply lines linking Baghdad with the strategic shipping lanes of
the Persian Gulf flew tight formations of Apache and Black Hawk helicopters. The designations attached to these agile mechanisms of military
force were taken from some of the warring opponents of the United States
during earlier phases of its imperial expansion. By identifying the original
resisters of American power with some of the US military's most efficient
killing machines, the superpower demonstrated its knack for cultural
appropriation. It demonstrated its propensity to incorporate the fighting
spirit of Old World Aboriginals into the arsenals and iconography of its
New World empire.

The original Black Hawk led an Aboriginal resistance movement in
1832 in the Illinois area. A group of pro-American Winnebego men eventually captured the besieged freedom fighter. They handed over their
captive to the top US officials at Prairie du Chien, a post that retained its
distinct character from its earlier days as an important fur-trade emporium

in both French and British imperial Canada. Black Hawk's incarceration can be seen as the final pre-emption by the United States of the sovereign aspirations of the Indian Confederacy. This legendary confederation of First Nations had extended its commercial ties with the Montreal-based traders into a military alliance with the British imperial government during the War of 1812. The Indian Confederacy's aim in allying itself with the British Army in North America was to achieve for its citizens sovereign recognition of an unextinguishable Aboriginal dominion in the heart of North America. In seeking a permanent national polity with fixed borders in their own ancestral hemisphere, the Indian Confederacy mounted the most concerted Aboriginal challenge ever to the expansionist policies of the United States. With the quelling of the Aboriginal resistance led by Black Hawk, a seasoned veteran on the British side in the War of 1812, the US government was, in a sense, mopping up the military remnants of Tecumseh's once-formidable Indian Confederacy.

After incarcerating Black Hawk for a short time, the American War Department decided to take its prize captive on a tour of major US cities in the nation's more heavily populated regions. The object of the exercise was to impress on Black Hawk and his oldest son, who also joined the tour, that it was futile for Aboriginal Americans to resist the power and might of the United States. Much to the surprise of the event's organizers, Black Hawk and his entourage created a minor sensation. Everywhere they went, Black Hawk and his son met with intense curiosity from large numbers of animated onlookers. The newspapers quickly joined and amplified the phenomenon, extending to Black Hawk a new kind of celebrity status. As this episode and others like it demonstrated, the American public were fascinated by defeated Aboriginal warriors. Ironically, in attempting to protect their own ancestral portions of the American homeland, these Indian patriots had contributed to the mythology of the seizure of the American West as a classic martial drama highlighting the hard-won character of civilization's conquest over doomed savagery.

In the years ahead there would be many variations on the themes of resistance, conquest, and celebrity in the glamorized myth making surrounding the westward movement of the American frontier. At Little Bighorn in Montana Territory in 1876, for instance, a well-armed Indian fighting force led by Crazy Horse and Sitting Bull beat the US Seventh Cavalry of General George Custer. Custer's military carelessness was partly attributable to his desire to parlay a major victory over Indians into winning the keys to the White House. In attempting to climb through military ranks to the ultimate prize of the US presidency, Custer had before him the example of Andrew Jackson and William Henry Harrison. Both were decorated Indian fighters who had shot to the top job in the United States largely through the fame they had garnered in leading frontier assaults portrayed and celebrated as part of America's benighted conquest of a dark and savage continent.

The setback for the US Army at Little Bighorn proved there could be significant military reversals in the course of Western civilization's onslaught on Indigenous peoples. The strange fate awaiting Sitting Bull was one marker of this realization. In the years before he was assassinated by a Siouan police officer in the employment of the US government, Sitting Bull briefly became the star attraction in Buffalo Bill Cody's Wild West Show. This populist extravaganza laid out the basic plotlines and script for literally hundreds of Hollywood "Westerns" in the years that followed. These lucrative early products of the Hollywood Dream Machine signalled to Americans, and increasingly to a growing global market as well, the seemingly inevitable course of the United States's leadership in vanquishing savagery and securing the West for civilization's ascendance. For many decades the various plots supporting this basic storyline remained largely unchanged. Only the deep political schisms generated by the heavy US involvement in the Vietnam War changed the symbolic geography that had given rise to the stark dichotomies dramatized in Hollywood Westerns. As the acrimony over Vietnam shattered a host of naïve certainties on which many pillars of American nationalism had been built, it became more difficult to recycle the standard mythology of the moving American frontier as an unwavering force for civilization's ascent over savagery. Some of the new realism proved more ephemeral than long lasting, however, when the Hollywood presidency of Ronald Reagan in the 1980s returned the United States to some of the more primal motifs in the representation of American patriotism.

The warriors for whom the Apache helicopters are named achieved this distinction by being among the most effective guerrilla fighters the world has ever known. "They are the tigers of the human species," observed Lieutenant-Colonel George Crook, the officer assigned the job of overseeing the US government's military hunt to disarm and to kill or incarcerate the last of the free Apaches in the Sierra Madre range in the Chihuahua region of Mexico.[2] From that remote mountain bastion the last of the Apache holdouts conducted a concerted armed resistance until the mid-1880s against the incursions of the acquisitors of their ancestral lands in Arizona, New Mexico, and Chihuahua. At the head of this small array of legendary resisters was Geronimo.

Geronimo and his group might never have been captured if Crook had not succeeded in hiring Apache scouts to track down their relatives in their secret mountain hideaways. In bringing Indian scouts into the US Army to advance American interests in the American Indian wars, the US government began to acquire expertise in the arts and science of divide and conquer. From Apacheria to India to Iraq and Afghanistan, the strategic techniques of infiltration, bribery, payoffs, and co-optation to open, widen, and exploit divisions between and within Aboriginal groups have been essential to the creation, expansion, and operation of virtually all imperial systems.

Geronimo gained an enduring reputation that remains securely lodged in the symbolic mystique of Americana. To this day the series of pictures taken by C.S. Fly when Geronimo and his small band of Chiricahua Apache were briefly captured remains among the best-known and frequently reproduced images in the history of photography. After posing for Fly, Geronimo and his group eluded their American captors one more time. Several months later they were apprehended by a force of 5,000 soldiers. They were immediately deported, along with some of the now-disfavoured Apache scouts, to a military prison in Pensacola, Florida. Like Sitting Bull, Geronimo was transformed by promoters into a popular attraction. He was allowed to sell autographs and souvenirs to tourists as his part of the bargain.

In 1904 Theodore Roosevelt invited Geronimo to join in the US president's inaugural procession down Pennsylvania Avenue in Washington, DC. Roosevelt's goal in selecting Geronimo was to present the famous old warrior as the "before" stage in a kind of before-and-after display designed to dramatize the civilizing ideals of the United States generally and of US Indian policy specifically. Geronimo was meant to embody an uncivilized contrast with Quanah Parker, a Comanche rancher and US magistrate who rode in the parade along with several graduates of the Carlisle Indian Boarding School. They had been selected to demonstrate the perceived success of American methods in elevating former savages to the refined heights of advanced civilization. Geronimo, however, generated a level of admiration not extended to Parker. The famed Apache, in fact, overshadowed all the participants save one. Only President Roosevelt was more applauded than Geronimo. According to Geronimo's biographer Angie Debo, as the onlookers threw their hats in the air, one is said to have exclaimed, "Hooray for Geronimo! Public Hero Number 2!"[3]

During the many years Geronimo spent in the custody of the American Army at Fort Pickens, Florida, and Fort Still, Oklahoma, there was always uncertainty about his precise legal status. This doubt anticipated a similar controversy that arose as the US government pursued the first stages of its War on Terrorism. A special prison was established at the American military base at Guantanamo Bay in Cuba to contain Taliban fighters taken captive in Afghanistan. These soldiers, it was believed, had close links with al-Qaeda, the group tagged by the Bush regime as the primary culprits responsible for the September 11 attacks on the Pentagon and the World Trade Center. Just as the Declaration of Independence placed "merciless Indian savages" in a kind of constitutional no man's land outside the domain of inalienable rights, so the prisoners at Guantanamo Bay were similarly denuded of all protections of law and due process. The "detainees" were denied access to the domestic criminal courts of the United States and to the international laws and procedures governing the treatment of prisoners of war.

The parallels between the case of Geronimo and the Guantanamo Bay incarcerees hint at the existence of many similar comparisons awaiting timely investigation. A central danger to be addressed in such investigation is how the US-led War on Terrorism holds the potential to renew some of the worst abuses of sovereign authority that Western civilization had seemingly surmounted in moving beyond European empire building, German fascism, Soviet totalitarianism, and South African apartheid. What is at stake is nothing less than the integrity of the rule of law, a tenuous, incomplete, and imperfect human creation even at the best of times. The rapid erosion of the rule of law has been closely connected to renewed patterns of imperial abuse that have placed some of those on the receiving end of modern-day colonialism, in a constitutional twilight zone without access to the remedies of both domestic and international law. Those so victimized are the contemporary descendants of the Declaration of Independence's "merciless Indian savages."

It could be argued, in fact, that many of the victims of the modern-day colonialism are actually worse off than some of the "savages" and "natives" on the receiving end of earlier versions of imperial rule. In the case of the British Empire, for instance, its subjects had frequently to contend with the alien authority of colonial institutions. For the most part, however, these institutions acted on the basis of public acts of the imperial Parliament and executive orders formulated through political procedures whose substance could usually be evaluated in the relatively clear light of day. Though these colonial institutions, along with the officials who administered them, often performed in repressive and unjust ways, the oppressive structure of this system was sufficiently clear that critics, such as Mahatma Gandhi, could advocate its replacement with indigenous instruments of home rule.

In the present constellation of global power, no such clarity exists. In the place of a world divided between imperial powers and their formal colonies, we now have a planet where the majority of citizens are effectively dominated by the domestic political whims, massive military establishment, transnational banking institutions, and prolific corporate progeny of a single superpower. There is no transparent constitutional shape, no tangible rule of law attending the methods of remote-control governance that have become the *modus operandi* of the informal American empire. While the staff of the American State Department, the Pentagon, the CIA, and its many related agencies might perform tasks similar to those that once took place in the British Colonial Office, very little of this activity directed at controlling events outside the American homeland has any basis in duly constituted law. The laissez-faire policies long favoured by American business enterprises, both at home and in their global operations, have been adopted as the primary technique of American *foreign* policy. This term, which seemingly recognizes the foreign and externalized character of the rest of the world as a domain lying beyond the jurisdictional scope of the United States, serves to disguise the global reach of American power. Underlying this thesis is the observation that the unilateralism of the United States is far more influential than the multilateralism of the United Nations in the way the world is actually governed.

The techniques of this global regime of remote-control governance are well documented and well known in some circles. They include forms of financial blackmail regularly practised in the poorer countries by the International Monetary Fund and the World Bank, the covert sponsorship of "regime change," such as those US-backed coups known to have taken place in Iran, Guatemala, and Chile, to name but a few, and the sponsorship of puppet regimes as epitomized by the royal dynasty in Saudi Arabia that is the local custodian of US-based oil and gas interests. Even the most superficial examination of the information freely available on the background of the September 11 tragedy reveals that the axis of evil behind the savage attack has most to do with the politics of the religious fundamentalism known to thrive among some clients of American power in Saudi Arabia. Compared with the intensity of the complex interplay among the religious fundamentalisms that came to dominate the executive branches of the governments of the United States, Israel, and Saudi Arabia, the role of the former regimes of Afghanistan and Iraq in the genesis of international terrorism was relatively insignificant.

Much of this project is devoted to explaining that the methods of indirect rule in the informal American empire are not new. They have evolved over an extended period, but especially since the devastation of Europe and Japan in the Second World War. What has changed with the Bush regime's leadership of the War on Terrorism is that the US government no longer hides and obfuscates its unwillingness to abide by the main tenets of multilateralism and international law. At the core of the international system as it existed on the eve of September 11 was the principle that the world's nation-states are each invested with a sovereign authority that cannot be legitimately breached. That principle evolved gradually after its rudimentary outlines were first articulated in 1648 in the Treaty of Westphalia. In place of the investment of the powers of self-governance in the agency of nations-states, the US government now asserts that it possesses a unique imperative to conduct "regime change," "pre-emptive strikes," and "anticipatory self-defense" to change the character of governments it does not like. It makes this assertion based on the conviction, frequently articulated by the president and his chief law enforcement officer, that the licence to violate the sovereign authority of foreign states has come to the United States by divine right.

In May 2003 the Bush White House shortened the name of the War on Terrorism to the War on Terror. It thereby highlighted the sharp internal contradiction within the phrase. War is, after all, a concentrated form of terror. The semantic adjustment was introduced in the course of a military victory ceremony on board a US aircraft carrier. "The Battle of Iraq," declared President George Bush from the deck of the USS *Abraham Lincoln*, "is one victory in the War on Terror that began on September 11, 2001."[4] Bush's speech was delivered amidst an event that was pure American show-manship, a finely honed spectacle of political propaganda designed to gen-erate those kinds of images that belong more to the realm of mythology than to articulate argument. In an era when software, public relations, and celebrity have become central currencies in the political economy of mass illusion, the event was a textbook example of artful advertising for the mil-itary-industrial complex. It served to help illustrate that the most conse-quential conflicts of our time are not those fought with the weaponry of physical violence but with the means of manipulating public opinion. The Bush White House seemingly acknowledged this aspect of contemporary warfare by referring on its website to "the largest media embed operation on any ship in naval history." In this operation, the *Lincoln*'s large crew played host to photographers and scribes representing the world's major media conglomerates. From Time-Warner to Disney-ABC, to General Elec-tric-MSNBC, to Westinghouse-CBS, to Rupert Murdoch's transnational media empire, these info-entertainment conglomerates are deeply embedded within the technopoly of the military-industrial complex.

The media spectacle married elements of the American sci-fi thriller *Independence Day* and Leni Riefenstahl's classic Nazi propaganda film, *Tri-umph of the Will*. In the opening scene of *Triumph*, Adolf Hitler is pictured approaching from the air the Nazi Party rally at Nuremberg in 1934. Pres-ident Bush began his big spectacle on board the *Abraham Lincoln* by touch-ing down on the vessel's deck in a S-3B Viking jet. Emblazoned on the windshield of the aircraft were the words "Commander-In-Chief." The US president then emerged in full fighter pilot garb, invoking the imagery of the dramatic concluding scenes in *Independence Day*. In those scenes, an American president leads a global coalition of armed forces from the cock-pit of a small jet fighter. The aim of this US-led operation is to defend the planet from the attacks of outer-space aliens.

The *Lincoln* and its crew provided the American president with a mon-umental setting for a stirring depiction of militarism triumphant. While the producers of the extravaganza borrowed heavily from the propagan-da techniques pioneered by Riefenstahl and her associates, however, the event was designed to conjur up the aura of Gettysburg rather than Nuremberg. A central element of the plan was to locate the ceremony on board the warship named after the American president who abolished the institution of slavery in the United States. In 1863 President Abraham Lincoln went to Gettysburg, the site of the Union's most pivotal victory over the slave-owning Confederacy. In his address, one of the most cele-brated orations of any American president, Lincoln invoked the rhetori-cal power of some of the most timeless phrases in the Declaration of Inde-pendence. Lincoln justified federal military actions in the American Civil

War as being dedicated to the proposition that "all men are created equal." The sacrifices of the Union side were dedicated to "a new birth of freedom; and that government of the people, by the people, and for the people, shall not perish from the earth." In 2003 George Bush attempted in his speech on the *Lincoln* to draw on the authority of these same principles. He described US operations in Iraq as serving the cause of freeing the Iraqi people from "enslavement." The purpose of the campaign, Bush asserted, was to produce a new regime "of, by, and for the Iraqi people."

In attempting to link the US objective of regime change in Iraq to the abolition of slavery throughout the course of the American Civil War, the Bush administration may have been responding to an interpretation initially suggested by British prime minister Tony Blair. Blair first connected the idea of the War on Terrorism with the abolition movement in a presentation he delivered at a Labour Party conference soon after the September 11 attacks. Oxford historian Niall Ferguson referred to this "messianic speech" in the concluding paragraphs of a survey text he wrote to accompany a BBC television series on the history of British imperialism. In Blair's early response to the terrorist attacks in New York and Washington, Ferguson comments, the British prime minister seemed burdened under the misapprehension that the United States was born "in a war against slavery" rather than "in a war against the British Empire."[5]

One of the main themes of Ferguson's prolific scholarship is that, on balance, the British Empire brought more advantages than disadvantages to humanity collectively in the course of that pluralistic polity's rise and fall. Among the positive legacies of what Ferguson refers to as "Anglobalization" are the pervasiveness of English as a worldwide medium of communication, the elaboration of expansive financial infrastructures favouring relatively unobstructed and abundant flows of international commerce, the spread of parliamentary institutions, and the benefits of the kind of social cohesion which arise from the ascendance of the rule of law over the rule of force.[6] Generally I agree with this aspect of Ferguson's work – and I believe I extend and support his thesis with many of the arguments I develop in these pages. I maintain, for instance, that the continuation into the twenty-first century of crown treaty negotiations with the Indigenous peoples of British Columbia, Quebec, and the federal territories of Northern Canada is directly attributable to the persistence of the imperial rule of law that was retained in what remained of British North America after the United States achieved sovereign independence in international law in the Treaty of Paris of 1783. A similar argument could be made about the political position of Indigenous peoples in Australia, especially in light of the Australian High Court's ruling in 1992 that they possess Aboriginal rights that cannot be unilaterally extinguished through application of the ethnocentric doctrine of *terra nullius* – of the strange legal precept that the land was unpeopled at the onset of European colonization.

Unlike in the remaining crown domain of North America, the United
States has, since 1871, simply denied the existence of an international law
of Aboriginal title, arguing at the UN and elsewhere that it derives its powers over Aboriginal Americans and their ancestral lands from the act of
conquering them. Between 1776 and 1871 the US government continued the constitutional inheritance codified for British North America in
the Royal Proclamation of 1763. The US government made and ratified
in Congress amost four hundred treaties with Indigenous peoples in
order to gain Aboriginal sanction for its expansions into Indian Country.
Most often, however, these treaty negotiations took place only after the
US military had conquered Indian fighting forces in the original
antecedents to the Battle of Iraq. The Treaty of Greenville, for instance,
was negotiated by American officials in 1795 only after the fledgling US
Army under General Anthony Wayne achieved a martial victory over the
Indian Confederacy in the Battle of Fallen Timbers in the Great Lakes
region. Before 1795 the fighting forces of Little Turtle, the leader who led
the negotiation on the Indian side in the making of the Treaty of
Greenville, had twice defeated the American Army in military conflicts
testing disputed claims to rich lands north of the Ohio River. The graduation years later of Little Turtle's grandson from the US Military Academy
at West Point serves to suggest the kind of advantages made available to
Aboriginal collaborators and their families once they changed sides to
become instruments rather than obstacles of US power.

The history of Aboriginal-US relations surrounding the making of the
Treaty of Greenville holds significant clues pointing towards possible outcomes from the US intervention aimed at bringing to power a new regime
for the governance of Iraq. This history of US expansion within North
America helps also to illuminate some of the relationships of power affecting conflicts over jurisdiction in lands and waters claimed simultaneously
by the Israeli state and the Palestinian people. From the perspective of
those parties dealing from the stronger position of entrenched state
power, the prerequisite for successful treaty negotiations seems to be a
decisive demonstration of armed superiority, making conquest the underlying basis of any peace settlement. This pattern links the aftermath of the
Battle of Fallen Timbers in 1794 with the aftermath of the Battle of Iraq in
2003. Both interventions by the US military established a balance of power
conducive to the subsequent installation of Aboriginal client regimes willing to sanction the transfer of control over the exploitation of natural
resources.

To realize this fundamental objective, the US government and its proxies can be expected to hold tenaciously in the future to the position that
they possess the prerogative of conquerors to decide who is or is not eligible to sit on the other side of the negotiating table. It seems likely that any
new treaties to emerge from such conditions on the superpower's imperial frontiers will be more like Indian treaties in the United States than the

constitutional instruments used to restore national governments in Western Europe and Japan after the Second World War. Accordingly, any agreement to recognize new polities in the occupied portions of the Middle East
will probably draw on the legacy of conquest in the American Indian wars.
Those in possession of the instruments of state terror will attempt to pressure selected representatives of Aboriginal groups to acknowledge formally that all their rights, titles, and jurisdictions flowing from their prior
possession of the (s)oil have been extinguished. The other side of this
same coin is the attempt to gain Aboriginal consent for the principle that
the authorities of the newly recognized regime flow from delegated powers transferred from the stronger to the weaker parties in treaty agreements. Hence the concept of extinguishing the Aboriginal rights and titles
of Indigenous peoples remains integral to the continuing expansion of the
New World Order that excluded the merciless Indian savages – in other
words the imagined enemies of civilization – from the liberties declared
universal at the moment of the future superpower's revolutionary inception in 1776.

My emphasis on Aboriginal title as an important element in the concept
of universal human rights leads me to support and amplify Ferguson's view
that the British Empire invested the process of globalization with many
redeeming features. I am less pleased, however, by his characterizations of
the rise of the United States from a civil war in British North America to its
current status as the planet's sole superpower. This weakness in Ferguson's
work reflects an analytical problem that cuts widely, I believe, across a
broad spectrum of British imperial and American historiography. The
basis of that problem is twofold. One weakness lies in the failure of most
historians to recognize the nature of so-called "Indian Affairs" as a prece-
dent-setting continuum of relations establishing underlying paradigms
and patterns for broader complexes of relationships between colonizers
and the colonized. The other weakness lies in the failure to situate the
American Revolution in its broader temporal context of violent clashes
between competing empires, competing interests, and competing theories
of sovereignty.

As I see it, the dates 1754 and 1814 are the most important temporal
bookmarks in framing the duration of the most violent phase of the
more extended American Revolution. The first date identifies the onset
of the Seven Years' War, when Great Britain and France tested the power
of the military force backing their overlapping imperial claims. The year
1814 saw the negotiation of the Treaty of Ghent, the agreement concluding the War of 1812. This war was the last time that the United States
and Great Britain, the present and past superpowers, clashed in violent
confrontation.

Throughout this period from 1754 to 1814 the Confederacy of Indigenous peoples in the Great Lakes–Ohio Valley area played a disproportionately large role in determining the course of imperial history in North

America, a saga whose pivotal effect on global history is now apparent. In conflict after conflict between colonial antagonists, the Aboriginal inhabitants of this contested region held the balance of power. At the core of the contention between Great Britain and France in the Seven Years' War, for instance, was the future of the strategic Aboriginal territories between the watersheds of the St Lawrence and the Mississippi rivers. Following British North America's incorporation of Canada, a disagreement over the character of Aboriginal rights and titles in the newly acquired territory was instrumental in expanding the schism between competing camps of British imperialists in the genesis of the American Revolution. In the War of 1812 it was the prospect that the citizens of the Indian Confederacy would achieve international recognition for their sovereign Aboriginal dominion in the heart of North America which infused the most profound ideological and geopolitical issues into that conflict. Prominent among the mobilized military forces in the War of 1812 was the Liberation Army of the Indian Confederacy. Under Tecumseh's inspired leadership, its military campaign amounted to an Aboriginal and British-backed version of the first American Revolution. The aim of this unfulfilled War of Aboriginal Independence – this second American Revolution – was to secure and hold jurisdictional ground for the First Nations. Such an outcome, if realized, would have set an international precedent that might well have moderated the ethnocentric extremes displayed in future expressions of European imperialism and American Manifest Destiny.

At the beginning of the twenty-first century these historical episodes acquire added meanings as the US government weighs the fate, for instance, of the Palestinians, the Kurds, and the diverse peoples arbitrarily grouped together as Iraqis following the First World War. One obvious place to look for indications of how these and other similarly oppressed groups will be treated in the American imperium is to look to the experiences of Indigenous peoples in North America, especially during the period when the United States emerged from its British imperial origins to claim and to colonize its own continental empire. Indeed, this process holds important keys to better understanding of many current phenomena, including the propensity of the American people and government to turn away from any approaches to global governance that might render the United States as a subject as well as a maker of international law. The roots of this pattern go back to the period before the American Civil War, when the US government rejected any external intervention into the sovereign authority of the southern states over the institution of slavery. Similarly, after the War of 1812, the US government deftly fended off all European involvement in the Indian wars and Indian removals that took place in the course of western expansion. This push found an extension in the Monroe Doctrine of 1823. In his most famous international pronouncement, President James Monroe articulated the intent of the US government to reserve the entire Western Hemisphere, save what remained of

British North America, essentially as a colonial hinterland of the imperial United States. One outcome has been to deny to the largely mestizo populations of Central and South America their inherent right to elaborate without US interference their own complex of foreign relations in the larger global community.

These historical vignettes are suggestive of the genesis of the near pathological unwillingness of the US government under President George W. Bush to acknowledge any secular law or authority on the planet higher than the power vested in the United States. They provide the contextual setting for a very consistent line of decision making connecting, for instance, the failure of the US government to join the League of Nations, the US refusal between 1948 and 1989 to ratify the United Nations Convention on the Prevention and Punishment of the Crime of Genocide, and the unqualified antagonism of the Bush regime towards any US involvement in the International Criminal Court. These and numerous other displays of American unilateralism have emerged in a country forged in the determination that its western expansion would not be impeded by either the resistance of Indigenous peoples or the constraints of imperial and international law.

From these beginnings, the United States and its corporate progeny have continued to expand in ways that eschew as much as possible the kind of elaborate constitutionalism that became an important factor in the evolution of the British Empire into the most pluralistic polity the world has ever seen. This nuanced constitutionalism placed a premium on flexible adaptation to the diversity of peoples, languages, cultures, and religions within Great Britain's imperial embrace. In contrast, the melting-pot liberalism of the United States has paradoxically made its informal empire far less tolerant than was the British Empire towards the eclectic character of subject peoples, but especially in the realm of economics and religion. The sense of Manifest Destiny permeating the expansionistic ethos of the United States has long imbued its version of the civilizing mission with a particularly strident strain of evangelism, one that has treated the universalization of capitalism almost as if the goal of commercial conformity was the product of divine revelation.

Much calculation and cunning has been employed in crafting the web of power behind the facade which gives the impression of the superpower's laissez-faire relations with the rest of the global community. The development of these relations outside the constraints of an overarching rule of imperial law is much less inadvertent than Ferguson indicates in his proposal that the United States should adopt a global personality more like that of Great Britain during the height of its imperial powers. Ferguson misleads his readers in picturing the United States as though its position in the world is currently similar to that of Great Britain at the moment when it began to transform its sphere of influence from an informal to a formal empire. As the most powerful outgrowth of the world's most sophis-

ticated imperial system, the informal American empire is best characterized as a distillation, rather than an unrefined version, of the most expansionistic elements of the British Empire. This pattern is especially clear
from my vantage point in Canada. My country emerges from the position
of those in North America who chose to stay with the British Empire
through the course of the American Revolution and the War of 1812.
Since 1776 it has become increasingly clear that the imperialism of those
on the Tory side of these conflicts was pale compared with the expansionary zeal of those who transformed the United States into the world's powerhouse of commercialism and militarization. Charles Darwin's theory of
the "survival of the fittest" meets Wal-Mart and Hiroshima.

In the *New York Times*, Niall Ferguson encourages his readers in the United States to move beyond the "tradition of organized hypocrisy" that prevails "so long as the American empire dare not speak its own name." As
part of the transition Ferguson advocates, he proposes that the best American universities should devote more attention and resources to cultivating
a class of graduates willing to serve overseas for long periods of time in a
US version of the British colonial service. In tendering this advice, Ferguson reflects on the importance of his own country's system of higher learning, which produced the "Oxbridge-educated, frock-coated mandarins"
that guided the British Empire from positions deep within the colonial
hinterland. "You simply cannot have an empire," he writes, "without imperialists – out there on the spot – to run it."[7]

I expect that Harvard University is as deeply engaged in the operation
of the informal American empire as Oxford University ever was in the
management of the British Empire. Where the older empire sent most of
its colonial agents out from the metropolis, however, the superpower
deploys its system of higher education mostly by importing students to
transform the offspring of foreign elites into willing agents of American
indirect rule. Advancement of this process has helped build the careers of
many American academics. For instance, Harvard professor Henry
Kissinger began his rise through the ranks by guiding many foreign
students through the assimilative process aimed at winning them over to
collaborate, when they returned to their home countries, in US-centred
networks of global command, both formal and informal, overt and covert.

This assimilative function was entrenched in Harvard's legal founda-
tions since its founding in the seventeenth century. Like several other Ivy
League universities in the former English colonies of the United States,
Harvard's charter includes a specific mandate to educate a class of Protes-
tant Indian missionaries equipped on graduation to evangelize their own
Aboriginal groups. A similar assimilative design seems evident in the deci-
sion of the US government to open a space at the prestigious West Point
Military Academy for Little Turtle's grandson after the Treaty of
Greenville. A cruder version of the same manipulative pedagogy devel-
oped in the training of Latin American military forces in the murderous

arts and sciences of "counterinsurgency" at the School of the Americas in
Fort Benning, Georgia.

As Ferguson should realize, the system of higher education in the United States has long since been recruited into many instrumental roles in the military-industrial complex that lies at the core of the informal American empire. Through the medium of consultant contracts, for instance, scores of academics have been as thoroughly embedded in the command structure of the American war machine as those CNN journalists who made their way to Baghdad inside US Army tanks. President Dwight D. Eisenhower devoted considerable attention to the perils of this infiltration of the academy in the speech where he first warned of the anti-democratic tendencies of the military-industrial complex. He cautioned that "a government contract becomes virtually a substitute for intellectual curiosity." He added: "The prospect of domination of the nation's scholars by federal employment, project allocations, and the power of money is ever present and is to be gravely regarded. Yet in holding scientific research and discovery in respect, as we should, we must also be alert to the equal and opposite danger that public policy could itself become the captive of a scientific-technological elite."[8] As should be clear by now, this text comes from outside the community of embedded academics in the military-industrial complex. Some of them have indeed substituted curiosity for government contracts, and the elusive ideal of scholarly objectivity for a chance to participate in the chain-of-command overseen by America's most overtly imperial presidency.

The frequent references by President Bush to the grace of God as the source of ultimate sanction for US policies has effectively rendered the world's most powerful country, for the time being at least, as a Christian theocracy. The division between church and state has been whittled away so that evangelical Protestantism, which has long vied with Enlightenment rationality for the heart, soul, and mind of America, has apparently prevailed. The sense of Manifest Destiny, which historically imbued the expansionistic ethos of the United States with Christian purpose, has been renewed, this time with a vengeance on a truly global scale. The old Manifest Destiny of the United States has been absorbed into the Born Again evangelism inspiring the unbridled zealotry of the War on Terrorism. Both currents of conviction and action have encouraged Americans to see themselves as God's Chosen People, assigned by the Creator to build a New Jerusalem on earth. Both currents of conviction and action draw heavily on the evangelical precepts that infused European imperialism with much of its messianic drive. That missionary enterprise began dramatically in 1493, just as the Christian Crusades against the peoples of Islam were coming to a close. With news of the "discoveries" of Christopher Columbus before him, the pope moved boldly to implement the doctrine that he was the exclusive instrument of universal power as Christ's sole vicar on earth. He did so by investing the sovereigns of Spain and

Portugal with a divinely sanctioned title to own and to govern the entire Western Hemisphere in the name of the Christian sovereigns' duty to elevate infidel savages to the higher glories of Christian civilization.

Most of this text and of the larger project of which it forms a part were conceived, researched, and written before the War on Terrorism began. Very quickly, however, the events that followed in the wake of September 11 have rendered one of its key propositions far less controversial: that the United States forms the metropolitan centre of a larger, more expansive polity that I choose to call the American empire or, sometimes, the American empire of private property. An essential dynamic animating this empire, I argue, was first set in motion when the United States was formed as an instrument to overcome British imperialism. The founders created a new kind of indigenous North American sovereignty for several reasons, including the objective of creating a more efficient agency of statecraft for the ingestion and privatization of the continent's vast and pluralistic Indian Country.

I first began developing this thesis in studying the Indian policies of my own country, a polity that absorbed and retained French-Aboriginal Canada even as it turned away from many of the principles animating most of the Anglo-Americans in the American Revolution and in the War of 1812. In both of these conflicts it was clear that the most zealous Indian fighters were on the supposedly liberal side of the clashes. In their Indian wars the founders and developers of the United States demonstrated attributes that help to clarify the nature of the dominant thrust in the complex of processes that have been recently described as globalization.

As I see it, one of the major themes in globalization is that the so-called decolonization movement, which unfolded with particular intensity in the 1960s, did not realize the promises of liberation during the dismantling of the old European empires. Instead, European imperialism was replaced by the form of unregulated, superpower hegemony that currently defines the main outlines of world order. The broad dissatisfaction with the failure of the decolonization movement to deliver genuine liberation may be difficult to apprehend from the perspective of the network of privileged enclaves that presently guides and exploits the continuing globalization of western dominance. But for 75 per cent of the world's population, the giant class of groups and individuals still sometimes referred to simply as "natives," the resentment mounts daily that the formal structure of empires, colonies, and subject peoples has not been replaced with a fairer means of organizing human relationships. We ignore at our peril this growing frustration with the continuity of colonialism. Surely the fate of "the West" and of the whole world does indeed depend on our capacity to formulate an application of Enlightenment ideals that is more just and progressive than the division of humanity between a small entitled minority and a large, disentitled majority.

Acknowledgments

Towards the end of the introductory chapter, I make some acknowledgments of the help and encouragement I received during the course of my work. There are specific expressions of gratitude, however, I want to register here. My friend and colleague Donald Boyd Smith has been an excellent collaborator at every step of our journey from Ontario to teaching positions in Alberta, Canada. Our shared endeavours on the academic borderlands of Indian Country go back to graduate school at the University of Toronto, where we were both fortunate to do our doctoral theses under the enlightened tutelage of J.M.S. Careless.

Sidney L. Harring at the City University of New York intervened strategically with encouragement and excellent suggestions at a crucial moment in the genesis of this project. I was introduced to Sidney by Lou Knafla at the University of Calgary. He made me aware of several references of relevance to this text. So too did Sarah Carter, also in the History Department at the U of C. Bruce Trigger insisted that I not allow my enthusiasm in favouring the Tory side in my account of the emergence of the United States to blind me to the importance of Enlightenment ideals, both historically and in our own times. In helping me to see some of the pitfalls of excessive cultural relativism, he enabled me to apprehend better the moral relativism that is becoming chronic in the problematic climax of the informal American empire. Olive Dickason and Boyce Richardson remained undaunted in expertly assessing the piles of thick manuscripts that were generated in working towards the text presented here and the second volume to come. Bruce Clark shared many of his rich insights both as a legal historian and as a seasoned freedom fighter who has earned the high honours marked on his person by many professional war wounds. I recall his insistence that the project retain its original title, "The Bowl with One Spoon."

My work on this text and on volume 2 has benefited from the incisive editing of Robin Mathews. I spent many hours with Robin discussing the work's broad thematic outlines as well as its textual details. I had similar experiences with the brilliant William Blackburn, who passed away just as he was hitting his stride on a second career teaching English literature in southern China. My student from Yellowknife, Chris Oram, worked for me on this project during one summer and unearthed rich material that helped to nourish this narrative, or at least its narrator. Carolyn Lastuka, Native American Studies Secretary at my university, typed drafts during the initial phase of this project.

I have discovered that there is considerable stamina, expertise, and artistry involved on the part of many people in making manuscripts into books. I have come to see why Philip Cercone at McGill-Queen's University Press is widely regarded as Canada's presiding magus in bringing together the many elements of a steady stream of consistently good and frequently great scholarly works. The point person in the transformation of my scriblings into published text was Rosemary Shipton, who is rightfully in high demand for her gifted editing and also for her prowess as a teacher of clear and precise writing. David Drummond would not quit until he captured the right image for the book jacket. The coordinating editor, Joan McGilvray, always commented congenially but decisively in giving me my orders to stop dilly dallying and move the project on to the next stage. Viola Cerezke-Schooler was the erudite angel who saved me as I was sinking into the abyss of a zillion index cards. I shall always be grateful for the time and effort she showed as a dedicated volunteer in our joint creation of the finding aid at the back of this volume. Check it out!

Publication of this text and the volume to follow has received substantial financial backing from the University of Lethbridge, which granted me a one-year study leave to take this project to its present stage. I want to thank Howard Tennant, the former president of the university, for making this outcome possible. Similarly, I am grateful to Brian Titley, the former president of my faculty association, and Bhagwan Dua, my former dean, who were instrumental in the planning and negotiation that prepared the way for this publication. As I understand it, the leaders of my university discussed at length the importance of intervening appropriately to adjust for the tendency of many public and private sector funders to direct scarce resources towards research in the hard sciences and technology rather than towards the academy's more traditional sanctums in the liberal arts, the humanities, and the social sciences. My current dean, Chris Nicol, and the current president of the university, Bill Cade, have maintained a steady hand in providing the resources and encouragement that have enabled me to reach publication.

All the help extended to me does not, of course, modify my final responsibility for the contents of this text. The fault for any errors which appear lies with me, and me alone. The person who knows my propensity for mistakes and error best, my wife, Charlotte Childforever Hall, has contributed in many ways to *The Bowl with One Spoon*. I thank her with all my heart.

Anthony J. Hall, May 2003
Lethbridge Alberta, Canada

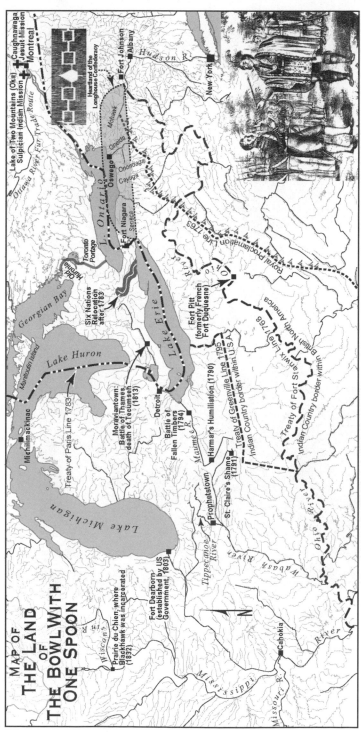

MAP OF THE LAND OF THE BOWL WITH ONE SPOON

Between 1754 and 1814 the Land of the Bowl with One Spoon was one of the most strategically placed and heavily contested regions on the planet. Until their defeat in the Seven Years War, French imperialists viewed the Ohio Valley as the key to joining their colonies along the St Lawrence and Mississippi River systems. For the leadership of the Indian Confederacy, the lands north of the Ohio River were transformed from a shared hunting ground into Aboriginal Indiana, a sovereign polity with fixed boundaries whose security would be backed by the might of the British Empire. For the fur-trade entrepreneurs of Montreal, the Land of the Bowl with One Spoon formed an old and integral part of the commercial hinterland of Canada's most important commercial metropolis. For the government of the United States, the territory north of the Ohio River formed the basis after 1787 of the Northwest Territory, an economic frontier of American expansionism and an internal colony of federal authority. All of these visions clashed violently in the War of 1812.

Sir William Johnson was the first Superintendent of the Northern Division of the British Imperial Indian Department. In 1763 he built Johnson Hall, which became an important centre in the diplomacy of the Covenant Chain. In 1992, the year of the 500th anniversary of Christopher Columbus's arrival in America, the author visited this historical site with his son Sampson. (Courtesy Albany Institute of History and Art [Edward Lawson Henry (1841–1919), *Johnson Hall*, oil on canvas, 1903]; photograph by author; and National Archives of Canada, c5197).

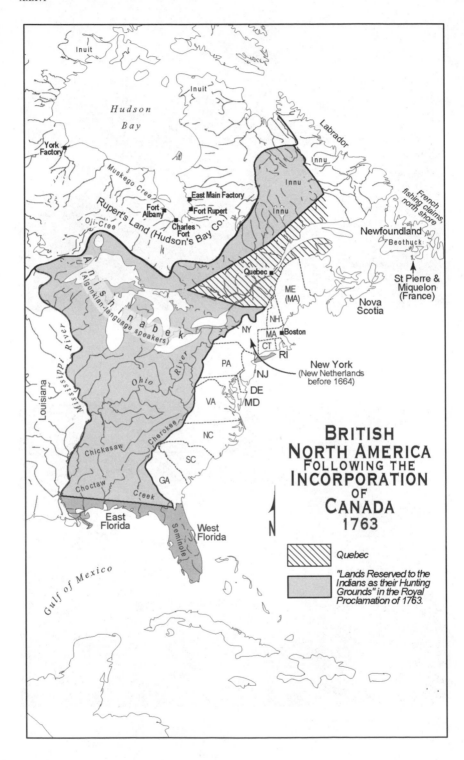

Inuit

Inuit

Hudson Bay

York Factory

Muskego Cree

Oji-Cree

Rupert's Land (Hudson's Bay Co.)

East Main Factory

Fort Albany

Fort Rupert

Charles Fort

A n i s h i n a b e k (Algonkian-language speakers)

Mississippi River

Louisiana

Ohio River

Ohio

Chickasaw

Cherokee

Choctaw

Creek

NC

SC

GA

East Florida

West Florida

Seminole

Gulf of Mexico

Labrador

Innu

Innu

Innu

French fishing claims, north shore

Newfoundland

Beothuck

Quebec

ME (MA)

NH

NY

MA Boston

CT

RI

PA

NJ

DE

MD

VA

New York (New Netherlands before 1664)

Nova Scotia

St Pierre & Miquelon (France)

N

BRITISH NORTH AMERICA FOLLOWING THE INCORPORATION OF CANADA 1763

Quebec

"Lands Reserved to the Indians as their Hunting Grounds" in the Royal Proclamation of 1763.

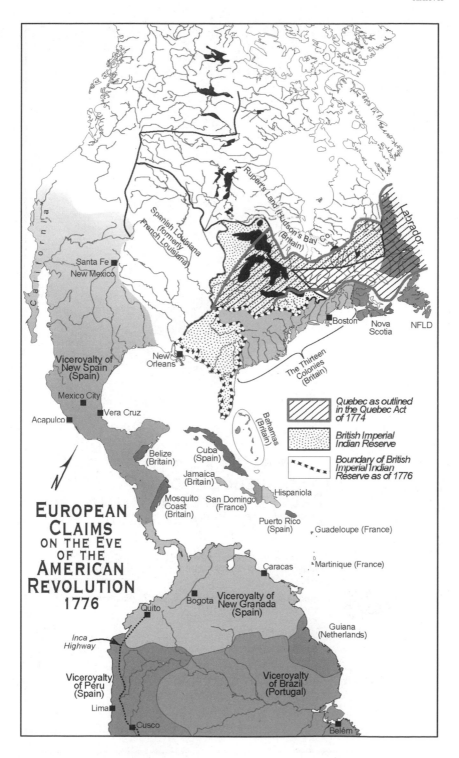

California

Rupert's Land (Hudson's Bay Co.)
(Britain)

Spanish Louisiana (formerly French Louisiana)

Labrador

Santa Fe
New Mexico

Boston

Nova Scotia

NFLD

Viceroyalty of New Spain (Spain)

New Orleans

The Thirteen Colonies (Britain)

Mexico City

Acapulco

Vera Cruz

Bahamas (Britain)

Quebec as outlined in the Quebec Act of 1774

British Imperial Indian Reserve

Boundary of British Imperial Indian Reserve as of 1776

Belize (Britain)

Cuba (Spain)

Jamaica (Britain)

Mosquito Coast (Britain)

San Domingo (France)

Hispaniola

EUROPEAN CLAIMS ON THE EVE OF THE AMERICAN REVOLUTION 1776

Puerto Rico (Spain)

Guadeloupe (France)

Martinique (France)

Caracas

Bogota

Viceroyalty of New Granada (Spain)

Quito

Guiana (Netherlands)

Inca Highway

Viceroyalty of Peru (Spain)

Viceroyalty of Brazil (Portugal)

Lima

Cusco

Belém

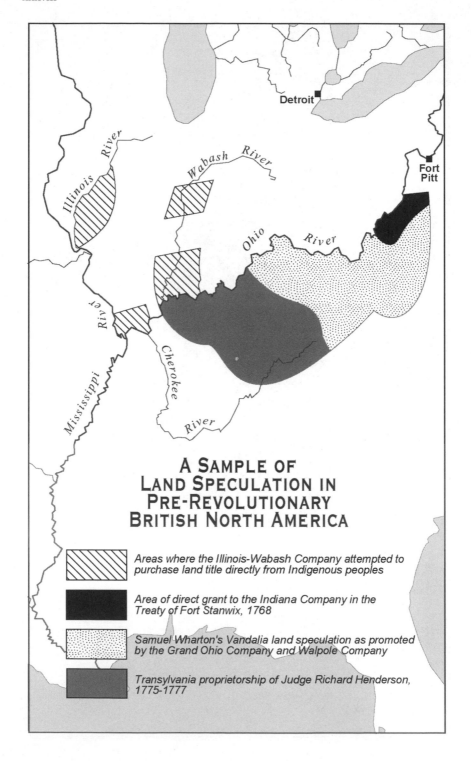

Detroit

Fort Pitt

Illinois River

Wabash River

Ohio River

Cherokee River

Mississippi River

A SAMPLE OF
LAND SPECULATION IN
PRE-REVOLUTIONARY
BRITISH NORTH AMERICA

Areas where the Illinois-Wabash Company attempted to purchase land title directly from Indigenous peoples

Area of direct grant to the Indiana Company in the Treaty of Fort Stanwix, 1768

Samuel Wharton's Vandalia land speculation as promoted by the Grand Ohio Company and Walpole Company

Transylvania proprietorship of Judge Richard Henderson, 1775-1777

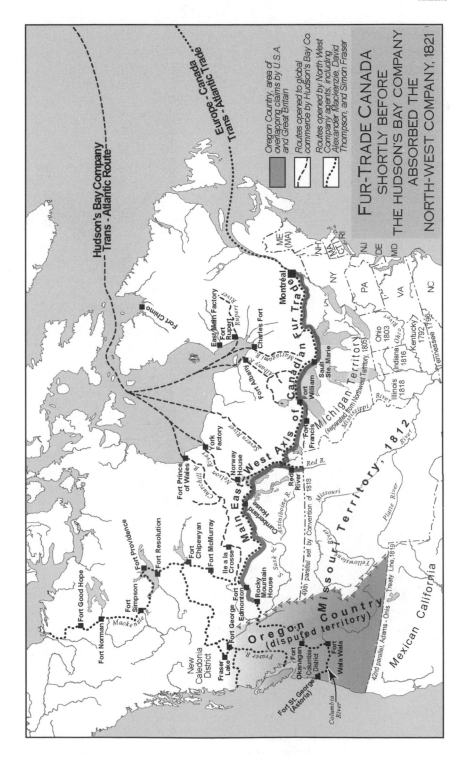

FUR-TRADE CANADA
SHORTLY BEFORE
THE HUDSON'S BAY COMPANY
ABSORBED THE
NORTH-WEST COMPANY, 1821

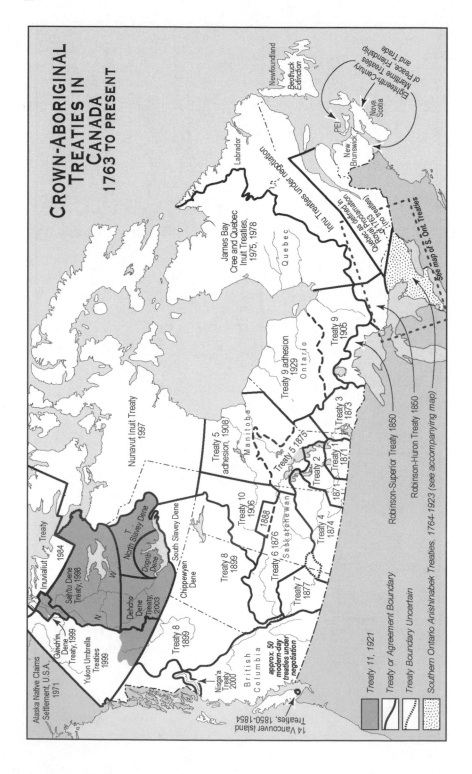

CROWN-ABORIGINAL TREATIES IN CANADA 1763 TO PRESENT

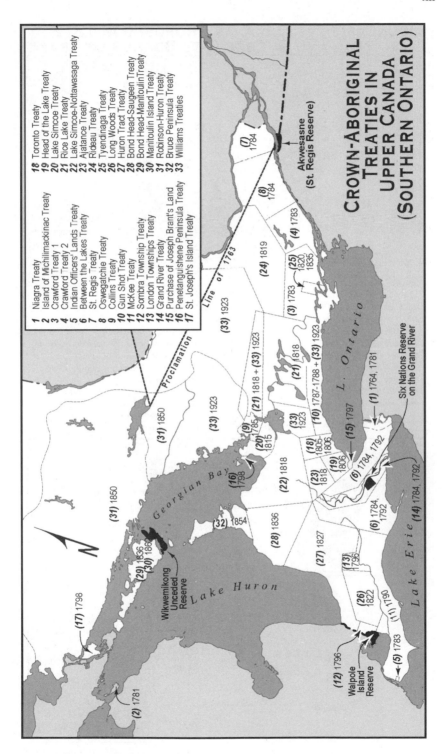

CROWN-ABORIGINAL TREATIES IN UPPER CANADA (SOUTHERN ONTARIO)

1 Niagra Treaty
2 Island of Michilimackinac Treaty
3 Crawford Treaty 1
4 Crawford Treaty 2
5 Indian Officers' Lands Treaty
6 Between the Lakes Treaty
7 St. Regis Treaty
8 Oswegatchie Treaty
9 Collins Treaty
10 Gun Shot Treaty
11 McKee Treaty
12 Sombra Township Treaty
13 London Townships Treaty
14 Grand River Treaty
15 Purchase of Joseph Brant's Land
16 Penetanguishene Peninsula Treaty
17 St. Joseph's Island Treaty

18 Toronto Treaty
19 Head of the Lake Treaty
20 Lake Simcoe Treaty
21 Rice Lake Treaty
22 Lake Simcoe-Nottawasaga Treaty
23 Ajatance Treaty
24 Rideau Treaty
25 Tyendinaga Treaty
26 Long Woods Treaty
27 Huron Tract Treaty
28 Bond Head-Saugeen Treaty
29 Bond Head-ManitoulinTreaty
30 Manitoulin Island Treaty
31 Robinson-Huron Treaty
32 Bruce Peninsula Treaty
33 Williams Treaties

BOUNDARIES OF U.S.A. AS PROPOSED IN 1812 BY MONTREAL AND QUEBEC CITY BOARDS OF TRADE

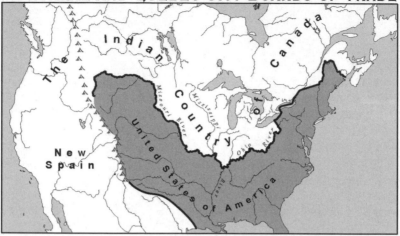

The Canadian Merchants argued that the Indians are *"the true proprietors of the territory. Their [Aboriginal] rights having never been acquired by us, could not be transferred to others without manifest injustice. This injustice was greatly aggravated by the consideration that those Aboriginal Nations had been our faithful allies during the American Rebellion now called Revolution – and yet no stipulation was made in their favour ... The boundary necessary for protection of Indian Rights and the Security of the Canadas in that quarter would be to run a line from the Sandusky on Lake Erie to the nearest waters running into the Ohio, then down that river and up the Mississippi to the mouth of the Missouri – then up the Missouri to its principal source and confining the American states to the Rocky Mountains as their western boundary, so that they can be excluded from at least all the country situated to the northward and westward of the line so designated and which country should remain wholly for the Indians and their hunting ground"* (See pages 400–2).

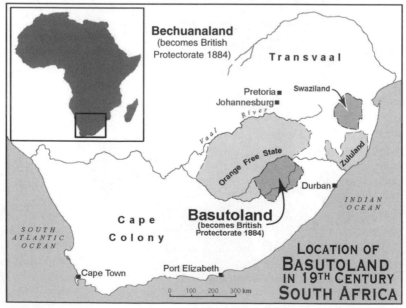

DARKENED AREAS INDICATE REGIONS OF THE UNITED STATES NOT COVERED BY RATIFIED INDIAN TREATIES

(AREAS WHERE NON-ABORIGINAL TITLES AND JURISDICTION REST ON THE DOCTRINE OF CONQUEST)

Tecumseh, Fred Loft, and George Manuel were all visionaries of the Fourth World who emphasized unity in diversity as the key to successful resistance against the inroads of colonization. (Courtesy Chicago Field Museum, neg. 3A93851.1C; National Archives of Canada, PA 7439; and the Union of British Columbia Indian Chiefs)

THE AMERICAN EMPIRE AND THE FOURTH WORLD

VOLUME ONE OF THE BOWL WITH ONE SPOON

The bowl with one spoon is an Aboriginal pictorial representation of the principle that certain hunting territories are to be held in common. In northeastern North America the image appeared frequently in the design of many wampum belts used to signify the terms of treaty agreements. In the era of Tecumseh the image came to signify the need for federal unity among Indigenous peoples if the shared Indian Country was ever to achieve sovereign recognition in international law.

Globalization
since 1492

What is new and what I find encouraging, is that national identity today is no longer tied to nation states, or even to aims of
creating states, but is often rooted in older kinds of community.
                    Erhard Eppler, West German Parliament, 1989

I pointed the yellow Pontiac Sunbird away from the interstate rush onto
the backroads just west of Albany, New York. As we left behind the smell of
burning tires and spewing diesel fumes, the air-borne scent of chemical
fertilizers filled our lungs. It was eased here and there by the fragrant
aroma of sweet grass. Beside me sat my eight-year old son, Sampson. I
glanced at him restlessly tugging at his tight-fitting Toronto Blue Jays baseball hat and rearranging big tufts of thick, black hair.

Sam was playing with the microphone device that enabled him to use
the car radio as a speaker system. He announced, "Next stop, the boring
history place where Daddy wants to go." Then he editorialized, "Daddy
should be staying on the highway so we can get to Marine Land in Niagara
Falls as soon as possible. I repeat, AS SOON AS POSSIBLE. Over and out." He
was impatient with me as I headed the car towards the community of Johnstown. Two weeks earlier I had pulled him out of school in Thunder Bay,
Ontario. I picked him up as I headed from my home in Lethbridge, Alberta, towards the Canadian east coast. I had negotiated with his mother and
his teacher to take him with me to the 1992 Learned Society conferences
at Charlottetown on Prince Edward Island.

"The Learneds" is the delightfully pretentious name given to a venera-
ble old institution in Canadian academia. Every year during those glorious
weeks when the winter term is over and summer is opening with all its fertile possibilities, most of the major professional associations of university
teachers in Canada arrange their annual meetings at a single institution.
The meetings continue, but the name has since been formally changed to
conform to the anti-elitist biases of the Politically Correct. Canadian academia is still miniature enough to allow for such a scholarly ritual, one that
would be unthinkable in the United States, given the vast size of the many-
faceted university culture there. The outcome of the Learned Society
assemblies in the crown dominion north of the American republic is a

national gathering of several thousand professors and graduate students from a variety of disciplines. Like academics everywhere, we Learned Canadians divide ourselves into a variety of groupings to read each other the papers on our most current research and to comment on one another's work.

Every year the organizers choose one topic as a unifying theme for the entire conference. In 1992 the interdisciplinary focus of the Learneds was the Indigenous peoples of the Americas in their five centuries of encounter with the colonists and non-Aboriginal settlers of their Aboriginal lands. The decision to set the Indigenous peoples of the hemisphere at the centre of professorial attention in 1992 was part of an international project of reconceptualizing the meaning of Europe's supposed discovery of the "New World."

Columbus's voyage of discovery 500 years before 1992 raised for all humanity profound questions, most of which remain far from resolved. Moreover, the quincentennary set the stage for the alignment of yet a larger number of zeroes in an anniversary – the beginning of the 2000th year since the death of Jesus Christ. The temporal end of that crucified man's days on earth was seized upon in Christendom to mark the end and the beginning of Western civilization's main means of calibrating the flow of time. For almost three-quarters of the years after the birth of Christ, the largest part of humanity was enclosed within separate localities, cut off from communication with all but neighbouring communities.

Although Columbus was certainly not the first transoceanic traveller to move between continents, his voyage in 1492 led to the most dramatic perceptual transformation in humanity's history. His well-publicized voyage confirmed that the world was not flat. Henceforth the realization passed from people to people that our celestial home is a globe, that its size is considerable, and that the planet hosts an amazingly diversified array of human societies as well as different plant and animal types almost beyond imagination. In *The Conquest of America*, Tzvetan Todorov commented on the unparalleled importance of the date 1492 as the marker of history's most monumental break with the past. He wrote, "even if every date that permits us to separate any two periods is arbitrary, none is more suitable, in order to mark the beginning of the modern era, than the year 1492, the year Columbus crosses the Atlantic Ocean."

We humans are still grappling with the problem of coming to terms with the magnitude of the change that occurred in the aftermath of Columbus's explorations. Without a doubt, his first voyage marked the moment when it started to become possible to conceive of anything like a single human family sharing a common fate. As Todorov noted, after 1492, humans discovered "the totality of which [we] are a part." Before that time, our ancestors "formed a part without a whole."[1] The date 1492 marks the moment when our current era of globalization began. More than five centuries after 1492 the variety of distinct species on the planet still has not been comprehensively counted and described. The pluralism of human culture offers a sociological equivalent to the biological diversity of life on the planet. The range of this cultural pluralism, like the extent of the globe's biodiversity, is thoroughly mind-boggling. Most of us will develop throughout our entire lifetime real familiarity with only a few of the thousands of different human cultures still existent on earth. Accordingly, we are still grappling with the problem of coming to terms with the magitude of the change that occurred in the aftermath of Columbus's explorations.

While a vast expansion of human knowledge of our environment took place in the early years of globalization, fiction as well as fact mingled together in what passed for truth.[2] The advent of 1992 presented the opportunity to address and correct some of the most persistent misinfor mation that attached itself to the original news that the world is round. Hence the quincentennary became a time when many of Columbus's original misapprehensions in 1492 finally received the serious, systematic, and sustained attention they deserve.[3]

Columbus initially thought that he had arrived at the outer islands of India rather than at the outlying archipelago of a huge double continent lying just beyond the horizons of Europe's official cosmologies. This mistake, which endures in the use of the term "Indian" to identify the hugely pluralistic range of Indigenous peoples of North, Central, and South America, is just one example of the persistent geographic, ethnographic, and legal confusions arising from Columbus's flawed cartography. In 1992 it was deemed no longer sensible or scientific to describe Columbus's transformative expedition in the Nina, the Pinta, and the Santa Maria as the discovery of a New World, as if the Old World of the ancient civilizations of the Americas somehow lay outside the authentic history of the human family. This acknowledgment led to the need to replace the historiography of European discovery, long a steady staple of social studies curricula for younger students, with narratives of *encounters* between distinct peoples.

Moreover, the prospect of *celebrating* the 500th anniversary of Columbus's arrival in the hemisphere, an idea initially advanced by officials in the United States and especially in Spain, soon became subject to doubt once various organizations of Indigenous peoples began to express their own views of what these last five centuries had meant for their societies. Clearly the year 1492 was the beginning of an era when four continents – Europe, Africa, and the Americas – began to merge into a transatlantic cultural complex. But the apportionment of the human costs and benefits from this convergence was disproportionately distributed, with the Europeans taking most of the assets, and the Africans and Aboriginal Americans taking most of the liabilities.

The various academic sessions on Aboriginal issues during the 1992 Learneds at Charlottetown were numbered among many similar exercises taking place at a variety of locales all over the planet. At all these events, and in the many publications that accompanied and elaborated what was said, the reality of the past and continuing colonization of Indigenous peoples was given serious intellectual attention. Their stories were inched away from the sidelines of humanity's collective memory to begin the process of becoming more fully integrated into the complex narrative weaves on the great themes of world history. The major unifying strand in this fabric is the process of *globalization,* a new word for an old process in dire need of careful historical interpretation.

In the eventful year of 1776, Adam Smith looked back in *The Wealth of Nations* on the process of globalization as it had developed up until his own day. His text is widely recognized as an intellectual marker of the transformation from mercantilism to capitalism, a transition with which the rise of the United States is paired. As a system of property law and as a philosophy of human interaction with the material realm, capitalism found its most efficient engine of expansion in the polity associated with the Declaration of Independence. That manifesto opened the way for the first exercise of decolonization in a European empire.

Introducing themes that Todorov would repeat centuries later, Smith wrote: "The discovery of America, and of the passage to the East Indies by the Cape of Good Hope, are the two greatest and most important events recorded in the history of mankind. Their consequences have been very great: but, in the short period of between two and three centuries which has elapsed since the discoveries were made, it is impossible that the whole extent of their consequences can have been seen. What benefits, or what misfortunes to mankind may hereafter result from these great events, no human wisdom can foresee." Smith continued by noting the disparity of power that enabled Europeans to commit "with impunity" great injustices on Indigenous peoples all over the planet. He expressed the hope that this tragedy would end. He speculated that "perhaps the natives of those countries may grow stronger, or those of Europe may grow weaker, and the inhabitants of all the different quarters of the world may arrive at that equality of courage and force which, by inspiring mutual fear, can alone overawe the justice of independent nations into some sort of respect for the rights of others."[4]

Smith rested these comments on a footnote, where he quoted in French a passage from Guillaume Raynal's new bestseller, *Histoire philosophique des establissements et du commerce des Européens dans les deux indes.* Raynal was one of those *philosophes* whose writings on all subjects invariably came back to condemnations directed at Europe's clerical and monarchical institutions. This attack on the ancient vested authority of the old regime contributed significantly to an atmosphere of unease that was about to become incarnate in extensive popular violence.

Like Smith's *Wealth of Nations,* Raynal's work was an integral part of the revolutionary tenor of those times of great intellectual and political fer-

ment that have come to be known as the Enlightenment. His anti-establishment influence would outlast the revolutionary culmination of the
eighteenth century. *Histoire philosophique*, which contained important contributions from the encyclopedist Denis Diderot, would become a vital text
behind the movement for the abolition of slavery in the nineteenth century.[5] The Enlightenment's domino effect on human rights activism, as
exemplified by the transformation in the 1830s of the British Anti-Slavery
Society into the Aborigines' Protection Society, would cast a long shadow
on our attempts to make a reckoning with history in 1992. Raynal saw in
the global transformations that began in 1492 "the beginning of a revolution in commerce, in the power of nations, in customs, in industry and the
government of all peoples – *le gouvernement de tous peuples.*"[6]

At Charlottetown in 1992, the legacy of 1492 offered a sharp focus for
observers to comment on the connection between Indigenous peoples
and the process of globalization that has joined all humanity into a single,
pluralistic polity. At no time before or since 1492, argued Todorov, has
there been an encounter as "astonishing" or as "intense" as that between
Europeans and the Indigenous peoples of the Americas.[7] The question of
what to make of that ongoing encounter or of others arising from similar
human interactions spurred by the global expansions of the Columbian
conquests after 1492 promises to loom as large for humanity in the second 500 years since Columbus's voyage as it did during the first 500 years.
In a small but significant way, this question would receive a major hearing
in Charlottetown in 1992, not only at the Learneds but in the deliberations surrounding a major proposal to change the constitution of the
last nation in the Americas to break its imperial ties with its European
mother country.

After our second or third day at the Charlottetown Learneds, Sam had
decided he wanted nothing more to do with the childcare facilities at the
University of Prince Edward Island. He opted instead to accompany me to
many sessions over the course of the week. I was impressed by his patience
and attentiveness. Together we took in talk after talk. We heard historians,
political scientists, law professsors, social workers, anthropologists, and
devotees of many other academic tribes give their interpretations of various aspects of the encounter between the First Nations and those who saw
this hemisphere primarily as a New World to be modelled as an extension
of Europe.

Some of the presenters, but primarily the law professors, were actively
engaged as consultants and advisers to various delegations in the negotiations that were piecing together the political compromise to elaborate and
renew the Canadian Constitution. One month later, again in Charlottetown, these fragments of legal tailoring were to be stitched together into a

major proposal for sweeping constitutional change that would, had it passed, have significantly altered the administrative structure of the largest country in the Americas. The political centre of gravity in the negotiations revolved around Quebec's relationship with Canada. By far the most unprecedented dimension of the process from the perspective of pan-American geopolitics, however, was the inclusion of four Aboriginal organizations in drawing up a blueprint for major changes in the governmental achitecture of a nation-state. Together these Aboriginal delegations, including the Inuit Tapirisat of Canada and the Assembly of First Nations, were making hemispheric and global history through their direct contributions to this effort.

The academic discussions at the Learneds on the legacy of 1492 found a direct and immediate conduit into a process of constitutional redesign – one of great potential significance not only to Canada but to all the countries and peoples affected by the ongoing course of the Columbian conquests. Many of the world's nation-states share a looming crisis of legitimacy if they fail to balance the New World heritage of the colonizing peoples and their descendants with the Old World continuity of those Indigenous peoples whose histories stretch back long before 1492. That crisis of legitimacy points with particular urgency at the United States, which is probably the least Indianized of all the countries of the Americas.

For his grace and good behaviour during the time we spent in Charlottetown, I had promised Sam that we would return to Thunder Bay via Niagara Falls and spend at least one day at the amusement park and aquatic zoo known as Marine Land. In planning our return route back from the Canadian Maritimes, I traced out a line on the roadmap running southwest through New England and straight west along the Mohawk Valley through the heart of New York state. My intentention was to make two stops along the journey, one for Sam at Niagara and one for me at Johnson Hall. As Sam and I approached Johnstown, I explained that this place name memorialized the British aristocrat, Sir William Johnson, the first superintendent of the Northern Division of the British Imperial Indian Department. The restored manor at the hub of Sir William's feudal estates, Johnson Hall, was the magnet pulling us forward. I learned from a tourist pamphlet that the site is one of five landmarks in the Saratoga Capital District Region maintained under the auspices of New York state's Office of Parks, Recreation and Historic Preservation.

Johnson Hall was raised in 1763. In the autumn of that year King George III of Great Britain signed a famous Royal Proclamation. Its effect was to make the lord of Johnson Hall, whose advice had influenced significantly the contents of the Royal Proclamation, one of the most influential men on the continent. Johnson's influence was connected to a tradition of treaty making with the Iroquois peoples indigenous to this region –

a tradition known as the Covenant Chain. I told Sam that Johnson Hall was one of the main shrines of both the Covenant Chain and British North America before the American revolt against British authority in 1776. Under the direction of the British sovereign, Sir William's responsibility was to extend the king's influence among the Indian nations through expanding trade and through elaborating the diplomatic protocols of the Covenant Chain. Because of the events leading up to the Royal Proclamation and what resulted from it, I had long come to think about Johnson Hall as one of North America's most significant historical sites, as important in its own way as anything we might see in Boston, Quebec City, Washington, D.C., New Orleans, Winnipeg, or San Francisco. Indeed, Johnson Hall was a primary site where the constitutional seeds of British imperial governance were germinated in preparation for their dissemination and cultivation throughout the transcontinental fur-trade empire centred on the St Lawrence–Great Lakes–Saskatchewan River axis.

Clearly, the officials in the United States who designate historical sites of national importance did not share my opinion. Johnson Hall was treated as a site of only secondary regional significance. The fact that it had belonged to a family on the Tory, conservative side of the American Revolution was part of the explanation why this place was not counted among the big-league monuments of America's national memory. The Johnsons were the heart and soul of Tory loyalty to the crown of Great Britain. Hence they were enemies rather than agents of republicanism. In their alliance both to the British monarch and to Indigenous peoples, the Johnsons were Old World obstacles to the expansionary agendas of Benjamin Franklin, Thomas Jefferson, George Washington, and the other aspiring makers of a New World empire constructed in the name of a sovereign people rather than a sovereign crown.

In my estimation, the lord of Johnson Hall personified many of the attributes that enabled the British Empire to expand so widely, often through flexible and ingenious adaptations to the pluralistic cultures of many Indigenous peoples. The diplomatic institution of the Covenant Chain, a complex of elaborate treaty protocols that connected the Six Nations Iroquois with the governors of New York colony, is a perfect example of the kind of transcultural invention through which the British Empire extended its web of influence around the planet.

As an aristocratic emigrant from Ireland who aspired to make his fortune in the fur trade and the land market of New York colony, Johnson identified business with the Six Nations and the diplomacy of the Covenant Chain as key centres of opportunity in the frontier economy surrounding him. With the backing of a rich uncle and the advice of Dutch merchants in the Albany area who had a long history of treaty diplomacy with the Six Nations, Johnson built up his estate in the 1740s and 1750s. As "Indian Affairs" became increasingly central to the outcome of the clash of the British and French empires in North America, Johnson's growing influence among the powerful Six Nations Iroquois was noticed with favour by imperial officials in London. It was reported that Johnson was "undefatigable among the Mohawks; he dressed himself after the Indian Manner, made frequent dances, according to their Custom when they excite to War."[8]

Johnson's influence among the Iroquois, and especially among certain Mohawk clans, was based on his reputation for dealing fairly with them and on his identification of British imperial interests in North America with the interests of this most famous of all Indian confederacies. In emphasizing the strategic importance of the Iroquois League to the security of British North America, Johnson built on principles and arguments already well advanced by former colonial officials, including Cadwallader Colden. Colden had previously been the British governor of New York who, in 1747, published an expanded edition of *The History of the Five Nations of Canada.*

Johnson backed up his assertions of friendship to the Iroquois in times of trouble by ordering the local militia under his command to fortify Iroquois villages. Similarly, he allowed Iroquois women and children to stay in the blockhouses of Fort Johnson, the forerunner of Johnson Hall, when Six Nations territories were under siege by the combined French and Indian forces that, until 1759, provided the military basis on which the fur-trade empire of Canada had coalesced.[9] A big part of Johnson's success in maintaining a degree of equilibrium between the Six Nations and the local non-Indian settlers on his estates was the persistence of the old feudal system of land tenure in that part of New York colony.[10] While Johnson's own fortune and his extensive patronage network were largely based on direct land grants from the Aboriginal inhabitants of the Mohawk Valley, the ethos of freehold land tenure – of private property – remained sufficiently in check to prevent many of the murderous, anti-Indian outrages that kept most of the Aboriginal groups along the frontiers of the Anglo-American settlements firm allies of the French.

The Mohawks gave Johnson the name *Warraghiyagey* – "he who does much business." A key aspect of creating the conditions for some of this business involved Johnson's ingratiating himself with the powerful women at the head of the Mohawks' matiarchal clan system. Johnson was famous for the presents he sent to Aboriginal clan mothers who could make or break the careers of many a fur trader. The nature of his attention to some of their daughters is, to this day, the subject of speculation and rumour, as Iroquois geneologists debate the number of people in Indian Country who can situate Sir William on their family tree.[11] Johnson's most important female partner in Mohawk Country was *Konwatsi'tsiaienne*, whose English name was Molly Brant.

Described in his personal records as "my faithful housekeeper," Molly Brant was Johnson's confidant, adviser, lover, and the acknowledged mother of several Johnson children. She was also a powerful matron

among the Mohawk, a woman who helped her clan and nation understand how they could best manipulate in their own self-interests the growing dependence of British imperialism in North America on the status,
image, and influence of the famed Six Nations League. Together, Molly
and William groomed her younger brother, *Thayendanegea*, or Joseph
Brant, for the pivotal role he would play in the politics of the Covenant
Chain and in the strategic defence of what would become British imperial Canada, especially after the outbreak of civil war in British North America after 1776.[12]

In 1755 the conduct of Indian Affairs was officially removed from the
jurisdiction of the local Anglo-American colonies and made an arm of
the imperial government under the direct authority of the British monarch.
As a result of this fateful reorganization, Johnson was given the top job
as the British sovereign's personal representative in the Northern Division of the British Imperial Indian Department. In my view, this new centre of imperial authority in northeastern North America became the
jurisdictional seed from which the growth of English-speaking Canada
began. The fact that the present-day federal Department of Indian
Affairs and Northern Development can be traced back directly to the
founding in 1755 of the British Imperial Indian Department provides
clear evidence that the essential origins of English-speaking Canada go
back to the politics of the Covenant Chain and the network of fur traders
and administrators whose activities revolved around the extraordinary
career of Sir William Johnson.[13]

Suddenly, the outlines of the imposing building I was looking for lay
straight ahead. These outlines were familiar to me from the often published painting of E.L. Henry. This image is reproduced, for instance, on
the cover of Francis Jennings's *Empire of Fortune*, the concluding volume of
the Covenant Chain trilogy, which has been a major influence on the interpretations presented here. Henry's work depicts a solemn treaty gathering,
complete with elaborately uniformed Red Coats and pipe-smoking
sachems, on the lawn between the blockhouses on either side of Johnson's
home. The parking lot we entered had only three or four cars. We walked
around the building and entered the main hallway from the back. The
woodwork of the well-maintained structure was hefty, yet finely crafted.
The carpenters' artisanship was especially evident in the durable engineering of the stairway and the utilitarian grace or Sir William's magnificent writing desk. The correspondence that had crossed this desk was
weighty in bulk, sophistication, and historical significance. The Johnson
Papers, which were published over a fourty-four-year interval, fill fifteen
dense volumes.[14]

Johnson's desk was the source of a rich stream of strategic advice vital to the imperial governance of British North America. When George III chose Johnson to lead the Northern Division of the newly created British Imperial Indian Department directly on his behalf, the thinking was that diplomacy with the Indigenous peoples was an essential feature of the mother country's foreign policy. Oversight of this area was too important to be left in the hands of officials who drew their authority from the local legislatures representing the land-hungry Anglo-American settlers.

If the alliance linking the Indians of Canada to the forces of French imperialism in North America was to be broken, Great Britain would have to coordinate and devote significant resources to this important area of statecraft. The wisdom of the new British imperial Indian policy was demonstrated during the course of the Seven Years' War, or the French and Indian War as the conflict is tellingly remembered in the United States. The most contested ground of this imperial war was the Ohio Valley.[15] Moreover, the primary prize for the military defeat of France's North American army in the Seven Years' War was the expansion of Britain's claims into the Indian Country of Canada, a vast domain emanating outwards in all directions from the Great Lakes. King George's Royal Proclamation of 1763 ushered in the new constitutional order, based in large measure on extending as peacefully as possible the diplomatic protocols of the Covenant Chain. The proclamation also established a new British colony called Quebec in the St Lawrence Valley heartland of the former New France. As well, it created a fixed boundary whose intent was to halt and then to regulate under imperial authority the westward expansion of the Anglo-American settlements and colonies into the Indian Country.

As Sam and I walked the site of Johnson Hall, a simplified picture began to coalesce in my imagination. I saw the fields and orchards of a multicultural mix of non-Indian settlers, including German speakers and Catholic Highlanders from Scotland, spread out around the east-facing front yard of Sir William's estate. As I walked around to the other side of the building, I looked westward along the length of the famous Mohawk Valley stretching out to Oswego, the Great Lakes, the Saskatchewan and Missouri River systems, and all the way to the Pacific and Arctic oceans. Sir William Johnson's backyard was, for one fleeting historical moment, a kind of gateway to the Indian Country of Canada. Moreover, the elaborate intricacies of the Covenant Chain, a laboratory of human relationships whose centres of advanced learning included Johnson Hall, seemed for Great Britain's imperial planners the key to building creatively on the heritage of Dutch-Iroquois relations. They hoped to extend the influence of the British Empire westward into the vast fur-trade country that had become a somewhat cohesive polity under the commercial and diplomatic influence of Montreal in the era of New France.

In 1763 the original Five Iroquois Nations – the Mohawk, the Oneida, the Onondaga, the Cayuga, and the Seneca – were still entrenched, if perilously, as the sovereign landlords of their strategic, trans-Appalachian pass between the Hudson River and Lake Ontario. This heartland they described metaphorically as their extended lodge, their longhouse. Beyond the Mohawk Valley lay the many predominantly Algonkian-speaking nations of the Great Lakes area, the great inland sea that lay at the heart of the Indian Country of Canada. In 1763 Sir William sought to extend the diplomacy of the Covenant Chain and of the British Empire to those Indian nations of Canada whose history for several generations had been that of enemies of both the Iroquois and the *Jogginosh*, the Algonkian term for the English.

As I absorbed the sweet summer rays, I projected myself back to the time when this spot was at the gateway of a new North American country whose mode of growth would be through the extension of trade and negotiated collaboration with the Indigenous peoples. Going back to the earliest beginnings of New France, Iroquoian speakers had given the name "Canada" to the world. Some of the immigrants from France and Holland had, together with their descendants, led the way in systematically adapting themselves to the languages, laws, and the cultures of the Indigenous peoples. They ceased to think of themselves so much as the creators of a *New* France or a *New* Netherlands and worked at finding middle ground with the Old World, Aboriginal peoples on their frontiers and in their midst.

One of the major adaptations that took place at Johnson Hall during the time of its most strategic importance for the British Empire was the process of borrowing from both the older colonial strategies of the Dutch and the French as well as from the cultures of the First Nations. The genius of Sir William Johnson was to shape, by means of his extended household, an adapted version of this means of expansion through collaboration with Indigenous peoples, but within the framework of the British imperialism.

What developed in the mid-eighteenth century in the Mohawk Valley was a complex of hybrid cultures linking Indians and newcomers with sufficient strength that they were able to move collectively into the vacuum of leadership after the French army was vanquished from the continent. These practitioners of the Covenant Chain were able to continue the development of Canada through the fur trade, much as Canada had evolved in the era of New France. Sir William Johnson was the key figure to oversee and facilitate the geopolitical continuity of the Indian Country of Canada after the defeat of the French military in 1759 on the towering heights of Fortress Quebec.

Some of those who migrated westward, but especially the Puritans, were inclined to look with intolerant disfavour at the prolific mixing and blending of cultures, values, and morals that characterized the assertive multiculturalism of Johnson Hall. In New England, unlike New France or New Netherlands, very little space was afforded to the development of any kind

of middle ground with the Indigenous peoples. The rebellion of those dis-
affected from the authority of the British Empire was in some measure an
effort to pre-empt the further development of the kind of country that was
developing in and around Johnson Hall, the crown's main fortress of Toryism in the North American interior. Accordingly, the American Revolution
facilitated the rejection by the emergent republic of the political, economic, and ideological complexes reflected in the transcultural democracy of the Covenant Chain and in the conservative brand of entrepreneurship cultivated at Johnson Hall. The American Revolution was similarly an
assault on the regime of crown property law that protected the hunting
grounds and the Aboriginal title of the Indigenous peoples in the Indian
Country west of the Appalachian Mountain chain. The primary crown official charged to protect these Aboriginal titles from the encroachment of
the Anglo-American colonists and their local governments was the lord at
Johnson Hall.

In 1991, the year before Sam and I visited Johnson Hall, some of these
ideas were elaborated by Heather Divine at a conference of academic specialists on the fur trade who assembled at historic Mackinac Island near the
strategic centre of the Great Lakes. Divine's paper focused on the links of
continuity between the society at Johnson Hall and the development of the
famous North West Company. In the decades following the American Revolution, this company, whose headquarters were in Montreal, would
extend the fur-trade empire of Canada northward to the Arctic Ocean and
westward and southward as far as the Pacific coast of what are now the
American states of Washington and Oregon.

Some of the families and individuals assimilated into the culture of Johnson Hall would go on to extend the Covenant Chain legacy of treaty alliances
with Indigenous peoples throughout the transcontinental extent of British
imperial Canada. One such individual was Simon McTavish. As Devine
explained, this most influential of Montreal entrepreneurs got his start in
the fur trade by working in the entourage of Sir William Johnson. Among
the most energetic of the Catholic Highlanders from Scotland to find profit in the fur trade as well as employment in the imperial Indian administration surrounding Sir William were the prolific Macdonnels. One of their offspring, Allan, would be instrumental in the mid-ninteenth century in
insisting on the importation of the constitutional regime of the Royal Proclamation into the Canadian North-West, even as the fur-trade economy gave
way to the economy of railways, mining, forestry, and privatized agriculture.

The northern Michigan location where Divine delivered her paper had
once been a strategic centre of the Canadian fur trade. In describing the
Tory multiculturalism that prevailed at Johnson Hall in the decade before
the American Revolution, she said:

The mansion itself was a hive of activity, with individuals of diverse race, color, and
creed – black slaves, Mohawk Indians, German tradespeople, British army officers

and Indian Department officials, Irish relatives and cronies, visiting gentry from
the cities – all going about their business in the entourage of Sir William Johnson.
Outside the mansion, militia units, comprised of Johnson's tenants and local community members, practised their drills under the watchful eye of Sir William Johnson himself. The regular activities of the Indian Department attracted groups of
Indians, who camped on the grounds of the estate. During his stay at Johnson
Hall, [Simon] McTavish would have observed the civil and even preferential treatment accorded to the Natives by Johnson and his non-Native associates, noting
they had free access to the house and surrounding property even though their
peaceable incursions would leave these areas in a perpetual state of untidiness. He
[McTavish] may have been personally acquainted with Molly and Joseph Brant,
the influential Mohawks so closely associated with Johnson's success in Indian
diplomacy. He may also have become acquainted with some of Johnson's mixed-
blood children, although Johnson sent most of his children away for formal
schooling until a local school was established to serve both tenant and Johnson-
family children.[16]

In her presentation, Divine spoke of the disapproving onlookers who felt
menaced by what they saw happening at Johnson Hall:

Even before Johnson's death [in 1774], there were rumblings of discontent in the
Mohawk Valley. New England freeholders who had recently moved into the area
resented both the royal sympathies of Johnson and his political, social, and economic domination of the entire region. They also distrusted the members of Johnson's immediate and extended "family" – his German, Irish, and Scottish tenants,
the functionaries within the Indian Department and the Mohawk Indians. Johnson's associates were disliked not only because they were culturally alien to the New
Englanders but because they posed a formidable military threat to the rebel
cause.[17]

Many of the founders of British imperial Canada were formed and influenced by the ambiance and activity in and around Johnson Hall. These
individuals provided some of the main personifications of those ideas and
principles opposed by the makers of the American Revolution. The oppo-
sitional forces aligned against this centre of British imperial Canada
helped establish the political and ideological basis of the coalition of interests that came together to form the United States of America. If the monocultural liberalism of the melting pot, together with the pre-eminence of
freehold land tenure, provided the thesis that gave rise to the American
empire, then the antithesis was the multicultural conservatism of Johnson
Hall. The feudal nature of Johnson's estates combined with the collectivist
orientation of the system of land tenure integral to the property relationship of both Indian Country and the fur trade of Canada.

These conservative principles were not extinguished in North America
by the success of the American Revolution. Instead, this Tory response to

the Whiggish ascendance embodied in the new republic found expression in the transcultural business regime of the North West Company and in the diplomatic protocols that extended the transcultural democracy of the Covenant Chain to the wider fields of crown recognition of existing Aboriginal and treaty rights.

❖

I was startled from my reverie by the menacing sounds emerging from the nearby wooded thicket where Sam and a couple of new-found American friends were playing. The happy tones of laughter had been given over to yells and whoops and guttural utterances connoting a reversion into some kind of war game. I approached the mock battle zone to investigate. The boys, I saw, were engaged in a variation on a game of cowboys and Indians. They switched roles from time to time, but always the nature of their playful interaction was as feigned enemies. The boy or boys in the cowboy role invariably swaggered. The would-be Indians' tactic of survival and revenge was concealment and surprise attack. After watching the action for a few minutes, I intervened. I tried to explain that the kind of interactions which had historically taken place on this famous treaty-council ground did not remotely resemble the kind of warring contest I had just witnessed between imagined cowboys and pretend Indians.

As I spoke, I could see Sam was quite embarrassed by my attempt to become his new friends' self-designated interpreter on the meaning of this place. Once again he rolled his dark brown eyes and stuck his tongue into his cheek in a way that signalled he did not approve. On the other hand, I thought I detected in his gesture a certain affectionate tolerance for his father's idiosyncratic preoccupation with "boring history places" like this one. "Let's hightail it outa here," Sam suggested, pulling down the peak of his Blue Jays baseball cap to indicate he meant business. By this time we stood alone on the edge of the woodlot. My historical interpretation, it seemed, was enough to scare away the two children who had re-enacted with Sam the primal fantasy of America's ascent from Indian to cowboy, from war zone to serene pasture land, from tee-pee to sky scraper, from Indian path to super highway, from tomahawks to nuclear weapons, from savagery to civilization.

There is very little in the iconography and vocabulary of North-America's popular culture to take into account the kind of treaty diplomacy with Indigenous peoples that provided the context for the original operation of Johnson Hall or for the extraordinary careers of those men and women, Indian and non-Indian, whose activities revolved around this essential shrine of North American history. It would take a lot of creative historical footwork in both the classroom and the media to envisage a day when treaty games between Red Coats and Indians might remotely approach the appeal of war games between cowboys and Indians. And what centre of influence could have greater effect on the consequential games we play as adults than the ostensibly harmless games we play as children?

I resisted Sam's blandishments that it was time to go. I wanted to learn what I could from the tour guide, who obviously took considerable pride in the responsibility he carried as the resident expert on Johnson Hall. I related my little story about the cowboy and Indian play fight I had just witnessed and how far removed this kind of imagined interaction was from what really happened here in the era before the American Revolution. The guide grinned and launched into his own account of the difficulty experienced by many visitors to Johnson Hall in envisaging the nature of this historic site. "You would not believe," he declared, "how many people who come here ask me to show them where the soldiers fired at the Indians." He continued, "when I tell them that this place had quite a different purpose, the visitors often don't seem to get it. They can't seem to imagine any kind of military installation on US territory whose purpose was anything other than advancing the war on Indian Country and securing the land from Indian retalliation."

As Sam and I drove away from Johnson Hall, I remembered the events of the train blockade at his home reserve of Long Lake 58, about 200 miles northeast of Thunder Bay. We both retained deep imprints from the week we had spent together in August 1990 at the protest camp on the main line of the Canadian National Railway. The spirit of our train blockade north of Lake Superior proved contagious. For a time, several Ojibway communities had effectively severed east-west rail communications in Canada. The actions were part of a wide mobilization of activist energy that broke out in many local confrontations identified collectively as the Indian summer of 1990.[18]

Two episodes started the domino effect that shaped the surprising events of that period. One was the stand of Elijah Harper, an Oji-Cree member of the Legislative Assembly in Manitoba. A fluke of history enabled Harper to block ratification of a significant contitutional amendment known as the Meech Lake accord.[19] The other episode was the armed Indian defence against the transformation of an Indian burial ground into an enlarged golf course at Oka, Quebec. That confrontation quickly escalated, to the point where it involved the blockage by the Mohawk Warriors of a major bridge in Montreal spanning the St Lawrence River. Several thousand Canadian soldiers eventually intervened as Canada came far closer to outright civil war than is generally recognized.

I had not taken Sam with me when I left the train blockade, along with Long Lake 58 band councillor Bernard Abraham, to confer in late August with various sides during the height of the Oka crisis. Earlier that summer, however, Sam and I and my other son, Riley, had been together in Winnipeg to witness the elaborate Aboriginal ceremonies attending the demise of the infamous Meech Lake accord. With us during that time of the summer solstice were perhaps 10,000 mobilized citizens of Indian Country. We had converged on the capital of the province founded by Métis leader Louis Riel to celebrate and substantiate with our physical presence the wide popular support behind Elijah Harper's stand.

The outpouring of creative energy from Indian Country during those heady days in June was wonderful to behold. In the parkland surrounding the Manitoba Legislature and at a number of hastily organized events at the Winnipeg Convention Centre there was an outburst of dancing, song-writing, T-shirt designing, speech making, pipe smoking, and sunrise ceremonies that combined with rare, hopeful synergy to announce all manner of personal and collective empowerment. Shock waves of inspiration as well as resentment burst on the rest of the country from that ground zero of ideological combustion – an explosion of thought and action that radically changed the course of subsequent Canadian history.

Although the events of the train blockade were certainly the most intense and deeply personal of the protest actions in which Sam and I had taken part, we had also shared each other's company at many other demonstrations of Indian Country's determined resolve to resist subjugation. We were, for instance, on the Red Squirrel Road in Temagami, Ontario, when First Nations peoples and non-Aboriginal environmentalists attempted to block the Ontario government from opening a thoroughfare into one of the last major stands of old-growth forest in that part of North America. Among those arrested was Bob Rae, who just months later was elected as premier of Ontario.[20]

The land dispute in Temagami was the testing ground for many careers, legal theories, and political strategies that would, in later years, make their influence felt at a number of sites throughout the continent where the assertion of existing Aboriginal and treaty rights met the drive to secularize and privatize natural resources.[21] Bruce Clark, the lawyer who spearheaded the legal effort to force the federal and provincial governments to address the existence of an unceded Aboriginal title in Temagami, was one of those schooled in the complexities of this important land dispute. He later applied many of the insights he gained in Temagami to a provocative interpretation of the very old and bitter dispute over Aboriginal rights that promises to dominate the politics, legal profession, and economy of British Columbia for many years to come.[22]

As with Clark and our mutual colleague Splitting The Sky, my own research energies were drawn after the summer of 1990 to the hotbed of contention and argument over the domestic and international status of Aboriginal title in British Columbia. On the basis of information supplied to me especially by Splitting The Sky, a veteran of the Mohawk Warriors and of the Attica prison uprising of 1971, I was pulled to investigate the complex circumstances and backgound of a major cover-up involving the intervention of the Canadian military, without parliamentary approval, at the Battle of Gustafsen Lake in 1995.[23] Splitting The Sky was the sundance captain of an Aboriginal religious ceremony that evolved into an armed confrontation involving the largest mobilization of government fighting forces in resource-rich western Canada since the crushing of the Métis resistance movement led by Louis Riel in 1885.

I found it telling that the Canadian government under Prime Minister Jean Chrétien would direct its military machinery so deeply into the centre of Canada's most complex and delicate human rights issue. This approach to modern-day Indian fighting was apparently acceptable to opposition politicians and the media, which cooperated with the police and their political masters to feed the public a steady stream of lies and distortions. "Not even the most professional and skilled of the scribes had the grit to step back and ask tough questions," noted *Vancouver Province* journalist Joey Thompson in her article "Media Should Apologize for Gullibility on Gustafsen Lake."[24]

My interest in the Gustafsen fiasco led to my invitation from the Federal Public Defender Office in Portland, Oregon, to give expert testimony in the extradition proceedings in the case of *USA* v. *James Pitawanakwat*. In her ruling on that case, Judge Janice Stewart overruled the us State Department – in other words, the executive branch of the us government. Citing the poltical offence exception in Article 4 of the Extradition Treaty between Canada and the United States, Judge Stewart denied the executive branch's request to send Pitawanakwat, an Indian veteran of the Battle of Gustafsen Lake, back to British Columbia. Judge Stewart's ruling in November 2000 essentially projected many constitutional issues surrounding the existence of Aboriginal and treaty rights in North America into the arena of us foreign policy.[25] Some of the evidence I brought forward in Pitawanakwat's trial was drawn from my research in preparing this text. Certain of my findings, presented here publically for the first time, have already made an impact, therefore, on American jurisprudence and on the content of us foreign policy, but especially as it relates to Canada.

The elevation of these matters to questions of foreign affairs for the world's sole superpower opened a Pandora's box of unresolved issues of international law pertaining to Aboriginal affairs in North America. These issues figured prominently in the War of 1812, in questions relating to Sitting Bull's legal status after his flight to Canada in 1876 after his military defeat of us forces at the Battle of Little Bighorn, and in the flawed legal proceedings leading to the extradition from Canada in 1976 of Indian activist Leonard Peltier. As Judge Stewart ruled in the Pitawanakwat case in commenting on Peltier's removal from Canada to face murder charges in the United States, his extradition was based on "false affidavits."

In her decision to extend us protection to Pitawanakwat against his politically motivated persecution by the government of Canada, Judge Stewart concluded that "the Gustafsen incident involved an organized group of native people rising up in their homeland against the occupation by the government of Canada of their sacred and unceded tribal land." She referred to 77,000 rounds of government fire shot into the protest camp, to the use of Canadian government land mines and to the deployment of an elaborate "smear and disinformation campaign."[26] This campaign was orchestrated by the Royal Canadian Mounted Police through their manipulation of Canada's print and broadcast media, including the crown-owned Canadian Broadcasting Corporation. The purpose of this campaign of officially sanctioned lies was to discredit the self-declared Ts'peten Defenders, including their lawyer of choice, Bruce Clark, and to divert attention away from the complex issues of constitutional and international law Clark had attempted to raise on behalf of his clients during their controversial stand.

As I drove westward with Sam along the Mohawk Valley Highway back in 1992, I wondered where the discussions initiated at the Charlottetown Learneds were pointing us. I wondered how the international dimension of the questions we had debated academically would be played out politically. As in many parts of North America, the road signs pointed to places with Indian names where few Aboriginal people live. I tried to picture this famous valley when in was dotted with corn fields and thick with busy villages, each one packed with longhouses dominated by the legendary matriarchs of the Haudonosaunee clans. The border up ahead beckoned – the *international* border. From the early times of colonization, Niagara Falls has been one of North America's most internationally acclaimed natural spectacles. Its historic importance, however, goes far beyond tourism. Niagara was one of those strategic places of power in North America where the empires of France and Britain, and then the New World empire of the United States, wrestled for geopolitical advantage. Often this quest for hegemony and control motivated the agents of empire to become deeply engrossed in the internal rivalries of the Indigenous peoples.

As twilight turned to night, the idea for this book began to coalesce. I resolved I would try to come up with a text expansive and comprehensive enough to demonstrate the richness of the connections linking the history of Johnson Hall, for example, to the dynamic eruptions of Indian Country that are integral to our own time.

On further reflection, it seemed that even the outlines of North America could not contain the kind of connections and transformations that are crying out for sustained and analytic synthesis. Although the historical rethinking that emerged from the 500th anniversary of 1492 tended to put the American hemisphere in the forefront, for example, the legacies of the interrelated imperialisms emanating from Spain, Portugal, England, France, Holland, Belgium, Russia, and Germany clearly advanced the imposition of foreign laws and institutions on Indigenous peoples all over the world. Without some reckoning with this larger frame of reference, much of the broader meaning of local instances of colonization and resistance will be lost.

As I began to conceive of this project, I reflected on the need to identify the connections linking transformations in Aboriginal identities to the construction of those imagined communities that have emerged from the expansion of European empires and from the Creole nationalisms dating from the earlier phases of the Columbian conquests. By and large these new nationalisms in the Americas were invented by transplanted Europeans who sought to distance themselves from both the metropolitan control of their imperial rulers and the claims of the Indigenous peoples of the hemisphere. This exercise in Creole identity politics has had important implications for the character and growth of the informal global empire that arose particularly from the frontier expansions of the United States. I determined I would describe this historical progression from my own vantage point in Canada, a country deeply integrated into the American empire but, for the time being at least, outside the federal framework of the United States.

As the project began to take form, I became increasingly interested in the economic dimensions of what happens when the expansionary forces of European empires and their successor states encroach on the lives and livelihoods of Indigenous peoples. In particular, the enormity of the philosphical, legal, cultural, and social changes suggested by the word "privatization" emerged for me as a powerful conceptual tool. The more I identified the notion of moving frontiers with the idea of globalization, the more central to my concerns became those specific historical processes involved in subjecting vast new realms of matter to the law and ethos of private property. The process of privatizing the commons, perhaps the most primal and essential legal procedure unifying more than five centuries of history in the Americas, pointed to the effort to imagine and then implement theories of sovereignty well suited to this task. Without a doubt, the emergence of the United States from the British Empire was in large measure a procedure to forge a new kind of sovereignty better suited to the task of rapidly and efficiently transforming new frontiers of matter into private property.

The way we construct sovereignty is deeply intertwined with our conceptualization and implementation of democracy. The more I thought about the dilemmas of democracy facing virtually all the world's peoples, the more the growing conflicts in and around Johnson Hall appeared to be seminal expressions of some of the most contentious and unresolved questions of our own times. How can democracy be made to conform better to the transcultural and intercultural realities that are integral to the process of globalization?

The tensions between two philosophies of law and governance that burst onto the world stage in 1776 were not resolved by the peace settlement that established the United States of America. Indeed, some of the most basic philosophical and economic contentions of the American Revolution remain almost as divisive today as at the time when George Washington and Sir William Johnson came to personify two different approaches to the governance of North America. In some of our most fundamental political choices in the new millennium, these contentions have been extended, amplified, and even globalized.

The war of values and ideas that once swirled in and around Johnson Hall was transported more deeply into the geography and psyche of North America in the War of 1812. That conflict included the most concerted military campaign ever undertaken by a confederacy of Aboriginal freedom fighters to resist the westward expansion of the United States. This campaign of peoples asserting their inherent rights of self-determination – a campaign waged against a country that saw itself as the world's beacon of liberty and democracy – takes on many new meanings in an era when the rhetoric of free trade is cited to justify the pre-emption of many old sovereignties and local idiosyncrasies. The Aboriginal freedom fighters of Tecumseh's generation endeavoured to escape the horrors of ethnic cleansing by seeking the protection of international law. This quest failed because, in that era no less than now, the franchise of those qualified to negotiate on the most extended frontiers of global geopolitics was extremely narrow. In Tecumseh's era, only the representatives of white Europeans and their far-flung progeny were considered eligible for recognized status at the imperial negotiating tables. There the world's borders were drawn and redrawn with virtually no say afforded to those Indigenous peoples whose ancestral lands were parcelled out.

The new imperialsim of the informal American empire is deeply rooted in the old imperialisms of Europe. The empires of Europe merge with the transnational empire of universalized capitalism in an increasingly globalized system of property law whose cumulative effect has been to privatize growing portions of the world's wealth in narrower and narrower circles of concentrated ownership and control. In the transformation to a single imperial regime of globalized commerce, Europe's most brash, rebellious, and ingenious of proteges, the United States, played a disproportionately large role. The influence and example of the United States contributed to the liberal rhetoric of free trade, which dominated the process leading to the creation of new agencies of supranational governance such as the World Trade Organization or the North American Free Trade Authority. The legal procedures used to legitimize these new instruments of standardized property law, however, were just as exclusionary in their own way as those high tables of imperialism that oversaw the division of the planet in earlier centuries.

In the tradition of the European imperialists and their New World proxies, the makers of these most recent institutional media of globalized commerce apportioned the lands and resources of Indigenous peoples as though there was little to distinguish these old human polities from the plants and animals of the earth's recolonized soil. The potential in this genre of injustice to activate resistance – to enliven broad social movements – was suggested in the wide public support that mobilized behind the Zapatista revolt in Mexico against NAFTA, the most recent extension of the Columbian conquests that began in 1492. The continuing resistance of Indigenous peoples to their own extinguishment may be emblematic of things to come if the disenfranchised and dispossessed majority of humanity rise up to oppose the further concentration of privatized wealth in fewer and fewer hands.

This line of thinking led me to devote considerable attention to the relationship of Indigenous peoples to corporations. For many generations after 1492 these legal inventions were the primary instruments to extend the jurisdiction of European sovereigns into foreign lands. One need only contemplate the names of the Hudson's Bay Company, the English East India Company, the African Lakes Company, the Levant Company, the Muscovy Company, the British South African Company, or the Dutch East India Company to gain a sense of the enormous influence of these enterprises in globalizing the culture, power, and acquisitive grasp of Europe. In its outreach to the world, the culture of European imperialism has largely been expressed as corporate culture. Like so many features of the American empire, the United States concentrated and distilled the expansive corporate culture it inherited from Europe.

This first generation of global corporation was born of the charter-making powers vested in their sovereign creators. The biggest of the corporate progeny of the original crown corporations, however, increasingly operate as if they have acquired a kind of free-standing sovereignty independent of any empire or nation-state. Indeed, the most powerful corporate conglomerates of capital, technology, and expertise have become a rule of law unto themselves, capable of avoiding or neutralizing the authorities of those public governments on whose chartering powers they still theoretically depend.

One of the aims I set in writing this text is to demonstrate how the interaction between corporations and Indigenous peoples, especially on the moving frontiers of the American empire, has been instrumental in the ascent of the largest of these institutions to their present position of global prominence. So influential have these truly global corporations collectively become that they have subordinated all other forms of human organization, including those nation-states that theoretically still monopolize the exercise of sovereignty in international law.

Corporate law has, in many instances, penetrated so deeply into the cultures and lands of Indigenous peoples that there is a growing trend to frame what is often identified as Aboriginal self-government in the legal wrappings of corporate charters emanating from the sovereign authority of national, state, or provincial governments. This effort to enwrap and express Aboriginal rights through the enterprise of business corporations was central to the Alaska Claims Settlement Act of 1971. It was also integral to a number of modern-day treaties, especially throughout northern Canada, including those with the Inuvialuit of the Beaufort Sea area and the Inuit of Nunavut. More recently, the Nisga'a Treaty in British Columbia described the Nisga'a governments to be established as "natural persons," the term that is frequently used in English-language law to identify corporations.

These kinds of adaptations, whose more flamboyant symbols include the Foxwood Casino of the Connecticut Pequots or the Rama Casino of the Ontario Anishinabek, are sometimes heralded as the dawning of a benvolent form of Aboriginal capitalism. However, the older pattern linking corporate expansion directly to the extinguished rights and titles of Indigenous peoples continues to prevail in most situations. As will be demonstrated in this project, the expansion of, for instance, the United Fruit Company, the International Nickel Corporation, Hydro-Quebec, Diashowa-Marubeni International, Monsanto, Eletronorte in Brazil, or Shell Oil in Nigeria have all been directly connected to the violated rights and freedoms of Indigenous peoples.

In writing about interactions and encounters on the frontiers where Indigenous peoples, along with their lands and resources, are subjected to alien regimes of governance and law, I am conscious that I am participating in the elaboration of very old and complex genres of literature. I trust that the richness of these branches of scholarship and reportage will become more familiar to those readers dedicated enough to survey or explore the research girding this project, as cited in the extensive notes accompanying each chapter. I believe I am entering a particularly fertile belt of interpretive tradition in arguing that early interactions between those on both sides of the expanding and imploding frontiers of empire are prone to have formative and lasting ramifications, especially for new societies that take shape on the foundations of these precedents. The patterns begun in the treatment of Indigenous peoples tend to carry over to influence and shape the genesis of many other kinds of relationship.

One of the most eloquent contributors to this way of looking at the process of culture change, especially in the Americas, is Wendell Berry. Since his *Unsettling of America: Culture and Agriculture* first appeared in 1977, it has been recognized as a classic contribution to that genre of writing devoted to explorations in the arts and sciences of ecology. Berry begins his text by explaining that the early urge to displace the Indigenous peoples from what became the United States initiated a pattern of sustained hostility towards any group that wove its way of life together with its sense of identity into the ecological fabric of a particular place. Berry argues that the United States was founded to facilitate successive waves of transient frontierism whose bias has been the extinguishment of all that is old, conservative, and aboriginal in order to clear the way for a perpetual "revolution of exploitation ... where statesmanship and craftsmanship are gradually replaced by salesmanship."27 This dynamic, Berry argues, has never been overcome. "The first and greatest American revolution has never been superseded," he writes. "It has been the coming of the people who did not look upon the land as a homeland ... If there is any law that has been operative in American history, it is that the members of any established people or group or community sooner or later become 'redskins' – that is, they become victims of an utterly ruthless, officially sanctioned and subsidized exploitation."28

Berry's commentary on the war on Indian Country as the formative, destabilizing event in American history speaks of the wider meanings and symbolisms attached to the continuing struggle of Indigenous peoples to stand their ground. This deeply conservative resistance, rooted in the oldest surviving polities known to humankind, represents the outer edges of a moving frontier of pluralistic restoration that points humanity towards alternative models of globalization radically different from the moving frontiers of standardized property law. This assertion of the contemporary existence of prior or pre-existing rights in turn represents the applied aspect of an evolving philosophy of ecological society – a philosophical complex that, in my estimation, constitutes the last ideological barrier to the totalitarian triumph of the unsustainable cult of possessive individualism.

Berry presents a critique of the excesses of American agribusiness, which often mines the soil and extinguishes biodiversity even as its ever expanding scale displaces farming families and whole communities. For contrast and inspiration, Berry looks to the sophisticated agriculturalists who cultivate the steep slopes of the Andes mountains in South America. He argues that these Indigenous peoples present a living example of a superior and sustainable approach to cultivating plants, especially the vast range of potato stocks that have their origin in the Aboriginal agriculture of that part of the world. "All the methods of the Andean farmers are based upon the one principle of diversity," Berry writes. The whole system is premised on assisting in the symbiosis between plant and habitat, where horticulturalists learn to make precise, localized responses to the variabilities of climate and soil in an environment where dramatic differences in altitude create a plethora of unique growing conditions. The bias of this system runs against the isolation and large-scale replication of monocultures. Instead, the seed stocks of the Andean farmers represent "a sort of genetic vocabulary in a state of continuous revision."29 Berry looks to the Indian farmers of the Andean mountains for examples of ways "to accommodate the diversity in the unity" of more integrated environments. In contrasting his own society with that of the First Nations horticulturalists in Peru, Berry asserts that "we may come to see how dangerous are our absolute divisions between city and farmland, farmland and wilderness, by which we exclude from our domestic enclosures everything for which we have foreseen no use or market."[30]

Many elements of my text explore further the connections touched on by Berry in equating the ability of humanity to sustain myriad pluralistic cultures with the ecological imperative to retain, protect, and enhance diverse habitats. Without these diverse habitats, this planet's vast array of plant and animal species, the earth's God-given richness, cannot be sustained. Moreover, the cultural identity and physical survival of whole peoples is no less doomed when the complex communities of plants and animals are displaced to make space for commercialized monocultures epitomized by the factory-like production of agribusiness and tree farms.

The name "ecocide" has been given to the impoverishment of biodiversity, largely through pollution or the transformation of diverse habitats to open space for the replication of identical life forms on vast industrial scales. One of the main hallmarks of ecocide, therefore, is species depletion. Its sociological equivalent is the death of culturally distinct human societies. Ecocide and genocide have often become paired manifestations of the same commercial processes in the increasingly globalized project of secularizing and privatizing nature along new frontiers of industrialized production.

Shepard Krech III has argued that Indigenous peoples in the Americas have sometimes had a broad and significant impact on the ecologies of their ancestral territories.[31] The scale and magnitude of their environmental interventions, however, have not approached those of the technological, military, and economic juggernaut that has assaulted and sometimes overwhelmed Aboriginal societies. Hence, the ecocidal destruction of plant and animal species through the commercialized elimination of their habitats has sometimes been more genocidally lethal for Indigenous peoples than either the military campaigns directed against them or the infamous gift blankets from the colonists' smallpox hospitals. As Indigenous peoples have been cut off from the complex plant and animal communities that have been integral to their nourishment, comfort, and physical and spiritual health, they have been effectively denied the underlying basis of their economic, cultural, and physical survival.

The lethal impact of the New World expansionism initiated with the Columbian conquests has been manifest in the early and violent demise of vast multitudes of Aboriginal individuals, together with the extermination of more than a thousand distinct Aboriginal societies. The extent of this cataclysm in the Americas, the primary frontier of Europe's most aggressive episodes of expansionary zeal, has been monumental. According to Todorov, the founding of New Spain and Portuguese Brazil in "the sixteenth century perpetuated the greatest genocide in human history."[32] In *Rivers of Blood, Rivers of Gold*, Mark Crocker goes further to argue that, "when viewed as a single process, the European consumption of tribal society could be said to represent the greatest, most persistent act of human destructiveness ever recorded."[33]

The effort to quantify the extent of the killing and death connected to the expansion of European imperialism is fraught with complexities, disagreements, and moral perplexities. Russell Thornton is one of those who has made a serious scholarly attempt to measure the extent of the cataclysm. In his controversial demography, he estimated that the Indian population in the Americas had shrunk by 1900 to about 6 per cent of its former size of around 72 million at the beginning of Europe's transatlantic leap. The sharpness of this decline, whose causes Thornton attributes primarily to disease as well as "warfare and genocide," was mitigated somewhat by the prolific mixing of Native and immigrant populations, especially in "Latin America."[34]

Although Aboriginal populations began to grow in the twentieth century, the precipitous demographic plunge during the first four centuries after Columbus highlights the monumental character of this central event in world history. Thornton's characterization of this tragic epic as a "holocaust" comes yet more sharply into focus when viewed alongside the extinction of more than three-quarters of the 2,200 or so Aboriginal languages and dialects spoken in the Americas in 1492.[35] At the beginning of the new millennium the pace of this impoverishment in human expressiveness continued to accelerate as part of a worldwide trend. The disappearance of so many linguistic windows of human understanding is robbing posterity of vital media of thought and articulation to convey, perpetuate, and augment our inherited cultural richness.[36]

While the centuries-old pattern of expropriation, subjugation, silencing, and extinguishment of Indigenous peoples in the Americas has long been treated as a shared skeleton to be kept in the adjoining closets of the empires and nation states that grew from the hemisphere's colonization, the law and politics surrounding the crime of genocide came sharply into focus in the final months of the twentieth century. With rationales that associated Serbian Yugoslavia with the master race fantasies of Nazi fascism, the North Atlantic Treaty Organization determined to bomb Yugoslavia as a way to check the "ethnic cleansing" directed largely at the ethnic Albanian population of Kosovo. Meanwhile Ward Churchill, in a manner anticipating a renewal of the controversies and debates that accompanied the legal proceedings at Nuremberg after the Second World War, published a sweeping and richly documented volume in 1998 under the provocative title *A Little Matter of Genocide: Holocaust and Denial in the Americas, 1492 to Present*.[37] Churchill's intent was to challenge the complicity of those intellectuals most responsible for maintaining the willed amnesia that prevents any real intellectual, ethical, or legal reckoning with the extent of the war crimes and crimes against humanity that have been integral to the colonization of North America by Europeans and Euro-Americans.

In North America in particular, the ethnic cleansing of Indigenous peoples has been so systematic, longstanding, and pervasive that it has been rendered all but invisible, except to the victims or their survivors and to those with the honesty and fortitude to face the stark evidence of the historical record. One marker of the extent and terrible effectiveness of this genocidal assault is Thornton's estimate that, between 1492 and 1900, the number of Indians and Inuit in the region covered by Canada and the United States dropped from around 7 million to fewer than 400,000.[38]

There can be no doubt that genocide, through direct killing, ecocide, and the assimilationist strategies of cultural genocide, has been instrumental in the colonization of the Indian Country. That colonization, largely through the strategy of indirect rule, continues to this day. There is also, however, a vital subtext in this story whose importance needs to be emphasized. The history that unfolded in and around Johnson Hall in the decade before the American Revolution speaks of the existence of an important tradition of legal and political formation both on this continent and in the world. This tradition has continued since that time, even though its roots precede the Royal Proclamation of 1763. Imperfect as this constitutional tradition is, it partially restrained the cold-blooded murder of Indigenous peoples and the unilateral extinguishment of their rights and titles to their Aboriginal lands. This constitutional heritage flows into the law of Canada and the United States from their shared roots in British North America. It also has origins in the imperial regimes of New Spain and New France, and in the treaty-making traditions of New Netherland. This constitutional heritage represents the primary hedge – albeit a relatively fragile one – against the assertion that Canada, the United States, and all the other non-Aboriginal polities of the New World were born of genocide and land theft on a monumental scale.

I cannot overstate the importance at this time of bringing to life the memory of how this legal heritage came into being and how it was sustained, however weakly or imperfectly, by those who lobbied and fought to check the incursions and aggressions of the continent's most zealous Indian fighters. The weapons of those who sought to expand the empire of possessive individualism through the quick extinguishment of the rights of Indigenous peoples were as likely to be legal paper and court rulings as guns and ammunition. The reality that the domestic and imperial courts were often used to clear the way for the expansion of empire should not be allowed to detract from the fact that, frequently, these procedures evaded the existing law of Aboriginal and treaty rights.

By emphasizing the actions of people who sought to slow or oppose the ethnic cleansing through the use of law, we strengthen the work of their descendants who try to continue this process today by affirming the human rights of Indigenous peoples. In clarifying that this stance is neither new nor unprecedented, we can help persuade the sceptical to recognize the solid constitutional backing behind the assertions of Indigenous peoples – to recognize the reality that the First Nations are protected by an existing regime of Aboriginal and treaty rights, one that is integral to both domestic and international law.

There are serious consequences in downplaying or denying the existence of this historical subtext, as Churchill is inclined to do in his zeal to clarify the scope and depth of the unaddressed realities of North American genocide. The outcome of such interpretation is that the First Nations appear to be poised on a weaker branch of the law than the constitutional trunk, which in reality supports their status not only in the domestic law of nation-states but in natural and international law as well. Moreover, Churchill's approach opens the way to the notion that Indigenous peoples in North America have been so thoroughly killed off that they can be discounted in contemporary processes of decision-making. While that outcome is certainly not what Churchill intended, his emphasis nevertheless lends itself to edifying the perception that First Nations exist in the past, but not in the present.

A key object of this text, therefore, is to chronicle and assess the historical genesis of the position that Indigenous peoples are invested with Aboriginal and treaty rights. These rights must be recognized and enforced in shaping our laws, institutions, and economic relationships, including our commercial trade treaties. The evolving ideas and instruments of what we have chosen to identify as Aboriginal and treaty rights converged with great impact in the years before the American Revolution, especially in the politics of the Covenant Chain, the content of the Royal Proclamation, and the multicultural character of life in and around Johnson Hall.

This convergence represented a kind of culminating expression of many principles and strategies that had developed over the first century and a half of English, Dutch and French colonization. It drew also on the legacies of the Spanish Empire. As in the British Empire, an axis of shared interest developed, linking Indigenous peoples and the imperial monarch. The basis of this strange alliance was the quest of both the king and the First Nations to protect the security of their respective Old World traditions against the quest of transplanted Europeans to control expanding frontiers of Creole jurisdiction. The formulation in Great Britain of the Royal Proclamation of 1763 stimulated and amplified a further parting of the ways in the theory of British imperialism in North America. This division led to the emergence of two transcontinental polities from the crucible of the American Revolution. The governments of both these polities evolved a legal theory of existing Aboriginal and treaty rights rooted in the constitutional principles most enduringly codified in the Royal Proclamation. The government of Canada continued to extend these principles through the making of the numbered treaties or, more recently, the Nisga'a Treaty and the establishment of Nunavut in 1999. The United States, in contrast, through an Act of Congress in 1871, unilaterally renounced its adherence to the international law of Aboriginal and treaty rights.

An important chapter of this saga took place in 1982 – the year the Canadian Constitution was patriated from Great Britain. The legal instrument of patriation described itself as the country's "supreme law." Section 35 of this document, entitled the Constitution Act, 1982, entrenched a provision recognizing and affirming "the existing Aboriginal and treaty rights of the Aboriginal peoples of Canada." This phrase was included not with the intention of creating new rights where no rights had existed before but of creating a bridge of continuity. It was meant to bring forward very old and elaborate constitutional traditions, from the time when only the government of Great Britain could change the constitutional architecture of Canada to a time when that authority was devolved to the federal parliament and the provincial legislatures. Hence, the concept of "existing Aboriginal and treaty rights" is prominently affirmed in Canada's supreme law. The judicial task of interpreting this phrase has been advanced in a number of cases, carrying, for instance, the names of *Guerin, Sioui, Sparrow, Badger, Delgamuukw,* and *Marshall.* That task, however, has only just begun, both in Canada and in many other jurisdictions. This book is intended to contribute constructively to that process of definition and interpretation – a process that, while centred on the courts, also belongs to society in general and especially to the public educators within society.

It remains to be seen if the conceptualization and enforcment of existing Aboriginal and treaty rights – a process whose origins lie more in 1492 than in 1982 – will be treated as an onus or as an adventure. One of my goals in writing this book has been to draw on my own studies and experiences to encourage my fellow citizens to see the process of imagining and implementing section 35 as an opportunity and a national adventure rather than as a national burden. In my estimation, Canada has a unique opportunity to show the world something both very new and very old, in living up to the challenge posed by our constitution, in opening up institutional space for the cultures and creative self-determination of Indigenous peoples in nation building, and in advancing ecological globalization in the new millennium.

Certainly, the principles of Aboriginal and treaty rights are as instrumental in the intellectual, political, and economic histories of the United States as they are of Canada. Indeed, as legal practioners, including Thomas Berger and Bruce Clark, were invited to the United States to give advice on the constitutional law of Aboriginal and treaty rights, the phrase began to enter the legal interpretation of the republic's supreme laws.[39] Moreover, as pressure grew to move beyond the North American Free Trade Agreement towards a common market or even a common currency, there were new political imperatives to emphasize the shared origins of Canada and the United States in British North America.

If Canada and the United States are unified by the fact that both countries share a common continent that has been, and continues to be, home to many Indigenous peoples, the same is true of all the Americas. I believe it is appropriate to apply the ideas and principles of existing Aboriginal and treaty rights to all the countries of North and South America. Accordingly, as the governments of all these countries move towards the creation of yet another commercial trade treaty, I believe that the would-be architects of this new commercial polity must address the existence of Aboriginal and treaty rights as a shared reality of the whole Western Hemisphere, derived from our shared experience of the ongoing Columbian conquests.

Indeed, I believe that the idea of Aboriginal and treaty rights, including those rights rooted in the principles of Aboriginal title, have contemporary applicability to every part of the planet that was claimed and appropriated after 1492 by European imperialism. A key legal instrument in establishing the precedents and frameworks for the interpretation of these legal and political principles is the Royal Proclamation of 1763, whose genesis and meanings will be extensivly explored in these pages. Accordingly, the legal and philosophical principles of Aboriginal and treaty rights, including Aboriginal title, point outward from the Americas to clarify a number of relationships in the world's other continents and islands. The utility of these terms arises because so many geopolitical boundaries on the planet go back to an era when diplomats in Europe divided and apportioned vast areas of the planet without reference to the rights, titles, wishes, cultures, beliefs, and interests of the Indigenous peoples of these lands.

The legal justification for this act of negation was termed the doctrine of *terra nullius*. The High Court of Australia addressed the obscenity of this negation when it announced in 1992, in the case of Torres Strait Islander Eddie Mabo, that the doctrine of *terra nullius* represents a blight on the history of Western civilization as abhorent as the legacy of slavery. Accordingly, the terms "Aboriginal rights" or "Aboriginal title" defy the idea of *terra nullius*. They describe those surviving principles of cultural, territorial, and legal configuration that have their origins in forms of human understanding and organization that predate the jurisdictional impositions of European imperialisms. In many instances these Aboriginal rights and titles were recognized in the course of gaining from Indigenous peoples what Dorothy Jones has described as a "license for empire."

Much of this text is devoted to tracing through one very old and sustained tradition of recognizing Aboriginal rights through treaty. While this book deals with the history of this recognition primarily in North America, treaties with Indigenous peoples were a commonly used means for European sovereigns to gain footholds in what became their colonies in many parts of the world, including South Africa, New Zealand, India, and Southeast Asia. These treaties with Indigenous peoples can be viewed from many perspectives and through many different interpretive lenses. In my view there is much to be learned about the difficult arts and sciences of negotiations across chasms of language, culture, and ecology in the huge range of interactions among individuals, peoples, sovereigns, and governments who combined their traditions of law and diplomacy to invent the protocols and procedures entailed in these treaties. In the northern part of North America this process of invention continues yet, not only in negotiating new treaties in British Columbia but in implementing the terms of old treaties, as is currently happening in the reorganization of Canada's east-coast fishery.

Although these agreements may have been viewed historically as licences for empire by those on the imperial side of the bargains, most often these instruments have been perceived on the Aboriginal side as charters of sharing and coexistence. A major goal of this text, and of the larger project of which it forms a part, is to demonstrate, document, and chronicle the genesis of this treaty tradition in North America, from its earliest beginnings until the present. I hope to present this chronicle with an eye to demonstrating the ongoing utility of these agreements in balancing unity with diversity, change with continuity. The case is made, for instance, that these agreements could inform various other mechanisms for transcultural democracy. Surely such means of securing mandates for cooperative action from culturally diverse constituencies is an aspect of public policy that is dangerously underdeveloped in an era when due process and the principle of consent are often sacrificed in the race to lead, or not to fall too far behind, on the globalization autobahn.

All in all, these treaties with Indigenous peoples present humanity with a rich record of the evolution of thought and negotiation on the character of Aboriginal rights specifically and, more generally, on the nature of inherent human rights. In my estimation, the extension and elaboration of this genre of treaty relations in the new millennium forms a living laboratory of negotiation and institution building that offers important alternatives to the crude tools of partition. This alternative to partition offers a way out of the usually violent dismemberment of complex societies in those many places on the planet where different peoples have overlapping claims of jurisdiction and sovereignty to common territory. The phrase "Aboriginal and treaty rights" could, in theory, be used to describe a particular complex of legal relationships that exists in many parts of the planet in various permutations and combinations. The existence of this stratum of imperial, constititional, and international law, however, came to the surface of legal scrutiny and political negotiation most overtly in Canada, largely because of the particular form of this country's most official act of decolonization. In Canada this formal break with the old imperial mother country in 1982 went by the name of patriation.

One objective of this book is to share with a broader readership, but particularly one in the United States, Central and South America, Australia, Oceana, Europe, India, and Africa, some of the fruits of the rich and many-faceted debate stimulated in Canada by the simmering and ongoing constitutional crisis here. This effort to redefine the legal character of the northern portion of North America has required considerable negotiation and debate on how to conceptualize and construct relations linking Indigenous peoples with other polities at the local, national, and international levels. In my view, this debate leads inexorably to a range of conclusions that call for the elaboration of a host of checks and balances to mitigate the domination by transnational corporations of the process of globalization. One of the most promising means of building new democratic checks into models of globalization is to create new international instruments and agencies for the protection and expression of the rights and responsibilities of "peoples," including Indigenous peoples.

Such initiatives would put real and substantial structures on top of theoretical constructs already well entrenched. The United Nations in many of its instruments refers to peoples as well as nation-states as primary units of collective self-determination. Moreover, the heritage of imperial Europe's treaties with Indigenous peoples forms a rich matrix that could anchor and legitimate the elaboration of new international laws and agencies. The goal of these edified institutions would be to help protect Indigenous peoples – indeed, *all* peoples – from the hostile and sometimes genocidal perils to which large parts of humanity have repeatedly been subjected. A more recent feature of these tragedies has been the confining of some of the world's oldest polities, often in the name of artificial and ill-conceived exercises of "decolonization," within the domestic constraints of nation-states that have been unreflective of, or outrightly antagonistic to, many Aboriginal cultures.

In his introduction to an anthology of court rulings, Native Studies professor Peter Kulchyski offers an explanation of a key phrase that runs through this volume: "Prior occupation is the historical ground upon which Aboriginal rights rest. 'They were here first' translates into: 'at one time, all this land was theirs. We rarely conquered them by force of arms. Now all this land is ours. We must owe them something.' That 'something' is Aboriginal rights."[40] The quest to define and deliver that "something" seemingly burst into the political and legal cultures of Canada in the events surrounding "patriation" of the Canadian Constitution from Great Britain. In 1973 a comparable discussion on the meaning of Aboriginal rights was generated in the United States by the intense media coverage afforded a military confrontation spurred by the symbolically charged return of the American Indian Movement to Wounded Knee on the Pine Ridge Reservation in South Dakota. A similar surge of changed consciousness bolted through Australian society in the mid-1990s, as the fuller implications of the High Court's *Mabo* ruling began to sink in.

One of the planet's most momentous, globalized versions of deliberation on Aboriginal rights arose from the transformation of the Zapatista

Liberation Army into a mass movement pressing for major constitutional reforms to better reflect the Aboriginal heritage and future of the world's most important Meso-American country. "We are all Indians of the world," a banner proclaimed paradoxically as it flew over the historic Zocalo Square in the heart of Mexico City. In masked anonymity, the pipe-smoking "Subcommandante Marcos" was among those in the Zapatour procession as it entered the city's central square to mingle with the crowds who had gathered there to meet the unorthodox movement's leaders. This political culmination of the Zapatista journey from Chiapas to the nation's capital in March 2001 aimed to rekindle the popular support once vested in Mexico's popular revolutionary Indian leader Emiliano Zapata.[41]

The inclusion in the patriated Canadian Constitution of section 35, referring to existing Aboriginal and treaty rights, created a specific focus for some of globalization's most fundamental ethical and legal problems. A key to understanding section 35 is that the words themselves do not profess to be the sole source of Aboriginal rights, although the document that contains them describes itself as the country's "supreme law." What section 35 affirms, instead, is the *recognition* of these rights, suggesting that they do not originate in Canadian law. This wording serves to underline that human rights are vested in people, or, collectively, in people*s*, rather than in governments. Accordingly, while governments have it in their power to recognize, facilitate, or block the exercise of human rights, they cannot give them or create them. Moreover, section 35 opens the door to the interpretation that the collective *rights* of Indigenous peoples draw their deepest legitimacy from sources rooted in many complex human histories that pre-exist Canada by many thousands of years. There are multiple implications in the idea that Canadian law recognizes Aboriginal rights, but that this legal regime does not – indeed, could not – create those rights any more than the government of Canada would have it in its power to create Aboriginal nationalities.

This interpretation seemingly opens the door to some reckoning with the principle that instruments of the Canadian state, or of the state mechanisms of all other New-World countries for that matter, are not the sole locus of law-making authority. Section 35 could be seen, therefore, as announcing the Canadian nation's willingness to embrace a form of jurisdiction not derived from the Canadian Constitution, the Canadian or British crown, parliament, or any of the provincial legislatures. It could also be seen as an instrument reserving for Aboriginal peoples, another name for Indigenous peoples, a distinct sphere of juridical and jurisdictional space of their own. Indigenous peoples retain the collective right, it could be argued, to elaborate or modify these recognized spheres of jurisdiction through their own legal processes, based on their own priorities, cultures, and beliefs, in their own good time as the need or will arises. Given the affirmation of the legal identification of the bearers of existing

Aboriginal and treaty rights as peoples, section 35 has clear implications that go beyond the geography and domestic law of Canada. This provision, for example, could be used to help develop further openings for Indigenous peoples from Canada and elsewhere to participate in the formulation and implementation of international law from a jurisdictional space of their own that Canada has recognized and affirmed.

It is possible, therefore, to see section 35 as affording recognition to the existence of forms of Aboriginal jurisdiction which pre-exist Canada and which retain legal force to this day. But this description includes only one of many possible ways to read and understand this constitutional provision. The provision does not grow so much out of Aboriginal heritages and experiences, although Aboriginal activists did lobby for its reinstatement after Canada's first ministers tried to remove it in November 1981 from the text of Canada's supreme law. Instead, the legal antecedents of section 35 lie primarily in traditions of governance expressed in the imperial elaboration of British North America, the jurisdictional seedbed from which both Canada and the United States have emerged.

In my view, it is the history of British North America's fragmentation into two polities after 1776 which holds many keys to understanding in a deeper way the historical resonance of Canada's declaration in 1982 of Aboriginal and treaty rights. The constitutional invocation of the rights connected to aboriginality reverberates with the sharp battle cries marking the revolutionary culmination of the eighteenth century, a period highlighted in this text. That transatlantic revolutionary event was the moment when the world-transforming current of thought known as the Enlightenment bolted from the realm of ideas into a violent struggle to overthrow old regimes and hierarchies. The word "Aboriginal" can be closely associated with ideologies on the conservative side of a revolutionary struggle that started with a civil war in British North America in 1776 and grew into a popular uprising in France in 1789. Indeed, the notion of aboriginality seems rooted in similar constitutional soil to the ideas and conventions that supported the existence of hereditary distinctions and titles embodied in the institutions of European monarchy and aristocracy.

Edmund Burke's classic denunciation in 1790 of the animating principles of revolutionary France provides perhaps the best literary defence of "hereditary property and hereditary distinction" as the fundamental basis for the sound organization of society. At the core of Burke's cherished system of governance – at the point of convergence where the titles, rights, and interests of society's different estates met – was the mediating authority of the sovereign crown. The constitutional stability and continuity embodied in the institution of British sovereignty, Burke wrote, required that the sovereign crown be passed along through "an hereditary descent in the same blood, through a hereditary descent qualified with protestantism."[42]

Recognition of the imperatives of aboriginality tend best to mirror the

arguments and convictions of those who resisted the most sweeping applications of the Enlightenment's revolutionary thrust, wherein the inherited
titles of monarchs and aristocrats were denounced in the name of the natural rights of human beings to equality before the law. The transatlantic
commonalities linking those holding similar conservative orientations
towards land and governance were reflected in the tendency for proponents of the embattled monarchies of Great Britain, and later Spain, to
move towards strategic alliances with Indigenous peoples in the Americas.
The linkages between monarchies and Indigenous peoples in the Americas and elsewhere in Europe's imperial realms tended to become especially elaborate at times when the colonial subjects of these European rulers
moved towards asserting their own sovereign powers of self-governing
independence. In the American empires of Spain, France, and Portugal,
many of the increasingly rebellious transplanted Europeans began to conceive of themselves as Creoles. As their Creole nationalisms, including that
of the Anglo-Americans, became increasing assertive, culminating in the
establishment of several new republics in the Americas, Indigenous peoples held the potential to become important checks on the expansionary
aggrandizement of the revolutionary challenges to the heritary principles
underpinning Europe's remaining monarchical regimes.

The book will explore the neglected histories of the old and elaborate
web of connections linking Indigenous peoples to the institution of
monarchy, but particularly the British monarchy. An essential key to a
deeper appreciation of First Nations understandings of the contemporary
meaning of existing Aboriginal and treaty rights can be found in this history.

There are many parallels and similarities between the modern-day legacies of this heritage and the way that Indigenous peoples in Australia and
New Zealand see their connections to the nation-states and the sovereign
crown of the old empire that has colonized their lands. As I shall demonstrate, the academic return to these histories as apt subjects for research
and analysis is beginning to have large implications for the content of judicial interpretations of domestic and international law.

The outcome of this inheritance is that the recognition of the imperatives of aboriginality can be conceptualized as a kind of New World variation on the laws and institutions supporting monarchy and landed gentries
in Europe. In this scheme, the First Nations can be conceptualized as cus-
todians of continuity and tradition in societies that otherwise are founded
in traumatic and dislocating breaks with the past. The essence of this break
is represented by the shared legacy of transoceanic immigration as the
major common denominator in the diverse experiences of non-Aboriginal
populations. The idea of First Nations as a kind of entrenched, entitled
aristocracy is far from the present realities of most Indigenous peoples,
whose day-to-day experiences are too often framed by the most serious
forms of racial discrimination, poverty, incarceration, suicide, addictions,

and violent death. Nevertheless, for those whose conservatism emphasizes clan and community as the key to social stability, Aboriginal and treaty rights could yet become a vital means for national governments and societies to realize some Burkean ideals about the need to balance cautiously the proper equilibrium between change and continuity.

In parts of the southwestern United States there are many living expressions of an informal recognition of Indigenous peoples as planters and keepers of the main tap roots of a pluralistic society's most vital, originating inspirations. Some of the regions acquired from Mexico in 1848 are unique in the United States, for the society of newcomers avoided the more pervasive urge to found their own societies on primal acts of aggression aimed at extinguishing the pre-existing cultures of Indigenous peoples. Instead, the growth of American civilization in parts of the republic's southwest developed in ways that have elaborated rather than denigrated or destroyed the motifs, technologies, and styles of the older, pre-existing cultures. In developing a society based on the creation of a New Mexico rather than on the elimination of the old Mexico, this part of the United States also adapted itself to the strong Indian dimension of its many faceted Mexican personality. The fruits of these synergetic adaptations are to be seen in the rich creativity that emanates prolifically, especially from the area of Sante Fe and Taos. In this densely-settled region, Peublo Indian architecture predominates even in the urban landscapes. And the application and elaboration of Native designs infuse the manufacture of all manner of art, craftsmanship, and industrial production, making this region rich in material and spiritual ways. Indeed, this region, with the ancient and adapting Taos Peublo at its cultural core, is one of the more important centres of literary and intellectual invention in the United States.

The imagery of Indian Country as the locale of America's natural aristocracy clashes with the facts at the basis of the revolutionary founding of the United States. The Thirteen Colonies broke away from the British mother country with the conviction that the hereditary titles of monarchs and the landed gentry must be struck down to clear the way for a more universal and egalitarian embrace of what Thomas Paine described in his famous answer to Edmund Burke as "The Rights of Man." In his reply, Paine brought his insights as one of the chief sloganeers of the American Revolution to an interpretation of the animating spirit of the French Revolution. Those who initiated Europe's most legendary revolutionary act sought to establish their transformed society on the extinguishment of hereditay titles rooted in feudal institutions. They announced their principles to the world in the Declaration of the Rights of Man and Citizen. "Men," the manifesto proclaimed, "are born, and remain, free and equal in rights."

The government of Pierrre Trudeau was seemingly more drawn to the legacy of Paine than of Burke when it articulated the imperatives of

Indian treaties and aboriginality in the language of rights. This affirmation of Aboriginal peoples' rights took place in the context of a constitutional change that nudged Canada yet further away from its conservative heritage as the country that emerged from the Tory side of the American Revolution. This constitutional change, which, ironically, was signed into law in a royal proclamation initialled by Queen Elizabeth II on Ottawa's Parliament Hill, separated Canada still more from the legal fabric of Great Britain. By adopting a written constitution with a charter of citizens' rights, the Trudeau regime moved Canada closer to the republican model pioneered by the founders of the United States.

The change in the Canadian Constitution in 1982 can be seen as part of a worldwide movement whose defining moment came with the adoption in 1948 by the United Nations of the Universal Declaration of Human Rights.[43] The transatlantic movement of Canada's constitution from Great Britain can be understood as one small part of a larger global process. Although this process is far more prolific of word than of action, its outcome has been to legislate many of the universalist and egalitarian principles originally proclaimed as justifications for the revolutionary movements emerging from the century of Enlightenment.

At the basis of this unfinished work of applied illumination is the recognition that all human beings are possessed of certain fundamental rights, liberties, and freedoms that must be afforded some basic recognitions and protections in both domestic and international law. Hence the guiding spirit of section 35, together with the Charter of Rights and Freedoms in Canada, seemed to have more to do with the revolutionary polemic of life, liberty, and the pursuit of happiness, or "liberté, égalité and fraternité", than with Burkean justifications of hereditary titles and distinctions. Accordingly, the legal and historical antecedants of the phrase "Aboriginal and treaty rights" straddle both the conservative and the liberal sides of some of the Enlightenment's great contentions. These contentions gave rise to the division of British North America after 1776 into a transcontinental republic and a transcontinental crown dominion that retained the old Iroquois name of Canada. The confusion wrought by the convergence of these different legal heritages could be seen on the eastern seabord of North America in the autumn of 1999, when Canada's Supreme Court gave a seemingly broad interpretation to a friendship treaty signed in 1760 between the British crown and the Mi'kmaq, Maliseet, and Passamaquoddy peoples.

The ruling found that a Mi'kmaq fisher, Donald Marshall Jr, was not guilty of any crime for selling $787 worth of eels he had caught out of season in 1993 in Pomquet Harbour, near Antigonish, NS.[44] As a result of this ruling, many Native fishers throughout Nova Scotia and New Brunswick took to their small boats to catch lobsters at a time of the year when this activity was otherwise prohibited by federal regulation. The Passamaquoddy of Maine intervened in the controversy, underlining that treaty issues

with Indigenous peoples often retain an international dimension. The Passamaquoddy reasoned that the crown's recognition of their treaty right to
fish still applied to them, even though their ancestral lands and some of
their ancestral fishing grounds had passed from the realm of Britain to
that of the United States in 1783.

The response of many non-Aboriginal lobster fishers was to characterize
the Supreme Court's ruling as a violation of their own rights to equal treatment before the law. With this explanation, some non-Aboriginal gangs
systematically pulled out many thousands of Aboriginal lobster traps and
harassed some Mi'kmaq people, even to the point of ramming and burning their automobiles, personal goods, and one Native house.[45] This
chaotic uncertainty over "rights" to the beleaguered fishery of the east
coast was paralleled in the forests of New Brunswick and British Columbia.
Some Aboriginal loggers interpreted Canadian law to mean that they had
existing Aboriginal and treaty rights to take trees from the extensive crown
lands in both provinces.

These episodes point to the polarizing implications of leading the struggle and the arbitration over the contemporary place of aboriginality and
Indian treaties into the forum of conflicting and contested rights. Rather
than framing the issue primarily as one involving the invention and elaboration of appropriate institutions to serve as media of continuing relations
between distinct peoples, the controversy is made to seem more like a fight
over how much stuff to put in a shopping cart of Aboriginal and treaty
rights. The east-coast fishery dispute, for instance, is made to seem like a
fight over how many tons of lobster or crab will be earmarked for Aboriginal use. Once it is established how many sea creatures will be apportioned
for this Aboriginal economic basket, the focus must shift to what proportion of the forests, mines, oil fields, and waters of the continent are needed to fulfil the outstanding debt and the ongoing cost of existing Aboriginal and treaty rights.

The prospect of putting quantities of trees, uranium, nickel, fresh water,
oil and gas, hydroelectricity, and the like into this shopping container of
rights would add bulk and substance to the items already in there. Among
the older items included in existing Aboriginal and treaty rights are federal transfer payments for housing, reserve infrastructure, health care, and
education, plus the myriad costs of First Nations governance, management, administration, and litigation. Not surprisingly, many non-Aboriginals watch with dismay the growing list of items passing through this container of Aboriginal and treaty rights. What they are prone to see is not
equality before the law but a form of special status based on reverse forms
of racial discrimination. They see a list of benefits whose sheer bulk sometimes seems to them to exceed any reasonable payment aimed at realizing
some sort of genuine equality before the law. This shopping-cart display of
rights serves for some non-Aboriginals as a provocation – as proof that
their own equal rights as citizens and tax payers are under attack. Their

more schooled members, including Tom Flanagan and Gordon Gibson, see the liberal ideals of Jefferson or Paine or Trudeau being struck down. The Enlightenment's old themes of revolutionary discourse are recycled to challenge the apparent return of government, under the guidance of the courts, to what can be perceived as Burkean justifications for hereditary titles and distinctions.

Because the contemporary controversies are so often removed from any sense of historical context, wild speculations proliferate about what is at issue and what should be done. For instance, former British Columbia premier Bill Vander Zalm raised the McCarthyesque spectre of the Red Scare to generate antagonism towards the Nisga'a Treaty, the first of about fifty modern-day land agreements in that province then working their way through the negotiation process. As a result of this deal, argued Vander Zalm in the autumn of 1999, "the Nisga'a will be a communist society." He proposed that every Indian man, woman, and child in British Columbia should be given a one-time grant of $250,000 to terminate their existing Aboriginal and treaty rights. The objective, he wrote, is "to emancipate our native people" and to "provide a means of individual ownership that will foster a sense of personal worth and value."[46]

There is nothing new or original in Vander Zalm's proposal for a final solution ending in the assimilation of Indian people, the termination of Indian nations and the final apportionment, privatization, and allocation of the remaining Indian Country under non-Aboriginal property law. What does seem novel is the magnitude of the amount he proposed to allocate for the realization of this process of extinguishment. His proposal to make millionaires of every Aboriginal family of four or more spoke to the imminence of the "communist" threat this pundit saw lurking in the remaining Indian Country, just beyond the frontiers of North America's capitalist bastion of private property.

A key objective of this text is to chronicle the missing context of past events so that proposals like that of Vander Zalm can be judged with the perspective, rigour, and insight that can only come from mastering some familiarity with history. By its very nature, the debate about the contemporary existence of Aboriginal and treaty rights in Canada, the United States, the Western Hemisphere, and the entire world is one that begins with the question of how history is to be understood. How are we to interpret the way the past impinges on the present so as to affect the shape of the inheritance we shall bequeath to posterity even seven generations hence? Will we grapple with the substance of our inheritances from history or will we continue to retreat into the black hole of memory loss, the willed amnesia that facilitates the ongoing neo-liberal revolution of the New World Order?

A major requirement to elevate the debate beyond disputes over what does or does not belong in the Aboriginal shopping cart is to widen the discussion beyond arguments over rights to include deliberations over the nature of relationships. There is no escaping the need of arriving at some

Capitalist ideology: If one has power, one MUST employ it for solely self-serving purposes. To do otherwise is to ignore both self & social interest. Exploitation by the powerful is to be the norm to "maximize efficiency" & "raise productivity."

sort of formula for sharing the natural resources, royalties, and jurisdictions as a means of concretely recognizing existing Aboriginal and treaty rights. There has been a marked tendency to put the cart before the horse, however: to haggle over prices, amounts, and things before properly clarifying the aims, procedures, and juridical status of all those parties involved in the process of renewing old covenant chains of treaty alliances and negotiating new agreements between peoples and governments based on the recognition of Aboriginal titles to lands and resources. This emphasis on procedures as well as things, this focus on the fluidity of verbs and processes to offset the fixed, static quality of subjects and objects, requires carefull attention to the historic genesis of the changing constructions of sovereignty and power. It requires close reading and thoughtful assessment of the evolving character of peoples, property, and governments in the New World.

The alternative to this approach is to let the debate become stuck and polarized in the land-mined quagmires of "rights talk."[47] So let's be clear on this point. The various discourses on the nature of rights gained such centrality and intensity in the Enlightenment that they have become essential and inescapable fixtures in the continuing quest to realize and implement more wisely constructed regimes aimed at ameliorating relationships linking human beings with one another and with the rest of nature. But this societal preoccupation with rights as a kind of moral equivalent to money in a marketplace of competing claims and imperatives has sapped the word and the ideas it contains of much of their former vigour. Accordingly, as inspirational as were the contentions in the era when it was revolutionary to insist that the divine right of kings must give way to the rights of people to choose their own governors, we can now witness the cheapened digressions arising from the seemingly unlimited extensions and trivializations of that original concept. As a result, the life-and-death struggle on which the future of some of the planet's oldest and most fragile human societies hinges can sometimes be cast for debate and arbitration into the same chattering rooms dominated by rights talk of far less consequence.

In this milieu, the existence of Aboriginal and treaty rights competes for space in forums of argument where the proponents of any number of other contestations seek to dignify their positions by adopting the language of rights. The controversies over what is known as Aboriginal rights are prone to end up in seemingly endless line-ups of contestations vying for time and attention. In the process, the same language that initiated the French Revolution ends up being harnassed, for instance, to the competing campaigns pitting smokers' rights against non-smokers' rights. The list of assertions and claims demanding the status of "rights" is almost infinite.

The attending "legalization of politics," which directs rights talk away from legislatures and towards the courts, tends to favour the interests of those who can command the best access to public or private wealth in order to pay the lawyers' bills derived from expensive litigation. While bold pronouncements in the constitutions of nation-states or international agencies may ostensibly provide protections for the weak and the marginalized against the arbitrary encroachments and onslaughts of the powerful, the economics of legal advocacy tend to commodify rights as a luxury available primarily to those with the capacity to purchase what it takes to achieve favourable court rulings.[48]

While the courts offer Indigenous peoples a prestigious venue to present their issues in a forum theoretically not directly subject to the majoritarian rule of the ballot box and the notoriously short-term imperatives of electoral politics, this strategy tends to tighten the control of those federal funding authorities who have a large role in deciding what cases and what issues will be brought forward into litigation. In this process, tight patronage networks of money and influence are prone to form around the determination of who will be funded to undertake the legal arguments posed on various sides of competing interpretations over what constitutes the legitimate sphere of existing Aboriginal and treaty rights. The effect of this legalization of the politics of Aboriginal rights is that the culture of litigation increasingly permeates the culture, tone, and substance of many branches of Aboriginal organizations. In this fashion, rights talk works its way into the inner dynamics of many relationships within Indian Country, so political disputes among Aboriginal groups and individuals tend to spill into the non-Aboriginal courts and create many new spins on old patterns of encouraged dependency.

The apportionment of the things being placed in the shopping cart of Aboriginal rights is adding significantly to the growing litigiousness surrounding the abundant schisms and divides *within* the First Nations. The great and growing uncertainties of the rules in the process of privatizing the collective inheritance of Indigenous peoples inevitably beg the questions suggested by Burke when he observed, "The characteristic essence of property, formed out of the combined principles of acquisition and conservation, is to be *unequal.*"[49]

The biggest problem with domestic courts of law as places to arbitrate the juridical meaning of existing Aboriginal and treaty rights is that these institutions as presently constituted have no basis in Aboriginal law, jurisdiction, and self-determination. Instead, the courts are exclusively rooted in a constitutional heritage that, in the case of Canada, for instance, draws all its legitimacy from the authority of the sovereign crown that established the framework for the colonization of the country. This heritage translates into a contemporary method of making judicial appointments that focuses all power in the executive branches of provincial and federal authority. Alternatively, it reserves no role at all for Aboriginal governments in the choosing of judges whose rulings have such broad-reaching influence on shaping the destiny of Aboriginal groups and individuals. Judges are exclusively beholden to federal and provincial politicians for their appointments. Moreover, they come up through a system of legal education and legal practice that does not require them to develop any expertise in the crown's tradition of making laws for Indigenous peoples, let alone in Indigenous peoples' own heritage of making, interpreting, implementing, and enforcing laws for their own self-governance.

The status of lawyers and judges as officers of the court and of the crown clarifies their own conflict of interest in any dispute involving arbitration over assertions testing different interpretations of where crown jurisdiction ends and Aboriginal jurisdiction begins. As institutions with deep roots in the colonization of Indian Country, the domestic courts are not presently constituted to act neutrally or disinterestedly as directing agents in the process of decolonizing the First Nations or as final arbiters in determining the extent of Aboriginal rights or titles to lands, resources, and self-governance.

The limitations of the domestic courts are especially apparent in the interpretation of treaties. If one accepts that these agreements represent commitments aimed ideally at facilitating coexistence between different peoples rooted in different cultures and legal traditions, how can a judiciary rooted exclusively in the crown's legal heritage credibly arbitrate disputes involving conflicting interpretations about the correct balances of power between Aboriginal and crown authorities? The same question arises in many republics, including the United States, where the authority of the courts is vested in sovereign peoples – in peoples who often excluded Indigenous peoples as groups and as individuals from the various regimes of Creole nationalism and citizenship that were the founding basis of self-governance throughout much of the New World. This conundrum points to the need to elaborate new types of cross-cultural courts to facilitate improved relationships between Indigenous peoples and the governing authorities of other polities. Woven throughout this text are rationales for this kind of innovation, both within nation-states and on the moving frontiers between domestic and international law, between the private and public spheres, between the imperatives of empire and the rights of groups and individuals.

It would be hard to underestimate the strength of the quiet determination in the governments of many nation-states to safeguard their "territorial integrity" by enclosing Indigenous peoples within the tight enclosures of the domestic law and courts. The very strength of this resolve is highly suggestive of the shared need of Indigenous peoples throughout the planet to break out of these constraints so they can speak, act, and trade on their own behalf in the global community. To exercise these inherent rights and freedoms, there is the need to construct more elaborate agencies of international law and mechanisms of enforcement to safeguard Indigenous peoples globally against the continuing cycles of the Columbian conquests.

This kind of innovation at the international level would provide some way to move beyond the present system of institutionalized conflict of interest that has developed ever since Indigenous peoples all over the planet were trapped and enclosed in small reserves of domestic law not of their own making. Frequently the governments of nation-states are so deeply implicated in the massive expropriations of Aboriginal lands, as well as in various instances of the interrelated crimes of genocide, ecocide, and ethnic cleansing, that there are tremendous constraints blocking domestic judiciaries from any objective reckoning with the root causes of the marginalized conditions plaguing surviving Indigenous peoples.

Grave conflicts of interest arise whenever the domestic courts of nation-states are left as the exclusive arbiters to deal with allegations that national governments or their corporate extensions have violated the human rights of Aboriginal groups and individuals. This failure to provide genuine third-party arbitration, the heart and soul of what is required for any society to be governed by the rule of law rather than the rule of politics, is especially clear when Indigenous peoples challenge the legal capacity of nation-states to monopolize jurisdiction over their ancestral lands. How can domestic judges, whose exercise of power constitutes a major expression of the sovereign status of nation-states, give credible rulings on cases that challenge the jurisdictional ground on which their own judicial benches sit?

The tension between Indigenous peoples and the domestic courts in many countries points to a larger phenomenon that has been manifest, for instance, in the killing fields of East Timor or Guatemala, or, similarly, in the flooded-out Aboriginal territories of northern Manitoba or Brazil. The violators of many varieties of human rights entailed in these episodes remain shielded from prosecution at the international level by the doctrine that the governments of nation-states retain sovereignty within their borders.

These same sovereign principles, however, are sharply eroded when the focus is shifted from the protection of human rights to the imperatives and powers of global corporations and the elaboration of global infrastructures to facilitate the flow of money or the protection of investment. The result is a huge and growing double standard that harnesses to corporate interests the language, philosophy, and enforcement mechanisms of universal "rights," even as violated human populations are frequently denied comparable protection and access to due process. There is, for instance, no equivalent in the international or supranational human-rights arena of anything like the World Trade Organization.

The World Trade Organization or, for example, the North American Free Trade Authority has provided means for corporations to challenge and sometimes override the policies and legislation of supposedly sovereign governments, even while whole populations can simultaneously be slaughtered and whole ecologies destroyed without any certain means to exact legal accountability from the perpetrators. While some might point as signs of positive change to NATO's punishment of Serbian Yugoslavia in

1999, followed by the trial of Slobodan Milosevic in 2002, the dubious legalities surrounding both the bombing raids and the war crimes tribunal serve to underline the absence of any reliable international mechanisms to arbitrate and uniformly enforce even the most basic protections for human rights. A key object of this text, therefore, is to show how globalization is proceeding without the elaboration at the international level of anything approaching a readily enforceable and uniform rule of law for the protection human rights. At the same time, the rise of global corporations has been instrumental in elevating the form of property law that coalesced in the North Atlantic community to near-planetary dimensions. The affirmation and recognition of existing Aboriginal and treaty rights, I believe, casts vital light on both these phenomena. Much as genocide represents an extension to a mass scale of the crime of murder, so ecocide represents a projection to larger proportions of the notion of suicide and self-destruction through the abuse of addictive and poisonous substances. One of the frequent signs that ecocide is occurring in a particular territory is when significant numbers of people indigenous to that land, but especially their youth, respond with extreme forms of self-abnegation. In impoverishing biodiversity, ecocide weakens the ecological integrity of surviving life forms, even as suicide often diminishes the existential quality of life of the human survivors left behind.

The affirmation of Aboriginal and treaty rights makes most sense when conceived in relation both to the international laws on self-determination and to the prohibition on genocide. Without the instruments of self-determination, peoples are deprived of their ability to develop the institutional tools they require to survive as distinct collectivities. The international laws on genocide and self-determination thus form the negative and positive aspects of the same judicial construct. They constitute the formative beginnings of a single judicial complex emphasizing the shared human rights of collectivities, but especially those peoples whose languages, cultures, and heritages are not well reflected in the constitutional design of existing nation-states.

Accordingly, large portions of this project are devoted to illuminating different contextual settings for the idea of existing Aboriginal and treaty rights as well as the idea of Aboriginal title. While the former phrase first appeared in 1982 in the Canadian Constitution as a means to project forward particular principles developed over several centuries in the crown's colonization of British North America, this way of describing a vital crossroads of history – past, present, and future – has application to the domestic laws of many nation states throughout what was once seen as a New World. Moreover, the meanings conjured up by the phrase coincides with the convergence of a number of international issues that are in some sense quite new, even as they are in other ways as old as the process of globalization. How are Indigenous peoples to be seen not only as objects of international law but also as participants in the process of formulating,

A relevant question for all peoples' rights to have a say over international agreements which will affect them.

interpreting and enforcing new global regimes for the protection of human rights and for the prevention of ecocide?

Although existing Aboriginal and treaty rights resonate with meaning at the level of international law and the domestic law of some nation-states, the phrase can gain full legitimacy only if it can also be seen as a code that speaks to Indigenous peoples' understanding of the contemporary extension of their own heritages, traditions, and decision-making processes. The strong roots of section 35 in the central contentions of the Enlightenment may help inspire some groups and individuals among the First Nations to see their own aspirations for freedom as part of a larger quest for human liberation. The provision seems to draw on both the conservative attachments to hereditary titles once explained so compellingly by Edmund Burke as well as on the liberal legacy derived largely from the eighteenth century's most revolutionary declarations concerning the universal character of human rights.

To interpret section 35 entirely through this Eurocentric lens, however, would be to do the provision an injustice. It would deprive section 35 of the full legitimacy it can acquire only by serving as a code that helps identify how the Aboriginal peoples specifically referred to would like to see themselves and their historical inheritance in relation to the rest of global society. For instance, some interpreters of section 35 are unwilling to accept any reading of existing Aboriginal and treaty rights that would limit its application to forms of municipal self-governance within closed frameworks of sovereign authority going back exclusively to the legacy of European "discovery," conquest, and expansion.[50] Instead, the natural inclination on the part of those who perceive section 35 as offering the legal and political potential for a break with contemporary forms of colonialism is to see the recognition as an acknowledgment that Indigenous peoples are not to be treated as inferior or subordinate polities; that their societies, however small in scale, have equal rights with other nationalities to exercise, enforce, and elaborate their own sovereign attributes.

The question is therefore raised whether the recognition of existing Aboriginal and treaty rights is anything more than a fine-sounding phrase to mask and justify the continuing colonial rule of dominant societies rooted primarily in the European heritage over smaller Aboriginal societies that have retained some modicum of their Aboriginal identities. Are the words contained in section 35 a genuine medium for pragmatic compromise and negotiation on the middle ground between different societies that, while disparate in magnitude and power, are equal in legal status? Can the recognition of existing Aboriginal and treaty rights help generate those attitudes and institutions needed to enhance the quality of human interaction on territory subject to overlapping claims of sovereign jurisdiction?

Inevitably, these questions point to disagreements that have their origins in different understandings of spirituality, different understandings of the

Creator and Her intentions for humanity. As this text will demonstrate, the extension into overseas empires of the sovereign claims of European monarchs was invariably justified in the language of religion. The theoretical rights thought to be derived from the discovery of overseas lands were advanced with the conviction that the authority of a Christian ruler must automatically overpower whatever rights that the "heathens" possessed to their own persons, self-governance, and lands. To this day, the legal systems of many parts of the world, including the United States, draw on these primal assertions of the right of Christian sovereigns to dominate the lands and lives of non-Christians. Only the negotiation of treaties with Indigenous peoples somewhat mitigated the starkness of the theological justifications for what were, in effect, simply raw power grabs.

Alexander Morris, lieutenant-governor of the North-West Territories in the era immediately following the Dominion of Canada's acquisition in 1869 of the extensive titles of the Hudson's Bay Company, gave explicit articulation to the religious justification for the legal transformation of British North America. While Morris was seeking treaty sanction in 1874 from the Cree and Saulteux inhabitants of Saskatchewan's Qu'Appelle Valley for the extension of the dominion's jurisdiction into the region, one Saulteaux negotiator known as the Gambler pressed him for an explanation of the legal theory behind the transaction. How was it, the Saulteaux diplomat asked, that the underlying title to his peoples' ancestral lands had already been transferred from a crown corporation to a crown dominion without Aboriginal consent? How was it that this Indian treaty was being negotiated only after the the major constitutional character of the land's new legal personality in international law had already been determined in a process where no representatives of the Aboriginal inhabitants of the territory had been present? In his effort to explain how the future of a vast Indian Country had already been decided in Europe in closed bargaining between a few European and Euro-Canadian men, Morris asserted, "The lands are the Queen's under the Great Spirit."[51] In other words, the right to exercise sovereign title in the land was to be based ultimately on a grant from God exclusively to the monarch of Great Britain.

In *Gustafsen Lake: Under Siege,* Janice G.A.E. Switlo addresses the reality that different interpretations of section 35 go back ultimately to different religious beliefs. She condemns many of her colleagues in the legal profession for failing to break from the lucrative confines of the federally sanctioned idea that constitutional affirmation of Aboriginal and treaty rights exists exclusively within the framework of crown law. She maintains that specialists in "Aboriginal law" are overwhelmingly inclined to frame their arguments from "the limited perspective of local domestic law," even though many Aboriginal clients originally go to court with the intention of asserting the sovereign character of their peoples' own legal systems.

The proposition that whole legal careers have been built in ways that may have won some cases even as the sovereign positions of Aboriginal litigants have been undermined and misrepresented leads Switlo to a startling conclusion. She maintains that "one of the most serious problems" for the First Nations peoples is their "lack of effective control over their lawyers."[52] Section 35, she argues, needs to be seen as a provision that identifies not only non-Aboriginal law but also identifies the conviction that the Great Spirit intended the lands of the Americas for the use and enjoyment of the Indigenous peoples. This belief extends to the legal position that the Great Spirit has granted to the Indigenous peoples a permanent and unextinguishable title in their own ancestral lands. Switlo identifies this position by introducing the term "Aboriginal allodial title," meaning the unalienable title that comes to Indigenous peoples from the Great Spirit. She argues that this phrase serves to help illuminate the widely felt Aboriginal rejection of the old legal theory articulated by Morris and others that God granted the underlying title to Indian land to the sovereign care of the British monarch. While the two positions are on one level irreconcilable, the key to co existence and even partnership is the wisdom to know when and how to "agree to disagree." If such accommodation is achieved, she cryptically adds, "only the lawyers lose."[53]

Switlo is far from alone in her contention that Canada's constitutional affirmation of existing Aboriginal and treaty rights is being abused to perpetuate old colonial doctrines that essentially divided humanity into superior and inferior orders, applying higher and lower forms of law to each one. For instance, Derek Rasmussen, a historian of education and a seasoned civil servant in the agencies in and around Canada's new territorial government of Nunavut,[54] consistently decries the way that very idea of aboriginality recycled old dichotomies posing modernity against primitiveness, civilization against savagery and barbarism. He advocates retiring the language of Aboriginality from the forum of the law and relegating the word and the concept to the history of ideas. Maybe then, he speculates, Euro–North Americans would be compelled to learn the correct names for what he calls the continent's "host peoples." What prevents this change from happening, says Rasmussen, is that "it may imperil some of the small compensations that 'aboriginal' peoples have begun to win from governments." By retiring the idea of aboriginality to the museum of outmoded concepts, the world would be left to grapple more frontally with the prinicple of the equality of all peoples – an equality that is clearly mocked by affording such different kinds of legal status to the Japanese or the Mi'kmaq. Rasmussen presses this comparison by asking rhetorically: "Japanese civilization is not older or more 'sophisticated' than Mi'kmaq civilization, so why is one Aboriginal and one not?"[55]

Any history of the treatment of Indigenous peoples within the framework of European empires and their successor states must address the phenomenon Rasmussen identifies. The way the world has been governed up to the present reflects the legacy of Europe's ordering of law to conform with the idea that peoples can be tiered between higher and lower orders of humanity. Some of the European Enlightenment's most brilliant conceptual rays did not extend to the high tables of international treaty making, where the whole planet was divided in ways that excluded any role whatsoever for representatives of those peoples deemed inferior according to any number of religious, racial, and civilizational theories.

As illustrated by the lack of Aboriginal representation in the bargaining to sell the vast lands claimed by the Hudson's Bay Company to the Dominion of Canada, Indigenous peoples were most often dealt with as if they were subject to a lower order of law. The questions posed by the Gambler to Morris speaks of a whole genre of criticism that applies to a host of international negotiations, right up to those involving the World Trade Organization or the proposed Free Trade Area of the Americas. By what right are some peoples and nations represented and others excluded in the highest level of international treaty making? This text comes back again and again to the historical genesis of those patterns of inclusion and exclusion in making and remaking the geopolitical map of the Americas and the rest of the world.

In reflecting on Canada's constitutional recognition of existing Aboriginal and treaty rights in 1982, Brian Slattery observed sceptically that this act substituted "impenetrable obscurity for what was formerly shadowy gloom."[56] I choose to be more optimistic. In my estimation, the identification and encapsulation in a few words of a whole complex of phenomena rooted in some of history's most infamous acts of injustice had a broad legal and political significance that went far beyond Canada. The declaration of the existence of this genre of human rights spoke directly to some of the most conspicuous dichotomies between rhetoric and action in many of those countries that saw, and that see, their liberal democracies as representing the best traditions of Enlightenment thought.

The idea of Aboriginal and treaty rights is best understood as an old but vital work-in-progress that calls attention to some of the most distilled legacies of those cycles of imperialism, colonization, and decolonization that have profoundly shaped the world all of us have inherited. Although the wording of section 35 seems biased towards conservative attachments to the importance of hereditary titles in the structuring of society, there is nothing to preclude interpretations that emphasize culture and language, for instance, rather than ancestry as the major determinant of who is to be included within the peoplehoods of the First Nations. Indeed, less emphasis on hereditary principles, and more grappling with the concept of pluralism, individualism, and minority rights within the First Nations, may be a key to a happier accommodation of section 35 (and all it entails) within more mainstream notions of liberalism. The essence of the problem is to find ways of creating and renewing middle grounds of negotiation between peoples without giving in to the homogenizing forces of monoculturalism. The expanding monocultures of mind and matter strip

humanity of vital perspectives on our own condition, even as they reflect
and facilitate an impoverishment of the ecological diversity essential to the
survival of all life forms on this planet.

Accordingly, this text, as well as the larger project of which this volume
forms the first part, is devoted to identifying the historical genesis of the
seemingly obvious idea that Indigenous peoples in the New World are
fully human and therefore invested with fundamental rights that must be
recognized in the structuring of all relevant legal, political, and economic relationships. As incomplete and tenuous as the application of this idea
has been so far, its advancement constitutes a vital aspect of the larger project inherited largely from the Enlightenment. A key element of this
unfinished effort to realize the Enlightenment's most timeless ideals is to
establish some sort of universal regime for the protection of basic human
rights. In my view the declaration by Canada in 1982 that Aboriginal and
treaty rights exist helped advance this cause. It established a strategic
point of reference for the analysis of those most complex and difficult
chapters of global history that form the subject matter of this text and this
project.

The second volume in this project will explore in detail how the construction of sovereignty is once again being changed to facilitate the extension of the frontiers of patent law and copyright law right into the genetic
blueprints of life. The information encoded in DNA is being claimed as
"intellectual property" by a growing array of biotechnogy companies whose
scientists are re-enacting in the inner realm of life's renewal the same ritual of "discovery" and patent that was the essence of European imperialism,
along with the subjugation and genocide of many Indigenous peoples.

Much like the era when their lands and resources were subjected to the
alien claims of European sovereigns, Indigenous peoples have been
among the most assertive resisters of this genetic equivalent of a gold
rush, partly because it is DNA from their own gene pools that is often
being patented as private property. Or, in other instances, it is the genetic harvests of Aboriginal horticultural science or the intimate familiarity
of some Indigenous people with the plants and animals of their Aboriginal lands that is providing much of the material and intellectual basis for
the American empire of private property's most recent surge of frontier
expansion.

The large and quick strides in constructing something approaching a
global rule of commerce to protect corporations and capital from acts of
perceived "discrimination" draws prolifically on the language of the civil
rights movement of the 1960s. There is something profoundly cynical
about appropriating the language of human rights – the language of "anti-
discrimination" – to serve the objective of moving power from the public
forums of democratic discourse to the closed realm of the so-called private
sector. While the commercial treaties that advance this process advertise
themselves as instruments of free trade, their larger purpose is primarily to

standardize property law and to hive off the wealth and privilege of the propertied and entitled minority from the effectively disempowered and largely disentitled majority.

The resulting worldwide trend of widening and accelerating polarities between rich and poor forms the larger context of the international struggle to create standards setting and enforcement remedies for the global expression of Aboriginal and treaty rights. The usual pattern of Indigenous peoples in virtually every country where they live and die is that they are numbered disproportionately among the most poor, the most criminalized, and the most suicidal components of national populations. The consistency of this demography constitutes searing proof of the profound inadequacies of leaving the protection of the rights of Indigenous peoples exclusively to the domestic laws and institutions of nation-states.

Some readers may find the organization and methodology employed in this text unusual or unorthodox. My approach to shaping the narrative has been heavily influenced by the examples set by many of the scholars and teachers of Indian Country who have been my tutors over the years. Among the best of them have been Arthur Solomon, Jim Dumont, Everett Soop, Peter O'Chiese, Casper Solomon, Edna and Liza Manitowabi, Susan and Joe Hare, Wilton Goodstriker, John Chief Moon, Basil Johnson, Francis Boots, Helen Piper, Joe Couture, Laurie Montour, Splitting The Sky, Tommy Porter, Ernest Benedict, Mike Bruised Head, Stanley Knowlton, Evelyn Kelman, Glen North Peigan, Yvonne Scout, Rayno Fisher, Ed Buller, Bernard and Frances Abraham, Verna Friday, Dan Pine, Herb Nabigon, Dave Melting Tallow, James Kelly, Harvey McCue, Georges Sioui, Bertha Onabigon, Melinda Bull Shields, Mike Little Moustache, William Ignace, Jean Morisset, Fred Suggashie, June Quipp, Olive Dickason, Antoine Lussier, Fred Wheatley, Jake Thomas, Mike Mitchell, Ovide Mercredi, Simon Winnipegtonga, Lewis Debassige, Leroy Little Bear, and, above all, Ernie Debassige. I also want to acknowledge the example set by some of my other teachers, who in their life and work clearly assimilated many of the best traditions and ideals of Indian Country. Among this group are Nahum Kanhai, Menno Boldt, Kenneth Kidd, Ed Newberry, Bruce Clark, Lyn Crompton, Jan Currie, Dave McNab, Brad Morse, Donald Smith, Janet Chute, Sam Corrigan, Malcolm Davidson, Brian Titley, John Milloy, Bruce Trigger, Peter Kulchyski, and Bruce Hodgins.

The more I listened to the oral narratives of these noted teachers, the more striking it became to me how their methods of communicating concepts and information varied from the kind of teaching and training I had received earlier in my formal education. One of the common motifs of my history teachers at the University of Toronto, as excellent as many of them were, was to identify a geographic region over a given period of time and

then develop a narrative within these temporal and spatial confines, more
or less in a chronological order. As opportunities increasingly opened to
me to watch some of Indian Country's best teachers in action, I was
increasingly struck by the way they drew on seemingly disparate, uncon-
nected subjects to weave together what turned out to be integrated and systematically developed elaborations of a particular idea or argument. The
heart and soul of the narrative was the idea or morale, and it was taken for
granted that one could carry the idea forwards or backwards through a
range of temporal, geographic, or episodic contexts to clarify the deeper
character of the animating principle at the narrative's core.

I am tempted to speculate that this narrative technique draws on the traditions of storytelling throughout Indian Country, where virtually every
nation recognizes an archetypal Trickster figure whose mischievous and
instructive exploits are the currency of much education, socialization, and
entertainment. In the Ojibway tradition of storytelling, for instance, that
Trickster is known as Nanabush or, sometimes, Nanabozoo. To the Cree he
is Weesageechak; to the Blackfoot, Napi. The Trickster can move instan-
teously anywhere he wants in time and space. He can change forms to
become any person, animal, plant, or inanimate object that serves his purposes. As Tomson Highway writes in *Kiss of the Fur Queen*, "he straddles the
consciousness of man and that of God, the Great Spirit."57 I don't think I
am making too big a leap to imagine that the contextual plasticity in relating the character development of Trickster can easily be translated into the
construction of other kinds of narratives as well.

My intent here, however, is not to tell a Trickster tale. My intent is to contribute constructively to the humanities and social sciences with a narrative
that employs the usual academic conventions of empirical proof and evidence. At the same time, however, I have made a conscious attempt to
draw from and adapt some of what I have learned from the range of ways
teachers in Indian Country construct their narratives of renewal and
encouragement.

I have consciously endeavoured to move beyond the conventions of
national histories towards a genre of historical elaboration that is more
consistent with the conceptual, territorial and organization configurations
of peoples rather than of states. At the same time, this text is at least as
much about the genesis and internal complexities of the American empire
as it is about Indigenous peoples and the Fourth World. Among the
narrative's goals is the illumination of how the organism known as Western
civilization has been shaped at its metropolitan cores by those precedent-
setting encounters on its expanding outer edges.

I have tried in this text to describe the changing chemistry of relationships among peoples, territories, ideas, and systems as they interact along
moving frontiers of geography, economics, and personality. In my effort to
clarify and illustrate the animating essence of transformative relationships,
I sometimes leave the familiar securities of linear treatment of time and

space to carry the reader backwards, forwards, or cyclically among different historical periods or across wide panoramas of geography and theory.

My goal in the writing has consistently been to achieve a creative discipline in illuminating the human condition, primarily through the study of history – past, present, and future. The finest of my teachers have repeatedly shown me in word as well as in deed that history is best understood as a complex of interactions among what has been, what is now, and what is yet to be. Nevertheless, most of this text is organized chronologically. At the same time, there is a good deal of temporal and topical overlap among the narratives developed in the different chapters as I attempt to identify, elaborate, draw together, and illustrate the interwoven nature of the text's various thematic strands.

As I moved from subject to subject, chapter to chapter, section to section, I sometimes pictured myself as Alice, falling through the looking glass of changed orientations to history. In the vocabulary of this text, the looking glass is transformed into frontiers of economic and cultural interaction. One such frontier is the place where Indigenous peoples and newcomers encounter one another. To elaborate the complex nature of this frontier, one must evaluate it from different vantage points. One prespective places the observer among those in the east, who look at the frontier as a westward-moving expansion of power and property. The observer then must try to break through to the other side of the looking-glass frontier to view this same space from the perspective of the west— as an imploding line of menacing aggression, narrowing horizons, diminished hopes, and, quite often, death and desecration.

This looking-glass trick of perceptual flipping worked for me in many different ways as I tried to make historical sense of the transformations from fur trade to free trade,[58] from Indian Country to federal territory to states and provinces. For me the history of the absorption of Canada into the American empire represented a particularly important frontier, with rich emanations of meaning radiating from both sides of the looking glass. This frontier of transformation has affected my own country deeply. The legacies of Johnson Hall, the Royal Proclamation, and the Covenant Chain were renewed and extended in 1982 by Canada's constitutional recognition of existing Aboriginal and treaty rights. This recognition paradoxically helped to safeguard, for as long as the sun shines and the grass grows, the very Indian Country that the American Revolution, the War of 1812, and Andrew Jackson's Indian removal policies of the 1830s were aimed at extinguishing.

I have the Royal Canadian Mounted Police to thank for their assistance in helping me to apprehend more clearly the looking-glass flips that occur on either side of the frontier of the criminal law. In 1990 I was charged by the Mounties for an alleged speech crime as a result of my involvement in a peaceful protest at a southern Alberta museum known as the Head-Smashed-In Buffalo Jump Interpretive Centre. Our protest was to call

attention to police tactics in quelling and discrediting the protest of a
Peigan group who identified themselves to the outside world as the Lonefighters. The aim of their protest was to make known what they asserted
was the illegal character of a controversial irrigation dam being built
upstream from their reserve on the Oldman River.[59]

The crown of Alberta eventually abandoned the criminal charge against
me after holding it over my head for a year and a half. The experience certainly clarified for me the extent of the power held by the criminal justice
system in establishing boundaries of what will be permitted and what will
be criminalized in negotiating and arbitrating the extent of existing Aboriginal and treaty rights. The possession of that power is the essence of
what it means to hold colonial authority over subject peoples. Certainly the
experience sensitized me to the tactics of "disinformation and smear" that
characterized the psychological warfare deployed by authorities to accompany the armed confrontation at Gustafsen Lake in 1995. With all of officialdom's apparent readiness to unleash instruments of state violence
inside or outside the law in order to hold the militant wing of the First
Nations' sovereignty movement on the margins of power, I believe the
essence of modern-day Indian fighting lies more in the weaponry of state
propaganda than in the machinery of physical violence.

This text is the first of two and possibly three volumes, each of which
reports on a larger research project I call *The Bowl with One Spoon*. The
intent is that each book can stand alone, even as it also forms part of a set.
In envisaging the prospect of a trilogy I have drawn on the example of
Francis Jennings' "Covenant Chain" series. I some ways I could characterize this project as an effort to extend and elaborate many of the themes
and approaches pioneered in "The Covenant Chain." Indeed, what I have
tried to bring together here builds on many of the ideas that first started
to coalesce in my imagination when I experienced the revelations that
came to me from my first reading of *The Invasion of America*.[60]

As "The Covenant Chain," along with Clarence Alvord's *Mississippi Valley
in British Politics*, showed me, the Royal Proclamation of 1763 embodied
the position of one side in a long process of polarization in British North
American imperialism which would eventually clash in the American Revolution.[61] The process of attempting to work through the legal applications of that same Royal Proclamation would become a major theme in my
main political encounters with my own country during some of my best
and most difficult experiences of both my professional and my personal
life. As I hope to demonstrate, the Royal Proclamation of 1763 is no less
momentous in its meaning for the world in these times than it was in the
era when it stood as one of the most symbolically potent provocations to
the civil war in British North America – a war that led to the emergence of
the American empire from the old British Empire.

I have used detailed subtitles within this volume's seven chapters. These
headings are designed to help readers who want to approach the book

selectively. In a narrative as ambitious as this one in the extent of the temporal and geographic space it covers as well as in the ethnographic diversity of the peoples it describes, I also felt it was important use these subtitles to help readers focus on the major changes of subject matter. I see them as a kind of literary cartography to a landscape of history, law, and politics that is probably not familiar to all but a few specialists.

A consistent challenge in writing this book has been the attempt to present a variety of comparative histories, emphasizing thematic as well as temporal or geographic unities. There is, however, a central narrative running through *The Bowl with One Spoon*: it describes the negotiation with Indigenous peoples in North America of rights and titles to lands through the medium of treaties. This narrative leads, for instance, from the dealings of the Dutch with the Longhouse peoples in the Mohawk Valley in the mid-seventeenth century to finalization of a treaty with the Nisga'a people in the twenty-first century. That process of bargaining continues yet, especially on the contested grounds and waters of the Indian Country of British Columbia.

This volume takes the narrative of extended negotiations as far as the height of land between the Great Lakes watershed and the continent's arctic watershed. Those negotiations took place before the Confederation of the Canadian dominion in 1867. By no means, however, is this volume's content delimited by these temporal and geographic markers. It devotes considerable space to developments up to the end of the twentieth century in a comparison between Indian affairs in North America and what was called "Native affairs" in South Africa. Similarly, it devotes attention to New Spain and to twentieth-century Mexico. It identifies a powerful tradition of Aboriginal leadership and philosophy in Tupac Amaru, in Tecumseh, and in George Manuel. It looks at the identity politics of Creole populations, majority cultures, and minority groups.

Part One of this book, "Surveying the Base Lines," introduces the range of subjects elaborated throughout *The Bowl with One Spoon* and it builds to explain the life and career of George Manuel, the founder in the mid-1970s of the World Council of Indigenous Peoples. Manuel left us a short volume describing the major outlines of his philosophy of the Fourth World. This philosophy represents a major point of departure and a recurrent motif running throughout this project.

PART ONE

Surveying the Base Lines

CHAPTER ONE

Charting Territory, Giving Names

I am distressed by the utter lack of interest in historical patterns
shown by so many of our economic and financial elites. Learning from the past is not easy, but history is still the only laboratory we have in which to study social change.
Stephen Blank, *The Literary Review of Canada*, 1999/2000

THE ECOLOGICAL IMPERATIVE: MONOCULTURES OR BIODIVERSITY AND CULTURAL PLURALISM?

Two immense, opposing forces are pulling at humanity as we move beyond
the millenarian fever during this time of great transformations. One historical impetus is tugging down old linguistic, cultural, national, economic, and political boundaries. The other pressure is seen in the struggle by
many of the world's peoples against assimilation and in support of those
values, institutions, and political rights they believe are essential to retain
or secure a distinct place on this planet. This fundamental divergence,
whose polarizing essence permeates almost every nuance of political decision making at this historical moment, is recognized by a growing chorus
of commentators as the great *yin* and *yang*, the primary thesis and antithesis, of global geopolitics.

To Boutros Boutros-Ghali, for instance, the former secretary general of
the United Nations, the essential tension of our time is between "globalization and fragmentation."[1] Michael Ignatieff characterized the same divergence as the last remaining big theme suitable for deep and extended coverage by that endangered species he identifies as "public intellectuals." With
the demise of the "Red Wheel" of Soviet-style communism, writes Ignatieff,
"the only grand narrative available is about the conflict between globalism
and particularism – between the forces of technology, capital, and science,
which are sweeping us towards global sameness, and the traditions of language, culture, religion, and identity, which maintain our differences
intact."[2] In the mid-1990s Benjamin Barber dramatized and popularized the
division in another way. He coined the phrase, "Jihad vs. McWorld" as a title
emphasizing the vast distance between the realms represented by fast food's
most iconographic franchise and the violence stereotypically connected to
the most violent outer fringes of religious and ethnic fanaticism.[3]

While the term "globalization" has emerged as an all-purpose signifier of
the border-piercing quality of developments in technology and economics

that compress space and devour the cultural ground of human difference, other descriptive variations on the same theme have competed for room in our lexicons of representation and imagination. One line of thought, stretching from Hegel to Alexander Kojeve to the Canadian philosopher George Grant,4 poses "the universal and homogenous state" as what Francis Fukuyama triumphantly popularized in 1992 as "The End of History."5

Fukuyama's book was written in victorious response to the disappearance of the Soviet Union and the dismantling of the Berlin Wall in 1989, events that seemed, in his estimation, to demonstrate that the great contentions of history had ended. He argued that the mortal blows delivered to fascism and then to Marxism left capitalism and liberal democracy as victorious for all time as the world's single viable ideological terrain from which to generate law, governance, and economic relations for all peoples. For Fukuyama and his patrons at the RAND Corporation and the business-sponsored John M. Olin Center at the University of Chicago, the internal inconsistencies within Western civilization had finally been resolved. This resolution, in turn, was hailed as the culmination of a global evolutionary process that had essentially eliminated all viable alternatives to the world-wide dominion of a way of life whose heartland is the United States and whose quintessential expression seemed at that time to lie in Japan.

The bias of the text presented here runs against the triumphalism of Fukuyama and towards the arguments and initiatives of those seeking to oppose the complete hegemony of the universal and homogenous state – global corporate rule – as the end of history. To this end I employ other vocabularies aimed at indentifying the genesis, character, and possible outcomes of the dialectic that remains our own era's most basic and influential animator. Often, for instance, I use language that comes in the first instance from biology, horticulture, and, most important, the strategically crucial field of ecology. I advance this language to explain various kinds of relationships whose descriptions have come to be far too monopolized by the professional jargon of economics and political science. To illustrate, I shall make reference to the "monocultural" attributes of global corporations against the "cultural pluralism" that is humanity's sociological equivalent to the God-given attribute of "biodiversity" in the plant and animal kingdoms.

The usefulness of applying terms drawn from agriculture to other forms of cultural expression is richly displayed in the writings of Vandana Shiva. An expert on seed science in India, Shiva outlined her broader analysis of political theory in her transitional volume *Monocultures of the Mind*. Her invocation of the limiting constraints of monocultural thinking dramatically cuts beyond the life cycles of plants to describe the universalist pretensions of the world's predominant economic regime.[6] Shiva reserves her most spirited condemnation for what she sees as a deluge of self-serving abuse of science's prestige. She identifies particularly those patriarchal agencies of capitalist accumulation in the northern hemisphere, alleging that their agents and allies sytematically discredit the local knowledge passed down and cultivated over thousands of years by many of the Indigenous peoples on the planet. Even as the insights and understanding contained in "folk" cultures are denigrated as unscientific, some of the most valuable fruits of this genre of knowledge are expropriated and patented as the "intellectual property" of global corporations, thereby furthering the concentration of power in narrowing circles of privatized wealth.

The abuse of science to favour some forms of knowledge and to delegitimize others, Shiva maintains, has been especially marked in the area of economics. Here there has been an extremely potent convergence of interests represented by commentators who justify and advocate the monopolization of power in fewer and fewer hands. They do so by cultivating the fiction that the property relations that grew out of a specific cultural context represent something more than mere human inventions. They characterize the kind of property relations that facilitated, first, the rise of European imperialism and, next, the planetary dominion of global corporations as being premised on the discovery and expanding application of universal natural laws. Some of the Enlightment's most influential assertions have been exploited to represent the expansionistic exploits rooted in one continent's history as the saga of revealed natural law universally applicable to the social organization of all peoples. Most often this intellectual slight of hand equates democracy itself, always an elusive ideal whose realization involves far more than the periodic appearance of ballot boxes, with the spread of an increasingly monocultural approach to the structuring of property relationships.

If monoculture represents one possible destiny at the end of history, then multiculturalism signifies another approach to the construction of society and the exercise of power. In the surprisingly strident intellectual resistance to the adoption of multiculturalism as government policy in North America, Allan Bloom, Arthur M. Schlesinger Jr, Robert Hughes, Samuel P. Huntington, J.L. Granatstein, and others have deployed potent arsenals of language that sought to discredit their opponents. They tend to paint multiculturalism's proponents indiscriminately as extremists whose advocacy of pluralistic educational and cultural policies amount to a virtual sanctioning of jihad, racism, tribalism, parochialism, and ethnic nationalism.[7]

Such condemnations emanating from within North America have reverberated globally. As Kay B. Warren comments in his reflections on the work of Mayan public intellectuals in Guatemala: "Throughout the world, ethnic mobilization and nationalist movements have been cast as a primary source of post–Cold War violent conflict. Groups that articulate their demands in ethnic terms are seen as dupes of cynical leaders seeking political power at any price."[8] Such alarmism drew heavily from the sweeping generalizations spawned in the 1990s by the authentic horrors of ethnic cleansing in Rwanda and in the fragmented former Yugoslavia.

The editorial writers at *The Economist* ruminated in 1991, for instance, that "the virus of tribalism risks becoming the AIDS of international politics – lying dormant for years, then flaring up to destroy countries."9

One of the objects of this book is to respond with equanimity to the brutalization of language and to the wild and uncritical generalizations that have sometimes been attached opportunistically to these debaucheries of history. The quest for appropriate language leads directly to the field of ecology, a realm of explanation where high esteem is afforded to attributes of balance, equilibrium, symbiosis, synergy, harmony, and recognition of the complexity of relationships between all species and organisms together with their habitats.10 In keeping with the underlying spirit of these demands, the arts and sciences of ecology require a far less human-centred view of experience and the development of intellectual frames of reference that place peoples inside, rather than outside, conceptions of how the web of life is sustained and renewed.

Among the most essential insights to emerge from the study of ecology is an emphasis on the verbs rather than on the nouns of experience – an emphasis that concentrates particularly on change, process, and relationships over long periods of time rather than on perspectives so fixated on isolated, static things and on dispassionate objectivity that few limits are placed on the secularization, objectification, and commodification of nature.11 Accordingly, ecological understanding places human nature within broader notions of the rest of nature, just as it positions politics and economics within larger environmental frames of reference. Alternatively, it eschews allocating the jurisdictional oddity known as "the environment" to a category of statecraft encompassed by the pre-eminent claims of politics or economics.

This ecological perspective embraces complexity, diversity, and almost unlimited variation as essential conditions for the healthy and successful renewal of plant and animal life on this planet. This same principle applies equally to human beings, whose basic media of social differentiation include the rich array of cultures inherited from history. The word "culture" has become one of the most elastic, all-purpose terms in the English language, an expression with a particularly rich and complex history in the social sciences.12 In using it, I emphasize those patterns of beliefs, manners, transmission of knowledge, and modes of human conceptualization that mediate all manner of community alignments linking human beings with one another as well as with our habitats and our plant and animal relatives. Culture is the most active ingredient in the ether of relationships that enables individuals to find for themselves, and to apportion to their fellows, unique places in the matrix of connections, bonds, rivalries, and antagonisms that constitue the changing configurations and moving constellations of human society.

The most ancient and precise instruments of human creativity and culture are the many thousands of distinct languages that have evolved over the millennia, carrying with them from one generation to the next, vast, adaptive accumulations of human insight. Nothing more graphically illustrates the impoverishment of the primary means for cultural diversity and pluralism than the muffling, silencing, and elimination of whole complexes of linguistic articulation from humanity's shared vocabulary of expressive media. The erosion and extinguishment of the conditions for linguistic pluralism can be seen as a cultural expression of the same complex of industrial and economic forces that lead to species depletion at a rate of about three distinct life forms an hour.[13] More species have disappeared from the planet in the last century and a half than since the last Ice Age.[14] As the ecological sage E.O. Wilson has been declaring for decades, the rapid and accelerating pace of this extinction of non-human life forms is a crisis of monumental proportions. More than any other index of ecological degradation, the impoverishment of biological diversity through species extinguishment exposes the suicidal unsustainability of contemporary civilization.[15]

The depletion and desecration of the web of life's pluralistic ambundance raises the deepest possible questions about our individual and collective responsibilities to one another, to our posterity, and to our plant and animal relatives. As one research team commented, "Death is one thing – an end to birth is something else."[16] The monumental implication of this murder of myriad life forms – this slow suicide from within as humanity collectively reduces the viability of our own successful renewal along with that of the planet's other animate beings – is beginning to be addressed on a variety of political and juridical fronts. In *Biodiversity and Democracy*, for instance, forester Paul Wood proposes to meet the crisis by amending national constitutions to afford the maintenance of biodiversity priority over other forms of interest and rights.[17]

The primary factors in the irreversible losses of biodiversity are industrial pollution, overharvesting, and, most devastating, the destruction of the habitats of many millions of unique life forms by allowing the commercial farming and reforestation of agricultural monocultures to monopolize arable space. The propensity of agribusinesses to take over vast areas of the planet for the commercial reproduction of commodified monocultures, including a very small number of domesticated animal species, expands the domain of an increasingly uniform regime of property relations. The sociological and anthropological equivalents to this monocultural monopolization of living space, including the world's oceans, is the disappearance of many of humanity's languages.

The mirror image of the widening fields of English, Spanish, German, French, Hindi, Cantonese, Arabic, and a few other languages lies in the narrowing or disappearing spaces left for the regeneration of the majority of humanity's pluralistic linguistic heritage. Over most of human history, the main repository of humanity's linguistic resources has been maintained, expanded, and renewed in the spoken communication of

Indigenous peoples spread throughout the planet. The densest concentration by far of linguistic resources on the planet in 1492 was in the Americas, the host continents for as many as 2,200 distinct tongues.[18]

One of the major outcomes of the Columbian conquests is that the majority of these Aboriginal languages in the Americas are no longer spoken. This silencing of the American holocaust's Indian victims helps facilitate the willed amnesia and the self-serving denial surrounding the prolonged horror of this continuing event in world history. The loss of languages in the Americas and in Australia marks the most extreme instances of a worldwide phenomenon. The monocultures of mind and matter that occupy more and more of the planet's space show up in the process that has already seen 6,000 distinct languages go silent, with 90 per cent of the world's remaining 6,000 languages facing sure extinction within one hundred years if present trends continue.[19]

The strong ecological links between and cultural pluralism in the human species and biodiversity in plants and animals is the cumulative outcome of at least tens of thousands of years of history. During long expanses of time, thousands of Aboriginal societies evolved their own sets of relationships with this planet's vast range of variegated geographies and bioregions, each one providing its own distinct combination of environmental niches for some of the many millions of life forms with which we share this earth.

The rich understandings derived from these long experiences of Indigenous peoples with the unique ecologies of their Aboriginal lands is often described as Indigenous knowledge, Aboriginal knowledge, Indigenous science, or Native science.[20] Although there have been sporadic cycles of interest in the power of Indigenous knowledge since the earliest encounters between Europeans and the Aboriginal inhabitants of the New World, the rush of botanists, entomologists, and other scientists to salvage information from the world's disappearing rain forests created the initial context for the most recent surge of effort to record and exploit the intricate understanding of plants and animals typically held by the Indigenous inhabitants of specific bioregions.[21] Indigenous languages are both rich repositories and tailor-made media for the dissemination and renewal of Indigenous knowledge. This way of passing along information and concepts draws heavily on the minute observation by countless generations of the distinct relationships between the life cycles of the plants, the animals (including the human ones), and whole complexes of geographic conditions indigenous to particular places.

Characteristically, Aboriginal languages tend to be ecologically constructed more around verbs than nouns – more around descriptions of processes than on categorizations of objectified things. This verb-noun dichotomy is graphically illustrated by the structure of Michif, a Cree-French trade language that developed along with the Métis identity from the intercultural fur trade of Canada. According to linguists Peter Bakker and Robert A. Papen, "with very few exceptions, the verbs in Michif are Cree and the nouns are French." [22]

In the final analysis, this priceless epistemological inheritance invested in Aboriginal languages is part of humanity's shared philosophical commonwealth. Indigenous knowledge, however, cannot long be sustained or renewed as a living force for human adaptation to the needs and requirements of other species while the relentless expansion continues of all forms of monoculture, whether environmental, psychological, political, or economic. As growing numbers of plant and animal species succumb to ecocide and as human society is pressed into increasingly monocultural moulds of social organization and property law, many words go silent in many different languages that once described existent beings, things, processes, and relationships. Their extinction becomes total, eliminated not only from living existence but also from the cerebral landscapes of human memory. Meanwhile, the new frontiers of verbal invention point humanity at the merging intersections of organism and machine, as biotechnology's corporate prospectors hurry to extract patents, products, and profits from the secularization and privatization of the genetic commons.

Accordingly, I see the complex of related issues pertaining to multiculturalism, biodiversity, ecology, and economics as the most fruitful grounds for the study of globalization. The very word "globalization" is itself reflective of a verb-poor language stretching the meaning of a noun – the globe – to describe a vast range of interrelated processes as they unfold through time.

To the extent that various aspects of globalization advance monocultures – the elimination of the conditions for pluralism and diversity among plant and animal species, including the human specie – we are looking at processes with vast environmental and sociological consequences in the twenty-first century. Our experience with genocide, species extinction, and linguistic impoverishment in the twentieth century may be mild compared with what is to come if we do not find ways and means to place limits and provisos on the incursions of McWorld and on the construction of the universal and homogenous state.

THE WORLD AS ONE BIG MARKET OR A PLANET OF DISTINCT PEOPLES?

The demise of European empires after the Second World War seemingly opened space for the liberated expression of the distinct peoples and the cultural pluralism of many societies that had previously suffered under the weight of various imperialisms. Beginning in the 1950s, many dozen former European colonies in Africa and Asia were recognized as sovereign nations in international law.[23] This accelerating movement of decolonization appeared for a time to be but one aspect of a wider process of liberating change in history. In the name of equality and self-determination, many old approaches to the apportionment of wealth and power shifted, with large ramifications for the relationship between men and women, labour and capital, and African-Americans and whites in the United States.

The extension of the instruments of self-government to many former colonies created the basis for a shift in the nature of ethnic and religious tensions within many of the new countries, whose borders were often more a product of European history than expressions of local conceptions of territorial configuration. Nevertheless, freedom's cry was heard and repeated in many thousands of communities where the Indigenous peoplehood of the inhabitants remained unreflected in the constitutional shape and design of the new nation-states or in many of the older ones in the Americas and elsewhere.[24]

The vast pluralistic potential that might have been liberated in widening the franchise of self-determination to thousands of Indigenous societies and dozens of nation-states was suggested in the opening words of the Charter of the United Nations. In that Charter, the primary unit of law and political organization was described as "peoplehood," with "We, the peoples of the United Nations," announcing "our" intention to avoid war and defend peace through a regime of respect for both the integrity of treaties and the existence of "fundamental human rights."

Even as the Old World empires of Europe withered, a New World empire emerged to place new constraints on decolonization and on the attending rights of diverse peoples to express freely the essential moral tenets of their distinct cultures. At the heart of this New World empire is not a country, although the leadership of the United States of America plays a singular role in the chain of command and in the policing structures of this global regime of increasingly standardized property relationships. What stands instead at the metropolitan core of this New World realm is an institutional complex of currency markets, bond markets, and transnational or global corporations. Together these denationalized centres of commerce, capital, and technology are becoming a supranational leviathan subject only to a law unto themselves. This leviathan of global corporatism is devoted to rendering universal the outcome of a very specific process of historical change and evolution, a process that gives rise to a narrow legal conception of how human beings should be governed in their conduct of relations with one another and with the rest of nature. It is the clash between the pluralistic forces of cultural diversity and the homogenizing thrust of global corporatism that constitutes the primary conflict of values, ideals, and purpose in these times. And, at the heart of this conflict, are two seemingly simple questions that remain as contentious now as at any time in history: What are the borders between the public domain and private property? And whose laws should define these distinctions?

The lack of any clear consensus about how to conceptualize property, especially on the genetic frontiers of biotechnology,[25] suggests that, instead of being at the end of history, we are at the awkward beginnings of an era whose essential character is still too close and pervasive to be ascertainable with real clarity. What is becoming apparent, however, is that the central conflicts of the new millennium are raising new questions about old geopolitical constructs as fundamental as sovereignty, peoplehood, private property, treaty relations, and the power to create and charter legal entities known as corporations. These central elements of domestic and international law are being subjected to a process of rethinking and reformulation even as nation-states are losing the powers and capacities to act authoritatively as viable agencies of self-determination and national sovereignty. Their role is increasingly pre-empted by the guiding force of speculation in currency, bond and stock markets, and the investment decisions of global corporations.[26] "The global financial marketplace," proclaimed the *New York Times Magazine* in 1998, "has emerged as the ruling international authority, more potent than any military or political power." In an article describing the financial markets as "the Nuke of the 1990s," the journalists at this magazine announced that "the global markets are the most powerful force the world has ever seen, capable of obliterating governments almost overnight."[27]

There is much confusion surrounding the consequences of further empowerment of the private sector to fill the vacuum left by the severe and rapid downsizing of public government. What is clear, however, is that the transformations under way are so basic as to constitute a revolution. Indeed, so fundamental are the shifts in the power structure that there is considerable uncertainty about exactly who, if anyone, is really in control. As David C. Korten observes, the main steering mechanism of global governance is a "system of autonomous rule by money and for money that functions on autopilot beyond the control of any human actor and is unresponsive to any human sensibility."[28]

The severe downturn beginning in 1997 among the former tigers of the "Asian economic miracle," for instance, seemed foreboding in ways that hinted at huge hidden fragilities on the global frontiers of particular forms of deregulation. Similar anxieties pulled at the smug confidences invested in a stock market when, in 2001, the high-tech engines of speculation sputtered into a free fall. Even the executives of the world's largest enterprises, elites who initiated the push during the Reagan-Thatcher years towards the wholesale privatization and downscaling of national governments, seemed uncertain of their capacity to control the whirlwind of forces unleashed by their growing influence. As William Grieder noted in *One World, Ready or Not,* "despite their supple strengths, the great multinationals are insecure themselves ... Behind corporate facades, the anxiety is genuine."[29]

In spite of the concealed nervousness even at the heights of financial and corporate power, the push continued on many fronts towards a universal regime of trade law and property law. Most movement in this

direction necessarily undermined democracy, as well as the conditions for
the maintenance of many of the cultural, economic, and political particu-
larities essential to the ecology of human diversity. The governments of
most nation-states served and advanced this agenda and strove to eliminate
all kinds of boundaries that might limit, restrict, or complicate the ability
of global corporations to conduct their transnational operations. In 1993
Akio Morita, the legendary driving force behind the global ascendance of
Sony Corporation, presented one of the clearest statements of what large
corporations expected from governments in the expansionary business
atmosphere generated by the end of the Cold War and the demise of the
Soviet Union. In an open letter to the leaders of the powerful G7 countries, Morita proposed that "we begin to seek ways of lowering *all* economic barriers between North America, Europe and Japan – trade, investment,
legal and so forth – in order to begin creating the nucleus of the new world
economic order that would include harmonized world business systems
with agreed rules and procedures that transcend national boundaries."
According to Mr Morita, the ultimate goal of this "harmonization" of law
to govern all property relations, was to make "the whole of the developed
world into one big market."[30]

The effort to organize the planet as one big market to provide a uniform
milieu of operations for global enterprises such as the Sony Corporation
assumes that economic forces should ultimately override cultural configurations as the primary principle of political organization. The unspoken
implication of such assumptions is that those peoples whose cultures do
not conform to the values of the Sony Corporation and its transnational
cousins cannot continue to survive, let alone thrive, in this world. Peoples,
no less than individuals, must either bend and assimilate to the ultimate
sovereignty of money and global technological innovation or die like modern-day dinosaurs to make room for those who have extended the legal
frontiers of corporate hegemony to the richest and most expansive fields
of private property.

My goal in this book is to present alternatives as I challenge the often-
unspoken genocidal assumptions of those who have, knowingly or not,
placed death sentences on so many of the world's distinct peoples. In challenging the underlying assumptions of neo-liberal modes of globalization,
I try to expose the dominant economic paradigm in the world today not as
the manifestation of some universal natural law[31] but as the historical outcome of Europe's colonization of the New World. In my view, the New
World imperialism of global corporations, headquartered primarily in the
United States, is derived in significant measure from the Old World imperialism of Europe. The colonizing power of this continuum of imperial
rule has fallen with especially severe force on the Indian Country of the
Americas.

A close look at this expansion into Indian Country exposes key episodes
in the early genesis of the processes currently disenfranchising and disin-

heriting a large portion of the world's people and peoples. The drive to expand the laws and ethos of private property westward into the vast expanse of Indian Country produced a New World Country known as the United States of America. In expanding westward, the United States became the essential heartland of a border-piercing entrepreneurial empire whose aggressive spirit has been internalized, renewed and extended by the likes of Mr Morita and his famous electronics company – a company that became a fitting symbol of the kind of institution Fukuyama saw as dominating the end of history.

In challenging the assumptions of "the New World Order," the phrase used by Morita and, in 1991, by President George Bush to justify the war on Iraq,[32] I condemn the crusade to impose a single global economic regime on all the world's peoples. I argue that, in a world where cultural pluralism and the self-determination of peoples is respected, there must be a wide range of different economic systems to support the ecology of human diversity in all its many manifestations. This way of viewing the world sees economics and technology as instruments of human will and invention, rather than as masters of most of the relationships linking human beings with each other and with the rest of nature. Instead of downgrading culture as a secondary feature of human organization that can be supported and expressed only when consistent with the requirements of a universalized system of economic relationships, my alternative view pictures cultural diversity, the human equivalent to biodiversity, as *the* essential condition of ecological equilibrium on the planet.[33] Only by respecting the rights of diverse peoples to chart their own distinct courses in history can cultural diversity be maintained. And there can be no true self-determination for the earth's distinct peoples unless they can defend and fashion diverse regimes of economic relations that both support and manifest the primary ideals inherent in each of the world's many cultures.[34] I argue that we should celebrate and facilitate the central contention of Samuel P. Huntington in *The Clash of Civilizations and the Remaking of World Order*. "In the post–Cold War world," he writes, "the most important distinctions among people are not ideological, political, or economic. They are cultural."[35]

In *A Canada of Light*, B.W. Powe adds a compelling voice to the growing conviction that the pluralistic cultural wealth of humanity cannot be sustained once those who wield political power primarily through the instrument of capital are allowed unrestricted latitude to complete their global regime of economic homogenization. "Culture must enfold economics," he states, "or there will be little purpose to the amassing of wealth and how that wealth is distributed." In advancing the image of Canada as a "communication state" where the ecological dynamics of process and "constant negotiation" are generally favoured over the single-minded attainment of absolute goals and fixed self-definitions, Powe argues that, "without a compelling case for cultural meaning ... everything becomes a financial arrangement, a soulless politics of deals."[36] His reflections are consistent with a great current of criticism running through many professions, disciplines, and schools of thought. The shared conviction animating this criticism is that the essential energy enlivening nature favours pluralism and diversity, and that planners of all sorts should strive to reflect rather than stiffle these ecological values in their work.

This theme permeates the reflections of Jane Jacobs, the urbanist who is best known for her influential observations on the evolution, character, and future of great cities. In an apparent departure from her main topic, Jacobs devoted a whole volume to making the case for the legal separation of the province of Quebec from the rest of Canada. She justified Quebec's independence as being consistent with the growing realization passed down from the Victorians that "nature was a force forever hostile to uniformity, a force that insisted on diversity." She added, "the belief [in diversity] has already influenced thought and action in a thousand different ways. And we can be as sure as we can be of anything that as long as our current understanding of nature prevails, the belief in diversity itself as a source of vitality will continue to be a powerful and growing influence on thought about all kinds of things."[37]

This current of thought stands at odds with the huge monocultural biases of prevailing orthodoxies in economic theory which drive and support the continuing frontier expansions of global corporatism. Among no other kind of group is opposition to this modern-day frontierism quite so visceral as in the struggle of several thousand surviving Indigenous societies on the planet to retain geographic, economic, and jurisdictional living space for themselves and their posterity. Collectively, Indigenous peoples constitute humanity's oldest and most linguistically diverse repositories of the cultural pluralism inherited from many tens of thousands of years of human history. In their fate lies an important key to the outcome of many fundamental processes of global transformation, especially as they pertain to the future of the planet's many distinct ecologies of biodiversity.

Since 1492 Indigenous peoples have faced history's most sustained, massive, and many-faceted drive to limit cultural and biological pluralism and to integrate us all into what we can now identify as a single global system whose primary medium is universalized capitalism. The impetus to create this regime has drawn on the expansionary energies of European empires and their successor states that emerged from the process of "decolonization." The first of these decolonized successor states, the United States, gave rise to an imperial regime of its own that afforded broad liberties to business enterprises. The largest of these enterprises formed the basis for most of the planet's global corporations. The drive of these commercial leviathans to expand their markets combined with their political interventions aimed at creating increasingly standardized structures of globalized property law. In the process, the corporate progeny of the informal American empire have become the world's most active promoters of planetary monoculturalism.

Seen in this light, the defence and the sustainability of aboriginality as a primary source of the right of distinct peoples to self-determination becomes, perhaps, the crucial test case for the defence of many other kinds of fundamental rights and freedoms. In success or failure, the character of Indigenous peoples' struggles to express and enhance the cultural pluralism of the Fourth World reveals much about the nature of those forces aligned against the continuation of many forms of community linking not only human beings but also the millions of plant and animal species with which we share our existence on this planet. The Columbian conquests that Indigenous peoples have endured since 1492 have been somewhat transmuted into more subtle, yet far more pervasive, forms of commercial imperialism. What remains consistent with earlier rounds of Europe's most genocidal bouts of frontier conquest, however, is the nature of the underlying justifications given in explaining the apportionment of expansionism's spoils.

No less than in the era of Europe's ascent to global dominance, the imperatives of commercial expansionism are advanced in language proclaiming that the outcome of history is inevitable, even as it frequently ascribes to very local and specific historical circumstances an unwarranted authority derived from false claims of universality. In this respect, Fukuyama's *End of History* is consistent with many older traditions of imperial self-justification that either explicitly or implicitly relegated the Aboriginal inhabitants of Europe's New World to the marginal status of doomed anachronisms in the way of narrow notions of Eurocentric progress.

In my estimation, the predominant motifs of globalization extend many of the basic patterns of the Columbian conquests which have remained since 1492 surprisingly consistent in their expropriative course. In order to move away from this old model towards more diversified forms of globalization, with plenty of room for the cultural pluralism that is the Fourth World's great hallmark, I believe we must favour cultural relationships over economic relationships as the primary medium of our interaction with each other and with the rest of nature.

I draw on the work of Karl Polanyi in challenging those sweeping claims that economics constitutes a pre-eminent system which encompasses and subordinates all other forms of social, cultural, and ecological interaction. In 1944 in *The Great Transformation*, Polanyi prophetically anticipated the intensity of the drive to push aside all resistance to the expanded dominion of markets, as if these institutions represented the realization of some form of universal natural law. In clarifying the huge and often violent interventions of governments in moving from one economic system to another, Polanyi rejected the "utopian" view that there is any such thing as a self-regulating market whose origins lie in attributes universal to the psychological makeup of all human beings. As he wrote, "man's economy, as a rule, is submerged in his social relationships."[38]

The exercise of economic self-determination to serve the cultural imperatives of distinct peoples would stand the program proposed by Morita in 1993 on its head. In the years that followed, this program was advanced with vigour by the governments of most countries.[39] The penalties from the International Monetary Fund, for instance, for not cooperating with the plan to retool the world as "one big market" were extremely harsh. The result of this subordination of self-governance and decolonization to the credit requirements of high finance was a rapid narrowing of the scope of real democracy, as limited and imperfect as our electoral devices have always been.[40] This reduction in the range of real electoral choices available to most citizens ccame as nation-states were increasingly being harnessed to the pre-eminent ideal of standardizing systems of global property law. This law can be envisaged as the whole complex of domestic and international provisions legitimizing ownership, exchange and taxation of lands, resources, goods, services, and money.

It should be emphasized that all forms of property ownership are arbitrary legal constructions created from the authority of a sovereign entity with the capacity to enforce its regimes of property relations through the power of its police and its criminal justice system. While the secure ownership of property depends on maintaining the stability of established sovereign authority, however, opportunities for the rapid acquisitions of new property are often available, especially to those riding the expansionary crest of new legal regimes and whose methods of rearranging heirarchies of power are sometimes revolutionary.

This phenomenon is illustrated in the processes that saw the establishment of all manner of New World proprietorships in the wake of the dispossession of Indigenous peoples. Between the old orders and the new ones have been many legal twilight zones, where genocide and bribery, extortion and influence peddling could co-exist with legally authorized transactions of sale and purchase. The repeated hauling out of great fortunes from such twilight zones on the kleptocratic borderlands of juridical order points to the fact that much of the world's financial capital is derived from primal expropriations on the frontiers of major transformations in sovereignty. This process is epitomized by the revolutionary emergence of the United States from the British Empire as a vehicle for, and prelude to, rapid westward expansion into Indian Country.

The growth of the United States has been instrumental in a global process of creating wider and wider zones for the application of standardized regimes of property law, often pushed forward in the name of free trade. By the late twentieth century the realization grew that the effect of this imposition of a dominant regime of property relations on most of the world's peoples was to further the universalization of the power of money over all other social, cultural, and humanitarian values. So expansive did the claims of capital become on the new frontiers of changing property relations that the genre of property law favoured by global corporations was extended into the farthest reaches of those reproductive forces that are at the basis of all life on this planet.

Even the genetic blueprints of living beings are being made the subject of individual and corporate ownership through the invention of a global regime of patent and copyright law covered under the rubric of "intellectual property." This frontier expansion of the laws of appropriation and "discovery" into the most sacred mysteries of life's renewal is a direct extension of the same historical processes by which European explorers in the name of their Christian monarchs once placed patents and charters on whole continents. These continents were thickly peopled with Indigenous peoples and densely covered with the intellectual and artistic edifaces representing the splendid achievements of their own Aboriginal civilizations. The cultural pluralism of Indigenous peoples symbolically marks the opposing pole from the pull to monoculturalism that is the hallmark of the rising dominance of global corporations.

The monocultural imperialism of global corporatism has been contested by the concurrent rise of non-governmental organizations (NGOs) as a growing force in the making of global history. These transnational agencies raise funds, organize citizens, and attempt to lobby poltiticians and business people, often in the name of international civil society. In so doing, the directors and members of these non-profit bodies have often endeavoured to mitigate the worst excesses of the empire of possessive individualism. In attaching themselves to missions such as environmental conservation, the lessening of world poverty and disease, or the protection of cultural pluralism, most NGOs have employed many of the organizational and communication techniques of those commercial conglomerates whose actions they often sought to stop or reform. Without a doubt, the networking potential of the Internet gave a powerful boost to the effectiveness of what their critics have dubbed "the NGO swarm."

In the 1990s the number of NGOs operating in two or more countries rose from 6,000 to over 26,000. The membership of these agencies grew correspondingly. For instance, by 1999 the Worldwide Fund for Nature could claim over 5 million members.[41] The NGOs flexed their muscles most effectively at the Rio Earth Summit in 1992, in the campaign to reform the World Bank, in the effective resistance to an expanded regime of commercial law promoted through the World Trade Organization, and in the failed effort to entrench a Multilateral Agreement on Investment. In all these campaigns, organizations representing Indigenous peoples played a significant role.

The British and Foreign Anti-Slavery Society, along with the closely connected Aborigines' Protection Society, were among the nineteenth-century forerunners of this genre of transnational organization. Although the ideals of Christian charity rather than the imperatives of cultural pluralism animated the activities of the broadly influential Aborigines' Protection Society, its methods of organization and many of its humanitarian goals set

patterns that still have relevance in efforts to further the democratic organization of more elaborate expressions of international civil society. The
contributions of this organization, whose activities are explored in this
text, speak of a broader phenomenon – that the legacies of the old British
Empire offer a range of legal, organizational, and institutional outgrowths
that can be deployed in checking the more monopolistic and monocultural propensities of the new American empire.

MANIFEST DESTINY AND "COLLATERAL DAMAGE": THE RECEDING FRONTIERS OF ANGLO-AMERICAN TRIUMPHALISM

As members of polities whose lands and identities represented the original
obstacles to the creation and consolidation of a New World Order emanating primarily from America, Indigenous peoples in the Western Hemisphere can speak with a kind of metropolitan authority about the experiences of those on the receiving end of a genre of imperialism whose scope
is now global. The very existence of Indigenous peoples in the heartland
of the empire of the United States can serve as a beacon or a warning to
other colonized classes and groups who are losing ground through the
transformation of the planet into "one big market." Indeed, the experience of First Nations in the Americas represents a kind of intense distillation of the meaning of colonialism in all its many manifestations. Their
strategies for survival in this new millennium ought to be viewed with the
utmost seriousness as plans that may have major implications and ramifications for many constituencies as we attempt to cope with an economic
and technological juggernaut that long ago crossed over the limits of environmental sustainability.

My own vantage point in this history is that of a Canadian whose professional life has unfolded within a relatively new academic field known as
Native American Studies. I write from the position of an observer outside
the United States, yet very much within the American empire. Further-
more, I write with an orientation to history that takes seriously the fact that
many of the earliest wars of the United States on Indian Country were also
wars on Canada. A key episode in this American campaign to extinguish
the Indian Country of Canada was the War of 1812, when the Shawnee
leader Tecumseh was martyred in his campaign to establish, with British
imperial support, a sovereign Aboriginal dominion in the interior of
North America.[42] This assault on Tecumseh and all he represented
marked the consolidation of a sense of manifest destiny in the United
States. This complex of conviction and belief has historically been used to
justify the dispossession of Native American peoples and to advance the
incorporation of large parts of Canada, Mexico, and all of Louisiana, the
Oregon Territory, and Alaska into the continental heartland of the American empire.[43]

A theme returned to frequently in these pages is the importance of the idea of manifest destiny in the rise of the United States to continental, hemispheric, and then world power. The essence of this infusion of religious conviction into public policy was that the will of God was manifest in the covenanted duty and destiny of the American people to expand their geographic, philosophical, and spiritual dominion in the world. This most potent of ideas in the shaping of global history developed its original shape and form on the frontiers of Puritan New England's encounters with Indian Country. From these beginnings, the idea was renewed and elaborated as the United States extended its secular power, together with its sense of providential mission, to ever wider spheres of geography. In the process, the revolutionary American republic gave rise to a multilingual American empire, just as the global reach of this same informal empire tremendously enlarged the power of the English-speaking world.

The phrase "manifest destiny" did not itself appear in print until 1845. It came in the form of a commentary on the United States's annexation of Texas penned in the *Democratic Review* by a New York journalist, John O'Sullivan. He coined the term in an editorial aimed at Great Britain and other alleged practitioners of "hostile interference" who, he asserted, were engaged in a conspiracy aimed at "limiting our greatness and checking the fulfillment of our manifest destiny to overspread the continent alloted by Providence for the free development of our yearly multiplying millions."[44] Much like the word "globalization," the phrase "manifest destiny" entered the world's vocabulary long after the process itself had embarked on its world-transforming course. Among those recognized for having given memorable articulation to the concept was the enigmatic Edmund Burke. Burke is best remembered for his classic defence of the principles of constitutional monarchy as he attacked the theories and actions of those who initiated the French Revolution. A generation earlier, however, the young politician gave powerful articulation in the British parliament to many of the grievances stimulating those on the Whig side of the arguments over the governance and destiny of British North America. These arguments laid the basis for a civil war popularly remembered as the American Revolution.

Although Burke culminated his illustrious career defending the hereditary institutions of the King in parliament and a landed gentry during the era of the French Revolution, he was highly critical of King George III for his imperial policies during the onset of the civil war in British North America. Burke was among those who alleged that the king had overreached the extent of his constitutional role by imposing the authority of the crown too aggressively into the Indian territories to the rear of the Anglo-American settlements. The effect of the Royal Proclamation of 1763 and, later, of the Quebec Act was to impose imperial authority as a barrier to the westward expansion of Anglo-American settlements and to set the British monarchy up as protector of the Aboriginal titles of the Indigenous peoples in the continent's interior. It was, accordingly, beyond the limits of

Burke's own political imagination to extend his attachment to the continuity of hereditary titles in Europe to the monarch's recognition of the hereditary titles invested in the Indigenous peoples within the crown's broadly expanded dominions in North America. In his celebrated speech advocating reconciliation with the rebellious elements in a polarized British North America, Burke criticized the Tory policy of imposing the authority of the crown as a defence of Indian Country and as an obstacle to check the rapid western expansion of Anglo-American settlements.

In articulating this important prototypical statement of manifest destiny, Burke referred to key passages in the Old Testament that the Puritans had used to justify the conquest and taking of Indian land in the expansion of their Calvinist theocracy. Burke deplored "the effect of [the imperial government's] attempting to forbid as a crime, and to suppress as an evil," what he saw as the fulfilment of a divine plan to people the continent with Protestant settlers. That westward expansion of population was nothing less than "the command and blessing of Providence," whose divine directive to His children was, "'Increase and multiply.'" For the crown to maintain the lands of British imperial Canada as a vast Indian reserve would be "to keep as a lair of wild beasts, that earth, which God, by an express Charter, has given to the children of men."[45]

The expansionary ethos of manifest destiny found one of its most effective advocates and instruments in President Thomas Jefferson. Conor Cruise O'Brien characterizes the Sage of Monticello as the "the prophet who wrote down the sacred scripture" of America's "civil religion."[46] As the primary author of the Declaration of Independence and the primary operative in the Louisiana Purchase, Jefferson was adept in situating his politics in the strategic transition zone between the sacred and the secular, between Bible and statute, between the Kingdom of Heaven and the republic of man. In his inaugural address in 1805, for instance, he invoked the Old Testament preoccupations of New England's Puritan founders as God's elect. "God led our forefathers," he said, "as Israel of old."[47]

The capacity of manifest destiny to cut through all contradictions and to surmount most logistical obstacles blocking its path finds its origins in the paradoxical marriage of the two major sources from which the United States draws its founding inspiration. One source lies in the messianic extremes of Calvinist protestantism. The other is the Enlightenment's more secular emphasis on reason and rationality, as well as on the natural rights that adhere universally to all people and peoples. In addressing this paradox as an essential feature of American expansionism, Albert K. Weinberg writes, "The alchemy which transmuted a natural right from a doctrine of democratic nationalism into a doctrine of imperialism was the very idea of manifest destiny which the doctrine of natural right created ... In the end the natural right was not a right universal, moderate, and innocuous, but a right special, exorbitant, and potentially aggressive."[48]

The expectation that not only North America but South America as well was destined to become a single, cohesive polity goes back at least to the presidency of Jefferson in the early years of the nineteenth century. Jefferson saw the emergence of his country as an "Empire of Liberty." As he declared, "Our confederacy must be viewed as the nest from which all America, North and South, is to be peopled." He looked forward with impatience to the day when the hemisphere would be settled by a people "speaking the same language, governed in similar forms, and by similar laws."[49] The claims and assertions of manifest destiny echoed through the generations. The doctrine began with many variations on the general theme that Indians had no right to the soil of their ancestry and birth because they were small in number and did not seemingly use the lands in ways that exploited its full potential to generate commercial wealth and support the expansion of Christian civilization. "Is one of the fairest portions of the globe," asked Indiana Territory governor William Henry Harrison rhetorically, "to remain in a state of nature, the haunt of a few wretched savages, when it seems destined by the Creator to give support to a large population and to be a seat of civilization, of science, and of true religion?"[50]

Similarly, the remaining claims and titles of the Old World empires of France, Spain, Portugal, Russia, and Great Britain were viewed by many American patriots as terminal holdings awaiting the assigned time to give ground before the superior rights of God's chosen ones. "It belongs of right to the United States," wrote an editorialist in the *New York Evening Post* on the eve of the Louisiana Purchase, "to regulate the future destiny of North America. The country is ours; ours is the right to its rivers and to all sources of future opulence, power and happiness which lay scattered at our feet."[51] The expectation that all of North America was the legitimate inheritance of the United States, has been common wisdom in many circles since the founding of the American republic. As John Adams wrote in 1776, "The Unanimous Voice of the Continent is that Canada must be ours."[52] A generation later, Congressman William Harper was articulating the shared assumptions of many in the United States when he declared, "To me it appears that the Author of Nature has marked out limits in the south, by the Gulf of Mexico; and on the north, by the regions of eternal frost."[53]

As with Jefferson, the geographical projectory of these predictions for the progress of manifest destiny could shift in a flash from a continent to a whole hemisphere. In the words of the *Democratic Review*, the goal was "to establish on earth the noblest temple ever dedicated to the worship of the Most High – the Sacred and the True. Its floor shall be a hemisphere – its roof the firmament of the star-studded heavens, and its congregation an Union of many Republics, comprising hundreds of happy millions."[54]

The expectation that some sort of continental union was both inevitable and desirable has not been the exclusive preserve of expansionists in the United States. There have been many champions in Canada as well of various forms of continentalism and Anglo-American manifest destiny.[55] One

of the most influential early Canadian voices to be raised in support of the
political and economic integration of North America was that of Goldwin
Smith, a Torontonian who, in 1891, layed out in *Canada and the Canadian
Question* one of the seminal arguments for the geopolitical unification of
the two countries. To Smith, it was clear that North America was an "Anglo-
Saxon continent." The American continent should therefore belong to
"the English tongue and to Anglo-Saxon civilization." Through "unification of the English-speaking race," the conditions would be sufficient "to
assimilate the French element or even to prevent the indefinite consolidation and growth of a French nation."[56]

If manifest destiny contained the kernel of the belief that the shared destiny of Anglo-Saxon peoples was to control all of North America, the
Indigenous peoples of the continent developed their own sets of principles
and symbols with the intent to secure for themselves and their progeny at
least some chance of collective survival. This planning was sporadically
applied with the most concerted effectiveness in the decades following the
American Revolution, when an Indian Confederacy coalesced along the
western frontiers of the fragile new republic. The objective of this most
prolific era of confederation building in Indian Country was for the federal council of this Aboriginal polity to assert its own sovereign jurisdiction
in international law over at least a portion of the First Nations' ancestral
lands.

One of the Aboriginal symbols that carried forward some of the central
theories of that geopolitical hope was the image of a bowl with one spoon
– a recurring motif running throughout this text. It began to appear with
particular regularity in the design of many Indian wampum belts in the
years when the Indian Confederacy achieved its most formidable scope,
especially through the articulated insights and organizational activities of
Tecumseh. These shell-beaded wampums were often adorned with picto-
graphic representations depicting the main contractual features of treaties
that Indian groups made with one another and sometimes with non-
Indian diplomats as well.[57] The bowl with one spoon was a representation
of the principle that certain hunting territories were to be shared in common. This concept of shared hunting territory became central to the sovereign strategy of the Indian Confederacy. The symbol conveyed the idea
that, because territory was shared by different Indian groups, no one
group could cede or sell land without the consent of the entire council of
federated Indian nations. The object was to block the northwesterly expansion of the United States in the decades following the American Revolution and to obtain international recognition for the fixed borders and the
sovereign geopolitical imperatives of the Indian Confederacy.

The Indian Confederacy's shared domain was, essentially, the southern
portion of the old Canada, a territory that would, in later years, become
the industrial heartland of the United States. The rise of major cities in the
Old Northwest of the United States, including Chicago, Milwaukee,

Detroit, Cleveland, Indianapolis, and Cincinati, bear witness to the ascendance of very different sovereign principles over lands once emblemized by the wampum symbol of the bowl with one spoon. Although the Indian Country of Canada gave way before the expansion of the American empire of private property, the old conflicts would find new proponents and new hunting grounds of discourse, argument, and confrontation.

The more recent treaties to formalize the incorporation of Canada into the American empire have been the Free Trade Agreement of 1988 and the North American Free Trade Agreement of 1993-94. Then, in 1998 and 2001, the leaders of the thirty-four nation-states in the Americas met first in Santiago, Chile, and then in Quebec City. The objective was to extend the kind of principles governing NAFTA to include all of South and Central America. These existing or contemplated trade treaties are geared to the expansion of a trading block governed by internal rules that are consistent with the basic outlines of the New World Economic Order as articulated by Akio Morita.[58] Moreover, these existing or contemplated constitutions of continental and hemispheric integration advance an agenda long advocated by proponents of Anglo-American Manifest Destiny.

The kind of explicit ethnocentrism expressed by William Henry Harrison and other proponents of manifest destiny has, by and large, been expunged from the official justifications for the advancement of the New World Economic Order. The intellectual progeny of Thomas Jefferson, James O'Sullivan, and Goldwin Smith, however, have largely retained the ethnocentric assumptions that have been historically essential to the psychology of manifest destiny and the drive to reorganize North America, and possibly all the Americas, as the domain of a single commercial polity.

The ethnocentric underpinnings of NAFTA were exposed clearly in January 1994, when the trade deal was identified by a largely Mayan fighting force in the Chiapas region of Mexico as the most recent weapon of oppression and dispossession in an extended war on Indian Country that began with Christopher Columbus and continues to this day.[59] From their base in a part of Mexico where the history, geography, and demographic mix of peoples still supports a vital and many-faceted Indian Country, the Zapatistas raised issues that stimulated resistance among several different types of constituencies. Evidence of the range of groups and individuals they inspired lit up throughout cyberspace, as more than 45,000 web sites in the United States, Europe, Japan, and elsewhere generated many explanations of the larger meanings embodied in the Indian stand. This outward-looking stand in Chiapas drew on the legacy of America's pre-Columbian past to identify and protest the continuing expropriative course of global corporatism.[60]

Although the protest began with the condemnation of a particularly corrupt *compradore* oligarchy whose long monopolization of the Mexican state led to NAFTA's dubious ratification, the Zapatistas directed a more widely broadcast critique against what is described in Central and South America as neo-liberalism. What the Zapatistas identified as neo-liberalism is often identified in the United States and Canada as neo-conservatism.[61] The movement to downsize and disempower the public sector, and to widen the frontiers of action available to the "private sector," has sometimes been tagged with the label the "New Right."[62] The patron saints of this evangelical return to old free trade orthodoxies, which in the nineteenth century were the stuff of classical liberalism, included F.A. Hayak, Milton Friedman, Barry Goldwater, Margaret Thatcher, and Ronald Reagan.

The cyberspace discussion of the Zapatistas' stand will probably be remembered as one of the first major episodes where the ubiquitous spread of interactive computer technolgy provided the means for a wide global exchange on the merits and demerits of the New Right's neo-liberal models for globalization. At the heart of this debate were many old questions about the meaning and methods of democracy. As well, many new questions were asked about how extending the frontiers of a particular genre of commercial relationships might affect the ecology of all relationships, both inside and outside the expanding matrix of the marketplace. Accordingly, in the course of this discussion, the Zapatista position on the rights of all peoples to self-determination became a significant flash point and reference point in the emergence of a new medium of global activism.

The pluralistic global community that began to coalesce around the resistance to neo-liberalism broke from this cyberspace nerve system on the Internet into active assembly and protest, with the demonstrations in many cities that accompanied efforts to initiate a new "millennial round" of the World Trade Organization (wto). This effort was centred on a meeting of the wto in Seattle in December 1999.[63] The protest in the streets led to a range of tough police responses, including the widespread use of tear gas, pepper spray, plastic bullets and concussion grenades. As a result, the wto's millennial round was transformed in the annals of history into the Battle of Seattle. This battle removed any doubt that the secretive, anti-democratic tactics employed in the neo-liberal retooling of the planet, especially since the demise of the Soviet Union, had generated huge pools of resentments among a wide range of constituencies and regular citizens. The spokespeople of these kernels of resistance to the unfettered planetary rule of money and global corporations – an approach to world governance that the wto seemed in 1999 to embody – sometimes identified themselves as representatives of "civil society."

The wto was born in 1995 as a kind of sovereign, governmental extension of the General Agreement on Trade and Tariffs. The lack of transparency in the organization's founding and in its early operations made it a potent symbol of the expanding hegemony of a globalized regime of monocultures and standardized property law such as that proposed by Akio Morita at the beginning of the decade. Among those protest groups locked outside the closed wto proceedings was a coalition of Indigenous peoples' organizations that issued its own declaration. This Indigenous

Peoples' Seattle Declaration accused the WTO of being integral to the advancement of a number of global agendas in the realms of agriculture, foresty, mining, and biotechnology. The combined effects of these initiatives, declared the authors, were "destroying Mother Earth and the cultural and biological diversity of which we are a part." The document identified the WTO as a vehicle for the promotion of industrial strategies that have led to "the scarcity of traditional foods and the dumping of junk foods into our communities." This process was alleged to have resulted in high levels of "diabetes, cancers, and hypertensions" among many Aboriginal groups.[64]

Drawing on their long experiences at the receiving end of imperialism, colonialism, and the ecological degradations associated with various forms of industrialialization, Indigenous peoples emerged as especially forceful witnesses and commentators on the future implications for the planet of adopting widened regimes of neo-liberalism. The importance of Indigenous voices in identifying the origins and character of neo-liberalism was made especially clear in the cyberspace activism connected to the Zapatista uprising in Mexico. That uprising was gradually transformed into a mass movement as symbolized by the public excitement stimulated by the "Zapatour" converging on Mexico City in March 2001. The rise of *Zapatismo* in Mexico and beyond can be understood as a broad embrace of America's Indian cultures. The geopolitical implication of securing conditions for the survival of these Aboriginal cultures is to create a check on the further incursions of the Columbian conquests as pressed forward especially by the neo-liberal expansions of the American empire.

The Zapatistas' electronic representations at the dawning of the Internet Age helped to clarify in the mid-1990s many emerging patterns of antagonisms, schisms, and alliances across a planet where the negotiation of commercial trade treaties provided the new high tables of geopolitical and geo-economic transformation. The emergence of the Zapatistas as leading-edge activists in the resistance against neo-liberal patterns of globalization harkened back to an earlier era of intellectual ferment on both sides of the frontier between Indian Country and the Anglo-American settlements in the era of the American Revolution and the War of 1812. In those times, the existence of Aboriginal and treaty rights was integrally connected to the range of issues most commonly associated with the events that transformed thirteen crown colonies into one federal republic. These issues included western expansion, commercial trade relationships, taxation, and the character and reach of sovereign authority in Britain and in several centres of power in North America.

Accordingly, the dispute over how to conduct relations of war or peace with Indigenous peoples was far more integral to the background, course, and aftermath of the American Revolution than has been widely appreciated. Moreover, the liberated ideals of those on the triumphant, liberal side of the American Revolution have run a course through history that has infused energy into the positions of those on both sides of the contemporary frontier between the expansion of monoculture and the survival of biodiversity together with cultural pluralism. On the side of the imperatives of pluralism are those who would assert the Aboriginal rights of Indigenous peoples. Pushing against the frontiers of existing Aboriginal and treaty rights are those seeking to cut down the boundaries of global multiculturalism in order to universalize a single, planetary regime of neoliberal property law.

The founders of the United States, who adopted the term "America" as part of the new country's name, could not embrace or even include the continent's original peoples in their conception of the republic's initial identity.[65] The founders of Canada, however, took the name of their country from Iroquoian people. This land of Canada, which was marked on many maps of the continent long before the United States existed, was established not through wars of extinguishment directed against Indigenous peoples. Canada was born in an atmosphere of intercultural collaboration, as trade, treaties, and intermarriage characterized many of the founding relationships between Native peoples and newcomers. It can truly be said that the real founding peoples of Canada in its first incarnation are not the English and the French. Instead, the genuine founders are those Indigenous peoples and their French-speaking partners who conducted their complex exchanges along the lake and river networks covering large expanses of the North American interior.

After the conquest of Canada by Great Britain, the English-speaking traders and imperialists who grafted their own interests onto those of the Native people in the Canadian fur trade were most likely to join the conservative side in the strategic disputes that gave rise to the American Revolution. Similarly, in the Indian wars that followed the "peace settlement" of 1783, the geopolitical interests of British imperial Canada depended on securing and extending treaty relations with the crown's Indian allies through the elaboration of broad principles entrenching the constitutional recognition and affirmation of Aboriginal rights and Indian title.

In this sense, the continuing extingushment of Indian Country, like the further integration of Canada into the American empire, are two aspects of the same historical process. Both ingestions feed the same appetites that once were proudly understood as expressions of America's Manifest Destiny. Given the nature of this inheritance from history, I believe that Canada cannot survive as a distinct society in North America without some kind of broadly supported formal return to the conditions of intercultural collaboration that were essential to the country's birth. In making such a return to its intercultural and mestizo origins, Canada would be following the lead of Mexico. In the 1920s in the course of its "revolution," Mexico's leaders incorporated in the name of *indigenismo* a relatively expansive embrace of the country's complex Aboriginal heritage. *Indigenismo* became an entrenched part of Mexico's national identity, purpose, and institutions.

George Grant tellingly observed in 1965 in his *Lament* for the demise of an independent Canada that the drive towards mastery of all of forms of nature, including human nature, eliminates space for the slow, organic growth of various local and indigenous communities favouring stability, continuity, and public order over the prerogatives of technological innovation.[66] The monocultural spread of the melting-pot liberalism centred in the United States, is inclined to squeeze out the more multicultural forms of social cohesion inherent in those conservative attributes that Grant associated with Canada's indigenous historical traditions

There are deep and obvious connections, therefore, between processes whose effect has been to extinguish the rights and identities of Old World societies and initiatives aimed at clearing the way for a New World Order.[67] Accordingly, the pronouncements of George Bush, Francis Fukuyama, Akio Morita, and others at the end of the Cold War played on very old themes, with particularly strong resonance in the history of the Americas. The demise of the Soviet Empire rekindled old passions from an earlier era when the United States first emerged from the revolutionary ferment within British imperialism. Ironically, while the new country grew in significant measure out of expectations that all which seemed most antiquated, anachronistic, and corrupt in Europe could be cast away, one of the larger implications of the republican experiment in North America was to extend, in a distilled and even exaggerated fashion, Europe's cultural influence throughout the entire planet.

In *The Cousins' Wars*, Kevin Phillips sketches a sweeping panorama of analysis that emphasizes the transatlantic continuity of developments leading to what he calls "The Triumph of Anglo-America." His narrative describes three conflicts internal to the English-speaking peoples – the English Civil War of the seventeenth century, the American Revolution of 1775–83, and the American Civil War of the 1860s. These brutal military contests, he argues, produced the ascent of an Anglo-American community on two continents that were bound together with the conviction that they were "a chosen people" with a "manifest destiny." Phillips argues that those leading this ascent of the cousins' beliefs, language, and influence from a civil war in England towards global dominance were, in the main, "commercially adept, militantly expansionist, Low Church Calvinistic Protestants" who were highly convinced of the divine sanction sanctifying their exploits in the world.[68] Alternatively, Phillips identifies not only agrarianism and "cavalier manor lords" such as Sir William Johnson as casualties of the great currents in history he paints with such bold literary strokes but also "the Irish, the blacks, and Native Americans" as "the collateral losers from the entire three-century sweep of the cousins' wars."[69]

This reference to "collateral losers" I find highly telling. It interjects into the language of historical interpretation the same sanitized term used by the perpetrators to explain the civilian casualties in the high-tech bombing missions directed against Iraq and later Serbian Yugoslavia in the 1990s.

The propaganda description of murdered civilians as "collateral damage" seemingly provided verbal gauze to veil from public understanding the full, bloody horrors arising from imperfect efforts to deploy more surgical styles of state violence. Is "the triumph of Anglo-America" to be surgically cut from its genocidal genesis through the deployment of language that would retroactively reclassify as collateral damage the experiences of Catholic Irishmen, Native Americans, and so many other Indigenous peoples on the moving frontiers of the English-speaking empire? Will the representational strategies of manifest destiny be extended to NATO, the military successor of the forces on the winning side of all those many conflicts that have opened the way for the creation of a North Atlantic community? After all, the sea lanes of NATO's ocean were the original highways for the expanding commerce, migration and geopolitical influence of the English-speaking peoples. It seems that Phillips's view of the past was written with a clear eye on the future, especially in his chapter on "Words as Weaponry," where he refers to "English, a Language of Victory."

Accordingly, Phillips's volume helps both to illuminate and to renew a revised and expanded form of manifest destiny. His text explains much about how Jefferson's oft-repeated agrarian vision of "a property-owning democracy" was overpowered with the force of a capitalist plutocracy. By the end of the nineteenth century, most of the really big decisions about how to construct America fell to a tiny inner circle of financiers dominated by the likes of J.D. Rockefeller, J.P. Morgan, and Andrew Carnegie. Building on the old Puritan legacy of the assumed "special right" of God's elect to extinguish and absorb Indian Country, these major transitional figures in the evolution of manifest destiny undertook many of the mergers and banking innovations that laid the groundwork for the rise of a newer generation of global corporations. This New World elite of high finance helped transmute the old imperialisms of Europe towards the kind of supranational agencies that have risen above the sovereign control of all the world's nation-states save one. Most often the border-piercing language of these global corporate entities is English, the familial tongue of the "cousins'" continuity between the British and the American empires.

Very often the predominantly English-language terminology employed by the CEO navigators of the high-tech, high-finance, high-politics world of global corporations resembles the kind of articulation that once was directed at claiming the Old Worlds of Indigenous peoples as New Worlds for expropriation and privatization under the charters and patents of European sovereigns. Where the insignia, crests, and imprimaturs of European monarchs gave the appearance of legitimacy to the old imperial claims, the new sovereigns of global commerce mark the outlines of their New World empires with the designs on their corporate logos.

From whence comes the theories of law and governance that invest a tiny elite on the planet with signing authority to direct whole corporate empires whose economies are sometimes far larger than those of the majority of nation-states? The flip side of this intense concentration of power in the executive hands of the patrician few is the corresponding dis-empowerment of the plebeian many. One important key to understanding the genesis of the narrowing franchise of directing authority in the New World Order lies in the historical genesis of the idea of Manifest Destiny. It lies in the Calvinist perception that God had given an "express Charter" to the earth to those Anglo-Americans who frequently perceived of them-selves as a special, elite breed who were the true "children of men."

CASH CENTRES IN NEON:
THE IRONIES OF THE SOVEREIGNTY MOVEMENT
AMONG FIRST NATIONS IN THE AMERICAS

In the spring of 1998 the *New York Times* ran as its cover story an account of the intentions and aspirations of the hundred member Skull Valley Goshute Nation in Utah. This group planned to bring new economic activ-ity to its small reservation by making it the site of a temporary civilian nuclear waste storage facility. Although the neighbouring non-Indian com-munities and their political representatives remained adamantly opposed to this development, the Goshute members were similarly determined that their assertions of sovereignty were powerful enough legally to overrule their detractors' objections.

As Leon Bear said in defence of the harsh economic realities behind his community's decision, "You can't eat wild rice anymore or you can't hunt around here." Referring to the two commercial toxic waste dumps in the vicinity, he continued, "They've poisoned the watering holes up in those mountains."[70]

The decision of some Indian groups in the United States and also in Canada to use portions of their remaining lands as the destination for their neighbours' cast-off toxins, poisons, and even nuclear waste marks dramatically the degree of desperation induced by Third World poverty in the heartland of First World prosperity. In some cases, resistance from within Indian Country has been enough to prevent the expansion of this phenomenon. In 1994, for instance, Cree activist Melvina Iron was instru-mental in leading a campaign of public education that helped to stop a plan that would have seen the Meadow Lake Tribal Council in uranium-rich northern Saskatchewan develop a storage facility to receive high-level nuclear waste. The architects of this scheme envisaged an Indian installa-tion that would have received a broad array of radioactive material, includ-ing plutonium, from many sources throughout the continent. The storage site on the Mescalero Apache reservation in New Mexico was meant to have been one of these sources.[71]

The tribal administration of the Campo Indians of southern California was at the centre of a similar controversy. In 1987 it developed plans to develop a landfill site for the solid wastes produced in and around San

Diego County. That decision set off a complex public struggle uniting Indian and non-Indian environmentalists. The plan went ahead, in spite of the stiff opposition. The outcome produced large revenues and high employment for the Campos, along with significant environmental and public health risks.[72]

There are many environmental achievements in Indian Country to offset the darker side of developments such as those listed above. In 1997, for instance, the Isleta Pueblo in New Mexico won a major court case that forced the City of Albuquerque, which is upstream from their community, to clean up the Rio Grande River. The Isleta people prevailed, having used their jurisdiction to set high water standards for reasons of public health as well as their use of the river for religious purposes.[73] The ground had been laid for this legal action by the action in the late 1980s of four Pueblo governments who collaborated through the All Indian Pueblo Council. They successfully opposed the building through New Mexico's Jemez Mountains of a high-voltage power line. Their oppsition to the project was based on the assertion of the importance of the Jamez area to their peoples' religious devotions.

The Blackfeet of northern Montana made similar arguments, based on the guarantee of religious freedom in the First Amendment of the American Constitution. The Blackfeet prevailed in their intervention to prevent the u.s. Forest Service from authorizing Chevron and Petrofina corporations to drill exploratory wells in a 100,000-acre site south of Glacier National Park. This territory continues to inspire premonitions of the divine among many who experience the grandeur of these sacred landscapes; they remain as places of worship and ceremony for the First Nations much as they have been for many thousands of years.[74] In northern California, ten small federally recognized Indian communities pooled their resources to purchase land for an intertribal park known as the Sinkyone Wilderness Project. Essential to the initiative are a number of experiments aimed at combining economic development with stewardship of the land in a way that maintains and stimulates the biodiversity native to the terrain.[75]

The relationship between Native people who still hunt and trap for a living and the proponents of various schools and traditions of environmentalism has not always been easy. For instance, the campaign of Greenpeace and other organizations directed against the continuation of the fur trade, especially as part of the European fashion industry, has at times been especially bitter.[76] Similar conflict has arisen between some environmentalists and First Nations people who seek to renew their traditions by harvesting whales in the way of their seafaring ancestors. This issue first arose in the international community in the 1970s, when some Inupiat of Alaska took to the sea to hunt bowhead whales. Their motivations were partly nutritional and partly economic, but their strongest arguments concerned the importance of this activity as a way to keep alive the spiritual and cultural rhythms they believed were vital to maintain the connection between their ancestors and their progeny. The Inupiat actions were initially opposed by the International Whaling Commission, which has played a significant role in preventing the total extinction of some of the world's most decimated whale populations. In the years that followed the Inupiat negotiated a settlement with the commission to harvest a small number of bowheads annually.[77]

A similar move in the late 1990s by some of the Makaw people of Washington state's Olympia Peninsula aroused global attention. The most outspoken critic of the Makaw's plan was Paul Watson, the legendary head of Sea Shepard Conservation, who threatened to use whatever tactics were necessary to stop this Aboriginal hunt of grey whale. His language, together with the equally strident defence of their decision by Makaw activists, was picked up widely in the media, creating the basis for an important discussion on the reality that the ethics of conservationism and of cultural survival sometimes clash. In the end the Makaw took a single whale without incident. Although they used a harpoon in the traditional way, they also, as negotiated, used a gun to minimize the animal's agony through a quick kill.[78]

The search for a substantial basis for an Aboriginal economy among First Nations in the United States crossed a new threshold in 1988, when Congress gave legislative force to the Indian Gaming Regulation Act. By the end of the century about one-third of the 554 federally recognized Indian nations in the United States had developed some sort of gambling enterprise. In 1997 those gaming businesses together generated $6 billion in gross revenues. About $1 billion of this amount was generated by one operation in Connecticut.[79] This establishment, the Foxwoods Resort Casino, opened for business in 1992, after a long struggle to obtain legal recognition for about 350 related individuals who asserted their collective identity as Mashantucket Pequots.[80]

Commenting in the *New York Times* on the rapid infusion of new money into some Indian communities in the United States, Timothy Egan wrote: "Indian country came alive, in ways both unintended and planned, with gambling. Suddenly, little patches of long-forgotten ground blossomed into cash centres in neon, which gave rise to cultural programs, language revival, scholarships, better schools."[81] But it would be naive to imagine that all or even most of the revenues from gaming were being used so benignly. By and large, the new casino money stayed within a narrow circle of power and privilege in Indian Country, compounding the propensity of many reservations to become miniature versions of American puppet regimes in Latin America. Among those exposed cases of embezzlement and fraud on Indian reservations in the United States were those involving the conviction and incarceration in 1996 of Wilbur Wilkinson, chairman of the Three Affiliated Tribes of the Fort Berthold reservation, and Darrell Wadena, tribal chairman of the White Earth reservation. They met in jail former Navajo chairman, Peter MacDonald, who is serving a fourteen-year sentence for his part in the complex saga of bribery, conspiracy, and fraud surrounding the dealings of the Native American Construction Company.[82]

The corruption, nepotism, and tight concentrations of wealth, which tend to be more overt in the most intensely colonized outposts of empire, gave exaggerated expression to the worldwide erosion of democracy accompanying the growing divisions between rich and poor almost everywhere on the planet. One result of the growing sophistication of neocolonialism and indirect rule in Indian Country has been that much of the available political energy has been consumed by inward-looking antagonisms. While such disputes were hardly new, the growing litigiousness of internal rivalries tended to devour resources and deform the anatomy of healthy activism. One of the towering examples of this kind of struggle between Indian groups was the Navajo-Hopi land dispute, a fight for the control of territory and resources that some would interpret as a thinly disguised manoeuvre on the part of those corporate interests working through Navajo jurisdiction to realize and extend their business plans. The combative jockeying for advantage between the Wisconsin-based Oneidas and the New York state–based Oneidas over potential benefits to be derived in the 1990s from a major land claim offers another variation on the same general theme.

While all these cases represent unique convergences of character and circumstance, they combined to contribute to a more general pattern that, almost certainly, is a factor in the near-absence of high-profile Native American activists and spokespersons with well-recognized places on the stage of national politics in the United States. There were no big and clear messages emanating from Indian Country in the 1990s with anything like the impact generated in the late 1960s and early 1970s by the occupation of Alcatraz Island or the return to Wounded Knee. Nor was there in the United States any equivalent to that group of Aboriginal politicians in Canada, including Ovide Mercredi, Elijah Harper, Georges Erasmus, Mathew Coon Come, Marilyn Buffalo, and Phil Fontaine, who in the late 1980s and 1990s became broadly recognized national figures and household names north of the international boundary.

The contrast requires some qualification. Cherokee leader Wilma Mankiller[83] and the Anishinabequai environmentalist Winona LaDuke, for instance, each generated some national attention. LaDuke achieved especially wide recognition through the accessibility of her ecological insights, which were disseminated by the Sierra Club. Her vice-presidential candidacy in two national elections as the Green Party running mate of Ralph Nader also gave her a high degree of public visibility on the stage of national politics in the United States. Similarly, the literary trail blazed by N. Scott Momaday was travelled by a particularly gifted group of Native American writers who, in the 1980s and 1990s, attracted major critical attention to the contemporary imaginative vitality of Indian Country. This group included James Welch, Leslie Marmon Silko, Louis Erdrich, the late Michael Dorris, Sherman Alexie, and the Cherokee author Tom King. In spite of King's roots in the United States, the majority of his stories were set primarily in the Canadian provinces of Blackfoot Country.

This blaze of creative writing in Indian Country United States represents a form of consulation for the apparent closure of genuine openings in American federalism to negotiate at the highest level of national politics any real reapportionment of power or any fundamental reckoning with the vast legacy of illegality involved in the theft of Aboriginal lands. This closure contrasted starkly with developments in Canada. Here, the decision in 1982 to sever some of the legal ties with Great Britain initiated a simmering constitutional crisis demanding some sort of domestically made redefinition of the country's "supreme law." Accordingly, in the late 1980s and early 1990s, "National Chiefs" Georges Erasmus, Ovide Mercredi, and their many colleagues working in and around several Ottawa-based Aboriginal organizations channelled their best creative efforts towards opening the text of Canada's constitution to the inherent right of Aboriginal self-government. At the same time, one of the few available forums for Native Americans in the United States to pose the possibility of major reforms in their relationship to power was in the venue of creative fiction. This literary realm of the imagination became the primary domain for the exercise of what Native American Studies professors Robert Warrior and Craig Womack described as "intellectual sovereignty."[84]

On those rare occasions in the United States where the info-entertainment industry explicitly connect breaking news with any serious consideration of history, the social, political, and economic legacies of slavery tend to be emphasized. The contemporary outgrowths of the theft and appropriation of Indian lands, an integral aspect of the rise of the American empire, are rarely explored. This blind spot was starkly evident, for instance, when, before a global TV audience, former president Bill Clinton fielded questions from students at Bejing University during his controversial trip to China in the summer of 1998. When Clinton was repeatedly asked by the Chinese students to give an accounting of the major human rights violations commited by his country, he emphasized urban violence and the racial tension in Black-white relations. He did not even mention the forced removal of Indian peoples from most of the lands and resources of the United States. Nor did he mention Leonard Peltier, the Anishinabe veteran of the American Indian Movement, who had become the clearest example of a political prisoner in the United States.

This large area of studied ignorance or willed amnesia in the national self-consciousness of most Americans is not based on any lack of research or scholarly activity in the United States. Since the 1960s there has been an impressive effort in academic circles to document and interpret the connection between the expansionistic ethos of the United States and the drive to eliminate and suppress Indian Country. Among the most prolific of the scholars to clarify the integral relationship between the rise of American expansionism and the dispossession of Native Americans are Francis Jennings, Richard Slotkin, Richard Drinnon, Francis Prucha, Jack Forbes, Wilcomb E. Washburn, Reginald Horsman, Dorothy Jones, Michael Paul Rogin, Ward Churchill, Richard White, Robert Williams Jr, Peter Matthiessen, John Sugden, Laurence Hauptman, Alvin M. Josephy, Patricia Limerick, William Hagan, Vine Deloria Jr, Robert Utley, Anthony F.C. Wallace, Dee Brown, Stephen Cornell, Edward Countryman, Donald Grinde Jr, Wilbur Jacobs, and Roy Harvey Pearce. How is it that the large body of work produced by these and many other scholars of the American Indian frontier has had such limited and marginal impact on the shape of the dominant political discourse of the United States at the end of the twentieth century? Perhaps it is naive even to ask such a question in a society where, as Jennings estimates, 1 per cent of the people own 90 per cent of the property.[85] Given such stark inequities in the heartland of the empire of possessive individialism, why would the narrow circle of business leaders at the top of the economy flirt with relaxing their tight control over the media of mainstream politics to allow a clear focus on the underlying alignments of interests at the geopolitical footings of American power?

There are many reasons why elites in the United States would want to avoid a sharp political focus on the contemporary implications of those cycles of genocide and dispossession that have been integral to the structuring of the steep pyramidical stuctures of wealth and power that gave both the American republic and the American empire their basic shape and form. Perhaps the imperial role of the United States has, ironically, made it the most European and the least Indian of all the countries of the Americas. In his geopolitical assessment of the central role of the United States in orchestrating the many forms of assault on Indian peoples throughout the American hemisphere, Jack Forbes has observed that "the USA can perhaps be regarded as the contemporary power most hostile to the interest of Native America." He goes further, predicting that a general upsurge of Indigenous peoples throughout the hemisphere "will create the greatest crisis in the history of the USA."[86]

The culture of casinos has had a temporary pacifying effect on the conduct of relationships between First Nations in the United States and the political branches of the federal government. Increasingly, however, the mobilization of Indigenous peoples outside the United States has signalled trouble ahead for institutions at the heart of the American empire. The rise of *Zapatismo* as the successor to *indigenismo* in Mexico, for instance, involved significant implications for the conduct of American foreign policy with its volatile southern neighbour. Similarly, the head offices of many US-based corporations have been confronted with the organized protests of Indigenous peoples living on the expanding frontiers of the American empire of private property. In 1999 at the annual meeting of the Occidental Petroleum Company in Los Angeles, for instance, the U'wa Indians of Colombia disrupted the proceedings. With the assistance of US-based environmental groups, their goal was to explain the devastating affects that would be visited on their lands and their Aboriginal livelihoods if Occidental pushed ahead its ecologically unsound resource-extraction schemes into U'wa territory. This ritual was re-enacted in 1999 at the annual meetings of a dozen major US corporations whose global activities have engendered the resistance of various combinations of Indigenous peoples' organizations with several networks of US- and Europe-based help and support.[87] Such transnational alliances across borders and cultures has greatly energized the activism of those who see their work as integral to the elaboration of transnational civil society.

The fact that many of the Indigenous peoples' protest movements are based in Central and South America points to the volatility of Aboriginal issues south of the Rio Grande. In many parts of this region, Indigenous peoples have suffered enormously under right-wing dictatorships whose murderous grasp of power has often been supported, formally or informally, by the US government through covert means, including the ruthless tactics of Operation Condor. Although much of the politics of these outright or quasi-police states has been wrapped in the rhetoric of the struggle between capitalism and communism, the deeper flow of history is often an extension of the old Indian wars that began in 1492.

Close to the core of the fight are competing visions of land tenure. Almost invariably the government of the United States has taken the side of all regimes in Latin America which are willing to lend state authority to the concentration of private ownership to land in very few hands. This propensity has been especially clear in Guatemala and Chile, where the CIA pulled the strings of pivotal *coup d'états* in both countries.[88] As a rule, the big land owners tend to be fair-skinned ladinos of primarily European descent. Their propertied privileges have depended over time on their willingness to collaborate closely with American corporations such as the notorious United Fruit Company.[89]

In describing her tragic, yet heroic, life in 1985 in an autobiography both celebrated and villified at different ends of the political spectrum,[90] Rigoberta Menchú did much to expose to international awareness the anti-Indian character of US involvement in the domestic politics of Central America. Her journey to winning the Nobel Peace Prize in 1992 was through the turmoil of the bitter civil war in Guatemala, where a small, US-supported ladino minority violently dominated an oil-rich country whose population is about 80 per cent Mayan.[91] Increasingly, Menchú saw the plight of her own people as a small part of a far larger pattern of unjust relations common not only to the Americas but to virtually all parts of the world where Indigenous peoples have been colonized and dispossessed.

The overt and covert military repression of many Indians south of the Rio Grande added pan-American meaning to the involvement of Indigenous peoples in attempts to rewrite the Canadian Constitution. In a sense,

Aboriginal activists in North America's northernmost country were asserting positions for more than themselves. They also acted as proxies for the
Indians elsewhere in the Americas, but especially for those who faced the
most severe recriminations for standing up to authority.[92] Similarly, there
were particularly broad pan-American implications in the specific inclusion of Métis in the content and negotiation of Canada's supreme law.

In Central and South America the vast majority of the population are, to
some extent, ancestrally mestizo. Indeed, it would not be exaggerating to
say that, of all the inhabitants of North, Central, and South America, there
are more people who have Indian ancestry than those who don't. This
largely unaddressed feature of the hemispheric culture of the Americas
constitutes a major wild card in the changing geopolitics of the western
hemisphere. Moreover, the porous, complex, and fluid relations between
Indian and mestizo groups throughout much of the Americas, but especially in Mexico, confounds the widely held perception of the Indian
Country of the Americas as a marginal or peripheral place.[93]

While Canada has emerged as a strategic centre for discussion and negotiation on the contemporary meaning of Aboriginal and treaty rights, there
have been other places in the Americas where major breakthroughs have
been made in raising aboriginality to the surface of national politics. In
1990, during Canada's most intense Indian summer, similar protests broke
out throughout Ecuador, where Indians also discovered the effectiveness of
blocking transportation corridors to draw attention to their grievances.[94]
Bolivia, too, was the scene of major pan-Indian demonstrations in 1990, as
Indigenous peoples there organized a mass march on the capital for what
they described as "land and dignity."[95] In 1994 the largely Mayan Zapitista
Liberation Army called attention to the anti-Indian character of Mexico's
integration into the "neo-liberal" empire of NAFTA and GATT.[96] The Zapatistas' mobilization was energized by the movement of over 100,000
Mayan refugees from the killing fields of nearby Guatemala.[97]

Just as the Assembly of First Nations was established in 1980 to express
unified Indian opposition to patriation and to further consolidate the otherwise scattered bargaining power of Indian bands vis-à-vis Canada's federal and provincial governments, so similar organizational innovations have
been instituted throughout Central and South America. The object has
been to create new openings for the exercise of Aboriginal political will at
the local, national, hemispheric, and international levels. Among the new
political associationss to emerge at the end of the twentieth century were
the Joint Council of Indigenous Peoples and Organizations of Brazil and
the Coalition of Indigenous Organizations of the Amazon (COICA). The latter became an especially innovative organization whose activities in the
global community have been seen as an important model for the emergence of transnational civil society. The organization was created in 1984 to
cover almost 2 million people, spread over about 400 distinct cultures, who,
collectively, have faced the intrusions of five different colonial traditions –

Spanish, Portuguese, French, Dutch, and English. While the complexities of representing such a complex diversity of Indigenous peoples have naturally generated some internal acrimony, COICA became a credible voice of an emerging pan-Amazonian Aboriginal identity, presenting its members as "the best guardians of the Amazon Rainforest." At different points, it has carried on negotiations with the World Bank, the Inter-American Development Bank, the European Parliament, the United Nations, and the International Labour Organization. In 1986 the Swedish parliament awarded COICA the "Right Livelihood Award" for the activities of its member federations in the field of evironmental protection.[98]

Although the physical assault on Indian lands continued unabated even in the face of this organized resistance, Aboriginal rights received some paper recognition in Brazil in 1988, Colombia in 1991, and Guatemala in 1996, to name but three.[99] These recognitions represent a move away from the "Hispanic" orientations of those Euro-American elites who followed Simon Bolivar in establishing the Creole nationalities of Central and South America. These non-Aboriginal polities were modelled on the ethnic nationalism integral to the founding and early growth of the United States. This ethnic nationalism in the United States found its strongest reflections in the continuation of slavery over the first century of the republic's existence and in the formal and informal Indian policies on the outward extremities of the United States's western expansions.

Among the most important centres of Aboriginal resistance to the continuing course of the Columbian conquests are the Mayan strongholds of Central America, including much of southern Mexico, and the Andean heartland of the old Inca Empire in Peru. Similarly, fur-trade history has helped make Canada the site of many resilient Indian and Inuit societies with long experience of holding their own ancestral grounds vis-à-vis the imported cultures and economies of the newcomers. This tendency is especially marked in the determination among many Six Nations peoples on both sides of the Canada-US border to assert their sovereign jurisdictions. It is also obvious in the determination of Indigenous peoples in British Columbia and Washington State to assert their continuing constitutional imperatives. The basis of those imperatives in Washington State are the Indian treaties of the 1850s. In British Columbia Aboriginal rights flow most prolifically from the uncompromised character of their Aboriginal titles in their ancestral lands and waters.

EAST AND WEST
IN THE CIVILIZATIONS OF THE AMERICAS

In April 1998 the heads of thirty-four nation-states met in Santiago, Chile, to establish the ground work aimed at creating a Free Trade Area of the Americas (FTAA). At this meeting, the government of Canada assumed responsibility for coordinating the next round of FTAA negotiations. The central event of those negotiations would take place in Quebec City in late April 2001. That summit would generate lively protests, which would lead to the incarceration of a number of demonstrators, including myself. My discussion of that episode forms the basis for my introduction of volume 2 of *The Bowl with One Spoon.*

Before leaving Santiago in 1998, Canada's prime minister, Jean Chrétien, explained that the socioeconomic condition of Indigenous peoples throughout the Americas was one of the matters requiring attention in the planning of the new hemispheric trading block. "We have discussed the situation of Indigenous people on our hemisphere," he said. "There are Indigenous people throughout our region. Too often, they are the most marginalized members of our society. We have a collective obligation to make their concerns a priority."[100] This small comment represented the first high-level acknowledgment that Aboriginal issues bear directly on the process of remaking the economic constitution of the Americas, a process whose most recent chapter began in 1988 with the making of the Free Trade Treaty between Canada and the United States. The extension of this trading block to Mexico in 1994 and then towards the rest of the hemisphere points at once forwards and backwards to an old saga of empire building whose real genesis began in 1492. Indeed, Chrétien's characterization of Indigenous people as marginal to "our society" clarified that all the governments represented at Santiago were basically non-Aboriginal in character and origin and therefore descended from the European side of the Columbian conquests.

Let us contemplate the enormity of the most recent variation in the old imperial project to re-engineer the outlines of culture and commerce on those two continents that have been the prize in what historian and US president Theodore Roosevelt called "The Winning of the West." The sheer speed and scope of the endeavour to structure the Americas as a single hemispheric trading block, which, in turn, is but one aspect of a larger, global process of geopolitical retooling, leaves us grasping for language, methodologies, and representational approaches expansive enough to respond to the new paradigms delivered to us daily by a global business culture that dominates so many media of mass communication. The enormous demands of the struggle to slow and reverse the ecological disaster of rampant monoculturalism require that we break loose from some of the more limiting conventions of chronology, linear thinking, and narrow specialization. We need new strategies of representation and scholarship to reverse the ongoing deconstruction of many local ecologies and Indigenous communities by the modern-day descendants of the conquistadors who act on behalf of tight conglomerates of global corporate sovereigns. Accordingly, the demands of this moment in globalization's history require that we find ways to move more easily between different intellectual realms. These realms can at once be located in very specific *indigenous* circumstances or, alternatively, at the outer reaches of those kinds of abstractions and generalizations that make it possible to conceptualize whole civilizations.

The kind of abstractions that are involved in conceiving of whole hemispheres as sites for single economic communities can lead in many directions, including sweeping generalizations about common historical patterns that cut across many old boundaries. The existence of NAFTA and the prospect of a Free Trade Area covering all the Americas help to focus attention on the single great theme of history universal to the hemispere. The most pervasive and persisting theme of more than five centuries of change throughout this region is the ongoing encounter between Indigenous peoples and those empires, economies, and nation-states whose expansions have continued the aggressions of the Columbian conquests.

With unflinching persistence, Jennings has argued that understanding of this vast matrix of human struggle and interaction has long been obscured and distorted by narratives that sought to depict the "Invasion of America" as a primal contest of *civilization* and *salvation* against *savagery* and *heathenism.*[101] Only by doing away with these lethal categories can we begin to grapple with the enormity of the misrepresentation presented to us for many generations in our Eurocentric national histories. Only then can we begin to look both backwards and forwards from 1492 with sufficient openness of mind to identify the continuities, discontinuities, convergences, fractures, and terminations that characterize human history over at least a hundred generations on lands that were christened as the Americas in a genocidal baptism of epic proportions. "The common history of the Americas," writes Jennings, "should be the history of the American Indians."[102]

Seen through the lens of ethnic specificity, the history of the American Indians is not one history but many, not one narrative but a plethora of diverse accounts whose narrators spoke an estimated total of 2,200 Aboriginal languages when Columbus first landed on the islands of the Arawaks and Caribs.[103] Seen through a macroscope rather than a microscope, however, many expressions of commonality and linkage emerge from the histories of the peoples who were all given the name "Indian" as a result of the geographic miscalculation of a disoriented Genoan navigator. To gain a sense of the shared civilization of Indian Country, it is necessary to take a wide view of past experience in the Americas similar to the perspective that identified the phenomenon known as "Western civilization."

This "Western civilization" is thought to have provided a degree of common heritage to many of the nations of people over vast temporal and geographic expanses. As emphasized in the teaching and writing of history over many generations, the identification of Western civilization as a shared heritage holds out the prospect of a shared destiny within the framework of broad general outlines. Acceptance of this shared heritage and common destiny helps to create bridges of empathy and cultural solidarity among peoples whose home localities might be in Paris or in Prague, Chicago or Cape Town, Lima or Lethbridge, Moose Jaw or Montreal, Auckland or Los Angeles. Within this overarching civilizational system, young people growing up in the suburbs of Miami, Oslo, or Edmonton, for instance, are encouraged to feel an interlinked sense of participatory engagement in a range of "Western" achievements. These achievements might range the field from the agricultural innovations of the Mesopotamians, to the law making of the ancient Greeks, to the plays of William Shakespeare, to the philosophical assertions of the American Declaration of Independence, to the musical compositions created by Beethoven, George Gershwin, or the Beatles.[104]

In the same fashion, it is possible to imagine a civilization of the Indigenous peoples of the Americas that, to some extent, transcends the many local, linguistic, and national distinctions of the shared Indian Country. Within the framework of this idea of civilization, Blackfoot, Dene, Pequot, Yanomami, and Canadian Métis have as much right to share in the agricultural achievements of Mesoamerica or Iroquoia as Philadelphians have a right to situate themselves in the legacy of the democratic achievements of ancient Athens. Similarly, Mayan people in Guatemala can as justly draw inspiration from the political culture of the Creek Confederacy as the city council of Sudbury, Ontario, can claim the English Magna Carta as one of the fountains of thought from which its civic ideals spring. Where much trouble starts is with the idea that "civilization" is a single historical complex whose most illustrious manifestations have moved progressively from early sources in Mesopotamia, and then to Egypt, Greece, Rome, Western Europe, the Americas, and especially to the United States. Within this interpretive framework, the westward expansion of Euro-American society into Indian Country – the "Winning of the West" for the United States – is made to seem like a recent extension of a far older projection of history whose course points ultimately towards the hegemony of a single world order.

The assumption that "Western civilization" is pointed towards inevitable ascendancy as the planet's "universal civilization" came under heavy criticism in 1996 from Samuel P. Huntington in *The Clash of Civilizations and the Remaking of World Order*.[105] Although Huntington joined the growing chorus of voices opposed to the simple-minded and wrongheaded pursuit of global monoculturalism,[106] he repeated and even elaborated many of the assumptions that, historically, have made the representation of Western civilization into an instrument of extinguishment aimed at Indigenous peoples in the Americas. In Huntington's view, the end of the Cold War and the demise of the former Soviet Union resulted in unwarranted expectations that the "end of history" was nigh and that "liberal democracy" must prevail everywhere. These hasty predictions led to unreasonable expectations that the cultural complex centred in Western Europe and the

United States was poised to become the universal cultural complex of the whole world.[107]

Drawing especially on the writings of former Canadian prime minister, Lester Pearson,[108] Huntington anticipated a world order aimed not at a universal civilization or anything like a global version of the American empire of private property. Instead, he anticipated a planetary future where diverse peoples will continue to return from the bipolar alignment of superpower rivalry in the Cold War back towards several major civilizational spheres of belief and social organization.[109] According to Huntington, most of these overarching civilizational spheres, which contain the fundamental values within which the governors of nation-states must endeavour to operate, are organized around major world religions, including Islamic, Hindu, and Orthodox Russian creeds. Except for a minor contributing role to the subordinate civilization of Latin America, however, there is no continuing and secure place in Huntington's multicivilizational paradigm for the Aboriginal civilization of the Americas.

Indeed, in Huntington's preferred scheme, the role of the United States as the obvious leader of "Western civilization" must be maintained by firm rejection of multiculturalism as state doctrine. According to this influential geopolitical thinker, the culture of the United States must continue to be aggressively and uniformly the culture of Europe,[110] a cultural orientation which, according to Huntington, is based on the premise that the Aboriginal cultures of the Americas have already been "wiped out" and "eliminated."[111]

Huntington's appeal to his largely American readership to abandon the quest for global hegemony and to accept, instead, a multicivilizational, multicultural destiny for humanity marks a move away from the kind of expectations advocated by Fukuyama and the other announcers of "an end to history" through the homogenizing ascendance of a New World Economic Order. Nevertheless, Huntington's insistence that the culture of his own country (and presumably of the rest of North America) must remain as firmly shut as possible to any official embrace of the cultures of all non-European societies, including Aboriginal societies, perpetuates the old genocidal tradition of literary extinguishment in representing the past, present, and future of Western civilization.

Huntington's semantic confusion in trying to hold Indigenous peoples of the Americas outside the cultural framework of American identity is especially apparent in his commentary on the assertions in Chiapas Mexico of the largely Mayan Zapatistas. To Huntington, this Indian resistance to NAFTA – a resistance supported by a considerable body of intellectual opinion in Mexico – marked "substantial resistance to North Americanization." How is it that the resistance of Indigenous peoples to a culture that Huntington insists is largely imported from Europe ends up being labelled as a rebellion against "North Americanization?"[112] By what strange alchemy of logic is such a reversal of roles advanced?

In some ways, Huntington's work demonstrates the implications of advancing the view, as Ward Churchill did in a very different kind of text,[113] that the genocide of the Indigenous peoples of the Americas was so near complete that Indian Country can essentially be ignored in negotiating the geopolitical future of the hemisphere. And if the Indigenous peoples of the Americas can be ignored, so too can all those Indigenous peoples globally who do not hold control of the machinery of any particular nation-state. In this sense, Huntington's text continues the tradition of denying Indigenous peoples cultural, political, and economic space by misrepresenting the past so as to write them out of history.

Huntington's work is a small but significant example of the kind of representation which, when replicated, amounts to a virtual ideological war directed against the contemporary existence of Indian Country. A key feature of that war of representation, whose main battle ground is the internal landscape of human imagination, has its origins in the failure to describe accurately and thoughtfully the place of the Aboriginal civilization of the Americas in more general surveys of human change and social development. From the vantage point of Indigenous peoples in the Americas, they are the true "Westerners" and their civilization is the true "Western" civilization. Those who imposed their foreign ways on Indian lands came primarily from the east. Their civilization is, from the perspective of Indian Country, an eastern, not a western, civilization.

The goal of these "easterners," who claimed as their own the destiny of "the West," was to suppress, deny, and ultimately replace the Aboriginal civilization of the Americas with the civilization whose origins lie in the Greco-Roman and Judeo-Christian heritages. Fundamental to the projection into the Americas of eastern civilization as "Western civilization" was the systematic negation of Aboriginal civilization through its depiction as savage, primitive, and even "prehistoric." In countless ways, this negation continues to this day, especially in consolidating the hegemonic monopolies of power derived initially from the semantic misrepresentation of Western civilization as if this cultural complex was the exclusive and original civilization of the Americas.

Words are the primary weapons in the apparent indigenization of a culture largely imported from Europe. This interhemispheric act of verbal appropriation is prone to depict the Indigenous peoples of the Americas, if and when they are treated at all, almost as phantoms whose existence has been and remains enclosed in some time and space disconnected to the new bastion of Western civilization. Accordingly, we need to become much more sensitive to the connection between words and deeds, between the apprehension of the thing and the thing itself, between the language of extinguishment and the act of genocide. Alternatively, there is great potential for human liberation in finding language that brings us closer to understanding our respective relationships to great streams of history and to wide expanses of geography. "Our very existence consists in our imagination of ourselves," writes Kiowa author Scott Momaday.[114] In a similar vein, the Shuswap sage George Manuel observed the semantic problems surrounding the representation of aboriginality: "Real recognition of our presence and humanity would require a genuine reconsideration of so many people's role in North American society that it would amount to a genuine leap of imagination. The greatest preservative for racial myths is the difficulty of developing a new language in which the truth can be spoken easily, quietly, and comfortably. Much of the distance we must travel to the Fourth World must be spent developing such a language."[115]

In his conclusion of *The End of History and the Last Man*, Francis Fukuyama gave a stunning display of the kind of language that perpetuates rather than overturns the "racial myths" that have been integral to what Jack P. Greene has decribed as "the intellectual construction of America."[116] In doing so, Fukuyama helps illuminate the underlying genocidal character of his preoccupation with a contemporary extension of American manifest destiny. He drew on some of the most infamously ethnocentric images of Hollywood "Westerns" to describe history's envisaged convergence in "one journey and one destination." His mixed metaphor not only predicted the demise of biodiversity but seized on the triumphal images of the conquest of American Indians as illustrative of the futility of resistance to the global ascent of the American empire of private property. "Rather than a thousand shoots blossoming into as many different flowering plants," Fukuyama wrote, "mankind will come to seem like a long wagon train strung out along the road. Some wagons will be pulling into town sharply and crisply, while other will be bivouacked back in the desert, or else stuck in the ruts in the final pass over the mountains. Several wagons, attacked by Indians, will have been set aflame and abandoned along the way."[117]

Fukuyama's incendiary reference to Indians as the enemies and antithesis of the American empire is telling. The resort of this celebrated propagandist to one of America's most deeply embedded clichés of primal conflict between cowboys and Indians is highly indicative of the nature of those hopes and expectations fanning the belief that neo-liberal models of globalization represent an inevitable end of history. Fukuyama's identification of Indian people as the pre-eminent "other" of civilizational progress marks a fitting point of introduction for the philosophy of the Fourth World as espoused by George Manuel.

THE ATTRIBUTES AND ACHIEVEMENTS
OF THE ABORIGINAL CIVILIZATION OF THE AMERICAS

A good place to start in the conceptual reconstruction of the hemisphere is by imagining all of North America as a single, cohesive geography – a view promoted in the geopolitical conception of NAFTA. More and more this continent of NAFTA is described throughout Indian Country as the Great Turtle Island.[118] The description comes about partly because the

geographic outlines of the continent resemble the outlines of a great turtle swimming to the northeast.

On a deeper level, however, the turtle is a central figure in a number of
Aboriginal creation stories. Indeed, as a long-lived animal of ancient origins
with the ability to survive in the dual environments of land and water, the
turtle's versatility has made it an object of veneration in many spiritual traditions. As it moves with purposeful poise between environments, the turtle
gives us clues on how best to balance our worldly existence in the realm of
matter with a psychic life in the unseen realm of spirits and dreams.

The imagery of North America as Turtle Island flows especially from
many of the creation stories told in a host of Aboriginal languages, including the Iroquoian tongues spoken by both the Six Nations of upper New
York state and the Hurons of the upper Great Lakes.[119] One version of the
story has been written down by Mike Myers, John Mohawk, and Mike
Mitchell, who in the 1970s worked in and around the influential and innovative North American Indian Travelling College based at Akwesasne. The
main features of this ancient creation story speak of a pregnant woman
who fell from the sky towards the realm that would become the earth. In
those days the whole world was covered in water. The woman fell through
the clouds after she became curious and started digging around the roots
of a huge and marvellous tree in her celestial domain. As the roots became
exposed, a large hole appeared, through which she fell. As she began her
plunge downward, she grasped a tobacco plant and a strawberry plant in
her two hands. Many birds flew together to create a large cushion to slow
her descent. The birds called to a giant sea turtle to swim beneath them so
the woman could land on its back.

Once the woman was securely sitting on the turtle, she talked with the
many creatures who were excitedly swimming around her. They asked her
how they could make her feel more secure and comfortable. "What I don't
see that is in my world," she said, "is land." The animals told her that there
was land far beneath the water. Some of them tried to swim down to bring
up some soil from down below. The beaver tried first. He failed. Then the
loon, the duck, and the seagull tried, but they failed too. Finally the otter
tried. He dove beneath the water and was gone a long time. When he finally hit the surface, the otter was dead, but in his tightly clenched paw was a
little bit of earth. The woman and her animal helpers took this earth and
put it on the back of the turtle. "Once this was done," write the authors, "a
strange transformation began to take place. The earth and the turtle
began to grow and spread. To keep the earth growing, the woman walked
in a circle, following the direction of the sun. It wasn't long before she had
a very large place to stand. All around her was land. This land began to
develop and take shape. Not long after the land formed, the woman gave
birth to a baby girl. This world was now their home."[120]

Many of the Algonkian-speaking peoples throughout much of North
America have similar stories that identify the turtle as the upholder of the

earth. When earthquakes come, it is sometimes said in Indian Country that the turtle is shifting position.[121] One of the most sacred spots for the Anishinabek in the Great Lakes area is Mackinaw Island, an island that takes its name from the Ojibway word for turtle. Mackinaw Island lies close to the place where Lake Huron and Lake Michigan meet, just south of Sault Ste. Marie.

In many Aboriginal nations, clans marked by the totem of the turtle hold proud and honoured places. Moreover, the turtle shell is often greatly esteemed in the practice of Aboriginal medicine, sometimes as a bowl and sometimes as the essential component of a ceremonial rattle. For our purposes here, the bowl with one spoon might well be imagined as a vessel constructed from the major part of the anatomy of one of the most primal, ancient, and longest-living species on earth. The global assault on turtles, frogs, and most other reptile populations marks a prescient symbol of the menaced state of the Old World Ecological Order, whose habitats are being destoyed by the favoured industrial techniques of the New World Economic Order.

The importance of the turtle as a teacher and as an icon of age, wisdom, and transcendence is represented in the designs of many sacred pipes and in the elaborate oral traditions that go with them.[122] In the late nineteenth century, for instance, James Mooney, an early ethnographer with the Smithsonian Institution, reported the close association of the turtle with the most important pipe of the northern Arapaho in Wyoming. According to the Arapahos' understanding, Mooney wrote, this pipe "was given to their ancestors at the beginning of the world after the Turtle had brought the earth up from under the water."[123] Such veneration of animal spirits, or sometimes of plant spirits, is a mark of the Fourth World that is fundamental to the cultures of most Indigenous peoples. In these societies, young people have been socialized over the generations to look at the lives of all other creatures as having meanings and purposes equal to those of human beings. Plants and animals even have the capacity to act as teachers – to give humans examples or direct advice on how to become integrated into the thick weave of relationships with other species that constitutes the web of life.

As relatively recent arrivals, the awkward humans are thought to be especially needful of help, advice, and instructions from those creatures who have been on the earth longer. From this attitude of familial connection with the other creatures arises a respectful attentiveness towards the unique characteristics of all fellow living beings, an attentiveness that extends back ultimately to the Earth Mother whose feminine nature has been acknowledged by most of the old cultures of the world. "Its hard to be an Indian in the white world," writes Jack Forbes, "but it is easy to be an Indian in nature, because the Earth, the plants, the animals, and the winged creatures provide companionship, love, or just authentic spontaneity unmarred by hate, jealousy or greed."[124]

This positioning of peoples inside life cycles rather than on top of biological and evolutionary heirarchies is supported by rich and complex traditions of storytelling which may have been muffled but never silenced. For many thousands of years these traditions of storytelling have been a primary way to socialize Turtle Island's rising generations as inheritors and makers of history. These cross-generational stories feature a mythological figure who reappears with different names in many Aboriginal traditions. To the Ojibway he is Nanabush or Nanaboozhoo. To the Cree he is Weesageechak. In other Aboriginal societies in North America he is known as Raven, Coyote, Napi, Hare, Sitconski, and by many other names as well. He is also known more widely simply as Trickster.[125]

Trickster can often be a teacher showing humans how to live in nature. There are many stories describing how Nanabush instructs the Anishnabek on how to use healing plants, harvest maple sugar, or use birchbark or other plant fibres to make vessels, mats, dyes, and teas. Yet Trickster can as easily teach through the mistakes he makes or the misdeeds he commits. He often creates havoc through his complex schemes to gain sexual favours from those he fancies. His exploits in countless guises cover a huge expanse of narrative and experiential ground, from high drama to low farce. In the words of Gerald Vizenor, "the trickster is comic in the sense that he does not reclaim idealistic ethics, but survives as part of the natural world." Vizenor continues, "he represents a spiritual balance in comic drama rather than the romantic elimination of human contradictions and evil."[126] In my view, Trickster shows humanity how to adapt to the apparent inhospitalities as well as to the ironies, paradoxes, and contradictions that permeate nature, including human nature. This message of acceptance, compromise, and adaptation contrasts starkly with the message of overcoming nature's contradictions and conquering or eliminating anything that is deemed evil or useless.

In this respect the moral ambivalence of Trickster stands in bold opposition to the perfectionism of the Christ figure in the Christian religion. The comparison between Christ and Trickster is identified directly by Cree novelist Tomson Highway.[127] This same centrality of meaning is alluded to in an article on the psychology of Trickster by Carl Jung, the celebrated colleague and critic of Sigmund Freud. "At the end of the Trickster myth," he wrote, "the saviour is hinted at."[128] Where the Christian saviour points human beings in the direction of exorcising or changing what is held to be evil or even less than perfect in nature, Trickster points us towards a more accepting relationship with the rest of creation.

In these days the living Trickster of Turtle Island can be expected to show up in all kinds of contemporary settings such as the bingo halls, gambling casinos, rodeos, skid rows, hockey tournaments, pow wows, and drug and alcohol programs of Indian Country. The living Trickster might show up disguised as a corporate lobbyist at the World Trade Organization headquarters in Geneva. Who knows what will befall Trickster as he changes form and connives to confound those who have borrowed his techniques for trans-species experimentation and cloning in the richly financed laboratories of the biotechnology industry?

Although there is in Indian Country a Fourth World propensity to adapt to the rest of nature rather than remake nature to conform to human impulses of self-centredness, it would be wrong to interpret this Aboriginal proclivity as passive resistance to the urge of inventiveness. Both North and South America have been the sites of monumental social and technological transformations whose substance in pre-Columbian times remains largely hidden by the myopic biases of ethnocentric pedagogy and Eurocentric historiography. In 1492, for instance, Tenochtitlan, the Aztec metropolis on the site of present-day Mexico City, was one of the largest human habitations in the world, estimated to be about four times larger than either London or Seville in that era. It was reported that the markets of Tenochtitlan were more extensive and grand in their diversity of products than anything that the first Spanish rapporteurs had seen in Europe.[129] The Aztec Empire of Mexico in 1492 was a relatively recent geopolitical adaptation that had been added on top of a long progression of powerful Mesoamerican cultures. The earlier influence of these Mesoamerican civilizations extended far into the northeast, up the Mississippi Valley and into the Ohio River area.

One of the most important trading centres in this northeastern hinterland of Mesoamerica has been given the name Cahokia. The site of Cahokia is in southern Illinois, across the river from St Louis, Missouri. Its population is estimated to have been somewhere between 20,000 and 75,000 inhabitants around 1,100 years ago. At its centre was a large, four-tiered earthen pyramid structure, much like those throughout Central America. The installations in the large palisade built around the central plaza included a sophisticated solar observatory built on similar principles to those at Stonehenge. They have been given the name "Woodhenge."[130] The Cahokia sky watchers were engaged in forms of astronomy that were highly developed in many Native American cultures. The calendar used by the Mayans was more precise and included more cycles of celestial change than the one that is most commonly used today.[131] This achievement was possible because of Mayan sophistication in the science of mathematics. Essential to Mayan mathematics was their invention and use of the concept of zero, a concept that had an independent genesis on the other side of the world, first in India, then in the Arab realm, and finally in Europe.[132]

Many of the engineering projects of the pre-Columbian Indian Country are still evident on the lands of North and South America. A thousand years ago the Anasazi civilization, the ancestor of the present-day Pueblo peoples in the southwestern United States, built large and elaborate apartment-like structures with as many as 800 dwellings in one complex. These structures had sophisticated systems of ventilation and climate control.[133] In the Andean region of South America, the Inca were renowned road builders, bridge builders, and stone masons. The Incas's Royal Road, which was carefully drained, graded, and paved over most of its length through some of the world's most mountainous terrain, ran 2,500 miles in distance.[134]

To the north, the Mound Builders of Turtle Island were members of Aboriginal cultures that archaeologists have identified by the imposed names of Adena and Hopewell. These busy peoples left tens of thousands of shaped earthwork projects, large and small, which often contain elaborate burial complexes. Some great plague or other natural disaster intervened around the year AD 1300 to end the engineering of those Mississippi Valley societies. The earthen monuments run north at least as far as the southern Ontario area. It is estimated that there are 5,000 mounds in southern Wisconsin alone. One of the most remarkable of these earthworks is near Locust Grove in Ohio. It is an effigy of a serpent, which stretches 200 metres from its extended jaws to its coiled tail.[135] In reflecting on the central motif to emerge from his survey of this whole body of earthen architecture, Roger G. Kennedy, the former director of the American History Museum at the Smithsonian Institution, writes, "Strict shapes and sizes were arranged in accordance with celestial lines. The eighteen-and-a-half-year lunar cycle, the twenty-eight-day monthly cycle, the cycles of the sun and seasons, all observed over many decades, were discerned to have patterns, patterns affirmed by the architecture."[136]

In *Hidden Cities: The Discovery and Loss of Ancient North American Civilization,* Kennedy devotes close attention to what he describes as the "monumental architecture" whose massive and elaborate outlines were still very evident throughout the Mississippi Valley in the early decades following the founding of the American republic. He outlines how some of the leading lights in the new country, including Thomas Jefferson and Albert Gallatin, chronicled and explored the achievements of those Aboriginal societies that built the pyramids, plazas, and other geometric structures that once dominated significant portions of the landscape of the present-day American Midwest. Moreover, Kennedy documents how this knowledge was distorted, put aside, and ignored later in the nineteenth century because of the consolidation of an approach to nation building in the United States that required the unqualified relegation of the Indigenous societies to a lowly post as the savage antithesis of the civilization of the newcomers. Kennedy points an accusing finger at those American "zealots" whom he finds guilty of "the wholesale obliteration of the evidence" chronicling the existence of ancient civilization in the Americas. He alleges that the national ideology of the United States was elaborated through the commission of intellectual crimes similar to those on which Spain constructed its New World empire. "In the 1530s," he writes, "the first archbishop of Mexico, Juan de Zumarraga, systematically destroyed whatever Aztec art, architecture, and literature fell into his hands, to reduce the competition offered by the testaments of the Indians to the New and Old Testaments of the Christians."[137]

The destruction of the architectural legacy of the Aboriginal civilization of the Mississippi Valley was, according to Kennedy, partly purposeful and partly inadvertent. He states that, in the course of US nation building, "thousands of mounds were falling to road builders, canal builders, and railway builders, to developers and farmers, to floods arising from the conversion of the sluiceways and valleys into recreational lakes. America's ancient past was being obliterated at a pace which, by 1948, had reduced by *ninety percent* the earthen architecture."[138]

Irrigation was another highly developed art and science throughout large areas of North and South America for many generations before the arrival of Columbus. Among the Incas, irrigation was integral to the productiveness of the terraced gardens along the steep mountain slopes of the Andes. Farther to the north, in Central America and in the more arid regions of what is now the southwestern United States, irrigation became essential for the maintenance of the large population centres that developed there.[139] And, of course, the existence of irrigation is built on the existence of elaborate systems of organized agriculture.

Without a doubt, it is the cumulative contributions of many generations of anonymous Indian horticulturalists who have made the most enduring and profound impact on the quality of life in virtually all the world's major civilizations. Among the crops produced from Amerindian food science are tomatoes, avocadoes, vanilla, pineapples, several peppers, and various kinds of groundnuts, beans, and gourds. Cotton and tobacco are two other Amerindian crops whose post-Columbian cultivation produced huge wealth and tremendous suffering. Added to this list are corn, potatoes, rubber, and coca, which has been called "the basis of modern anesthetics."[140] Corn and potatoes are especially rich and prolific sources of food, and they rapidly changed the face of many societies that adopted these most characteristic emblems of Amerindian agriculture. Corn or maize, along with groundnuts, were said by Levi-Strauss to have "completely transformed the African economy."[141] Similarly, Betty Fussell has identified corn as "America's quinessential crop." "So quickly did the American corn revolution of [the twentieth century] spread," she writes, "that not only was the Great American Desert transformed, but also barren lands in Egypt, South Africa, India and China; today China, after the United States, is the world's largest producer of corn."[142]

The transformative effects of the spread of potatoes, a gift to the world from the agricultural science of the Incas, has been comparable to the spread of corn.[143] So central did this domesticated plant become to the food economy of Ireland that the country was absolutely traumatized by the potato famine of the 1840s. This event helped set off a major wave of transatlantic migration just as the traffic of the transatlantic slave trade was abating. Accordingly, the adoption of Amerindian crops throughout much of Europe, Africa, and later Asia stimulated a steady rise in population as the new foods supported far higher densities of settlement. Much of this enlarged population ended up migrating to the Americas, a process that continues yet. Hence, one effect of the dissemination of the agricultural innovativeness central to the Aboriginal civilization of the Americas has been to help stimulate population increases beyond the hemisphere. These enlarged populations have tended to produce huge numbers of immigrants to the Americas. On the whole, their tendency has been to displace, murder and vandalize many of the hemisphere's Indigenous societies. Very often these episodes of "ethnic cleansing" were advanced with paradoxical rationales for the takeover of resources that condemned Indian societies for their alleged backwardness in agriculture.

The changes brought about by corn and potatoes are rivalled by those of Amerindian crops associated with dismal chapters in humanity's history. For generations, African American slaves, part of the founding capital of the American empire of private property, laboured on plantations devoted to the cultivation of cotton and tobacco, both domesticated plants that had their origins in Amerindian horticulture. The transformation of tobacco from a plant used most frequently for religious ceremonies to a pervasively marketed consumer product is a saga of vast significance in the political economy and public health of global society.

While the domestication of plants was integral to the Aboriginal civilization of the Americas, the same was not true of the domestication of animals. One outcome of this marked tendency of Indigenous peoples in the Americas not to breed animals in the same manipulative fashion that they scientifically intervened in the intergenerational evolution of plant life was to solidify the image of Indians in Europe primarily as hunters. Large parts of present-day Canada have historically supported many of those Aboriginal societies closely identified with the political economy of animal hunting.

Most of Canada is no more suitable today for large-scale farming than its lands were in pre-Columbian times. This key characteristic of Canada's largely arctic and subarctic geography is mainly responsible for the country's prominence, to this day, in the world's trade in animal furs. Even in Canada, however, Aboriginal agriculture was well established in various locales when French explorers, including Samuel de Champlain, arrived in the early seventeenth century in the upper Great Lakes. A key centre of Aboriginal farming was Huronia, a thriving domain of 20,000 to 30,000 Iroquoian-speaking people who grew corn, beans, and squash in their territory between what is now Lake Simcoe and Georgian Bay, just south of the rocky Canadian Shield.

Until the demise of Huronia in 1649, the French commercial and evangelical incursions into the Indian Country of Canada were largely based on efforts to infuse French influence and French products into the Hurons's pre-existing trade network. This Aboriginal trade and diplomatic network was centred on the ability of the Hurons to produce large agricultural surpluses for export to their many Algonkian-speaking allies whose own indigenous productivity was mostly set in the rocky geography of the Canadian Shield. Thus the French-Aboriginal fur trade, the primal commerce on which Canada is founded, depended in its early genesis on the Aboriginal vitality of exchange between economically diverse Indian societies whose cultures were centred on the harvesting of domesticated plants and wild animals.[144] Much distortion has arisen from the tendency to generalize the imagery of Aboriginal hunters as if their way of life was typical of all the Indigenous peoples of the Americas. As we shall see, the political philosophy of John Locke has been an extremely influential source of this distortion.

This association of Indian societies with hunting rather than horticulture has tended to disguise a central fact in the planet's political economy: over half of the world's agricultural products come from crops first domesticated by Amerindian farmers and plant breeders.[145] The diffusion of these regenerative resources into the scientific commonwealth of humanity constitutes a gift from the Aboriginal civilization of the Americas whose longterm value far surpasses that of all the gold and silver stripped from Mesoamerica in the first waves of European theft from the New World. According to Francis Jennings, in 1492 most Indians lived by planting.[146]

THE ECOLOGY OF CONTRASTING RELATIONS LINKING HUMANS AND PLANTS

Many questions arise from the contention that the Americas are the site of two major global civilizations, one indigenous and one largely imported from Europe. What, for instance, are the major points of contrast that differentiate these two cultural complexes? In my estimation, different approaches to the use and manipulation of plant life represent one of the most illustrative markers pointing to a whole range of philosophical distinctions between the Aboriginal civilization of the Americas and the civilization imported largely from Europe.

Where Aboriginal horticulturalists developed agriculture based on biological diversity and careful attention to the relationship between and among different species, the more recently imposed industrial approaches to plant domestication emphasize the selection, isolation, enclosure, and extended reproduction of commodified monocultures. The bias towards cultivated diversity rather than compartmentalized conformity is exemplified in the vast range of corn types and potato types that were nurtured by the Indigenous farmers of the Americas. Inca potato breeders, for instance, are known to have developed hybrids resulting in many hundreds, and possibly thousands, of distinct varieties of the nutritious plant.[147] Aboriginal horticulturalists have cultivated yet a larger range of strains from the rich gene pool of maize or corn. "It is not accidental," writes Carl O. Sauer in *Seeds, Spades, Hearths, and Herds*, "that a single native village [in the Americas] may maintain more kinds of maize than the [US]

Corn Belt ever heard of, each having a special place in the household and field economy."[148]

The cultural complexes surrounding the cultivation of corn are representative of the contrasts and continuities between the industrial civilization of the newcomers and the Aboriginal civilization of the Indigenous peoples, especially in the United States. For instance, the title of J.B. Longone's *Mother Maize and King Corn: The Persistence of Corn in the American Ethos* is highly suggestive. It speaks of a basic transformation in the predominant motifs of spirituality and gender relations, supported by the dominance of the same family of cultivated plants on the same territory that gave rise to both the old and the new civilizations of a hemisphere.[149] From the corn flakes of the Kellogg brothers of Battle Creek, Michigan, to the ever expanding cornucopia of processed foods and industrial products created from corn starch, corn syrup and dextrose, there has been no end to the plurality of uses invented for Indian maize in the American empire. These industrial innovations have been derived from the fruits of the tireless agricultural experiments of Indian peoples who reaped prolific results, especially in the legendary corn fields of the Arikara, Mandan, and Hidatsa on the Upper Missouri River Valley.[150]

A common technique among Aboriginal farmers in many parts of the Americas has been the cultivation of beans and squash along with maize. To their Iroquoian cultivators, this agricultural triad is revered and celebrated in ceremonial life as "the three sisters."[151] The formidable powers that Haudonosaunee or Iroquois people attribute to this plant complex has a strong basis in mainstream science. The biological relationship of corn, beans, and squash is one of the foremost examples in world horticuture of a botanical relationship that is classically symbiotic.[152]

To conceptualize the evolution of Aboriginal agriculture in the Americas over the two thousand years before 1492 is to imagine a different approach to farming and ecology from the methods of the "Green Revolution." Instead of drawing a sharp dicotomy between field and forest, for instance, Aboriginal agriculturists in the treed portions of North America were inclined to see a continuum of interrelated life forms in the delicate relationships between forested areas and grasslands. Instead of seeing forests as obstacles to agriculture that must be almost entirely eliminated, treed areas were viewed as models to be partially emulated in the planning and cultivation of gardens.[153]

Many Indigenous peoples in the Americas, as well as in many other parts of the planet, learned to use fire carefully, deliberately, and scientifically in the development of their distinctive forms of agriculture. Generally speaking, their goal was to maintain and stimulate the dense web of ecological connections linking life in the forest and life in the grasslands.[154] They wanted to encourage the development of variable habitats for the rich range of plant and animal species that thrive along transition zones between differing geographical areas. In *Americans and Their Forests*, Michael Williams describes this Aboriginal application of fire technology:

Indians made an impact on the forest by clearing it periodically for cultivation, but in all probability they made even greater impact with the widespread use of fire. Fire was used not only for cooking and heating but for opening up the land for cultivation and also to provide additional fertilizer by recycling debris and its stored nutrients. Fire was used to maintain and extend already open grassland by preventing forest growth and thus encouraging game; to promote the growth of fresh grass in already open areas; and to promote the growth of plants bearing nuts and berries ... All the evidence points to the fact that Indians were careful users of fire as a tool to manage the land and promote their welfare. Cereal grasses were fired annually, basket grasses and nuts about every three years, brush and undergrowth in the forest about every 7 to 10 years, large timbers in swidden rotation every 15 to 30 years or more ... Fire was a natural and integral – even sacred – part of the Indian landscape and livelihood.[155]

The creative employment of fire as an agent of regeneration and biodiversity marks a clear line of technological and philosophical demarcation between the Aboriginal civilization of the Americas and the "New World" civilization of this hemisphere. Where fire was a tool of agricultural experimentation and innovation for many Indigenous societies, land fires were perceived for most of the newcomers and their descendants as chaotic eruptions menacing human control over nature, as represented most characteristically in the monocultural conformity of tree plantations.[156] Indian people also employed fire for reasons other than biodiversity. According to Roger Williams, the Puritan maverick who founded the colony of Rhode Island, the Indian people of that region "burnt up all the underwoods in the countrey, once or twice a yeare" to achieve "expedition of their hunting voyages."[157] Other observers noted that Indian people sometimes used fire as a weapon to force their enemies from hiding. Similarly, the legends are legion concerning the signals that Indian people sometimes communicated over distances through their calculated manipulation of smoke.[158]

The systematic application of fire as a means for restoring the optimal regenerative conditions for biodiversity was an important expression of the Aboriginal quest for ecological vigour and equilibrium. The encouragement of biodiversity among plants, especially in the multiplication of transition zones between forest and grasslands, helped to increase many animal populations – including, in eastern North America, elk, deer, beaver, hare, pocupine, turkey, quail, and ruffed grouse. When these populations increased, so did those of many carnivors, such as wolves, foxes, eagles, hawks, and lynxs. By these means, William Cronon notes, Indigenous peoples in the New England region "were harvesting a foodstuff which they had been consciously instrumental in creating."[159] They were engaged in forms of calculated burning that seem to have been shared by many of the world's Indigenous peoples, including, for instance, the Indigenous peoples of the Pacific Northwest and the Aborigines throughout many parts of Australia.[160]

At the philosophic core of this approach to domestic economy is a view of human relations with other species that emphasizes the attributes of liberated pluralism over the enclosure of commercialized monocultures, of biodiversity over the imposition of standardized forms in life's repro- ductive processes. Accordingly, this preference for what Vandana Shiva calls "the democracy of all life"[161] can be seen as a fundamental and enduring hallmark of the Fourth World generally and of the Aboriginal civilization of the Americas more specifically.

One of the most prolific and eloquent commentators on the subtlety and complexity of Aboriginal adaptations to particular places in North and South America has been Claude Lévi-Strauss. Throughout his great anthropological treatises on "the science of mythology," he depicts the thick complex of structural interconnections linking the philosophical currency of Aboriginal storytellers to the ecological dangers and opportu- nities of local environments. What emerges is a montage of images that fre- quently demonstrate how phrases such as "hunter/gatherer" fail to convey a sense of the complexities in the Aboriginal political economies of Indige- nous people. Of the Klamath and Modoc peoples in the west-coast area of the present-day United States, for instance, Lévi-Strauss writes:

In Klamath and to a lesser extent Modoc territory, swamps provided a supply of pond or water lilies *Nufar polysepalum*. Natural beds of these plants covered several thousand hectares of the Klamath Marshes, where fallen seeds formed a viscous mass, which could be harvested by canoe. The importance of these seeds, known as *wocas*, in the diet of the Kamath can be judged from the fact that these Indians referred to them by no fewer than five different names, according to their degree of ripeness and the fresh or rotten state of their outer casing. In order to remove their gummy secretion, the kernels had either to be left to ferment in water, or pre- cooked in steam, after which they were shaken up ... Then baked ... In addition to the lily seeds, the Kamath and Modoc made use of all kinds of roots, bulbs, tubers and rhizomes, the chief of which belonged to the liliacae (*Camassia quamash, escu- lenta*) and the umbelliferae, the falses caraway (*Carum oregonum*). They gathered berries, seeds, wild fruits and edible lichens, and extracted sweet resin from certain conifers. In April and May they removed and ate the soft cambium underneath tree bark. From the lakes and marshes they took rushes, bulrushes, reeds and cats'-tail grass for the weaving of mats, caps and baskets.[162]

To appreciate the living essence of Aboriginal civilization in the Ameri- cas, we need to remove the confusing fog of misrepresentation generated by overly sharp and simplistic distinctions between farmers and hunters, between sedentary societies and nomadic tribes. In place of these labels, we might pose, instead, the distinction between integrated biodiversity and enclosed monocultures as the two major defining poles of civilizational organization in the Americas. Where most of the agricultural or semi-agri- cultural economies of Indigenous peoples tend to emphasize the former, the civilizational thrust of New World America is decidedly biased towards the latter. Indeed, the drive to extinguish the Aboriginal civilization of the

Americas can be seen as the definitive expression of the urge towards monocultural universalism that characterizes the most expansionary, frontier spirit inherent in Western civilization.

Among the most vital living expressions of Aboriginal agriculture in North America are those activities carried on by the Anishinaabaig [Anishinabek] peoples, a part of whom are known as the Ojibway. Many of them in the area of present-day northwestern Ontario, Manitoba, Minnesota, and Wisconsin still harvest "wild rice." The English name of this plant is misleading. There is abundant evidence to indicate that Ojibway people have planted and cared for this vegetable for countless generations.[163] In their own language, the Anishinaabaig describe wild rice as "Manito Gitigaan," as "the gift from the Creator's garden." More commonly they refer to it as "manomin." A variation on the word "manomin" was used by Ojibway people to identify their closely related Anishinaabaig neighbours in the Minnesota area, the Menominee.[164]

Historically, the life cycle of many Ojibway bands has been closely connected with the life cycle of manomin, a North American rice that can thrive only in very specific types of aquatic environment. In 1992 a council of Ojibway elders and political representatives enacted at Wabigoon, Ontario, their own legal declaration aimed at formalizing their people's specific rights and responsibilities in relation to manomin. Their actions were conceived in part as a response to the decision of a Manitoba court, which ealier struck down a policy of the Manitoba government aimed at recognizing the special relationship of First Nations peoples to the cultivation and harvesting of wild rice.[165] "Manomin," the Aboriginal legislators at the Wabigoon Council declared, "is of fundamental spiritual, cultural, and economic importance to the Anishinaabaig people, and the ownership is in the Creator." They continued, declaring "the intent and purpose of this legislation is to begin the process of codifying the laws which the Anishinaabaig have followed throughout our history to care for and use this sacred gift."[166]

The Ojibways' Manomin Law of 1992 draws specifically on the authority of Treaty 3 in Canada. "The treaty promise," says the enactment, "amounts to an exclusive right of use and management of the resource." The legislation created the basis for a Treaty 3 Anishinaabaig Manomin Management Board. Moreover, the law stipulates that the manomin regime will include provision for "spiritual ceremonies, ricing committees and the role of Elders in management, and any other activity undertaken by Anishinaabaig to protect the rice for present use and future generations."

The Manomin Law of the Anishinaabaig puts in bold perspective the kind of societal priorities advanced in constitutional phrases such as "the inherent right of Aboriginal self-government" or "Aboriginal government as one of three orders of Canadian government." The legislation very specifically draws the connection between the role of manomin in Ojibway economics and the role of the Ojibway-manomin relationship in the former's spiritual and cultural life as well. By clearly articulating this position, the Anishinaabaig Council at Wabigoon pointedly called into question the "Western" view that would secularize "the gift from the Creator's garden" as a "natural resource" whose primary values are determined in the commercial marketplace.[167] Although the Manomin Law did not restrict Ojibway people from earning their livelihood from the commercial sale of wild rice or from "extending the territory of wild rice," the declaration asserted the importance of maintaining a degree of continuity in an ancient relationship that is integral to the cultural identity of the Ojibway and to the unique ecology of their ancestral lands and waters. The Mandomin Law took the concept of Aboriginal rights beyond the realm of "reserves" and other forms of territorial demarcation towards a more fundamental reckoning with the jurisdictional requirements of maintaining and defending a way of life on the interfaces where economics, culture, and biodiversity meet.

No less than the Cree struggle against Hydro-Québec, the Sioux crusade to prevent the continued desecration of the sacred Black Hills,[168] the Zapatista condemnation of NAFTA, or the Yanomami campaign against the intensified destruction of the remaining Amazonian rain forest, the Manomin Law of the Ojibway calls into question some of the most fundamental and sacrosanct principles animating the American empire of private property. By forcing the question of whether wild rice is to be treated as part of the cultural inheritance of a people or simply as a cash crop like any other, the assertions of the Anishinaabaig Council at Wabigoon serve as an apt contemporary symbol of the centrality of conflicting treatments of plants that historically have differentiated the Aboriginal civilization of the Americas from the "Western" civilization of the newcomers and their descendants.

For governments or courts to ignore, belittle, or oppose Aboriginal laws like those covering manomin is to maintain the monocultural hold of a regime whose ecological effect has been to diminish biodiversity and undermine cultural pluralism in the service of the more favoured gods of technological efficiency, together with a single civilization of universalized property law.

A HIERARCHY OF NARRATIVES: MYTH AND ENLIGHTENMENT IN GLOBALIZING THE WORLD'S STORIES

Richard White has written eloquently and insightfully to challenge the distortions and inaccuracies entailed in "the recent canonization of Indians into environmental sainthood."[169] Shepard Kreech III took up this same subject, illustrating how the idealized imagery of what he calls the "Ecological Indian" plays on far older themes in European and North American literature. From the earliest stages of the European exploration of the

Americas, idealized characterizations of the "Noble Indian" have been put forward to serve as witness and proof of the perceived inadequacies and corruptions of European society. Both White and Kreech take aim at what they view as the self-indulgent and distorting romanticism of those who would perpetuate the mythology of noble savagery by depicting Indian peoples as archetypal environmentalists whose Aboriginal societies in no way changed or disrupted the natural milieu around them. They assert that this approach demeans and dehumanizes Indigenous peoples by failing to acknowledge the fact that, at every stage in history, they have transformed the earth in ways that reflect and influence their constantly changing cultures.

Kreech, for instance, devotes a chapter to exploring whether the Indigenous peoples of North America were responsible for the extinction of a variety of large mammal species during the Pleistocene era. Similarly, he delves into the problem of whether the former Hohokam inhabitants of the old ruins along the Salt River in Arizona "irrigated themselves to death." In their time no less than our own, agricultural land could be destroyed by too much dependence on watering techniques that brought heavy concentrations of subterranean salt to the surface. Kreech carries his theme into more recent times, chronicling how Indian peoples have repeatedly overhunted mammals such as beaver, buffalo, and deer once their pelts became commodities in the global trading system.[170]

In his study of the encounter of Choctaw, Pawnee, and Navajo peoples with the various newcomers to their territories, White chronicled how assertively Indigenous peoples tried to escape the dependency that came with their subordination within the exploitative framework of the global economy. "Among Indians themselves," White wrote, "market relations were such a threatening and destructive relationship that all these nations resisted them, with temporary success, for generations." This finding led White to conclude that "culture here controlled economics," a comment that butresses one of the central propositions of my text. White added that those who seek genuine understanding of the generation of dependencies on the frontiers of global trade systems must eshew dogmatic attachment to "finding the invisible hand of economic interests." What is required, instead, is scholarly commitment to "finding the reciprocal influences of culture, politics, economics, and the environment."[171]

There is, of course, a dark, ignoble parallel to the deep veins of literary and artistic misrepresentation that support the contemporary stereotypes of Indians as noble, pristine environmentalists who never seriously modified the ecology of their ancestral lands. Just like the imagery of noble Indians, the imagery of ignoble and diabolical savagery is based on archetypes rooted in very old strains of storytelling that run through the writings and imagination of European thinkers from classical to medieval to Renaissance times. From 1492 until the present, the effect of this consistent pattern of pressing the Indigenous peoples of the Americas into representational moulds foreign to their own civilization has been to stimulate some of the world's most infamous episodes of dehumanization as reflected in both the depictions and deeds of their non-Aboriginal oppressors. The persistence of the misrepresentation is emblemized in the word "Indian," the marker of a huge geographic mistake that foreshadowed many representational gaffes to come.

One of the most persistent ancient mythologies to appear in the representation of Aboriginal America is that their societies embodied in pre-Columbian times the idyllic qualities of the Garden of Eden before Adam and Eve fell from grace. Closely connected to the imagery of pre-Columbian America as an Eden on Earth was the belief that this "New World" hosted peoples who personified many of the best attributes of the ancient world, but especially those characteristics rooted in the classical cultures of Greece and Rome.[172] The mirror image of this schizophrenic mythology was embodied in the view of North American Indians as heathens and pagans who were in league with the devil himself. This view of Indian Country as a kind of Hell on Earth would become all too real as the evangelical zealotry of Western civilization urged forward the colonizing onslaught.[173]

The European imposition on the peoples of the New World of their most primal, Old World images of heaven and hell, classical enlightenment and primitive savagery, illustrates one of the most basic aspects of the phase of globalization that began in 1492 and continues yet. This dynamic lies in the expanded dissemination and convergence of humanity's resources of historical memory and creative imagination through the telling of stories. Accordingly, much of this text is devoted to the exploration of those connections and relationships that continue to come into being through storytelling, an activity that is an essential cultural basis in the bonding and transformation of all peoples, countries, and civilizations. It advances the thesis that the accelerated conveyance and convergence of stories is one of globalization's great hallmarks. The process is as essential a feature of globalization as, for instance, the expansion of immigration and commerce, the elaboration and extension of technological innovations, and the movement of plants, animals, and micro-organisms in what Alfred Crosby identified as *The Columbian Exchange*.[174]

There is great potential for surges of inventiveness and interpretive illumination in the examination, analysis, and possible synthesis of those stories whose renewal and is essential to the process of reproducing and adaptating the genesis of all human societies. How can any kind of true human community be self-perpetuating, or how can new ones come into existence, unless its members adhere to minimal codes of shared conduct and shared belief? Even those communities formed primarily around markets require some sort of common system of belief in order to afford legitimacy to the rules of property relations and currency exchange on which commercial institutions depend.[175] One usual means of transmitting and conveying the most basic principles, archetypes, and assumptions that help bond individuals into wider associations of culture, country, commerce, and creed is through the relation of certain kinds of stories that are needed to help explain a community's internal coherence to its own members. Most often this kind of story takes the form of historical narratives describing the founding acts that brought a community into being, as well as the subsequent actions of those leaders deemed best to embody a society's most fundamental values.

Great historical flux is the probable result when humanity's most archetypal stories are changed or synthesized. Since 1492, for instance, this process of narrative change has been manifest in the religious syncretism of many Indigenous peoples throughout the Americas. For generations their storytellers have been grafting together narratives that combine Christian teachings with older Aboriginal accounts of human and natural history. This blending of stories has continued to bring light from darkness; these hybrid narratives have continued to offer insight, for instance, into the origins of the world, the weaving together of all creatures and species into the web of life, the impact of great floods, and the coming of great teachers and prophets who speak of Creation's Divine Order and remind humanity of higher ethical ideals.

The best storytelling traditions originating in the heritage of 1492 speak of the great opportunities in globalization for the widening of human understanding through epistemological cross-fertilization. This same process can also represent a great liability if the outcome eliminates yet more grounds for cultural pluralism or continues homogenization of people and peoples into monolingual, monocultural masses. The danger here is that the individual imaginations of these masses have become, in effect, the collective manufactured product of a global entertainment conglomerate whose highest ideal is to perpetuate the kind of property relations that best serve the American empire of possessive individualism.

The great opportunities of transcultural blending are exemplified in the melding of inspirations that have resulted in the emergence of the blues, jazz, and rock and roll from the cross-fertilization in America of African and European musical forms. The more stiffling effect of this same process is manifest in the commercial dissemination of a narrow spectrum of this creative output as a medium for the expansion and consolidation of mass markets through the activities of an increasingly global music business. This industry tends to eliminate space for musical diversity as it blankets the planet with the reproduction on commercial radio of a small number of "hit" tunes put together by a revolving retinue of performers whose aggressively promoted songs become the currency and capital of large corporations. The ultimate parody of this process lies in the recycling of the great protest anthems of the 1960s into advertising jingles for global corporations.

In *Culture and Imperialism,* Edward Said actively promotes a more creative synthesis incorporating the storytelling creativity of those on both the expansionary and the receiving ends of Europe's colonization of the planet. He does so by careful examination of the literature that has driven and justified imperialism and the corresponding movements for decolonization. These two genres of narrative, Said asserts, present very different ways of explaining what is, in fact, the same process of globalization. The path towards reconciliation lies in removing the false dichotomies that prepetuate such antagonistic ways of dealing with shared legacies inherited from history. In making this case, Said's moral compass seems pointed towards the need for a democratic synthesis between a kind of global citizenship open to everyone and the necessity of maintaining narrower, more particular kinds of political community that enable individuals to express themselves as members of more circumscribed types of national, linguistic, ethnic, and religious collectivities. Above all, Said argues for a fluid, many-faceted concept of personal and collective identity that can embrace the reality that "no one today is purely *one* thing."[176]

My goal here is to make a contribution to the needed synthesis called for by Said. One method is to describe and evaluate the storytelling that has helped animate the actions of those on both sides of the moving frontier of what I have identified as the American empire of private property. The expansion of this empire continues yet as the most active element in that mix of processes and patterns that go by the name of globalization. These processes grow from older imperial histories that again and again saw Europeans and their far-flung heirs in complex encounters with peoples who, to this day, are frequently identified simply as "*the natives.*" Often the stories of Native-newcomer encounter take on near-mythological meaning in the elaboration of those tales of self-justification or, more recently, self-reproach used to explain the genesis of a progressively enlarging series of New World, post-Columbian societies.

From James Fenimore Cooper to Frederick Jackson Turner, from Bartolome de Las Casas to John Collier, from Francis Jennings to Bruce Clark, the language of those who relate what has happened on the expanding frontiers of the New World empire is frequently brimming with moral intensity. This intensity is based on knowledge of the high ethical and interpretive stakes that depend on how these encounters are popularly and officially viewed. So integral are the early episodes of Native-newcomer relations in the founding myths of most New World societies that the colouring of these events can help tint the basic psychology of very basic forms of collective self-understanding.[177] Seminal patterns are established affecting the preception of all kinds of "others" beyond many different kinds of "frontier," real or imagined.

The mythological meanings in these stories of encounter are explored in this text. My own narrative will identify the thick webs of connections between, for instance, the founding and genesis of New England, British North America, and the American empire. Clearly, the culmination of this continuum in the ascent to unparalleled global power of the American empire has acquired heightened significance in recent times. The stories of the emergence of the United States from the British Empire have taken on added meaning as so many currents of change have followed patterns heavily influenced by this most important transition in the flow of Anglo-American and world history.

While British North America proved to be a kind of dual creation that both permeated and opposed the animating energy of the American empire, the British imperial government has been paradoxically connected at different times to the coalition of peoples united in resistance to the most aggressive variants of New World colonialism. The stories that tell of the mounting of this sporadic resistance speak of the connections linking, for instance, the founding and genesis of French-Aboriginal Canada, the Indian Confederacy of Canada, and what George Manuel entitled the Fourth World. Interspersed among the stories of extreme antagonism are those that tell of many efforts at compromise and negotiation between those on both sides of this frontier dividing imperial expansion from indigenous resistance. A major legacy of this effort to find middle ground lies in the many hundreds of treaties negotiated with Indigenous peoples.

The Vatican's "donation" of the entire American hemisphere to Spain and Portugal in 1493 was a major factor in the development of the treaty tradition in European colonization outside these imperial regimes. Because the American colonies of France, England, the Netherlands, and Sweden were pressed forwards without a papal grant, there was added incentive to gain from Indigenous peoples through treaty what Dorothy Jones has described as "a license for empire."[178] The evolution of treaty diplomacy, especially with the Indigenous peoples whose lands provided the basis for New France, New England, New Netherlands, and New Sweden, represented flawed but ground-breaking efforts in transcultural negotiations. One of the early motivations for Europeans to initiate this process was to gain juridical legitimacy *from* Indians. Among the early English-speaking jurisdictions in North America to garner treaty legitimacy from Indians were Rhode Island, New York, and Pennsylvania. The use of this genre of negotiation to gain Aboriginal sanction for settler societies was repeated in negotiations with Indigenous peoples in, for instance, India, South Africa, West Africa, and New Zealand. The negotiations with the Maori of New Zealand produced, in 1840, the Treaty of Waitangi, which is probably the best-known example of this type of agreement in the world today.

From the North American variant of this saga of globalization emerged the idea of a Covenant Chain of treaty connections between Indigenous peoples and Anglo-American colonies. This Covenant Chain of experimentation on the domestic and international frontiers of intercultural democracy runs all the way from the council grounds at Johnson Hall to the establishment of Nunavut in the eastern Arctic and the contemporary treaty negotiations with the First Nations peoples of British Columbia. One of the objects of this text is to lay out the bare outlines of the story that shows the connections between the earlier history of the American empire and the new round of treaty making. Some critics of the most recent treaties charge that the primary purpose of these deals is to simplify and standardize property law according to neo-liberal principles.

Narratives of resistance to this most recent wave of expansion along new frontiers of private property tell of the events of the bitterly contested, 1988 federal election in Canada, which turned largely on the question of whether to ratify the Free Tade Agreement with the United States. In 1994 the Indians of Chiapas helped write the next chapter in this struggle through the Zapatistas' acts of defiance against the further incorporation of Mexico into the American empire through the neo-liberal vehicle of NAFTA. Then, in 1999, the Millennial Round of the World Trade Organization was disrupted by the outbreak of the Battle of Seattle.[179] In the eclectic mix of protestors who clashed with police, I saw the multicultural *avant-guarde* of the Fourth World, a movement at once conservative and revolutionary whose shared motivation is to realize models of globalization different from the monocultures of enclosed privatization advocated by the proponents of global corporatism.

The history presented in this text turns largely on the relations between different peoples and between the various stories from which we derive our sense of integration into, or antagonism towards, different communities. The same kind of forces that converge in the establishment of different hierarchies of peoples also influence gradations in the prestige and power attached to different stories essential to the internal coherence of different societies. One of the obvious factors affecting this hierarchy of stories is whether they are conveyed primarily through oral or literary traditions of socialization and scholarship.

The disadvantaged status of those stories belonging primarily to the oral cultures of Indigenous peoples has been the subject of considerable attention in the academy. Similarly, problems about the nature of historical proof and evidence in relating the histories of the First Nations have attracted the attention of many Commonwealth jurists, including those who penned Australia's *Mabo* ruling in 1992 and Canada's *Delgamuukw* ruling in 1997. The reparative reversals called for by these rulings have global historical significance. With all their importance, however, the reparations they envisage are minimal compared with the magnitude of the thefts originally justified by relegating so much of the world's pre-Columbian history to the inarticulate darkness implied in the word "pre-history" or to the fictional emptiness declared in the doctrine of *terra nullius*.

One of the great challenges in the continuing process of globalization will be to make better sense of the implosion of stories from around the world that bear on basic questions of the ordering of the legal, economic, and political relationships between and among different peoples. The history of how different courts have handled litigation arising from the expansion of European empires and New World nations into the lands of Indigenous peoples presents endless examples of the inequities that flow from denigrating Aboriginal stories, even as those of the newcomers are elevated to the constitutional heights of enforced law. With some few exceptions, this legal history presents a sorry monument to the distance between theory and practice even in those societies that style themselves as liberal democracies. As disputes arose between Indigenous peoples and newcomers, the courts of the latter have frequently been closed even to hearing the grievances of the former, who, as wards of the state, have often been locked under the trusteeship of those very state agencies overseeing their dispossession.

In the rare instances where Aboriginal litigants and witnesses have been afforded the opportunity to tell their side of different stories, the usual response of the newcomers' courts has been to protect the interests of the powerful by dismissing Aboriginal narratives as unempirical, unauthoritative, or irrelevant. The rationales for this invalidation of Indigenous knowledge are often presented through resort to the most vile imperial traditions of religious and racial prejudice dressed up in the Darwinian language of the emerging social sciences.[180] This legal history has produced a mountain of precedent that has nothing whatsoever to do with the principle of equal treatment before the law. It remains to be seen how this mass of precedent will inform the many new kinds of courts that are being invented on the commercial frontiers of globalization's new jurisdictional frameworks. The signs are not good, however, if the shape of things to come is evidenced in the closed procedures for the creation of new supranational agencies such as NAFTA, the World Trade Organization, and the Free Trade Area of the Americas.

The anti-democratic biases in the procedures used to create these agencies have been reflected and compounded in the secretive procedures and inequitable rulings that have been hobbled together by the technocratic judiciaries at the WTO and at the North American Free Trade Authority. As will be discussed in more detail in volume 2, the arbitration panels of these supranational bodies have been inclined to revert back to some of the most objectionable approaches of the old imperial courts. They have been prone to apply their judicial weight consistently to support the claims of the powerful over the narratives of those seeking to testify about officialdom's violations of the rule of law, particularly at those points where the weakest and most marginalized members of society are brushed aside even further towards the fringes of the New World Order.

The profound unease generated by these pioneering efforts to construct the infrastructures of a global rule of commerce came into harsh focus at the Battle of Seattle in 1999. The activism and violence in the streets was suggestive of the anger and resentments generated from handing over such expansive realms of decision making to supranational judiciaries

selected through processes and subject to pressures that are anything but
transparent. The dawning realization of many citizenries that we are being
subjected to an aggressive assertion of jurisdictional authority we had no
hand in creating or shaping replicates and further globalizes the long
experiences of Indigenous peoples. That tendency compounds the effective disenfranchisement of the most chronically dispossessed. It extends to
wider constituencies the experience of those myriad peoples indigenous to
vast portions of the planet once claimed as the overseas realms of Eur-
poean sovereigns – peoples who fell under the control of empires and of
nation-states not of their own making, under the power of regimes imper-
vious to their own exercises and expressions of political will.

There are profound ecological and political problems pointing to the
unsustainability of this approach to constructing what is probably better
understood as a global rule of commerce rather than a global rule of law.
For instance, the destruction of biodiversity on the monocultural frontiers
of global privatization is part of the same expansion of institutionalized
extinguishment that has closed the high courts and high councils of imperial globalization to all advice but the trickle of analysis coming from a narrow clique of neo-liberal courtiers, technocrats, and functionaries. In this
fashion, forms of globalization are advanced without popular sanction.
Huge transformations are initiated on the planet without so much as a
hearing for those voices and stories that have much to convey about a global ecological crisis. When attention is drawn to the speedy impoverishment
of biodiversity, the lethal consequences of this crisis belie the rosy futures
promised in the unsustainable pyramid schemes that have become the
prime currency of neo-liberal economics.

The disqualification of so many narratives and voices has much the same
nonsensical effect as the despoilation of species at a time when it is well
understood that the genetic chemistry of any seemingly obscure fungus,
plant, virus, or insect may turn out to have vast medicinal or industrial
applications. In much the same way, there is no telling what stories or voices in any part of the planet may end up providing vital answers to some of
science's most perplexing technical riddles or humankind's most pressing
moral dilemmas. That the rules and protocols of the Wabigoon Council on
the cultivation of wild rice, for instance, may turn out to have broad applications in restoring ecological harmony to all kinds of imbalances in the
relationship of agriculture to many other aspects of human culture. And
maybe Trickster has some insights to offer us all on how to achieve poise
and grace in dealing with both the tragic and the regenerative elements of
life on the frontiers of an uncertain future.

It is vital to keep insisting, therefore, that any advancement of globalization must take into account the rights and responsibilities of all people, as
well the juridical implications arising from the founding stories of all peoples. A key to the realization of this ideal would be the elaboration of
transnational or, perhaps, supranational courts capable of assessing and

balancing the juridical implications woven into those narratives of renewal that are most essential to the equilibrium between continuity and adaptation in the perpetuation of all human cultures.

THE CONVERGENCE OF PROPERTY RIGHTS AND THE IDEA OF FREEDOM IN THE TRANSMUTATION OF ENLIGHTENMENT THOUGHT INTO AMERICAN NATIONALISM

The intergenerational passing on of founding stories is essential to the viability and continuity of virtually all peoples, communities, or nationalities. In the course of globalization, some of the world's vast store of national histories, myths, legends, and folklore have acquired a kind of unassailable pre-eminence in humanity's hierarchy of narratives. The story of the founding of the United States is one of these narratives of power.

Many vital messages are conveyed in the repeated telling of how the United States came to acquire its unique place in the world. These messages have many strategic roles in generating those popular attitudes on which major laws, institutions, and forms of property relationships depend not only in the United States, but, increasingly, throughout the rest of the planet as well. There exists a huge weight of vested interest biased against any radical tampering with the way the major outlines of this pivotal event in world history is to be popularly explained and interpreted. While the interpretive controversies over how best to relate the story of this genesis have been contained within intellectual frameworks that do not seriously challenge the fundamental constitutional shape of the United States, a more deeply disruptive war of ideas has been waged on the contested ground of that monumental event in Western civilization that gave rise to the American Revolution. That event is known as the Enlightenment, unquestionably the brightest, most precious, and most multi-faceted gem of inspiration to arise in the last millennium of European experience.

The main chapters of the Enlightenment were written during the course of European and Anglo-American history, especially in the eighteenth century. What culminated in revolutions against monarchical regimes began as a gradual revolution of thought that challenged many old orthodoxies in epistemology, statecraft, and religion. The inquiring thinkers who made the Enlightenment cast aside what they increasingly saw as the anachronistic hold of dogma and superstition. Their ideal was to embrace, instead, the principle that human reason and rationality constitute the most reliable means of identifying truth.[181] Accordingly, the veracity of humanity's inherited stories would have to be tested in the clear light of reason.

The biblical narratives celebrating the religious revelations of Adam and Eve, Abraham, Moses, and Jesus Christ were a major source of privileged stories whose veracity became the subject of increased scrutiny and debate. While many of the Enlightenment's most shining beacons of erudition remained devout Christians throughout their lives, the primary thrust of their intellectual quest led inevitably towards more secular forms of human conceptualization. The goal was to eliminate what was untrue from the cosmology of human understanding so that the way could be cleared for the construction of new edifices of science and social well-being in unobstructed conformity with revealed principles of natural law.

The most fundamental laws of nature were seen to permeate the entire universe uniformly. Their essence, therefore, was identified as universal. If universal laws applied throughout that part of nature outside the human realm, these same universal principles should be made to prevail in the ordering of human societies through the instrument of law and human governance. There were many sweeping implications in the attending idea that natural law could be logically extended to the identification of natural rights as the just possessions of all human beings.[182] As this line of reasoning caught hold, there was a growing inclination to question all sorts of dstinctions in legal status dividing, for instance, royalty and aristocracy from commoners, slaves from citizens, and men from women.

Efforts to apply such ideals to human institutions have clarified the existence of several sharp contradictions in the range of contentions advanced in the name of differing visions of the Enlightenment's truth. What is decribed as "the Enlightenment" actually embraces not one story but many, not one pre-eminent narrative but a host of competing conceptualizations about how best to pursue human knowledge and to order human society. The most fundamental insight that unifies the eclectic range of ideals advanced under the banner of the Enlightenment's heritage is that the amazing cognitive instrument of human reason must be afforded recognition as the highest arbiter in differentiating what is true from what is untrue.

Many of the Enlightenment's ideals were ardently embraced, particularly by the descendants of New England's Puritan founders. These most lionized of pilgrims had crossed the Atlantic as militant activists of the Reformation, seeking to secure liberty for the exercise of their own theocratic version of religious freedom. The creative tensions between the secular biases inherent in Enlightenment thought and the religious enthusiasms of the founders of the United States have remained essential to the republic's character ever since. As Conor Cruise O'Brien has wryly observed, "the American Enlightenment resists decay because it is pickled in holy brine."[183]

The element of Enlightenment thought that has most thrived in the United States is the complex of theory whose proponents insist that society must be organized to allow maximum latitude to individuals to acquire and hold private property. Accordingly, the pursuit of private property became the most popular way in the United States to realize that pursuit of happiness which is promised to American citizens as an inalienable right in the opening phrases of the Declaration of Independence. From the very moment the American people announced to the world their existence in their legendary founding scripture, the right to possess property was treated as one of the most vital expressions of human rights.

The centrality of material acquisition to the realization of many American Dreams can be starkly illustrated by observing how much of American history has to do with the annexation of new territories in North America and with the development of new markets hemispherically and globally. The course of much of the planet's history since 1776 illustrates the powerful nature of the axis linking the course of American manifest destiny to the global dissemination of expansive approaches to the formulation of property law. The primary tendency in this legal history is to legitimize the transformation of the earth's vital elements into material commodities susceptible of being bought and sold as private property. It is a classic chicken-or-egg problem to decide whether this history was the result or the cause of the preoccupation of those in the American heartland with the ownership of property as the highest expression of human individualism. What is impossible to ignore, however, is that history presented the American people with unparalleled opportunities for proprietary expansion and aggrandizement, ones they have clearly exploited in elaborate and gigantic ways.

This American preoccupation with possessive individualism takes some of its cues from the importance of the institution of slavery during the early generations of the republic's existence. The usual response to the arguments of those who opposed the enslavement of African Americans in the southern states was to advocate the pre-eminent status of the slave owners' property rights over the inherent human rights of that most infamously privatized class of Black people.[184]

The need to bend the ideals of the Enlightenment to the requirements of Western expansion presented another forum of intellectual contortion as a vast Indian Country was transformed into transferable capital available primarily to a relatively circumscribed constituency of white, Protestant males. In my estimation it was the Puritan legacy, rather than the Enlightenment legacy, of the United States that was drawn on most heavily in fashioning this most characteristic feature of early American property law.

The rights thought to be invested in Anglo-American individuals were largely organized, advanced, and pre-empted by an increasingly sophisticated array of corporate entities whose main commercial metiers were land speculation and, later, railway construction. As this text will demonstrate, it was the leaders of these corporate entities who best capitalized on the emphasis on property ownership as the foremost expression of American individualism. Through their success in manipulating the claims of manifest destiny to expand the power and assets of their corporations, they made themselves the most prolifically rewarded beneficiaries from the extinguishment of Indian Country. This legacy from the transformation of Indian lands into private property has helped ever since to shape the expansionary ethos and methods of American corporate culture.[185]

The United States's great political and ideological showdown with the Soviet Union further cemented the tight connections linking fundamentalist Christianity with the emphasis on property rights as the most vital expression of the American ideal of freedom. The framing of this global struggle as one between capitalism and Marxist communism heightened the impression in the American republic that private property was a religious institution sanctioned by God Himself. This fervour was generated vis-à-vis a Soviet state that officially embraced atheism. This attribute of Soviet ideology can be seen as an extension of the most secularizing, materialistic thrust of Enlightenment thought as interpreted particularly by Karl Marx and his close associate Frederick Engels. Unlike the elements of Enlightenment inspiration adopted by the American revolutionaries, who took much of their intellectual orientation from John Locke, the Marxist makers of the Russian Revolution were more influenced by the ideological reveries of Jean-Jacques Rousseau.

Along with figures such as Voltaire, Diderot, Hume, and Kant, Rousseau was one of the major literary figures of eighteenth-century Europe. His writings affected many thinkers in the Anglo-American colonies who would incorporate into their republican experiment some of Rousseau's evocative visions. The American founders could not help but be influenced by Rousseau's emphasis on the idea of a "social contract" as the basis of the state, and on his advancement of "the people" as the only legitimate source of sovereign authority. Where Rousseau veered away from the preoccupations of the founders of the United States was in his argument that Native Americans and other Indigenous peoples beyond Europe were in a state of harmony with nature uncorrupted by the distortions engendered by layer upon layer of European social artifice. This preoccupation made Rousseau one of the primary literary elaborators of the mythological "noble savage." This great mythological figure striding through the pages of European literature was made to act as both the witness and the proof of what Rousseau and his disciples saw as the rotting, overly ripe condition of a plagued European society.

Rousseau's embrace of uncorrupted nature as the antithesis and antidote of civilization's imbalances made him extremely distrustful of the institution of private property. The most famous passage expressing this distrust would cut through history to define one of the arguments about the role of property and the role of the state in the expression of human culture and political economy. In his essay on *The Origins of Inequality*, Rousseau wrote:

The first man who, having enclosed a piece of ground, bethought himself of saying "This is mine," and found people simple enough to believe him, was the real founder of civil society. From how many crimes, wars, and murders, and from how many horrors and misfortunes might not one have saved mankind, by pulling up the stakes, or filling up the ditch, and crying to his fellows: "Beware of listening to this imposter; you are undone if you once forget that the fruits of the earth belong to us all, and the earth itself to nobody."[186]

UNIVERSALITY AND RELATIVISM
IN ENVISAGING THE FOURTH WORLD

The Enlightenment's encouragement to understand human society in the light of natural law established the basis for what would later come to be called the social sciences. In large measure the social sciences were founded in the effort to study the character of all those Indigenous peoples whose existence became known in the metropolises of Europe largely as a result of the vast global explorations that mapped out the expanding realms of European imperialisms. The broadening of perspectives from globalization's genesis after 1492 opened many new conceptual frontiers, as Aboriginal and European thinkers on both sides of the colonial divide examined their own societies in light of the expanding information available about the range of variations and possibilities in the human condition.

The developing study of Indigenous peoples beyond Europe, but especially in the Americas, was particularly instrumental in the genesis of thought justifying often antagonistic conceptions of how human beings should structure their relationships with their material environments through the medium of property law. Indeed, as chapter 2 will demonstrate, it would not be stretching the evidence too far to argue that the theoretical roots of both American-style capitalism and Soviet-style communism drew on different conceptions of how Native Americans related to one another and to their earthly environments. Where Locke's theories about Native American interaction inspired the former, Rousseau's imaginary journeys in Indian Country informed communist traditions of thought and analysis.

With the expanding exploration of the planet's geography and ethnography, the pioneers of social science claimed the legacy of the Enlightenment in their advancement of increasingly ambitious theories of human nature and human change. By the second half of the nineteenth century, the work of Charles Darwin became an ideological lightening rod flashing the apparent authority of high science on a broad intellectual consensus that it was possible to situate all human societies over all human history within the stucture of a single grand theory of evolutionary change. A transformation from savagery to barbarism to civilization, or from stone age to bronze age to iron age, was widely accepted as the conceptual basis for a universal projectory of ascent from lower to higher forms of human organization.

In the twentieth century a cloud of disrepute gradually settled over this

Darwinian project, which advanced one of the most potent conceptions of universality to emerge from the Enlightenment. A growing number of voices were raised, especially after the global cataclysm of the Second World War, to question the principle that all human societies were subject to a universal law of human change. This reaction against the application of universal theories to the totality of all human relationships drew particular zeal from those critics who identified the racial character of much of the dominant thinking in evolutionary theory.

Johann Gottfried Herder anticipated such criticisms by presenting contemporaneous critiques of the universalist claims that were integral to the main currents of philosophy in Europe during the century of Enlightenment.[187] Most often, however, the beginnings of the contemporary rejection of universalist evolutionary theory are attributed to Franz Boas and his many students in anthropology. Generally speaking, Boas and his intellectual progeny abandoned the efforts of many of their discipline's founders to fit all societies into grand conceptual grids based on ideas of universally applicable criteria for organizational, racial, or technological gradations of human development. Instead, they advanced the idea that all societies are oriented around unique configurations of stories, beliefs, and practices that form the basis of unique cultures. The ideal was to attempt to study and understand each culture as a unique human creation, rather than as a manifestation of some universal principles governing the organization of all humanity.[188]

The idea of cultural relativity that began in anthropology moved quickly to the rest of the social sciences, just as Einstein's theory of relativity indicated that even time and space could not be treated as fixed universals in the hard sciences. In the name of postmodernism, a vast assault was mounted on the idea that there is any single, privileged vantage point from which to view, judge, and classify objectively all human experience.[189] From this proposition it seemed to follow that all stories of human change, all cultures and all conceptions of morality, were equally valid or invalid and equally susceptible to being selected by individuals or groups, in much the same way as commodities can be picked or rejected for purchase in the marketplace.

More extreme rejections of the continuing influence of Eurocentric Social Darwinism went so far as to change the identities of those on the imagined evolutionary scale. At its worst, this genre of analysis simply replaced one form of ethnocentric chauvinism with another. In *Black Athena*, for instance, Martin Bernal dismissed all Eurocentric interpretations of historical progress as outright racist propaganda and then offered an alternative interpretation, making extremely overblown claims that the main tap roots of humanity's civilizational heritage lie primarily in Africa.[190]

The nihilism, amoralism, and outright speciousness attributed by some to the postmodernist stance – or to the attending intellectual trends of poststructuralism or post-colonialism – has generated a variety of negative responses, from both the right and the left wings of the political spectrum. The rejection of relativism was particularly strong among those most committed to various forms of religious, intellectual, and moral fundamentalism. In 1987 Allan Bloom lent his erudite voice to a spirited critique of relativism by focusing particularly on what he saw as the disastrous new orthodoxy in the curricula of many American universities.[191] In *The Closing of the American Mind*, he asserted that too much ground was being given in the curricula to the study of peoples and second-rate thinkers outside the Enlightenment traditions. These traditions, he argued, marked the highest intellectual achievements of Europe and its cultural outgrowths, especially in the United States.[192]

In Canada, Tom Flanagan specifically cited cultural relativism as a contributing factor in his more general attack on the conclusions of the massive report done in 1996 by the Royal Commission on Aboriginal Peoples (RCAP). After outlining the roots of relativism in the anthropological scholarship of Franz Boas, Ruth Benedict, Margaret Mead, and others, Flanagan directed his criticism at RCAP's authors for their alleged failure to take into account what he described as "the civilization gap" between Europeans and Indigenous peoples in the Americas. Flanagan based this critique on what he argued were the many ways that relativist blindness prevented RCAP's authors from addressing what he alleged was the evolutionary retardation of Aboriginal societies. In posing an alternative both to the work of RCAP and to what he described as the new "aboriginal orthodoxy," Flanagan attempted to rehabilitate the old evolutionary principles of societal hierarchy so integral to the pre-Boasian scholarship of Morgan, Marx, Schoolcraft, and many others. Accordingly, he lauded the assimilationist direction of Indian policy in Canada before 1969. He defended this approach as a necessary expedient to deal with the legacy stemming from his contention that, in 1492, "the Old World was about five thousand years ahead of the New World on the path of civilization."[193]

The attack on relativism has extended far beyond the academy to exert great influence on the contest for power in the main theatres of electoral politics. For instance, in the United States the New Right was particularly energized, in the Reagan years, by the hostility of Protestant fundamentalists towards the ethical eclecticism of what was denigrated as the undisciplined tribe of the "politically correct" – the peaceniks, cultural relativists, feminists, and outright anarchists – who seemed to be undermining the moral fabric of the American republic.

Indeed, the political landscape of many countries was dramatically altered by the coordinated reactions against the diverse range of intellectual pursuits and moral conducts that found legitimating shelter under the huge tent of relativism. For instance, the flirtations of many social democrats with some of postmodernism's more balkanizing preoccupations resulted in the Left's corresponding failure to maintain the sharpness of its traditional focus on commonalities that most ordinary men and women share, but especially in their identity as both workers and consumers.

Building on the perspectives introduced by critic Robert Hughes in his engaging commentary on the alleged excesses of "multi-culti" fanaticism in the art world, Todd Gitlin in *The Twilight of Common Dreams* bemoaned the balkanization of the Left's political mission. Gitlin thoughtfully criticized its leadership for too uncritically embracing even the most chauvinistic excesses of multicultural and gender politics. The failure of social democrats to balance judicious accommodation of cultural pluralism with unifying visions of common goals, purposes, and ideals helped clear the way for the New Right to seize from its opponents the populist high ground as champions of the Enlightenment's most potent assertions of humanity's universal attributes and needs.[194]

In a volume entitled *Sociocultural Evolution,* Bruce Trigger added his voice to those of a growing range of left-leaning thinkers, including Gitlin's and Hughes's, who cautioned that the preoccupation of so many social scientists with cultural relativity and postmodernism represented a great betrayal of the Enlightenment's most important legacies. The abandonment of the idea that it is possible for human reason to identify certain universal truths applicable to all human beings left the New Right and the business interests on neo-liberalism's frontiers almost entirely free to direct the process of globalization in their own image. In this fashion, argued Trigger, many of global corporatism's greatest critics "become unwittingly complicitous in promoting it, and postmodernism, willingly or unwillingly, becomes the culture of transnational capitalism."[195] Trigger attempted to disengage both the racist and the relativist baggage that has attached itself to the basic premise of sociocultural evolution. This evolutionary premise holds that, through the application of human reason, human societies can self-consciously evolve towards higher, more sophisticated, and more inclusive forms of organization so as to ameliorate the overall human condition as well as the ecological health of the planet.

According to Trigger, it is vital to restore confidence that human beings can work together so as to bring closer various visions of planned progress. Only in this way can viable alternatives be generated to counter the neo-liberal preoccupation with markets as the sole valid arbiter of what on the planet is valuable and what is expendable. By embracing the Enlightenment's promise that certain universal needs, rights, and characteristics unify the entire human condition, it becomes possible to plan for the future in ways that recognize people and peoples as something far greater than mere economic animals. This process of planning requires the elaboration of many new political agencies at both local and global levels to express democratically the plurality of cultures, interests, opinions, and beliefs that mark humanity in both our diversity and what we share in common.

Many bitter contestations, therefore, continue to swirl around the question of the contemporary relevance of the Enlightenment and who can most authentically claim to represent and advance its brightest ideals. As has long been the case, many aspects of this argument are significantly affected by the ways in which relations between Indigenous peoples and Western civilization are represented and understood. One school alleges that too much pedagogical emphasis on multiculturalism and too much politically correct identification with the most brutalized and marginalized victims of New World colonialism threaten to sap Western civilization of its expansionary confidence.

A major subtext of this argument, advanced with particular vehemence by Bloom, Schlesinger, Huntington, Fukuyama, and others, emphasizes the strategic importance of the United States in defending the Enlightenment's heritage against menaces thought to be lurking within and beyond the frontiers of the American empire. The Irish statesman and scholar Conor Cruise O'Brien summed up this position in a series of lectures prepared for the Canadian Broadcasting Corporation. He identified what he saw as the Enlightenment's enemies, a list that included the Vatican, the most fundamentalist branches of Islam, the deceitfulness and trivialization of image-driven electoral politics, and what he dismissively tagged as "PCM – 'politically correct' and multiculturalism." The strength of the United States, argued O'Brien, stands as the major force aligned against these perceived elements of doctrinaire reaction and social decline. The American republic remains, in O'Brien's estimation, "the heart and soul of the Western value system, the Enlightenment tradition, which sustains and permeates the Western intellectual framework of democracy, freedom of expression, and the rule of law." He concluded that "the continued predominance of the Enlightenment tradition in the West depends on its continued predominance in the United States."[196]

In my estimation there are clear hints of xenophobic exclusiveness in such narrow characterizations of the Enlightenment as a system of understanding and governance whose brightest illuminations are contained, or can be contained, within a tightly defended citadel of American strength. This approach seems to privilege an inward-looking reflex whose narrowness of vision betrays the Enlightenment's boldest invitation to engage all people and peoples in a ceaseless challenging of all kinds of arbitrary power that cannot be justified in the light of human reason, in all its many complex manifestations.

The inward-looking dynamic of this reactionary mentality was symbolized by President George W. Bush's initiative in the early years of the twenty-first century to further the militarization of space by raising a "Star-Wars" protective shield over a privileged North American enclave. The stunning limitations of this scheme, which the United States's young president inherited from the regime of Ronald Reagan, was graphically demonstrated on September 11, 2001, when three hijacked commercial airliners slammed into the Pentagon and the twin towers of the World Trade Center. The vulnerability of these classic symbols of American commercial and military might to terrorist attack highlighted the pre-eminence of the power of ideas over the power of military arsenals. No expanded infrastructure of Star Wars defence coupled with "Homeland Security" can protect against the power of the idea that all people and peoples have an equal human right to self-determination. No laser shield can defend the United States against the implications of some contemporary reckoning in the global community with the crimes against humanity commited against Indigenous peoples to clear the way for the expansion of European empires and their successor states. The first of these successor states, Western civilization's original prototype of "decolonization," was the United States.

One of the most striking symbols of political inequality in the world today is marked in the us government's position that it is entitled to militarize space unilaterally, exclusively for its own protection. It asserts that imperative even as the world's sole superpower maintains a vast military apparatus whose design is premised on the principle that the us government retains the right to intervene with armed force virtually everywhere on the planet at a moment's notice. Added to the United States's unparalleled capacity for military intervention is an elaborate network of covert "national security" operations whose history has been to help destabilize and overthrow many foreign regimes not to the United States's liking. These capacities for covert and often illegal interventions were returned to Cold War levels after the events of September 11 provided the opening to replace the many-faceted war against "international communism" with a similarly constructed war on "international terrorism." In both instances, the us government eschewed all forms of international due process that might limit its unilateral capacity to identify, try, convict, and punish the real or imagined enemy forces in its global crusades. The resulting reinforcement of a world order based on the pre-eminence of the rule of force over the rule of law constitutes a huge vote of nonconfidence in humanity's capacity for a more democratic future. In my view, it weakens rather than strengthens the integrity of the United States as the imagined citadel of the Enlightenment's core values.

The fate of the West's civilizational projectory depends primarily on its capacity to find viable resolutions for its deepest and most complex ideological contradictions. Its fate depends on widening the franchise of the Enlightenment's most challenging democratic principles, including the ideal of the inherent right of all peoples to self-determination. The Enlightenment's global fate depends on the outcome of some authentic grappling in the global community with the principles of equality, human rights, and the necessity to subordinate the exercise of temporal power to the force of democratic law rather than the imperatives of military or commercial might.

There has been great resistance, centred primarily in the United States, to the elaboration of any agency or agencies sufficiently funded and empowered in the international community for the effective protection of the human rights of people and peoples. Indeed, the experience of Africa with "decolonization" suggests a distinctly racial tint in the determination of who is eligible to receive international protection when the sovereign powers of nation-states are engulfed by the violence of ethnic conflict.[197] NATO's bombing war on Yugoslavia in 1999 without the sanction of the UN Security Council marked a telling illustration of the poverty of international instruments available for forceful intervention within the rule of law to prevent human-rights violations. The United States must bear the lion's share of the responsibility for the gross lack of a global regime of consistent, rules-based intervention when it is *peoples* rather than *money* and *oil*, the pre-eminent grease of the global economy, requiring the enforced protection of international law.

The subordination of the global rights of people and peoples to the global imperatives of money and commerce is more than accidental. It is rooted in the continuity of the ongoing Columbian conquests which has made made universalist, neo-liberal economics the primary medium to perpetuate the gross inequities born of European imperialism. Beginning in 1492, the powers directing these imperial ventures apportioned global resources among themselves and divided humanity by military force and by international laws whose structures reflected and formalized many imagined hierachies of racial and civilizational order. The global banking regimes, as epitomized by the role of the World Bank or the International Monetary Fund, have been primary devices for maintaining continuity in the structural apportionments of credits and liabilities inherited from the era of European imperialism.

Until the United States lends its pivotal weight to the elaboration of a global rule of law *by which it too is governed*, the Enlightenment's highest ideals will have been betrayed. In that sense, recognition of the international dimension of relations between the world's sole superpower and First Nations within the United States's own borders is symbolically strategic in terms of sending a clear signal of the American republic's willingness to embrace the sanctity of the rule of law over the rule of conquest in international affairs.

Until such a reckoning with history occurs, the United States, with all its potential for good and for evil, will withdraw further into the nostalgia of its laser-protected self-image. That self-understanding has been based on reliving again and again the heady intoxicatation of the moment when the liberated United States was seemingly designated as the natural successor of the Roman Empire, when the revolutionary founders of the American republic became Europe's appointed agents for the westward expansion of Western civilization. From that moment, the leading lights of the United States began to conceive of their country as the planet's chief warrior in the ongoing battle of civilization's ascent over savagery in a global Indian Country.

It is important not to be too categoric in deciding who is friend or who is foe to the Enlightenment, in much the same fashion that the infamous Committe on Un-American Activities once rushed to similar ideological judgments about who was friend or foe to the United States. After all, none other than Michel Foucault, one of the seminal figures on the early frontiers of postmodernist scholarship, toiled prodigiously to understand the responsibilities of intellectual work within the Enlightenment's tradition. Foucault saw the Enlightenment as "an enterprise for linking the progress of truth and the history of liberty in a bond of direct relation."[198]

For my own part, I see the quest to give concrete political expression to the recognition and affirmation of existing Aboriginal and treaty rights as a project entirely consistent with the best traditions of the Enlightenment. Similarly, I see the cautious recognition of official multiculturalism at the national level, and the accommodation of the principle in the global community that all peoples have an inherent right to self-determination, as logical emodiments of Enlightenment inspiration. Both these ideals extend urges to liberty that earlier found expression in the movements for the abolition of slavery, the attainment of the universal franchise, and the freedom of workers to engage in collective bargaining.

Because of the overlapping histories of Canada and Indian Country as major obstacles to the early revolutionary expansion of the American empire, the rights and liberties of First Nations have been more likely to find recognition and protection among non-Aboriginals on the conservative side of the Enlightenment's continuing projectory through history. As this text documents, the conservative alliance between Indigenous peoples and Euro-Americans can be traced from French-Aboriginal Canada to the alignment of ideas and interests codified in the Royal Proclamation of 1763 to the crown-Indian alliances during the era of the American Revolution and the War of 1812. This historic pattern found distilled expression particularly in the more conservative branches of Canada'a religious organizations. For instance, the Roman Catholic Church, whose metropolitan power was centred in Quebec, intervened to defend Indian rights on Manitoulin Island and Métis rights in Red River in the 1860s. In the Church of England the Reverend E.F. Wilson pioneered the advocacy of Indian government as one of three orders of Canadian government in the 1890s. Similarly, in the early years of the twentieth century, Arthur O'Meara, a lawyer and Anglican clergyman, gave important advice to the nascent First Nations political organizations of British Columbia on the constitutional status of Indian title in crown law. This seminal work, aimed at extending the constitutional principles of the Royal Proclamation of 1763 across the Rocky Mountains, enhanced what came to be called the Red Tory tradition in Canadian politics.

The conservative bias in this particular stream of enlightened observance of the human rights of Indigenous peoples exposes many of the frailties in the New Right's careless assumptions about the movement's own true positioning vis-à-vis the history of ideas. In the maintenance of their own self-delusions, New Right proponents have often been politically incorrect.

By now it should be clear that I do not see this text as emanating from a relativist rejection of the "Enlightenment Project."[199] Quite the contrary, I believe it celebrates the urges to human freedom and liberation that are at once the Enlightenment's most enduring legacies as well as the markers of its greatest failures and most unrealized potentials. In embracing the heritage of European Enlightenment as one framework for advancing the ideals of cultural pluralism and biodiversity, I naturally favour some Enlightenment narratives over others. These narratives seem to me to be more true in the light of my own powers of human reason, however subjective and idiosyncratic my own media of perception and conceptualization may arguably be.

While the Enlightenment establishes many of the moving frontiers of history and understanding that run through this text, it could not be true to its larger objectives without affording attentive consideration to the creative muses, declarations, and science of many Aboriginal thinkers who were socialized in traditions that drew only secondarily on the European intellectual heritage. Many of the most persistent themes in the changing constellations of Aboriginal thought are informed by an understanding of the genocides and ecocides that have destroyed many groups and individuals.

Even more profound condemnations spring from an awareness of the ways that the protagonists of imperialism attempted to justify their impositions as a positive service to Indigenous peoples, whose alleged inferiorities were proclaimed as the applied findings and manifestations of universal natural law. The vile comparisons emanating from this genre of justification for land theft and genocide tend to persist in the popular imagination even as evidence of the crime is papered over by the treatises of social science. One unfortunate effect is to obscure the continuing force of racism, along with antiquated theories of racial hierarchy. Their unextinguished power has been only partially reduced by the cultural relativism of Boas and those who followed in his professional footsteps.[200]

Rejection of these false pretensions of universality still leaves room to embrace the more general principle that nature is governed by some universal codes that need to be observed and respected to achieve ecological harmony. In their propensity to advocate, if not always to live by, this most fundamental principle of natural law, First Nations spokespeople, knowingly or not, make common cause with some of the Enlightenment's most versatile and characteristic claims. Indeed, there is much implicit recognition of the universal attributes and requirements of all life forms in the contention that the legal, economic, and political institutions of the planet need to be remade in order to afford more latitude for the renewal of cultural pluralism and the maintenance of biodiversity.

Accordingly, I view George Manuel's Aboriginal vision of the Fourth

World as a conception that emanates from outside the European heritage but that is consistent with many aspects of the Enlightenment. I see the Fourth World as a major contributor to the growing case advancing the need for new agencies at the global level to enforce uniform codes recognizing the inherent rights of diverse human communities to express their cultural differences, especially through the medium of pluralistic property relationships. In her denunciation of cultural relativists for not facing many of globalization's harshest environmental and geo-economic degradations, Vandana Shiva's work is also illustrative of the urge to embrace more sophisticated means of determining what is universal in the ecology of human relations and what is the appropriate sphere of indigenous knowledge and local autonomy.

MORAL RELATIVISM AND THE JUSTIFICATION OF MANIFEST DESTINY, EMPIRE, AND CAPITALISM

The related phenomena of language loss and accelerating species extinguishment call attention to the proximity of ecological holocaust on the planet. This prospect should cast a clear light on the existence of some inescapable absolutes that bind humanity in a common plight requiring concerted action through the agency of many different kinds of political and juridical institutions, some already in existence and some yet to be invented.

Ecocide, no less than genocide, constitutes a type of crime whose perpetration must be removed from the obfuscations of the kind of moral relativism that has thrived in justifying the expanding frontiers of the American empire and of global capitalism. The containment of much dark experience, past and present, in the black hole of invisibility, collective amnesia, and official indifference has depended on historiographical traditions clothing some of colonialism's most wanton episodes of ethnic and species murder in the redemptive language of natural law. Very often the alibi of natural law in human affairs has been used to rationalize holy jihads of atomizing privatization. The fundamentalist aim of the neoliberal crusade is to replace multicultural pluralism and biodiversity with an expanding civilization of possessive individualism and commodified monocultures.

In *Guns, Germs, and Steel,* Jared Diamond illustrates an extreme version of the moral relativism that is being elevated so as to downplay the violence involved in the transformation of the Americas and other colonized lands where Indigenous peoples have been overwhelmed and marginalized. He notes that "the original Native American population has been reduced by a debated large percentage: estimates for North America range up to 95 percent. But the total human population of the Americas is now approximately ten times what it was in 1492, because of the arrival of Old World peoples." This observation gives scientific gloss to the classic defence of moral relativism – that the means are insignificant when the outcome is worthy.

Diamond pushes further the moral relativism underlying his Pulitzer Prize–winning text. In an interpretation that simply waves away as predestined the genocide and ethnic cleansing carried out in what he describes as "the most massive demographic shift on any continent except Australia," the author effectively absolves the major protagonists in this transformation. In a chilling display of the dark expediency of an interpretation that privileges geographical determinism over the idea of human beings as responsible and accountable agents of our own actions, Diamond asserts that the marginalization of Indigenous peoples in the Americas "has its ultimate roots in developments between about 11,000 B.C. and A.D. 1." In this fashion, the history of encounter between Natives and newcomers since 1492 is made to seem as the performance of a drama whose plot and outcome were long decided before the commencement of the Columbian conquests.²⁰¹

I see Diamond's much-celebrated resort to geographic determinism as emblematic of the zeal, especially in the United States, to find a way around a major interpretive dilemma in rationalizing the power of the American empire. Where Francis Fukuyama, Allan Bloom, and many others give voice to the wish of a powerful, right-wing constituency to claim the Enlightenment's universalist high ground as the basis of what they see as their own moral absolutism, problems arise about how to rationalize the crimes commited on the frontiers of manifest's destiny's imperial march through history. This dilemma is central to the existence of all empires whose apologists must seek to justify the extension of imperial power as a means of spreading the verities of law, truth, and morality. How can it be explained, however, when the very laws and morality espoused in the justification of empire are violated with impunity in imperialism's expansion and maintenance? Generally the transgressions, large and small, are explained away as necessary in the service of a higher good. Such rationalizations, however, most often serve influence more than truth. This bias implicates apologists of power in forms of moral relativism that often go far beyond the milder, less cynical, and less self-serving forms of relativism associated with Boas and his postmodern, intellectual progeny. What form of relativism could be more extreme than that which seeks to downplay the murder of some kinds of people as less of a crime than the murder of other kinds of people?

By giving the nod of science to an interpretation that would characterize the post-1492 history of the Americas not as an expression of human decisions and actions but as a fulfilment of natural law, Diamond presents a minor variation on Darwinian explanations of imperialism that he professes to hate. Diamond's argument is simply too convenient to the exercise of capitalist power in replacing old preoccupations with "race" with new attachments to "the environment" as the ultimate explanatory factor to justify the dominance of some kinds of human beings over other kinds of human beings.

Some human stories are simply less true than other human stories. Among the truest are those that identify the web of ecological interconnectedness animating the web of life as well as those that support the egalitarian view that all human beings are more alike than they are different. Among the most implausible historical explanations ever attempted are those that would downplay the prevalence of murder and forced relocation of Indian peoples, especially east of the Mississippi, by citing the higher needs of a nation founded in the conviction that all men are created equal. Any effort to describe this expansionary process, or others like it, as an expression of natural law mandated by race, geography, economics, or God represents an exercise of moral relativism of the highest order.

While it is important to identify the universal attributes we share as humans not only with each other but with all other living organisms, the healthy maintenance and procreation of life also require broad latitude for the expression of difference and infinite variation within larger thematic structures and rhythms. This need for diversity is no less true in the political economy of human societies than in the ecology of our plant and animal relatives. As Karl Popper has argued with great insight and erudition, fundamentalist faiths and totalitarian regimes of any stripe are true enemies of the openness on which pluralism thrives.[202]

The conditions of this culture of openness and diversity cannot be maintained on a planet where utopian obsessions with market fundamentalism establish the conditions for a new totalitarianism. Nor can they be maintained in a monocultural milieu where seemingly limitless industrial enclosures and privatizations of the global commons eliminate the basis for substantial pluralism among peoples, even as the secularizing power of money is extended into the deepest genetic recesses from whence spring the sacred rejuvenative forces essential to the renewal of all species and all ecological communities.

CHAPTER TWO

Imagining Civilization
on the Frontiers of Aboriginality

In the world of the mighty only the great and their servants fit.
In the world we want we all fit. The world we want is one where
many worlds fit.
> Fourth Declaration of the Southern Liberation Army,
> Emiliano Zapta, 1996

INDIGENOUS PEOPLES ON THE GLOBAL FRONTIERS
OF ACTIVISM AND IMAGINATION

In the spring of 2000 about a quarter of a million Australians converged on Sydney to create the country's largest demonstration ever. At the symbolic heart of the event was the walk across the Harbour Bridge. There, at the mid-point, the Australian national flag flew alongside the black, red, and yellow Aboriginal flag. As the walkers passed by they reflected on the goal of achieving reconciliation between the country's non-Aboriginal majority and the country's half-million Indigenous peoples. Overhead, a sky writer printed "SORRY" from the white vapour flowing from behind his small plane.[1]

The scope of the demonstration illustrated how the issues at its core had captured the attention and energies of a significant proportion of Australia's population. What had begun in 1991 with the establishment by the Australian parliament of the Council of Aboriginal Reconciliation had moved well beyond the confines of government and its attending academic and technocratic agencies. Instead, the challenge of reconciliation with Australia's First Nations has become a matter that has stimulated a diverse range of groups and individuals who have effectively begun to reinvent the Australian nation by grappling with its oldest, most profound, and most notoriously neglected human-rights issue.

By addressing the current legacies of the crimes against humanity that were integral to the country's historical genesis, many fresh perspectives on the future presented themselves to Australia's national imagination. One of the key animators and chroniclers of this process has been Henry Reynolds, a historian whose treatises on the history of Aboriginal policy proved instrumental in persuading the High Court to recognize the existence of Aboriginal title in Australia's *Mabo* ruling of 1992.[2] In recounting

his own experience in some of the hundreds of community meetings that
led to the mass passage across the Sydney Harbour Bridge, Reynolds wrote:

Almost everywhere I have been, no matter how large or small the community,
whether the meeting was at lunchtime or at night, on almost every occasion I was
impressed by the size of the audience. But there was something else about the audiences and that was their deep concern, their intensity, their obvious concentration
on the subject, their clear sense that this was an important thing they were involved
in. The significant thing is that the reconciliation process has spread right across
Australia. It is no longer just a movement of educated middle-class people. It is no
longer just an urban movement. There are reconciliation groups all across the
country.

These groups are doing many interesting things. They are meeting together with
local Indigenous people. The degree of Indigenous participation varies widely, but
in some places it is very substantial. In communities right across Australia, there are
people meeting, thinking, researching, talking and coming up quite often with
extremely interesting and creative proposals to try and reach reconciliation there
in their own communities.[3]

The intensity of activism and debate on the place of the First Nations was
an essential element of a many-faceted quest to fashion a decolonized
identity for Australia that transcended the mean narrowness of its white
supremist origins. This contemporary quest for a national identity has
included intense contestation over the role of the monarchy in a revised
constitution. The movement to transform the Australian Constitution and
the movement aimed at reconciliation with Indigenous peoples were clearly approaching the same kind of convergence that made Aboriginal and
treaty rights a major factor in the patriation of the Canadian Constitution
in 1982.

The timing of the Harbour Bridge demonstration came on the eve of
the Sydney Olympics and on the cusp of the country's centennial celebra-
tions of the creation of the Australian federation in 1901. Clearly the
mood was propitious for some kind of sweeping declaration of national
purpose, looking both forward and backward at the country's defining and
most fundamental relationships. The reconciliation movement presented
an ideal opening to announce that Australia was entering the third millennium with the confidence to face even the darkest chapters of its own
history as a necessary condition of genuine maturation and renewal. "If
achieved," announced Senator Aden Ridgeway, a Gumbayyngirr Aboriginal from New South Wales, "reconciliation can become a crucial factor in
giving the gift of national social cohesion."[4] Australia's quest for a more
pluralistic form of self-determination through the elaboration of a more
edifying range of relations with the country's First Nations gives recent
expression to a very old process in the history of Western civilization.[5]
Again and again, Indigenous peoples have figured prominently in the

labours and imaginative endeavours of those whose goal has been to expand the frontiers of old civilizations or to invent new ones in the New World.

A key to understanding Australia's quest to grow out of the most racist aspects of its colonial heritage involves the legal and philosophical rejection of the doctrine of *terra nullius* as the basis of the country's system of apportioning land tenure and jurisdiction. Australia was not empty at the time of its incorporation into the British Empire, and the land was the home of an extremely diverse range of peoples. The pluralism of these peoples was reflected in the existence of approximately 600 dialects spread out over 270 languages at the time when European expansion drew Australia into the process of globalization at the end of the eighteenth century. The vast majority of Australia's Indigenous languages have gone silent in the course of colonization. Among those twenty or so languages that remain vital are Pitjantjatjari, Yolngu, Bundjalung, and Kaurna, all of which have been incorporated into the country's curricula of higher education.[6]

A strike in 1966 by Aboriginal workers in Australia's Northern Territory proved to be pivotal in casting the first rays of national doubt on the doctrine of *terra nullius*. That strike was led by the Gurindji sage Vincent Lingiari. With Lingiari as their spokesman, Gurindji workers in the expansive ranching operations owned by Lord Vestey withdrew their labour. While the dispute with the employer began over issues of pay and work conditions, Lingiari asserted the existence of an unceded Aboriginal title to the ancestral lands of the Gurindji people. This stand resonated with many groups and individuals throughout Australia. It does so still. The activism led to a referendum that theoretically opened the door of Australian citizenship for the first time to the country's Indigenous peoples.[7]

The idea of the existence of an Aboriginal title in the lands of Australia has slowly percolated into political and juridical thinking about the country's constitutional character.[8] In 1988, the year of Australia's Bicentenary, the Labor government of Prime Minister Bob Hawke broke what has sometimes been referred to as "the great Australian silence." He raised and quickly abandoned the idea of a new treaty with Indigenous peoples. This initiative followed a brief but intense effort on the part of the Labor Party to incorporate what it called "Aboriginal self-determination" into Australia's governmental system. Between 1983 and 1985 the National Aboriginal Conference, a body of elected Aboriginal representatives, was elevated to a more instrumental role in directing the process of policy formation in the Ministry of Aboriginal Affairs.[9]

The High Court of Australia dramatically increased the pressure for some kind of fundamental reckoning with the country's Indigenous peoples with two rulings in 1992 and 1996. Both unequivocally overturned the old doctrine of *terra nullius*. The *Mabo* decision and the more recent *Wik* decision rejected the principle that Australia was an empty land when Captain Cook first arrived. The *Mabo* ruling represented one of the most cathartic and powerful statements to emerge from the 500th anniversary of 1492. Much as in the Nisga'a ruling of Canada's Supreme Court in 1973, Australia's top judges essentially pointed the political wing of government at the need to initiate negotiations with Indigenous peoples on the issue of land title. In the *Mabo* ruling, this appeal was made in language that went beyond technicalities to identify the extent of the moral cancer that had gripped the soul of Australia from the time of its founding.

The High Court made it clear that it was dealing with nothing less than "the assessment of the legitimacy of the propositions that the continent was unoccupied for legal purposes and that the unqualified legal and beneficial ownership of all the lands of the continent were vested in the Crown." The magnitude of what was at stake justified them, the judges argued, in the use of "unrestrained language." The ruling described "the conflagration of oppression and conflict" that "spread across the continent to dispossess, degrade and devastate the Aboriginal peoples and leave a national legacy of unutterable shame." The exploitation of the doctrine of *terra nullius* to justify the unilateral dispossession of Indigenous peoples constituted "the darkest aspect of the history of this nation." And, the court judges added, "the nation as a whole must remain diminished unless and until there is an acknowledgement of and retreat from, those past injustices."[10]

The evocative court ruling made Aboriginal rights by far the most polarizing issue in the political culture of Australia. The decision of the High Court was initially embraced by the Labor government of Australian prime minister Paul Keating. In moving towards the enactment in 1993 of the Native Title Act to bring Australian legislation into more comfortable conformity with the High Court's jurisprudence, Keating characterized the *Mabo* ruling as a "practical building block of change." He added, "by doing away with the bizarre conceit that this continent had no owners prior to the settlement of Europeans, *Mabo* establishes a fundamental truth and lays the basis for justice."[11]

Those supporting some sort of fundamental reconciliation with Australia's First Nations organized themselves in groups such as Women for Wik or Wik Ed. By 1998 observers were noting that the debate in and around the work of the Council of Aboriginal Reconciliation had generated "the largest people's movement since the Vietnam War."[12] The mobilization of popular will in defence of Aboriginal rights drew particularly from the shocking details outlined in a report on *Stolen Generation Aborigines* released in 1997 by the Australian Human Rights and Equal Opportunity Commission. That report chronicled how, until the 1970s, many Aboriginal children were seized from their families and subjected to all kinds of abuse in the name of the country's assimilationist policies. Many young Aborigines were fostered out and used essentially as slave labour or even as sex slaves by their overseers.[13] Australia's governor-general, Sir William Deane, issued a formal apology to the country's Indigenous peoples for the wrongdoing exposed in *Stolen Generation*[14] – an apology backed by hundreds of thousands of Australian citizens' signatures in what were dubbed the "Sorry Books."

The movement to reshape Australia's identity through the embrace, rather than the negation, of Aboriginal rights drew vitality from many sources. First among these was the Koori Renaissance, led by a number of gifted Aboriginal artists, activists, and educators including Kevin Gilbert, Noel Pearson, Faith Bandler, Geraldine Briggs, Rob Riley, and Galarrway Yunupingu.[15] Their efforts were supported and complemented by a host of non-Aboriginal academics and journalists who added to the literary depth and scope of the reconciliation movement. For instance, John Pilger, an Australian filmmaker and investigative journalist based in London, did much to widen appreciation of the international implications of the struggle to realize the rights and titles of Aboriginal peoples in Australia.[16]

The proponents of reconciliation in Australia advanced contemporary variations on a number of themes that have long formed a significant, if subordinate, text in the saga of European colonization. This subtext was historically advanced by organizations such as the British-based Aborigines' Protection Society. The more recent interventions in Australia helped to energize the response of some whose position on Aboriginal rights lay squarely within the ongoing continuum of imperial expansion as it has dominated global history since at least 1492. The reactionary power of these unbroken imperial patterns was realized in the election in 1996 of the government of Prime Minister John Howard. That government represented the fullest application to Australia of the neo-liberal policies of Margaret Thatcher and Ronald Reagan.

One of the first acts of the new Howard regime was to cut $400 million from the Aboriginal Affairs budget. Condemning what he referred to as "the guilt industry," Howard dramatized the government's policy shift away from the Keating legacy by refusing to add his own initials to the hundreds of thousands of signatures collected in the Sorry Books.[17]

Howard's Aboriginal policies drew on the right-wing populism of Pauline Hanson and her One Nation Party as well as on the writings of historian Geoffrey Blainey. Hanson came to political prominence in the Australian state of Queensland by co-opting the language of individual equality to oppose what her campaign literature referred to as "immigrationism, multiculturalism, Asianisation and Aboriginalism (romantic primitivism)." All these trends, Hanson alleged, "ultimately divided and weakened the unified cohesion of the Australian nation.[18] Social scientist Geoffrey Blainey reinforced this perspective by referring derisively to the writings of Henry Reynolds and John Pilger, for instance, as "black armband history."[19]

Incorporating the provocative language of Hanson and Blainey in justifying government policy, the Howard government bent before the pressure exerted by several powerful lobbies, but especially that of the Australian mining industry. In 1998 the Howard government enacted a series of amendments to the Native Title Act of 1993. These amendments all had the effect of undermining the bargaining position of Aboriginal groups and strengthening the hand of all parties who derived many of their entitlements to the minerals, waters, and pastoral lands of Australia from the state governments. These controversial modifications of the country's fundamental laws attracted severe condemnations from a number of sources, including Australia's Law Reform Commission and the United Nations Committee on the Elimination of Racial Discrimination. These bodies were among the most prominent proponents of the position that the Howard government's amendments to the Native Title Act violated Australia's Racial Discrimination Act. The passing of the Racial Discrimination Act in 1975 signalled Australia's adhesion to the International Convention on the Elimination of All Forms of Racial Discrimination.

The rising influence in Australia of right-wing fringe groups such as Hanson's One Nation Party foreshadowed the growth of xenophobic nationalism throughout many countries in the West. In France, for instance, this phenomenon found expression in the ascent to political prominence of Jean-Marie Le Pen. In Canada this tendency was embodied in the mid–1990s in the emergence of the Reform Party from the resources-rich western provinces. The Reform Party was subsequently renamed the Alliance Party. Like their fellow right-wing populists in Australia, members of Canada's Reform Party advocated the invocation of parliamentary supremacy to negate judicial recognition of Aboriginal title.[20] In the spring of 2002 the Alliance party worked closely with the government of Canada's westernmost province to implement a modified application of the scheme to extinguish Aboriginal rights by mobilizing the electoral force of a non-Aboriginal majority. Citing the imperatives of "direct democracy," Canada's right-wing politicians collaborated in organizing a provincial referendum whose object was to create a legal and political mandate intended to narrow the jurisdictional scope of treaty negotiations with the Indigenous peoples in British Columbia.[21]

Most of the proponents of the referendum in British Columbia hoped to reverse the outcome of the Supreme Court of Canada's *Delgamuukw* ruling in 1997. That decision gave greater clarity to the Supreme Court's earlier ruling on the Nisga'a case in 1973, one that seminally identified the existence of an unextinguished Indian title in most of British Columbia. The *Mabo* and the *Delgamuukw* rulings can be conceptualized as two manifestations of the same inconsistencies in the application of crown law to the colonization of Indigenous peoples' lands in many regions of the British Commonwealth.

As I see it, the mass march in Sydney during the spring of 2000 represented one of many significant rituals in the worldwide movement emphasizing the need for major initiatives, both domestically and internationally, to reverse the destructive course of the ongoing Columbia conquests through various forms of reconciliation with Indigenous peoples. Another major ceremony in this same process took place in Mexico City a year later, as the leaders of the Zapatista Liberation Army left their strongholds in the Mayan highlands of Chiapas.

The Zapatistas had first gained international prominence when these Indian freedom fighters timed their initial brief assertion of armed control over several centres in Chiapas to coincide with the inauguration in 1994 of the North American Free Trade Agreement. With this founding act, one soon reinforced by a pioneering mobilization of the communications potential of the Internet and of home computers, the Zapatistas initiated an unorthodox campaign for political change that was simultaneously locally rooted and globally oriented.

In moving towards the centre of Mexico's political process in the spring of 2001, the Zapatistas renewed and elaborated in a different context many of the same themes of social justice publicized a year earlier by the quarter-million marchers on Sydney Harbour Bridge. The leaders of this procession sought to broaden the base of *Zapatismo* in Mexico and globally through a dramatic movement over a 3,500-kilometre route, culminating in a mass gathering at the Zócalo Plaza. This central ceremonial place can be envisaged as the site where the imperial regime of New Spain and the new Mexico meet the old capital of Mesoamerica – namely the Aztec metropolis of Tenochitlan which lies beneath modern-day Mexico City. The Zapatistas characterized their triumphant arrival in Zócalo Plaza as the first entry of a rebel group onto this sacred site since Pancho Villa and Emiliano Zapata arrived in 1914 to participate in the revolutionary transformation of a Mexico traumatized by US military intervention at Veracruz earlier that year.

In claiming to represent the true heritage of Emiliano Zapata and the Mexican Revolution, the Zapatistas aroused a huge fascination over a surprisingly wide spectrum of world public opinion. As illustrated by the geographic distribution of over 45,000 Zapatista-related web sites, Zapatista cells and support groups proliferated, especially in the urban centres of Europe and North America. The international celebrity of some of those who greeted the Zapatista leadership in their dramatic entry in Zócalo Plaza attests to the exuberant hopes attached to a movement that first caught root among the Mayan peasantry of southern Mexico. Among those in attendance were American film icons Robert Redford and Oliver Stone. Also present were Spain's most prominent writer, Manuel Vasquez Montalbán, and Portugal's Nobel Prize–winning author, José Saramago.[22] "I have to be in Mexico City on March 11," declared Canada's Naomi Klein, author of a best-selling text condemning neo-liberal globalization.²³ "It's like Martin Luther King Jr.'s March on Washington."²⁴

How did the Zapatistas transform their stand from an armed resistance in an obscure corner of Mexico into a genuinely transnational intellectual movement aimed at global transformation? Certainly timing was a key factor. Their uprising came at a moment when the globalization of a particularly unrestrained form of corporate capitalism seemed so invincible that Fukuyama and others were triumphantly proclaiming a virtual end to history. The Zapatistas provided intellectual asylum and a big, many-coloured ideological tent for a diverse array of thinkers and activists desperate to explore viable alternatives to an universal regime of unfettered corporate rule. This refuge for neo-liberalism's dissenters was placed squarely in the context of the world's oldest, most pervasive, and most multicultural resistance movement. The basis of this resistance is the ongoing struggle against the continuing conquest of Aboriginal lands and Indigenous peoples that began in 1492 when Europe first christened the Americas as a New World and as its primary frontier of colonial expansion.

In seeking to justify his own participation in the rise of Zapatismo in North America, the prominent Californian activist and politician Tom Hayden explained that the movement "suggested we could reclaim the indigenous roots that lie mangled beneath the architecture of our modern selves." He added, "We of the North were invited, challenged, to do our part in resisting a Conquest 500 years old."²⁵

The attraction of the Zapatistas was closely connected to the mystique generated by the movement's main spokesperson, a masked figure identified to the world simply as Subcommandante Marcos. In the sketchy outlines of his publicized biography, the story is told of how he first came to the jungles and mountains of Chiapas to enlist the Indians in Marxist class struggle. Instead of indoctrinating the Mayans, it was Marcos who is said to have been assimilated into the decentralized democracy of Indian approaches to consensus building. The results of this transformation showed up following the Zapatista's initial successes in asserting their presence in Chiapas. Rather than making moves to insert their own representatives directly into Mexico's governing system, the Zapatistas, through Subcommandante Marcos's rhetorical interventions, embarked on a cultural campaign aimed at remaking the very framework of power politics. In this way the Zapatistas were able to combine their pro-Indian stance with an agenda for change that transcended the limitations of ethnic fundamentalism and identity politics. In contributing to this feat, Marcos cunningly crafted a media image directed at knitting together a broad coalition of those shut out of neo-liberalism's narrow enclave of concentrated privilege. In elaborating this theme, the masked enigma is reported to have said:

Marcos is gay in San Francisco, black in South Africa, an Asian in Europe, a Chicano in San Ysidro, an anarchist in Spain, a Palestinian in Israel, a Mayan Indian in the streets of San Cristóbal, a Jew in Germany, a Gypsy in Poland, a Mohawk in Quebec, a pacifist in Bosnia, a single woman on the Metro at 10:00 PM, a peasant without land, a gang member in the slums, an unemployed worker, an unhappy student, and, of course, a Zapatista in the mountains.[26]

The Zapatistas arrived in Zócalo Plaza just months after a new Mexican president, Vicente Fox, had taken office. With the election of Fox, the notoriously corrupt hold of the Party of the Institutionalized Revolution, which had monopolized the national government of Mexico for most of the twentieth century, was finally broken. In his presidential campaign, Fox had vowed that he would be able to arrive at a peace settlement with the Zapatistas based on some accommodation of their assertions and claims concerning Aboriginal rights. When they entered Zócalo Plaza, Fox referred to their masked leader, saying, "Welcome Subcommandante Marcos, welcome to the Zapatistas, welcome to the political arena, the arena of the discussion of ideas." As a former president of the local branchplant of Coca-Cola, the company whose global expansion served over the course of the twentieth century as an icon for the growth of the American empire as well as the export of the American way of life, President Fox embodied many of the attributes of neo-liberal globalization that had given the Zapatistas a worldwide platform to present their alternatives. Marcos emphasized the ideological distance between the two main visions of the future that were struggling for the hearts and souls of humanity in the opening years of the twenty-first century. As he said of his group's governing philosophy, compared with that of Fox: "We are part of the world moving toward recognizing differences, and he [Fox] is working toward hegemony and homogenizing, not just the country, but the world."[27]

The Zapatistas sought entrenchment of major reforms in the laws, policies, and institutions of Mexico to facilitate more effective forms of Aboriginal self-governance for the Indians of Mexico. Building on significant reforms achieved by Mayan activists in Guatemala,[28] the Zapatistas made the renewal of Indian languages through pedagogical reform and ambitious schemes of Aboriginal broadcasting a priority. In an interview with Ignacio Ramonet of *Le Monde*, Marcos described the Zapatistas vision of Aboriginal rights:

Our principal object is that the Mexican Congress will recognize Indigenous peoples as collective subjects of law. The Constitution of Mexico doesn't now recognize Indianness. We want the state to admit that Mexico is composed of different peoples; that Indigenous people possess their own political, social and economic organizations. And that they retain a strong relationship with the land and with their community, their roots and their history ... We don't want to proclaim the birth of the Maya nation, or split up the country into a multiplicity of small Aboriginal countries. We want rather that the laws recognize an important part of Mexican society, which possesses its own form of organization and which demands that its Aboriginal characteristics be recognized.

Marcos moved easily between this agenda for Mexico and a larger critique of neo-liberal models of globalization. "To some degree," he maintained, "economic globalization signifies the globalization of the way of life in the United States." This approach to human organization, he asserted, is imposed on every facet of life. Even the proposal of an alternative is made to seem "utopian, unrealistic," and a denial of the "inevitable" course of history. Neo-liberal forms of globalization, he added, come to reign "not only in the functioning of government, but also in the media, in the school and in the family." They lead in particular to the elimination of those societies based not on mobility but on complex attachments to the local ecology of particular places. "And that concerns all the Indigenous peoples of Latin America," Marcos said. "Globalization demands their elimination."[29]

One of the explanations for the attractiveness of *Zapatismo* in Mexico lay in its renewal and elaboration of themes already well developed in nationalist discourse. The movement renewed ideals and concepts raised particularly in the 1920s by Manuel Gamio, José Vasconcelos, and others. Through *indigenismo* they sought to direct the course of the Mexican revolution towards the official embrace of Mexico's distinct Indian and mestizo personality in a country where a large majority of the country's citizens have some Indian ancestry.[30]

The Zapatista entry into Zócalo Plaza took place on the eve of the clash of hemispheric agendas that converged dramatically in Quebec City in April 2001. The meeting was planned to help initiate a Free Trade Area of the Americas (FTAA), which some saw as a vehicle for the entrenchment of the pan-American empire centred in the United States. In the early years of the twenty-first century, no less than in the 1920s, increased emphasis on Mexico's Indian character continued to represent an obvious strategy of resistance against the incursions, enticements, and absorptions of the "gringo" empire of the United States.

This pan-American empire had grown from the Old World empires of Spain, France, Holland, Russia, Portugal, and, in particular, Great Britain. The United States was the primary inheritor of the imperial missions of these powers to remake the Americas in the image of Europe and Western Civilization. The emergence of the American republic from the British Empire constituted the formation of the first and the most influential of the Creole nationalisms that had formed in the American colonies to replace European empires. The Columbian conquests found expression in these Creole nationalisms whose shared aim was to empower the transplanted European populations even as the Indian populations were, in

varying degrees, shunned, persecuted, and pushed aside. They were seen
as impediments to the progress of those new nation-states whose first prototype was the United States.

The secret negotiations aimed at establishing a Free Trade Area of the
Americas seemingly continued a well-established pattern of New World
imperialism whose pan-American dimensions were first revealed in 1823
when the United States in its Monroe Doctrine laid claim to the entire
Western Hemisphere as its exclusive domain of remote-control hegemony.
While the United States embodied a potent blend of Creole decolonization and New World imperialism, the transplanted majority populations of
Canada, Australia, and New Zealand gradually negotiated their transition
to self-government and qualified independence within the constitutional
framework of continuing crown sovereignty.

Australia has been one of the most tardy of the Commonwealth countries to address the deep legal and moral questions derived from the
unextinguished existence of Aboriginal rights and titles in the ancestral
lands of Indigenous peoples. New Zealand, however, evolved in a very different way.[31] For the Maori, the Indigenous peoples of that country, New
Zealand has been Aotearoa since time immemmorial. In 1840 the British
government sought to gain the sanction from the Maori for the transformation of New Zealand into a colony whose main role in the empire was
to receive and host European settlers. These settlers would acquire the
rights of local self-government in a jurisdiction that also afforded the
rights and responsibilities of New Zealand citizenship to the Maori. The
Treaty of Waitangi can be perceived as the founding charter on which the
legal and moral legitimacy of New Zealand is ultimately grounded. This
interpretation has broad implications. Like the ideas embodied in the
Royal Proclamation of 1763, the role of the Waitangi Treaty in New
Zealand's legal make-up raises the idea that Indigenous peoples throughout the planet have retained the constitutional power to give or withhold
sanction to the empires and nation-states that have developed and
evolved on their ancestral lands. A key feature of the Waitangi Treaty,
which was viewed as being very enlightened in the era of its negotiation,
was the extension to adult Maori males of New Zealand citizenship and,
with it, the franchise in national elections. In later years this legal innovation was expressed by the creation of several seats in the New Zealand parliament specifically to represent Maori electors.[32]

In 1975 the Treaty of Waitangi Act established the Waitangi Treaty Tribunal as an intercultural institution for hearing and ruling on allegations
that the terms of the original agreement between the crown and the
Maori have not been fulfilled. Since 1975 the mandate and membership
of the tribunal have been gradually expanded towards the evolution of a
highly innovative diplomatic protocol for the unfolding negotiation of
crown-Maori relations.[33] This process has made the Waitangi Treaty the
most important founding agreement with an Aboriginal group in the

construction, organization, and evolution of a modern-day nation-state. In 1987 Mr Justice Richardson ruled on the treaty's centrality in the legal and political culture of New Zealand. He said: "The Treaty must be viewed as a solemn compact between two identifiable parties, the Crown and the Maori, through which the colonization of New Zealand was to become possible. For its part the Crown sought legitimacy from indigenous people for its acquisition of sovereignty and in return it gave certain guarantees."[34]

The legal and political muscle the Maori retain in their own governments and in the government of New Zealand stems from their firm insistence on the constitutional pre-eminence of the Treaty of Waitangi. From this treaty flow the founding recognitions that have afforded Maori voters direct representation in the New Zealand parliament. From this political base, some Maori activists have questioned the New Zealand government's power to open the country's natural resources to yet further exploitation by foreign investors as long as these same resources remain the subject of unresolved negotiations with Indigenous peoples.

This Maori response came in reaction to those dramatic neo-liberal transformations in New Zealand that prompted some critics to compare the country's right-wing governors to the Pinochet regime: to them, New Zealand became "Chile without the gun." Beginning in the early 1980s, this bloodless coup saw the rapid slashing of social programs, quick government downsizing, and the elimination of almost all restrictions on foreign investment. As a result, between 1988 and 1993, New Zealand led the world in the sale of government-owned assets. These changes had dramatic implications for the Maori, who were deeply integrated into New Zealand's welfare state. The new investment regime affected the course of many disputes over title to extensive parts of the country's lands and fisheries. It biased the economy against broad interpretations of the Treaty of Waitangi. The active enticement of foreign investment into the disputed resources, therefore, seemed to prejudice the possibility of mutually satisfactory resolutions.

Maori participation in the mainstream of New Zealand's political culture resulted in some modest effort on the part of the government to consult with Native organizations in deliberations concerning the country's economic relations with the outside world. In 1997, for instance, the Ministry of Maori Development announced a process of talks to consider the significance for Maori people of New Zealand's participation in the controversial Mutilateral Agreement on Investment (MAI). Maori resistance to the proposed global treaty was part of a larger wave of opposition that contributed to the temporary retreat of MAI's proponents.[35]

While some Maori activists have been prominent in the identification of neo-liberalism's dark side, they have tended to look with suspicion at certain varieties of *Pakeha,* or non-Indigenous, opposition to the new inroads and agencies of global corporatism. "It is not enough," Aziz

Choudry observed, "to seek to nostalgically return to the golden age of the strong nation state." Moreover, said he, "a true peoples' sovereignty cannot be based on the denial of the sovereign rights of others." At the basis of the new coalition needed to promote viable alternatives to the kind of global corporate rule advanced through agencies like the World Trade Organization or the Asian-Pacific Economic Co-operation (APEC), Aziz envisaged a regime that would take seriously "the work of women, the exploitation of workers, the lack of government accountability, and the enormous contributions made by Indigenous peoples and peoples of the South."[36]

The rise of Fourth World politics in Australia, New Zealand, Mexico, Canada, and many other parts of the Americas has been paralleled by the prominence of Indigenous peoples elsewhere as significant centres of resistance against the integration of nation-states and global corporations in the privatized commodification of natural resources. This importance has grown as understanding has developed that the governments of many nation-states have become so subordinate to the power of global capital that the key levers of decision making are less and less accessible to the democratic controls of ordinary men and women. As the democratic flexibility of national governments became progressively crippled through the handing off of powers to the unaccountable private sector – and especially to the transnational private sector that operates increasingly through the instruments of supranational sovereignty such as the World Trade Organization[37] – Indigenous peoples have emerged as an older form of polity and as alternative centres of legal jurisdiction with long histories of resistance to assimilation into colonial structures not of their own making.

Hence, when the phenomenon of globalization is understood as a continuation of the major forces in history unleashed in 1492, the societies of Indigenous peoples emerge by virtue of the longevity of their struggles as key centres of activism in the arts and sciences of resistance. The continuity of their resistance represents a mirror image to the continuity of the forces of expansion whose instruments have been European empires, the successor states of European empires, and those corporate conglomerates of capital and technology that have moved beyond the power and control of single national governments. From the Massachusetts Company to the East India Company to the Hudson's Bay Company, from the Ohio, Indiana, and other land speculation companies to the railway companies, from the ranching enterprise of Lord Vestey, to the commercial activities of Hydro-Québec, Shell Oil, Weyerhauser, Carghill, Monsanto, and Diashowa-Marubeni International, the expanding frontiers of corporate culture have often pushed at the imploding territorial and jurisdictional frontiers of Indigenous peoples.

The rising transnational influence of Zapatismo at the dawning of the twenty-first century has been especially influential in clarifying the continuities in a five-centuries-old cycle of colonialism whose present incarnation is most succinctly described as neo-liberal globalization. With the growth of this understanding has come widening appreciation that the pre-Columbian sources of aboriginality make the laws and institutions of Indigenous peoples the last line of defence against various forms of extinguishment, disempowerment, and dispossession which began with European imperialism and continued under the authority of new law givers whose primary fealty is to corporations rather than countries. These law givers often used the rhetoric of free trade even as the hidden agenda has been to bind both peoples and national governments to the higher authority of huge regional and global commercial regimes whose overwhelming tendency is to monopolize and centralize power in tighter and tighter circles of concentrated wealth.

When the issues are framed in this way, the struggle of Indigenous peoples to exercise self-determination and to defend their Aboriginal lands and resources takes on many larger meanings at the symbolic frontiers of a more inclusive, transcultural democratic movement. Activists in this movement may march under many banners, but they are inclined to find common cause in a shared commitment to defend the ecology of diversity among human beings and among our plant and animal relatives. This defence of biodiversity and cultural pluralism leads inevitably to various expressions of opposition to the inroads of monoculturalism through the standardization of property law and the unlimited commodification of nature.[38]

The opposition of Ogoni activists to the environmental desecration of their ancestral land in the Niger Delta region of West Africa constituted one of the clearest examples of an Aboriginal group on the cutting edge of protest against the more violent aggressions of global corporatism. Their resistance movement attracted international attention to the corporate tactics of the Shell Oil Company, whose operations in Nigeria depended on their close collaboration with that country's military dictatorship under General Sani Abacha. In 1995 this oil-rich regime executed author Ken Saro-Wiwa and eight other Ogoni activists in an effort to silence Ogoni criticism of Shell's exploitation and desecration of Ogoni lands.[39] Although the Nigerian government subsequently declared its intention to move away from the extremes of military dictatorship, these reforms had minimal effect on the plight of the Ogoni, whose ancestral lands were still exploited primarily for the benefit of foreign oil producers. Most of the pipelines, for instance, continued to be unburied, and heath problems abounded from the open flaring of toxic chemical soups. Similarly, the Ogoni lands were poisoned by oil spills, involving over 47,000 barrels from the operations of Shell alone over a six-month period in 1997.[40]

The Ogoni resistance movement inspired scores of Fouth World struggles on every continent, where various kinds of coalitions have protested and lobbied in a variety of ways to prevent Indigenous peoples from being further uprooted and rendered even more marginal and powerless in their Aboriginal lands. More often than not a key dimension of the continuing struggle included new tensions created by growing class differences within many Aboriginal communities. This tension unfolded against a background where many of the old colonial policies of forced cultural assimilation – as implemented, for instance, by the work of Christian boarding schools – had been formally abandoned.[41] The new colonialism became manifest primarily in the pressures to assimilate Indigenous peoples into the economies, legal systems, and corporate structures that grew out of the old colonialism.

While the governments of many nation-states endeavoured to treat issues arising from their relations with Indigenous peoples as topics of domestic politics to be constrained as much as possible within the boundaries of domestic law, the international and global character of the questions involved came increasingly to the surface.[42] Local activism pushing for the recognition and implementation of Aboriginal and treaty rights was mirrored in various international forums, including the United Nations, the International Labour Organization, the European Parliament, and the World Bank. Within the United Nations since the early 1980s, a Working Group on Indigenous Populations has hosted an important annual forum in Geneva to bring forward new models of self-determination that might modify the monopolization of sovereign authority by nation-states and their corporate clients and patrons. The formal aim of this working group is to bring about UN ratification of an instrument establishing international standards for the protection of the rights and titles of Indigenous peoples.[43] In 2002 this working group was upgraded from a subcommittee of the UN Human Rights Commission to become a more self-contained agency, the Permanent Forum on Indigenous Issues.

George Manuel, an erudite and energetic Shuswap leader from British Columbia, did much of the essential groundwork in the 1970s to establish the intellectual and organizational framework for the globalization of Indigenous peoples' issues.[44] A contemporary of Vincent Lingiari, Manuel was part of that generation of First Nations leaders who threw off the verdict of Social Darwinism that had defined Indigenous peoples' societies as primitive, archaic, and dying forces without relevance to the future genesis of the world's economic, political, and cultural organization. As the primary founder of the World Council of Indigenous Peoples, Manuel had a clear vision on the threat posed by the unfettered dominion of global corporatism. In the years before his death in 1989, he foresaw the genesis of a great debate on globalization that was taking shape on the horizons of humanity's imagination. Manuel conceived of plans for fundamental reforms, beginning with his own peoples but extending beyond politics and economics towards the more all-encompassing field of global ecology.

For these reasons, Manuel is treated in this volume as an emblematic figure with roots in the land of the bowl with one spoon. He stands in the tradition of Tupac Amaru and Tecumseh, as a bridge builder between peoples. His endeavours to advance the ideals of what he called the Fourth World amounted to a fundamental reckoning with basic definitions of progress. In bringing his perspectives from the frontiers of aboriginality to the task of imagining what constitutes a truly civilized society, Manuel stood prominently within an old tradition of reflection. This tradition of thought has developed especially in that transition zone of ideas, law, geography, and politics where Indigenous peoples encountered, first, European imperialism and, then, the accelerated, New World form of empire building most dramatically illustrated by the westward expansion of theUnited States. The intellectual intensity of the thought to emerge from this frontier region of cross-cultural conflict and intercultural collaboration represents an ideological equivalent to the biodiversity that tends to flourish in zones of transition between significantly different ecological regions.

As a nation-state that came into colonial existence first as a fur-trade preserve of Indigenous peoples and then as a commercial hinterland of the American empire centred in the United States, Canada offers many examples of how those on both sides of the frontiers of aboriginality, including George Manuel, used their vantage points to develop all sorts of visions of the way civilization should be imagined and organized.45

ABORIGINAL AND TREATY RIGHTS
IN THE MAKING OF NORTH AMERICAN HISTORY

In *Rec-onciliation,* an anthology of readings published in 2000 in Australia, Canadian social scientist Peter Jull drew on his extensive experience working on land title and constitutional issues with various Aboriginal groups in Canada, but especially the Inuit. He argued that negotiations over Aboriginal titles and rights in the northern half of North America presented some examples that Australians might learn from in their own quest to constitute a more just regime of relations between non-Aboriginals and First Nations. In comments that presented the Canadian experience perhaps too favourably, Jull wrote that, "For over a generation and a half, indigenous and non-indigenous Canadians have negotiated or re-negotiated the fundamental assumptions of national political culture. It was bracing and produced a larger, richer, more complex, more interesting, and more satisfying country. Narrow late Victorianism and British Empire triumphalism were a straightjacket. Canada became a new country."46

Stephen Leacock, the McGill University professor who is best remembered as a humorist and as a pioneering "Red Tory," 47 left a memorable illustration of the stifling attributes of British Empire triumphalism. It, along with ideas of manifest destiny centred in the United States, came to characterize much of the verbiage on race and power in the English-speaking world during the early twentieth century.[48] Leacock's humanitarian approaches to most social policies did not extend to an enlightened conception of Indigenous peoples in shaping Canada's past, present, or future. In his introduction to the memoires of baron de Lahontan, one of New France's more prolific writers who produced abundant commentaries on Canada's Aboriginal inhabitants, Leacock wrote:

In this boundless wilderness, which surrounded the infant settlement of French Canada, there was little if any trace of the hand of man. The Indian had no control over it. He wielded a tomahawk that would crack a skull, but could not fell a tree. Nor had he the energy or the industry to initiate, even if he had the means, the economic struggle that ultimately created the North America we know. From the incoming whites he eagerly demanded brandy and gunpowder; but a plough, never. Lazy and arrogant, his life was spent in the pleasures of the chase, the cruelties of his cannibal warfare, the gluttony of his feasts, and the stoical endurance of his winter starvation. These miserable creatures roamed over, but did not occupy, the beautiful forest land and the prairies of North America. Their numbers were, as we have seen, insignificant; their claim to ownership scarcely even more than a general and comprehensive claim to live and nowhere reinforced by the visible results of accumulated toil and efforts of preceding generations.[49]

The ideological attack on Indian Country of Canada was sometimes explicit, but more often it was simply ignored in most representations in prose, poetry, politics, and painting. Similarly, whole complexes of contemporary Aboriginal social and cultural expression were often treated as invisible, nonexistent, or irrelevant, and therefore not a factor in planning, shaping, and manipulating the basis of future history. This way of extinguishing aboriginality from the imaginative constructs of the newcomers and their descendants can be seen in the work of the Group of Seven. In the 1920s, members of this group of painters began to achieve recognition for their bold, engaging renditions of the primal landscapes located in and around the massive Precambrian Shield.[50] What they showed was a vast domain – an ancient Indian Country – empty of its Aboriginal inhabitants. What they displayed was a finely textured geography of northern North America as a territory devoid of its Aboriginal presence and lacking human history before the arrival of the newcomers. Their paintings marked the artistic equivalent in Canada of the legal concept in Australia that the land was *terra nullius* at the time of its exploration by Europeans.

In 1946 historian Arthur Lower reached out in a similar way to appropriate the energy of the Canadian landscape. "From the land of Canada," he wrote, "must come the soul of Canada."[51] But how could Canada or any other New World country claim this terrestial soul without its citizens coming to accept and even embrace the regenerative force of those cultures that have evolved with the land for tens of thousands of years? How could the Creole nationalisms of the Americas, including that of twentieth-century Canada, claim as their own the living spirit of their adopted territories while sanctioning policies aimed at extinguishing the legal connection of Indigenous peoples to their Aboriginal lands? In Lower's time, such questions rarely arose in serious debates in literature, politics, and the arts. Even today huge prejudices hold the discussion on the place of Indian Country and Indigenous peoples within narrow enclaves of political and intellectual debate. Many of us are constrained by the attitude towards evolutionary progress inherent in the title of Lower's *Colony to Nation* – a phrase that describes the experience in reverse of those Indigenous peoples whose freedoms have most frequently been extinguished and curtailed in the rush to create a New World Order.

The attitude towards the land held by Leacock, Lower, or the Group of Seven not only misrepresented the Aboriginal presence but also missed some of the fundamental attributes of the imperial enterprise so essential to the genesis of their own country. Unlike Australia, where Britain faced little competition from European rivals, the history of Canada grew out of intense rivalry between competing empires. Until 1759, France and Britain vied for dominance. For fourteen years after the end of the Seven Years' War in 1763, two antagonistic schools of British imperialism clashed within the increasingly unstable constitutional framework of British North America. After this conflict broke into the open in 1776, the quest for hegemony set the New World republic of the United States against the Old World coalition of conservatives on both sides of the Atlantic. This coalition joined in the defence of British imperial Canada, especially during the War of 1812.

Throughout this development of the North Atlantic community, First Nations peoples in the heart of the continent played strategic and sometimes decisive roles. Their strongest fighting contingents were generally allied with the conservative side of the conflicts, pitting first a Protestant empire against a Roman Catholic empire, and then the British Empire against the Born-Again New World empire that would emerge from the founding and expansion of the United States. Accordingly, while the Aboriginal land issue remained unaddressed in Australia until the 1990s, the constitutional status of Aboriginal and treaty rights in Canada was an important strategic issue in the prolonged competition to secure the collaboration of those Indigenous peoples who held the balance of power in North America's interior. As Harold Innis, Donald Creighton, Bruce Trigger, Richard White, and many others have documented, the need to construct viable networks of alliance with the First Nations was given powerful geopolitical expression in the imperial strategies of New France and in the corporate operations of both the London-based Hudson's Bay Company and the Montreal-based North West Company.[52] Constitutionally, the vision of Canada as a land reserved for the Indians as their hunting grounds was entrenched in the Royal Proclamation of 1763, the document that established many of the underlying principles of crown-Aboriginal treaties which are still being negotiated today.

The original Canada was founded through the establishment, extension, and consolidation of an elaborate fur trade linking Indigenous peoples with a relatively small number of Roman Catholic, French-speaking colonists. As the seemingly horizonless possibilities of this primal exchange between peoples drew the more adventurous francophones deeper into Indian Country, they began to identify so closely with the land of their Aboriginal hosts that they described themselves as *canadiens*. In the opinion of Jean Morisset, a *canadien* nationalist and geographer who steadfastly insists on proclaiming the Métis character of *les peuples canadiens*, the central role played by Indigenous peoples in the founding of the original Canada "bespeaks the Indians' permanent geopolitical importance." He adds, "the fact that a country called Canada could exist was obviously less owing to France's effort than to the sociological and strategical alliances of the *canadiens* with the *Indians*. And besides, without the *canadiens* there cannot be any Canada. I think I can go as far as to say that the *canadiens* as a people would have ceased to exist sometime in the eighteenth century if it had not been for the *Indians*."53

The rich blending of Aboriginal and French Canadian cultures was noticed by Claude Levi-Strauss in his *Introduction to a Science of Mythology*. In this monumental survey of the oral traditions of Indigenous peoples in South and North America, the inventor of structural anthropology noticed that "so many features of French folklore, transmitted orally to the Indians by Canadian trappers, came to occupy a privileged place" in the story-telling of some of his Aboriginal subjects. This pattern was especially evident, he wrote, among the peoples he studied in the northwesterly portions of North America.54

The transcultural orientation of French-Aboriginal Canada was retained and even elaborated upon after 1763, when the Tory architects of British imperial Canada announced their intentions in a Royal Proclamation to polish and extend a Covenant Chain of treaty alliances with First Nations. In 1764 Sir William Johnson called together a major gathering of Indian leaders at Niagara to explain and confirm those principles in the Royal Proclamation designed to make allies of former enemies of the British imperial crown. It is said that Aboriginal delegates at this council attended from as far west as the Mississippi, as far north as Hudson Bay, and as far east as Nova Scotia. The reciprocal nature of these negotiations, to entrench a regime of crown recognition of existing Aboriginal and treaty rights, was marked by the imperial government's presentation of a beaded wampum belt. Its acceptance on the Indian side represented a determination to live within the constitutional framework outlined in King George's promises.55

This Royal Proclamation reserved the interior of North America to Indian nations as their hunting grounds. King George's royal words, which
remain entrenched as the constitutional foundation of Canada to this
day,[56] stipulated further that no non-Aboriginal colonial privatization of
Indian hunting territories could take place without the explicit, formal
consent of the British sovereign's Indian allies.[57] The king further prohibited private individuals from purchasing reserved Indian land, declaring
that this unique power of negotiation belonged exclusively to Him and His
Royal Heirs.

The proclamation was the essential strategic and ideological marker
that divided the course of British colonization on the continent towards
the forging of the new American republic on the one hand and the
consolidation of a counterrevolutionary British North America on the
other.[58] The North American realm that emerged from the Loyalist side
of the American Revolution retained its identity as an Indian Country
long after the peace treaty of 1783. During the War of 1812, for
instance, James McGill, the Montreal fur-trade baron, wrote to colonial
authorities in Great Britain as follows: "The Indians are the only Allies
who can aught avail in the defence of the Canadas. They have the same
interest as us, and alike are objects of American subjugation, if not
extermination."[59]

The Royal Proclamation also outlined the essential constitutional principles governing the making of treaties between the crown and the Indigenous peoples in Canada. These principles, first articulated in 1763, are still
working their way through the political machinery of the Canadian state,
so the system of crown-Aboriginal treaties is being extended to this day
into British Columbia, Quebec, and large areas in the north. If crown
treaties with the First Nations of Canada are truly to last for as long as the
sun shines and the waters flow, they commit those governed by these agreements to accept a more conservative orientation to history and community than the restless transience of those seeking to regenerate themselves
again and again on the moving frontiers of an ever-expanding New World
Order.[60]

Crown-Aboriginal treaties, therefore, point to a tradition of North American history different from that of the obsessive newcomer frontierism
expressed in the need to be born again and again in a steady cycle of physical, psychological, religious, and ideological conquest.[61] As instruments
symbolizing an aptitude for compromise and coexistence rather than conquest, these treaties are suggestive of the paradigm of different peoples
exercizing overlapping sovereignties in shared enjoyment of commonly
held territory. The crown-Aboriginal treaties of the northern dominion are
a vital medium of intercultural communication as essential to Canada's
genesis as the establishment of east-west transportation links in the fur-
trade and the railway eras.

Much depends on the ability of all sorts of people to share in Aboriginal perspectives of these agreements not as land surrenders but as sacred covenants that emphasize the intergenerational, transcultural, and cross-species continuity of relationships linking human communities with the Indigenous ecology of their Aboriginal or adopted lands.[62] The fact that crown-Aboriginal treaty making is being renewed in Canada in the new millennium suggests the possibility of a more widespread application of this highly adaptable medium of intercultural democracy. A key episode in widening the franchise of groups capable of making, renewing, and implementing treaties took place at the Earth Summit in Rio de Janiero in 1992. At a forum of non-governmental organizations, thirty-nine "people's treaties" were initiated to stress the need for the wider involvement of "civil society" in efforts to slow and reverse the deterioration of the global biosphere.[63] The use of treaties as a vehicle to protect biodiversity in the environment complements the use of treaties as a medium to affirm and celebrate the rich cultural diversity that is so essential to the social, psychological, and spiritual equilibrium of the human species.

The existence of treaties with the Indigenous peoples of North America constitutes an essential marker in the contemporary debate on whether civil society is most fruitfully viewed as a melting pot or as a multicultural mosaic. In the same fashion that the Royal Proclamation of 1763 marked an original parting of the ways on this fundamental question, so was this strategic division in colonizing practice reaffirmed in 1871. In that year the American Congress passed a law prohibiting the making of further treaties with Indian nations inside the borders of the United States.

The decision in 1871 to outlaw the extension of the system of federal-Indian treaties followed a period when federal officials had depended heavily on this device for incorporating Indian lands into the republic. After the American Revolution, the new federal authority of the United States asserted its constitutional pre-eminence over state governments by exercising the exclusive power to make treaties or to make war with Indian nations on the republic's western frontiers. Through this strategy, which effectively replaced the Royal Proclamation with a similar American constitutional convention, the central government made itself the master of western expansion.[64]

By 1871 the constitutional pre-eminence of the federal government in the United States was no longer in question. The federal army had defeated the secessionist states in the South and there seemed little doubt that this same fighting force would be invincible in finalizing the military suppression of the remaining Indian Country north of the Rio Grande and south of the 49th parallel. With the triumphant militarism of the federal government and of manifest destiny in the background, the American Congress declared "that hereafter no Indian nation or tribe within the territory of the United States shall be acknowledged as an independent nation, tribe or power with whom the United States may contract by treaty."[65] The wording of this law recognized that the very act of making treaties with Indigenous peoples confirmed their legal status as independent nations, tribes, or powers. From what source would First Nations derive their capacity to enter into treaties with another sovereign other than from their own inherent sovereignty and their own inherent rights to make and implement their own laws?

Even with the details of the American law before them, authorities of the Dominion of Canada embarked in 1871 on one of the country's most concerted and expansive eras of crown-Aboriginal treaty making. Between 1871 and 1877, seven numbered treaties were made with Saulteaux, Cree, Assiniboine, Dene, and Blackfoot peoples whose territories stretch from the Lake Superior region westward to the Rocky Mountains.[66] The negotiation of the numbered treaties continued until 1929, when Canadian and provincial officials emerged from the smokey roar of their pontooned bush planes at Big Trout Lake in northern Ontario. For many of the Crees who had assembled there to consider their adhesion to an expanded Treaty 9, this was the first time they had seen the aeronautical device that was about to transform dramatically so many facets of life in the Canadian North.[67]

The principles of crown treaty making with the Indians of Canada as articulated in 1763 and as renewed in 1871 were confirmed and extended again after 1973. That year an ambivalent ruling of the Supreme Court forced the government of Canada to recognize that the requirements of the Royal Proclamation had not been met in opening large parts of Indian Country to exploitation and ownership by non-Aboriginal settlers and corporations. Although their findings had significant ramifications in all parts of Canada not covered by crown-Aboriginal treaties, the judges' attention was centred on the assertions of the Nisga'a Indians of the Nass Valley of northwestern British Columbia. Like many other Aboriginal groups in Canada's westernmost province, the Nisga'a had long argued that the government of British Columbia was in fundamental breach of the crown laws of colonial expansion in North America. Their contention stemmed from the fact that officers of the crown had never obtained Indian consent for the provincially controlled exploitation of their ancestral lands.[68]

After 1973 the federal government opened new offices, with the goal of resolving outstanding disputes over Aboriginal land title in Canada. This initiative effectively reopened the stream of crown treaty negotiations with First Nations that had been dammed up since 1929.[69] The renewed process led to the making of modern-day treaties primarily in those situations where large vested interests were focused on opening up new economic frontiers of resource extraction in the Canadian North.

In those parts of Canada where there was not a pressing economic imperative to fulfil the legal requirements of the Royal Proclamation of 1763, the negotiations tended to get bogged down in bureaucratic quagmires. In 1997 the Supreme Court intervened in an ambivalent ruling on what is known as the *Delgamuukw* case. The decision gave qualified reaffirmation to the relatively strong legal position of Indigenous peoples, especially in British Columbia, who asserted that their Aboriginal title had not been extinguished.

The majority of Canadians have failed to look beyond the local aspects of Aboriginal land claims to the broader global context of modern-day treaty making with Indigenous peoples. This failure is largely one of political imagination in a country whose government developed as a colony of Great Britain and whose economy and foreign policy developed in the twentieth century as a satellite of the United States. In such a nation, it is assumed that the really important decisions are made elsewhere.[70] There has been a slowness to appreciate how history has converged to make Canada one of the primary test cases in the world on the position of Indigenous peoples in global geopolitics. At the nub of that history lie the geopolitical legacy of the fur trade, an enterprise that placed the constitutional principals of Aboriginal title and treaty alliances with Indigenous peoples near the strategic core of successive struggles over the site of imperial dominance in North America's interior.

The historical depth of questions connected to the constitutionality of Aboriginal and treaty rights in Canada can be illustrated by way of a comparison with recent controversies over the formulation and amendment of the Native Title Act in Australia. Those controversies have rarely penetrated beneath the level of legislative debate to a genuine grappling with the constitutional nature and fundamental constituent parts of the Australian nation. They have rarely been framed to acknowledge the idea of Aboriginal title as a principle of international law that is derived from sources which pre-exist the sovereign authority at the basis of the Australian federation's flawed and incomplete legal structure. They have rarely incorporated the idea of Aboriginal rights and titles not as add-ons to Australia's self-government but rather as unextinguishable principles situated at the very origins of Australia's national identity. Those controversies have not begun to incorporate the necessary discussion which must take place on how the British imperial monarch's fiduciary responsibilities to Indigenous peoples will be passed on. Historically the imperial sovereign in the British Empire has been vested with ultimate responsibility to safeguard the rights and titles of the crown's Aboriginal allies from the unlawful incursions of the crown's subjects and their corporate extensions.

As these volumes will demonstrate, such issues have been prolifically addressed, especially in the surge of academic literature that accompanied the political push to patriate and elaborate Canada's constitution. The profound questions raised by such issues, however, have rarely been allowed to enter the mainstream of debate in the political culture of the United State's northern neighbour. Hence the largest part of the

Australian public are hardly alone in lacking the opportunity to appreciate how closely the evolving definition of the sovereign title of their own country is connected to the status afforded Aboriginal title in domestic law, in international law, and in the changing balances of power in global geopolitics. The political repression of issues of such wide-ranging importance, however, cannot be indefinitely perpetuated.

The experiences of Canada, Australia, New Zealand, Mexico, Norway, Fiji, Nigeria, and many other countries will tell us much about whether nation-states can be reconfigured to conform with the principal outlines of the Fourth World. The great question to be addressed in this historical reckoning is whether the appropriations and extinguishments connected with the ongoing Columbian conquests can be reversed.

The expansions of the United States towards a global empire epitomized the ethos and methods of the Columbian conquests. Given the depth and scope of the history the United States shares with its northern neighbour, especially with respect to their common inheritances from British North America, the way the northern dominion treats the continuing existence of Aboriginal and treaty rights has significant ramifications for the world's only superpower. While the United States is a country, it is also the primary metropolis and heartland of an empire of proprietorship based on the idea that the frontiers of private property can be indefinitely extended across the lands and waters of the planet and even into the deepest genetic recesses of life's procreative energy. In such an empire, the sanctity of contracts and the capacity of human and corporate individuals to own and exchange property reigns supreme. Hence there is a great deal riding on how the United States, the world's primary symbol, proponent, and policeman of capitalism, handles the reality that its own pre-eminent position was largely achieved through the unilateral appropriation of Aboriginal lands and of the very persons of those legally designated as slaves. In its failure or success in sorting through the basic internal contradictions embedded in its origins, the United States bears much of the responsibility for determining whether the global promise of Europe's Age of Enlightenment will be fulfilled or whether we are entering a new Dark Age characterized by the culmination of the Columbian conquests in a worldwide tyranny of unjust property relationships.

LAHONTAN, ADARIO, AND GREY OWL: THE IDEAS AND IMAGERY OF INDIGENOUS PEOPLES IN THE CONTINUING ILLUMINATION OF ENLIGHTENMENT THOUGHT

The military alliance governed by the North Atlantic Treaty Organization stands as a symbol of the assimilative processes that unfolded over more than five centuries to make two continents appear to be the site of a single civilization. Will modern-day treaties in Canada become legal and political instruments simply to advance further the process of extinguishing what remains of Indian Country, as if Aboriginal nations were terminal nations whose eventual destiny is to be incorporated and absorbed into the domineering Euro-American societies around them? Or will these treaties lead to the further invention of a resurgent Indian Country based on intercultural democracy and a sharing of land, resources, and jurisdictions? Will the modern-day treaties of Canada with Indigenous peoples renew the transcultural character of the original, mestizo Canada and lead away from the crusading, genocidal course of the evangelical American empire? How, then, might the making of modern-day treaties in Canada affect the genesis of the American empire generally or of the United States more particularly?

Will the ongoing negotiations in Canada, but especially those in British Columbia, nudge the United States towards some reckoning with those surviving Indigenous peoples in parts of the American republic, including California, where the existence of unceded Aboriginal title has never been formalized through the ratification of treaty negotiations? Will treaty negotiations in Canada suggest the necessity of the United States's return to the facts of its retreat from even the minimal requirements of international law when it decided in 1871 to end treaty negotiations with Indigenous peoples before Indian or Inuit consent was secured for the imposition of US jurisdiction on large parts of the republic's territorial base? Will the United States's abysmal record as a violator of treaties with Indigenous peoples yet have diplomatic ramifications affecting how other nation's view the world's superpower? Will the appropriate connections be drawn between the United States's history of violating Indian treaties and its government's unwillingness to live with the framework of any international law that it cannot dominate? Will links be made, for instance, between the United States's many roles in the Middle East and the lawlessness entailed in the treatment of Indigenous peoples throughout its own history of territorial expansion? Might international concern about these linkages affect the United States's capacity to oversee, for example, the negotiation and implementation of a treaty to bring about the consolidation of a Palestinian state on Israel's frontiers? Why should any power in the Americas trust the United States to live within the framework of continental and hemispheric trade treaties when it has consistently refused to adhere to the treaties negotiated to legitimize the assertion of sovereign title over its own territorial base?

Very specific questions such as these should be posed in the context of more general contentions about the nature of democracy and human rights. These contentions ignited passions that burned most brilliantly in the political culture of the century that produced the American Revolution and the French Revolution, events that transformed the fundamental framework of Western civilization. During the century of Enlightenment,

France became a primary laboratory for a particularly potent mix of anti-authoritarian ideas. The spirit of rising resistance in France to the arbitrary rule of monarchs and priests was vitalized and enhanced by the examples flowing from Europe's expanding imperial frontiers. News of the discoveries and observations of European explorers, together with the widening extent of colonial enterprise, helped stimulate an atmosphere of rapid transformation in the self-understanding of many in the heartland of imperial adventure.[71] France's vast imperial claims throughout the fur-trade domain of Aboriginal Canada provided a particularly rich ground for the cultivation of those cultural and intellectual exchanges which cast growing doubts on the old orthodoxies of church and state.

A major medium for this infusion of news and observations from the Indian Country of Canada into the intellectual pulse of the French Enlightenment were the annual reports from the Society of Jesus, generally referred to as *The Jesuit Relations*.[72] As the appointed shock troops leading the Roman Catholic response to the Protestant Reformation, the Jesuit Order counted the empire of France in North America as one of its important theatres of evangelical enterprise. The Jesuits' favoured style of evangelism was to learn the cultures and languages of their Aboriginal hosts and to introduce images of and references to, the Christian God as gently as possible into existing motifs of belief and ritual. In this sense the main missionary impulse in the Indian Country of Canada during the era of New France tended towards a multicultural approach, with the view that Aboriginal societies could be reformed rather than radically remade to reflect the religious and civilizational ideals of Christendom. The Jesuits' goal was not to prepare the ground for a huge influx of European immigration into Indian Country but to cultivate the development of Christian Indian theocracies, with Roman Catholic clergy as the directing lights of the reconstituted societies.

In justifying this approach to evangelization, many Jesuit missionaries produced a steady stream of published literature emphasizing, with some significant exceptions, the positive and benevolent qualities of Aboriginal societies in the Americas as well as the kind personalities these cultures most regularly produced. The underlying motive was to advance the deistic idea that human beings in their natural state are born with an innate inclination to be decent and conscious of the divine. Alternatively, other writers used depictions of Indigenous peoples in the Americas to argue that human nature without the influence of Christian revelation was naturally evil and diabolical. Accordingly, the deists' object was to demonstrate that the coming of Christianity to Aboriginal societies would give their citizens an improved opportunity to live in harmony with God's divine plan. While the effect of conversion for the Jesuits was to improve an already healthy human condition, rather than to overturn a reign of diabolical debauchery,[73] some of New England's more militant Puritan preachers viewed unconverted Indians as unredeemed sinners. Reverend John Eliot, for example, was the prime architect and overseer of the "praying towns" of the Protestant Indians of Massachusetts.[74]

The more worldly, open-minded view of Indian Country flowed into Europe especially from the pens of the Jesuit fathers Jean de Brébeuf, Joseph François Lafitau, and Pierre de Charlevoix, all of whom were accomplished students of both the literature and the diverse cultures of the Indigenous peoples of Canada.[75] Their writings were used by Raynal, Diderot, Voltaire, Rousseau, and many others as primary sources of ethnographic observation that detailed the character of "natural law" among those peoples who lived beyond the achievements and corruptions of European civilization.

The most intellectually potent of the ethnographies transported to Europe, however, were those by the baron de Lahontan, a French soldier of anti-clerical persuasion who, at the end of the seventeenth century, was deeply involved in the political intrigues of the fur trade in the Great Lakes area. Lahontan recorded many criticisms of the French that he claimed were regularly made by the "natural philosophers" he met in Indian Country. Some Aboriginal groups in North America, he concluded, had applied "the true rules of justice and reason" in ways that made the French seem poor and unethical by comparison.[76] The basic themes of these criticisms found a large European readership through several editions of his writings and through translation into many languages.[77]

According to Lahontan's Indian informants, the French suffered particularly from the tyranny embodied in monarchy, from the inequitable distribution of wealth, and from all manner of ills brought about from irrational approaches to health, marriage, class distinctions, law enforcement, and religion. "They brand us for slaves, and call us miserable Souls, whose life is not worth having, alledging that we degrade ourselves in subjecting ourselves to one Man who possesses the whole Power and is bound by no Law but his own will ... They think it unaccountable," wrote the baron, "that one Man should have more than another and that the rich should have more respect than the poor." Rather than wealth, it was "Wisdom, Reason and Equity" that was most esteemed in Indian Country. This love of equality and personal autonomy extended across genders, for "the Women are entitled to the same Liberty with Men." In short, asserted the author, "they say that the name of Savages which we bestow upon them would fit ourselves better, since there is nothing in our actions that bears an appearance of wisdom." Underlying all these distinctions was Lahontan's ironic contention that his Aboriginal associates in Canada tended to live their lives in a way that respected the sanctity of human reason over the Christian ideal of faith. "They maintain that Man ought never to strip himself of the Privileges of reason, that being the noblest faculty with which God has enriched him," he wrote. "The word Faith is enough to choak them."[78]

This emphasis on human reason as the most important means of distinguishing truth from superstition went to the heart of that complex of ideas that would open Europe to the surge of intellectual illumination known as the Enlightenment. If Lahontan has credence as an ethnographer and a pioneering *philosophe*, then, there was a real infusion of Indian ideas into the identity crisis that would radically transform Europe, but especially France, by the end of the eighteenth century. Accordingly, the ideological power of globalization is suggested by the apparent impact of Native American stories and critiques on what would become the most revolutionary currents of European thought and opinion.

Many sceptics have discounted the possibility that Lahontan was a conduit for the movement of genuine thought and observations from Indian Country into that ferment of ideas that ultimately found expression in the revolutionary fervour which overtook Europe after 1789. The common approach has been to treat as fiction that part of Lahontan's work which professes to translate Native North American opinion; to assume, instead, that Lahontan put his frustrations with his own society into the mouths of Indians. This rejection is especially marked when it comes to that part of his writings which I view as a masterpiece of cross-cultural Enlightenment studies. This work is constructed as a dialogue between Lahontan and a Huron leader known variously as Adario, Kondiaronk, or the Rat. The two men debate the respective merits of their own societies and, not surprisingly, the Huron sage gets the upper hand in most of the arguments.

Among those to relegate this Huron critique of European society to the realm of fiction was Stephen Leacock, who wrote the anti-Indian diatribe already cited in his introduction to a new edition of Lahontan's works. A similar judgment was rendered by Henry Steele Commanger, who stated in his study subtitled *How Europe Imagined and America Realized the Enlightenment*, "Lahontan created Adario."[79] This unsupported contention that one of the seminal articulations of democratic and egalitarian principles in Enlightenment thought had a European rather than an Aboriginal North American origin is consistent with other strategic exclusions blocking the existence of the Aboriginal civilization of the Americas from memory and awareness. Such erasure, to support the image of civilization's progress as a one-way affair moving only from east to west, reflects the same amnesia that has obscured recognition of the importance of Amerindian horticulture. This pattern of blinkered recollection is integral to the view of the North Atlantic community not as one based on ethnic cleansing but as a simple ascent of civilization over savagery.

Adario, or Kondiaronk, as he is more frequently identified, emerges from many historical records as an extremely important person in the Indian Country of Canada, a man who was widely recognized as having precisely those kinds of skills in oratory and debate that Lahontan attributes to him.[80] Charlevoix, for instance, noted that Kondiaronk made a celebrated speech shortly before being poisoned at the crucial meeting near Montreal in 1701 to renegotiate the terms of the fur trade.[81] Charlevoix explained further that Kondiaronk's speeches were almost always accompanied by heavy applause, "even from those who disliked him." The Huron, he continued, "was not less brilliant in conversation in private." Many officials in New France "often took pleasure in provoking him to hear his repartees, always animated, full of wit, and generally unanswerable." Kondiaronk's skills in debate and conversation made him one of Canada's most sought-after dinner guests at the governor's chateau in Quebec. In fact, Charlevoix counted Kondiaronk as "the only man in Canada who was a match for the Count de Frontenac."[82]

In my view, this characterization of Lahontan's opponent in the *Dialogues* goes far to indicate that Kondiaronk, as well as other Native people throughout New France, were articulate contributors to the revolution of ideas and understanding in the Enlightenment. The celebrated German philosopher Leibnitz, who briefly became Lahontan's scholarly patron during their stay at the court of Hanover, added further testimony to support this view. Leibnitz acknowledged that Lahontan almost certainly allowed himself some artistic licence in his writing, but he gave qualified support to the authenticity of his colleague's work. "Lahontan's Dialogue," he wrote in a letter to a friend, "even if not true in every point, as you easily understand, is nevertheless not altogether fictional." Leibnitz refers to Adario as "a real person from the tribe of the Hurons, who came to France several years ago, yet approved his institutions before ours."[83]

One of Lahontan's most remarkable intellectual successors on the transcultural frontiers of the Indian Country was the twentieth-century conservationist known to the world as Grey Owl. Like Lahontan, Grey Owl combined real familiarity with the inner worlds and environments of Indigenous peoples in the Great Lakes area with his own creative inventiveness and talent for publicity. He also produced a blend of authentic observation and fictional representation, which combined to form a potent, if more cunningly disguised, challenge to the *status quo* of his times. Where Lahontan let Kondiaronk speak to the inequities of pre-revolutionary France, however, Grey Owl responded to his immigration into Indian Country by taking on himself the identity of a Native critic of the destructive excesses of industrial society.[84]

Grey Owl came into the world in 1888 as Archie Belaney. The son of a child bride and a severely alcoholic father, Archie was raised by close relatives in Hastings, England. He migrated to Canada in 1906 as part of the largest of all waves of European immigration to North America. After a short stay in Toronto, the tall, agile Englishman moved northwards into the Temagami area, a particularly rich zone of ecological biodiversity around the watershed dividing the Arctic from the Great Lakes basins.[85] Intent on becoming a guide, Belaney learned all he could about survival in the primal geography of the Canadian Shield. As the years passed, he gravitated towards life among those First Nations people in northern Ontario and Quebec who lived outside the geographic confines of reserves and the legal constraints of the federal Indian Act. During the formative phase of his apprenticeship as a trapper, Belaney was adopted through marriage into the Egwuna clan, part of the Ojibway community that, in later years, would settle on Bear Island in Lake Temagami.

Belaney left his first wife and enlisted as a Canadian soldier in the First World War. On returning to Canada he took up his woodsman's way of life once again, this time in northern Quebec. In 1925 at Mattawa he met a nineteen-year-old waitress whose family roots lay in the Mohawk community of Oka. Her name was Gertrude Bernard, but after she moved into Archie's cabin, he referred to her increasingly as Anahareo. Under Anahareo's influence, the accomplished bushman was gradually convinced to put aside his traps and to start raising beaver cubs. Slowly Grey Owl absorbed his wife's deep empathy for the feelings of wild animals and a corresponding distaste for the way they were being decimated and tortured by their human hunters. This conviction became an obsession for Belaney, who, meanwhile, had been concocting a story about his origins as the offspring of a Scots father and an Apache mother born south of the Rio Grande.

The woodsman began to weave together these strands of fact and fiction into literature, first in a series of short articles written for the Canadian Foresty Association and then into more ambitious projects. By 1931, when his first book, *The Men of the Last Frontier* was published, the transformation was complete. Grey Owl and Anahareo's efforts to conserve the beaver, an animal that was almost completely trapped out in Canada after many generations of fur-trade dominance, captured the attention of a society that had recently been plunged into the Great Depression. Their crusade to save the animal that had become one of Canada's most ubiquitous national emblems was quickly joined by James Harkin, the commissioner of Canada's growing network of National Parks. Under Harkin's imaginative direction the couple were filmed, publicized, and supported in their work to understand the life cycle and the personalities of what they called "the beaver people."[86]

In the 1930s Grey Owl, Anahareo, and their conservation work in Canada's National Parks attracted enormous attention. The films, the publications, and especially Grey Owl's lecture tours fed off one another, producing a wave of popular identification with wildlife conservation in the transatlantic world. Grey Owl created a sensation with his *Pilgrims of the Wild*, published in 1934, and his speaking engagements in Britain, rekindling the mass fascination with various types of Native North American performers in the major metropolises of the British Empire. This trend had begun in 1710 with the public frenzy generated by the visit to London of several Iroquois ambassadors billed as the "Four Kings of Canada."[87] It continued with the hugely popular speaking and preaching tours featuring a host of literate Indian evangelists, including Samson Occum, Peter Jones, and, in the late nineteenth century, Buhkwujjenene. A son of

Shingwaukonse, Buhkwujjenene travelled to England to raise funds for the establishment of an Anglican Native boarding school in Sault Ste Marie, Ontario.[88]

Grey Owl's story and imagery were embellished and promoted by a whole legion of journalists, publicists, publishers, filmmakers, agents, and park officials who had their own reasons for complicity in the making of this living legend. In his biography of the man who came to symbolize the effort to protect some of the last extensive and relatively undisturbed environments of the Americas, Lovat Dickson, Grey Owl's publisher, said: "This voice from the forest momentarily released us from some spell. In contrast with Hitler's screaming, ranting voice, and the remorseless clang of modern technology, Grey Owl's voice evoked an unforgettable charm, lighting in our minds the vision of a cool, quiet place, where animals and men lived in love and trust together."[89]

The disguise began to come apart shortly before Grey Owl's death in 1938. While his image as an impostor proved dominant for a time, his real achievements as a pioneering voice for wildlife conservation and as an advocate for recognition of Indigenous peoples' rights and titles have gradually come to refurbish his reputation. As a headline in the Montreal *Gazette* in 1972 put it: "Ecology Fad Returns Grey Owl to Fashion."[90] The transformation of Grey Owl's life into a major motion picture by Sir Richard Attenborough in 1999 added further to the mystique around the individual known variously as "Beaver Man" or "Wilderness Man." To coincide with the release *Grey Owl*, a speech Belaney delivered to the Empire Club in Toronto in 1936 was republished. In that talk, Grey Owl criticized Canadian Indian policy and outlined a proposal for reform, thereby linking the joint ideals of biodiversity and cultural pluralism.

Grey Owl focused in his speech on the Canadian North, which he identified as Canada's "great heritage." Most Canadians, he alleged, knew almost nothing of their country beyond the quarter part associated with "civilization." "The other three-quarters," he continued, "are in the hands of the Indians, for all anybody dare tell them it isn't. That is the richest part of Canada." The "destruction" brought about by careless industrial encroachment was, he claimed, "wiping" Canada's great northern heritage "off the face of the earth." Closely related to this phenomenon was Canada's ill-considered Indian policy, which was transforming the Native people into "hoboes and misfits," a ruinous process that "has made the Indian an outcast in his own country." To rectify these human and environmental abominations, the conservationist proposed that the Canadian government undertake to employ Indigenous peoples as keepers of the ecological health of the North. Grey Owl concluded his speech by outlining his vision:

it is costing a lot of money to keep us [Indians] in idleness and watch us disintegrate and slowly fade away. We have our place in the economic scheme of life in

Canada and we want the same jobs we had before. We can do it. And it is worth trying one more experiment on that great job after the many failures you have already had. Put the Indian where he can do the most work and the most good for the country, a 50 – 50 proposition. You give us education, give us recognition, and we will look after your north country for you. [Applause] ... I want to arouse in the Canadian people a sense of responsibility, the great responsibility they have for that north country and its inhabitants, human and animal.[91]

MARGARET ATWOOD'S "GREY OWL SYNDROME" AND FREDERICK JACKSON TURNER'S FRONTIER THESIS

The literary imagery produced from Grey Owl's pilgrimage into the Indian Country of Canada continues to help globalize the consciousness required to understand the connections linking cultural pluralism to the maintenance of biodiversity through the preservation of wildlife habitat. Moreover, the outcome of Grey Owl's immigration into North America stands as a stark embodiment of the distinctions between the United States and the two neighbouring polities within which the transformed Englishman constructed both the learned and the imagined parts of his complex Aboriginal identity. Indeed, by situating his imagined Indian identity in both Mexico and Canada, two polities with a strong Native ambiance that contrasts dramatically with the country that Indian observers have described as "the new white nation," Grey Owl made himself into a potent symbol of transcultural transformation. In imagining for himself an Indian heritage in the mestizo polities of Canada and Mexico, Grey Owl created a legend representing the antithesis of one of the central mythologies fundamental to the "victory culture" of the United States.[92]

This victory culture, whose most classic popular expression lay in those Hollywood "Westerns" produced before the Vietnam War, found seminal academic articulation in the famous paper delivered in Chicago's Columbian Exposition in 1893 by Frederick Jackson Turner. Turner delivered this essay, "the most influential piece of historical writing ever done in the United States," at one of the world's major events to celebrate the 400th anniversary of the "discoveries" of 1492. According to frontier historian Walter Prescott Webb, the paper "altered the whole course of American historical scholarship."[93] Turner subsequently became the founder and guiding light of the "frontier school" of American historiography. His thesis provided the basis for an interpretation of the country's past which retained considerable authority until the fervour of American self-confidence was dampened by the anti-war movement of the late 1960s and early 1970s.

This frontier thesis was built around the belief that Europeans were dramatically remade at the outer edge of America's westward-moving frontier. In both their absorption and conquest of the primitive essence of a dwindling Indian Country, migrants from the "Old World" of Europe were thought to be reconstituted as a new type of self-reliant individual. The resulting process of democratization was said to have produced a genuinely American form of civilization along with the expansionistic ethos of a New World empire headed for global domination. Turner captured the basic elements of this perception of American manifest destiny when he defined the American frontier as "the meeting point of savagery and civilization" and "the line of most rapid and effective Americanization."

Turner would have his archetypal frontiersman taken from the railway car and put in a canoe. The power of the frontier "strips off the garments of civilization and arrays" his idealized subject "in the hunting shirt and the moccasin." The frontier then puts the pioneer "in the log cabin of the Cherokee or Iroquois and runs an Indian palisade around him." The new comer "fits himself into the Indian clearings and follows the Indian trails." "Before long," wrote Turner, "he has gone to planting Indian corn and ploughing with a sharp stick; he shouts the war cry and takes the scalp in orthodox Indian fashion." Having both assimilated and overcome the Aboriginal heritage of the frontier, the pioneer "little by little transforms the wilderness, but the outcome is not the old Europe." Instead, "at the frontier, the bonds of custom are broken," giving the makers of the American experiment in New World living "a gate of escape from the bondage of the past."[94]

The life of Grey Owl challenged the transformative forces thought to govern emigration from the Old World civilization of Europe to the New World civilization of America. Like Lahontan, Archie Belaney entered the Great Northern Forest of the continent to learn from its Indigenous inhabitants, both human and animal, that some of the most rapacious forms of savagery lay not beyond the frontiers of what is called civilization, but at the very centres of power and control where the conquest of nature is mandated. In achieving a genuine transformation of spirit from the Old World of Europe to the Old Indian World of the Americas, Grey Owl scouted a path towards an effective Americanization with implications far more revolutionary than the frontier transformation eulogized by Turner.

Grey Owl's story demonstrated that, well into the twentieth century, First Nations cultures in Canada still retained their power to assimilate newcomers within their own systems of loyalty and conviction.[95] The continuation of Indian Country's porous boundaries of culture and identity represents a moving frontier of the mind with generous rules of immigration into its psychic geography. The immigration of so many transcultural travellers into Indian Country stands as proof of the Aboriginal realm's ability to transcend the limitations of ethnic nationalism. Indeed, a vital mark of the Fourth World's adaptive capacity to resist colonization by expanding its own frontiers of intercultural innovation lies in the capacity of Indigenous peoples globally to absorb and assimilate a portion of colonialism's emigrants.

Novelist and literary critic Margaret Atwood seized on Grey Owl's story as a beacon of something deep and pervasive in the character of Canada. She identified Belaney's experience as emblematic of "the Grey Owl syndrome." She described this condition as "the desire among non-Natives to turn themselves into Natives, a desire which becomes intertwined in a version of wilderness itself ... as the repository of salvation and new life."[96] Atwood hangs this theory on the literary careers of two writers: John Richardson and Ernest Thompson Seaton.

Seaton was the Canadian author of children's books that gave flattering and informative descriptions of useful aspects of North American Indian life and lore. The books created the basis for the Woodcraft Indian movement, a network of camps and clubs for boys of all backgrounds. Almost certainly Seaton's publications were instrumental in helping to stimulate in the young Archie Belaney some of his fascination with, and understanding of, the symbolic power of animal stories emanating from Indian Country. According to Atwood, Seton was far more ambitious in his idea of transcultural migration than Grey Owl. Seton "did not attempt the rather modest feat of turning himself into an Indian, but pursued the greater ambition of turning everyone else into an Indian."[97]

Atwood identified John Richardson as significant primarily for his authorship of *Wacousta,* a novel first published in 1832.[98] The book described life in and around Forts Detroit and Michilimackinac at the time when Pontiac and the Algonkian peoples with him made their assertive stand. The main character is a noble Cornishman who disguises himself as an Indian in order to seek revenge on a rival who stole his fiancé. *Wacousta* enjoyed broad popularity for over a century. According to Atwood, the plot was based partially on the real life of Major John Norton (Teyoninhokarawen), another important transcultural figure of Scots-Cherokee background who became a key deputy of Joseph Brant among the Six Nations people in Upper Canada in the early nineteenth century.[99] At the end of the novel Wacousta's mistress, who is white and pregnant with his child, walks off into Indian Country to have the baby. "The audience are invited," wrote Atwood, "to become Indians too ... to join her on the Indian side."[100]

Atwood draws considerable meaning from the fact that John Richardson was himself of Aboriginal ancestry through his maternal grandmother – an Ottawa women named Manette, the wife of fur trader John Askin. In his partial Indian ancestry, Richardson was far from unusual among many of the English-speaking elites of British imperial Canada.

The first superintendent and founding patriarch of the British Imperial Indian Department was the lord of the manor at Johnson Hall. Indeed, Sir William Johnson's role in polishing and extending the Covenant Chain of crown-Indian alliances beyond the Six Nations into the Algonkian-speaking domain of the Great Lakes makes him one of the essential founding fathers of English-speaking Canada. Sir William marked his fatherhood by many means, both direct and indirect. One of the most direct expressions was in the children he conceived with several Aboriginal women, including his most famous partnership with Molly Brant. The number of his children is still a subject of debate, though the estimate by some Six Nations people of around one hundred is probably a gross exaggeration.[101] Johnson generally acknowledged and helped his children in ways that seemed decent and acceptable to their mothers and their extended Indian families. Some of Johnson's Aboriginal descendants acquired important posts in the Indian Department. There they worked alongside other men and women who shared the mixed family trees typical of the fur-trade heritage of Canada.

Among the mixed-ancestry families who enjoyed prominence and relative influence in the era following the American Revolution, when English-speaking settlers attempted to graft themselves onto the earlier Aboriginal and French roots of Canada, were the Askins, the Richardsons, the Girtys, the McKees, the Caldwells, the Elliots, the Hamiltons, the Ironsides, the Nortons, the Robertsons, and the Dicksons.[102] The advantages available to the enterprising among these families were many, including the lucrative contracts to supply and provision the Indian Department – whose negotiations and politics depended on their maintaining a steady flow of "presents" to Indian Country. They also had an inside track on patenting some of the most valuable land north of the Great Lakes.[103] Although the Royal Proclamation technically prevented direct land transfers from Aboriginal groups to individuals, the rules were sometimes bent, especially by Joseph Brant in the Grand River Valley and by other adept opportunists in the area of present-day Windsor, where many of the leading families had many Aboriginal branches in their family trees. In terms of the fledgling patronage networks of British imperial Canada and the prevailing Tory orientations of power in the remaining crown domain, political connections with the Indian Department and family connections in Indian Country could be valuable assets in the society that developed in opposition to the republican experiment of the American revolutionaries.

This theme of creative blending on the middle ground of compromise and coexistence runs through Janet Chute's *Legacy of Shingwaukonse: A Century of Native Leadership*.[104] The book provides a clear interpretive window into the leading figures and ideas that animated the rich genesis of Native life in the Sault Ste Marie area, historically one of North America's most important hubs of the fur trade and the attending culture of métissage. Chute illustrates how this transcultural heritage runs through the history of the Pine family, whose lasting influence was largely secured in the era of the War of 1812 by the Ojibway leader Shingwaukonse (or Little Pine, in English). Among Shingwaukonse's sons was John Askin, an important figure in the early twentieth century. The significance of the Askin name among the elite families of both Indian Country and Tory Canada illustrates the thick web of intercultural connections that added to the influence of those inter-married clans that straddled both sides of a frontier society. The nature of this frontier during the earlier phases of Canadian nation building was very different from the one imagined by Frederick Jackson Turner in his theory on the genesis of American exceptionalism.

The defining moment for this multicultural and often transcultural society beyond the frontiers of US control was the War of 1812. More than any other event, that life-or-death conflict crystallized the pivotal importance of the principles of alliance between the crown and the First Nations. This relationship between military allies was the central sinew of a strategic connection essential to the geopolitical survival of Canada. A key constitutional legacy of this defensive action against the course of US manifest destiny is the legal provision recognizing the existence of Aboriginal and treaty rights in Canada's "supreme law." One of the most observant chroniclers of the Indian role in keeping Canada from "the triumphant arms of the United States" was Major John Richardson, who in his service with the Right Division of the Canadian Army worked closely with Tecumseh and the fighting forces of the Indian Confederacy. After his success with *Wacousta*, Richardson wrote a chronicle of his military memories in 1842, *The War of 1812*, a volume he hoped would become a basic text for teaching Canadian patriotism to Canadian students.[105]

The abundant family ties securing various paths of immigration towards the frontiers or into the heartlands of Indian Country widen the definition of what Atwood described as "the Grey Owl syndome." In early Canada, transcultural migration between European and Aboriginal identities was relatively common and strategically essential to the health of the fur trade and to the defence of territory against the westward-moving wave of Anglo-American settlement. In the decades following 1776 this wave of Euro-American migration surged forward most aggressively through the agency of the United States. A key factor in the Native resistance to this movement lay in the rich transcultural exchanges and innovation on the middle ground of trade and negotiation between peoples on the other side of the United States's shifting frontier. Among the most influential media of the pluralistic diversification of the Indian Country of Canada was the frequency of successful intercultural marriages.[106]

The raising by Indian families of Anglo-Americans taken as captives in infancy or childhood is another important theme of experience among some of those who learned to move most easily and adeptly between potentially formidable barriers of culture and language. Simon Girty, an official with the British Imperial Indian Department in the late eighteenth century, is a good example of a former captive who thrived in the multicultural atmosphere of Canada.[107] A generation later John Tanner, or Shaw-shaw-wa Be-na-se, who wrote in rich detail of thirty years spent among the Ojibway, had a far more difficult time adapting later in life to the culture from which he was taken as a child.[108]

Where intermarriage and childhood captivity opened the way for some movement into Indian Country, many newcomers and their descendants have simply extended the experience of immigration into the continent by moving beyond the European outposts and the Euro–North American overlay of culture into the deeper terrain of identification with the continent's Aboriginal civilization. Thus, the man for whom the Grey Owl syndrome is named was following a well-beaten path from Europe into the Indian Country of North America. Over hundreds of years this journey has assimilated in varying degrees many transcultural travellers whose experience of transformation on the absorptive frontiers of the First Nations confounds the Turner myth.

The traffic on this transcultural path diminished somewhat after the War of 1812 in eastern Canada and after the completion of the Canadian Pacific Railway in western Canada, when the sharp decline in the economic health of the fur trade limited the viability of this key medium of transcultural migration. Where men were the primary migrants into Indian Country in early Canada, the federal Indian Act created a legal vehicle until 1985 for thousands of non-Aboriginal women married to Indian men to acquire the legal personality of registered Indians. The story of this means of immigration into Indian Country – one travelled, for instance, by the war brides that some of the Indian soldiers brought back with them from Europe after both world wars – remains largely untold.

THE CIVILIZING MISSION
AND THE GENESIS OF SOCIAL ENGINEERING

The word "civilization" is mentioned frequently in the voluminous literature devoted to the description of Indigenous peoples once their geopolitical importance in North America diminished with the demise of the fur trade and once non-Aboriginal laws and institutions began increasingly to constrain their lives. It was used, for example, to identify, explain, and justify the changed direction of the British imperial government's Indian policy after 1830. Rather than emphasize the role of Indian peoples in the fur trade and in the defence of Canada, the authors of the new policy sought to encourage Indian peoples in Canada to become Christians and sedentary farmers within small reserve enclaves.[109]

In 1857 the provincial legislature of the province of Canada moved to take over from Great Britain the local governance of both this "civilizing" mission and practical control of the province's Indian reserves. The outcome of this ironic devolution to non-Aboriginal colonists of the power to govern Native peoples was a statute called An Act for the Gradual Civilization of the Indian Tribes in Canada. That statute, whose aims and intentions were soundly rejected by an assembly of Iroquoian and Algonkian leaders who gathered in 1858 at Onondaga Council House on the Six Nations reserve near Brantford,[110] established a procedure for

Aboriginal individuals to extinguish their registered Indian status by becoming enfranchised citizens of Canada. Although the concerted Indian resistance to the transfer of authority for "Indian Affairs" from the imperial to the provincial governments led to some modifications, this first Indian Act established many of the key patterns of parliamentary authority over Indian reserves in Canada that have been extended and modified by the federal government until the present day. Indeed, Canada's Indian Act stands as a legislative artifact of many different systems of subordinating Indigenous peoples as wards of central authority during the most oppressive stages in the genesis of European empires and their successor states.

While it was one thing to drape the expression "civilization" over various initiatives aimed at constraining, absorbing, and extinguishing Indian Country, it was something quite different to establish a consensus about the precise content and meaning of this civilizational mission. Was the preferred model of civilization, for instance, Protestant or Roman Catholic, French-speaking or English-speaking, capitalist or socialist? The study of the various initiatives to bring civilization to Indigenous peoples tends to be most instructive not for what we learn about the objects of these attempts at social engineering but for what it reveals about the attitudes, preoccupations, and antagonisms of those who saw themselves as makers of a New World or as instruments of the expansion of Western civilization – or some combination of the two.

Viewed in this way, the abundant writings and pronouncements of those engaged in different aspects of this internally complex civilizing mission often render explicit what would otherwise be left vague or implicit about the intentions and contentions of those seeking to transform parts of the planet into a *New* France, a *New* England, a *New* South Wales, a *New* Zealand, a *New* Spain, a *New* Netherlands, the Dominion of Canada, or, for that matter, a sovereign Quebec. As Francis Jennings writes of his own research in a comment that could as easily apply to non-Aboriginals throughout the rest of the *New* World as it does to citizens of the United States, "my underlying motive for studying the history of Amerindians and Euroamericans has been to discover my own people."[111]

The emerging heartland of English-speaking Canada provides a small example of how the main contentions of power and control in colonial society were played out in efforts to control Aboriginal policy.[112] In the 1830s one of the most hotly contested issues in the crown colony north of the Great Lakes was whether the Church of England would be afforded privileged status and exclusive access to those rich parcels of land set up for the support of a "Protestant clergy." The leading advocate in Upper Canada of the Anglican Church as a kind of state church was the Reverend John Strachan, an arch conservative who set his mark on the colonial elite through his influence as a teacher. Strachan's chief opponent of Anglicanism as a state church was the Reverend Egerton Ryerson. Ryerson began his career as a missionary in Upper Canada's successful Methodist Indian missions.[113]

While the struggle to control the future status of the clergy reserves in Upper Canada was at the core of the conflict to decide what would be the relationship between church and state in the primarily Protestant, English-speaking crown colony taking shape west of Quebec, Strachan and Ryerson also waged a propaganda war over the direction of Indian policy. Strachan maintained that the Church of England should be afforded favoured status by those Indian Department officials with the responsibility of administering the imperial government's civilizing policy. Ryerson, in contrast, spoke and wrote of the need to allow Indian people some degree of religious freedom in deciding what Christian denomination they would belong to.

This controversy led Ryerson to advocate that Methodist evangelists should be allowed to continue to act as teachers and preachers at those Indian missions specifically set up by Methodist evangelists. The best known of these missions was the successful agricultural community created by Mississauga converts at the mouth of the Credit River, just east of Toronto.[114] Ryerson also maintained that government support should be extended to the Methodist teachers and preachers at the new crown Indian reserve established at Coldwater and the Narrows in 1830. This reserve had been established with the intention of making it a showpiece for Indian people and colonists alike – to demonstrate the direction of the imperial government's new "civilizing" policy.

There was little chance in the long run that Strachan's vision of Upper Canada as a Church of England theocracy could prevail. Instead, Ryerson's view dominated, especially as he carried his vision of religious politics into his role as the chief architect of the public education system in what would become Ontario after 1867.[115] It is tempting to see Ryerson's advocacy of the importance of mandatory, publically supported education in his province as an outgrowth of the kind of perceptions he developed in his early involvement with the Methodist missions, whose declared purpose was to civilize the Aboriginal "savages" of Upper Canada. How far was the intellectual journey between the Indian missions and the idea that all children, Aboriginal or not, come into the world as savages and require state intervention through public education to bridge the transition to civilization? This assertion of state control over the education of young people was apparently established to create a sort of safety net aimed at assimilating all children at least partially into the rhythms and mores of industrial civilization. Public education was based on an extension of the state's authority to maintain an imagined continuity in the process of civilizational renewal, regardless of whether parents were effective participants in this broader societal mission.

As superintendent of education in Ontario, Ryerson held to the position he developed in his work in the Indian missions – that the government oversight of public education should engender Protestant values without favouring one denomination over another. Similarly, his recognition of the inescapable distinctiveness of the Roman Catholic missions among the Indigenous peoples of Upper Canada contributed significantly to his conviction that the public-supported education system must allow for the development of a separate stream of pedagogy overseen by the Roman Catholic clergy. Not surprisingly, Ryerson never lost his interest in Indian education even after he became responsible for Canada West's system of pubic education. Accordingly, in 1847 he wrote a report that became the essential blueprint for the development of the system of government-funded and Christian Indian residential schools.[116]

Indian Country has attracted the attention and enthusiasm of all manner of social engineers who have tried, in the name of civilization, many sorts of crusades and experiments in evangelization and political economy. Ryerson was one of the most ambitious of these social engineers. His career, aimed at drawing civilization from savagery, first through Christian evangelization among Indigenous peoples and then through public education for everyone, embodies a persistent tendency that manifests itself in a variety of ways. This pattern is based on the propensity for large processes of pervasive social change to begin on the Aboriginal frontiers of Western civilization's most active field of expansion and transformation in the Americas. It is this phenomenon that places the historical experiences of Indigenous peoples, especially in North America, seemingly at the forefront of what many other groups may expect in the age of global corporatism. In an earlier era this same pattern made various efforts to transform Aboriginal societies anticipatory of larger schemes to build up the machinery of the social welfare state.

In many instances, influential non-Aboriginals have tested their various theories about the preferred shape and design of "New World" societies in their efforts to transform the identities and cultures of Indigenous peoples. These ventures in social engineering have been situated on the expanding frontiers of Western civilization's geography, imagination, and claims to legal and moral legitimacy.

ECONOMISTS, ANTHROPOLOGISTS, AND REVOLUTIONARIES: STAKING IDEOLOGICAL CLAIMS ON THE IMAGINATIVE FRONTIERS BETWEEN INDIAN COUNTRY AND WESTERN CIVILIZATION

While Indian Country has long been a place one can point to on some maps of the Americas, it can also be perceived as a realm of imagination that has been visited by many writers and thinkers who have played major and minor roles in shaping the intellectual content of Western civilization over hundreds of years. It has been a place whose imagined character has been grist for the artistic and scientific mills of many theorists, philosophers, novelists, playwrights, and poets: What constitutes a state of nature, they have asked, or How is property is to be conceived and apportioned?

Much of this mind travel was absolutely disconnected or only haphazardly connected to any real familiarity with the genuine condition of Indigenous peoples in the Americas. Among those major figures who illustrated some of their fundamental contentions with largely illusory examples of how Indian people live were John Locke, Thomas Hobbes, Jean-Jacques Rousseau, François Voltaire, Frederick Engels, and Karl Marx. For them and for many others whose impressions of Indian Country came almost exclusively from reading, the existence of Indigenous peoples beyond Europe's older spheres of influence and understanding provided a site to conceptualize and construct idealized states of nature. This imagined association of Aboriginal Americans with pure and unaltered nature provided the perceptual place in which to situate and consider fundamental ideas such as freedom, liberty, family, state, superstition, deism, property, or, in the pessimistic mind of Hobbes, the "war of all against all" in a ungoverned realm where life was "nasty, brutish and short."

By referring to commentaries coming in from the New World, these idealized conceptions could be embellished and presented not as abstractions involving a resort to "pre-history" or to some long-gone dawning of humanity, but as reports on current affairs with an aura of scientific authority. They could be presented as descriptions of actual peoples that had been observed and documented in recent or contemporary times. The geographic and ethnographic "discoveries" encountered during the age of European exploration helped stimulate the creation of many new landscapes of literature and ideology based on combinations of fact, fiction, and speculation about the conditions of Indigenous peoples at the outlying edges of the new empires. The literary device of Europeans situating their make-believe realms somewhere across the Atlantic in the New World of their imaginations goes back at least to the first half of the sixteenth century. William Shakespeare set his play *The Tempest* on the edges of America. Similarly, in 1516 Thomas More set his literary rendition of *Utopia* in roughly the same geographic region.[117]

This kind of speculative philosophizing at the edge of Indian Country gradually gave way to more informed commentaries among authors whose accounts were derived largely from first-hand observation – from field work and from library sources. The development of this kind of reporting and analysis was integral to the emergence of the social sciences and, in particular, of the discipline of anthropology. Indeed, it could almost be said that anthropology as a professional field was invented on the intellectual frontiers of Indian Country. Among the more prominent figures in this effort to produce reliable descriptions and interpretations of life among Indigenous peoples in North America were Joseph-François Lafitau, Lewis Henry Morgan, Henry Rowe Schoolcraft, Franz Boas, Frank

Hamilton Cushing, Paul Radin,, Marius Barbeau, Ruth Benedict, Alfred Kroeber, Claude Levi-Strauss, Irving Hallowell, William Fenton, and Sally Weaver.

These major pioneers and contributors to the anthropology of Indian Country tended to stand on a middle ground between those who used fully or partially fictional Native Americans to advance their theories and those who came to identify so closely with the struggles of Indigenous peoples that they eschewed the more dispassionate language of science to advocate the protection of Aboriginal rights. Bartholome de Las Casas, the great bishop of Chiapas, was the most important founder of this tradition of documenting the violent incursions on Indian Country and advocating a regime of repect for the human rights of Indigenous peoples. As he argued in his writings directed at refuting those in Spain who supported the exploitation of Indigenous peoples in the slave trade, the Indians of New Spain must not "be deprived of their freedom or their possession and ownership of their property that nature has granted them for their lawful use and enjoyment."[118] In the famous trail at Valladolid in 1550 and in a stream of publications, Las Casas exposed to public view the crimes against humanity on which New Spain was founded and the sheer insanity of devaluing, destroying, or ignoring the stunning achievements of the Aboriginal civilization of the Americas.[119] Among those who continued in various ways some of the traditions of thought and argument pioneered by Las Casas were Lahontan, John Dunn Hunter, the Reverends Jeremiah Evarts and E.F. Wilson, Helen Hunt Jackson, John Collier, Grey Owl, Thomas Berger, Peter Matthiessen, Ronald Wright, Bruce Clark, Tom Hayden, and Hugh Brody.

Even in the writings of those field workers in Indian Country who tried to situate their work on the ground of science, the pillar of Western civilization's most compelling claims to universalism, there is plenty that cannot be properly understood apart from the subjective perspectives of the observers. Consequently, many of the tenets in the professional anthropology of Indian Country resemble the theological controversies that permeate the literature of the civilizing mission. Missionaries often preoccupied themselves, for instance, with the debate on deism. That debate was concerned with the question of whether the Aboriginal objects of their evangelism had an innate awareness of the divine. Professional anthropologists, however, were more likely to use reportage from Indian Country as currency for other, more secular varieties of argument. These anthropological controversies included elaborate discussions over whether humanity can be arranged along hierarchies of evolutionary development or whether there are basic structures of cognition, belief, and mythology that cut across lines of culture and language.[120]

The point of these comments is not to dismiss or devalue the worth of the extensive literatures created by non-Indian observers and chroniclers of Indian Country, whether inside or outside the tradition of professional anthropology. Without doubt these writings represent a huge repository of insight and data recording both major and minor episodes in the history of the difficult and delicate human endeavour of trying to understand one another better. Often, however, many of the primary sources of non-Indian observation of Indian Country contain hidden codes whose meanings cannot be properly understood without reference to debates and controversies that have little to do with the people being written about and much to do with the self-images and self-doubts of the people doing the writing. Large portions of the extensive literature written in the debate about the identity of Indigenous peoples beyond Europe and what they should become is, in fact, most valuable for what it can tell us about the history of anxiety concerning the character and destiny of Western civilization. In this sense, one of Indian Country's significant attributes is the space it has provided to help pilgrims from within the colonizing societies move across threshholds of territory, law, and imagination to look back at their own people, sometimes triumphantly and sometimes with dismay, disappointment, anger, apprehension, or contempt.

To illustrate the importance of the imaginary Indian Country as a place of intellectual inspiration and contention, it is useful to compare the contrasting approaches to the formulation of property law that can be traced back to the radically different interpretations of Locke and Rousseau. Locke's musings on the imagined relationship between Native Americans and land helped establish the capitalist twist of that variant of Enlightenment thought running through US history. Rousseau's idealization of the imagined communism of Indigenous peoples helped give rise to the communist ideology used to justify the revolutionary overthrow of old regimes in both Russia and China. Engels's *Origin of the Family, Private Property and the State* is one of the great markers in the convergence between the political history and the intellectual history flowing from Rousseau's seminal hostility towards the institution of private property. In writing the book, which he published in 1884, Engels claimed to have relied heavily on the notes of his recently deceased colleague Karl Marx.

Engels's effort to lay out the basic framework for a communist school of social science demonstrated the general pattern of overlap and interaction between the fields of anthropology and political economy. The origins of these two disciplines in intertwined rivulets of Enlightenment inspiration continued for generations, as ethnographic observation formed the basis of much economic theory well into the twentieth century.

The Origin of the Family is a pithy little volume intended to present and interpret the conclusions outlined in a longer work, *Ancient Society*, by pioneer anthropologist Lewis Henry Morgan.[121] Engels's book recognized Morgan's effort to compile a general theory of human evolution as "one of the few epoch-making works of our time." *Ancient Society* according to Engels, has "the same importance for anthropology as Darwin's theory of evolution has for biology and Marx's theory of surplus value has for

political economy."[122] Morgan's work was said to have vindicated many of
Marx's main findings in the explanation it offered of how different societies journied at different rates along a single evolutionary pathway divided into three main levels – savagery, barbarism, and civilization. Engels
claimed that Morgan had identified the convergence of changes that
marked the transition from the higher stages of barbarism to the earlier
stages of civilization.

Central among the markers identified by Morgan was the emergence of
the institution of patriarchal monogamy from older clan systems. These
clans, or "gentes" as Morgan also referred to them, were governed by principles where the paternity of children was uncertain, even as very strong
taboos prohibited sex within the members of these extensive groupings of
familially bonded individuals. According to Morgan and to Engels, the
beginnings of patriarchal monogamy facilitated the evolution of social systems emphasizing ownership of property passed from generation to generation through the father's line. With this innovation came the concept
of individual title to land, the invention of money as "the commodity of
commodities," and the development of economic classes.[123]

The state had developed as a "machine" to facilitate the "holding down
of the oppressed, exploited class" by the ruling class. This relationship was
theorized to have begun with men's oppressive domestication of their
wives in particular and of women in general. As gender exploitation
expanded to class exploitation, the state was said to have been elaborated
as a means of "giving one class practically all the rights and the other class
practically all the duties."[124]

In common with Rousseau, Engels characterized the development of
the institutions of private property as at once an advancement and a
tragedy for the largest number of people oppressed by the complexities of
civilization. "Monogamous marriage," he wrote, "was a great historical step
forward; nevertheless, together with slavery and private wealth, it opens
the period which has lasted until today in which every step forward is also
relatively a step backward, in which prosperity and development for some
is won through misery and frustration for others."[125] Engels repeated this
lament in his conclusion, arguing that "from its first day, sheer greed was
the driving spirit of civilization; wealth and again wealth and once more
wealth, not of society but of the single scurvy individual – here was its one
and final aim."[126]

The author to whom Engels attributed this vindication and extension of
Marxist theory was a successful corporate lawyer in Rochester, New York,
whose formative anthropological field work was done among the Six
Nations Iroquois indigenous to that part of the United States. In 1851
Morgan first published the main findings of his investigative journey into
the elaborate patterns of custom and law linking the matriarchal clan
structures of the Iroquois Confederacy to the intricate complexities of

Longhouse self-governance.[127] Morgan's study constitutes an important element of a complex intellectual history that has made the governing principles embodied in the Six Nations' Longhouse the most deeply studied and celebrated constitution in the Aboriginal world of the Americas. His original text, which is widely claimed by the discipline of anthropology as one of its seminal works, captured broad attention among pioneering social scientists in many countries, including the busy bibliophile Karl Marx.

As revealed by his published notebook compiled between 1880 and 1882, Marx devoted careful attention to the ethnographic studies of Morgan as well as to those of Henry Sumner Maine, John Lubbock (Lord Avebury), and John Budd Phear.[128] In seeking to draw from ethnology general theories of human change, Marx was much immersed in the Victorian project of expanding on Darwin's insights on the laws thought to govern the evolutionary ascent of species from lower to higher forms. Along with Morgan, Edward Tyler, Herbert Spencer, and many others, Marx and Engels embodied the Enlightenment's confidence that all of humanity was ultimately subject to universal laws whose identification was a key to achieving greater and faster feats of progress.

In his conclusion of *The Origins of the Family*, Engels presented a telling passage from *Ancient Society* as the pre-eminent proof that Morgan "had discovered afresh in America the materialist conception of history [originally] discovered by Marx."[129] Morgan's analysis of the place of private property in modern civilization returns to the major themes animating much of the thinking of Rousseau. Along with Morgan, Marx, and Engels, Rousseau shared a vision of progress not as a simple linear ascent to higher and better ways of life but as a cyclical movement in history. This cyclical process, they believed, was destined to lead to the revival of some aspects of the imagined purity and ecological balance of less complex forms of human organization, such as those thought to be manifest in the imagined Indian Country. Morgan declared, for example, that the most oppressive burden from which humanity would have to free itself was the investment of so much human creativity in the institution of individual ownership. The passage that Engels chose to cite concludes with a phrase invoking both the Declaration of the Rights of Man and Morgan's own observations on the genius of Longhouse governance:

Since the advent of civilization, the outgrowth of property has been so immense, its forms so diversified, its uses so expanding and its management so intelligent in the interest of its owners, that it has become, on the part of people, an unmanageable power. The human mind stands bewildered in the presence of its own creation. The time will come, nevertheless, when human intelligence will rise to the mastery over property, and define the relations of the state to the property it protects, as well as the obligations and the limits of the rights of its owners. The interests of society are paramount to individual interests, and the two must be brought into just and harmonious relations. A mere property career is not the final destiny of mankind, if progress is to be the law of the future as it has been of the past ... The dissolution of society bids fair to become the termination of a career of which property is the end and aim; because such a career contains the elements of self-destruction. Democracy in government, brotherhood in society, equality in rights and privileges, and universal education, foreshadow the next higher plane of society to which experience, intelligence and knowledge are steadily tending. It will be a revival, in a higher form, of the liberty, equality and fraternity of the ancient gentes.[130]

While a clear projectory of thought and history links the reflections of Rousseau, Marx, Morgan, and Engels to the communist revolutions of the twentieth century, Locke's literary depictions of Native Americans have broad importance amid the complex of ideas and interests that fused to form the world's other major revolutionary tradition. The formative event in this revolutionary disjuncture – the emergence of the United States from British North America – is also often characterized as the primary threshhold between mercantilistic and capitalistic forms of economic organization.

The publication in 1776 of Adam Smith's *Wealth of Nations* is widely seen as the main text signifying this commercial transition. Locke's *Two Treaties of Government*, however, probably played a more seminal role in providing the formative justifications for that revolutionary projectory through world history that has made capitalism and the American empire the pre-eminent systems of governance and law in the structuring of global economic relations. *Two Treatises* first appeared in England in 1690, around the time that William of Orange left Holland with his wife, Mary, to take possession of the English throne in the culminating act of "the Glorious Revolution." Like *The Wealth of Nations*, *Two Treatises* encapsulated much of the ascendant thinking in its time and place of publication. Both volumes captured the philosophical spirit of the winning side of the respective "cousins' war" with which each was associated.

Locke's commentary on law and governance gave ample justification to the rising fortunes and whiggish ambitions of an emergent middle class in England and in the Anglo-American colonies. This class of tradesmen, merchants, and land owners, whose bastion of political influence in England became the House of Commons, had recently subordinated the monarch to the principle of parliamentary supremacy, even as the recent military conflagrations had reaffirmed the identity of their country as primarily a Protestant Kingdom under a Protestant sovereign.

Locke, like Sir Isaac Newton, whose scientific achievements he greatly admired, became one of the major players in the rise of England as a centre of scholarly industry during the Enlightenment. He combined a strong devotion to Protestant Christianity with an insistence that human reason, coupled to sound logic, must serve as the essential arbiter of truth. In synthesizing the secular and the divine, Locke pointed the way to that paradox that would make the United States at once a profoundly religious and overwhelmingly Protestant country where church and state were technically disconnected. Locke personified that paradoxical synthesis of Reformation zealotry combined with Enlightenment rationality that has characterized the United States from its inception.

In *Two Treatises*, Locke illustrated many of his major theories by making abundant references to the Indigenous peoples Europeans met in their global explorations, but especially to the imagined character of the Aboriginal societies adjacent to England's early colonies in North America. By virtue of his broad responsibilities as secretary to the Earl of Shaftesbury, a Lord Proprietor of Carolina, Locke was one of about six or eight men primarily in charge of shaping England's colonial system in North America during the Restoration.[131] As a result of this work, Locke poured over much of the early literature describing the Indigenous peoples on the other side of the Atlantic. Like Hobbes, Locke pictured Native Americans in a "state of nature," existing outside history at the beginning point of human progress. "In the beginning all the world was *America*," wrote Locke, assigning metaphorically that continent's Aboriginal inhabitants to the status of infants before entering the process of civilizational maturation.[132] His ethnography, therefore, lacks the ironies inherent in the characterizations of Rousseau and his intellectual progeny, who saw principles to emulate as well as practices to transcend in Aboriginal relationships with land, with each other, and with the rest of nature.

Lock's view of progress is rigidly linear rather than cyclical. While Locke uses references to imaginary Native Americans to illustrate those theoretical universals he associates with a state of nature, these imagined Indians are mostly referred to as negative examples whose practices must be left behind in the cause of human progress.

One of Locke's main starting points in *Two Treatises* is that human beings are owners of their own persons and thus the owners of their own labour. Locke then made a great leap. He argued that by virtue of their investment of labour in the shared domain beyond the frontiers of private property, individuals could claim rights of ownership in that part of nature transformed by their work. In illustrating this point, he made one of his most frequently cited observations, describing how he thought Indian hunters in America exercised ownership in the animals they hunted: "This Law of reason makes the Deer, that Indian's who hath killed it: 'tis allowed to be his goods who hath bestowed his labour on it, though before it was the common right of everyone." Locke then compared the relationship between the imagined dead deer and its imagined Indian killer to the process of transforming land into private property. Just as a hunted animal could be transformed into the private possession of its hunter, so could the work of agricultural improvement transform "the wild woods and uncultivated waste of America" into private property. In developing this idea, Locke set up a comparison between what he referred to as "the wild Indian, who knows no Inclosure," with the farming communities of Devonshire in England.[133] Amid passages with frequent references to biblical instructions directing men to "subdue the Earth," to "improve it," and to exercise mastery over her "inferior Creatures," Locke wrote: "For I aske whether in the wild woods and uncultivated waste of America left to Nature, without any improvement, tillage or husbandry, a thousand acres will yield the needy and wretched inhabitants as many conveniences of life as ten acres equally fertile land does in Devonshire where they are well cultivated." Elsewhere Locke argued that "all the profit an Indian received" from one acre of land in America would not be worth "1/1000" of the profits derived from a comparable acre in England.[134]

More than any other single text, Locke's *Two Treatises* set the idea that Native Americans were exclusively hunters who were entirely without their own Aboriginal forms of agriculture. These writings were instrumental in the process that has blocked from the memory of those on the expansionary side of the Columbian conquests clear recognition of the importance of Amerindian horticulture in the genesis of many commercialized crops.

Locke's theories on the relationship between government and property were embraced enthusiastically in the Anglo-American colonies.[135] A major factor in the elevation of *Two Treatises* among the generation of colonists who would revolt from crown authority in the American Revolution was the fact that Locke's justification conformed so well with the experiences, expectations, and interests of those Anglo-American colonists who had derived wealth and prosperity from expanding their settlements westward into Indian Country. Locke's marriage of ethnography to political economy offered a clear rationale for the continuing unilateral expropriation of Indian lands. In addition, he offered the Anglo-American colonists' a philosophical justification to take up arms and to revolt against an imperial regime that seemed, with the Royal Proclamation of 1763, to be preventing them from realizing their providentially ordained manifest destiny to expand and to multiply.

The importance of Locke's ideas in the genesis of the American Revolution will be explored in more detail in chapter 4. For now it can be said that when King George issued his Royal Proclamation in 1763, the imperial government seemed to betray Lockean principles by setting up imperial obstacles to colonial expansion into Indian Country. This severe limitation on the perceived right of the Anglo-Americans to push their settlements unrestrictedly westward was compared to the kinds of monarchical tyranny that Locke's generation and, before it, Cromwell's generation had faced and defeated in the revolutionary genesis of parliamentary supremacy. Clearly Locke's protestantism helped inform his conviction that "the great and *chief end*, therefore, of Mens uniting into Commonwealths, and putting themselves under Government, *is the Preservation of their Property*."[136] The emphasis on private property as society's pre-eminent institution was integral to the Reformation from its inception. This way of organizing the material realm seemed to those who led the early protests against Roman Catholicism an extension of the asserted right of *individuals* to relate to God directly, rather than indirectly through the old priestly hierarchy under the Vatican. As Martin Luther contended, "the possession of private property was an essential difference between men and beasts."[137]

Luther's view that those societies based primarily on communal rather than individualistic orientations to property were something less than human suggests one of several reasons why the Indian frontiers of Protestant New England were so much more violent than those of Roman Catholic New France. Indeed, Locke's parable of Indian life, deer hunting, and the creation of private property may have been extrapolated in the minds of some Anglo-Americans to support the notion that the investment of work involved in hunting and killing Indians made their former lands the rightful possession of the person or persons who had cleared the ground of the Aboriginal people. It should not be surprising, therefore, that the US government reiterated to the United Nations Human Rights Commission as recently as 1987 the doctrine of "conquest" as the basis of the republic's claim to the possession of title and sovereign jurisdiction in large parts of the republic's land base.[138] The Old Testament associations invested in the idea of taking land through the violent vanquishment of its original possessors was emphasized in Congress by Thomas Hart Benton in 1839. In sponsoring a bill that would have granted title in the lands of Florida to individuals who would agree to defend it from the Seminoles, Benton proclaimed, "Armed occupation was the true way of settling a conquered country." He continued, "The children of Israel entered the promised land, with implements of husbandry in one hand, and the weapons of war in the other."[139]

The propensity of many Anglo-American settlers to compare their Aboriginal neighbours to animals has been noted by Richard Drinnon. He wrote that "in times of trouble natives were always [described as] wild animals that had to be rooted out of their dens, swamps and jungles." Not only were they wild animals but they were often "vermin,"[140] a term describing the mammalian equivalent of "weeds." Accordingly, many kinds of pluralism were depleted in the outbursts of work and violence aimed sometimes at rooting out the imagined human "vermin" on the edges of the Anglo-American frontier and sometimes at weeding out biodiversity to make way for the cultivation of commercialized monocultures.

Locke's *Two Treatises* have been among the most influential texts ever written to provide legal or moral justification for the dispossession and genocide of Indigenous peoples. Lockean rationales for the extinguishment of Aboriginal and treaty rights have been used against First Nations not only in North America but in many other parts of the planet as well.[141]

Locke's own preference, however, was to press Indian individuals into systems of private property under the legal authority of colonial governments. To advance this principle, Locke introduced a law for Carolina in 1672 that set aside individual plots for Indian farmers. The Anglo-American colonists, however, refused to respect this legal innovation.[142]

Locke's law for Carolina foreshadowed many other laws whose object was to integrate Native people into individualistic land tenure under non-Aboriginal law. For instance, the application of the Dawes Act in 1887 to Indian reservations in the United States was aimed at privatizing communal forms of land tenure. Similarly, the Canadian government's White Paper on Indian policy in 1969 was aimed at privatizing Indian reserves and making them normal municipalities under the provincial laws of possessive individualism.

This effort to place *The Origins of the Family* and *Two Treatises of Government* in the context of political and intellectual history demonstrates the common roots of political economy and anthropology in the genesis of the social sciences. Moreover, the role of these texts in the world's two most important revolutionary traditions illustrates the ideological significance of the way Indigenous peoples have been represented in literature, but most particularly in depictions of their imagined relationships to land, to other creatures, and to the institution of property, both private and communal. When it comes to picturing the goals and purposes of whole societies, different civilizational complexes have been instrumentally shaped on the imagined frontiers of aboriginality.

On the one hand is the Lockean tradition, justifying capitalist expansion through primal expropriations, displacements, and extinguishments of those Indigenous peoples who fail to conform with the culture of possessive individualism as the primary ingredient of imagined progress. On the other is the tradition leading from Rousseau and to Marx, Morgan, and Engels. That tradition sees the institution of private property as civilization's most prolific source of internal conflicts. These conflicts can only be transcended, it was argued, through a revival in more complex technological and social milieus of the mores imagined to have animated Aboriginal societies, such as those that Morgan identified among the Six Nation Iroquois. The most essential element of the imagined liberty, equality, and fraternity of what Morgan referred to as "the ancient gentes" was their collectivist orientation to land and other forms of property.

The French Revolution sits somewhere on the middle ground between the two revolutionary traditions embodied in the founding of the United States and the Soviet Union. This revolt against the old regime began in 1789 with the Declaration of the Rights of Man; it culminated in the military dictatorship of Napoleon. The concepts articulated by both Lahontan and his eloquent Huron debating partner, Kondiaronk, anticipated many of the most powerful ideas flowing through France's revolutionary era, even as Locke's and Morgan's studies of North American Indians anticipated some of the main tenets of the ideological conflict in the twentieth century between the American and the Soviet empires. Similarly, it would be hard to overestimate the ideological force of the ideas infused into the Enlightenment's heartland by Lahontan and also by Lafitau, Charlevoix, and other agents of French and Roman Catholic imperialism in North America who found much to praise and admire in the Indian Country of Canada.

Clearly the intellectual legacy of this rich record of ethnographic exploration in the New World of Europe's imagination was instrumental in helping to shape the perspectives of many brilliant contemporary critics, but none more so than Jean-Jacques Rousseau. His warning echoes down through the generations about the past and future horrors imposed on humanity by the first "imposter" who carved off a piece of the earth and called it his private property. Rousseau's caution that "you are undone if you forget that the fruits of the earth belong to us all, and the earth itself to nobody" still resonates.

In 1944 in *The Great Transformation*, Karl Polanyi returned to the scholarly tradition that had once linked ethnography and political economy so seamlessly. He argued that the "utopian" elevation of market relations to pre-eminence over all other kinds of social relations represented idiosyncratic preoccupations of particular interests within particular societies, rather than the expression of universal human attributes. Similarly, Polanyi viewed the isolation of parcels of land as a market commodity as "perhaps the wierdest of all undertakings of our ancestors." He wrote: "We might as well imagine man's being born without hands and feet as carrying on his life without land ... it is the site of his habitation; it is the condition of his physical safety; it is the landscape and the seasons." Polanyi maintained that colonization revealed the true significance of this drive "to separate land from man and organize society in such a way as to satisfy the requirements of the real-estate market." In each and every colonial situation where this process is extended to new frontiers, he maintained, "the social and cultural system of native life must be first shattered."[143]

Polanyi was extremely critical of his colleagues in the discipline of economics. He alleged that they had cut themselves off from their field's own intellectual history when this heritage threatened their own utopian preoccupations. The growing sophistication of anthropology in the twentieth century, he argued, disproved many of the old theories built on the premise that the literature of exploration showed that all human beings were motivated by similar economic instincts, irrespective of their cultural socialization. According to Polanyi, when the evidence would no longer support the view that market relations were based on universal human attributes rather than on specific historical phenomena, the economists simply neglected to acknowledge the evidence that undermined their most cherished biases. He detailed this accusation as follows:

The same bias which made Adam Smith's generation view primeval man as bent on barter and truck induced their successors to disavow all interest in early man, as he was now known *not* to have indulged in those laudible passions. The tradition of the classical economists, who attempted to base the law of the market on the alleged propensities of man in a state of nature, was replaced by the abandonment of all interest in the cultures of "uncivilized" man as irrelevant to an understanding of the problems of our age.[144]

In the decades that followed, the guild of professional economists, with some few exceptions, continued to cut themselves off from the other social sciences and from the intellectual heritage of their own discipline. In draping their analysis of the human condition in the mystique of the most essentialist and discredited aspects of Enlightenment universalism, many practitioners of the "dismal science" continued down the dinosaur's path of overspecialization. They seemed caught in a time warp, as their most prominent members elevated a narrow view of materialism to the doctrinal stature of divine revelation. The dogmatism of this intellectual vision was especially marked among the neo-liberal proponents of the New Right. In his musing on what he calls "post-liberalism," for instance, English political philosopher John Gray noted that this class of theorists "failed to grasp the historical and cultural presuppositions and limits of the civil society they seek to maintain, restore or enhance." Hence, in their preoccupation "with securing the legal and economic conditions of market competition ... [they] only rarely and inadequately addressed the cultural conditions that undergird and sustain a stable market order."[145]

While the return to simplified and stylized versions of classic, mid-nineteenth century economic liberalism was most pronounced among the ideological shock troops of the New Right, the largest part of the whole economic profession failed to heed Polanyi's warning. Rather, they withdrew yet further into the fantasy world of unsullied quantification of human interactions with their physical and social environments, as if the ecological complexities of cultural pluralism and biodiversity could be relegated to insignificance outside the framework of the pre-eminent, universalist claims implied in endless variations on the study of relationships between product supply and customer demand. The overwhelming tendency of professional economists since the writing of *The Great Transformation* has been to attach themselves even more uniformly to a rigid adherence to the secular religion of materialism and ownership as the highest expression of individualism. While claiming the secularizing heritage of the Enlightenment as justification for their preoccupation with markets, as if these media for the negotiation of power were expressions of natural law, neo-liberalism's proponents tended concurrently to advance their pet profession's free-trade certitudes with all the monotheistic certainty of Counter Reformation clerics.

The high priests of privatization, downloading, deregulation, and further extinguishment and commodification of the global commons, therefore, seemed religiously convinced of the heretical nature of any competing visions. As the Reagan-Thatcher years elevated neo-liberalism almost to the status of holy revelation in government and business, professional economists became increasingly dogmatic in their certainties about how property relations should be structured. There was less and less willingness to tolerate, let alone encourage, diversified conceptions and constructions of property law in order to serve the healthy, pluralistic renewal of all peoples and all species who must share our small planet.[146]

As governments and large corporations increasingly employed economists as propagandists and apologists for their neo-liberal platforms, the discipline's academic practitioners tended to shy away from any systematic reckoning with the rich findings emanating from the exercises in self-reflection undertaken especially in anthropology, but also in many other precincts of the social sciences. The reaction to the intellectual isolationism of too many professional economists in the academy might be compared to that of kin when a family member falls prey to Alzheimer's disease. "In the twentieth century," exclaimed sociologist Patricia Marchak in her pioneering study of the restructuring of nation-states to serve global markets, "the science of economics has lost all sense of reality."[147]

THE CULTURES OF ENFORCED DEPENDENCY AND THE RHETORIC OF SELF-SUFFICIENCY

In the decades following the Second World War, the protagonists engaged in the Cold War through a number of venues, including bitter ideological contention between the American and the Soviet empires. Much of this acrimony centred on arguments attempting to explain the "underdevelopment" in the Third World. Were less-industrialized countries simply slower-moving travellers along an evolutionary course of upward economic progress or was their subordinate position the result of an enforced dependency serving the interests of distant metropolitan centres? Among the terms used to explain theories of forced subordination in the world's economic hierarchy were the "development of underdevelopment," the "structure of dependence," "unequal exchange," and "global apartheid."[148]

The experience since 1492 of Indian Country specifically, or of Indigenous peoples more generally, presents a classic panorama of variations on a consistent theme of imposed and resisted dependency. The history of European trade with First Nations in North America, for instance, reveals a consistent pattern aimed sometimes successfully, sometimes not, at creating dependencies among Indigenous peoples on the specific goods and products they received. A classic example of such dependence was for agents of European empires to supply Aboriginal individuals and groups with specific types of guns in the expectation that they would be forced to return to representatives of the same imperial system for replacement parts. Once Aboriginal groups and individuals were ensnared within the technological net of a particular regime of colonial power, they became vulnerable to widening ranges of dependence as their arts and sciences of production gave way to a growing range of imported goods in what Emmanuel Wallerstein has identified as "the modern world-system."

The large-scale distribution of "presents" by imperial agencies seeking strategic advantages from Indigenous peoples, especially in periods when the First Nations held the balance of power in military contests between European or Euro-American rivals, became another essential strategy in efforts to stimulate and encourage cultures of dependency on the frontiers of empire. This practice continued in North America until well into the nineteenth century, though it reached its pinnacle in the era of the Seven Years' War, the American Revolution, and the War of 1812.[149] Some might see a clear connection between this earlier phase of efforts to Europeanize Indian Country and the culture of welfare and social assistance that presently determines many aspects of the family and community life of up to 80 per cent of the residents of many reserves and reservations in Canada and the United States.

The theme of enforced dependencies merges with the theme of ecocide in those many instances where environmental degradation was purposely advanced or inadvertently perpetrated, with the outcome of denying Indigenous peoples their traditional means of economic self-sufficiency and political independence. The officially sanctioned plundering of the great buffalo herds is the superlative demonstration of purposeful ecocide as a deliberate means to bring about forced dependency and to realize the necessary preconditions for confining Indigenous peoples within the tight physical and jurisdictional enclaves of reserves and reservations.[150]

In *The Roots of Dependence,* Richard White looked at the history of Choctaw, Pawnee, and Navajo strategies to resist losing their autonomy through the incursions of an alien market system. For generations, White shows, these peoples' exchanges of goods with other Indian groups, with Europeans, and with Euro-Americans often retained elements of traditional gift exchanges. White was very specific about the two most potent influences that ultimately undermined Aboriginal efforts to resist incorporation into a system of economic and political relations they knew would cripple their capacity for self-determination: credit and alcohol. He wrote,

Liquor created exactly the insatiable demand the traders sought while loosening cultural restraints against overhunting. Credit put the Indians quickly into debt, and furthered the traders' control. When given full rein, the credit-liquor combination could lead to rapid overhunting, the loss of wild-food supplies, the institution of market economy, the growth of market relations inside the society, eventual turmoil, and complete dependence on Europeans and Americans.[151]

An eloquent commentary on the means and implications of the cultivation of dependencies in Indian Country is found in Anna Jameson's
narrative of her travels in the Great Lakes of North America in 1837. In
Winter Studies and Summer Rambles in Canada, this adventurous women
includes an account of her visit to the present-giving ceremonies at Manitowaning on Manitoulin Island. She stopped at this place together with
many of the citizens of what remained of Tecumseh's old Indian Confederacy. One of the motivations of the several thousand Native people who
camped there was to receive their annual tribute of "presents" – a sort of
Aboriginal-style military pension – from representatives of the British
crown. In that era many Aboriginal participants in these major gatherings
still moved relatively freely throughout their ancestral domain on both
sides of the Great Lakes and in the northern reaches of the Mississippi
Valley. Those Aboriginal groups, however, whose principal residences
were on the US side of the international boundary were under growing
pressure either to migrate permanently to Canada or to withdraw to the
area of present-day Oklahoma, as dictated by the Indian removal policies
of President Andrew Jackson.

Jameson's observations are a typical blend of remarks describing both
the manners and appearances of the Indians she met together with her
own reflections on the comparative attributes of her own people. She
begins by explaining her unease with the culture of dependency she saw
before her. "For the natural progress of arts and civilization springing from
within" her Aboriginal hosts, writes Jameson, "and from their own intelligence and resources, we have substituted a sort of civilization from without, foreign to their habits, manners, organization." She elaborates, "I
have seen dresses of mountain sheep and young buffalo skins, richly
embroidered, and almost equal in beauty and softness to a Cashmere
shawl." After listing other similar objects, she continues, "It is reasonable
to presume that as these manufactures must have progressively improved,
there might have been farther progression, had we not substituted for articles they could procure or fabricate, those which we fabricate; we have
taken work out of their hands, and all motive to work, while we have created wants they cannot supply." Thus, writes Jameson, "We have clothed
them in blankets – we have not taught them to weave blankets. We have
substituted guns for bows and arrows – but they cannot make guns." The
outcome is "we are making paupers of them, and this by a kind of terrible
necessity."[152]

In this fashion, Jameson's account of the displacement of a civilization
from within by a civilization from without anticipated many major features
of the culture of dependency facing most human societies currently on the
planet. This pattern emerges from the drive of transnational companies
and their local agencies to transform marketing and manufacturing in
ways that render all sorts of traditions of indigenous invention, productivity, and distribution unworkable in the context of "one big market" and a

single, standardized regime of property law. Of all the economic transformations connected with the ongoing Columbian conquests, it is this dynamic of change that lies at the core of most conceptions and definitions of globalization.

Jameson then turned her attention to the condition and the role of women in those Algonkian-speaking societies with which she was most familiar. She addressed the broadly held opinion in Britain at that time that Aboriginal women were treated poorly by Aboriginal men because of the amount of heavy labour seemingly expected of them by their families and communities. Her comments made an effective critique of the relationship between gender and class among her own people.

When we speak of the *drudgery* of the women we must note the equal division of labour; there is no class of women privileged to sit still while others work. Every squaw makes the clothing, mats, moccasins, and boils the kettle for her own family. Compare her life with the refined leisure of an elegant woman of the higher classes of our society, and it is wretched and abject; but compare her life with that of a servant-maid of all work, or a factory girl – I do say that the condition of the squaw is gracious in comparison, dignified by domestic feelings, and by equality with all around her. If women are to be exempted from toil in reverence to the sex, and as *women*, I can understand this, though I think it unreasonable; but if it be merely a privilege of station, and confined to a certain set, while the great primeval penalty is doubled on the rest, then I do not see where is the great gallantry and consistency of this our Christendom, nor what right we have to look down upon the barbarism of the Indian savages who make *drudges* of their women.[153]

In eschewing the language of the Christian "civilizing" mission, Jameson was a rare voice of conscience for her time, place, and social class.

The discussion of extending civilization to "savages" or "heathens" to "emancipate many minds from their littleness"[154] served many purposes. For instance, it advertised in Europe or Euro–North America the aims and objectives of westward expansionism. While in the United States the publicized heroes of western colonization were often military figures, including Colonel Christopher "Kit" Carson, General William Tecumseh Sherman, and General George Crook, in the British Empire and in British North America especially the advertised leaders of the expansion of Western civilization were often missionaries.

In *Vanguards of Canada* the Reverend John Maclean illustrated the close connection between the publicization of Christian evangelization in Indian Country and the promotion of westward emigration. Maclean was part of a large contingent of Methodist missionaries employed by the Canadian Conference of the Weslayan Methodist Church. In 1853 the British Wesleyans passed over to their Canadian branch responsibility for the Indian missions throughout the domain of the Hudson's Bay Company.[155] This transfer of ecclesiastical authority was a clear prelude to the transfer to the

Dominion of Canada of civil jurisdiction over Rupert's Land and the North-West Territories a decade and a half later. When *Vanguards* appeared in 1918, it was one volume among a large stream of similar texts generated from the busy missionary presses to celebrate what had been achieved by those evangelical men and women who had prepared "the West" for an influx of non-Indian settlers and for an English-speaking and Protestant variety of Canadian civilization.

After devoting separate hagiographies to the Reverends Peter Jones, John Sunday, James Evans, Henry Steinhauer, and George and John McDougall as the first among his would-be saints of Protestant expansion into Indian Country, Maclean lays out a map with the clear intention of promoting emigration to western Canada. On this map he superimposes the "journies of the vanguards" on markers illustrating the location of Canada's natural resources – livestock, oil, and gas in Alberta; iron, coal, wheat, and mixed farming in Saskatchewan and Manitoba; and minerals, lumber, and farming in Ontario. At the corner of the map an advertisement reads: "Lantern and Lantern Slides for Sale or Rent. TRAVEL with the vanguards, STUDY with beautiful pictures of Canada's resources and scenic beauty, SEE our mission fields throughout the Dominion. Send for a catalogue. Methodist Mission Room. Toronto."[156] Elsewhere, Maclean elaborated his view of Protestant missionaries as part of "the standing army of the Dominion" and the groundbreakers of a uniquely Canadian variety of civilization. "The work of educated and pious men," he detailed, "prepares new districts for the advent of the settler, and the grand heritage that God has given us is made accessible for the enterprising poor who seek their fortunes in the west." He concluded: "It pays to send the Gospel to the Indians, and to maintain our work among the aborigines of *our own land.*"[157]

Almost invariably the switchover from the era of trade and warfare in Indian Country to the era of reserves and "civilization" involved a great deal of rhetoric about how to break the dependencies of Indigenous peoples on outside support and on ways to generate economic self-sufficiency. Ironically, the proposals for generating self-sufficiency among Indian people were based almost invariably on the idea of integrating them more deeply into those systems of market relations that had been instrumental in their earlier loss of autonomy. Moreover, the administrators and proponents of these "civilizing" policies held out the prospect that the outcome of their activities would be to make themselves redundant and thus rid the government of the expense of governing Indigenous peoples. This rationale lives on to this day in official justifications for programs of Aboriginal "self-governance" in virtually all countries where Indigenous peoples form a small, marginalized component of larger national entities.

In nearly every case, the tension between the older traditions of generating dependencies and the newer ideals of generating self-sufficiency have been resolved in favour of the former. This outcome is consistent with the fact that the First Nations, if they were to achieve real economic self-determination and political liberation in their ancestral lands, would challenge the stability of all sorts of hierarchies of wealth and power at their very base.

ABORIGINAL VOICES IN THE ARTICULATED IRONIES OF THE CIVILIZING MISSION IN INDIAN COUNTRY

Aboriginal authors contributed a number of works to the body of writings and publications devoted to promoting, chronicling, or criticizing the expansion of Western civilization into Indian Country. Much of this Aboriginal literature had a decidedly Christian twist until well after the Second World War. Among the Aboriginal evangelists of Indian Country were a particularly vibrant group to emerge from the Methodist Indian missions of Upper Canada. The leader of this group was Kahkewaquonaby, or the Reverend Peter Jones, who wrote a history of his own Ojibway people.[158] Also prominent among these Aboriginal evangelists were the Reverends John Sunday, Peter Jacobs, George Copway, and George Henry. Copway left the church in the 1840s and entered the lecture circuit in the United States under the patronage of Francis Parkman, James Fenimore Cooper, Washington Irving, Lewis Henry Morgan, and others.[159] Meanwhile, George Henry also broke from his missionary background to join George Catlin's troupe of performing Indians.[160]

In Minnesota in 1852–53 William Warren wrote an extremely rich narrative based primarily on the oral histories of his mother's people. He attempted to resolve his great admiration for the elaborate teachings of the Midewiwin Society, the primary keepers of much of the Aboriginal religious philosophy of the Anishnabek people of the Great Lakes area, with his own Christian convictions. He sought to achieve this feat by arguing for a common Jewish source for both the Christian and the Midewiwin heritages. Warren's manuscript, *History of the Ojibway People,* was not published until 1885, over three decades after his death.[161] Another Aboriginal proponent of the Asian origins of Native American society was Francis Assiginack, who contributed three scholarly papers to the newly created Canadian Institute in the 1850s.[162] Assiginack's work was calculated to take advantage of the opportunity developing for a few Aboriginal practitioners within the emerging disciplines of anthropology and ethnography. Among the other early pioneers from Indian Country to move into the field of professional anthropology were John Brinton Hewitt, a Tuscorora man, and Francis La Flesche, an Omaha man. They began their careers as interpreters and field assistants. From there, in the 1880s, they joined the regular staff of the Smithsonian Institution's newly formed Ethnology Bureau.[163]

There is growing recognition that the key informants of most major Euro–North American anthropologists should be acknowledged as scholars and literary collaborators in their own right. Prominent among this group was Ely S. Parker, the Seneca military figure and future commissioner of the US Indian Bureau who worked closely in his younger years with Lewis Henry Morgan in developing the text of what became the classic *League of the Ho-de-no-sau-nee.*[164] In Kwakiutl Country on the west coast of British Columbia, George Hunt and Henry Tate were the key figures in opening up to Franz Boas many facets of life in a small group of Indian communities that has attracted huge anthropological interest over the years.[165]

In the years before the First World War, Pauline Johnson, an aristocratic Mohawk woman from the Six Nations reserve in southern Ontario, travelled widely in the transatlantic world as a poet whose modest celebrity was based largely on her dramatic readings while dressed in her traditional garb. In her literary performances, Johnson played on a number of themes drawn from her heritage in the Six Nations, a group whose history is intertwined with the genesis of both the British and the American empires. By combining many of the classic motifs of noble savagery with broader appeals to nationalistic progress, Johnson was able, in an era when imperialism was draped in a readily exploitable mystique, to attract the patronage of her Victorian admirers.[166]

The twentieth century saw the emergence of a number of prolific activists in Indian Country, including Carlos Montezuma, Andy Paull, the Reverend Peter Kelly, Alice Lee Jemison, Vine Deloria Jr, and Harold Cardinal. Their work is explored in more detail in next chapter 3, which is centred around the philosophical contributions of George Manuel in his classic text *The Fourth World.* The literary creativity associated with the Fourth World movement and the American Indian Movement was carried on in Canada in more recent times by a newer group of Aboriginal writers. Their fiction, short stories, histories, and autobiographies both reflected and announced the emergence in a fresh form of many of the old themes of the struggle to defend and even expand the frontiers of the Indian Country of Canada. For the most part this new generation, including Maria Campbell, Howard Adams, Jeanette Armstrong, George Kenny, Tomson Highway, Troy Twigg, and Beth Brant, threw off the Christian or anthropological approaches of their literary predecessors to develop their own unique approaches, genres, and voices.

A major impetus in the search for new terminologies to explain and transform the relationships of Indigenous peoples with others in Canada was the emergence of "the constitution" in the 1980s and the early 1990s as the symbolic core of Canadian politics. Accordingly, the effort to transform Canada's supreme law in light of the disappearance of the British Empire created the political context within which the old Indian Country rose like a phoenix to challenge the imagination of the civilization of northern North America. The task of moving beyond the imperial structures of British North America to articulate a domestic, made-in-Canada

legal definition for Canadian nationhood created the basis for the emergence of a new kind of ideological frontier separating the perspectives of
those who looked to the land as part of a New World and those of more
conservative orientation.

IMAGINING CANADIAN CIVILIZATION: INDIGENOUS PEOPLES AND THE MAKING OF CONSTITUTIONAL LAW

Many Native people who found themselves caught squarely between New
World and Old World orientations to history held up the Royal Proclamation and their treaties with the British sovereign as a protection against the
most recent attempt to widen the American empire through further extinguishment of crown recognition of their legal status as the First Nations of
Canada. As a result, Aboriginal leaders were drawn into a new kind of
treaty making with federal and provincial officials. The process began with
Aboriginal efforts to prevent the British government from delegating further constitutional powers to non-Aboriginal governments in Canada without First Nations' consent. Between 1979 and 1982, therefore, Indigenous
peoples sent delegations of elders, chiefs, and support personnel to Great
Britain to explain their opposition to patriation of the Canadian Constitution.[167]

The Canadian government intervened to prevent Aboriginal leaders
from gaining a direct audience with Queen Elizabeth II. Canadian officials, however, could not prevent the Indian lobby in London from attracting considerable sympathetic attention in the media, in parliament, and
among the British judiciary. Consequently, when the Canada Act was finally debated at Westminster, fully twenty-seven of the thirty hours of discussion in the British House of Commons were devoted to the question of
how patriation would affect the legal and political position of Indigenous
peoples.[168]

The fears that drove the First Nations delegations to Great Britain were
substantially realized several years later when Canada's eleven first ministers met in private at a government retreat on the shores of Meech Lake,
just to the north of Ottawa. In 1987 the premiers of Canada's ten provincial governments, together with Prime Minister Brian Mulroney, produced
a political accord designed to amend the Canadian Constitution in several significant ways. The Meech Lake accord would have entrenched a definition of Canada's "fundamental characteristic" that was mute on the existence of Indigenous peoples and unresponsive to the exercise of
Aboriginal and treaty rights as a living dynamic in the negotiation and
implementation of Canadian federalism.[169] Aboriginal frustration with the
process and content of the Meech Lake accord was compounded because
of the previous experience of their own representatives as non-voting participants in constitutional discussions. Largely as a result of their high-pro-

file, international resistance in Great Britain and elsewhere to patriation, "Aboriginal matters" were marked as the first item on the post-patriation constitutional agenda of Canada's first ministers.[170]

Between 1983 and 1987 four constitutional conferences took place in Ottawa where leaders of four Aboriginal organizations sat across the table from leaders of Canada's federal, provincial, and territorial governments. All these two-day meetings were televised live, in their entirety, on the full network of the Canadian Broadcasting Corporation. In format, method, and subject matter, these gatherings were unprecedented in the history of the Americas. Never before had the nature of the relationship between Indigenous peoples and an American nation-state been given such high-level, sustained political attention at such a seminal moment of national reconceptualization. The central idea to emerge from these conferences was the need for new institutional arrangements to allow Aboriginal communities wider jurisdictional latitude to pursue their own self-government. Only thus could the colonizing, extinguishing momentum of federal Indian policy be reversed. Only thus could the broader meaning of "existing Aboriginal and treaty rights" be practically and meaningfully realized.

As the process unfolded, Aboriginal leaders lectured the Canadian first ministers, the national television audience, and their own peoples on the need to construct a basic institutional infrastructure of Aboriginal self-governance. The basic rationale for constructing these institutions would be to preserve and promote the distinct character of Indigenous cultures in fields as diverse as education, health care, social services, and economic development.[171] It soon became clear that most of the provincial delegations had no real interest in opening jurisdictional space within Canadian federalism to include a permanent and clearly defined jurisdictional compartment for the exercise of Aboriginal self-government. Indeed, the western premiers in particular demonstrated that their primary concern was to protect the ability of their own governments to maintain their lucrative monopolies over the exploitation of natural resources within provincial boundaries. With these concerns at the forefront of their negotiating strategies, most of the premiers baulked at any proposal to define Aboriginal and treaty rights in ways that even hinted at the ability of Indigenous peoples to retain and exercise a continuing, unextinguishable Aboriginal interest in their ancestral lands.

The four-year process of constitutional conferences on Aboriginal matters came to an end without a constitutional amendment on Aboriginal self-determination. Canada's failure to take advantage of this unique opportunity to begin the post-patriation reinvention of the country with a bold, unambiguous embrace of Aboriginal and treaty rights prepared the ground for a looming constitutional crisis. There were ominous signs of deep and fundamental disagreements about the nature and purpose of Canadian self-government in the first ministers' inability to recognize

Aboriginal self-government as a foundational aspect of Canadian democracy.

The fifth constitutional conference in post-patriation Canada took place at Meech Lake. This meeting grew out of the earlier exclusion of the government of Quebec from the process that led to patriation. To gain the Quebec government's sanction for Canada's new legal structure, the first ministers agreed to amend the Canadian Constitution to recognize Quebec as a "distinct society." Moreover, they agreed to recognize that the National Assembly of Quebec should have legislative powers to preserve and promote the distinct identity of the only major jurisdiction on the continent where the primary language of communication is French.

To many thoughtful observers, the first ministers' overnight recognition of Quebec's special cultural imperatives seemed to scream of a glaring double standard. The people and government of Quebec, it appeared, were being extended precisely the kind of recognition that First Nations had been repeatedly denied over a four-year process of public consultations. Indeed, one could almost see the closed bargaining session at Meech Lake as a cynical appropriation of the best ideas to emerge from the unsuccessful conferences on Aboriginal matters.

These were some of the factors that created the symbolic terrain for the eventual demise of the Meech Lake accord, first in the public opinion of English-speaking Canada and then in the legislative process of constitutional amendment. Indeed, the Aboriginal rejection of the Meech Lake accord grew into a full-fledged opposition movement that culminated in 1990 with the accord's final death ritual on the floor of the Manitoba legislature. A key figure in this popular movement to claim the Canadian Constitution as the democratic domain of peoples rather than as the exclusive monopoly of governments was Elijah Harper, a soft-spoken Oji-Cree parliamentarian who represented a largely Aboriginal riding in northern Manitoba.[172]

The huge wave of support for Harper's legendary "no" to the Meech Lake process was instrumental in the decision to include four Aboriginal delegations in the subsequent round of constitutional negotiations. This next process led to the elaboration of yet another proposal for sweeping constitutional change, a proposal that included some truly historic innovations to make room for Aboriginal peoples as distinct constituencies with an inherent right to their own self-government within the framework of Canadian democracy.[173]

The outcome of this third political process was presented in 1992 to the Canadian people for their approval or disapproval in a national referendum. Their rejection of the proposal, known generally as the Charlottetown accord, brought to an end one of the most creative, yet frustrating and ultimately unfulfilled, periods of geopolitical experimentation in the history of Canadian statecraft.[174] The failure to make viable constitutional compromises in the Aboriginal process, in both the Meech Lake and the

Charlottetown processes, had many serious implications. These interrelated failures effectively shut down the immediate possibility of using the instrument of constitutional amendment to bring the nation-state of Canada into closer conformity with the changing configurations of international and domestic forces it faces. Prominent among these forces was the rising tide of support for motifs of statecraft consistent with the ideals of the Fourth World. Pushing against this Fourth World tide were commercial pressures to further accommodate neo-liberal models of globalization.

The Liberal government of Prime Minister Jean Chrétien seemed to confirm the federal abandonment of constitutional amendment as an instrument of Canadian statecraft in 1995, when it extended further veto powers to the provincial governments in Canada. As one former premier quipped, "the Constitution is in a crystal cave, and it won't emerge for 500 years."[175] By effectively sabotaging the machinery of constitutional amendment, the Canadian government may have advanced the day when the only available means of elaborating the Canadian Constitution will be through the formulation of a national treaty. The makers of such a treaty would not be governments but a grand council composed of representatives of those peoples deemed most essential to the fundamental character of Canada.

Obviously First Nations, the only constituencies to be identified in Canada's supreme law as "peoples," would have to play a prominent and symbolically foundational role among these constituencies. The authority to elaborate the Canadian Constitution through a process of treaty making could be derived from various provisions in section 35 of the Constitution Act, 1982. These provisions, which remain suggestively vague on issues of representation and process, afford constitutional status and protection to future treaties as well as to past treaties with Aboriginal peoples.

The prospect of reconstituting Canada through some sort of process of treaty federalism may be attractive to those in Quebec who seek to escape the straight-jacket of provincehood in order to restore a more national character to the French-speaking heartland of North America.[176] As Jean Morisset has engagingly argued, there is a fundamental connection rooted deeply in history which necessarily links the North American destinies of Aboriginal peoples and the French-speaking descendants of the original *canadiens*.

The often paradoxical synergy linking these issues was dramatically exposed in 1990, when the Aboriginal resistance to the Meech Lake accord in Louis Riel's province led with a brutal yet poetic historical logic to the armed confrontation at Oka between Mohawk Warriors and the assault team of the Quebec provincial police.[177] The ensuing anti-Indian vigilantiism in the greater Montreal area manifested in visceral, physical terms the harsh tensions between nationalist movements that share much in common and yet whose different orientations to sovereignty are pointed antagonistically on a collision course.

CONVERGING SOVEREIGNTIES:
FIRST NATIONS, QUEBEC, AND CANADA IN THE CHANGING
GEOPOLITICAL MAP OF THE AMERICAS

The hostile convergence between the competing geopolitical visions of
First Nations patriots and Québécois nationalists is nowhere so clear as in
the legal, political, and propaganda battle over the future of the James Bay
watershed in Quebec. For the indigenous Cree of the region, their land is
Eeyou Estchee, a beautiful and bountiful hunting ground whose destiny as
an Indian Country lies within Canada. For the government of Quebec, the
James Bay watershed is a rich source of hydroelectricity whose harnessing,
export, and domestic exploitation are crucial to building up the technocratic and economic viability of the Quebec state, whether inside or outside Canada.[178]

There are haunting echoes of the old French and Indian War in the
prospect of further violent confrontations over disputed Aboriginal territories in Quebec. A key Anglo-American strategy in the old French and
Indian War had been to neutralize and diplomatically break the alliance of
Aboriginal peoples and the *canadien* which had been a primary geopolitical bastion of New France. The British conquest of Canada in 1759 led in
rapid succession to the Royal Proclamation of 1763 and the Quebec Act of
1774. Both these constitutional transformations, in turn, compounded
fundamental disagreements over the legal status of the Indian Country to
the rear of the Anglo-American settlements. That disagreement was instrumental in the genesis of the civil war in British North America that developed into the American Revolution.[179]

Might conflicts over different visions of how to partition Canada after the
secession of Quebec lead to a similar chain of rapid-fire changes in the way
North America is governed? The possibility of a different kind of French
and Indian War in an imprecisely partitioned Canada raised a number of
old issues whose fundamental importance first became clear during the
eighteenth century when the borders of the Indian Country of North American were repeatedly redrawn in the diplomatic salons of Europe.

Given the pivotal power of the American government in the event of an
outbreak of hostilities in Canada, strategic thinkers in the United States
would be under particular pressure to confront some of the most central
questions that arose in the early genesis of their own country.[180] Would the
US government see in a Quebec declaration of independence a reflection
of the United States's own history in the American Revolution or of the
secessionist states in the American Civil War? Would Québécois colonization of the Indian and Inuit Country in the arctic watershed north of the
St Lawrence Valley be interpreted as a violation of the territorial rights of
Indigenous peoples or as a continuation of the same process of frontier
expansion that was essential in creating and sustaining a sense of confident
manifest destiny in the United States?

The circumstances of the British crown's original assertion of sovereignty over Canada established some of the most fundamental legal distinctions that would have to be revisited in North America in the event that the government of Quebec declared independence. The British extended crown law to the Indian Country of Canada through the military defeat of French imperialism as well as through the making of treaties of friendship and alliance with First Nations in the Great Lakes–Ohio Valley area.[181] While the British imperial government briefly deviated from this courting of Indian favour, the militant stance taken by Pontiac and the Indian Confederacy impressed on the crown the importance of cultivating good relations with the First Nations in North America's interior.[182] An outcome of this history is that Indigenous peoples in Canada tend to perceive sovereignty as an essence they have retained rather than a goal to be achieved through a referendum or a similar demonstration of political will.

Where many Québécois nationalists seek to overcome the legacy of conquest by striving to achieve international recognition of Quebec's sovereignty, First Nations in Canada tend to see themselves as undefeated peoples whose primary basis of official relations with the Canadian state is through treaties and other instruments of sovereign alliance with the crown. In this Aboriginal view, what is lacking is not First Nations' sovereignty but practical recognition by non-Aboriginal officialdom of the unextinguished, living character of their existing Aboriginal and treaty rights.[183] The struggle of the Aboriginal leadership to gain recognition of their rights and international status tends to translate into a political struggle to enter the inner sanctum of power and decision making at the core of Canadian federalism. Hence the essential dynamic of this First Nations movement is to enter the process of building and designing Canada, albeit as distinct, autonomous constituencies with a permanent and unextinguishable Aboriginal title to the country. This quest for recognition and inclusion leads in precisely the opposite direction from the drive of those whose basic political motivation is to partition the Canadian state and to withdraw Quebec from the Canadian federation.

The effort to partriate and then elaborate the constitution of Canada at the end of the twentieth century revealed much about the awkward relationship of the country's founding groups – French Canadians and Indigenous peoples – to the federal state. The fact that the only provincial government excluded from the patriation agreement was Quebec's clarified that Quebec is not a province like the nine others in Canada. It clarified that Quebec's unique culture is accompanied by a unique legal and political personality outside the framework of the relationships put in place by the authors of The Constitution Act, 1982. The repeated failure to integrate the Quebec government into the patriated Canadian Constitution opened much political ground for those nationalists who sought to reconstitute their province as a sovereign, independent country in North America. The political uncertainty created by the formidable movement for an independent Quebec, whether in government or in opposition, is certain to continue generating the kind of fundamental instability in Canada that has prevented the national downgrading of Aboriginal issues.

The continuing high profile of Aboriginal issues in Canada has been maintained to a significant extent because of the nature of the issues raised by the Quebec sovereignty movement. This reality was highlighted by a contrast with the virtual invisibility on the national stage after the 1970s of fundamental issues pertaining to the legal and political status of Indigenous peoples in the United States. That marginalization of Indian Country outside the main venues of national political life in the United States came about along with the creation of the culture of casinos. Another factor in creating this black hole of national invisibility was the devastating impact of the US government's secret war of dirty tricks on the more militant wing of the First Nations sovereignty movement. The American Indian Movement was the group most systematically targeted in a secret campaign of disinformation and assassination that easily qualifies as state terrorism conducted within the United States.

The relationship of Indigenous peoples to the process of attempted constitutional amendment in Canada has clarified much about the ambivalent position of First Nations *vis-à-vis* the laws and politics of the federation in the northern dominion. In two of three rounds of attempted constitutional amendment since 1982, Aboriginal organizations have been given seats at the first ministers' negotiating table. Aboriginal representatives, however, have sat in these chairs essentially as consultants rather than as voting delegates in the process of changing the constitution. Their non-voting status in the deliberations demonstrates the formal exclusion of First Nations from the inner circle of Canadian Confederation. The constitutional amending formula as formalized in 1982 gives parliament and provincial legislatures a virtual monopoly over the process of changing Canada's highest law. First Nations have no formal say as distinct constituencies when it comes to determining the very architecture of Canadian self-governance.

The disenfranchised status of First Nations in the central voting structure of the Canadian federation was especially apparent between 1983 and 1987. Even though Aboriginal and treaty rights were the subject of the constitutional deliberations, the final decision on the definition of these rights lay entirely with the uniformly Euro-Canadian first ministers and with their legislatures; alternatively, it lay not at all with the Aboriginal politicians at the other end of the table. Hence, the apparent equality implied in the seating arrangement was misleading. Indigenous peoples were still being treated essentially as objects to be governed rather than as human beings with an inherent democratic right to a collective say in their own self-governance as citizens with a dual attachment to the First Nations and to Canada.

The presence of Aboriginal organizations at the first ministers' negotiating table raised a number of questions about the formal legal and political status of these delegations. Where these four Aboriginal organizations, including the Assembly of First Nations, provisional governments-in-waiting or were they lobbying groups for Indian, Métis, and Inuit governments not at the table? What was the nature of the negotiating mandate given to the leadership of these Aboriginal organizations by different First Nations, by Canada's six hundred Indian bands, by regional tribal councils, and by Aboriginal men and women both on and off the federal lands that have been reserved for them? What was the role of the federal Indian Act in structuring procedures for choosing the leadership of the Aboriginal organizations? What consideration was afforded to Aboriginal groups such as the Coalition of First Nations who opposed the entire format of the negotiations?[184] Who were the Métis and what was the nature of the relationship between their organization and the Indian, Inuit, and federal, provincial, and territorial delegations? Were the Aboriginal constituencies represented at the table legally situated inside or outside Canadian citizenship, inside or outside the Canadian federation? How did Aboriginal involvement in this forum of federal-provincial negotiations affect the constitutional content and political perception of First Nations' treaty relationships with the old imperial crown of Great Britain and the newer federal crown of Canada? What changing conceptions of sovereignty were expressed in a process of bringing together elected representatives of federal, provincial, territorial, and Aboriginal politics – a procedure whose very legitimacy was formally challenged by the government of Quebec?

These questions, and others like them, continue to present a number of hard choices, especially in the Indian Country of Canada. Given the continued centrality of the Indian Act in the federal structure of both direct and indirect rule over Indian reserves,[185] it is no small problem for Aboriginal peoples to decide who should be negotiating on their behalf and how their leaders should be conducting relations with other orders of government. The problem is complicated by the heavy dependence of Indian bands and Aboriginal organizations on federal funding, a system that produces almost infinite scope for conflicts of interest, petty corruption, and federal resort to divide-and-conquer tactics.

While many Aboriginal people have opted to work within the federally funded structures of Indian Act representation, there is a growing movement within the First Nations which insists that Aboriginal leadership must be derived from indigenous traditions of Aboriginal law, custom, and convention. Internal disagreements between Aboriginal groups on either side of this strategic divide have been integral to the politics of the Mohawk crisis at Oka in 1990 and the confrontations in 1995 at the Indian ceremonial and burial sites of Gustafsen Lake, British Columbia, and Ipperwash, Ontario.[186] Another wave of internal dissent has emanated from various coalitions of Aboriginal women. They accused the male-dominated band councils under the umbrella of the Assembly of First Nations of having internalized the paternalistic oppressiveness of their Euro-Canadian colonizers.[187]

The constitutional transformation at the end of the twentieth century of the largest nation-state in the Americas heightened both the internal strife as well as the ideological and political dynamism of the Indian and Inuit Country of Canada. During the era of the fur trade, this northern polity was well on its way to becoming a mestizo polity in much the same tradition as Mexico. The renewal of this older version of Canada was highlighted by the presence of a national organization representing the Métis among the four Aboriginal organizations that participated directly in the effort to come up with a domestically made elaboration of the country's supreme law.

On the one hand, the move to formalize Canada's legal makeover from a colony of the British Empire to an ostensibly independent, North American country has created a pretext for a further extinguishment of Aboriginal and treaty rights in the name of constitutional renewal and "equality of citizenship." On the other hand, the emergence of the Canadian Constitution as a central subject of political debate and negotiation produced, as George Manuel predicted, a major new forum to address the place of Indigenous peoples in Canada's genesis – past, present, and future. This text serves to illustrate some of the connections between that domestic process and some of the larger currents of global transformation pointing towards the Fourth World.

Because Canada was the last major country on the mainland of the Americas to sever constitutional ties with its European mother country, the direct involvement of Indigenous peoples in the effort to rewrite a national constitution is of particular historical significance. Notwithstanding all the problems inherent in their non-voting status in the process of constitutional amendment, the articulate presence of Aboriginal representatives at several of the first ministers' constitutional bargaining sessions has set important precedents for many other countries in the Americas. Although the governments of these countries have long since formalized their independence from the Spanish, Portuguese, French, or British empires, in 1982 no nation-state in the Americas had deviated far enough from its European heritage to acknowledge and embrace in a fundamental way an Aboriginal heritage and future as a major projectory of national legitimacy. No nation-state in the Americas was able to make the claim that its government was more rooted in the Indian than the European side of the Columbian conquests.

In 1992 Canada stood on the threshold of such a fundamental recognition, which was long overdue in the Americas. The Charlottetown accord would have acknowledged Aboriginal peoples as founding peoples[188] and advanced an understanding of Aboriginal title as the permanent and unextinguishable tap root from which all other kinds of titles and jurisdictions emanate in the Americas. Philosophical reconciliation with the legal principles of Aboriginal title is basic to our imaginative reconstruction of a more realistically grounded interpretation of the history of the Americas. By looking at the continuing force of the legal principles bound up in the idea of Aboriginal title, we must address the living legacies emanating from the inescapable fact that these two continents were the basis of a very old world when Christopher Columbus began what David E. Stannard has called the American Holocaust.[189]

The failure to implement Aboriginal and treaty rights fairly cuts at the geopolitical base of Canada in a way that undermines the social compact on which many other kinds of relationship depend as well. The clearest example of the interconnection of Aboriginal issues to other areas of statecraft was manifest in the way the failure of the constitutional process between 1983 and 1987 created the conditions for the demise of the Meech Lake accord. The famous images of a resolute Elijah Harper, feather in hand, calmly blocking the passage of the accord through the Manitoba legislature should have clarified that no effort to reshape Canada's legal architecture will be viable without the active collaboration of Indigenous peoples and First Nations in this task of geopolitical reconfiguration.

The active, if fundamentally flawed, involvement of Indigenous peoples in the effort to articulate a constitutional definition of Canada outside the British Empire underlined and highlighted the contrasting lack of any similar Aboriginal involvement in the founding of the United States. Sooner or later the citizens of the that nation will have to address the fact that their country's constitution was formulated without the input or consent of Indigenous peoples whose lands still provide the territorial basis for the republic. Similarly, they will have to address the reality that African American slaves were also unrepresented in the constitutional structuring of a country where the racial outlines of socioeconomic inequality are still the most striking characteristic to outside observers.

Until the deep implications of these two conspicuous omissions are squarely confronted, both in international law and in some sort of national return to the country's founding instruments, the US Constitution will always have a kind of provisional status and a tenuous legitimacy. Perhaps the role of Indigenous peoples in remaking Canada's constitution can be seen as part of the process of reconstituting a more democratic American empire. Perhaps this Aboriginal involvement, however problematic, will enliven some basic principles of human rights that will eventually resonate in the juridical restructuring of the country.

The involvement of Aboriginal representatives in attempts to remake the constitution of the United States's closest satellite and largest trading partner has particularly significant meaning for the evolution of the American empire through NAFTA and through other instruments of hemispheric integration and global corporatism, including the proposed Free Trade Area of the Americas.[190] Along with the legacy of slavery, the Indian question represents the most profound challenge to the sagacity, morality, and capacity for justice of the imperial heartland of the American empire.

Many First Nations have lived and died in the dark, genocidal shadow of manifest destiny. The drive towards extinguishment of Aboriginality is implicit in the motto *E pluribus unum* or in Crèvecoeur's ideal of a republic where "individuals of all nations are melted into a new race of men."[191] Some rays of deflected illumination are pointed towards this shadowy zone in the genesis of the United States by the imperfect yet partially successful efforts to renew constitutionally the northern portion of the continent as a multicultural land, one where Quebec is a distinct society and where Indigenous peoples are free in theory, if not yet in practice, to exercise their existing Aboriginal and treaty rights.

INDIAN COUNTRY IN THE EVOLUTION OF RELATIONS BETWEEN CANADA AND THE UNITED STATES OF AMERICA

Like Mexico and Australia, Canada has become an important theatre of tension between the cultural pluralism of the Fourth World and the monoculturalism inherent in the empire of possessive individualism. A powerful symbol of Canada as a medium of expression for a revitalized Indian Country in a changing American empire has been situated since 1991 in the courtyard of the Canadian Embassy on Pennsylvania Avenue in Washington, DC. The work, entitled *The Spirit of Haida Gwaii,* is set in black bronze. Measuring 19 feet long, 11 feet wide, and 12 feet high, the piece represents a tightly packed group of animal and human spirit creatures who are navigating together in a crowded Haida canoe.[192] The sculptor is Bill Reid, a former radio announcer of Haida-Scots background who later in his career took the carving styles of West Coast Indians to new heights of artistic expression and critical recognition. Reid's work on the project was interrupted when he left his studio to take part in his people's protests against the incursions of the BC logging industry into the sacred centre of Haida Gwaii, otherwise known as the Queen Charlotte Islands.[193]

In the view of political philosopher James Tully, who sees in the piece a fitting icon of "the age of cultural diversity," *The Spirit of Haida Gwaii* "is destined to become one of the major artistic landmarks of the Americas."[194] From my perspective, the work announces with stately authority the entry onto the international stage of an ecological vision of protected biodiversity through transcultural treaties linking peoples and generations. In its conception, genesis, and its geographic setting on Canada's most important diplomatic site at the core of the American capital, *The Spirit of Haida Gwaii* is in every way a vital Fourth World expression of the continuing struggle against the assimilation of Indian Country into the monocultural empire of private property. Much depends on this struggle. Ultimately the whole world is a shared hunting ground, a realm of land and water still rightly signified by the bowl with one spoon. We must navigate together in our crowded vessel or perish together in our failure to keep the craft afloat. All landing points in our journey are unique and yet part of the same Old World, a world that will die rather than be made new again by encouraging monocultures and extinguishing the diversity of our plant, animal, and human relatives.

In "Darling Don't Cry,"[195] Buffy Sainte-Marie has put her own recording trademark on a Cree round-dance song that was originally part of the repertoire of the Red Bull singers from the Little Pine reserve in Saskatchewan. In the heartbeat rhythm of the words, written by Edmund Bull, I hear tones and inclinations that come from deep within the soul of the Indian Country of Canada. In the undulating Cree syllabics of the English-language phrases, I hear the whispers of tens of thousands of Native American people who headed north to escape the extinguishing fervour of the new white nation:

Darliiiing Doooon't Cryyyy
When I Leeeeave
The USAAAAA
If You Like
I'll Take You Home
When I
Go Back
To Ca naaaa daaaa
Hay yih ya ho

As the penetrating tones of the song sink deep, I imagine the Six Nations people who left old villages and started new ones in order to maintain their alliance with the crown. I imagine the many Algonkian-speaking groups – Potawatomi, Ojibway, Ottawa, and others – who moved north of the Great Lakes after the hopes of North America's most powerful Indian Confederacy dimmed with the martyrdom of Tecumseh. I think of the many Sioux migrations across the medicine line, including the flight of the forces of Sitting Bull after their victory over General George Custer's army at the Battle of Little Bighorn. I think of Chief Joseph and the Nez Percés' intercepted run for asylum in Canada.[196]

In November 2000 a reversal apparently began of this Indian refugee flow from the United States to Canada. In Portland, Oregon, Judge Janice Stewart refused to allow the executive branch of the American government to extradite back to Canada the Odawa activist, James Pitawanakwat, a veteran of the Battle of Gustafsen Lake. For the first time in the history of Canada–US relations, a US judge invoked the legal authority of the political offences exception in Article 4 of the Extradition Treaty. Where Sitting Bull and Leonard Peltier had been forced by Canadian authorities to return to the United States to meet their persecutors, Pitawankwat was afforded the protection of the US government against his politically motivated persecution by Canadian officials in the covert continuation of North America's ongoing Indian wars.[197]

I reflect on such episodes as the basis of history made and of history yet to be made. I situate myself, my country, my continent, and my hemisphere in the global flow of events as I join hands with the other round dancers in a moving circle of unbroken rhythm. At the centre are the drummers and singers who give beat, melody, and harmony to their songs of the Fourth World.

CHAPTER THREE

Globalization, Decolonization, and the Fourth World

The steady illumination of his genius, dim only because distant,
is like the faint but satisfying light of the stars compared with the
dazzling but ineffectual and short-lived blaze of candles.
Henry David Thoreau,
A Week on the Concord and Merrimack Rivers, 1849

IMPERIALISM AND ITS ENEMIES: TUPAC AMARU AND "THE GEORGE WASHINGTON OF SOUTH AMERICA"

There are many ironies in the revolutionary struggle against imperialism that began in North America in 1776. In that year, many of the colonial people of eastern North America combined to declare their inherent rights of self-government outside the sovereign claims of the British government. The American Revolution, in turn, supplied the model for many future revolutionaries. Its example proved particularly compelling for the Creole populations in "Latin America" who sought liberty from the imperial authority of Spain and Portugal.[1] While many among the transplanted European populations of the Spanish, Portuguese, and French empires in the Americas developed a self-image as Creoles *(criollo, crioula)*, the Anglo-American pioneers of British North America and the United States were more inclined to develop images of themselves as members of a white race.[2] One of the definitions of the term "Creole" in the Oxford English dictionary is particularly instructive. It defines the Creole as a "naturalized" person of European origin who was born neither in Europe nor of "aboriginal" descent.

The transfer of constitutional authority from the imperial capitals of Western Europe to the new national capitals in the Americas had profound effects on the apportionment of political and economic power within the western hemisphere. No sooner were the constitutional ties with Europe cut than the peoples of South and Central America were drawn into the orbit of a new kind of informal empire. And the commercial, ideological, and political metropolis of this strange New World empire was located in the United States.[3] The overthrow of Spain's and Portugal's imperial rule in the Americas was treated in the United States as an extension and fulfilment of that nation's own revolutionary founding. The

American historian Samuel Flagg Bemis gave voice to this perception by identifying the Creole revolts against Spain and Portugal in the early nineteenth century as a "heroic and magnificent climax of the Anglo-American Revolution itself: the achievement of that American system for which the North American Revolution had pointed the way."[4]

The towering figure of the Creole revolt against Spain was Simon Bolivar, whom many American textbooks touted as "the George Washington of Spanish America." He emerged as the key figure in the creation of a new polity known as Gran Columbia. It covered a region in New Spain that had formerly been the viceroyalty of New Granada. The federal regime founded by Bolivar was later divided to become what is now Venezula, Colombia, Panama, and Ecuador. Along with Peru and Bolivia, scholars sometimes refer to these countries as "the Bolivarian bloc."[5]

Bolivar's revolutionary equivalent in Argentina and Chile was José de San Martín. In the global transformations instigated by Europe's Napoleonic Wars, the Creoles of Brazil also broke away from their Portuguese constitutional moorings. Their break with tradition, however, was not as great as among the Spanish-speaking Creoles, for they retained a member of the Portuguese royal family as their constitutional monarch.[6] Finally Mexico, then a vast domain extending far into the southwest portion of the present-day United States and southward to Panama, became an independent republic in 1821.[7]

One explanation of the affinity in the United States for the independence struggles in the rest of the hemisphere is that these revolutionary movements were self-consciously centred in the transplanted European population rather than in the still-numerous and powerful Aboriginal societies. The ideological gymnastics needed to invent these New World nationalities in opposition to both the European identities and the Aboriginal identities of the Native peoples have been considerable. Bemis details the busy and anxious diplomatic manœuvres undertaken by the US government to transform the Creole rebels in New Spain into the leaders of recognized governments and to usher them into the closed circle of sovereign polities capable of making international law:

At the outset of the revolt the United States – in contrast to Great Britain – sent agents to the rebel governments; at first, in 1810, "agents for seamen and commerce," who were political observers; then, in 1811, actual consuls appointed by the President and duly confirmed by the Senate, officials who accepted formal exequaturs from *de facto* governments. This was as close to recognition *de jure* of the new states as it was possible to go. Representatives from Venezuela (1810), Buenos Aires (1811), and especially Mexico (1811) met in Washington a friendly and solicitous, if technically informal, welcome by the President and Secretary of State.[8]

While there were clearly many similarities linking the Creole populations that constructed the new national identities of both the United States and

Latin America, Bolivar himself was alert to the dangers of being drawn into the peripheries of a new Pan-American empire dominated by the United States. To fend off this tendency, he sought closer links with Great Britain, whose business interests were quickly moving into Spain's and Portugal's old empires with trade and investment. With a prophetic eye, Bolivar confided to a British diplomat that the United States appeared "destined by Providence to plague America with torments in the name of freedom."9

Although large parts of the Aboriginal populations played no role whatsoever in the legal "decolonization" of their ancestral lands, the majority of those Indian people who did become involved in the struggle between European imperialism and Creole nationalism took the monarchical side in the conflict. In doing so, they tended to re-enact the pattern among those Indigenous peoples who had become enmeshed in the Anglo-American revolution against Great Britain. In both British North America and in New Spain, the imperial monarchies had come to be seen by a good number of Aboriginal groups and individuals as a kind of arbiter of last resort in their struggles with the colonial populations over land and resources.

In New England the legal intervention of Queen Anne and her Privy Council in 1704 on the Indian side in the case of *Mohegan Indians* v. *Connectcut Colony* was emblematic of this pattern.10 Similarly in New Spain, Indians acquired and frequently used access to the royal courts to such an extent that they were sometimes characterized as unusually litigious.11 In invoking the authority of Spanish laws for their protection, many of the Aboriginal litigants moved into processes opened up especially by Dominican clerics, including Brother Bartholme de Las Casas. The members of that religious order had been influential in making the rights and titles of Indigenous peoples a matter of considerable juridical controversy in the imperial centre of the Court of Castille, a realm renowned for its obsessive preoccupations with legal contestation. So habituated had the Pueblo Indians become to the use of royal courts in New Spain that they quickly and expertly sought access to the US judiciary to protect their rights and titles following the transfer of their New Mexico homelands from the Mexican republic to the American republic in 1848.12 Pueblo litigiousness continues to this day in that part of the United States where Indigenous peoples are numerically and politically powerful, and reasonably well integrated into the surrounding economy.13

Litigation, however, provided the Indigenous peoples of New Spain with only one of many strategies in their efforts to resist various forms of colonization. Clearly these strategies had to be revised when constitutional authority in the non-Aboriginal polities of government shifted from the imperial capitals to the new national capitals in the Americas. This withdrawal of the European sovereigns tended to narrow rather than expand the range of strategic options available to First Nations peoples in defending their Aboriginal rights and titles. It tended to move questions about the place of Indigenous peoples in the global community away from the theatre of international law towards the more restrictive confines of domestic politics. There were, however, some advantages as well as disadvantages in the early initiatives made by some of the new Latin American governments to lower or eliminate legal barriers between the Indian and the Creole populations.

Such formal legal modifications were often only remotely connected to actual practices in highly stratified societies where powerful distinctions of class were embedded in the cultural distinctions among ladinos, mestizos, zambos (African Indians), mulattos, and indios, who were sometimes also known as *naturales*. Undergirding and facilitating the economics of this tightly tiered system was the institution of slavery. The human currency in this system was drawn initially from Indian societies and then, increasingly, from the transatlantic trade in human chattel which made Americans out of millions of violently uprooted Africans. As for the "Creoles," this term was slowly replaced by the idea of a broadly based Hispanic identity that Simon Bolivar laboured to express in a federal Pan-American polity that was politically independent from Spain but culturally connected to the language and heritage of the Iberian Peninsula. While many local particularisms within Central and South America stymied Bolivar's quest, Gerald Torres argues that the United States would eventually offer the most promising site for the pragmatic negotiation of a multicultural Hispanic identity.[14]

With the transformation of New Spain and Brazil into Latin American nations and with the transformation of Louisiana into a part of the United States, the word *Creole* acquired a broader range of added or changed meanings. It would prove to have a rich and varied life throughout many of the world's trading routes, where linguistic invention has been especially quick and creative. Among its many usages it became a term to describe European languages as they were transformed in the West Indies through local usage, especially by indigenized Africans, into various forms of "patois."[15] The common thread of meaning in these transformations seems to be that the word has been consistently attached to the peoples, languages, and processes that were once alien to a place but made themselves local. Because the usage also connoted a hybridization between new and old, between local and imported, the term also took on nuances that had formerly been the exclusive domain of *mestizaje*. In the Russian colony of Alaska, for instance, the name Creole was attached to the mixed-ancestry children of Russian fathers and Aboriginal mothers. The term acquired powerful legal meaning, for Creoles, but not Indians or Inuit, were admitted into the laws and institutions reserved in Alaska for Russian subjects.[16]

Just as the nature of Creole identity has gone through many adaptations, so, too, the Indigenous peoples of the Americas have adapted different strategies and motifs of self-identification over the centuries. Their challenge has been to find ways to hold ground even in the shared physical, cultural, and jurisdictional spaces of their colonizers; to retain this ground even as they negotiated middle grounds of exchange and compromise; and to understand and to some extent integrate the new-comers, even as they developed strategies to remain outside the trans-formative tactics and schemes employed by Creoles to indigenize their own identities.

In spite of a certain malleability in Aboriginal self-identification, howev-er, the unchanging requirement of Aboriginal survival over more than five centuries has been the resistance of Indigenous peoples to the complete annihilation of their physical persons as well as resistance to the legal and political extinguishment of their shared titles to their ancestral lands. Without some intergenerational continuity of shared identification with the local ecology of particular places, the cultural and legal constructions of aboriginality make little sense. There can be great flexibility, however, in locating and conceptualizing these Aboriginal places. They can cover everything, for instance, from a small Indian reserve to the entire Ameri-can hemisphere.

The designation of a large part of the western hemisphere as "Latin America" signifies the idea that its major cultural motifs are rooted in the Roman Empire and in the continuing influence of the Roman Catholic Church. Indigenous resistance towards the remaking of their Aboriginal domains as Latin America was directed first at the imperial-ism of Spain and Portugal and then against the nationalisms growing out of the transformative shock waves generated by the American and French revolutions.[17] As Grimaldo Rengifo Vasquez observed in his dis-cussion of alternative forms of Aboriginal agriculture prevalent among the Inca peasantry in the diverse ecologies of the Andean Mountains, "decolonization began the day after the European invasion and it has lasted until today."[18]

That spirit of resistance has been and remains especially strong and many-faceted among the Inca peoples of Peru. As early as 1609, Garcilas-co de la Vega employed the medium of Spanish-language literature to pre-sent an Inca perspective on the pre-Columbian and post-contact history of his mother's people. This classic work, entitled *Royal Commentaries of the Incas and a General History of Peru*,[19] has been influential in many ways. One of its readers in the second half of the eighteenth century was Jose Gabriel Kunturkani Tupac Amaru. This sleekly handsome Aboriginal aristocrat was the great-great-great-grandson of the gruesomely beheaded sovereign of the Inca royal family. The regal ancestor had been executed by the Span-ish imperial government in 1572, following the cycles of tragedy initiated for the Inca by the legendary conquests of Francisco Pizzaro. In the 1770s this living personification of the Inca royal line, whose family had retained the old Inca title of Tupac Amaru as their Christian name, began a move-ment that grew into a major uprising. It ended with the deaths of over 150,000 people, most of them Indian.

Tupac Amaru was part of an elite Indian group in Peru – the *caciques* – vested with considerable powers of local governance from the Spanish crown. This charming and erudite leader lived in an era when Inca culture was resurgent and to some extent integrated into Spanish imperial practice in Peru. Fluent in both Spanish and classical Quechua, Tupac Amaru attempted various court actions aimed at obtaining some relief for his peoples from high taxes and forced labour requirements. When these processes failed, he led an increasingly strident opposition to the established regime. It is said he began his patriotic uprising by addressing his people with the words "From this day forth, no longer shall the Spanish feast on your poverty!"[20]

This Indian leader reached out to Peru's Creole, mestizo, and slave populations. He sought to attract the support of slaves by promising to free them if his movement was successful. Initially this strategy seemed to work. Tupac Amaru began attracting many Creole and mestizo supporters who seemed prepared to see their liberated country transcend the indignities of slavery. Some were attracted to his cause when Tupac Amaru proposed that Peruvians "should live as brothers, congregated in one body." In his manifesto, the Indian leader called on "*Gente Peruna*" and "*gente nacional*" to join him in opposing the "*Gente Europea*." The Peruvian nationals invited to join his movement included all those who were born in the Inca territitories and those who, regardless of ancestry, identified with the indigenous interests of his country.[21] Tupac Amaru took great pains initially to clarify that his protest was not against the Spanish sovereign but against bad government and bad crown officials who violated the imperial law to their own advantage. He declared that his stand was to end the abuses "against the unfortunate Indians and other persons, and against the provisions of the very kings of Spain, whose [beneficial] laws I know from experience have been suppressed and ignored."

Variations on this same charge have been repeated many times in Aboriginal stands throughout the New World. The substance of the charge is that the newcomers' wrongdoing directed at Indigenous peoples constitutes not only a moral crime but an elaborate pattern of criminal violation of the imperial sovereign's own laws and juridical integrity. The intensity of Creole revolts in both Anglo and Latin America drew some of their intensity from the desire of colonial peoples to be free of such accusations from Indian peoples and to avert the prospect of imperial intervention on behalf of Aboriginal rights. This theme of Aboriginal protest persists to this day – for instance in Canada, Australia, and New Zealand. In these Commonwealth coutnries the British monarch remains the head of state.

Tupac Amaro did not relent from his quest for justice. The proof of European wrongdoing, he asserted, was "the tears that have flowed for three centuries from the eyes of my unhappy people." Restitution, he insisted, required an end to official corruption, extortion, and unjust monopolies. "In each province," he demanded, "there shall be a chief magistrate [chosen] from the Indian nation itself and that in this city [Cusco] a Royal Audience shall be established with a resident viceroy presiding, so that Indians may have ready access and recourse."[22]

In spite of Tupac Amaru's care to base his movement on an inclusive, multicultural vision of the Peruvian people, the uprising soon spun out of control. His campaign to bring an end to the foreign expoitation of his country set off a bloody race war, with atrocities commited on all sides. His sometimes subtle distinctions in differentiating friend from foe were lost in the atmosphere of uncontrollable violence that quickly developed. Then the Spanish military forces intervened with great brutality, resorting to the murder of Indians in their multitudes even as government officials tortured and dismembered the movement's leaders. As the tide turned, almost all of Tupac Amaru's Creole supporters quickly abandoned him. While he had promised to respect their landed property rights, the reforms he proposed were simply too menacing to the economic status quo, especially to the institution of slavery. The Creoles' abandonment of this Indian-based liberation movement confirmed the reversion back to the oppressive dynamics of the Columbian conquests. When the Creole populations did give their backing to the decolonization struggles led by Bolivar and San Martín a few decades later, their energies were channelled into a narrower, more ethnocentric movement of revolutionary nationalism based on the model provided in the founding of the United States. In order to bring about some Pan-American unity in this process of transforming Spanish subjects into liberated citizens of their own indigenized polities, Bolivar advanced the ideal of a shared Hispanic identity.

Like the Anglo-Americans who established the United States, the founders and shapers of the new Hispanic nationalities would seek many ways of securing their political and economic advantages. They would seek ways of securing their legal and political rights in their adopted hemisphere through methods that would enhance rather than minimize the racial and civilizational advantages they claimed for themselves by virtue of their ancestral and cultural inheritances from Europe.[23] They would seek in their European antecedants justifications to uproot, push aside, kill, or assimilate the Indigenous peoples. Those who pursued this agenda gave little thought to the internal contradictions within a genre of nationalism aimed simultaneously against the imperialism of Europe and the continuing sovereignty of Indigenous people. In 1808, for instance, Thomas Jefferson pointed the way towards the Monroe Doctrine of 1823 when he called for "the expulsion of European influence from the New World."[24] As the leader of a new nation engaged in the expansionary displacement of Native American by Euro-American populations, Jefferson seems blind to the irony of his pronouncement when viewed from an Aboriginal perspective.

The Anglo-American colonies and the United States were initially drawn into the politics of New Spain primarily because of the strong influence of that polity on the Indigenous peoples in the border regions of North America's English-speaking settlements. This pattern was especially clear around the northern regions of Florida. After the early sixteenth century, Florida was an integral part of the Spanish Empire. Although it was briefly attached to the British Empire between 1763 and 1783, the region reverted back to Spanish control until General Andrew Jackson asserted US jurisdiction militarily in the region in 1819. His aggressions against the Indian, British, and Spanish enemies of the United States propelled Jackson into the White House, and they also helped intensify a prolonged, guerrilla-type struggle with the zamboized Seminoles of the Florida Everglades.

A good example of a First Nations leader who expertly exploited the tensions between Spain and the United States to advance the strategic position of his own peoples was the wiley Alexander McGillivray. At the end of the eighteenth century McGillivray found ways to embody the aspirations of the loose but elaborate confederacy of Muskogean-speaking peoples who were mostly identified by others as the Creeks. Their national territories were also among the most contested borderlands between the old Spanish Empire and the nascent American empire. In 1784 McGillivray and several other Creek leaders signed the Treaty of Pensacola with the Spanish imperial sovereign. This agreement opened up the flow of trade between the Creeks and an enterprise staffed primarily by United Empire Loyalists – Anglo-Americans who took the pro-Tory, anti-revolutionary side in the American War of Independence. Some of these Loyalists retained their lucrative trade connections with Great Britain, despite Florida's reversion back to Spanish control.

As these trade relationships brought prosperity to Creek Country, the Spanish governor of Louisiana, Estavan Miro, appointed McGillivray as Spain's commissary to the Creeks. A salary attached to the title. From this strong position of continuing attachment to Spain, the Creeks fought against Anglo-American settlers pushing into their Aboriginal territories from the state of Georgia. The Creek stance against these frontier interlopers was so succcessful that officials of both New Spain and the United States became alarmed.

As a result of the demonstration of Creek strength in battle and in diplomacy, McGillivray and a large Creek delegation were invited to New York to treat with President George Washington and Secretary of War Henry Knox. The delegations spent the summer negotiating the Treaty of New York. It gave the Creeks a federal commitment to protect their territories from the incursions of the state of Georgia even as the Creeks retained their capacity to continue diplomatic relations with the Spanish.[25]

These few episodes are suggestive of the larger nature of New Spain's capacities to reach into the internal and foreign affairs of the United States. The intensity of interaction might have been even greater except for the transformation of the French Revolution into the Napoleonic Wars in Europe. That rapid series of events moved the vague and ill-defined European claims to Louisiana from Spain to France and then to the United States in 1803. This acquisition of a European title to the vast Indian Country across the Mississippi River, the site of what would become the most mythologized of all the USA's westward-moving frontiers, slowed but did not end the extension of Spanish influence into North America's interior.

Although it was often diffuse and uneven, the sheer extent of the geographic reach of New Spain at its peak was tremendous. In 1794, for instance, a panic spread throughout the little capital of Upper Canada, a newly created British colony taking shape along the northern shores of Lake Ontario and Lake Erie. The local Indians, it was feared, were preparing an attack. They were thought to be with some Spanish allies moving malevolently through the dense surrounding forests.[26] The attack never took place, but the mere apprehension that it might have is revealing. A joint Spanish-Indian action so far away from New Orleans and Mexico would have been an enormous logistical feat. The perception in Upper Canada, a colony on the northwest boundaries of the empire state of New York, was highly suggestive of the hemispheric extent of the physical and psychological power of New Spain as friend or foe of the Indigenous peoples, of America's other European empires, and of the United States.

The importance of New Spain to the United States is reflected in the fact that much of the American republic presently sits on land formerly governed by the Court of Castille. This recognition of Spain's principal colony as a foundational polity of "America" is signified by the pervasiveness of the founder of New Spain's name, which is attached to so many of the American nation's places and institutions. The geographic placement of the nation's capital, Washington, on the lands of the District of Columbia is illustrative of New Spain's foundational status in what Jack Greene has described as "the intellectual construction of America."[27] By making such direct claims on the legacy of Columbus, New Spain, and Latin America, the United States of America confirmed its place along that projectory of history going back to the vast expansions of imperial Rome.

Not only does the United States sit on the territories of several hundred old Aboriginal polities, many of them now extinct, but it can also be conceptualized as a jurisdictional overlay on large parts of the older Roman Catholic and mestizo realms of Mexico and of French Aboriginal Canada. Beyond that, the United States covers grounds that were once, in whole or in part, the North American domains of France, the Netherlands, Sweden, and Russia. Hence the heartland of the American empire incorporated and extended the capacity of the British Empire, from which it grew, to absorb, co-opt, and amalgamate the efforts of other European colonizers of Indigenous peoples and their lands. This attribute of the United States would become especially significant after the Second World War. That was the era when the American empire effectively moved into the vacuum of imperial power left by the withdrawal of several European nations from their colonial control of the territories and persons of Indigenous peoples all over the planet. The labour, lands, resources, markets, and religious souls of these many thousands of Indigenous peoples had long been the prize of the imperial expansion of Europe that began in 1492.

These colonized lands are the same sites where, over thousands of years, the vast plurality of humanity's many thousands of Aboriginal languages developed. These Aboriginal languages, in which are invested the largest part of humanity's capacities to describe the indigenous details of thousands of local ecologies, act also as hallmarks and proofs of the survival of the world's oldest polities. The memory, territory, and culture that make up these Aboriginal landscapes are often unrelated to the borders of the world's two hundred or so nation-states. Many of these borders have no correspondence at all to the histories of Indigenous peoples before the Columbian conquests. Instead, they reflect the outlines of the colonial land apportionments as the planet was divided up among the imperial aggressors from Europe in the formative stages of the Columbian conquests.

These primary sources of humanity's immense linguistic pluralism are becoming mute as fast as the industrialized destruction of the world's wild fisheries and old-growth forests. The most obvious biological comparison to this linguistic impoverishment of cultural pluralism lies in the near extinction of North America's great buffalo herds. The orgy of ecocide in their mass slaughter stands as the pre-eminent symbol of the genocidal assault on Indigenous people through the elimination of the ecological basis of their political economy. At least 90 per cent of the world's languages are falling silent as quickly as the industrial despoliation of what remains of the planet's land-based and sea-based biodiversity. This process of linguistic impoverishment has been strongly connected to the capitalist hunger to expand the size and cultural homogeneity of markets. One of the most strategic exports shipped to these markets has been the products of the American info-entertainment industry, a densely merged set of cloned conglomerates that has manufactured and replicated much of the imagery most instrumental in the creation of those monocultures of mind and matter on which mass consumerism depends.

By the end of the twentieth century it had become clear that the corporate images and logos of consumerism were worth far more to the economy of illusion and speculation than the infrastructure of trade necessary to feed, cloth, house, and doctor the largest part of the planet's population. So invasive did the contest become to colonize commercially the external landscapes of urbanization and communications as well as the internal landscapes of imagination that the iconography of global corporations effectively overwhelmed many expressions of human culture not directly connected to the generation of mass markets. Much as the empire builders of Europe and Creole America long tried to compromise and to co-opt the leaders of the peoples they wished to colonize and rule, so the marketers of global neo-liberalism manoeuvred to buy and co-opt the embodiments of global celebrity. As Torontonian Naomi Klein has argued, the aim was to "make the brand the star." The aim was no longer "to sponsor culture but to *be* the culture."[28] In capturing the intangibles of culture itself as the pre-eminent currency of commodification, the American empire of private property conquered yet another frontier in its amazing ascent to global hegemony.

The globalization of neo-liberal economics went forward during an era when European empires were being dismantled in the name of decolonization. As the world's first polity to emerge from the imperial control of a European empire, the government of the United States benefited enormously from the global penetration of this paradigm of "decolonization." The ability of the United States to combine the idealized imagery of its own decolonization with the busy substance of empire building was probably the twentieth century's most effective feat of paradox and illusion. It further entrenched the central irony of a hemisphere and a world still grappling to absorb the transformative shock waves that burst on global history with the geopolitical earthquake known as the American Revolution. In commenting on the irony of the United States's own penchant for paradox, Hannah Arendt has written that "the American Republic [dared] realize equality on the basis of the most unequal population in the world, physically and historically."[29]

This integration of the imagery of decolonization into the refinement of empire building could not have succeeded by guile alone; the feat required an external slight of hand on a vast scale along with a good measure of self-delusion within the United States. Such self-delusion, however, was far from accidental. It depended for its effectiveness on carefully crafted acts of selective memory and willed amnesia. It remains to be seen how much longer this deployment of strategic forgetfulness can be sustained.[30]

INDIAN, MESTIZO, AND *INDIGENISMO*

The French-speaking republic of Haiti emerged from a seminally important slave revolt in San Domingo in 1803.[31] Except for Haiti and a sprinkling of smaller, French-speaking polities in the Caribbean region, French America failed to generate any independent nation-states of its own to join the English-speaking, Spanish-speaking, and Portuguese-speaking republics of the hemisphere. As subsequent developments would confirm, the cataclysm of 1759 irreversibly diminished the fate of French power in North America. There would be no substantial recovery from the outcome of the Seven Years' War, when, in achieving a near total triumph over

French imperialism, British imperialism set the stage for the emergence of a new sovereign republic in North America.[32]

There was some small consolation in the fact that, over much of the third quarter of the twentieth century, the party of the Quebec independence movement would create the government of North America's only predominantly French-speaking jurisdiction. The Parti Québécois, however, could not obtain a mandate from its constituents to move Quebec out of the constitutional monarchy containing the federation and parliamentary democracy of Canada. The would-be liberators of *les québécois* did not realize their dream of setting up their own sovereignty to replace that of Queen Elizabeth II, the queen of Canada. Where her predecessor, Queen Elizabeth I, had started the rise of England by granting Sir Walter Raleigh in 1584 a charter to "conquer and possess" overseas territory not yet in Christian hands,[33] the reign of Queen Elizabeth II, which began in 1952, would see the formal abandonment of British imperialism. What was left behind was a huge institutional, historical, and cultural legacy, the pervasiveness of the English language, and the most pliable and resilient sinews of a decolonized empire, of which Canada, New Zealand, Australia, and the rest of the Commonwealth still form a part.

America's Creole nationalisms continued to advance the extinguishment, rather than the embrace, of Aboriginal rights and titles in pursuit of their own forms of indigenization. Although there have been exceptions, modifications, and qualifications to this general pattern, at the beginning of the third millennium not one nation-state in the Americas could make an authentic claim to have its primary constitutional and ideological roots on the Indian rather than the European side of the Columbian conquests. Nevertheless, the most significant deviation away from the pattern of nation building through the destruction, containment, or absorption of the First Nations occurred in Mexico as an outgrowth of the revolutionary transformation that began in 1910.

As the corrupt entrenchment of Mexico's Institutional Revolutionary Party (PRI) over most of the twentieth century came to symbolize, the Mexican revolution was compromised and co-opted from its inception. Nevertheless, one of its most enduring and authentic features was its incorporation of an idealized conception of the country's pre-Columbian Indian past and, to a lesser extent, its living Indian present, into the structures, motifs, and ideologies of the Mexican state. Emiliano Zapata was the most striking personification of the strong Indian facets that were part of the Mexican revolution. This legendary figure was a Nahuatl-speaking activist from the hills south of Mexico City. Zapata used the political capital he gained from significantly widening the base of the revolution by pushing to entrench in the Mexican constitution one of its most popular provisions. Section 27 of this constitutional instrument codified forms of land tenure that were well adapted to the traditional agriculture of the country's large Indian populations, especially in the south. It established the "inalienability of village lands," whereas the NAFTA-related amendments allowed for the privatization of these territories and their use as collateral in obtaining loans.[34]

The constitutional modification of the symbolically potent section 27 by the government of Mexican president Carlos Salinas would provide the platform for the entry onto Mexico's political stage in 1994 of the Zapatista Liberation Army. Through "zapatismo," these activists would help give continuity to the movement of *indigenismo* that began during the revolutionary transformations of the early twentieth century. The intellectual leaders who formulated their country's revolutionary program included the goal of moving Mexico away from the Creole forms of nationalism that characterized the Latin America republics established, with strong US help, during the early decades of the nineteenth century.[35]

The indigenismo movement did not find its most significant manifestations in legislation or constitutional change, although some of its substance finally found reflection in significant institutional reforms that took place once Lazaro Cardenas became the Mexican president in 1934. The heart of this indigenismo movement lay, rather, in the conceptual push to reimagine Mexico as a mestizo country that drew much of its genius and pluralistic culture from the Indian roots that ran through the family heritages of the vast majority of Mexico's citizens. This cultural movement was expressed in a variety of ways, from the massive murals of Diega Rivera, Clemente Orzozo, and David Siqueiros to the productions of the Ballet Folklorico and the elaborate pursuits of Mexico City's Museum of Anthropology.

One of the key figures in this movement, Manuel Gamio, was a pioneer anthropologist and archaeologist as well as a top-ranking official in Mexico's education system.[36] The heart of his ideological endeavour was to create a coherent sense of Mexican nationalism by stressing the Indian and mestizo character of the country. As Allan Knight has described it, the ideal was "to mestiz-ize the Indians and, at the same time, to Indianize the mestizos, to create a national synthesis on the basis of reciprocal contributions."[37] Gamio began to outline his proposal in 1916 in a classic work entitled *Forjando patria*. With metaphors that embodied the urge to combine new and old in the pace and form of Mexico's industrialization – in language that introduced the ideal of realizing a new kind of Aboriginal-newcomer synthesis in the national identity of an American country – he began by writing, "In the great forge of America, on the giant anvil of the Andes, virile races of bronze and iron have struggled for centuries." Out of this struggle emerged the mestizo identity, the carrier of "the national culture of the future." Now the time had come for Mexico's new governors to "take up the hammer and gird themselves with the blacksmith's apron, so that they may rise from the patria of blended bronze and iron."[38]

There are many explanations for this optimism that Mexico could define for itself a unique and independent future by drawing on the creative dynamism of the country's many First Nations, including the Nahua, the Zapotec, and the Otomi. Issues of national pride, national reconciliation, and national self-respect were clearly central. Similarly, the mobilization of Indiannness as an element of Mexican statecraft could well have major implications in terms of the country's ambivalent relationships with its patron, customer, enemy, and expansionistic neighbour, the United States. Where the mestizo and Roman Catholic character of Mexico's national personality were unmistakable, the majority community in the United States clearly did not share those attributes. As Roy Harvey Pearce, Richard Drinnon, and many others have chronicled, among all the polities of the New World, the United States acted most assertively and self-consciously during its first 150 years not only to de-Indianize its national personality but to develop a version of American civilization that defined itself as the very antithesis of Indianness.[39]

In an era when the white supremacy inherent in European imperialism had reached its pinnacle, the equivalent of this phenomenon in the United States went by the name of "manifest destiny." Indeed, the insecurities generated in Mexico from the expressions of manifest destiny helped drive the politics of the Mexican revolution, including its emphasis on the country's mestizo and Indian character. This emphasis had important geopolitical implications in terms of its symbolic importance in helping to fend off the claims and assertions of American expansionism. The oil industry in the United States had been especially forceful in pushing its way past all obstacles to gain access to Mexico's vast store of fossil fuel resources, especially around Tampico, and on the Yucatan and Baja peninsulas.[40] As the growing instabilities of the Mexican revolution threatened the imperial role of US business interests in Mexico, the American navy in 1914 landed about 6,000 Marines on Mexican soil. With the script of their previous military intervention in Nicaragua in mind, the US Marines took control of the port of Veracruz, one of Mexico's oldest and busiest commercial centres.[41]

In taking this action, President Woodrow Wilson demonstrated that the ideas he would later espouse about the self-determination of all peoples did not seem to apply to the American republic's own backyard. This blatent violation of its southern neighbour's national sovereignty sent shock waves through virtually every facet of Mexican society. It seemed to many to be the first step in the making of a new Mexican-US war and it reminded many irrate citizens that Mexico had already lost at least half of its territory to the United States in 1848. No doubt this dramatic display of what seemed to be the next object of manifest destiny had a catalytic effect on the idea that the country's Indianness represented a natural shield against the capitalist, Protestant gringo incursions of the United States.

The easy embrace in Mexico of the country's Indian and mestizo heritage contrasted dramatically with the harsh suppression of a similar movement in the northwestern quarter of North America. In the second half of the nineteenth century that region saw the rise of a nationalist movement among the self-identifying Métis of the Canadian prairies. Their increasingly self-confident movement took concrete constitutional and geopolitical shape especially in the years after the Métis heartland at Red River (on the site of present-day Winnipeg) was included in the huge British North American land transfer of 1869. In a backroom business transaction in London, England, the European title to the continent's northwest was moved from the crown entity known as the Hudson's Bay Company to the crown entity known as the Dominion of Canada. The Métis movement's well-schooled leader, Louis Riel, embodied in his own person the successful mixture of Indian, French, Scottish, and Roman Catholic backgrounds whose combination had long provided the mestizo formula for the smooth, intercultural operations of the Canadian fur trade. The government of the newly created dominion, however, executed Riel in 1885, demonstrating its subservience to the Ontario-based power of an Orange Protestant coalition of transplanted Ulstermen.

In politics, attitudes, and aspirations, these Creole Ulstermen resembled many of their individualistic American brethen, who tended to be overrepresented on the most extended frontiers of the United States's sometimes genocidal expansions. The members of the fraternal order calling for the hanging of Louis Riel identified themselves by the colour signifying William of Orange's Protestant accession to the throne of England in 1688. In acting so quickly and aggressively to replace the Catholic, mestizo fur-trade society that had arisen over more than two centuries during Canada's earlier incarnations, the Orangemen repeated that powerful projectory of Western expansion inspired by Cromwell's Puritan conquests of Catholic Ireland.

Throughout Central and South America there were echoes and reflections of the transformations taking place in Mexico. In spite of the execution of Tupac Amaru in 1781, for instance, the Indian and mestizo dimensions of Peru never ceased to be integral to the character of that nationality. The existence of the Peruvian state has been juxtaposed onto a land that was and is the imperial heartland of the Inca Empire, one of the most renowned centres of the Aboriginal civilization of the Americas. In the early twentieth century Haya de la Torre and Jose Carlos Mariategui dramatically infused this consciousness more deeply into Peruvian politics. They helped prepare the cultural ground for the writing of Jose Maria Arguedas, whose work, according to Ronald Wright, "is widely regarded as indigenismo's highest literary expression."[42]

While indigenismo helped to define Mexico's difference from the United States and to announce its unwillingness to submit to the idea of manifest destiny, the United States also gave rise to some important variations on this theme. At the centre of that movement was John Collier, whom President Franklin D. Roosevelt elevated to be the top civil servant in the Bureau of Indian Affairs. Collier's assignment was to invent an Indian version of the New Deal, a task that resulted in the Indian Reorganization Act of 1934. This legislation was pressed forward to reverse the assimilationist thrust of American Indian policy and to stop the breakup and privatization of Indian reserves. Collier shared with Mexico's Manuel Gamio an intellectual variety of Indianism. Their activism arose largely from the scholarly study of Aboriginal cultures, histories, and civilization. Like Gamio, Collier argued with erudition and enthusiasm that it would be impossible to construct sophisticated and mature forms of nationalism in America until the Indian heritages of the hemisphere were acknowledged and embraced by everyone who had found new homes on the western hemisphere's Aboriginal lands.

Collier is viewed as one of the key figues in the professionalization of "applied anthropolgy," a discipline that, in the mid-war years, was influenced by academic collaborations with British imperial theoreticians, but especially by those involved in efforts to formalize "indirect rule" in Nigeria. Collier saw in the "Indian question" potential answers and responses to some of the world's most pressing problems. His analysis revolved around the idea that the tensions and synergies of "ethnic relations" would become more instrumental in the quickening processes of globalization. At times Collier's enthusiasms could approach messianism. His convictions were only partly secular, for at Taos, New Mexico, where he was a regular guest along with D.H. Lawrence in the legendary literary salon of the Mabel Dodge Luhan, Collier went through an experience of spiritual awakening. His participation in a traditional Tiwa ceremony left him transformed. Of the Indians of the Americas, he wrote, "they had what the world has lost. They have it still."[43]

Collier was among those who participated in the founding of the Interamerican Indigenista Institute. The first executive director of this organization was Manuel Gamio. The institute, which drew assistance from the Organization of American States, included among its member countries Argentina, Guatemala, Bolivia, Brazil, Chile, Colombia, Nicauragua, Panama, Paraguay, Peru, Venezula, Honduras, Mexico, and the United States. It encouraged the governments of each of these countries to establish a national unit to advance the interests and knowledge of Indian groups. It facilitated the collecting and exchange of information, especially through the organization of regular conferences and through its mostly Spanish-language publication, *America Indigena*.[44]

Many questions arose about the propensity of some proponents of indigenismo to romanticize the issues or to be more preoccupied with the achievements of dead Indians in the past than with the problems of living Indians in the present. Throughout Central and South America, where mestizo identity is often the rule rather than the exception, it was often difficult to say whether indigenismo enhanced or merely exploited and co-opted the politics of Indian culture and experience. In the United States and Canada, a variation of this same debate is centred in the long and elaborate history of government registration and certification of Indian identity. The Indian registries maintained by these governments have tended to institutionalize under federal control the main means of determining who can or cannot claim "status" inside the legal enclaves of official Indianness. It remains to be seen if the application of Indian registries to the more fluid politics of Aboriginal affairs would help or hinder the rise of Fourth World activism in Latin America.

The writings of Jose Vasconcelos represent one of the most ambitious efforts to extend the indigenismo movement beyond the confines of Mexico or even of the American hemisphere. A close colleague of Gamio, Vasconcelos saw the blending of ancestries in Mexico as a metaphor for global transformations. He saw the global mixing of peoples, cultures, and ideas as a prelude to "cosmic" *mestizaje*.[45] His views anticipated some of the more recent reflections of Edward Said in *Culture and Imperialism* and other writings. Said's literary quest has been to draw synthesis from the critical analysis of the stories, histories, and other cultural forms that express and motivate imperialism and decolonization.

The urge to both imperialism and decolonization has created the larger framework for the proliferation of those ideological and technological forces that drew previously isolated Indigenous peoples into global systems of commerce, evangelism, politics, and communications. The nineteenth century and the first decades of the twentieth century, in particular, were important times when the histories of the colonized and the colonizers became inextricably linked in converging projectories of intermeshed experience that continue to this day.[46] As Vasconcelos, Gamio, and Collier predicted in reflecting on the meeting of Native and newcomer in their own countries and in their own hemisphere, the ethos of *mestizaje* and indigenismo would help both to explain the accelerated pace of globalization and to offer alternatives and antidotes for the replication and amplification of its most imperialistic attributes.

IMPERIALISM, CAPITALISM, SOCIAL DARWINISM, AND THE EXHAUSTION OF EUROPEAN EMPIRES

The power of elite Europeans to decide the future of Indigenous peoples elsewhere in the world was clearly manifest in the scramble after the Berlin Conference of 1885 to partition Africa into many separate colonies. The European diplomats who carved up the map of Africa afforded no consideration to what African peoples themselves wanted for their political destinies.[47] Europe's rapid partition of Africa helps to illustrate the reality that, in many other parts of the planet, Indigenous peoples were legally transformed in the eyes of their imperial governors into various kinds of wards of colonial authority. This pattern was as true in the western portion of North America as it was in sub-Saharan Africa and in many other parts of the colonized world. From Texas to Tuktoyaktuk, from Argentina to

Alert, Indigenous peoples had little say in determining the terms of their incorporation into the territory and empire of the United States or into the transformation of British North America from many distinctive colonies into a federal dominion and an independent country.

A particularly compelling idea emerged in the nascent social sciences to provide apparent justification for the ascendance of Europeans or their geographically far-flung descendants over the dark-skinned peoples of the world. During the reign of Queen Victoria many influential voices were raised in the academy to provide legitimizing support for the construction of global systems that situated all human societies along hierarchical ladders of sophistication and worth. The claims of evolutionary social science were breathtaking in the completeness of the explanations they offered for the existence of human diversity. All human beings through all of human history, it seemed, could be made to fit into niches of development that spanned the field from stone age to bronze age to iron age to industrial age; from tribe to colony to nation to empire; from feudalism to capitalism; from animism to Christianity; from hunter to agriculturalist to city dweller; from dark skin to light skin; from savagery to barbarism to civilization.[48]

Charles Darwin provided the primary theory underlying the profusion of evolutionary paradigms that so characterized the latter part of the nineteenth century. In 1859 he published his ground-breaking volume, *The Origin of Species*. In it he described how organisms over time reproduced, mutated, evolved, and differentiated themselves towards higher and higher levels of adaptation to their specific environments. "This preservation of favourable individual differences and variations," he wrote, "and the destruction of those which are injurious, I have called Natural Selection, or the Survival of the Fittest."[49] This evolutionary concept was elaborated by Darwin in *The Descent of Man* and integrated more fully into the emerging social sciences of the era by Herbert Spencer, Edward Tylor, and many others. Their resulting sythesis, later labelled as Social Darwinism, provided the key for an interpretation of history that seemed to ennoble capitalism along with Europe's imperial impositions on the cultures, identities, and free will of Indigenous peoples elsewhere on the planet.

Suddenly the worldwide expansion of Europe's power, especially through the imperial export of the capitalist system that seemed to epitomize the principle of the Survival of the Fittest, was made to seem like a realization of natural law. Suddenly the apparent mandate of this natural law could be cited as reason for the bestowment of special rights of possession and special duties of decision making on those who had emerged with the greatest share of the world's spoils. Suddenly the legitimizing aura of science was available to those who advocated the elimination, either directly through murder or indirectly through cultural genocide, of peoples whose distinct identities were deemed to represent the primitive, the childlike, the backward, the unfit, or the savage elements of the evolving human species. Suddenly a huge ethical obstacle was seemingly removed to continuing the forced imposition of Europe's image of itself on the rest of the world. Social Darwinism provided apparent justification for phenomena that would go by many euphemisms, including Manifest Destiny, pacification, counter-insurgency, regime change, and ethnic cleansing.

The past and present exploitation of evolutionary theory should not be allowed to detract from the wide embrace of humanity's genuine capacity for social and ecological self-improvement through the application of reason, argument, and truth to the elaboration of technologies and democratic institutions to improve our collective lot. At the core of the argument about how best to evolve must be the debate over what constitutes authentic progress. But neither should this acknowledgment obscure the huge and sometimes lethal manipulations of evolutionary theory to justify the raw exercise of power in all its many manifeststions. In making this case, Gertrude Himmelfarb has written: "Darwinism has exalted competition over convention, ethics, and religion. Thus it has become a portmanteau of nationalism, imperialism, militarism, of the cult of the hero, the superman and the master race."[50]

The theory of progress through natural selection provided tremendous authority to the emissaries of empire who sought to categorize peoples along the lines of race and ethnicity. Those on the fair-skinned, imperial side of moving frontiers were declared the inheritors and instruments of historical progress, while those on the receiving end of imperial expansion were characterized as hindrances and impediments to progress as long as they did not assimilate the ways of their colonizers. For the proponents of Social Darwinism, the rewards of history naturally belonged to the strongest. All others were deemed worthy of nothing but obsolescence and death, the necessary sacrifices for the Darwinian ascendance of human civilization.[51]

But Europe was not a monolith; nor were Europeans a single people. The energy for Europe's career of global expansion was derived in part from the intensity of conflicts within that continent. Conflicts over religion, ideology, territory, and the succession rights of competing dynasties – all these points of tension were the crucible from which the nation-states of Europe emerged. With the consolidation of European nation-states, the receptacles of internally complex national bureaucracies, warfare reached new levels of sophisticated ruthlessness in that part of the world that showed itself to be deeply divided within itself. Given this heritage of unrelenting military, economic, and ideological fighting, it is small wonder that many Europeans and their far-flung progeny found such resonance in the Darwinian view that virtually all of natural as well as human history could be encapsulated in the single theme of the survival of the fittest.

Accordingly, the global extension of Europe's influence was in many instances driven forward by competition between European nations for new markets, new sources of raw materials, new pools of labour and new fields of souls to save through missionary enterprise.[52] The global extent of the rivalries between and among European nations became absolutely clear with the two world wars that engulfed the planet during the first half of the twentieth century.

The First and the Second World Wars exhausted Europe. Even Great Britain, the ostensible winner, emerged from the conflagrations essentially bankrupt. Under these conditions, the hold of the European powers on their overseas empires faltered. The logistical breakdown of the old imperialism was accompanied by changes of attitude and perception among those both on the delivering and the receiving end of colonialism.[53] The murderous career of Nazi Germany, it seemed, had thoroughly discredited the racist applications of Social Darwinism as an acceptable principle for the ordering of international geopolitics.[54] The dangerous propensities of "master race" fantasies had been exposed in the nightmare of a vast eugenics experiment gone totally mad. New theories of global governance were required at the dawning of an era when the imagery of the planet photographed from space provided new icons for the old processes of globalization.

"PEOPLES" AND SELF-DETERMINATION: CHALLENGES TO THE MONOPOLIZATION OF SOVEREIGNTY BY NATION-STATES

The Age of Europe lasted from 1492 to 1945. Thereafter the United States completed its emergence as the dominant world power. It did so by replacing Nazi Germany as capitalism's shield of resistance against the communist ideology of the Soviet Union. The ascent of the Soviet Union after the Russian Revolution of 1917 can be conceived as the final project of global imperialism centred in Europe. The ascent of the United States to the status of the world's pre-eminent superpower, with primary responsibility for defending and expanding the system of property relations on which the planet's major transnational corporations depended, was confirmed through its lead role in implementing the Marshall Plan to strengthen Western Europe. Similarly, the United States confirmed its dominant position as the chief sponsor and director of global opposition to communism in the Korean War, in the operation of the North Atlantic Treaty Organization, and in virtually every scientific, political, military, ideological, and psychological aspect of the Cold War.

At the dawning of what was anticipated by many to become "the American Century," the United States, along with its contrary mirror-image superpower, the Soviet Union, moved quickly to fill the vacuum of global authority created by the dismantling of Europe's older overseas empires.[55] The rush of the United States to pick up where Europe left off was particularly apparent in Vietnam. There the American imperial army replaced the French imperial army in the name of defending an Aboriginal society from the perils, real or imagined, of international communism.[56] As both superpowers vied for favourable political, economic, and ideological positioning in an increasingly bipolar world, the domineering foreign policies of both polities were often masked in rhetoric claiming for each the moral high ground associated with the defence of human rights and the fight against racism, colonialism and discriminatory oppression in all its forms. This exercise of superpower dominance converged with an outpouring of global public opinion aimed at creating a world with sufficient safeguards to prevent a repetition of the savage aggressions and atrocities that had marked the first half of the twentieth century.[57]

The United Nations became a primary forum where many of the highest and most idealistic urgings of humanity for a better, more harmonious planet mixed daily with the sometimes opportunistic or self-interested jockeying of national governments for strategic advantage. The founding Charter reflects much from that moment of efflorescent optimism at the end of the Second World War, a moment when it seemed possible for humanity to exorcize from itself the most cruel forms of tyranny and to affirm "the principle of equal rights and self-determination of peoples."

The relatively open atmosphere in which the UN Charter took shape was described in his memoires by John P. Humphrey, the quiet Canadian from McGill University in Montreal who was instrumental in drafting the document that would become the UN's Universal Declaration of Human Rights. Humphrey detailed how a variety of non-governmental organizations took part in the proceedings at the founding UN conference at San Francisco in 1946:

The United States government had invited forty-two private organizations representing various aspects of American life – the churches, trade unions, ethnic groups, peace groups, etc. – to send representatives to San Francisco, where they acted as consutants to its delegations. These people, aided by the delegations of some of the smaller countries, conducted a lobby in favor of human rights for which there is no parallel in the history of international relations, and which is largely reponsible for the human rights provisions in the Charter ... The experiment has never been repeated on the same scale in the halls of the United Nations.[58]

It is revealing that he does not think to comment on the fact that this representation of civil society was drawn exclusively from the United States. His silence on the issue suggests that Humphrey, who worked closely with Eleanor Roosevelt, must have accepted the idea of the United Nations as a global extension of the United States and the New Deal. Nevertheless, even this limited expression of pluralism in the process of founding the United Nations would contrast dramatically with the closed procedures that gave rise to the next generation of international agencies, whose central icon and coordinating dynamo is the World Trade Organization. With almost no public debate in its member countries, it emerged in near secrecy from the General Agreement on Tariffs and Trade in 1995.

The Preamble to the Charter of the United Nations places great emphasis on the word "peoples" as the primary political unit of the world order it announces. This emphasis, which builds on the famous opening phrase of the American Declaration of Independence, seems to point in a very different direction from an international system where the legal motifs of nation-states and global corporations have dominated the juridical landscape. There are other phrases in the Preamble that resonate with powerful meaning and suggestion in relationship to many of the issues central to this text. Among those phrases are "nations large and small," "justice and respect for the obligations arising from treaties," and "the promotion of the economic and social advancement of all peoples." Given the significance of the Charter and especially its Preamble, the opening sentences are reproduced here. On behalf of the global community, the founders of the United Nations proclaim:

WE THE PEOPLES OF THE UNITED NATIONS determined to save succeeding generations from the scourage of war, which twice in our lifetime has brought untold sorrow to mankind, and to reaffirm faith in fundamental human rights, in the dignity and worth of the human person, in the equal rights of men and women and of nations large and small, and to establish conditions under which justice and respect for obligations arising from treaties and other sources of international law can be maintained, and to promote social progress and better standards of life in larger freedom

AND FOR THESE ENDS to practice tolerance and live together in peace with one another as good neighbours, and to unite our strength to maintain international peace and security, and to ensure, by the acceptance of principles and the institution of methods, that armed force shall not be used, save in the common interest, and to employ international machinery for the promotion of the economic and social advancement of all peoples.[59]

The emphasis on peoplehood as the primary locus of collective self-determination presents a major opening in international law for the liberation of those groups that have been most ruthlessly oppressed by earlier episodes of imperialism and colonization. Such peoples – those Indigenous peoples beyond Europe whose Aboriginal lands provided the hinterlands for the global extension of European imperialism after 1492 – have often lacked access to and control of nation-states – the sole available instrument of sovereignty following the demise of the European empires.

The identification of "peoples" as the primary unit of self-determination in the founding instrument of the United Nations renewed a key element of the European Enlightenment. Some of the activists who best embodied the spirit of the Enlightenment affirmed the imperatives of peoplehood, not nationhood, as the starting point for the shared expression of democracy among connected individuals. In 1795, for instance, the authors of the French Declaration of Rights defined the character and jurisdictional rights of the world's peoples in the following terms: "Each people is independent and sovereign, whatever the number of individuals who compose it and the extent of territory it occupies. This sovereignty is inalienable."[60] In the nineteenth century the ideological abstractions invested in the elaboration of nationalism drew on the more primal conception – the more *aboriginal* conception – invested in the idea of peoplehood. Thus the widespread deployment of nationalism as a catalyst of citizens' homogeneity is most properly understood as an outgrowth of earlier notions given explicit articlation during the Enlightenment; modern nationalism is more a derivation from, than an embodiment of, the ideals of the sovereign people. It was in the name of this sovereignty that the polity of France was transformed through revolution.

This ideological construction is reflected in Thomas Guillaume Raynal's *Histoire philosophique et politique des établissements et du commerce des Européens dans les deux Indes.* That work was among the clearest embodiments of the animating ideals of the French Revolution. It had enormous influence, for instance, on identifying slavery as a great crime of European imperialism.[61] Raynal saw the circumnavigation of the planet as the beginning of a revolution in "le governement de tous peuples." His image of a global revolution in the governance of all peoples has been cited again and again, including by Adam Smith in the *Wealth of Nations.*[62]

This inheritance from the Enlightenment was renewed in 1982 when the Canadian Constitution was patriated from Great Britain with a provision recognizing Indians, Inuit, and Métis as the Aboriginal peoples of Canada. Given the significance attached to the word "peoples," not only in Enlightenment thought but in those juridical instruments poised on the most idealistic frontiers of international law, this constitutional reference is highly significant. The affirmation of the constitutional existence of the Aboriginal and treaty rights of the Aboriginal peoples of Canada can be seen as a seminal event in the growth of a global movement aimed at recognizing and implementing the principle that all peoples have an inherent right of self-determination.

There were powerful forces at play in the processes that led to the formulation of such strong language in international law linking decolonization with the self-determination of all peoples. These forces developed in the atmosphere of the Cold War dominated by the United States and the Soviet Union. One of the most significant, ground-breaking UN declarations was made in 1960 shortly after John F. Kennedy became president of the United States. The beginning of his presidency coincided with the height of the Cold War and with a proliferation of stately ceremonies or hasty getaways, as the European powers continued to pull their imperial governors out of their colonies to open the way for the self-government of their former colonial subjects. The UN Declaration on the Granting of Independence to Colonial Countries and Peoples spoke of "the necessity of bringing to a speedy and unconditional end colonialism in all its forms and manifestations." In phrases that elaborated aspects of the Charter, the UN General Assembly proclaimed that "all peoples have the right to self-determination; by virtue of that right they freely determine their political status and freely pursue their economic, social and cultural development." This wording on the self-determination of peoples was repeated in 1966 in two International Covenants adopted by the UN General Assembly.[63]

The formulation of such language reflected strong aspects of self-understanding among key constituencies of both the United States and the Soviet Union. Both polities were founded in revolutions against imperial regimes. The founder of the Soviet Union, Vladimir I. Lenin, had come to power having published a text in 1916 entitled *Imperialism, the Highest Stage of Capitalism.*[64] Among Lenin's first global pronouncements on behalf of the communist state was his articulation of the principle that Soviet internationalism offered humanity a means of escaping the various oppressions and exploitations embedded in both capitalism and colonialism. In the era of decolonization after the Second World War, Soviet officials would repeat and elaborate these themes again and again. Similarly, the United States could present its form of government as the world's original prototype of decolonization. It could offer its leadership to those peoples seeking to break the hold of European dominance by pointing to the way the United States had been the world's first polity to gain sovereignty by opposing the imperial jurisdiction of an Old World power. Given the intensity of the competition between the governments of the United States and the USSR to present themselves as the obvious friends, allies, and role models to those peoples emerging from European imperialism, there were strong motivations for each superpower to try to outdo the other in its formal condemnations of colonialism.

The rapidly changing character of membership in the United Nations seemed to reflect the content of those international declarations that labelled colonialism a crime and self-determination a virtue.[65] Where fifty nation-states had been represented in the San Francisco conference that gave birth to the United Nations in 1945, the number of countries represented in the UN General Assembly over the next half-century almost quadrupled. There are many ways to interpret this rush to afford recognition in international law to a broadening array of sovereign states. On the one hand, the widening range of linguistic, cultural, and ethnic identities represented in the United Nations points to the image of a post-colonial world stretching to widen and diversify the rules of eligibility for national self-determination. On the other, the expanding membership of the UN club can be seen to mask a more fundamental imposition of standardized political models on diverse peoples who have been pressed to adopt the conventions of the nation-state as the exclusive legitimate instrument of sovereignty.

The international system sanctioned by the charter members of the United Nations came to resemble the legal motifs of land ownership that emerged primarily from the specific historical conditions of both Western Europe and the Creole nationalisms of America.[66] In this model, the government of each state recognized at the United Nations was afforded an internationally recognized status similar to that of the owner of a title deed to a specific plot of land. The motifs of Lockean possessive individualism came to permeate the qualifications for acquiring those sovereign proprietorships on which the UN system was based. Where the genesis of this form of proprietorship led back to authorities asserted by European monarchs in granting charters for imperial colonization, much of this power had been devolved to the succesor states of European empires, whose first and leading member was the United States. The United States had originally exercised its newly acquired role in replicating its sovereign power by being the first to offer international recognition to the new Creole nationalisms that replaced the old imperialism of New Spain. After the Second World War the United Nations became the primary instrument in the process of formally recognizing and certifying the new nations in the process of widening the franchise and dropping the colour bars of those deemed qualified to sit at the high tables where international law is made.

It was the United Nations, rather than the United States, that formally acquired the chartering powers that the sovereign monarchs of imperial Europe had once monopolized. Much more careful attention needs to be devoted, however, to determining how much the United Nations served to disguise the power of the United States during the era of decolonization. How much power was monopolized by the United States as the final arbiter in controlling who could be admitted, or who would be barred, from the widening franchise of the United Nations's sovereignty club?

Certainly a key to this debate lies in widening the terms of the discussion about the role of transnational financial institutions in setting the terms for the distribution of those new national charters that entitled and empowered their recipients to exercise sovereign jurisdiction over the UN-titled proprietorships dividing the earth's surface. The granting and mortgaging of these UN-granted titles through the operations of a US-based global banking regime circumscribed, contained, and truncated the process of "decolonization" in much the same way that the tight legal, financial, and geographical constraints of Indian reservations enclosed whatever theoretical powers of self-government Indian tribes in the United States might have retained.

In this scheme, various sovereign countries might from time to time be partitioned to open ground for new nation-states. Indeed, this process of partition was initially embraced and facilitated by the major international powers in Yugoslavia, when they responded quickly to the fast decolonization of the Soviet Empire with early recognition of several new Balkan polities. In spite of the heavy rhetoric of human rights deployed by the NATO powers during their bombing campaign in 1999, the preferred model for sorting out the cultural and religious complexities in the Balkans seemed to be the establishment of ethnic enclaves organized on much the same principles as was done in balkanizing Indian Country through the structuring of North America's reserve system.

The dependence on partition as the highest form of international response to ethnic conflict reflects the prominence of Lockean ideals of possessive individualism in the Darwinian structuring of global geopolitics. Indeed, in some instances, ethnic tensions have provided the pretext for forms of partition whose effect is to deprive Indigenous peoples of forms of genuine intercultural self-determination, based on the formulation of local innovations, to meet local problems. Accordingly, a central feature of this emphasis on partition has been to pre-empt Aboriginal responses to ethnic tensions based on the fundamental principle that concurrent assertions of sovereignty can be – indeed, must be – accommodated within commonly shared territory. Such innovations would have implications for the organizational and ideological frameworks of freehold systems of land tenure. These systems found prototypical expression in the westward expansion of the United States. The role of the United States as the leading polity of globalization is marked in the growing integration of the legal motifs of freehold land tenure into the mix of power relationships that constitute the basis of the international system.[67]

The insistence that only nation-states are eligible for full admission into the United Nations marginalizes approaches to human governance that might encourage different peoples to share ground and jurisdiction through the elaboration of overlapping structures of concurrent sovereignty. Except for the internal organization of federal states,[68] overlapping sovereignties remain an anathema to an international system whose primary mechanism for accommodating human diversity is to run new boundary lines on the planet. The stately boundary lines subdivide the world's land in a proprietary mode that reflects many of the same principles manifest in the organization of a huge suburban real estate project.

How is it determined what peoples must stay in the subordinate global ghettos of inferior political status and what peoples will be granted entry into the more priviledged suburbs of internationally recognized self-government? A key criterion for admission into the closed monopoly of the United Nations's exclusive sovereignty club lies in the willingness and capacity of subject peoples' new governors to mimic the organizational form of the nation-state. By pointing the decolonized peoples of the planet towards the nation-state as the only internationally acceptable instrument of sovereign self-determination, these same peoples have, in many instances, been pointed away from many of their own local sources of Aboriginal philosophical and political understanding.

They have been pressed, instead, into a mould of human development not of their own making. They have been pressed to fit, however awkwardly, into institutions of national governance whose prototypes first appeared to liberate the entrepreneurial energies of the emerging middle classes in the European coastal regions of the North Atlantic Ocean. They have been shoved and contorted to conform to the shape of proprietary nation-states whose original purpose was to replace the communal conservatism of European feudalism with the more individualistic and liberal orientation of European and Anglo-American capitalism.[69] They have been turned away from the Aboriginal dynamics of their own local histories and set up to relive on a reduced scale the historical evolution of their former imperial rulers. In this way, the globalization of the European heritage continues, especially through the expansion and intensification of that hierarchical, highly privatized genre of property relationship on which the informal American empire thrives. It continues even though most of the formal structures of European imperialism have been dismantled and phased out.

In *Nation against State*, Gideon Gottlieb decries the failure on the part of the United Nations and other international organizations to create a range of new instruments for distinct peoples without states of their own to express various forms of recognized self-determination. To avoid "loosening fearful anarchy and disorder on a planetary scale," he argues, "the international system needs additional concepts and a richer vocabulary to accommodate the national claims that cannot be expressed by existing state structures."[70] It is hardly surprising that most of those who led the initial push for decolonization, especially after the Second World War, adopted the forms and structures of the European nation-state even as they rejected the authority of European countries to rule their peoples. After all, those individuals who both organized and articulated the urge of subject peoples for self-determination were often educated in mission schools and later in the great universities of Europe and the United States. Their visions of human liberty and freedom were more likely to draw on the principles of Christ, Jean-Jacques Rousseau, Thomas Jefferson, Karl Marx, or John Stuart Mill than on thinkers whose cultural and philosophical roots lay outside the intellectual traditions of Europe.

Surprisingly few voices were raised to question the wisdom of dismantling European imperialism without coming to terms with the continuing legacy of European approaches to the ordering of relationships linking human beings to each other and to the rest of nature. One of those who endeavoured to go beyond the claims of national independence towards a higher order of human liberation was Mahatma Gandhi, though he was not inherently against European traditions of thought and politics for their own sake. He is known to have praised the "spiritual foundations" of the British Constitution[71] and, on one occasion, he wrote: "I hate the distinction between foreign and indigenous." But while Gandhi acknowledged that much could be learned from India's encounter with Europe, he aspired to a form of decolonization for his people that would transcend the oppressiveness of European nationalism. "I am not interested in freeing India merely from the English yoke," he said. "I am bent on freeing India from any yolk whatsoever ... Hence for me the movement of swaraj is a movement of self-purification."[72] Gandhi's campaign for swaraj – for home-rule through self-purification – was evident in every aspect of his seamlessly intertwined personal and political life. It was evident, for instance, in his rejection of violence as a instrument of national liberation, in his frequent fasting as a demonstration of his preference for self-respect over food, and in his advancement of the spinning wheel as a symbol of an India that abjured the centralized industrialism of Europe for the local self-sufficiency of the village.[73]

In 1960 Frantz Fanon advanced a more strident and extravagant rejection of "European achievements, European techniques, and the European style" as the basis for the decolonization of Africa and the other four-fifths of humanity he ironically referred to as "natives."[74] A Black psychiatrist from Martinique, Fanon emerged as one of the most formidable theorists of the Algerian revolution against French imperial rule.[75] In *The Wretched of the Earth*, Fanon encouraged the opponents of colonialism to come up with blueprints and examples of development that would avoid what he called the pitfalls of national consciousness. "Let us not pay tribute to Europe by creating states, institutions, and societies which draw their inspiration from her," he wrote. "Humanity is waiting for something from us other than such an imitation, which would be almost an obscene caricature." [76]

When he penned *The Wretched of the Earth*, or *Les damnés de la terre*, Fanon could already see that the liberating spirit of decolonization was in the process of being betrayed. As European rulers left their colonial estates, the power and privilege they left behind was being taken up not by broadly rooted democratic movements but by small, self-serving groups who consciously modelled themselves in the image of the middle classes of Europe and the United States. According to Fanon, however, these new, aspiring middle classes of decolonized nations lacked the means and the diversity of the groups they sought to imitate. "Neither financiers nor industrial magnates are to be found within this national middle class," he wrote. "The national bourgeoisie of underdeveloped countries is not engaged in production, nor invention, nor building, nor labour; it is completely canalized into activities of the intermediary type." The highest goal of this class of nationalist was "to take on the role of manager for Western enterprise" and to transfer "into their own native hands" those "unfair advantages which are the legacy of the colonial period."[77]

Fanon's worst fears were to be realized throughout much of Africa and in many other quarters of the supposedly decolonized world. These regions often became host to a variety of one-party, dictatorial regimes that maintained a ruthless hold on power through violent exploitation and repression of the largest mass of people within the boundaries of their UN-sanctioned, US-approved national proprietorships. In the materialistic ostentatiousness of their personal lives and in their unrestrained use of state violence to safeguard hierarchical allocations of privatized wealth, privilege, and power, many of the dictatorial heirs of decolonization became "not even the replica of Europe, but its caricature."[78]

In *The Black Man's Burden: Africa and the Curse of the Nation State*, Basil Davidson documents some of the lethal outcomes of a process that has alienated many Indigenous peoples in Africa not only from their governors but also from the genius of their own Aboriginal systems of self-determined organization.[79] Faced with a poor range of options, African groups have sometimes resorted to very crude and brutalized forms of myopic tribalism to combat the military reigns of terror of their nationalistic opponents. The genocidal clashes of peoples in the former French colonies of Rwanda and Burundi mark the bloody extremes of bedlam that can occur when the politics of decolonization and ethnic nationalism gruesomely converge.[80]

In placing the severity of these crimes against humanity in context, however, it is important to recall the extremes of ethnic nationalism embodied in the early Indian policies of the United States. These Indian policies reflect the outcomes of forms of decolonization where Anglo-Americans took powers unto themselves that previously had been vested in the imperial government. This transfer of power, which was ultimately sanctioned and legitimized by the British government, subjected the Indigenous peoples on the western frontiers of the United States to a new intensity of violent aggression on their own imploding frontiers. This expression of ethnically based nationalism established many prototypical patterns. Only rarely would decolonization devolve powers in an equal and balanced way to all those groups and individuals affected by the transfer of power. Those peoples excluded from the constitutional formulae for power sharing after decolonization have consistently suffered oppression under the weight of privilege extended to favoured groups by departing imperial rulers. An iconographic illustration of this phenomenon lies in the crisis facing Native American peoples after they were left in an ill-defined constitutional twilight zone following Great Britain's recognition of the sovereign authority of the United States in the Treaty of Paris of 1783.

While the burden of African history has fallen heavily on many of her peoples, one of the African liberation struggles became a bright beacon of inspiration for an Indian leader who has been called "Canada's greatest prophet."[81] A Shuswap activist from the interior of British Columbia, George Manuel imagined, described, and enlivened a realm he identified as the Fourth World. His vision of this Fourth World foresaw a fundamental reorientation of global politics and economics to open space for

Indigenous peoples to grow and develop in ways consistent with the underlying order of their own Aboriginal cultures and traditions. By advancing an agenda of global change emphasizing the self-determination of peoples rather than the sovereign authorities of nation-states or the prerogatives of global corporations, Manuel went far to fulfil Fanon's plea for blueprints of decolonization that transcend the constraining bias of Eurocentric models.

GEORGE MANUEL, THE FOURTH WORLD, AND THE MAKING OF A NEW MIDDLE GROUND

During the 1970s George Manuel consolidated an international network of friends and associates who together formed a movement to express and realize the ideals of the Fourth World. A key person in the genesis of this movement was Marie Smallface Marule, a Blood Indian from southern Alberta who worked in Ottawa with Manuel after he became national chief of the National Indian Brotherhood, Canada's most influential Indian organization in 1970. In the years before she moved to Ottawa, Smallface had worked in Zambia on behalf of Canadian University Students Overseas (CUSO), Canada's equivalent to the United States Peace Corps. There she became deeply involved in the struggles of the African National Congress, an involvement that included her marriage to an ANC activist named Jake Marule.[82] While in Ottawa, the Marules arranged many social and political gatherings involving George Manuel and diplomats from Tanzania and a number of other African countries. It was at one of these gatherings that Manuel first heard Mbuto Milando, first secretary of the Tanzanian High Commission, utter the novel phrase "the Fourth World." As Manuel writes in his book *The Fourth World: An Indian Reality*, the Tanzanian diplomat remarked to him, "When Native peoples come into their own, on the basis of their own cultures and traditions, that will be the Fourth World."[83]

As leader of the National Indian Brotherhood, an essential element of Manuel's work was to derive political unity from the broad mosaic of Aboriginal nations, bands, organizations, and individuals that, together, give contemporary shape and form to the Indian Country of Canada. As he ascended the ladder of political influence, the Shuswap activist learned to study, join, and represent the struggles of many distinct Indian societies beyond his own, including the Dene of the Mackenzie River Basin, the Ojibway and Six Nations of the Great Lakes region, the Micmac [Mi'qmak] of Atlantic Canada, and the far-flung Cree, whose various territories stretch from the foothills of the Rockies to the eastern shores of James Bay in northern Quebec. Manuel's success in politically spanning these cultural, linguistic, and geographic spaces made him a leading proponent in his generation of pan-Indianism, a movement with deep roots going back at least to Pontiac and Tecumseh in the long history of Aboriginal resistance to the Europeanization of North America.[84] Manuel went far beyond pan-Indianism, however, when he conceptualized the struggle of his own peoples in Gandhian terms as part of a worldwide movement aimed at global liberation from many forms of repression and tyranny.

Manuel developed his global view of the Fourth World during visits with Maori people in New Zealand, Aborigines in Australia, and Saami in Scandinavia. It was during the trip to Tanzania to participate in that country's tenth anniversary of independence, however, that his conception of the Fourth World seems to have coalesced. "Of all the models of economic and social development I have seen, Tanzania is the closest example to my understanding of the way that Indian people want to develop, he wrote. "Tanzania is such a good example of the difference between the Third World and the Fourth World because neither the people nor their leaders have been content to produce a new society that is merely a darker imitation of the world of their colonial masters."[85]

In Tanzania, Manuel seems to have found the hope that it was possible for subject Indigenous peoples to throw off the weight of European dominance and to forge ahead in a manner that balances the conservatism of their pre-colonial pasts with the revolutionary potential of their post-colonial futures. A powerful figure who helped impress this understanding him was Julius Nyerere, the president of Tanzania and one of the principal thinkers and activists in the larger movement for African decolonization after the Second World War.[86] After meeting Nyerere personally, Manuel saw in him the essential animating spirit of his own ancestors and of the looming struggle to realize the Fourth World. Nyerere personified the animating impetus of egalitarian sharing and cooperation, he said, one starkly in contrast to that of "destruction, conquest and suppression" which had been integral to the European colonization of the New World.[87] "We have only to watch Julius Nyerere taking time from his executive duties to work alongside the day labourers in a small village," he said, "to know that the traditions of our grandfathers have a place in the modern, technological world."[88]

For Manuel, the Tanzanian approach to independence demonstrated that sovereign self-determination is more a means to an end than an end in itself. "Here was a people who were fortunate enough in their leadership to realize that political independence was not the coming of the Messiah," he stated; "it was only the beginning of the struggle for economic and social self-sufficiency. Political independence only gave them the tools of sovereignty with which to begin to build their nation." Manuel concluded, "Julius Nyerere finds ways of reminding his audience of this every time he speaks." Clearly, Nyerere's forward-looking approach spoke strongly to Manuel's own preoccupation with articulating a philosophy aimed at presenting North American Indian cultures not as dead museum relics but as vital, living communities with important roles to play in

shaping the future. "Indian institutions are as capable of growth and adaptation as any others," Manuel insisted, adding, "We are neither the beginning nor the end." With this conviction as an anchor, Manuel predicted
that the strength and the enduring capacity of the Fourth World "lies more
with our grandchildren than with our ancestors."[89]

The strategic efforts of Nyerere and many of his peers to unseat European empires from their African and Asian colonies were accompanied by
a major ideological attack on the intellectual foundations of Social Darwinism. Manuel and the other champions of the Fourth World took that
ideological campaign one step further. By insisting on the right of their
peoples to a place of influence in the future of the planet, the activists of
the Fourth World rejected the virtual death sentence cast on most "Native"
societies by the proponents of Darwinian politics and social science. They
refused to accept the judgment heaped on them explicitly or implicitly by
"modernization" theorists and others that their cultural roots were nestled
in earlier, lower, or more primitive phases of human evolution. Nor would
they agree that their Aboriginal identities were of a lower order of importance to the destiny of the world than those of societies derived from the
nation-states of Europe and the Creole nationalisms of America. They
rejected the notion that most "Native" societies could be classified and relegated to virtual obsolescence through the imposition of pseudo-scientific
terms such as "savage," "barbaric," "stone age," or "tribal." And they dismissed the idea that the Indigenous peoples of the planet are any less capable of change, adaptation, innovation, and creative contribution than
those societies organized to reflect and extend the archetype of the European nation-state.

An essential theme running through the seminal conception of the
Fourth World was a rejection of the models of social, technological, and
economic development implicit in the idea of the Third World, where the
imagery of underdevelopment is the underlying premise. Once a nation or
people comes to accept a view of itself as underdeveloped, it is adopting
the assumptions of Social Darwinism. It is accepting a view of human social
evolution which assumes there is a set of universally applicable stages that
all human societies must go through. Beyond the adoption of these shared
assumptions, however, there was much disagreement among Third World
thinkers over which group of nations represented the highest model of
development, a disagreement that existed as long as the First World of
American-dominated countries competed with the Soviet-dominated
regimes of the Second World.

While superpower rivalry made the Third World a zone of intense political, ideological, economic, and sometimes even military conflict between
two competing geopolitical systems, Third World thinking left little room
for recognition of the value, worth, and contemporary applicability of
Indigenous knowledge and philosophy. Fourth World thinking is necessarily antagonistic to the bias of Third World thinking, a mode of con-

ceptualization that promotes external models of change for most of humanity to mimic and duplicate.[90]. Unlike Third World thinking, with its emphasis on imposing standardized, monocultural moulds of growth and development on different societies, Fourth World thinking emphasizes the freedom of diverse peoples to chart their own distinct courses of social, legal, economic, technological, and political change. The object of this change is to ameliorate the pluralistic ecology of human relationships in ways that reflect and project forward the Aboriginal inspiration and dynamics of First Nations cultures. Fourth World thinking emphasizes the importance of human adaptation to, and integration with, the distinct ecologies of particular places rather than large-scale manipulation of geography, society, and biology by powerful elites concentrated in a few metropolitan centres.

In moving beyond the Social Darwinism of Third World thinking, George Manuel and his associates gave expression to principles whose ideological thrust had been anticipated by some anthropologists and ethnographers at least since Franz Boas broke from the Darwinian preoccupations of his colleagues in the early twentieth century.[91] Indeed, Manuel specifically honoured Boas in his book, noting how this unrelenting critic of simple-minded theories of human evolution defended the legitimacy of the potlatch against those in church and state who were intent on snuffing out this famous West Coast Indian ceremony.[92] Manuel balanced his tribute to Boas and several other students of Indigenous peoples with cautionary remarks about the self-serving excesses of many contemporary anthropologists. He charged that they sometimes advanced their own careers without contributing anything back to the Aboriginal communities they studied.[93]

Notwithstanding these criticisms, Manuel was able to establish fruitful relations with a small but energetic circle of progressive anthropologists and ethnographers connected especially to Survival International and a Copenhagen-based association known as the International Work Group on Indigenous Affairs.[94] Some of the Scandanavian anthropologists, but especially Helge Kleivan, contributed significantly to the transformation of Fourth World thinking into an organizing principle of political action and social science research. Kleivan helped, for instance, to organize a conference in 1973 of Inuit, Saami, Dene, and Cree representatives which Manuel also attended.[95] In 1975 Manuel built on this work and organized a broader gathering of Aboriginal representatives in Port Alberni, British Columbia. At that meeting the World Council of Indigenous Peoples was officially founded.

The work of the Scandanavian anthropologists in their own countries was energized by the rise of Fourth World politics in Saami country, a territory that was familiar to Manuel in his most nomadic years. Anthropologist Robert Paine of the Institute of Social and Economic Research at Memorial University in St John's, Newfoundland, joined in the transatlantic discussions generated by the rise of Saami assertiveness, especially in Norway.[96] Paine's Canadian colleague, anthropologist Sally Weaver, brought similar attentiveness to her assessments of the emergence of Aboriginal issues in mainstream politics in Australia.[97] Meanwhile law professor Douglas E. Saunders, who had apprenticed under Manuel when he worked at the National Indian Brotherhood, helped to infuse the language and thought of the Fourth World into a number of legal and academic venues, but especially those loosely affiliated with the formation and work of the United Nations Working Group on Indigenous Populations.[98]

The emphasis on the activism of the Saami, who are indigenous to Europe, helped to clarify that the activists of the Fourth World were not in the first instance preoccupied with "race relations" but with issues arising from colonization and the appropriation of the Aboriginal territories of Indigenous peoples in every part of the planet. As many Saami people see it, their territories have been colonized by the northern expansions of the Scandanavian countries in much the same way that the Indian and Inuit lands in the Americas have been colonized by European empires and their successor states. The activism of the Saami and their allies helped many Europeans to see that the colonization of Indigenous peoples was not some remote phenomenon situated exclusively in the past on the overeas frontiers of their former empires. Rather, the dispossession and disempowerment of Indigenous peoples is an ongoing, contemporary phenomenon happening even within Europe. The formative era of Saami activism culminated in a hunger strike of the Saami Action Group, conducted with great publicity in Oslo in 1979. The immediate goal was to draw attention to the flooding of Saami lands in Norway through the building of a massive hydroelectric dam known as the Alta project.[99]

The involvement of anthropologists and ethnographers in the Fourth World movement called into play many motifs of intellect and action that had been integral to the rise of *indigenismo*, especially in Mexico and then in the circle of ideological activism centred on John Collier, Manuel Gamio, and the Interamerican Indigenista Institute. This development can be seen, in a way, as another stage in the growth of "applied anthropology." In 1976 some social scientists in the United States, but especially at Harvard University, joined the trend. They founded Cultural Survival, an organization to promote publications that stimulated changes in public policy so as to safeguard cultural pluralism.[100] In contrast to the anthropologists, who had developed their discipline along the imperial side of the moving frontiers of colonization, a small but influential constituency of social scientists applied their professional energies to bringing some corrections to the gross imbalances of power rooted in historical and contemporary injustices. The emergence of the Fourth World politics of Indigenous peoples therefore had a symbiotic relationship with the changing politics of the academy generally and of the discipline of anthropology more specifically.[101]

Like other Aboriginal representatives of the Fourth World in his generation, George Manuel had an ambivalent relationship to academic politics.
There was nothing in his wariness towards some anthropologists, however,
that detracted from an approach that was inclusive rather than exclusive,
intercultural and transcultural rather than parochial. Manuel was no
preacher of ethnic fundamentalism. "The Fourth World is no less open to
others than to us," he told his non-Aboriginal readers. "We know we cannot move very far [towards the Fourth World] unless you also choose to
move ... We cannot become equal members in *your* society. We *can* become
a member of a new society in which everyone chooses to share. But that
cannot happen until you begin to consider and reformulate your understanding, and your view of the world, as we have begun to reformulate
ours."[102]

Manuel's politics were founded on his conviction that Aboriginal societies remain rich repositories of knowledge and attitudes, with wide applicability to many of the dilemmas facing all humankind. This belief was rooted in Manuel's deep understanding that the world of his Indian ancestors
in the Americas had already bequeathed to human civilization a vast array
of lasting innovations, especially in horticulture, architecture and political
science.[103] "Our cultures," he explained, "possess a strength and a vitality
with which the visitors to our continent have not yet been prepared to
credit us." He anticipated that the Aboriginal societies of the future would
continue to challenge and transform their neighbours just as earlier generations of Indigenous peoples had done in the past. Moreover, he foresaw
a broadening of the transformative capacity of the Fourth World as the old
colonialism gradually ground itself down. "The Western World is gradually working its way out of its former value system," he wrote, "and into the
value system of the Aboriginal World."[104]

When Manuel wrote *The Fourth World* with the assistance of Michael
Posluns, a talented young admirer from Toronto, the Shuswap activist had
ample cause for his optimism that history was opening cultural and intellectual space for an infusion of ideas from Indian Country. As a speaker,
he was much in demand to address college and church audiences in the
late 1960s and early 1970s. These were years when members of the postwar baby boom generation – the Woodstock Generation – were coming of
age. In their massive opposition to the Vietnam War, their rejection of the
most overt forms of American apartheid, and their search for less exploitative means of relating to one another and to the natural environment, the
young people who surged into the electorate and marketplace of many
countries seemed poised to overturn many of the orthodoxies of their parents.[105] It was among this generation of Indians and non-Indians that
Manuel found his most attentive audience and his most conspicuous
encouragement that a true decolonization of Indigenous peoples was possible. It was among this uneasy, searching generation, whose long-haired
demeanour borrowed so heavily from the emblems of Indian Country, that

he crafted and articulated an alternative vision of globalization, one where the New World of the newcomers and their descendants would be brought into greater harmony with the Old World of Indigenous peoples.

There were many factors at work to stimulate the dynamic, transcultural vibrancy that Manuel's writing and career epitomized and advanced. The 1960s and 1970s were a time of large-scale migration of many Native people from their reserves and reservations to urban centres. Paralleling this move came the end of the now-infamous Christian Indian boarding schools, to be replaced by the federally financed integration of most Native students into regular public or denominational schools in non-Indian communities. While "integration" constituted the overriding theme of Indian education during the period, some First Nations groups began to design and operate their own pedagogical institutes at, for instance, the Rough Rock Demonstration School on the Navajo Reservation, the Blue Quills School near St Paul, Alberta, the Little Red Schoolhouse in St Paul–Minneapolis, and the Wandering Spirit Survival School in Toronto.[106]

The peak of Manuel's career coincided also with the period when many of the remote Native communities of northern Canada were brought within the reach of telephone, radio, and television. This opening of electronic highways of communications took place around the time that the Arab oil embargo of 1973 stimulated a great surge of commercial pressure to exploit what remained of the untapped energy resources in North America. The resulting expansions of North America's energy resource frontiers led, for instance, to the extension of massive hydroelectric works into northern Manitoba and northern Quebec.[107] It led also to a rush to capitalize on the remaining coal, oil, and uranium deposits in the American midwest and southwest[108] and to a proposal to build a pipeline through the relatively undisturbed Dene and Inuit hunting teritories in the western arctic.[109]

Fourth World politics developed during a time when there was some relaxing of more than a century of government repression aimed at holding many Native people within the tight legal and geographic constrainsts of North America's Indian reserves and reservations. As the forces of economic, social, and technological transformation broke down many of the old lines of clear demarcation between the experiences of Native and non-Aboriginal, the extended borderlands of cultural mixture, overlap, and improvisation gave rise to new forms of indigenismo that some have characterized as rebirth, revitalization, and resurgence. In the words of Gordon Brotherston in *Book of the Fourth World*, the era of George Manuel was a time of renovation from within.[110] This hybrid expressiveness showed up in the paintings and sculptures of many celebrated Aboriginal artists, including Allan Houser, Norval Morrisseau, Daphne Odjig, R.C. Gorman, Joshim Kagegamic, Bill Reid, Fritz Scholder, and Carl Ray. Their art often blended representations of the ancient, animating spirit beings of the

American continent with a graphic sensibility derived, in part at least, from newer influences such as Morrisseau's long exposure to the mythic realm of Christian stained-glass windows.[111].

In literature, the Kiowa author N. Scott Momaday emerged as the towering figure, winning the Pulitzer Prize in 1969 with his *House Made of Dawn*.[112] As would become clear over subsequent decades, Momaday's achievement helped inspire many younger Native Americans to pursue careers as writers and as literary critics. Many of them found openings especially in the English Departments of North American universities, where the emphasis on "post-colonial literature" had a considerable effect on hiring strategies.[113] In music, the energy of the powwow trail influenced a growing number of recording artists, but none more so than Cree songwriter Buffy Sainte-Marie. Some of her compositions became virtual anthems for a protest movement whose leading thinkers increasingly saw the conflict in Vietnam as an extension of earlier American wars on Indian Country.[114]

In trying to explain the importance he attached to the rise of Zapatismo, Tom Hayden has left a telling account of his political coming of age after he began to place the US military involvement in Vietnam in the historical context of the Indian wars. He wrote:

It was not until the 1960s jarred my own sense of identity, and an Indian band seized Alcatraz Island, that I sat down on a Berkeley floor to read *Bury My Heart at Wounded Knee* and experienced a life-altering realization that America and the West had been destroying native people for 500 years. I then saw Vietnam for what it was, not a mistake or a Cold War confrontation, but a continuation of the conquest of the indigenous. The US bombing campaigns had names like "Rolling Thunder," our helicopters were called Apaches. The jargon was the same, with only the labels changed: "the only good gook is a dead gook." The defoliation of crops had begun long before William Westmorland, with Kit Carson. The Harvard-based doctrine of "forced urbanization" and the Pentagon strategy of "fighting the birth rate" was aimed at destroying ancient cultures attached spiritually to land and ancestors.[115]

Manuel's original political philosophy of the Fourth World was part of this creative surge of energy aimed at achieving some sort of reckoning with five centuries of conquest and some way to infuse the worldwide decolonization movement with the impetus of renovation emanating from within North America. His work soon became a recognized landmark in an emerging terrain of published, First Nations scholarship produced in and around the colleges and universities of North America. By far the most prolific of this new generation of Aboriginal academics was Vine Deloria Jr, a Souian scholar who applied his expertise in law and theology to a study of the changing experiences of Native Americans over the course of the history of the United States.[116] In Canada, Trent University professor Harvey McCue, whose Ojibway name is Waubageshig, helped to publish the work of several Aboriginal colleagues while producing an analysis of the relationship of Canadian Indian policy to Frantz Fanon's theories of colonial oppression and native liberation.[117] Other key activists in the movement of intellectual renewal from within Aboriginal societies included Jack Forbes, Howard Adams, Rupert Custo, and Roxanne Dunbar Ortiz. These historians of politics documented and explained many complex interactions between colonialism and resistance. Beatrice Medicine, Bob Thomas, Leroy Little Bear, Alfonso Ortiz, Verna Kirkness, Jeanette Henry, and Elizabeth Cook-Lynne fought to widen the social sciences to an array of Aboriginal voices far beyond their own. Fred Wheatley and Basil Johnson gained recognition in the academy as accomplished scholars whose deepest wells of erudition lay in their sophisticated mastery of Aboriginal languages. Emma LaRoque confronted the patriarchal character of colonialization even as it extended to the gender inequities embedded in Indian Country. Arthur Soloman helped to transform some of Canada's major prisons into sites of learning and spiritual devotion for many Aboriginal inmates. And, as always, Iroquois Country contributed prolifically to the thought, literature, and activist energy of the larger Indian Country. Prominent among the makers and shapers of the Iroquois renaissance were Ernest Benedict, Oren Lyons, Shirley Hill Witt, Ray Fadden, John Mohawk, Kahn-Tineta Horn, Louis Hall, Jacob Thomas, Philip Deer, Marlene Brant-Castellano, and later Mike Mitchell, Tommy Porter, Francis Boots, Splitting the Sky, Ellen Gabriel, Dan David, Brian Maracle, Tom Hill, Roberta Jamison, Gerald Alfred, and many, many more.

What meanings are to be derived from this group's orientation to North America as Aboriginal witnesses and observers of the course of history in the quintessential land of immigrants, the continent of the Statue of Liberty? What meanings are to be derived from their reflections on the colonization of their peoples in that part of the planet where European societies asserted their most prolonged, intensive, and successful drives to remake overseas lands in their own image? What role would they play in criticizing the underlying assumptions on which the Creole nationalisms of the American hemisphere have been constructed? To what extent would they be a vehicle to channel or transform currents of indigenismo from South and Central America into the North American heartland of the American empire?

Here was a group of articulate commentators whose own peoples' dispossession and subjugation had opened vast territories for the consolidation of the most aggressively expansionistic system of economic, social, and political relationships the world has ever seen. Here was a group of commentators in a unique position to clarify how colonial settlers had been transformed themselves into citizens of sovereign, independent states – states that had connected their own claims of legitimacy on legal and ideological efforts to delegitimize and extinguish the First Nations. Here was a group of commentators in the strongest position to relate the circumstances of their own lives to a 500-year cycle of history linking, for instance, the Spanish conquest of Mexico to the flooding of Cree lands by Crown corporations in northern Quebec or northern Manitoba. Here was a group of commentators who had grown up in, but not fully of, the very heartland of conspicuous consumption, advertising, mass communications, obsessive technological fetishism, and corporate dominance over the civic sphere. What were the aesthetic, social, and political implications of this rapid multiplication of recorded Aboriginal voices, some of whom spoke and published with the backing of academies whose intellectual authority had previously been lent to legitimizing the ideological machinery of Aboriginal extinguishment and dispossession?

Beneath the apparent novelty of this Aboriginal surge towards the mainstream of North American art, literature, academia, mass media, and politics lay an old and resilient pattern of Aboriginal renovation from within. This pattern of adaptation to, and compromise with, the aggressive cultures of the newcomers has been described in great detail by Richard White in his book *The Middle Ground: Indians, Empires, and Republics in the Great Lakes Region, 1650–1815*. For White, the archetypal middle ground of compromise and mediation between Indigenous peoples and newcomers was the Great Lakes area until the end of the War of 1812. For almost two centuries before the War of 1812, this region gave form and substance to a geopolitical entity known as Canada, where the fur trade was the primary glue of intercultural collaboration among Indigenous peoples, French Canadians, and the businessmen and Tory governors of British imperial Canada. This zone of intense exchange, mediation, and cultural blending between Indigenous peoples and newcomers, this mestizo middle ground, lasted until the defeat of Tecumseh's Indian Confederacy by the army of the United States. According to White, thereafter "the middle ground withered and died"; thereafter the Indians became "objects of study;" thereafter scholars "reinvented the Indian as the other;" thereafter "the Americans arrived and dictated."[118]

But the basis for the middle ground did not disappear as surely as Canada withstood the claims and acquisitive assertions of American manifest destiny. In many ways Manuel's articulation of the present and future propsects of the Fourth World marks a fitting announcement of the return of the middle ground. The fact that this announcement emerged from British Columbia, the site of some of North America's most contentious continuing battles over the contemporary meaning of Aboriginal title, was especially significant.[119] In the philosophy of George Manuel lay a contemporary manifestation of renovation from within. As White wrote, "The meeting of sea and continent, like the meeting of whites and Indians, creates as well as destroys. Contact was not a battle of primal forces in which only one could survive. Something new could appear."[120] The Fourth World was the name given to one such initiative in the ongoing process of renewing and renovating the world's oldest human polities. Proponents of the Fourth World held up to humanity the vision of a global possibility that was pristinely new yet concurrently rooted in eons of careful adaptations to the planet's most primal Aboriginal ecologies.

As a realm of human creativity at once universal yet locally rooted, open to innovation yet respectful of tradition, Manuel's conception of the Fourth World was in every sense a middle ground of paradox and compromise. As the National Indian Brotherhood proclaimed in preparing the way for the founding of the World Council of Indigenous People: "Neither apartheid nor assimilation can be allowed to discolour the community of man in the Fourth World. An integration of free communities and the free exchange of people between those communities according to their talents and their temperaments is the only kind of confederation that is not an imperial domination."[121]

One of the most enticing features of the Fourth World in the late 1960s and early 1970s, a time of intense, youth-driven quests for alternatives, was the possibility that the old ways of Indigenous peoples offered a new ethos of environmental sensitivity in North America and beyond. According to Manuel, this quest for a more enlightened regime of ecological relationships among human beings, technology, and the rest of the natural environment created the larger context for the struggle by Indigenous peoples to gain recognition and respect from their neighbours. North America, he asserted, "is our Promised land," the source of the "medicines" used by his peoples over countless generations to heal their ailments. By accepting and recognizing the deep bonds between Indigenous peoples and their ancestral territories – by reversing a trend aimed at "the separation of the people from the land"[122] – the non-Aboriginals would in turn be opening the way for their own development of a more secure, mature, and spiritually enlightened relationship with their adopted territories. The ongoing experience of immigration would continue to move beyond Europe's frontier outposts towards the Old World soul of Aboriginal America. The newcomers would merge their energies and aspirations with indigenismo's steady current. They would beget Métis, either through the hybridization of family lines or through the more fundamental act of reimagining the meaning of ancestral traditions as well as the horizons of hope awaiting generations yet unborn. The newcomers and their descendants would follow the lead of the First Nations in developing fuller, more anchored senses of the animating spirit of the Aboriginal hemisphere. They would put aside the frontier ethos of conquest, victory, and ascendancy *over* the land to cultivate a more reverential and familial connection *with* the land. They, too, would enter the Fourth World.

In making this case, Manuel insisted that the ecological sensibility still retained by some citizens of the First Nations was more practical than romantic, more essential than ephemeral, more grounded in common sense than abstractly adrift in the etherial realm of high idealism. He explained, for instance, that the traditional relationship of Indian people with the land, the water, the air, and the sun has often been praised because of its spiritual nature. People seeking their own roots have praised it because it is a tradition they can grasp. But its real strength historically for our people, and its growing appeal today both for our own young people and for non-Indian people concerned for the generations still coming towards us, is not a romantic notion. Its strength lies in the accuracy of the description it offers of the proper and natural relationship of people to their environment and to the larger universe. It offers a description of the spiritual world that is parallel to, and in fact part of, the material universe that is the basis of all our experience. The land, the water, the air, and the sun are sacred because they are the source of all life. They are the limbs of the Guardian Spirit. Their sanctity is recognized because of their importance to our survival.[123]

RENOVATION FROM WITHIN: THE APPRENTICESHIP OF GEORGE MANUEL AND THE POLITICAL ORGANIZATION OF INDIAN COUNTRY IN THE TWENTIETH CENTURY

In rooting his political program in a broad and inclusive approach to ecology and spirituality, George Manuel created a synthesis combining the ideas and motifs of many earlier eras of organized activism in Indian Country. On the one hand, his references to the metaphysical or supernatural realm as offering the highest form of justification for enacting the principles of the Fourth World harkened back to the kind of Aboriginally based religious fervour generated in the eighteenth and nineteenth centuries by the Aboriginal resistance struggles associated with figures such as Pontiac, Tecumseh, Black Hawk, Sitting Bull, and Wovoka. On the other hand, Manuel's more gentle form of Aboriginal evangelism was not so extreme as to alienate the many Christians among his own constituents and allies, nor did it preclude the more secular preoccupations that tended increasingly to dominate the activites of Aboriginal political organizations in the twentieth century.

Manuel's central point was that Aboriginal spirituality was not a force that opposed the materialism of everyday experience. Rather, it offered the basis for a more sane and ultimately sustainable approach to materialism than that embodied in those kinds of market relationships that disregard or even revile and defile the sanctity of the most elemental life forces in nature, including human nature. Accordingly, Manuel, as the chief philosopher of the Fourth World, continued the tradition of renovation from within the First Nations by recasting and adapting old ideas from his Aboriginal heritage in new language imbued with fresh insight gained from his encounters with the many novelties unique to his own generation of Native North Americans. As a student, a practitioner, and, ultimately, as a synthesizer of both old and new kinds of political activism of Indigenous peoples, Manuel's project cannot readily be understood outside the various political milieus that nurtured him, engaged him, and bound him within the constraints he sought to transcend.

In his years as an apprentice activist, Manuel's most influential teacher and mentor was Andy Paull, the wiley Squamish legal expert, journalist, and sports coach who founded and spoke for the North American Indian Brotherhood until shortly before his death in 1959. In his tribute to Paull in *The Fourth World*, Manuel remarks that there was "never a moment" when this beloved politician "was not organizing something" and reaching into "every aspect of Indian community life." One of his frequent tactics was to bring Indian workers in various economic sectors together through potlatch ceremonies he organized. On one occasion with hop-pickers, for instance, he "formed what amounted to an employment agency to match up workers with jobs, keep tabs on people who might get lost in an area that was new to them, and see that everyone got home at the end of the season."[124]

Paull's application of the ancient institution of the potlatch to the changing economic circumstances of his people represents an essential lesson for Fourth World politics. This renovation from within suggests the forces of continuity linking Manuel's work globally with the ideological and political currents that, for more than a century, have surged up with particular power from the unresolved issues of Aboriginal title at the basis of British Columbia's system of land tenure. The ongoing legal and political controversies surrounding the issue of Indian title to Canada's westernmost province highlight the shared experiences of many Indigenous peoples throughout the course of the Columbian conquests. These controversies illustrate the character of the colonization faced by the First Nations as well as the strategies of decolonization that are integral to the Fourth World. It would be difficult to overstate Paull's importance in keeping the Indian title question alive in the shared political imagination of many Aboriginal individuals and groups. Similarly, it would be difficult to overstate his significance as a teacher, mentor, and guide in helping Manuel grow into the ideas and historical struggles that would become the basis of his work.[125]

The most important of these organizations was the Allied Indian Tribes of British Columbia. This body, which was representative of the ethnically diverse Aboriginal population in the province, was founded in 1916 at a gathering at Andy Paull's Mission Reserve 1 in North Vancouver. The insistent lobbying of the Allied Tribes, with Paull as the organization's secretary, led to the creation in 1927 of a Special Committee of the Senate and House of Commons. The committee's investigation of the Indian title issue in British Columbia pointed a spotlight of national visibility at Paull as well as at the Reverend Peter Kelly. A Haida aristocrat and a Methodist missionary, Kelly, like Paull, studied and reflected on the failure of the crown to apply the constitutional principles of the Royal Proclamation of 1763 to the non-Indian colonization and settlement of British Columbia. [126]

Although the committee members commended both Paull and Kelly for the quality of their presentations, in their final report they denied the validity of the Allied Tribes' position. Their recommendations led to an outright legal prohibition on any paid legal work having to do with research or litigation to advance any Aboriginal claim in Canada.[127] This provision, one of the more repressive features of the dominion government's increasingly pervasive subjugation of Indian reserves and Indian peoples during the 1920s and 1930s, was not lifted until 1951. Moreover, it was not until 1973, during Manuel's term of leadership at the National Indian Brotherhood, and again in 1997, that the Supreme Court of Canada finally pronounced on the existence of Indian land title in a province that is rich in natural resources, cultural pluralism, and biodiversity.

The defence of land and resources is almost always a primary impetus in Indian politics, but it has unfolded with particular force in British Columbia.[128] In part it comes as a response to the aggressive legal manipulation by both the provincial and the federal governments to suppress and even prohibit peaceful Aboriginal resistance to their unilateral dispossession. The Aboriginal peoples' counterattack to this tactic has depended heavily on the innovative strategy demonstrated by the careers of Paull and Manuel. These two men drew not only on their own peoples' traditions of Aboriginal law but also on the imperial law of Great Britain to counteract the extinguishment implicit in the recent overlay, without Indian consent, of provincial and federal powers on the ancestral lands of First Nations. For several generations this strategy of counterattack has received broad support from the many Aboriginal communities in British Columbia, but especially from the Nisga'a people of the Nass Valley in the northwestern section of the province. Since the late nineteenth century the Nisga'a have often been at the forefront of efforts to force the federal and provincial governments into recognizing Indian title as the necessary prior condition for the initiation of authentic treaty negotiations. The consistency of that stance resulted in the making of the Nisga'a treaty in the final years of the twentieth century.

With the virtual outlawing of overt organizing on the Indian title issue in British Columbia after 1927, the public face of Aboriginal politics in the province changed considerably. During the Depression, the Indian fishermen and cannery workers invented new vehicles of Aboriginal trade unionism, especially through the formation of the Native Brotherhood of British Columbia and, later, of the Pacific Coast Native Fisherman's Association. Paull was instrumental in bringing about an amalgamation of the two groups during the Second World War, largely through his ability to rally Indian opposition against the extension of federal income tax to off-reserve Indians, including many engaged in the lucrative West Coast fishery.[129]

The Christian religion was a major influence on the organizational work of Paull's generation of Indian activists. By the twentieth century both Protestantism and Roman Catholicism had become dominant forces in the community life of most Aboriginal groups on the continent. The wide-spread federal establishment of Christian boarding schools for Indian youth in Canada and the United States was a crucial factor in the emergence of Christianity as the primary religion of Indian Country. Although these institutions have been the subject of a growing wave of condemnation as a result of their assimilationist objectives and the high rates of mental and physical abuse that often took place there, some commentators have pointed out that the development of the kind of cross-cultural activism carried on by men like Paull and Kelly would have been unthinkable outside of the pan-Indian networking and consciousness created by these schools. As Paul Tennant has noted in his study of Aboriginal politics in British Columbia: "By bringing together children from different tribal groups and by keeping them together for long periods away from traditional influences, while at the same time isolating them from white society, the schools promoted ... pan-Indian identity and provided future leaders with essential political resources."[130]

The establishment of English as a *lingua franca* throughout Indian Country, together with the widespread acceptance of Christianity, created the basis for all sorts of new associations across old lines of language, culture, and ethnicity distinguishing one Aboriginal nation from another. The divisions associated with denominational politics, however, laid the groundwork for different forms of acrimony both within and among First Nations communities. The lines of distinction dividing, for instance, Roman Catholics from Anglicans from Methodists in Indian Country were often crossed and transcended in efforts to forge common positions on key issues. It would be wrong, however, to underestimate the sometimes disunifying influences of the Christian churches on those generations of Indian politicians who created the organizational infrastructure inherited by George Manuel, first in his activism in British Columbia and then at the healm of the most important Indian organization in Canada.

A large part of Andy Paull's education and career was shaped through his close association with the Roman Catholic Church. This association was marked in 1955 when the Vatican awarded Paull with the *Bene Merenti* Medal. Paull's personal and public life was especially intertwined with the work of the Oblate Order, whose missionary and pedagogical vocation has figured strategically in the community life of many Indian societies throughout western and northern Canada.[131] The fact that the Oblate missionaries to the Indians were often French-speaking adds a particularly interesting twist in the cross-cultural complexities of Roman Catholic evangelization over large sections of Canada, where the most powerful legions of colonization and assimilation did their business in English and prayed in Protestant churches.

In *Andy Paull: As I Knew Him and Understood His Times*, the Oblate Father Francis Dunlop left an affectionate and realistic, if sometimes paternalistic, biography.[132] Paull's home was right beside the boarding school on

Mission Reserve 1, a similar situation to that of Jules Sioui, the Huron activist from the Quebec City area who worked closely with Paull at the end of the Second World War to help found the North American Indian Brotherhood. Although Sioui shared Paull's attachment to the Roman Catholic Church, the former was seen as a more uncompromisingly militant than Paull in his hostility towards the government.[133] This hostility was augmented by the pervasive French Canadian aversion to conscription during the war, a position that prompted Sioui to explore the prohibition in Canadian Indian treaties against forcing Native people into mandatory military service.[134]

This same hybrid marriage of Aboriginal patriotism and French Canadian nationalism probably led Sioui to imagine a form of Indian independence that went far beyond the scope of what many Native people were prepared to entertain. Sioui's unqualified hostility to the Canadian state would prove especially suspect among those several thousands of Indian men who returned from active service in the Canadian military during the Second World War.[135] Sioui disseminated many of his key ideas in a small pamphlet entitled, provocatively, *War... Peace in Canada: The Invaders Responsible for the Death of Louis Riel.* He concluded this essay with the following words:

Since four centuries, you, the invaders, ever since you set foot on our soil, you have attempted to do everything for the purpose of annihilating our race; you have taken all our heritage from us; you have impaired our morale and patriotism. Yet you are not satisfied, and you would like to see us give up all hope as to the future of our national survival ... We must obtain our national independence and the right to make use of our own currency. We must obtain vast territories, in order to administer our own natural, political and economic resources. Barring that we will count for nothing and we will go to nothing.[136]

Sioui had many Native followers in Quebec and Ontario. The axis of understanding between Sioui and Paull also attracted a certain amount of supportive interest from the prairies. In this heartland of the numbered treaties, various forms of Aboriginal political activism had taken strong hold since the early 1920s in spite of concerted federal hostility directed particularly at certain key organizers such as Lieutenant Fred Loft, the founder of the League of Indians of Canada.[137]

John Tootoosis, the Cree leader from Saskatchewan, was among those who headed to Ottawa in 1944 in the hopes of fulfilling the unrealized potential inherent in some organization similar to the old League, an organization that had briefly been willed into existence in the fluid political atmosphere following the First World War. Now that the defeat of Nazism was in sight, the time seemed right to try once again to forge some sort of pan-Canadian or even pan-North American association that would give First Nations peoples a more unified, and thus more influential, voice in shaping those government policies that most affect them. Many of these hopes, personalities, and tendencies came together at the meeting in Ottawa in 1944. The minister of Indian Affairs, T.A. Crear, agreed to visit this assembly, the first tacit signal ever from the dominion government that it was ready to recognize some sort of organizational mouthpiece for Indian peoples from coast to coast in Canada. Crear's condition, however, was that Sioui not attend. Sioui reluctantly agreed, opening the way for the more moderate Andy Paull to assume the responsibilities of the top job in the North American Indian Brotherhood.[138] Tellingly, the Native Brotherhood of British Columbia, an organization dominated by Protestant leadership, failed to support Paull in his new capacity at the head of an organization that remained throughout its lifetime more its leader's personal vehicle of public pronouncement than an institution cutting wide and deep in Indian Country. It was more a blueprint for future action than an instrument of a realized political coalition.[139]

Even as the North American Indian Brotherhood attempted to put an organizational umbrella over a large and diverse Aboriginal constituency, a host of local Native organizations emerged after the Second World War. One of the most enduring was the Indian Federation of Saskatchewan, which continues to this day under the name of the Federated Saskatchewan Indian Nations. The impetus to establish this provincially based Indian entity came largely from the Co-operative Commonwealth Federation government of Premier Tommy Douglas.[140] The election of this Baptist minister and social democrat to Saskatchewan's top political job in 1944 represented a significant shift towards the left wing of the political spectrum and the tentative beginnings in Canada of a willingness to start constructing the rudimentary outlines of a social welfare state. The Métis and the Indians, the poorest constituencies in the province, naturally attracted the attention of a government dedicated to overcome the most blatant examples of social and economic inequality. Despite the distrust among many Aboriginal people in Saskatchewan who resisted working closely with any non-Aboriginal government, Douglas's genuine commitment to democratic ideals gradually disarmed some of his opponents. They began to use the province's most influential Indian organization to achieve some pragmatic solutions to real problems.

By rejecting the blatantly assimilationist objectives proclaimed in that era by most officials of church and state with a role in the formulation of Canadian Indian policy, the CCF government in Saskatchewan moved closer to the philosophical ground of John Collier's Indian New Deal in the United States. As an official of the Douglas government explained in 1946, "The Indian must first be free to develop his own culture and not merely imbibe ours; to learn his own history, and not to rely on our interpretation of it; to practise his own religion, and not be coerced into another; to devise his own means of self-government, and not be cowed by ours."[141]

The growing importance of the Indian Federation of Saskatchewan was perceived as a threat in some branches of the Roman Catholic Church, whose adherents were jealous to maintain their own ecclesiastical hold over the organizational work of their Aboriginal adherents. Like Andy Paull and Jules Sioui, John Tootoosis was Roman Catholic. Tootoosis told the story of how John Henry Agecoutay from Pasqua was approached by a Roman Catholic priest in the early days of the federation. The priest offered Agecoutay money to start up a competing organization with the promise that the Catholic missionaries would work with him to cultivate his leadership role.[142]

Denominational antagonisms within Christianity created the basis for new categories of factionalism among Aboriginal activists. The central arguments within Indian Country, however, continued to revolve around the issue of how far to go towards integration or even assimilation into the increasingly dominant culture and institutions of non-Aboriginal society. For much of the twentieth century this debate centred on the relationship of First Nations people to enfranchisement and citizenship in the nation-states dominating their lands. While the segregationist-integrationist dichotomy has been integral to the politics of decolonization in almost every colonized society, the demographics of Indianness in Canada and the United States in this period were quite different from those of Mexico and many other parts of Central and South America. In the predominantly Protestant and English-speaking parts of the continent, the Indigenous peoples have constituted a much smaller percentage of the overall population than in large, overwhelmingly Roman Catholic districts of the former New Spain and New Portugal.

The prospect of Indigenous peoples being effectively absorbed and assimilated into the non-Aboriginal majority has been made to seem more menacing in Canada and the United States. Indeed, this kind of extinction through displacement as well as through assimilation and absorption into the majority population has been re-enacted again and again, especially in the United States east of the Mississippi. Even counting the self-identifying mestizo population, all the Indigenous peoples collectively still constitute a small minority of the total population, although they are less of a minority in Canada than in the United States. The sheer weight of numbers is stacked against the use of integrationist strategies by Indigenous peoples to pull the mainstream population towards identifying more closely with the land's Indian heritages.

Until 1960, when the federal government of Prime Minister John Diefenbaker finally extended the vote to registered Indians, the debate over whether to accept the franchise in elections was by far the most hotly contested issue in both the Indian Federation of Saskatchewan and the Indian Association of Alberta. The extension of the franchise quickly cast a spotlight of attention on the legality of the provision in the Canadian Indian Act that outlawed the purchasing and consumption of alcohol by registered Indians. The issue of the franchise was, and still is, at the symbolic core of some of the central strategic questions facing virtually all Indigenous peoples in nation-states not of their own making. Are First Nations peoples, for instance, best served by maintaining their collective legal personalities inside or outside the constitutional structures of those countries whose place in the world was founded on ongoing appropriations of Aboriginal lands? Or could some compromises be worked out so that First Nations citizens can integrate into the citizenship stuctures of the newcomers without subordinating their sense of attachment to, and participation in, the cultural, legal, political, and economic evolution of their own Aboriginal communities and polities?

These questions have repeatedly generated the tensions in Indian politics that have created the basis for the middle ground usually sought by Andy Paull and his most accomplished protégé, George Manuel. At the one extreme of the ideological and tactical spectrum has been Indian separatism, as advocated, for instance, by Jules Sioui during the Second World War. At the opposite strategic pole are the integrationist or even assimilationist outcomes sought, for example, by the Reverend Peter Kelly. His primary aim in Indian politics was to cut down the barriers of discrimination preventing his generation of Native people from taking a more equitable place in North American society. Each side of this debate grows out of particular historical experiences that need to be looked at and evaluated in their own terms. It would be inappropriate, therefore, to dismiss or trivialize the infusion into Indian Country of convictions and ideas contributed either by the more nationalistic proponents of sovereign independence or by those activists such as Kelly who sought to dissolve or transcend some of the more abhorent forms of racial discrimination and forced segregation that have disfigured the Americas since the arrival of the first conquistadors.

Perhaps the most insistent and influential person of the integrationist movement in Indian North America in the twentieth century was Carlos Montezuma.[143] Born to Yavapai parents in the area of Phoenix, Arizona, Montezuma was raised by non-Indians and became a medical doctor. He worked closely with Richard H. Pratt, the founder and guiding light of the Carlisle Indian Boarding School in Carlisle, Pennsylvania. With Pratt's steady encouragement, Dr Montezuma initiated what would become a lifelong crusade to dismantle the Bureau of Indian Affairs in the United States. His ultimate goal was to remove all the ideological, institutional, and legal constructions that prevented Native Americans from acquiring full citizenship and participating from this base of recognized equality across the whole spectrum of professional, economic, intellectual, artistic, and political domains of national life in the United States.

Montezuma's primary vehicle for disseminating his views was his monthly newsletter, *Wassaja: Freedom's Signal for the Indian*. He published this periodical, whose title was his own Indian name, from 1916 until shortly before his death in 1922. The "sole purpose" of the journal, he announced, "is Freedom for the Indians through the abolishment of the Indian Bureau." The Chicago-based editor of *Wassaja* kept hammering away on this theme in texts and cartoons that borrowed heavily from abolitionists who, several decades earlier, had dedicated themselves to bringing slavery to an end. "Let My People Go," proclaimed one of his many editorials.[144]

The doctor was at different times both a detractor and a proponent of the Society of American Indians, an association made up largely of graduates of Indian boarding schools. Some of their most gifted members gathered in 1911 to assess the condition of their peoples and to lobby for various agendas of amelioration. Among the more prominent of the early members were the Sioux author Charles A. Eastman, the Seneca ethnologist Arthur C. Parker, the Sioux musician and activist Gertrude Bonnin (or Zitkala-sa), and the Yale-educated Winnebago minister, Henry Roe Cloud. Montezuma was unrelenting in his criticism of the society during those periods when he believed its policies were dominated by Native Americans either directly employed by, or in any way beholden to, the federal Bureau of Indian Affairs. As with similar political organizations that would develop among Native people in Canada, the overlapping issues of citizenship, enfranchisement, treaties, and self-determination of Indigenous peoples always aroused grave controversy and conflict – conflict that effectively crippled the Society of American Indians after 1919.[145]

The ideas and convictions set out by Montezuma in *Wassaja* found renewed expression during the Depression in the work of the American Indian Federation. This organization developed in direct opposition to the commissioner of the Bureau of Indian Affairs, John Collier, who, with the Indian Reorganization Act of 1934, attempted to reverse the extinguishment and privatization of the remaining Indian domain in the United States. One of the dominant voices in the American Federation of Indians was Seneca activist Alice Lee Jemison. She believed that Collier's work represented a cynical ploy to continue, and even to extend, the power of the Bureau over Indian lives. "We are weary unto death," she said, "of the propaganda for a continuance of the bureau to further 'protect' the Indian."[146]

In the charged ideological atmoshere leading to the Second World War, Jemison's extreme right-wing libertarianism and anti-communism made her group vulnerable to allegations that her movement bordered on fascism. The extreme nationalism of Jules Sioui made his activism susceptible to similar suspicions. The fascistic shading of their Aboriginal politics antipated patterns that would subsequently arise in the final decades of the twentieth century. With the greater dependence of many countries on high levels of immigration, and with the increased mobility of some categories of worker, various nativist movements, but especially those in Western Europe, moved to the far right of the political spectrum. Certainly the politics of

Sioui and Jemison were considerably different from the positions of more moderate Aboriginal activists, including, for instance, Fred Loft, Andy Paull, John Callihoo, and the many Native Americans aligned with the Indian New Deal as promoted by Collier. While the moderates criticized past and present abuses of federal authority in the treatment of Native people, they also demanded more positive applications of government power to improve the lives of First Nations groups and individuals in practical ways. One of the great ironies adhering to this perspective on Indian-government relations stems from the desire of many Native critics to use the federal state as an instrument not only for the protection of Aboriginal rights but also for their implementation through the delivery of services. The nature of such expectations highlights a paradox: criticism of federal authority also implies a defence of the capacity of the federal government to intervene as a constructive agent of socioeconomic amelioration.

There has been one big idea that has tended to unify Aboriginal activists: it is that First Nations treaties with non-Aboriginal governments hold central importance in defining the place of Indigenous peoples in North American life. Certainly this view was central to Jemison's politics as she looked to the Treaty of Canandaigua of 1794 as the primary legal instrument that recognized and entrenched the sovereignty of her people in upstate New York. For Jemison, the attack on the Bureau of Indian Affairs was the other side of her assertion of treaty rights. "We have always had self-government among the New York Indians," she asserted.[147]

This preponderance of informed opinion in Indian Country on the centrality of treaties has given broad significance to the old struggle to make new treaties in British Columbia. In affirming the applicability of old imperial laws acknowledging the existence of Indian title in their ancestral territories, Aboriginal activists in that province have figured prominently among those who have stimulated greater appreciation of the force of existing treaties with First Nations. In theory these treaty agreements established the terms and conditions for non-Indian expansion, colonization, and settlement in North America. The unifying power of this idea helped make it possible for Andy Paull and George Manuel to build bridges to larger coalitions of Indigenous peoples located in Quebec, the rest of Canada, the United States, Mexico, and, tentatively, the larger world. As Manuel wrote, "recognition of native title is to be the mainspring of responsible government for Indigenous peoples."[148] Certainly some elements of the reconciliation movement in Australia at the beginning of the new millennium recognized the negotiation of treaties with Indigenous peoples as a primary constitutional medium for the renewal of the larger Australian nation. The rise of *zapatismo* in Mexico seems to be pointed in a similar direction. Among the central fixtures and key points of reference in this quest for intercultural relations are the Royal Proclamation of 1763 and the Treaty of Waitangi of 1840, the treaty that formalized crown recognition of the Maori foundations of New Zealand.

In 1944, just as the North American Indian Brotherhood was forming in Canada, a similar organization was founded in the United States – the National Congress of American Indians, which continues to this day. Its constitution was modelled on the Indian Reorganization Act, the primary legal instrument of the Indian New Deal. Although many of its initial members were employees of the Bureau of Indian Affairs, its architects sought to give some lobbying leverage to the new organization by establishing an arm's-length relationship with the federal government. Until 1999 the pan-Indianism of the Congress did not extend beyond the borders of the United States.[149] This orientation shifted somewhat during the summer of 1999, when its representatives met with delegates of the Assembly of First Nations in the territories of the Sto: lo and the Musqueam peoples. The city of Vancouver sits on these Aboriginal territories. At this gathering in Vancouver, representatives of both the NCAI and the AFN acknowledged the other with the objective of helping Indigenous peoples throughout North America gain their "full and rightfull place in the community of all nations." In pursuit of this objective the delegations ratified a Declaration of Kinship and Cooperation among the Indigenous Peoples and Nations of North America. Among its key passages was the following:

Others' hands have drawn boundaries between Canada and the United States. These arbitrary lines have not served, and never will, the ties of kinship among our peoples. We hereby resolve to affirm and to strengthen those bonds of mutual respect, cooperation and affection. As friends and allies, we Indigenous Peoples and Nations will go forward with greater strength and wisdom as we interact with other governments in our region, our hemisphere and our world ... We affirm that the Assembly of First Nations and the National Congress of American Indians each derive their authority from their constituent nations and shall continue to represent them in a constitutional and democratic manner. We authorize our national organizations, to inform, assist and support each other in areas of common concern, including:

Achieving full recognition, protection and implementation of our existing legal and political rights of our constituent nations, including those founded on our own national laws, the laws of Canada and the United States, and the laws of the wider international community;

Ensuring that as laws and institutions further develop in various domestic and international forums and councils, the voices of our nations are included and respected.[150]

Throughout this gathering there were repeated references to the need to renew the Indian Confederacy as it had existed in the era when Tecumseh provided his inspired leadership.[151] Similarly, the declaration helped invest substance into initiatives undertaken earlier in the twentieth century. The goal of these initiatives was to establish a continental framework for political organization among Indigenous peoples.

One such initiative was centred in Oakland, California. In the 1930s Lawrence Twoaxe, a Mohawk from the Caughnawaga reserve (Kanewake) who lived in Oakland, succeeded in establishing several chapters of an organization called the League of Nations of North American Indians. Among his most engaged collaborators were John Tootoosis and Chief Albert Ed Thompson on the Peguis reserve in southern Manitoba. Like many of his Indian colleagues and associates who engaged in organizational work among their own people in that era, Chief Thompson faced reprisals, threats, and intimidation from members of the Royal Canadian Mounted Police. The purpose of the League, as articulated by Twoaxe, was "to perpetuate and preserve our posterity as a sovereign people."[152]

The continental framework called for in 1999 can be seen as an extension of both the League of Nations of North America and the North American Indian Brotherhood, the British Columbia–based organization that drew much of its form and substance from the politicking of Andy Paull. Although the name of the North American Indian Brotherhood suggested it had broad geographical reach, there were too few resources available in the years after the Second World War to organize effectively throughout the vast Indian Country of Canada, let alone throughout the continent. This same limitation of resources circumscribed the activities of the successor to the North American Indian Brotherhood, the National Indian Council of Canada, which was founded in 1961 in Saskatchewan House in Regina.

In 1968 the NCI also came to an end. It succumbed to the tensions between those Native people recognized by the federal government in Canada as registered Indians and those Native people, including the ubiquitous Métis, who live outside Indian reserves and outside the narrow legal definitions of Indian "status," as determined by federal statute. The result of this split was the creation of the Native Council of Canada and, for registered Indians, the National Indian Brotherhood. Beginning in 1970 the national chief of the NIB was George Manuel.[153] In 1980 the Assembly of First Nations was created by the NIB leaders, with Delbert Riley as the first national chief. The AFN drew its legitimacy from Indian sources rather than from the chartering powers of federal or provincial authority. The initial purpose of this Indian entity was to provide a base for First Nations to respond collectively to the propect that the Canadian Constitution would be patriated from Great Britain. "The rights and responsibilities given to us by the Creator," declared the makers of the AFN in their founding Declaration, "cannot be altered or taken away by any other Nation."[154]

THE GENESIS OF THE AMERICAN INDIAN MOVEMENT, THE MILITANT WING OF *INDIGENISMO* IN CANADA AND THE UNITED STATES

A recurrent theme in the history of the Indian Country of North America since 1783 has been the struggle to maintain and develop coalitions of

Indigenous peoples that are not constrained by the domestic laws or international boundaries of Canada and the United States. The most serious challenge to this process of domestication was mounted by the Confederacy of Indian Nations in the Great Lakes–Ohio Valley area in the early 1790s and again in the War of 1812.

In the second half of the nineteenth century Indigenous peoples on the prairies of North America made similar, if less fully realized, attempts to join forces in defiance of the new borders imposed on their ancestral lands. These Aboriginal struggles to resist the power of alien federal authorities led to the hanging of Louis Riel and the incarceration of Big Bear and Poundmaker in 1885 in Canada. They led also to the massacre at Wounded Knee in 1890 of Siouian ghost dancers. The US Army's Seventh Cavalry committed this atrocity, whose victims were mostly unarmed women, children, and elders.[155] The slaughter was, in some measure at least, an act of vengeance by the Seventh Cavalry for the humiliation it had suffered in 1876 at the Battle of Little Bighorn. In that legendary clash, Siouian warriors directed by Crazy Horse and Sitting Bull defeated and killed General George Armstrong Custer as well as most of his soldiers. The Seventh Cavalry's revenge at Wounded Knee is generally seen as the final ritual in the military crushing of Aboriginal independence in North America. At the time of this massacre the Indian population in the area of the present-day United States had been reduced to 290,000 from an estimated pre-Columbian population of between 10 and 20 million.[156]

The most repressive era of Indian administration continued in the United States until John Collier's Indian New Deal beginning in 1934. In Canada it was not until after the Second World War that there was some relaxation of the prohibitions constraining political organizing among Indigenous peoples. Andy Paull's North American Indian Brotherhood renewed in name, if not in elaborate substance, a continentalist vision of Indian Country. In the 1960s and early 1970s, the period when George Manuel grew to political maturity, First Nations activism was drawn towards not only more continentalist frames of refererence but also more hemispheric and genuinely international forms of politics and diplomacy. While Manuel's work in Canada and beyond represented one facet of this trend, there were many groups and organizations moving in similar directions. By far the most flamboyant of these proponents of an expanded and more mobilized and cosmopolitan Indian Country were the activists who gathered around the American Indian Movement.

The movement took much of its initial energy from the formal and informal associations of Native people in Canadian and US prisons. One of the rallying points of activism inside the jails was the struggle of Aboriginal inmates to gain the right to conduct the rituals of Aboriginal spirituality, including pipe ceremonies and sweat lodge ceremonies. These assertions were based on the principle that the religious freedom of Indigenous peoples was at issue and that Native traditionalists and ceremonialists must be granted the same kinds of freedom to attend to the spiritual needs of Aboriginal inmates as was allowed, for instance, to Christian clergy or Jewish rabbis. The politicization of Aboriginal inmates in prison also involved the creation of many formal and informal study groups. Research and discussion in these small study circles focused on the nature of current and historical processes that led many First Nations people towards their criminalization and incarceration. How was it that First Nations citizens had been so marginalized that they appeared to be outsiders and misfits in their own Aboriginal lands? As with many other national liberation stuggles, the concentration of so many subject people in the jails of their oppressors gave Aboriginal inmates the opportunity to see that there might be larger patterns at work in the genesis of their families' personal misfortunes and difficulties. There might be forces of history at play whose origins ran far deeper than the twists and turns of their own individual lives.

The warehousing of so many Aboriginal inmates in the jails, especially in mid-western jurisdictions including Minnesota, the two Dakotas, Manitoba, and Saskatchewan, provided the institutional setting for First Nations people from many different backgrounds and regions to establish bonds of friendship and cooperation. As had sometimes transpired inside the Indian residential schools, shared initiatives now led some Aboriginal inmates inside prison to work to achieve common political objectives once they were released from jail. Indeed, many of AIM's leading lights, including Eddie Benton Benai, Clyde Bellecourt, and Art Solomon, have stated that the conditions in jail and penitentaries in North America provided fertile ground for the germination and cultivation of the more militant forms of Aboriginal activism. In the early 1970s the renewed militance emanating from this particular part of Indian Country helped ignite broad controversy.[157] This heavily publicized militance, in turn, helped set the stage for Manuel's more conciliatory endeavours in championing the ideals of the Fourth World.

By the late 1960s the activism in the jails began to be felt in some of the urban ghettos where many First Nations congregated. This activism was particularly organized and aggressive in the twin cities of St Paul and Minneapolis, where AIM was given its formal start in campaigns against police racism and in initiatives to put in place viable and culturally appropriate forms of social services. The energy and enthusism that came to be associated with the AIM also has important roots on university campuses in the United States and Canada. At a major conference at the University of Chicago in 1961, Aboriginal college and university students gathered to create the National Indian Youth Council. Along with the mobilization of Indian inmates in North America's prisons, the NIYC became one of the key sites of discussion, collaboration, and controversy from which AIM would later emerge.

Very quickly the NIYC emerged as a focus for the activities of First

Nations people who had become impatient with the milder lobbying tactics of organizations such as the National Congress of American Indians. Prominent among the student activists was Clyde Warrior, a Ponca satirist who was one of the primary founders of the NIYC. Warrior's witty yet inspirational speeches helped motivate a younger generation to challenge the more gentle tactics of their parents and grandparents in taking up the struggle for recognition of Aboriginal and treaty rights. Too many of the older generation of Indian politicians, according to Warrior, acted like "Uncle Tomahawks."[158] This type of characterization foreshadowed the polarization in Indian Country with which AIM would come to be identified. Warrior found many attentive audiences during the vibrant annual meetings of the NIYC in the early 1960s. As remembered by Shirley Hill Witt, a Mohawk scholar and influential member of the organization, the assemblies and conferences began to take on an "international flavour" when planning sessions included Indian delegations from every Canadian province except Saskatchewan.[159]

The essential tactic of the National Indian Youth Council was to create broad support in the larger Indian Country for the activities of local activists seeking to accomplish the goals of particular nations and communities. The great protypes for this kind of strategy were the fish-ins that took place in the mid–1960s in Washington state. According to the terms of major treaties transacted in the 1850s with the Yakima and with other First Nations in the region, the Indigenous peoples of the Washington state area retained extensive rights to fisheries that the state government refused to respect. The basic tactic of the fish-ins was to create media events where Aboriginal individuals would exercise their treaty rights and defy state fishing laws. The objective was to create the context for public arrests that would test the law and generate debate both inside and outside Indian Country.

The fish-ins attracted the support of some powerful non-Indian allies, including the film star Marlon Brando. At a fish-in rally in the Washington state capital of Olympia, Brando joined the other speakers on the podium to denounce the consitent violation of Indian treaties by the government and people of the United States. "Not one of [the treaties] has been kept," he charged. "In every case, money has been the ruling factor in the dispute with the Indian, and every time money has won out."[160] Brando worked closely with Robert Satiacum, a colleague of George Manuel. Satiacum repeatedly challenged the status quo in his determined innovations to deploy the reference in the US Constitution to "Indians not taxed" as the legal basis for Native Americans to develop new kinds of viable Aboriginal economies. Brando's role was significant. It transcended the gilded glitz of Hollywood philanthropy to offer substantial intellectual content in bringing wider public attention to the oldest and deepest human rights issue in the Americas. Brando articulated in an American context a principle that was heard frequently in white activism against the apartheid regime in

South Africa: that racial oppression in all its manifestations dehumanizes the perpetrators as well as the recipients of the injustice.

The fish-ins served to widen recognition that the integrity and credibility of the rule of law was at stake in matters concerning Aboriginal and treaty rights. As Brando, Satiacum, Warrior, and others argued, when governments advanced their own political agendas by violating treaties with First Nations, or when they evaded the laws of Aboriginal title altogether, they sacrificed any pretext that society is rules based rather than power based. They sacrificed any pretext that democracy and civility prevailed over tyranny and force as the basis of society's hierarchical structures.

In his condemnation of the treatment of Native Americans, Brando renewed a tradition in US intellectual life that dates back to the work of Helen Hunt Jackson and many activists before her. In 1881 Jackson published a searing indictment of American Indian policy entitled *A Century of Dishonor*.[161] Although Brando and Jackson shared common ground in their condemnation of the systematic fraud and criminality that has characterized the taking of Indian land, they were poles apart in their thinking about what should be done to correct this legacy of injustice. Where Jackson emphasized the extension of the rights of American citizenship to Native Americans as a panacea for the injustices they faced, Brando was more inclined to embrace a strengthened regime of Aboriginal self-governance as the appropriate corrective. The philosophical divide between these two activists was matched by a similar divide within Indian Country. Among First Nations people there has long been strategic clashes over the appropriate balances to be struck between integration into their surrounding societies and the ideal of autonomy through Aboriginal self-determination.

Jackson was prominent among those non-Aboriginals who helped form various organizations, including the Indian Rights Association, to press government to tear down the legal walls of discrimination and to open the way for Native Americans to participate in all aspects of society from a position of equal citizenship.[162] Brando, in contrast, was more in line with the intellectual tradition of the American Indian Defense Association, founded by John Collier in 1923. Its policies, which were sometimes branded by critics as "sentimentalist," emphasized the importance of cultural pluralism and the need for small nations, including those composed of Native Americans, to retain and develop tools of self-governance, including the capacity to hold land in common.

In Canada the Toronto-based Indian-Eskimo Association, which had its origins in the Canadian Association for Adult Education, offered the most substantial organizational framework in the early 1960s for activists of many backgrounds, Aboriginal and non-Aboriginal, to engage in the debate over the nature and meaning of Aboriginal rights in contemporary society.[163] This discussion, both in Canada and the United States, usually involved a good deal of controversy over emphasis. Should activists highlight the need for the lessening of racial discrimination, or the plague of Aboriginal poverty, or the ideal of self-determination through a wider application of Aboriginal and treaty rights? As these discussions engaged more attention, in anticipation of the reopening of the unresolved land and constitutional issues in Canada, the extensive library collection of the Indian-Eskimo Association became an increasingly strategic resource.

H.B. Hawthorne of the University of British Columbia figured prominently among the scholars who were involved in the political and legal dealings. On behalf of the federal government, in 1963–66 he oversaw a major academic study of the socioeconomic conditions of Indian peoples in Canada.[164] Later, Douglas Saunders and Peter A. Cumming presided over the publication for the Indian-Eskimo Association of different editions of the ground-breaking *Native Rights in Canada*.[165] Like the legal scholarship of Thomas Berger and the anthropological work of Wilson Duff, the contributions in *Native Rights* proved instrumental in bringing forward the legal and ethnographic arguments that led to the reopening of negotiations on Aboriginal title to lands and resources throughout Canada, but especially in British Columbia.[166]

The process of designing, building, and staffing the Indian Pavilion at Montreal's Expo 67 was a major flash point of contention and argument among academics, politicians, bureaucrats and artists holding a variety of visions on how to conceive of and present the place of First Nations in North American society. This world's fair was the major spectacle marking the 100th anniversary of Canada's Confederation. The controversies over the representation of Indian life at Expo were so sensitive that the files on this subject in the National Archives of Canada were still marked "secret" in the opening years of the twenty-first century.

The hearings of the Royal Commission on Bilingualism and Biculturalism provided another highly charged forum for the expression of grievances and alternative perspectives on Aboriginal policies.[167] This commission was initiated in 1963 to address the growing uncertainty over Quebec's place in Confederation. The frames of reference of the investigation provided a clear target for some Native politicians, including Kahn-Tineta Horn, the Kanewake fashion model and outspoken AIM activist. A disciple of Louis Hall, whose teachings would later give rise to the formation of the Mohawk Warriors' Society, Horn intervened to question the exclusion of Indigenous peoples from the Two Founding Nations paradigm of Canadian history.[168]

The growing prominence of the Indian-Eskimo Association as a centre of research, public activism, and political debate was increasingly challenged, especially after 1968, when the National Indian Brotherhood was created. The charge, made by Harold Cardinal and others, was that the cross-cultural IEA was depriving exclusively Aboriginal organizations such as the National Indian Brotherhood of potential funding and of the capacity to speak on Aboriginal issues with unfiltered or unmediated Aboriginal voices. Accordingly, in 1972 the IEA, under the guidance of its president, Thomas H.B. Symons, changed its mandate as well as its name. Henceforth the organization was known as the Canadian Association in Support of the Native Peoples, or CASNP. The determination to keep the organization alive in a different form was based on the recognition that "there is still a strong need for citizen allies in the struggle of native people for their right to self-determination and an end to crushing poverty."[169]

At the time of this transition, Thomas Symons, the founding president of CASNP and of Trent University in Peterborough, Ontario, was hard at work on a major study for the Association of Universities and Colleges of Canada. The outcome of this study was a document entitled *To Know Ourselves,* a sharp condemnation of the Americanization of Canadian post-secondary institutions. The extensive recommendations called for various forms of indigenization of higher education.[170] This agenda, in the name of enhanced Canadian Studies, was a decisive factor in the establishment at Trent University in 1972 of the first Department of Native Studies in Canada.[171] By this time, similar pressures in the United States had led to the establishment of a Native American Studies Department at the University of Minnesota, in the heartland of the American Indian Movement. The subsequent establishment of Native Studies at a growing number of North American universities, including UCLA, created a new genre of academic activity for an increasingly politicized Indian Country, whose most aggressive and flamboyant demonstrations of "Red Power" were embodied in the image and tactics of AIM.

The event that most effectively focused, synthesized, and launched these converging forces of social activism coming from the prisons, universities, reservations, and urban centres of Indian America was the occupation in 1969 of Alcatraz Island in San Francisco Bay. This action drew considerable support from the large group of Aboriginal people in urban California, a large proportion of whom had migrated to the West Coast as a result of federal relocation and termination policies pursued during the Eisenhower presidency. As the occupation of Alcatraz Island continued, however, it became the destination for the pilgrimage of many Native and non-Native people from other parts of North America.

Robert Warrior and Paul Chaat Smith indicate in the opening chapters of their narrative *Like A Hurricane: The Indian Movement from Alcatraz to Wounded Knee* that there was no master plan to orchestrate the takeover of the abandoned site of the United States's most infamous federal prison.[172] Rather, the action arose concurrently from several sources. Alcatraz Island became, simultaneously, a marker of the inequitable conditions permeating Indian Country and a rallying point for a more promising collective future.

Calling themselves the Indians of All Tribes, the occupiers announced their stand to the world in the following terms:

PROCLAMATION TO THE GREAT WHITE FATHER AND ALL HIS PEOPLE

We, the native Americans, reclaim the land known as Alcatraz Island in the name of all American Indians by right of discovery ... We feel this Alcatraz Island is more than suitable for an Indian Reservation, as determined by the white man's own standard. By this we mean that this place resembles most Indian reservations in that:

1. It is isolated from modern facilities, and without adequate means of transportation.
2. It has no fresh running water.
3. It has inadequate sanitation facilities.
4. It has no oil or mineral rights.
5. There is no industry, and so unemployment is very great.
6. There are no health care facilities.
7. The soil is rocky and unproductive; and the land does not support game.
8. There are no educational facilities.
9. The population has exceeded the land base.
10. The population has always been held as prisoners and kept dependent upon others.

Further, it would be fitting and symbolic that ships from all over the world, entering the Golden Gate, would first see Indian land, and thus be reminded of the true history of this nation. This tiny island would be a symbol of the great lands once ruled by free and noble Indians.[173]

The combination of words, personalities, and images that came together under the banner of the Indians of All Tribes tantalized the appetites of media hungry for fresh perspectives on the politics of protest. Alcatraz became the perfect backdrop to dramatize the idea that incarceration, either literally or metaphorically, marked the characteristic fate of Indigenous peoples as subjects of the historic and continuing colonization of the New World.

As the occupiers persisted month after month, many proposals, both serious and whimsical, were floated about what to do with the island. One of the most frequently offered ideas was that Alcatraz should be remade as an Indian institution of higher learning – a "Thunderbird University." Such an monument of higher education in Indian Country, it was thought, would make a fitting west-coast counterpoise to the underlying message of the Statue of Liberty. This insistence on the importance of Indian education as the strategic core of Native American revitalization and improved on public education as the primary antidote to the injustice visited on First Nations is a theme born of struggle which resonates with growing force right up to this day.[174]

The informal spokesperson of the occupation was Richard Oakes, a young Mohawk iron worker who lived in San Francisco but whose home community was the Akwesasne reserve that straddles the border of New York state, Ontario, and Quebec. Among the other leaders to emerge from the Alcatraz occupation were Grace Thorpe, the daughter of Olympic athlete Jim Thorpe, and the legendary Wallace "Mad Bear" Anderson, the group's Tuscorora mentor. Anderson had been a merchant seaman, with wide contacts among Indian groups throughout the Americas. In the late 1950s he returned home to lead the resistance against the New York Power Authority's flooding of Seneca lands in the Niagara Falls area. From there he gave inspiration and direction to the traditionalists who tried to reassert Longhouse procedures and protocols on the governing council of the Six Nations reserve near Brantford, Ontario.[175]

The leading role played by Richard Oakes and Anderson in the activities of the Indians of All Tribes is consistent with the importance of Six Nations activists on both sides of the Canada–US border in setting examples and in acting as catalysts in the larger struggle for fundamental reforms in relations between Indigenous peoples and non-Aboriginals in North America. Especially in their assertion of the sovereign authority of the Great Law on which their old Hau-de-no-sau-nee (Longhouse) League is based, the traditionalist Six Nations leadership has consistently refused to be engulfed in the domestic regimes of two countries whose own early histories are intertwined with the commercial, diplomatic, political, and intellectual evolution of North America's most famous and deeply studied Aboriginal Confederacy. As the Indigenous peoples with the most complex, elaborate, and many-layered experience of treaty diplomacy with a variety of non-Indian governments in North America, the domestic and external politics of the Six Nations Iroquois have had important echoes and repercussions throughout the Indian Country. Indeed, this formidable Longhouse influence has often gone beyond the American hemisphere both to inspire Indigenous peoples globally and to call attention to the oppressions they frequently face.[176]

Among the major twentieth-century preludes to the pan-Indian action at Alcatraz were a number of stands taken by the members of the Six Nations Iroquois when they protested treaty violations resulting in their unlawful subjugation under the power of governments not of their own making. After the First World War, for instance, Levi General, whose Indian name was Deskahe, visited the League of Nations in Geneva. He attended as the ambassador of the Longhouse League, which had resolved to register the unwillingness of the Longhouse government to submit to Canada's assertions of sovereign jurisdiction over the Six Nations.[177] Other Six Nations demonstrations of their status in internation law included the annual marches beginning in 1926 across the international bridge between Buffalo, New York, and Fort Erie, Ontario. Tuscarora leader Clinton Rickard was the driving force behind this demonstration of the Indian Defense League of America.[178] Similar, if less orderly, events took place on a fairly regular basis at the transborder reserve known as Akwesasne. Demonstrators there persistently called attention to claims of an Indian right of free movement of goods across the Canada–us boundary as guaranteed by Jay's Treaty, an old agreement from fur-trade days. In 1968 a group of Akwesasne Mohawks underlined their opposition to what they saw as the illegal imposition of customs levies on goods carried within their community. They blocked the Seaway International Bridge and took control of Cornwall Island. The action was important in setting the stage for the seizure during the following summer of Alcatraz Island.[179]

One clear expression of Longhouse League sovereignty has been in the creation and use of Six Nations Iroquois passports. One of the first countries to recognize these documents was Cuba, shortly after Fidel Castro's revolution. In 1958, at a ceremony on their Liberation Day in Havanna, the government of Cuba formally acknowledged the international sovereignty of both the Six Nations Confederacy and the Miccosukees of Florida. Mad Bear Anderson was given an official state welcome at this event, including "police escort in Cadillacs, bands and machete-waving campisinos." The flamboyance of this diplomatic event at the height of the Cold War marks one extreme in a continuum of displays at the United Nations and in many other international venues, where various delegations of Longhouse League ambassadors consistently demonstrated their refusal to be contained within the domestic laws of either Canada or the United States.[180]

The unbroken assertion of Iroquois sovereignty outside the framework of the domestic laws of Canada and the United States has been an essential inspirational element in establishing the continent-wide orientation of the American Indian Movement. In the early 1970s AIM captured the imagination (or ire) of a wide constituency in Indian Country. Its members and supporters had been galvanized and mobilized through the organizational endeavours of many forerunners, including the National Indian Youth Council and the Indians of All Tribes. AIM's effectiveness grew from many of its organizers' ability to cross and transcend some of the barriers of place, nationality, class, and belief that have sometimes divided a very pluralistic Indian Country. At the heart of the alliances that gave AIM its timeliness were the connections between urban-based Aboriginal activists and reservation-based traditionalists. These "traditionalists," who were sometimes referred to according to the race-based preoccupations of some as "full-bloods," tended to remain outside the patronage networks of jobs and limited upward economic mobility available on most Indian reservations. They tended not to be the ones most prone to benefit directly from those programs and payments on which the federal governments of North America depended to maintain their control over Indian Country.

The important place of Iroquois nationalism in the emergence of both AIM-style militance and Fourth World–style global awareness is forever captured in the pages of *Akwesasne Notes*, a Mohawk publication named after the transborder community where the newspaper was put together. By the mid–1970s *Akwesasne Notes* had replaced the NIYC's *America before Columbus*, or *ABC*, as the journal of record chronicling the struggle of Indian peoples in the Americas for land and self-determination. Indeed, *Akwesasne Notes* pushed its coverage beyond the western hemisphere to a more global perspective on the urge to decolonization in all its manifestations. Both of these publications were instrumental in enabling readers to see the common themes linking the struggles of many Indigenous peoples for liberation through the expanded recognition at home and abroad of Aboriginal and treaty rights.

As the movement for renovation from within Indian Country gathered force, support, and sophistication, leaders focused increasingly on the existence and persistent violations of Indian treaties in both the United States and Canada. This strategy was founded on the principle that Indian treaties represent a compelling genre of evidence that Indian nations were, historically, recognized as sovereign peoples with the authority to make transactions at the level of international law. Alternatively, the failure of the governments of Canada and the United States to respect and uphold treaties pointed to the vast distance between the pretensions and the underlying realities of the political regimes in both countries. By placing treaties at the forefront of controversy about the place of First Nations in contemporary North America, the activists in and around AIM captured sensitive geopolitical turf with strategic implications for both the foreign and the domestic policies of the United States, and Canada in the Cold War atmosphere of the 1970s.[181]

THE TRAIL OF BROKEN TREATIES, WOUNDED KNEE, ANICINABE PARK, THE NATIVE PEOPLES' CARAVAN, AND THE SUICIDE OF NELSON SMALL LEGS JR

In 1972 AIM organizers brought together a cross-country caravan known as the Trail of Broken Treaties. Their purpose was to mobilize Aboriginal support behind a twenty-point plan advocating that the US federal government return to treaty making and treaty implementation as the primary instrument of formal relations with Indian peoples. One of the key drafters of the document was Hank Adams, a brilliant and accomplished veteran of the NIYC and the fish-ins. His activism was increasingly directed at extensive research in the archival sources of American Indian policy.[182] The twenty-point plan was later explained and elaborated more fully by Vine Deloria Jr, especially in his *Behind the Trail of Broken Treaties: An Indian Declaration of Independence.* According to Deloria, many Indian groups in the United States had reservations whose size compared with that of small nations such as Luxenbourg, Mauritius, Kuwait, and Trinidad.[183] These countries fit the ideal of small nations referred to in the Preamble of the UN Charter. Deloria saw in the viability of these small nations both proofs and illustrations of what Indian societies might achieve if given a chance to build up their own governments within the framework of international law. The key to this recognition could be secured if the United States government respected its own laws as entrenched in almost four hundred Indian treaties negotiated over the first century of the republic's existence.[184] As Deloria looked to the future, he imagined a further harmonization and rationalization of American Indian policy through a new round of treaty making that would afford Indigenous peoples a more clearly defined place of security and equality in a rejuvenated country that was finally liberated from its genocidal origins and heritage.

The Trail of Broken Treaties ended in the occupation and partial destruction of the Bureau of Indian Affairs headquarters in Washington, DC. During this action the occupiers of the building draped a banner from the ediface renaming it the Native American Embassy. According to Deloria, the property destruction was largely attributable to the infiltration of federal secret agents with the object of fomenting violence in order to obscure the protestors' message and deny them public sympathy.[185] Robert Warrior and Paul Chaat Smith, however, offer a many-faceted and less conspiratorial explanation of the vandalism. Whatever the truth of the matter, there is a growing mass of evidence documenting the subsequent covert efforts of federal agents to infiltrate, destabilize, discredit, and ultimately destroy AIM.[186]

After the Trail of Broken Treaties, many AIM leaders continued to gravitate towards Souian spiritual teachers such as Frank Fools Crow. The prayers, meditations, and ceremonies of these spiritual leaders provided an ancient unbroken cycle of Souian veneration of the Sacred Black Hills in South Dakota.[187] These hills are part of the vast area that the United States government had agreed to protect for Sioux people according to the terms of the Fort Laramie Treaty of 1868. In choosing to emphasize the violations of the Fort Laramie Treaty as representative of American treaty violations generally, and to emphasize the desecration of the Black Hills as representative of the American assault on the environment generally and on Indian religious freedom specifically, AIM framed the essential underlying issues for what was to become its most famous and characteristic stand.

In 1973 AIM activists occupied the tiny hamlet of Wounded Knee on the large Pine Ridge reservation in South Dakota. They chose this site because Wounded Knee had been the place where the American army in 1890 had massacred an unarmed Sioux band, including many women and children. The ensuing armed clash between Indians and federal forces focused the attention of the US media on Native American issues as never before in the twentieth century. Large segments of public opinion were mobilized both for and against the positions advocated by AIM. This polarization of opinion became most severe on the Pine Ridge reservation itself. AIM and its supporters opposed the federally funded tribal administration of Chief

Richard Wilson. According to his opponents, Wilson was a puppet of the federal Bureau of Indian Affairs. His power was seen to rest not on Siouian traditions but on federal money, legislation, and coercion. According to Wilson and his supporters, however, AIM was composed primarily of seditious outside agitators whose ultimate goal was to participate in the overthrow of legitimate elected authority in the United States.

The factional divisions on the Pine Ridge reservation became an extreme prototype of many internal conflicts that would characterize the struggle to decolonize the Indian Country of the United States and Canada in the years ahead. AIM leaders such as Russell Means or Dennis Banks would characterize the Pine Ridge tribal administration as "Vichy Indians" or "hang-around-the-fort Indians." In the view of the militants, their Pine Ridge opponents were representative of a class of assimilated Native Americans they derided as "apples" – red on the outside and white on the inside. To this group, the perceived affluence and influence of some of their Indian opponents was based on their formal or informal collaboration with an alien federal regime – one that continued the legacy of the Columbian conquests that began in 1492. It entrenched inequality, they claimed, and blocked Indian communities from making, renewing, and implementing authentic Aboriginal law based on Aboriginal constitutions older than those of the United States or Canada. Of all Native American organizations, they said, the National Tribal Chairmen's Association was the most vulnerable to manipulation through federal funding.[188]

This fundamental disagreement on basic principles flared into a virtual civil war that saw the Pine Ridge tribal police – the core of the more informal, paramilitary "Goon squad" – supported by the FBI and other federal agencies in a concerted attack on AIM. According to AIM academic Ward Churchill, this "reign of terror" on the Pine Ridge reservation between 1973 and 1976 resulted in sixty-nine murders of AIM members and their sympathizers.[189] Most of these killings have not been properly investigated to this day. At the same time, masses of state evidence of the most dubious kind were marshalled to convict AIM organizer Leonard Peltier for the killing of two FBI agents in one of the most controversial shooting incidents during the troubles at Pine Ridge.

AIM's ideas and tactics moved across the international border. In 1974 a group of Ojibway activists, many of whom had visited Wounded Knee the previous summer, chose to assert Indian title to a small park in the town of Kenora in northwestern Ontario. In previous years Kenora had become infamous for the antagonistic relations between local non-Aboriginals and Aboriginal people. Kenora was frequented by visitors from many surrounding reserves whose citizens were numerically dominant in the larger region, yet the city itself – a relatively isolated Euro-Canadian enclave – commanded a form of political dominance over many aspects of the area's frontier economy. There was considerable potential for violence, then, when an armed group calling itself the Ojibway Warriors' Society decided to seize control of Anicinabe Park.

The leader of the Ojibway Warriors' Society was a forceful young militant named Louis Cameron. He came from the nearby White Dog reserve, whose citizens, along with those of Grassy Narrows, were losing their fishing economy, their health, and their social cohesion as a result of the mercury poisoning emanating from the huge Reed Pulp and Paper facility coming on stream in the neighbouring community of Dryden. In an interview from Anicinabe Park, Cameron made it clear that the American Indian Movement provided the inspiration for his group's action. "We looked around," he said, "and the only organization we saw that had the kind of feeling that served the people is AIM. So we went to AIM conferences," he continued, "we went across the country and met people from different countries – people from Angola, friends from Algeria and South America – friends who were getting it on in their own country."[190]

Referring to AIM's stand at Wounded Knee and the criminal charges held over the organization's leadership, Cameron had this to say:

There's Indian leadership – great people great men and women who did something for their people ... And these men, these great men, Russell Means and Dennis Banks, they're charged as criminals because they spoke out on behalf of their people. They spoke of freedom, they spoke of dignity and pride and life, and now they're considered as criminals by the courts of the United States of America. These people they're not criminals. They're courageous Indian people, courageous human beings. And all Indian people have to confront the system. Like the United States government, the United States laws, we have to face the Canadian courts, we have to face the Canadian law, we have to face the Canadian police.[191]

Cameron's analysis graphically captured the sense of urgency and determination that gave the stands at Wounded Knee and Anicinabe Park national and international significance. In seeking to justify the confrontational stance his group had adopted, Cameron explained:

The government is trying to put our people in an economy which separates the individual himself into two separate beings and separates groups, separates society and confuses and divides and controls. Our people, who are still directly connected to the land and still have direct communications with each other – very horizontal type of social relations – we cannot go into capitalist society and start ripping each other off. The government does not understand this, particularly that this is not the only economic structure available in the world ...

All these things – with the education system, the churches – are pushing our people. You know, everyone knows, that people have to be free to express human freedom. They have to laugh, they have to yell and they have to be free to move around. But when you push people into a group like that a lot of that expression turns inside. It's what you call internal aggression. And as a result Indians live a very dangerous style of life. They fight each other, they drink alot. And the tendency of suicide is higher.

This is the crime, the injustice that is being commited by the government and by the business around the country. They are taking one segment of society and pushing it violently inwards. Now we have to live that style of life which is detrimental to human beings. So we, the Ojibway Warriors' Society, believe the only way is to bring the internal aggression outwards. It must go out, we must break out through the same way we got in. We got in by violence, we must go out by confrontation.[192]

Cameron placed a great deal of emphasis on his peoples' treaties with the crown. He articulated his sense of their character and the extent to which the treaties have been violated and abused in the following terms:

We want free government. We want self-determination, we want our own land back, our own nations, our own governments. The treaties have been signed and they've been violated – they just use them for manipulation purposes.

When we signed the treaties, the treaties were a different kind of law – an Aboriginal law, a hereditary law. It's a moral law, a sacred law. They don't understand that. They think they can take one government, and transfer it to another government, and therefore they can breach the contract because they have a transfer of leadership.[193]

No one was killed during the standoff at Anicinabe Park. The Ojibway Warriors' Society, the Ontario Provincial Police, and the aroused townsfolk all managed to find a way to avoid the tragedy that several times seemed to have arrived when some rounds of gunfire were exchanged. Teaming up with other activists from across Canada, some of whom had been involved in another AIM-inspired blockade at Cache Creek in British Columbia, Louis Cameron went to Ottawa leading what became known as the Native Peoples' Caravan. When they arrived for what was planned as a peaceful demonstration on Parliament Hill, the group was greeted with the first mobilization of the Royal Canadian Mounted Police's newly organized riot squad. The episode did not prevent the demonstrators from delivering their list of demands, which included the following points:

1. THE HEREDITARY AND TREATY RIGHTS OF ALL NATIVE PEOPLES IN CANADA, INCLUDING INDIAN, METIS, NON-STATUS AND INUIT, MUST BE RECOGNIZED AND RESPECTED IN THE CONSTITUTION OF CANADA. It is the continuing violation of our hereditary rights that has resulted in the destruction of the self-reliance of the Native peoples. We are no longer content to be the most impoverished people in Canada,
2. WE DEMAND THE REPEAL OF THE PRESENT INDIAN ACT AND THE CREATION BY NATIVE PEOPLE OF NEW LEGISLATION RECOGNIZING OUR RIGHT TO SELF-DETERMINATION AND SOVEREIGNTY OVER OUR LANDS.

The Department of Indian Affairs operates to serve business and government interests – not the interests of the Indian people.

3. WE DEMAND A COMPLETE INVESTIGATION OF THE DEPARTMENT OF
INDIAN AFFAIRS BY NATIVE PEOPLE AND THE TRANSFER OF ITS POWER
AND RESOURCES TO NATIVE COMMUNITIES. *Indian Affairs must belong to the
Indian people.* Indian Affairs must be separated from the Department of Northern
Development.

4. WE DEMAND ANNUAL PAYMENTS IN PERPETUITY FROM ALL LEVELS OF
GOVERNMENT. Canadian wealth is derived from the land and the natural
resources of the land. *The time has come for Canadian governments to pay their debts to
Native peoples.*

5. WE DEMAND AN END TO THE DESTRUCTION OF OUR NATIVE
ECONOMIES.[194]

The group that came to Ottawa in the autumn of 1974 ended up occupying a vacant government building on Victoria Island in the middle of the
Ottawa River. They named their encampment the Native Peoples'
Embassy. Under George Manuel's leadership, the National Indian Brother
injected themselves between the Canadian cabinet and and the AIM-
inspired group that had gathered around Cameron. The outcome was an
agreement to give the NIB more access to the executive branch of the
Canadian government. This decision began a series of unsuccessful
attempts aimed at the creating some sort of cooperation between the most
influential Indian organization in the country and the top politicians in
the Trudeau government.[195]

Although the system of political representation created by the Indian
Act continued to predominate in most Indian reserves and at the National Indian Brotherhood, much of the political leverage giving bargaining
power to the more moderate federally funded Aboriginal leaders, including George Manuel, continued to be generated by the activities of the militant, AIM-related groups such as the Native Peoples' Caravan. AIM's loyal
constituency in Indian Country always remained a minority, but there is no
denying their success in politicizing issues of significance to all Native peoples in ways that would never have taken place without their infusion of
energy. In Vancouver, for instance, Aboriginal activists organized themselves as the Native Alliance for Red Power. Like AIM in its earliest days in
St Paul–Minneapolis, NARP's activities started with the monitoring and
investigating of police treatment of Indians in the skid-row section of
town.[196] NARP organizers called their work the Beothuck Patrol, making
poignant reference to the Indigenous people of Newfoundland who have
long been extinct, owing, in part, to the campaigns of terror directed at
them by lawless non-Indian settlers.[197]

In Toronto, the Nishnawbe Institute on the eighteenth floor of the legendary Rochdale College was one of the seminal centres of Aboriginal
resurgence during the period. With a large building on the downtown

campus of the University of Toronto, Rochdale had grown by the early 1970s into one of the most influential bastions of North America's "counter culture." Nowhere was the exchange of beliefs and attitudes between young Indian idealists and "hippie" activists more clear and direct.[198] The more militant cousin of the Nishnawbe Institute was the Toronto chapter of AIM. The elder of the group was Art Solomon, a former trade unionist from the Sudbury area whose influence among Aboriginal youth initially grew from his leading role in the Indian Hall of Fame at the Canadian National Exhibition.[199] The Toronto "AIMsters" called themselves Wenjack, a reference to the last name of the young Ojibway boy who froze to death as he tried to return home after escaping from an Indian residential school.[200] One of AIM Toronto's most potent and controversial protests was directed at archaeologists whose excavations unearthed Indian burial grounds. Part of the effort to politicize this issue involved an occupation of the vault holding the North American Indian collection at the Royal Ontario Museum. In the activists' view, the excavation of Indian graves, undertaken in the name of an omnipotent science, was symbolic of the dominant society's disrespect towards the spirituality, cultural integrity, and shared humanity of Indigenous peoples.[201]

In Calgary, the major AIM-related initiative centred on the need for appropriate social services for Aboriginal people living in the city. Among the most prominent proponents of this initiative, based in the Calgary Urban Treaty Indian Alliance (CUTIA), were Roy Little Chief, Ed Burnstick, Urban Calling Last and Nelson Small Legs Jr. The group called attention to the urgency of their issues through the occupation of Indian Affairs offices and an incompletely realized effort to redirect the idealized cowboy and Indian imagery of the Calgary Stampede to more authentic representations of the harsh realities facing First Nations people in the skid-row culture of urban Canada. The activism came to an abrupt and tragic transition when Nelson Small Legs Jr apparently took his own life in an act of ritual suicide. He killed himself in full regalia to protest the inaction and inertia represented by the "wall of words" holding his people down.[202] The suicide created a brief wave of controversy, prompting various politicians, including Prime Minister Pierre Trudeau, to comment publically on the sad affair. The burial of the well-liked activist from the Peigan reserve south of Calgary generated especially intense introspection within AIM. In their struggle to achieve both the internal and external conditions of decolonization, AIM's members tended to cultivate a life-and-death language to reflect a life-or-death struggle for collective survival through self-determination.

One of the most zealous contributions to this discussion came from Louis Hall, who later emerged as a central figure among the Mohawk Warriors at Oka in 1990. Hall was a controversial Longhouse traditionalist from Kanewake, Quebec, and a powerful voice for AIM during this period. He disseminated his uncompromisingly militant messages through art work and through mimeographed newsletters that he sent to Native activists around the continent. In his work as an artist, Hall was responsible for much of AIM's most provocative and characteristic iconography. In an essay entitled "Suicide as a Weapon against Oppression," Hall commented:

The aftermath of the demise of Nelson Small Legs Jr. by self-destruction reached its uproar all the way to Ganienkeh (Mohawk Land). The conditions which the victim fought against is an old story. For 400 years an all out psychological warfare has been waged by the white race against the Native Americans. It has caused untold suffering among the Red Indians. Numerous suicides, among other casualties, like alcoholism and drug addiction, have resulted from the mind warfare. Other Indians are merely dispirited, demoralized and see no future for Indians as far as surviving as Indians is concerned. They only see Indians surviving as imitation white people and part of the white nation to be eventually absorbed until no traces remain of the Red race. They have reconciled themselves to extinction. This is the desired result of psychological warfare.

   This type of warfare is every bit as deadly as the one with guns. Brainwash the Indians, make them feel inferior, create conditions worse than death and the victims may destroy themselves ... Not all Indians will be destroyed in this way. Some will fight on and on. As they go along, they learn to fight this insidious and subtle struggle. There is a right way to fight and a wrong way to fight ... Self-destruction is not the answer. Of all the types of destroyed Indians (casualties of psychological warfare), the "establishment" prefers suicides. They solve better the "establishment's" Indian problems. Drunks and dope addicts who stay alive represent no threat to the dominant society's rule, just a pain in the ass. Indians who commit suicide play right into the establishment's hand. That's what they want. A lot of dead Indians. The more the better. Indian suicides arouse no sympathy from the people who created the intolerable conditions. These suicides only please them as they see their plan of genocide succeed.[203]

INDEPENDENCE OR INDIRECT RULE?
GOVERNMENT FUNDING OF ABORIGINAL ORGANIZATIONS
AND THE DILEMMA OF ABORIGINAL SELF-GOVERNMENT

The class conflicts in the Indian Country of Canada did not emerge at this time as divisively or as acrimoniously as those in the Indian Country of the United States, especially on the Pine Ridge reservation. This difference was largely attributable to the administrative integrity, ideological orientation, and political finesse of George Manuel during his years with the National Indian Brotherhood. Although Manuel eschewed violent protest himself, he refused to condemn those Indian activists who emphasized strident confrontation as the necessary response to overcome the oppression of a regime that had colonized and expropriated Aboriginal lands, Indian economies, and First Nations cultures. Indeed,

Manuel invited Louis Cameron of the Ojibway Warriors' Society to speak at the book launching of *The Fourth World* in 1974. At this event Manuel noted that the choice facing non-Indian society was to respond either to his own pen or to his militant friend's gun.[204] "Change cannot come about without conflict," he said, adding, "but conflict does not have to go the road of violence."[205]

Manuel had risen to the head of Canada's foremost Indian organization on a wave of Aboriginal resistance to a major shift in Indian policy proposed by the Trudeau government in 1969. Through Jean Chrétien, Trudeau's young minister of Indian Affairs and Northern Development, the prime minister proposed in the name of "equality" to do away with the legal and institutional infrastructure that treated Indians as a distinct subject of federal jurisdiction. In particular, Trudeau was anxious to eliminate Indian treaties as permanent instruments of relationship between Indian societies and Canadian authorities. As a leader who had built his political career in opposition to the idea of the Québécois as a distinct nationality *vis-à-vis* the rest of Canada, Trudeau was predisposed to oppose Indian treaties as permanent fixtures of Canadian statescraft. He was against anything that would secure for Indigenous peoples, or for any other constituency in Canada, their own distinct place in domestic and international law.[206]

As Trudeau told a largely Indian audience in Vancouver in 1969, "It is inconceivable ... that in a given society one section of the society have a treaty with the other section of society. We must all be equal under the laws and we must not sign treaties among ourselves."[207] These principles were clearly evident in Chrétien's policy statement, which proposed that "once Indian lands are securely within Indian control, the anomaly of treaties between groups within society and the government of that society will require that these treaties be reviewed to see how they can be equitably ended."[208]

In the process of rejecting the Trudeau/Chrétien White Paper, Indian politicians and some of their constituents entered into a new era of organized assertiveness that helped propel Aboriginal activism to genuine innovation on the frontiers of the Fourth World. That process continues to this day. Indeed, the White Paper represented a major point of departure in the political life of Canadians in that its intent was to entrench a constitutional definition of the country as an officially bilingual, multicultural state based on the equality of individuals, rather than on the shared prerogatives of historically bound groups or communities.[209] In this sense, Trudeau's effort to bring Indian treaties to an end foreshadowed a concerted attack from Ottawa on the distinct character of the relationship between the government and people of Quebec and the larger Canadian federal system. Moreover, the emphasis of the White Paper on the equality of individuals signalled Trudeau's intention to direct Canada towards more thorough integration into the neo-liberal orientation of the American empire and away from the conservative orientation of Canada's crown heritage as a community of legally distinct communities.

As the Aboriginal rejection of the White Paper coalesced, Harold Cardinal, a Cree from the Sucker Creek reserve in Alberta, emerged along with George Manual as one of the primary architects and spokespersons of the Indian rights movement in Canada. Cardinal left his work as a student activist in 1968 to become president of the Indian Association of Alberta. It was in this capacity that he led the fight against the White Paper, a fight that helped consolidate the viability of the National Indian Brotherhood as a major locus of Aboriginal political will. As a part of his campaign to expose Trudeau's plan as a betrayal of the principles on which Canada was founded, Cardinal penned a short manifesto entitled *The Unjust Society*. In this volume, he outlined his own views of the central importance of Indian treaties for the future of the First Nations as well as Canada. These agreements, he contended, are important "not so much for their content as for the principles they imply in their very existence." "As far as we are concerned," Cardinal said, "our treaty rights represent a sacred, honourable agreement between ourselves and the Canadian government that cannot be unilaterally abrogated by the government at the whim of one of its leaders unless the government is prepared to give us back title to our country ... To regain the confidence of our people, the government of Canada must reinstate our treaties. Upon this foundation and upon this foundation only, the government of Canada still can embark on an honourable understanding with the Indian peoples."[210]

In another presentation, Cardinal elaborated on and clarified his conception of treaties by explaining how these agreements are viewed by older Indian people both now and in the past.

In many respects our elders perceived the treaties as a process whereby the white society, with its legal systems, with its system of law, would guarantee to our people the right to continue practising their beliefs, the right to continue fulfilling their responsibilities to the Creator as agreed upon since time began. Our elders intended that the treaties would tell the guests who came to our country that while we welcomed them to our country, and while we wanted to build a nation in partnership with other nations so that our children could grow up in a better environment, we also by the process of our treaties wanted to let other people know that our first allegiance, our first commitment, was not to a temporal power, but to our Creator.[211]

The overwhelming attachment of most Indigenous peoples in Canada to their treaties with the crown was reflected in a corresponding hostility to the White Paper. This broadly based Indian rejection of the White Paper caused the government to renounce it, ostensibly at least. The initiative of 1969 was further undermined by a decision of the Supreme Court of Canada on a case brought forward by the Nisga'a Indians of British Columbia.

In an ambivalent ruling in 1973, the country's top judges implicitly instructed the Canadian government to seek political agreements with those Aboriginal groups residing on territories that had never been the subject of Indian treaty negotiations.[212] Consequently, in 1973 the federal government opened a new era of treaty making, specifically with some of those Aboriginal communities that had never sanctioned the imposition of non-Aboriginal titles and jurisdictions on their ancestral lands. The first of these modern-day treaties, which fulfilled the requirements of the Royal Proclamation of 1763, was formalized in 1975 between the governments of Quebec and Canada and the Cree and Inuit of the James Bay region of northern Québec.[213]

The federal government's renunciation of the White Paper policy and the reopening of the land issue in British Columbia and in the rest of Canada marked tremendously important policy shifts achieved during Manuel's term as national chief of the National Indian Brotherhood. In lobbying for these transformations, Manuel's generation of Indian politicians, whose most prominent members include Harold Cardinal, Dave Courchene of Manitoba, and Fred Plain and Harry Muskokomon of Ontario, built on the organizational work of many who laboured during darker times when activism in Indian Country was actively discouraged and sometimes even criminalized. A few of those who contributed to the legacy inherited by Manuel and the other founders of the National Indian Brotherhood are Lieutenant Fred Loft, the Reverend Edward Ahenakew, Mike Mountain Horse, Dan Kennedy, Augustine Steinhauer, Joe Dion, Joe Sampson, Johnny Callihoo, Omer Peters, the Reverend Ahab Spence, the Reverend Stanley Cuthand, Senator James Gladstone, Joe Dreaver, Henry Jackson, Gus Debassige, William Scow, Guy Williams, Frank Calder, and Senator Len Marchand. By and large, the political activities of those engaged in Indian politics before the White Paper of 1969 worked on a volunteer basis. Manuel's discussion of the always precarious condition of Andrew Paull's personal finances is indicative of how Aboriginal activism was mostly conducted and paid for over the largest part of the twentieth century. "Wherever Paull went," wrote Manuel, "the blanket or the hat was passed to keep Andy travelling and working ... Often, on his later trips to Ottawa, when I was old enough to remember and be active, we would raise enough money to just get him to Ottawa. A week or so later we would get a wire from him. It was time to chip in again and help him get back home."[214]

The ethos of volunteerism that characterized Aboriginal politics until 1969 changed dramatically during Manuels's term at the National Indian Brotherhood. Taking the position that, in a modern nation-state, many different kinds of constituencies must be assisted by government to organize and articulate shared positions, the Trudeau regime ushered in a period where Ottawa's financing of Indian Affairs in Canada was made to conform more fully with the institutional arrangements that had prevailed in the United States since the era of the Great Depression and the Indian New Deal. Beginning in the 1970s it became possible for Aboriginal activists to develop careers in the expanding political, bureaucratic, and technocratic branches of federally funded Aboriginal governments and organizations. While this change opened many new opportunities for those First Nations people in a position to profit from the professionalization of what would increasingly be known as Aboriginal self-government, many viewed with suspicion the various strings attached to the new infusions of federal and provincial money into Indian Country. In explaining opposition to the new financing mechanisms, for instance, Wilmer Nadjiwon, a former president of the Union of Ontario Indians, commented: "How can we be expected to negotiate competently and honestly with the very party that is providing our funding? In allowing the federal and provincial governments to take over the purse strings of our own political organizations, we gave up too much and opened the door to a very insidious process that tends to compromise or even subvert our own leadership."[215]

The issues raised after 1969, when expanded core funding became available for a wider array of Aboriginal organizations and institutions, renewed in a fresh context a very old debate in Indian Country. This debate revolves around the observation that virtually all the colonial powers in the Americas have at different times used presents, medals, honours, or outright bribery to engender dependencies and cultivate a class of Aboriginal leadership willing to collaborate in facilitating various forms of indirect rule on behalf of non-Aboriginal authority. Indeed, the manipulation of patronage to subvert, undermine, demoralize, or compromise the leadership and resistance of subject peoples has long been a staple tactic of imperialists and empire builders around the world. It constitutes a facet in the exercise of power which, as Frantz Fanon and many others have observed, was integral to undermining the authenticity and legitimacy of the "decolonization" movements proceeding from the dismantling of European empires after the Second World War.

The internal dynamics of the informal American empire were confirmed and extended in the process of co-opting or sabatoging the liberation stuggles of many Indigenous peoples in Africa and Asia. Fanon's observations on the course of events on these frontiers of political transformation were replicated in the ideas of those leading the rise of the American Indian Movement. Some of its proponents looked to Indian reservations as internal laboratories of federal power where systems of indirect rule were developed through the cultivation of a comprador class of Native people. As illustrated by the civil war on the Pine Ridge reservation in the mid–1970s, the class privileges of reservation-based elites were sometimes backed by federal authority in their resort to violent or even lethal repression in silencing the criticisms of the system's detractors.

Variations on these themes of internal colonialism were, it was argued, reproduced hemispherically and even globally in the rise of the American empire. In commenting on the consistency of this pattern in the growth and consolidation of the American power, Jack Forbes noted in 1978 that "it is certainly not surprising that the United States has always supported the European-oriented ruling cliques in every Native American nation." He then extrapolated how this pattern was extended throughout Latin America, writing that "almost everywhere the United States supports (and, today, maintains in power) the minority European ruling classes [act] against the native and mixed-blood masses."[216] The American Indian Movement addressed within North America a central problem of virtually every struggle for decolonization. From the struggle led by Tecumseh to that of Nelson Mandela, that problem has been how to guard against the co-optation of leadership in the fight to counter colonialism. Given the vast disparities of power and numerical strength in North America, that problem has been particularly perplexing for Indigenous peoples in Canada and and the United States.

In the early 1920s the Canadian government illustrated the extent of its determination to deny Indigenous peoples an independent political base of their own in its response to an attempt made by Lieutenant Fred Loft and his Indian colleagues in Ontario and the prairie provinces who worked hard to establish the League of Indians of Canada. An integral feature of the organization was the plan to fund it independently with dues from local bands. Only in this way could the organization be placed beyond the financial control of the dominion government. The bureaucracy of the Indian Department did everything in its power to counter the establishment of this pan-Canadian Indian association. In 1927 the government passed an amendment to the Indian Act prohibiting any soliciting or payment of funds aimed at "the recovery of any claim ... for the benefit" of any "band or tribe."[217]

Although this provision of the Indian Act was repealed in 1951, the legacy of this pre-emptive attack on the financial independance of virtually all federally-recognized Aboriginal organizations continues to this day. Leaders such as Andy Paull became accustomed to carrying on their organizational work in Indian Country within the severe constraints imposed by federal authority. George Manuel carried on this tradition of activism, eschewing the more independent courses of action advocated by Carlos Montezuma, Alice Lee Jemison, Jules Sioui, and the proponents of AIM and the Ojiway Warriors' Society. While Manuel could partially identify with the grievances and aspirations that motivated his more radical cousins, he negotiated his differences with non-Aboriginal authorities from within the framework of the institutions that these same authorities were willing to sanction and to facilitate through the agency of federal dollars.

Manuel was extremely conscientious in his refusal to exploit for unwarrented personal gain his leadership position within the Ottawa-based

National Indian Brotherhood. He also insisted that those who worked for him must adhere to his unbending regime of honest public service. In this way he avoided being targeted by the allegations regularly flung by AIM members at the National Congress of American Indians and the more recent National Tribal Chairmens' Association. While Manuel's personal honesty, however, may have helped Indigenous peoples in Canada avoid the kind of violent class conflict that exploded into a virtual civil war on the Pine Ridge reservation, no amount of honest bookkeeping could hold back the widening of the class divisions in Indian Country that the policies of his NIB helped to facilitate. The unresolved tensions stemming from class and economic relations in the Fourth World are suggested in the following passage from Manuel's book. "We also know," he writes, "that the kind of integration based on mutual respect and acceptance of each other's values *as valid for the other* will never happen until Indian people achieve the same standard of living as that enjoyed by city-dwelling, middle-class, white Canadians."[218] The questions raised by this reference to social class, integration, and standards of economic well-being are perhaps best put into perspective through consideration of the activism of African Americans in the 1960s and early 1970s.

The more radical wings of this activism included the Black Panthers and the Student Nonviolent Coordinating Committee (SNCC). More moderate opinion tended to rally around the leadership of Dr Martin Luther King from the Southern Christan Leadership Conference. In many ways the mobilization of African Americans set the stage for the emergence of the American Indian Movement. The direct attack on the most obvious manifestations of racial apartheid in the United States helped create the climate of opinion that was receptive to precisely the kind of manifesto outlined by George Manuel in *The Fourth World*.

During this remarkable era of politicization among African Americans, and, indeed, among all Americans, the way was opened for a Black minority to enter into, and partially to integrate with, the Euro-American middle class. As Cornel West writes, "beneath the rhetoric of Black Power, black control and black self-determination was a budding 'new,' black middle class hungry for power and starving for status ... the 'new' black business, professional and political elites heard the bourgeois melody behind the radical rhetoric and manipulated the movement for their own benefit."[219] The surge of upward mobility for some African Americans during the height of the civil rights movement had many complex outcomes. One effect was to draw off some of the natural leadership from the poor Black working class and the unemployed underclass in the United States. The conditions of their continuing ghettoization in urban enclaves of poverty, violent crime, drug addiction, and modern-day plagues, including HIV infection, arguably became worse rather than better.

There are a number of dissimilarities in the legal, political, and socio-economic positions of Indigenous peoples and African Americans, whose oppressed condition on the continent goes back largely to the legacy of slavery. Nevertheless, there is also much to link the circumstances of both groups. Each must live with the continuing consequences of primal acts of dispossession and expropriation grounded in systems of property law that afforded European colonists and their progeny superior rights to amass wealth through the exercise of dominion over Black slaves as well as over the continent's Aboriginal lands and waters. Thus, Indigenous peoples and African Americans have both had to contend during formative stages of their histories with regimes that disadvantaged them legally, economically, and politically by deeming them to be inferior, based on imagined constructions of racial and civilizational hierarchy. Within this shared frame of reference there were significant commonalities and unities linking the social, political, and economic analysis presented by both the Black Panthers and the American Indian Movement during the era when the civil rights movement converged forcefully with the movement to end the United States' military involvement in Vietnam. The Fourth World ideas and proposals of a George Manuel, a relative moderate of his time compared with some of the more militant proponents of Aboriginal nationalism, can fruitfully be placed in the continuum of options posed during this rare moment when it seemed as though a major reconfiguration in North America's legal, political, social, and economic structures was possible. The larger ideological frames of reference of this debate were primarily set by the greatest of the African Americans orators, from the integrationist Martin Luther King to the Black separatist Malcolm x.

A careful consideration of Manuel's work, especially when seen in the light of the African American liberation struggle of his era, helps to illustrate the view that there was little in either his philosophy of the Fourth World or his oversight of the National Indian Brotherhood to protect against the self-interested exploitation of the rhetoric of self-determination by an emerging Aboriginal middle class. Accordingly, it was naive at best, negligent at worst, for Manuel not to have given more careful consideration to the long-term implications of allowing the expansion of Aboriginal organizations and institutions to become completely dependent on transfer payments from the federal government. In making this criticism it is fair to consider the fundamental problem Manuel faced – the lack of any substantial economic base in Indian Country apart from the possibility of increased federal transfer payments. In this milieu of limited choice, what options did Manuel have but to take advantage of the one major source of financing available for building and elaborating the institutions that Indigenous peoples needed? Perhaps he reasoned that accepting this expedient would lead to a healthier situation where First Nations would gain governmental tools to lobby for a more secure economic base, especially through the capacity to share substantially in the revenues, royalties, and employment generated from the extraction of natural resources from the continent's Aboriginal lands.

Although Manuel the man may have been inured to the temptations and corruptions of extreme possessive individualism, the fact that he did not address directly the assimilative potential inherent in the Aboriginal technocracies and institutions he helped create unfortunately detracts from his legacy. It is lamentable that he did not grapple more conscientiously with the serious critiques of the growing hierarchies of power and class *within* Indian Country that were essential to the insights and motivations of groups like the NYCI, AIM, CUTIA, and the Ojibway Warriors' Society. These groups helped to bring forward into contemporary times some of the ethos and energy from the older Indian confederacies, whose collective rights to shared property and jurisdiction were frequently signified in the wampum symbol of the bowl with one spoon.

The approach to institution building in Indian Country since Manuel's time has tended to advance the creation of a small Native middle class that, in the style of the urban elites of Black America, has become farther removed from the most downtrodden and increasingly demoralized underclass in overcrowded ghettos or on reserves and reservations. Moreover, the post–White Paper funding structures have tended to compound a situation where success in Aboriginal politics is increasingly dependent on the capacity of candidates for leadership positions to learn and assimilate the attitudes, procedures, and protocols that predominate in non-Aborginal governments.[220] The outcome is a system of Aboriginal governance that has appropriated much of the language and imagery of decolonization and self-determination, but which continues many of the old cycles of oppression, often in expanded and more sophisticated forms. Indeed, the motifs of neo-colonialism in North America's Indian Country tend to replicate or even lead the development of more general patterns of indirect rule that are pervasive throughout the formal and informal structures of the American empire.

As elsewhere in the Third World, the continuing politics of neo-colonial repression in North America's Indian Country have frequently been manifest in the uneasy state of relations between Aboriginal elites and the most marginalized citizens of reserves, reservations, and the skid-row sections of many urban centres. The elites heading the top-down structures of federally funded systems of Aboriginal governance have tended, with some notable exceptions, to muzzle, interrupt, or pre-empt those sometimes weak voices seeking to articulate directly the struggles of the homeless urban poor, the victims of domestic violence and child abuse, the physically disabled or the mentally ill, the drug addicted, the recurringly incarcerated, the gays and lesbians, and various associations of women seeking a greater say in what are ostensibly their own First Nations governments.

It would be unfair to attribute the responsibility for this tendency on the legacy of George Manuel alone. After all, there is certainly a good deal of truth to his observation that there can be no authentic form of constructive, reciprocal integration between different societies sharing the same land base unless principles of economic parity in some way govern their relations. Similarly, who would deny the correctness of Manuel's insistance that there could be no liberation for Indigenous peoples through self-determination until First Nations have been released from the bondage brought about by disproportionately high rates of poverty, substance addictions, and incarceration? While the foremost champion of the Fourth World eloquently advanced these points, however, Manuel failed to leave a clear map of the precise nature of economic reforms needed to realize and enhance his vision of cultural pluralism. In particular, he failed to address the problem of how to integrate First Nations into the predominant class structures of the Euro–North American majority while maintaining some level of resistance against the assimilative force of a regime of property relations that had historically evolved in the very process of extinguishing and privatizing the largest part of the collectively held Indian Country.

George Manuel went only part of the way to fulfil Frantz Fanon's call for blueprints of political and economic relations that transcend the limitations of European models. What was most undeveloped in Manuel's analysis was a fuller explanation of how Indigenous peoples can go about liberating their own entrepreneurial energies and technological inventiveness within recognized regimes of diversified Aboriginal property law capable of expressing and supporting Aboriginal cultures rooted in the local ecologies of particular places.

GEORGE MANUEL'S ORIENTATION TO THE BRITISH EMPIRE, THE AMERICAN EMPIRE, AND THE WORLD

Many of the strengths and weaknesses of George Manuel's reflections on the process of decolonization were intimately connected to his growth to political maturity in a Canada whose constitutional fabric was still closely intertwined with that of Great Britiain. Like Andy Paull and many other Indian politicians in Canada who went before him, Manuel could be highly critical of local officialdom while affirming his attachment to the constitutional monarchy in which the sovereign authority of Canada was and still is invested. This way of characterizing violations of Indigenous peoples as violations of the imperial law was at least as old as the stand taken by Tupac Amaru in New Spain in 1781. He had described the treatment of the Indians of Peru as a breach "against the provisions of the very kings of Spain."

Manuel took the lessons he drew from Canada's place in the declining British Empire a great deal further than most of his peers. He elaborated his conception of Aboriginal self-government or Aboriginal dominion within the same constitutional continuum that had allowed for broadening the horizons of Canadian self-government or Canadian dominion, first within the framework of the British Empire and then within the framework of the British Commonwealth of Nations.[221] Indeed, in his use of language, Manuel demonstrated the extent to which his sense of place and purpose in history was connected to his understanding of the process of devolution, decentralization, and eventual dismemberment of the old British Empire. Throughout *The Fourth World*, he made repeated references not only to "responsible government" but also to "home rule" as the desired outcome of his own peoples' liberation struggles. Similarly, the central importance of the Aboriginal title question in his home province of British Columbia was integral to his appreciation of the broader international significance for the Fouth World of the unextinguished imperial law of British North America and of the Canadian dominion. The Royal Proclamation of 1763 was at the core of this complex of imperial law underlying crown recognition of Aboriginal and treaty rights.

Generally speaking, the term "responsible government" described the constitutional basis of self-government in those parts of the empire, such as Canada, Australia, and New Zealand, where the vast majority of inhabitants are non-Aboriginal. The term "home rule" was used most often to identify more limited forms of decolonization in those parts of the empire, such as India and West Africa, where the colonial immigrants and their descendants remained a small minority compared with the population of the Indigenous peoples. By invoking the names of both traditions as descriptive of the preferred course of future history for his own peoples, Manuel conferred a broader level of legitimacy and a heightened level of coherence on the Aboriginal agenda. He presented Aboriginal aspirations for decolonization as a manifestation and extension of the same urges motivating colonized peoples throughout Europe's overseas realms, including those liberal-minded Canadians who have been encouraged to celebrate the constitutional evolution of their own country "from colony to nation."[222]

What has frequently been omitted from this more liberal view of Canadian history, however, has been a conservative perspective on the country's transformation from a formal constitutional colony of Great Britain to an economic and cultural colony of the United States. Indeed, as the initial site for many of the first branch plants of major US corporations, Canada has tended to be the testing ground and the first hinterland of the global system of economic relationships essential to the make-up of the informal American empire. Thus the clash of politics and law between the British Empire and the American empire in the contested Indian Country of Canada has broad implications for the future course of globalization and the attending fate of many other peoples throughout the planet. The emergence of the idea of the Fourth World from the most contested province of this most contested ground is far from coincidental.

Manuel's sense of engagement in the constitutional transformation of the remnant structures of the old British Empire was certainly a key factor in his ability to see the larger international patterns of oppression and resistance animating Indigenous peoples globally. His international orientation has been built upon by subsequent Aboriginal leaders in Canada who tend to be more active at the United Nations and other international forums than their Native American counterparts in the United States.[223] Indeed, whether they have constituted majorities or minorities in their territories, Indigenous peoples from all the old British Empire have been more inclined to seek international remedies for their grievances. This orientation was cultivated over those centuries when the British Empire grew to become the largest and most pluralistic polity the world has ever seen. While the American empire has transcended the scope and magnitude of the British Empire, its informal structures and more monocultural orientations have presented obstacles to the elaboration of various kinds of associations among the diverse subjects of the world's new leviathan.

Manuel's perception of the connection between the ascendance of the Fourth World and the decline of old European empires had particularly interesting implications for Canadian politics in the 1970s. In those years virtually all the major legal instruments that had created and shaped Canadian parliamentary institutions drew their ultimate legitimacy from the authority of the British government, which technically retained the exclusive power to amend the Canadian Constitution. In the era when George Manuel was at the helm of the National Indian Brotherhood, Canadian citizens still had not claimed or asserted the power to reshape internally the foundational structures of Canadian federalism. To this extent Canada retained a kind of quasi-colonial status under the higher authority of Great Britain, even if the Mother Country had gradually handed over so many powers of self-government that most Canadians had come to perceive themselves as citizens of a sovereign, democratic federation with full, independent status in the international community.[224]

Manuel's quest for widened spheres of self-determination for Indigenous peoples therefore unfolded in a country overwhelmingly dominated by non-Aboriginals who had yet to formalize fully their own decolonized status outside the framework of the British Empire. For Manuel, the resulting imminence of major constitutional change in Canada was both a danger and an opportunity. The transformation could be dangerous for his Aboriginal constituents in that most of the major constitutional promises to recognize and protect the legal titles and distinct cultures of Indigenous peoples had been articulated directly in the name of various British monarchs in their sovereign capacity as the highest authority in the British Empire. If federal and provincial authorities in Canada were to acquire the capacity to amend the Canadian Constitution domestically, what certainty could there be that Canadians would exercise their widened powers of self-government in ways that conformed to the promises and commitments made by the British sovereign, especially in the Royal Proclamation of 1763 or in treaties with Indian nations?

Certainly there were no conditions placed on these promises that identified them as qualified or terminal commitments subject to the political tastes and whims of future electorates. Instead, many of the crown's treaty commissioners had encouraged Indigenous peoples in Canada and elsewhere in the British Empire to see their agreements with the British sovereign as sacred covenants that established a formal basis of legal, social, and economic relations between different societies for as long as the sun shines, the grass grows, and the rivers flow to the ocean.[225]

There was a compelling historical basis to the fears that would later push Manuel and many of his fellow Indian leaders to oppose patriation of the Canadian Constitution from Great Britain. Time and time again, in virtually all parts of the empire where immigrants and their descendants outnumbered the Indigenous peoples, liberated colonials exploited their widened powers of self-government to oppress, subjugate, and dispossess Aboriginal groups in their midst and on their frontiers. The pattern was consistent, whether in the newly independent United States, the Creole nationalities of Latin America, New Zealand, Australia, South Africa, or even the pre-Confederation province of Canada after the colony was granted responsible government in 1840s and 1850s. In all these instances and many others as well, the non-Aboriginal settlers used their expanded autonomy to negate or overpower the promises and guarantees that Indigenous peoples had been able to extract from the European sovereigns whose agents first colonized their lands. Hence, in almost every instance, any evacuation of imperial jurisdiction by European governments has led non-Aboriginals in colonies and former colonies to widen their jurisdictional frontiers at the direct expense of those Indigenous peoples whose resources and territories have always been the primary prize of New World expansionism.[226]

Given the experience of Manuel and his Indian colleagues, there was little reason for them to expect that the Canadians would act any differently towards the rights and titles of Indigenous peoples once the government of Great Britain gave up its exclusive power to amend the Canadian Constitution. There was little reason to have confidence that Canadian authorities would respect with consistency and enthusiasm the constitutional and international character of Indian treaties. Nor was there much basis for Indian confidence that Canadian officials would live up to the constitutionality of the Royal Proclamation of 1763. This major monument of North American history established the legal framework for treaty making in British North America, including future treaty making in those parts of the continent where Aboriginal title had never been the subject of crown negotiations with the Indigenous peoples.

While the prospect of constitutional change represented a possible menace to Indigenous peoples in Canada, Manuel could also see in 1974 a measure of opportunity in the probable imminence of a major transformation in the structure of the Canadian federation. In *The Fourth World* he recorded "the demand that Indian people be allowed to sit at the table where our lives are being negotiated, where our resources are being carved up like a pie." With an eye on the likelihood that Canada was about to be reordered and reshaped into a new political form through the writing of a new constitution, he echoed the premier demand brought to Ottawa by Louis Cameron and the Native Peoples' Caravan. "Our identity as Indian peoples," Manuel wrote, "must be enshrined in the fundamental law of Canada."[227]

As the last large country in both the Americas to move towards severing formal legal ties with its imperial parent in Europe, Canada stood well placed to participate in the new phase of the discourse on decolonization which came with the entry of so many new African and Asian countries into the United Nations world system. The circumstances of Quebec as the heartland of the last remaining organized and large French-speaking community in the Americas, apart from Haiti, added urgency and complexity to the impending negotiations in Canada on independence, self-government, human rights, and cultural pluralism. As it would turn out, the efforts to articulate and elaborate a new constitutional framework for Canada proved to be the prelude for a broader push aimed at formulating new forms of hemispheric and global constitutions through the media of commercial trade and investment treaties. In this new generation of commercial negotiation, the same questions about the inclusion or exclusion of Indigenous peoples could be pressed just as appropriately. In the establishment, for instance, of NAFTA, or of the Free Trade Area of the Americas, or of the World Trade Organization, it could legitimately be said that representatives of Indigenous peoples were entitled to sit at the table where their futures were being charted and their resources being carved up.

It was George Manuel's hope, therefore, that the constitutional plasticity of Canada opened the prospect that this country could be the scene of a major breakthrough in the global advancement of the ideals of the Fourth World. Similarly, the same arguments justifying a distinct, First Nations role in elaborating the Canadian constitution – an ethos of inclusiveness personified by Elijah Harper's popular stance in 1990 on Canadian constitutional reform – could as easily be invoked to assert the inherent right of Indigenous peoples globally to a say in reforming or stopping the commercial trade treaties that are transforming the arena of international law. These trade treaties were technically established through the international sovereignty of national governments. However, some have viewed these agreements more as the outcome of negotiations where the agents of global corporations pulled many of the strings in directing the actions of puppet client states. The new supranational agencies that emerged from these deals were designed to change the shape of economic and political relations *within* countries as well as between countries.

This use of the instruments of international law to affect transformations in national law enabled proponents of neo-liberal forms of globalization to evade direct reckoning with their opponents on the more elaborately organized home turfs of domestic politics. Moreover, the negotiation of these agreements without Aboriginal consent arguably continued the same dubious approach to international law that resulted in the dividing up of much of Africa and the Americas without input from the Indigenous peoples of those continents. In this respect the negotiation without Aboriginal involvement of NAFTA continued the same brand of unjust exclusion that saw, for example, Louisiana transferred from France to the United States in 1803 without even superficial consultations with the Indigenous peoples of the transferred territory. It continued the legacy of exclusion originated in the pope's "donation" of the entire western hemisphere to the sovereigns of Spain and Portugal in 1493.

Manuel's vision of the Fourth World continues to offer humanity a very different future from the monocultural organization of the world's resources as an American empire of private property under a regime of transnational corporate rule. The Fourth World envisages a pluralistic global village without the tyranny of a universal and homogenous state. In articulating this ecological vision when he did, Manuel captured some of the essence of a particularly creative moment in the cultural, intellectual, and political ferment of First Nations in North America and of Indigenous peoples around the world. In this way, Manuel stands in the tradition of Tupac Amaru and Tecumseh. While these leaders died in the struggle to realize their own versions of the Fourth World, they left behind a legacy on which others, including Manuel, could constuctively build and elaborate.

The fuller significance of Manuel's inspiration would emerge only gradually in the years after his death when huge conglomerates of wealth and political influence pushed agendas that pointed the world towards monocultural models of globalization. The unsustainability of the dominant model demanded the formulation of alternative approaches. The idea of the Fourth World provided the seeds of a viable philosophy and strategy of resistance to the dominant models of globalization; it pointed towards the need for the replacement of neo-liberal geo-economics with forms of globalization more attuned to the natural ecology of inter-human and cross-species relationships. As Vine Deloria Jr, the Lakota theologian who for at least a generation served as the unofficial dean of Native American Studies, exclaimed, "I believe George Manuel has opened a whole new chapter in the experiences of mankind:"

He calls the institutions of the world to re-examine their origins, the beliefs which brought them into being, and the basis that lies beneath their formal structures ... What makes a "nation"? How do peoples come into existence? How do peoples relate to each other? These are some of the questions that plague us today. If we continue to view the world as the combination of political and economic forces of recent vintage which seem to control our lives and properties, we do violence to the very core of our existence. Thus it is that the Fourth World of George Manuel offers a vision of human existence beyond that of expediency and the balancing of powers and speaks to the identity crisis that has gripped every land and its peoples.[228]

PART TWO

Patenting the Land

CHAPTER FOUR

Revolution and Empire

Heedless of theories, Americans began the building of their
empire with an inheritance of ethnocentric semantics that made
logic valid to themselves out of the strange proposition that invasion, conquest, and dispossession of other peoples support the
principle that all men are created equal.

Francis Jennings, *Empire of Fortune*, 1988

INDIAN COUNTRY IN HISTORY, GEOGRAPHY, LAW, AND LORE

Indian Country is a place located as much in the geography of the mind as
in the geography of land and jurisdiction. In the genesis of both Canada
and the United States, the phrase "Indian Country," or "Indian Territory,"
has been assigned various constitutional meanings. In the lexicon of colonial North America, Indian Country describes a finite domain with precisely set yet notoriously movable borders. The colonial destiny of this Indian Country was to shrink and eventually disappear as the more "civilized,"
advanced Euro-American societies grew and expanded. A large legal
machinery was developed seemingly to legitimize the gradual extinguishment of Indian Country until it was completely terminated. This system
has a momentum that continues to this day. The cold, Darwinian assumption beneath it is that Indian societies are terminal societies which, in the
interest of progress, must give way to those whose inheritance from history is a superior way of life and the right to shape the world of tomorrow.

The assumptions beneath the machinery of extinguishment cut against
another view of Indian Country as an extremely versatile realm of personality, imagination, law, and territory. Indian Country can at times be a place
and at other times a social network, a frame of reference, a complex of
allegiances, or a relationship with history, nature, knowledge, and society.
To the American army in Vietnam, enemy territory, which could be almost
anywhere, was regularly described as "Indian Country."[1] To Fred Ragsdale,
a Chemehuevi professor of law from California, "Indian Country is a
romantic phrase that evokes nostalgia for the Old West as depicted in the
movies. Indian Country once meant exactly that, the country of Indians, a
place where Indians lived ... It was a geographical definition with clearcut
jurisdictional overtones. It could be marked on a map with some accuracy." Ragsdale goes on to describe a US court case in 1882 that changed

Indian Country "from a geographical concept to something else – exactly what else is a difficult question." He adds, "Indian Country is about as provisional as Marlboro Country, that is, it is an image, or a state of mind, or a sociological phenomenon to many. Indian Country is an incredibly complex jurisdictional issue disguised in a colorful phrase."[2]

A key idea that animates this text is that, for much of its history, Canada was perceived, organized, and defended essentially as a vast North American Indian Country. The primary element in this formula was the fur trade, one of the few vehicles of interaction that fostered some degree of cooperation, alliance, and reciprocity between Indigenous peoples and European newcomers – rather than the more usual cycles of conquest, dispossession, and genocide. The fur trade was allowed to grow and expand throughout most of Canada as the primary economic activity from the early seventeenth century until the late nineteenth century. The region was widely perceived to be a frigid zone, mostly inhospitable to agriculture, and unfriendly to settlement by all but a few hardy Euro-American mercantilists and their Aboriginal neighbours, wives, in-laws, business partners, suppliers, and customers.

In his filmed and literary commentary on *America*, British Broadcasting Corporation eminence Alistair Cooke demonstrated the dogged persistence of old European assumptions about the relationship between climate and ethnography in North America. According to Cooke, the territory north of the US border is composed of notoriously "bleak and unproductive lands." Similarly, the land south of the United States is subject to a climate that "debilitates the white man when its diseases do not enfeeble him." Cooke's America is, therefore, an ethnically divided place where "the United States spans the limits of the climate where white men can live and work."[3] In imagining a continental division with a single zone of "white" predominance, together with north and south zones of Aboriginal persistence, Cooke's geographic generalizations, like Grey Owl's invented life, suggest the continuing power of the identification of Canada and Mexico with Indian Country. Of course, the power and intensity of that identification grows the farther one goes back in time.

From the perspective of most English-speaking settlers along much of the eastern seaboard until the era of the American Revolution, for example, Canada was the Indian Country behind their settlements. As Canada's Aboriginal inhabitants became increasingly well armed, they became more dangerous and a formidable obstacle to western expansion. From the perspective of the French-speaking settlers clustered along the St Lawrence, Canada included the vast Indian Country upriver from their Catholic seigneuries, a domain open to French trade, evangelism, diplomatic contact, and even familial connection as long as the French emissaries adapted themselves to Aboriginal cultures, manners, protocols, languages, and laws. In integrating themselves into the diverse and elaborate mores of Indian Country, some of the French-speaking colonists transformed themselves into canadiens long before the more Eurocentric New Englanders began to adopt the name of the lands known by the designation of America.

This identification of Canada as an Indian Country continued long after the British conquest of New France on the Plains of Abraham in 1759. The rise of Montreal as a significant commercial centre, the home of the North West Company, and the major hub of the North American fur trade stands as a testament to the viability of Canada as a domain reserved by the British sovereign to the Indians as their hunting grounds. After a civil war erupted in British North America in 1776, the British imperial government held onto much of Canada largely by appeasing the Roman Catholic clergy of Quebec and by encouraging Indian fighting forces to defend their Indian Country against encroachment by the people and government of the United States.

This alliance of Indians, French Canadians, and British imperialists in defence of Canada as a bastion of Roman Catholicism, as an Indian Country, and as a hinterland of the Montreal fur trade culminated in the War of 1812. Shortly thereafter the Hudson's Bay Company, already in business since 1670, became, through merger with the North West Company in 1821, the primary agency charged with asserting the crown's presence through the maintenance of the northern part of North America as an Indian Country. The Charter of that most famous of all fur-trade companies described the domain of the HBC commercial monopoly as all the lands drained by rivers flowing into Hudson Bay, a territorial assertion whose southwestern outline roughly approximates the 49th parallel. The western border between Canada and the United States, the medicine line that distinguishes the arctic watershed from the broad Mississippi Valley, has its origins in the reservation of land as an Indian Country and as a fur-trade preserve, two sides of the same geopolitical coin. As Harold Innis wrote in 1930, "it is no mere accident that the present Dominion [of Canada] coincides roughly with the fur-trade areas of northern North America."4

While the British North American provinces underwent a major constitutional reorganization after 1867 with the aim of diversifying the Canadian economy through the transformation of Indian Country into regions suitable for mechanized agriculture, mining, oil and gas extraction, forestry, and hydroelectric development, this transformation remains spotty and uneven. To this day the permanent population of the Canadian North remains predominantly or significantly Aboriginal in many localities, a result of the choice of most non-Aboriginal citizens to locate themselves in a few cities along a single narrow band of relatively dense settlement that hugs the country's southern border. Although Aboriginal peoples – Indians, Inuit, and Métis – constitute only about 5 per cent of the total Canadian population of approximately 30 million, they nevertheless represent a numerical majority over the largest part of the vast, sparsely settled Canadian land mass. Moreover, in recent decades, the Aboriginal population has been growing at a rate over twice that of the overall Canadian population, even taking into account the non-Aboriginal increase through immigration.[5]

Accordingly, when George Manuel looked forward in 1974 to the prospect of a major reworking of the Canadian Constitution, he could realistically anticipate that Indigenous peoples would have some influence on the process both as the fastest-growing group in Canada and as members of Aboriginal societies who have played a major role in the commercial, strategic, and constitutional evolution of Canada over a long and formative period of the country's history. One of the challenges facing Manuel's generation of Fourth World activists and those who followed was how to revivify, rather than invent anew, some of the old strengths of Canada as an Indian Country founded on cooperation and reciprocity, however imperfect, between Indigenous peoples and non-Aboriginals. Clearly the days are gone when the fur trade can be looked to as the primary medium of exchange to animate the old alliances on which the original Canada and several subsequent incarnations took shape. But just as Innis's pioneering study *The Fur Trade in Canada* led to some surprising outcomes, so perhaps the study of Canada as an Indian Country and as a Fourth World frontier might hold unexpected capacities to generate new perspectives on some of the oldest and most pervasive issues arising from the accelerating pace of globalization.

For Innis, the fur trade provided a prototypical "empire of communications," a network of commercial, social, and political interaction not only across wide geographic spaces but across broad diversities of culture as well. Anticipating the coming of cyberspace, Marshall McLuhan extended Innis's pioneering work on communications theory, concentrating on the transformation of a print-based culture into an electronically wired world.[6] This genesis of thought arose in a North American setting where the Indigenous peoples had been brought into the process of globalization primarily through the complex of intercultural negotiations on which the viability of the fur trade depended. As Richard White suggests in *The Middle Ground*, a kind of belated sequel to *The Fur Trade in Canada*, this history of cultural innovation and experimentation in pluralism represents an approach to the generation of social cohesion very different from the monoculturalism emphasized in neo-liberal forms of globalization.[7]

Like Innis, McLuhan, and also George Grant, George Manuel found patterns and precedents in the history of Canada that informed his critique of American expansionism as the dominant force in globalization. As a Shuswap activist from British Columbia, Manuel had been shaped in a milieu where the quest of his own peoples for decolonization took form in a country characterized by the expanding commercial frontiers of the American empire and by constitutional motifs inherited from a dwindling British Empire. Manuel's vision of the Fourth World drew from these different facets of local, national, and global history. To these strands he added an assessment of the importance of the knowledge retained by some Indigenous peoples in addressing the ecological crisis looming on the horizon, a crisis whose hallmark would be the replacement of biological and cultural diversity with vulnerable and unsustainable monocultures.

In presenting the Fourth World as an alternative model of globalization, Manuel looked backwards and forwards in time and outward across cultures with a breathtaking imaginative sweep. In developing a broad, integrated conception of global change from a deep sense of rootedness in the heritages of Canada, Manuel's intellectual achievement is rivalled among his generation of thinkers writing in English only by Northrop Frye, George Grant, and Marshall McLuhan.

THE ACQUISITION OF INDIAN LANDS IN THE RISE AND FALL OF EMPIRES AND IN THE INVENTION OF NEW SOVEREIGNTIES

At various points in this text I have referred to something I call the American empire of private property as the enemy and antithesis of the Indian Country of Canada. I see the past experiences of Indian Country's citizens as a kind of forerunner for those of many other peoples and nationalities whose old connections to their ancestral lands and their inherited communities are being severed and atomized through the expansion of neoliberalism throughout the planet. My method in tracing the dialectical tension between these two opposing realms has been largely historical. While much of my study has been directed at episodes and events that happened long before my lifetime, I have witnessed many contemporary clashes continuing, ideologically, some of the central contentions of the old wars between the Indian Country of Canada and the American empire of private property.

As Manuel anticipated, the struggle to define and shape the constitution of Canada became a particularly important forum of contestation between competing visions whose origins go back to the earliest times of European colonization in the Americas. Negotiations to determine the relationship of Quebec and the First Nations to the federal state set Fourth World principles against the deeper integration of Canada into the empire of private property that emerged from the revolutionary side of the American War of Independence.

If the Indian Country of Canada was long tilted towards the orientations and even the place names of the Indigenous peoples of northern North America, the American empire of private property collected much of its original impetus as well as its name from the European origins of the United States. "America," writes Fernand Braudel in the third volume of *Civilization and Capitalism*, "was the achievement by which Europe most truly revealed her own nature."[8] In *The Wretched of the Earth*, Frantz Fanon makes essentially the same observation, but from a more pointedly critical stance. He writes, "The United States of America became a monster, in which the taints, the sickness, and the inhumanity of Europe have grown to appalling dimensions."[9]

More recently Samuel Huntington, Arthur Schlesinger Jr, and others have argued with great vehemence that the identity of the United States is derived almost exclusively from its European heritage.[10] This position, which marks a fundamental dismissal of Frederick Jackson Turner's frontier school of American historiography, has been developed as part of the arsenal of ideas pointed against the adoption of multiculturalism as government policy. An obvious illustration of this view of the United States as a kind of distilled or exaggerated expression of Europe is to equate the historical process that produced the American empire with the process that produced the Roman Empire. Just as ancient Greece was the site of the intellectual and cultural birth of many of the underlying principles that were adapted, extended, and built upon in Rome's ascent to dominance over much of the Mediterranean and European world, so England can be said to have provided the language and many of the seed ideas given expanded global currency by the United States.

If we find validity in this genre of comparison, questions arise about the nature of the point of compression in the hour glass of history that led to the emergence of the empire of the United States from the North American empire of Great Britain. What were the lines of unbroken continuity and what were the obstacles of irreconcilable difference that caused Europe's most expansionistic country to lose most of its American colonies, only to see these born-again offspring of British imperialism become the founders of a reconstituted, second-generation empire and later a global superpower?

Disagreements over how to govern and acquire Indian lands were integral to the transition from one form of empire to the another, from one form of colonization to another. Essential to the process of breakdown and reconstitution in the machinery of one of Western civilization's most dramatic surges of westward expansion was the push in the Anglo-American world to widen the legal, political, and commercial frontiers of chartered corporations through the extinguishment and privatization of Indian Country. Accordingly, one of the major outcomes of the American Revolution was to put in place a new political and ideological framework for the generation of a regime of property and corporate law more closely geared than the old imperial system to the expropriation and reconstitution of Indian lands as real estate and as capital. This phenomenon represented at once a break with, and an extension of, principles whose origins and wellsprings lie in Europe. It therefore helped to establish some of the ironies and paradoxes that came to characterize the American nation, republic, and empire.

As a regime that would thrive on the mastery of illusion and on the cre-

ative deployment of contradictions, the United States moved to monopolize the imagery of "America," a polity that could concurrently be a country, a continent, or a whole hemisphere. It became Europe's principal
agent, extension, and land speculation, even as its leaders also claimed to
represent the whole of the imagined New World to the imagined Old
World. Similarly, the United States came to embody both the acquisitive
aggressions of the colonizing world just its spokespeople laid claim to the
imperative of representing the colonized portion of the planet. At the
roots of this amazing enterprise in spanning ideological distance between
seemingly irresolvable opposites were the origins of the United States as a
synthesis of the religious zealotry invested in the Reformation and the secularizing force of the European Enlightenment.

In the same way that the United States absorbed and refined some of the
most expansionary qualities of European imperialism generally and of
British imperialism specifically, the creation of the American republic also
constituted the world's first episode of decolonization. How have subsequent rounds of decolonization followed patterns pioneered by the first
successor state of a European empire?[11] To what extent, for instance, did
the ethnic violence along the United States's westward-moving frontier
anticipate the ethnic conflict that would come to characterized the decolonized world after the dismantling of European empires, including that of
the Soviet Union in 1989? To what extent was the ethnic nationalism manifest in the Indian policies of the newly independent United States a forerunner of the ethnic nationalism that would see those groups most
empowered by the process of decolonization use their new-found powers
to undermine, dispossess, or vanquish those not so favoured?

The expansion of European empires and their successor states into the
Aboriginal territories of Indigenous peoples has historically provided an
extremely crucial zone of contestation, testing various strategies, theories,
and exercises of sovereignty. Underlying the success or failure of these
various assertions of sovereign authority was a relatively simple question:
Who could acquire the lands and titles from the Indigenous peoples and
what legal constraints, protocols, or procedures, if any, should govern this
transfer?

Many other questions arise from this first one. Could individuals or corporate bodies, for instance, acquire land directly through purchase from
Indigenous peoples, or was this basic right of transfer to be restricted to
the sovereign agencies of the non-Aboriginals? If the latter was true, how
would the vital power to acquire Indian land be apportioned between
local and central governments, or between the monarchial and representative branches of these governments? What were the rules, if any, governing wars of conquest of Indigenous peoples or the unilateral dispossession of their lands, their identities, or their persons through the
institution of slavery? If it was deemed that Indigenous peoples retained
an inherent human right not to be unilaterally dispossessed of their lives,

their land, their personhood, or their cultures, who would enforce this aspect of the law?

From the time of earliest colonization until the present day, issues surrounding the enforcement of Aboriginal and treaty rights continue to pose a particularly challenging set of questions going to the root of the fundamental legitimacy of the rule of law in many parts of the world, but especially in the Americas, in Australasia, in Southeast Asia, and in many parts of Africa. When, for instance, Indigenous peoples are rendered as minorities in their ancestral lands, even as they retain some semblance of their Aboriginal title and law-making authority within the framework of empires or their successor states, what agencies should enforce and defend the integrity of various forms of Aboriginal jurisdiction? Who should be liable, criminally or otherwise, when existing Aboriginal and treaty rights are not enforced? When questions arise about conflicts between Aboriginal and non-Aboriginal assertions of jurisdiction, who can with credibility on all sides arbitrate the disputes? Much of the history of the New World has been tied up with the conflicts surrounding these questions. Their outcome has generated many of the key answers to questions about where power is concentrated to dominate, rule, and own large portions of the earth.

CHRISTIANITY, LAW, AND POSSESSIVE INDIVIDUALISM IN THE EARLY PHASES OF EUROPE'S TRANSATLANTIC EXPANSION

As navigators, traders, missionaries, military men, and monarchs moved to expand their influence in the era of globalization that began in 1492, the broadening horizons of Eurocentric power stimulated many innovations. The Columbian conquests generated the need to legitimate the nascent imperialisms of Europe with revised and extended theories of law. This theorizing about the exercise of power in the global arena was often explained as "the law of nations." Gradually, however, the opening of the New World necessitated the development of fields of study, enactment, litigation, and arbitration identified as international law.

There is much irony in the fact that the treatment of Indigenous peoples in the Americas and elsewhere was a major topic of analysis and debate in the genesis of international law. This irony arises because of the tremendous contemporary antagonisms among the governing authorities in most nation-states against the expansive interpretation of Aboriginal and treaty rights. This antagonism is often expressed in the tendency not to allow questions concerning the titles, rights, and well-being of Indigenous peoples to seep into forums of legal consideration beyond the local realm. The inclination is to contain Aboriginal issues within circumscribed domestic confines; to prevent these matters from being highlighted as legal questions of international, transnational, or supranational concern.

This bias on the part of national governments is inherent in a world where the "territorial integrity" of so many countries has been based on negating the Aboriginal title of Indigenous peoples. The effort to domesticate rather than internationalize the legal arbitration of Aboriginal and treaty rights also serves the neo-liberal aim of maintaining emphasis on commercial treaties as the pre-eminent concern of global geopolitics. The other side of this subordination of the power of people to the power of money has been to downgrade both human rights and environmental issues as pre-eminent issues to be addressed by international, transnational, or supranational agencies.

The European land grabs and power grabs that began in 1492 were often justified and rationalized as evangelical enterprises whose major object was to expand the realm of Christendom. While the aim of advancing the global supremacy of the universal Christian church was proclaimed as the primary justification for colonization of large parts of the planet, however, the business of exploration, conquest, and trade tended to provide the ascendant monarchies of Europe with means to flex their more secular authorities even as they moved to distance themselves from the absolutist pretensions of ecclesiastical control from the Vatican. In New Spain, in fact, the powers invested in the Spanish monarchy tended to overshadow the powers of the papacy, for the sovereign acquired the right to present candidates for all levels of ecclesiastical office, an unprecedented form of patronage that centralized great authority in the Court of Castile.[12]

This monarchical push in Europe towards forms of sovereignty independent from the totalitarian power of popes coincided with the Reformation that broke the Christian monopoly of the Roman Catholic Church. The Reformation was a revolution of thought and conviction tied closely to the proliferation of published literature, but particularly the Bible, as facilitated through the invention of the printing press. The Reformation resulted in making England and the Netherlands major bastions of Protestantism, a decentralized complex of Christian devotion well suited to the individualistic ethos of a nascent middle class bent on pushing the frontiers of private ownership into the tradition-bound collectivism of feudal institutions. The merchant classes in these ascendant centres of emergent capitalism moved aggressively to derive commercial advantage from the Eurocentric forms of globalization that developed following the transformative "discoveries" beginning in 1492.

The Holy See in Rome responded to the new era of globalization by issuing a Papal Bull of Demarcation in 1493. Working on the principle that the whole world was the Christian God's rightful domain, the pope moved as Christ's vicar on earth to delegate authority over the whole hemisphere on the other side of the Atlantic to the Castillian crown of Spain.[13] When the government in Lisbon raised a legal challenge, the Vatican apportioned the eastern extremity of South America to Portugal. One outcome

of this means of dividing the Americas is that the Spanish language predominates over most of the territory south of the Rio Grande, whereas the
Portuguese language persists to this day as the official tongue of Brazil.

The Papal Bull of 1493 also originated the pattern wherein virtually all
the empires and nation-states of the Americas, including the United States,
do not derive their founding legal authority primarily from the Indigenous
peoples. Instead, virtually all the post-Columbian jurisdictions in the Americas, even those set up through acts of revolutionary defiance aimed at Old
World mother countries, looked ultimately towards European sponsors or
their appointed agents as important sources of their legal legitimacy. The
one qualifier in this Eurocentric pattern lies in the history of treaty negotiations with the First Nations peoples. The development of this means of
creating a licence for empire reached its highest and most long-lived
expression in the colonization of British North America and the Dominion of Canada.

In 1537 Pope Paul III issued a second decree reflecting the Vatican's
move towards a more enlightened embrace of the shared humanity of the
Indigenous peoples of the Americas. In a Papal Bull entitled *Sublimus deus
sic dilexit*, the Pope proclaimed that the Native people were not to be treated "as dumb brutes created for our service ... [but] as true men ... capable
of understanding the Catholic faith ... [Moreover] the said Indians and
other people who may be discovered by the Christians, are by no means to
be deprived of their liberty or the possession of their property, even
though they be outside the faith of Jesus Christ ... nor should they be in
any way enslaved."[14] This bull embodied insights emerging primarily from
that part of the church that had attached itself to the establishment and
expansion of New Spain. Among the most important of the contributors
to the discussion of how the Spanish crown should structure and justify its
imperial expansion was Francisco de Vitoria, the Dominican holder of the
chair of theology at Salamanca University. In 1532 this teacher, whose students were prominent among the early waves of Roman Catholic missionaries sent to evangelize the Indigenous peoples of the Americas, presented a series of influential lectures entitled *On the Indians Lately Discovered.*

Vitoria's contributions in the nascent field of international law supported the rise of the Spanish monarch's influence in the Americas along with
the placement of some restrictions on the near-absolute claims of the Vatican. Vitoria advanced a model of transatlantic relations that envisaged the
subordination of Indian peoples under a kind of benevolent Christian
guardianship until their conversion was realized. He rejected the extremist doctrine of discovery and advocated a qualified respect for the free will
of Indian peoples and their basic human right not to be dispossessed or
enslaved. He argued, for instance, that the Native inhabitants of the Americas were the "true owners" of their property, including their ancestral
lands. Moreover, they held a "true dominion" over themselves and their
possessions that "cannot be denied to them." Vitoria buttressed these asser-

tions with cautions that pre-empted Spaniards from seizing the territory or other possessions of the Indigenous peoples on the claim that they were guilty "of the sin of unbelief or any other mortal sin." The implication of this position was that Indians possessed the power to negotiate treaties with Christian sovereigns, as long as these treaties conformed to the divine linkages among God, people, and the Law of Nations connecting all humanity in a *societas naturalis.*[15]

Vitoria's reflections on the status of Indigenous peoples in the Americas figure prominently in the history of the idea that human rights are central to the conceptualization and implementation of international law. His theories were adopted and extended by the Dominican missionary Brother Bartolome de Las Casas, whose manifestoes on the need to recognize Aboriginal rights and titles have resonated through subsequent centuries and across many boundaries of language and culture.

The climax of Las Casas's career occurred at Valladolid, Spain, in 1550–51. That year he met Juan Gines de Sepulveda in the world's first major court action to arbitrate the extent of Aboriginal rights in the imperial law of a major European power. Where Las Casas argued that Indigenous peoples could not be legally enslaved, Sepulveda maintained before a council of theologians and jurists that Indians were in a condition of "natural servitude" in relation to the people and government of Spain. In making this case, Sepulveda drew heavily on the theories of Aristotle, whose writings were frequently employed in that era by those who argued that the unilateral dispossession and subjugation of Indigenous peoples was the just expression of a natural hierarchy of power, sophistication, and worth.[16]

While the colonization of New Spain provided many openings for legal and philosophical arguments supporting the theory of Aboriginal rights, the actual process of transforming some of the richest and most extensive Indian societies on the planet proved catastrophic for the Indigenous peoples. Thus began the world's most ruthless and sustained episode of ethnic cleansing, one that many believe continues yet. From its earliest stages, this drive aimed to extinguish the Aboriginal civilization of the Americas and to replace it with an expanded transatlantic domain for the culture of Europe and for Western civilization. In his effort to halt or reverse the tragedy of this terrible genocide, Las Casas looked to the Spanish monarchy as the only agency capable of setting up a regime of protection for the Indigenous peoples. While the Spanish sovereign sporadically placed some checks on the murderous excesses of the Spanish colonists, the interventions of the central authority were generally too weak to moderate significantly the acquisitive zeal that attracted fortune-seeking migrants from Europe to their New World.[17]

Protestant authorities were fast to exploit for their own purposes the startling news about the severity of Spanish crimes against the humanity of Indigenous peoples. The resulting Protestant condemnation established the basis for what became known as the Black Legend. This legend lent claims of urgency to advocates of Protestant expansionism who advanced their own imperial designs with claims about the benefits that would flow to Indians from Protestant evangelism.

While England's early colonial enterprises in North America were shrouded in the language of Christian evangelization, a more pressing spur to join in Europe's transatlantic expansion was the fear that, if action was not quickly taken, Roman Catholic powers, including Portugal and France, would soon monopolize and control the apparently vast wealth of the so-called New World. A primary legal device employed by the English monarchs in advancing their overseas enterprises was to issue Royal charters authorizing the creation of corporations. These corporations were delegated specific trade and proprietary monopolies whose legitimacy lay ultimately in nothing more than the geopolitical ability of the charter giver to project the scope of his or her sovereign claims beyond the boundaries of the home country. By and large, these companies were owned by a number of shareholders who combined their capital to undertake the specified enterprise. This model was somewhat modified in 1629 with the creation of the Massachusetts Bay Company. The controlling owners of this Puritan company were also the settlers who laid the foundations of New England.[18]

Although there was reference to the object of Christianizing the Indigenous peoples in the territories to be colonized, in none of these early English charters was there any acknowledgment that the Aboriginal inhabitants of the lands covered by the crown grants held any rights or titles in their ancestral lands. The English crown depended almost entirely on the legal theory of "discovery" in the earliest phases of that regime's transatlantic expansion. The ideas of Vitoria, it seemed, found no early reflection in the court of the English monarchy. Nor were the beginnings of English colonization accompanied by anything like, for instance, the Spanish *Leyes de la Indias*, which in 1512 and 1542 established some theoretical protections for Aboriginal rights in New Spain. This paucity of central direction in the genesis of the English empire in America allowed for a good deal of autonomy within the different colonies.[19] The Spanish realm, in contrast, was theoretically a single, homogenous domain governed from the centre. The structure of the Spanish Empire made the imperial authority unafraid to make laws for all of New Spain governing relations with the Indigenous peoples.[20]

The charter granted to Lord Baltimore by King Charles I to create Maryland in 1632 reads in part like the rules of engagement for a holy crusade on infidels. This document referred to "savages having no knowledge of the Divine Being" and whose ancestral territories were "hitherto uncultivated." Against these "barbarians," the colonists were authorized to wage war and "to pursue them even beyond the limits of their province." The new settlers were further instructed, "if God shall grant it, to vanquish and captivate [the Indians]; and the captives to put to death, or, according to their discretion, to save."[21]

Many of those engaged in colonization interpreted the plagues and diseases that had dramatically thinned much of the Aboriginal population along the eastern seabord as divine sanction for the effective extinguishment of Indian rights and titles in the early charters. In 1631, for instance, Governor John Winthrop of Massachusetts explained, "God hath consumed the natives with a miraculous plague, whereby the greater part of the countrey is left voide of inhabitants."[22] These early justifications were accompanied by increasingly elaborate biblical explanations, developed especially among the Puritans, to support the transformation of parts of Indian Country into what would become the initial living space of the American empire of private property. One of the most frequently cited biblical passage used to justify the early English colonization of North America was verse 28 of the first chapter of Genesis. In that passage God instructs his children to "multiply and replenish the earth, and subdue it." According to Patricia Seed, the English, more than any other European nationality, connected these instructions primarily with agriculture rather than human procreation.

Although the Puritans and other Anglo-American settlers could see that Indian peoples, like themselves, also planted gardens, this apparent fulfilment of God's divine plan was discounted in a number of ways. The fact that Indians, for instance, generally did not build fences around their garden plots as the English did in their "ceremony of possession" was sometimes taken as evidence that Indigenous peoples lacked true and binding ownership of their ancestral lands. And the fact that Indian peoples generally did not fertilize the soil with the manure of domesticated animals was sometimes used as an argument to remove biblical sanction from their forms of agriculture.[23] Both of these rationales appeared in 1631 in John Winthrop's seminal justification for the colonization of New England. His commentary includes a specific reference to chapter 115, verse 16, of Psalms, where biblical sanction is given to the principle that the Lord gave the earth "to the sons of men." Many founders of New England, as well as Edmund Burke at the onset of the American Revolution, interpreted the "sons of men" to exclude the First Nations. Of the Indigenous peoples, Winthrop wrote: "this savage people ruleth over many lands without title or property; for they inclose no ground, neither have they cattell to maintayne it ... why may not Christians have liberty to go and dwell among them in their waste lands and woods (leaving them such places as they have manured for their corn) as lawfully as Abraham did among the Sodomites? For God hath given to the sons of men a two-fould right to the earth; there is the natural right and the civil right."[24]

Winthrop's equation of both "natural right" and "civil right" with the imagined property rights of God's Chosen People echoes along the historical genesis of the American empire from its origins in the early seventh

century. The effects of the Puritan founders of New England on the future
course of American manifest destiny were immense. Near the heart of the
Puritans' Calvinist convictions was their Old Testament belief in the existence of a Covenant between them and the Lord. The Puritan zeal to realize their destiny as a people chartered by God for a special purpose in the
world – as a people divinely sanctioned to dominate and expand – gave
their quest to construct a New Israel a degree of earnest determination
and zealotry that has remained an essential feature of the psychology of
the United States ever since.[25]

This Puritan fundamentalism played an important role in the imperial
metropolis as well as in the colonial hinterland of what would become
British North America. The growing influence of Puritanism in England,
as personified most concretely in the military career of Oliver Cromwell,
was an important part of the civil wars whose outcome after 1688 was the
constitutional subordination of future English monarchs to the financial
discipline of parliament. This transformation, in turn, marked a move
away from feudal institutions based on old complexes of rights and obligations between serfs, nobility, and royalty with shared interests in commonly held estates. Instead, the revolutionary turmoils of seventeenth-century England advanced its economic reorganization and that of its North
American colonies through enclosure and the legal transformation of
expanding portions of the natural world as privately held property.

In a classic volume entitled *The Political Theory of Possessive Individualism*,
C.B. Macpherson has detailed the philosophic arguments supporting the
growing entrenchment and influence of privatized wealth in the prelude
to the European Enlightenment. At the heart of this theory of possessive
individualism, he argued, is a view of natural law where "society consists of
relations of exchange between proprietors" and "political society becomes
a calculated device for the protection of this property and for the maintenance of an orderly relation of exchange."[26] Macpherson explained how
this way of viewing human relationships with one another and with the rest
of nature was most clearly developed in the writings of John Locke.

As we saw in chapter 2, Locke set many of his theoretical discussions on
the institution of private property in the America of his imagination. Central to his analysis was his comparison of fictional Native Americans
hunters with English farmers. The Indian hunter, he said, demonstrated
how by investing work in the killing of a deer, what was once held in common was transformed into a private possession. Locke extended this same
principle to the investment by individuals of human labour in the agricultural domestication and privatization of "waste" land. The influence of
Locke's reflections on the connections between American Indians and private property was made explicit in Thomas Pownall's musings on the
administration of the Anglo-American colonies. A governor of Massachusetts from 1757 to 1760 and a speculator in western lands, Pownall wrote
that the Indigenous peoples of North America were "not landowners, but

hunters, not settlers but wanderers, with no idea of property in land, of that property which arises from a man's mixing his labour with it."[27]

Locke's writings on America largely reproduced in more secular language many of the same rationales for the pre-emption of Indian Country that Puritan theologists been developing since the beginnings of New England. In 1630, for instance, Puritan writer John Cotton busily churned out a text that pointed the way towards Lockean outlines of possessive individualism, asserting, "in a vacant soyle, hee that taketh possession of it, and bestoweth culture and husbandry upon it, his Right it is."[28] Some variants of this Puritan prejudice incorporated harsh assumptions, especially those maintaining that First Nations were not "the sons of men" and that they lived instead outside the protections, privileges, and rights afforded God's chosen ones. Cotton Mather, the Puritan preacher whose zealousness inflamed the witch burnings in Salem, Massachusetts, preached that "probably the devil decoyed those miserable [Indian] savages [to America] in the hopes that the Gospel of Jesus Christ would never come here to destroy or disturb his *absolute empire* over them."[29] "What is not useful is vicious,"[30] he declared in a related observation that anticipated the monocultural swaths to be cut through history by possessive individualism's expanding empire. The God-given manifest destiny for some meant genocide and ecocide for those deemed vicious rather than of use to the unlimited commodification of Mother Earth.

While Mather's sermons marked the extremes of Puritan zealotry, his condemnation of Indigenous peoples as diabolical represented a pervasive mode of thought in the justifications and rationalizations of European imperialism. As long as First Nations were seen to stand outside Christendom and outside the system of knowledge deemed scientific and universal by the recognized sages of Europe, they were regarded as societies without law and without the inherent right to maintain, cultivate, and defend their own ways of life. Only rarely was the Eurocentric rule of imperialism relaxed, as in the Indian Country of Canada during the fur trade.

The paternalistic rejection of the ecological egalitarianism of Native people was revealed in the eighteenth century by the celebrated English scientist Robert Boyle. As Governor of the New England Company, one of the Church of England's missionary branches,[31] he announced his organization's intention to lead the few surviving Indian people of the New England area away from their conviction that the human species is but one element in the web of life, rather than the lord and master of the rest of Creation. Boyle denounced the tendency of Indigenous peoples to perceive of nature "as a kind of goddess." "The veneration, wherewith men are imbued for what they call nature," he said, "has been a discouraging impediment to the empire of man over the inferior creatures of God."[32]

This potent blend of theology, philosophy, and scientific theory emanating from the imagined frontiers of Protestant civilization gave theoretical legitimacy to a powerful surge of privatizing zeal. While the mobilized forces of possessive individualism still had to contend with the entrenched conservatism of feudal interests and institutions in Europe, the circumstances in the Anglo-American colonies were very different. The vast lands and resources of the "New" World appeared to present limitless horizons of opportunity for rugged frontiersmen to express their own religious and secular images of themselves as God's Chosen People and as unrestrained agents of possessive individualism. All that stood in the way were the Indigenous peoples who claimed their land as their own rightful inheritance.

JOHN LOCKE, THE KING, AND THE INDIANS IN THE IDEOLOGY OF THE AMERICAN REVOLUTIONARIES

Locke's commentaries on property in *Two Treatises on Government* were well known and useful to that generation of Anglo-Americans who broke free from the British Empire. As Anthony Pagden has written, that text "was to become a foundational document for North American republicanism."[33] Locke's analysis rang true for many of its Anglo-American readers because the process he described of privatizing the commons seemed to explain their own experience of wresting valuable property from nature on the frontiers of colonization.[34] By imagining themselves not as pre-emptors of other peoples' rights and titles but as instruments of civilization, salvaging wealth and prosperity from "the wild woods and uncultivated waste of America,"[35] they derived essential justification from Locke for their genocidal mode of colonization. They were seemingly supported in their shared determination to throw off the might of British imperialism in order to pick up and deploy the more potent ideological arsenals of the rising American empire of possessive individualism.

Revolutionary fervour in the Anglo-American colonies grew dramatically after 1763, when the imperial army of King George III retained its heavy presence in the Indian Country of Canada even after it had vanquished the military forces of France from the interior of the continent.[36] The announcement in the Royal Proclamation of 1763 that the frontier expansion of the Anglo-American colonists would be outlawed in favour of retaining Canada as an Indian hunting ground and as a fur trade hinterland of Montreal appeared to be a grave violation of common sense. The prospect that the interior of North America would be organized as a realm of shared jurisdiction between Indigenous peoples and a class of officials under the direct patronage of the British king seemed provocative and tyrannical to many Protestant colonists, who regarded Catholic-Aboriginal Canada as a conquered realm and as their rightful inheritance by natural law.

The Royal Proclamation and the Quebec Act, which in 1774 confirmed the exclusion of the Indian Country of Canada from Anglo-American control, seemed to signal that the British king was set on reversing the outcome of the English civil wars of the seventeenth century and reasserting

Tory dominance over America and the Whig ascendance in the British parliament. The Virginian, Thomas Jefferson, played a decisive role in marshalling Anglo-American hostility to the British monarch towards a revolutionary march to independence. In a pamphlet entitled *A Summary View of the Rights of British America*, Jefferson elaborated the widely held theory that the powers of the British monarch were illegitimately seized from free Saxons in the Norman Conquest of 1066. Where the pre-conquest Saxons were thought to have governed themselves according to natural law and to have held their lands individually in a form of free tenure unencumbered by the claims of any higher authority, this liberty was imagined to have to be broken by the feudal imposition of the "Norman Yolk." This violation of natural law was now being re-enacted, Jefferson charged, as the rights and liberties of the free Saxons of America were subjected to an illegitimate feudal alliance of Indians and the British king blocking the westward expansion and proprietary progress of a free citizenry.[37]

The belief that the British North American Indian policy of King George III was a violation of natural law and a betrayal of common sense was extremely influential in the process leading to the Declaration of Independence in 1776. The primary author of that document was Jefferson, who drew much of its content directly from Locke's writings. Indeed, so resonant were Locke's phrases in the Declaration that Richard Lee raised the objection that it was almost a plagiarism.[38] A telling example of this influence is found in the passage asserting the "inalienable rights" of "all men" to "life, liberty, and the pursuit of happiness." Locke had written of men united "for the mutual *Preservation* of their Lives, Liberties and Estates, which I call by the general Name, *Property*."[39] The striking overlap between the pursuit of happiness and the quest for property points insistently to the paradox of making the expropriation and privatization of Indian Country the instrumental means of realizing so many proprietary American Dreams.

British North American Indian policy after 1763 did indeed obstruct the concurrent pursuit of happiness and private property by many British subjects in the Anglo-American colonies. The antagonism towards a developing alliance of Indians and imperial Red Coats on the western frontiers of the Anglo-American settlements was registered most directly in the text of the nascent American empire's founding manifesto. An allegation clearly pertaining to King George's recognition of Indian land rights in the Royal Proclamation of 1763 completed the Declaration's elaborate list of justifications for the Anglo-American revolt. King George was accused of endeavouring "to bring on the inhabitants of our frontiers, the merciless Indian Savages, whose known rule of warfare, is undistinguished destruction of all ages, sexes and conditions."[40]

The American Revolution of 1776 to 1783 unleashed new rounds of violence which saw Aboriginal groups and individuals, but especially those under the command of Mohawk Captain Joseph Brant, inflict severe casualties on the outlying settlements of the exposed Anglo-American colonies, excluding Loyalist Nova Scotia.[41] In one sense this conflict represented merely the latest episode in a recurring saga of expansion and resistance, one that saw Indian people attempt various forms of alliance and association to increase their military effectiveness. The Declaration of Independence established a fundamental point of reference in determining whether Aboriginal military campaigns such as these would be interpreted as legitimate acts of self-defence or as illegal acts of savage terrorism. To this day this interpretive dichotomy has rarely been seriously addressed, let alone satisfactorily resolved, through a formal return to the founding principles of the United States. The distinction drawn in the US founding manifesto between "men" and "merciless Indian savages" has never been conscientiously faced with anything like the resolve once required to bring slavery to an end.

Various linguistic codes have been developed to justify the reservation of authority to outlaw different forms of Aboriginal resistance in North America, the western hemisphere, and the rest of the world as well. During the Cold War, for instance, this tactic of deligitimization widened communism's definition to include any group or individual proposing forms of indigenous self-determination that would place limits on the transnational operations of globalized capitalism. The so-called War on Terrorism was vulnerable to the same type of abuses that had seen the old Cold Warriors' assault on communism expanded into a covert war directed at virtually all forms of dissent.[42] Especially after the murderous demolition of New York's World Trade Center in September 2001, the appetite for revenge in the United States helped to stimulate a direct return to the conceptual division of humanity along the lines articulated in the superpower's founding instrument. In the ideological underpinnings of the US War on Terrorism there were strong reverberations of Locke's intellectual legacy as lodged in the American Declaration of Independence. That legacy was marked in the exclusion of "merciless Indian savages" from those deemed to be invested with an equal human right to life, liberty, and the pursuit of happiness.

With the continuation of European imperialism after 1776, with the expansion of the United States, and with the rise of the informal American empire, larger and larger swaths of humanity were relegated to the status once reserved for the Indigenous peoples referred to in the Declaration of Independence. These far-flung relatives of the Native North Americans have been classified as savages and barbarians and as peoples fit only for a perpetuity of existence on the margins of the world's pre-eminent system of economic relations. They have thereby been excluded from those deemed eligible to exercise the inherent right of self-defence and self-determination by the minority of humanity whose governors have claimed a superior level of attachment to, and responsibility for, the fate and destiny of global civilization.

THE AMERICAN REVOLUTION AS AN EPISODE
IN A LONG ANGLO-AMERICAN WAR ON INDIAN COUNTRY

The outbreaks of violence and bloodshed along the edges of the Anglo-American settlements during the American Revolution can easily be pictured as the continuation of a generations-old struggle along one of history's most notoriously volatile frontiers. Among the earliest and most severe of these recurring rounds of warfare on the frontiers between Indian Country and the nascent Anglo-American settlements were the Pequot War of 1637[43] and what became known as King Phillip's War of 1675–76.[44] On the Aboriginal side, these conflicts widened appreciation of the role the French could play as arms-supplying allies in the resistance against Anglo-American expansion, just as the casualties suffered underlined the importance of confederacy-building to draw a degree of military unity from the ethnic diversity of Indian Country. On the New England side, the war on the tenuous pan-Indian alliance surrounding the Wampanoag sachem Metacom, who was known to the non-Indians as King Phillip, had an especially profound effect on confirming Puritan hostilities towards Aboriginal peoples and dampening their enthusiasm for westward expansion for another century.[45] Moreover, the conflict confirmed the utility of maintaining some sort of common front in dealings with the Indians, a strategy that began with the creation in 1643 of the United Colonies of New England[46] and persisted intermittently until a broader, more binding Confederation was seriously considered at the Albany Conference of 1754.[47]

Before 1776 many conflicts occurred as well on the frontiers of Anglo-American settlements to the south. Concurrent with King Phillip's War in New England, a rebel faction in Virginia, led by Nathaniel Bacon, embarked on a campaign of ethnic cleansing directed not only at Native people beyond the frontiers of the English plantations but at friendly Christian Indians within the colony as well. In North Carolina in 1711 the Tuscaroras reacted with concerted militarism to defend their dwindling land base and to stop the enslavement of some of their people at the hands of British traders. The Yamasee War involved complex military and diplomatic negotiations between many constituencies, including factions of Creeks, Catawbas, Cherokees, and Floridian Spaniards. Their manoeuvres kept the aggressive Carolinians on a disorganized military footing from 1715 to 1728.[48] Increasingly these defensive stances on the part of Indigenous peoples were intertwined with the development of North American theatres of European military conflicts including the War of the Austrian Succession in 1744 and the Seven Years' War. The termination in 1763 of this conflict, which is sometimes remembered as the French and Indian War in the United States, set the stage for the American Revolution by eliminating the hostile power of the French army from the Indian Country at the rear of the Anglo-American settlements.[49]

From the perspective of Aboriginal peoples on the upper reaches of the Ohio River, the American Revolution really began in 1774, when the Virginian governor, Lord Dunmore, effectively declared war on the Shawnee. This conflict was part of a complex series of machinations among land speculators manoeuvring for advantage on the geographic, commercial, political, and military frontiers of the American empire of private property.[50]

The British engagement and encouragement of Indian fighting forces during the American Revolution became a major subject of propaganda on the side of the rebels. The controversy was inflamed by British General John Burgoyne, who attempted to intimidate his enemies with exaggerated assertions about the dangers posed by the "thousands" of Indian warriors under his command (or so he claimed). One of the outcomes was a British parliamentary debate where Edmund Burke and others berated Lord North's government for allegedly turning on "Protestant brethren" the "torturing, mangling" fury of "the cannibal savage," whose glory was "roasting alive by slow fires and frequently even devouring their captives."[51]

The fighting forces rallied behind the Continental Congress attempted to counter the British influence in Indian Country by making overtures to Native groups. In this fashion the common front of the old Longhouse League was effectively broken, as some Oneida and Tuscaroras joined the rebels' side. Other Aboriginal groups, including the Roman Catholic Iroquois, Abenaki, Huron, and Malecite people in the heartland of what had been New France and Acadia, responded, with some few exceptions, by maintaining a studied neutrality outside the cross-fire between non-Indian enemies.[52] Many First Nations peoples, however, did not have the option of neutrality in what they well understood was yet another major episode in a life-and-death struggle to defend their homes, their families, and their nations from extermination. The implacability of hostility among some factions of the Anglo-American enemy was demonstrated when the government of North Carolina offered a £50 bounty for every Cherokee scalp.[53] William Henry Drayton announced a similar intent in South Carolina in 1776 when he ordered: "Burn every Indian town and every Indian taken shall be the slave and property of the taker and ... the nation [shall] be extirpated and the lands become the property of the public."[54]

QUAKER, VIRGINIAN, PURITAN, DUTCH, FRENCH, AND BRITISH IMPERIAL ELEMENTS IN THE INDIAN HISTORY OF COLONIAL NORTH AMERICA

The polarization in the American Revolution over the issue of Aboriginal and treaty rights had developed during several generations of Anglo-American colonization along the Atlantic seabord. The disagreement over the place of Indian Country in the development of British North America became particularly grave and acrimonious after the incorporation of

Canada into the crown's domain in 1763. By the time of the Royal Proclamation, however, the basic arguments were already well advanced between
competing schools advancing differing strategies of British imperialism in
North America.

These arguments went back to questions about the charters and patents
that had been granted by the English monarch to the corporate founders
of the Anglo-American colonies. As conveyances of rights resting on the
doctrine of "discovery," such legal instruments, and many similar devices
to come, were increasingly exposed as insufficient to serve as the sole
sources of constitutional legitimacy for the new European and
Euro–North American settlements.[55] For all sorts of reasons, some altru-
istic, some self-serving, the case was developed that the legal procedures
of Anglo-American colonization must include provisions to take into
account the rights and titles inherent in the shared humanity of the peoples indigenous to the colonized territories. Accordingly, one of the most
consistently frustrated, yet doggedly reoccurring impetuses in this history
is the effort to correct the ongoing ethical and legal inequities flowing
from the institutionalized theft entrenched in the founding acts of America. The often imperfectly or hazily perceived aim of those seeking to shift
the newcomers' society away from its original sin was to add to the legal
ediface of America some basic guarantees of the inherent human right of
Indigenous peoples not to be robbed of their lives, their lands, or their
collective capacities for self-determination.

The creation and edification of a regime of recognition for what has
come to be called Aboriginal and treaty rights demanded, therefore, that
Indigenous peoples not be stripped of possession of their ancestral territories without their consent and without agreements giving them just compensation. In order for such agreements to point at destinations other
than termination or cultural extinguishment, these political accords –
these treaties – with Indigenous peoples would have to include provisions
enabling them to retain and develop jurisdictional and economic infrastructures of their own within the new society of immigrants to take shape
around them. The basic political problem to be faced in realizing such an
ideal was the pervasiveness and tenacity of an assumption that often
remained unconscious and inarticulate – that empire-building or nation-
building in America required the extinguishment and privatization of
Indian Country.

The civil war that erupted in Virginia in 1675–76 embodied many of the
fundamental arguments over Indian policy in the Anglo-American
colonies in the century and a half before the American Revolution. At the
heart of the dispute were the charges levelled against Sir William Berkeley,
the governor of Virginia, by rebel leader Nathaniel Bacon. In their manifesto, the rebels charged the representative of the crown with improperly
treating "the protected and Darling Indians" within the colony as if they
were subject to the laws of England. According to Bacon, all Native people

were "outlaws" – "Robbers and Theeves and Invaders of His Majesty's Right
and our Interest and Estates." All Indians, he said, Christian or not, were
deemed "wholly unqualified for the benefitt and Protection of the law."[56]
With a clear conviction that the only good Indian was a dead Indian,
Bacon and his followers went on a genocidal crusade directed at all Native
people, whether inside and beyond the Anglo-American settlements of the
colony. Many of their victims were Iroquoian-speaking Susquehannock.
The head Indian fighter met his death in Berkeley's successful campaign
to crush the rebellion.

The episode foreshadowed patterns of conflict that would emerge in a
more elaborate way a century later, when revolutionaries in the Thirteen
Colonies revolted against a rule of law that included what they saw as
repressive Crown barriers of protection against Anglo-American expansion
into Indian Country.[57] Wilcombe E. Washburn, who wrote an important
seminal work about Bacon's rebellion,[58] noted, "the most fundamental
issue of the most significant colonial rebellion in America's history prior to
the American Revolution was over the status of the Indian."[59]

Roger Williams was the first settler in the Anglo-American colonies to
give clear expression to the principle that Indigenous peoples retained a
title to their ancestral lands that could not be unilaterally extinguished by
any charter of the English monarch. Williams developed this position as
his contacts grew with Massachusetts' Aboriginal neighbours. An indication of the depth of these contacts is to be found in Williams's publication
of New England's first major account of the grammar and vocabularies of
the region's Algonkian languages and dialects.[60] His empathetic understanding of this Aboriginal mode of communications extended to his conviction that it was no more justifiable to force Christianity on Indigenous
peoples than to strip them unilaterally of ownership and control of their
Aboriginal territories.[61] This latter conviction led him to the conclusion
that it was a "National sinne" for the magistrates of Massachusetts to claim
jurisdiction and ownership in Indian lands by virtue of a royal patent
alone.[62] Neither the English king nor the recipients of his royal grants of
colonizing rights could with legitimacy "take and give away the Lands and
Countries of other men."[63]

For these positions, Williams and his followers were briefly classified as
heretics by the patriarchs in charge of the Puritan theocracy of Massachusetts. One of the most outspoken of them, John Cotton, charged that
Williams saw it as a "National duty to renounce the patent on which the
legal legitimacy of the colony of Massachusetts was based." To accept this
position, alleged Cotton, "would have subverted the fundamental State
and Government of the Country."[64]

Williams and his followers put their theories about Aboriginal rights and
titles into practice once they left Massachusetts in 1635 to found the new
Anglo-American settlement of Rhode Island. Lacking a royal charter for
this community they went to the Indigenous Narragansett people to seek

official sanction from them for their new colonizing venture. Thus they founded Rhode Island on the basis of an Indian treaty where an Aboriginal nation endowed the immigrants with a grant of legitimacy for their initiating act.

The resulting rift in Puritan society was quickly papered over when the English king intervened to endow Rhode Island with a royal charter, an act that served to obfuscate the monarch's position on the legal status of Aboriginal and treaty rights in his fledgling North American empire. This intervention was part of a complex chain of manoeuvres essential to winning over Williams and his Narragansett allies to the Puritans' side in the Pequot War of 1637 and King Phillip's War of 1675–76.[65] In spite of the self-serving nature of the successful bid to integrate Williams and his Indian friends into the Puritans' military strategies, the precedents set by the negotiation of the Rhode Island Treaty had some impact on the subsequent constitutional history of British North America. Into this saga of Protestant expansionism crept some of the principles outlined in the sixteenth century by Vitoria and Las Casas in their efforts to place some legal constraints on Spain's imperial exploitation of Indigenous peoples and their Aboriginal lands in the Americas. Gradually and sporadically, the constitutional principle developed in imperial and international law that various crown-derived jurisdictions and titles to the soil of colonized countries could not be finalized until some sort of purchase from the Aboriginal inhabitants had been transacted.

Along with this deeply problematic proposition of arranging negotiated settlements with First Nations specifying the terms for extinguishing their land title, other even darker precedents were set by the Puritan-Narragansett alliance during the colonists' bloody conquest of Connecticut in 1637. One precedent clarified what later generations would label as genocide as another means of clearing the land of the "burden" or "incumbrance" of Aboriginal title. The other precedent marked the import into the English colonies of the divide-and-conquer strategies of imperial expansion that were first used with such lethal efficacy by Hernan Cortes in the Spanish conquest of Mexico. From the founding of New Spain to the support rendered to the Northern Alliance in the us-led war against the Taliban regime in Afghanistan, ethnic and other divisions among Indigenous peoples have provided the colonizing powers wide openings to expand their influence through the provision of military support to Aboriginal fighting forces.

William Penn, the "Great Proprietor" and Quaker founder of Pennsylvania, was another key figure who was instrumental in steering the law of English colonization towards some small accommodations with the constitutional principles of Aboriginal and treaty rights. Although Penn received a royal charter for Pennsylvania much like that for Maryland, he brought the Christian theology of the Society of Friends to the construction of laws and policies for relations with Pennsylvania's Aboriginal inhabitants and neighbours. In a series of letters, Penn outlined how these relations were to be founded on attributes of friendship, brotherly love, and fundamental justice. Between 1682 and 1701, efforts were made to moderate Quaker expansionism with these ideals in a series of treaties with the Lenni Lapi Indians indigenous to the territory. This group, who around this period gave rise to a wise and legendary leader known as Tamanend, has sometimes been identified by the name of the Delaware River flowing through their ancestral lands. The early Quaker treaties with the Lenni Lapi, or Delawares, established a regime of relations between Natives and newcomers that apportioned territory and outlined the design of a judicial process – one that was to have afforded Indian people equitable representation on juries when allegations of criminality were directed at their countrymen.[66]

In advocating the constitutional practice of negotiating treaties with Indigenous peoples to formalize the transfer of title from First Nations to Anglo-Americans, Williams and Penn were influenced not only by their face-to-face encounters with Indigenous peoples in America but also by their wide reading and travel, especially in the Netherlands. Given the importance of that country as a centre of learning, it is entirely possible that Williams and Penn were exposed to the thought of Vitoria. That exposure may have come through the writings of Hugo Grotius. Grotius was one of the most influential and prolific Dutch intellectuals. He helped expand the boundaries of international law to include the ideas of those Spanish priests who had first criticized the means and the theory employed in subjugating the Indians of the Americas. Drawing on the literature of the Spanish conquest and on the more obscure records of Scandinavia's old Viking involvement in America, Grotius edged towards the principle in the early seventeenth century that all peoples of the world are invested with sovereign rights.[67] The scholastic traditions of the Dutch, however, were probably less influential than more pragmatic calculations of strategic interest in the founding of New Netherlands on the principle that all colonization in North America must be based on the purchase of lands from the Indigenous peoples. The records of these purchases, the proprietors of the Dutch West India Company correctly perceived, would be instrumental in fortifying Holland's territorial claims on the continent against the rival claims of the English.

The entrepreneurs of the Dutch Empire in North America eased their colony into the space between Virginia and New England along the river that Henry Hudson had mapped in 1609 while searching for a route to the Orient for the Dutch East India Company. The negotiation of land agreements with Indigenous peoples proved advantageous in producing documentation to bolster the colony's claims to legal legitimacy against European competitors.[68] It was also instrumental in creating, after some early hostilities, bonds of relatively friendly association with Indigenous peoples which were vital to the development of trade with them. The original sinews of these tenuous bonds of friendship were more the diplomatic motifs of Aboriginal gift exchanges than the Dutch practice of land purchase. One of the early staples of exchange in the Dutch-Indian trade network were the wampum shells that briefly served as currency to facilitate commerce in the cash-poor settlements of New England, New Netherlands, and the tiny and short-lived colony of New Sweden.[69] Before long, however, the major staple of commerce in New Netherlands became beaver skins, which were obtained in large numbers from Mohawk Indians who conducted their trading around the Dutch posts of Fort Orange and Fort Nassau near the northern end of the Hudson River. There were vast and significant geopolitical implications for the continent in the establishment of strong links of diplomatic and commercial collaboration between the Dutch and the Mohawks, the easternmost group in the Longhouse Confederacy.

This remarkable invention of political science was known to the Five Iroquois Nations allied within the institution as the *Haudenosaunee*. That word signifies the extended lodge – the *Longhouse*.[70] News of the existence of this resilient and powerful federation has been disseminated to the world through, among others, the writings of Lahontan, Cadwallader Colden, and Lewis Henry Morgan. The negotiating protocols practised within the Longhouse League were gradually learned, adapted, and extended to broader associations of Indians and colonists in what became known as the Covenant Chain. This chain, the basis of what Francis Jennings has called "the ambiguous Iroquois empire," was to become a vital motif in the establishment of British imperial Canada, both before and after the American Revolution.[71]

The strategic importance of the Dutch alliance with key constituencies in the Longhouse League was dramatically illustrated in the late 1640s, when a large Iroquois war party used several hundred guns obtained from Dutch traders to unseat their major, Iroquois-speaking rivals, the Hurons. Governor Samuel de Champlain had chosen this prolific trading confederacy, whose large pallisaded towns lay on the shores of Georgian Bay in what is now southern Ontario, with the view that the Hurons held the key to France's imperial domination of the continent. Champlain's plan had to be significantly altered when the Hurons, already diminished and suffering terribly from diseases introduced unknowingly by the Jesuit priests who wintered among them, were totally unrooted from their strongholds by the well-armed Iroquois enemies. These military pioneers of the ambiguous Iroquois empire subsequently claimed for the Five Nations the former Huron hunting territory, along with that of the similarly vanquished Eries and Neutrals, north of the Great Lakes. Moreover, the Longhouse people enlarged their numbers by absorbing, rather than murdering, many of the defeated people through their elaborate ceremonies of adoption.[72]

The debacle in Huronia pointed the way to many patterns of history whose full meaning would unfold only gradually in the years ahead.

Certainly the experience of the Dutch with the Five Nations demonstrated what the French had already grasped – that the Indigenous peoples of North America held the capacity to be instruments of, as well as obstacles to, European imperialism. In order to exploit the opportunities of empire building in Indian Country, however, it was necessary for agents of imperialism to learn the Indigenous languages, assimilate and follow the Indigenous laws and customs, enter the intrigues of changing relationships between and among Aboriginal clans, nations, and confederacies, and carry on trade with Native people in ways that met their own evolving conceptions of fairness, utility, style, pleasure, and strategic advantage. This dawning understanding corresponded with the apprehension that much of the subsequent history of the continent would develop as a contest between two strategic east-west routes into the interior of the continent. One route, whose major metropolis was Montreal, would develop as an Aboriginal/Roman Catholic/French-speaking cultural complex projected outward from the St Lawrence–Great Lakes axis. The other route, whose metropolis was New York, would develop outward from the Hudson River–Mohawk Valley corridor to Lake Ontario as an Aboriginal/Protestant/English and Dutch-speaking cultural complex.

The competition between these two systems would heighten as the empire of France in North America increasingly hemmed in the Anglo-American colonies by building, sporadically, on Robert Cavelier de La Salle's initiative to link, commercially and militarily, the fur trade domain of Canada with a Mississippi River–based colony named Louisiana.[73] The ensuing clash of imperialisms focused increasingly on the question of who would control the lands of the Ohio River valley, the rich, arable zone that would either link or sever connections between Canada and Louisiana The outcome of the Seven Years' War settled this issue of power between empires, only to widen the schism between antagonistic camps of British imperialists and plant the seeds of civil war in British North America.

Moreover, the outcome of the Seven Years' War removed a source of division in Indian Country, establishing the basis for a formidable effort on the part of Indian nations to put aside their animosities as the necessary condition for establishing a wide, multicultural confederacy with sovereign council fires and fixed territorial boundaries protected by international law. In the wake of the American Revolution, this bold geopolitical ideal would come to replace the procedures of mere land purchases in the elaboration of the treaty alliances between the Indian Confederacy of Canada and the sovereign authority of the British Empire.

The gradual expansion towards this broader and broader definition of the meaning of Aboriginal and treaty rights – a conception most fully expressed in the alignments of power and politics in the era of the War of 1812 – began in the central sanctums of the English monarchy in 1664. That was the year when King Charles ii, his family newly restored to royal authority after the Interregnum, sent a military expedition across the

Atlantic to take over New Netherlands and reconstitute the jurisdiction as New York. Along with the expedition, he sent several royal commissioners whose task it was to discipline the Puritan oligarchies of New England and to reaffirm the authority of the crown, especially in the apportionment of land tenures and in the governance of relations with Indigenous peoples.

Building on their experience of the Pequot War in 1637, the Puritan leaders had resolved to expand their power base through the conquest of Indian lands. To advance this object, the Puritan patriarchs built up the United Colonies of New England explicitly as a military body designed for wars of aggression on Indian Country and for the reapportionment of former Indian lands to non-Indian colonists. The royal commissioners struck down the legal and biblical interpretations supporting the effort to expand local jurisdiction in this way. The representatives of the king dictated, "No colony hath any just right to dispose of any lands conquered from the natives, unless both the cause of the conquest be just and the land lye within the bounds which the king by his charter hath given, nor yet to exercise any authority beyond these bounds."[74] The commissioners elaborated this ruling by denying the way the local Calvinist authorities were interpreting Psalms 115:16 of the Old Testament. In keeping with their view of themselves as members of an elect group, uniquely covenanted by God as his chosen people, the Puritan magistrates had deemed that Indians were excluded from the biblical direction that the Lord had given the earth "to the children of men." The commissioners butressed the outlines of the English sovereign's Indian policy by stipulating that the phrase, "'children of men' comprehends Indians as well as English; and no doubt the country is theirs till they give it or sell it, though it not be improoved."[75]

In this fashion the royal commissioners introduced, in 1664, the beginnings of a policy that, one century later, would be more fully entrenched, expanded, and elaborated upon by King George III in his famous Royal Proclamation. However, it was one thing to pronounce that Indian peoples retained a title in their Aboriginal lands until they voluntarily decided to sell this interest, but quite another, in 1664 or in 1763, for agents of the crown to enforce this limitation on the insistent, expansionist designs motivating many of the Anglo-American colonists. Accordingly, the British monarchy no less than the imperial authority of New Spain experienced huge logistical problems when it came to imposing on the American colonists any European scheme for the protection of Aboriginal and treaty rights.

The royal commissioners left largely unaddressed many legal questions arising from the issue of transferring title from Indians to non-Indian individuals, companies, or colonies. Who, for instance, should have the authority to purchase the title to Indian lands? Who should be responsible for arbitrating competing claims arising from overlapping purchases of the same parcels of territory? How should the legal construct of land ownership be resolved with broader questions of government jurisdiction in the general process of transferring title on the frontiers between Indian Country and the Anglo-American settlements? These and many other related questions were left to the trial and error of subsequent generations. As the royal commissioners brought their work to a close in New England, the English imperial machinery of New York quickly and easily displaced the Dutch imperial machinery of New Netherlands. At the head of the expedition was the Duke of York, the future King James II. For a decade, the colony drifted in commercial and political uncertainty, with the Dutch briefly reasserting control of the jurisdiction. After 1675, however, New York quickly emerged as a powerhouse of business and expanding political influence under the able governorship of Edmond Andros, who, together with his associates in the Five Nations, elaborated the treaty protocols known as the Covenant Chain. The protocols of this diplomatic invention were founded on an alliance of colonies and Aboriginal polities. At the central nexus of this surprisingly adaptable and resilient chain of relationships were the Five Nations, but especially the Mohawks, and the New York representatives of the English Crown.[76]

In many ways the crown's takeover of New Netherlands was a kind of dress rehearsal for the British imperial government's annexation of Canada a century later. In both instances crown officials, after some early uncertainty, opted not to displace or disown the colonists in the defeated empires. Moreover, in the conquest of both New Netherlands and Canada, Crown officials sought to employ, elaborate, and even extend the old commercial and diplomatic relationships that their European predecessors had built up with Indigenous peoples on the frontiers of Indian Country. In this way the Dutch and the French played a major role in educating the architects of the evolving British Empire in North America on the importance of Indian policy as an instrument of imperialism. Similarly, the pioneering involvement in Indian Country of Dutch and French officials was instrumental in inculcating the realization that an expanded regime of Aboriginal and treaty rights could actually widen the sphere of centralized authority in the process of expanding the British Empire.

Recognition of the strategic utility of placing jurisdictional responsibility for Indian affairs under a single imperial authority developed throughout the eighteenth century as skirmishes between the French and the British empires in North America built to a final showdown of military might that was truly global in extent. This understanding flowed from a number of sources into the Lords of Trade and Plantations, who were then responsible for the imperial oversight of the Anglo-American colonies. The 1755 report of a Charleston-based fur trader named Edmond Aitken expressed the growing controversies and contentions surrounding Indian Affairs succinctly and eloquently:

It is universally known that the Indian [Affairs] have been managed and conducted on one general plan, steadily pursued throughout Canada and Louisiana, under the immediate direction of the Crown; the chief object of which is to exclude us not only from the Mississippi but from all Indian nations on this side of it. In execution whereof are employed Men of the greatest Knowledge and Experience, by early and long service, from among the Officers and the Missionaries; who are supported out of the trade with the Indians, who rest their hopes for preferment on their own Behavior, and who on all Occasions support the Honour and the Dignity of the French Nation, and watch for all opportunities to turn every Occurrence to the Disadvantage of Great Britain and her Colonies. And every opening where they can obtain the least opening for it, they fail not either by Consent or Compulsion, to place forts however small, under the pretense of protecting those Indians against their enemies, (which are sometimes of their own creating for the purpose) but with a real intention to establish a Claim of Possession, and to fix Boundaries to us.

Aitkin contrasted the importance afforded by the French to the conduct of relations with Indian nations to what he saw and experienced in the Anglo-American colonies:

Some of the colonies have made no regulations at all in the Indian Affairs; others have made different ones, and some but seldom if at all sent proper persons to look into them. But the management of them has often been left to the Traders, who have no skill in Public Affairs, are directed only in their own interest, and being generally the loosest kind of People, are despis'd and held in great Contempt by the Indians as Liars, and Persons regarding nothing but their own Gain.

Aitkin's report contributed significantly to the establishment in 1755 of the British Imperial Indian Department as an adjunct of the military establishment under the direct patronage of the king. His analysis made it clear that Indian Affairs was integral to the crown's conduct of foreign policy and that there would be grave consequences by leaving the management of relations with Indian nations to the jurisdiction of the individual Anglo-American colonies or even to individual Anglo-American traders:

The importance of Indians is now generally known and understood. A Doubt remains not, that the prosperity of our Colonies, will stand or fall with our Interest and favour among them. When they are our Friends, they are the Cheapest and strongest Barrier for the Protection of our Settlements; when Enemies, they are capable of ravaging in their methods of War, in spite of all we can do, to render those Possessions almost useless. Of this the French are sensible, as well as of our Natural Advantages beyond their own, that they have employed all their Art, not only to embroil us with the Indians ... but to destroy and utterly extirpate those Nations whose Affections they could not gain, by setting one against another, and themselves assisting to do it. The same reason should certainly make it our Policy, to support and preserve them.[77]

Aitkin's characterization of the disarray that prevailed in the Anglo-American management of relations with Indian peoples was no exaggeration. The ameliorative efforts, such as those of Roger Williams, William Penn, or the royal commissioners in 1664, to elaborate and enforce more just and equitable approaches to Aboriginal and treaty rights were overwhelmingly the exception rather than the rule. Even in New York the institution of the Covenant Chain had been allowed to become rusty and decrepit. In 1753, for instance, a delegation of Mohawks visited Fort George to complain how the British had left the Six Nations "exposed" to French enemies who "held a knife over our heads to destroy us."

The seriousness of the message was underlined by the reputation of its deliverer – the sachem Hendrick (Theyanoguin). As a young man, Hendrick had been part of the celebrated delegation known as the Four Kings of Canada, who visited London in 1710. Since that time the sachem had developed a reputation as one of the strongest supporters of the English–Six Nations alliance in Mohawk Country. Hendrick reminded his attentive listeners of "the ancient alliance between our respective Forefathers." "We were united by a Covenant Chain," he continued, "and it seems likely to be broken not from our Fault but yours." He warned, "As soon as we come home, we will send up a belt of Wampum to our Brothers the 5 Nations to acquaint them the Covenant Chain is broken between you and us."[78]

News of Hendrick's words was taken very seriously in London and throughout the Anglo-American colonies. It led to the conference in Albany in 1754 where local officials tried unsuccessfully to establish a more coordinated approach to Indian Affairs. In 1755 the British government finally filled this void of policy and administration when it established a northern and a southern division of a centrally controlled imperial Indian Department.[79] Edmond Aitkin was rewarded for drafting his powerful report by being appointed superintendent of the southern division. His responsibility was to establish a more stable foundation of crown relations with several large Indian constituencies, including the Creek, Cherokee, Chickasaw, Choctaw, and Catawba confederacies.

The creation in 1755 of the northern division of the British Imperial Indian Department established the first governmental seed in North America for what would become English-speaking Canada. The first superintendent of Indian Affairs in the department that continues to operate to this day within the federal government of Canada was Colonel William Johnson. For much of his career this wealthy fur trader, crown official, and land speculator, whom Duncan Campbell Scott labelled as "the great prototype of all Indian officials,"[80] attempted to establish a middle ground of compromise to avert a full-scale war between the Indian Country of Canada and the Anglo-American colonies.

The vigorous and gregarious Johnson came to New York colony from Ireland in 1738 to oversee the Mohawk Valley estates of his wealthy uncle,

Vice-Admiral Sir Peter Warren. Very quickly, Johnson's major efforts were absorbed into the commercial and political intrigues of the ambitious Mohawks, gave him the name Warraghiyagey, meaning "he who does much business." Part of this business involved opening a road through the Mohawk Valley to Oswego, the strategic post on the southern shores of Lake Ontario. As Warraghiyagey developed a reputation among the Mohawks for his generosity and fair dealings, new opportunities opened up for him to obtain Mohawk land in a colony where feudal-like institutions of land tenure contributed to the maintenance of a stable western frontier of Anglo-American and Dutch-American settlement.[81]

Johnson looked to the example of New France in shaping his career in Indian Country. He explained in a letter to New York governor George Clinton, for instance, that the French "would never employ a Trader to negotiate any matters with the Indians but a King's officer, who in whatever Rank or capacity is attended by a Retinue of Soldiers accordingly to denote his consequence."[82] With this example in mind, he proceeded to absorb and imitate the customs, laws, and protocols of the Six Nations peoples. He seems to have derived tremendous pleasure as well as remarkable influence from his widely noticed transcultural transformations on the frontiers between Indian Country and the Anglo-American settlements.

Johnson easily picked up the several Iroquoian dialects of his Six Nations associates. He often dressed himself according to their fashions, danced with them in the prescribed Mohawk style, and displayed the patience required to join them in their complex religious ceremonies and elaborate political deliberations. When he went to battle with the Iroquois against the French and their Indian allies, he had himself painted in the Mohawk style and donned the clothing of a Mohawk war captain. When he sought favours or sought to reassure his Indian hosts of his friendly intentions, he distributed presents appropriate to the rank, status, and personal tastes of the recipients.[83] When he sought an audience with his Longhouse Confederacy associates, Johnson was diligent in the performance of the correct protocols of condolence, metaphorically wiping the tears away from the eyes of those in attendance for the loss of all their recently deceased relatives as the necessary prelude to substantive negotiations. Moreover, he well understood that to proceed successfully with any significant negotiations, it was crucial to make sure that the appropriate wampum belts were identified, designed, manufactured, and exchanged in the process of reaching binding agreements. In 1753 an Onondaga sachem by the name of Ononwarogo, otherwise known as Red Head, acknowledged Johnson for addressing the Six Nations "in our own way, which is more Intelligible to us, because more conformable to the Customs and Manners of our Fore Fathers."[84]

As Johnson's influence grew, he was afforded increasing responsibilities in carrying on New York's responsibilities in the old Covent Chain. In 1746 Governor Clinton had appointed him colonel of the forces of the Six

Nations, a post he quit in 1751 in protest against the failure of the New York legislature to reimburse him the cost of presents he had distributed in encouraging Six Nations fighting forces to join in King George's War. His comments about the preoccupations of local politicians compared with the demands of war and diplomacy in Indian Country, are telling. Johnson referred to "the expenses I am dayly obliged to be at in treating with all sorts of Indians – The well ordering of whom is of much more importance to the Welfare of His Majesty's Government than the whole act of governing the unruly Inhabitants [of New York]."[85]

Colonel Johnson's energetic and impassioned rallying of Six Nations' involvement in the early stages of the Seven Years' War, confirmed his importance in the eyes of the British military establishment in North America. The official title granted him in the new imperial machinery of crown authority over Indian Affairs was "Colonel, Agent and Sole Superintendent of the affairs of the Six Nations and other Northern Indians." Along with this appointment, he was made a baronet by King George II, who included a gift of £5,000 for long and faithful service. This amount, a large fortune according to the standards of the eighteenth century, helped defray the expenses of £17,000 he is reported to have incurred in distributing presents to the Six Nations during 1755 and 1756. Soon after, with Sir William now entrenched as one of the most influential officers of the crown in British North America, the king's personal representative to the Indians of Canada began work on Johnson Hall.

ABORIGINAL AND TREATY RIGHTS IN THE SEVEN YEARS' WAR AND IN THE INDIAN RESISTANCE MOVEMENT ASSOCIATED WITH PONTIAC

Johnson's stand in 1755 at the battle of Lake George, following the defeat of British officer George Washington at Fort Necessity, was one small reversal in a campaign that initially went against the Anglo-American army. In 1758 the weight of British naval strength began to turn the tide, with the British capture of Louisbourg on Isle Royal, now Cape Breton Island. While the Seven Years' War was partly a contest of military force, it also developed as a test of prowess in the arts and sciences of diplomacy and treaty making in Indian Country.

The institutions of the refurbished Covenant Chain were one centre of this diplomatic activity, with another key site of negotiations in the upper Ohio Valley. Fort Duquesne, the strategically vital French post, was situated on a promontory near the source of the Ohio River. In 1758 the French surrendered this stronghold, directly as a result of the British negotiation of a treaty stipulating that the land titles of the Indian nations in the interior would be observed and respected by the Anglo-American colonists. This treaty promise constituted the basis for the transformation of Fort Duquesne into Fort Pitt on the site of present-day Pittsburgh.[86]

The campaign to defeat the French army in North America therefore served as a stimulant and a catalyst in the development of a form of British imperial Indian policy with widened provision to recognize and affirm existing Aboriginal and treaty rights. While many of these policies had been suggested or even applied in different periods and localities over the course of several previous generations of Anglo-American colonization, the climax of the life-or-death struggle with the French Empire created the context for the elevation of Indian Affairs to the highest level of statecraft and constitution making in British North America. Sir William Johnson and the Longhouse League contributed many principles to this development. Another important, yet less readily recognized, source of the crown Indian policy that would coalesce and become entrenched in the Royal Proclamation of 1763 were those Quaker pacifists who formed themselves as the Friendly Association of Pennsylvania.

It was this Quaker group, as represented especially by Israel Pemberton, which was largely responsible for pulling together the many delegations of Native people and colonists who assembled in Easton Pennsylvania in 1758 to negotiate and ratify a major Indian treaty. The Treaty of Easton included sufficient guarantees for the Native participants to withdrew their support of the French control of Fort Duquesne on the condition that the Anglo-Americans would respect the right of Indian peoples in the upper Ohio Valley to enjoy security of land tenure in their ancestral territories. This withdrawal of Aboriginal sanction for the French control of the easternmost reaches of the Ohio River Valley allowed the British army of Brigadier General John Forbes simply to take over Fort Duquesne without a shot being fired.

In lobbying the governor of Pennsylvania to support their contentions in the Easton Treaty, the members of the Quakers' Friendly Association drew on their prior experience of negotiations with the Delaware people, who in that era were represented by a sachem known as Teedyuscung.[87] They noted the "Strong, Clear and Certain" quality of the Delawares' stipulation that the making of a treaty in 1757 must include "the fixing of a boundary between the English settlements and the Tract of Land which the Indians desired to be secured to them and their Posterity forever."[88] This same provision, the Quakers insisted, must be entrenched in the broader, more encompassing, and more elaborate treaty proposal then working its way towards final ratification on the council grounds of Easton. Against the opposition of the influential and many-tentacled land speculator Benjamin Franklin, among others, the Quaker conservatives gained their point.[89]

The principle of establishing a fixed boundary was carried over into the treaty made at Easton in 1758. The negotiations extended the protocols of the Covenant Chain by confirming, in effect, that the Six Nations were essentially the landlords of the territories that the crown promised to protect for the Indian nations of the upper Ohio Valley. While this legal construction was resented by those "subordinate" Indian groups in the ambiguous Iroquois empire, the arrangement was accepted as an expedient of power and security in an unstable and highly volatile milieu.

The history beneath the founding of Pittsburgh as an Anglo-American settlement represents the demise of Canada as a French domain based on trade and alliance with Indigenous peoples. This old alliance was not neutralized through the conquest of the French and the Indians, as the mythology of the American empire of private property would suggest, but through an expanded British imperial regime of recognition and affirmation of Aboriginal and treaty rights. In taking over from the French crown the commitment to exclude dense Anglo-American settlement from the Indian Country of the Ohio Valley, the British crown had already in 1758 moved across a frontier of law and imagination that would become the stuff of civil war and then revolution in the intensified struggle between the Indian Country of Canada and the American empire of private property.

Accordingly, by the mid-eighteenth century, the principle that Vitoria had articulated in the early 1500s and that Williams had articulated in the early 1600s began to penetrate deeply into the constitutional framework of British North America. The basis of the principle was the idea that First Nations retained titles of collective ownership and self-governance in their ancestral lands. These titles, it was increasingly acknowledged, could only be transferred or transformed through negotiations reflecting Indian consent. The embrace of this principle, primarily by those on the more conservative wing of the growing controversy over how British North America should be governed, would have broad consequences. This alignment of ideas and interests illustrates that those on the Tory side of the growing divide in the transatlantic, English-speaking world were, in some ironic ways, closer to the egalitarian spirit of the Enlightenment that future historians would associate primarily with the experiences of those who instigated and sustained the American Revolution.

While the treaty making at Easton Pennsylvania represented one of the major themes of the Seven Years' War, much of the conflict came down to more conventional military turmoil. The central drama of the more orthodox test of military muscle occurred in 1759 on the Plains of Abraham, when the army of General Wolfe overwhelmed the army of General Montcalm in a battle where both military leaders were fatally wounded. The following spring the British navy was the first to reach Quebec, leading to the French surrender of Montreal. Point 40 of the Articles of Montreal's Capitulation stipulated that "the Savages or Indian allies of His Most Christian Majesty [the King of France] shall be maintained in the lands they inhabit, if they choose to reside there; they shall not be molested on any pretence whatever for having carried arms and served His Most Christian Majesty; they shall have, as well as the French, liberty of religion, and shall keep their missionaries."[90] This provision applied most directly to the

Aboriginal inhabitants of the Roman Catholic missions in the settled heartland of New France. The largest of these missions were Sault-Saint Louis and St Regis, settlements established under Jesuit auspices. To their Mohawk residents they became known, respectively, as Kanewake and Akwesasne. Also prominent among the Indian missions established in French-Aboriginal Canada was Lac des Deux-Montagnes, to which the Sulpician founders of Montreal had moved in the seventeenth century with their Indian adherents. While the Sulpician mission, which developed in and around the French Canadian community of Oka, was known as Kanesatake to the Mohawks, it also attracted some Roman Catholic Nipissing and Algonquin settlers. The remaining members of what were known as the Seven Nations of Canada were the Hurons of Ancienne Lorette and the Abenaki at Saint-François, or Odenak, along with an attending smaller Abenaki community at Becancour across from Trois-Rivières.[91]

The Seven Years' War included a range of atrocities committed on both sides of the conflict. In some instances these violent episodes erupted in spontaneous fury, and in others the bloody incursions were carefully conceived and planned. In the orders that preceded the attack in 1758 on the Abenaki stronghold of Saint-François-de-Sales, for instance, Massachusetts governor William Shirley directed the Rangers under the command of Captain Robert Rogers, to "distress the French and their allies, by sacking, burning and destroying their houses, barns, barracks, canoes, battoes etc. and by killing cattle of every kind; and at all times to endeavour to way-lay, attack, and destroy their convoys of provisions by land and water, in any part of the country."[92]

The rapid military collapse of the French Empire in North America proved particularly traumatic in many districts and communities in the Indian Country of Canada. When the Treaty of Easton had been confirmed in 1758, the expectation among the First Nations people who negotiated the deal was that the French would be weakened, but not altogether vanquished, from their strongholds in the interior of the continent. But that vanquishment – or perhaps it would be more accurate to say abandonment – is exactly what transpired. Onontio, the Iroquois name for the governor of New France, seemed to have vacated the country, leaving it open to another occupying army under the banner of the Union Jack. This title, Onontio, is believed to have been derived from the name of Charles Huault de Montmagny, the governor of New France between 1636 and 1648. Picking up the French nuance of Montmagny's name, the Five Nations Iroquois dubbed this official as the "Great Mountain," or Onontio in their own language. Over the years this term was widely accepted among both Iroquoian and Algonkian speakers as the title attributed to the leading official of the French empire in Canada.[93]

By 1759, after the battle of La Belle Famille, the Union Jack was hoisted over the old French post at Niagara. Within months, Onontio's forces left their other installations throughout the Great Lakes area, as well as the eastern half of the Mississippi Valley. The British army quickly moved to fill the strategic void, with little overt opposition from the Indigenous peoples or from the French traders and settlers who remained.[94] A factor in this Indigenous acquiescence was the suggestion that these British troops would bring in their wake a richer and more ample trade.

As the British army and the Anglo-American soldiers claimed the upper hand, the kind of attentiveness to the concerns and demands centred in Indian Country gave way to less accommodating and more overbearing attitudes. At Fort Pitt the British military engineers built a more imposing installation than had been promised. Moreover, Pennsylvanians in the vicinity continued to hack away at the forest to establish homesteads and hamlets in spite of half-hearted British efforts to enforce on them the boundary provisions detailed in the Treaty of Easton. In the Great Lakes area the founding orders of British imperial Canada emanated not from persons imbued with the century of experience gained from the Covenant Chain but from a major-general who, in the words of Richard White, combined "the moral vision of a shopkeeper and the arrogance of a victorious soldier."[95] This officer, Jeffrey Amherst, ignored Sir William Johnson's advice to continue the traditions of Onontio in the conduct of his relations with his Indian allies. These traditions included the feeding of Indian delegations when they came to visit the posts, providing them with parts to repair their guns and other implements, and the generous distribution of presents in ways that would inject various forms of non-Aboriginal influence – essentially British patronage – into the leadership structure of Indian Country. Amherst's orders also cut back the flow of alcohol to Indian consumers, always a contentious and controversial subject in the regulation of relations with Indigenous peoples.[96] Amherst renounced these practices and conventions as hostile to his cost-cutting measures. Moreover, the diplomatic protocols surrounding the traditions of alliance with Indian nations offended his preoccupation with setting the fur trade on what he saw as firmer, more businesslike footings, where Indians governed their actions according to the dictates of the market rather than the artificial supports of an interventionist state.

Throughout Indian Country, rumours abounded that Onontio would return and liberate the people from a regime that seemed hostile, arrogant, and set on subjugation rather than alliance. A steady traffic of wampum belts moved throughout the Great Lakes and deep into the Mississippi River Valley, as different Indigenous groups called out for help and assistance to throw off the weight of the British occupier. One theme of resistance was based on the effort to recreate the Canada of alliance and reciprocity with Onontio, and another came from the teachings of Neolin, sometimes known as the Delaware prophet. Neolin preached a turning away by Indian people from European forms of dress, technology, and alcohol. The "Good Road" could be found by learning to live "without any trade or Connection with ye White people."[97] Although this message advanced a form of Aboriginal separatism, there is little doubt that the teachings represented a rich tapestry of philosophies, including influences derived from the activities of Quaker, Moravian, and other Christian evangelists, including some Aboriginal preachers. All of these agents of conversion were active and influential among the Delaware during the era when Neolin developed his theological interpretation.[98]

The universalist scope of the Christian teachings was probably influential in leading Neolin, and those who found sustenance in his message, to the position that God had specific expectations for all Indian peoples as a group distinct from other nationalities. Moreover, there was a notion in the teachings that Indian people had themselves partly to blame for the hardships that had befallen them. Their subjugation was the result of their failure to follow the Creator's divine plan for Indians. Just as their sins could be absolved by returning to a more righteous way of life in Indian Country, so the British oppressor could be vanquished by rejecting their ways and their dominance. This religious movement had powerful political potential, for, as White has written, "to take the blame is, in a sense, to take control."[99]

An Ottawa strategist from the Detroit area by the name of Pontiac was instrumental in marrying into a shared battle cry the force of hope in Neolin's message together with the resentments directed towards the British occupiers. In an upsurge that was partially planned and partially spontaneous, the ethnically diverse Aboriginal and French population of the Indian Country of Canada rose up in the spring and summer of 1763 to take control of virtually every newly acquired British military post except those of Detroit, Niagara, and Fort Pitt.[100] This display of a combined fighting muscle, which was strong enough to impose a high level of Aboriginal control over much of their remaining territory, caught large parts of the British imperial military and political establishment off guard. Certainly this Indian resistance movement, soon associated with the growing mystique of Pontiac's name, illustrated for many in the higher echelons of imperial command in British North America the gross inadequacies of Amherst's Indian policies. Inversely, the news from the interior suggested the apparent superiority of the regime advocated by Sir William Johnson through his long familiarity with the Covenant Chain.

The timing was significant for this display of the consequences of failing to recognize and affirm the regime of Aboriginal and treaty rights that the Indians of Canada had come to expect – a regime that some of their spokesmen, including Pontiac, were quite capable of articulating and demanding with lawyer-like precision. News of the dramatic reversal in the conditions in the interior reached London just as the final draft was being prepared under Lord Halifax of King George III's Royal Proclamation. The purpose of this proclamation was to outline the constitutional principles that would guide the governing bodies and officials of the North American territory from which the French crown had formally withdrawn its claims in the recent Treaty of Paris. With knowledge of the new menace to the "Public Peace, Welfare, and Good Government,"[101] the king's advisers in the Lords of Trade inserted added provisions to appease and disarm the Aboriginal resistance associated with Pontiac's name. The episode had demonstrated the negative consequences that might result from failing to extend some constitutionally entrenched guarantees to the Indians of Canada that their Aboriginal titles and rights would be recognized and protected by the crown.[102]

While news of the turnaround in British policy for the interior was gathered and sent on its slow, transatlantic voyage, Major-General Amherst attempted to respond to Pontiac with the ruthless severity that had stimulated the Aboriginal resistance in the first place. In a written request that resonates to this day with the genocidal terror of biological warfare, Amherst exclaimed, "Could it not be contrived to send some small pox among the tribes of Indians? We must on this occasion use every strategem in our power to reduce them."[103] Colonel Henry Bouquet, to whom Amherst directed his proposal, advanced his own suggestion to "extirpate or remove that [Indian] vermin by using bloodhounds to hunt them down."[104] The question awaits definitive proof of whether the waging of germ warfare was carried out through the making of lethal gifts to Indians of blankets obtained secretly from the smallpox hospital.

The central contention of the resistance movement in and around Pontiac's changing orbits of influence was that the Indigenous peoples had never been the subjects of French rule nor had they ever transferred their Aboriginal titles in their ancestral lands to French proprietorship. Since the Indians of Canada retained an unextinguished right in their Aboriginal lands, it followed that the French government lacked the capacity to transfer ownership of these territories to Britain.[105] The Aboriginal view of the British position in Indian Country was that the Englishmen were there more as tenants than owners. This assertion foreshadowed a similar controversy twenty years later, when many challenged the legality of the decision of the British government in the Treaty of Paris to hand over huge tracts of unceded Indian land to the new republic of the United States. The basic outlines of this position were explained to independent fur trader Alexander Henry, who travelled the Great Lakes shortly after the British takeover of the old French posts. At Michilimackinac, an Ojibway leader by the name of Minavavana held a conference with Henry, chastising him for his countrymen's failure to understand the true nature of their legal and political relationship to Indian Country. Minavavana declared, "Englishman, your king has never sent us any presents, nor entered into a treaty with us, wherefore he and we are still at war." He continued:

Englishman, although you have conquered the French, you have not yet conquered us! We are not your slaves. These lakes, these woods and mountains, were left to us by our ancestors. They are our inheritance; and we will part with them to none. Your nations suppose that we, like the white people, cannot live without bread – and pork – and beef! But you ought to know, that He, the Great Spirit and Master of Life, has provided food for us, in these spacious lakes, and on these woody mountains.[106]

In 1764 Charlot Kaske outlined a similar interpretation that emanated from the francophile attachments that were especially strong in many of the Algonkian-speaking communities along the Illinois and Wabash rivers south of Lake Michigan: "The English come here and say that the land is theirs and that the French have sold it to them. You know well our fathers have always told us that the land was ours, that we were free there, that the French came to settle there only to protect us and defend us as a good father protects and defends his children."[107]

The great display of Indian resistance to the British occupiers flared quickly and then gave way to less overt forms of defiance. With the departure of Amherst and with Sir William Johnson increasingly in charge of crown relations with Indigenous peoples in Canada, an uneasy equilibrium developed once again. Johnson's own legal analysis led him to conclusions similar to those of Pontiac and many of the other Indian activists, who insisted that the crown recognize and affirm a more expansive regime of Aboriginal and treaty rights. In a letter to a colleague in New York in 1765, Johnson explained, "Strictly speaking our rights of soil Extend no farther than they are actually purchased by Consent of the natives, tho in a political sense our Claims are much more extensive ... but these claims are kept up by European powers to prevent Encroachments or pretensions of each other, nor can it be consistent with the Justice of our Constitution to extend it further."[108] A year earlier Johnson had written to the Board of Trade, explaining, "I must beg leave to observe that the Six Nations, Western Indians, etc., have never been conquered, either by the English or the French, nor subject to Laws, consider themselves as a free people."[109]

Johnson set himself to the task of winning over Pontiac himself to become a proponent of the British connection and a crown-authorized "chief" of the Indian peoples in Canada. In 1764 he wrote to General Thomas Gage that Pontiac was "a Person of extraordinary abilities." He added, "this fellow should be gained to our Interest or knocked on the head."[110] By 1766 Johnson seemed to have won over the man he considered essential to the stability of the new order in the Indian Country of Canada. Apparently Pontiac was vulnerable to British blandishments, leading him to adopt a kind of magisterial manner that predictably pointed towards trouble among some of the Algonkian-speaking peoples. In his zeal to set Pontiac up as an instrument of British Indian policy, Johnson displayed a kind of awkwardness at variance with his firm grasp of the nuances necessary to the exercise of power and influence among the Longhouse peoples of the Mohawk Valley.

As Sir William moved beyond the elaborate cultural complexities of Johnson Hall both to follow and to lead the extension of the crown's authority into the truly vast domain of the Indian Country of Canada, he was faced with a sometimes daunting multiplicity of distinct peoples coming within his expanding governmental orbit. The Indigenous peoples in the larger Great Lakes area numbered in total around 60,000, a figure roughly comparable to the size of the entire French Canadian population in that era. Another point of comparison was the number used a generation later, when a territory of the United States was transformed into a state once the population of non-Indians exceeded 60,000.

Among the "Western Indians" listed by Johnson in an estimate he made in 1763 of his department's clients was the small but influential Huron, or Wyandot, community at Detroit. This site was also home to small Ottawa, Ojibway, and Potawatomi settlements. In their largest aggregate, these three powerful Indian nations formed the basis of the Three Fires Confederacy. In the Ohio Valley were the Shawnee, whose name simply refers to "the south." They shared ground with various factions of Delawares and the Miami Confederacy. The "Far Indians" included Three Fires peoples, together with Sauk, Fox, Winnebago, Menominee, Illinois, Kickapoo, Mascouten, Weas, Piankeshaw, and others. A breakaway faction of Senecas in the west were sometimes referred to as Mingos.[111] Beyond the Far Indians were various Siouian-speaking groups, some of whom had gradually been pushed from the northern Woodlands to the prairies by Ojibway and Cree peoples with better access to guns from the English posts on the shores of Hudson Bay.[112]

Pontiac's move into the orbit of British imperial Canada alienated the most stubbornly conservative and francophile elements in Indian Country, especially in the Illinois and Wabash countries where Charlot Kaske was a dominant figure. The hopes harboured there for the return of Onontio, the French governor, were struck a double blow when the French sovereign withdrew his claims to Canada and transferred his imperial claims to the region west of the Mississippi River to Spain. In the decades ahead, the Mississippi served as the eastern boundary of Louisiana, a boundary that Thomas Jefferson and many other future architects of the United States looked to as the logical geographic line of demarcation for a continental apartheid project aimed at separating the New World Americans and their slaves from the Old World Indigenous peoples.

In 1769 Pontiac visited family members around the Mississippi River, a part of Indian Country where the level of disappointment ran high that France had departed and Britain was installing its own agents of indirect rule among the First Nations. In this charged atmosphere, Pontiac was assassinated under circumstances that still leave room for speculation about who might have been behind the killing. The man who clubbed Pontiac from behind and then stabbed him was a well-known Peoria leader. The execution took place as Pontiac was leaving a store in the French Canadian settlement of Cahokia.[113]

The store was owned and operated by the company of Baynton, Wharton, and Morgan, a firm that was to figure prominently in the financial and political deal-making that provided vital mortgages for the making of the American Revolution. In this huge transaction with history, Indian Country served as the ultimate prize and the primary seed capital to be leveraged in the expectation that a new, more efficient legal, military, and ideological machinery of westward expansion could be constructed around the authority of a local, North American sovereignty. As Thomas Paine wrote, "lands are the real riches of the habitable world, and the natural funds of America."[114]

Pontiac excited the imaginations of many who knew him in life and, by reputation, after his death. He seems to have engendered a fascination similar to that built up around Lahontan's great informant, Kondiaronk. Both of these Indian intellectuals have been hailed as gifted, yet doomed, law givers from the forests of Canada whose legacy is to serve as evocative symbols of what was, what might have been, and what could yet be. Their roles foreshadowed the blaze of insights that would burst into history through the agency of Tecumseh and, later, that of George Manuel. The lineage of thought and action personified in the activism of these four First Nations leaders gives temporal and philosophical depth to the genesis of the Fourth World. Among the literary origins of the sense of mystique and melodrama surrounding the defiant Ottawa resister was *Ponteach; or, the Savages of America: A Tragedy*. This play, written in whole or in part by Captain Robert Rogers, was first published in Great Britain in 1766 to very caustic reviews.[115] In 1898 Francis Parkman, the popular historian of impeccable Bostonian Puritan pedigree, made Pontiac the title character in his most famous and characteristic narrative of doomed Aboriginal savagery and backward Roman Catholic feudalism giving way before the Darwinian rise of the Protestant individualism driving American civilization.[116]

In life as well as in literature, Pontiac's image loomed large and influential. Sir William Johnson cast Pontiac as the essential figure in his scheme to extend the protocols of the Covenant Chain and the Extended Lodge outward into the Algonkian-speaking heartland around the Great Lakes. To Tecumseh, Pontiac's primary genius lay in his guidance of the religious enthusiasms generated by Neolin towards confederacy building and the generation of North American Indian constitutional law. There can be little doubt that the precedents set by Pontiac and Neolin were the primary example for Tecumseh when he attempted a similar feat in turning his brother's theology towards more secular, geopolitical ends. In his legendary speeches to urge Indian peoples to forge the common citizenry of a single, sovereign federation, Tecumseh is reported to have reminded his varied audiences that the thin and menaced protections for their existing Aboriginal and treaty rights – protections that he sought to edify in the forum of international law – were directly attributable to Pontiac.

THE ROYAL PROCLAMATION OF 1763
AND THE GROWING DIVISION BETWEEN ANTAGONISTIC
CAMPS OF BRITISH IMPERIALISTS

The Royal Proclamation of 1763 created the legal provisions for governing the Caribbean Island of Grenada within the British Empire. Similarly, the document laid out the borders and governing principles for a new British province named Quebec. It established East Florida and West Florida at the southerly extremes of a vastly expanded British North America. The fifth jurisdiction described by King George III in 1763 was by far the largest. This territory, encompassing the region south of Quebec and west of the rivers draining into the Atlantic, was "reserved" to the "Indian nations" as "their Hunting Grounds."[117]

The proclamation's provisions creating Quebec from the St Lawrence Valley heartland of what had been New France, along with the reservation of the North American interior as an Indian hunting ground, established the constitutional foundation of British imperial Canada. Similarly, because it embodied so many of the principles and theories against which many Anglo-Americans revolted, the Royal Proclamation established a kind of constitutional antithesis of what would become the United States of America, at least in its early decades of existence.

In putting in place the constitutional foundations of crown authority in territories new to the presence of British law, the sovereign in this single instance could act with a kind of monarchical independence. Such unilateral action on the part of the king seemed to some like a regression back to the era before Parliament had established its constitutional supremacy through the English civil wars. While the legality of this unusual feature of British imperial law was supported in 1774 in the famous case of *Campbell* v. *Hall*,[118] the monarchical character of the Royal Proclamation made it a source of Anglo-American suspicion as an apparent display of the British sovereign's alleged hostility to democracy and his alleged bent towards tyranny. The initial antagonisms intensified over time. The jurisdictional divisions outlined in the proclamation compounded the differences in interest and ideology that emerged at the centre of the warfare between the old Indian Country of Canada and the emergent American empire of private property.

The Royal Proclamation of 1763 entrenched in the constitution of British North America a number of principles essential to the recognition and affirmation of Aboriginal and treaty rights. The principles on which these recognitions were based had gradually penetrated the legal imagination and constitution construction of those responsible for shaping the imperial framework within which British North America was situated. Articulation of these principles had emanated from a number of different sources. One of them was based on the experience of a century and a half of crown colonization of the Anglo-American provinces. From a process of trial and error in the westward extension of the Anglo-American settlements, the fragile notion had gradually developed in a variety of contexts that it was strategically wise to obtain some sort of documented Aboriginal sanction for the transfer of lands away from Indian control. Nowhere was the imperial learning curve higher than in New York colony on the utility of developing sound protocols and procedures to signify crown recognitions of Aboriginal rights. In establishing the foundations of what later generations would describe as "the empire state," both the neighbouring Six Nations peoples and some of the Dutch residents educated elements of Anglo-American officialdom into the advantages to be derived from elaborating approaches to the rule of law based on trade, collaboration, and treaty making with Indigenous peoples. The Indian policies of the pacific wing of Quakerism in Pennsylvania contributed as well to the evolution of the Anglo-American constitutional principles that found confirmation and entrenchment in the Royal Proclamation.

The proclamation can also be seen as what Anthony Pagden referred to as "the final resolution" to a specific constitutional dispute that had simmered since the late seventeenth century in a legal contest pitting a group of Mohegan Indians against the government of Connecticut colony.[119] In 1705 the Mohegans and their friends and allies in England achieved a major victory in this dispute. Their many-faceted legal argument with Connecticut's local government was widely viewed as the most important case decided in the eighteenth century by the Judicial Committee of the Privy Council.[120] That judicial body was the highest imperial court in the British Empire. While some of the Anglo-American colonists lobbied hard to fight back the sweeping legal consequences of this Indian win, the Privy Council ultimately solidified its original decision. The jurists maintained that Indians in North America constituted a "distinct people" who were the possessors of "the property of the soil" until such time as they ceded their ancestral lands. Moreover, the institution of a special imperial court with judicial representation from outside North America was deemed necessary to assure genuine third-party adjudication of Indian disputes with the local colonial governments. Similarly, Indigenous peoples within British colonies or adjacent to them were found not to be under the direct authority of English law. They were, rather, subject to "a law equal to both parties," a juridical regime referred to by one of the jurists involved in the case as "the law of nature and nations."[121]

According to Pagden, one of the aims of the Royal Proclamation's drafters was to entrench some of the constitutional principles that had emerged from the case of *Mohegan Indians* v. *Connecticut Colony*. The goal was to entrench, in the form of an irrevocable royal decree, the legal prohibition preventing colonial officials from unilaterally extinguishing those Aboriginal and treaty rights whose recognition and protection had been promised by the imperial government. Another source of examples for the drafters of the proclamation were the Indian policies of New France, but

especially the marriage in Canada of the fur trade with the centralization
of imperial control over the power to make peace or war with the citizens
of Indian Country. Finally, as we have seen, those Indian peoples who
threw in their lot with Pontiac influenced the context of imperial decision
making in 1763 dramatically by demonstrating their capacity to make
Canada ungovernable. They dramatized the fact that they could be kept in
check only through the outlay of huge military spending for the fighting
of protracted Indian wars, or, alternatively, through the institution of measures that went part of the way towards meeting Aboriginal expectations of
what constituted a fair regime for the recognition of Aboriginal and treaty
rights.

Many inferences can be drawn from the role of Indigenous peoples in
North America as influential participants in determining the Royal Proclamation's contents. Their integral involvement in shaping the constitutional
landscape of a tremendously expanded British North America exposes the
wrongheadedness of conceptions that see imperialism simply as a system of
commands pointing one way from the metropolitan centre towards the hinterland of empire. As Eric Hinderaker has argued in his study of the series of
empires that played roles in the governance of the Ohio Valley until 1800,
these media of intercultural relations are best understood as "processes
rather than structures," as "negotiated systems" where Indigenous peoples
retained considerable power to "shape, challenge, or resist colonialism."[122]
Accordingly, no less than in its expansion of empire into Africa throughout
the nineteenth century, the expansion of Great Britain's empire in North
America in 1763 was largely a matter of adaptation to, and accommodation
of, local conditions on the frontiers of crown authority. As Robinson and Gallagher have argued in assessing a more recent chapter of British imperial history, the new colonial policy embodied in the Royal Proclamation was
"improvised by the official mind"; it was a reflection of "the hopes, the memories and the neuroses which inform the strategists' picture of the world ... A
government's view of who may be trusted and who must be feared."[123]

In the Royal Proclamation, King George prohibited the purchase of the
Indians' reserved lands by private individuals. Instead, the sovereign
claimed his own royal monopoly as the sole agent with legal authority to
make such transactions. Using the royal "we," the king asserted this exclusive power for himself and his royal heirs with reference to a long history
where there had been no clear and uniform policies for the expansion of
Anglo-American settlements into Indian Country. Without established procedures for the transfer of title from Indians to non-Indians, all manner of
travesties had transpired, including many variations on the theme of
bribery, coercion, or getting Native people drunk before asking them to
sign deeds. With this history as a background, the king proclaimed:

And whereas great Frauds and Abuses have been commited in purchasing Lands
of the Indians, to the great Prejudice of our Interest, and to the great Dissatisfac-

tion of the said Indians; In order, therefore, to prevent such Irregularities in the future, and to the End that the Indians may be convinced of our Justice and determined Resolution to remove all reasonable cause of Discontent, We do, with the advice of our Privy Council strictly enjoin and require, that no private Person do presume to make any purchase from the said Indians, within those parts of our Colonies where, We have thought Proper to allow Settlement; but that, if at any Time any of the Said Indians should be inclined to dispose of the said Lands, the same shall be Purchased only for Us, in our Name, at some public Meeting or Assembly of the said Indians, to be held for that Purpose by the Governor or Commander in Chief of our Colony respectively within which they shall lie.[124]

The "great Frauds" to which the king referred had affected the British imperial interests in many ways. The oldest and most spectacular example had been in the rise of New France largely through French imperial exploitation of the severe hostility shared by many Indian groups and individuals towards the Anglo-American colonists and towards some of their Longhouse League allies as well. The Indian takeover of the British posts in Canada in 1763 had demonstrated that the defeat of the French army had in no way brought an end to the deep suspicions and resentments in Indian Country that the drafters of the Royal Proclamation hoped at least partially to repair.

While the great frauds perpetrated by Anglo-Americans in Indian Country had hurt British imperial interests at the highest level of foreign policy, the negative ramifications of the lack of any clear and uniform procedures in the purchasing of Indian land had created an atmosphere of instability and chaos on the frontier that undermined the viability of the crown's colonizing enterprise. One of the major sources of this instability was the fact that many single parcels of land were the subject of two or more transactions with different Indian groups, resulting in many overlapping claims. Francis Jennings has referred to this phenomenon in early colonial New England as the "deeds game."[125] The key to the game among Anglo-Americans was to find a group of Indians ready to sanction a land sale without much concern for whether that particular group really was indigenous to the land in question. This kind of approach often led to an outcome where the same parcel of land could be ceded again and again by different Indian sellers, sometimes without the true Aboriginal inhabitants even being involved or informed. The cumulative result of this unregulated free-for-all in the purchase of Indian land was a proliferation of competing claims. Not only did these divisions create or compound animosities among some Aboriginal groups but they pitted many non-Indians against one another, whether as individuals, as shareholders in specific colonizing companies, or as citizens of different Anglo-American jurisdictions with conflicting intentions to expand into the same territory.

As was the case in the genesis of the famous case of *Mohegan* v. *Connecticut*, sometimes the imperial government was pulled into these land disputes as the ultimate arbiter, a tendency that demonstrated over time the importance of asserting centralized control and a common regime of rules over the stimulation or restraint of the western movement of Anglo-American settlements. Another key consideration on the part of the imperial government involved legal concerns that, when individuals or corporate entities bought lands directly from Indian people, the rights of the purchasers were arguably held within the law of the Aboriginal sellers rather than within the law of the crown. In other words, when the purchaser of Indian land was anything other than a sovereign entity, that purchaser could, theoretically, acquire only a form of title created by the legal authority of the Indian nation sanctioning the sale. The perceived antidote to combat all manner of uses to which this argument might be put was for the king himself, as the ultimate receptacle of sovereignty in the British Empire, to reserve the right to purchase parcels of Indian Country as an exclusive monarchical prerogative.

The Royal Proclamation specifically excluded from its application those lands covered by the Hudson's Bay Company Charter. It ordered all non-Indian settlers living west of the new border along the height of land dividing the watershed of the Atlantic Ocean from the Mississippi Valley to remove themselves from the Indians' reserved territory. King George stipulated as well that the non-Indian fur traders would be allowed to conduct business in the protected Indian Country, but only within the regulatory framework to be established under the authority of the imperial government.

The Royal Proclamation is rich in the paradoxes surrounding different conceptions of democracy. In stipulating that the interest of Indian people in their ancestral lands could not be changed without their voluntary agreement, the king confirmed and expanded the principle that the law of British colonization prohibited the unilateral dispossession of Indigenous peoples without their consent. The declaration that this consent could only be obtained at "some public meeting or Assembly of the said Indians, to be held for the Purpose," seemed to provide a degree of protection against the manipulation in private of a few individual Indians, who might be secretly bribed or coerced to sell for personal gain or mere survival their peoples' collective interests. While the proclamation seemed to advance some limited recognition of the democratic rights of Indigenous peoples, this acknowledgement was perceived by some Anglo-American colonists as an authoritarian constraint on their own right and that of their local governments to establish direct relations with Indian peoples on the western frontiers. By imposing centralized, monarchical authority as a barrier of protection against unchecked, unregulated, and decentralized non-Indian expansion into a clearly outlined Indian Country, the king seemed to be creating a huge obstacle boxing in the acquisitive liberties of the restless Anglo-Americans.[126]

King George was careful to be clear and explicit about the nature of his

own "Interest" and his own "Dominion" in this historic constitutional confirmation of existing Aboriginal and treaty rights in British North America. The key passage balancing the rights of Indians within a framework of
law centred on the sovereign's own monarchical authority is a study in the
creative ambivalence necessary to the assertion of power in a milieu distrustful of crown authority. The king proclaimed: "And whereas it is just
and reasonable, and essential to our Interest, and the Security of our
Colonies, that the several Nations or Tribes of Indians with whom We are
connected, and who live under our Protection, should not be molested or
disturbed in the Possession of such Parts of Our Dominions and Territories as, not having been ceded or purchased by Us, are reserved to them,
or any of them, as their Hunting Ground."[127] While the Royal Proclamation of 1763 laid out the basic design for a significantly altered British
North America, the document left unanswered a large number of questions about how the principles it contained would actually be administered
and enforced. Moreover, major controversies would inevitably arise about
how to pay for the system of governance outlined by the king. Issues of
finance were especially contentious when they concerned the regulation
and patrolling of the long eastern border of Indian Country, whose very
existence was resented and largely ignored by many of the Anglo-American colonists.

In 1764 the Lords of Trade issued a plan to administer Indian Country
according to the principles of the Royal Proclamation. The following year
the British government attempted to impose a new tax known as the
Stamp Act to help defray the high cost of maintaining a large military
establishment in the North American interior.[128] The resistance to the
Stamp Act became a flash point of Anglo-Americans resentment that they
were seemingly being asked to pay for the instruments of their own
repression and constraint. Faced with outright rioting in the streets and
with the cry of "no taxation without representation," the British government backed away from the Stamp Act, but not from the basic principles
of the Royal Proclamation.

In 1768 the Lords of Trade outlined a modification on their plan of
1764. While some of the imperial regulations on the fur trade were lifted,
the authors of this revised Indian policy made it very clear that Indian
Department officials had a major responsibility for the "setting aside of all
local interfering of particular Provinces" from the conduct of diplomacy,
war, or trade with Indian nations in the continent's interior.[129] The Lords
advised the king further that more resources should be allocated to train
and develop a class of crown Indian agents "acting under your Majesty's
immediate Authority; and which, as they have reference to the general
Interests of the Indians, independent of their connection with any particular Colony, cannot be provided for by the Provincial Laws." Among the
particular tasks that the crown's Indian agents were expected to perform
in the vast, crown-protected Indian Country to the rear of the Anglo-

American settlements were "the renewal of antient Compacts or Covenant-Chains made between the Crown and the principle Tribes of Savages in that Country; the reconciling of Differences and Disputes between one body of Indians and another; the agreeing with them for the sale or surrender of Lands for publick purposes not lying within the limits of any particular Colony; and the holding of Interviews with them for these and a variety of other general Purposes, which are merely Objects of Negotiation between Your Majesty and the Indians."[130]

The effort to carve out a domain of shared imperial and Aboriginal jurisdiction in British North America was part of a larger complex of geopolitical calculations rooted largely in English history and in the intricacies of British domestic politics.[131] Almost certainly, for instance, the conceptualization of the interior of the continent as a vast Indian hunting domain under crown protection drew from the English tradition embodied in the existence of extensive royal hunting preserves in the mother country. Moreover, the desire to discourage Anglo-American settlers from moving far into the North American interior was partially based on old mercantilistic justifications for the creation and edification of an overseas empire. For proponents of these mercantilistic views, the purpose of colonies was primarily to consume the surplus from British manufacturing industries and to supply relatively unprocessed raw materials to the more labour-intensive, secondary industries of the home country. Accordingly, the prospect of Anglo-American settlers moving westward away from the Atlantic seemed to challenge the very reason for establishing colonies in the first place.

The fear was that the further the colonists moved inland, the more likely they would be to respond to the higher transportation costs of importing British goods by setting up their own indigenous manufacturing enterprises. As an adviser to the secretary of state detailed in a memorandum to his superior, any course of colonization should be avoided that encouraged the Anglo-Americans to plant "themselves in the Heart of America, out of reach of [the imperial] Government, and where, from the difficulty of procuring European Commodities, they would be compelled to commence Manufactures to the infinite prejudice of Britain."[132]

This form of rapid, relatively unregulated westward-moving colonization was regarded as antagonistic rather than complementary to British imperial interests because it seemed more likely to expand the competition to, rather than consumption of, products emanating from British factories. Alternatively, the commercial interests involved in the fur trade appeared to be more worthy of political support through instruments such as the Royal Proclamation and, later, the Quebec Act because the nature of this primal exchange was more clearly in line with the classic principles used to explain and justify mercantilistic expansion.[133]

The British imperial decision to protect and administer Indian Country as a domain of shared monarchical and Aboriginal jurisdiction, therefore,

was the other side of the decision to discourage the westward expansion of
Anglo-American settlement. This imperial desire to maintain an essentially eastward-looking commercial orientation in the English-speaking settlements of British North America was advanced by efforts to point the forces
of growth in the colonies towards northward and southward expansion
along the Atlantic seabord. In the north this thrust in policy resulted in
efforts to build up Nova Scotia not only as a bastion of the British navy on
the North Atlantic but as a settlement colony as well. A prelude to this
strategy was the British wartime decision in 1755 to deport the French-
speaking, Catholic population of Acadia. Running alongside the politics of
deportation, one of the darker reflections of the British imperial mind of
that era, were crown efforts to disengage the Mi'kmaq (Micmac), Maliseet,
Abenaki, and Passamaquoddy peoples of the region from their old
alliances with the Church of Rome and the empire of France. This concerted effort to gain acquiescence from the Roman Catholic Indian communities in the region for the expansion of the British Empire onto their
lands resulted in the extended negotiation of important treaty cycles in the
mid-eighteenth century.

This cycle built on the terms of the agreement made in 1726, when
Mi'kmaq, Maliseet, and Abenaki people met at Boston and then at
Annapolis to negotiate the terms of a peace settlement.[134] This early treaty
was repeatedly referred to in subsequent negotiations in 1749, and again
in 1760 and 1761, when the First Nations of the region renewed their
promises to local crown officials that they would accept as permanent the
British presence in their midst. This most recent Aboriginal acceptance of
the British role in the region seemed inescapable after the French naval
stronghold of Louisbourg succumbed a second time to British militarism
in one of the more decisive engagements of the Seven Years' War. In return
for the Aboriginal commitment to eschew further aggression, the British
sovereign promised the Indigenous peoples enjoyment of religious freedom as well as recognition of the First Nations' capacity to continue to
hunt, trap, fish, gather, and plant as they had been in the custom of doing.
The treaty also referred to the crown's intention to establish a system of
"truckhouses" that would be the basis of a government-regulated trade system designed to hold Native commercial alliances securely within the
British orbit. As Lieutenant-Governor Jonathan Belcher promised the
assembled First Nations delegates at his farm near Halifax during the
negotiations, "The Laws will be like a great Hedge about your Rights and
properties."[135]

In spite of the lieutenant-governor's reference to the protection of
Aboriginal property, these agreements were primarily about peace, religion, and trade. They did not touch directly on questions concerning
the underlying Aboriginal title to all the lands of what are today the Maritime provinces of Canada as well as portions of the eastern seabord of
the United States. Hence these Maritime Indian treaties lie outside the

constitutional tradition that runs through the agreements negotiated according to the principles codified in the Royal Proclamation of 1763. In 1999 the treaty of 1760–61 became the subject of an especially controversial Supreme Court ruling in Canada. Responding to criminal charges brought against Mi'kmaq fisher Donald Marshall Jr, the court interpreted the agreement to mean that the Indigenous peoples of the region retained an Aboriginal right to a portion of the local fishery. The decision set off a series of angry, non-Aboriginal responses verging on vigilantism. This harsh collision of attitudes and interests pointed to the potent ramifications involved in interpreting history on the frontiers where Indian Country meets the contemporary extensions of the empire of possessive individualism.[136]

The British government's move to impose taxation on the crown's subjects in British North America was stimulated by the doubling of Great Britain's national debt as a result of the vast expenses incurred over the course of the Seven Years' War. The question of how to pay down this debt, together with how to pay for the administration of government over a vastly expanded extent of North American territory, greatly perplexed the imaginative resources of those in both the metropolis and the hinterlands of an enlarged empire. As the British government increasingly looked to the Anglo-American colonies for revenue to help support the machinery of imperial control, profound questions arose about the legitimacy of a system where Anglo-American citizens would be taxed by an imperial regime within which they had no direct democratic representation.

The withdrawal of the first Stamp Act in 1765 did not resolve the problem but only left the contention simmering towards the day, in 1774, when the revellers at the Boston Tea Party defiantly threw this valuable commodity overboard even as they dressed themselves up as Mohawks. The nature of their disguise perhaps referred to the thick web of connections linking issues of Indian Affairs, taxation, and democracy in the Anglo-American colonies on the eve of the revolution.[137]

The prospect of being taxed to support a costly military establishment whose primary purpose was to fend off Anglo-American expansion into Indian Country was particularly galling to many in the Thirteen Colonies as well as to some of their financial backers and political allies on the other side of the Atlantic. From the perspective of many English-speaking Protestants in the restless jurisdictions along the Atlantic seabord, they had sacrificed and contributed mightily to Britain's victory over France in the acquisition of Canada, a polity that was perceived as a bastion not only of hostile Indians but of the godless Roman Catholic *canadiens* as well. In facing these local enemies, along with the imperial forces of France, many Anglo-Americans had participated in most aspects of the largest war ever mounted until that time in the expansion of the British Empire. The role of the colonists was so large that Fred Anderson has argued that "to a degree virtually unknown in the eighteenth century, every colony north of

Virginia had experienced the conflict as a people's war."[138] The prospect of having the perceived territorial fruits of this popular victory placed beyond the boundaries of fast and easy Euro-American colonization seemed hard to accept. The prospect that this newly annexed territory would be transformed from a colonial asset into a financial liability seemed almost unfathomable to many of those Anglo-American colonists, who maintained, with some legitimacy, that they had sacrificed much to achieve ascendance in the French and Indian War.

The issue of how the imperial government could obtain revenue in British North America was burdened with huge symbolic baggage as long as the crown's Anglo-American subjects thought that the purpose of any new imperial tax was to pay for an imperial army that would keep English-speaking Protestants from exploiting their hard-won commercial opportunities in the trans-Appalachian West. The other side of this prohibition on rapid western expansion of the Anglo-American settlements was the protection of Indigenous peoples and their Aboriginal rights as well as the promotion of the mercantilistic interests that were fast converging on Montreal as the commercial hub of British imperial Canada and as the main fur-trade metropolis of the North American continent.

Accordingly, while issues concerning taxation and democratic representation were the most visible points of argumentation in the division between those two factions whose diverging interests would ultimately give rise to the civil war in British North America, beneath these public controversies lay a far deeper conflict. At issue in the jostling over responsibility for local taxation and Indian Affairs was the question of who would acquire the capacity to determine the pace and form of Euro-American expansion into Indian Country.[139] With the Royal Proclamation of 1763 the imperial government – indeed the monarch himself – had reserved the exclusive authority to purchase and acquire Aboriginal title in the lands he had reserved for Indian peoples as their hunting preserve. Through this single provision, the British sovereign had made himself and his royal heirs the sole authority empowered to transfer land from Indians to non-Indians – in other words, the British sovereign had monopolized in imperial hands the exclusive constitutional power to regulate the westward expansion of Anglo-American settlements. In the issue of control of relations with Indian peoples, therefore, lay an inestimably wide power to determine who would own America. From there it followed, as John Jay declared, "that the people who own the country ought to govern it."[140]

The Royal Proclamation of 1763 served as a catalyst to widen a major split between two contending camps seeking to control the course of British imperialism in North America. These two factions divided along the lines of decentralization and centralization, monoculturalism and multiculturalism. The decentralists sought to expand the power and jurisdiction of the local governments in British North America. This push towards expansion demanded that large portions of Indian Country be absorbed and privatized into existing colonies or new colonies as quickly as possible. The inescapable attending violations of the rights of Indian peoples could be rationalized within this more monocultural camp as the necessary price of progress and as a geopolitical expression of the kind of economic principles of "laissez-faire, laissez-aller" that Adam Smith was about to express in the fateful year of 1776 in his *Wealth of Nations*. Later in the nineteenth century, social Darwinism would provide an even more evolved rationalization for extinguishing Indigenous peoples as the sometimes necessary cost of "civilization's" expansion.

The proponents of a widened base of local, Anglo-American jurisdiction in a decentralized British Empire tended to have an exceptionally self-aggrandizing conception of themselves as the pre-eminent and naturally dominant group on the continent. From this conviction, which drew heavily on the ideological legacy of John Locke and on the Calvinist roots of their mostly Protestant devotions, flowed the certainty that they should be afforded favoured status and maximum latitude by the British authorities to express their competitive advantages in forging a new society. For those who saw the empire from this ethnocentric perspective, it made little sense to hold back the enterprise of the Protestant Anglo-Americans by subjecting them to the restraints that would flow from crown protection for Aboriginal and treaty rights or for the rights of French-speaking Roman Catholics in Quebec or elsewhere in Canada.

The other side of this debate on imperialism favoured a more centrally controlled British North America where the Anglo-American settlements would be held within the limits of a fixed western boundary. The lands on the western side of this boundary were to be left as an Indian Country and as a fur-trade preserve, where the rule of law was based on the establishment and elaboration of alliances linking Indigenous peoples directly with the central government of the British Empire. While the decentralists anticipated the ascendance of Anglo-American Protestants as the dominant group on the continent, the more conservative imperialists sought a balance that emphasized a more pluralistic or multicultural organization of society. The proponents of a more centrally controlled British North American empire not only afforded some latitude for the recognition of Aboriginal rights and titles but also made provision in the Quebec Act of 1774 to accommodate the Roman Catholic religion and the old civil code of the *canadien* inhabitants of the newly created British province of Quebec.[141]

LAND SPECULATORS AND THE QUEST FOR "FREE TRADE" IN INDIAN LANDS ON THE EVE OF THE AMERICAN REVOLUTION

In addition to these two camps of British imperialists, one emphasizing a strong central government and the other emphasizing dramatically expanded jurisdiction for local governments, a powerful lobby advocating a third option emerged. Although proponents of this third option favoured rapid western expansion of the Anglo-American settlements into Indian Country, they preferred to work primarily through new types of corporations rather than depend too heavily on government as the major guiding instrument of colonization. While the architects of these corporate vehicles would work either with the British government or, as seemed appropriate, with the local law makers of the Anglo-American colonies, in the years before the American Revolution their preferred means of acquiring the most coveted commodity on the continent was by purchasing land titles directly from Indian peoples in open violation of the major provisions of the Royal Proclamation of 1763. In turning away from the crown and towards the Indians as the primary source of the land tenure they sought to acquire, the directors of these land-speculation companies endeavoured to move their enterprises away from the imperial monopoly of colonizing authority implied in many of the founding charters of the original corporations granted territorial patents in North America.

Accordingly, there are rich veins of contemporary meaning in the history surrounding the actions of those who sought to create and develop this class of Anglo-American corporate entity. Their tactic was to lobby for, and to speculate in, various agendas for transforming Indian lands into non-Indian settlements and privately held capital. The land-speculation companies that emerged from these initiatives became major vehicles of experimentation in the development of forms of property law that vastly expanded the geographic frontiers and the internal sophistication of Lockean expressions of possessive individualism. When the owners and executives of these companies were repeatedly frustrated in their various efforts to privatize the commons that the British crown had reserved to the Indians as their hunting grounds, they contributed significantly to the revolutionary creation of a new sovereign entity that would give the aura of legal legitimacy to their huge development schemes.

The important web of connections linking the genesis of the American Revolution to the political and commercial manoeuvres of those engaged in land speculation beyond the boundaries of the Anglo-American settlements has been elaborately chronicled by a number of scholars, including Clarence Alvord, Thomas Perkins Abernathy, Dorothy Jones, Robert A. Williams Jr, Jack Sosin, Ray Allen Billington, and Francis Jennings.[142] To the extent that these and other historians have cogently demonstrated the importance of land speculators in the revolutionary act of pushing aside crown restrictions shielding Indian Country from Anglo-American privatization, what we see is a precedent of signal importance to the privatization of other sorts of commons in our own times. This history suggests the emergence of new types of entrepreneurship capable of affecting the creation of new sorts of sovereign authority in situations where older mechanisms of government fail to generate the kinds of laws required to legitimize an expanded empire of possessive individualism.

A clear focus on the role of the British North American land specula-tion companies in the genesis and outcome of the American Revolution helps to illuminate the enormous commercial ramifications flowing from the invention of a new kind of indigenous sovereignty in the western hemisphere. As the primary laboratory for a variety of seminal experi-ments in the constitution of human governance, the United States pro-vided a far more efficient institutional machinery for Euro-American expansion than the imperial structures of the British Empire. An essential element of this saga of experimentation with the instruments of sover-eignty involved the spawning of a new breed of business corporation capa-ble of leading and exploiting the process of transforming a large portion of the earth's surface into privatized wealth, the liquid medium facilitat-ing the emergence of global capitalism. Indeed, so influential was this process that the image and role of the United States in the global com-munity would become over time almost completely synonymous with the image and role of capitalism itself. It is this dynamic of capitalism's histo-ry which gives the pre-revolutionary land-speculation companies their larger significance as harbingers of vital developments to come.

While the land companies were prototypes of more general trends in the evolution of American corporate culture, their energy projects out-ward with particular linear force towards the speculative schemes of the North American railway companies and towards the global operations of the us-based oil and gas companies. The corporate frontiersmen at the vanguard of this particular projectory of capitalist expansion have been especially aggressive and influential agents in the process of shaping the world's pre-eminent regime of economic relationships. A spotlight on their actions helps shed light on that dynamic of corporate history which has seen many business enterprises originating in the United States acquire more and more attributes of sovereignty as they have grown from national to transnational proportions. A key to understanding this pro-cess lies in the us government's persistent refusal to elaborate any formal legal structures that might give definitive constitutional shape to the worldwide expansion of the United States's commercial, political, and military influence.

In this respect the American empire has developed on dramatically dif-ferent principles from the British imperial parent of the United States. Where the architects of the British Empire constructed a complex legal infrastructure in an effort to give the expanding worldwide claims of the British sovereign concrete constitutional substance, the architects of the American empire decided against this strategy. Instead, they chose quite deliberately to avoid setting in place any overarching infrastructure of clear-ly articulated laws that might set limits on the United States's ability to adapt to the changing conditions of power politics in any part of the planet.

The decision to opt for laissez-faire deregulation and against the rule of law in constructing the complex global machinery of American power was closely connected to the preferred agenda for the transnational expansions of US-based companies. In eschewing the old model of European colonialism, the United States avoided any direct reckoning with the central contradiction embodied in its status as both the world's sole surviving "superpower" and as a republic founded on anti-imperialist ideals. Moreover, US-based global corporations have been left more free to move into the vacuum of sovereign authority created by the US government's refusal to surround many of its instruments of global power with the formal constitutional attire of international law. This approach to world order, affording such extensive, sovereign-like powers to global corporations, was anticipated by the corporate attempt in pre-revolutionary North America to purchase land titles from Indigenous peoples on a sovereign-to-sovereign basis.

One of the busiest speculators in Indian lands in the era after the Seven Years' War was General George Washington. His original entry into the field was through buying up the land-grant certificates that the crown distributed to war veterans according to a mathematical formula detailed in the Royal Proclamation of 1763.[143] In this fashion, Washington assembled extensive claims to western territories with the view of obtaining crown charters for his proposed Anglo-American settlements. Like several other prominent land speculators, Washington maintained agents both in London and in Indian Country to promote his various ventures, as carried forward by vehicles such as the Mississippi Company.[144]

On both sides of the Atlantic, investors assumed, along with George Washington, that the Royal Proclamation was only a "temporary expedient" and that the time was right to "hunt out good lands" in the areas reserved to the Indians as their hunting grounds.[145] Those touched by this speculative frenzy devoted significant amounts of monetary, political, and imaginative capital to the task of anticipating or manipulating how different portions of Indian Country would be brought into the marketplace for exploitation and development by non-Indians. While much of this activity was centred in London, England, some speculators, such as William Murray, headed west with the view that the Royal Proclamation was unconstitutional and that direct purchases of land from Indian groups would ultimately establish a valid form of title. With this expectation, Murray paid $24,000 directly to Aboriginal groups for two parcels of land at the junctions of the Ohio River and the Illinois River with the Mississippi River. He did so in the name of a syndicate of investors who had formed themselves as the Illinois-Wabash Company.[146]

Judge Richard Henderson of North Carolina was another major land speculator of the era. He worked closely with Daniel Boone, who on hunting expeditions scouted out prime lands for possible purchase and development in the Kentucky area. After some initial experimentation,

Henderson organized the Transylvania Company as a joint stock enterprise with the view of buying lands directly from the Cherokee. In 1775, on the eve of the American Revolution, Transylvania was hastily established as a kind of independent corporate proprietorship. Responding to this act, the House of Burgesses of Virginia formally rescinded Transylvania's status in 1777, reconstituting it as Kentucky County.[147]

By far the most influential speculations in British North America in the pre-revolutionary era began with the activities of a Philadelphia fur-trading enterprise by the name of Baynton, Wharton and Morgan. The officials of this company increasingly entered the political realm of those with the power to affect the pace and shape of Anglo-American expansion into the Indian Country of Canada. Samuel Wharton was the guiding figure in making the transition from a business based on purchasing furs from Indian peoples to an enterprise founded on purchasing land titles from them. It was Wharton who first got the idea of turning to advantage the loses incurred by his company during the Indian resistance struggle associated with Pontiac. By requesting reparations in the form of Indian lands, the firm of Baynton, Wharton and Morgan set in motion the events that led to the negotiation of the Treaty of Fort Stanwix in 1768. One of the natural allies of Samuel Wharton was Benjamin Franklin, who kept a close eye on the progress of all speculations in western lands and sought to include himself as a shareholder and political operative in the most promising of all these ventures.[148] Another key speculator with his own network of associates and collaborators in Indian Country was George Croghan, who worked directly for Indian Affairs superintendent Sir William Johnson.[149] In this era, Croghan and Johnson were the indispensable intermediaries between the citizens of Indian Country and those speculative entrepreneurs centred primarily in metropolitan centres including Philadelphia, New York, and London, England.

Johnson set himself the task of negotiating on behalf of the king a treaty that would provide a major new supply of commodity to the land speculators, among whom he himself can be counted. His object was to conduct this negotiation in a manner consistent with the principles of the Royal Proclamation of 1763 and in a way that would demonstrate the dominance in Indian Country of the Six Nations Iroquois. The diplomatic instrument of this power relationship was the Covenant Chain, an institution whose influence he sought to extend in negotiations to readjust the boundary between the Anglo-American colonies and the territory reserved by the king for the Indians as their hunting territory.

At Fort Stanwix in 1768 the agendas of many land speculators converged with those seeking affirmation of the dominance of the imperial government, the Six Nations Iroquois, and the Covenant Chain. There a major Indian treaty was formalized in the presence of over three thousand individuals composing myriad delegations on both the Indian and non-Indian sides. Although the vast tracts of land being given up, comprising much of present-day Kentucky, Tennessee, West Virginia, and western Pennsylvania, were largely the ancestral domain of Shawnee, Delaware, and Cherokee peoples, it was Six Nations representatives who signed the treaty with their clan symbols. Moreover, much of the £10,460 paid for the lands went to Six Nations peoples, who together with their close associate, Sir William Johnson, had successfully advanced their image and reputation, for the time being at least, as the enforcers of a viable peace between Indian Country and the Anglo-American colonies. The Treaty of Fort Stanwix shifted the boundary of the Indian Country of Canada westward to run along the Allegheny and Ohio rivers as far as the mouth of the Tennessee River. The Treaty of Hard Labor and the Treaty of Lochaber brought about a corresponding westward shift in the boundaries of the Indian groups who maintained relations with the southern division of the British Imperial Indian Department.

Although the sacrifice of territory on the Aboriginal side was enormous, one of the seemingly positive outcomes, especially in the north, was to establish a boundary line that corresponded with a clear and identifiable geographic feature, the Ohio River. The Royal Proclamation line might be indistinguishable in many locales without benefit of surveys and markers, but the same could not be said of the largest part of the Fort Stanwix line. In the decades ahead until the peace settlement ending the War of 1812, there would be recurring surges of conviction emanating from both Indian Country and the leadership of British imperial Canada that the Ohio River should be maintained as the fixed boundary of a permanent, internationally recognized Aboriginal dominion.

Johnson's expectation in negotiating the Treaty of Fort Stanwix was that the opening of so much new territory to land speculators would decrease the pressure to extinguish and privatize yet more of the remaining Indian domain. He was wrong. The events of 1768 stimulated rather than stifled a new wave of speculative activity. Near the heart of the action was Samuel Wharton and his growing array of business associates, who had joined the scheme to seek Indian lands in reparation for the losses suffered during the Aboriginal resistance associated with Pontiac. The new vehicle of the plan was the Indiana Company, whose shareholders included George Croghan, Joseph Galloway of Pennsylvania, Governor William Franklin of New Jersey, Benjamin Franklin, as well as the Philadelphia firm of Baynton, Wharton and Morgan.

The Indiana Company succeeded in gaining Six Nations sanction at Fort Stanwix for the principle that this corporation of "suffering traders" should receive the "Indiana grant" as a form of reparation for earlier losses.[150] In 1769 Wharton travelled to London to seek parliamentary approval for the company's Indian-derived land claim. On arrival he began distributing shares to garner political support for the colonizing project. Moreover, he manoeuvred adeptly to disarm opponents by incorporating rival projects, such as those being promoted by George Washington, into his scheme. The resulting complex of commercial and political transactions gave rise to successively bigger and more ambitious schemes, known, respectively, as the Grand Ohio Company and the Walpole Company. At its peak, this corporate and political juggernaut of possessive individualism, based entirely on the prospect of transforming huge tracts of Indian land into real estate, encompassed many of Britain's most powerful and illustrious figures in government and high finance. Among them were Thomas Walpole and Thomas Pownall. Also prominent among the shareholders were the counsellor to the Board of Trade, Richard Jackson; the undersecretary of the Treasury, John Robinson; Postmaster General Anthony Todd; East India Company director Sir George Colebrook; together with Privy Councillors Lord Gower, Lord Rockford, Lord Chamberlain, Lord Hertford, George Grenville, and Lord Camden.[151]

The object of this expanded enterprise was to create a whole new colony named Vandalia in the interior of British North America. While the project's powerful political backers forced the resignation of its major opponent, Colonial Secretary Lord Hillsborough, the scheme began to fall apart after 1772 as disruptions in the Anglo-American colonies dampened the expansionistic enthusiasms in the British government.[152] Wharton responded to this setback by shifting his lobbying efforts on behalf of the Vandalia project to the newly created Continental Congress in Philadelphia. In making this transatlantic shift, Wharton, along with many other land speculators of his ilk, anticipated the rise of a new sovereign authority that would take control of the larger project of expanding an American empire of private property into Indian Country. In moving their lobbying operations from the British parliament to the Continental Congress on the eve of the American Revolution, the land speculators brought to the nascent government a profusion of new thinking on how to liberate corporate expansion by breaching new boundaries of crown property law in the unregulated extinguishment and privatization of Indian Country.

One of the animating urges of many important land speculators in the years immediately before the American Revolution was to challenge those provisions of the Royal Proclamation of 1763 which prohibited Indian groups from selling their lands directly to any party other than the British sovereign. To do so they elaborated calculated arguments that Indian people were invested with a natural right to possess property and a corresponding capacity to sell their interests in their ancestral lands to whomever they might choose. For the advocates of this interpretation, including Samuel Wharton, the king went beyond his jurisdiction in the Royal Proclamation of 1763. It was illegal, they asserted, for the British sovereign to limit Indian "sovereignty" by imposing on them the force of a monarchical monopoly in the purchase of their Aboriginal title. And, it was argued, the king also violated the right of his subjects, both as individuals or as shareholders of corporations, in outlawing their capacity to purchase Indian land titles directly from Indigenous peoples at whatever price they could negotiate.

This embellishment in the criticism of the Royal Proclamation was consistent with the increasingly irrate denunciations of the British monarchy in the prelude to the American Revolution. In 1772 William Trent, a major partner in the Grand Ohio Company, added the gloss of expert authority to the proposition that crown subjects could obtain a valid and perfect title by purchasing land directly from Indian people. The vehicle of this authority was a slightly edited legal opinion given the title of its authors, Lord Camden and Charles York. The Camden-York opinion was initially written in 1757 to cover the situation of the East India Company in its dealings with local leaders in its principal field of operation. The authors postulated, "in respect to such places, as have been or shall be acquired by treaty or grant from the Grand Mogul or any of the Indian princes or governments, your Majesty's letters patent are not necessary, the property of the soil vesting in the grantees of the Indian-grants."[153] Trent revised the text slightly by removing the term, "Grand Mogul." He therefore introduced the impression that the Camden-York opinion applied to North America rather than East India. This view of the opinion was accepted and actively advanced by many land speculators, especially in the Continental Congress. Certainly the existence of the opinion and the inclination of so many British and Anglo-Americans land speculators to see its contents as common sense played a significant role in the decision of William Murray to push ahead with the colonization plans of the Illinois-Wabash Company. Similarly the Camden-York opinion was the instrumental factor in persuading Judge Richard Henderson to put aside the more modest plans of the Louisa Company and to push ahead, instead, the Transylvania project by purchasing land directly in 1775 from a group of compliant Cherokee in the Treaty of Sycamore Shoals.

THE PLACE IN WORLD HISTORY OF THE ROYAL PROCLAMATION AND THE AMERICAN REVOLUTION

In 1996 Edward Countryman attempted to incorporate reflections on the experiences of Indian peoples, together with those of African Americans, into the historiography of the American Revolution's making and outcomes. In this effort he strangely neglected the frequent references to Indigenous peoples in the abundant literature generated by those land speculators seeking to discredit and overturn the constitutional principles outlined in the Royal Proclamation of 1763.[154] This genre of criticism, together with more general reflections on the powerful symbolism embodied in King George's effort to monopolize the conduct of official relations with First Nations in North America's interior, involved some apparently sympathetic consideration of the natural rights of Indigenous peoples.

The underlying motivations for such expressions of sympathy, however, were extremely self-serving. Basically this analysis, advanced by Samuel Wharton and others, dealt with only one dimension of Aboriginal self-determination – the capacity of Indigenous peoples to sell their property according to the rules of market relations in the Anglo-American colonies. There was no serious consideration of the right of Indigenous peoples not to sell their land; their right to opt, instead, to maintain their own legal integrity as free citizens of their own unmolested and territorially secure polities; or their right to situate their own complexes of property relations within jurisdictional and cultural frameworks of their own making rather than within the framework of Anglo-American law.

Nor did the land speculators' attentiveness to the theoretical rights of Indian peoples extend seriously to the idea of protecting their persons, let alone their unceded ancestral lands. On the eve of the American Revolution, George Croghan reported that so many Indians were being murdered by the backwoodsmen of Pennsylvania that it was dangerous for Native people even to come close to the Anglo-American settlements in the area. One of the few murderers actually brought to trial for taking an Indian life, reported Croghan, "thought it a meritorious act to kill Heathens whenever they are found." According to William Johnson, this viewpoint was not an aberration but "the opinion of the common people."[155]

The huge double standards of the Anglo-Americans in dealing with the application of law to Aboriginal people was a source of enormous consternation in Indian Country. In a comment that resonates right up to the present day,[156] Croghan was asked by a group of Delaware how it was that their people were so often killed by whites without anyone being charged, let alone convicted, yet "every little Crime which any [Indians] commited in their drink – was taken great Notice of."[157] Viewing this trend, the Delaware prophet Neolin was heard to have warned his Indian audience that the Anglo-Americans with their diseases and with "their imprisoning you, will totally destroy you."[158]

To understand and appreciate the broader historical significance of the Royal Proclamation of 1763, therefore, the general character of the Anglo-American society into which this pronouncement was delivered needs to be carefully considered. Among the sociological attributes of this society was a marked propensity for frequent murders of Indians by colonists to go unpunished and as well as a pervasive obsession with the hope of capitalizing on the transformation of Indian lands into private property. In *Surviving as Indians: The Challenge of Self-Government*, Menno Boldt provides an assessment of the Royal Proclamation which entirely divorces the document from the life and times of its production. In his otherwise thoughtful and engaging text, Boldt repeatedly dams the proclamation as "villainous" and, "even by the then prevailing standards that then governed European domestic and international relations," as a "corruption of justice." "The Royal Proclamation" he writes, "was uniquely framed to dispossess Indians of their sovereignty and their lands."[159] Without a doubt, the Royal Proclamation embodied a paternalistic attitude to Indian peoples based on Eurocentric assumptions placing the king and his immediate subjects at the pinnacle of elaborate hierarchies of peoples and laws. While its authors did not entirely escape the Eurocentric assumptions of the society that produced them, they did, nevertheless, break new ground in entrenching important principles of human rights whose full implications have yet to be reckoned with in the arena of international law. While the most immediate implications of the Royal Proclamation belong to Canada and the United States by virtue of their shared constitutional roots in British North America, there are global dimensions to this seminal prohibition outlawing acts that would unilaterally dispossess Indigenous peoples of their ancestral lands.

In the Royal Proclamation the central government in the British Empire undertook the legal responsibility to protect the lives, lands, and jurisdictions of Indigenous peoples from non-Indians and their corporate extensions, as well as from the incursions of the local governments in the colonies. These local governments were almost always dominated by interests seeking to expand the frontiers of private property through the extinguishment, absorption, and commodification of Indian Country. On the Indian side there were difficult tradeoffs to contemplate in accepting or rejecting the legal regime set in place by the Royal Proclamation. In accepting the protective role of the central authority as a shield against the incursions of land-hungry colonists and their corporate and governmental extensions, Indian peoples were also accepting a degree of subservience under the central authority of the imperial sovereign. They were accepting some limitations on the principle of Aboriginal sovereignty in favour of forms of imperial trusteeship within the framework of their membership as distinct peoples within the British Empire.[160]

Almost invariably this form of trusteeship was grossly abused in the process of devolving powers in the British Empire. Throughout this process, responsibility for safeguarding the rights and titles of Indigenous peoples was folded into sweeping delegations of constitutional power away from the imperial centre. The result was that Indigenous peoples in both the United States and Britain's "White Dominions" – Canada, Australia, New Zealand, and South Africa – were transformed from allies of the Crown into wards of the state. As wards they were precluded from voting or running for elected office in the non-Aboriginal systems of self-governance. Moreover, they were precluded from making contracts, participating in land markets, and obtaining ready access to pursue civil litigation in the courts. In other words, they were subjected to the unmediated control of precisely that genre of local government against whose incursions the Royal Proclamation was originally meant to be a shield.

This outcome continued a persistent pattern that has made the Royal Proclamation, since its inception, the basis of a kind schizophrenic regime – one where there has been considerable distance between the theory and practise of crown law. The nature of this regime was very evident in Canada, for instance, after the main constitutional instrument of Confederation was patriated from Great Britain in 1982. In section 25 of that act, wherein the British parliament granted to the parliament and provincial legislatures of Canada authority to amend the Canadian Constitution, the binding nature of the Royal Proclamation of 1763 was declared.

The unsevered character of the Royal Proclamation's recognition of the existence of Aboriginal title was given further substance in section 35 of the patriation enactment, where the existence of Aboriginal and treaty rights was recognized and affirmed. In spite of that recognition, however, the Canadian government generally sided with the provincial governments in pushing to negate the principles declared in section 35 by presenting arguments in court whose intent was effectively to extinguish and negate, rather than recognize and affirm, the existence of Aboriginal and treaty rights. Similarly, in the making of modern-day treaties with the First Nations of Canada beginning in 1975, the Canadian government continued to seek provisions based on the principle of extinguishing rather than recognizing and affirming the existence of Aboriginal title. In so doing, the Canadian government blatantly violated its fiduciary responsibilities by pressuring Aboriginal groups to extinguish their Aboriginal titles rather than seeking ways to negotiate practical means whereby Indigenous peoples could exercise their Aboriginal titles with due regard for the rights and titles of other groups and individuals. This exercise of Aboriginal title might be expressed, for instance, in the investment of new taxing powers in edified regimes of Aboriginal government that are accountable to their own constituents. Or it might be expressed in the development of more pluralistic arrays of property law that include the power of Aboriginal governments to charter corporate entities designed to give new form to old traditions of culture and custom.

Nevertheless, the very persistence of treaty making in Canada, but especially in the contested ground of British Columbia, is a testament to the continuing relevance of the legal principles articulated by King George as he and his advisers struggled to apply what they understood as the main lessons of the Seven Years' War. In specifying the necessity of obtaining Indian consent for any change in the legal status of their protected Aboriginal lands, the authors of the Royal Proclamation broached the subject, however tentatively, of the need to respect the democratic rights of the citizens of Indian Country to a say in determining their own destiny. This provision suggests the importance of bringing about modifications in the terms of relationships between peoples through negotiated settlements rather than through unilaterally imposed dictates. The reference to the need to conduct all land transactions in "public meetings" points to the need for transparency, so that citizens on both sides of the moving boundaries of Indian Country could have the opportunity to see and understand what is being done on their behalf.

While it is important to give close attention to these emanations of enlightenment in the Royal Proclamation, it is also vital to see the dark side of a document that both reflected and codified many of the gross inequities of power that constituted the essence of empire building and imperialism in eighteenth-century North America. The Royal Proclamation is mired in the ethnocentricism that was the most characteristic attribute of Europe's aggressive expansion in the post-Columbian era, even as there are elements within it that reflect the more redeeming features of Enlightenment thought. Seen in this light, those provisions pointing towards recognition of the democratic rights of Indigenous peoples mark a significant breakthrough pointing towards a more humane and ecologically sensitive form of statecraft.

Thus, the Royal Proclamation of 1763 can be seen as a significant marker in the broadening stream of recognition that *all* human beings and peoples are entitled to the protections of a rule of law which recognizes and affirms their individual and collective rights to life, liberty, and the pursuit of happiness. It can be seen as one of the juridical and inspirational sources of the principles articulated by President Woodrow Wilson in engaging the military power of the United States in the First World War. In seeking to clarify his country's opposition to imperialism in any form, he outlined a vision of global geopolitics based on the starting principle that all peoples, small or large, rich or poor, have a right of self-determination.

One way to conceptualize the inherent rights of all peoples to their own place is through a more expansive global application of the principles entailed in the idea of Aboriginal title. After all, the decolonization of old imperial systems, especially after the Second World War, can easily be interpreted as a form of recognition that Indigenous peoples retained an unextinguished title in themselves and in the lands of their ancestors in spite of several generations of colonial rule. Aboriginal title can be understood, therefore, as a continuing inheritance of history that has survived, along with the Indigenous peoples in whom it is collectively vested, the extinguishing force of the Columbian conquests that began in 1492.

The Declaration of Independence is certainly one of the most important documents articulating the urge to synthesize both empire building and decolonization, two of the most important impulses that characterize large aspects of the human condition over the second half of the last millennium. As we have seen, the declaration's affirmation of the inalienable right to pursue happiness was drawn from Locke's ideas about the centrality of the institution of private property in state formation. Locke's vision of the construction of property gave legitimizing force to the appropriation of Indian lands as the seed capital for England's rise to global influence through the making and expansion of colonies in North America.

If the old dichotomy raised in the Declaration of Independence between "men" and "savages" is to be transcended, the seminal principles outlined in the Royal Proclamation need to be extended towards new frontiers of decolonization. Only in this way can the principle be acted upon that the world's diverse peoples have an inherent right to pursue their own eclectic visions of happiness through instituting various regimes of property relations that are supportive and reflective of their own distinctive Aboriginal cultures. To advance towards the reciprocal pluralism of the Fourth World, our notion of human rights will have to expand into new frontiers of ecology as people and peoples seek new means to fend off the forces of monculturalism that are severely impoverishing the planet's store of biological, cultural, and linguistic diversity. There are parallels, then, between the Royal Proclamation of 1763 and the acts that abolished slavery, extended the franchise to women, or secured the right of collective bargaining. While the formal end to the institution of slavery, for instance, pointed the way towards the liberation of those suffering under its burden, abolition alone was not enough to bring about true equality between peoples previously subjected to such dramatically different treatment under the rule of racist laws. The fact that it was often the slave owners, rather than the former slaves, who were compensated for the transformations brought about by abolition pointed the way to many new inequities to come. In a similar fashion the limited and qualified recognitions afforded to Indigenous peoples in the Royal Proclamation pointed the way towards, yet did not adequately fulfil, a truly just and comprehensive regime for the realization of Aboriginal and treaty rights.

There are more than a few ironies in advancing an image of the Royal Proclamation, in many ways a quintessential expression of eighteenth-century British imperialism, as a purveyor of Enlightenment thought and as a marker pointing the way to what George Manuel termed the Fourth World. Many of these ironies emerge from the fact that the proclamation came to symbolize for some extremely influential figures the monarchical tyranny against which one of the archetypal events of the European Enlightenment – the American Revolution – was fought. The outbreak of this revolutionary war along the unstable boundaries of Indian Country and along the ideological fault lines of a profound schism in British imperialism speaks to the complexities of meaning in the emergence of the New World empire of the United States from the Old World empire that was its parent.

Ultimately the American Revolution looms as too large an event in human affairs to be patented and enclosed as a monopolistic intellectual property belonging to the developers of any single historical interpretation.[161] As an episode at the epicentre of so many vast and pervasive forces in human thought and social experimentation, the creation of the United States is a project with simply too many facets to be explained or contained within the framework of arithmetic calculations on either the plus or minus side of any single moral ledger. The outcome of the American Revolution was to prove so important to the history of all the world's peoples that it would be unseemly to characterize the event with any single ethical judgment.

Notions of liberty and freedom are such vital, fragile, and elusive ideals that they deserve to be weighed seriously whenever they are proclaimed. Too much is at stake to dismiss the claims and assertions of any self-declared freedom fighters, including the founding fathers of the United States. If they sometimes failed to realize, or even betrayed, the high-minded conceptions they articulated, it remains for us to act assertively on those aspects of Enlightenment thought that projected a beacon of universal liberty for humankind on the horizons of our shared global destiny. The challenges posed by Kondiaronk, Pontiac, Tecumseh, Grey Owl, George Manuel, and even by King George in the Royal Proclamation still remain to be grappled with seriously in extending the inspiration of Enlightenment and Fourth World thought to the ecology and architecture of human society.

The American Revolution was a complex event animated by individuals whose moral compasses pointed in many different directions. Without a doubt, however, a forensic focus on the event as the prelude and facilitator of one of the hugest land grabs in human history imbues this moment with large and continuing implications for every human being – indeed for every living organism – on the planet. In the act of pushing aside the structures of crown laws and institutions that provided even a porous and flimsy edifice for the protection of Indian Country, the makers of the American Revolution crossed a major threshold in a process of privatizing and enclosing the global commons. They moved assertively to expand the ideological boundaries of the English Revolution into an American Revolution whose ultimate aim was to create a new global framework to widen the Lockean frontiers of a New World empire of possessive individualism. As Countryman has written in his assessment of the American Revolution as a "disaster" for Indigenous peoples, "the western land that Indians held on their own terms under the old order became the huge trove of free capital that was the basis for the young republic's commercial agricultural expansion, north and south alike."[162]

The Royal Proclamation acquires a significant place in world history as the document at the symbolic core of those crown institutions the American revolutionaries sought to extinguish in their rush to liberate their own expansionary freedoms through the quick acquisition and privatization of Indian Country. It emerges as a kind of constitutional antithesis in the process of first imagining and then inventing the United States. The British subjects on both sides of the Atlantic who criticized the Royal Proclamation did so from an entirely different base of assumptions than Menno Boldt. These critics were preoccupied with the limitations it placed on Anglo-Americans rather than the Indians. They rejected the idea of a protected region in North America of shared Aboriginal and imperial control, and they rejected the Royal Proclamation because it went too far towards the recognition of Aboriginal rights.

In 1781 the irrepressible Samuel Wharton developed this perspective more fully in a pamphlet entitled *Plain Facts: Being an Examination into the Rights of the Indian Nations in America.* The purpose of this pamphlet was, in the first instance, to persuade delegates in the Continental Congress that the Indiana grant made by the Six Nations to the Indiana Company at Fort Stanwix in 1768 should be recognized. More generally, Wharton sought to ground the new republic in the principle that land titles purchased from Indian people would be recognized as valid. In making this assertion, he had allies as well as enemies in the Continental Congress. His opponents were composed largely of coalitions of competing land speculators, especially from the old dominion of Virginia, who had staked their claims in the west on the expectation of some sort of continuity in the transatlantic passing from the crown of rights to colonize and assert good title on the frontiers of non-Indian settlement.[163]

The conception of Aboriginal rights advanced by Wharton and by others was based on the notion that Indian people could be made to conform to the Lockean grids of land enclosures, private property, and possessive individualism that formed the material and ideological basis of the American Revolution. When efforts were made to turn this theory into actual practice, as happened often in that era, the outcome most often was for land speculators to cultivate a few compliant Indians to receive what amounted to bribes so that they would sign land transfer agreements on behalf of large numbers of First Nations people. In other words, what most often took place in these land purchases were transactions whereby a very few Native individuals were enriched personally as they signed away and privatized land rights that, in reality, were collectively held. This process of overcoming the resistance of Indigenous peoples through an elaborate process of bribing, demoralization, and co-opting Aboriginal leadership would become the preferred means of extinguishing Aboriginal title and expanding the empire of possessive individualism along one frontier after the next. Indeed, this process of informal colonization through the very deliberate cultivation of huge class differences within Aboriginal societies would become the hallmark of the American empire along its ascent from continental to hemispheric to global proportions.

The Camden-York opinion, which seemed to assert a limited form of sovereignty for Indigenous peoples, illustrated that the culture of possessive individualism in Indian Country was often defended in the language of Aboriginal rights. Among the most committed patriots of Indian Country, however, the preferred tactics of men like Samuel Wharton, William Murray, or Judge Richard Henderson were correctly perceived as the most insidious and corrosive means of destroying the First Nations. The subsequent rise of Tecumseh to influence among the people and peoples of many Indian nations was largely based on a wave of hostility against all those in the Native comprador class who were responsible for advancing the break-up of the Aboriginal commons – as frequently symbolized in pictorial representations of a bowl with one spoon.

The point of view of the land speculators in pre-revolutionary British North America was compellingly and sympathetically presented by Clarence Walworth Alvord in 1917 in *The Mississippi Valley in British Politics: A Study of Trade, Land Speculation, and Experiments in Imperialism Culminating in the American Revolution*. This two-volume publication systematically condemns the Royal Proclamation, though for radically different reasons from those of Menno Boldt.[164] Alvord was one of the most erudite and creative of that school of American historians whose work was inspired and guided by the frontier theory of Frederick Jackson Turner. He continued the search for the spirit of the American frontier, a place Turner had previously defined as the meeting ground of "savagery and civilization" as well as "the line of most rapid and effective Americanization."[165] This search took the mid-western scholar to England for research in the papers of Lord Shelburne, a close contemporary and colleague of Benjamin Franklin and a major directing force in the success and expansion of the American empire of private property. Alvord's ringing endorsements of the ideas and visions that animated the land speculators vividly illustrates how important their conceptions have been in shaping the ethos of the continuing American Revolution.

This continuing revolution can be conceived as the line of most rapid and effective privatization of the global commons, a movement through world history which was to broaden the monocultural motifs of Lockean possessive individualism. Alvord's interpretive metaphors eloquently embody the frontier-breaching aggressions that gave rise to the expansionary career of the United States. Accordingly, he represents a fitting personification of the forces and influences against which Tecumseh and George Manuel aligned themselves in their respective defences of Indian Country and of the Fourth World. Alvord demonstrated how the fundamental division in British imperialism before 1776 was based largely on two opposing orientations to the rights and titles of Indigenous peoples beyond the Appalachians. His reading of this conflict is founded in pure Social Darwinism. In drafting his assessment of the role of land speculators as agents of revolutionary change, Alvord asserted that North America represented the great prototype of economic development and political organization for that part of humanity who deserved a place in the future. Among the first peoples who had to be moved aside or eliminated to make way for the expansion of the emergent American way of life were the peoples indigenous to the eastern half of the Mississippi Valley. Their displacement, he argued, was a realization of "the inexorable forces of nature." He added, "the logic of history was fulfilled in the occupation by the better endowed people of the territory so inadequately utilized by the inferior race."[166]

Alvord characterized the imperial opponents of the US founders as unrealistic and visionless individuals who failed to grasp the essence of the predominant North American experiment in political economy. In fact, however, the constituencies who opposed the revolutionary Americans established the foundations of a second transcontinental nation-state on the continent. While this other sea-to-sea country, Canada, has lacked the commercial dynamism and expansionary zeal of the United States, its more easy embrace of multiculturalism from its more conservative inheritance in British imperialism may yet emerge in the new millennium as a decided advantage.[167]

The heroes of Alvord's well-chronicled drama are Lord Shelburne and Benjamin Franklin, two politicians who, he demonstrated, co-operated closely in all manner of speculative schemes to open the Indian Country of Canada to Anglo-American settlement. Like "prophets," both men had "caught a vision of the inexorable march of white men across the American continent." They were both among the "advance guard" of politicians, speculators, and pioneers who foresaw "that mighty host of emigrants which was to march with irresistible force across the great inland valley, scale the Rocky Mountains and take possession of the West."[168]

According to Alvord, the axis of understanding between Lord Shelburne and Benjamin Franklin was most instrumental in the outcome of the Treaty of Paris, which formally ended the American Revolution in 1783. A major feature of the agreement was to establish a new international boundary along the Great Lakes. This part of the bargain, which gave the new republic a large part of the Indian country of Canada, was calculated to entice the United States away from its French allies. Commenting on the agreement in a paper he delivered before the British Academy in 1924, Avord exclaimed, "The bribe was magnificent." He continued, "The giving and taking of it belong to the realm of high finance, not petty crimes"[169] If, as Tom Paine claimed, land was "the natural funds of America," then the Treaty of Paris enabled the United States to begin its journey in world history with a huge reserve of capital to be mortgaged against the possibility of yet further expansion. But whose lands had been offered in this bribe to draw the new republic into closer and more harmonious relations with Great Britain? By what right did the government of Britain hand over these properties to a foreign country, albeit a foreign country whose grant of legitimacy a future US Supreme Court would deem was derived ultimately from the British crown? How could it be that the British government handed over to the United States the vast territories north of Ohio River, the very lands that the king's agent, Sir William Johnson, had contracted directly on the British sovereign's behalf to reserve and protect as an Indian hunting ground? How could the Treaty of Paris of 1783 so flagrantly violate the terms of the Treaty of Fort Stanwix of 1768?

More vicerally, how could this great betrayal of so many of the crown's Aboriginal allies in the American Revolution be justified or explained?

Until the termination of the War of 1812, controversy over the nature and legitimacy of the land transfer in 1783 would become one of the central points of dispute between Great Britain, the United States, and the Indigenous peoples of the North American interior. This contention would come to lie at the centre of the uncertainty over the legal status to be afforded the Indian Confederacy of Canada and, by implication, to all the Indigenous peoples of the New World at the high tables of international diplomacy and international law.

Notwithstanding the years of sporadic conflict culminating in the War of 1812, the new North American boundaries created in 1783 resisted all efforts to make the Ohio River the marker of a permanent Aboriginal dominion in the continent's interior. The transfer of the richest part of the Indian Country of Canada from the old British Empire to the nascent American empire affirmed a transatlantic familial affinity that would persist and grow into a new form of global manifest destiny – one Kevin Phillips would describe at the end of the twentieth century as "the triumph of Anglo-America."[170]

UNIVERSALITY AND THE GLOBALIZATION
OF THE AMERICAN EMPIRE

Before 1776 the Anglo-American colonists of British North America were important contributors to the building and expansion of the British Empire. The magnitude of this infusion of Anglo-American energy into the building and expansion of the British Empire reached a climax during the Seven Years' War, an enormous mobilization of imperial activity culminating in the incorporation of Canada into British North America.

After the peace settlement of 1763, many of the Anglo-American settlers watched with dismay as British imperialists went about co-opting and incorporating into their global geopolitical system many former enemies whose identity is captured in the name the Americans apply to this conflict: the French and Indian War. In incorporating the citizens of French-Aboriginal Canada into the economic and constitutional structures of the British Empire, the architects of British imperialism re-enacted and refined a similar scenario to the one that, a century earlier, transformed New Netherlands into New York. Part of this colonial transformation entailed co-optation of that complex of Dutch-Aboriginal alliances which were incorporated and modified in the British Empire as the basis of the Covenant Chain.

Through their revolt from Great Britain in the American Revolution, the more powerful constituencies of Anglo-Americans sought to break away from the parental authority of an empire they had been instrumental in creating. They did so largely to take more direct, unmediated control of their own empire of western expansion.[171] They sought to conquer, co-opt, colonize, relocate, or extinguish Indigenous peoples on their own western frontiers in a more aggressive fashion than the Old World imperialism that had shaped their orientation to their adopted hemisphere. As Richard W. Van Alstyne first observed in 1960 in *The Rising of the American Empire*, the leaders of the nascent American republic quickly adopted the language of imperialism in describing the objects of their new polity. In fact, the title of his book comes directly from the words of George Washington, a former British general, a speculator in Indian lands, and the first president of the United States. Van Alstyne wrote that Washington's vision of the rising American empire accurately described what he and many of his fellow citizens had in mind – "an *imperium* – a dominion, state or sovereignty that would expand in population and territory, and increase in strength and power."[172]

Indian Country provided the first frontiers for the emergence of the nascent American empire from the British Empire and from the American republic. The United States moved quickly from a seminal test of its military muscle in the War of 1812 to clarify the hemispheric dimensions of its imperial aspirations in the Monroe Doctrine of 1823 and in the developing enthusiasms for territorial expansion that went by the name of "manifest destiny."[173] In Cuba and in the Philippines at the turn of the century, the United States continued a long process of moving into the imperial vacuum left by the shrinkage of the Spanish Empire. When the United States tried to move after 1954 into the vacuum left by the shrinkage of the French Empire in Vietnam, the American empire met the most intense domestic crisis of its history.[174]

The American empire revealed its nature most clearly in many covert and overt operations in Central America and the Caribbean during the early decades of the twentieth century. It was the American Marine Corps that first cynically dubbed these myriad operations as the Banana Wars, a name that has stuck.[175] While these episodes in the expansion of the American empire re-enacted on a different scale many of the same patterns that first arose in the conquest, subjugation, or co-optation of Indian Country, it was not until the decades following the Second World War that the ironies and paradoxes of the American empire were exposed on a global scale. The contrast between the assessments of President John F. Kennedy and British historian Arnold Toynbee during the height of the Cold War highlighted the paradoxes permeating the role of the United States in the global community. Those paradoxes arose from the simultaneous identity of the United States as the first successor state of a European empire – as the world's prototype of decolonization – and as the centre of a new kind of commercial and military empire. The imagery of the United States as the world's pioneer leading the way along the road of decolonization and democracy was invoked by Kennedy during the presidential campaign of 1960. He declared, "The cause of all mankind is the cause of America ... We are responsible for the maintenance of freedom all around the world."[176]

This interpretation of the US role on the planet contrasted dramatically with the interpretation delivered by Toynbee at an American university in 1961: "America is today the leader of a world-wide anti-revolutionary movement in defence of vested interests. She now stands for what Rome stood for. Rome consistently supported the rich against the poor in all foreign communities that fell under her sway; and since the poor, so far, have always and everywhere been more numerous than the rich, Rome's policy made for inequality, for injustice, and for the least happiness of the greatest number. America's decision to adopt Rome's role has been deliberate, if I gauged it right."[177] Both Toynbee's and Kennedy's view took as their major point of reference those justifications for the American empire derived from the rise of the Soviet Union as the mirrored superpower to the United States in the Cold War.[178] During this era the US government ascribed both the details and the grand outlines of its foreign policy to its leadership in a global crusade. Beginning with the presidency of Harry Truman, the "the world-wide Soviet Communist conspiracy" was the perceived threat against which this crusade was directed. The extent of the US international interventions transacted in the name of containing or combating this "conspiracy" is almost beyond imagination. It could involve everything from a campaign of psychological warfare waged against the Communist Party of Italy[179] to engineering the transfers of power in the wake of Belgium's withdrawal from the Congo.[180]

As part of these operations, the US Central Intelligence Agency engineered a *coup d'état* in Guatemala in 1954 against the democratically elected government of Jacabo Arbentz.[181] The American decision to overthrow the Arbenz regime was based on the State Department's assessment that it had undermined through land reform the dominant role of the United Fruit Company in Guatemala's economy. As a result of Arbentz's reforms, asserted Piero Gleijes, "for the first time in the history of Guatemala, the Indians were offered land rather than being robbed of it."[182] There was no allegation that Arbenz was himself a communist. From the perspective of the US State Department, his perceived crime was that his government "implicitly accepts the Communists as an authentic political party and not as part of the world-wide Soviet Communist conspiracy."[183] The intervention of the Central Intelligence Agency (CIA) to impose a military dictatorship contributed to the genesis of a lethal civil war in Guatemala that saw US-backed military regimes commit mass executions of civilians, including many tens of thousands of Mayan peasant farmers. The violence reached especially ruthless extremes in the mid–1980s, when 440 villages were entirely destroyed, more than a million refugees were uprooted, and about 200,000 people, most of them Maya Indians, were outright killed by death squads.[184] As with most of the atrocities on the long list of crimes against humanity committed by US-backed puppet regimes in Latin America, the School of the Americas in Fort Benning, Georgia, provided much of the military training for those in charge of Guatemala's genocide campaign.[185]

Some of the worst atrocities occurred during the regimes of Guatemalan president General Efrain Rios Montt and US president Ronald Reagan. The Reagan government's support for right-wing regimes throughout Central and South America was so unqualified that, in 1983, it described Amnesty International's condemnations of their propensities for murder and torture as a "Communist-backed disinformation plan."[186] Reagan himself told the world that General Montt had received a "bum rap" just as the systematic murder, torture, and rape in Guatemala was reaching its most violent extremes.[187] When the atrocities of the Guatemala government were condemned in a United Nations resolution in December 1982, only the United States, Argentina, Chile, Israel, El Salvador, the Philippines, and Haiti voted against that motion.

The strategy to aim much of the counter-insurgency violence at Maya communities was purposeful and systematic. In the eyes of Susanne Jonas, the Guatemalan war "took on the character of an assault by the ladino state against the Indian population."[188] In *Petrotyranny*, John Bacher characterized the debacle as "ethnic cleansing for the [American] oil industry."[189] Another explanation was penned by Cultural Survival's David Maybury-Lewis. In accounting for this "genocide" in the colonial hinterland of the American empire of private property, he wrote in the early 1980s during the height of the atrocities, "even Indians who are apolitical are perceived as a threat to the regime, since it is clear they have a grievance. It is the centuries of injustice done to them which makes them a threat. But the presence of Indians, even their self-consciousness, in both Guatemala and the Andean countries does not so much threaten the state as it does the profoundly inequitable relations within the state."[190]

Complaints arose even from within the Guatemalan government about how the Cold War was exploited as a pretext simply to advance the interests of the rich at the expense of the poor – to recreate in the American empire the same biases that Toynbee attributed also to the Roman Empire. The source of that complaint was Hector Gramajo, the Guatemalan defence minister in 1987. At a meeting where a wealthy land owner urged the US-trained military to get on with its campaign of counter-insurgency, a frustrated Gramajo is reported to have exclaimed, "You people have been asking us to kill your Marxists for you for the past four hundred years."[191]

What is to be made of this image of a four-hundred-year campaign against a political ideology that Karl Marx and Frederich Engels did not formulate until the middle decades of the nineteeth century? The inference to be drawn is that the Cold War provided a cover for many raw assertions of American economic interests that were usually defined in terms of the global profitability and viability of US-based corporations. The Indian wars of North America have been more seminally influential than the geopolitical calculations of the Cold War in shaping the ascendant form of the American empire as the predominant instrument and expression of globalization. In this scheme of historical interpretation, the United Fruit Company can be seen as emblematic of a kind of successor enterprise that realized some of the same genre of aspirations that led to the formation and activities of the land speculation companies in pre-revolutionary British North America. Indeed, the importance of these corporate vehicles of land speculation in helping to foment the civil war that divided British North America serves as a prelude or even a model for the shape of things to come in the worldwide genesis of the American empire. The formative encounter that most influenced the underlying character of this empire was not so much the wars with Great Britain. It was, rather, the encounters with the Indigenous peoples, including the many Indian wars that preceded, accompanied, and followed the American War of Independence. As Reginald Horsman has written in *Race and Manifest Destiny*, "In dealing with the Indians the United States began to formulate a rationale of expansion which was readily adaptable to the needs of an advance over other peoples and to a world role."[192]

The cyclone of pressures and events that whirled around Pontiac during the last decade of his life were highly suggestive of the coming patterns of resistance, co-optation, and assassination in building and expanding the empire of possessive individualism. Similarly, the cycles of bribery and intimidation aimed at cultivating a class of Native compradors on the American frontier was especially influential in creating the climate of hostility in which the pan-Indian movement spearheaded by Tecumseh arose.

Tecumseh's struggle against the expansion of the American empire into Indian Country started with an internal crusade. The object of that self-policing within Indian Country was to end the wholesale selling of Indian lands and Indian resources to agents of the United States largely through the covert device of secret payoffs to corrupt Indian individuals. As Tecumseh, the Indian sovereigntist, well understood, these compradors were in the process of forming a propped-up class of collaborators who would derive personal advantages for themselves and their families by facilitating federal control of the remaining Indian Country through the political expedient of indirect rule. The agents of the American empire had much to learn from witnessing the potency among his own peoples of Tecumseh's protest against those Indian traitors who had enriched themselves personally by selling away the collective rights and titles of the First Nations. The lessons learned from fighting this Aboriginal resistance movement were eagerly seized upon after the War of 1812, when the US government began its career of infiltrating and redirecting different freedom struggles beyond its territorial boundaries.

From Latin America to Haiti to Saudi Arabia to Iran to Indonesia and to Central Africa, the US government, along with its corporate clients, built upon the American republic's earlier experience of how to turn decolonization into a dynamo for their own empire building.[193] No rising Tecumsehs would be permitted to overcome the propped-up, comprador elites who were deemed most favourable towards, and most emblematic of, the great disparities of wealth that have become the most consistent hallmark of the empire of possessive individualism. Indeed, the atheistic communism that was the official doctrine of the Soviet Empire served only to invest the institution of private property with a more potent religious symbolism in the life of the older, revolutionary empire founded in 1776. The imperial heartland of this American empire uniquely combined the zealotry of the Reformation with the secular prestige of the Enlightenment.

In spite of its idealization of the principle of *E Pluribus Unum,* a country as big, as rich, and as free wheeling as the United States has at times given rise to genuinely pluralistic political cultures. For instance, President Woodrow Wilson's international bid to remake the world order to integrate the self-determination of all peoples arose from the context of an earlier contest with Teddy Roosevelt and the Progressive Movement. That movement had coalesced around the convictions of many Americans that significant remedies were required to limit the power of business cartels and industrial monopolies that concentrated so much power in so few hands. During the Great Depression of the 1930s, Franklin D. Roosevelt won the presidency and proceeded to moderate with his New Deal the most devastating inequities generated by unregulated, laissez-faire capitalism. Included in Roosevelt's program of social and economic reform was an especially innovative Indian New Deal overseen by social activist John Collier. Collier's rejection of the assimilationist assumptions of Indian policy anticipated a looming debate that would see the old melting-pot symbolism of the American nation increasingly called into question. The alternative posed to the American melting pot was official multiculturalism, an option that some Americans welcomed as the domestic equivalent of the global movement for decolonization after the Second World War.[194]

In the heartland of the American empire, therefore, domestic politics have been a site of considerable contention. Indeed, during the second half of the nineteenth century that contention became manifest in one of history's most bitter and lethal civil wars. What has been consistent, however, is the straight line of policy with regard to the frontier expansions and foreign policies of those polities leading up to, including, and emanating from the United States of America. Edward Said has commented on the apparent consistency of this American stance towards the non-European world in reflecting on the United States's hostility to Arab culture, generally, and to the Iraqi regime of Saddam Hussein, in particular. The US-led attack of UN forces on this regime was dubbed by President George Bush Sr in 1991 as an illustration of the existence of a "New World Order." In describing the uncritical reporting of this military action, Said mused that "Arabs are only an attenuated recent example of the Other who have incurred the wrath of a stern White Man, a kind of Puritan superego whose errand into the wilderness knows few boundaries and who will go to great lengths to make his points."[195]

After the United States emerged from the destruction of Europe in the Second World War as the planet's most powerful nation,[196] the proliferation of new nation-states and international agencies created the impression that humanity was governed by what Adlai Stevenson described as "a pluralistic world order."[197] The United States helped to advance this impression by situating much of its military strength in Europe within the framework of the North Atlantic Treaty Organization. It similarly cloaked some of its financial clout in the World Bank and the International Monetary Fund organizations that emerged from the conference at Bretton Woods in 1944. In 1988 the Free Trade Agreement between Canada and the United States ushered in a new era of global trade deals, leading to the transformation of the General Agreement on Tariffs and Trade into the World Trade Organization in 1995.

While the broad franchise of national memberships in many of these organizations has been calculated to convey the sense that democracy, the rule of law, and pluralism were alive and well in the international community, even such elaborate institutional ornaments could only thinly disguise the vast clout of the United States government in world affairs. As early as 1972 Richard Barnet commented on the global scope of American military and political supremacy, including over China and the Soviet Union. "Uniquely blessed with surpassing riches and an exceptional history," Barnet wrote, the United States "stands above the international system, not within it. Supreme among nations, she stands ready to be the bearer of the Law."[198] At the crucible of this would-be universal law of the American empire is capitalism and the Lockean ideals of private property. From the ascent of New England to the ascent of the World Trade Organization, the one constant of this continuum of expansionism has been to remove space for the existence of alternative systems of property relations and property law.

It is the consistency of this quest to achieve a universal framework for economic relationships that marks the continuities linking, for instance, the American treatment of the "Red Indians" on its geographic frontiers and the American treatment of Red communists on its ideological frontiers. The consistent aim has been to deprive space on the planet for the maintenance and renewal of any system or systems of economic relationship which hold alternatives to the Lockean ideals that animate the American empire of private property. It is the overwhelmingly successful fulfilment of this single aim which is leading to the global impoverishment of cultural pluralism and biodiversity as well as the corresponding monopolization of monocultures.

Anthony Pagden concluded *Lords of All the World* with some reflections on the persistence of the universalist assumptions that were exported from Europe to the rest of the planet beginning in 1492. The monotheistic convictions of Christianity were initially a primary medium and product of this export. It seems, however, that the new monotheism on the advancing frontiers of the ongoing Columbian conquests is faith in the omnipotence of capitalism. Here, the convergence of ideas, attitudes, and laws that constitute capitalism are said to express a universal natural law rather than a manifestation of several local histories that merged with particular force in the creation and expansion of the United States. Pagden writes:

But the price of joining the new world order – now represented by international monetary organizations – is still the willingness to live by a law whose force is assumed to be not, as is all other legislation, local, but universal. It is marked, too, by the claims that the premises upon which this law are based are self-evident. They require no explanation, much less defence, and they are, by their very nature, applicable to all peoples everywhere ... The modern moral, cultural and political worlds we currently inhabit are all, in the first instance, the creation of the Enlightenment, and the Enlightenment was, perhaps more than has been recognized, the product of a world which was in the process of ridding itself of the first – although by no means, alas, its last – imperial legacy.[199]

CHAPTER FIVE

The Bowl with One Spoon

The Great Spirit gave this great island to his red children; he
placed the whites on the other side of the big water; they were
not contented with their own, but came to take ours from us.
They have driven us from the sea to the lakes: we can go no
further. They have taken upon them to say, this tract belongs to
the Miamis, this to the Delawares, and so on; but the Great Spirit
intended it as the common property of us all. Our father tells us,
that we have no business upon the Wabash, the land belongs to
other tribes; but the Great Spirit ordered us to come here, and
here we will stay.
    The Prophet's Speech to Governor Harrison in Benjamin Drake,
        Life of Tecumseh, and of His Brother The Prophet, 1858

THE NORTHWEST TERRITORIES
IN THE TRANSFORMATION OF INDIAN COUNTRY INTO
NORTH AMERICAN STATES AND PROVINCES

The centrality of Indian Affairs in the genesis of property law and federalism in both Canada and the United States is nowhere so clearly convergent
as in the history of the territory north of the Ohio River and south of the
Great Lakes in the three decades following the end of the American Revolution. This contested ground was the site of three widely differing
geopolitical visions: that of the indigenous peoples, of the fur-trade interests of British imperial Canada, and of the victors of the American War of
Independence.

The vision that would later prevail was the one shared by most citizens of
the United States. For them, this region was the major prize of victory for
having emerged successfully from the American Revolution. Under their
influence, the region north of the Ohio River became the archetypal frontier – indeed, the prototypical experiment – of national expansion. It
became the first of many regions in North America that were transformed
into internal colonies of federal authority. After its establishment in 1867,
the dominion government of Canada would copy this model in extending
its jurisdictional reach into the part of North America that formerly had
been both a pluralistic Indian Country and the fur-trade preserve of the
Hudson's Bay Company. The creation of the Northwest Territory by the US
government in 1787, therefore, was the first such action to be followed by

the establishment of many more federal territories in both the United
States and Canada. Among these federal territories has been a series of
jurisdictions, covering shifting portions of the continent, which, at one time
or another, have been called the Northwest Territories. This name persists
on the map of North America until the present day. Hence, in a very real
sense, the first Northwest Territory north of the Ohio is the constitutional
parent of today's Northwest Territories in Canada's western Arctic.

The legal instrument that created the first Northwest Territory was the
Northwest Ordinance of 1787. Although it was a legislative, rather than
constitutional, instrument of the US government, it acquired over time a
kind of mystique, giving it the aura of one of the republic's supreme laws.[1]
According to Goldwin Smith, one of the foremost proponents in the late
nineteenth century of continental integration, the Northwest Ordinance
was "second in importance only to the constitution,"[2] which emerged that
same year from the famous convention in Philadelphia. Similarly, in the
eyes of Stephen A. Ambrose, a chronicler of Thomas Jefferson's role in US
westward expansion, the Northwest Ordinance was as "revolutionary a document as the Declaration of Independence."[3]

The Northwest Ordinance formalized the answer to one of the central
controversies that divided the makers of the new republic in the era of the
American Revolution. By placing sole responsibility for the conduct of
relations with Indian nations in the jurisdictional sphere of the central government, the framers determined that the federal authority, as opposed to
the state governments, would acquire sole jurisdiction over westward
expansion. As a result, the US central government began to emerge as pre-
eminent over state authorities. Thus the governing bodies of the original
Anglo-American colonies finally accepted, in their new-found sovereignty,
some of the huge constraints earlier imposed on their ambitions by the
Royal Proclamation of 1763. The most prominent of these constraints was
that the original states along the Atlantic seabord would have fixed western boundaries.

The other side of the limitations placed on state jurisdiction was that the
new federal government acquired the power to carve out states from what
was deemed to be the "public domain" beyond these clarified boundaries
of the original Anglo-American colonies. Hence the republic's young capital city, whose site was chosen by Congress in 1790, became the primary
centre in the United States where the private profit to be derived from the
legal transmutation of the American earth would be apportioned and distributed. The elected officials and their appointees in the bureaucracy of
Washington, DC, would negotiate the trade in political capital and in the
huge monetary gains to be derived from the transformation of the former
Indian Country into private property – in other words, into real estate. The
centralization in the national capital of control over western expansion was
a formative step in the ascent of Washington, DC, to its prominent role in
global geopolitics.

This federal control over the wealth and opportunity generated through the privatization of Indian lands would reach a zenith in the mid-nineteenth century. Among the main agencies and beneficiaries of this expansion of federal influence were the railway companies which provided the technological means to realize more fully many of the ambitions of those land speculation companies whose influence in the revolutionary achievement of American independence Clarence Alvord has so engagingly described.[4] As Miriam Beard wrote in her sweeping account of the ascent of American business during the "Gilded Age," when the railway companies were central engines of commercial expansion, "merely from his office in Boston or New York, or in a lobby chamber in the capital, the speculator could purchase forests, prairies or mountain ranges, and trust to the United States Army to clear the way for him by removing Indians and squatters."[5]

Some of the key provisions of the Northwest Ordinance were worded in the language that symbolized the intention to situate the United States in the continuum of Europe's civilizational mission which began with the Vatican's "donation" of the Americas in 1493 to the Spanish and portuguese Crowns. Article 3 of the Ordinance repeated the traditional rationalizations for bringing Indigenous peoples under the power and authority of Christian regimes:

Religion, morality, and knowledge, being necessary to good government and the happiness of mankind, schools and the means of education shall forever be encouraged. The utmost good faith shall always be observed towards the Indians; their land and property shall never be taken from them without their consent; and in their property, rights, and liberty, they shall never be invaded or disturbed, unless in just and lawful wars authorized by Congress; but laws founded in justice and humanity shall from time to time be made, for preventing wrongs being done to them, and for preserving peace and friendship with them.[6]

The transformation of an evangelical mission into a pedagogical one in the Northwest Ordinance anticipated the merging of church and state in the field of Indian education. As a mission statement arising from the world's first formal exercise of decolonization, the Northwest Ordinance also suggested the limits of the US move away from its own European antecedents. Although American independence would translate into forms of self-governance for the republic's citizenry, the American government fully intended to continue the forceful projection of the European heritage westward into Indian Country. In adopting as its own a North American variation of imperial mission, the central government reserved the power to resort to violence and warfare to achieve its expansionary aim. In elaborating the new law of western expansion in the language of Christian and educational mission, the US government clarified its conception of the relationship of the American republic to Indian Country. A structure of laws was set in place to govern the republic's acquisition of the Indigenous peoples' territories. With all its high-minded tone, however, the powers said to be invested in the Indians would not be interpreted to allow them to favour their own Aboriginal heritage or to retain in peace their own Aboriginal lands. Once again, the inevitability of their submission to the "manifest destiny" of Western civilization was simply taken for granted.

The evangelical character of this mission took its first and most prototypical form in New Spain, whose missionary responsibilities were integral in the crown of Castile's grant from Pope Alexander VI. Clearly the Spanish intention to expand the domain of Christendom throughout the Americas drew on the example of the principle established many centuries earlier after the conversion of the Roman emperor, Constantine. He began an assault on all manner of devotions deemed "pagan" in order to make Christianity the universal church of the Roman Empire.[7] The fact that the Spanish monarch also bore the title of Holy Roman Emperor during the era of New Spain's fastest expansion speaks eloquently of the powerful influences of antiquity on the imperial mission begun in Spain and continued by other powers, including the United States of America.[8]

The French and English sovereigns countered Spain's sweeping claims with bold statements of their own evangelical missions. In establishing the Company of One Hundred Associates for the Commerce of Canada, for instance, France's King Louis XIII, on Cardinal Richelieu's advice, authorized the members of that enterprise to "discover in those lands and countries of New France, called Canada, some habitation capable of sustaining colonies, for the purpose of attempting, with divine assistance, to bring the [Indigenous] peoples who inhabit them to the knowledge of the true God, to civilize them and to instruct them in the faith and apostolic, Catholic and Roman religion."[9] The Charter of the Virginia Company issued in 1609 also included very explicit language describing the missionary purposes of the new English polity. Its purpose was to serve in "propagating of Christian religion to such people, as yet live in darkness and miserable ignorance of the true knowledge and worship of God, and may in time bring the infidels and savages living in these parts to humane civility and to a settled and quiet government."[10] The founding seal of the original Massachusetts Company depicted a similar objective. The seal contained a picture with an Indian man imploring, "Come Over and Help Us."[11]

With the Northwest Ordinance of 1787, the new government of the United States announced its intention to continue the westerly projection of the same missionary project begun by the European sovereigns who looked to the Americas for new frontiers of imperial expansion. In that sense the United States declared itself to be an instrument of a projectory in history rooted first in the Roman Empire and then in Christendom's violent Crusades against the power of Islam in the Middle East. The ordi-

nance formalized the creation of the first American Northwest Territory
north of the Ohio River. Moreover, it created the prototypical model of a
constitutional procedure for the legal transformation of Indian Country
into North American states and provinces. In these jurisdictions, non-Indian settlers and corporations could acquire land as private property and
establish, when sufficiently numerous, powers of local taxation and self-
government.

The idea of the original Northwest Territory was to establish on the
frontiers of non-Indian settlement a colonial extension of federal authority during that intermediate phase when Indian people were being
removed from the lands by wars, ceding treaties, relocation, or by any
combination of these three basic techniques for the extinguishment of
Aboriginal title. This constitutional procedure for western expansion was
re-enacted again and again in the westward movement of Euro-American
settlement across the United States, as Ohio Territory became the state of
Ohio, Indiana Territory became the state of Indiana, Michigan Territito-
ry became Michigan state, Dakota Territory became the states of North
and South Dakota, Montana Territory became the state of Montana, and
so on.

This same constitutional procedure was also adopted by the Dominion
of Canada after the annexation in 1869 of the huge Indian Country where
the British imperial presence had been established by the trading activities
of the North West Company and the Hudson's Bay Company. Much of the
provincial domain of Canada, including the prairie provinces and much of
northern Ontario and Quebec, were created from lands once designated
as the Northwest Territories. The federalization of Aboriginal territories in
preparation for their transformation into future provinces is still being
implemented with some modifications in what remains of the Canadian
Northwest Territories as well as in Yukon and Nunavut.

THE UNITED STATES, GREAT BRITAIN
AND THE ABORIGINAL "RIGHT OF THE SOIL"
NORTH OF THE OHIO RIVER

What US officials saw as the first Northwest Territory of their republic persisted as the southern part of Greater Canada in the geopolitical imaginations of the fur-trade community based in Montreal and Great Britain.
This region, after all, was a key territory in the fur-trade empire of New
France. Moreover, after 1763, the northern half of the Mississippi Valley
continued to be an integral fur-trade hinterland of the commercial empire
of the St Lawrence.

The desire to reverse the outcome of the Treaty of Paris of 1783 was
especially marked among those who identified their own commercial
interests with the metropolitan interests of Montreal. Following the Seven
Years' War, Montreal's commercial leadership was provided primarily by a

number of Scottish entrepreneurs, many of whom first settled in Canada's commercial hub with the aim of supplying the expanding operations of the British imperial military establishment in North America. The most ambitious of these Scots entrepreneurs soon learned of the commercial rewards to be gained from working cooperatively with those *canadiens* who possessed extensive knowledge of the Aboriginal inhabitants and transportation corridors in the Indian Country of Canada. Oftentimes these *canadien* fur traders had close familial connections with those Aboriginal groups in the interior, who had formerly been allied with the interests of French imperialism in North America.[12] The result of this amalgam of peoples and commercial interests was to renew and edify the old fur-trade community of New France in the context of an enormously expanded British North America. This edified fur-trade community centred in Montreal tended to share the conviction that the British government had acted in 1783 with grievous disregard for Canada's geopolitical integrity and for the interests of the crown's Canadian subjects when it handed over the rich territory south of the Great Lakes to the sovereign jurisdiction of the new republic.

The most deeply rooted of the three geopolitical visions for the future of the lands north of the Ohio River was that of the Indigenous peoples. The predominant reaction among them when they learned in 1783 that the British government had handed over their lands and themselves to the sovereign jurisdiction of the United States was indignation and the shared conviction that the transaction was illegal. In the minds of their leadership there was a clear memory that, in the Treaty of Fort Stanwix of 1768, the first treaty following the principles outlined in the Royal Proclamation of 1763, crown and Aboriginal negotiators had fixed the southeastern boundary of Indian Country at the banks of the Ohio River.[13] As Governor Frederick Haldimand reported from Canada to Lord North in 1783, "These [Indian] People my Lord, have, as enlightened Ideas of the nature and Obligations of Treaties as the most Civilized Nations have, and know that no infringement of the Treaty in 1768 ... can be binding upon them without their Express Concurrence and Consent."[14] The determination of Indian peoples to affirm the territorial provisions of the Treaty of Fort Stanwix and, ultimately, to retain their lives, their lands, and the sovereignty of their nations became for three decades the primary obstacle to the realization of American plans to privatize the Northwest Territory as a domain of non-Indian settlements and states. The Indian determination to make the necessary geopolitical transformations in order to defend these goals attracted considerable support from the non-Aboriginal fur traders of Canada and their allies in the British imperial government.

This solidarity of purpose to check the expansion of the United States after the American Revolution became the basis for one of the Canadian Indian Country's most dynamic and constitutionally inventive periods.

From 1783 until the making of Jay's Treaty in 1794, the British government signalled its apparent renunciation of key parts of the Treaty of Paris, together with its continuing alliance with the Indigenous peoples of Canada, by retaining the British military posts south of the Great Lakes. These posts also doubled as fur-trade emporiums. The maintenance of this continuity conveyed to Indian nations in North America's interior that the British crown was prepared to continue the alliances forged in the era when Sir William Johnson and the Royal Proclamation of 1763 were the primary beacons of imperial Indian policy.

While the territorial provisions of the Treaty of Paris of 1783 represented a profound betrayal of many Indian nations, the implications were particularly grave for those Indian groups that had opposed the assertions of American independence most directly. None had battled harder on the frontiers between Indian Country and the Anglo-American settlements than the Mohawk fighting forces connected to Colonel Joseph Brant. In 1784 crown officials in Canada tried to respond to the damage inflicted by the Treaty of Paris on Brant's people. Accordingly, the imperial government purchased two plots for the Six Nations from Mississauga Indians north of Lakes Erie and Ontario. The larger of these plots was situated on the rich, fertile soils around the Grand River, where Brant, along with about 2,000 other Indian migrants, moved to escape the affront of falling subject to the jurisdiction of New York State and their enemies in the federal government of the United States.[15]

These migrants were sufficiently representative of all groups in the Six Nations Confederacy to establish the basis for a new Longhouse in what would become Upper Canada. The Six Nations reserve, which would become in later years the largest Indian settlement in Canada in terms of population, also received some Delaware, Nanticoke, Tutelo, Creek, and Cherokee settlers who had not yet been entirely assimilated into the national identies of their hosts. The second plot of land to receive Indian migrants from the old Mohawk Valley was in the Bay of Quinte area. This reserve, known subsequently as Tyendinaga, become home primarily to Mohawks who moved along with a larger wave of United Empire Loyalist seeking to maintain continuity in their relationship with Great Britain. In 1791 the newly created crown colony of Upper Canada became home to a third group of Indians seeking refuge from the severe hostilities they had encountered in the new republic. This Christian Delaware group were pacifist Moravians, and they established the town of Fairfield on the Thames River with the help of their missionary, David Zeisberger.[16]

With large supplies of guns and ammunition supplied by officials in the British posts south of the Great Lakes, the Indian peoples of the region became increasingly assertive of what they were encouraged to view as their unceded Aboriginal and treaty rights. Their defence of their ancestral lands led in 1790 and 1791 to two major defeats of the weak and

unorganized army of the United States government. The first of these
Indian victories was based on a small-scale battle with soldiers under the
command of Brigadier General Josiah Harmar. The second defeat was far
more decisive, as a thousand soldiers under the command of Northwest
Territories Governor Arthur St Clair were either killed or wounded on the
Wabash River, though with minimal Indian casualties.[17] These two Indian
successes in defeating the US army are sometimes referred to as Harmar's
Humiliation and St Clair's Shame.

This reversal gave growing confidence to the patriotic, pan-Indian movement among Indigenous peoples, just as it awakened the imaginations of
many imperial strategists on both sides of the Atlantic to the potential
strategic importance of an Indian buffer state in the North American interior. Among the most enthusiastic proponents of the plan to bolster the
consolidation of an Indian polity in the interior of North America were
Lord Dorchester, the governor general of Canada, and Sir John Graves
Simcoe, the first lieutenant-governor of the crown colony of Upper Canada.[18] Upper Canada had been carved in 1791 from greater Quebec as a
new jurisdiction west of the Ottawa River. Its geopolitical purpose in the
British Empire was to provide a secure home for Aboriginal refugees from
the United States, together with an influx of more conservative, largely
Protestant, and often multicultural United Empire Loyalists, including
many Quakers, Menonites, and former slaves.[19]

To understand the attraction of an Indian buffer state at this juncture in
history, it is necessary to see it in the context of the factors that had
enabled the founders of the United States to move from the margins of
anti-establishment revolt to the realm of recognized sovereignty in international law. If France had been able to impede British imperialism in
North America by offering support to the revolutionary Anglo-American
opponents of continuing crown rule, why shouldn't Great Britain respond
by supporting Aboriginal opponents of American republicanism in the
creation of their own Aboriginal nation-state? Why not use Aboriginal
resistance to US expansionism as a check on the growth of a potentially
powerful competitor and as a shield and a buffer to protect those vulnerable British North American settlements north of the Great Lakes?[20]

While support for the creation of an Indian buffer state became the
official yet secret policy of the British government, crown diplomats publicly responded to the strength of the Indian Confederacy by trying to
lead the United States to recognize that Indian peoples retain an Aboriginal title in their ancestral lands until such time as they voluntarily
agree to exchange this interest for various forms of negotiated compensation. By asserting this position the British government was essentially
promoting the idea that the United States should take over the laws and
principles that King George had proclaimed in 1763 and that his agents
had renewed and confirmed through the negotiation of the Treaty of
Fort Stanwix in 1768. In asserting this position, the British government

was attempting to repair some of the damage done to its Indian allies in 1783.

The essence of this effort was to advance the idea that the crown had not actually ceded those Indian lands south of the Great Lakes to the United States in 1783. All that had been handed over was the sovereign's exclusive authority to purchase those lands, a capacity of pre-emption that the Royal Proclamation had articulated in 1763 and one that had been exercised by Sir William Johnson in the name of the king at Fort Stanwix in 1768. In 1793, with two humiliating military defeats to the Indian Confederacy behind them, American officials agreed to the British interpretation of Aboriginal and treaty rights in those disputed lands north of the Ohio River that were federal territories for some, an integral part of Canada to others, and a protected Indian Country to those who remembered and believed the crown's promises to Indian peoples in 1763 and 1768.

Given the international background of the American adoption of these principles, the formal declaration on behalf of the US president in 1793 can be interpreted as a move towards a kind of uniform law for the continent, or at least for that part of the continent whose constituent parts share common colonial roots in the British Empire even as they emanate from opposing sides of the American Revolution. The presentation was overseen and witnessed by officials of the British Imperial Indian Department, who recorded the proceedings. The delegation of commissioners representing the US president made their proclamation to an assembly on the Miamis River. The presenters addressed their Indian audience as "the Deputies of the Confederate Indian Nations." To them, the US delegation explained:

BROTHERS —
We do know very well that at the Treaty of Fort Stanwix, twenty-five years ago, the Ohio River was agreed on as the boundary between you and the White People of the British Colonies. And we know that about seven years after that Boundary was fixed, a quarrel broke out between your Father the King of Great Britain, and the People of those Colonies, which are now the United States. This quarrel was ended by the Treaty Of Peace made with the King about ten years ago, by which the Great Lakes and the waters which unite them, were by him declared to be the boundaries of the United States.

Having outlined this history, the US officials went on to acknowledge the inadequacy of the United States's view of the boundary agreement as previously interpreted:

BROTHERS —
We therefore frankly tell you, that we think those Commissioners put an erroneous construction on that part of our treaty with the King, as he had not purchased the

Country of you, of course he could not give it away. He only relinquished to the United States his claim to it. That claim was founded on a right acquired by treaty, with other White Nations to exclude them from purchasing or settling any part of the country; and it is a right which the King granted to the United States.

The delegation then went on to clarify the decision of the US government to harmonize its position on the question of Indian title north of the Ohio River with the position the British government had publicly adopted:

BROTHERS —
We now concede this great point; We by the express authority of the President of the United States, acknowledge the property or right of the soil of the great Country above described, to be in Indian Nations so long as they desire, to occupy the same. We only claim particular tracts in it, as before mentioned, and the right granted by the King, and which is well known to the English and the Americans, and called the right to pre-emption, or the right of purchasing of the Indian Nations disposed to sell their lands, to the exclusion of all other White people whatever.[21]

While this approach seemed to hold out an olive branch to the Indian Confederacy, in fact the US government was preparing to attack the Aboriginal defenders of the Indian Country of Canada in yet another frontier campaign. George Washington fended off those who feared that his office could give rise to another Cromwell if too much power over the US army was allowed to reside in the presidency. His raising of an American army of sufficient strength to check the rising might of the Indian Confederacy in the Battle of Fallen Timbers was a significant turning point in the military history of the United States. As military historian Dave Palmer observed, "The modern defense establishment of the United States emerged in embryonic but recognizable shape in the climactic year of 1794."[22]

The British government responded to the resulting change in the balance of power on the contested ground north of the Ohio River by agreeing to Jay's Treaty. This agreement involved the commitment to withdraw crown forces by 1796 from those military posts south of the Great Lakes. The bargain also included provision to enable Indigenous peoples to cross unimpeded over the international boundary and to continue to participate in the commercial life of the fur-trade empire centred in Montreal.[23]

FROM COVENANT CHAIN TO THE CONFEDERATE INDIAN NATIONS: JOSEPH BRANT AND THE REVOLUTIONARY FERMENT IN THE LAND OF THE BOWL WITH ONE SPOON

While the quest for a sovereign Aboriginal Indiana suffered a setback after the Indian defeat at the battle of Fallen Timbers in 1794, the vision of a fixed Indian state north of Ohio River was renewed and rekindled through the inspiration of Tecumseh in the era of the War of 1812. As Gregory Evans Dowd demonstrated in *A Spirited Resistance: The North American Indian Struggle for Unity, 1745–1815*, Tecumseh's advancement of a sovereign Indian state based on a federal union of Indian nations was the outcome of at least two generations of persistent pan-Indian activism among diverse Indian peoples from the Hudson's Bay to the Gulf of Mexico. Tecumseh, he writes, "drew upon traditions of nativism and networks of intertribal relations that had been vibrant throughout the trans-Appalachain borderlands, reaching back into the past beyond the time of Neolin and Pontiac."[24]

The economics of Indian Country in this era were far more complex and many faceted than can readily be apprehended from the seemingly one-dimensional term "the fur trade." In Indian Country, for instance, agriculture remained an important component of work, exchange, and nourishment even in the era when the trapping and trade of animal pelts tended to predominate. This agriculture could take the form of gardening the symbiotic plant community of corn, beans, and squash, or it could involve the complex harvesting and ceremonial protocols associated with mandamin, or wild rice, as it was called by the newcomers. As we discussed in chapter 1, the Indian cultivation and use of plants as food, medicine, and construction materials emphasized the drawing of vegetable diversity from ecologically complex environments maintained and enhanced through the sophisticated human application of fire technology. This approach to agriculture contrasted starkly with the emphasis on cultivated monocultures in the American empire of private property.

The inventive and pluralistic character of the Indian Country of the Great Lakes before 1815 is the subject of Richard White's *The Middle Ground*. Although White uses the French term *pays d'en haute* to describe the geographic subject of his study, what he has written is basically an ethnohistory of the Indian Country of Canada during one of its most creative eras of adaptation to European immigrants and to agents of Euro-American empires.[25] This exchange also affected profoundly the non-Aboriginal groups and individuals who managed to assimilate themselves with varying degrees of success into the Indian Country of Canada. These adoptees chose immigration rather than expansion into Indian Territory.

In the Euro–North American part of the Indian Country of Canada a geographic and ethnographic revolution took place once the newcomers adopted the transportation technology of Native peoples in the continent's interior. The knowledge of how to make and navigate canoes, a craft at once both simple and sophisticated, became essential to modes of inland mobility that had no real equivalent on the other side of the Atlantic. For this reason the canoe quickly became an icon of Canada, a country that, from its inception, has depended on human capacity to communicate effectively over wide expanses of space and between markedly different realms of culture and language.

The Indian domain of Canada was not a place of simple or uniform identities. Indian Country was many countries, with linguistic, cultural, and political variations in many respects as wide as those marking the distinction between different European nations. One of the most basic ethnic distinctions in the southern portion of eighteenth-century Aboriginal Canada was between Iroquoian-speaking peoples and Algonkian-speaking peoples. The traditional territories of the former were largely in the more arable domain south of the Canadian Shield, while the latter made up a diverse complex of societies whose traditional territories cover ground between the Atlantic coast and the foothills of the Rocky Mountains.[26] The bitter animosity that once divided the Iroquoian-speaking Hurons against the Iroquoian-speaking Five Nations shows, however, that the lines of animosity or alliance in Aboriginal Canada often transcended boundaries of language and culture. Issues of war and peace, trade and diplomacy often turned on questions beyond the natural inclination to identify most with those who speak a common language and who share a similar way of life.

While the Indian Country of Canada was a place of diverse identities, these identities could at times be very elastic and even porous. When the Five Nations Iroquois vanquished the peoples of the Huron Confederacy from Huronia in 1649 many of the latter were absorbed and assimilated into former. Around 1,000 Tahontaenrat Hurons, for instance, established a new community among the Seneca in 1651. This immigration led the way for several thousand other Hurons who were absorbed into the cultures and clans of the Iroquois Confederacy, but most especially into the Mohawk and Onondaga nations.[27]

In the eighteenth century it was common practice for many Indian communities living to the back of the Anglo-American settlements to adopt Euro-Americans of many backgrounds into their societies. In many instances Indian raiding parties took captives to build up their people's waning numbers. These captives were adopted into Indian families and fully incorporated into the life of their new communities. It was a source of great anxiety in the Anglo-American settlements when these adopted Indians chose to stay in Indian Country, even when they had the opportunity to return to their biological families.[28] As Hector St John de Crevecoeur observed in 1782, "thousands of Europeans are Indians, and we have no examples of even one of those Aborigines having from choice become European!" He speculated that there must be in the Indians' "social bond something singularly captivating and far superior to anything to be boasted of among us ... There must be something more congenial to our native dispositions, than the fictitious society in which we live ... There must be something bewitching in their manners, something indelible and marked by the very hands of nature." De Crevecoeur claimed to have discussed with some Indianized former captives their decision to remain with their adopted Aboriginal relatives rather than to return to their biological, Euro-American families. He reported that they gave as their reason the existence among the Indigenous peoples of "the most perfect freedom, the ease of living, the absence of those cares and corroding solicitudes which so often prevail with us; the peculiar goodness of the soil they cultivated, for they did not trust altogether to hunting; all these, and many more motives, which I have forgot, made them prefer that life of which we entertain such dreadful opinions."[29]

The adopted Indians from the Anglo-American settlements moved into a realm where the *canadiens*, with settlements at Kaskaskia, Detroit, Vincennes, and Michilimackinac, seemed to some observers almost indistinguishable from Indians. As one English officer remarked, these French-speaking people "adopted the very Principles and Ideas of the Indians and differ from them only a Little in color."[30] According to a Pennsylvanian land speculator, George Croghan, the French and Indians of Canada had been "bred up together like children in that Country, and the French have always adopted the Indians' Customs and Manners."[31] The *canadiens* blended into the rhythms and cultures of Indian Country in North America's deep interior in part because there were few enough of them that they did not seriously challenge the jurisdiction and control of the First Nations in their ancestral lands. Before 1763, when the French imperial government formally withdrew its claims to North America, the French style of colonization involved especially attentive rounds of diplomacy and treaty councils. This treaty diplomacy developed within the framework of an imperial policy where Christianized Indians were to be afforded the status of full-fledged French subjects with full rights to live in France if they chose. While this recognition was of insignificant worth to most First Nations citizens, it may have helped discourage the native-born French population from psychologically distancing themselves from the Indigenous peoples.

In the era of New France, the French paid what amounted to rent for the use of small plots of land on which a number of rudimentary French military posts were situated.[32] These payments, and the treaty rituals that accompanied them, helped to disarm any Indian resistance to the presence of *canadien* travellers, traders, and settlers in their midst. The posts were integrated into the politics and commerce of the fur trade, the primary medium of commercial and diplomatic reciprocity on which the genesis of French-Aboriginal Canada as well as British imperial Canada depended. Indian Country therefore provided comfortable and amiable homes for many individuals and families of partial or full European ancestry who chose to adapt themselves to the mores of the First Nations. The Indian Country of Canada was also the home of some African and African-American people who had escaped the bondage of slavery on southern plantations. Like many Euro-Americans who had assimilated into Aboriginal life, the propensity of African-Americans to assimilate smoothly into Indian Country became more marked once they married into Aboriginal clans.[33]

The Indian Country north of the Ohio River, therefore, was a domain of prolific transcultural exchange and fertile innovation. The rhythms of life on the middle ground were further vivified by the emergence of what the French called "republics." These republics were Indian villages inhabited by individuals from a number of different nations. Some of these people had migrated from the east away from ruined hunting grounds and the bloody violence of the westward-moving, Anglo-American frontier. Others were people of mixed ancestry who felt more at ease in the multicultural milieu of these Aboriginal republics. Some were innovators or opportunists, anxious to exploit new possibilities for profit and power in Aboriginal societies breaking loose from some of the conventions and orthodoxies of Aboriginal traditions.[34] Hence, the Indian Country of Canada was by no means a static, unchanging milieu. Instead, this realm was alive with social tumult, ideological ferment, and radical political energies as intense in their own ways as the revolutionary forces that transformed the Thirteen Colonies into the United States.

As the politics of Indian Country changed, new kinds of leadership emerged to give articulation and structure to the strategies made necessary by the emergence on the continent of an independent, Anglo-American republic born as a military and legal engine for the ingestion and privitization of Indian lands. Joseph Brant and Tecumseh, who advocated similar goals but adopted varying strategies in the Indian Country of Canada, became the most influential articulators of the new politics of Aboriginality after American independence. Brant was a Mohawk born outside the aristocratic circle of clans whose offspring were eligible to receive names from among the fifty permanent titles integral to the system of representative government in the Six Nations' Longhouse League.[35] This League, whose central governing institution was situated at Onondaga, had increased its strength by absorbing many groups and individuals besides the defeated Hurons. In the early eighteenth century the Confederacy, whose main symbol was the Great White Pine of Peace, absorbed a new national polity, the Tuscorora. The former Five Nations was reconstituted as the Six Nations.

Brant, an interloper on the traditional power structures of his own peoples, was a colonel in the British Army. In spite of his humble origins, he had come to be the primary custodian of the memories and protocols associated with the old system of alliances linking the politics of several British colonies along the Atlantic seaboard with the politics of several Indian nations in the interior.[36] This famed political invention, centred on the council grounds near Johnson Hall, was known as the Covenant Chain. The making of the treaties at Easton, Pennsylvania, in 1758 and at Fort Stanwix, New York, in 1768 represented the high points in the political influence of this important intercultural institution. Like many institutions and polities whose legitimacy and viability depend on the maintenance of particular interpretations of history, the power of the Covenant Chain was largely psychological. Although it gave rise to a realm of paradox described by Francis Jennings in his book as *The Ambiguous Iroquois Empire*, it lay at the centre of some very tangible exercises of authority.[37]

When Sir William Johnson became the first superintendent of Indian Affairs of the northern section of the British Imperial Indian Department in 1755, he went to work to renew, to revitalize, and "to polish" the links in the Covenant Chain.[38] In treaties that advanced the principle that the Iroquois League was at the head of a more extended Indian empire, Johnson sought to advance the legal theory that the British alliance with the Six Nations gave the crown an indirect jurisdictional claim throughout the Indian Country of Canada. In advancing this strategy, Johnson worked closely with his lover and confidante, Molly Brant.[39] Molly's younger brother was Joseph Brant, who was educated and groomed to play a key diplomatic and military role in the renewal within British imperial auspices of the old Covenant Chain. The site of young Joseph's early formal education, Moor's Indian Charity School in Lebanon, Connecticut, was later transformed into Dartmouth University, primarily through the successful fundraising efforts of one of its Native graduates.[40]

As Dorothy Jones outlines in her book *License for Empire: Colonialism by Treaty in Early America*, Great Britain depended far more heavily than any other European imperial power on the making of formal, written treaties with Indigenous peoples, not only in North America but in Africa and the subcontinent of India as well.[41] While agents of the French Empire in the Americas had depended on the rituals of treaty making in securing good relations with Indigenous peoples, including those in the coastal regions of Brazil during the sixteenth century, these agreements were frequently left unwritten.[42] The British approach to imperial expansion into Indian Country was more formal and more obsessed with the legalistic precision of the written word. Between 1763 and 1774 the name of the sovereign of Great Britain was invoked in more than two dozen Indian treaties with Aboriginal groups in the continent's interior. Throughout the negotiations leading to these agreements, the politics of the Covenant Chain and of the Longhouse Confederacy came to dominate British imperial thinking about the geopolitics of Indian Country in North America. As the Covenant Chain's most experienced Indian practitioner, Joseph Brant carried a weighty legacy of history with him to the disputed terrain beyond the Ohio River after the American Revolution.

All the important transactions of both the Longhouse League and the Covenant Chain were marked with wampum belts, a form of shellwork tapestry containing pictorial representations of the key concepts of particular agreements.[43] In 1786 at a large assembly of people representing communities from throughout the Indian Country north of the Ohio

River, Brant referred to an important wampum describing the political
character of that territory. At the Huron village of Brownstone on the western side of the Detroit River, Brant told the assembled delegates, a hundred years ago a "Moon of Wampum was placed in this country with four
roads leading to the centre for the convenience of Indians from different
quarters to come and settle and hunt here. A dish with one spoon was like-
wise put here with the Moon of Wampum."[44] The bowl with one spoon was
a well-known symbol among Brant's audience for the principle that land
would be held in common, that all the hunting and fishing rights to a specific territory would be shared by those subscribing to a given agreement.
The bowl with one spoon supplied an essential metaphor for the emerging
Indian Confederacy of Canada. The diverse assembly of Aboriginal delegates at the Brownstown meeting heard Brant and other Longhouse veterans advise, "If we make a War with any Nation, let it result from the Great
Council fire, if we make peace, let it proceed from our unanimous Councils. But whilst we remain disunited, every inconvenience attends us. The
Interest of any one Nation should be Interests of us all, the welfare of one
should be the welfare of all others."[45]

Brant and his Longhouse associates, however, were not ideal champions
of unity in this group. To most of their audience, these appeals were too
reminiscent of the politics of the Covenant Chain. Adherents of the
Covenant Chain had developed the habit of looking at the western Indian
nations beyond the Ohio River as if they were subservient to the rule of the
Longhouse, a subservience that, in most instances, was more fiction than
fact. The animosity of many Algonkian-speaking peoples towards Six
Nations peoples had antecedents that were deeper than the historical genesis of the Covenant Chain. In most Algonkian languages the Six Nations
peoples were known as *Nahdoways,* a phrase that can be translated to mean
snakes.[46] This unflattering characterization is suggestive of Algonkian distaste for traditional enemies whose heartland was the Mohawk Valley
between Albany and Lake Ontario.

The Longhouse League, or the Haudonosaunee as the confederacy is
described by its own members, was an effective federation of five Iroquoian nations, and, after the Tuscarora were adopted in 1721, six
nations. In the view of Stephen Saunders Webb, the Haudonosaunee
became so influential by the end of the seventeenth century that the
league's capital, Onondaga, was the most important political centre in
eastern North America.[47] By the time that Brant addressed the Brownstown gathering in 1786, however, the Longhouse had been split by the
American Revolution and the Covenant Chain was largely a spent force in
the strategic calculations of the governors of British imperial Canada. As
the centre of geopolitical conflict moved westward, Algonkian-speaking
peoples increasingly moved into the political role once held by the Longhouse League.

The marriage of several British Indian Department officials to

Shawnee women was a sign of the ascendant importance of that group in the Indian Confederacy of the bowl with one spoon.[48] The emergence from the Shawnee of leadership directed at the organization of a pan-Indian confederacy was noticed by the British general, Thomas Gage, even before the American Revolution. In 1770 he wrote of the "plan formed by the Shawnese, of uniting the Nations in one general Confederacy." He thought the idea "a Sensible Scheme, and dangerous for us."[49]

Brant's personal politics further undermined his credibility as a champion of the aims of the Indian Confederacy. If the Confederacy was to hold land in common, it followed that groups and individuals within the Confederacy could not sell land on their own. Brant, however, would follow precisely that course in administering the Six Nations' land holdings around the Grand River north of Lake Erie. Brant's approach was to sell land parcels in the Grand Valley directly to Euro-American settlers, especially to Loyalists from the Butler's Rangers unit who had fought with him during the American Revolution. In selling land directly, Brant seemed to be circumventing the Royal Proclamation's stipulation that only the British sovereign could purchase the title to Indian lands. In Brant's view, however, the Six Nations had full title to their land grants north of the Great Lakes and he, as their leader, was entitled to sell parcels of real estate directly to individual purchasers at the full market value.[50]

Brant's own deep involvement in the real estate market made it difficult for him to be credible when advising others to hold and defend land in common. Indeed, Brant's membership in the fraternity of North American land speculators was almost certainly a factor in the fragmentation of the Indian Confederacy in 1793. That split was between hard liners, who insisted on maintaining the Ohio River as Indian Country's eastern boundary, and Brant's Six Nations people, who were prepared to accept a more westerly boundary marked by the Muskingum River. This divisiveness in turn contributed to the disastrous reversal of the Indian Confederacy's military fortunes in 1794 in the Battle of Fallen Timbers.[51]

After the Confederacy's defeat by the American army, Brant largely withdrew from the realm of high North American geopolitics into the more local intrigues of Six Nations governance in the new British colony of Upper Canada.[52] In later years, Brant retired to his mansion on the shores of Burlington Bay, the site of present-day Hamilton, Ontario. His mansion was clearly built to resemble Johnson Hall, the home of his initial mentor and benefactor and the site of his formative schooling in the politics of the Covenant Chain.[53] While Brant had, personally, been tied too tightly into the legal knots of private property to reflect and represent the ethos of the bowl with one spoon, he nevertheless played the key role in establishing a direct line of continuity between the politics of the Covenant Chain and the politics of the Indian Confederacy of Canada.

TENSKWATAWA, TECUMSEH, AND THE VISION OF
AN ABORIGINAL DOMINION OF UNITED INDIAN NATIONS

The outcome of the skirmish at Fallen Timbers led to the negotiation of Jay's Treaty between Great Britain and the United States.[54] At this agreement's heart was the British government's commitment to withdraw its troops in 1796 from the Indian Country south of the Great Lakes. To soften the blow of this withdrawal on the fur-trade interests of Montreal, the British negotiators insisted on a further provision ensuring Indians the right of free passage across the international boundary created by the Treaty of Paris in 1783. While this stipulation kept some lines of communication and commerce open between the heartland of the commercial empire of the St Lawrence and its southern hinterland, the British withdrawal of a military presence south of the Great Lakes seemed to formalize the end of a policy to cultivate the growth of an Indian state from the territory and from the political, social, economic, and cultural ingredients of the Indian Confederacy of Canada.

Although British policy makers ceased temporarily to treat the establishment of an Indian state as a practical possibility, the concept had taken deeper root among some Aboriginal groups and individuals who refused to treat as inevitable the demise of their societies and the loss of their lands before the rising power of the United States. If the Thirteen Colonies had found strength in unity, why should Indian nations not employ unity to secure their own recognition as a full-fledged nation state in international law? This recognition, the strategists of the Indian Confederacy understood, could probably not be achieved without helpful and influential allies. After all, had the American rebels not depended heavily on support from the government of France to achieve their objectives? Just as the "thirteen fires" in their revolution had depended on France, why shouldn't a united council of Indian nations look to British allies for help along the way to achieving international recognition as a sovereign Aboriginal dominion with firm and protected international borders?

These concepts formed the basis of a political strategy advanced with eloquence and strategic acumen by the Shawnee man named Tecumseh. The Shawnee are one branch of a large group of Algonkian speakers who call themselves *Anishinabek*. In their language, the name Shawnee refers simply to the people of the south. As southerners in the Algonkian-speaking world, the Shawnee had felt the brunt of the Virginians' territorial push towards their northwest. It was Shawnee people who had been forced from their ancestral lands by the notorious Indian fighters who established first the county and then the state of Kentucky.[55] Among these founders of Kentucky was land-speculator Richard Henderson's chief agent and operative, Daniel Boone. In later years Boone would be romanticized, especially by the Turnerian historians, as the archetype of the American frontier's conquering spirit.[56] By the time the Shawnee arrived in the land of the bowl with one spoon, therefore, their political culture had been profoundly influenced by prolonged exposure to the persistent ruthlessness of the American invasion of Indian Country.

While Shawnee history shaped Tecumseh's interpretation of events, it was the intertribal milieu of the village republics north of the Ohio River that established the political and ideological context for the formative stages of his work. In the early years of the nineteenth century, Tecumseh stayed on the edges of a religious movement generated by the visions of his brother, Tenskwatawa.[57] Much like Neolin two generations earlier, Tenskwatawa preached that all Indians should stop drinking alcohol, stop beating their spouses, and stop using European clothing and technology. Instead, they should revert to their old ways of making tools, weapons, and garments. Similarly, they should cultivate corn and other Indian foods in the fashion of their ancestors. Tenskwatawa proclaimed that by following this course, Indian people could regain harmony with their spiritual overseers. The spirits would then be drawn to intervene and remove from Indian Country the acquisitive newcomers who were overrunning their land.

In the early years of this movement, Tecumseh seems hardly to have been noticed by the American and British officials who closely monitored Tenskwatawa's rise.[58] After 1809, however, Tecumseh quickly emerged as the movement's most articulate and influential voice. His strategy seems to have drawn heavily on the example of Pontiac's turning of Neolin's teachings towards more secular, geopolitical objectives.[59] The Indian resistance movement of Pontiac's time was said to have held particular significance for Tecumseh, for his own relatives had been killed in the struggle to maintain the liberty of Indian peoples even as their lands were absorbed into the British Empire.[60]

Much of the most dynamic activity of the rejuvenated Indian Confederacy of Canada in the early nineteenth century was centred in the volatile world of the intertribal communities which the French had termed republics. Tenskwatawa's followers created several of these multicultural villages. One of them became the independence movement's main capital. It was known as Prophetstown or, sometimes, Tippecanoe, because the town was situated at the confluence of the Tippecanoe and Wabash rivers. Increasingly, Tenskwatawa's teachings were directed against the American people and the American government. In one of the Shawnee prophet's transcendental states, he was said to have been seized by the Great Spirit who proclaimed, "I am the Father of the English, of the French, of the Spaniards and of the Indians ... But the Americans I did not make. They are not my children but the children of the Evil Spirit. They grew from the scum of the great water when it was troubled by the Evil Spirit and the froth was driven into the woods by a strong east wind. They are very numerous but I hate them. They are unjust – they have taken away our lands which were not made for them."[61]

If the world of the intertribal villages west of the Anglo-American settlements created the immediate context for Tecumseh's work, British imperial Canada created the larger geopolitical framework within which he manoeuvred. Although the British had withdrawn their posts from south of the Great Lakes, they built a new chain of military establishments around the perimeter of the frontier province of Upper Canada. From these military bases, members of the British Imperial Indian Department retained active alliances with Indian groups throughout the land of the bowl with one spoon.[62] By and large these officials, including Mathew Elliot,[63] Alexander and Thomas McKee, Daniel and William Claus, George, James and Simon Girty,[64] George Ironside, and Robert Dickson,[65] were former fur traders who were fluent in Aboriginal languages and connected through marriage to Indian families. Some, like Alexander McKee, were themselves of mixed ancestry. These connections sometimes tended to draw that generation of Indian Department employees towards a deeper sense of loyalty to their Aboriginal families, friends and business associates than to the remote hierarchy of British imperial officials above them.

The prestige and budget of the British Indian Department was elevated after 1807, when an incident on the high seas known as the Chesapeake Affair increased the likelihood of war with the United States.[66] In the heightened state of military alert along the international boundary, Indigenous peoples were once again eyed for their potential as allies or enemies in the eventuality of renewed hostilities between the empires of Canada and the United States. As war became more imminent, British Indian Department officials distributed large quantities of presents to Aboriginal visitors at the crown's military establishments. And crown officials encouraged the renewal of the old Indian Confederacy in the land of the bowl with one spoon. The men with the responsibility to administer crown Indian policy in the years before the War of 1812 were therefore given a very fine line to walk. Their assignment was to retain and develop alliances with Indian nations, whose defence of their lands would provide a defensive shield for British North America in the eventuality of an outbreak of international conflict. While the strategy on the British side was to encourage Aboriginal animosity towards the United States, this projection of will fell short of the commitment to go into full-fledged war with the republic specifically over the issue of Aboriginal and treaty rights.

Like Joseph Brant, Tecumseh had learned from hard experience that the British had a propensity to back away from their commitments to Indigenous peoples at decisive moments – as in their betrayal of their Indian allies in the Treaty of Paris, or in Tecumseh's own experience after he participated in 1794 in the Battle of Fallen Timbers. After the fighting forces of the Indian Confederacy had been checked by the American army, some warriors, including the young Tecumseh, sought to enter the safety of the British fort in the area. Its commander, however, refused the Indians entry. He feared that their admission might spark a full-scale war between Great Britain and the United States. On many occasions, Tecumseh reminded crown officials of his own experience of seeing the gates of Fort Miami shut in his face.[67]

As long as British interests ran contrary to those of the United States, British interests were in large measure compatible with the shared interests of Indian peoples in the North American interior. It was this middle ground of shared geopolitical interests that provided Tecumseh with manoeuvring space to advance and refine the objectives of the Indian Confederacy. Why not manipulate the British into renewing their support for an inviolate Indian Country capable of checking the westward expansion of the United States? Why not elaborate and extend the old politics of the Covenant Chain and the Indian Confederacy of Canada to bring about the emergence of an Aboriginal dominion of United Indian Nations? While in later years Aboriginal strategists such as Black Hawk, Sitting Bull, and Big Bear would contemplate similar strategies, never again would such a split among North America's non-Aboriginal colonizers provide the possibility for First Nations freedom fighters to resist American expansionism in overt military conjunction with the British Empire.

Tecumseh imagined the Aboriginal dominion as a flexible federation – as a community of communities – that stressed the commonalities of shared Indian heritage. The key to his political program was to establish the principle that particular Indian groups lacked the authority to sell particular parcels of territory in ceding treaties. The land was the common property of all Indian nations together. Only a council of United Indian Nations had the true authority to negotiate the boundaries of Indian Country.[68] This council would emerge as the central authority of the Aboriginal dominion. As Tecumseh explained to his American nemesis, William Henry Harrison, the governor of Indiana Territory, officials of the United States had "taken upon themselves to say this tract belongs to the Miamis, this to the Delawares and so on, but the Great Spirit intended it as the common property of all Tribes, nor can it be sold without the consent of all."[69] The vision of First Nations holding shared title and jurisdiction in their ancestral lands extended the metaphoric meaning of the bowl with one spoon. Only by strictly adhering to the principle of collective land rights could the Indian Confederacy break the cycle of divide-and-conquer that had been used with such devastating effect against them. Only by adhering to the principle of collective Aboriginal title could Indigenous peoples reverse their subordination under the domestic law of their colonizers to assert, instead, their sovereign capacities of self-determination in international law.

From 1808 to 1813, when the Shawnee leader was killed by the bullet of an American soldier at the Battle of the Thames in Upper Canada,[70] Tecumseh was constantly on the move as the Indian Confederacy's chief strategist and ambassador. Some accounts say he travelled from the Gulf of Mexico to present-day northern Ontario seeking adherents for his politi-

cal principles. While some of the accounts are exaggerated, he certainly
travelled south to urge the Mushkogee or Creeks, together with the
Choctaw, Chickasaw, Cherokee, Seminole, and Osage peoples, to join the
Indian Confederacy.[71]

As the council fires of the Indian Confederacy were rekindled with the
tacit and sometimes overt encouragement of the British Imperial Indian
Department, the new developments caught the attention of Indian groups
far towards the west, including some who lived near the open prairies. In
1803 their lands became subject to the Louisiana Purchase, when
Napoleon sold to the United States government France's claims to the territory beyond the Mississippi River. The Sioux in particular, who would
play a significant role in the War of 1812,[72] were stirring towards confrontation with what they called "this new white nation now encroaching
on our Lands and wishing to be considered our father." Acting through
Sauk intermediaries in 1805, a Sioux delegation conveyed to the Confederacy's councils their people's wish to add their lands to the domain of the
bowl with one spoon.[73]

As the strength of the Confederacy grew, Tecumseh looked with growing
disdain on a number of chiefs whom he considered co-opted agents of the
American government. One of these was Little Turtle, the Shawnee leader
who had played a major role in the Confederacy's victories over the American army in 1790 and 1791.[74] After the Treaty of Greenville in 1795, Little Turtle began to live much as the Americans did. Black Hoof was another former war leader of the Shawnee who attempted to make his peace
with the government of the United States. He worked closely with the
Quaker missionary, William Kirk, to establish the Indian village of
Wapakoneta on the Auglaize River south of Lake Erie. In 1807 Wapakoneta's inhabitants cleared 430 acres for cultivation. They planted orchards,
acquired breeding stock of cattle and pigs, built mills, and hired a blacksmith. In spite of their promising start, however, the American federal
government refused to grant a title deed to Black Hoof's people. And the
administration of President Thomas Jefferson withdrew support for the
community's Quaker missionary,[75] suggesting that bullets and ceding
treaties rather than ploughs and title deeds remained the preferred instruments of American Indian policy.[76]

The failure of the American government to accommodate Black Hoof's
effort to blend in quietly into American society was duly noted by many
Indian observers. This episode served to strengthen the hand of Tecumseh
and the other proponents of Indian unity, shared land holding, and common resistance to the expansion of the United States. Tecumseh's growing
confidence was expressed in his reaction to the making in 1809 of yet
another ceding treaty in Indiana Territory. He labelled the Aboriginal men
who made the Treaty of Fort Wayne traitors who had been bribed and
intimidated to act against the laws of their own peoples.

The use of threats, coercion, whiskey, and secret payoffs to obtain Aboriginal land sessions was an old practice that undermined the legitimacy of the transfers and badly demoralized the First Nations. Tecumseh resolved that this genre of treason and fraud must stop. He told Harrison that the United States's so-called land purchase of 1809 was not valid and that he intended to kill those who had collaborated with the American governor in the transaction.[77] In condemning those who had signed the Treaty of Fort Wayne, Tecumseh responded much as Palestinian or Black South African patriots might have responded in more recent times to those among their own people who were seen to be too closely connected with the agencies of their own peoples' oppression. In every decolonization movement, one of the most difficult tasks is to confront the reality of internalized oppression. That oppression might be reflected in the cultivation of castes of indigenous collaborators who are willing to participate in regimes of indirect rule on behalf of alien empires. Or it might be expressed in the psycholgy of self-doubt or even self-contempt that sometimes comes from being socialized in colonized societies where the means of collective self-determination have been extinguished or badly damaged.

As one of the most gifted and insightful proponents of decolonization that the Americas has ever produced, Tecumseh understood that the liberation of his own peoples required more than a straight fight against the acquisitive expansionism of the United States. He knew that the success of his cause required some hard reckoning with forms of internalized colonization that stood in the way of elevating his peoples' shared polity to recognized sovereign status in the international community. And, like many leaders of the worldwide decolonization struggle to come, Tecumseh, no less than Gandhi or Nelson Mandela, was faced with the need to instill a sense of shared purpose and identity among an array of diverse peoples facing a common oppressor. Tecumseh could see that the United States was essentially grooming a caste of Indian collaborators to give the appearance of legitimacy to a system of land transfer that built up the power of the federal government primarily at Indian expense. Governor Harrison was proud of the fact that he had been able to obtain land from the Indians at an average price of about 2 cents an acre. The American government sold the same land for about $2 an acre.[78]

For Tecumseh, the only way to break this disastrous cycle was for Indian peoples to stand together, to discipline their own would-be comprador elements, and to demand that their shared territories be treated as the inviolate realm of a sovereign Aboriginal dominion. Until the Indian Confederacy obtained this form of international recognition, reasoned Tecumseh, the American government would continue to treat Indian peoples as some lower order of humanity that could be uprooted, cheated, killed, or robbed outside the usual constraints of the rule of law.

Tecumseh's gifts as an orator were legendary. Many who heard him speak in his Algonkian tongue said that his manner of description was often too subtle to allow for precise translation. In 1899 *Harper's Magazine* published Simon Pokagan's account of one of Tecumseh's characteristic speeches, given to a gathering of Anishinabek in the Chicago area shortly before the commencement of the War of 1812.[79] The account comes from Pokagan's father, Leopold, who heard Tecumseh's oratory many times. The text is interesting because of its author's bilingual approach. In those days, writes Pokagan, Tecumseh "and two other chiefs went from tribe to tribe, riding spirited black ponies finely equipped, and themselves gayly dressed. When he arose in the council-house his bearing was so noble that cheer on cheer would be given before he would open his mouth to speak."[80]

As he often did, Tecumseh began his presentation with an assessment of the environmental damage, especially the deforestation, that accompanied the Euro-American style of settlement:

Before me stands the rightful owners of kwaw-notchi-we aukee [this beautiful land]. The Great Spirit in His Wisdom gave it to you and your children to defend, and placed you here. But a-te-wa! [alas] the incoming race, like a huge serpent, is coiling closer and closer around you .... As sure as waw-kwen-og [the heavens] are above you they are determined to destroy you and your children and occupy this goodly land themselves.

Then they will destroy these forests, whose branches wave in the winds above the graves of your fathers, chanting their praises. If you doubt it, come, go with me east-ward or southward a few days journey along your ancient mi-kan-og [trails], and I will show you a land made desolate. There the forests of untold years have been hewn down and cast into the fire! There the be-sheck-kee and the wa-mawsh-ka-she [the buffalo and the deer], pre-nay-shen and ke-gon [the fowl and fish], are all gone. There the woodland birds, whose sweet songs once pleased your ears, have forsaken the land, never to return; and waw-bi-gon-ag [the wild flowers], which your maidens once loved to wear, have all withered and died.

After recounting the case of an American frontiersman who was rewarded for murdering in cold blood many peaceful Indians, on their way to make a treaty, Tecumseh continued:

When we were many and strong, and they were few and weak, they reached out their hands for wido-kaw-ke-win [help], and we filled them with wie-ans and maw-daw-min [meat and corn]; we lived wa-naw-kiwen [in peace] together; but now they are many and strong, and we are getting few and weak, they waw-nen-dam [have forgotten] the deep debt of mawmo-i-wendam [gratitude] they owe us, and are now scheming to drive us towards ke-so [the setting sun], into desert places far from ke-win and da-na ki aukee [our native land]. Eh [yes], they come to us with lips smoother than bi-me-da [oil], and words sweeter than amose-poma [honey], but beware of them! The venomous amo[wasp] is in their odaw [heart]! and their dealing with us, when we have not tamely submitted, has ever been maw-kaw-te and ashki-koman [powder and lead]; against such mau-tchi aunene [wicked men] our only pagos-seni-ma [hope], our only inin-ijim [safety], is in joining all our tribes, and then, and not until then, will we be able to drive the souless invaders back. Fail in this and awak-ani-win [slavery] and ne-baw [death] are ours!

Tecumseh finished by reminding his audience that the few rights and liberties they still held had not been retained cheaply:

And lastly, do not forget what peace you have enjoyed the past fifty years in your homes and on your hunting grounds you entirely owe to the brave Pontiac, who at risk to his own life, destroyed the forts of your enemies around the Great Lakes, driving the white invaders back.[81]

Even before the commencement of the War of 1812, Tecumseh's comportment marked him among opponents as a formidable individual with a great potential to change the course of history. As Harrison said of him:

The implicit obedience and respect which the followers of Tecumseh pay to him is really astonishing and more than any other circumstance bespeaks him one of those uncommon geniuses, which spring up occasionally to produce revolutions and overturn the established order of things. If it were not for the vicinity of the United States, he would perhaps be the founder of an Empire that would rival in glory that of Mexico or Peru. No difficulties deter him. His activity and industry supply the want of letters. For four years he has been in constant motion. You see him today on the Wabash and in a short time you hear of him on the banks of Lake Erie or Michigan, or on the banks of the Mississippi and wherever he goes he makes an impression favourable to his purposes.[82]

Harrison made these comments in a letter stating his intention to dislodge the inhabitants of Tippecanoe from their stronghold while Tecumseh was journeying southward to confer with the Mushkogees [Creeks] and others. In the days ahead the governor of Indiana Territory led a force that accomplished this design in an otherwise inconclusive melee. The Battle of Tippecanoe, the incident that in later years proved to be Harrison's ticket to the White House, was a significant setback, but not a full-fledged disaster for Tecumseh. One result of the loss to the US army of the Indian Confederacy's capital was that the Shawnee leader was forced by strategic necessity into closer military collaboration with the British army than he would have otherwise preferred.[83]

Just as the Indian Confederacy was drawn into closer alliance with the British Empire, so too was the United States drawn more deeply into the geopolitical orbit of its old ally, France. France had been the main European sponsor of the revolutionary forces during the American War of Independence. In preparing for his European conquests, Napoleon Bonaparte had continued France's tradition of support for the United States by transferring the European title to Louisiana to the American republic. By the summer of 1812, Napoleon had reached the zenith of his dictatorial power in his paradoxical campaign to export the liberating ideas of the French Revolution through the application of military force. With the spread of the Napoleonic wars to North America from the European continent and from the high seas, the Indian Confederacy and the United States entered the conflict on opposite sides of the conflagration between Britain and France. The war of 1812 began only months before the tenacity of the Russian army at Borodino together with the severity of the Russian winter set in motion the beginning of the end of Napoleon's quest to dominate all of Europe and much of that continent's colonial holdings as well.

The US attack on Canada began when Michigan Territory's governor, General William Hull, led an American force of 1,500 troops towards Detroit from Dayton, Ohio. On reaching his destination, Hull learned that Indian fighting forces had defeated an American contingent based at Michilimackinac. With calculated prodding from both Tecumseh and the British general, Sir Isaac Brock, Hull concluded that the soldiers and civilians under his authority faced the full onslaught of an Indian massacre. In the following language, Hull justified his resulting decision to surrender the American post of Detroit:

After the surrender of Michilimackinac, almost every tribe and nation of Indians, excepting a part of the Miamis and Delawares, north from beyond Lake Superior, West from beyond the Mississippi, south from the Ohio and Wabash, and east from every part of Upper Canada and from all the intermediate country, joined in open hostility, under the British standard against the Army I commanded ... the surrender of Michilimackinac opened the northern hive of Indians, and they were swarming down in every direction.[84]

The Aboriginal struggle in the War of 1812 went far beyond the Great Lakes–Mississippi Valley area. A faction of Creeks known as Red Sticks rose up against the Americans.[85] Their stand gave the rising politician, Andrew Jackson, his first major opportunity to gain public celebrity as an Indian fighter. A Red Stick refugee to the Seminoles by the name of Osceola went on to lead a more prolonged resistance of Native people and African-American maroons in the Florida Everglades.[86]

The conflict between Great Britain and the United States describes only one dimension of the War of 1812. A related but very distinct component of the conflagration was a virtual war of liberation undertaken by the Indian Confederacy with very specific geopolitical objectives. This Indian War of Independence amounted to an Aboriginal response to, and mirror image of, the American War of Independence. The Confederacy's primary objective was to gain international recognition as a nation state with secure, internationally recognized borders. The most prolific sources of the animating sparks of revolutionary excitement running through the Indian Country of Canada were the multicultural villages that the French had labelled "republics." While these communities retained a degree of ecological conservatism derived from the Aboriginality of the majority of their citizens, they also generated many new expressions of unity in diversity in the changing political economy of the First Nations. The War of 1812 was, in a sense, the Indian "revolution" predicted by Harrison. And the "uncommon genius" who inspired this American war for First Nations sovereign self-determination was Tecumseh.

FOR THE PROTECTION OF INDIAN RIGHTS AND THE SECURITY OF THE CANADAS: PERSPECTIVES ON THE SIGNIFICANCE OF INDIAN COUNTRY IN THE WAR OF 1812

If the actions of the Indian Confederacy in the War of 1812 are viewed as those of patriots fighting a war of national liberation, their American opponents emerge from the conflict as reactionaries intent on crushing Indian independence and absorbing the Indian Country of Canada in a single campaign. Richard Johnson, the Kentucky Congressman who took credit for shooting Tecumseh in the Battle of the Thames, described his hopes for the war in the following terms: "The waters of the St. Lawrence and the Mississippi interlock in a number of places, and the great disposer of Human Events intended those two rivers should belong to the same people."[87] "The British in Canada," wrote Julius W. Pratt, an American chronicler looking back on the era, "were in unholy alliance with the Western Indians, and that only by cutting off the Indians from British support could the West gain peace and security."[88] The War of 1812 renewed many of the hostilities in the United States which, during the revolutionary era, had been focused directly on King George III as an alleged instigator and agitator of Indian hostility against the Anglo-American colonies. In the Declaration of Independence Thomas Jefferson had turned his accusations against the monarch into charges that the British sovereign had encouraged "merciless Indian savages" to attack Anglo-American frontier settlements, and in 1813 he wrote of the "unprincipled policy of England" to "seduce the greater part of the tribes within our neighborhood to take up the hatchet against us."

This apportionment of blame seemed to assuage any reservations Jefferson may have harboured about abandoning his professed advancement of the "civilizing mission" and to renew, instead, his call to pursue Indian people "to extermination, or to drive them to new seats beyond our reach." In an exchange of correspondence with John Quincey Adams, Jefferson lamented that, as president, he had not authorized an earlier plan to arrange for the asssassination by Native agents of Tenskwatawa, but had opted instead to "let him go." The outcome, Jefferson wrote, was the us government "shall be obliged to drive them [the Indians], with the beasts of the forest into the Stony [Rocky] Mountains." He predicted, however, that "they will be conquered in Canada. The possession of that country," he continued, "secures our women and children for ever from the tomahawk and the scalping knife, by removing those who excite them." To this assessment Adams agreed, writing, "Another Conquest of Canada will quiet the Indians forever and be a great Blessing to them and to us."[89]

The early days of the War of 1812 were the decisive moment when "Upper Canada – nay both the Canadas – must have yielded to the triumphant arms of the United States" if it had not been for the rapid mobilization of the Indian Confederacy's fighting forces. Because of the Aboriginal role in the rapid British capture of Michilimackinac and Detroit from the army of the United States in the summer of 1812, "Canada was saved." The words are those of Major John Richardson, one of those authors identified by Margaret Atwood as a personification of the "Grey Owl syndrome." A soldier of partial Aboriginal ancestry, Richardson served directly under Major-General Isaac Brock and Tecumseh, who was given the commission of brigadier-general in the British army once hostilities began. In Richardson's view, the British alliance with the fighting forces of the Indian Confederacy was "a measure which alone secured us possession of Upper Canada."[90]

The importance of the Indian Confederacy in the defence of Canada is underlined by the demographics of the conflict. The United States had over seven million citizens in 1812. The concurrent population of British North America was less than half a million. Where the United States army had 7,000 officers and men, there were fewer than 5,000 British regulars in North America. Only 1,200 of these professional soldiers were posted in Upper Canada, a frontier colony whose non-Aboriginal inhabitants were mostly recent immigrants from the United States. These comparisons highlight the strategic significance of the 10,000 Aboriginal fighting men ready for military mobilization at the commencement of hostilities with the United States. About 8,000 of the Indian Confederacy's forces lived in territories claimed by the United States.[91] With these kinds of numbers at their disposal, and with the Confederacy's army defending the home territories they knew intimately, there can be no doubt about the pivotal importance of the Indian role in the War of 1812.

As in 1792, the initial Indian military successes revived interest in London in the idea of the Indian state. As A.L. Burt writes in his classic study of diplomatic relations between the United States and Britain during these years: "The idea [of the Indian state] was practically accomplished in 1812, and 1813 saw no change. Through the Indians, the British were in control of the American Northwest, the American military efforts in that direction being confined to the limited objective of protecting frontier settlements, thanks to the local dread of massacre by savages and to the pitifully inadequate support provided by a harassed Washington."[92] Major General Isaac

Brock, the commander of the King's forces in the early days of the War of
1812, was a powerful proponent of the creation of an Indian state before
his death at Queenston Heights. After the taking of Michilimackinac and
Detroit and the fall of Northwest army, Brock proclaimed that the Michigan Territory had been ceded to the crown. This tactic was calculated to
scuttle the peace plans of British doves and help prepare the constitutional gound for the Aboriginal dominion. He advised his superiors to give
careful attention to the status of the First Nations in all future negotiations
and thereby "attach them to us forever." Admiral Sir John Borlase Warren,
commander of the North American Naval Station, was another srong military proponent of the viability and desireability of an Aboriginal dominion with the Ohio River for its southern boundary.[93]

The peace negotiations to end the War of 1812 took place in 1814 in
Ghent, the former capital of East Flanders. The Americans entered the
negotiations from a position of considerable weakness. Although Tecumseh was dead, the Indian Confederacy still controlled much of the domain
of the bowl with one spoon. Moreover, Napoleon was defeated. The Americans could no longer depend on the strength of France to bolster their
bargaining position. According to Burt, in the early stages of the bargaining the British sought to make the establishment of the Indian state the
"*sine qua non* of any treaty." That innovation would help protect British
North America on its most vulnerable flank. "The embarrassing and costly
blunder of 1783, when [Britain] forgot her red allies," writes Burt, "was at
last to be repaired by the creation of an Indian buffer state. The project
which had been dropped in 1794, when an American war threatened to
come on top of a French war just begun, was thus revived twenty years later
by the collapse of the long French war coming on top of the delayed American war."[94]

Not surprisingly, the American negotiators balked at the proposal. Their
aversion to the principle of the Indian state was sufficient for them to continue the war. The British resolve on behalf of the Indian state was not of
the same order of magnitude, so the project was abandoned. Instead, an
article was inserted into the British peace proposal requiring the Americans to cease hostilities with the Indians and to restore to them the status
and titles they held in 1811 before hostilities began. The hollowness of the
provision was marked by the fact that the Americans accepted it so readily. "The American acceptance of the Indian article," writes Burt, "was the
great turning point."[95] Once the primary business of Indian Affairs was
resolved (without the hint of any direct involvement of any living Native
person), the way was cleared for British and American negotiators to move
on to a host of secondary issues. Rather than repairing the damage done
to His Majesty's Indian allies in the Treaty of Paris, the Treaty of Ghent
essentially entrenched what was done in 1783. Yet again the limits of
Britain's Aboriginal policies were demonstrated. When the legal and moral
strength of Aboriginal title, Aboriginal treaties, or Aboriginal hostilities

towards the Americans could be exploited as a shield of defence for British imperial Canada, Indigenous peoples were encouraged to express their nationalistic aspirations to the fullest. But when conditions required that the British government invest its own political and military capital in the defence of Indian Country, a different rule applied.

In spite of the British government's retreat from its role as champions of the Indian Confederacy's national right to sovereign self-determination, however, the peace negotiations of the Treaty of Ghent once again demonstrated the centrality of what is currently known as "Aboriginal and treaty rights" in the high diplomacy of both Great Britain and the United States during that era. Questions involving the relationship of Indian peoples to the sovereign crown of the United Kingdom or to the sovereign people of the United States were questions that belonged largely to the realm of foreign rather than domestic policy. In their war and diplomacy with the United States, the governors of British imperial Canada repeatedly insisted that the titles, treaties, and self-governing rights of the Indigenous peoples were extensive enough to place severe limitations on what the American government could or could not do, especially on the western frontiers of Euro-American settlement. The legacy of this pressure from Great Britain on the United States to adopt broader constitutional definitions of Aboriginal and treaty rights is recorded in many documents. For instance, it appears in the acknowledgment rendered in 1793 to the Confederate Indian Nations on behalf of President George Washington that Aboriginal peoples retain "the right of the soil" in their ancestral lands until such time as they change their legal status through treaty negotiations.

More than any other issue, the conflicting attitudes towards the prospect of an Aboriginal dominion in the heart of North America marked the fundamental political, ideological, and economic differences between the founders of pre-Confederation Canada and the founders of the American empire of private property. The different philosophies of political economy manifested in these two strategic orientations to the rights and titles of Indigenous peoples have replicated themselves on many ideological frontiers until the present day. The axis of history and understanding linking Tecumseh's vision to George Manuel's conception of the Fourth World, for example, represents a very different approach to the planning of globalization than the agendas advanced by the World Trade Organization or by Sony Corporation's Akio Morita's advocacy of "the whole of the developed world as one big market."

The rudimentary outlines of many great debates to come were present in the streams of advice directed to the negotiators meeting at Ghent in 1814 with the aim of ending the conflict in North America. Among the most important and telling of the dispatches directed at the British diplomats was one from the Montreal- and London-based entrepreneurs of the Canadian fur trade. Indeed, their letters to the imperial government during the War of 1812 provide an extremely vivid portrayal of the status and strategic importance of Indian Country in the geopolitics of British imperial Canada. These reports equated "the protection of Indian Rights and the Security of the Canadas"[96] and "the blended Interests of His Majesty's Canadian Subjects and His faithful Indian Allies."[97] As noted by James McGill, a leading Montreal philanthropist and trader in the North West Company: "The Indians are the Only Allies who can aught avail in the defence of the Canadas. They have the same interest as us, and alike are objects of American subjugation, if not extermination."[98]

These British and Canadian proponents of a strong and independent Indian Country charge repeatedly that their American enemies were intent on the usurpation and destruction of the First Nations. In a memorial of the Boards of Trade of both Montreal and Quebec City, for instance, the American government is accused of "pursuing an unrelenting and systematic plan of despoiling [Indian peoples] of their Lands by every kind of chicanery and injustice." The "real object" of that government and of the "rapacious Land Jobbers" who control it is the "extirmination" of Indian peoples. The merchants went on to outline their view of the wrongheadedness and dubious legality of the border provision in the Paris Treaty of 1783 between the United States and Great Britain. Referring to the lands south of the Great Lakes, they note: "That country was inhabited by numerous tribes and Nations of Indians independent of us. They are the true proprietors of the territory. Their rights having never been acquired by us, could not be transferred to others without manifest injustice. This injustice was greatly aggravated by the consideration that those Aboriginal Nations had been our faithful allies during the American Rebellion now called Revolution – and yet no stipulation was made in their favour."

The Canadian merchants pressed the British government to undo the injustice of 1783 by pushing the American government into a new treaty to recognize a sovereign and independent Indian nation state. They outline the geographic scope of this envisaged Indian Country as follows:

The boundary necessary for the protection of Indian Rights and the Security of the Canadas in that quarter would be to run a line from Sandusky on Lake Erie to the nearest waters falling into the Ohio, then down that River and up the Mississippi to the Mouth of the Missouri – then up the Missouri to its principal source and confining the American states to the Rocky Mountains as their western boundary, so that they can be excluded from at least all the Country situated to the northward and westward of the line so designated and which country should remain wholly for the Indians and their hunting ground.[99]

A similar proposal was drafted in London in 1814 by the officers of Inglis, Ellis and Company, which, along with McTavish, Fraser and Company, was the most influential financial centre of the Canadian fur trade. In outlining their concern for the future "Independence and Freedom" of their Indian customers, suppliers, and partners, they proposed that the United

States should cede the southern zone of Greater Canada back to the crown: "If it is found impossible or inexpedient to insist upon the Cession to His Majesty of the sovereignty of the Countries within the proposed Boundary the Sovereignty of it should be left to the Indians who are originally entitled to it and your Memorialists have no hesitation in trusting that property with the Natives which they have so much reason to dread again placing under the power of their Oppressors."[100]

Like the events that led the US government to acknowledge in 1793 that Indian nations retained "the right of the soil" in their unceded ancestral lands, the geopolitical commentaries on the legal status of Indian Country during the War of 1812 are essential testimonies in the elaboration of a continental law of existing Aboriginal and treaty rights. The commentaries of those who perceived of Indians as allies rather than enemies reflect the evolutionary thrust of a Canadian nation whose geopolitical position in North America depended in the early nineteenth century on recognizing, rather than extinguishing, the Aboriginal title and political rights of the First Nations. In outlining the outcome of this policy, the merchants of Montreal and Quebec City detailed "the results of Indian friendship" as reflected in the initial conflicts of the War of 1812. "Had [the Indians] acted against us," the traders argued, "or even had they been neutral, Upper Canada must surely have fallen under the American yolk." They concluded, "Honour, humanity and Justice enjoin it as an imperious duty that such men as are our Indian Allies, who have proved themselves *our friends in need*, ought for no consideration whatsoever to be abandoned to the merciless oppressor."[101]

INDIAN REMOVAL AFTER THE WAR OF 1812: FEDERAL ACTIVISM INSIDE AND OUTSIDE THE RULE OF LAW IN THE UNITED STATES

The extended Aboriginal resistance in the domain of the bowl with one spoon prevented the government of the United States from mastering control of that area until after the completion of the War of 1812. Although Ohio had become a state in 1803, the year of the Louisiana Purchase, Indiana didn't enter the union as a state until 1816, when the hostilities around the international border had subsided. The opening of the Erie Canal in 1825 along the Mohawk Valley between Albany and Lake Ontario resulted in a major surge of Euro-American settlement south of the Great Lakes.

With the industrial transformation of the Six Nations' traditional stronghold into a major transportation corridor, Tecumseh's most dire predictions came true. The trans-Appalachain west was finally rendered wide open to become the site of one of the busiest resettlement projects the world has ever witnessed. The huge traffic in people, produce, and manufactured imports along the Erie facilitated the rise of the empire state and the ascendance of the port of New York as the premier point of arrival for wave after wave of immigrants. Many of these newcomers joined with the Anglo-Americans in a migration that finished the transformation of America's "Old Northwest" into a conquered frontier as well as the site of the world's pre-eminent experiment in applied possessive individualism.

The New World baptismal rites culminated in the trans-Appalachain west with initiatives aimed not only at exorcising the land of its Indian title but also at permanently displacing the Aboriginal bearers of that collective territorial right. As Tecumseh had predicted, Indigenous peoples from the Great Lakes to the Gulf of Mexico were to be pushed away from their Native lands towards the setting sun. In 1830 Congress moved to enact President Andrew Jackson's Indian removal policies as legislation. Those policies enviasged the Mississippi as a boundary between non-Aboriginal Americans east of the great river and non-American Aboriginals to the west. There was stunning symmetry and simplicity in such a sweeping continental conceptualization of how race and territory should be divided. The idea had originated with the regime of Thomas Jefferson when he contemplated mass deportation of Indian peoples to points west of the Mississippi or even "with the beasts of the forest into the Stony [Rocky] Mountains." Jackson's ascent to the presidency was closely associated with his role in the extinguishment and privatization of Indian Country. As the victorious American general in the Battle of New Orleans, Jackson had emerged from the War of 1812 as a hero. A large part of the fame he had gained as an Indian fighter originated in his quelling the assertions of the Creek Red Sticks. The Red Sticks had answered Tecumseh's plea to join in the campaign of unified Indian resistance to the western expansion of the United States.

General Jackson continued to wage military actions on Indian Country, pursing Seminole freedom fighters into the Florida Everglades in 1818. When he subsequently parlayed his military fame to become the country's new chief executive, he was not about to renounce the tactics that had brought him to high office. His political ascent was fuelled partly by the power of patronage he derived from asserting control over the network of land agents who redistributed to non-Indians the Indian territory taken through his conquistadorial style of frontier administration.[102] Jackson's sponsorship of Congressional legislation to remove all Indians from lands east of the Mississippi illustrates the tremendous hold of segregationist thinking on American public policy.[103] The sheer scope of the scheme gives credence to the characterization that the Sioux had prophetically given to the United States when one of their diplomats described the country in 1805 as "the new white nation." The push to enforce the laws of Indian removal became one of the truly epic sagas of what the frontier school of American historians often described, unfortunately without irony, as "Jacksonian democracy."[104]

Although some Aboriginal groups, together with their Christian missionaries, accepted their westward relocation as inevitable, there was major resistance to the scheme, especially in the southeast. In this region several powerful Indian confederacies, sometimes known as the "Five Civilized Tribes," had developed effective strongholds based on pragmatic marriages of their own Aboriginal laws and traditions with the forms of political economy cultivated by their Euro-American neighbours. In particular, the largest constituency of Cherokees, as well as their missionaries, opposed relocation, just as adamantly as they resisted all attempts by the state of Georgia to impose its jurisdiction on them.[105]

The resulting litigation pitting the state of Georgia against the Cherokee Nation and their agents produced what Charles Warren described as the most serious crisis ever faced by the Supreme Court in the United States.[106] In his classic ruling in 1832 in the case of *Worcester* v. *Georgia*, Chief Justice John Marshall asserted the pre-eminence of the treaty relations linking the Cherokee to the federal government. Georgia's efforts to impose its jurisdiction on Cherokee Country were "repugnant to the Constitution, laws and treaties of the United States." Moreover, the federalist judge described the status of Indians as a "distinct people, divided into separate nations, independent of each other, and the rest of the world, having institutions of their own, and governing themselves by their own laws."[107] This ruling is one of the most expansive interpretaions in the history of American jurisprudence on the legal extent in constitutional law of existing Aboriginal and treaty rights. The judgment is often cited to advance various arguments in support of the principles of First Nations' sovereignty; the ruling re-orients, or reconciles, the main thrust of many of Marshall's earlier pronouncements on the legal status of Indian peoples. In his finding on the case of *Cherokee Nation* v. *Georgia* written in 1831, he described Indian peoples as "domestic dependent nations." He ruled that they are in "a state of pupilage" and that "their relationship with the United States resembles that of a ward to his guardian."[108]

In determining the deeper issue of the source of the rights to land on which the United States sits, Marshall turned ultimately away from the First Nations to the doctrine of "discovery" and to the sovereign powers asserted by the English king in granting North American lands to the crown's subjects. Marshall's ruling in 1823 on the case of *Johnson* v. *McIntosh* was the vehicle for the formal transplanting of these Eurocentric legal theories into the interpretation of the law of the United States. This case involved a conflict over lands, with one claimant asserting legitimacy of his title going back to the original federal grant and the other claimant asserting the pre-eminence of his title based on an earlier purchase immediately before the American Revolution by the Illinois-Wabash Land Company. As discussed in detail in chapter 4, the Illinois-Wabash Company was one of those enterprises which acted on the legal theory that private companies could purchase land directly from the First Nations. The case was rooted directly in those controversies about the legitimacy of the Royal Proclamation of 1763 and the applicability of the Camden-York opinion of 1772.[109]

In his finding in 1823 and especially in 1832, Judge Marshall basically gave the force of jurisprudence to much of the content of the Northwest Ordinance of 1787, legislation that clarified the federal government's paramount role in the governance, acquisition, and redistribution of Indian lands beyond the boundaries of state jurisdiction. This authority over Indians, he ruled, was derived from the Treaty of Paris of 1783, whereby "the powers of government and the right of the soil, which had previously been in Great Britain, passed definitely to these States." He added, "It has never been doubted, that either the United States, or the several States had a clear title to all lands within the boundary line described in the treaty [of Paris], subject only to the Indian right of occupying, and that exclusive power to extinguish that right, was vested in that government which might constitutionally exercise it." In the view of Robert A. Williams, the outcome of the legal dispute between Johnson and McIntosh completed the process of judicial confirmation that American law drew its structures and legitimacy from English rather than indigenous sources. The case, Williams argued, continued "the discourse of the Norman Yoke and its fiction that European monarchs acquired feudally conceived rights of conquest upon their discovery of infidel-held territories in America."[110]

The Marshall rulings overwhelmingly favoured the pre-eminence of federal over state authority. It was the federal government of the United States that had moved into the role in Indian Country previously asserted by King George in the Royal Proclamation in 1763. Accordingly, Marshall left no doubt whatsoever that the state of Georgia was overstepping its jurisdiction by trying to impose its laws on the Cherokee Nation. Such encroachment was declared illegal. It represented a violation of the Indians' federally guaranteed Aboriginal and treaty rights. The clear implication was that the federal government would be violating its own laws as well as advancing the illegitimate designs harboured by the government of Georgia in enforcing the Indian removal laws on the Cherokee.

President Jackson refused to adhere to the federal government's constitutional responsibilities to protect the Cherokee and other Aboriginal groups from the incursions of state governments and their citizens. Instead, the Indian removal schemes were pushed ahead with disregard for the rulings and jurisdiction of the Supreme Court. In responding to criticism about the apparent carelessness of the Jackson administration in enforcing the rule of law, the president is reputed to have said, "John Marshall has made his decision, now let him enforce it."[111]

Jackson turned to that faction of Cherokees who had fought along with him against the Creek Red Sticks in the War of 1812. While this group made a treaty agreement with the federal government to relocate, the largest part of the Cherokee, whose leader was John Ross, concertedly opposed the federal determination to remove them illegally from their homes. In 1838 the federal government finally used the army to force the resisters to pick up stakes. The outcome was a long and arduous march at gun point across the country to the designated Indian Territory west of the Mississippi on lands that today constitute the basis of Oklahoma. This migration of about 15,000 people, including some Black slaves held by the Cherokee, has acquired the evocative name of the Trail of Tears. About a fifth of the travellers died on the walk to a legislatively promised land that the federal government covenanted to "forever secure and guaranty to them, and their heirs and successors."[112] The Trail of Tears was the centrepiece of a complex series of episodes that saw many Indian groups indigenous to lands east of the Mississippi either relocate to the territory apportioned to them by the federal government or else migrate to Canada or to Mexico to escape the jurisdiction of the United States altogether. While the Potawatomi were prominent among the Aboriginal migrants to Upper Canada, some of the Kickapoo sought new homes in Mexico.[113]

The forced relocation of Indians east of the Mississippi to the Aboriginal territories of other Indian nations west of the Mississippi was a raw assertion of federal muscle that awaited some sort of retroactive legal rationalization. As a single episode, it is probably the most blatant example in US history of "ethnic cleansing." This phrase, which crossed over from the Serbian language into English to describe the ethnic chaos in the Balkans following the demise of the Soviet empire, lacks any clear legal definition. However, the Trail of Tears must surely qualify as a textbook example of the phenomenon, especially in the context of the sweeping scheme of apportioning territory to divide different peoples in Jacksonian America.

The task of creating legal theory to justify the unilateral dispossession of Indians became even larger after 1871, when the American federal government abandoned even the legal fiction of obtaining Indian consent through treaty for the transport, enclosure, and subjugation of the First Nations. Until there is some basic constitutional reckoning with this fundamental flaw at the nation's foundation – some honest effort to address politically the reality that the United States's position in the world is founded on a primal exercise of power over Indians that was exerted without legal justifications – the American republic will continue to lack the capacity to pose without hypocrisy as a proponent, let alone as an enforcer, of the rule of law in the international community.

In the late nineteenth century Chief Joseph, the Nez Percé leader who became one of the most celebrated resisters of the policy of containing Indian peoples on reserves, challenged directly the legal basis of American Indian policy. In commenting on the refusal of government officials to allow him to return from the Colville reservation in Washington to his ancestral territory in the Idaho area, Chief Joseph remarked, "I have asked some of the great white chiefs where they get the authority to say to the Indian that he shall stay in one place. They cannot tell me."[114]

One of the most lucid and candid commentaries on the legal thinking underlying American Indian policy after the War of 1812 was penned by Benjamin Drake. Drake's commentary first appeared in 1858 as part of his biography of Tecumseh, a work of considerable authority that was based largely on the author's interviews with individuals who knew the famous Aboriginal patriot. In contrasting Tecumseh's legal interpretation of his peoples' status with that of the US government, Drake stipulates explicitly the dependence of the latter on the doctrine of "discovery" and on the view of Indian peoples as "savage hordes not sufficiently advanced in civilization to be admitted into the family of nations":

In acquisition of these [Indian] lands, however, our government has held that its title was perfect when it had purchased of the tribe in actual possession. It seems, indeed, to have gone further and admitted that a tribe might acquire lands by conquest which it did not occupy, as in the case of the Iroquois, and sell the same to us; and, that the title thus acquired, would be valid. Thus we have recognized the principles of international law as operative between the Indians and us on this particular point, while in some others, as in not allowing them to sell to individuals, and giving them tracts used as hunting grounds by other tribes beyond the Mississippi, we have treated them as savage hordes, not sufficiently advanced in civilization to be admitted into the family of nations. Our claim to forbid their selling to individuals, and our guarantying [sic] to tribes who would not sell to us in our corporate capacity, portions of country occupied as hunting grounds, by more distant tribes, can only be based on the right of discovery, taken in connection with a right conferred by our superior civilization.[115]

Drake goes on to explain how these doctrines were never accepted as the basis of law by many Indian groups encompassed by the jurisdictional claims of the United States. The rejection of these rationales for the taking of Indian land was particularly clear and concerted among those who were inspired by the ideas of Tecumseh. About Tecumseh's legal theory of Aboriginal and treaty rights, Drake writes:

His doctrine seems to have been that we acquired no rights over the Indians or their country either by discovery or superior civilization; and that the possession and jurisdiction can only be obtained by conquest or negotiation. In regard to the latter he held that purchase from a single tribe, although at the time sojourners on the lands sold, was not valid as it respected other tribes. That no particular portion of the country belonged to the tribe then within its limits – though in reference to other tribes, its title was perfect; that is, possession excluded other tribes, and would exclude them forever; but did not confer on the tribe having it, the right to sell the soil to us; for that was the common property of all the tribes who were near enough to occupy or hunt upon it, in the event of its being at any time vacated, and could only be vacated by *the consent of the whole*. As a conclusion from these premises, he insisted that certain sales made in the west were invalid, and protested against new ones on any other than his own principles.[116]

"TERRITORY IN THE ACTUAL POSSESSION OF ABORIGINAL AND POWERFUL NATIONS": THE CASE OF *CONNOLLY* V. *WOOLICH*

The relationship between the jurisdiction of the crown and the First Nations in the Indian Country of Canada was clarified in the courts by a case known as *Connolly* v. *Woolich*.[117] Although the ruling was not given until 1867, the dispute involved the legal status of a marriage conducted in 1803 at Rivière-aux-Rats near Lake Athabaska in what is now the northern Alberta region. The groom was William Connolly, a seventeen-year-old novice fur trader seeking to make his fortune within the extensive commercial empire of Montreal's North West Company. The bride is recorded in history as Susanne "Pas-de-nom," clearly a mark of the failure to identify her real Indian name. When she married William, Susanne was fifteen. She was the daughter of a prominent and influential Cree leader in the rich fur-trade country of Athabaska.

The marriage's prelude involved considerable negotiation between William and his future wife's extended family. When he finally succeeded in gaining their agreement for the union, the marriage ceremony itself was apparently also very elaborate. It took place *à la façon du pays,* in other words, according to the Aboriginal customs and traditions of Susanne's people. Susanne and William Connolly were for many years very devoted to one another. They travelled together throughout the vast fur-trade domain of Canada, spending time, for instance, at Île-à-la-Crosse, Cumberland House, Fort Chippewayan, Rainy Lake, Lake of the Woods, York Factory, Norway House, and Fort William. Over twenty-eight years of married life they had seven children. One of them, Amelia, married Jame Douglas in 1828. In 1851 he became the second governor of the crown colony of Vancouver Island. That colony provided the jurisdictional seed for British Columbia.

William Connolly struck up a relationship with a distant cousin named Julia Woolrich when he was in Montreal to arrange for an English education for one of his sons. In 1832 he married this woman in a Roman Catholic ceremony. The legal dispute arose when John Connolly, the part Cree son of Susanne and William, challenged in court his legal exclusion from his father's sizeable estate. On William's death that estate went entirely to Julia, who died in 1864. The case received considerable publicity in Montreal and Great Britain. Both sides in the dispute were able to afford the highest calibre of legal talent available in Montreal during that era.

The decision was rendered in 1867 by Judge Samuel Cornwallis Monk of the Lower Canada Superior Court in Montreal. He did extensive research preparing his ruling, including examination of the charters of the Canadian fur-trade companies centred in Montreal and London, the rulings of Chief Justice John Marshall in the United States, some treatises on international law and considerable documentation of the law of marriage throughout the

British Empire. Judge Monk decided that the Cree law governing the marriage of William and Susanne was binding and legitimate in a way his court must recognize. Accordingly, William's second marriage to Julia was deemed illegitimate. The outcome was that John Connolly and, by implication, his brothers and sisters born of Susanne would share in their father's estate.

Judge Monk's ruling went far in elaborating that, in 1803, the laws of the fur-trade domain of Canada were essentially Indian in origin and character. Moreover, this sphere of Aboriginal jurisdiction could be recognized and enforced in the crown's courts. "Indian political and territorial rights, laws, and useages remained in full force," he wrote.[118] To some extent even the European and Euro-Canadian traders were governed by Aboriginal law; in one of the ruling's most memorable phrases, Judge Monk deemed it was not possible for William Connolly "to carry with him the common law of England to Rat River in his knapsack." Judge Monk went so far as to question the legal viability of the sweeping terms of the Hudson's Bay Company's charter, granted in 1670. He suggested that "it was not in the power of the Crown" to grant the company proprietary rights in "such extensive regions of territory in the actual possession of aboriginal and powerful nations." This act seemed to him like "a violation of the plainest principles of public international law."[119]

The ruling was appealed in Canada, where the Appeals Court upheld Judge Monk's ruling. The next and final level of judicial arbitration in those days was the Privy Council of the House of Lords in Great Britain. The litigants made an out-of-court settlement, however, before taking it to the highest imperial court in the British Empire.

Judge Monk's ruling seems entirely consistent with the principles outlined by the Canadian fur-trade executives during the War of 1812. In both the diplomatic correspondence of the executives and Judge Monk's ruling, the Indian territory is not to be understood as some kind of subject realm where the crown's legal presence extinguished the pre-existing Aboriginal law of Indigenous peoples. Instead, the viability of the fur trade in which William Connolly was engaged depended on the capacity of Euro-Canadians to comport themselves within the rules of conduct and relationship that constituted the unwritten laws and constitutions of the Indigenous peoples. Indeed, the unwritten character of those Aboriginal constitutions was consistent with British constitutional law, which remains to this day largely unwritten. In recognizing that Indigenous peoples retained their own Aboriginal sphere of law and jurisdiction within the larger framework of the British Empire, Judge Monk addressed directly the principal problem that permeates all other problems in the jurisprudence of Aboriginal and treaty rights. That problem is how to find a balance that incorporates the rights and titles of Indigenous peoples with the legal regimes that have colonized their ancestral lands.

In the Canadian context, this problem amounts to protecting the principle that existing Aboriginal and treaty rights are not monopolized within the sphere of domestic jurisdiction created by the crown. While the rights and titles of First Nations must be afforded room for genuine integration into crown laws and institutions, ways must be found concurrently to adhere to Judge Monk's recognition that the jurisdiction of Indian Country also retains an integrity of its own that is distinct from crown law even if it is also recognizable by crown law.

The quest for this balance has been a major influence on the course of North American history. Without a doubt the most ambitious attempt to achieve such a balance came in the form of the idea to found a sovereign Aboriginal dominion in the heart of North America with backing and recocognition from the British imperial government. As we have seen, that innovation was embraced by Tecumseh as the only way he could see to avoid the subjugation and ultimate destruction of his own peoples under the alien, domestic rule of the United States. The future of the continent was dramatically altered by Tecumseh's crusade in the War of 1812 to elevate his peoples' treaty making from small, land-for-money deals to the stature of international relations between sovereign powers. This conflict did not produce the outcome envisaged by Tecumseh – the achievement of a lasting and viable equilibrium in Native-newcomer relations in North America. Ironically, however, the Indian role in the War of 1812 was instrumental in contributing to a subsequent equilibrium in Canada-US relations.

The genesis of treaty making with First Nations can be seen as the history of legal innovation to find ways to recognize Indigenous peoples as polities whose rights and titles belong simultaneously to the realms of domestic and international law. The effort to announce the existence of this fine legal balance appears in the repeated characterizations throughout the history of British North America of Indian nations as *allies* of the crown, as polities with which the imperial government was, in the words of the Royal Proclamation, "connected."

In 1794 Lord Dorchester, the governor general of British imperial Canada, gave explicit instructions about the importance of conducting all negotiations with Indigenous peoples in ways that left no doubt about the crown's recognition of the Aboriginal integrity of their own jurisdictionl sphere. These instructions were directed at members of the British Imperial Indian Department to clarify that, in future, the laws, customs, protocols, and conventions of the First Nations must be treated as paramount in all their treaty negotiations with the crown. Dorchester stipulated that all treaties "are to be made in public council with Great Solemnity and Ceremony according to the Ancient Usages and Customs of the Indians, the Principal Chiefs and leading Men of the Nation or Nations *to whom the lands belong* being first assembled."[120] These instructions represented part of the process of applying and elaborating the principles of intercultural democracy whose legal antecedants were in the Royal Proclamation and the diplomacy of the Covenant Chain. This instruction renewed the corporate memory of the Indian Department, providing the protocol almost a century later for the negotiation of the numbered treaties.

There is a large scholarly literature elaborating on the kind of principles that Judge Monk adressed in his ruling. Janet Switlo, for instance, has coined the term "Aboriginal allodial title" to mark the principle that jurisdiction of First Nations in their own ancestral territories is derived from sources outside the law of the crown. The crown can recognize this title, but it cannot create it, expropriate it, or extinguish it. Similarly, the persistent theme running through both *White Man's Law* and *Crow Dog's Case* by Sidney L. Harring is that Indigenous peoples have their own legal traditions that they continue to make, elaborate, revise, and enforce independently of how the governments of the United States and Canada structure their own legal regimes.[121] A key element of the arts and science of law making and jurisprudence in these countries is to integrate the evolving reality of Aboriginal law into the continent's overarching juridical systems. This process is essential in creating "a new common law of all peoples" in societies whose essence is multicultural and pluralistic.[122]

Alan Cairns expresses a similar vision. He views the paradigm of "nation-to-nation" treaty relations as too divisive in terms of its effect on the unity and viability of the evolving Canadian nation. His preferred metaphor to describe the character of Aboriginal status in Canada is that of *citizens plus*.[123] The phrase was introduced in 1966, in the first comprehensive study of the political, legal, and socioeconomic conditions of registered Indians in Canada.[124] While Harry B. Hawthorne was the chief researcher on the project, Cairns was part of his staff. In his own book published over thirty years later, Cairns returns to the phrase *citizens plus* to describe his vision of the appropriate legal positioning of First Nations people both inside and outside the regular structures of Canadian citizenship.

By emphasizing the treaty negotiations that took place at Niagara in 1764, legal historian John Borrows adds his voice to those opposing the notion of the crown's absolute domestication of existing Aboriginal and treaty rights. Borrows demonstrates that, in 1764, the terms of the Royal Proclamation of 1763 were discussed in the framework of an elaborate negotiation near one of the world's most renowned geographic features. The meaning of the Royal Proclamation was discussed in English and in many Aboriginal languages, with the view that First Nations would elaborate a relationship with the imperial government emphasizing peace and frienship, alliance with the crown, free trade, and the necessity of Aboriginal consent for any land cession in the protected Indian territories. Recognition that the Royal Proclamation was subjected to a consensual political process of give and take between crown officials and a representative array of Aboriginal delegations, argues Borrows, "would go a long way to dispelling notions found in Canadian legal and political discourse that regard First Nations as subservient to or dependent upon the Crown in pressing and preserving their rights." Such acknowledgment helps establish that First Nations should be regarded "as active participants in the formulation and ratification of their rights."[125]

Borrows devotes considerable attention to the patterns on the "Great Wampum" recording the substance of the treaty understandings formulated at the Niagara Council. In *A Wampum Denied*, Sandy Antal also emphasizes the diplomatic importance two generations later of this same shelled record that was brandished by Tecumseh in the crucial negotiations leading to the military alliance between the crown and the First Nations in the War of 1812.[126] Emphasis on the adoption of wampum protocols by all the colonial powers in eastern North America constitute a rich form of illustration that the newcomers incorporated into their own systems of law and diplomacy constitutional conventions derived from the legal traditions of First Nations peoples.

One of the recurring motifs in the wampum recordings of treaty agreements are the two parallel rows, symbolizing different boats travelling the same stream. The two-row wampum, which first appeared as a metaphor of Longhouse–New Netherlands relations, became a symbol of dual autonomy in shared territory, an alliance between equals moving along parallel paths of history, or sovereignty-association.

The necessary metaphors of pragmatic cooperation and co-existence in the fur-trade domain of Canada were clearly accessible to Judge Samuel Monk. Like many Tory elites among his generation of Canadians, Monk had family roots in the British Imperial Indian administration. The patriarch of his family, George Henry Monk, had served for twenty years, starting in 1783, as the Indian commissioner of Nova Scotia.[127] This background may have been a factor helping Judge Monk to make the imaginative leap when he pointed out the absurdity of the idea of William Connolly carrying the common law of England with him in his knapsack to the Athabaska district in 1803. With this comment, the judge acknowledged that Connolly's movement into Indian Country represented a demanding process of deep immigration into a distinct and powerful realm that subordinated most European influences, including legal ones, to the pre-eminent authority of the First Nations. This process of genuine immigration into the all-encompassing embrace of Indian Country, with the attending need of the immigrants to assimilate and absorb the prevailing motifs of Aboriginal cultures, was, and is, an experience shared by many influential Canadians. It is an experience of immigration that belonged to Archie Belaney no less than to William Connolly, the baron de Lahontan, Sir William Johnson, or Anna Jameson. It is this history whose deep roots give continuing vitality to the "Grey Owl" syndrome. This willing assimilation into the Old World of the Americas is expressed in an attitude to culture and ecology embodied in the will to recognize and renew, rather than deny and extinguish the existence of Aboriginal and treaty rights.

The case of *Connolly* v. *Woolich* brings to light the character of a North American civilization including many mixed-ancestry families who lived out their lives on the middle ground where the imported cultures of Europe and the indigenous cultures of North America merged. Clearly the children of William and Susanne were thoroughly integrated into the colonial culture of Canada. As the wife of James Douglas, Amelia Connolly Douglas was the matriarch of British Columbia's first family. John Connolly was just one of many prominent figures in Lower and Upper Canada, with family trees leading up country into the lineages of the First Nations. These individuals belong to an important class of mixed-ancestry people in every colonial empire who have supplied much of the intercultural expertise on the middle grounds that are essential staging grounds for most imperial enterprises.

Like French-Aboriginal Canada, British imperial Canada was founded on a heritage of strategic alliances with Indigenous peoples. The economics of the fur trade, together with the strategic implications of war and conflict with the United States, necessitated a practical emphasis on cooperation with, rather than conquest of, the First Nations. Ultimately, however, the ethos of alliance and equality in diversity would stretch only so far. The failure of the British government to make room for First Nations' representation at the highest level of negotiations on North America's boundaries could only be based on legal assumptions similar to those of the American government.

The decidedly Eurocentric nature of all those major transactions where the map of North America was drawn and redrawn without direct Aboriginal involvement or consent could be rationalized only through resort to theories of civilizational hierarchy. These theories distinguished "savage hordes" from "civilized" Europeans and their "advanced" American descendants. This ranking of human societies was deemed sufficient to disqualify Indigenous peoples in the Americas from direct involvement at the high tables of international treaty making. There is no escaping the dark reality that, beneath the policy distinguishing international treaty making from the making of treaties with Indigenous peoples, lies a theory of government distinguishing higher from lower orders of humanity. Among those international agreements that decided Aboriginal futures without Aboriginal representation or consent were the Treaties of Paris in 1763 and 1783, as well as the Treaty of Ghent in 1814. In 1818 the tradition of elaborating in Europe the geopolitical map of North America was continued. According to the "Convention" of that year, the 49th parallel was established as the border between the United States and British North America from the Lake of the Woods to the Rocky Mountains.

One of Tecumseh's great objectives was to overcome the Eurocentric exclusion of Indigenous peoples in North America from the highest level of involvement in the making of international law. In seeking to alter the framework of international law in this way, Tecumseh was acting consistently with the egalitarian spirit of Enlightenment thought. His quest to gain sovereign representation for the Indian Confederacy at the high tables of international diplomacy added another dimension to the political revolution sought by Toussaint L'Overture. L'Overture was the leader of the slave revolt that remade the french sugar colony of San Domingo into the republic of Haiti.[128] Both Tecumseh and Tousaint L'Overture had come of age in an era when the Declaration of the Rights of Man raised hopes and expectations not only among oppressed Europeans, but also among many subject peoples in the colonized world. Each leader was martyred in the midst of his struggle to find a middle ground of resolution between his own peoples' quest for liberation and the egalitarian ideals used to justify the revolutions that transformed the transatlantic world at the end of the eighteenth century.

In a different way, Chief Justice John Marshall in the case of *Worcester* v. *Georgia* and Judge Samuel Monk in the case of *Connolly* v. *Woolrich* translated some of the central ideals of Enlightenment thought into their interpretations of US and British North American law. Monk's ruling was especially innovative in laying out a vision of an extremely pluralistic British Empire where Indigenous peoples retained wide jurisdictions over themselves, over their territories, and even over visitors to their territories. He left us a picture of how the imperatives of commerce could be exercised without the heavy imposition of imperial rule on societies entering into networks of globalized trade.

In the late nineteenth century the highest court in the British Empire passed down another, very different ruling that symbolized the subordination of Enlightenment egalitarianism beneath the emerging role of Darwinian social science as the ideological handmaiden of imperial rule. The West's accelerating retreat from the idealism inherent in the cry of "liberty, equality and fraternity" would later culminate in the rise of nationalist extremism as most notoriously manifested in the eugenic fantasies animating Nazi fascism.[129] The imperial court's ruling came in 1888 in response to a constitutional dispute between the governments of Canada and Ontario. The provincial arguments in this dispute, known as the *St. Catherine's Milling and Lumber* case, drew heavily on a line of legal precedent running back to the juridical justifications for Christendom's attacks on the Muslim realms during the Crusades.

In advancing the imagery of Indigenous peoples as childlike wards of federal authority, the *St. Catherine's Milling* case promoted the same ideology the European powers were concurrently using to justify their extension of ownership and control throughout their proliferating colonies in Africa and Asia. The litigation moved through the courts at roughly the same time, for instance, as a series of complex transactions enabling King Leopold II of Belgium to claim sovereign jurisdiction over the vast Congo River basin in the name of an imagined mandate vested in the world's civilized nations to exercise a benign tutelage over peoples deemed to be primitive and barbarian.[130] Like the establishment in 1885 under Leopold's personal proprietorship of the state of Congo, the outcome of the *St. Catherine's Milling* case set in motion patterns of economic exploitation that proved disastrous for many Aboriginal groups and individuals. In North America, Africa, and most other parts of the colonized world, the civil, political, and human rights of Indigenous peoples were further repressed beneath the resurgent claims of western civilization's old missionary imperative. This resort during the declining years of the Victorian era to the most chauvinistic rationales for nationalism and empire building marked a tragic renunciation of the Enlightenment's most radical challenge to humanity to construct a world order based on reciprocity, equality, and democracy.

GEORGIA AND ONTARIO
VERSUS ABORIGINAL AND TREATY RIGHTS:
INDIAN AFFAIRS AND THE BALANCE OF POWER IN THE
FEDERALISMS OF CANADA AND THE UNITED STATES

The *St. Catherines* case wound its way between 1885 and 1888 from the Ontario court to the Supreme Court of Canada and then to the highest court in the British Empire, the Judicial Committee of the Privy Council.[131] The case was based on a crisis in Canadian federalism similar to the divisions addressed by John Marshall in *Johnson* v. *McIntosh* and in the Cherokee cases of the early 1830s. Where Marshall had to deal with a constitutional conflict between the jurisdictional spheres of Georgia and the federal government in the United States, the *St. Catherine's* case pitted the governments of Ontario and Canada against each other in their conflicting interpretations of the scope and depth of Aboriginal and treaty rights.

In the Canadian case this division in federalism came down to different views of the constitutional meaning of a single phrase in the British North America (BNA) Act, legislation of the British parliament which brought about Canadian Confederation in 1867 as a federal union of provincial and dominion jurisdictions. The provision at issue was section 91(24), which specifically assigned "Indians and lands reserved for the Indians" to the legislative authority of the dominion government.

In pushing for a broad constitutional interpretation of section 91(24), the dominion government of Prime Minister John A. Macdonald hoped to assert federal capacity to control and tax the exploitation of natural resources over those vast expanses of Canada not covered by Indian treaties at the time of Confederation. His government had extended a licence to the St. Catherine's Milling Company to cut trees in the area of present-day Kenora, Ontario, a move that prompted the provincial government of Premier Oliver Mowat to charge the loggers, and, by extension, the federal authority with the commission of a crime. The object of the Mowat government in this and other legal confrontations with the dominion government was to advance a constitutional vision of provincial sovereignty within the boundaries of provincial jurisdiction, including the strategically vital area of control over the use, exploitation and possible privatization of what were known as crown lands.[132] The question to be answered was whether the proprietary interest in the largest part of the country would adhere to the provincial crowns or the dominion crown in Canada's federal system.

The case reproduced many of the conflicts and tensions that made Indian Affairs the object of major controversy between the imperial government and the local governments of the Anglo-American colonies, especially in the decade and a half leading up to the American Revolution. An indication of the persistence of similar themes of conflict between local and central authorities on the jurisdictional frontiers of Euro-American expansion is illustrated by the constitutional prelude to the *St. Catherine's* case. Before embarking on their courtroom fight over the jurisdictional boundaries of constitutional responsibility for Indians and lands reserved for the Indians, the federal and provincial governments fought one another over the location of the western boundary between Ontario and the federal lands of Manitoba and the Canadian North West Territories.[133] The *St. Catherine's* case bore considerable resemblance to the case of *Johnson* v. *McIntosh*, in that both trials involved two non-Indian litigants making claims of their own. Their antagonistic arguments were made in a forum where no living Indian people were present to observe or give their views and opinions about the nature of their legal status. Nevertheless, questions of immense import for the First Nations as well as for millions of Canadian citizens, living and unborn, turned on testimony regarding two different interpretations of the nature of Indian rights, Indian titles, and crown-Aboriginal treaties.

In asserting the exclusive power of the central authority to conduct relations with First Nations, the dominion government of Canada was restating an old constitutional principle emerging from many generations of colonization in North America. The central government of the United States had asserted this same imperative with its enactment of the Northwest Ordinance of 1787. Before that, King George had declared the pre-eminence of imperial authority over local authority in designing and implementing the Indian policy of British North America. King George's Royal Proclamation, in turn, gave renewed expression to a tradition of English colonial law that began to coalesce as early as 1664. That year the Royal Commissioners accompanying the English forces who conquered New Netherlands used the occasion to reign in the expansionary tactics of the United Colonies of New England. The king's representatives stipulated that the colonists' local governments in North America could not acquire Indian lands through conquest or purchase without the monarch's explicit sanction.

In developing their arguments for the *St. Catherine's Milling* case, the lawyers for the dominion government placed particular emphasis on the Royal Proclamation of 1763. By virtue of the wording of section 91 (24) of the BNA Act, the treaty-making prerogative once vested in the imperial government had shifted, they maintained, to the central government of Canada. This interpretation led the dominion government's lawyers to conclude that their client was the recipient, and thus the current holder, of the rights and titles passed from Saulteaux people to the crown in the making in 1873 of Treaty 3 in the Kenora area.

The lawyers for the Ontario government, including Edward Blake, countered the dominion's position by arguing for a very narrow constitutional interpretation of the phrase "lands reserved for the Indians." If Indians held no rights, or very limited, fragile, and easily extinguishable rights to their ancestral lands, then little of substance would have changed hands in the treaty negotiations of 1873. The essence of the Mowat government's position was that, since property was a creation of law, and since Indian people were alleged to be primitive and savage and therefore without law, they had no binding claim to any substantial title in their ancestral lands.

In developing their arguments, which were unformly based on negating any notion that the crown had historically recognized and affirmed an expansive understanding of existing Aboriginal and treaty rights, the lawyers for Ontario resorted to all the old rationales for Indian dispossession. Many strands of this argument went back to the precedents set in *Calvin's* case in 1608, when English Lord Chief Justice Edward Coke articulated legal principles integral in the justification of Europe's Holy Crusades in the Islam world. Drawing on the long line of precedents going back to *Calvin's* case – arguments that in the early history of Virginia reinforced the zealousness of Nathaniel Bacon's murderous campaign directed at Indians both inside and outside the colony – the lawyers for Ontario asserted, "At the time of the discovery of America, and long after, it was an accepted rule that heathen and infidel nations were perpetual enemies, and that the Christian prince or people first discovering and taking possession of the country became its absolute proprietor, and could deal with the land as such."[134]

There is more than coincidence in the similarities in the constitutional arguments of the governments of Georgia in the 1830s and of Ontario in the 1880s. In both localities, officials advanced arguments to extinguish and negate Aboriginal and treaty rights in order to realize the expansion of their own governments' jurisdictions. This parallel points to the propensity in the federal systems of both the United States and Canada for state governments and provincial governments to advance their own agendas in terms that are sometimes fundamentally hostile to the protection of the human rights of populations outside the majoritarian culture of the dominant group. This pattern was clear in the southeastern quarter of the United States, where the assertion of "states' rights" has historically disguised

not only the most aggressive demands for Cherokee dispossession but also
the defence of the institution of slavery and, after the Civil War, of the legitimacy of racial segregation through the elaboration of the Jim Crow
laws.[135] In Canada the role of provincial authorities as agents of majoritarian hostily to the human rights of marginalized peoples was dramatically illustrated in November 1981. At that time, nine of Canada's ten provincial premiers temporarily succeeded in stripping the positive recognition
and affirmation of Aboriginal and treaty rights from the text of the document that detailed the terms for the patriation of the Canadian Constitution from Great Britain.[136]

In the United States, the Civil War began in 1861 primarily as a military
crisis born of conflicting constitutional interpretations of the relationship
between federal and state authority. By the end of the conflagration in
1865, President Abraham Lincoln's Emancipation Proclamation transformed the conflict into a great moral crusade as the federal government,
in opposition to the Confederacy of American States, abolished slavery. A
century later the federal government employed the American army once
again to enforce federal laws on those southern states that had fallen back
into various practices of racial segregation, including in public education.
These episodes illustrate the reality that jurisdictional conflicts in federalism tend to lie on the surface of more fundamental arguments about the
recognition or denial of the most basic human rights.

No less than the conflicts over the institution of slavery in the United
States in the nineteenth century, the legal tests over the existence or
absence of Aboriginal and treaty rights went to the roots of the most fundamental questions of human rights. On the outcome of this issue hinged
the answer to whether the agency of American self-governance would
become a shield of defence for human dignity or a weapon of vanquishment and dispossession in the hands of a conquering army of possessive
individualism.

Chief Justice Marshall's interpretation of the American Constitution
elaborated the principle that the central government retained the legal
power – indeed, it inherited the legal obligation – to push aside and overrule all incursions emanating from state authority on the remaining Indian Country. In spite of this directive from the highest court in the land, the
federal government proved unwilling in the 1830s to shield Native people
and a remnant of their ancestral lands and resources east of the Mississippi from the aggression of the people and government of Georgia. There
were many betrayals arising from the federal enactment and implementation of Indian removal in the 1830s. Not only were Indian peoples east and
west of the Mississippi betrayed but soo too was federal power undermined
along with the credibility of the federal authority as a maker and upholder of treaties. Put plainly, in advancing Indian removal, the federal government purposely and systematically violated the authority of the
Supreme Court and of the American Constitution itself. Jacksonian Indian

removal thus signalled that both within the United States and in its relations with the international community, the rule of law would be treated as
a contingent apparatus to be used or discarded according to the higher
needs of political expediency.

Over time, John Marshall's decisions asserted with growing insistence
the exclusivity of the constitutional bond between Indian peoples and the
federal government. Presumably this trend reflected Marshall's growing
appreciation of the fundamental constitutional importance of the federal
role in Indian Affairs in affirming the sovereign pre-eminence of the central government over the state governments.[137] As Francis Jennings has
written: "Even after defeat the Indians retained importance because they
held the key to whether the United States should only be a confederation
of equal states or should become an empire with sovereign central jurisdiction ... In a very real sense, even within the arbitrarily fictional domain
of the law, the empire of the United States has derived its authority from
power over Indians."[138]

While the government of the state of Georgia failed in its legal efforts
before Chief Justice Marshall to negate the Aboriginal and treaty rights of
the Cherokee, the lawyers for the government of Ontario won most of
their constitutional arguments with the dominion government in the
court's judgment on the *St. Catherine's Milling* case. The central government of Canada suffered a major constitutional setback in 1888 that weakened it severely on a number of legal fronts. Because of the ruling, provincial governments have been able to assert broad powers of ownership in,
and control over, the largest part of Canada's land base. Most often provincial governments have exercised this control by extending licences to
transnational corporations, enabling them to exploit the country's mineral, fossil fuel, and forestry wealth without regard for the existence of Aboriginal and treaty rights. While the federal government retained much of
the responsibility to enforce these rights, its incentive and capacity to do
so were diminished by the judges' pronouncements in this seminal episode
of constitutional interpretation.

In the lower court's ruling on the *St. Catherine's* case, Chancellor John
Boyd outlined a narrow interpretation of the constitutional phrase "lands
reserved for the Indians." He referred to the small plots known as Indian
reserves, as places where "Indians are regarded no longer as in a wild and
primitive state, but in a condition of transition from barbarism to civilization."[139] On appeal, the Judicial Committee of the Privy Council in Great
Britain ruled that Indians' title to their ancestral lands existed, but that this
right was "personal and usufructory," "dependent on the goodwill of the
Sovereign." Further, it ruled that "the right of the Provinces to a beneficial
interest" in the lands in question were "available to them as a source of revenue whenever the estate of the Crown is disencumbered of the Indian
title."[140]

Where the centre of the *St. Catherine's* case revolved around section

91 (24) of the British North American Act, another key question at issue was the constitutional meaning of section 109 of that same document. That provision stipulates that the "lands, mines, minerals, and royalties belonging to the several provinces of Canada" are "*subject to* any trusts existing in respect thereof, and to any interest other than that of the province in the same" [added emphasis]. This limitation on the constitutional powers of provinces projects into Canadian federalism a limitation similar to the United States's qualified right to the soil as confirmed even in the ruling on the case of *Johnson* v. *McIntosh*. As noted above, in Marshall's decision in 1823, the two powerful words "subject to" are invoked to draw limits on the sovereign capacity of non-Aboriginal authorities to displace or disinherit Indian peoples without their consent.

Accordingly, this potent constitutional mantra, "subject to," resonates throughout the generations over much of North America, a land that has been subjected to some of the most systematic and methodical applications of ethnic cleansing that the world has ever seen. What else is an Indian reserve or reservation other than a souvenir of the drive to clear the land of Indigenous peoples as a preparation for its repopulation with resettled immigrants? While no one can turn back the clock, the powerful phrase "subject to" presents the interpreters of the constitutional law of both Canada and the United States with a clear opening to throw off the onerous weight of some of the most dubious precedents on the books. This line of precedent goes back to the justifications for Christendom's violent Crusades in the Islam world. Its history is one of bloody violation of the most rudimentary rights of other peoples. Alternatively, the line of precedents that ease the absolutism of the New World conquests with the qualifying proviso "subject to" draw on some of the most inspiring emanations of the human spirit illuminated by the continuing rays of the Enlightenment. These rays of liberty find contemporary reflection particularly in those beacons of international law recognizing that the right of self-determination belongs to *all* peoples, large and small.

One of two dissenting decisions on the *St. Catherine's* case was written in the newly created Supreme Court of Canada by Judge Samuel Henry Strong. Rather than confining himself to narrow analysis of the "black letter law" of existing statutes and the legal rulings of other courts, Strong looked to the broad sweep of Canadian history in coming to the conclusion that the existing constitution reflected most of the dominion government's arguments in defence of its interpretation of existing Aboriginal and treaty rights. In approaching the law in this way, Judge Strong looked at the Canadian Constitution in a manner consistent with a more encompassing view of the British Constitution as a complex of laws and conventions that are largely unwritten. This constitution grew out of shared memory of certain key events and processes; it emanated not so much from words on paper as from the wellspring of what had happened in the genesis of that society.

In his dissenting opinion, Judge Strong reached back to the strategic importance of the Royal Proclamation of 1763 and of crown alliances with Indian nations in the struggle to withhold the northern part of the continent from absorption into the United States. His way of looking at the BNA Act renewed the easy connections made by the fur-trade executives who, during the War of 1812, equated the protection of Indian rights and the security of the Canadas. In his effort to illuminate the spirit, nature, and intent of Canada's constitution, he wrote:

From the memorable year 1763, when Detroit was besieged and all the Indian tribes were in revolt, down to the date of confederation, Indian wars and massacres entirely ceased in the British possessions in North America, although powerful Indian nations still continued for some time after that former date to inhabit those territories. That this peaceful conduct of the Indians is in a great degree to be attributed to the recognition of their rights to land unsurrendered by them, and to the guarantee of their protection in the possession and enjoyment of such lands given [sic] by the Crown in the Proclamation of October, 1763, hereafter to be more fully noticed, is a well known fact of Canadian history which cannot be controverted. The Indian nations from that time became and have since continued to be firm and faithful allies of the Crown and rendered it important military service in two wars – the war of the Revolution and that of 1812.[141]

Of all the individuals and groups who peopled the history described by Judge Strong, none personified better than Tecumseh the animating principles of the idea of Indigenous peoples as makers, not mere objects, of international law. Tecumseh's fate, however, was to be a martyr rather than a founder of the pan-Indian state. But his tireless efforts as ambassador, military recruiter, historian, law giver, strategist, and general of the Indian Confederacy were crucial to the survival of the Indian Country of Canada, the deeper polity onto which British North America had been grafted in 1763 through the legal authority of King George's Royal Proclamation. Without Tecumseh's intellectual and logistical mobilization of Indian peoples throughout much of North America to make their most concerted united stand ever against the enemy Long Knives, Upper Canada would certainly have fallen to the United States. And the fall of Upper Canada would in all probability have led to the American annexation of Rupert's Land and the North-West Territories, an Indian and Inuit territory covering the largest part of present-day Canada.

THE LEGACY OF TECUMSEH
AND OF THE BOWL WITH ONE SPOON

In the United States, Tecumseh has been afforded the role of worthy Indian opponent whose intelligent, principled, and spirited opposition to the westward expansion of the republic helped give nobility and valour to the growth of a great nation.[142] This genre of acknowledgment runs throughout the pages of the biography by Benjamin Drake, who set the mould for many laudatory studies to follow in the United States. Tecumseh's "genius should neither be tested by the magnitude of his scheme nor the failure in its execution, but by the extraordinary success that crowned his patriotic labours," Drake wrote. "By the battle of Tippecanoe ... the great object of his ambition was frustrated, the golden bowl was broken at the fountain; that ardent enthusiasm which for years had sustained him, in the hour of peril and privation, was extinguished."[143]

The Indian Confederacy's great setback in the loss of Tippecanoe in 1811 forced Tecumseh towards a more open alliance with the British, whom he never entirely trusted. The memory of the confrontation at Tippecanoe would resonate in years ahead to provide an entry to the White House for Tecumseh's nemesis, William Henry Harrison. In their effort to cast a candidate in the image of "Old Hickory" – President Andrew Jackson – the Whigs turned to the man they dubbed "Old Tippecanoe." With Harrison as their prime candidate, the Whigs succeeded in this electoral venture, making the hero of Tippecanoe the second veteran Indian fighter from the War of 1812 era to reach the highest office in the United States. On his way to victory, a huge rally was organized in Harrison's home state of Ohio on the very site of the old Indian Confederacy's envisaged national capital. This place was known as Tippecanoe in the national lore of the United States, but Prophetstown to those whose revolutionary hopes were directed at the creation of a united council fire for an inclusive Aboriginal dominion of United Indian Nations. The crushing of these hopes for a sovereign Indian federation would be glorified in the Whigs' slogan for the presidential campaign of 1840: "Tippecanoe and Tyler too."[144]

While Tecumseh served in the role of worthy opponent to the builders and shapers of the American empire of private property, in Canada the Shawnee leader's work and aspirations are preserved in the fact that the country exists, apart from the realm of the Stars and Stripes. Tecumseh is as indispensable to the course of Canadian history as Samuel de Champlain or John A. Macdonald, Louis Riel or Henri Bourassa, René Lévesque or J.S. Woodsworth, Pierre Trudeau or John Diefenbaker. And the legacy of the Indian Confederacy continues to find expression in the peoples and institutions of the Canadian federation, whose constitution was renewed in 1982 to recognize and affirm existing Aboriginal and treaty rights.

If the legacy of Tecumseh and the Indian Confederacy is acknowledged as a fundamental legacy of Canada, so too is the philosophy of the bowl with one spoon part of Canada's living essence. The wampum representation of this bowl symbolizes shared land and shared access to shared resources. It is consistent with the creative and humane use of the state to achieve a variety of shared purposes. For instance, the Canadian Broadcasting Corporation and publicly financed universal health care extend in another context some of the the general principles of the bowl with one spoon. Attacks on this genre of public enterprise in the name of privatization and deregulation project forward many of the same hostilities to the role of an activist central government that originally animated the revolutionary rejection of British imperialism as the regulatory agency of Anglo-American colonization.

Moreover, the principles of the bowl with one spoon give added historical and cultural context to the political evolution that once carried Canada along the path largely charted by those who have come to be known as Red Tories. This tradition of Canadian nationalism has drawn heavily from conservative Anglicans, Anabaptists, and Roman Catholics, as well as from those social democrats whose quest for the authority to govern led from the League for Social Reconstruction to the Co-operative Commonwealth Federation to the New Democratic Party.

In the United States the convergence of conservatism and social democracy has been hampered by the violent exorcism of the Tory tradition from the new republic's array of acceptable political philosophies. After the American Revolution, British North America became the major preserve for the kind of conservatism that had been cultivated in the manor of Sir William Johnson, in the far-flung North West Company, in the British Imperial Indian Department, and in the quest of Tecumseh to entrench a permanent Indian Country in the heart of his peoples' Aboriginal continent. In the words of George Grant, the prophetic sage of Red Toryism, the founders of English-speaking Canada responded to their experience on the losing side of the American Revolution by joining with the Native people and the French Canadians in their "desire to build a political society with a clearer and firmer doctrine of the common good than that at the heart of the liberal democracy to the south."[145] Nevertheless, in the United States, too, there is a growing movement seeking a conservatism that is genuinely conservationist rather than neo-liberal in its approach to ecology, cultural pluralism, and the building of an economy that eschews vast, polarizing inequities between rich and poor.

At the core of Tecumseh's political program, which would find indirect expression in the Red Tory approach to Canadian nationalism, was a strict prohibition against "free trade" in lands and natural resources. In affirming the principle that lands and resources beyond the Ohio River belonged collectively to all the peoples of the Indian Confederacy, Tecumseh was essentially affirming the strategic importance of a system of land tenure and property law in Indian territory that was internal to the legal authority of a united council of First Nations. That ability to govern property relationships, Tecumseh understood, was the most indispensable and strategic tool of sovereign self-determination for any confederacy of self-governing peoples.

Without this internalization of a system of property relations within the collective jurisdiction of the Indian Confederacy, the Aboriginal domain in North America would continue to be fragmented, splintered, and devoured. It would continue to be atomized by the legal, administrative, and military machinery of an interlocked system of business and government designed for the transformation of Indian lands into new capital, real estate, and living space for the human and corporate citizens of the New World republic. Resistance to the transformation of the land of the bowl with one spoon foreshadowed an extended resistance to the thoroughgoing integration of what remained of Canada into the American empire.[146] It forshadowed the global ascendance of the decolonization movement. That movement for decolonization has, in turn, blended inexorably into the movement of those opposed to neo-liberal forms of globalization. One of the growing convictions unifying this otherwise eclectic movement is the belief that neo-liberalism promotes the continuation of the Columbian conquests, whose main agencies of expansionism include European imperialism, the Aboriginal and foreign policies of the United States, and global corporations. Similarly, the emergence in 2003 of a global movement of opposition to a US-led invasion of Iraq advanced a tradition of resistance consistent with the principles invoked by the Wampum imagery of the bowl with one spoon.

In current times no less than in the era of Tecumseh, some Aboriginal individuals might enrich themselves by helping to bring the shared First Nations domain under the laws of the empire of possessive individualism. But their personal gains have been based on the most ruthless and destructive kind of theft from their own peoples. They have acted on behalf of a system that, in the words of Eduardo Galeano, believes "communal cultures that do not separate human beings from one another and from nature are enemy cultures."[147]

Without a system of land tenure under the recognized authority of a sovereign Aboriginal nation-state, Tecumseh understood that Indigenous peoples would continue to be treated as a lower order of humanity whose rights and titles to their territories (and ultimately to themselves) were subject to a lower order of law. And in order to achieve recognition in international law, it was crucial in Tecumseh's estimation for Indian nations to demonstrate a common front in their relations with the outside world. For Tecumseh, the career of the United States demonstrated the point graphically. As he told William Henry Harrison, "the U. States had set him the example by forming a strict union amongst all the Fires that compose their confederacy."[148] Without federal unity, the United States could not have achieved recognition in international law. And without recognition in international law, the American rebels would have been seen as terrorists and criminals rather than as founders of a new country.

While Tecumseh recognized that the Indian Confederacy must act on the international stage to achieve a degree of security and stature in international law, there were still tremendous obstacles barring his people from direct participation in the highest level of geopolitical negotiations governing their lands. Direct Aboriginal representation was totally absent in the bargaining leading to the drawing of the map of North America in its present major geopolitical outlines. Among these international transactions were the Treaties of Paris of 1763 and 1783, the Louisiana Purchase in 1803, the Treaty of Ghent of 1814, and the Convention of 1818. The fact that all these negotiations on the apportionment of North American lands took place in Europe is illustrative of the Eurocentric orientation even of the United States during this era. In many ways the American republic remained throughout its early career a colonizing venture whose legitimacy ultimately depended on the power of influential European sponsors. The major outlines of the geopolitical map of North America were drawn up much like the major outlines of the geopolitical map of Africa. They were drawn largely by Europeans whose decisions had reference to the interests of different European powers rather than the interests and rights of Indigenous peoples of the reconfigured territories.

The consistent exclusion of Indian nations from the most basic territorial negotiations on the future of the lands of North America was perpetuated in the making of the Treaty of Guadalupe Hidalgo in 1848, in the Dominion of Canada's purchase of the Hudson's Bay Company titles in 1869, in the addition to Canada of British Columbia in 1871, and in the United States's purchase from Russia of Alaska in 1867. The treatment of Indigenous peoples as inferior and as subjects of an inferior order of law, continued with the negotiation of the Free Trade Agreement of 1988 and the North American Free Trade Agreement of 1994.[149] The same politics of exclusion project the legacy of the Columbian conquests into the system of representation to create a Free Trade Area of all the Americas. In these negotiations the principle parties simply ignored and continue to ignore the reality that the lands of Canada, the United States, Mexico, and the rest of the hemisphere are already subject to various forms of Aboriginal title, as well as to imperial and state treaties, conventions, and accords with Indigenous peoples.

However flawed or imperfect, these imperial and state agreements with Indigenous peoples set terms, requirements, and limitations for the subsequent European and Euro-American colonization of the so-called New World. The formulation of any new treaties that go forward without specific legal provisions to conform to the legal requirements of the older layer of treaties with the hemisphere's Indigenous peoples should be seen as invalid. Any such deals, including the proposed treaty to create a Free Trade Area of the Americas, should be seen as violations of existing law of Aboriginal and treaty rights and thus as unconstitutional transgressions of both domestic and international law. Accordingly, the recent trade treaties' neo-liberal reconfigurations of the hemisphere repeat the same patterns that have prevailed since the map of North America was shaped and reshaped primarily in the diplomatic salons of Europe. Just as Tecumseh and the Indian Confederacy went to war with the United States to assert their right to a say in determining the international identity of their own country, so the Zapatista National Liberation Army went to war with the compador government of Mexico on 1 January 1994 to assert much the same principle. That was the day the North American Free Trade Treaty came into force. "We want a world with all the many worlds that the world needs to really be the world," the Zapatistas proclaimed in their banners.

CHAPTER SIX

Expansion or Immigration into Indian Country?

On such spots, the Indians might be perpetuated in Canada, as
the Welsh have been in this country, or the Basques in Spain and
France.

Aborigines' Protection Society,
Report on the Indians of Upper Canada, 1839

IMAGINING CIVILIZATION
ON THE ABORIGINAL FRONTIERS OF UPPER CANADA

In establishing the new jurisdiction of Upper Canada in 1791, the British
imperial government finally adapted itself to the principle that it would
sanction and oversee the development of an inland colony in North
America whose primary function was to host agricultural settlements for
non-Indians. For many years before the American Revolution, it had
resisted pressure to allow such a form of colonial enterprise. This resistance was essential to the institution of the Royal Proclamation of 1763
and the Quebec Act of 1774, just as it also led to the slide towards civil war
and revolution in the Anglo-American colonies.

The influx of settlers into Quebec and Nova Scotia both during and
immediately following the American Revolution forced the hand of the
British imperial government. The northward migration in the interior of
a sizeable population of United Empire Loyalists with a need for land to
begin new lives in what remained of British North America persuaded the
colonial administration to moderate its dependence on the fur trade as
the exclusive vehicle of inland colonization.

By dividing Quebec into an older, predominantly Roman Catholic and
French-speaking colony named Lower Canada and a new, predominantly
Protestant and English-speaking colony named Upper Canada, British
imperial Canada was geographically and constitutionally rearranged
along the lines of its primary, non-Aboriginal duality. This duality has
been integral to the organization of the Canadian federation ever since.
The portrayal of Canada as a partnership of two language-based communities has served one vision of pluralism, even if it also symbolically and
actually excluded First Nations from many aspects of the federation's
basic institutional framework.

The central role of Sir John Johnson in the genesis of Upper Canada

illustrates the importance of Johnson Hall and the northern division
of the British Imperial Indian Department in the genesis of English-
speaking Canada. John Johnson was the son of Sir William Johnson. As a
young man, John Johnson participated actively with his father in the protocols of the Covenant Chain, including the negotiation in 1768 of the
Treaty of Fort Stanwix. Sir John inherited many of his father's responsibilities in the Indian branch of Britain's North American military establishment. His role in the aftermath of the American Revolution was such
that he has been referred to in one text as "Minister of Loyalists and Indian Affairs."[1] As members of the King's Royal Regiment of New York as well
as other United Empire Loyalists began to settle along the north shore of
the upper St Lawrence and of Lake Ontario, Sir John became their main
spokesperson to the imperial government. In 1785 he issued on the Loyalists' behalf the key request that would soon be acted upon in Great
Britain to divide what remained of Quebec into Lower and Upper Canada. Sir John argued that a new frontier jurisdiction was needed to the west
of Quebec's old seigneuries to provide the growing influx of English-
speaking Protestants with a framework of familiar institutions, including
freehold land tenure.[2]

The creation of a crown colony in the deep interior of the continent
necessitated some reworking of Indian policies to persuade Indigenous
peoples in the heartland of the old Indian Country of Canada to accept
significant numbers of property-owning Euro-North American farmers in
their midst. This necessity grew quickly and dramatically after the War of
1812, when a new level of tranquillity along the international border led
to the rapid influx of non-Indian settlers, including some miners and promoters of lumbering ventures on both sides of the Great Lakes. Accordingly, pressures mounted in the crown domain north of the Great Lakes
to convince, cajole, or coerce Indigenous peoples to back away from the
resources in wider and wider portions of their ancestral lands. And, in
short order these economic pressures led various crown agents to advance
tactics for the extinguishment and privatization of Indian Country –
tactics which, in an earlier era, the officialdom of British imperial Canada
would have opposed.

The history of crown Indian policy in the Upper Canada area after the
War of 1812 is deeply intertwined with efforts of a new kind of Anglo-
American society to imagine and invent itself on the Aboriginal frontiers
of its version of civilization. The citizens of this frontier society, the jurisdictional seed of what would become Ontario after 1867, identified
strongly with the immensity and the seemingly unlimited scope for
exploitation of their North American setting. But the continuing colonial
identity of Upper Canada, or Canada West as it was technically known
after 1840, acted as a check on the exuberant development of New World
enthusiasms such as those that saturated the national ethos of the United

States. Accordingly, the position eventually taken in the *St. Catherine's Milling* case by the government of Ontario marks a major move away from the heritage of imperial myths and legends associated with the coming of the United Empire Loyalists. The decision of the Mowat government to attack the animating spirit of the principles connected with the Royal Proclamation of 1763 constituted the crossing of a major threshhold towards deeper integration of English Canada into the American empire of private property.

Nevertheless, the unbroken Old World pull of the constitutional connection to Great Britain, even though in an increasingly tenuous fashion, continued to place some brakes on those who wanted to extinguish the Old World reality of the continuing Indian Country. Of all the Aboriginal communities north of the Great Lakes, none came to reflect more truly the Indian aspect of the British imperial personality of Upper Canada than the Anglican members of the Six Nations settlement near Brant's Ford and the Mohawk settlement at Tyendinaga.[3] The small but exquisitely preserved Anglican chapel built in 1786 by Joseph Brant and his friends in the Mohawk Village of Upper Canada still stands as a kind of monument to the British imperial heritage of the Indian Country of Canada.[4] The chapel holds the Queen Anne Silver Communion Plate and Bible presented by the English sovereign to the "Four Kings of Canada" in 1710, when the young Hendrick and his companions were celebrated in London as the exotic ambassadors of a friendly Aboriginal realm.

THE CONTINUING INDIAN COUNTRY IN THE OLDER, MORE EASTERLY DISTRICTS OF BRITISH NORTH AMERICA

The reactions of Indigenous peoples meeting the outer edges of expanding Euro-American settlements, such as the growing frontier districts of Upper Canada, were inevitably more volatile than those of Indian communities in colonial settings where there was a long history of Aboriginal and non-Aboriginal settlers living side by side. For instance, in the Maritime colonies of Nova Scotia, Prince Edward Island, and, after 1784, New Brunswick, Micmac [Mikmaw, Mi'kmaq] groups continued quietly to favour their own Aboriginal language and their unique version of Roman Catholicism. In this way they were able to maintain effectively their own cultural spaces in the increasingly circumscribed geographic places left to them by the British colonial authorities.[5]

In commenting on the successful cultivation in the nineteenth century of broad Micmac literacy in the reading and writing of special scripts designed, with the help of their missionaries, to represent the sounds of the Micmac language, Micmac educator Marie Battiste remarked: "Micmac society continually rejected the English language, the Protestant worldview, and its individualistic society as demonic in nature. They believed that British society rested on the Protestant legacy of a losing fight against evil."[6]

In the nineteenth century most of the First Nations peoples of the province of Lower Canada continued, like the Micmac, to retain many of the legacies from their long histories of relations with the French Empire in North America. By and large the Roman Catholic orders that established the Indian missions in the St Lawrence Valley retained legal title to these communities. In future years this twist in the regime of land tenure would engender considerable tension, especially among the Aboriginal inhabitants in and around the Sulpician seigneury at Oka.[7] In Lower Canada, officials of the Roman Catholic Church tended to perform many governmental functions, both on Indian reserves and among the French Canadian population generally, that elsewhere in British North America developed under the direct auspices of the state.

While Roman Catholicism and the unique land laws of Lower Canada set quite narrow boundaries around the lives of some Indian people, many adventurous younger folks from these old Christian communities could not be so easily constrained. Hundreds of individuals from these missions, but particularly the large Mohawk communities of Kanewake and Akwesasne, were especially active as traders, voyageurs, and trappers in the far-flung activities of Montreal's North West Company.[8] Iroquois men were prominent, for instance, in the activity of attaching the Oregon area around the Columbia River basin to the fur-trade economics of Canada. When the Hudson's Bay Company took over the commercial domination of the Oregon region from the North West Company in 1821, Mohawk men stayed on in the area throughout the transition.[9] Some Mohawk men in the West, including Michel and Baptiste Callihoo, married Cree women and settled down in the Edmonton area, obtaining their own Indian reserve through participation in Treaty 6 in 1876.[10] The legendary skills of many Kanewake men as voyageurs made a number of them the first candidates selected when Colonel Garnet Wolsey recruited the most experienced boatmen available in Canada to transport troops and supplies up the Nile River in Egypt as part of Britain's widening imperial adventures in Africa in the 1880s and 1890s.[11]

Some of the children and grandchildren of the famous Iroquois voyageurs also travelled widely throughout North America as part of the growing contingent of Mohawk steel workers. Beginning in the late nineteenth century, they were much sought after to help raise the bridges and the skyscrapers that became some of the most spectacular symbols of American dominance and power in the world.[12] Another attraction that took many Iroquois men away from their Indian communities in Quebec, as well as in Ontario and New York, was the growth of the sport of lacrosse, or *baggataway* as the game is known in the language of its founders. Although lacrosse was traditionally played by many Indian nations, it was the excitement aroused by the sportsmen at Kanewake that set the example for the creation of a larger league in the Montreal area in the 1850s. From there the game caught on quickly, especially after the Prince of Wales established the National Lacrosse Association in 1867.[13]

One of the hot spots of lacrosse in the twentieth century was British Columbia, and one of that province's most legendary teams was Andy Paull's North Shore Indians. In the 1930s this team could sometimes attract more than 10,000 spectators to its games in Denman Street Arena.[14] No doubt Paull's reputation in promoting the games of lacrosse and hockey helped this Indian politician to cultivate wide connections throughout the Indian world, including among Iroquois athletes and their families in Ontario and Quebec.

In the mid-nineteenth century French Canadians began pushing the boundaries of their settlements further north into the territory of the Innu [Montagnais] and Algonquin peoples and eastward towards Micmac Country. As a result, eleven new reserves were created, including Temiskaming, Maniwaki, Manouane, Restigouche, Doncaster, and Coucoucache.[15] Where in Ontario and the prairie provinces Indian reserves were generally set aside through the negotiation of treaties with First Nations, in Quebec, as in the Maritime provinces and British Columbia, reserves were simply assigned without formal negotiations. In Quebec, the issue of Aboriginal title to land and resources was not addressed seriously until the building by Hydro-Québec of the James Bay project in the early 1970s. Much to the dismay of the dam builders, a lower court in Quebec granted the Cree an injunction to stop construction on the massive hydro project. Although this work stoppage was quickly overturned in appeal, the court's initial ruling effectively forced the provincial and federal governments to the negotiation table. The James Bay and Northern Quebec Agreement, signed in 1975, was the first modern-day treaty in Canada.

THE PRIVATIZATION OF INDIAN COUNTRY
AND THE MAKING OF A CROWN LAND SPECULATOR:
THE ABORIGINAL POLICIES OF SIR FRANCIS BOND HEAD

The Treaty of Ghent ending the War of 1812 did not immediately change the reality that the largest number of the crown's Aboriginal allies in the interior of North America continued to reside principally south of the Great Lakes in the northern reaches of the vast Mississippi Valley. For about one generation following 1814, many thousands of these Indian people continued to gather at British military posts on the Great Lakes to receive "presents" from personnel of the British Imperial Indian Department. These presents were in a sense military pensions for veterans of the War of 1812 and earlier conflicts with the United States. They could also be seen as payments in fulfilment of treaty obligations incurred by the

crown in earlier years.[16] Included among the items distributed at the
British posts after the War of 1812 were guns and ammunition, cooking
utensils, jewellery, blankets, cloth, tobacco, beaver traps, eye glasses, scis-
sors, needles, shoes, fishing hooks, rope – and, always, medals, flags, and
British military uniforms for the leading men of each nation.[17] As the
years passed, the elaborate ceremonies accompanying the distribution of
presents attracted growing numbers of adventurous tourists and missionaries of several denominations who jealously competed with each other in
the saving of souls. And, in spite of official efforts to keep them away,
there were usually a number of American whiskey traders whose object
was to depart the scene with as many Indian presents as possible.

In the early 1830s major present distribution ceremonies took place at
the British navel base of Penetanguishene in the heart of old Huronia.
Several miles away was a newly established Indian reserve along the
famous Toronto portage route between Lake Simcoe and Georgian Bay.
At this reserve, known as Coldwater and the Narrows, the British imperial government attempted to establish a model Aboriginal community
attractive enough to entice the First Nations visitors at Penetanguishene
to adopt a different way of life. Essentially the new policy followed the
assimilationist strategies earlier articulated by President Thomas Jefferson
in the United States. Indians were to be encouraged to become Christians, to take up farming, and to learn to read and write. In the ethnocentric language of the time, they were encouraged to become
"civilized."[18]

The new Indian policy grew largely from the expectation that the era of
war with the United States had passed and that Indian fighting strength
was no longer crucial to the military security of Upper Canada. As the military importance of Indian affairs diminished, the desire grew in the colonial administration to be free of the expense of purchasing and distributing large quantities of the "presents" on which the crown's Indian allies
had come to depend. A primary driving force of the Indian civilizing policy was the desire to encourage Indian self-sufficiency and to reduce the
expenditures of the Indian Department.[19] This motivation for the strategy of assimilation has remained relatively constant ever since the civilizing
course of Canadian Indian policy was adopted in 1830. The hope of
escaping the expense of a distinct political and administrative apparatus
for Indian Affairs has often been the catalyst for government efforts
aimed at making Indigenous peoples more like Euro-American settlers.[20]

While the assimilationist shift in 1830 set the primary direction of
Canadian Indian policy right up to contemporary times, there was a brief
reversal in the stated intent of the imperial government in 1836 and
1837. During that short period Sir Francis Bond Head was lieutenant-
governor of Upper Canada. In those years British colonial administrators
tried to apply to the conduct of Indian policy in Canada lessons they

thought they had learned from the treatment of Indigenous peoples in South Africa. The generic name given to Black South Africans in that era was Kaffirs, a pejorative term in today's usage.

Bond Head's dramatic reversal on the civilizing policies attracted the attention and ire of the highly vocal and elaborately organized coalition in Great Britain that had coalesced primarily in the movement to abolish slavery. In the 1830s that celebrated lobby increasingly drew a connection between the injustice of slavery and the injustice facing Indigenous peoples who were losing their lands to British emigrants.[21]

The seeds of the controversy were planted in 1836 at the present distribution ceremonies that took place at Manitowaning, the site of the new Indian Department station on Manitoulin Island. At the event, the new lieutenant-governor of Upper Canada tried to put together the essential pieces of a scheme to separate Aboriginal settlement from Euro-American settlement in a fashion similar to the approach then being promoted in both the United States and South Africa. Bond Head advanced this plan by asserting his conviction that whenever Indian people and Europeans lived side by side, it was disastrous for the Indians. "Whenever and wherever the Two Races come into contact with each other," he wrote, "it is sure to prove fatal to the Red Man."[22]

This opinion led Bond Head to the conclusion that Indian people should leave their missions and reserves in the arable portions of Upper Canada south of the Canadian Shield. They should move, instead, to Manitoulin Island and pursue a way of life that he believed was more reflective of their natural inclinations. He justified his plan in the following terms:

It was evident to me that we should reap a very great Benefit, if we could persuade those Indians, who are now impeding the Progress of Civilization in Upper Canada, to resort to a Place [Manitoulin] possessing the double advantage of being admirably adapted to *them* (insomuch as it affords, Fishing, Hunting, Bird-shooting and Fruit), and yet in no Way adapted to the White population ... I felt convinced that a vast Benefit would be conferred upon the Indians and the Province by prevailing on them to migrate to this place.[23]

Bond Head was obviously attracted to the personal power available to him if he could exploit the crown's authority to transform Indian lands into real estate. By the time he arrived in Upper Canada the empire of private property had taken firm hold north of the Great Lakes. Land speculation ruled the local economy and local politics. Bond Head, in fact, worried that speculators were keeping the price of land artificially high. Real settlers were opting to go to the United States, where they could get land more cheaply or sometimes for free as homesteaders. The Lieutenant-Governor reasoned that an increased supply of land on the open market would lower prices and prevent the haemorrhaging of *bona fide* settlers to the United States. Yet more pressing for Bond Head was the need to open new lands to increase the power of his office, an office under increasing attack by reformers whose political stronghold was the province's elected assembly.[24] Without fresh territories to sell and distribute to political friends, the crown's representative complained that he was "like a Statue on the Land Market, deprived of the activity of those who surround [me]."[25]

Although lacking the element of coercion, Bond Head's scheme was similar to the Indian removal policy then being implemented in the United States. Manitoulin was to be the Canadian equivalent of the designated Indian Territory that the regime of President Andrew Jackson was staking out west of the Mississippi River. In fact, the two schemes were connected in that Manitoulin was seen as one of the destinations for Indian people from south of the Great Lakes who chose to settle in the familiar domain of their imperial ally rather than in the unfamiliar domain allocated to them by Congress. Most of the groups that Bond Head met in Manitowaning in 1836 had travelled from territories south of the Great Lakes in the upper Mississippi Valley. Their solemn gathering continued many of the traditions of the Indian Confederacy that only twenty-four years earlier had prevented the Canadas from falling under the yolk of the United States. The assembled leaders sat in about twenty rows opposite the crown's representative. A pipe-smoking ceremony began the proceedings. In recounting the moment years later, Bond Head wrote, "passions of all sorts had time to subside; and the judgement, divested of its enemy, was thus enabled calmly to consider and prepare the subject of the approaching discourse."[26]

The opening speeches were given by Aboriginal delegates, who spoke to the lieutenant-governor through interpreters. Bond Head seems to have been genuinely moved by the manner of presentation. "In composition and mode of utterance," he wrote, their oratory "would have done credit to any legislative assembly in the civilized world." "The calm, high-bred dignity of their demeanour," he continued, "the scientific manner in which they progressively construct the framework of whatever subject they undertake to explain – the sound arguments by which they connect, as well as support it – and the beautiful wild flowers of eloquence with which, as they proceed, they adorn every portion of the moral architecture they are constructing, form altogether an exhibition of grave interest."[27]

Then came Bond Head's turn to speak. The moment had come for him to mark Manitoulin and the 23,000 adjacent islands as a permanent Indian sanctuary where Indians could be "totally separated from the whites." In introducing this topic, he referred to the "wampum of friendship" that long had connected the king and the Indian nations of Canada. That wampum served to record in First Nations fashion the proceedings at the great council at Niagara in 1764, when the contents of the Royal Proclamation of 1763 had undergone a process of two-way treaty negotiations.

Having given diplomatic lip service to this shared constitutional history, the lieutenant-governor continued:

In all parts of the world farmers seek for uncultivated land as eagerly as you, my red children, hunt in your forest for game. If you would cultivate your land it would be considered your property, in the same way as your dogs are considered among yourselves to belong to those who have reared them; but uncultivated land is like wild animals, and your Great Father, who has hitherto protected you, now has great difficulty in securing it for you from the whites, who are hunting to cultivate it.[28]

The metaphors employed in this speech are drawn in all probability directly from some of the most famous passages in John Locke's *Second Treatise on Government.* For instance, Bond Head's comparison of farmers to hunters extends concepts that were introduced by Locke when he wrote, "This Law of reason makes the Deer, that Indian's who hath killed it: 'tis allowed to be his goods who hath bestowed his labour on it, though before it was the common right of everyone."[29]

Bond Head's use of Lockean motifs reflects much about the ironies of this crown official who aimed to defend British imperialism in North America by making the executive branch of government resemble that of the republic to the south. He hoped to make the crown's domain north of the Great Lakes as attractive to immigrants as the lands of the United States. The success of the lieutenant-governor's plan clearly depended on further attacks on the battered remnant of land remaining in Aboriginal hands. Bond Head's paradoxical politics made him a significant participant in the process of advancing the integration of Canada into the American empire of private property. By evoking metaphors drawn from Locke in the conduct of his Indian policy, he moved onto ideological turf cultivated with particular effectiveness by Thomas Jefferson. It was Jefferson who was most responsible for weaving Lockean concepts into the fabric of the American Declaration of Independence and into the republic whose existence that document announced.

Bond Head's rhetorical flourishes, then, belonged more to the theoretical realm of the empire of possessive individualism than to the old traditions of crown-Aboriginal alliance as embodied in the diplomacy of the Covenant Chain and the envisaged Indian buffer state. With the conclusion of the War of 1812, the nature of British imperial Canada had irrevocably changed. The Colonial Office increasingly contemplated decentralizing the old imperial system by devolving jurisdictions and control over the privatization of lands to the colonial populations in the empire. The transfer of control over the process of privatizing Indian lands had the potential to become a significant source of local revenue to finance the expenses of a decentralized empire.

One of the great constitutional and moral problems that officials in the imperial metropolis had to address, however, was how the devolution of powers to edify the self-government of non-Aboriginals in the colonies would affect the Indigenous peoples. Would the latitude of First Nations' self-governance be diminished by expanding the jurisdictional field available for colonial self-rule, or "responsible government" as it came to be called? Would colonial citizens use their broadened self-government to undermine and negate the imperial government's earlier recognitions of Aboriginal and treaty rights? Bond Head's importation into Canada of us-style tactics to open Indian lands for new Anglo-American settlements forced a reckoning in Great Britain with some of these most basic issues inherent in the creation of an overseas empire based largely on emigration from the mother country.

This reckoning occurred when news reached Great Britain about how Bond Head had gone about leaving his role as "a statue in the land market." To acquire title to new territories that could be parcelled out in the development of his own Tory patronage network, Bond Head turned to those Indian communities in Upper Canada who had already adopted the economics of commercialized agriculture. Among these groups were the Moravian Delaware on the Thames River, the Methodist Mississauga at the Credit mission just east of Toronto, the Methodist Mississauga at the Grape Island mission in the Bay of Quinte area, the three Ojibway bands at Coldwater and the Narrows (the site of present-day Orillia), and the large Six Nations settlement near Brantford.[30] As the fate of the successful Cherokee agriculturalists in Georgia illustrated, there were no automatic protections anywhere in North America for land cultivated in Euro-North American style by Indian communities. This lack of any regular and secure form of land tenure for Indian groups living adjacent to non-Aboriginal settlements was exploited by Bond Head as a bargaining tactic to gain major concessions from the Saugeen Anishinabek, whose leaders attended the distribution ceremonies at Manitoulin Island in 1836.

As the council entered its most serious phase, Bond Head turned to the Ottawa and Ojibway inhabitants of world's largest fresh-water Island. He asked: "Are you willing to relinquish your respective claims to these islands and make them the property (under your Great Father's control) of all Indians whom he shall allow to reside on them?" He asked the appropriate representatives to come forward and mark their totems – their clan emblems – on a transcript of the speech he had just given. Several delegates responded affirmatively to the lieutenant-governor's request.[31] With this part of the proceedings complete, most of the delegates left. Bond Head then called into council the leaders of the Saugeen, a small group of Anishinabek that gave their name to their home territory and that controlled the last major section of arable land in Upper Canada not subject to any previous treaty.[32] Bond Head proposed to the Saugeen representatives that they cede their land and move to Manitoulin

Island. This option they flatly refused to consider. A Wesleyan missionary in attendance observed that Bond Head persisted in subjecting the Saugeen to a continuing cycle of "proposals, persuasions, and threats," all to no avail.

The lieutenant-governor then changed strategies. He promised to help the Saugeen build houses. And he promised to secure for them "forever" their possession of all land north of Owen's Sound, a peninsula projecting about 50 miles out into Lake Huron. According to this Wesleyan observer: "To *this*, the poor Indians did readily acede, with tears in their eyes: their hopes revived, and their countenances beamed with joy. This is what they wanted – land secured to them, from which they could not be removed, where they could have help to build houses and settle their families, and where they could at length rest their bones."[33] Not all the principal leaders of the Saugeen agreed to the deal. Chiefs Newash, Wahbahdick, and Wahwahnosh did not give their assent.[34] The transaction, therefore, was controversial even at the time it was made. For those who did agree, however, the tradeoffs they made are a classic illustration of the basic dynamics of many treaty negotiations that would follow.

Bond Head made it clear that the Indian land in question would continue to be encroached upon whether or not the group agreed to a treaty. White settlers were coming in large numbers, and some of them would continue clearing and fencing uncultivated land even without any official authorization. The choice before the Saugeen, then, was whether to continue as they had in the past. Should they continue with an uncertain kind of claim to extensive territories – a claim that was difficult to enforce actively – or should they withdraw to a narrower domain that the crown would explicitly promise to protect for them as their own?

The Saugeen Treaty is stark in its simplicity and directness. It captures in a few words the essential deal that the Canadian government would offer again and again after 1870, when trying to confirm the crown's full title to the land purchased by the dominion from the Hudson's Bay Company. Unlike the texts of the later treaties, however, the text of the Saugeen transaction is not written in lawyer's language. Unlike the numbered treaties, it is possible to hypothesize that there was actually some concurrence between what the Indians were told and what the official text says. The treaty reads as follows:

I now propose to you that you should surrender to your Great Father the Sauking territory you at present occupy, and that you should repair either to this island or to that part of your territory which lies on the north of Owen Sound, upon which proper houses shall be built for you, and proper assistance given to enable you to become civilized and to cultivate land, which your Great Father engages forever to protect for you from the encroachments of whites.[35]

The promise to help the Saugeen become "civilized" could mean much or little. It is doubtful that the Saugeen thought of themselves as "uncivilized," if that term implied some kind of inferiority. What was clear to the Saugeen and many other Aboriginal groups at the time they made treaties, however, was that the world they had known was in rapid flux. Major changes were inevitable once large numbers of newcomers arrived in their lands. There was no way people could live in the future as they had lived in the past. Given this expectation, the Saugeen sought concrete forms of assistance from the government in helping them adapt to the changes that were coming. Certainly this help would have to include various kinds of schooling that would assist Indian youth to prepare for the kind of economic and social milieu awaiting them. According to the Wesleyan observer of the treaty negotiations, the Saugeen told Bond Head they "wanted to have their children taught to read."[36]

The subject of education was absolutely central to most of the treaty negotiations that would take place in the generations ahead. Again and again the record makes it clear that First Nations peoples were anxious to receive all manner of technical training. Similarly, they repeatedly used whatever bargaining leverage they had in negotiations with Crown officials to gain access to the tools of literacy required for the pursuit of higher-level learning in many branches of the arts and sciences. Formal education in the ways of the newcomers was widely seen among First Nations peoples in the nineteenth century as essential for the defence, advancement, and enhancement of the rights, titles and interests of Aboriginal communities. There was no desire on their part to transform Indian education into a device for indoctrination and assimilation. As is now well known, however, this assimilationist strategy would eventually come to dominate the pedagogical methods employed in most church-run Indian residential schools. These Christian institutions would in later years be funded and chartered by the Dominion of Canada to make good on the crown's treaty promises to institute appropriate programs for Indian education.

At a gathering in Orillia in Canada West in 1846, many Aboriginal activists commented on the importance of using education as a means of holding ground for First Nations societies in the midst of colonial society. A Tyendinaga Mohawk by the name of John Hill called on his people to donate money for an early Indian boarding school by promoting the envisaged institution in terms of its importance for self-determination and self-realization. "We must all join hands in the great cause of Indian improvement," he asserted. "This is our only hope to prevent our race from perishing, and to enable us to stand on the same ground as the White man."[37] Like Hill, the Saugeen people in all probability saw in 1836 the promise of education through formal schooling as a strategic means of retaining a distinct place of relative autonomy within colonial society. They saw this treaty promise as a key to self-determination and some measure of prosperity in a rapidly changing milieu. Accordingly, a particularly horrible betrayal of good faith occurred when this sweet crown promise of education in the treaties was transformed.

At its most radical extreme, the overzealousness of the civilization mission became an evangelical crusade aimed at severing the intergenerational continuity in the transfer of Aboriginal heritages, traditions, and languages. The Indian residential schools would become the primary sites of this evangelical drive to induce a kind of forced amnesia to wipe away the cultural inheritance of the First Nations and to reorient Aboriginal youth to accept, instead, the Christian heritage of Europe. The tendency of these institutions to become places where indoctrination and extreme abuse of power overwhelmed the aims of genuine education resulted in many dark consequences for students and former students, and also for their children and even their grandchildren. There is tragic irony in so many damaged lives stemming from these early hopeful discussions about education and the access it would provide to the arts and sciences of the newcomers.

THE MISSIONARIES AND THEIR EMPIRE: THE MOVEMENT TO PROTECT "ABORIGINES IN BRITISH SETTLEMENTS"

In the Saugeen Treaty, Bond Head obtained territory that he described as "an immense Portion of the most valuable land, more than sufficient to defray the whole Expense of the Indians and the Indian Department in the province." The transaction opened about 3 million acres for Euro-American settlement. In the days ahead, Bond Head conducted further negotiations that opened smaller parcels of territory comprising part of the Wyandot reserve near Windsor and part of the Moravian Delaware reserve at the place on the Thames River where Tecumseh had been killed. In another transaction of especially dubious quality, Bond Head obtained totems on a document marking Indian agreement to abandon the reserve at Coldwater and the Narrows.[38] In reporting his deeds to the Colonial Office, Bond Head asked to be released from as many imperial restrictions as possible, "particularly as regards the Land-granting Department." This request was closely related to his intention to take an active role in the forthcoming election in the province. In his view, the power of the executive to distribute land at cheap prices was an indispensable political tool in the campaign to counter electorally the growing influence of "republican Principles" emanating from the United States.[39]

Bond Head's approach to Indian Affairs jealously guarded the royal prerogative. Although he referred to Indian peoples as "allies" of the crown who enjoyed a degree of self-government within their own communities, the lieutenant governor adopted a paternalistic tone that hinted at the shape of things to come. The legal construction of Indigenous peoples as wards of the state under the trusteeship of central governments

would become a major fixture of nineteenth-century imperialism in its
many manifestations.[40]

This theory of benevolent Christian trusteeship has deep roots going
back at least as far as Vitoria. The idea acquired force in the United States
within the framework of Jefferson's policy to promote the civilization of
Aboriginal peoples. Bond Head outlined the principles of Aboriginal governance at this transitional stage in British North America's evolution. His
explanation came in the context of an effort to fend off the intervention
of the local legislature in a dispute involving rival Wyandot groups:

In Upper Canada the Indians have hitherto been under the exclusive care of His
Majesty, the territories they inhabit being tracts of Crown Land devoted to their
sole use as "His allies." Over these Lands His Majesty has never exercised his paramount right, except at their request, and for their manifest advantage – within
their own communities they have hitherto governed themselves by their own
unwritten laws and customs. Their lands and property have never been subject to
tax or assessment of themselves liable to personal service. The Superintendents,
Missionaries, Schoolmasters and others who reside among them for their protection and civilization are appointed and paid by the King – to His representative all
appeals have until now been made, and with him has the responsibility rested – in
every respect they appear to be constitutionally within the jurisdiction and prerogative of the Crown.[41]

Bond Head's intense intervention on the frontiers of Indian Country in
North America proved to be a study in paradox. On the one hand he
played the role of the quintessential North American land grabber, using
ceding treaties cynically to deal the executive branch of the colonial government into the political poker game of land speculation. On the other
hand he was a true romanticist, one of those observers of the human condition who shared with Jean Jacques Rousseau a deep sense of ambivalence about the losses accompanying the gains incurred in channelling
the growth of Western civilization into narrow conceptions of progress.
There is little doubt that Bond Head was sincere in his conviction that
the people he had met at Manitowaning personified many precious and
fragile traits that were disappearing in the commonwealth of human
attributes. In recording these opinions, he contributed significantly to an
important heritage of self-critical introspection in imagining Western
civilization on the frontiers of Aboriginality. Of the Indigenous people he
met at Manitowaning, Bond Head wrote, "They hear more distinctly – see
farther – smell clearer – can bear more fatigue – can subsist on less food
– and have altogether fewer wants than their white brethren."[42]

Since Aboriginal peoples in their "natural" state were, in Bond Head's
view, superior to Europeans in so many ways, they should not be subjected to the contaminating influence of Europeans, even to the well-
intentioned evangelism of Christian missionaries. "Our Philanthropy, like

our friendship," he wrote, "has failed in its professions." "The greatest kindness we can do [the Indians]," he advised the British Colonial Office, "is to induce them, as I have done, to retreat before what I may justly term the accursed Progress of Civilization."[43]

Bond Head's Indian policy enabled him to combine the appearance of pragmatism with an eloquently expressed sentimentalism. He was able to pay homage to what he saw as the majesty of a passing era in humanity's march through history even as he helped cut the executive branch of the colonial government into the continent's hottest gambling game – betting on different scenarios for the transformation of Indian lands into real estate. Bond Head was no pioneer in his manipulation of crown authority to achieve advantage in the North American game of land speculation. In the years following the Seven Years' War, both Sir William Johnson and George Washington derived considerable personal wealth and powerful patronage networks from adept manoeuvres on the frontier between Indian Country and the empire of private property. Where Johnson had drawn on the diplomacy of the Covenant Chain to balance Indian interests with Anglo-American hunger for new territories to capitalize in the land market, Bond Head was more like Washington in his haste to push aside all Indian and imperial obstacles to westward expansion

Initially Bond Head's engagingly literate genre of dispatches from Upper Canada met a favourable reception in the Colonial Office in Great Britain. The colonial secretary, Lord Glenelg, reported from London that King William IV had taken a personal interest in what the lieutenant-governor had done. "His Majesty regards, with peculiar approbation," he wrote, "the humane consideration for their national habits and feelings, which appear to have directed your negotiations with them." On his own behalf Lord Glenelg observed, "We must abandon the hope of imparting to the Indians the blessings of Christianity, on the ground that these blessings were necessarily more than counterbalanced by the evils with which they have hitherto been unhappily associated."[44]

In Glenelg's view, Bond Head's initiatives conformed with the line of policy that the imperial government had decided to pursue in South Africa. A series of increasingly bloody conflicts with the Xhosa peple on the expanding frontiers of Cape Colony persuaded officials in the Colonial Office that the wisest course of British South African policy would be to restrain the movement of the colonial population into the continent's interior. The thinking behind this decision resembled that in the formulation in 1763 of the Royal Proclamation. That legal instrument had been formulated with the aim of restraining Anglo-American colonists from extending their settlements too rapidly into the Indian Country of North America.

The Protestant missionary societies in Great Britain, which were about to marshal considerable influence over crown Indian policy in Upper Canada, played an instrumental role in persuading Glenelg to restrain colonial expansion in South Africa. This decision was embodied in instructions that reached Cape Colony in the spring of 1836. On behalf of the British government, Lord Glenelg directed local officials to abandon the newly created province of Queen Adelaide and to hand control back to the Indigenous people, the Xhosa. Lieutenant-Governor Andries Stockenstrom was further instructed to consolidate this arrangement with a series of crown treaties with the chiefs of the Xhosa people.

In his monumental history *Frontiers: The Epic of South Africa's Creation and the Tragedy of the Xhosa People,* Noel Mostert compares the colonial response to Glenelg's decision with the unrest that swept over the Anglo-American colonies after British subjects were blocked from expansion into the interior and then taxed in 1765 to enforce the imperial regime for their own containment.[45] The decision generated especially grave antagonisms among the Dutch Boer inhabitants of Cape Colony. Like the self-declared Americans who, in asserting their independence from Europe, took the name of their adopted continent, the Dutch Boers emerged from their assertions of independence as Afrikaners. As Calvinists with a strong sense of mission as God's Chosen People, Afrikaners drew on the same theological roots as those Americans who traced their lineage back to the Puritan founders of New England. The ending of slavery in the British Empire in 1834, together with the apparent retreat of the British in 1836 from Xhosa territory, only increased the determination of many Afrikaners to move deep into the interior to escape British intervention into the Boer approach to racial hierarchy and self-government.[46]

Thus, the politics that led to the Afrikaner exodus from Cape Colony – the Great Trek of 1836–38 – was driven by pressures similar to those that caused the Anglo-American revolt in 1776 against the British prohibitions on the colonization, acquisition, and privatization of Indian Country. As geopolitical expressions of indigenized settler resistance to Great Britain's efforts to enforce protective Aboriginal policies, therefore, the Afrikaner founding of the republics of Transvaal and Orange Free State bear some resemblance to the American founding of the US republic.

Sir Francis Bond Head's reports on his new Indian policies in Upper Canada arrived at the Colonial Office just as Lord Glenelg had decided to restrain the expansionism of the colonial population in South Africa. As the conviction grew at headquarters that the British interest lay in containing the frontiers of Euro-African settlement in Cape Colony, Bond Head's news seemed to substantiate Lord Glenelg's own reading of how best to govern relations between Indigenous peoples and emigrants from Europe. Indeed, it almost appears as if Bond Head had borrowed some of his lines directly from his superior in the Colonial Office, who wrote to his Cape Colony colleagues in 1835:

it is a melancholy and humiliating but an undisputable truth, that the contiguity of the subjects of the nations of Christendom with uncivilized tribes has invariably produced the wretchedness and decay, and not seldom the utter extirmination of the weaker party ... Of all the chapters in the history of mankind, this is perhaps the most degrading. Nor is there any one course of events on which every human mind dwells with such settled aversion and shame, as on that which records the intercourse between the Christian States of Europe and the heathen nations of America and Africa. I know not a greater calamity could befall Great Britain than that of adding Southern Africa to the list of the regions which have seen their aboriginal inhabitants disappear under the withering influence of European neighbourhood. It is indeed a calamity reducible to no certain standard or positive measurement, but it involves whatever is most to be dreaded, in bringing upon ourselves at once the reproaches of mankind and the weight of national guilt.[47]

Lord Glenelg's approach offended many of the British missionary societies that had devoted considerable energy to evangelical work among the Indigenous peoples of South Africa. Rather than supporting the endeavours of the Christian vanguard, which included actions to prevent the worst of the terrible atrocities against Aboriginal South Africans, the British government seemed instead to be undermining the work of Protestant humanitarians. The Protestant missionary societies, which had demonstrated their parliamentary muscle with the passage of the Emancipation Act in 1833, quickly organized to counter the Colonial Office's apparent unwillingness to commit the British government to an expansive policy of Christian evangelization in South Africa. The primary instrument used to realize the parliamentary objectives of the missionary societies was the British House of Commons Select Committee on Aborigines in British Settlement. The chair of the committee, which was established in 1835, was Thomas Fowell Buxton, a British brewer who had replaced William Wilberforce as the effective leader of the anti-slavery lobby.[48]

The Aborigines' Protection Society, which was modelled on the British Anti-Slavery Association, was quickly formed to help facilitate the work of the Select Committee. Bond Head's new Indian policy immediately captured the attention of the mobilized activists. Their condemnation of the lieutenant-governor's work was intense, broadly supported, well organized, and sustained.[49] Bond Head's critics drew on the strength of Christian altruism and resolve, and deeply entrenched institutional interests were also at stake. The implications of both Glenelg's and Bond Head's approach seemed to call into question the legitimacy of missionary endeavour among Indigenous peoples throughout the British Empire. Moreover, Bond Head's ceding treaties with the Saugeen and other Aboriginal groups seemed to exemplify the worst excesses of colonial administration when unrestrained land hunger became the primary motivation of policy. In one of a stream of representations to Lord Glenelg, the officers of the Aborigines' Protection Society wrote:

Never, perhaps, was the simple and unsuspecting Confidence of the Indians more
clearly exhibited, and seldom has the Confidence been more abused, than in the
late Exchange of 3,000,000 Acres of the richest Land in Upper Canada for 23,000
barren unproductive Islands remote from the Seat of Civilization and unfit for the
Residence of Europeans. We object then to the Treaty on the Ground of its Injustice, because we regard it as taking an unfair Advantage of the Ignorance and Simplicity of those who have unhappily been led to give their Assent.

But further, we object to the Treaty on account of its obvious Tendency to hinder the Progress of Civilization. The mere circumstance that but a few of the
Tribes of Upper Canada have as yet become civilized is assuredly no Proof that
their Civilization is impracticable. The Experiment has never yet been fairly tried
... when Experience has so frequently taught them that the Cultivation of the Soil
will in their Case prove only a preparatory Step to its Seizure by the Europeans.[50]

The Reverends Peter Jones and John Sunday, Mississauga preachers
from Upper Canada with a wide following in evangelical circles in the
United States and Great Britain, both gave testimony to the Select Committee. Their cross-cultural expertise seemed to provide abundant evidence that Indigenous peoples in Upper Canada were fully capable of
becoming "civilized." That point, however, was not among the priorities
of Sunday and Jones. Their prime interest was to lobby the imperial government to put in place a system of land tenure that would entrench
their own agricultural communities as permanent and secure. The Aboriginal evangelists wanted some kind of concrete assurance that their
people would receive protection from both land-hungry neighbours and
policies like those of Lieutenant-Governor Sir Francis Bond Head and
President Andrew Jackson.[51]

The Select Committee on Aborigines in British Settlements reported in
1837, just as Queen Victoria ascended to the imperial throne. The committee's words proved to be a fitting opening to the Victorian era. The
authors endowed the British Empire with a religious purpose similar to
the animating spirit of manifest destiny in the United States:

It is not to be doubted that this country has been invested with wealth and power,
with arts and knowledge, with the sway of different lands, and the mastery of the
restless waters, for some great and important purpose in the government of the
world. Can we suppose otherwise than that it is our office to carry civilization and
humanity, peace and good government, and, above all, the knowledge of the true
God, to the uttermost end of the earth?[52]

While the Select Committee's report raised imperialistic paternalism to
the level of a religious calling this message was qualified with many sensible proposals to protect Indigenous peoples from the land-grabbing
excesses of colonial populations. Repeating themes that echoed many old
debates in British imperialism, the committee noted the dangers of

affording local representative bodies a directing role in the conduct of relations with Indigenous peoples. So often, they observed, "the representative body is virtually a party" to "disputes to adjust with native tribes" that they "ought not to be the judge of such controversies." The potential for conflict of interest was simply too great. Rather, "the protection of the aborigines should be considered as a duty particularly belonging and appropriate to the Executive Government, as administered either in this country or by the Governors of the respective colonies." By following such advice, the British government could avoid "the guilt of conniving at oppression."[53]

This identification of the importance of using the authority of the central government to shield the rights and titles of Indigenous peoples from the incursions of local governments renewed the articulation of one of the oldest and most basic principles to emerge from imperial colonization of the New World. As early as 1664 the English government had enforced this principle in an effort to hold back the United Colonies of New England from expanding their boundaries into Indian Country through local wars of conquest. In 1755 the Edmund Aitkin report had led to a similar outcome. Imperial authority was centralized in a department of Indian Affairs. This policy decision was confirmed after the Seven Years' War in the Royal Proclamation of 1763 and in the Quebec Act of 1774. The American Revolution and the War of 1812 stand for all time as illustrations of the intensity of will among the non-Aboriginal population – among the transplanted Europeans who have been referred to as *Creoles* throughout much of the Americas – to overcome all imperial regulations aimed at protecting lands reserved for Indigenous peoples. This history, in turn, demonstrates the continuing relevance of the recommendation of the Aborigines Committee that the protection of Aboriginal and treaty rights is a responsibility belonging to the executive branch of central authority in imperial and, by implication, federal forms of government.

According to Mostert, "The Aborigines Committee remains one of the most striking and impressive examples of public enquiry in nineteenth-century Britain, its massive report one of the most absorbing public documents of that century."[54] The careful and detailed study and analysis it embodied stand in stark contrast to many of the early justifications of manifest destiny in the United States. In explaining his own theory for the "justifiable extinguishment" of Aboriginal rights, for instance, William Henry Harrison asked rhetorically, "Is one of the fairest portions of the globe to remain in a state of nature, the haunt of a few wretched savages, when it seems destined by the Creator to give support to a large population, and to be the seat of civilization, of science, and of the religion?"[55] In contrast, the Select Committee discussed British imperial expansionism in the following terms: "The moment [has come] for the nation to declare, that with all its desire to give encouragement to emigration, and to find a soil to which our surplus population may retreat, it will tolerate no scheme which implies violence or fraud in taking possession of such a territory."[56]

The year 1837 also witnessed armed uprisings in Upper and Lower Canada. In Upper Canada the resistance to British imperialism, which was led by William Lyon Mackenzie, was relatively weak. In Lower Canada the uprising had a wider base, drawing as it did on the French Canadian nationalism of those who looked to Louis-Joseph Papineau for leadership. Both Mackenzie and Papineau were republicans who sought American intervention to "liberate" Canada from what they saw as the oppressiveness of British rule. In spite of the resentment towards Bond Head's Indian policies among many Aboriginal people in Upper Canada, some of the Indian veterans from the War of 1812 joined the British military in their manoeuvres to quell the insurrection. The old military alliance with the crown still persisted.[57]

RESPONSIBLE GOVERNMENT, THE EARLY MINING FRONTIER, AND THE ASSERTIONS OF ABORIGINAL TITLE: THE GENESIS OF THE ROBINSON TREATIES OF 1850

Although the uprisings were easily crushed, the British government responded to this display of discontent in the Canadas by devolving power from the imperial government to the representative bodies in British North America. The two Canadas – Upper Canada and Lower Canada – were united and given a single legislature. That legislature in turn was given broader responsibilities through an innovation known as responsible government. Essentially, Canada's governor general stopped taking direction in domestic affairs from Great Britain and instead, accepted the direction of the party holding the majority of seats in the local legislature. The executive branch of government was controlled by a cabinet, composed of individuals chosen by a prime minister from the elected caucus of the majority party. The crown's representative was responsible to the legislature, which in turn was responsible to the electorate. In this way the voting population of British North America – the adult males who owned land – acquired broader powers of self-government.[58]

In the late 1840s the British government opened various fields of jurisdiction to the workings of responsible government. Because of the unique character of British imperial responsibilities for Indian Affairs, however, this branch of colonial administration continued to operate directly under British authority until the mid-1850s.[59] At that point, even this jurisdictional domain was formally devolved to the legislatures of British North America.

In the province of Canada, the mark of this devolution to local control was the first Indian Act, which was formally entitled An Act to Encourage the Gradual Civilization of the Indian Tribes in Canada and to Amend Laws Respecting Indians. In this statute the legislature of

Canada asserted authority to break off pieces of land from the collective domain of an Indian reserve. The legislature also claimed the authority to decide the official criteria for distinguishing (civilized) citizens from (uncivilized) Indians. To meet these criteria, an adult Indian male applying for enfranchisement had to demonstrate himself to be competent in French or English, free from debt, and capable of passing a "civilization test" to be established by a board created for the purpose. The first civilization test asked Indian applicants to name the continents of the world, to demonstrate sufficient general knowledge to qualify for Canadian citizenship. In this remarkably telling exercise of power, local officials revealed that an expanded domain of self-government for the non-Indian citizens of Canada had been accompanied by a corresponding diminishment in the domain of self-government available to the non-citizen Indians of Canada.[60]

The advice of the Select Committee on Aborigines in British Settlements had not been followed: the representative body of the local government had been given the directing role in the management of Indian Affairs. The first action of that legislature was to put in place legislation whose objective was, ultimately, to break up the reserves and to destroy the collective cultural and legal identities of distinct Indian societies. Canadian citizenship and the institution of private property under Canadian law were to be the primary instruments for atomizing the domain of Aboriginal peoples.

The widened sphere of self-government for the male citizens of the Province of Canada unfolded in the context of a steady dismantling of the old mercantile structures on which British imperial Canada had been constructed after 1763. This transformation had particularly harsh consequences for many of the Montreal merchants who had largely severed their business attachments to the Indian Country of Canada after 1821. That year their primary entrepreneurial vehicle in the fur trade, the North West Company, was purchased by the London-based Hudson's Bay Company. British exchange with the huge Indian Country of northern North American was henceforth mostly funnelled through the northern ports on Hudson's Bay rather than the inland port of Montreal.

The decline of the North West Company had been difficult during the last decade of its existence. The Treaty of Ghent in 1814 and the border settlement of 1818 resulted in the transfer of considerable business from the Nor' Westers to John Jacob Astor's American Fur Company.[61] Moreover, the Hudson's Bay Company placed a major obstacle in the heart of the Nor' Westers' main east-west transportation route when it opened the way in 1811 for Lord Selkirk to establish a Scots farming settlement at Red River. This settlement was planned around the site of present-day Winnipeg. The conflicts between the HBC-sanctioned settlers and the emerging Métis community connected to Montreal's most important enterprise broke into open violence at Seven Oaks in 1816.[62] A half

decade later the Montreal-based fur trade finally succumbed to the natural superiority of the commercial system whose monopoly of Fort
Churchill, an ocean port in the deep interior of northern North America,
ultimately proved decisive.

By the 1840s the merchants of what Donald Creighton entitled "Commercial Empire of the St. Lawrence" were further alienated from Great
Britain by a change in the tariff structure premised on the ascendant principles of free-trade liberalism.[63] The Second British Empire in North
America was severely shaken as the British government moved to restruc-
ture the mother country's political relationships with Canada along the
economic lines championed by Adam Smith and partially implemented,
especially by Lord Shelburne, in laying down the commercial rules for the
emergence of the United States from the downfall of the first British
Empire. In 1849 some of the Montreal business class responded dramatically to the removal of Canada from favoured trading status in a more
decentralized, increasingly *laissez-faire* British Empire. They participated
in the vandalization and burning of Canada's Legislative Assembly building in Montreal. Thus, some of the children of those merchants who, in
the War of 1812, had condemned the American government as a regime
of rapacious land jobbers and murderous Indian fighters now clamoured
for the Province of Canada to be annexed to the United States.[64] In 1854
this push for closer commercial ties and greater political integration with
the American empire was partially appeased when Great Britain negotiated a treaty eliminating most tariff barriers between Canada and the
republic to the south.[65]

These constitutional and commercial changes established the broader
framework within which the non-Indian governors and settlers of the
Province of Canada and the Maritime provinces set about transforming
the land either as an extension or as a British North American clone of
the American empire of private property. After the War of 1812, for
instance, the Canada Company in Upper Canada and the British-American Land Company in Lower Canada were established in much the same
fashion as those British enterprises that speculated on the opening of
Indian Country in the years leading up to the American Revolution.

As in the United States the most direct legal and commercial extensions
of the earlier land-speculation companies were railway companies.[66] In an
era of "free trade" and colonial self-government, the charters for these
enterprises came not from Great Britain but from the local legislatures of
British North America. These legislatures became the hub of tremendous
speculative activity prompting Allan McNab, a Tory parliamentarian from
the Hamilton area, to proclaim, "Railways are my politics."[67] The rush to
use the new institutions of local self-government to privatize the lands and
resources of Canada inevitably led the new regime into direct confrontation with those who projected forward the old imperial laws and ethos of
the Indian Country of Canada.

The major sites of this confrontation were the mineral-rich lands north of the Great Lakes, lands which, in later years, would support the mining economy of northern Ontario. Some of these non-Indian mines were developed on sites where Indigenous peoples had for thousands of years chipped raw copper directly from the rock faces of the Canadian Shield. This raw copper they pounded into various tools and ornaments.[68] In the late 1840s the provincial legislature of Canada began to issue permits to mining companies to conduct their extractive operations at several sites along the northern shores of Lake Superior. These licences were extended without any consent whatsoever from the local Ojibway in a region that, for many generations, had been pivotal to the transportation and communications networks of the North American fur trade. By opening a portion of Indian Country to non-Indian exploitation without the agreement of the Indigenous peoples, the provincial government soon faced allegations that it had violated some of the key provisions of the Royal Proclamation of 1763.[69]

Shingwaukonse, whose Ojibway name can be translated as Little Pine,[70] was the most prominent Indian leader to protest this failure on the part of local authorities to live up to the crown's own law of Aboriginal and treaty rights. By the time mining operations began in his territory, this renowned figure of the Sault Ste Marie area was already in his mid-seventies. Shingwaukonse and the father of Nebennigoebing, another key protagonist in the events leading up to the making of the Robinson Treaties of 1850, had both been awarded medals for their heroism on the side of the crown in the War of 1812. The memory of Indian peoples as active allies of the crown in the recent conflict with the United States would increasingly colour the debate, pitting those who saw the Indian Country of Canada as an integral part of the emerging nation against those who argued that existing Aboriginal and treaty rights need not be addressed in the development of new resource frontiers.

Another key figure to intervene on the side of the Indians was Lord Elgin. As governor general of Canada, he clearly understood his constitutional responsibilities to defend the honour of the crown in maintaining those sacred covenants, including the Royal Proclamation of 1763 and the wampum representation of it. Lord Elgin knew that the British sovereign was ultimately directly implicated in all transactions involving Aboriginal title.

Shingwaukonse and Nebennigoebing chose Allan Macdonell as their lawyer. Macdonell was a Tory, a mining promoter, and later a railway promoter.[71] The Macdonell clansfolk had been prominent among those Roman Catholic Highland Scots who migrated to British North America in the eighteenth century. While many migrated in response to economic pressures, they were also adapting to the frustrated resistance aimed at preventing England's colonization of Scotland. The outmigration of Scotland's Aboriginal clansfolk had increased after 1745, when the defeat of

Bonnie Prince Charlie in the Battle of Culloden destroyed Jacobite hopes of replacing the Hanoverian hold on the British throne with a Stuart-controlled monarchy. This transatlantic movement was part of a larger pattern that saw many of the Highlanders become soldiers in the British Empire's worldwide military system.

Before the American Revolution, many of the Macdonells migrated along with other Highland Scots to become tenants in the feudal estates of Sir William Johnson in New York colony. There they were often inducted into service in the local militia and into the British Imperial Indian Department. This experience prepared them to join the crown's side in the American Revolution and, in some cases, to participate in the expansion of Montreal's fur-trade empire through the entrepreneurial medium of the North West Company. In commenting on the seminal stage of this genesis, one chronicle noted, "The Macdonells of the Mohawk Valley were steady in their devotion to Sir William Johnson, and accepted his political views as their own." This same account noted that, in the War of American Independence, sixteen Macdonells were officers in New York's three Loyalist regiments. They were prominent in the group surrounding Sir John Johnson during the era of the founding of Upper Canada.[72]

Of all the influential Macdonells in Canada's history, Allan played the primary role in carrying forward the diplomatic legacy of Johnson Hall, the Covenant Chain, the Royal Proclamation, and the Indian buffer state to the frontiers of the Province of Canada in the mid-nineteenth century. Macdonell's father, Alexander, had been a tenant on Sir William's estate and had served, along with Captain Joseph Brant, in Butler's Rangers, the unit whose military operations had so terrorized the outlying Anglo-American settlements during the American Revolution. After the war, Alexander was appointed sheriff of the Home District of Upper Canada by Lieutenant-Governor John Graves Simcoe. Later, the elder Macdonell became assistant superintendent of the British Imperial Indian Department.[73]

Alexander's son, Allan, became a student of the province's most zealously conservative schoolmaster, the Reverend John Strachan, an education that, along with his family background, should have made him a charter member of Upper Canada's closely knit Family Compact, Roman Catholic branch. From this background and education Allan Macdonell crafted, along with Shingwaukonse, an extremely versatile contemporary interpretation of Aboriginal and treaty rights. This constitutional interpretation combined Tory tradition with adaptation to the era's entrepreneurial ethos. It recognized the capacity of Indian nations to develop their own regimes of property law and to charter corporations directly accountable to them.

There is no doubt that this interpretation was partly self-serving on Macdonell's part. He himself was the recipient of one of several 999-year mining leases given out by the Ojibway of the Sault Ste Marie area in the era before the Robinson Treaties. In accepting this lease, Macdonell promised to hire Indian people as miners and to train them in drilling operations so they could develop their own resource companies.[74] In advancing this policy, Macdonell argued that, without a treaty, the provincial government had "no power over the land and that the Indians had a perfect right to work the mines, cultivate the land or employ any Agent or servant to do it for them." He added, with a precautionary eye towards the kind of thinking that was becoming integral to Indian policies of both Canada and the United States, "the Indians are not to be regarded as minors in law."[75]

In anticipating a future that would include a clear constitutional space for Indigenous peoples to participate in the economic, corporate, and political development of the country as distinct societies, the vision of Shingwaukonse and Allan Macdonell was at sharp variance with the policies that would unfold in the years ahead. The tragedy of crown-Aboriginal treaty making since the War of 1812 has been that the outcome failed to give Indigenous peoples a viable way to participate as self-determining collectivities in the economic transformation of Canada away from the fur trade and towards other kinds of activities. This twisted exploitation of treaties as instruments to extinguish Aboriginal title rather than as vehicles to protect and develop the ingredients for viable Aboriginal economies, marks the same tragic trend that Tecumseh so effectively identified two generations earlier. One of the keys to a form of economic viability for First Nations government then, no less than now, would have been the capacity to reap a percentage of the royalties coming from key forms of commercial activity on the full extent of their ancestral lands, not merely on their narrowly circumscribed reserves. As Shingwaukonse commented of the entry of mining enterprises into his people's territory: "The Great Spirit, we think, placed these rich mines on our lands, for the benefit of his red children, so that their rising generation might get support for them when the animals of the woods should have grown too scarce for our subsistence ... We want pay for every pound of mineral that has been taken off our lands, as well as that which may hereafter be carried away."[76]

In 1847 the Ojibway of the Lake Superior region petitioned the governor general with their position. A year later a delegation, including Shingwaukonse, Nebennigoebing, and Allan Macdonell, travelled to Montreal, where they delivered their message personally to Lord Elgin. In a report to the legislature, Denis-Benjamin Papineau, commissioner of crown lands, rejected the Ojibway assertions. He argued that the petitioners, "being only a small tribe they do not form a Nation and therefore cannot claim the Territory."[77] Some of the affected Ojibway, together with Métis relatives and non-Indian allies, responded to these various slights in 1849 by occupying and closing down the operations of the Quebec Mining Company at Mica Bay near Michipicoten. For their actions, the occupiers, including Shingwaukonse and Allan Macdonell, were arrested and briefly incarcerated in Toronto. At this point Lord Elgin intervened, by essentially ordering the provincial government to proceed with treaty negotiations as quickly as possible.[78] Thus the crown's representative in Canada demonstrated that the new principles of responsible government would have to conform with the continuing imperial responsibilities with respect to Indian Affairs.

In December of 1849 Allan Macdonell presented in the pages of the Tory newspaper *The Patriot* a wide-ranging commentary on Ojibway history and on the crown law of Aboriginal and treaty rights.[79] The most aggressive opponents of Macdonell's Tory preoccupation with the continuing relevance of Indian Country to the development of Canada were to be found in the Reform Party, whose liberal enthusiasts rallied around the Clear Grit leader George Brown and his publishing vehicle, *The Globe*.[80] As the journalistic centre of the Toronto business community's desire to develop a commercial empire of its own in the continent's North-West – a desire shared by Allan Macdonell – *The Globe* had published large portions of Papineau's rejection of the principles supporting the Ojibway assertions of titles to lands north of the upper great Lakes. Macdonell explained:

Mr. Papineau says, "being only a small tribe they do not form a nation, therefore cannot claim territory." During the last war they were not then considered so insignificant. Their assistance as allies was eagerly sought for, and readily given: not to fight for their own territories, but, as they say, "to help you keep what we have given you." And the old Chief Shingwaukonse, now a prisoner here, with the father of Negennigoebing came down with *seven hundred* warriors to our assistance and served during the war... at no period in the history of the country has the Government ever attempted to possess itself of an inch of Indian lands without a treaty first being had: and so far back as 1763 so careful was the Crown, that the Indian tribes with whom it is connected should not be molested or disturbed in the possession of territory unceded to the Crown, that it was by the Royal Proclamation declared and expressly forbidden to any Governor General or Commander-in-Chief etc, to grant warrants of survey, or pass patents for any lands whatsoever, which had not been ceded or purchased by the Crown ... Thus the Royal Proclamation which guaranteed to these people security in their possessions, and induced them to become allies of the Crown, which they have ever since served with fidelity and truth is now utterly disregarded and forgotten: – and our own Provincial statutes set at defiance by the Government itself.[81]

In 1850 William Benjamin Robinson negotiated two treaties on behalf of the crown with twenty-one Ojibway bands north of the upper Great Lakes. The Robinson-Huron Treaty covered 35,700 square miles around Georgian Bay. The Robinson-Superior Treaty covered 16,700 square miles north of Lake Superior. Twenty-one reserves were established by these agreements, eighteen in the former treaty area and three in the latter. The fact that the crown negotiators failed to include several bands indigenous to the treaty areas created the conditions for a number of future land disputes. The Robinson Treaties also failed to create a clear opening for Indigenous peoples to participate from a position of strength in the new kinds of economic activities that would come to dominate their ancestral lands in the future. Instead, provincial officials tended to be backward-looking in their expectations for First Nations, as indicated, for instance, in excerpts from the document William Robinson sent to his superiors:

The lands now ceded are notoriously barren and sterile, and will in all probability never be settled except in a few localities by mining companies, whose establishments among the Indians, instead of being prejudicial, would prove of great benefit as they would afford a market for any things they may have to sell, and bring provisions and stores of all kinds among them at reasonable prices ... In allowing the Indians to retain reservations of land for their own use I was governed by the fact that they in most cases asked for such tracts as they had heretofore been in the habit of using for purposes of residence and cultivation, and by securing these to them and the right of hunting and fishing over the ceded territory, they cannot say that the Government takes their usual means of subsistence and therefore [they] have no claims for support.[82]

EXPANSION OR IMMIGRATION INTO INDIAN COUNTRY?
ALLIANCES ACROSS CULTURES
IN THE MAKING OF THE FOURTH WORLD

While Tories in pre-revolutionary British North America and in post-revolutionary British imperial Canada were far from unanimous in adopting the principles of Aboriginal and treaty rights as an essential feature of empire building, what recognition there has been of these ideals was far more likely to come from the conservative than the liberal parts of the political spectrum. This Tory tendency towards identification with the Indian Country of Canada was deeply rooted in the history of the North American struggle to check, both militarily and ideologically, the spread of republicanism and to counter the expansive claims of American manifest destiny.

The other main bastion of support among non-Indians for the rights and titles of Indigenous peoples was centred in some branches of the Roman Catholic Church. This identification, however paternalistic, with the conservative, collectivist orientation of Indian Country was founded in the missionary enterprises that were integral to the history of New France.[83] The legacy of this evangelization was marked in the Catholic missions. These missions included Kanewake and Lake of Two Mountains, near Montreal and Oka, respectively, as well as at Village des Hurons near Quebec City.[84]

In the 1840s and 1850s an emboldened and rejuvenated Jesuit Order reached back towards their old missionary stronghold in the upper Great Lakes. After an aborted effort to establish a stronghold on Walpole Island near Detroit, the Jesuits set up a new base of operations among the Odawa (Ottawa) community at Wikwemikong on the eastern end of Manitoulin Island.[85] Like the Ojibway, the Odawa are part of the large family of Algonkian speakers in North America's interior who refer to themselves to this day as Anishinabek.

This Jesuit-Odawa connection proved to be a major axis of resistance in 1862, when officials from the provincial legislature tried to force a ceding treaty onto the Indian people of Manitoulin Island. Although Crown Lands Commissioner William McDougall gained the signatures, through dubious tactics, of several Indian men from the western portion of the island, the Wikwemikong people, with the solid backing of their predominantly French-speaking priests, resisted all efforts to break their common front against the machinations of the government of land speculators dominating the Province of Canada. As a result, the Wikwemikong community to this day proclaim the status of their lands as an "unceded reserve."[86]

In seeking in 1863 to undo the damage of the previous year, the Wikwemikong leadership tried to convince their Indian neighbours to renounce the Manitoulin Treaty. In making this case to an agitated Aboriginal assembly composed of treaty proponents and treaty resisters, the Odawa spokesperson, Wah-kai-keghik, employed the image of a single eating vessel as a metaphor for the need to draw sustenance from the bowl of Indian unity. Moreover, he referred in his speech to population increases among his own people, a demographic observation corroborated five years earlier by a special commission entrusted to prepare the ground for the provincial takeover of jurisdictional responsibility for Indian Affairs from the imperial government.[87] Wah-kai-keghik, confirmed in his belief that Indigenous peoples in his district were now increasing rather than decreasing in numbers, said:

We know what will be the result when the whites come and live among us. They will do the labour that is required on the Island, and will of course make money and to you, my friends, will be given the lowest meanest work to do as servants – such as, carrying water, cutting up wood, cleaning the stables, making baskets, and when the land you have ceded shall have been divided among yourselves and white settlers, what land will your children have? Our families are increasing. The Indians are increasing in number. How can our descendants be provided for? We have no other reserve besides this. My friends, we want to eat out of one dish as it were; we do not wish to break a part of it to give away. All of us who met together at Me-tche-wedig-nong, and held a grand council there, agreed that we should eat out of one dish. We feel convinced that the Indians would be better off if they kept the Island for themselves than if they surrendered part of it.[88]

Chief Misheguong-pai replied to Wah-kai-keghik on behalf of those Aboriginal groups on Manitoulin Island who were resolved to accept the future held out by the treaty, a future where they would be subject to a different rule of law from that of their ancestors and a future where their children would grow up in close proximity to non-Indians. There were resonant echoes of past history and history yet to be made in the exchange between these two men advocating profoundly different strategies on how to respond to the prospect of becoming a small minority in their own ancestral lands. Misheguong-pai answered:

The future will tell what Indians will be better off. You who oppose to make a treaty or we who consent to make it. We have hitherto obeyed the Queen and Her officers, we mean to do so still. We place ourself in the good keeping of the Government. My friends, we are no longer independent people. We cannot live as our forefathers did. We are dependent on the white man for many things essential to our welfare. The Queen is our monarch. She has authority over us. My friends, I cannot agree with what you have said. I tell you plainly I shall not aid your projects ... My friends, we cannot resist the tide of immigration. The whites are coming nearer and nearer to us. They will at last surround us, but they will not drive us away before them.[89]

The Catholic-Aboriginal resistance to the Manitoulin Treaty set the stage for a similar resistance movement aimed against the Dominion of Canada's annexation of the Hudson's Bay Company lands. While the Reform politician and land speculator William McDougall went to Manitoulin in 1862 as treaty commissioner, in 1869 he travelled to the Red River settlement as the new lieutenant-governor of the newly annexed dominion territories. In this second role as the representative of the Crown, the Toronto businessman again found himself facing a strong coalition of Indigenous people and their Roman Catholic clergy, only in this instance his Native opponents were Métis who looked to Louis Riel as their spokesperson. With the powerful Roman Catholic Church of Quebec playing the role of intermediary, the provisional government led by Riel negotiated with the dominion government of Prime Minister John A. Macdonald the terms of what the Métis leader later described as "a treaty."[90] This treaty was given legislative and constitutional articulation as the Manitoba Act, the instrument that created a new Canadian province on a land base that was to have included 1.4 million acres to be "set apart for the half-breed children."[91]

The development of a Métis identity in and around the Red River crossroads of the Canadian fur trade represented one of many cultural outcomes arising from European and Euro-American immigration into Indian Country. Another variation developed among the Cherokee during the era of the American Revolution. In that conflict a number of committed Tories sought sanctuary among the crown's Cherokee allies. While a subsequent Cherokee treaty with the new American republic set out the terms for returning the non-Aboriginal refugees, an exception was made to allow those Tories who had intermarried, or who had otherwise been adopted, to remain with their host communities. Many availed themselves of this provision.[92] The adoption of Tory refugees during the era of the American Revolution was part of a significant immigration of Europeans, especially into Cherokee and Creek country. Among the most successful immigrants into Indian Country were the Scots, whose own clans were being cleared from their ancestral lands in the process of transforming the tribal titles of the Highlands into more privatized holdings under the property law of Great Britain.

The blending of cultures on the middle ground of Scots–First Nations relations became essential to the survival strategies of Creek and Chero-kee peoples especially in the early decades of the nineteenth century. The importance of intercultural adaptation were personified in the regimes of Aboriginal leadership provided by Alexander McGillivray of the Creeks and John Ross of the Cherokee, both of whom, as their family names sug-gest, had many European ancestors on their family trees.[93] Among the Cherokee, the names of the Rogers, the Macphersons, the McClamores, the Campbells, the McDonalds, the Adairs, and the Lowrys identified a transatlantic communion of clans, a process of immigration that pressed beyond Europe's palisaded frontier outposts into the Aboriginal heart of the continent's older human heritages.[94]

Similarly, many Scots immigrants into the vast fur-trade domain of Canada, but especially the Roman Catholic Highlanders, tended to follow in the footsteps of the *canadiens* who had been absorbed in varying degrees into Indian Country. The direction of French imperial policy in North America was one factor among several that contributed to the rel-atively seamless blending of *canadien* identity into Métis identity, and Métis identity into Indian identities. Some of the architects of this policy had looked largely to the Indigenous peoples, rather than to transplant-ed Europeans, to provide the major population base of the French Empire.[95] Intermarriage was sporadically encouraged to promote the adoption of French culture by the Aboriginal population. According to the Marquis de Mirabeau, however, just the opposite outcome had proven the norm. He believed that the pursuit of this policy in New France, "instead of Frenchifying the savages ... had savagized the French." In fact, the enticements and liberties of Indian Country had made the *canadiens* increasingly "incapable of that subordination which is the soul of all colonies."[96]

The Roman Catholic Highlanders were especially prone to follow the lead of the *canadien* pathfinders in their propensity to assimilate them-selves into the pluralistic cultures of Indian Country. In some instances this process stopped short of full-fledged integration, involving, rather, various forms of identification through advocacy of the rights and titles of

First Nations. Certainly Allan Macdonell embodied this tradition, as did his fellow clansman Simon J. Dawson. Dawson was a Canadian parliamentarian representing northern Ontario who took the side of Native people in many of their struggles over fishing rights and in support of their various struggles with the Department of Indian Affairs.[97]

While the politics of Macdonell and Dawson represented one approach to alliance with the First Nations, intermarriage was the primary vehicle for yet deeper processes of immigration into Indian Country. The Orkney Islands to the north of the Scottish mainland were one of the main sites of departure for those whose process of immigration was very different from the one described by Frederick Jackson Turner in his invention of the American frontier thesis. In their anxiousness to avoid impressment into the British Navy, Orkneymen often sought and gained employment, especially in the transportation brigades of the Hudson's Bay Company. Many never returned, but instead established in Canada families whose mixed-ancestry offspring augmented the First Nations, the colonial society and those who were most comfortable in the fertile middle ground between the two.[98]

Race-based paradigms in the social sciences, but especially the lens of "Indian-white relations," obscure full appreciation of the fact that European immigration into the Americas could take many forms. An important subtext of this process of immigration was epitomized by the experiences of many Highland Scots on both sides of the Atlantic. They can be envisaged as Indigenous peoples uprooted from their lands, their traditions, and their Aboriginal laws by the colonization of an alien imperial system. This experience inclined some of them to find common ground with First Nations peoples in their adopted land. Their inclination to identify with the First Nations foreshadowed a different kind of ecological identification pioneered by Archie Belaney in his transformation into Grey Owl.

The life of John Norton, whose Mohawk name was Teyoninhokarawen, serves to illustrate the richness of the adaptations made in the process of immigration into Indian Country. Norton is believed to have been the true-life inspiration for one of the main characters in John Richardson's novel *Wacousta*. His father was Cherokee, and his mother was a Scot. Born in 1760, Norton was adopted into the Six Nations community in Upper Canada, where he became one of its most prominent citizens. He maintained throughout his life close connections with both his Scottish and his Cherokee relatives, visiting them frequently in his travels on both sides of the Atlantic.[99] On his many sojourns to Great Britain, Norton participated actively in the movement for the abolition of slavery, helping to expand the interests of that powerful lobby to include the dilemmas and struggles of Indigenous peoples throughout the British Empire. His activism was instrumental in the genesis of the Aborigines' Protection Society, whose work originally coincided with that of the parliamentary inquiry in 1837 on Aborigines in British settlements. Like Grey Owl or George Manuel, Norton's intercultural defence of an outword-looking and pluralistic alliance of First Nations peoples, whatever their ancestry, made him a pioneering proponent of the Fourth World.

The easy assimilation, especially of many Scots into the clans of the Creek, the Cherokee, and the First Nations of Canada, illuminates a dimension of the Fourth World that cuts beneath many subsequently constructed boundaries of race and ethnicity. It is a phenomenon that goes far beyond anything envisaged by Margaret Atwood in her hypothesis on the Grey Owl syndrome.

The sporadic armistices in the Columbian conquests established the basis for some fertile middle grounds between Aboriginal and immigrant populations. Among the motivativating factors for alliance and liaison at these points of intercultural experimentation were common experiences of displacement, dispossession, and subordination in the expansion of possessive individualism's transatlantic empire. That expansion had victimized many, as the process of making privatized, domestic enclosures extinguished old feudal estates. That enclosure movement, which marks the beginnings of the biotechnology industry through the selective breeding of livestock, uprooted many ancient Aboriginal communities in Europe, whose members were forced to seek new homes and new alliances in adopted lands. Sometimes the immigrants found they had more in common with the continent's Indigenous peoples than they had with those who represented New World counterparts of the same social and economic classes who had uprooted their clans in the old country.

Reciprocal bonds of business, intermarriage, and shared experience with various forms of marginalization and dispossession made the phenomenon of immigration into Indian Country a very different process from the form of expansionism aimed at extinguishing Indian Country. That process of immigration and assimilation *into* Indian Country has been essential in the emergence of the Fourth World as a pluralistic realm of prolific intercultural inventiveness on the middle ground of compromise, negotiation, and exchange.

THE BIBLE, THE STATE, AND THE SATELLITE DISH: RELIGION AND CULTURE ON MOVING FRONTIERS OF IDENTITY AND EMPIRE

In Asia and Africa, the Christian bearers of European imperialism have faced stiff missionary competition, especially from those travelling the global pathways and highways of Islam. In the Americas, however, the world religion locating salvation in Jesus Christ encountered its most open field for rapid expansion. While many Indigenous peoples in the Americas actively resisted Christian evangelization, over several centuries most Indian and Inuit societies eventually arrived at some sort of synthesis, weaving aspects of their own inherited traditions of spiritual observance into the rituals and devotions of both Protestantism and Roman Catholicism.

One general observation is that the societies forged by English-speaking Protestants were most prone to push for complete or near elimination of Indian Country. Similarly, except for those Anglo-Americans taken in childhood as captives of Aboriginal societies, there were comparatively fewer Protestants than Roman Catholics who sought acceptance in Indian Country through intermarriage or through various forms of assimilation. There were, of course, many exceptions to this rule. There might have been more exceptions except for the decisions made by the government of the United States and later by the government of Canada. In the Dominion of Canada the United States' assimilationist brand of Indian policy was seized upon, especially after a transcontinental railway was built across British North America largely to prevent the fur-trade domain of the Hudson's Bay Company from being absorbed into the American republic.

Up until the late 1820s, the Protestant religion had become integral to large parts of the culturally and ethnically plural society that made up the citizenry of the Cherokee Nation. On behalf of the American Board of Commissioners for Foreign Missions, the Reverend Jeremiah Evarts led a major drive to mobilize public opinion against the strategy of Indian removal as proposed and later implemented by President Andrew Jackson. Evart's church-based crusade, however, failed to generate sufficient political will to save even the Cherokee from being coercively and illegally uprooted by the federal government in its coercive journey culminating in the Trail of Tears.[100] The Cherokee spokesperson John Ridge highlighted the implications of enforcing Indian removal even on the Indian society in North America that went the farthest in adapting itself to the mores of Anglo-American life. In 1832 he declared to a Protestant audience: "You asked us to throw off the hunter and warrior state: We did so – you asked us to form a republican government: We did so – adopting your own as a model. You asked us to cultivate the earth, and learn the mechanical arts: We did so. You asked us to learn to read: We did so. You asked us to cast away our idols, and worship your God: We did so."[101] The unhappy outcome of Evart's crusade can be seen as a marker not only of the failure of the United States to accommodate even those Aboriginal societies that had been most open to accept the immigration of peoples, ideas, and techniques from the larger Anglo-American world but as a failure of American Protestantism. The crux of that failure was manifest in the unwillingness of regular church members to heed the advice of Protestantism's most outspoken champions of Aboriginal and treaty rights as an integral feature of American democracy.

While Georgia's appropriation of the remaining Cherokee Territory represented a major defeat for of some of the most powerful centres of

Protestant influence, British Columbia was the site of some very successful Protestant adaptations to Aboriginal societies. These adaptations were
especially rich in the coastal regions south of Alaska. In the 1950s Philip
Drucker reported that potlatch ceremonies had been largely imported,
with some few modifications and disguises, into Protestant ceremonies.
Drucker observed further that the old clan systems among coastal peoples
seemed to have been incorporated into the structures of local church governance.[102] The blending of Protestant and Aboriginal cultures on the
West Coast, however, tells only part of the story. A more discordant element lies in the role of some Protestant missionaries in pushing for an
amendment to the Indian Act that would criminalize participants in traditional potlaches conducted outside the framework of Christianity.[103]

While Protestants can point to a number of their missionaries who
made genuine attempts to absorp rather than eliminate many of the cultural attributes of Indian Country, the intercultural blending of peoples
and identities has taken place on a far larger scale within the framework
of the Roman Catholicism of the American hemisphere. Since 1492 that
tradition has been the predominant Christian force throughout the
Americas, except for those phases of colonization and decolonization
resulting in the creation and growth of the United States. While much of
Canada shares a similar Protestant heritage, the Roman Catholic Church
maintained until recently an integral involvement in the genesis and protection of French Canadian culture.

To understand the deep integration of the Roman Catholic Church
into those many Central and South American countries to emerge from
New Spain, it is vital to understand the unprecedented quality of the marriage of church and state throughout the decisive stages of Spanish imperialism. As J. Lloyd Mecham has written, "never before or since did a
sovereign with the consent of the pope so completely control the Catholic
Church as did the Spanish kings in their American possessions."[104]
Unlike the rulers of the other European empires in the Americas, the
Spanish and the Portuguese sovereigns derived all their titles in the hemisphere from a "donation" given by the papal head of the Roman Catholic
Church. In the case of Spain, this grant went so far that the Catholic monarchs of Spain acquired the power of patronage to present all candidates
for ecclesiastical office, high and low. The clergy of New Spain, therefore,
owed their positions more to the Spanish court than to the Vatican.

While this marriage of church and state could often be acrimonious, it
also created the basis for considerable convergence of monarchical and
ecclesiastical authority in the expansion of New Spain's influence into
Indian societies. When conquistadors seized control of this expansion,
the outcomes were frequently lethal for Indigenous peoples. But from
these horrors emerged a growing partnership between the Spanish crown
and some ecclesiastical orders, but especially the Dominicans. Increasingly the intertwined authority of clergy and crown developed coherent

approaches to the protection of the Indians against depredations by the transplanted European populations.[105] There can be no doubt that the ethos of Roman Catholicism has been far more conducive than Protestantism in the genesis of mestizo identities. Similarly, although the aim of winning Indian converts has rarely been absent from such ventures, Roman Catholicism in the Americas has been far more comfortable in adapting to the process, or leading the process, of various kinds of immigration into Indian Country.

The complex psychology of many mestizo people is sometimes manifest in extreme prejudices or even violence pointed towards their relatives on the Indian branches of America's family tree. As Demietrio Cojti Cuxil, a Mayan professor of communications at the San Carlos University has commented, the notion of mestizo identity has sometimes conjured up images of the "sexual violence" of Spanish conquistadors against Indian woman. He adds, "Nobody wants to dig into this kind of beginning; there is a profound resistance against studying and accepting it." According to Cuxil, the impulse of the most ladinoized of the mestizo has often been to press on self-identifying Indian peoples the idea that "you must forget your language. You must abandon your culture. You must become like us to release us from the responsibility of discriminating against you."[106] While mestizo identity can sometimes take on a decidedly hostile disposition towards Indian cultures, however, the mixed-ancestry population can also give rise to prolific adaptations on the fertile middle ground of intercultural innovation. From the large mestizo populations of the Americas have emerged many of those intermediaries and interpreters who have helped to provide First Nations with both protection and a strategic range of economic, political, and cultural connections integral to adaptation and survival.

In the region of the United States that once belonged to Mexico stand many powerful symbols of Roman Catholicism's capacity to graft itself seamlessly onto the Old World heritages of the Americas. One such symbol is the chapel structure that is well integrated into the sacred architecture as well as the elaborate ceremonial life of the Pueblo in New Mexico's Ranchos de Taos. The Taos Pueblo is one of the oldest continually occupied settlements in the Americas. Its origins go back well before the arrival of the Europeans in the region. The site stands as one of America's most important shrines celebrating the adaptive resilience of the human spirit. Its antiquity, together with its contemporary vitality, serve to symbolize the superficiality of the perception that America is a New World.

While there has been much creative synergy between Roman Catholicism and many spiritual and cultural heritages of Aboriginal America, there have, of course, been many betrayals of this heritage. One of the most recent took place during the final decade of the Cold War. The root of this betrayal was the active role of Pope John Paul II as an ally and agent of the United States' efforts to topple the Soviet Empire from within. The pope's proud adherence to Polish nationalism was a significant contributing factor in his becoming an especially active participant in the making and implementation of American foreign policy during the final phase of the Cold War. In siding so forcefully with the world's ascendant superpower, however, the Vatican became decidedly derelict in its treatment of those priests and nuns who attempted to grapple with the injustice and inequity embedded in some of the American empire's most notorious client regimes

Among the Roman Catholic clergy who sided most fearlessly with the poorest of the poor (who in Latin American are disproportionately Aboriginal) were Archbishop Oscar Romero of El Salvador and Bishop Samuel Ruíz of Chiapas. Bishop Ruíz acted as the main intermediary in early negotiations between the Mexican government and the Zapatista Liberation Army. Like Bishop Carlos Filipe Belo, the clergyman who stood shoulder to shoulder with the Indigenous peoples of East Timor during the darkest hours of repression under the genocidal thuggery of the us-backed Suharto regime in Indonesia, Bishop Ruíz and Archbishop Romero personified the contemporary legacy of Bartolome de las Casas. Their work embodied the essence of Liberation Theology, an element of Roman Catholicism that was stunted by the Vatican's very active role as a participant in the Cold War.[107]

Pope Paul's unease with the activists of Liberation Theology was directed especially harshly at Archbishop Oscar Romero. Archbishop Romero was treated rudely and then criticized by the pope during his visit to the Vatican in 1981. This papal snub was closely watched by agents of many right-wing regimes throughout Latin America. The elites of these regimes interpreted Pope John Paul's slighting of Archbishop Romero as a signal that they could discount clerical opposition to the repressive tactics often executed in the name of "counterinsurgency."[108] All these tactics were regularly taught to the military and police agents of us hegemony in Central and South America at the infamous School of the Americas in Fort Benning, Georgia. The academy's Spanish-language manuals included instruction in "counterinsurgency" through "motivation by fear, payment of bounties for enemy dead, false imprisonment, executions, and the use of truth serums."[109] With awareness that the pope was displeased with Archbishop Romero, the El Salvadorian death squads of Roberto D'Aubisson, a graduate of the School of the Americas, assassinated the controversial cleric within one month of his return from Rome. Romero's murder was one among tens of thousands of assassinations which the archbishop's successor described as "a war of extermination and genocide against a defenceless civilian population."[110]

The repression of right-wing regimes in Latin America during the Cold War fell especially lethally on many Indian groups. In the 1980s, for instance, Guatemala was the site of an array of government assaults directed by General Rios Montt primarily against his country's traditional

Mayan population. That dictator, like a number of his key advisers, was among the many us-backed operatives in Latin America who broke with the Roman Catholic Church to join the most evangelical branches of us-centred Protestantism. Indeed, Montt had experienced his "born again" conversion at the Gospel Outreach Church in Eureka, California. As John Bacher and many other have reported, some us-based oil companies with extensive investments in Guatemala and throughout many other parts of Central and South America have been among the main corporate donors channelling funds into the missionary work of evangelical Protestants. From the earliest stages of its founding in New England to the rise of the United States as a superpower, the American empire has been far more attuned to the individualistic ethos of the more fundamentalist branches of Protestant Christianity than the more collectivist orientations of Roman Catholicism, even during the vehemently anti-communist papacy of Pope John Paul II.[111]

The right-wing governments of Latin America have had no monopoly on anti-Indian actions and ideas. After it came to power in Nicaragua in 1979, the left-leaning Sandinista regime took harsh actions aimed at imposing national norms on the Miskito Indians on the Atlantic coast. The Miskito resistance to Sandinista land reform received some support from CIA operatives who continued the tradition of us involvement in the internal politics of the region, a tradition as old as the Monroe Doctrine. Covert us involvement in this Indian resistance movement should not be allowed to detract from an appreciation of the genuineness of Miskito opposition to some of the more doctrinaire applications of socialist policies. These socialist policies have sometimes advanced a kind of collectivist mirror-image of the monocultural universalism inherent in the economic assumptions of possessive individualism.[112]

While Rigobertu Menchu was instrumental in bringing the wholesale slaughters of Mayan peoples in Guatemala to wide public attention, the atrocities against Indians in her country were part of a more pervasive pattern, both regionally and hemispherically.[113] In Chile, after the us-backed coup in 1973, for instance, some of those Mapuche Indian people who resisted the policies of General Augusto Pinochet were eliminated in murderous forms of reprisal that became the hallmark of that ruthless regime. The aim of the Pinochet government was to further divide and privatize the remaining Mapuche lands – to continue the assault of the American empire on yet another frontier of the land of the bowl with one spoon.[114]

On the frontiers between Protestantism and Roman Catholicism lies the unique history of the Church of England in North America. For much of the nineteenth and twentieth centuries that denomination dominated much of the Christian religious life around the coasts of Hudson Bay and its southern projectory, James Bay. In many respects, the Church of England long enjoyed more pervasive and unchallenged influence in that region than it did in England itself, and it would be no exaggeration to

say that in large parts of this region, it formed the basis of a kind of Anglican theocracy. Technically this region was part of the vast domain shifted
from the proprietorship of the Hudson's Bay Company to the jurisdiction
of the Dominion of Canada in 1869. In practice, however, the old English
Company, like the Church of England, remained integral to the governance of the region for many decades after the formal transfer of titles
from the crown company to the crown dominion. The directness of the
transatlantic connections had much to do with this reality. Until the era
of bush-plane transport and radio communications throughout that huge
part of Canada not directly connected to the hemisphere's networks of
road and rail, many of the small ports on Hudson Bay and the river systems they supplied were connected more directly with Europe than with
North America's major urban centres.

The enduring importance of England's most famous fur-trade enterprise as well as the Church of England were reflective of the region's basic
transatlantic orientation to the outside world. The direct links to Europe,
but especially to the culture of Scotland, were reflected in many aspects
of the Aboriginal culture – in the strong celtic tones and rhythms of the
local fiddle music, for instance, or in the prominence of bright tartan
plaids in the clothing of the Aboriginal matrons, who moved with ease
between long periods on the trap lines to periods of sedentary life centred
in the Anglican missions and Hudson's Bay Company trade emporiums.

The Cree and Ojibway, like the Inuit in the more northerly reaches of
the region, gradually integrated the commercial and religious culture of
their trading partners in Great Britain into their Aboriginal cultures and
identities. Because the Indigenous peoples remained the majority population and long retained viable economic bases through their central role
in various aspects of the fur trade, they were able to incorporate these
English institutions into their Aboriginal lifeways largely on their own
terms. In other words, they were able to exercise considerable control
over what they would incorporate or reject from the outside world. Certainly the traditional spiritual observances of these hunting people
remained vital, even as most of them also incorporated Christianity into
their lives in varying degrees.[115]

It was not until the 1960s that Canada's Indian Affairs administration
began to assert from Ottawa strong governmental authority in this region.
Before that time the Indian missions of the Church of England represented, albeit on a far smaller scale, a kind of variation on the marriage of
church and state that characterized the government structures of New
Spain. That blending of religious and secular authority is built into the
structure of the British monarchy, which combines in the person of the
sovereign the duties of both head of state and head of England's National Church.

A striking image of that convergence is to be seen in the design of St
James's Anglican Church in the Cree community of Wunniman Lake in

the northern reaches of Ontario. Jeremiah Shinnawap personally constructed this landmark in the early 1960s. A deacon in the Anglican
Church and a signer of the adhesion to Treaty 9 in 1929, this Cree leader
designed the pointed steeple, which includes in its structure a very clear
representation of a crown.

In relating his discussions with Sewyn Dewdney of the Royal Ontario
Museum, John Webster Grant presented the following account of the Oji-
Cree community of Kasabonika as it was in 1965. "Clearly visible from the
air," he wrote, "was a large rectangular enclosure with a puzzling extension in the form of a cross. The enclosure, it turned out, was modelled on
the New Jerusalem as described in Revelation 21. Streets were laid out in
crosses and diagonals to conform to the design of the Union Jack, a
reminder of the community's Anglicanism."[116] Grant also referred to the
existence in the community of a mysterious document that he characterized as a 3,000-page "Cree-Ojibway Talmud." It was written in the local
language in the syllabic script. The Cree syllabic script was developed during the mid-1800s by the Methodist missionary, James Evans. Among the
publications issued by the Church of England in Cree syllabics were the
Bible as well as a rich assortment of Anglican hymns. From Country and
Western to Rhythm and Blues, there have been many stylistic variations
over the years in the way these same Anglican hymns have been rendered
in the local Aboriginal language to reflect changing styles.

The rich spiritual expressiveness arising from the Indigenous peoples
in the coastal regions of Hudson Bay can be interpreted, in part, as creative responses to the way that officialdom frequently merged the secular
and religious symbolism of the British monarchy. Their aim was to
encourage First Nations to accept and join the imperial mystique of the
British Empire. A similar instance of this Anglican marriage of church
and state was embodied in the short but famous life of Metlakata, a village theocracy built near Alaska by and for Tsimshian people.[117] In commenting on the broad influence in Indian Country of some Anglican
missionaries, including Metlakalta's Reverend William Duncan, Paul
Tennat has observed, "the British monarch was head of the church, the
fountain of British justice, and the author of the Royal Proclamation of
1763."[118]

In the final two decades of the twentieth century the sounds of Aboriginal Gospel, Aboriginal Country, and Aboriginal Rock music from, for
instance, the Innu band *Kashtin* were bounced throughout the satellite
systems that quickly filled the airwaves of northern Canada with Native-
language broadcasting. While the Inuit Broadcasting Corporation was the
pioneer in the field, a number of other Aboriginal media societies soon
joined it.[119] Thus the Indian Country of Canada, whose archetypal icon
was the canoe, gained a new symbol. The satellite dish became the totem
to signify the existence a new empire of communications in Indian and
Inuit Country.

One of the more successful Aboriginal communications societies to spring up in the Canadian north in this period was named *Wawatay*, a word meaning northern lights. The Wawatay Communications Society dissiminated print and broadcast media to a large area in northern Ontario and northern Manitoba where the people describe themselves and their language as Oji-Cree. Just as the name implies, the Oji-Cree inhabit the broad frontier zone between the more southerly heartland of the Ojibway and the more northerly Muskego Cree. The primary domain of the Muskego Cree – sometimes known also as the Swampy Cree – is the coastal lowlands. Like many thousands of words and place names in English, the term *muskeg* has its origins in an Indian source – the Muskego Crees' way of describing their swampy terrain along the coastal region of Hudson Bay. The emergence of the Oji-Cree language in the borderlands between different Indigenous peoples points to the fact that the blending of cultures can take place along many different kinds of frontier, including those *within* Indian Country. This blending of identities points to the multiplicity of possible cultural constructions embraced in the simple terms, Métis or mestizo. In an era when the accelerating pace of globalization translates into accelerating forms of blending along a mind-boggling array of frontiers between and within societies, the experience of being mestizo describes an increasingly central part of the broader human condition.

The same satellite systems that carried Aboriginal-language broadcasts also delivered unrelenting waves of imagery generated largely by the info-entertainment industry of the United States. Throughout the planet the huge volume of this cargo of imagery has profoundly affected the perceptual landscapes of Indigenous peoples – indeed, virtually all peoples, everywhere. The same empire that began with the export of the King James Bible took to the airwaves to communicate the Dow Jones stock market quotations, the entertainment product of the World Wrestling Federation, or the antics of the Jerry Springer Show.

These cultural products were exported as agents of the American empire developed new frontiers of resource extraction in the coastal regions of the Hudson Bay. They developed under the auspices of provincial governments in Canada. In northern Manitoba and Quebec, the Hudson Bay/James Bay watershed was dramatically transformed to produce hydroelectricity to energize North America's urban centres.[120] The massive flooding associated with these hydro works amounted to a major assault on the hunting and fishing economies of the region's Indigenous peoples. There were portents of larger disruptions to come as Canada's northward-flowing watershed was eyed as the source of a new supply of fresh water for commodified export, especially to the arid southwestern portions of the United States.[121]

Except for the Maritime provinces, Canada's geography east of the Rockies is roughly composed of the northern portion of the St

Lawrence–Great Lakes drainage basin along with the continent's arctic watershed. Much of this arctic watershed established the territorial extent of the Hudson's Bay Company, whose Charter was granted in 1670. The restructuring of this drainage basin began during the Second World War, when the northward flow into Hudson Bay of the Long Lake drainage basin was redirected southwards at Ogoki to run into the Great Lakes. The most immediate aim was to serve us pulp and paper companies operating in northern Ontario.[122]

A former premier of Quebec, Robert Bourassa, was in the 1980s an active promoter of the large-scale export of fresh water from the Hudson Bay watershed to the arid regions of the United States.[123] In large measure Bourassa was the main architect of the expansion of Hydro-Québec specifically and, more generally, of the Quebec government's infusion of influence into the traditional territories of the Cree, the Algonquin, the Innu, and the Inuit. These territories, an important part of the old fur-trade hinterland of the Hudson's Bay Company, lay to the north of the historical St Lawrence Valley heartland of New France.[124]

The clash between the Quebec government and the Cree peoples of Quebec was especially intense. This encounter involved not only antagonism over access to natural resources but also the meeting of two traditions of European imperialism in Indian Country. While the historical roots of the majority constituency represented by the Quebec government lay in the Roman Catholic, French-speaking heritage of North America, the Crees had woven into their many-faceted Aboriginal identities the ethos of the English-speaking Hudson's Bay Company as well as the unique culture of the Church of England. Hence, the fight between the armies of France and Britain on the Plains of Abraham during the Seven Years' War established patterns and motifs which persisted as the American empire continued to penetrate the Indian Country of Canada. Where the Anglo-American colonies began their transformation into the United States of America during the course of the French and Indian War, the building of the massive James Bay Hydroelectric project furthered the splitting of the very alliance on which the founding of French-Aboriginal Canada had been based.

Like many Native people throughout the Canadian North, a significant constituency of Cree, Ojibway, and Inuit in the Hudson Bay coastal regions have responded to the growing secularization of society by joining more evangelical varieties of Protestantism. For instance, Billy Diamond and Matthew Coon Come, the leading figures of their respective generations in the vibrant Cree politics in Quebec, both left their Anglican heritage to join Pentecostal churches.[125] Elijah Harper went through a similar process of religious conversion away from the Roman Catholicism of his youth. This former Oji-Cree member of the Manitoba legislature achieved wide national fame in 1990 as the legendary slayer of the controversial constitutional deal named after Meech Lake.[126]

One explanation for this movement away from Anglicanism and Roman Catholicism to extreme Protestant fundamentalism lies in the qualified rejection of those theocratic structures which, with all their problems and shortcomings, had provided viable strategies of survival for a number of First Nations communities over several generations. The most tragic hallmark of the breakdown of the old order in many of Canada's northern communities is to be seen in the tragic epidemics of suicide, murder, and substance abuse which have disproportionately plagued the region's Aboriginal youth.

CHAPTER SEVEN

Two Legal Countries

I do not like the Natives at all and I wish we had no Black men in South Africa. But there they are, our lot is cast with them by an overruling Providence and the only question is how to shape our course so as to maintain the supremacy of our race and at the same time to do our duty.

Memorandum of J.X. Merriam, prime minister of Cape Colony, to General J.C. Smuts, 1906

So far as the Natives are concerned, politics will, to my mind, only have an unsettling influence. I would therefore not give them the franchise.

Reply of General Smuts to Prime Minister Merriam

CREOLE IDENTITY POLITICS AS A CATALYST OF GLOBALIZATION

For most of the period since 1492, European imperialism has been the driving agency of globalization. The Atlantic Ocean gave the powers of Western Europe a shared window of global expansion, one they used, both competitively and cooperatively, in an unusually aggressive fashion. In history's most sweeping saga of global transformation, Europe imposed and exported many of its attributes through the media of militarism, commerce, Christian evangelization, and technological innovation. The most influential agency in this outburst of expansionism, however, was Europe's export of surplus people to the far corners of the earth. As transplanted populations of European origin took root, new generations of Creoles emerged that simultaneously claimed the civilizational heritage of their ancestors even as they increasingly resented and rejected the colonial rule of their imperial parents. Many of these Creole groups, but especially those in the more tropical districts of the Americas, expanded the agricultural domain of commercialized monocultures by creating and exploiting a vastly expanded market for African slaves. The transplanted slave populations, primarily from West and Central Africa, experienced their own unique process of creolization, as America's native-born Blacks gradually adapted to the indigenous conditions of their new milieus. The slave revolt in the French colony of San Domingo, which culminated in 1803 in the creation of the republic of Haiti, was a pivotal moment in the transformation of transplanted Africans into people of the New World.

The founders of Haiti, the second republic of the Americas, adopted an Aboriginal name for their new polity. The white Creoles who founded the United States, however, made it very clear that the first republic of the Americas was established on principles antagonistic to what the Declaration of Independence referred to as "the merciless Indian savages." The transformation of transplanted Europeans into indigenized "Americans" began a process of profound change in global geopolitics whose sweeping consequences for all humanity are only now becoming fully apparent. The appropriation of the European name of a whole hemisphere to describe "America's" national identity was paralleled most closely by the transformation of the Dutch Creoles of South Africa into "Afrikaners." Both the self-identifying "Americans" and "Afrikaners" drew heavily on the same Calvinist tradition of Protestant fundamentalism. They shared a potent preoccupation with the contemporary meaning of those portions of the Old Testament assigning a providentially chartered mission to God's "chosen people." This imagined grant of divine sanction proved instrumental in helping to spark the revolts of both the Americans and the Afrikaners against the constraints of British rule. In both British North America and British South Africa the attempt of the imperial government to limit Creole expansionism intensified the climate of political rebellion.

The worldwide exodus of Europeans from their Aboriginal lands set in motion particularly complex cycles of identity politics as Creoles coalesced to form many new nationalities patterned on variations of the American prototype. Where Creole numbers and identity have been strongest, so too has the propensity to invent anthropological categories and laws to subordinate, contain, or eliminate "the natives," "the aborigines," or "the autochtones." Indeed, the very idea of "the native" helps clarify much about the thinking and orientation of those who would invent such a category. Clearly the indigenized Creoles of European ancestry have tended to see themselves as sharing a common identity that transcends the spatial outlines of their new nations. They feel they are citizens of a transnational community whose global proportions stand in opposition to the place-based orientation of the world's "natives."[1] Long before the spread of transnational corporations headquartered primarily in the United States, "America" was at the centre of a transnational network of Creole societies that made themselves contrapuntally both vehicles and critics of European imperialism.

A major ingredient in the chemistry of globalization since 1492, therefore, has been the complex identity politics of the world's Creole populations. The Creole descendants of imperialism's agents and emigrants have recognized no such thing as a Diaspora. The Creoles have endeavoured to indigenize themselves and their new nationalities in ways that simultaneously embrace and reject their antecedents and in ways that appropriate idealized imageries of Aboriginal culture even as Aboriginal peoples are rarely incorporated as distinct, self-governing constituencies in the Creole federations of New World polities.

Even before its recognition in 1783 in the treaty of Paris as a country sovereign in international law, the polity that became the United States has consistently been, both in its pre- and post-revolutionary incarnations, the world's busiest laboratory of Creole identity politics. The deeper dynamics of this political genesis, however, have often been obscured by the American preoccupation with race. This preoccupation has tended to veil the shared Creole identity of those whose ancestors immigrated voluntarily and those whose ancestors were forced to immigrate through the complex of commerce, coercion, politics, and law that went by the name of slavery.

In spite of the legacy of slavery, civil war, and the elimination or removal of many Aboriginal groups, "America" has been invented and reinvented along lines which, in the words of Román de la Campa, have rarely deviated "far from the lines of utopia and nostalgia."[2] This process of invention has depended heavily on the idea of America as an oasis of freedom, far removed from humanity's most violent sites of conflict. This notion was tremendously reinforced by the geography of two world wars in the twentieth century. The US government resisted entering both conflicts until each was already well advanced. This hesitation was rooted in the conception of America as a refuge of liberty, providentially remote from the seemingly pathological antagonisms plaguing the indigenous peoples of Europe. Even when Americans were most inclined to see themselves as isolationist, however, the drive to expand the international frontiers of American business has rarely let up. The propensity of American business interests to indigenize their expanding operations – to re-enact the cultural transformation of Creoles in the commercial sphere of high finance and industrial expansion – became clear in the heavy dependence of Nazi Germany on American business, American technology, and American expertise. Edwin Black, for instance, has meticulously chronicled the key role played by the German extension of the IBM Company in providing the computing technology that was integral to the Nazi campaign to enslave and then eliminate the Jews of Europe.[3] The I.G. Farben Chemical Company, one of the biggest exploiters of Jewish slavery, similarly extended the commercial operations of the Standard Oil Company of the United States into the strategic industrial core of the Third Reich.[4]

Ever since the United States entered the Second World War it has maintained the planet's most active and elaborate apparatus of global intervention. The Cold War provided the rationale for the continuing military mobilization of the United States on a global scale. As the US military machinery was increasingly crafted as capitalism's ultimate police force, the American business community continued its worldwide quest for new

markets, new sources of cheap labour, and new sources of raw material.
The quest to remove any and all regimes that might limit capitalism's global reach culminated in the implosion of the Soviet Union in 1989, a development which, in turn, enabled many large enterprises mostly headquartered in the United States to complete their metamorphosis from
multinational corporations to transnational corporations to global corporations. Again this commercial transformation approximated earlier patterns, which saw Creole populations displace and marginalize Aboriginal
groups on many frontiers of globalization. The more recent process
involves the extinguishment and marginalization of the world's diverse,
local political economies by an increasingly universalized regime of
monopoly capitalism. The chain of command in this new kind of worldwide command economy leads in most instances to those interlocked
groups in government and business that control the towering heights of
the power structure in the United States.

   Throughout the second half of the twentieth century the United States
was able to maintain the fantasy that it could simultaneously maintain its
isolation from the world's most violent conflagrations even as it intervened,
both overtly and covertly, throughout the rest of the planet to advance capitalism's global hegemony. That fantasy came crashing to earth on 11 September 2001. The televised spectacle of two commercial jet airliners
exploding into the twin towers of the World Trade Center in New York dramatically changed the conceptual framework of global geopolitics. Almost
immediately Osama bin Laden, a maverick member of the United States's
puppet regime in the oil-rich principality of Saudi Arabia, was depicted as
the ultimate personification of the many conspirators who executed this
crime against humanity. This most concerted media depiction compelled
the world to ask, "Who is this man bin Laden?" Was he some new kind of
messiah figure among colonized peoples, rising like the Delaware prophet
or Tenskwatawa from behind the frontiers of the American empire's newest
Indian Country? Was someone waiting in the Arab and Muslim worlds to
take over this religious movement to give it a more secular geopolitical
direction? Would some modern-day Tecumseh attempt to take charge in an
effort to forge unity from the factionalized chaos dividing those oppressed
peoples whose commercially colonized lands provide the bulk of the oil
fuelling the American empire of possessive individualism?

   A big part of the trauma of 9/11 for most Americans was the end of the
delusion that the isolationist tradition of the United States could coexist
with the expansive reach of American foreign policy. In his early response
to the tragedy President George W. Bush, a committed evangelical Protestant, provided America's enemies in the Arab and Muslim worlds with a
propaganda bonanza. The US president introduced his government's new
"War on Terrorism" by referring to it as "this crusade."[5] Not only did
Bush's apocalyptic language invoke the ethos of the Crusades, Christendom's expansionary prelude to the Columbian conquests beginning in

1492, but his stark division of the world between the brightness of civilization and the darkness of barbarism invoked the most striking contradiction within the American Declaration of Independence. The president's depiction of America's new enemies was extremely close to the Declaration's references to "the merciless Indian savages, whose known rule of warfare is an undistinguished destruction of all ages, sexes and conditions."

The Creole construction of Bush's cosmology was further illuminated as the world approached the first anniversary of the attacks by the suicide hijackers on the twin towers in New York and on the Pentagon in Washington, DC. "The battlefield has now shifted to America," declared the US president, "so there's a different dynamic than we've ever faced before."[6] The most telling marker of Bush's Creole thinking lay in the assumptions beneath his use of the word "we." Since 1492 America has been the site of one conflict after the next for embattled Indigenous peoples. In that respect the western hemisphere has never ceased to be a battlefield. For instance, Guatemala was the site of repeated massacres of many tens of thousands of innocent Mayan farmers during the Cold War presidency of Ronald Reagan. The number of people killed by US-backed forces in that one small Central American country alone dwarfs the number of people brutally murdered in the twin towers. Surely in a world where we truly embrace the principle that all people are created equal, we would not have to grapple with such blatant double standards, with such stunning moral relativism. We would be free, instead, to enforce uniformly a universal set of legal principles to punish all those proven responsible for perpetrating crimes against humanity, in whatever place and in whatever numbers.

In the United States the transplanted peoples of Europe and Africa built a polity that stands in a class of its own in terms of the scope and effectiveness of its expansionary impulse. In much of the remainder of the wstern hemisphere, however, Creole identity did not so thoroughly overpower Indian identity. Creole identity, rather, tended to be channelled more narrowly into Ladino identity and Hispanic identity. These identities came to be contained, in turn, within the framework of a more pervasive, all-embracing mestizo melting pot, one that has not entirely engulfed the remaining Indian societies in Central and South America. While this mestizo culture dominates the Chicano culture of California and the heavy Mexican presence throughout the American Southwest, for the most part the relationship between the Creole society and the Aboriginal societies of the United States more closely resembles conditions in Canada, Australia, and New Zealand. Indeed, in the case of Canada, we can trace in its Aboriginal policies until the present an unbroken course of constitutional history going back to the beginnings of English colonization in North America. That continuity, as expressed particularly in the continuing negotiation of crown treaties with Indigenous peoples in Canada, might in due course provide something of a matrix and marker to help guide the reintegration of the United States into those aspects of international law that the US government began to leave behind with Jacksonian Indian removal.

The decision of many in the Thirteen Colonies to break loose from the British Empire in 1776 made it more thinkable in the years that followed to exempt the United States from the international law governing the conduct of relations with Indigenous peoples. That break from even the pretence of recognizing the rule of law in dealing with the civil, political, and territorial rights of weaker Aboriginal societies established patterns that would be replicated again and again in the global rise of the American empire. It confirmed an approach that Thucydides attributed to the Athenians as they were preparing in 416 BC to impose their rule on the Melians. "The question of justice only enters where the pressure of necessity is equal," declared the Athenian spokesman. "The powerful exact what they can, and the weak grant what they must."[7]

THE CANADIAN INDIAN ACT, CITIZENSHIP, AND THE PARLIAMENTARY DEBATE ON INDIAN PEOPLE AND THE RIGHT TO VOTE IN FEDERAL ELECTIONS

By the time of the Confederation of the first four Canadian provinces in 1867, most of the Indian groups north of the Great Lakes and along the St Lawrence Valley were enclosed within the narrow geographic and legal boundaries of reserves. A similar regime was also in place among the Micmac and Malecite of Nova Scotia and New Brunswick when these jurisdictions were joined to Ontario and Quebec, the former Upper Canada and Lower Canada, to form the new dominion. Just as a major thrust of Canada's westward expansion has been to reproduce the prairie provinces into rough constitutional clones of Ontario, so the Indian policies developed in Upper Canada proved to set the basic prototype for the administration of Indian Affairs over much of the vast region acquired from the Hudson's Bay Company in 1869.

This transaction, one of the largest land transfers ever in world history, left the issue of Aboriginal and treaty rights to be dealt with at a later date. The purchase by the Dominion of Canada of the HBC rights and titles expanded the land mass of the dominion by about 400 per cent. Moreover, the deal opened the way in 1871 to the adhesion of the crown colony of British Columbia to the dominion on the condition that a transcontinental railway be built to connect that province to the other British North American settlements in the Maritime provinces and in the Great Lakes–St Lawrence watershed.

In 1871 crown commissioners began applying the constitutional principles outlined in the Royal Proclamation of 1763 to treaty negotiations with the Indigenous peoples in portions of the annexed territories. The extension of the system of crown-Aboriginal treaties based in the founding legal instrument of British imperial Canada continues to this day to work its way through the political institutions of the federation. While the negotiation of treaties represented the constitutional arm of dominion Indian policy, however, crown officials elaborated federal legislation for the governance of Indians once they were enclosed on reserves. This complex of legislation, known generally as the Indian Act, grew out of the old statute enacted in 1857 by the Legislative Assembly of the Province of Canada.

The dominion parliament's Indian Act of 1876 revised the rules for enfranchisement outlined in the earlier Act for the Gradual Civilization of the Indian Tribes in Canada, but the essential principle was seemingly reaffirmed: Native people, once registered by the Indian Department, were to be treated as wards, or guardians, of federal authority.[8] This mode of infantilizing First Nations individuals as minors of the parent state was a consistent motif of Aboriginal policy in Canada, Australia, and the United States. Aboriginal wards were prevented from participating directly in legislatures, courts, and, of course, land markets. The resulting disempowerment helped to create the conditions for some of the most severe violations against the human rights of Indigenous peoples, including the "stolen generations" fiasco in Australia and the high incidences of involuntary sterilization directed at Native women in North America. The law of wardship made it extremely difficult for Aboriginal parents to defend their children against various forms of violation such as the physical and emotional abuse in Canada's church-run Indian residential schools. Mothers and fathers were restricted in their ability to perform their parental responsibilities because in the eyes of the state, they too were classified as the legal equivalent of children under the authoritarian rule of the central government.

In the late nineteenth century the conception of Indigenous individuals and groups as government wards in a state of tutelage increasingly dominated the legal characterization of subject peoples in virtually all European colonies in Africa and Asia. Moreover, this model of relations was adopted in South Africa by the government of the minority white population to formalize and justify its control over the majority Indigenous population. Accordingly, the Canadian Indian Act captures in miniature and precise ways the general outlines of larger juridical constructs of subordination that, at one time, were applied to the greater portion of human beings throughout the planet.

The construction of the legal walls separating registered Indian people from Canadian citizenship and from direct participation in Canadian politics did not happen all at once or without resistance and protest. By far the most substantial debate in the new dominion over the place and legal status of Indian people occurred in the late nineteenth century in the House of Commons. That far-ranging parliamentary exchange included reference to many disadvantaged groups, including women and black slaves before abolition. Both these groups were considered, like registered Indians, to be alien to the legal requirements of the franchise. As such, the exchange offers a broad and clear window into Victorian conceptions of many topics, including race, gender, and the perceived relationship between citizenship and civilization

In 1885 Canada's Conservative prime minister, John A. Macdonald, introduced the Dominion Electoral Franchise Act, proposing various criteria for elegibility to vote in federal elections. The requirements of being an adult male resident with property worth at least $150 were presented to parliament as the central qualifications for a "person" to exercise *his* democratic rights. In the wording of the proposed statute, "person means male person, including an Indian." Macdonald's initiative challenged a basic principle outlined in the federal Indian Act, which the Liberal government of Alexander Mackenzie had instituted in 1876. That legislation identified a legal "person" as an "individual other than an Indian."[9] In an address to the House of Commons, Macdonald introduced in a political context the basic arguments that lawyers for the dominion were preparing to elaborate in court in the *St Catherine's* case. He asserted, "here are Indians, aboriginal Indians, formerly the lords of the soil, formerly owning the whole of this country. Here they are in their own land, prevented from either sitting in the House, or voting for men to come here and represent their interests. There are one hundred and twenty five thousand of these people, who are virtually and actually disenfranchised, who complain, and justly complain, that they have no representation."[10] In supporting his party's position, another Conservative MP explained that the extension of the franchise to Indian males would be "but an infinitesimal part of their own rights, which they have surrendered to us, that we return to them."[11]

The prospect of extending the vote to registered Indians drew heavy fire from the oppposition party. Many Liberal members of parliament stood up in the House to declare their explanations why Indian men should not be allowed to vote in federal elections. There was much talk of the alleged childlike character of Aboriginal adults and the inability of many of them to read, write, or speak either of the country's two official languages. One MP said that to extend the vote to Indians would be as foolish as to enfranchise women. "To give the franchise to women," Mr Fairbanks indicated, "would interfere with their proper position: it would be a burden instead of a benefit to them." He added, "This, I believe, would be the case as regards the Indian ... as a ward of the government, it will be doing him an injury rather than a benefit to give him a power which neither by training, education nor instinct is he able to appreciate or to wisely exercise."[12]

The attack was led by David Mills, who, as a former minister of the interior, had been in charge of the Indian Department during the years when the Liberal government was in power. Mills was one of the most knowledgeable and inventive proponents of "provincial rights" in the early years of Confederation. He gained much of his expertise as Ontario's former boundary commissioner, a position he used to become conversant with the old controversies that situated different legal interpretations of Indian title at the centre of many historic power struggles between central and local governments in British North America. With this expertise to draw on, Mills in 1885 was deeply involved in the *St. Catherine's Milling* case. He was instrumental in helping Liberal premier Oliver Mowat lay the groundwork for the province's constitutional attack on Aboriginal and treaty rights as a means of boxing in the jurisdictional reach of the central government. When Mills criticized Macdonald in the parliamentary debate on Indians and the federal franchise, he, no less than the prime minister himself, was airing the political dimension of a much larger legal argument headed for the highest court in the British Empire.[13]

The core of the position presented by Mills was that Indians lacked the legal prerequisites to assume the rights and responsibilities embodied in the federal franchise because they were wards of the state. He asserted that registered Indians were individuals who were unqualified to own land as private property. Moreover, they could not be taxed for their reserves, which were held in trust on their behalf by the queen. "The very reasons that prevent a guardian from dealing with a ward's property," he said, "ought to prevent the Indian from voting as a free man, while he continues to be a ward of the government." Mills compared the legal condition of Indians in Canada to slaves in the United States before emancipation. As one of Canada's leading exponents of "provincial rights," he was inclined to look with some sympathy at the constitutional position of the southern states in maintaining the legal force of their most characteristic and controversial institution before 1865. According to Mills, the idea of extending the franchise to registered Indians was "a proposition no less absurd than it would have been to have conferred the franchise on the slaves of the South, while they were still in a state of slavery."[14]

Edward Blake, a former Liberal premier of Ontario, provided yet another demonstration of the strong connections between the parliamentary debates on Indians and the franchise in 1885 and the constitutional contentions that emerged as central to the *St. Catherine's Milling* case.[15] He was the lead lawyer who later presented Ontario's winning arguments to the Judicial Committee of the Privy Council in Great Britain. In that forum and in parliament, Blake emphasized the allegation that the government of Canada was in a conflict of interest in seeking to empower itself both as the Indians' guardian and as the beneficiary of any transfer of titles or of any bundle of easily manipulable votes.

In the parliamentary debate Blake developed the political side of the broader legal position he would later elaborate in Great Britain He accused Macdonald of exploiting the franchise bill to acquire political control of Indian votes. Blake made this accusation with knowledge that, since 1878, Macdonald had held the position of superintendent general of Indian

Affairs, with a network of Indian agents under his direct patronage and
control. With his eyes on the prime minister, Blake referred to the sweeping powers over Indian people available to Macdonald personally. "You
have your local superintendent, the sub-officer of the Superintendent
General, over them," he said, "controlling them, deciding in tangible
terms what should be done in daily concerns of their life." He concluded
that Macdonald was, in his capacity as superintendent general, "the person
who is arbiter of [registered Indians] destinies." Macdonald was "acting in
the belief he can control their votes; and I say that a more infamous proposal was never made to any Legislature."[16]

News of the turmoil in the North Saskatchewan River Valley in 1885 drastically changed the political context of the debate. Canadians in the east
learned that about twenty non-Indians had been killed by Indian people in a
complex outbreak of violence connected indirectly to the Métis stand against
the Macdonald government's tactics in dispossessing them of their lands.[17]
The imagery generated by this news enabled Mills to speak of Indian people
going from "a scalping party to the polls."[18] Another Liberal commented:

We find by the Indian Report, that a majority of [Indian people in the west] are
still pagans; not only are they pagans but we find from recent events that they still
have in them the savage and ferocious disposition of ordinary barbarians. That
they are ready, on the slightest pretext, to return to their ancient habits of rapine,
pillage, and murder, and yet the right hon. gentleman proposes to give the franchise to Indians, most of whom are in Rebellion against the Government.[19]

Much of the criticism of Macdonald's proposal was informed by the old
and familiar explanations of the imagined distinctions between savagery
and civilization. Another telling part was framed by the increasingly potent
and pervasive language of *race*. In the century leading up to the eugenic
totalitarianism of the Third Reich, a formidable and growing constituency
were attracted to the notion of history as the outcome not so much of a battle between inferior and superior *ideas*, but as the result of the ascendance
of superior races over inferior races of people. The growing obsession with
the struggle between races as the most potent animating force in human
evolution was boldly announced in Theodore Roosevelt's multi-volume
series *The Winning of the West*.[20] This history was penned by a future American president. Its account of the "Germanic race's" westward expansion in
North America set the tone for the era when Rudyard Kipling would eulo-
gize imperialism as the expression of "the White Man's Burden."

The development of Indian policy in both the United States and Canada was one area of public policy where this growing juxtaposition of theories of race, imperial mission, and "manifest destiny" became sharply
demonstrable. It is an area of statecraft where explicit theories about race
and the supposedly scientific basis of relations between different branches
of humanity are often rendered in explicit ways.[21] In joining the debate

over Indian people and the right to vote, the member of parliament for Quebec, Mr. Casgrain, drew heavily on the language of scientific racism to support his contentions:

Now, if we examine the position of the Indian race in Canada, and even in the whole of British North Americas, it is easy to see that it is not a race capable of being civilized ... Their natural instincts, propagated from race to race, and which in medical term, is called atavism, are maintained within them a peculiar manner and renders them unfit to become an element of any kind of civilization, such as it is understood in the European and other countries – unfit to till the land. This study, which I have had occasion to make, on the habits of the Indian, shows that his intelligence is not developed to a sufficient degree to allow him to use the vote in such a manner as to render it useful to himself and to the country.[22]

In much the same way that Premier Tommy Douglas ran into a wall of Indian resistance when he tried to extend the provincial franchise to Indian people in Saskatchewan after the Second World War, John A. Macdonald met a similar phenomenon when his initiative was not enthusiastically embraced by many Indian people. While their criticisms were entirely different from those of the Liberals, the effect was to strengthen the hand of the opposition party. The basis of the resistance in some branches of Indian Country was outlined in a letter from Chief Jones of the Six Nations reserve near Brantford to the prime minister: "Many of the Indians on the Grand River have been told, that in case they received the vote, then Treaty Rights with the Government would not be able to compel the Government to observe and carry out the treaties. They have been told that the granting of the Franchise to them, was a scheme of the Government with the object of imposing direct taxation on them."[23]

A variation on this argument was carried into the House of Commons by Mr. Paterson, the member of parliament for Brant. He explained that band members of the Six Nations reserve in his constituency did not want the vote "because they take the position that they are not subjects of the Crown, but allies." Another parliamentarian from the Bay of Quinte reported that he was told by a member of the Tyendinaga band that this Mohawk community "considered this attempted legislation as being part of a scheme to place their reserve under ordinary municipal control and taxation, and finally to deprive them and their children of their birthright." The reserve lands of Indian people were characterized as "secured to them by treaty with the Crown, free from all taxation – a perpetual inheritance."[24]

The effect of these criticisms were amendments that greatly circumscribed the number of registered Indians eligible to vote in federal elections. The legislation was made to apply only to the more long-established reserve communities in eastern and central Canada, and only to those adult Indian males within these communities who possessed substantial wealth apart from the lands held in trust for their use and benefit by the crown. In 1898 even this small window of direct participation in the mainstream political culture of Canada was shut down, as a new Liberal government in Ottawa repealed the Electoral Franchise Act and put in place another set of arrangements based on the systems of voter registration in the provinces. This reform had the effect of shuting out entirely all registered Indians from participation in the larger electoral process in Canada.

THE INDIAN ACT AND THE COLONIAL RULE
OF INDIAN BANDS AS MUNICIPAL EXTENSIONS
OF DOMINION AUTHORITY

There were major implications in the outcome of this failed quest to find some sort of middle ground for Indian people between three quite distinct legal identities. First among these legal personalities is the way many Indian men and women see themselves as members of nations of peoples with treaty relations with the crown. The second identity is that of Indians as wards of the state subject to the sweeping authorities of both the Indian Act and the superintendent general of Indian Affairs. Finally, there is the view of Indians as Canadian citizens with recognized rights and responsibilities to participate directly in the democratic life of the new dominion.

The formal and complete exclusion of Indian people from the electoral process of choosing federal governments ushered in a period when the Indian Act enclosed the life of Indian people on reserves, with few political checks and balances. In the first half of the twentieth century this regime of near total control was left increasingly to the government of a largely unmonitored and unaccountable federal bureaucracy. This corps of permanent civil servants, whose most powerful and characteristic representative was the well-known Canadian poet Duncan Campbell Scott,[25] ruled the country's Indian reserves secure in the knowledge that there were few political costs and liabilities to be incurred by their elected overseers if bad results flowed from their decisions.

This combination of wardship and bureaucratic control resulted in Canada's establishing, before 1951, one of the world's most notorious regimes of near total domination of Indigenous peoples. At the centre of this regime was the federal Indian Act, which, as Blake clearly explained in 1885, placed the most elaborate kinds of power over the day-to-day lives of registered Indians in the superintendent general of Indian Affairs. This official, or, as he was later called, minister of Indian Affairs, delegated many authorities to local Indian agents. With these powers, Ottawa's agents governed Indian reserves as miniature colonies of dominion authority, or, to put it another way, as municipal extensions of the federal government. The job of these agents, who often gained their positions as patronage rewards, was modelled on the role of colonial governors from Great Britain who ruled Canada in the days before responsible government. Similarly, the Indian Department was a kind of scaled-down clone of the old Colonial Office, whose personnel directed the governance of Canada in the days before its non-Aboriginal male inhabitants were granted some degree of self-government. It can truly be said, therefore, that the Indian Act and the Indian Department together generated a culture that was an extreme distillation of Canada's colonial heritage and, at times, a veritable caricature of the most grotesque features of colonialism in action.

Ella Cork, the brilliant New Englander who observed and documented the constitutional complexities of Six Nations politics in the 1950s, has written a particularly clear and succinct characterization of the Indian Act. "It defines Indians," she notes, "as having a status separate and particular from other Canadians with a whole body of law applicable only to them, rendering them dependant, incompetent and subject to arbitrary decree in almost every aspect of their economic and political lives."[26]

The Indian Act allowed for local elections to install elected chiefs and councillors in the image of the elected mayors and town councillors of municipalities. The role of these elected people in Indian bands was almost totally an advisory one, however, with real power being vested in the local Indian agent. Indeed, every feature of an Indian "band" drew its legal personality as a distinct polity not from the First Nation that provided its membership but from the increasingly elaborate provisions of the Canadian Indian Act. The purpose of that Act was to provide a uniform system of administration, even as the original First Nations of the country were effectively balkanized into tiny, isolated Indian towns cut off from easy access to the full extent of traditional territories and allied peoples.

As officers of the dominion, Indian agents maintained almost complete discretionary power over every formal transaction on a reserve, including what could be bought or sold or who was eligible to run in band elections. The calculated design of the federal government was to marginalize the traditional forms of leadership and law making rooted in the Aboriginal inheritance and to put in its place Indian agents and their elected advisers who acted as adminstratators of policies formulated in the Ministry of Indian Affairs.

There were few political checks to prevent the bureaucrats from extending their influence over Indian reserves by proposing amendments to the Indian Act which concentrated greater and greater powers in the hands of a minister not elected by Indian people or formally accountable to them in any way. From the days of the takeover of legislative responsibility for Indian Affairs by the Province of Canada, through the evocatively titled Act for the Gradual Civilization of the Indian Tribes, the main preoccupation of officialdom has been to siffle and discourage any expression of Aboriginal heritage. In the twentieth century the Indian Act was extended to prohibit and actually outlaw many forms of Indigenous cultural expression.

The Indian Act, for instance, criminalized the continuation of traditional forms of Aboriginal governance and spiritual observance. The prohibitions on Indian "giveaways" and on "Indian dancing' were directed particularly at the potlatch ceremonies of west coast peoples and the sun dances or thirst dances of prairie peoples.[27] Moreover, Indian agents on many western reserves acquired the power to give or withhold passes that Indian people needed to leave their communities.[28] In 1927 section 141 was added to the Indian Act. It outlawed any exchange of money for the pursuit of any Indian claim or interest without the explicit approval of the officers of the Indian Department. This provision effectively extended the jurisdiction of the Indian Act even to non-Indians, including researchers and lawyers. Henceforth they were prohibited from receiving funds to advance Indian positions in court or in any other venues of decision making. This imposition of dominion power between Indian bands and potential non-Aboriginal advocates was extremely dehabilitating during an era when, as wards of the state, First Nations people could not technically represent themselves directly in the crown's courts.

This provision in the Indian Act also effectively prohibited the work of any Indian politicians operating without the approval of officials in the Indian Department. By this means the dominion government essentially outlawed the politics of any Indian resistance involving the need of money, even for travelling, mailing, paper, or the reproduction of documents. Section 141, therefore, was almost certainly a factor in the tactics of Andy Paull and others who used sports or cultural activities as a cover for their continuing political work. Paull's activities as a hockey and lacrosse coach in British Columbia enabled him to maintain and expand his network of connections throughout the closely policed domain of Indian Country at a time when the political activism of First Nations people was often treated as a criminal act. Paull's tactics serve as a reminder of the kind of resourcefulness on the part of many Aboriginal people that enabled some to defy even the most oppressive constraints and restrictions formally imposed on Indian Country during the years of the Indian Department's most draconian reign.[29]

During this era the Indian Affairs bureaucracy pushed parliament to pass a law enabling civil servants to remove registered status involuntarily from any Indian person deemed sufficiently "civilized" to enter Canadian citizenship. This measure was designed as a tactic to undermine through forced enfranchisement the efforts of Indian activists such as Lieutenant Fred Loft. As detailed in chapter 3, Loft achieved considerable success after the First World War in his efforts to organize Indigenous peoples regionally and across Canada into pan-Indian associations. These associations were modelled partly on the principles of labour unions and partly on those of the old Indian Confederacy.[30]

RESISTANCE AND VOICES OF CRITICISM
AGAINST THE IRON RULE OF THE DOMINION
OVER INDIAN COUNTRY

Given the lack of orthodox political tools avilable to Aboriginal and non-Aboriginal critics of the oppressive regime of Indian governance, what opposition there was deserves careful attention. Some of it has been observed in chapter 3, where the seminal importance of Indian resistance movements, especially in British Columbia, is noted. Another great centre of Indian resistance to be explored in more detail in volume 2 is the challenge to the extension of Canada's jurisdiction into the prairies led particularly by Big Bear and Poundmaker.

In central Canada, too, political organizers like Lieutenent Fred Loft, Jules Sioui, and Henry Jackson, as well as non-Indian activists like those who worked in and around the Indian-Eskimo Association in the 1960s, stood on the shoulders of many others. These critics and sceptics questioned and challenged the growing tyranny of the federal Indian Department and its virtual hundred years' war on the cultural and spiritual expressions of Aboriginal identities. The rules of engagement for this assault on Aboriginal cultures were in the Indian Act. The institutional stronghold for the crusaders of assimilation, however, was the network of church-run, federally funded residential schools that became key centres in the continuation of the old quest to extinguish Indian Country by indoctrinating its citizens to renounce their own Aboriginal heritage.

The passage of the Act for the Gradual Civilization of the Indian Tribes in Canada in 1857 led to the organization of a major gathering in 1858 centred on the Six Nations reserve at the Onondaga Council House. Delegations attended from all parts of Iroquois Country, including the Mohawks of Tyendinaga, Kanewake, and Akwesasne and as well as those Oneida people who had recently left New York state to take up residence in Upper Canada on territory they had purchased with their own funds. The Anishinabek of the Algonkian-speaking communities in the province of Canada were also well represented, with delegations from Walpole Island, Rice Lake, Manitoulin Island, and several other places as well.

John Smoke Johnson, the grandfather of the poet Pauline Johnson, acted as spokesman to convey the outcome of the deliberations to government officials in attendance. He noted the unanimous view of all delegations that "they do not wish to be given over from the care of the Imperial government to the care of the provincial one." Moreover, Johnson clarified the profound depth of Indian resentment against those provisions of the new Indian Act setting forth a procedure whereby Indian individuals could become enfranchised citizens of the Province of Canada, and thereby acquire pieces of their old collectively held Indian reserves as private property to be bought or sold in the open market. The delegation from Akwesasne declared with particular vehemence the destructive potential of the enfranchisement provisions to splinter their people and to destroy the special body of imperial laws for the protection of existing Aboriginal and treaty rights. "There is nothing in it to be of benefit," they said, but "only to break us to pieces." It "blasts our dearest hope as a race," said another speaker, noting that the wampum marking relations with the government had turned black with the odium of broken promises. In responding to round after round of "hearty receptions" to "the unanimous voice" of those against the new legislation, Johnson reiterated: "They pray for a Repeal of sections of the Civilization Act which would admit the Enfranchisement." Moreover, they profoundly resented "being abandoned by the Imperial government."[31]

There were many implications, large and small, which accompanied the devolution of power over Indian Affairs from the imperial government to the provincial government in the late 1850s. Some of these changes swirled around the issue of intermarriage between Aboriginal women and Euro-Canadian men, a common practice when these kinds of familial bonds were instrumental during the fur trade. The old ways, however, were increasingly challenged as the new legal regime of the empire of private property cast its shadow across the remaining Indian estates north of the Great Lakes. As part of this transformation, a committee of the legislature investigating Indian Affairs deemed in 1858 that "an Indian woman marrying a white loses her rights as a member of the tribe, and her children have no claim to the land or moneys belonging to their mother's nation."[32]

By 1860 sexual politics became an element in the bold protest of an Ojibway woman named Nah-nee-ba-we-quay, or Mrs Catherine Sutton. As the wife of a non-Indian Methodist clergyman, Mrs Sutton found herself stripped of any legal capacity to participate directly in the Aboriginal land transaction affecting the site of her family's agricultural operation in the Owen's Sound area of Upper Canada.[33] Nah-nee-ba-we-quay watched helplessly in 1854 as a few Indian men made a dubious treaty ceding lands that included her family's farm, complete with barn, farm house, fencing, and large, laboriously cleared fields. Being Indian, Nah-nee-ba-we-quay was legally disqualified even from buying the farm back as private property on the open market. This experience underlined for the Aboriginal activist the huge injustice inherent in reducing registered Indians to the legal status of wards of the state and in situating them outside the framework of the rights and responsibilities of citizenship. In her widely distributed commentary, Nah-nee-ba-we-quay declared

1. That their [reserve] land is held by tribal tenure; by which arrangement it appears the members of the tribe have no individual rights; so that, if the chiefs of the tribe can be gained over, by whatever means, their holdings may be sold away from them at any time, without redress or compensation.
2. That being in law minors ... they [registered Indians] have no legal powers of action – cannot vote for members of Parliament, or contract or enforce debts; are

excluded from Government schools, and, in other respects, placed under disabilities, which are not known as regards any other class of persons in the colonies, whether fugitive slaves, or settlers, or refugees from any part of the world, and which do not exist as regards Indian settlers in the United States.[34]

Nah-nee-ba-we-quay found a receptive audience for her arguments in Canada, the United States, and Great Britain. She addressed many Quaker audiences, who drew her issues to the attention of the Aborigines' Protection Society. As a result of her connections to these influential groups, Nah-nee-ba-we-quay was given the opportunity to express her grievances directly to Queen Victoria. The queen, in turn, referred Nah-nee-ba-we-quay to the Duke of Newcastle, the secretary of state for the colonies.

This activism seemed headed towards success when Nah-nee-ba-we-quay prepared to confer with the Duke of Newcastle and the Prince of Wales on the event of their major tour of Canada in 1860. Two obstacles to the meeting were imposed, however, one by the superintendent general of Indian affairs in the Province of Canada and the other by a council of male Indian chiefs. The latter, whose leader was David Wawanosh, was determined that the main issues to be emphasized at any Indian meeting with the heir apparent of the British royal family were encroachments on the Indian fisheries, the need for firm legal protections for unceded Indian lands, and allegations about fraud and theft of Indian monies held in trust by officials of the local Indian Department. The Indian delegation insisted, therefore, that the Ojibway woman's advocacy of individual rights within the larger Aboriginal collectivity were matters of "concern to private individuals rather than of the Council as a whole."[35] As for the Prince of Wales, the superintendent general of Indian affairs intervened to convince the royal visitor not to get involved.

Any intercession on behalf of either Nah-nee-ba-we-quay or the Wawanosh delegation would amount, so the Prince of Wales was told, to an infringement on the jurisdiction of the local legislature and a violation of responsible government. The prerogatives of colonial self-rule were used aggressively as justification for negating the old alliance between First Nations and the crown, the principle that had once been essential to the defence of Canada. Consequently, both Indian efforts to call on the royal authority of British North America were blocked in the name of responsible government.

Although she failed to realize her political objectives, Nah-nee-ba-we-quay was far ahead of her time, drawing broad publicity to a range of issues surprisingly similar to those that would preoccupy the Native Women's Association of Canada over a century later. In the last decades of the twentieth century, issues pertaining to gender and to the relationship of First Nations people with Canadian citizenship focused increasingly on the status of the Canadian Charter of Rights and Freedoms in Indian Country. These matters, however, and the modern-day role of the Native Women's Association are addressed more fully in volume 2.

Another seminal and articulate voice of protest raised against the dominion government's Indian policy was that of the Reverend E.F. Wilson, the Anglican missionary who worked closely with the Anishinabek people of the Sault Ste Marie area to found the Shingwauk residential school for boys and the Wawanosh school for girls. Wilson learned the Ojibway language and wrote a useful dictionary, giving English translations from that important Aboriginal tongue. While he spent much of his life as a proponent of the civilizing mission in Indian Country, in later years he began to doubt seriously the sagacity of using the power of church and state to try to eliminate all signs of Aboriginal cultures and identities.[36] Wilson's onset of doubt came about partly through his collaboration with pioneer anthropologist Horatio Hale and partly through his visit in 1888 to the Cherokee Nation in the Indian Territory established following the Indian removal policies of President Andrew Jackson. Wilson was deeply impressed by the sucess of the Cherokee in developing a whole range of institutions, including courts, schools, hospitals, businesses, and a legislature. These institutions, he maintained, incorporated many of the best features of the society of the United States with methods and philosophies that were genuinely Cherokee in origin and development. With this example before him, Wilson became convinced that the assimilationist principles of Canadian Indian policy were drastically wrongheaded.[37]

Wilson outlined his critique under the pen name of "Fair Play." He did so in a series of four articles published in 1891 in a small publication known as *The Canadian Indian*.[38] He wrote:

We have not considered [the Indians'] feelings; we have not given him sufficient credit for intelligence, we have not sufficiently considered that the love of fatherland, the love of the old traditions of the past, the love of the old language, and the old stories and songs, is as strong in the Indian as in any Englishman or Frenchman or Italian. A highly educated Mohawk Indian said to me only the other day – and I must confess I was surprised to hear him say it – "the last thing I would wish to give up is our language" ... Why should we expect that Indians alone, of all people, should be ready to give up all old customs and traditions and language, and adopt those of the aggressor upon their soil? The change we expect the Indian to make, and to make so quickly ... is a radical one – a change of dress, a change of dwelling, a change in mode of gaining livelihood, a social change, a religious change, an educational change, a *totum in toto* change. And this – not so much for his own benefit, as for our convenience. We want the land. We cannot have Indian hunters annoying our farmers and settlers. If the Indian is to remain he must learn to be a decent neighbour; and to be a decent neighbour, we expect him to accept our religion, our education, our laws, and our customs. We allow him no choice, and we allow him no time.

In questioning the orthodoxy of assimilation as the cornerstone of Indian policy, Wilson detailed his fear that this approach to nation building served no one's interests well in the long run. Again he advanced points by asking a number of rhetorical questions:

Is there nothing – nothing whatever – in the past history of this ancient people to merit our esteem, or call forth our praise? Were their laws in the past all mere childishness? Were there no great minds among their noted chiefs? Do the ruins of their ancient cities show no marks of intelligence, energy or persevereance, in the people that planned and constructed them? While taking steps to preserve their ancient relics in our museums, and while studying their past history and their many and diverse languages, were it not well, as a matter of justice and Christian kindness to them, as well as out of respect for their part and but little-understood history, to allow them to preserve their own nationality, and, under certain restrictions, to enact their own laws? Would it not be pleasanter, and even safer to us, to have living in our midst a contented, well-to-do, self-respecting, thriving community of Indians, rather than a set of dependent, dissatisfied, half-educated and half-Anglicanized paupers?

Some of Wilson's proposals were directed at establishing a self-directed and self-governing Indian community within the organizational structure of the Church of England. The clergyman also recommended that Indian people be given their own legislature with an Aboriginal lieutenant-governor capable of extending crown authority to Indian-made laws. These laws would be debated and enacted in Aboriginal languages. Moreover, this Aborginal legislation would reflect and enhance Aboriginal cultures, including forms of collective land tenure that, in Wilson's estimation, were integral to the Indigenous way of life of Indian peoples. Wilson even went so far as to advocate the designation of an Indian capital city and the institution of Indian government as a third order of Canadian government.

As Wilson's career suggests, the genesis and development of the system of Indian industrial and residential schools in Canada has a complex history. While the system by and large carried forward a coercive campaign of psychological warfare aimed at breaking the continuity of Aboriginal systems of belief and spirituality, the people who worked in and around the schools displayed the whole spectrum of good and bad human attributes. Wilson's essays put him in a class of his own among the more enlightened personnel to work in the boarding schools; Samuel Blake was another maverick within the Anglican Church who questioned and criticized the work of both his denomination and his government in the field of Indian education.

Blake was a prominent lawyer in Toronto who, in the early twentieth century, was on the executive committee of the Church of England's Missionary Society of the Canadian Church. In this capacity he developed a wide-ranging criticism of the boarding schools, institutions that too often

were places of death, disease, physical abuse, and psychological torture for
their young Aboriginal inmates. Blake advocated a major move away from
the boarding schools to day schools, with Indian pupils by and large staying at home with their families.[39] In 1908 Blake outlined many of his criticisms in a pamphlet provocatively entitled *The Call of the Red Man as
Answered by the Commissioner of Indian Affairs of the United States of America:
What Will Be the Answer of the Dominion of Canada?* This document was written in the form of a commentary on large excerpts taken from a recent
report produced by the US Bureau of Indian Affairs. The following passage
gives an illustration of the kind of principles Blake sought to stimulate in
Canada's system of Indian education:

The notion must be driven away that you must thrust everything out of the Indian
and turn him into a white man in order to make him fit for citizenship. I denounce
that as pure heresy; it is contrary to every law of nature. What we should do is to
stir up in him the proper pride of race, not rob him of his language, not rob him
of his traditions, not rob him of all that has made him love his home, and cemented the tie between himself and his parents. How much wiser to let him expand
along natural lines – to build on what we find already founded. You cannot if you
try, change an Indian into a white man, so what is the use of trying? Why not,
instead, try to make a good Indian of him.[40]

Given the connection of Canadian Indian policy to similar projects of
assimilation aimed at other Indigenous groups throughout the colonial
world, there were surprisingly few thoughtful voices raised to identify the
larger patterns and make the appropriate comparisons. One of the exceptions to this rule was provided by R.V. Sinclair, who, in 1910, wrote a series
of letters to the *Ottawa Evening Journal* condemning the dominion's Indian
policies. With acknowledgement in his subsequent book of the "Fair Play"
of the paper who published his original letters, a reference perhaps to the
pseudonym "Fair Play" used by Wilson in his seminal letters published in
The Canadian Indian almost two decades earlier, Sinclair compared Canada's treatment of "native races" unfavourably with that of other "civilized"
countries. His critique echoed many of the points outlined by Nah-nee-ba-
we-quay a half-century earlier. His comparative analysis also underlines the
extremism of the Canadian government in building the Indian Act into an
apartheid-like structure – indeed, one of the prototypes for South African
apartheid. As Sinclair poignantly observed, this most distilled of all legislative instruments of colonialism separated Indian individuals from any semblance of official recognition for their rights and responsibilities of legal
"personhood," otherwise known as citizenship.

A Chinaman, a Hindoo, the most ignorant and unsophisticated new settler can
assume obligations, can procure credit, impossible for the red man, the original
occupant of the country ... It has remained for Canada alone, among the civilized

people who have native races, to more and more encroach on such rights and, as
I have said before, to deprive him of his primordial rights as a man.

Other countries and colonies furnish no such example. The policy of the United States government is very different. In their dealings with the aborigines, other
colonies have set Canada a glorious example. Take New Zealand with the Maoris.
We find a complete process of amalgamation. Several Maoris are members of the
New Zealand Parliament, and are distinguished not only for their ability, but their
loyalty to the Crown. In Africa we find the native races have all the rights that other
subjects of the Crown enjoy. We find the black man prominent not only in the
political life of the different colonies of that continent, but filling important positions in the church, at the bar, in fact in all the different ranks of life which go to
make up the various orders of municipal authorities or activities. From Cape to
Cairo, the "native" is treated, with few insignificant exceptions, as an equal in so far
as his opportunities are concerned. The Indian has no such opportunity here ...
Simply because the effect of the Indian Act and its administration has been to
deprive the Indian [of that which] goes to make a man and a citizen.[41]

By far the most broadly significant conflict over Indian policy in Canada
in the first half of the twentieth century involved resistance to the dominion's drive to outlaw the Longhouse government on the Six Nation reserve
near Brantford and to put in its place the municipal-type structures outlined in the federal Indian Act. The conflict unfolded in the context of two
large events that established the frames of reference for an important convergence of different views on the locations of sovereignty in the British
Empire after the First World War. One event was the creation in the early
1920s of the League of Nations, with its headquarters in Geneva. The
other big event was the development in Canada of more assertive forms of
local nationalism born largely of shared investments in a huge war effort
that gave ordinary Canadians a heightened sense of citizen participation in
an emerging country. The newly elected Liberal government of Prime
Minister William Lyon Mackenzie King chose to direct this mood of mobilized self-confidence towards breaking Canada loose from some of the
imperial structures of the British Empire and edging the country instead
towards deeper integration into the structures of the informal American
empire.

The constitutional implications of this geopolitical repositioning of
Canada were felt closely and acutely by the Longhouse traditionalists
among the Six Nations peoples of Canada. As they demonstrated again
and again, they retained a clear picture of themselves as situated within
their own sovereign sphere, a jurisdictional integrity that was protected
and represented by their long tradition of treaty relations with the sovereign of the British Empire. They saw themselves then as many see themselves now, as allies of the crown rather than as subjects of the crown. The
clear leader of the reinvigorated Longhouse traditionalists after the Great
War was Levi General. He was the holder of the name Deskahe, one of the

leadership titles belonging to a clan of the Cayuga nation. Deskahe, in turn, was one of the original fifty names adopted by the founders of the Longhouse League, otherwise known as the Haudonosaunee. That famous old Confederacy has been extensively studied for the genius of its combination of federal, democratic, and hereditary principles.

A powerful and compelling speaker, Deskahe gave impassioned yet diplomatic articulation to the sentiments of those peoples who had been worried that the Longhouse government of the Six Nations people near Brantford had become too permeated by the influence of Christian sachems. The fact that the Longhouse continued in the early 1920s to be recognized by dominion officials as the official governing body of the Six Nations is indicative of the unique place of this Aboriginal Confederacy and of the Covenant Chain in British North America's constitutional genesis.

The Longhouse League sovereigntists at first directed their attention to Ottawa. They hired an Ontario lawyer, Andrew G. Chisholm, and sent Deskahe to the nation's capital to protest the dominion's intervention in the land tenure system on the Six Nations reserve as well as its intiative to implement involuntary enfranchisement. When a registered Indian was enfranchised, he or she became a regular citizen and ceased to be an Indian for the purposes of the Indian Act. Deskahe quickly discovered that Ottawa was essentially closed to any exercise of First Nations political will. Moreover, it was impossible to bring a civil case before the Canadian courts without the sanction of the Justice Department. In those years its political masters were entirely hostile to the arguments of those seeking recognition of the Longhouse League as a sovereign government with a long heritage of treaty alliances with the imperial crown.

There was no real forum within Canada, or within any other of the emerging nation-states in the colonized world, for any even-handed testing of competing visions of sovereignty before neutral, third-party ajudicators. The rights and titles of many Indigenous peoples around the world were thus closely bound up with the quest of the defenders of the Longhouse Confederacy. Their aim after the Great War was to find or invent some means of achieving legal or political access to the international arena to prevent Canada's tightening grip of domestic jurisdiction on the relative independence of a famous Aboriginal polity that had figured prominently in the career of the British Empire in North America. Accordingly, the Longhouse activists fired their Canadian lawyer and hired an American lawyer, George Decker, with the aim of taking their case beyond North America to the League of Nations.[42] Their understanding of the futility of trying to advance their case in Canada was hastened by a negative ruling handed down in 1921 in Ontario in a fishing case involving a Mohawk citizen, Eliza Sero. With Andrew Chisholm as her lawyer, Sero attempted unsuccessfully to defend herself against a criminal charge for fishing out of season by invoking the argument of the sovereign alliance between her people and the crown.[43]

With mounting evidence before him that that there were no domestic remedies for the grievances of adherents to the Longhouse Confederacy, Deskahe travelled in 1920 and 1923 to Europe, making extended visits to London and Geneva.[44] His object was to act as an ambassador of his peoples and to participate on their behalf in the making of the new global system of international relations trying to take form, as thinking men and women from many backgounds grappled with the meaning of the Great War and the problem of how to avoid its like ever again.[45] In entering the discussions and negotiations that accompanied the establishment of the League of Nations, the aspirations of Deskahe's constituency were reflective of what some optimists had hoped the war had been fought to achieve.[46] As the president of the United States, Woodrow Wilson, had proclaimed in commiting his country to enter the war in 1917: "We shall fight for the things we have always carried nearest our hearts – for democracy, for the right of those who submit to authority to have a voice in their own government, for the rights and liberties of small nations, for a universal dominion of right by such a concert of free peoples as shall bring peace and safety to all nations and make the world at last free."[47]

At Geneva Deskahe called attention to the government of Canada's failure to respect the complex of treaties and international law that situated the Six Nations as sovereign peoples within the framewok of the British Empire. Particularly galling to the Longhouse traditionalists was the dominion's allocation of individual land titles to returning Six Nations war veterans, a tactic that was seen as a provocative encroachment on the control of the Confederacy over their remaining sovereign territory. Deskahe found many sympathetic eyes and ears in Geneva and London for his meticulously argued allegations against the government of Canada. Dutch officials, with memories of New Netherland's old connections to the Longhouse League in the seventeenth century, were cautiously helpful in creating a forum for the status of the Six Nations to be discussed. Delegations from the governments of Persia, Estonia, Ireland, and Panama were also attentive. These diplomats represented constituencies that had struggled with their own hard experiences of colonization and decolonization. They were, in a sense, pioneers in the discussion of a global issue slowly but inexorably moving onto the world stage. A major ally of Deskahe in Geneva was René Claparede, who was the driving force of an influential organization known as the Bureau internationale pour la défense des Indigenes.[48] Under Claparede's guidance, this bureau gave rise to a committee called the "Commission des Iroquois," which was instrumental in gaining official acknowledgment from the League of Nations of a submission entitled *The Red Man's Appeal for Justice.*[49]

Officials in Canada reacted with severity to Deskahe's mission, illustrating vividly the ethnocentric biases of the dominion government. The government of Mackenzie King moved to isolate the sachem from his constituency and to dislodge the Longhouse from the position of governing authority on the Six Nations reserve. First, Colonel C.E. Morgan, a veteran of the Boer War and a former colonial administrator of the Kaffirs of South Africa, was appointed superintendent of the Six Nations. Next, the King government installed a detachment of the Royal Canadian Mounted Police at Oshwegan, the administrative centre of the Six Nations reserve. This action was the prelude to the enforcement of an order in council of the federal cabinet outlawing the old Longhouse government and instituting, instead, a government derived from the authority of the federal Indian Act. No provision was made for a referendum in the Iroquois community to decide the matter. This strategic omission was certainly motivated by the knowledge that the outcome would have been to reject the dominion's imposition of its own legal authority over that of the Longhouse League and its Great Law.

Shortly after this unilateral imposition of an Indian Act regime, essentially at the end of the guns of the RCMP in Oshwegan, the King government responded in Geneva to answer the submission of the Longhouse government to the League of Nations. The response was published in the league's *Official Journal*. The government of Canada rejected the allegation of the Longhouse people that they had been subjected to an "act of war" when "an armed force" pre-empted the proceedings of their own Aboriginal governing system to impose the alien regime of the Indian Act. In their submission, the Canadian officials maintained that it was not "necessary" for the Six Nations to continue their "antiquated form of government." Instead, the dominon government "provides machinery for a simple elective system on Indian reserves" through the Indian Act. The officials denied that the presence of the RCMP at Oswegan was connected with the imposed change of regime. The Canadian government stated, "It has been necessary, from time to time, to send Dominion police on the reserve. They are a civil force acting under civil authority. Their presence on the reserve has been for the purpose of suppressing illicit distilling and maintaining law and order for the protection of the law-abiding Indian populace."[50]

In October 1924 the RCMP supervised elections for the selection of a chief and council who would advise Colonel Morgan in his capacity as federal Indian agent. The vast majority of adult males boycotted the election, a decision whose most important enforcers were members of the Mohawk Workers Club. The main function of this club was to provide financing for Deskahe's activities in Europe, a role they fulfilled largely by sponsoring lacrosse matches. One year later Deskahe died.[51] His funeral was watched closely by agents of the dominion's police force, who by this time had succeeded in planting an undercover agent to report secretly on the workings of the Mohawk Workers Club. The activists continued to draw their case to the attention of sympathetic officials in Europe. But without the brilliance of Deskahe's interpretations of international law and in the face of a concerted effort on the part of the governments of Canada and Great Britain to discredit the proponents of Six Nations sovereignty, the scope of their effectiveness was contained.[52]

The episode, however, had exposed a major problem in the workings of the dominion's Indian Department, where a dull bureaucratic ineptness combined with a quick willingness to avoid negotiation by invoking, instead, the instruments of state coercion. As the editorialists at the Montreal *Family Herald and Weekly Star* lamented, Indian people could now clearly see that their historic access to the sovereign of Great Britain had been severely curtailed, to be replaced by "a departmental Jack-In-Office in Ottawa." The grievances of Indian people would now have to wait "upon the leisurely convenience of bumptuous officials, who displayed far less zeal for Indian rights, than for their own convenience, and the political interests of their party."[53]

Accordingly, the Dominion government's efforts in the 1920s to assert the sovereign independence of Canada translated into a corresponding push to subjugate Indian nations more forcefully under an alien rule of law whose increasingly monocultural bias was antagonistic to the exercise of genuine Aboriginal jurisdiction. This expansion of dominion self-government, concurrently with an attack on the self-government of Indigenous peoples, re-enacted the patterns established when the local government in Canada took over legislative responsibility for Indian Affairs from the imperial government in Great Britain, through passage of the Act for the Gradual Civilization of the Indian Tribes. As was the case in 1857, the principle was again demonstrated in 1924 that in almost all instances where New World countries are dominated by immigrants and their Creole descendants, enhanced autonomy for the majority population translates into the extinguishment of sovereign space remaining to Indigenous peoples.

The attack on the Longhouse League by the King government was also an attack on the continuing identity of Canada as British North America. The double-barrelled quality of the attack was derived from the centrality of the Longhouse League and its attending diplomatic polity – the Covenant Chain – in the establishment of British imperial Canada. From the politics of Johnson Hall to the ascent of Montreal's North West Company as a medium of transcontinental influence, the dual heritage of the Longhouse League and the Covenant Chain had helped to infuse British imperial Canada with a sufficient dynamism in Indian Country to continue crown governance in North America, even after the etablishment of the United States as an independent republic. The other side of King's attack on the country's British constitutional heritage was his desire to nudge Canada towards a deeper integration into the American empire. As a former adviser to New York's Rockefeller conglomerate, King's pro-American and anti-British biases were deeply rooted. His grandfather, William Lyon Mackenzie, had led an unsuccessful revolt, centred in Toronto in 1837, seeking termination of

Canada's legal connection with Britain as a prelude to its possible annexation to the United States.[54]

Canada's move away from the Old World orientation of the Royal Proclamation and the British North American Act and towards the New World orientation of the United States advanced the impetus that has been integral to the genesis of the American empire from its inception. Ever since the Declaration of Independence drew a distinction between "men" and the "merciless savages" that King George was accused of inciting to violence, there has been a deep bias in the American empire against the perpetuation of all forms of diplomacy and negotiations with Indigenous peoples which recognize the continuity of their inherited polities and Aboriginal titles. Accordingly, the constitutional principles of crown recognition of the existence of Aboriginal and treaty rights were to be almost completely submerged after 1924 by the legislative hegemony of the Indian Act. That underlying feature of the country's constitution remained drowned until the Nisga'a people brought Canada's older legal heritage to the surface when they obtained a somewhat favourable ruling on the existence of Indian title from the Supreme Court of Canada in 1973.

The dominion's outlawing of the Longhouse government marked a clear moment of transition when the instruments of state coercion were used aggressively to isolate Indigenous peoples from any access to the international community and to contain them within the constraints of domestic law. The bare-faced disinformation disseminated at the League of Nations about the nature of the police intervention on the reserve is telling. So, too, is the justification of the police actions as a requirement to maintain "law and order" for the protection of the "law-abiding Indians." The implication of this statement is that those Longhouse people seeking recognition for their government in the international community were not law-abiding. The sovereigntists among the Six Nations peoples were effectively criminalized in the very process that saw the government of Canada violate its own rule of law by unilaterally transgressing the crown's recognition of existing Aboriginal and treaty rights. This criminalization of Indigenous law at Oshwegan would be followed in 1927 by an outright prohibition of all forms of Indian political activity involving any exchange of money.

The criminalization of Aboriginal law and custom, as well as the criminalization of the will to defend these most fundamental attributes of self-determination, demonstrates the clear character of the Indian Act regime as a genuine machinery of colonial repression. Its primary purpose was to enable the Canadian federation to monopolize the exercise of sovereign authority in the lands, waters, courts, and legislatures covering the northern half of North America. The provisions it made for the governance of Indian peoples on Indian reserves, which in total covered much less than 1 per cent of the total Canadian land mass, were secondary to the larger purpose of pushing aside and isolating the First Nations to make way for the ascendant sovereignty of the Canadian nation.

The treatment of the heritage of the Covenant Chain and of the tradition of crown-Aboriginal alliances as subversive established basic patterns that have continued until this day. That transformation effectively made Blue Jackets of the Red Coats, as the tradition of Indian fighting that had shaped the us military from its inception increasingly permeated the ethos of Canada's federal police force. In the name of law and order, the RCMP would intervene again and again to quell various acts done in the name of exercising existing Aboriginal and treaty rights. The confrontations at Oka in 1990 and at Gustafsen Lake in 1995, both involving First Nations activists who looked to the Covenant Chain and the Longhouse League as sources of legal and political legitimacy, renewed some of the issues left festering in 1924. That was the moment when the coercive muscle of the state was most overtly invoked to negate and deny the existence of an old Aboriginal constitution and an old treaty tradition integral to the constitutional integrity of British North America outside the constitutional framework of the American republic.

THE BRITISH IMPERIAL BACKGROUND OF APARTHEID AS EXPRESSED PARTICULARLY IN THE HISTORIES OF CANADA, SOUTH AFRICA, AND THE UNITED STATES

Until the amendments of 1951, the federal Indian Act of the Dominion of Canada was one of the most oppressive instruments in the world for the governance of Indigenous peoples. That year the recommendations of a parliamentary committee were adopted, lifting the most overtly repressive features of the legislation, including its prohibition on Indian dancing, Indian giveaways, and the raising of money to pursue an Aboriginal claim. Not only was the underlying philosophy of the Act largely discredited by what Nazism had revealed about the gross inhumanities lurking in "the West's" Darwinistic fantasies of master-race hegemony. But Indian peoples themselves had contributed in a variety of ways, including through extremely high levels of military enlistment, to the mobilization of the Allied Forces during both world wars.[55]

This enlistment was entirely voluntary, for in both wars the dominion government had decided that, as wards of the state rather than as citizens, Indian men could not be conscripted. What developed informally after 1951, then, was an approach where some registered Indians acquired two distinct legal personalities, one as tax-paying Canadian citizens in their transactions off their reserves and another as subjects of indirect rule and as partial wards of the state in their legal lives on their reserves. Neither of these legal personalities took into account in any substantial way the underlying constitutionality of the Indian Country of Canada as expressed in both the Royal Proclamation of 1763 and the legacy of Indian nations as allies of the crown, some nations with treaties and some with an Aboriginal title that remains unaddressed.

When the right to vote in federal elections was finally extended to registered Indians in 1960 under Prime Minister John Diefenbaker, some Indian people resisted, predicting that future federal regimes would view First Nations simply as interest groups rather than as original peoples with Aboriginal title or with treaty agreements allying them to the crown.[56] Six Nations peoples had first resisted accepting the franchise to vote in dominion elections in 1885, when Macdonald had tried to change Canada's electoral law to include registered Indians. After the Second World War Saskatchewan premier Tommy Douglas met similar resistance when he tried to extend the provincial vote to treaty Indians. That initiative stimulated many important discussions in North America's first popularly elected socialist government. Provincial officials, together with a diverse group of Aboriginal politicians and pundits, looked carefully at the interrelationships between a host of laws, categories, and statuses, including Canadian citizenship, the Indian Act, Indian treaties, the franchise, taxation, and a possible suspension of the provisions prohibiting registered Indians from purchasing or consuming alcohol.[57]

In 1960, when the Diefenbaker government moved to extend the franchise to registered Indian adults, there were a number of protests and complaints from the more conservative branches of Indian Country. Demonstrations against enfranchisement took place among the Micmac and at Kanewake and Akwesasne. Cree Elder Albert Lightning from the Treaty 6 area in Alberta announced that many First Nations people in Alberta were "absolutely" hostile to the move. "This is a trick to rob us of what we have left," declared a leader from Kanewake. Particular criticism was levelled at James Gladstone from the Blood reserve in the Treaty 7 area. He had been brought into the Senate by Diefenbaker to prepare the ground for the coming change. "Senator Gladstone is a yes-man for Ottawa," proclaimed one of the placards at Akwesasne. The outcry was sufficiently intense that the prime minister offered personal assurances that the change in the electoral laws would not have any negative effect on the integrity of what would later come to be known as Aboriginal and treaty rights.[58]

This scepticism in Indian Country proved prophetic. In 1969 the government of Prime Minister Pierre Trudeau moved to privatize and municipalize reserves, to terminate Indian treaties, and to dismantle the federal infrastructure of Indian Affairs, all in the name of the equality of Canadian citizens. When this initiative was strongly resisted by many Indian people, whose leaders labelled the policy "cultural genocide," the Trudeau government renounced the approach, leaving in limbo until this day the question of how Indian peoples are connected to citizenship in both Canada and their First Nations.[59] Moreover, there is no clear understanding on where the points of connection, if any, bring these dual citizenships together or how treaties with the crown figure in the broad outlines of Canadian federalism.

Trudeau's initiative, soon dubbed the White Paper, was originally promoted in language that drew on the compelling activism of the civil rights movement in the United States. The federal government's call for an end to all legal "discrimination" differentiating Indian people from others in Canada seemed in line with the great social movement given timeless articulation by Dr Martin Luther King in particular. Where Trudeau promoted the White Paper as a break with the heritage of the Indian Act, the government proposal was more correctly characterized as a fulfilment and a realization of the assimilationist objectives of the authors of the Indian Act. From the time of its inception, the goal of this legislative device had been the eventual removal of all formal legal markers of Indian Country and the cultural and legal absorption of Indigenous people as equal citizens in the civilization of possessive individualism.

The White Paper came to represent the dark side of the extension of the language and laws of "equal" Canadian citizenship to Aboriginal peoples in Canada. Yet the fact that it took until 1960 before registered Indians in Canada were extended the right to vote, the most obvious hallmark of citizenship in a democracy, raises questions about how the handling of this issue compares with that of other countries, especially those that share the heritage of the British Empire. More precisely, the timing raises obvious questions about the comparisons, similarities, and possible connections linking Aboriginal Affairs in Canada to the "Native" policies of that country where the disenfranchised condition of Indigenous Africans grew into a controversy of global proportions in the final decades of the twentieth century. That country is South Africa.

Not surprisingly, insistent protests of denial tend to arise, especially in government circles, when issues are raised linking the administration of Indian Affairs in Canada with the development of the infamous apartheid regime in South Africa. Prime Minister Brian Mulroney gave clear expression to this sentiment of denial in 1987, when he was asked a question while leaving the Vatican. After visiting the pope and just before a tour of Africa to consult and encourage the opponents of South African apartheid, the Canadian leader was asked a question suggesting some hypocrisy on his part for not doing more at home to ameliorate the condition of Indigenous peoples. Mulroney responded indignantly, saying "there is no comparison at all between the difficulties of our aboriginal peoples and the system of evil that exists in South Africa."[60] It is hardly surprising that Mulroney, like many other Western leaders, preferred to view South African apartheid during that vile regime's most ruthless final years as an aberration rather than as the most stark illustration of a far more pervasive and permeating legacy emanating from Europe's colonization of the planet. The desire not to see in apartheid the mirror of something deep in the heritage of Western civilization is similar to the desire not to see in the

Nazism of the Third Reich the expression of something powerful and potent in the imperfectly understood psyche of Europe and its political progeny.

The need to put distance between the liberal democracies of the West and what transpired in South Africa before 1993 is met by demonizing the White Afrikaners as the Hitler of "civilized" nations, just as German Nazism is explained away as "the hallucinatory patchwork of warped, half-baked, and self-contradictory notions" imposed on an unwitting people by "the definitive monster" – by the ultimate "über-egotist" of all time.[61] The truth, of course, is not nearly so simple. While the dark forces embodied in South African apartheid and German Nazism have seemingly been wrestled to the margins of global society, the roots from which these movements emerged remain deeply planted in the living history even of those largely English-speaking nations who see themselves as beacons and pillars of liberal democracy. The distance between the rhetoric of equality and the maintenance of privilege rooted in institutionalized racism is most transparent in the Aboriginal policies of countries like Canada, the United States, New Zealand, and Australia.

The regime that grew around the Indian Act of Canada was founded on the principle that peoples should be kept both separate and unequal until such time as the inferior group, or individuals within that group, become sufficiently tutored in the arts of "civilization" to receive citizenship as the final mark of extinguishment of their Aboriginal cultures and identities. Even in those reserves where the Indian Act is being reformed in favour of newer federal and provincial legislation delegating municipal-like powers to Indian bands and their local governments, this legal reform is still consistent with assimilationist philosophy from which the Indian Act was conceived. The statutes extending the powers of self-administration to the Sechelt people of British Columbia in 1988,[62] for instance, represent more an extension of, than a break with, the ideology of the White Paper of 1969 and, for that matter, the Act for the Gradual Civilization of the Indian Tribes in Canada.

The enfranchisement provisions of the first Indian Act in 1857 marked a curious marriage of apartheid thinking with a liberal optimism in the malleability of human nature. More significant than what the law did on reserves, however, was the confirmation of relationships of power and property in the society of citizens living off Indian reserves. By enclosing Indigenous peoples within the legal category of wardship apart from the rights and responsibilities of citizenship, the first Indian Act set the direction for its many legislative cousins in the colonies and former colonies of Great Britain. This body of law gave legitimacy to local regimes of non-Aboriginal control over land apportionment and land ownership; it eliminated altogether the original proprietors from direct participation in those most primal transactions creating the heirarchies of wealth and power whose structures became the framework of the empire of possessive individualism. When the focus is placed on the evolution of the rules for the distribution of land during the formative phase in the development of the United States, Canada, New Zealand, Australia, and South Africa, it becomes abundantly clear that the Dutch Africaners were only embellishing pre-existing principles of apartheid that were essential to the nation building of all these geopolitical outgrowths of British colonial rule.

The British imperial propensity to make different laws for the governance of different populations, and then to confirm these legal distinctictions in the organization of territory, was most dramatically illustrated in the crown's revised cartography of North America as outlined in the Royal Proclamation of 1763. In 1830 the government of the United States appropriated and extended the most self-serving aspects of these British principles in developing its own approach to national expansion. This distilled application of the worst features of the Royal Proclamation became incarnate in what was surely one of the boldest schemes of partition and apartheid ever imposed on human geography – President Andrew Jackson's scheme to divide the United States along the Mississippi, with citizens of "the new white nation" in the east to be segregated from relocated Indian nations in the west.

The lasting legacy of this scheme of American apartheid is clearly marked in the near absence of federal Indian reservations east of the Mississippi. The only significant exceptions to this campaign of ethnic cleansing east of the Mississippi are in New York, Maine, Florida, and Wisconsin. In Wisconsin, some Indian people were allowed to hold ground as a result of their importance as labourers in the region's lucrative lumber industry.

As outlined in chapter 6, Sir Francis Bond Head attempted to create a British North American equivalent of this ethnically cleansed American empire of private property. His attempt at Indian removal focused on Manitoulin Island as the refuge for the Aboriginal survivors of the shrinking Indian Country. Lord Glenelg initially approved of Bond Head's plan because it was consistent with the Colonial Office Native policies in South Africa. But the linkage between events in these two colonies led to the hostile reception given to the scheme by the British missionary societies, the Aborigines' Protection Society, and the Parliamentary Committee on Aborigines in British Settlements. This convergence points to the importance of picturing local histories of the treatment of Indigenous peoples in the context of larger patterns of empire, ideology, and policy making.

The linkages connecting the treatment of Indigenous peoples in different quarters of globe persisted throughout the nineteenth century and the early twentieth century. The importance of these global relationships are emphasized in Bernard Makhosezwe Magubane's *Making of a Racist State*.[63] This chronicle of relatively recent South African history details the role of the British imperial government in the manipulation of law to cut Indigenous and other people of colour from the ownership and governance of their own country. In Magubane's view, the outcome of this process of dispossession and disempowerment of Black South Africans – apartheid – was not an isolated phenomenon but the culmination of a long experience in the British Empire of the crown claiming powers of trusteeship over Indigenous peoples as a means to facilitate the appropriation of their land and, in some instances, their work. Magubane advances this interpretation with the view of correcting the impressions left by Leonard Thompson and others that South African apartheid reflected almost exclusively the mythology and local preoccupations of the Afrikaner population.[64]

Mugubane outlines the zealousness of British efforts to appease and enlist the Dutch Afrikaner population of South Africa following their defeat in 1902 in the Boer War. The zeal to accommodate and integrate the expansionary tactics of a defeated White settler population vis-à-vis an Indigenous population, into the imperial culture reproduced some of the crown's strategic manoeuvres following the conquest of New Netherlands after 1664 and the conquest of French imperialism in Canada in 1759. In New York and Canada this mode of colonization translated into extending the commercial relations with the Indigenous peoples by building on the fur-trade diplomacy of New Netherlands and New France. In South Africa, however, this form of empire buiding meant capitalizing further on the Afrikaner exploitation of the so-called Kaffir as cheap, local labour forces, especially in the fantastically promising mining sector.

To be effective, however, this strategy to appropriate the land and cheap labour of the Indigenous peoples of South Africa meant enlisting the Afrikaner leadership in what was described as "the mission of the Newer World." This mission was, according to General J.C. Smuts, the key Boer convert to British imperialism, to consolidate to "a grand racial aristocracy." "Unless the White race closes ranks," Smuts advised, "its position will become untenable in the face of the overwhelming majority of prolific barbarism."[65]

The Union of South Africa was thus constituted as a self-governing dominion within the British Empire in 1910. As in the case of another "White Dominion" of the British Empire – Canada – the Indigenous population, with some few exceptions, were excluded from the right to vote in national elections or the right to own land as private property. Accordingly, with the advice and approval of their Afrikaner allies, the British lawgivers founded the new polity on a system of suffrage which, again with some small exceptions, was limited to white males.

The decision to lay the foundations in this way for what was to become the world's most notorious "racist state" was done with a steady, admiring gaze on the legacy of the British Empire as an instrument for the dominant Europeans and their descendants over Indigenous peoples throughout the world. It was this ethos that animated in Canada the genre of imperialism preached by Stephen Leacock and enabled one of the primary prophets of the movement, Lord Milner, to conceive of himself as a "Liberal Imperialist."[66] To Lord Milner, the extension of crown dominion beyond Cape

Colony to the larger South Africa was motivated out of a "religious faith" in the necessity of "preserving the unity of a great race, of enabling it, by maintaining that unity, to develop freely on its own lines, and to continue to fulfill its distinct mission in the world."[67]

As would be the case when the British parliament debated the bill to patriate the Canadian Constitution seventy years later, most of the discussion on the Union of South Africa Act in 1910 was devoted to the "Native question." In a remarkably telling speech, Lord Balfour tried to situate the issue of the relationship between the Indigenous population of South Africa and the vote in the context of the larger history of European expansion:

The Red Indians are gradually dying out. The Australian Aborigines are even more predestined to early extinction. But with the black races of Africa and those same races transported to America, for the first time we have the problem of races as vigorous in constitution, as capable of increasing in number, in contact with white civilization. For the first time, that problem has to be dealt with by peoples determinedly attached to all the constitutional traditions of liberty and freedom. That problem is new. It is coming before the brethren in the United States in a form which they, no doubt for solid reasons, made unnecessarily embarrassing since the American Constitution started with a very crude *a priori* statement about the equality of mankind and a brutal application of the most rigid principles of slavery ... All men are, from some points of view, equal; but to suppose that the races of Africa are in any sense equals of men of European descent, so far as government, as society, as the higher interest of civilization are concerned, is really ... an absurdity which every man who looks at this most difficult problem must put out of his mind if he is to solve the problem at all.[68]

The exclusion until recently of the large Aboriginal majority from the franchise in South Africa has placed the "native question" front and centre of that country's consciousness about its own internal nature as well as its place in the world. Accordingly, the thick complex of issues raised by the exclusion of Indigenous peoples from the country's framework of self-governance could not be pressed to the sidelines of national identity in South Africa. The issues could not so easily be subordinated and forgotten, as tended to happen in countries like the United States, Canada, or Australia, where the legal and political status of First Nations was made to seem of little significance compared with other facets of national life. The numerical strength and physical power of the Indigenous peoples of South Africa made it impossible to enforce forms of "ethnic cleansing," especially as happened in North America. In the United States and Canada, First Nations were enclosed within such narrow enclaves that they became largely invisible to most of the non-Aboriginal population. Although apartheid involved a similar approach to organizing physical and jurisdictional space in order to segregate different populations, the

Black, Aboriginal sector of South Africa was simply too prominent to be hidden away.

Moreover, the importance of this Aboriginal population to the dominant minority as a cheap labour pool illustrates the close convergence between issues originating in slavery and issues concerning the protection of the rights, titles, and resources of Indigenous peoples. This convergence was essential to the birth of the Aborigines' Protection Society and the work of the parliamentary committee on Aborigines in British settlements, both agencies whose global orientation gave them importance in the genesis of international civil society and Fourth World thinking.

The centrality of "the native question" in South Africa is illustrated in a text written in 1910 by a South African parliamentarian named P.A. Silburn. In *The Governance of Empire*, Silburn joined his voice with that of Stephen Leacock in Canada, as well as many other would-be architects of an imperial federation to replace the British Empire. One of the missions Silburn proposed for a new imperial federation was the creation of a more democratic imperial centre capable of taking on the responsibility of conducting relations with Indigenous peoples in a way that would mediate their contacts with local non-Aboriginal populations and governments. At the core of an imperial federation would be a new kind of parliament or council, with appropriate representation from all the imperial crown's self-governing jurisdictions.

Silburn's proposal can be seen as a return to some of the ideas expressed in 1837 by the Aborigines' committee in Great Britain. Similarly, in proposing that relations with Indigenous peoples most properly belong in the jurisdiction of central authority rather than local authority, Silburn invoked the basic elements of a controversy that had been integral to the breakdown of the first British Empire through the rebellion in the Anglo-American colonies. Much of his attention focused on what he referred to as "the Native races of British Africa." There were also ample references throughout his text to the treatment of Indigenous peoples in Canada, the United States, New Zealand, Fiji, the West Indies, Australia, and many other parts of the British Empire.

Silburn used the history of the Basuto people to illustrate his ideal of vesting constutional responsibility for the conduct of crown-Aboriginal relations in the central authority of an imperial federation. In 1871 Basutoland was placed under the direct authority of the government of Cape Colony in South Africa. However, Chief Mairosi led a determined resistance movement against this subordination of his people under the authority of neighbouring jurisdiction dominated by a non-Aboriginal settler population. The success of this armed resistance led to the withdrawal of the Cape Colony's claims to Basuto lands. As a result, the imperial government in Great Britain negotiated through treaty an agreement in 1884 with the Indigenous people of Basutoland.[69] For Silburn, the mediating force of this imperial intervention provided the model for the kind of role he envisaged for the central authority of an imperial federation. Among its responsibilities would be the need to make provisions for the protection of Indigenous peoples from the more zealous incursions and exploitations emanating from non-Aboriginal populations.

Silburn's proposal was not exempt from the paternalism and racist assumptions that permeated his time and place in history. These attitudes were clearly demonstrated, for instance, in the plans he outlined for the creation of native assemblies that would enable the Indigenous peoples to elect their own representatives in parliamentary bodies. Much like the Indian Act in Canada, however, the apportionment of the franchise in this way would afford Aboriginal electors "representation, not responsibility." In other words, the role of the elective bodies would be primarily to give advice rather than to exercise real power. In this fashion the Indigenous peoples could be placated "without giving them a voice in the government of the Europeans."[70] Although Silburn clearly did not transcend the prejudices of the society that made him, his analysis illustrates the continuity of many grand themes concerning the relationships between Indigenous peoples and non-Aboriginal settler populations. These themes were central in the shaping of the broad outlines of North American history in the late eighteenth and early nineteenth centuries, and many of the same themes dominated the politics of South Africa in the late nineteenth and early twentieth centuries.

Silburn was clearly reaching for a model of globalization that, with all its paternalism, nevertheless held substantial spaces for Indigenous peoples in the geopolitics of world governance. His proposal adds to the deep body of evidence on the importance of developing regimes of governance where Indigenous peoples retain relations with levels of authority above the domestic regimes of law and jurisdiction dominated by the national governments of Creole settlers. There are elements in Silman's analysis, therefore, that lead towards the conception of the Fourth World. The conceptual journey to the Fourth World has many pathways that run along both sides of the moving frontiers between Indigenous peoples and those whose sense of orientation to world history is more derived from Europe's originating role in the Columbian conquests.

THE THEORETICAL, OFFICIAL AND INFORMAL CONNECTIONS BETWEEN THE REGULATORY REGIMES OF "NATIVE AFFAIRS" IN SOUTH AFRICA AND CANADA

Throughout much of the twentieth century the governments of Canada and South Africa collaborated on a number of levels, especially in settling on the compromise of the Commonwealth as an alternative to imperial federation within a fading British Empire. One aspect of the developing sense of shared interest between the governments of these two "white dominions" was the development of a close relationship between the

Canadian Department of Indian Affairs and the Union of South Africa's Department of Native Affairs. Personnel in both departments kept up an active correspondence, and they regularly exchanged many reports and studies of mutual interest.[71] Moreover, officials from both countries, at least until 1963, visited each other's Native "reserves," where they borrowed ideas and compared notes on the governance of the "tribes" living under the authority of their respective regimes.

In 1906 and 1907, for instance, Oswin Boys Bull, an administrator of South Africa's school system, visited Canada to study the partnership of the dominion government and the churches in the running of the residential school system for Aboriginal people.[72] In 1945 C.J. Burchell, the high commissioner for Canada in South Africa, travelled to Transkei, which he described as the largest Native reserve in the Union. Although the South African government would not institute its most extreme expressions of what it called "separate development" until after 1948, by the time Burchell visited Tanskei most of the major fixtures of apartheid, especially those pertaining to the rules of eligibility for land ownership and the franchise, were already in place.[73] Perhaps with a view to passing along suggestions for Canada's Indian policies, Burchell was attracted to learn as much as he could about the institutions of self-administration for the Transkei inhabitants. He explored how the reserve's system of land tenure was structured as well as the workings of the "Bunga" or "native parliament," which dated back to 1895. Moreover, he studied how the local law system was administered by "native magistrates."[74]

While Burchell in his official correspondence wrote with the eye of an optimistic and devoted functionary in the task of holding up the White Man's Burden, in his private letters he abandoned any pretense of being anything other than a paternalistic arbiter of racial hierarchy. He referred to the Black South Africans as being of "a very low type." They were described as "perfectly dumb" with "little brain capacity." He predicted, moreover, that, if "given advancement," they would probably "create more trouble in this country than the negroes do in the United States."[75]

The exchanges of ideas and personnel worked both ways. In 1956, for instance, the Carnegie Corporation of New York sponsored the visit to Canada of F.J. Van Wyk, the director of the South African Institute of Race Relations. J.S. Cross, Canada's deputy minister of citizenship and immigration, informed his subordinate, Colonel H.M. Jones, director of Indian affairs, that he should make himself and some of this staff available for meetings with the South African dignitary. Van Wyk was said to be especially interested to learn of "the steps which are being taken to integrate [Indian people] into the Canadian economic and social structure."[76]

The presence of the thick files of reports from the South African Department of Native Affairs that are preserved in the records of the Canadian Department of Indian Affairs literally speaks volumes. Many of these glossy and well-illustrated publications begin with a picture of the longtime minister of the department, Dr Hendrik Frensch Verwoerd. Verwoerd held the Native Affairs portfolio from 1950 to 1958, before becoming prime minister of South Africa from 1958 to 1966. The report of the Native Affairs branch for 1953–54 is indicative of the kind of explanations given during the years when Verwoerd was a key figure in elaborating the laws and the rationales for the most extreme forms of apartheid, or, as the South African government preferred, "separate development."

The department described its constituency as being composed of several "ethnic groups," defined by "clearly distinguishable Bantu languages." These groups were enumerated as Xhosa, Zulu, Swazi, Ndobele, Tsonga, Southern Sotho, Tswana, Northern Sotho, and Venda. The predominant rhetoric in the text is that of a benevolent guardian advancing civilization by patiently encouraging "the gradual assumption of responsibility by the Bantu for the development of their own areas." This gradual extension from the white government of power to Bantu wards was referred to as "autogenous development." In his introduction to the report, Dr Verwoerd described this form of autogenous development as including the "diversion of Bantu manpower to the most promising labour markets, thereby eliminating waste of time and energy for workseekers on the one hand and supplying employers with the necessary labour on an efficient basis on the other." This explanation for regulating the movements of Bantu "ethnic groups" was to include "influx control measures and the gradual removal of foreign Natives from urban areas." The section of the report describing the governance of "Bantu areas" refers to several laws passed to widen the police powers of the "Bantu authorities." These quasi-government bodies were said to have been "established with the object of giving the Bantu a certain measure of internal control of their own areas" – control that allegedly had suffered for want "of that inherent authority which the people know and understand."[77]

In 1960 the nature of Prime Minister Verwoerd's understanding of the "inherent authority which the people know and understand" was flashed to the world with news of the Sharpeville massacre. This event began as a protest against the tyranny of the "pass laws," one of the instruments of control over "Native affairs" that the governments of Canada and South Africa shared throughout much of the twentieth century. When sixty-seven Africans were shot by South African police outside Johannesburg, there could no longer be any doubt about the vicious realities disguised behind seemingly innocuous legislative labels such as the Promotion of Bantu Self-Government Act of 1959.

As long as Indigenous peoples in Canada lacked the franchise, Canada's government was in no position to take a leading role in condemning the regime of apartheid in South Africa. In 1960, however, Prime Minister John Diefenbaker passed his Canadian Bill of Rights, an initiative whose broader meaning for Canadian society was evocatively suggested by extending the vote to registered Indians and fulfilling the plan

John A. Macdonald had introduced in 1885. "There can no longer be a relationship of master and servant anywhere in the world," Diefenbaker proclaimed during a year that would see many former colonies in Africa and Asia acquire the powers of self-rule. These episodes created the stage for one of Diefenbaker's finest hours. At the Commomwealth Conference in 1961, the Canadian prime minister joined ranks with the leaders of the Asian and African nations to eject Verweord's government from the organization.[78]

Old habits and attitudes die hard. In the summer of 1962 Colonel Jones organized a full-fledged tour of the prairie Indian reserves for the South African ambassador to Canada, W. Dirkse-van-Schalwyk. This gesture may well have represented an internal signal within the powerful bureaucracy of the Indian Affairs Department to protest Diefenbaker's perceived snub of a group in South Africa who were generally perceived as esteemed colleagues in this particular quarter of the civil service. The South African ambassador, whom the Indian agents commonly referred to as "His Excellency," visited the Morley Indian Residential School, the Sarcee reserve near Calgary, the Hobbema reserves near Wetaskiwin, the Ermineskin reserve near Edmonton, the Duck Lake Agency and Beardy's reserve in Saskatchewan, and the Fort Alexander and Brokenhead reserves in Manitoba. An Indian agent in Manitoba wrote of the visit, "it was most interesting to hear [the ambassador's] observations on the native people of South Africa and the seeming points of resemblance and dis-similarity between them and our Indian people."[79] W.F.B. Pugh, the superintendent of the Morley and Sarcee Indian Agency, quipped in his report to Colonel Jones, "There was to have been a barbeque at the [Morley] school at 3:00 pm, but in good old fashion Indian timing when we left at 4:00 pm, it was still not underway."[80] Writing after the completion of his tour from the South African Embassy in Ottawa, Dirkse-van-Schalwyk thanked his hosts for their gracious hospitality. Of the officials he had met in the Indian Affairs Branch, he commented to the deputy minister of citizenship and immigration, they were "most interesting and enlightening" and all in all "are a fine lot of fellows."[81]

The ease with which officialdom compared the native question in Canada and South Africa during the decades following the Second World War was as evident in the public school teaching of social studies as it was in the conduct of diplomacy. Here, for instance, is how one of Dent's school texts described South Africa's apartheid regime to Ontario's students. The volume, entitled *Canada and the Commonwealth*, was written in 1953 by a school principle and three University of Toronto historians, George W. Brown, J.M.S. Careless and Gerald M. Craig. The authors wrote:

There is one great difference between South Africa and Canadian life: that of South Africa is built on native labour. Imagine a Canada where the English and French-speaking groups were a small minority, dwelling among millions, let us say, of North American Indians far more primitive than our Indians of today; where these same tribesmen performed all the basic work of the country; and where our neighbours across the border were not people very much like ourselves but were, instead, a hundred and fifty million even more primitive Indians!

Such a strange imaginary picture may help us not only to understand South Africa's racial problem, but to recognize how far this land of great problems has come, despite its difficulties. For the Union of South Africa is still the most modern and highly developed country on the African continent, modern in its fine buildings, roads, railways, and airways, in its schools and universities, and in its system of social legislation. It may yet lead the rest of Africa to civilization.[82]

Apologists for the white minority regime in South Africa continued until its final years to defend racism's stronghold by making unflattering comparisons to the treatment of Aboriginal peoples in Canada. In 1989, for instance, Angus M. Gunn, a Professor Emeritus at the University of British Columbia and a friend of the Hoover Institute at Stanford University, contrasted the Sechelt self-government legislation in Canada with what he argued were more sweeping and more democratic changes then taking place on the old Bantustans of South Africa:

As part of the process of dismantling apartheid, the [South African] government has given new powers and autonomy to the self-governing states. Functions such as planning, development, administration and maintenance of townships, all are examples of the new functions being handed over to local authorities. Meanwhile, in Canada, a 1988 measure of self-government, for one group, has been acclaimed as a breakthrough for native rights, despite the fact that it falls short of the autonomy given by the South African government to its native peoples.[83]

Gunn's discussion of the the the P.W. Botha government's treatment of South Africa's Indigenous peoples leaves out the harsh details of the violence, bribery, and intimidation involved in the cultivation of a class of Black collaborators willing to cooperate with the white minority regime in presenting as self-government what in reality was indirect rule. Ironically this tactic of subjugation, whose ruthless workings would in later years come partially to light through the investigations of the Truth and Reconciliation Commission chaired by Bishop Desmond Tutu, was justified in the name of equality and of the universal franchise. "The principle of one man, one vote has long been accepted in South Africa," argued South African president P.W. Botha in 1986. He added, "It all depends in which structure you want to apply it."[84]

There is scope for vast manipulations of conflicting meanings in the language of citizenship, enfranchisement, and self-government for Indigenous peoples. The extension of citizenship to Indigenous peoples in nation-states not of their own makings and unreflective of their own languages and cultures can become a two-sided sword over time. The essential consideration in determining if this form of citizenship is a means of defence or a weapon of aggression turns on whether Indigenous peoples constitute a majority or a small minority of the population of the nation-states that have coalesced on their lands. In South Africa, for instance, where Indigenous peoples collectively far outnumber their colonizers by at least six to one, the mandate of apartheid was to direct the political actions of "tribal" peoples away from the white government of the South African Union towards "self-government" on reserves, or Bantustans or homelands, comprising less than one-quarter of the country's land mass.

In countries such as Canada or the United States, where Indigenous peoples have become a small portion of the overall population, the politics of citizenship cut in different directions. To enwrap Indigenous peoples in the legal clothing of normal citizenship after they have been pushed from their lands and after they have been economically and politically marginalized can be to advance the fiction that the newly enfranchised groups somehow have sanctioned the legal regime that has dispossessed them. Moreover, the entry of already marginalized First Nations people into regular citizenship can seem to further their legal assimilation as individuals, undermining their cohesiveness as groups – as peoples – in political regimes whose course and direction they have little chance to influence or substantially to steer.

In one of his final speeches before he was defeated by Phil Fontaine in his 1997 bid for re-election as national chief of the Assembly of First Nations in Canada, Ovide Mercredi underlined the way the concept of equality can be used as a political and legal weapon against Indigenous peoples. "They talk of equality *after* they've taken our land," Mercredi said. "They talk of equality *after* they've taken our resources."[85] This blurring of legal lines between citizenship in a nation-state and citizenship in a First Nation has particularly complex implications for those Aboriginal societies whose members hold and esteem their treaties with other sovereign authorities. How can Indigenous peoples in Canada retain their status as "allies" of the crown if they are concurrently subject to crown law under a uniform regime of "equal" Canadian citizenship?

In South Africa the question of citizenship was decided by 1994 when the country ushered in "majority rule" under the new regime led by President Nelson Mandela.[86] In the United States, American citizenship was formally extended to Indians in 1924 by an Act of Congress. In Australia a referendum sanctioned the admission of Aborigines into citizenship in 1967.[87] In Canada the relationship of Indians, Inuit, and Métis peoples to citizenship remains ambivalent and unclear to this day, a function in part of the growing number of question marks surrounding the reality of a country where the constitution was patriated from Great Britain against the explicit objections of both the government of Quebec and several coalitions of First Nations.[88] For the half million people in Canada registered by the federal government as status Indians, no less than for the seven million citizens of Quebec, their official relationship to the laws and institutions of Canada are matters of ambivalence and contestation. For Aboriginal people – both for those who are registered by the federal government as well as for the potentially larger group who are unregistered but self-identifying – this contention grows out of the uncertainty of living amid what might be described as two legal countries.

INDIGENOUS PEOPLES, LIBERALISM, AND THE IRONIC LEGACIES OF BRITISH IMPERIALISM

The Aboriginal reserves and reservations that have been set aside in the course of European imperialism and in the rise of Creole nationalism stand as monuments to the central place afforded to partition and to "ethnic cleansing" in the expansion of Western civilization. These remaining plots stand as markers of deeply held convictions of how the apportionment of land should be made to conform to imagined hierarchies of race and Creole progress. To appreciate this way of viewing reserves more fully it is necessary to remind ourselves what they tell us about the history of the territories outside these remnant fragments of once-cohesive Aboriginal realms. The extension of the principles of private property to these reserved areas is the culminating sleight of hand in the push to create a New World of tiered materialism in the place of many Old Worlds.[89] In the Aboriginal ecologies of these Old Worlds, humans, plants, and other creatures share the land through a plurality of unwritten legal tenures and covenants linking different species as well as past and future generations.

To privatize under non-Aboriginal law the last of the remaining Aboriginal domains in the name of equal citizenship is to perpetuate and extend the ecological extinguishment embodied in the monoculture of possessive individualism. This termination, however, is still widely promoted as the final solution to the Aboriginal question throughout many parts of the Western world. In 1997, for instance, the Reform Party was elected as Canada's official opposition on a platform that included a recycling of Trudeau's 1969 plan to terminate reserves and complete the legal assimilation of Indian status and Indian institutions into the matrix of regular Canadian citizenship. A similar policy was promoted, concurrently, in Australia by the One Nation Party. The parallelism between the polarization of mainstream politics around the Aboriginal title question, especially in Australia and British Columbia, suggests that the expanding network of alliances embodied in the Fourth World has stimulated an increasingly global rejection of the recognition of Indigenous peoples as self-governing polities bridging domestic and international law.

Uncertainty over the meaning of liberalism is one of the main sources of confusion surrounding the push to eliminate cultural pluralism

through the extinguishment of the collective Aboriginal titles of Indigenous peoples. While the primary bias of liberalism points towards the
equality of individuals before the law, this attribute is increasingly at odds
with liberalism's other great preoccupation – self-determination and, especially, the self-determination of peoples. The conflict between these two
competing centres of liberal thought is intensified as global corporations
claim the rights of individuals and of naturalized citizenship in all the
nation-states in which they do business. At the same time the largest corporations claim forms of transnational citizens' rights at the global level
which are not available to human "persons" in their capacity as citizens of
national governments.[90]

This new breed of global corporate citizen gains standing not available
to individual human beings through its ability to acquire direct access to
the supranational courts being established at the World Trade Organization and in the complex of trading blocks that are becoming the *de facto*
regional branches of an inchoate planetary commercial federation. This
global trade federation is proving to reach far beyond the boundaries of
even the most ambitious architects of the imperial federation that once
captured the imagination of those seeking to further the democratization
of a transformed British Empire.

The historic wording of the Indian Act in Canada, which defined a
"person" – a citizen – as "an individual other than an Indian," casts a
revealing light on a broad range of legal manipulations that disqualified
large portions of the world's population from participating as equals in
the formative stages of the capital accumulation that formed the material basis of the planet's dominant financial system. Where racial and civilizational definitions were historically integrated into the law to legitimate the dispossession of Indigenous peoples of their ancestral lands
and resources, it is increasingly clear in the current era that possession
of significant wealth is the real requirement for the exercise of citizens'
(corporate) rights. The ability to hire and retain influential lawyers represents the effective entry point in the process of transforming theoretical rights into implemented rights. That requirement creates a huge
bias against precisely those groups whose vulnerability to arbitrary
actions by the powerful often provided the original rationale for the
formulation of domestic and international instruments of protection for
human rights.

The appropriation by business corporations of the legal personality of
personhood increasingly makes the theory of liberal democracy a facade
for the tyranny of a corporate command economy on a global scale. As
proponents of the totalitarian globalization of possessive individualism
seek to legitimate this system through invoking the language of the
Enlightenment's most evocative declarations on the equality of individuals,
Indigenous peoples acquire enhanced strategic importance as personifications the planet's oldest surviving polities. The antiquity and continuity

of group-based Aboriginal identities, titles, and rights gives Indigenous peoples important legal anchors to provide political and juridical resistance against those who would atomize all forms of cohesive community not assimilated into neo-liberal paradigms of unfettered commercialization. Similarly, old imperial structures emerge with new meaning and new relevance as legal instruments to help check the seemingly limitless frontier expansionism of neo-liberal forms of globalization.

Pre-eminent among such instruments is the Royal Proclamation of 1763 and the associated tradition of treaty making and treaty renewal that is interconnected with this extending Covenant Chain of transcultural negotiations and communications. While the Royal Proclamation has its origins in the British colonization of North America, the key provision it entrenches offers seminal constitutional articulation of a principle that should be as integral to international law as the prohibition on slavery. This provision stipulates that Indigenous peoples have a basic democratic right to a collective say in how their Aboriginal lands will be apportioned, employed, exploited, or developed by newer societies moving into their ancestral territories.

In *Native Liberty, Crown Sovereignty*, Bruce Clark presents a legal analysis of the constitutional substance of imperial structures as they relate to Indigenous peoples. A major legacy from the Royal Proclamation are "*imperial* enclaves of Indian jurisdiction in *constitutional* law." These enclaves of Indian jurisdiction have in some instances never been extinguished, although this old structure of recognition of Aboriginal titles and rights has been papered over with contradictory domestic legislation, starting with the Province of Canada's first Indian Act. In reflecting on the alleged unwillingness of the judiciary to bring out in their jurisprudence the contemporary implications of the imperial recognition of the existing right of Aboriginal self-government, Clark writes:

One is left to conjecture the reason for this overlooking of the imperially made constitutional law. The suggestion has been that litigators and legal analysts have tended to adopt a regional rather than an imperial perspective, which has precluded identification of the uniformity of the imperial scheme. The further surmise offered here is that the integration ethic has so dominated the psychology of recent jurists that the existence of enclaves, resting upon ancient segregation ideology, was mentally excluded from consideration. The overall scheme of the imperial legislation, incorporating the segregation ideology by confirming or constituting separate governments for the natives and colonizing races, was simply not addressed. It remained out of sight and out of mind. The paradox is that not only has the twentieth-century democratic ethos fostered the integration ethic which has pre-empted a ready recognition of the existing aboriginal right of self-government, but this same liberal democratic ethos has also fostered the self-determination ethic, which now demands for its satisfaction the establishment of the right as if it were a new idea.[91]

The strategic geopolitical role of Indigenous peoples, especially in

North America, is confirmed by Will Kymlicka in his treatise *Liberalism, Community, and Culture.* His object is to clarify liberalism's ability to balance the distinct existence of "cultural communities" with the individual rights and responsibilities implied by citizenship in a state. In making this argument, the situation of Indigenous peoples in Canada emerges as the author's classic case in point. How can First Nations individuals be truly free, Kymlicka asks, unless their rights are respected to sustain and develop together their own Aboriginal communities of shared heritage, language, culture, law, and politics? In attempting to resolve liberalism with the existing Aboriginal and treaty rights entrenched in the Canadian constitution, Kymlicka seems to imply that a tradeoff is also necessary to tailor these same rights to liberalism's unalterable requirements. He justifies the inescapably assimilationist cut of this proposal in terms which invoke the imperatives of political adaptation in the real world. "Aboriginal rights," he argues," at least in their most robust form, will only be secure when they are viewed, not as competing with liberalism, but as an essential component of liberal political practice."

Kymlicka is especially critical of liberal juridical enterprise in the United States, where the preoccupation with a "colour-blind constitution" associated with the American civil rights movement has tended to result in the failure to give serious legal and philosophical attention to Aboriginal rights as anything other than a sideshow or anomaly of American statecraft. "The refusal to consider the distinct situation of Indians," he writes, "is a common affliction of modern American liberal thought." Kymlicka closes his book by arguing that, in a global context, the situation of Blacks in America is more of an anomaly than the situation of Indians. Neglecting to mention that in some countries such as Guatemala, Indigenous people are a majority, Kymlicka writes: "Far more of the world's minorities are in a similar position to the American Indians (i.e. as a stable and geographically distinct historical community with separate language and culture rendered a minority by conquest or immigration or the redrawing of political boundaries) ... The issues raised by Indian status are confronted daily in countries all over the world."[92]

In the closing years of the First World War, US president Woodrow Wilson contributed a series of seminal ideas to the global community, joined as never before in the trauma of a truly global war. These concepts, built around the core affirmation that all *peoples* have a right to self-determination, still hold great potential to extend the boundaries of liberalism to express, rather than atomize, the principles of cultural pluralism. This pluralism could find vigorous expression in the recognition of existing Aboriginal and treaty rights as an integral feature of global geopolitics. The recognition that the inherent democratic right to self-determination applies to *peoples* as well as to individuals extends the idea of equality before the law. Moreover, the legal conception of "peoples" remains, for the time being at least, beyond the grasp of those who seek to expand the powers and profits of their corporations by appropriating the juridical identity and rights of "persons."

This sleight of hand, which treats human persons and corporate persons as equal citizens, constitutes one of the central problems of our ailing liberal democracies. Unlike human persons, who are mortal, corporate persons are potentially immortal. While corporations are agencies chartered by the state to negotiate market forces and political forces, they are exempt from the biological forces of birth, death, and procreation. The treatment of Aboriginal humans as non-persons – as wards of the state – highlights the importance of the legal constructions attached to the idea of personhood in the present architecture of world order. It underlines why, for instance, the Zapatistes characterize their opponents as proponents of neo-liberalism.

The developing controversies and contradictions swirling around the word "liberalism" were anticipated by President Wilson's emphasis on the inherent right of all peoples to self-determination. To some extent his ideas were advanced in response to the position taken by the new Soviet regime led by Vladimir Illich Lenin. Lenin's assertions that the revolutionary movement in his country was antagonistic to imperialism in all its manifestations helped push Wilson to clarify that the United States, too, was a revolutionary country that had been born into the world from a liberal revolt against imperialism. He wanted to clarify why the United States was bringing its enormous military might into what was, up until then, primarily a European conflagration. He wanted to emphasize that the United States's intervention was not to bolster one empire's power over another but to liberate and democratize the diverse societies of central Europe in particular.[93] Wilson's focus on *peoples* as the primary unit of self-determination on a more democratized planet was resisted in his home country and, subsequently, at the League of Nations, which the United States did not join. After the Second World War, however, the United Nations became a forum where the principle that all peoples have a right of self-determination was repeated again and again in many of the international body's key declarations and conventions.[94]

Indeed, the United Nations entered the world in its founding charter as an assembly of peoples. Where the United States announced its legitimacy by declaring its source emanating from "we the people," the United Nations announced the source of its legitimacy as emanating from "we the peoples." The course of history running between these two declarations can thus be interpreted as an extension of the classical illumination of the Enlightenment from the liberalism of individual equality to the liberalism of equity among peoples; and from the democratization of nations states to the democratization of the global community. Although the principle of the self-determination of peoples has been one of the most powerful animating notions in recent world history, especially during the decolonization of the old European empires, the idea has been applied very selectively. One of the strongest forces against the principle's wider application has been the shared interest of the governments of nation-states to retain their theoretical monopolization of the exercise of sovereignty in the international community. The other side of this shared interest has been a common inclination on the part of national governments to hold all questions pertaining to the titles and rights of Indigenous peoples within the framework of domestic laws, courts, and policies.

This shared inclination tends to be reflected in the way resistance movements of Indigenous peoples are covered and reported in the media. Occasionally, however, incidents such as the flare up at Wounded Knee in 1973, the standoff at Oka in 1990, the Zapatista uprising in Chiapas in 1994, or the resistance of the Indigenous peoples of East Timor to Indonesia's genocidal assaults resonate with such forceful global meaning that the institutional pressures to restrain Aboriginal issues within domestic frameworks is temporarily transcended. The march for reconciliation with Indigenous peoples across Sydney Harbour Bridge in May 2000 was clearly one of those moments when events transpired in a way that went beyond the politics of one particular country. The fact that the walk attracted 250,000 marchers, a group that represents a significant proportion of Australia's population, suggested that an especially potent idea had been liberated with the power to mobilize large numbers of people.

Another episode that transcended domestic boundaries occurred when Louis Stevenson, chief of the Peguis Band in Manitoba, responded with a dramatic gesture to Prime Minister Mulroney's dismissal in 1987 of any link between Indian Affairs in Canada and apartheid in South Africa. Chief Stevenson challenged this interpretation by inviting Glenn Babb, South Africa's ambassador to Canada, to visit his reserve and compare its poverty and poor housing with the conditions of South African homelands.[95] Babb accepted. On his tour he was accompanied by representatives of several right-wing coalitions and associations in western Canada, Aboriginal and non-Aboriginal. Among these self-declared friends of the South African government were several members of the Saskatchewan Indian Business Development Association. Linda Freeman wrote of them: "Like the class that was created to run the governments of South African bantustans, this group of native leaders emerged from institutions established by provincial and federal governments in Canada to manage aboriginal and social development."[96] The visit was treated as front-page news in Canada and South Africa. In South Africa the episode gave a propaganda coup to the white minority regime's efforts to characterize Mulroney's anti-apartheid diplomacy, especially in the Commonwealth, as hypocritical.

The Peguis episode caused a rush of exchanges between the Assembly of First Nations and the James Bay Cree with officials of the African National Congress. The visit was ultimately matched in 1990 when Chiefs Roy Kaminawash and Gerry Mackay took ANC delegate Bishop Desmond Tutu on a tour of the Osnaburgh, an Indian reserve in northern Ontario that displayed many of the pathologies of poverty and unemployment characterizing the most marginalized parts of Indian Country. Moreover, like many Aboriginal communities, Osnaburgh's biggest problems originated primarily in a massive industrial intervention into the indigenous ecology of its citizens' Aboriginal domain. In this case, the intervention led to massive flooding of the old settlements, together with destruction of the wild rice gardens.

The historical record leaves no doubt, therefore, that the evolution of Aboriginal policies in Canada and South Africa converged at many points in the context of the British Empire, the Commonwealth, and, later, in the resistance movements of Indigenous peoples in both countries.[97] While there are similarities, there are also tremendous discontinuities in both national histories: the central difference is that newcomers to Canada and their descendants – the Creoles – usually outnumbered the Indigenous peoples, whereas a key factor in the construction of South African apartheid was the imposition by a minority population of political rule over an Aboriginal majority.

The numerical domination of Indigenous peoples in Canada has been less marked than in the United States, a country whose elaborate legacy of "race relations" from slavery has taken this most powerful of New World polities, especially in its early years, along many roads similar to those travelled by the white government in South Africa.[98] These distinctions and parallels aside, however, all three countries share the fundamental reality of the massive appropriation of lands and resources from the Old World Aboriginal societies, which were either eliminated or contained on comparatively small reserves. Moreover, the Indigenous people were precluded by law, with some few exceptions, from participation as groups or individuals in the land market, in corporation building, and in the process of drafting and implementing the overarching political architecture of those Creole states that developed on their ancestral territories. In all three countries, as in most of the "West" beyond Europe, these sweeping acts of dispossession and disenfranchisement were justified by defining Indigenous peoples as primitive and uncivilized, and, therefore, as wards and guardians under the higher trusteeship and tutelage of the state.[99] Moreover, even this act of paternalistic rationalization often disguised far harsher realities. As Samuel Huntington reminds us in *The Clash of Civilizations*, the growth of Western civilization was achieved "not by the superiority of its ideas or values or religion ... but rather by its superiority in applying organized violence."[100]

THE ORIGINS OF PROPERTY AND CAPITAL IN THE RACIALIZED ECONOMY OF GLOBAL APARTHEID

The complexity and rawness of the long encounter in South Africa between Aboriginal Africans and Europeans and their Creole descendants has produced some of colonialism's most dramatic outcomes. Similarly, the study of this monumental encounter has resulted in major works of literature and scholarship that illuminate many of the larger implications of Europe's incredibly aggressive expansion of influence into the cultures, territories, and economies of many thousands of Indigenous peoples all over the planet. One such work was J.A. Hobson's *Imperialism: A Study,* published in 1902.

Hobson was an English journalist who covered the Boer War. He wrote of this experience as "a turning point in my career and an illumination to my understanding of the real relations between economics and politics." He connected imperialism, as epitomized by the activities of Cecil Rhodes and the British South Africa Company, primarily to the science of economics. Hobson argued that in the metropolitan countries, capitalists looked to their governments to push their way into new markets for their surplus production, resulting from the low pay to workers and the consequent "underconsumption" at home. Much like Silburn in *The Governance of Empire,* Hobson characterized the governance of Basutoland after 1884 as an example of what he called "sane imperialism." He lauded the imperial government's administration of Basutoland, which concentrated on the education of Basuto youth and on the protection of Basuto resources. Beyond these aspects of imperial rule, most aspects of colonial governance, including Basutoland's system of land tenure, were left within the internal jurisdiction of the Basuto people's own traditional structures. Hobson compared this approach with what he called "insane imperialism ... which hands over these [Aboriginal] races to the economic exploitation of white colonists who will use them as 'live tools' and their lands as repositories of mining or other profitable treasure."[101]

By contrasting the imperialism embodied in the governance of Basutoland with the other extreme represented by the unfettered control over Indigenous peoples by the white business interests of "Johannesburg and Rhodesia," Hobson invoked a more recent manifestation of an old controversy in the Aboriginal policies of the British Empire. The same dichotomy of interests and philosophies came into conflict in the rift between British imperial Canada, whose administrators left a large degree of self-governance to the First Nations, and the pre-revolutionary Anglo-American colonies. Where the former was organized around the principle that the imperial government was a protector of Aboriginal rights and titles, the latter tended to be dominated by land speculators and frontiersmen seeking to extinguish all imperial and Aboriginal restraints to the westward expansion of their privatized titles and settlements.

Lenin seized on Hobson's *Imperialism* as a major source of interpretation for his more polemical *Imperialism, the Highest Stage of Capitalism,* published in 1916.[102] As we have seen, the politicization of theories of imperialism played a role in the propaganda contest between Wilson and Lenin to appeal to world public opinion, as their diplomats vied with one another to influence the shape of global geopolitics after the First World War. The very first episode of ideological conflict between the capitalist United States and the communist Soviet Union created the strategic opening to introduce the concept that the planet should be reorganized to express democratically the self-determination of all *peoples*. As we have seen, the state philosophies of these competing regimes were derived, respectively, in part at least, from the Enlightenment traditions of Locke and Rousseau, both of whom presented themselves as authorities on natural law as manifested in the lives of Indigenous peoples beyond Europe.

In the years ahead, Hobson's and Lenin's texts generated detractors who advanced many other theories to explain the workings of imperialism.[103] The extent of this revision, however, forms a testament to the intellectual influence of Hobson's original theories. In 1996 Titus Alexander published a work that carried forward the legacy of Hobson's *Imperialism* by again characterizing South Africa as an illustration in miniature of some of the main political and economic forces at work in the world. In an elaborately documented fashion, he argued that the international systems governing the generation and apportionment of wealth and property duplicate similar kinds of enforced inequities to those maintained in South Africa before 1993. While the concept of race is not emphasized in what Alexander calls "global apartheid," the legacy of the racial hierarchies created by the old imperialisms of Europe are a central factor in the new hierarchies of wealth and power supported by bodies such as the World Trade Organization, the International Monetary Fund, the World Bank, the UN Security Council, the G8, and the Organization for Economic Co-operation and Development.

White South Africa was one of the world's richest states in the midst of poor African peoples. Three-quarters of the land and all its natural resources could only be owned by whites, a sixth of the population. The West also has a sixth of the world's population and commands over three-quarters of global resources. Not only did Europeans colonize large parts of the world's arable lands, particularly in the Americas, but they control most of the rest through market forces.

Alexander presents a compelling picture of an international system designed to facilitate the extraction of wealth from what he calls "the Majority World" and to concentrate wealth in "the West." The prevailing tendency in this regime of global apartheid is, Alexander argues, to further impoverish the poor in order to further enrich the rich. Among the statistics presented to illustrate this point are those from the World Bank, showing that between 1960 and 1993 the disparity between the richest and the poorest 20 per cent of the world's population rose from 30:1 to 70:1, in other words by 250 per cent![104] Canada's prime minister, Jean Chrétien, referred to the growing disparities in the global economy in his televised reflections on the first anniversary of the events of 11 September 2001. "I do think the Western world is getting too rich in relation to the poor world," he said. "And necessarily, we're looked upon as being arrogant, self-satisfied, greedy and with no limits. And the 11th of September is an occasion for me to realize it even more."[105]

This rapid concentration of wealth in fewer and fewer hands is polarizing economic relations *within* the West in much the same way that the process is increasing tension between the "industrial countries" and the "developing countries." Lester Thurow, an economist from the Massachusetts Institute of Technology, presented dramatic evidence of this process in 1999. He demonstrated that the real wages of 60 per cent of the population of the United States in the previous two decades had dropped by 20 per cent.[106] This erosion of middle-class status for working people was paralleled by a startling rise in the growth of a massive, largely privatized prison industry to incarcerate a large part of the American underclass. Between 1977 and 2000 the number of people in jail in the United States jumped from 300,000 to almost 2 million.[107] With this huge increase in inmates, the United States led the world, except for Russia and Rwanda, in its rate of locking up its own people. In most European countries the percentage of people incarcerated is about one-seventh of that in the world's sole remaining superpower. Black males are about seven times as likely as white males to spend time in prison. In fourteen states, inmates lose their right to vote for the rest of their lives. In most other states, incarcerees and former incarcerees are disenfranchised until their parole comes to an end. The result is that almost 4 million adult citizens of the United States have been denied the most emblematic hallmark of a democracy – the right to cast electoral ballots for candidates of their choice. Almost half of these disenfranchised Americans are Black, a factor that was decisive in the controversial outcome of the US presidential election in 2000.[108] By the end of the twentieth century, the 550 or so of the world's billionaires owned property equivalent to that owned by the poorest 50 per cent of the planet's entire population![109] A key factor in this pattern of intensifying inequities was the transformation of transnational corporations into global corporations. In their growing domination of the world's economy, these immense conglomerates acquired new capacities to dominate the political branches of most nation-states. Their consistent aim was to privatize much of the remaining public sphere as well as to manipulate property law in ways that furthered neo-liberal patterns of globalization.

At the dawn of the new millennium, slightly over half of the world's 100 richest economies were corporations. In terms of money changing hands, General Motors was larger than Denmark, Ford was larger than South Africa, and Mitsubishi, the world's biggest corporation, was larger than Indonesia even before the onset of political instability and the economic recession in that part of Asia in 1997–98. The world's 200 largest corporations sold more annually than the combined gross domestic product of 182 countries – in other words, of all nation-states in the world except the nine largest![110] Although the world's top 200 corporations had combined sales equivalent to 28 per cent of the world's entire gross domestic product, they employed only one-third of 1 per cent of the planet's population.[111]

The growing disparities of wealth were highlighted and dramatized when the bankruptcy of Enron Corporation in the United States in 2001 helped to bring to light a number of other corporate scandals. The common theme to emerge from the mounting revelations was the extent to which many chief executive officers had exploited the deregulatory cycles initiated in the era of Thatcherism and Reaganomics. CEO pay in many of the United States's largest corporations had increased in the 1990s in the order of 500 per cent. According to the United States's largest labour organization, between 1980 and 2000 the pay differential between an average CEO in one of America's larger corporations and an average blue-collar worker had jumped from about 42:1 to about 531:1.[112] The pay increases sometimes dwarfed the vast fortunes derived from the combination of dubious accounting practices and lucrative stock option deals.[113] The revelations in 2002 contributed to the view that too many corporate insiders had stolen large chucks of the modest wealth of regular stock market investors. The resulting decline in the value of stock markets, the most dynamic agencies of possessive individualism in our current era, created added unease about the broader implications of allowing unlimited latitude to neo-liberal forms of globalization.

In spite of the conditions of increased austerity and heightened militarism at the beginning of the twenty-first century, entrenched habits and patterns proved resistant to change. Many large corporations continued to rid themselves of staff and manufacturing capacity to become specialists in the marketing of brand names rather than the selling of products. More and more the actual goods to which the megamarketed brand names adhered were produced in milieus where low-wage labour in sweatshop conditions was maintained through the coercive enforcement of strict anti-union regimes. What has emerged from these geoeconomic transformations is a global society where the logos of planetary corporations increasingly dominate physical and imaginative space to such an extent that these ubiquitous symbols of corporate differentiation are made to seem pre-eminent; they are made to seem as though they have already overwhelmed all other forms of ecological diversity in the human, plant, and animal realms; they are made to seem like nature's pre-eminent display of pluralism.[114]

The huge concentration of wealth in fewer and fewer hands has developed in a world where the total production of goods and services between 1950 and 1997 grew from $5 trillion to $29 trillion. In spite of this statistical expansion of wealth 33,000 children under five, almost all of them

poor, die every day. As one observer has commented, "in no act of genocide, in no act of war, are so many people killed per minute, per hour, and
per day as those who are killed by hunger and poverty on this planet." The
speaker was Fidel Castro, the longstanding president of Cuba and the
quintessential *bête noire* of the American empire of private property.[115] In
his acceptance speech for an award from the World Health Organization,
Castro continued:

Why in this world which produces almost $30 trillion worth of goods and services
per year, do one billion three hundred million human beings live in absolute
poverty, receiving less than a dollar a day – when there are those who receive more
than a million dollars a day? Why do 800 million lack the most basic health services
when the cost of providing a minimal level of health care protection to all the citizens of the world – an amount estimated in 1998 dollars at $25 billion – amounts
to just 3% of the amount devoted annually to armaments. Why are there 250 million children in the world forced to work? Why do 2 million girls become prosti-
tutes every year? Why do 15% of the world's population consume 82% of the
world's medicine while the whole rest of the world have access to only 18%?[116]

Huge historical questions lurk just beneath the surface of these
immense and growing divisions in the world, where the ecomomy has
been structured so that a small number of human beings are afforded a
measure of material worth many millions of times higher than the largest
mass of poor individuals. There is simply no escaping some kind of fundamental reckoning with the origins of the basic divisions splitting win-
ners from losers in this global economy of vast polarities between an entitled minority and a disentitled, disenfranchised, and dispossessed
majority. There is, for instance, no escaping some reckoning with the fact
that the peoples most radically marginalized and dispossessed in the elaboration of the global economy tend overwhelmingly to be the children
and grandchildren of those most negatively affected by earlier acts of dispossession and disenfranchisement on which the overseas empires of
Europe were founded. Similarly, there is no escaping some reckoning
with the fact that the busy structuring of the global economy as an increasingly moncultural empire of private property tends to favour the children
and grandchildren of those who benefited most from the original transformation into capital of the lands and resources of Indigenous peoples
beyond Europe's shores.

There is much that is disingenuous in the neo-liberal justification of
"free trade" in terms that emphasize the *political* equality of citizens (and
corporations) but which stridently avoid any fundamental grappling with
the origins and genesis of such gargantuan *economic* inequalities in society.
Although this issue is pervasively global, the historical issues that surround it are highlighted particularly in the study of slavery and the dispossession of Indigenous peoples, not only in the Americas, but around

the world. One variant of the growing movement to address these inequities in public policy has introduced the legal concept of "vicarious liability" to identify the onus of responsibility held by the recipients of wrongfully appropriated labour and resources. South Africa provides a clear window on the extent to which humanity is coping, or not, with the contemporary legacy of an economy founded on such stunning acts of legalized theft. What statutes of limitation are to be observed in the laundering of that part of the capital in the global ecomony whose origins lie in primal acts of appropriation and privatization of whole continents and populations that were rendered as the currency and basic staple of the slave trade? How much of the global economy, as monopolized increasingly by a merging concentration of global megacorporations, is based on an amassment of wealth facilitated originally by the creation of laws that divided humanity along lines of race, culture, and the imagined dichotomy between savagery and civilization? To what extent is the global economy still a planetary kleptocracy?

In December 1997, as he prepared to step down from the leadership of the African National Congress, Nelson Mandela said in a speech in Mafikeng that real democracy in his country was still in its early and most vulnerable infancy. The extension of the franchise to the Black majority was just the beginning, rather than the end, of a process where the most difficult problem would be to address the *economic* disparities arising from apartheid. Accordingly, Mandella insisted that "a major and determined effort will have to be made by both the public and private sectors to realize this objective of deracializing the economy."[117] Mandela's implicit identification of a *racialized economy* has a powerful, broadly felt resonance. What real reconciliation can there be when the dominant group in a racially structured society agree that their criteria of political and legal discrimination were wrong, but they then hold onto their economic advantages without acknowledging that the source of this wealth is connected to the original dispossession, disenfranchisement, or enslavement of racially stigmatized people on which the system of property relations was founded? Surely this question is one that can as easily be posed in all those nation-states on the planet whose development depended, and in many cases still does depend, on a primal expropriation of Aboriginal lands. Such states include Canada and the United States, Mexico and Guatemala, New Zealand and Australia, Norway and Sweden, Nigeria and Indonesia, northern Russia and Chinese Tibet.

Some important episodes in globalization's more recent sagas are unfolding around initiatives to protect the owners of capital acquired from those racialized economies that have their origins in the worldwide expansions of European empires. The effort to create what was known as the Multilateral Agreement on Investment presented a classic example of one such iniative. A big part of the rationale for integrating nation-states into the global regime of this proposed treaty was to protect investors –

the owners of capital – from the possibility of having their assets expropriated in any way through the legislative enactments of any participating government.

The irony of the MAI was that so much of its language was appropriated from the terminology of the civil rights movement. One of its major objects was to outlaw all forms of "discrimination" by governments that might be tempted to extend various kinds of preferred treatment to local rather than foreign corporations. This effort to standardize global property law and shield monetary investment from any form of "expropriation" calls attention to the lack of any similar safeguards for Indigenous peoples facing expropriation of their Aboriginal lands and resources. Indeed, the MAI would have created global law whose effect would have been to protect the owners of that part of the world's financial capital that is derived, in part at least, from the extinguishment and privitization of Aboriginal territories. The MAI would have outlawed many forms of democratic effort to break down what Titus Alexander terms global apartheid. The effort to institute a global law to prohibit some forms of expropriation and to further the protections for those forms of legalized theft rooted in the racialized economy revealed a double standard whose injustice goes far beyond South Africa.

The political organization of groups and individuals opposed to the Multilateral Agreement on Investment represented the consolidation of many new alliances and coalitions. These coalitions found shared purpose in opposing the continuing privatization of the global commons and the further monopolization of the political and economic power by agents of global corporations. The early signs of this resistance caused those interests behind MAI to move the initiative in the mid–1990s from the World Trade Organization to the Paris-based Organization for Economic Co-operation and Development. This change in venue excluded the world's poorer countries, narrowing the negotiations to twenty-eight of the world's richest countries.

In 1998, resistance by organized lobbies within these richer countries, including France and Canada, caused an apparent retreat of governments away from negotiations of the MAI. This retreat was accompanied by suggestions that the would-be law givers behind MAI will return to the World Trade Organization in order to realize a global regime where the investments of global corporations will be put beyond the legislative control of nation-states, Indigenous peoples, and other centres of possible democratic resistance to the economic inequities at the base of global apartheid.[118]

TWO LEGAL COUNTRIES:
THE AMERICAN EMPIRE AND THE FOURTH WORLD

In *Latin America: At War with the Past*, Carlos Fuentes reflected on the distinction between "the two nations" that live in the heart of every Latin American polity. The great dichotomies he saw in the history of his peoples pose "revolutionary populism versus monarchical authority," for instance, or the grant to Indians everywhere of "full civil liberties and equality" even as they remain "victims of serfdom." He describes these two nations as "the legal country and the real country."[119]

While the old superpower polarization between the United States and the Soviet Union has passed into history, a new duality of conviction and philosophy has emerged to apportion the planet between what might be called two legal countries of perception, philosophy, and history. The dominant global country can be characterized as the empire of possessive individualism. Its most characteristic features were illustrated in the creation and expansion of the United States as the New World instrument of an imagined Manifest Destiny to extend to global proportions the Columbian conquests. As Fred Anderson has argued, the Seven Years' War was the most decisive event in global history that created the conditions from which the United States emerged.[120] That event, frequently described in the United States as the French and Indian War, led to the reorientation of imperial power in ways without which the national history of the American republic could never have begun. The United States's own national history began later, with the revolt in the Thirteen Anglo-American colonies against the British imperial parent.

The Seven Years' War began with a clash of conflicting visions over how to structure intercultural relations with Indigenous peoples in the Ohio Valley, a strategic region that presented a major key to North American hegemony for both the French and British empires. The strategists of the Longhouse Confederacy, whose capital was Onondaga, had long played these two conflicting empires off against each other to maximize their own commercial and geopolitical advantage in what Francis Jennings has called the ambiguous Iroquois empire. The breakdown of the tenuous balance of power centred in Iroquoia, however, was clarified by the failure to polish and renew the Covenant Chain at the Albany Conference of 1754.

Subsequently, the British imperial sovereign stepped more deeply into colonial politics to centralize authority over diplomatic relations with Indigenous peoples on the frontiers of the Anglo-American settlements. That assertion of imperial jurisdiction to the west of the Anglo-American settlements was integral to the genesis of the American Revolution in the years ahead. Meanwhile, the outbreak of international hostilities in the Ohio Valley after 1754 so destabilized world order that it set off a global military conflict among Europe's competing imperial powers. The instability over the geopolitical status of the Ohio Valley, a matter closely connected to uncertainty over the international status to be afforded to that region's Indigenous peoples, continued until the termination of the War of 1812.

The formal withdrawal from North America of the French imperial antagonists in the French and Indian War removed one of the rationales in the Anglo-American settlements to retain their colonial ties with Great

Britain. This geopolitical change encouraged the most expansionistic factions in British North America to reject the constraints of British imperialism and to seek an empire of their own by quickly absorbing, extinguishing, and privatizing the vast Western Indian Country. With the formation of the United States between 1776 and 1783, the sovereign machinery was developed to implement this plan of rapid and largely unregulated western expansion. The creation of the American republic as the first successor state of a European empire and as a prototype of decolonization set many patterns for the genesis of many new nationalities to come. The process of decolonization that started with the establishment of the United States continued what Bendict Anderson has descibed as the establishment of "the Creole nationalisms of the Americas." In the Spanish Empire and Brazil especially, the formation of Creole cultures involved the genesis of identities composed of peoples of European and African ancestry who were born and raised in the Americas. The revolutionary movement started by the Euro-American people who founded the United States soon spread to similar Euro-American communities in the central and southern sections of the western hemisphere. With Simon Bolivar as their primary inspirational leader, these Creole sovereigntists asserted the independence of their former colonial societies in constitutions often closely modelled on that of the United States. Meanwhile, the French Revolution, which began in 1789, embodied a kind of Europeanization of the movement of decolonization and nationalism first acted upon in the United States. The growing force of west-to-east influences in the transatlantic community prompted Anderson to argue that "nationalism emerged first in the New World, not in the Old."[121]

The exclusion of Indigenous peoples from the Creole nationalism of the United States was seminal in helping to point the global movement of decolonization towards extreme forms of ethnic nationalism. The full force of those ethnic nationalisms did not become fully clear until the last decades of the twentieth century following the major dismantling of European empires after the Second World War. The genocidal tragedies in Rwanda, Sudan, Sierra Leone, and the Balkans, for instance, defined some of the extremes of the ethnic conflicts ushered in by formal decolonization.[122] Very few of the "new nationalisms" emerging from the formal end of European empire were exempt from ethnic strife. Again and again this transfer of power from imperial to local hands privileged some ethnic groups to the disadvantage of other communities that did not share some or all of the cultural, linguistic, or religious characteristics of the new governing authorities.[123] The resulting proliferation of ethnic turmoil at the end of the twentieth century continued patterns of decolonization whose character was originally revealed in the way that the nascent American empire emerged from the British Empire.

There must be no double standards in passing judgment on those who commit crimes against humanity in what has come to be informally described as "ethnic cleansing." It is vital to remember, however, that the early Indian policies of the United States involved elaborate and sweeping forms of ethnic nationalism.[124] That attribute of both nationalism and decolonization in the world's first successor state of European imperialism established patterns and precedents that have often accompanied the dismantling of European empires, including that of the former Soviet Union, right up to this day.

The military course of the American Revolution represented in part a continuation and a heightening of the old heritage of Indian wars that had long characterized the frontier regions of the Anglo-American colonies. After the United States was formally granted its independence by the European powers in 1783, the leadership in the republic worked to edify the powers of a new central authority by investing it with the power to make peace with, or war on, the Indigenous peoples on the western frontiers of Euro-American settlements. In its early years, the central government in the world's first decolonized country made some show of attempting to adhere to the principles of international law, such as it was in that era, by purchasing Aboriginal title from Indigenous peoples in treaty negotiations. While the American republic developed its own variation on the principles codified in the Royal Proclamation of 1763, the new country gave rise to a distilled version of the most expansionary dynamic within British imperialism.[125] This aggressiveness was reflected in the United States's resort after 1871 to its own domestic interpretations of "conquest" as a primary legal explanation for the subordination and extinguishment of Indian Country to clear the way for the expansion of the quintessential New World nation.

The preference for repeated rituals of bloodletting in the western expansion of the United States became integral to the culture of the world's prototypical new nationality. The careers of two American presidents, Andrew Jackson and William Henry Harrison, serve as clear indicators of the symbolic importance of military triumph over Indians as a hallmark of worthiness for leadership during the American republic's first century. Both men achieved fame in the complex of Indian wars connected to the War of 1812.

In 1987 the US government clarified and formalized the centrality of the doctrine of "conquest" in its geopolitical formation and in its diplomatic relations with the rest of the world. That clarification came in the form of a reply from the US State Department to the United Nations Human Rights Commission. The State Department was responding to a complaint brought forward by Hopi traditionalists. Like some of the key activists of the Western Shoshone and Six Nations peoples, Hopi people have been among the most active intervenors in venues of international law.[126] In answering the Hopi complaint, the executive branch of the American government declared, "conquest renders the tribes subject to the legislative powers of the United States and, in substance, terminates the external powers of the sovereignty of the tribe."[127]

This dependence on "conquest" as the basis for the United States's claim of title and jurisdiction in its own national territory sheds a puzzling light on the status of the 367 treaties made by the government of the United States with the Indigenous peoples within its international boundaries.[128] Unlike the treaties made with the First Nations of Canada, which until 1975 were not formalized in legislative enactments by either the Canadian or the British parliaments, all similar agreements in the United States were ratified through the same process as treaties with foreign nations. That process required ratification by the American president and a two-thirds plurality of the senators in Congress.[129] As the Reverend Jeremiah Evarts detailed and elaborated in the late 1820s in an important series of articles distributed widely throughout his country,[130] one of the most serious blows ever to the integrity of the rule of law within the United States and to the country's international standing was the policy of Indian removal mounted by the administration of President Jackson in 1830. That initiative went forward in defiance of the provisions of over a hundred treaties negotiated up until that time with Indigenous peoples east of the Mississippi River. Moreover, Indian removal was advanced in defiance of the authority of the Supreme Court of the United States. In the case of *Worcester* v. *Georgia*, Chief Justice John Marshall had clarified in 1832 the pre-eminence of the federal government's responsibilities as transacted in treaties to protect Indigenous peoples from the encroachments of state governments.

While the United States violated its older treaties with Indigenous peoples, it made many new treaties with the goal of gaining some appearance of Indian sanction for the establishment of the Indian Territory west of the Mississippi on the site of present-day Oklahoma. There was a further surge of treaty activity in the years immediately following the American Civil War. In 1871, however, the nation at the emerging imperial centre of the American empire of private property went far in defining itself as a polity favouring the Darwinistic ethos of conquest over the consolidation of the rule of law both in domestic affairs and in the international community. In 1871 Congress passed a law stipulating that "no Indian nation or tribe within the territory of the United States shall be acknowledged or recognized as an independent nation, tribe, or power with whom the United States may contract by treaty."[131] The United States thus renounced the constititional heritage of the Royal Proclamation of 1763 and of the Northwest Ordinance of 1787, two legal instruments that can be interpreted as pre- and post-revolutionary markers clarifying the law of western expansion in the emergence of North America's most powerful new Creole nationality. In putting aside even the fiction that the United States's relationship with the First Nations within its boundaries was based on voluntary association through treaty, rather than on coercive subordination through conquest, the United States sent a powerful signal to the international community. As John R. Wunder has written, "The Resolution of 1871 not only represented an end to pretense in Indian relations, but it also meant a serious modification and violation of international law and a threat to the diplomacy of the United States."[132]

In 2000 and 2001 the United States Commission on National Security (USCNS), co-chaired by Gary Hart and Warren B. Rudman, issued three reports, the first of which was entitled *New World Coming*. The contents of these documents highlighted some of the internal anxieties felt within the United States as its national government grappled with its imperial role in the formal and informal structures of the American empire.[133] Central to these anxieties was the contention that "the security of the American Homeland" was menaced by a host of enemies. This anxiety over the security of "the Homeland" came at a moment when the United States was seemingly unassailable in its superpower dominance over the rest of the planet. As Phase III of the report warned, however, "just below the enormous power and prestige of the United States is a neglected and, in some cases, decaying institutional base." This anxiety over the United States's vulnerability led the reports' authors to propose the creation of a "New National Homeland Security Agency." Like so many other government plans that were rushed into implementation after the events of 11 September 2001, a Homeland security agency has since been created and elaborated. The establishment of this new bureaucracy helps to clarify that the realm of US government activity misleadingly dubbed as "national security" has all along been geared more to foreign affairs than to the United States's own domestic sphere. The report's authors argued that a big part of "homeland security" involved the militarization of space. "Space," they declared, "will become a critical and competitive military environment."[134] The commission's proposal to further the militarization of space was warmly embraced by the administration of President George W. Bush. On taking office on the basis of a dubious Supreme Court ruling, Bush's government left no doubt where it stood. The US executive branch had clearly joined the powerful lobby promoting an agenda of massive government spending to appropriate the heavens as a space-age extension of American frontierism. The decision to militarize space, regardless of its destabilizing effect on world order, marked the attainment of yet another stage of coercive domination in the genesis of what Richard Slotkin has dubbed "the Gunfighter Nation."[135] As in the decision to eschew further treaty making with Indigenous peoples in 1871, there were major geopolitical implications in the United States's move to appropriate control of space through the exercise of further military force rather than through, for instance, negotiated international settlements at the United Nations. The United States's warrior posture towards the heavens clarified its preference for continuing the legacy of conquest as the preferred means of both winning and maintaining control of "the American Homeland."

The Creole nationality at the core of the American empire thus fell back on its old dependence on "manifest destiny" as justification enough for its unilateral assertions of control over new frontiers of the terrestial and celestial commons. No amount of space-age hardware orbiting the planet, however, could provide the kind of real national security that can only come from the construction of a world order where the rule of law prevails over the rule of force as the most decisive determinant of international relations. As Jean Jacques Rousseau, one of the early sceptics of the empire of private property, mused in *The Social Contract*, "The right of conquest has no other foundation than the right of the strongest."[136]

The title of John Wunder's article on the end of Indian treaties in the United States refers to "the Alteration of Indian Rights to Their Homelands." The descriptive term "Homelands" was also used by the white minority regime to describe some of the "Bantustans" assigned to Black South Africans before the formal ending of apartheid in the early 1990s.[137] Regardless of whether one choses to read such evocative historical associations into the contemporary useage of a charged word, the USCNS's emphasis on the security of the "American Homeland" seemed discordant with an outward-gazing orientation on the part of the world's only superpower. The imagery of this homeland as a enclave set apart from the rest of the world by an elaborate infrastructure of space-bound weaponry hardly seemed like a propitious way for the United States to greet the new millennium. The plan sent the message that the rest of the planet would remain the site of potential US military operations, whereas the United States itself would become the sole jurisdiction protected with the laser equivalent of a medieval moat around a menaced castle. What was to account for the marked sense of anxiety and insecurity that seemingly took hold of the United States at the very moment of its ascent to unparalleled and unprecedented power in the global community?

According to Sha Zukang, China's chief nuclear disarmament negotiator, the United States's plans to extend the frontiers of Star Wars came "from some kind of Cold War psyche in America. People are searching for some sort of enemy, and maybe it can be China."[138] Zukang's government was given at least a temporary reprieve from being America's primary enemy when the events of 11 September 2001 turned the ire of the United States towards Osama bin Laden's al Qaeda and towards the Iraqui regime of Saddam Hussein. For all the talk of the need to fight a new kind of war, however, the new "terrorist" enemy was made to appear surprisingly similar to the old "communist" enemy of the Cold War. In the mobilization to rid the world of both threats, the US government reserved complete discretion to identify, try, and eliminate its opponents according to techniques and criteria entirely of its own choosing. When any conflicts would arise between the authority of the US government and the constraints of international law, the former would always prevail.

The attacks on the Pentagon and the World Trade Center demonstrated the lethal limitations of the envisaged Star Wars Shield that had been the centrepiece of the Bush regime's military agenda. Yet that priority was retained even as the United States moved to augment many of its other military, police, and intelligence-gathering functions. Then the objective of "regime change" in Iraq was thrust into the foreign policy spotlight of the American empire's imperial presidency. The larger symbolism of this many-faceted display of global dominance was not lost on Canada's prime minister. As Jean Chrétien looked towards his own retirement after a decade of serving as prime minister, he reflected, "You cannot exercise your powers to the point of humiliation of others. And that is what the Western world – not only the Americans but the Western world – has to realize. Because they are human beings too."[139]

Any move to embrace such principles in a viable and enduring way would have to adopt the inescapable principle that all peoples have an inherent right to self-determination. In this principle lies the core Enlightenment ideal that the power of governors can only be legitimate when based on the consent of the governed. A global rule of law based on the ideal of consent rather than on the military and economic might of the United States would have to start with a renunciation by the superpower's own governors of dependence on the force of conquest in securing the underlying title to us national territory. Accordingly, there would be vast symbolic implications in the edification of any international regime for recognizing and enforcing the principles of Aboriginal and treaty rights, including within the United States itself. Without the development of such a regime, many Indigenous peoples globally will continue to face the unbroken tyranny of the Columbian conquests. The key to breaking or maintaining this conquistadorial cycle lies in the willingness of Europe's first successor state to let go of superpower privilege to make way for a multilateral global democracy of diverse peoples.

The first major test of the American empire of possessive individualism was invested in its resolve to break up the Indian Confederacy in the land of the bowl with one spoon. In place of that bowl, American authors of the reports on national security introduced their readers in 2001 to something they identified as "the international security commons." "As the prime keepers of the international security commons," they wrote, the United States "must speak and act in ways that lead others, by dint of their own interests, to ally with American goals."[140] This reference to the politics of "interest" marks a striking move away from the kind of outward-looking optimism that the founders of the United States displayed in invoking the Enlightenment ideal of America as all humanity's land of promise and hope.

While the American empire was the dominant legal country at the beginning of the new millennium, the Fourth World emerged from the resisting side of the world's most legendary saga of frontier expansion. The Fourth World emerged as the inheritor and embodiment of the principles of global geopolitics once defended by Tecumseh and by the freedom fighters of the land of the bowl with one spoon. They fought to break the mould of Creole decolonization established by the United States and to form, instead, their own Aboriginal dominion in the heart of North America. This other legal country has embraced the Fourth World pluralism embodied in the reality that the planet is still home to an amazing array of human cultures, with 6,000 distinct languages still alive in the consciousness and communications of Indigenous peoples. This other global country is one whose citizens defend habitat and jurisdiction for the millions of plant and animal species with whom we share this planet.[141] In this global country, the idea of the Fourth World provides a kind of broad ideological umbrella to cover the changing coalitions of pluralistic resistance aimed at preventing the monocultural transformation of the entire planet at "the end of history" into "one big market."

The Indian Country of Canada has been one site where the struggle between the empire of possessive individualism and the Fourth World has been long and particularly elaborate. The changing map of Canada has been both a zone of frontier expansion for the American empire and a vast fur-trade preserve, reserved by the British sovereign to the Indians as their hunting grounds. The nascent empire of the United States was only partly successful in its military campaign directed at annexing the Indian Country of Canada during the War of 1812.

The Indian Country of Canada has been defended internationally by Deskahe. He went to Europe to infuse the League of Nations with principles from the Longhouse League and from the Covenant Chain, both models for the diplomacy and protocols of Tecumseh's Indian Confederacy. Deskahe's international initiatives were coercively countered by the actions of Prime Minister Mackenzie King, a former employee of the Rockefeller Corporation in New York. King favoured the destiny of Canada as part of the American empire, rather than as British North America, when he deployed the federal police in 1924 to crush the institutions of the Covenant Chain and of Longhouse governance, two major sites in the historic expansion of British imperial influence into the Indian Country of Canada.

While the political integrity of Indian Country has found many proponents, its ecological integrity was creatively advanced by Grey Owl. Moreover, its power as a force of transcendant artistic inspiration was captured and celebrated especially in the carvings of Bill Reid or in the paintings of Norval Morisseau. Singwaukonse, Allan Macdonell, the Reverend E.F. Wilson, and Nah-nee-ba-we-quay all brought forward powerful visions of how to blend and mix the interests of Canada and Indian Country in the difficult era when the mercantilistic culture of the fur trade gave way to the more capitalist culture of railways.

The legacy of alliance between the Indigenous peoples and the British imperial sovereign found contemporary expression when the Canadian Constitution was patriated in 1982 with a provision recognizing and affirming the existence of Aboriginal and treaty rights. The recognition of Indians, Inuit, and Métis in the constitution as Aboriginal peoples seemed calculated to become a bridge between domestic law and the United Nations covenants that projected Woodrow Wilson's thinking on the self-determination of all peoples into the frontier regions of international law.

The Indian Country of Canada provided both the contested battle ground and much of the prize to be seized in the war of convictions, philosophies, and soldiers that resulted in the birth of the new American empire from an angry revolt against the old British imperial parent. The continuing Indian Country within the United States temporarily found some relatively secure places, especially on the contested frontiers of New Spain. Creek diplomat Alexander McGillvray adeptly manoeuvred on these frontiers in the closing years of the eighteenth century. His experiences, however, were not typical. The oppressive or even lethal consistency linking, for instance, Black Hawk to Sitting Bull to Richard Oakes to Robert Satiacum to Leonard Peltier and to the American Indian Movement demonstrates the harsh intensity of those forces that conspire to constrain Indian Country within tight domestic bounds in the heartland of the American empire. The suppression of these leaders, who in different ways all resisted the continuing colonization of their peoples within the United States, was mirrored in the US government's external interventions to overthrow foreign governments considered less than friendly to the global ascent of US-based capitalism. Among those so sacrificed were the regimes of Mohammed Mossadegh in Iran, Jacabo Arbenz in Guatemala, Patrice Lumumba in the Congo, General Sukarno in Indonesia, Kwame Nkrumah in Ghana, and Salvadore Allende in Chile.

An essential aim of this text has been to clarify that there is a long history since 1492 of historical struggle to resist or modify those modes of globalization which have advanced the ascent of the empire of possesive individualism. A major marker of transformation in the changing cyberspace politics of this broadening movement was announced to the world during the confrontations between protesters and police in the last days of the twentieth century. The site of this clash of interests and ideals was the Seattle meeting of the World Trade Organization. From the large demononstrations during a meeting of the World Bank in Prague to the convergence of activists in Quebec City in 2001 to question the means, constitution, and purposes of a Free Trade Area of the Americas, such confrontations became for a time a basic motif at any official gathering where the project of neo-liberal globalization was raised.[142] The huge global protests against a US-led invasion of Iraq massively broadened the base of this worldwide movement.

The philosophy of the Fourth World has the potential to help give added coherence to the quests of those seeking alternatives to a militaristic world order and to neo-liberal models of globalization. The character of these models is most fully revealed in the sometimes violent expansion of commercialized monocultures. The philosophy of the Fourth World fulfils Frantz Fanon's quest for models of decolonization emanating from sources of human imagination outside the intellectual traditions expressed in Europe's imperialistic drives for global dominance. Fourth World inspiration can be found, however, in many sources both inside and outside the European tradition. It can be found, for instance, in the teachings of the Inca leader, Tupac Amaru, or in the historical writings of Henry Reynolds, one of the the sages of the Australian reconciliation movement.

The Fourth World is consistent with many of the most egalitarian principles of the Enlightenment, especially in the extension of the projection of the idea of rights beyond the human realm into broader spheres of ecological relationships. This advancement of "the democracy of all life" finds expression in the work of Vandana Shiva as much as it does in the writings of Grey Owl, John Collier, or George Manuel. When Manuel articulated the essential philosophy of the Fourth World in the mid–1970s, he gave renewed and broadened articulation to ideas and principles that were rooted in thousands of years of Aboriginal history in the Americas. Some of these ideas found their way into the great controversies of the European Enlightenment, especially by way of the reports of baron de Lahontan. Lahontan provided a chronicle of Aboriginal criticisms of French civilization. One of the great specialists in this genre of critique was the Huron diplomat and sage Kondarionk. His legendary abilities as a diplomat and as an astute scholar of constitutional relationships is said to have set the stage for the erudite activism of Pontiac.

Pontiac's influence is forever entrenched in the content of the Royal Proclamation of 1763. He infused his will into that crucial constitutional document by providing the Indian Confederacy with the leadership it needed to intervene strategically in the founding acts of British imperial Canada. The other figure whose advice was decisive in the making of the Royal Proclamation was Sir William Johnson. His principal teachers included his soulmate, the Mohawk matron Molly Brant. Johnson's object was to extend the Covenant Chain of treaty alliances between the British crown and the Longhouse Confederacy's ambivalent empire and to expand the crown's influence throughout the Indian Country of Canada, a land of receding horizons of mercantilistic colonization pointing towards the Northwest – a land of struggle and transformation on the moving frontiers between the shared hunting grounds of the bowl with one spoon and the possessive individualism of the American empire.

In its codification of the principle that Indigenous peoples must be afforded a say in any change in the legal tenure of their ancestral lands, the Royal Proclamation has a permanent place in the genesis of the Fourth World and of international law. With all its paternalistic limitations, King George's seminal recognition of the democratic rights of Indigenous peoples not to be unilaterally dispossessed demonstrates that liberals had no monopoly on introducing the central illuminations of Enlightenment thought into constitutional practice. The continuing role of the monarchy in this, the world's most significant constitutional recognition of the existence of Aboriginal and treaty rights, may yet prove decisive as humanity grapples with changing notions of the meaning of sovereignty.

The heritage of alliances between the British imperial Crown and First Nations was most dramatically expressed in the War of 1812. That was the moment when the great geopolitical questions about the future place and status of Indigenous peoples in North America and the world became central to the clash of principles between the United States and Great Britain. Tecumseh, the erudite sage of that conflict, died protecting his Aboriginal mother country. Like the martyrdom of Toussaint L'Overture in the quest to transform the slaving colony of San Domingo into the free republic of Haiti, Tecumseh was killed in his effort to defend his peoples by changing the framework of international law. The great man left behind him a compelling vision that would merge with other strands of inspiration in the genesis of the Fourth World. Tecumseh's quest to draw a pluralistic unity from diversity found earlier expression in the intercultural resistance movement led by Tupac Amaru in Peru and by Pontiac in the Great Lakes region of North America. A global extension of that same quest became manifest in the founding by George Manuel in 1975 of the World Council of Indigenous Peoples.

Tecumseh's determination was decisive when he urged his peoples to rise up in defence of their territories against the acquisitive expansionism of the American Long Knives. A contemporary observer of a key council in 1812 where Tecumseh defended the necessity of this course transcribed his speech as follows: "Here," said Tecumseh, "is a chance presented to us; yes such as will never occur again for us Indians of North America to form ourselves into one great combination and cast our lot with the British in this war. Should they [the British] conquer and again get mastery over the whole of North America, our rights, at least to a portion of the lands of our fathers, would be respected by the King."[143]

As demonstrated, for instance, by the rise of *Zapatismo* in Mexico, the principles at issue in the War of 1812 are very much with us today, as the empire of possessive individualism and the Fourth World vie for legitimacy and space. In the War of 1812 North America's Indigenous peoples amassed the most substantial resistance ever to stop the westward expansion of the United States. Indeed, not until the Battle of Little Bighorn and, later, its undeclared war in Vietnam, would the US military incur a setback comparable to that meted out by the fighting forces of the Indian Confederacy in the War of 1812. The Aboriginal aim was to stop the ethnic cleansing and the extinguishment of Aboriginal title in North America's interior, and to entrench a constitutionalized alliance with the British crown to secure a pluralistic Aboriginal dominion with fixed, immoveable borders. The creation of such a sovereign Indian Country within the framework of the British Empire would have represented a definitive reversal of the Columbian conquests. It would have broken the monopoly of the "White Nations" in the making of that genre of international law by which vast regions of the planet were apportioned as if these territories, as well as their Aboriginal inhabitants, were Europe's rightful inheritance. That global apportionment of power over peoples and land would later provide the basis for what Rudyard Kipling would choose paradoxically to popularize as "the White Man's Burden."

The questions raised for the hemisphere and for the world by Tecumseh remain central on two continents where, as Subcommandante Marcos attested, there is still not one nation-state, sovereign in international law, whose constitution definitively embraces the heritage of Indigenous peoples as the primary tap root of juridical legitimacy. The politics of this exclusion stand as stark evidence of the continuing force of the Columbian conquests as the most oppressive, ongoing projectory in the process of globalization that began in 1492.

Notes

PREFACE

1 See Neil Postman, *Technopoly: The Surrender of Culture to Technology* (New York: Vintage Books, 1993).

2 Lieutenant-Colonel George Crook, cited in Dan L. Thrapp, *The Conquest of Apacheria* (Norman: University of Oklahoma Press, 1967), 256

3 Angie Debo, *Geronimo: The Man, His Time, His Place* (Norman: University of Oklahoma Press, 1982), 418–19

4 President George W. Bush's speech of 1 May 2003, as posted on the White House website

5 Niall Ferguson, *Empire: The Rise and Demise of the British World Order and the Lessons for Global Power* (New York: Basic Books, 2002), 368

6 See Niall Ferguson, *Cash Nexus: Money and Power in the Modern World, 1700–2000* (New York: Basic Books, 2001), 390–418

7 Niall Ferguson, "The Empire Slinks Back: Why Americans Don't Really Have What It Takes to Rule the World," *New York Times Magazine*, 27 April 2003, 56–7

8 Dwight D. Eisenhower, "Farewell Address," in Bruce Young, *Hotel California* (North Vancouver: The Good Earth, 1979), 213–15

INTRODUCTION

1 Tzvetan Todorov, *The Conquest of America: The Question of the Other*, trans. Richard Howard (New York: Harper & Row, 1984), 5

2 See Edmundo O. Gorman, *The Invention of America: An Inquiry into the Historical Nature of the New World and the Meaning of History* (Westport, Conn.: Greenwood Press, 1961); Howard M. Jones, *O Strange New World: American Culture; The Formative Years* (New York: Viking Press, 1964); John H. Elliot, *The Old World and the New, 1492–1650* (Cambridge: Cambridge University Press, 1970); Jack P. Greene, *The Intellectual Construction of America: Exceptionalism*

and Identity from 1492 to 1800 (Chapel Hill: University of North Carolina Press, 1993).

3 For a discussion of some of the events and projects associated with the Quincentenary in the United States, see Howard Zinn, *A People's History of the United States, 1492–Present,* Twentieth Anniversary Edition (New York: Harper-Collins, 1999), 624–9. See also Claudia L. Bushman, *America Discovers Columbus: How and Italian Explorer Became an American Hero* (Hanover: University Press of New England, 1992); Ronald Wright, *Stolen Continents: The "New World" through Indian Eyes since 1492* (Toronto: Viking, 1992); Thomas R. Berger, *A Long and Terrible Shadow: White Values, Native Rights in the Americas, 1492–1992* (Vancouver: Douglas & McIntyre, 1991); Ron Bourgeault et.al., *1492–1992: Five Centuries of Imperialism and Resistance* (Winnipeg/Halifax: Society for Socialist Studies/Fernwood Publishing, 1992); Djelal Kadir, *Columbus and the Ends of the Earth* (Berkeley: University of California Press, 1992).

4 Adam Smith, *An Inquiry into the Nature of Causes of the Wealth of Nations,* ed. Edwin Cannan (New York: The Modern Library, 1937), 590.

5 Anthony Pagden, *Lords of All the World: Ideologies of Empire in Spain, Britain and France, c.1500–c.1800* (New Haven: Yale University Press, 1995), 163–77.

6 Ibid., my translation

7 Todorov, *The Conquest of America,* 4–5.

8 Cadwallader Colden, *The History of the Five Nations of Canada: Which Are Dependant on the Province of New York, and Are a Barrier between the English and the French in that Part of the World,* 2 vols. (1727, 1747; New York: A.S. Barnes, 1904), 2: 218.

9 Heather Divine, "Roots in the Mohawk Valley: Sir William Johnson's Legacy in the North West Company," in Jennifer S.H. Brown, W.J. Eccles, and Donald P. Heldman, eds., *The Fur Trade Revisited: Selected Papers of the Sixth North American Fur Trade Conference, Mackinac Island, Michigan 1991* (East Lansing/Mackinac Island: Michigan State University Press and Mackinac State Historic Parks, 1994), 223–4.

10 See Patricia U. Bonomi, *A Factious People: Politics and Society in Colonial New York* (New York: Columbia University Press, 1971).

11 See Francis Jennings, *Empire of Fortune: Crowns, Colonies and Tribes in the Seven Years' War in America* (New York: W.W. Norton, 1988), 77.

12 See Isabel Thompson Kelsay, *Joseph Brant, 1743–1807: Man of Two Worlds* (Syracuse: Syracuse University Press, 1984).

13 Duncan Campbell Scott, "Indian Affairs, 1763–1841," in Adam Shortt and Arthur G. Doughty, eds., *Canada and Its Provinces* (Toronto: Glasgow Brooks, 1914), vol. 4; Scott, "Indian Affairs, 1840–1867," ibid, vol. 5

14 Sir William Johnson, *The Papers of Sir William Johnson,* 15 vols., ed. James Sullivan et al. (Albany: University of the State of New York, 1921–65)

15 See Eric Hinderaker, *Elusive Empires: Constructing Colonialism in the Ohio Valley, 1673–1800* (New York: Cambridge University Press, 1997).

16 Divine, "Roots in the Mohawk Valley," 228

17 Ibid., 231

18 Anthony J. Hall, "Treaties, Trains and Troubled National Dreams: Reflections on the Indian Summer in Northern Ontario, 1990," in Louis Knafla and Susan W.S. Binnie, eds., *Law, Society, and the State: Essays in Modern Legal History* (Toronto: University of Toronto Press, 1995), 291–319

19 On the background of Indian resistance to the Meech Lake accord, see Tony Hall, "What Are We? Chopped Liver? Aboriginal Affairs and the Constitutional Politics of Canada in the 1980s," in Michael D. Beheils, ed., *The Meech Lake Primer: Conflicting Views of the 1987 Constitutional Accord* (Ottawa: University of Ottawa Press, 1989), 423–456

20 See Bruce W. Hodgins and Jamie Benidickson, *The Temagami Experience* (Toronto: University of Toronto Press, 1989).

21 See Tony Hall, "Where Justice Lies: Aboriginal Rights and Wrongs in Temagami," in Matt Bray and Ashley Thomson, eds., *Temagami: A Debate on Wilderness* (Toronto: Dundurn Press, 1990), 223–53.

22 See Bruce Clark, *Native Liberty, Crown Sovereignty: The Existing Aboriginal Right of Self-Government in Canada* (Montreal: McGill-Queen's University Press, 1990); Bruce Clark, *Justice in Paradise* (Montreal: McGill-Queen's University Press, 1999).

23 See Tony Hall, "The Philosophical Conflict that Animates Gustafsen Lake," *Globe and Mail*, 5 September, 1995; Splitting the Sky (a.k.a. John Boncore Hill, Dacajeweiah), with She keeps The Door (a.k.a. Sandra Bruderer, Iskwatem Ekanawetak), *From Attica to Gustafsen Lake* (Chase, BC: John Pasquale Boncore, 2001).

24 Joey Thompson, "Media Should Apolgize for Gullibility on Gustafsen Lake," *Vancouver Province*, 26 September 1997

25 Kirk Makin, "U.S. Judge Won't Extradite Canadian Native Activist," *Globe and Mail*, 23 November 2000, A1, A5

26 United States District Court for the District of Oregon, *United States of America v. James Allen Scott Pitawanakwat*, 15 November, 2000, Judgment 00-M–489-ST. Published in *Canadian Native Law Reporter*, no. 1 (2001): 340–60

27 Wendell Berry, *The Unsettling of America: Culture and Agriculture* (San Francisco: Sierra Club Books, 1996), 11

28 Ibid., 4

29 Ibid., 177–8

30 Ibid., 179

31 Shepard Krech III, *The Ecological Indian: Myth and History* (New York: W.W. Norton, 1999)

32 Todorov, *The Conquest of America*, 5

33 Mark Crocker, *Rivers of Blood, Rivers of Gold: Europe's Conquest of Indigenous Peoples* (New York: Grove Press, 1998), xiii

34 Russell Thornton, *American Indian Holocaust and Survival* (Norman: University of Oklahoma Press, 1987), 42–3. For a full discussion of the academic litera-

ture on pre-Columbian demography in the Americas, see Kreech III, *The Eco-logical Indian*, 73–99.

35 See Barbara J. Boeseker, "The Disappearance of American Indian Lan-guages," *Journal of Multilingual and Multicultural Development* 15, 2 and 3 (1994): 147–60

36 See Robert St Clair and William Leap, eds., *Language Renewal among American Indian Tribes: Issues, Problems, and Prospects* (Rosslyn, Va: National Clearing-house for Bilingual Education, 1982).

37 Ward Churchill, *A Little Matter of Genocide: Holocaust and Denial in the Americas, 1492 to Present* (Winnipeg: Arbeiter Ring Publishing, 1998)

38 Thornton, *American Indian Holocaust and Survival*, 42–3

39 See Thomas R. Berger, *Village Journey: The Report of the Alaska Native Review Commission* (New York: Hill and Wang, 1985); Clark, *Justice in Paradise.*

40 Peter Kulchyski, ed., *Unjust Relations: Aboriginal Rights in Canadian Courts* (Toronto: Oxford University Press, 1994), 7

41 Patrick Moser, " Marcos Cheered in Mexico City, *The Globe and Mail*, 12 March, 2001, A3

42 Edmund Burke, *Reflections on the Revolution in France* in *Two Classics of the Frence Revolution* (New York: Doubleday, 1989), 64, 34

43 John Humphrey, *Human Rights and the United Nations: A Great Adventure* (Dobbs Ferry, NY: Transnational Publishers, 1984)

44 Bob Beal, "Don't Blame the Mi'kmaq, Blame History," *Globe and Mail*, 10 November 1999, A17; Ken Coates, *The Marshall Decision and Native Rights* (Montreal and Kingston: McGill-Queen's University Press, 2000)

45 Daniel LeBlanc, "Ottawa Gropes for Response to Fish Battle,"ibid., 5 October 1999, A1, A4; Paul Barnsley, "Decision Looms Large," *Windspeaker* 17, 7 (November 1999):1–2

46 Bill Vander Zalm, "Let's Pay Off the Nisga'a," *Globe and Mail*, 12 November 1999, A15

47 Jeffrey Simpson, "Rights Talk: The Effect of the Charter on Canadian Political Discourse," in Philip Bryden, Steven Davis, and John Russell, eds., *Protecting Rights and Freedoms: Essays on the Charter's Place in Canada's Political, Legal, and Intellectual Life* (Toronto: University of Toronto Press, 1994), 52–9. For an Aboriginal critique of the narrow and Eurocentric biases of rights talk, see Patricia Monture-Angus, *Journeying Forward: Dreaming First Nations' Indepen-dence* (Halifax: Fernwood Publishing, 1999).

48 See Michael Mandel, *The Charter of Rights and the Legalization of Politics in Canada* (Toronto: Wall and Thompson, 1989).

49 Edmund Burke, *Reflections on the Revolution in France*, 63 (emphasis in origi-nal)

50 Michael Asch and Patrick Macklem, "Aboriginal Rights and Canadian Sover-eignty: An Essay on *R. v. Sparrow*," *Alberta Law Review* 29 2 (1991): 498–517; Catherine Bell and Michael Asch, "Challenging Assumptions: The Impact of Precedent on Aboriginal Rights Litigation," in Michael Asch, ed., *Aboriginal and Treaty Rights in Canada* (Vancouver: UBC Press, 1997), 38–74

51 Alexander Morris, *The Treaties of Canada with the Indians of Manitoba and the North-West Territories* (Toronto: Belfords, Clarke and Co., 1880), 102

52 Janice G.A.E. Switlo, *Gustafsen Lake: Under Siege, Exposing the Truth behind the Gustafsen Lake Stand-Off* (Peachland, BC: TIAC Communications, 1997), 274, 134

53 Ibid., 255–60, 279

54 Derek Rasmussen, "'The Queen Wishes Her Red Children to Have the Cunning of the White Man': The Myth of Educating Inuit Out of 'Primitive Childhood' and into Economic Adulthood" (MA thesis, Simon Fraser University, 1999)

55 Personal communication from Derek Rasmussen, 12 November 1999

56 Brian Slattery, "The Constitutional Guarantees of Aboriginal and Treaty Rights," *Queen's Law Journal* 8 (1983): 232

57 Tomson Highway, *Kiss of the Fur Queen* (Toronto: Doubleday Canada, 1999), 1

58 Randall White, *Fur Trade to Free Trade: Putting the Canada–U.S. Trade Agreement in Historical Perspective* (Toronto: Dundurn Press, 1988)

59 See Jack Glenn, *Once upon an Oldman: Special Interest Politics and the Oldman River Dam* (Vancouver: UBC Press, 1999)

60 Francis Jennings, *The Invasion of America: Indians, Colonialism and the Cant of Conquest* (Chapel Hill: University of North Carolina Press, 1975); Jennings, *The Ambiguous Iroquois Empire: The Covenant Chain Confederation of Indian Tribes with English Colonies from Its Beginnings to the Lancaster Treaty of 1744* (New York: W.W. Norton, 1984); Jennings, *Empire of Fortune*

61 Clarence Walworth Alvord, *The Mississippi Valley in British Politics: A Study of the Trade, Land Speculation, and Experiments in Imperialism Culminating in the American Revolution*, 2 vols. (Cleveland: Arthur H. Clark, 1917)

CHAPTER ONE

1 Boutros Boutros-Ghali, "Global Leadership after the Cold War," *Foreign Affairs* 75, 2 (March–April 1996): 87

2 Michael Ignatieff, "The Decline and Fall of the Public Intellectual," *Queen's Quarterly* 104, 3 (1997): 400–1

3 Benjamin R. Barber, *Jihad vs. McWorld* (New York: Random House, 1995)

4 George Grant, *Technology and Empire* (Toronto: Anasi, 1969); Alexander Kojeve, "Tyranny and Wisdom," in Leo Strauss, *On Tyranny* (Ithaca: Cornell University Press, 1968)

5 Francis Fukuyama, *The End of History and the Last Man* (New York: Avon Books, 1992)

6 Vandana Shiva, *Monocultures of the Mind: Perspectives on Biodiversity and Biotechnology* (London, Zed Books, 1993); Vandana Shiva and Maria Miles, *Ecofeminism* (London: Zed Books, 1993); Vandana Shiva, *Biopiracy: The Plunder of Nature and Knowledge* (Toronto: Between the Lines, 1997)

7 Allan Bloom, *The Closing of the American Mind* (New York: Simon & Schuster,

1987); Arthur M. Schlesinger Jr, *The Disuniting of America: Reflections on a Multicultural Society* (New York: W.W. Norton, 1992); Robert Hughes, *Culture of Complaint: The Fraying of America* (New York: Oxford University Press, 1993); Samuel Huntington, *The Clash of Civilizations and the Remaking of World Order* (New York: Simon and Schuster, 1996); J.L. Granatstein, *Who Killed Canadian History?* (Toronto: HarperCollins, 1998)

8 Kay B. Warren, *Indigenous Movements and Their Critics: Pan-Maya Activism in Guatemala* (Princeton: Princeton University Press, 1998), xiii–xiv

9 "War in Europe," *The Economist,* 6 July 1991

10 See Ian Angus, *A Border Within: National Identity, Cultural Plurality and Wilderness* (Montreal: McGill-Queen's University Press, 1997), 170–204.

11 On the history of the idea of ecology, see Stephen Bocking, *Ecologists and Environmental Politics: A History of Contemporary Ecology* (New Haven: Yale University Press, 1997).

12 See Kamala Visweswaran, "Race and the Culture of Anthropology," *The American Anthropologist* 100, 1 (1998): 70–83. For a penetrating critique of the failure to root cultural studies within the framework of evidence-based history, see Keith Windschuttle, *The Killing of History: How Literary Critics and Social Theorists Are Murdering Our Past* (San Francisco: Encounter Books, 1996).

13 See Niles Eldredge, *Life in the Balance: Humanity and the Biodiversity Crisis* (Princeton: Princeton University Press, 1998)

14 Winowna LaDuke, *All Our Relations: Native Struggles for Land and Life* (Cambridge, Mass.: South End Press, 1999), 1

15 E.O. Wilson, *The Diversity of Life* (Cambridge, Mass.: Harvard University Press, 1992)

16 M. Soule and B.A. Wilcox, eds., *Conservation Biology: An Evolutionary-Ecological Perspective* (Sunderland, Mass.: Sinauer, 1980), 8

17 Paul M. Wood, *Biodiversity and Democracy: Rethinking Society and Nature* (Vancouver: UBC Press, 2000)

18 Lyle Campbell and Marianne Mithun, *The Languages of Native America* (Austin: University of Texas Press, 1979)

19 Robert Robins and Eugenius Uhlenback, *Endangered Languages* (Providence: Berg, 1991); Joshua Fishman, *Reversing Language Shift* (Clevedon: Multilingual Matters, 1991); Michael Kraus, "The World's Languages in Crisis," *Language* 68 (1992): 4–10; see Stephen A. Wurm, ed., *Atlas of the World's Languages in Danger of Disappearing* (Paris: UNESCO Publishing, 1996); Rodger Doyle, "Languages, Disappearing and Dead," *Scientific American,* March 1998, 26; Barbara J. Boseker, "The Disappearance of American Indian Languages," *Journal of Multilingual and Multicultural Development* 15, 2 and 3 (1994): 147–60

20 Marie Battiste and James (Sa'ke'j) Youngblood Henderson, *Protecting Indigenous Knowledge and Heritage* (Saskatoon: Purich Publishing, 2000); Gregory Cajete, *Native Science: Natural Laws of Interdependence* (Sante Fe: Clear Light Publishers, 2000).

21 See, for instance, Darrell A. Posey, "Ethnoentomology of the Kayapo Indians

of Central Brazil," *Journal of Ethnobiology* 1, 1 (1981): 165–74; Posey, "Indigenous Ecological Knowledge and the Development of the Amazon," in E. Moran, ed., *The Dilemma of Amazonian Development* (Boulder: Westview Press, 1983); Posex, "Indigenous Management of Tropical Forest Ecosystems: The Case of the Kayapo Indians of the Brazilian Amazon," *Agroforestry Systems* 3, 2 (1985): 139–58.

22 Peter Bakker and Robert A. Papen, "Michif: A Mixed Language Based on Cree and French," in Sarah G. Thomason, ed., *Contact Languages: A Wider Perspective* (Amsterdam: John Benjamins Publishing Company, 1997), 295

23 R.F. Holland, *European Decolonization, 1918–1981: An Introductory Survey* (London: Macmillan, 1981); Gifford Prosser and William Roger Louis, eds., *The Transfer of Power in Africa: Decolonization, 1940–1960* (New Haven: Yale University Press, 1982); W.H. Morris-Jones and Georges Fischer, eds., *Decolonization and After: The British and French Experience* (London: F. Cass, 1980); A.P. Thornton, *Imperialism in the Twentieth Century* (London: Macmillan, 1978)

24 See Richard J. Perry, *From Time Immemorial: Indigenous Peoples and State Systems* (Austin: University of Texas Press, 1996).

25 Jeremy Rifkin, *The Biotech Century: Harnessing the Gene and Remaking the World* (New York: Penguin Putnam, 1998)

26 See Hans-Peter Martin and Harald Schumann, *The Global Trap: Globalization and the Assault on Democracy and Prosperity*, trans. Patrick Camiller (Montreal: Black Rose Books, 1997); John Dunn, ed., *Crisis of the Nation State?* (Oxford: Oxford University Press, 1995); Joseph A. Camilleri and Jim Falk, *The End of Sovereignty? The Politics of a Shrinking and Fragmented World* (Aldershot: Edward Arnold, 1992); Susan Strange, *The Retreat of the State: The Diffusion of Power in the World Economy* (Cambridge: Cambridge University Press, 1996); Jean-Marie Guehenno, *The End of the Nation State*, trans. Victoria Elliot (Minneapolis: University of Minneapolis Press, 1995).

27 Roger C. Altman, "The Nuke of the 1990s," *New York Times Magazine*, 1 March 1998, 34

28 David C. Korten, "Life after Capitalism," paper presented at Edmonton, Calgary, and Saskatoon, November 1998, 3

29 William Grieder, *One World, Ready or Not: The Manic Logic of Global Capitalism* (New York: Touchstone, 1998), 25

30 Akio Morita, "Toward A New World Economic Order," *The Atlantic Monthly*, June 1993, 88

31 See George Soros, "The Capitalist Threat," ibid., February 1997.

32 See Ward Churchill, "'Gaining "Moral High Ground': An Ode to George Bush and the 'New World Order,'" in Churchill, *Since Predator Came: Notes from the Struggle for American Indian liberation* (Littleton, Col.: Aigis Press, 1995), 297–309; Noam Chomsky, *Year 501 – The Conquest Continues* (Montréal: Black Rose Books, 1993), 33–64; Richard J. Barnet and John Cavanagh, *Global Dreams: Imperial Corporations and the New World Order* (New York: Simon & Schuster, 1994).

33 See Michael Carrithers, *Why Humans Have Cultures: Explaining Anthropology*

and Social History (Oxford: Oxford University Press, 1992); Ruth Benedict, *Patterns of Culture* (1934; Boston: Houghton Mifflin, 1959).

34 See C. Tomushat, ed., *Modern Law of Self-Determination* (Boston: Martinus Nijhoff Publishers, 1993); Umozurike Oji Umozurike, *Self-Determination in International Law* (Hamden, Conn.: Archon Books, 1972).

35 Samuel Huntington, *The Clash of Civilizations and the Remaking of World Order* (New York: Simon & Schuster, 1996), 21

36 B.W. Powe, *A Canada of Light* (Toronto: Somerville House, 1997), 89, 146–7, 152

37 Jane Jacobs, *The Question of Separatism: Quebec and the Struggle Over Sovereignty* (New York: Random House, 1980), 113–14

38 Karl Polanyi, *The Great Transformation: The Political and Economic Origins of Our Time* (Boston: Beacon Press, 1957), 46

39 See Howard M. Wachtel, *The Money Mandarins: The Making of a Supranational Economic Order* (Armonk, NY: M.E. Sharpe, 1990); David C. Korten, *When Corporations Rule the World* (West Hartford, Conn. and San Francisco: Kumarian Press and Berrett-Koehler Publishers, 1995).

40 Arthur MacEwan, *Neo-Liberalism or Democracy: Economic Strategy, Markets, and Alternatives for the 21st Century* (Sydney: Pluto Press, 1999).

41 Anonymous, "The Non-Governmental Order: Will NGOs Democratise, or Merely Disrupt Global Governance?" *The Economist*, 11–17 December 1999, 20–1

42 Robert S. Allen, *His Majesty's Indian Allies: British Indian Policy in Defence of Canada, 1774–1815* (Toronto: Dundurn Press, 1992), 88–166; Colin C. Calloway, *Crown and Calumet: British-Indian Relations, 1783–1815* (Norman: University of Oklahoma Press, 1987). On the genesis of the Indian Confederacy, see Gregory Evans Dowd, *A Spirited Resistance: The North American Indian Struggle for Unity, 1745–1815* (Baltimore: Johns Hopkins Press, 1992).

43 See Reginald Horsman, *Race and Manifest Destiny: The Origins of American Racial Anglo-Saxonism* (Cambridge, Mass.: Harvard University Press, 1981); Reginald C. Stuart, *United States Expansionism and British North America, 1775–1871* (Chapel Hill: University of North Carolina Press, 1988).

44 John O'Sullivan, editorial, *The Democratic Review,* July/August 1845

45 Edmund Burke, cited in John A, Hawgood, "Manifest Destiny," in H.C. Allen and C.P. Hill, eds., *British Essays in American History* (Crawley, Sussex: Bookprint, 1969), 126

46 Conor Cruise O'Brien, *On the Eve of the Millennium* (Toronto: Anansi, 1994), 58–9

47 Thomas Jefferson, cited in Albert K. Weinberg, *Manifest Destiny: A Study of Nationalist Expansion in American History* (Chicago: Quadrangle Books, 1963), 40

48 Ibid., 41

49 Thomas Jefferson, cited in Stephen E. Ambrose, *Undaunted Courage: Meriwether Lewis, Thomas Jefferson and the Opening of the American West* (New York: Simon and Schuster, 1996), 56

50 William Henry Harrison, cited in Weiberg, *Manifest Destiny,* 79

51 *New York Evening Post*, 28 January 1803, cited ibid., 31

52 John Adams, cited ibid., 19

53 Congressman William Harper, cited ibid., 54

54 *Democratic Review*, 1838, cited ibid., 107

55 Donald F. Warner, *The Idea of Continental Union: Agitation for the Annexation of Canada to the United States, 1849–1893* (np: University of Kentucky Press for the Mississippi Valley Historical Association, 1960)

56 Goldwin Smith, *Canada and the Canadian Question* (London: Macmillan, 1891), 275. This theme of the unifying the Anglo-Saxon people of North America was quite common at the turn of the century. See John R. Dos Passos, *The Anglo-Saxon Century and the Unification of the English-Speaking People* (New York and London, 1903); Samuel E. Moffett, *The Americanization of Canada* (1907; Toronto: University of Toronto Press, 1972).

57 Tehanetorens, *Wampum Belts* (Onchiota, NY: Six Nations Indian Museum, nd); Michael Foster, "Another Look at the Function of Wampum in Iroquois-White Councils," in Francis Jennings et al., *The History and Culture of Iroquois Diplomacy* (Syracuse, NY: University of Syracuse Press, 1985), 99–144; Jerry Martien, *Shell Game: A True Account of Beads and Money in North America* (San Francisco: Mercury House, 1996)

58 Ralph Nader et.al., *The Case against Free Trade: GATT, NAFTA and the Globalization of Corporate Power* (San Francisco and Berkeley: Earth Island Press and North Atlantic Books, 1993); Gary C. Hufbauer and Jeffrey J. Schott, *NAFTA: An Assessment* (Washington, DC: Institute for International Economics, 1993)

59 Ward Churchill, "The Meaning of Chiapas: A North American Indigenist View," in Churchill, *Since Predator Came*, 354–67; Neil Harvey, *Rebellion in Chiapas: Rural Reforms, Campesino Radicalism, and the Limits to Salinismo*, Transformation of Mexico Series no. 5 (San Diego: Ejido Reform Research Project, Center for US–Mexico Studies, University of California, 1994)

60 Naomi Klein, "The Unknown Icon," in Tom Hayden, ed., *The Zapatista Reader* (New York: Thunder's Mouth Press/Nation Books, 2002), 120

61 Subcommandante Marcos outlines his view of neo-liberalism in "The Fourth World War Has Begun," ibid., 270–85.

62 See Patricia Marchak, *The Integrated Circus: The New Right and the Restructuring of Global Markets* (Montreal: McGill-Queen's University Press, 1993).

63 Rod Mickleburgh, "Protests Turn Seattle into a War Zone," *Globe and Mail*, 1 December 1999, A1; Paul Sullivan, "Battling the Global Bogeyman," ibid., A17

64 Indigenous Peoples' Seattle Declaration on the occasion of the Third Ministerial Meeting of the World Trade Organization, 30 November–3 December 1999

65 The commonly accepted view is that the term "America" has its origins in explorer Amerigo Vespucci's name. Olive Patricia Dickason, however, challenges this interpretation. She believes the word might be derived from a descriptive term given by Native people to Europeans. See Dickason, *The Myth of the Savage and the Beginnings of French Colonialism in the Americas* (Edmonton:

University of Alberta Press, 1984), 8. On conceptions of Indian peoples as the antithesis of the constructed identity of American nationhood, see Roy Harvey Pearce, *Savagism and Civilization: A Study of the Indian and the American Mind* (Baltimore: Johns Hopkins University Press, 1965).

66 George Grant, *Lament for a Nation: The Defeat of Canadian Nationalism* (Toronto: McClelland & Stewart, 1965)

67 See David Horowitz, *The First Frontier: The Indian Wars and Americas Origins* (New York: Simon & Schuster, 1978); Richard Slotkin, *Regeneration through Violence: The Mythology of the American Frontier, 1600–1860* (Middleton, Conn.: Wesleyan University Press, 1973); Richard Slotkin, *The Fatal Environment: The Myth of the Frontier in the Age of Industrialization, 1800–1890* (New York: Atheneum, 1985); Ward Churchill, "Like Sand in the Wind: The Making of the American Indian Diaspora," in Churchill, *Since Predator Came*, 167–202. For a critique of the Jacksonian School of American historians, who have contributed heavily to the conception of the United States as a New World country founded on the conquest of Indian Country, see Jack Forbes, "Frontiers in American History and the Role of the Frontier Historian," *Ethnohistory* 15, 1 (1968): 203–35. On the subject of the Old World/New World connections, see Fred Chiappelli, ed., *The First Images of America: The Impact of the New World on the Old*, 2 vols. (Berkeley: University of California Press, 1976); John H. Elliot, *The Old World and the New, 1492–1650* (Cambridge: Cambridge University Press, 1970); Germán Arciniegas, *America in Europe: A History of the New World in Reverse* (New York: Harcourt Brace Jovanovich, 1986); William Brandon, *New Worlds for Old: Reports from the New World and Their Effect on Social Thought in Europe, 1500–1800* (Athens: Ohio University Press, 1986)

68 Kevin Phillips, *The Cousins' War: Religion, Politics, and the Triumph of Anglo-America* (New York: Basic Books, 1999), xv

69 Ibid., 459

70 Timothy Egan, "New Prosperity Brings New Conflicy to Indian Country," *New York Times*, 8 March 1998, 1, 22

71 See Dan Westell, "First Step Taken by Indians for Saskatchewan A-Dump," *Globe and Mail*, 15 October 1994, A3; Erik Eckholm, "The Native – and Not So Native – Way: The Apaches," *New York Times Magazine*, 27 February 1994, 45–8

72 See Dan McGovern, *The Campo Indian Landfill Wars: The Fight for Gold in California's Garbage* (Norman: University of Oklahoma Press, 1995).

73 Egan, "New Prosperity Brings New Confict to Indian Country," 22

74 Shepard Kreech III, *The Ecological Indian: Myth and History* (New York: W.W. Norton, 1999), 218–19; Robert H. Keller and Michael F. Turek, *American Indians and National Parks* (Tucson: University of Arizona Press, 1998), 43–64

75 William Poole, "Return of the Sinkyone," *Sierra* 81, 6 (1996): 52–5

76 See George Wenzel, *Animal Rights, Human Rights: Ecology, Economy and Ideology in the Canadian Arctic* (Toronto: University of Toronto Press, 1991).

77 Sam W. Stoker and Igor I. Krupnik, "Subsistance Whaling," in John J. Burns, J. Jerome Montague, and Cleveland J. Cowles, eds., *The Bowhead Whale,*

Special Publication no. 2 (Lawrence, Kan.: The Society for Marine Mammalogy, 1993), 579–629

78 Richard Blow, "The Great American Whale Hunt," *Mother Jones* 23, 5 (1998): 49–53, 86–7; Krech III, *The Ecological Indian*, 222–3

79 Egan, "New Prosperity Brings New Conflict to Indian Country," 22

80 See Laurence Hauptman and James D. Wherry, eds., *The Pequots in Southern New England: The Fall and Rise of an American Indian Nation* (Norman: University of Oklahoma Press, 1990).

81 Egan, "New Prosperity Bring New Conflict to Indian Country," 22

82 Paula Mitchell Marks, *In a Barren Land: American Indian Dispossession and Survival* (New York: William Morrow, 1998), 350–80

83 See Wilma Mankiller and Michael Wallis, *Mankiller: A Chief and Her People* (New York: St Martin's Press, 1993).

84 Robert Allen Warrior, *Tribal Secrets: Recovering American Indian Intellectual Traditions* (Minneapolis: University of Minnesota Press, 1995); Craig S. Womack, *Red on Red: Native American Literary Separatism* (Minneapolis: University of Minnesota Press, 1999)

85 Jennings, *The Founders of America*, 377

86 Jack D. Forbes, "The United States and Native America: The Colossus at the Crossroads," in Forbes, *Tribes and Masses: Explorations in Red, White and Black* (Davis, Cal.: D-Q University Press, 1978), 83–5

87 Peter Walman, "Colombia's U'wa: Giving Corporate America Hell," *Globe and Mail*, 10 June 1999, A12

88 Nick Cullather, *Secret History: The CIA's Classified Account of Its Operations in Guatemala, 1952–1954* (Stanford, Cal.: Stanford University Press, 1999); Susanne Jonas, *The Battle for Guatemala: Rebels, Death Squads, and U.S. Power* (Boulder, Col.: Westview Press, 1991); Mark Ensalaco, *Chile under Pinochet: Recovering the Truth* (Philadelphia: University of Pennsylvania Press, 2000)

89 Noam Chomsky, *Turning the Tide: US Intervention in Central America and the Struggle for Peace* (Boston: South End Press, 1985); Chomsky, *Year 501*, 3–96, 155–95; Michael McClintock, *The American Connection: State Terror and Popular Resistance in El Salvador*, 2 vols. (London: Zed, 1985)

90 Rigoberta Menchú, *I, Rogoberto Menchú, An Indian Woman in Guatemala*, ed. Elisabeth Burgos-Debray, trans. Anne Wright (London: Verso, 1985). The use of Menchú's book in survey courses of Western civilization was made a symbol of allegedly "politically correct" subversion in Dinesh D'Sousa, *Illiberal Education: The Politics of Race and Sex on Campus* (New York: Free Press, 1991).

91 See John Bacher, *Petrotyranny* (Toronto: Dundurn Press, 2000), 210–11

92 For a statistical calculation of the number of Indians in the Americas see *Report on the Americas*, Special Edition: *The First Nations, 1492–1992* 25, 3 (1991): 16.

93 See Carlos Fuentes, *Latin America at War with the Past*, CBC Massey Lectures (Toronto: CBC Enterprises, 1985). See Eduardo Galeano, "The Blue Tiger and the Promised Land," *Report on the Americas*, Special Edition: *Inventing America 1492–1992* 24, 5 (1991): 13–17.

94 Les Field, "Ecuador's Pan-Indian Uprising," *Report on the Americas* 25, 3 (1991): 39–44

95 Phillip Wearne, *Return of the Indian: Conquest and Revival in the Americas* (London: Cassell/Latin American Bureau, 1996), chapter 6

96 On the Zapatista Movement, see the special edition of *Cultural Survival Quarterly* 18, 1 (1994). N On the Zapatista opposition to "neo-liberalism," see Louise Boivin, "Mexican Rebels in Chiapas Globalize Their Resistance to Neo-Liberalism," *Solidarity with Native People*, issue 56–7, October 1996

97 See Richard Wilson, *Maya Resurgence in Guatemala* (Norman: University of Oklahoma Press, 1995).

98 Françoise Morin and Bernard Saladin d'Anglure, "Ethnicity as a Political Tool for Indigenous Peoples," in Cora Govers and Hans Vermeulen, eds., *The Politics of Ethnic Consciousness* (London and New York: Macmillan and St Martin's Press, 1997), 157–93

99 Wearne, *Return of the Indian*, chapter 6. See also Donna Lee Van Cott, ed., *Indigenous Peoples and Democracy in Latin America* (London: Macmillan, 1994); Ward Churchill, "Genocide in the Americas, Landmarks from 'Latin America Since 1492,'" in Churchill, *Since Predator Came*, 41–73; Greg Urban and Joel Sherzer, eds., *Nation-States and Indians in Latin America* (Austin: University of Texas Press, 1992); Marie Léger, ed., *Aboriginal Peoples: Toward Self-Government* (Montreal: Black Rose Books, 1994)

100 Cited in *Globe and Mail*, 24 April 1998, A21

101 See, for instance, Francis Jennings, *The Founders of America: How Indians Discovered the Land, Pioneered in It, and Created Great Classical Civilizations; How They Were Plunged into a Dark Age by Invasion and Conquest; And How They Are Reviving* (New York: W.W. Norton, 1993), 82; Francis Jennings, *The Invasion of America: Indians, Colonialism, and the Cant of Conquest* (New York: W.W. Norton, 1976).

102 Jennings, *The Founders of America*, 15

103 See Peter Hulme, *Europe and the Native Caribbean, 1492–1797* (London: Methuen, 1986); Eric Williams, *From Columbus to Castro: The History of the Caribbean, 1492–1969* (New York: Harper and Row, 1970).

104 See William H. McNeill, *The Rise of the West: A History of the Human Community* (Chicago: University of Chicago Press, 1963); Adda B. Bozeman, *Politics and Culture in International History: From the Ancient Near East to the Opening of the Modern Age* (New Brunswick, NJ: Transaction Publishers, 1994); Daniel D. McGarry and Clarence L. Hohl Jr, *Sources of Western Civilization* 2 vols. (Boston: Houghton Mifflin, 1963); Emile Durkheim and Marcel Mauss, "Note on the Notion of Civilization," *Social Research* 38 (1971): 808–13; 1. Schapera, ed., *Western Civilization and the Natives of South Africa: Studies in Culture Contact (London: Routledges and Kegan Paul , 1967)*

105 Samuel Huntington, *The Clash of Civilizations and the Remaking of World Order* (New York: Simon & Schuster, 1996)

106 See, for instance, George Soros, "The Capitalist Threat," *The Atlantic Monthly* February 1997, 45–58.

107 Francis Fukuyama, *The End of History and the Last Man* (New York: Free Press, 1992)

108 Lester B. Pearson, *Democracy in World Politics* (Princeton: Princeton University Press, 1955), 82–3

109 Huntington's multicivilizational approach also draws significantly on the work of Fernand Brandel. See Brandel, *A History of Civilizations*, trans. Richard Mayne (New York: Penguin Books, 1993).

110 Huntington, *The Clash of Civilizations*, 301–21

111 Ibid., 46, 51

112 Ibid., 151

113 Ward Churchill, *A Little Matter of Genocide: Holocaust and Denial in the Americas, 1492 to the Present* (Winnipeg: Arbeiter Ring Publishing, 1998)

114 N. Scott Momaday, "The Man of Words," in The Indian Historian Press, *Indian Voices: The First Convocation of American Indian Scholars* (San Francisco: The Indian Historian Press, 1970), 55

115 George Manuel and Michael Posluns, *The Fourth World: An Indian Reality* (Don Mills: Collier-Macmillan, 1974), 224

116 Jack Greene, *The Intellectual Construction of America: Exceptionalism and Identity from 1492 to 1800* (Chapel Hill: University of North Carolina Press, 1993)

117 Fukuyama, *The End of History*, 338–9

118 First Nations International Court of Justice, *The First Nations of Turtle Island and Her Majesty the Queen in the Right of Canada* (Toronto: FNICJ Justice Department, 1996)

119 See Bruce G. Trigger, *The Children of Aataentsic: A History of Huron People to 1660*, 2 vols. (Montreal: McGill-Queen's University Press, 1976), 1: 77–8.

120 Michael Myers, John Mohawk, and Michael Mitchell, "Creation Story," North American Indian Travelling College, Akwesasne, nd, 1–3

121 Tehanetorens, *Tales of the Iroquois* (Rooseveltown, NY: Akwesasne Notes, 1976), 18

122 James Mooney, *The Ghost-Dance Religion and Wounded Knee* (New York: Dover Publications, 1973), 976. First published as "The Ghost Dance Religion and the Sioux Outbreak of 1890," *Fourteenth Annual Report (Part 2) of the Bureau of Ethnology to the Smithsonian Institution, 1892–93, by J.W. Powell, Director* (Washington, DC: Government Printing Office, 1896), 959

123 Ibid.

124 Jack D. Forbes, *Columbus and Other Cannibals: The Wétiko Disease of Exploitation, Imperialism and Terrorism* (Brooklyn, NY: Automedia, 1992), 8

125 See Paul Radin, *The Trickster: A Study of American Indian Mythology* (New York: Greenwood Press, 1975).

126 Gerald Vizenor, *The People Named Chippewa: Narrative Histories* (Minneapolis: University of Minnesota Press, 1984), 4

127 Tomson Highway, *Kiss of the Fur Queen* (Toronto: Doubleday, 1999), i

128 C.G. Jung, "On the Psychology of the Trickster Figure," in Radin, *The Trickster*, 211

129 Bernal Diaz del Castillo, *The Discovery and Conquest of Mexico, 1519–1810*

(London: George Routledge and Sons, 1928), 268; Rudolph van Zantwijk, *The Aztec Arrangement: The Social History of Pre-Spanish Mexico* (Norman: University of Oklahoma Press, 1985)

130 Jennings, *The Founders of America*, 56–67

131 See Anthony Aveni, *Empires of Time: Calendars, Clocks and Cultures* (New York: Basic Books, 1989); D. Duran, *Books of Gods and Rites and the Ancient Calendar* (Norman: University of Oklahoma Press, 1971).

132 Claude Lévi-Strauss, "Race and History," in Lévi-Strauss, *Structural Anthropology*, trans. Monique Layton (New York: Basic Books, 1976), 338; Robert M. Carmack, *Quichean Civilization* (Berkeley: University of California Press, 1973)

133 Francis Jennings, *The Founders of America*, 52–5. See alsoPeter Nabokov and Robert Easton, *American Indian Architecture* (New York: Oxford University Press, 1988); Buddy Mays, *Ancient Cities of the Southwest* (San Francisco: Chronicle Books, 196); Robert H. And Florence C. Lister, *Chaco Canyon: Archaeology and Archaeologists* (Albuquerquie: University of New Mexico Press, 1962); Kendrick Frazier, *People of the Chaco: A Canyon and Its Culture* (New York: W.W. Norton, 1986).

134 Victor Von Hagan, *The Royal Road of the Inca* (London: Gordon and Cremonesi, 1976)

135 Jennings, *The Founding of America*, 56–8

136 Roger G. Kennedy, *Hidden Cities: The Discovery and Loss of Ancient North American Civilization* (New York: Penguin, 1996), 277

137 Ibid., 224

138 Ibid., 239

139 Emil W. Haury, *The Hohakam: Desert Farmers and Craftsmen* (Tucson: University of Arizona Press, 1976)

140 Lévi-Strauss, "Race and History," 338. See Carl O. Sauer, *Seeds, Spades, Hearths, and Herds: The Domestication of Animals and Foodstuffs* (Cambridge, Mass.: The MIT Press, 1972); Linda S. Cordell and Bruce D. Smith, "Indigenous Farmers," in Bruce G. Trigger and Wilcomb E. Washburn, eds., *The Cambridge History of Native Peoples*, vol. 1: *North America*, Part 1 (Cambridge: Cambridge University Press, 1996), 201–66; R. Douglas Hurt, *Indian Agriculture in America* (Lawrence: University Press of Kansas, 1987); William E. Doolittle, "Agriculture in North America on the Eve of Contact: A Reassessment," *Annals of the Association of American Geographers* 82, 3 (1992): 386–401

141 Levi-Strauss, "Race and History," 338

142 Betty Fussell, *The Story of Corn: The Myths and History, the Culture and Agriculture, the Art and Science of America's Quinessential Crop* (New York: North Point Press, 1992), 7

143 Redcliffe N. Salaman, *The History and Social Influence of the Potato* (Cambridge: Cambridge University Press, 1985), 188–343

144 See Trigger, *The Children of Aataentsic*; Conrad Heidenrich, *Huronia: A History*

and Geography of the Huron Indians, 1600–1650 (Toronto: McClelland & Stewart, 1971); Olive Patricia Dickason, "For Every Plant There Is a Use: The Botanical World of Mexicans and Iroquoians," in Kerry Abel and Jean Friesen, eds., *Aboriginal Resource Use in Canada: Historical and Legal Aspects* (Winnipeg: University of Manitoba Press, 1991), 11–34.

145 Ward Churchill, "White Studies: The Intellectual Imperialism of U.S. Higher Education," in Churchill, *Since Predator Came: Notes from the Struggle for American Indian Liberation* (Littleton, Col.: Aigis Publication, 1995), 249; Barrie Kavasch, *Native Harvests* (New York: Random House, 1979)

146 Jennings, *The Founders of America,* 41

147 Salaman, *The History and Social Influence of the Potatoe,* 159

148 Sauer, *Seeds, Spades, Hearths, and Herds,* 65

149 J. B. Longone, *Mother Maize and King Corn: The Persistence of Corn in the American Ethos* (Ann Arbor, Mich.: William L. Clements Library, 1986)

150 G.F. Will and G.E. Hyde, *Corn among the Indians of the Upper Missouri* (St Louis: W.H. Miner, 1917); G.L. Wilson, *Buffalo Bird Woman's Garden: Agriculture of the Hidatsa Indians* (1917; St Paul: Minnesota Historical Society, 1987)

151 Dickason, "For Every Plant There Is a Use," 91

152 Sauer, *Seeds, Spades, Hearths, and Herds,* 64

153 See, for instance, J. Donald Hughes, *American Indian Ecology* (El Paso: Texas Western Press, 1983); T.C. Blackburn and M.K. Anderson, eds., *Before the Wilderness: Environmental Management by Native Californians* (Menlo Park, Cal.: Ballena Press, 1993)

154 See P.J. Crutzen and J.G. Goldhammer, eds., *Fire and the Environment: The Ecological, Atmospheric, and Climatic Importance of Vegetation Fires* (Chichester: John Wiley and Sons, 1993); L. Trabaud, ed., *The Role of Fire in Ecological Systems* (The Hague: SPB Academic Publishing, 1987).

155 Michael Williams, *Americans and Their Forests: A Historical Geography* (Cambridge: Cambridge University Press, 1990), 43

156 Stephen J. Pyne, *Vestal Fire: An Environmental History, Told through Fire, of Europe and Europe's Encounter with the World* (Seattle: University of Washington Press, 1998)

157 Roger Williams, cited in James Tully, "Rediscovering America: The Two Treatises and Aboriginal Rights," in Tully, *An Approach to Political Philosophy: Locke in Contexts* (Cambridge: Cambridge University Press, 1993), 150

158 Kreech III, *The Ecological Indian: Myth and Legend,* 101–22

159 William Cronon, *Changes in the Land: Indians, Colonists, and the Ecology of New England* (New York: Hill and Wang, 1983), 51

160 See Robert Boyd, ed., *Indians, Fire, and the Land in the Pacific Northwest* (Corvallis: Oregon State University Press, 1999); James L. Kohen, *Aboriginal Environmental Impacts* (Sydney, Australia: UNSW Press, 1995), 35–42

161 Vandana Shiva, "Decolonizing the North," in Shiva and Maria Mies, *Ecofeminism* (London and Halifax: Zed Books and Fernwood Publications, 1993), 265

162 Claude Lévi-Strauss, *The Naked Man: Introduction to a Science of Mythology,* vol.
     4, trans. John and Doreen Weightman (New York: Harper and Row, 1981),
     17–18
163 See D. Wayne Moodie, "Manomin: Historical-Geographical Perspectives on
     the Ojibwa Production of Wild Rice," in Kerry Abel and Jean Friesen, eds.,
     Aboriginal Resource Use in Canada: Historical and Legal Aspects" (Winnipeg:
     University of Manitoba Press, 1997), 71–9; Frances Densmore, "Use of
     Plants by the Chippewa Indians," *Bureau of Ethnology, Fourty Fourth Annual
     Report,* 1928, 275–397.
164 Thomas Vennum Jr, *Wild Rice and the Ojibway People* (St Paul: Minnesota
     Historical Society Press, 1988)
165 Allan McChesney, "Aboriginal Communities, Aboriginal Rights, and the
     Human Rights System in Canada," in Abdullahi Ahemed An-Na'im, ed.,
     Human Rights in Cross-Cultural Perspectives (Philadelphia: University of Penn-
     sylvania Press, 1992), 235–6
166 The Treaty 3 Anishinaabe Manomin Law, 1995, 5 October 1992
167 For a study of wild rice as a cash crop, see S.G. Aitken, P.F. Lee et al., *Wild
     Rice in Canada* (Toronto: NC Press, 1988).
168 Edward Lazrus, *Black Hills White Justice: The Sioux Nation Versus the United
     States, 1775 to the Present* (New York: HarperCollins, 1991)
169 Richard White, *The Roots of Dependency: Subsistence, Environment, and Social
     Change among the Choctaws, Pawnees, and Navajos* (Lincoln: University of
     Nebraska Press, 1983), xiii
170 Kreech III, *The Ecological Indian,* 29–43, 45, chapters 5, 6, and 7
171 White, *The Roots of Dependence,* xv
172 See especially Joseph-Francois Lafitau, *Customs of the American Indians Com-
     pared with the Customs of Primitive Times,* 2 vols., ed. and trans. William N. Fen-
     ton and Elizabeth L. Moore (1724; Toronto: The Champlain Society, 1974,
     1977).
173 John F. Moffitt and Santiago Sebastian, *O Brave New People: The European
     Invention of the American Indian* (Albuquerque: University of New Mexico
     Press, 1996); Robert F. Berkhofer Jr, *The White Man's Indian: Images of the
     American Indian from Columbus to Present* (New York: Alfred A. Knopf, 1972)
174 Alfred W. Crosby, *The Columbian Exchange: Biological and Cultural Conse-
     quences of 1492* (Westport, Conn.: The Greenwood Press, 1972)
175 See John Gray, *Post-Liberalism: Studies in Political Thought* (London: Rout-
     ledge, 1996), 253–82
176 Edward W. Said, *Culture and Imperialism* (New York: Vintage Books, 1994),
     336
177 See Roy Harvey Pearce, *Savagism and Civilization: A Study of the Indian and the
     American Mind* (Baltimore: Johns Hopkins University Press, 1965); Elemire
     Zolla, *The Writer and the Shaman: A Morphology of the American Indian,* trans.
     Raymond Rosenthal (New York: Harcourt, Brace, Janovich, 1973).
178 Dorothy V. Jones, *License for Empire: Colonialism by Treaty in Early America*
     (Chicago: University of Chicago Press, 1982)

179 Alexander Cockburn and Jeffrey St Clair, *Five Days That Shook the World: Seattle and Beyond* (London: Verso, 2000)

180 See, for instance, Sidney L. Harring, *White Man's Law: Native People in Nineteenth-Century Canadian Jurisprudence* (Toronto: University of Toronto Press, 1998); Bruce Clark, *Justice in Paradise* (Montreal: McGill-Queen's University Press, 1999).

181 Paul Hazard, *The European Mind [1680–1715]*, trans. J. Lewis May (New York: The New American Library, 1963); Norman Hampson, *The Enlightenment* (New York: Penguin, 1979)

182 See Richard Tuck, *Natural Rights Theories: Their Origin and Development* (Cambridge: Cambridge University Press, 1993)

183 O'Brien, *On The Eve of the Millennium*, 59

184 Eugene D. Genovese, *Roll, Jordan, Roll: The World the Slaves Made* (New York: Pantheon Books, 1974), 25–48

185 See Winowna LaDuke, *All Our Relations: Native Struggles for Land and Life* (Cambridge, Mass.: South End Press, 1999).

186 Jean-Jacques Rousseau, *A Discourse on a Subject Proposed by the Academy of Dijon: What is the Origin of Inequality among Men, and Is It Authorized by Natural Law?* (1755), in Rousseau, *The Social Contract and Discourses*, trans. G.D.H. Cole (London: J.M. Dent, 1986), 84

187 Isaiah Berlin, "Herder and the Enlightenment," in Berlin, *Vico and Herder: Two Studies in the History of Ideas* (London: The Hogarth Press, 1976), 143–216

188 Franz Boas, *The Mind of Primitive Man* (New York: Macmillan, 1911); Vernon Williams, *Rethinking Race: Franz Boas and His Contemporaries* (University of Kentucky Press, 1996); Herbert S. Lewis, "The Misrepresentation of Anthropology and Its Consequences," *American Anthropologist* 100, 3 (1998): 716–33

189 See Pauline M. Roseneau, *Post-Modernism and the Social Sciences: Insights, Inroads, and Intrusions* (Princeton, NJ: Princeton University Press, 1992).

190 Martin Bernal, *Black Athena: The Afroasiatic Roots of Classical Civilization*, 2 vols. (New Brunswick, NJ: Rutgers University Press, 1987, 1991)

191 The Eurocentrism of most interpretations of Western civilization were countered with the particularly excessive claims, for instance, advanced in Martin Bernal, *Black Athena: The Afroasiatic Roots of Classical Civilization*, 2 Vols. (New Brunswick N.J.: Rutgers University Press, 1987, 1991)

192 Allan Bloom, *The Closing of the American Mind: How Higher Education Has Failed Democracy and Impoverished the Souls of Today's Students* (New York: Simon & Schuster, 1987)

193 Tom Flanagan, *First Nations? Second Thoughts* (Montreal: McGill-Queen's University Press, 2000), 36, 46

194 Robert Hughes coined the phrase "multi-culti" in *Culture of Complaint: The Fraying of America* (New York: Oxford University Press, 1993). Todd Gitlin, *The Twilight of Common Dreams: Why America is Wracked with the Culture Wars* (New York: Henry Holt, 1995)

195 Bruce G. Trigger, *Sociocultural Evolution: Calculation and Contingency* (Oxford: Blackwell, 1998), 245

196 O'Brien, *On the Eve of the Millennium*, 150, 153, 157.

197 See Jack David Eller, *From Culture to Ethnicity to Conflict: An Anthropological Perspective on International Ethnic Conflict* (Ann Arbor: Univerrsity of Michigan Press, 1999).

198 Michel Foucault, "What Is Enlightenment? (Was ist Aufklarung?)," in Paul Rabinow, ed., *The Foucault Reader* (New York: Pantheon Books, 1984), 42–3

199 Roseneau, *Post-Modernism and the Social Sciences*, 26, 76, 86; John Gray, *Enlightenment's Wake: Politics and Culture at the Close of the Modern Age* (London: Routledge, 1995); Robert Darnton, "George Washington's False Teeth," *New York Review of Books* 44, 5 (1997): 34–8

200 Karmala Visweswaran, "Race and the Culture of Anthropology," *American Anthropologist* 100, 1 (1998): 70–83

201 Jared Diamond, *Guns, Germs, and Steel: The Fates of Human Societies* (New York: W.W. Norton, 1999), 375

202 Karl R. Popper, *The Open Society and Its Enemies*, 2 vols. (Princeton, NJ: Princeton University Press, 1963)

CHAPTER TWO

1 *Edmonton Journal*, 29 May 2000, A3; Harvey Goldberg, "The Wisdom of Oz: Canada can learn from Australia's gestures of reconciliation to its First Nations," *Globe and Mail*, 1 June 2000, A17

2 Henry Reynolds, *Aborigines and Settlers: The Australian Experience, 1788–1839* (Melbourne: Cassell Australia, 1972); Reynolds, *The Other Side of the Frontier: Aboriginal Resistance to the European Invasion of Australia* (Ringwood, Australia: Penguin, 1981); Reynolds, *Dispossession: Black Australians and White Invaders* (Sydney: Allen and Unwin, 1989)

3 Reynolds, "A Crossroads of Conscience," in Michelle Grattan, ed., *Rec-onciliation: Essays on Australian Reconciliation* (Melbourne: Black, 2000), 54

4 Aden Ridgeway, "An Impasse or a Relationship in the Making," ibid., 16

5 See Herbert Cole Coombs, *Aboriginal Autonomy: Issues and Strategies* (Cambridge: Cambridge University Press, 1994); Robert Tonkinson and Myrna Tonkinson, "Aborigines of Australia," *Cultural Survival Quarterly* 17, 3 (1993).

6 House of Representatives Standing Committee on Aboriginal and Torres Strait Islander Affairs, *Language and Culture: A Matter of Survival*. Report into Aboriginal and Torres Strait Islander Language Maintenance (Canberra: Australian Government Printing Service, 1992); Collin Yallop and Michael Walsh, *Language and Culture in Aboriginal Australia* (Canberra: Aboriginal Studies Press, 1993); Rob Amery and Colin Bourke, "Australian Languages: Our Heritage," in Colin Bourke, Eleanor Bourke, and Bill Edwards, eds., *Aboriginal*

Australia: An Introductory Reader in Aboriginal Studies, 2nd ed. (St Lucia: University of Queensland Press, 1998), 122–45

7 Patrick Dodson, "Lingiari: Until the Chains Are Broken," in Grattan, ed., *Reconciliation*, 264–74

8 G. Cowlishaw and V. Kondos, eds., *Mabo and Australia: On Recognizing Native Title After Two Hundred Years* (Sydney: Anthropological Society of New South Wales, 1995)

9 Sally Weaver, "Self-Determination, National Pressure Groups, and Australian Aborigines: The National Aboriginal Conference, 1983–1985," in Michael D. Levin, ed., *Ethnicity and Aboriginality: Case Studies in Ethnonationalism* (Toronto: University of Toronto Press, 1993), 53–74

10 Cited in Raimond Gaitla, "Guilt, Shame and Collective Responsibility," in *Reconciliation*, 276. See P.J. Butt and R. Eagleson, *Mabo: What the High Court Said and What the Government Did*, 2nd ed. (Sydney: Federation Press, 1996); John Bastien, "Recent Developments in Native Title Law and Practice: Issues for the High Court," in *Land, Rights, Laws: Issues of Native Title*, Issues Paper 13 (Canberra, February 2002); Christine Choo and Margaret O'Connell, "Historical Narrative and Proof of Native Title," in *Land, Rights, Laws: Issues of Native Title*, Issues Paper 3 (Canberra, September 1999); Ian Keen, "Cultural Continuity and Native Title Claims," in *Land, Rights, Laws: Issues of Native Title*, Issues Paper 28 (Canberra, July 1999).

11 Speech by Prime Minister Paul Keating, December 1992, cited on the worldwide web site of Oxfam, Community Aid Abroad, August 1993

12 Michael Perry, "Public support for Aborigines booming in Australia," *Globe and Mail*, 10 June 1998, A5

13 Human Rights and Equal Opportunity Commission, *Bringing Them Home: A Guide to the Findings of the National Inquiry into the Separation of the Aboriginal and Torres Strait Islander Children from Their Families* (Sydney: The Commission, 1997)

14 "An Open Letter to Her Majesty Queen Elizabeth II, Queen of Australia, from Australians for Native Title et al.," 23 June 1997

15 Noel Pearson, "The Concept of Native Title in Common Law," in Galarrway Yunupingu, ed., *Our Land Is Our Life: Land Rights Past, Present, Future* (St Lucia: University of Queensland Press, 1996); Kevin Gilbert, *Living Blacks: Blacks Talk to Kevin Gilbert* (Sydney: Penguin, 1984); Gilbert, *Because a White Man'll Never Do It* (Sydney: HarperCollins, 1994)

16 John Pilger, *A Secret Country* (London: Vintage, 1990); Pilger, "Secret Waters," in Pilger, *Hidden Agendas* (London: Vintage, 1999), 223–48

17 Pilger, "Secret Waters," 232

18 Cited in Hansonism: We Are All Australians," www.gwb.com.au/onenation/truth/conclus.html

19 Geoffrey Blainey, *A Shorter History of Australia* (Port Melbourne: William Heinemann, 1994); Blainey, *Blainey: Eye on Australia. Speeches and Essays of Geoffrey Blainey* (Melbourne: Schwartz Books, 1991)

20 Preston Manning, "Parliament, not judges, must make the laws of the land,"
    Globe and Mail, 16 June 1998, A23
21 Anthony J. Hall, "The Denigration of a Great National Question,"
    Windspeaker, April 2002, 4-6
22 Ignacio Ramonet, "Maros Marches on Mexico City," in Tom Hayden, ed., *The
    Zapatista Reader* (New York: Thunder's Mouth Press/Nation Books, 2002),
    133-41
23 Naomi Klein, *No Logo: Taking Aim at the Brand Bullies* (Toronto: Alfred A.
    Knopf, 2000)
24 Naomi Klein, "The Unknown Icon," in Hayden, ed., *The Zapatista Reader*,
    122
25 Tom Hayden, "In Chiapas," ibid., 83, 78
26 Subcommandante Maros, cited in Naomi Klein, "The Unknown Icon," 118
27 John Rice, "Zapatista Rebels Ride into Mexico City,"*National Post*, 12 March
    2001, A16
28 Kay B. Warren, *Indigenous Movements and Their Critics: Pan-Mayan Activism in
    Guatemala* (Princeton: Princeton University Press, 1998)
29 Ignacio Ramonet, "Marcos marche sur Mexico," *Le Monde*, March 2001. See
    also Dan Tschirgi, "Des islamistes aux zapatistes, la revolte des 'marginaux de
    la terre,'" *Le Monde*, January 2000; Carlos Pardo, "Resistances zapatistes," *Le
    Monde*, August 1998
30 Alan Knight, "Racism, Revolution, and *Indigenismo*: Mexico, 1910-1940," in
    Richard Graham, ed., *The Idea of Race in Latin America, 1870-1940* (Austin:
    University of Texas Press, 1990), 71-114
31 Augie Fleras and Paul Spoonley, *Recalling Aotearoa: Ethnic Relations and Indige-
    nous Politics in New Zealand* (Auckland: Oxford, 1999)
32 See Paul McHugh, *The Maori Magna Carta: New Zealand Law and the Treaty of
    Waitangi* (Auckland: Oxford University Press, 1991).
33 Alan Ward, *An Unsettled History: Treaty Claims in New Zealand Today* (Welling-
    ton: Bridget William, 1999); Paul Havemann and Kaye Turner, "The Wait-
    angi Tribunal: Theorising Its Place in the Re-Design of the New Zealand
    State," *Australian Journal of Law and Society* 10 (1994): 165-94; Roger Maaka
    and Augie Fleras, "Treaty Settlements and Social Change: The Treaty of
    Waitangi, the Waitangi Tribunal, and the Re-scripting of Maori-Crown Rela-
    tions in New Zealand," paper presented to the Canadian Indigenous/
    Native Studies Association (CINSA) conference at the University of Alberta,
    28-31 May 2000
34 *New Zealand Law Reports* (1987): 673
35 Ministry of Maori Development, Government of New Zealand, "New Zealand
    Government Consults with Maori on MAI," 5 November 1997, press release
36 Aziz Choudry, "APEC, Free Trade and Economic Sovereignty," paper present-
    ed at a conference in Davao, the Philippines, before the Manila People's
    Forum on APEC, 14 November 1996
37 See Anthony J. Hall, "Magazine Meglomania: Are World Trade Rulings the
    New Indian Act?" *Canadian Forum*, March 1997, 5-6

38 See David Korten, *When Corporations Rule the World* (West Hartford, Conn.: Kumarian Press / San Francisco: Berrett-Koehler Publishers, 1995)

39 Ken Saro-Wiwa, *Genocide in Nigeria: The Ogoni Tragedy* (Port Harcourt, 1992); "Testimony of Dr. Owens Wiwa before the Joint Briefing of the Congressional Human Rights Caucus and the Congressional Black Caucus," Washington, DC, 30 January 1996, published electronically by the Sierra Club; Ken Wiwa, *In the Shadow of a Saint* (Toronto: Knopf Canada, 2000).

40 Mark MacKinnon, "Saro-Wiwa's Battle Still Being Fought," *Globe and Mail*, 10 June 1999, A13

41 See Andrew Armitage, *Comparing the Policy of Assimilation: Australia, Canada, and New Zealand* (Vancouver: UBC Press, 1995)

42 For different perspectives on Indigenous peoples' struggles around the world, see Roger Moody, ed., *The Indigenous Voice: Visions and Realities* (Utrecht: International Books, 1993); Patricia Morales, ed., *Indigenous Peoples, Human Rights and Global Interdependence* (Tilburg: International Centre for Human and Public Affairs, 1994); Julian Berger, *Report from the Frontier: The State of the World's Indigenous Peoples* (London: Zed Books, 1987); Independent Commission on International Humanitarian Issues, *Indigenous Peoples: A Global Quest for Justice* (London: Zed Books, 1987); Noel Dyck, *Indigenous People and the Nation State: Fourth World Politics in Canada, Australia and Norway* (St John's: Institute of Social and Economic Research, Memorial University of Newfoundland, 1985); Jens Brøsted et al., *Native Power: The Quest for Autonomy and Nationhood of Indigenous Peoples* (Gergen: Universitetforlaget AS, 1985); William Renwick, ed., *Sovereignty and Indigenous Rights: The Treaty of Waitangi in International Contexts* (Wellington: Victoria University Press, 1991); Augie Fleras and Jean Leonard Elliot, *The Nations Within: Aboriginal-State Relations in Canada, the United States and New Zealand* (Toronto: Oxford University Press, 1992).

43 See Dean B. Suagee, "Human Rights of Indigenous Peoples: Will the United States Rise to the Occasion?" *American Indian Law Review* 21, 2 (1997): 365–90; Russel Lawrence Barsh, "Indigenous Peoples in the 1990s: From Object to Subject of International Law?" *Harvard Human Rights Journal* 7 (1994): 35–86

44 Jeff Sallot, "Indigenous Issues Topic of UN Forum," *Globe and Mail*, 13 May 2002, A8

45 Peter McFarlane, *Brotherhood to Nationhood: George Manuel and the Making of the Modern Indian Movement* (Toronto: Between the Lines, 1993)

46 Peter Jull, "Embracing New Voices: Reconciliation in Canada," in Grattan, ed., *Rec-onciliation*, 227

47 Ron Dart, *The Red Tory Tradition: Ancient Roots, New Routes* (Dewdney, BC: Synaxis Press, 1999), 69–83

48 See Carl Berger, *The Sense of Power: Studies in the Ideas of Canadian Imperialism, 1967–1914* (Toronto: University of Toronto Press, 1973); Reginald Horsman, *Race and Manifest Destiny: The Origins of American Racial Anglo-Saxonism* (Cambridge Mass.: Harvard University Press, 1981).

49 Stephen Leacock, ed., *Lahontan's Voyages* (Ottawa: Graphic Publishers, 1932), vii–viii

50 F.B. Housser, *A Canadian Art Movement: The Story of the Group of Seven* (Toronto: Macmillan, 1926)

51 Arthur R.M. Lower, *Colony to Nation: A History of Canada* (1946; Don Mills: Longmans Canada, 1969), 564

52 Richard White, *The Middle Ground: Indians, Empires, and Republics in the Great Lakes Area, 1650–1815* (Cambridge: Cambridge University Press, 1991); Harold Innis, *The Fur Trade in Canada: An Introduction to Canadian Economic History* (New Haven: Yale University Press, 1930); W.J. Eccles, "The Fur Trade in Eighteenth-Century Imperialism," in Olive Patricia Dickason, ed., *The Native Imprint*, vol. 1: *The Contribution of First Peoples to Canada's Character* (Np: Athabasca University Educational Enterprises, 1995), 345–70; Bruce G. Trigger, *Natives and Newcomers: Canada's "Heroic Age" Reconsidered* (Montreal: McGill-Queen's University Press, 1985); Alfred Goldsworthy Bailey, *The Conflict of European and Eastern Algonkian Culture 1504–1700: A Study in Canadian Civilization*, 2nd ed. (1937; Toronto: University of Toronto Press 1969)

53 Jean Morisset, "La Conquête du Nord-Ouest, 1885–1985: Or the Imperial Quest of British North America," in Ian A.L. Getty and Antoine S. Lussier, eds., *As Long as the Sun Shines and the Water Flows: A Reader in Canadian Native Studies* (Vancouver: UBC Press, 1983), 282. See also Morisset, *L'identité usurpée: L'amerique écartée* (Montreal: Nouvelle Optique, 1989); W.J. Eccles, *The Canadian Frontier, 1534–1760* (Albuquerque: University of New Mexico Press, 1974); Cornelius J. Jaenen, *Friend and Foe: Aspects of French-Amerindian Cultural Contact in the Sixteenth and Seventeenth Centuries* (Toronto: McClelland & Stewart, 1976); Denys Delâge, *Le pays renversé: Amérindiennes et européens en Amérique du nord-est, 1600–1664* (Montreal: Boréal Express, 1985); Trigger, *Natives and Newcomers*

54 Claude Levi-Strauss, *The Naked Man: Introduction to a Science of Mythology, vol. 4*, trans. John and Doreen Weightman (New York: Harper & Row, 1981), 23

55 See John Borrows, "Wampum at Niagara: The Royal Proclamation, Canadian Legal History, and Self-Governance," in Michael Asch, ed., *Aboriginal and Treaty Rights in Canada* (Vancouver: UBC Press, 1997), 155–72.

56 The continuing force of the Royal Proclamation is specifically affirmed in section 25 of the *Constitution Act, 1982*.

57 On the Royal Proclamation, see Brian Slattery, "The Hidden Constitution: Aboriginal Rights in Canada," in Menno Boldt and J. Anthony Long, eds., *The Quest for Justice: Aboriginal Peoples and Aboriginal Rights* (Toronto: University of Toronto Press, 1985), 114–38. The Proclamation is published in its entirety in Getty and Lussier, eds., *As Long as the Sun Shines*, 29–37

58 Francis Jennings, *Empire of Fortune: Crowns, Colonies, and Tribes in the Seven Years War in America* (New York: W.W. Norton, 1988); Robert J. Clinton, "The Proclamation of 1763: Colonial Prelude to Two Centuries of Federal-State Conflict over the Management of Indian Affairs," *Boston University Law Review* 69 (1989): 329–81

59 James McGill, cited in G.F.G. Stanley, "The Indians in the War of 1812," in Morris Zaslow, ed., *The Defended Border: Upper Canada and the War of 1812* (Toronto: Macmillan, 1964), 178

60 For a commentary on the conservatism of Canada and the liberalism of the United States, see Gad Horowitz, "Conservatism, Liberalism, and Socialism in Canada: An Interpretation," *Canadian Journal of Economics and Political Science* 32, 2 (1966): 143–71

61 Slotkin, *Regeneration through Violence.* On the rise of the American empire, see Richard W. Van Alstyne, *The Rising American Empire* (New York: W.W. Norton, 1974); V.G. Kiernan, *America, the New Imperialism: From White Settlement to World Hegemony* (London: Zed, 1978); Robert V. Remini, *Andrew Jackson and the Course of American Empire*, 3 vols. (New York: Harper and Row, 1977–84); Albert K. Weinberg, *Manifest Destiny: A Study of Nationist Expansion in American History* (Baltimore: Johns Hopkins University Press, 1935); Robin W. Winks, "A System of Commands: The Infrastructure of Race Contact," in Gordon Martel, ed., *Studies in British Imperial History: Essays in Honour of A.P. Thornton* (London: Macmillan, 1986), 8–48

62 On Aboriginal perspectives on treaties, see Richard Price, ed., *The Spirit of the Alberta Indian Treaties* (Edmonton: Pica Pica Press, 1987); John Snow, *These Mountains Are Our Sacred Places: The Story of the Stoney Indians* (Toronto: Samuel Stevens, 1977); Treaty 7 Elders and Tribal Council, with Walter Hildebrandt, Sarah Carter, and Dorothy First Rider, *The True Spirit and Original Intent of Treaty 7* (Montreal: McGill-Queen's University Press, 1996).

63 Peter Padbury, "UNCED and the Globalization of Civil Society," in Eric Fawcett and Hanna Newcombe, eds, *United Nations Reform: Looking Ahead after Fifty Years* (Toronto: Dundurn, 1995), 209

64 Francis Jennings, *The Founders of America* (New York: W.W. Norton, 1993), 313–19

65 Cited in Francis Paul Prucha, *The Great Father: The United States Government and the American Indians*, abridged ed. (Lincoln: University of Nebraska Press, 1986), 165

66 Anthony J. Hall, "Indian Treaties," in *The 1997 Canadian Encyclopedia Plus. CD-Rom Edition* (Toronto: McClelland & Stewart, 1996)

67 Charlotte Childs interview in the Oji-Cree language with Mary-Ann Anderson, who was present at the adhesion ceremonies in 1929. Broadcast on "Indian Faces," CBQ Radio, Thunder Bay, Ontario, November 1990

68 Thomas Berger, "The Nishga Indians and Aboriginal Rights," in Berger, *Fragile Freedoms: Human Rights and Dissent in Canada* (Toronto: Clark, Irwin, 1981); Daniel Raunet, *Without Surrender, without Consent: A History of Nishga Land Claims* (Vancouver: Douglas and McIntyre, 1984); Paul Tennant, *Aboriginal Peoples and Politics: The Indian Land Question in British Columbiua, 1849–1989* (Vancouver: UBC Press, 1990)

69 See Ken Coates, ed., *Aboriginal Land Claims in Canada: A Regional Perspective* (Toronto: Copp Clark Pitman, 1992); Robert M. Galois, "Reclaiming the

Land: Aboriginal Title, Treaty Rights and Land Claims in Canada," *Applied Geography* 12 (1992): 109–32.

70 See J.J. Brown, *Ideas in Exile: A History of Canadian Invention* (Toronto: McClelland & Stewart, 1967).

71 Francois Marie A. Voltaire, *Le Huron; ou, l'Ingenue.* 2ND ed. (Lausanne, Switzerland, 1767); Jean-Jacques Rousseau, *Discours sur l'origine et les fondements de l'inégalité parmi les hommes* (Amsterdam: M.M. Rey, 1755); Gibert Chinard, *Amérique et le rêve exotique dans le littérature française au XVIIe et au XVIII siecle* (Paris: Librairie E. Droz, 1934)

72 Reuben Gold Thwaites, ed., *The Jesuit Relations and Allied Documents*, 73 vols. (Cleveland: Burrows Brothers, 1896–1901)

73 George R. Healy, "The French Jesuits and the Idea of the Noble Savage," *William and Mary Quarterly*, 3rd series, vol. 15, 2 (1958): 143–67

74 See Neal E. Salisbury, "Red Puritans: The 'Praying Indians' of Massachusetts Bay and John Eliot," ibid., vol. 31, 1 (1974): 27–54

75 Father Joseph François Lafitau, *Customs of the American Indians Compared with the Customs of Primitive Times*, 2 vols., ed. and trans. William N. Fenton and Elizabeth L. Moore (Toronto: The Champlain Society, 1974–77); P.F.X. Charlevoix, *History and General Description of New France*, 5 vols., ed. and trans. John Gilmary Shea (New York: Francis Harper, 1900)

76 Louis Armand de Lom d'Arce de Lahontan, *New Voyages to North America by the Baron de Lahontan*, 2 vols., ed. Reuben Gold Thwaites (1703; Chicago: A.C. McClurg, 1905), 426

77 A.H. Greenly, "Lahontan: An Essay and Bibliography," *The Papers of the Bibliographical Society of America* 48 (1954): 334–89

78 Lahontan, *New Voyages to North America*, 420–1, 572, 613, 439

79 Henry Steele Commager, *The Empire of Reason: How Europe Imagined and America Realized the Enlightenment* ,(New York: Anchor Books, 1978), 81

80 See, for instance, Nicola Perrot, *Mémoire sur les mœurs, coustumes et religion des sauvages de l'Amérique septrionale*, ed. R.P.J. Tailhan (Montreal: Editions Élysées, 1973), 142–5, 309

81 On "The Grand Settlement at Montreal, 1701," see William N. Fenton, *The Great Law and the Longhouse: A Political History of the Iroquois Confederacy* (Norman: University of Oklahoma Press, 1998), 330–60

82 Charlevoix, *History and General Description of New France*, 5: 146. See also ibid., 4: 12; 5: 142–5.

83 Leibnitz to Bierling, 30 January 1711, Hanover, in *Gothofredi Guillelmi Leinniti, Opera Omnia, Nunc primum collecta, in Classes distributa, praefationibus et indicibus exornata, studio* (Fratres de Tournes, 1768), 5: 363–4. The letter was translated from the original Latin for me by Walter Beringer of York University, Toronto.

84 Donald B. Smith, *From the Land of Shadows: The Making of Grey Owl* (Saskatoon: Western Producer Prairie Books, 1990)

85 See Bruce W. Hodgins and Jamie Benedickson, *The Temagami Experiece: Recre-*

ation, Resources, and Aboriginal Rights in the Northwestern Ontario Wilderness (Toronto: University of Toronto Press, 1989).

86 Grey Owl, *The Adventures of Sajo and Her Beaver People* (London: Lovat Dickson and Thompson Ltd, 1935)

87 See Fenton, *The Great Law and the Longhouse,* 363–81

88 See Carolyn T. Foreman, *Indians Abroad, 1493–1938* (Norman: University of Oklahoma Press, 1943).

89 Lovat Dickson, *Wilderness Man: The Strange Story of Grey Owl* (Toronto: Macmillan, 1973), 5

90 *Montreal Gazette,* 8 April 1972

91 Grey Owl, "Grey Owl: 'After a Thing Like That a Man Doesn't Mind Missing a Meal,'" *Globe and Mail,* 1 October 1999, A9

92 See Tom Englehardt, *The End of Victory Culture: Cold War America and the Disillusioning of a Generation* (New York: HarperCollins, 1995)

93 Walter Prescott Webb, "The Frontier Thesis and the 400 Year Boom," in George Roger Taylor, ed., *The Turner Thesis, Concerning the Role of the Frontier in American History* (Lexington, Mass.: D.C. Heath, 1972), 132

94 Frederick Jackson Turner, "The Significance of the Frontier in American History," reprinted in Walker D. Wyman and Clifton B. Kroeber, eds., *The Frontier in Perspective* (Madison: University of Wisconsin Press, 1965), 2

95 See James A. Clifton, ed., *Being and Becoming Indian: Biographical Studies of North American Frontiers* (Chicago: The Dorsey Press, 1989).

96 Margaret Atwood, *Strange Things: The Malevolent North in Canadian Literature* (Oxford: The Clarendon Press,1995), 35

97 Ibid., 42. See also Ernest T. Seton, *Two Little Savages: Being the Adventures of Two Boys Who Lived as Indians and What They Learned* (New York: Doubleday,
1903); *The Birchbark Roll of Woodcraft* (New York: A.S. Barnes, 1902); *The Book of Woodcraft and Indian Lore* (Garden City, NY: Doubleday, 1912).

98 Major John Richardson, *Wacousta: A Tale of the Pontiac Conspiracy* (Toronto: McClelland & Stewart, 1923); see David R. Beasley, "John Richardson," *Dictionary of Canadian Biography,* vol. 8: 1851–1860 (Toronto: University of Toronto Press, 1985), 743–8.

99 See Carl F. Klinck and James J. Talman, eds., *The Journal of Major John Norton* (Toronto: The Champlain Society, 1970).

100 Atwood, *Strange Things,* 44

101 See Milton W. Hamilton, "Myths and Legends of Sir William Johnson," *New York History* 34, 1 (1953): 3–26; Hamilton, "Sir William Johnson's Wives," ibid., 38, 1 (1957): 18–28.

102 See Robert S. Allen, *The British Indian Department and the Frontier in North America, 1755–1830* (Ottawa: Department of Indian and Northern Affairs, 1975).

103 J. Clark, "The Role of Position and Family and Economic Linkage in Land Speculation in the Western District of Upper Canada, 1788–1815," *Canadian Geographer* 19 (spring 1975): 18–34

104 Janet E. Chute, *The Legacy of Shingwaukonse: A Century of Native Leadership* (Toronto: University of Toronto Press, 1998)

105 Major John Richardson, *The War of 1812. First Series. Containing a Full and Detailed Narrative of the Operations of the Right Division of the Canadian Army* published by the author (1842; Toronto: Coles, 1974)

106 Jacqueline Peterson, "Many Roads to Red River: Metis Genesis in the Great Lakes, 1680–1815," in Jacqueline Peterson and Jennifer S.H. Brown, eds., *The New Peoples: Being and Becoming Metis in North America* (Winnipeg: University of Manitoba Press, 1985), 37–73

107 See Reginald Horsman, *Mathew Elliot, British Indian Agent* (Detroit: Wayne State University Press, 1964).

108 John Tanner, *A Narrative of the Captivity and Adventures of John Tanner during Thirty Years Residence among the Indians of the Interior of North America*, ed. Edwin James (1830; Minneapolis: Ross and Haines, 1956)

109 John Sheridan Milloy, "The Era of Civilization – British Policy for the Indian of Canada" (PhD thesis, University of Oxford, 1978)

110 National Archives of Canada, Record Group 10 (Indian Department Records) vol. 245, D. Thornburn to R. Pennefather, 13 October 1858

111 Francis Jennings, *Empire of Fortune: Crowns, Colonies, and Tribes in the Seven Years War in America* (New York: W.W. Norton, 1988), 482

112 Anthony J. Hall, "The Red Man's Burden: Land Law and the Lord in the Indian Affairs of Upper Canada, 1791–1858" (PhD thesis, University of Toronto, 1984), 76–127

113 Egerton Ryerson, *Letters from the Rev. Egerton Ryerson to the Hon. and Rev. Doctor Strachan* (Kingston: The Herald Office, 1828)

114 Donald B. Smith, *Sacred Feathers: The Reverend Peter Jones (Kahkewaquonaby) and the Mississauga Indians* (Toronto: University of Toronto Press, 1987)

115 See Alison Prentice, *The School Promoters: Education and Social Class in Mid-Nineteenth Century Upper Canada* (Toronto: McClelland & Stewart, 1977); Egerton Ryerson, *The Story of My Life by the Late Egerton Ryerson D.D., L.L.D. (Being Reminiscences of Sixty Years Public Service in Canada)*, ed. J. George Hodgins (Toronto: William Briggs, 1883); Neil McDonald and Alf Chaiton, eds., *Egerton Ryerson and His Times* (Toronto: Macmillan, 1978).

116 Canada, *Statistics Respecting Indian Schools with D. Ryerson's Report of 1847 Attached* (Ottawa: Government Printing Bureau, 1890), appendix A

117 Athur J. Slavin, "The American Principle from More to Locke," in Fredi Chiappelli, ed., *First images of America: The Impact of the New World on the Old*, 2 vols. (Berkeley: University of California Press, 1976); Henri Baudet, *Paradise on Earth: Some Thoughts on European Images of Non-European Man*, trans. Elizabeth Wenholt (New Haven: Yale University Press, 1965); Benjamin Bissell, *The American Indian in English Literature of the Eighteenth Century* (New Haven: Yale University Press, 1925); Hoxie Neal Fairchild, *The Noble Savage: A Study in Romantic Naturalism* (New York: Columbia University Press, 1928)

118 Bartholome de Las Casas, *In Defense of the Indians*, ed. and trans. Stafford Poole (DeKalb: Northern Illinois University Press, 1974), 102–3

119 See Lewis Hanke, *The Spanish Struggle for Justice in the Conquest of America* (Boston: Little Brown, 1965).

120 See Harris, *The Rise of Anthropoligical Theory;* Renalto Rosaldo, *Culture and Truth: The Remaking of Social Analysis* (Boston: Beacon Press, 1993).

121 Lewis Henry Morgan, *Ancient Society, or Researches in the Lines of Human Progress from Savagery through Barbarism to Civilization* (1877; New York: Gordon Press, 1976)

122 Frederick Engels, *The Origins of the Family, Private Property and the State In Light of the Researches of Lewis Henry Morgan* (New York: International Publishers, 1972), 72, 83

123 Ibid., 225

124 Ibid., 235–6

125 Ibid., 129

126 Ibid., 235

127 Lewis Henry Morgan, *League of the Ho-de-no-sau-nee or Iroquois* (New York: Sage Books, 1851); Thomas R. Trautmann, *Lewis Henry Morgan and the Invention of Kinship* (Berkeley: University of California Press, 1987)

128 Karl Marx, *The Ethnological Notebooks of Karl Marx (Studies of Morgan, Phear, Maine, Lubbock)*, 2nd ed., ed. Lawrence Krader (Assen, The Netherlands: Van Gorcum, 1974)

129 Engels, *The Origin of the Family*, 71

130 Ibid, 236–7

131 James Tully, "Rediscovering America: The Two Treatises and Aboriginal Rights," in Tully, *An Approach to Political Philosophy: Locke in Context* (Cambridge: Cambridge University Press, 1993), 140–1

132 John Locke, *Two Treatises of Government*, ed. Peter Laslett (New York: New American Library, 1965), 343

133 Ibid., 331, 336, 328

134 Ibid., 336, 340

135 Daniel Harvcy Gottesman, "The Expense of Spirit: Indians, Ideology and the Origins of National Identity in British North America, 1630–1776" (PhD Thesis, University of Toronto, 1979)

136 Ibid., 395 (emphasis in original)

137 Martin Luther paraphrased in David E. Stannard, *American Holocaust: Columbus and the Conquest of the New World* (New York: Oxford University Press, 1992), 233

138 Franke Wilmer, *The Indigenous Voice in World Politics* (Newbury Park: Sage Publications, 1993), 58

139 Thomas Hart Benton cited in Michael Paul Rogin, *Fathers and Children: Andrew Jackson and the Subjugation of the American Indian* (New Brunswick: Transaction Publishers, 1991), 129

140 Richard Drinnon, *Facing West: The Metaphysics of Indian-Hating and Empire-Building* (New York: New American Library, 1980), 53, 54–5, 199, 220–1, 223, 337, 344, 448–9, 501–3. See also Jack Jack D. Forbes, *Columbus and Other Cannibals* (Brooklyn, NY: Autonomedia, 1992), 101

141 See L.C. Green and Olive Dickason, *The Law of Nations and the New World* (Edmonton: University of Alberta Press, 1989); Wilcombe E. Washburn, "The Moral and Legal Justification for the Dispossessing the Indians," in James M. Smith, ed., *Seventeenth-Century America: Essays in Colonial History* (Chapel Hill: University of North Carolina, 1959); Ruth Barnes Moynihan, "The Patent and the Indians: The Problem of Jurisdiction in 17th Century New England," *American Indian Culture and Research* 2, 1 (1977): 8–18; Chester Eisenger, "The Puritan Justification for Taking the Land," *Essex Institute Historical Collections* 84 (1948): 131–43; Robert A. Williams Jr, *The American Indian in Western Legal Thought: The Discourse of Conquest* (Oxford: Oxford University Press, 1991).

142 Tully, "Rediscovering America," 144

143 Karl Polanyi, *The Great Transformation* (Boston: Beacon Press, 1957), 178

144 Ibid., 45

145 John Gray, *Post-Liberalism: Studies in Political Thought* (London: Routledge, 1993), 274

146 See Arthur MacEwan, *Neo-Liberalism or Democracy? Economic Strategy, Markets, and Alternatives for the 21st Century* (Sydney: Pluto Press, 1999).

147 M. Patricia Marchak, *The Integrated Circus: The New Right and the Restructuring of Global Markets* (Montreal: McGill-Queen's University Press, 1991), 268

148 See Immanuel Wallerstein, "The Present State of Debate on World Inequality," in Wallerstein, ed., *World Inequality: Origins and Perspectives on the World System* (Montreal: Black Rose Books, 1975), 16; Titus Alexander, *Unravelling Global Apartheid: An Overview of World Politics* (Cambridge: Polity Press, 1996); Arturo Escobar, *Encountering Development: The Making of the Third World* (Princeton, NJ: Princeton University Press, 1995); Mike Mason, *Development and Disorder: A History of the Third World since 1945* (Toronto: Between the Lines, 1997)

149 See Wilbur R. Jacobs, *Wilderness Politics and Indian Gifts: The Northern Colonial Frontier* (Lincoln: University of Nebraska Press, 1966).

150 See Frank Gilbert Roe, *The North American Buffalo: A Critical Study of the Species in Its Wild State*, 2nd ed. (Toronto: University of Toronto Press, 1970).

151 Richard White, *The Roots of Dependency: Subsistence, Environment, and Social Change among the Choctaws, Pawnees, and Navajos* (Lincoln: University of Nebraska Press, 1983), 318–19

152 Anna Jameson, *Winter Studies and Summer Rambles in Canada*, 3 vols. (1838; Toronto: Coles, 1972), 3: 309–310

153 Ibid, 305–6

154 The phrase is from John Ryerson, *Hudson's Bay; or, A Missionary Tour in the Territory of the Hon. Hudson's Bay Company* (Toronto: Missionary Society of the Wesleyan Methodist Church, 1855), xiv–xv

155 See John Webster Grant, *Moon of Wintertime: Missionaries and the Government of Canada in Encounter since 1534* (Toronto: University of Toronto Press, 1992), 143–66

156 John Maclean, *Vanguards of Canada* (Toronto: The Missionary Society of the Methodist Church, 1918), inside back cover

157 John Maclean [Robin Rustler], *The Indians: Their Manners, Their Customs* (Toronto: William Briggs, 1889), 329 (emphasis added)

158 Peter Jones, *History of the Ojebway Indians, with especially Reference To Their Conversion to Christianity* (London: A.W. Bennett, 1861)

159 George Copway, *Indian Life and Indian History by an Indian Author* (Boston: Albert Colby, 1858)

160 Maungwudaus (George Henry), *An Account of the Chippewa Indians, Who Have Been Travelling among the Whites, in the United States, England, Ireland, Scotland, France and Belgium* (Boston: Published by the author, 1848)

161 William W. Warren, *History of the Ojibway People* (1885; St Paul: Minnesota Historical Society, 1984)

162 Francis Assiginack, "Legends and Traditions of the Odahwah Indians," *Canadian Journal of Industry, Science, and Art* 3 (1858): 115–25; "The Odahwah Indian Language," ibid., 481–5; "Remarks on the Paper Headed 'The Odahwah Indian Language," ibid. (1860): 182–6; "Social and Warlike Customs of Odahwah Indians," ibid., 3 (1858): 297–309

163 Nancy Oestreich Lurie, "Relations between Indians and Anthropologists," in Wilcombe E. Washburn, ed., *Handbook of North American Indians*, vol. 4: *History of Indian-White Relations* (Washington: Smithsonian Institution, 1988), 549

164 Lewis Henry Morgan, *League of the Ho-de-no-sau-nee or Iroquois* (Rochester: Sage Books, 1851), reprinted as *League of the Iroquois* (New York: Corinth Books, 1962)

165 See Ronald Rohner, "Franz Boas: Ethnographer of the Northwest Coast," in June Helm, ed., *Pioneers of American Anthropology: Monographs of the American Ethnological Society, 43* (Seattle: University of Washington Press, 1966), 149–222.

166 See Betty Keller, *Pauline: A Biography of Pauline Johnson* (Vancouver: Douglas and McIntyre, 1981).

167 National Indian Brotherhood, "The Chiefs Visit England," *The National Indian* 2, 10 (1979):

168 See Douglas E. Sanders, "The Indian Lobby," in Keith Banting and Richard Simeon, eds., *And No One Cheered: Federalism, Democracy and the Constitution Act* (Toronto: Methuen, 1983), 301–32.

169 Hall, "What Are We? Chopped Liver? Aboriginal Affairs in the Constitutional Politics of Canada in the 1980s," in Michael Behiels, ed., *The Meech Lake Primer: Conflicting Views of the 1987 Constitutional Accord* (Ottawa: University of Ottawa Press, 1989), 424–56

170 Douglas E. Sanders, "An Uncertain Path: The Aboriginal Constitutional Conferences," in Joseph M. Weiler and Robin M. Elliot, eds, *Litigating the Values of a Nation: The Canadian Charter of Rights and Freedoms* (Toronto: Carswell, 1986), 63–7

171 See Menno Boldt, *Surviving as Indians: The Challenge of Self-Government* (Toronto: University of Toronto Press, 1993); D.C. Hawkes, *Negotiating Aboriginal Self-Government: Developments Surrounding the First Ministers Conference*

(Kingston: Institute of Intergovernmental Relations, Queen's University, 1985) Frank Cassidy and R.L. Bish, *Indian Government: Its Meaning in Practice* (Halifax: Institute for Research on Public Policy, 1989); Frank Cassidy, ed., *Aboriginal Self-Determination: Proceedings of a Conference Held September 30–October 3, 1990* (Halifax: Institute for Research on Public Policy, 1991).

172 Pauline Comeau, *Elijah: No Ordinary Hero* (Vancouver: Douglas & McIntyre, 1993)

173 Peter H. Russell, *Constitutional Odyssey: Can Canadians Become a Sovereign People*, 2nd ed. (Toronto: University of Toronto Press, 1993), 154–263; Susan Delacourt, *United We Fall: The Crisis of Democracy in Canada* (Toronto: Viking, 1993)

174 See, for instance, Curtis Cook, ed., *Constitutional Predicament: Canada after the Referendum of 1992* (Montreal: McGill-Queen's University Press, 1994); Kenneth McRoberts and Patrick Monahan, eds., *The Charlottetown Accord, the Referendum and the Future of Canada* (Toronto: University of Toronto Press, 1993); Jeremy Webber, *Reimagining Canada: Language, Culture, Community and the Canadian Constitution* (Montreal: McGill-Queen's University Press, 1994).

175 Peter Lougheed, cited in Robert Mason Lee, "Ruminations on Quebec from Lougheed, Sage of the West," *Globe and Mail*, 21 December, 1996, D2

176 See Guy Laforest, Louis Balthazar, and Vincent Lemieux, eds., *Le Québec et la restructuration du Canada, 1980–1992* (Sillery, Quebec: Les editions de Septentrion, 1991); Charles Taylor, *Reconciling the Solitudes: Essays on Canadian Federalism and Nationalism* (Montreal: McGill-Queen's University Press, 1993)

177 Geoffrey York and Laureen Pindera, *People of the Pines: The Warriors and the Legacy of Oka* (Toronto: Little Brown, 1991); Tony Hall, "Indian Summer, Canadian Winter," *Report on the Americas* 25, 3 (1991): 34–7

178 Sean McCutcheon, *Electric Rivers: The Story of the James Bay Project* (Montreal: Black Rose Books, 1991); Robert Bourassa, *Power from the North* (Toronto: Prentice Hall, 1985); Ward Churchill, "The Water Plot: Hydrological Rape in North Canada," in Churchill, *Struggle for the Land: Indigenous Resistance to Genocide, Ecocide and Expropriation in Contemporary North America* (Toronto: Between the Lines, 1992), 329–74; Bruce W. Hodgins and Kerry A. Cannon, eds., *On the Land: Confronting the Challenges to Aboriginal Self-Determination in Northern Quebec and Labrador* (Toronto: Betelgeuse Books, 1995); Ronald Niezan, *Defending the Land: Sovereignty and Forest Life in James Bay Cree Society* (Boston: Allyn and Bacon, 1998).

179 Francis Jennings, *Empire of Fortune*; Charles H. Metzger, *The Quebec Act: A Primary Cause of the American Revolution* (New York: United States Catholic Historical Society, 1936); I.R. Christie, *Crisis of Empire: Great Britain and the American Colonies, 1754–1783* (New York: W.W. Norton, 1967); Jack M. Sosin, *Whitehall and the Wilderness: The Middle West in British Colonial Policy, 1760–1775* (Lincoln: University of Nebraska Press, 1961); Lawrence H. Gip-

son, *The British Empire before the American Revolution*, 15 vols. (New York: Alfred A. Knopf, 1936–70)

180 See Lansing Lamont, *Breakup: The Coming End of Canada and the Stakes for America* (New York: W.W. Norton, 1994).

181 After taking over several British posts in the Great Lakes area in 1763, the leader of the coordinated Indian action, Pontiac, is reported to have said: "Englishmen, although you have conquered the French, you have not conquered us. We are not your slaves." Pontiac, quoted in Alexander Henry, *Travels and Adventures in Canada and the Indian Territories between the Years 1760 and 1776*, ed. James Bain (Edmonton: Hurtig, 1969), 44. See Howard Peckham, *Pontiac and the Indian Uprising* (Chicago: University of Chicago Press, 1947); Eric Hinderaker, *Elusive Empires: Constructing Colonialism in the Ohio Valley, 1673–1800* (New York: Columbia University Press, 1997).

182 See especially Richard White, *The Middle Ground, Indians, Empires and Republics in the Great Lakes Region, 1650–1815* (Cambridge: Cambridge University Press, 1991), 315–17.

183 On Aboriginal sovereignty, see Diane Engelstad and John Bird, eds., *Nation to Nation: Aboriginal Sovereignty and the Future of Canada* (Concord, Ont.: Anansi, 1992).

184 The position of the Coalition of First Nations is outlined in Eric Robinson and Henry Bird Quinney, *The Infested Blanket: Canada's Constitution – Genocide of Canada's Indians* (Winnipeg: Queenston House, 1985).

185 On the genesis of the federal Indian Act in Canada, see John L. Tobias, "Protection, Civilization, Assimilation: An Outline History of Canada's Indian Policy," in Getty and Lussier, eds., *As Long as the Sun Shines*, 39–55; Chief Joe Mathias and Gary R. Yabsky, "Conspiracy of Legislation: The Suppression of Indian Rights in Canada," *BC Studies* 89 (1991): 34–45.

186 On this conflict of strategies in the Indian Country of Canada, see Anthony J. Hall, "The Politics of Aboriginality: Political Fault Lines in Indian Country," *Canadian Dimension* 27, 1 (1993): 6–10; Hall, "Who Killed Dudley George? Reflections on Ipperwash and Gustafsen Lake," ibid., 29, 6 (1995/1996): 8–12.

187 See Lillianne Ernestine Krosenbrink-Gelissen, *Sexual Equality as an Aboriginal Right: The Native Women's Association of Canada and the Constitutional Process on Aboriginal Matters*, Nijmegen Studies in Development and Cultural Change, vol. 7 (Saarbrücken, Fort Lauderdale: Verlag breitenbach Publishers, 1991). On the genesis of the Indian women's movement, see Janet Silman, *Enough Is Enough: Aboriginal Women Speak Out* (Toronto: The Women's Press, 1987).

188 Recognition of Aboriginal peoples as founding peoples was announced in the title of Olive Patricia Dickason's important survey text, which was published just as the Charlottetown accord was formulated. See Dickason, *Canada's First Nations: A History of Founding Peoples from Earliest Times* (Toronto: McClelland & Stewart, 1992).

189 David E. Stannard, *American Holocaust: Columbus and the Conquest of the New World* (New York: Oxford University Press, 1992)

190 The relationships between the constitutions of Canada, the United States, and, to a lesser extent, Mexico are considered in Marian C. McKenna, ed., *The Canadian and American Constitutions in Comparative Perspective* (Calgary: University of Calgary Press, 1993). None of these essays addresses seriously the relationship of First Nations to the process of constitution making, including the constitution of NAFTA. According to Kenneth M. Holland, NAFTA's existence "raises the prospect of political as well as economic integration of North America." See Holland, "Federalism in a North American Context: The Contribution of the Supreme Courts of Canada, the United States and Mexico," ibid., 87.

191 Hector St John de Crévecoeur, *Letters from an American Farmer*, 1782, letter 3. Cited in Schlesinger Jr, *The Disuniting of America*, 12

192 Robert Bringhurst and Ulli Steltzer, *The Black Canoe: Bill Reid and the Spirit of Haida Gwaii* (Vancouver: Douglas & McIntyre, 1991)

193 Doris Shadbolt, *Bill Reid* (Vancouver: Douglas & McIntyre, 1986)

194 James Tully, *Strange Multiplicity: Constitutionalism in the Age of Diversity* (Cambridge: Cambridge University Press, 1995), 18

195 "Darling Don't Cry" is on Buffy Sainte-Marie's CD *Up Where We Belong*, EMI, 1996.

196 Isabel Thompson Kelsay, *Joseph Brant, 1743–1807: Man of Two Worlds* (Syracuse: Syracuse University Press, 1984); Charles M. Johnson, ed., *The Valley of the Six Nations: A Collection of Documents on the Indian Lands of the Grant River* (Toronto: University of Toronto Press, 1964); James A. Clifton, *A Place of Refuge for All Times: Migration of the American Potawatomi into Canada, 1830 to 1850*, National Museum of Man Mercury Series, Canadian Ethnology Service Paper no. 26 (Ottawa, 1975); Robert F. Bauman, "Kansas Canada or Starvation?" *Michigan History* 36 (1952); Bauman, "The Migration of the Ottawa Indians from the Maumee Vallee to Walpole Island," *Northwest Ohio Quarterly* 21 (1949); Ian Johnson, "The Promised Land," *Ontario Indian* 5, 7 (1982): 22–5, 54–6; Peter Douglas Elias, *The Dakota of the Canadian Northwest: Lessons for Survival* (Winnipeg: University of Manitoba Press, 1988); Roy W. Meyer, "The Canadian Sioux Refugees from Minnesota," *Minnesota History* 41 (1968): 13–28; W.R. Wrightman, *Forever on the Fringe: Six Studies in the Development of Manitoulin Island* (Toronto: University of Toronto Press, 1982), 20–56; Grant MacEwan, *Sitting Bull: The Years in Canada* (Edmonton: Hurtig, 1973); C. Frank Turner, *Across the Medicine Line: The Epic Confrontation between Sitting Bull and the North-West Mounted Police* (Toronto: McClelland & Stewart, 1973); Merrill D. Beal, *"I Will Fight No More Forever": Chief Joseph and the Nez Pérce War* (New York: Ballantine Books, 1971)

197 See the introduction, 18–20; *United States v. Pitawanakwat*, United States District Court for District of Oregon, Steward Mag. J., 15 November 2000, court file number 00-M-489-ST, ruling published in *Canadian Native Law*

Reporter 1 (2001): 340–60; Kirk Makin, "US Judge Won't Extradite Canadian Native Activist," *Globe and Mail*, 23 November 2000, a1.

CHAPTER THREE

1 Benedict Anderson, *Imagined Communities: Reflections on the Origin and Spread of Nationalism*, rev. ed. (London: Verso, 1991)
2 Theodore W. Allen, *The Invention of the White Race*, vol. 1: *Racial Oppression and Social Control* (London: Verso, 1994); vol. 2: *The Origin of Racial Oppression in Anglo-America* (London: Verso, 1997)
3 See John Lynch, *The Spanish American Revolutions, 1808–1826*, 2nd ed. (New York: W.W. Norton, 1986).
4 Samuel Flagg Bemis, *The Latin American Policy of the United States* (New York: Harcourt, Brace and World, 1943), 39–40
5 Arthur Whitaker, *The United States and South America: The Northern Republics* (Cambridge, Mass.: Harvard University Press, 1948), 6
6 Leslie Bethell, "The Independence of Brazil," in Bethell, ed., *The Independence of Latin America* (Cambridge: Cambridge University Press, 1987), 155–94
7 David Bushnell, "The Independence of Mexico and Central America," ibid., 49–94
8 Bemis, *The Latin American Policy of the United States*, 32
9 Simon Bolivar, cited in David Bushnell and Neill Macaulay, *The Emergence of Latin America in the Nineteenth Century* (New York: Oxford University Press, 1988), 25
10 J.H. Smith, *Appeals to the Privy Council from the American Plantations* (New York: Columbia University Press, 1950), 417–41
11 Anthony Pagden, *Lords of All the World: Ideologies of Empire in Spain, Britain and France, c. 1500–c. 1800* (New Haven: Yale University Press, 1995), 138
12 Charles R. Cutter, *The Protector de Indios in Colonial New Mexico, 1659–1821* (Albuquerque: University of New Mexico Press, 1986), 105–110
13 Edward H. Spicer, *Cycles of Conquest: The Impact of Spain, Mexico and the United States on the Indians of the Southwest, 1533–1960* (Tucson: University of Arizona Press, 1967); Roxanne Dunbar Ortiz, *Roots of Resistence: Land Tenure in New Mexico, 1680–1980* (Los Angeles: University of California Press, 1960)
14 Geral Torres, "The Legacy of Conquest and Discovery: Mediations on Ethnicity, Race and American Politics," in Frank Bonilla et al., eds., *Borderless Borders: U.S. Latinos, Latin Americams and the Paradox of Interdependence* (Philadelphia: Temple University Press, 1998), 153–68
15 See Dell Hymes, ed., *Pidginization and Creolization of Languages* (Cambridge: Cambridge University Press, 1971).
16 Richard A. Pierce, "Russian and Soviet Eskimo and Indian Policies," in Wilcomb E. Washburn, ed., *Handbook of North American Indians*, vol. 4: *History of Indian-White Relations* (Washington: Smithsonian Institution, 1988), 122

17 Miguel Jorrin and John D. Martz, *Latin-American Political Thought and Ideology* (Chapel Hill: University of North Carolina Press, 1970)

18 Grimaldo Rengifo Vasquez, "The Ayllu," in Frederique Apffel-Marglin with PRATEC, eds., *The Spirit of Regeneration: Andean Culture Confronting Western Notions of Development* (London: Zed Books, 1998), 118

19 Garcilasco de la Vega, *Royal Commentaries of the Incas and a General History of Peru*, 2 vols., trans. Harold V. Livermore (Austin: University of Texas Press, 1966)

20 Tupac Amaru, cited in Ronald Wright, *Stolen Continents: The New World through Indian Eyes* (Toronto: Viking, 1992), 197

21 John Lynch, "The Origins of Spanish American Independence," in Bethell, ed., *The Independence of Latin America*, 38

22 Tupac Amaru to the town council of Cusco, 3 January 1781, cited in Wright, *Stolen Continents*, 197

23 See D.A. Brading, *The First America: The Spanish Monarchy, Creole Patriots, and the Liberal State, 1492–1867* (Cambridge: Cambridge University Press, 1991).

24 Samuel Flagg Bemis, paraphrasing Thomas Jefferson in 1808, in Bemis, *The Latin American Policy of the United States*, 27

25 Michael D. Green, "Alexander McGillivray," in R. David Edmunds, *American Leaders: Studies in Diversity* (Lincoln: University of Nebraska Press, 1980), 41–63

26 Charles M. Johnson, "Joseph Brant, the Grand River Lands, and the Northwest Crisis," *Ontario History* 55 (1963): 276–80

27 Jack Greene, *The Intellectual Construction of America: Exceptionalism and Identity from 1492 to 1800* (Chapel Hill: University of North Carolina Press, 1993)

28 Naomi Klein, *No Logo: Taking Aim at the Brand Bullies* (emphasis in original) (Toronto: Vintage Canada, 2000), 30

29 Hannah Arendt, *The Origins of Totalitarianism* (New York: Harcourt Brace, 1976), 55

30 On the strategic deployment of memory and amnesis, see Victoria Freeman, *Distant Relations: How My Ancestors Colonized North America* (Toronto: McClelland & Stewart, 2000)

31 C.L.R. James, *The Black Jacobins: Toussaint L'Ouverture and the San Domingo Revolt*, 2nd ed. (New York: Random House, 1963)

32 Fred Anderson, *Crucible of War: The Seven Years War and the Fate of Empire in British North America, 1754–1766* (New York: Vintage Books, 2000)

33 Pagden, *Lords of All the World*, 64

34 Bill Weinberg, "Mexico's Dirty War," in Tom Hayden, ed., *The Zapatista Reader* (New York: Thunder's Mouth Press/Nation Books, 2002), 98

35 John Ross, *The Annexation of Mexico: From the Aztecs to the I.M.F.* (Monroe, Me: Common Courage Press, 1998), 193

36 See Manuel Gamio, *La Poblacion del Valle de Teotihuacan*, 3 vols. (Mexico City: Departmento de Antropologia, Instituto Nacional, 1922).

37 Allan Knight, "Racism, Revolution, and *Indigenismo*: Mexico, 1910–1940," in

Richard Graham, ed., *The Idea of Race in Latin America, 1870–1940* (Austin: University of Texas Press, 1990), 86

38 Manuel Gamio, *Forjando patria* (Mexico City: Editorial Porrua, 1960), 5–6, 98

39 Roy Harvey Pearce, *Savagism and Civilization: A Study of the Indian and the American Mind* (Baltimore: Johns Hopkins University Press, 1965); Richard Drinnon, *Facing West: The Metaphysics of Indian-Hating and Empire Building* (Minneapolis: University of Minnesota Press, 1980)

40 Ross, *The Annexation of Mexico*, 49–80

41 Lester D. Langely, *The Banana Wars: An Inner History of the American Empire, 1900–1934* (Lexington: University of Kentucky Press, 1983), 77–116

42 Wright, *Stolen Continents*, 278

43 John Collier, *Indians of the Americas* (New York: W.W. Norton, 1947), 15

44 Roxanne Dunbar Ortiz, *Indians and the Americas: Human Rights and Self-Determination* (New York: Praeger, 1984), 46–7

45 Jose Vasconcelos, "The Latin American Basis of Mexican Civilization," in Vasconcelos and Manuel Gamio, *Aspects of Mexican Civilization* (Chicago: University of Chicago Press, 1926), 83

46 Edward W. Said, *Culture and Imperialism* (New York: Vintage, 1994). See also Eric Wolf, *Europe and the People without History* (Berkeley: University of California Press, 1982)

47 See Ronald Robinson and John Gallagher, *Africa and the Victorians: The Official Mind of Imperialism* (London: Macmillan, 1961); Robert O. Collins, ed., *The Partition of Africa: Illusion or Necessity* (New York: John Wiley and Sons, 1969).

48 On Social Darwinism, see Richard Hofstadter, *Social Darwinism in American Thought*, rev. ed. (Boston: Beacon Press, 1955); Loren Eiseley, *Darwin's Century: Evolution and the Men Who Discovered It* (New York: Doubleday, 1958); Christian Bolt, *Victorian Attitudes to Race* (Toronto: University of Toronto Press, 1971); Marvin Harris, *The Rise of Anthropological Theory* (New York: Thomas Y. Crowell, 1968); Robert F. Berkhofer, *The White Man's Indian* (New York: Vintage, 1979); Carl Berger, *Science, God and Nature in Victorian Canada* (Toronto: University of Toronto Press, 1983); Robert E. Bieder, *Science Encounters the Indian, 1820–1880* (Norman: University of Oklahoma Press, 1986).

49 Charles Darwin, *The Origin of the Species, Chapters I–VI, XV* (Chicago: The Great Books Foundation, 1957), 82

50 Gertrude Himmelfarb, *Darwin and the Darwinian Revolution* (New York: W.W. Norton, 1959), 416

51 On Darwinism and on the applications of Social Darwinism to justify empire building and subjugation of various groups, see particularly Stephen Jay Gould, *The Structure of Evolutionary Theory* (Cambridge, Mass.: Harvard University Press, 2002); Reginald Horsman, *Race and Manifest Destiny: The Origins of American Racial Anglo-Saxonism* (Cambridge, Mass.: Harvard University Press, 1981); Hofstadter, *Social Darwinism in American Thought*, especially chapter 9. For racist interpretations of history which rest on the assumptions of Social

Darwinism, see especially Theodore Roosevelt, *The Winning of the West*, 6 vols. (New York: G.P. Putnam's Sons, 1906); Goldwin Smith, *Canada and the Canadian Question* (London: Macmillan, 1891); Benjamin Kidd, *Principles of Western Civilization* (New York: Macmillan, 1902); John Fiske, *Outlines of Cosmic Philosophy*, 2 vols. (Boston: Houghton Mifflin, 1874). On Social Darwinism and Naziism, see Michael R. Marrus, *The Holocaust in History* (Hanover, NH: University Press of New England, 1987). On the idea and history of genocide, see Frank Chalk and Kurt Jonassohn, *The History and Sociology of Genocide: Analyses and Case Studies* (New Haven: Yale University Press, 1990); Robert Davis and Mark Zannis, *The Genocide Machine in Canada: The Pacification of the North* (Montreal: Black Rose Books, 1973); Ward Churchill, "Genocide: Towards a Functional Defintion," in Churchill, *Sinsce Predator Came: Notes from the Struggle for American Indian Liberation* (Littleton, Col.: Aigis Publications, 1995), 75–106; Jean-Paul Sartre, *On Genocide* (Boston: Beacon Press, 1968); Leo Kuper, *The Prevention of Genocide* (New Haven: Yale University Press, 1985).

52 J.H. Parry, *Trade and Dominion: The European Overseas Empires in the Eighteenth Century* (London: Weidenfeld and Nocolson, 1971). See Bernard Semmel, *The Rise of Free Trade Imperialism: Classical Political Economy, the Empire of Free Trade and Imperialism, 1750–1850* (Cambridge: Cambridge University Press, 1970); D.K. Fieldhouse, *The Theory of Capitalist Imperialism* (London: Longmans, 1967); Fieldhouse, *Economics and Empire, 1830–1914* (London: Weidenfeld and Nicolson, 1973); Brian Stanley, "Commerce and Christianity: Providence Theory, the Missionary Movement, and the Imperialism of Free Trade, 1842–1860," *Historical Journal* 26, 1 (1983): 71–94; Andrew Porter, "Commerce and Christianity: The Rise and Fall of a Nineteenth-Century Missionary Slogan," *Historical Journal* 28, 3 (1985): 597–621.

53 See, for instance, Kumar Goshal, *People in Colonies* (New York: Sheridan House, 1948); Harold Macmillan, *Tides of Fortune, 1945–1955* (London: Macmillan, 1969); Bernard Semmel, *Imperialism and Social Reform* (London: Allen and Unwin, 1960); Frank H. Tucker, *The White Conscience* (New York: Frederick Ungar Publishing, 1968).

54 See, for instance, Raphael Lemkin, *Axis Rule in Occupied Europe* (Concord, NH: Rumford Press, 1944). Reflecting on the experience of Nazi rule in Europe, Lemkin invented the term "genocide" to describe the policies of the Third Reich. See also Aimé Césaire, *Discourse on Colonialism*, trans. Joan Pinkham (1955; New York: Monthly Review Press, 1972); Albert Memmi, *The Colonizer and the Colonized* (1957; Boston: Beacon Press, 1967).

55 See Rupert Emerson, *From Empire to Nation: The Rise to Self-Assertion of Asian and African Peoples* (Cambridge, Mass.: Harvard University Press, 1967).

56 See Drinnon, *Facing West*, 355–467; Isabel Molyneux, *The Vietnam Connection* (Edmonton: Molyneux Books, 1991); Howard Zinn, *Postwar America, 1945–1971* (Indianapolis: Bobbs-Merrill Publishers, 1973).

57 See Evan Luard, *A History of the United Nations*, vol. 1: *The Years of Western Dominance, 1945–1955* (New York: St Martin's Press, 1982); Adam Bartos and

Christopher Hitchens, *International Territory: The United Nations, 1945–95* (London: Verso, 1994).

58 John P. Humphrey, *Human Rights and the United Nations: A Great Adventure* (Dobbs Ferry, NY: Transnational Publishers, 1984), 12–13

59 See Leland M. Goodrich, Edvard Hambro, and Anne Patricia Simons, *Charter of the United Nations: Commentary and Documents*, 3rd and rev. ed. (New York: Columbia University Press, 1969); The United Nations, *A Vision of Hope: The Fiftieth Anniversary of the United Nations* (London: Regency Corporation, 1995), 290.

60 French Declaration of Rights, 1795, cited in E.J. Hobsbawm, *Nations and Nationalism since 1780: Programme, Myth, Reality* (Cambridge: Cambridge University Press, 1990), 19

61 See Pagden, *Lords of All the World*, 162–77.

62 Adam Smith, *An Inquiry into the Nature and Causes of the Wealth of Nations*, ed. Edwin Cannan (New York: The Modern Library, 1937), 590

63 The UN Declaration on the Granting of Independence to Colonial Countries and peoples. The wording on the self-determination of Peoples was repeated in 1966 in the International Covenant on Civil and Political Rights and in the International Covenant on Economic, Social and Cultural Rights. See Roxanne Dunbar Ortiz, *Indians of the Americas: Human Rights and Self-Determination* (New York: Praeger, 1984), 29–72.

64 V.I. Lenin, *Imperialism, the Highest Stage of Capitalism: A Popular Outline* (1916; Moscow: Progress Publishers, 1966)

65 See David A. Kay, *The New Nations in the United Nations, 1960–1967* (New York: Columbia University Press, 1970); Kay, "The United Nations and Decolonization," in James Barros, ed., *The United Nations: Past, Present and Future* (London: Collier-Macmillan, 1972), 143–70; Antonio Cassese, *Self-Determination of Peoples: A Legal Reappraisal* (Cambridge: Cambridge University Press, 1996); Christian Tomuschat, "Self-Determination in the Post-Colonial World," in C. Tomuschat, ed., *Modern Law of Self-Determination* (Boston: Martinus Mihhoff Publishers, 1993); U. Umozurike, *Self-Determination in International Law* (Hamden, Conn.: Archon Books, 1972); Rosemary Righter, *Utopia Lost: The United Nations and World Order* (New York: The Twentieth Century Fund Press, 1995); Erica-Irene Daes, "Some Considerations on the Right of Indigenous Peoples to Self-Determination," *Transnational Law and Contemporary Problems* 3, 1 (1993): 35–45.

66 Anderson, *Imagined Communities;* Joseph William Singer, "Sovereignty and Property," *Northwestern University Law Journal* 86, 1 (1991): 1–55

67 See Amos Yoder, *The Evolution of the United Nations System* (New York: Crane Russak, 1989); Thomas M. Frank, *The Power of Legitimacy among Nations* (New York: Oxford University Press, 1990); Joseph R. Rudolph Jr and Robert J. Thompson, eds., *Ethnoterritorial Politics, Policy and the Western World* (Boulder: Lynne Rienner Publishers, 1989).

68 See Stephen J. Randall and Roger Gibbins, eds., *Federalism and the New World*

Order (Calgary: University of Calgary Press, 1995); Graham Smith, ed., *Federalism: The Multi-Ethnic Challenge* (New York: Longmans, 1996).

69 See Charles Tilley, ed., *The Formation of National States in Western Europe* (Princeton: Princeton University Press, 1975); C.B. Macpherson, *The Political Theory of Possessive Individualism: Hobbes to Locke* (Oxford: Oxford University Press, 1962); Immanuel Maurice Wallerstein, *The Modern World-System: Capitalistic Agriculture and the Origins of the European World Economy in the Sixteenth Century* (New York: Academic Press, 1974); James Tully, "Aboriginal Property and Western Theory: Recovering a Middle Ground," in Ellen Frankel Paul et al., eds., *Property Rights* (Cambridge University Press, 1994).

70 Gideon Gottlieb, *Nation against State: A New Approach to Ethnic Conflicts and the Decline of Sovereignty* (New York: Council on Foreign Relations, 1993), 26, 35

71 M.K. Gandhi, *The Collected Works of Mahatma Gandhi*, 12: 505, cited in Robert A. Huttenback, *Racism and Empire: White Settlers and Colored Immigrants in the British Self-Governing Colonies* (Ithaca: Cornell University Press, 1976), 14

72 Louis Fischer, ed. *The Essential Gandhi: His Life, Work, and Ideas* (New York: Vintage, 1983), 197, 191

73 Erik H. Erikson, *Gandhi's Truth: On the Origins of Militant Nonviolence* (New York: W.W. Norton, 1969)

74 Frantz Fanon, *The Wretched of the Earth*, trans. Constance Farrington (New York: Grove Press, 1968), 312–13

75 See Peter Geismar, *Fanon: The Revolutionary as Prophet* (New York: Grove Press, 1971); Ato Sekyi-Otu, *Fanon's Dialectic of Experience* (Cambridge, Mass.: Harvard University Press, 1996)

76 Fanon, *The Wretched of the Earth*, 315

77 Ibid., 149–50, 152

78 Ibid., 175

79 Basil Davidson, *The Black Man's Burden: Africa and the Curse of the Nation State* (New York: Times Books, 1992)

80 See Taisier M. Ali and Robert O. Matthews, eds., *Civil Wars in Africa: Roots and Resolution* (Montreal: McGill-Queen's University Press, 1999).

81 Vine Deloria Jr., Foreword to George Manuel and Michael Posluns, *The Fourth World: An Indian Reality* (Toronto: Collier-Macmillan Canada, 1974), xii

82 Personal conversations with Marie Smallface Marule in Lethbridge, Alberta. See Peter McFarlane, *Brotherhood to Nationhood: George Manuel and the Making of the Modern Indian Movement* (Toronto: Between the Lines, 1993), 129–71

83 Manuel and Posluns, *The Fourth World*, 236

84 On pan-Indianism in North American colonial history, see Gregory Evans Dowd, *A Spirited Resistance: The North American Indian Struggle for Unity, 1745–1815* (Baltimore: Johns Hopkins University Press, 1992). On pan-Indianism in the United States early in the twentieth century, see Hazel W. Hertzberg, *The Search for an American Indian Identity* (Syracuse: Syracuse University Press, 1971). On Canada, see Peter Kulchyski, "A Considerable Unrest: F.O. Loft and the League of Indians," *Native Studies Review* 4, 1 and 2 (1988):

95–117; Stephen Cornell, *The Return of the Native: American Indian Political Resurgence* (New York: Oxford University Press, 1988), 106–48.

85 Manuel and Posluns, *The Fourth World*, 246, 245

86 See Julius K. Nyerere, *Nyerere on Socialism* (Dar es Salaam: Oxford University Press, 1969); Nyerere, *Freedom and Socialism: A Selection from Writings and Speeches, 1965–1967* (Dar es Salaam: Oxford University Press, 1968); Cranford Pratt, *The Critical Phase in Tanzania, 1945–1968: Nyerere and the Emergence of a Socialist Strategy* (Cambridge: Cambridge University Press, 1976).

87 Canadian Press report, Calgary, 13 May 1971, cited in McFarlane, *From Brotherhood to Nationhood*, 160

88 Speech of George Manuel, 25 October 1974, cited ibid., 164

89 Manuel and Posluns, *The Fourth World*, 244, 216, 214

90 Vine Deloria Jr compares Third World thinking to Fourth World thinking in his foreword to Manuel and Posluns, *The Fourth World*, ix–xii.

91 See George W. Stocking Jr, *The Shaping of American Anthropology, 1883–1911: A Franz Boas Reader* (New York: Basic Books, 1974).

92 Manuel and Posluns, *The Fourth World*, 77–8. See Marshall Hyatt, *Franz Boas, Social Actiavist: The Dynamics of Ethnicity* (New York: Greenwood Press, 1990).

93 Manuel and Posluns, *The Fourth World*, 158–61

94 McFarlane, *Brotherhood to Nationhood*, 164–71

95 Francois Morin and Bernard Saladin d'Anglure, "Ethnicity as a Tool for Indigenous Peoples," in Cora Govers and Hans Vermeulen, eds., *The Politics of Ethnic Consciousness* (London: Macmillan; New York: St Martin's Press, 1997), 163

96 Robert Paine, *Dam a River, Dam a People? Saami (Lapp) Livelihood and the Alta/Kautokeino Hydro-Electric Project and the Norwegian Parliament*, IWGIA Document 45 (Copenhagen: International Work Group for Indigenous Affairs, 1982); Paine, "Norwegians and Saami: Nation State and Fourth World," in Gerald Gold, ed., *Minorities and Mother Country Imagery* (St John's: Institute of Social and Economic Research, Memorial University of Newfoundland, 1985); Paine, "Ethnodrama and the 'Fourth World'; The Saami Action Group in Norway, 1979–1981," in Noel Dyck, ed., *Indigenous Peoples and the Nation-State: Fourth World Politics in Canada, Australia and Norway* (St John's: Institute of Social and Economic Research, Memorial University of Newfoundland, 1985), 190–235

97 Sally Weaver, "Political Representitivity and Indigenous Minorities in Canada and Australia," Dyck, ed., *Indigenous Peoples*, 113–50; Weaver, "Self-Determination, National Pressure Groups, and Australian Aborigines: The National Aboriginal Conference, 1983–1985," in Michael D. Levin, ed., *Ethnicity and Aboriginality: Case Studies in Ethnonationalism* (Toronto: University of Toronto Press, 1993), 53–74

98 Douglas Saunders, "The Indian Lobby and the Canadian Constitution, 1978–82," in Levin, ed., *Ethnicity and Aboriginality*, 151–89; Saunders, *The Formation of the World Council of Indigenous Peoples*, IWGIA Document 29 (Copenhagen: International Work Group for Indigenous Affairs, 1977); Saunders,

"Aboriginal Rights: The Search for Recognition in International Law," in Menno Boldt and J. Anthony Long, eds., *The Quest for Justice: Aboriginal Peoples and Aboriginal Rights* (Toronto: University of Toronto Press, 1985), 292–303

99 Paine, "Ethnodrama and the 'Fourth World,'" 190–235

100 Franke Wilmer, *The Indigenous Voice in World Politics* (Newbury Park: Sage, 1993), 140–2; David Maybury-Lewis, *Indigenous Peoples, Ethnic Groups, and the State* (Boston: Allyn and Bacon, 1997)

101 Robert Paine, ed., *Advocacy and Anthropology: First Encounters* (St John's: Institute of Social and Economic Research, Memorial University of Newfoundland, 1985); James B. Waldram, ed., *Anthropology, Public Policy and Native Peoples in Canada* (Montreal: McGill-Queen's University Press, 1993); Dara Culhane, *The Pleasure of the Crown: Anthropology, Law and First Nations* (Burnaby, BC: Talonbooks, 1996)

102 Manuel and Posluns, *The Fourth World*, 261 (emphasis in original)

103 There is a large and growing literature on the many influences and contributions of American Indian societies on the evolution of Western and world civilization. See, for instance, Felix Cohen's "Americanizing the White Man," in Lucy Kramer Cohen, ed., *The Legal Conscience: Selected Papers of Felix S. Cohen* (Np: Archon Books, 1970), 315–27; Irving A. Hallowell, "The Backwash of Frontier: The Impact of the Indian on American Culture," in W.D. Wyman and C.B. Kroeber, eds., *The Frontier in Perspective* (Madison: University of Wisconsin Press, 1957), 229–58. For more contemporary accounts of the transfer of ideas, culture, and technology from Indian sources, see Warren Lowes, *Indian Giver: The Legacy of North American Native Peoples* (Toronto: Canadian Alliance in Solidarity with Native Peoples, 1986); Jack Weatherford, *Indian Givers: How Indians of the Americas Transformed the World* (New York: Crown Publishers, 1988); Gordon Brotherston, *Book of the Fourth World: Reading the Native Americas through Their Literature* (Cambridge: Cambridge University Press, 1992). There is a large literature presenting contending arguments about the impact, or lack thereof, of the Iroquois Constitution on the Constitution of the United States. See, for instance, Donald A. Grinde Jr, "Iroquois Political Theory and the Roots of American Democracy," in Oren Lyons, John Mohawk, et al., *Exiled in the Land of the Free* (Santa Fe: Five Rings Corporation, 1992), 228–80; Elizabeth Tooker, "The United States Constitution and the Iroquois League," *Ethnohistory* 35, 4 (1988): 305–36; Grinde and Bruce E. Johansen, *Exemplar of Liberty: Native America and the Evolution of Democracy* (Los Angeles: University of California Regents and UCLA American Indian Studies Center, 1991).

104 Manuel and Posluns, *The Fourth World*, 11

105 See, for instance, Myrna Kostash, *Long Way from Home: The Story of the Sixties Generation in Canada* (Toronto: James Lorimer, 1980); Harold Jaffe and John Tytell, eds., *The American Experience: A Radical Reader* (New York: Harper & Row, 1970): Theodore Roszak, *The Making of the Counter Culture* (New

York: Anchor Books, 1969), Roderick Aya and Norman Miller, eds, *The New American Revolution* (London: Collier-Macmillan, 1971).

106 Many of these changes are described in Harvey McCue, "The Modern Age, 1945–1980," in Edward S. Rogers and Donald B. Smith, eds, *Aboriginal Ontario: Historical Perspectives on the First Nations* (Toronto: Dundurn, 1994), 377–417. On Indian education, see Margaret Connell Szasz, *Education and the American Indian: The Road to Self-Determination, 1928–1973* (Albuquerque: University of New Mexico Press, 1974); Jean Barman, Yvonne Hébert, and Don McCaskill, eds., *Indian Education in Canada*, 2 vols. (Vancouver: UBC Press, 1986); Mick Fedullo, *Light of the Feather: A Teacher's Journey into Native American Classrooms and Culture* (New York: Doubleday, 1992); Marie Battiste and Jean Barman, eds., *First Nations Education in Canada: The Circle Unfolds* (Vancouver: UBC Press, 1995).

107 See James B. Waldram, *As Long as the Rivers Run: Hydroelectric Development and Native Communities in Western Canada* (Winnipeg: University of Manitoba Press, 1988); Boyce Richardson, *Strangers Devour the Land* (Vancouver: Douglas & MacIntyre, 1979); Sean McCutcheon, *Electric Rivers: The Story of the James Bay Project* (Montreal: Black Rose Books, 1991).

108 See Rex Wyler, *Blood of the Land: The Government and Corporate War against the American Indian Movement* (New York: Vintage Books, 1984); Joseph G. Jorgensen, ed., *Native Americans and Energy Development* (Boston: Anthropology Resource Center and Seventh Generation Fund, 1984); Donald A. Grinde and Bruce E. Johansen, eds., *Ecocide of Native America: Environmental Destruction of Indian Lands and People* (Santa Fe, NM: Clear Light, 1995).

109 Karmel McCullum and John Olthius, *Moratorium: Justice Energy, the North, and the Native People* (Toronto: Anglican Book Centre, 1977); Thomas R. Berger, *Northern Frontier, Northern Homeland: The Report of the Mackenzie Valley Pipeline Inquiry*, 2 vols. (Ottawa: Department of Supply and Services, 1977). See also Robert Davis and Mark Zannis, *The Genocide Machine in Canada: The Pacification of the North* (Montreal: Black Rose Books, 1975).

110 Brotherston, *Book of the Fourth World*, 6

111 See, for instance, Lister Sinclair and Jack Pollock, *The Art of Norval Morrisseau* (Toronto: Methuen, 1979); Duane Champagne, *Native America: Portrait of the Peoples* (Detroit: Visible Ink, 1994), 609–31

112 N. Scott Momaday, *House Made of Dawn* (New York: Harper & Row, 1968)

113 See Arnold Krupat, ed., *New Voices in Native American Literary Criticism* (Washington: Smithsonian Institution, 1993).

114 Richard Drinnon, *Facing West: The Metaphysics of Indian-Hating and Empire Building* (New York: New American Library, 1980)

115 Tom Hayden, "In Chiapas," in Hayden, ed., *The Zapatista Reader* (New York: Thunder's Mouth Press/Nation Books, 2002), 77

116 A thoughtful commentary on the literature of Vine Deloria Jr is presented in Robert Allen Warrior, *Tribal Secrets: Recovering American Indian Intellectual Traditions* (Minneapolis: University of Minnesota Press, 1995)

117 Waubageshig, "The Comfortable Crisis," in Waubageshig, ed., *The Only Good Indian: Essays by Canadian Indians* (Toronto: New Press, 1970). See Rupert Costo and Scott Momaday et al., *Indian Voices: The First Convocation of American Indian Scholars* (San Francisco: Indian Historian Press, 1970).

118 Richard White, *The Middle Ground: Indians, Empires, and Republics in the Great Lakes Region, 1650–1815* (Cambridge: Cambridge University Press, 1991), 523, xv

119 See Paul Tennant, *Aboriginal Peoples and Politics: The Indian Land Question in British Columbia, 1849–1989* (Vancouver: UBC Press, 1990).

120 White, *The Middle Ground*, ix

121 Manuel and Posluns, *The Fourth World*, 12, 219–20

122 Ibid., 12

123 Ibid., 256

124 Ibid., 84

125 On Paull see E. Palmer Patterson II, "Andrew Paull and Canadian Indian Resurgence" (PhD Thesis, University of Washington, 1962).

126 See Alan Morley, *Roar of the Breakers: A Biography of Peter Kelly* (Toronto: Ryerson Press, 1967).

127 Patterson II, "Andrew Paull," 139–73

128 See Paul Tennant, *Aboriginal Peoples and Politics: The Indian Land Question in British Columbia, 1849–1989* (Vancouver: UBC Press, 1990).

129 Patterson II, "Andrew Paull," 174–224

130 Tennant, *Aboriginal Peoples and Politics*, 81

131 See Raymond J.A. Huel, *Proclaiming the Gospel to the Indians and Metis* (Edmonton: University of Alberta Press, 1996); Anne Hélène Kerbirious, *Les indiens dans l'ouest canadien vus par les oblats, 1885–1930* (Sillery: Les editions du Septenrion, 1996).

132 Herbert Francis Dunlop, *Andy Paull: As I Knew Him and Understood His Times* (Vancouver: Standard Press, 1989)

133 I met and interviewed Jules Sioui at his home on the Huron reserve at Loretteville in the late 1970s.

134 Norma Slulman and Jean Goodwill, *John Tootoosis: A Biography of a Cree Leader* (Ottawa: Golden Dog Press, 1982), 177–85

135 See Fred Gaffen, *Forgotten Soldiers* (Penticton, BC: Theytus Books, 1985).

136 Jules Sioui, *War ... Peace in Canada: The Invaders Responsible for the Death of Louis Riel* (Np, nd), cited in Donald B. Smith, "Amerindians in Quebec and Canada, Half-a-Century Ago— And Today," in Laurier Turgeon, Denys Delâge, et Real Oulette, eds., *Transferts culturels et métissages Amérique/Europe, XVIe-XXe siècle/Cultural Transfer, America and Europe: 500 Years of Interculturation* (Quebec: Les Presses de l'Université Laval, 1996), 135

137 See Stan Cuthand, "The Native Peoples of the Prairie Provinces in the 1920s and 1930s," in J.R. Miller, ed., *Sweet Promises: A Reader in Native-White Relations in Canada* (Toronto: University of Toronto Press, 1991), 381–92; Peter Kulchyski, "'A Considerable Unrest': F.O. Loft and the League of Indians," *Native Studies Review* 4, 1 and 2 (1988): 95–117; Delia Opekokew, *The*

First Nations: Indian Government and the Canadian Confederation (Saskatoon: Federation of Saskatchewan Indians, 1980), 28–38; Murray Dobbin, *The One-and-a-Half Men* (Vancouver: New Star Books, 1981); Joseph F. Dion, *My People the Cree* (Calgary: Glenbow Museum, 1979); Edward Ahenakew, *Voices of the Plains Cree* (Toronto: McClelland & Stewart, 1973)

138 Sluman and Goodwill, *John Tootoosis*, 1981

139 Patterson ii, "Andrew Paul," 225–49

140 See James M. Pitsula, "The Saskatchewan CCF Government and Treaty Indians, 1944–64," *Canadian Historical Review* 75, 1 (1994): 21–52; F. Laurie Barron, *Walking in Indian Moccasins: The Native Policies of Tommy Douglas and the CCF* (Vancouver: UBC Press, 1997).

141 Morris Shumiatcher, cited in Barron, *Walking in Indian Moccasins*, 61

142 Barron, *Walking in Indian Moccasins*, 79

143 See Peter Iverson, *Carlos Montezuma and the Changing World of American Indians* (Albuquerque: University of New Mexico Press, 1982).

144 Ibid., 106, 148

145 See Hazel Whitman Hertzberg, "Indian Rights Movement, 1887–1973," in Washburn, cd., *History of Indian–White Relations*, 308.

146 Jemison, cited in Laurence M. Hauptman, *The Iroquois and the New Deal* (Syracuse: Syracuse University Press, 1981), 43

147 Ibid, 54

148 Manuel and Poslums, *The Fourth World*, 229

149 See Hazel W. Hertzberg, *The Search of an American Indian Identity: Modern Pan-Indian Movements* (Syracuse: Syracuse University Press, 1971).

150 Declaration of Kinship and Cooperation among the Indigenous Peoples and Nations of North America through the Assembly of First Nations and the National Congress of American Indians, Vancouver, 23 July 1999

151 Tasha Hubbard, "Protocol Accord Signed by First Nations on Both Sides of Artificial Border," *First Nations Messenger* 1, 5 (September/October 1999), 1–2

152 Cited in Sluman and Goodwill, *John Tootoosis*, 163

153 Ibid., 208–15

154 A Declaration of the First Nations, December 1980, in Ian A.L. Getty and Antoine S. Lussier, eds., *As Long as the Sun Shines and Water Flows: A Reader in Canadian Native Studies* (Vancouver: UBC Press, 1983), 337

155 See Dee Brown, *Bury My Heart at Wounded Knee: An Indian History of the American West* (New York: Holt, Rinehart and Winston, 1970), 415–50

156 Wilmer, *The Indigenous Voice in World Politics*, 84

157 I base these observations largely on my discussions with Art Solomon, an AIM elder who worked in the prisons, especially in the area of Kingston, Ontario, in the late 1960s and the 1970s. See also Peter Matthiessen, *In the Spirit of Crazy Horse* (New York: Viking, 1983), 35–58.

158 See Robert Allen Warrior, *Tribal Secrets: Recovering American Indian Intellectual Traditions* (Minneapolis: University of Minnesota Press, 1995), 28–9

159 Shirley Hill Witt, "Nationalist Trends among American Indians," in Stuart

Levine and Nancy Oestreich Lurie, eds., *The American Indian Today* (Baltimore: Penguin, 1968), 118

160 Marlon Brando, cited in Stan Steiner, *The New Indians* (New York: Dell Publishing, 1968), 57

161 Helen Hunt Jackson, *A Century of Dishonour: The Early Crusade for Indian Reform*, ed. Andrew F. Rolle (New York: Harper & Row, 1965)

162 See William T. Hagan, *The Indian Rights Association: The Herbert Walsh Years, 1882–1904* (Tucson: University of Arizona Press, 1985).

163 For a full discussion of aspects of the history of the Indian-Eskimo Association and of Canadian Association in Support of Native People (CASNP) see J. Rick Ponting and Roger Gibbins, *Out of Irrelevance: A Socio-Political Introduction to Indian Affairs in Canada* (Toronto: Butterworths, 1980), 298–309. Since 1983, the name has been the Canadian Alliance in Solidarity with the Native Peoples.

164 H.B. Hawthorn, *A Survey of the Contemporary Indians of Canada: Economic, Political, Educational Needs and Policies*, 2 vols (Ottawa: Queen's Printer, 1967). See also Sally M. Weaver, "The Hawthorn Report: Its Use in the Making of Canadian Indian Policy," in Noel Dyck and James B. Waldram, eds., *Anthropology, Public Policy and Native Peoples in Canada* (Montreal: McGill-Queen's University Press, 1993), 75–97; Alan C. Cairns, *Citizens Plus: Aboriginal Peoples and the Canadian State* (Vancouver: UBC Press, 2000).

165 Peter A. Cumming et al., eds., *Native Rights in Canada*, 2nd ed. (Toronto: Indian-Eskimo Association, 1972)

166 See Carolyn Swayze, *Hard Choices: A Life of Tom Berger* (Vancouver: Douglas & McIntyre, 1987); Donald N. Abbott, ed., *The World Is as Sharp as a Knife: An Anthology in Honour of Wilson Duff* (Victoria: British Columbia Provincial Museum, 1981).

167 See Sally M. Weaver, *Making Canadian Indian Policy: The Hidden Agenda 1968–1970* (Toronto: University of Toronto Press, 1981), 12–50.

168 I discussed this presentation with Ms Horn when she visited Lethbridge in 1996.

169 *Indian-Eskimo Association of Canada Bulletin* 13, 1 (1972), 2

170 Thomas H.B. Symons, *To Know Ourselves* (Toronto: McClelland & Stewart, 1978)

171 See Hall, "The Genesis of Native Studies in Canada," in Peter Adams and Doug Parker, eds., *Canada's Subarctic Universities* (Ottawa: Association of Canadian Universities for Northern Studies, 1987), 192–205.

172 Paul Chaat Smith and Robert Allen Warrior, *Like a Hurricane: The Indian Movement from Alcatraz to Wounded Knee* (New York: The New Press, 1996), 1–86

173 Cited in Matthiessen, *In The Spirit of Crazy Horse*, 37–8

174 See Peter Bluecloud, ed., *Alcatraz is Not an Island* (Berkeley: Wingbow Press, 1972).

175 See Edmund Wilson, *Apologies to the Iroquois, with a Study of the Mohawks in High Steel by Joseph Mitchell* (New York: Farrar, Straus & Giroux, 1960); Ella

Cork, *"The Worst of the Bargain,"* concerning the Dilemmas Inherited from the Fore-fathers along with Their Lands by the Iroquois Nation of the Grand River Reserve (San Jacinto, Cal.: Foundation for Social Research, 1962).

176 See, for instance, Francis Jennings, ed., *The History and Culture of Iroquois Diplomacy* (Syracuse: Syracuse University Press, 1985).

177 See E. Brian Titley, *A Narrow Vision: Duncan Campbell Scott and the Administration of Indian Affairs in Canada* (Vancouver: UBC Press, 1986), 110–34.

178 See Clinton Rickard, *Fighting Tuscorora: The Autobiography of Chief Clinton Rickard*, ed. Barbara Graymont (Syracuse: Syracuse University Press, 1973).

179 Ernest Benedict, "Indians and a Treaty" in Waubageshig, ed., *The Only Good Indiana*, 157–60. On the history of Jay's Treaty, see Samuel Flagg Bemis, *Jay's Treaty: A Study in Commerce and Diplomacy*, rev. ed. (New Haven: Yale University Press, 1962); A.L. Burt, *The United States, Great Britain, and British North America from the Revolution to the Establishment of Peace after the War of 1812* (New Haven: Yale University Press, 1940), 140–65; Geoffrey York and Lau-reen Pindera, *People of the Pines* (Toronto: Little, Brown, 1991), 167–8.

180 Wilson, *Apologies to the Iroquois*, 272

181 See Rupert Custo and Jeanette Henry, eds, *Indian Treaties: Two Centuries of Dishonor* (San Francisco: The Indian Historian Press, 1977).

182 Smith and Warrior, *Like a Hurricane*, passim.

183 Vine Deloria Jr, *Behind the Trail of Broken Treaties: An Indian Declaration of Independence* (New York: Delta, 1974), 160–86

184 These treaties are surveyed in Francis Prucha, *American Indian Treaties: The History of a Political Anomaly* (Berkeley: University of California Press, 1994). In his review of Prucha's book, Deloria describes "the history of treaties as *the* definitive context within which Indian policy should be understood." See Deloria, "The Subject Nobody Knows," *American Indian Quarterly* 19, 1 (1995): 143–7. The texts of the US Indian treaties are published in Charles J. Kappler, comp., *Indian Treaties, 1778–1883* (New York: Interland Publishing, 1973). See also Julian Boyd, ed., *Indian Treaties Published by Benjamin Franklin* (Philadelphia: Historical Society of Pennsylvania, 1938).

185 Deloria, *Behind the Trail of Broken Treaties*, 57–8

186 Peter Matthiessen, *In the Spirit of Crazy Horse* (New York: Penguin Books, 1992); *Voices from Wounded Knee* (Rooseveltoon: Akwesasne Notes, 1974); Ward Churchill and Jim Vander Wall, *The Cointelpro Papers: Documents from the FBI's Secret Wars against Dissent in the USA* (Boston: South End Press, 1990). For a first-person account of the trials and tribulations of AIM, see Russell Means with Marvin J. Wolf, *Where White Men Fear to Tread: The Autobiography of Russell Means* (New York: St Martin's Press, 1995).

187 See Edward Lazarus, *Black Hills White Justice: The Sioux Nation versus the United States, 1775 to the Present* (New York: HarperCollins, 1991). Mario Ganza-lez and Elizabeth Cook-Lynne, *The Politics of Hallowed Ground: Wounded Knee and the Struggle for Indian Sovereignty* (Urbana and Chicago: University of Illinois Press, 1999).

188 See Jack D. Forbes, *Native Americans and Nixon: Presidential Politics and Minority Self-Determination, 1969–1972* (Albuquerque: University of New Mexico Press, 1986).

189 Ward Churchill and Jim Vander Wall, "AIM Casualties on Pine Ridge, 1973–1976," in Churchill, *Indians Are Us? Culture and Genocide in Native North America* (Toronto: Between the Line, 1994), 197–206

190 Louis Cameron (interview), *The Ojibway Warriors Society in Occupied Anicinabe Park, Kenora, Ontario, August 1974* (Toronto: Better Read Graphics Collective, 1974), p.13

191 Ibid., 10

192 Ibid., 4–5

193 Ibid., 6

194 The Demands of the Native Peoples' Caravan, published ibid., 32

195 On the failure of this effort at collaboration, see J.W. Beaver, *To Have What Is One's Own* (Ottawa: National Indian Socio-Economic Development Committee, 1979).

196 See Henry Jack, "Native Alliance for Red Power," in Waubageshig, ed, *The Only Good Indian*, 162–80.

197 See L.F.S. Upton, "The Extermination of the Beothucks of Newfoundland," *Canadian Historical Review* 58 (1977): 133–53.

198 The co-founder of the Nishnawbe Institute was Wilfred Pelletier. See Pelletier and Ted Poole, *No Foreign Land: The Biography of a North American Indian* (Toronto: McClelland & Stewart, 1973). My major source on the Nishnawbe Institute during this era was the late Jan Currie, who moved from Rochdale to the Native Studies Department at Laurentian University in Sudbury, where I first worked in 1982.

199 See Michael Posluns, ed., *Songs for the People: Teachings on the Natural Way, Poems and Essays of Arthur Solomon* (Toronto: NC Press, 1990).

200 John A. Price, *Native Studies: American and Canadian Indians* (Toronto: McGraw-Hill Ryerson, 1978), 244–6. Willie Dunn recorded a song about Charlie Wenjack.

201 Harvey McCue, "The Modern Age, 1945–1980," in *Aboriginal Ontario*, 413. Also based on the author's discussion with Sherman Butler in July 1998.

202 Joan Ryan, *Wall of Words: The Betrayal of Urban Indians* (Toronto: PMA Books, 1978)

203 Louis Hall, "Suicide as a Weapon against Oppression," mimeographed newsletter, 11, 22 June 1976

204 Telephone interview with Michael Posluns conducted in March 1996.

205 George Manuel, "Statement," in Waubageshig, ed., *The Only Good Indian*, 3

206 The most authoritative work on the White Paper is Sally M. Weaver's *Making Canadian Indian Policy: The Hidden Agenda, 1968–1970* (Toronto: University of Toronto Press, 1981). See also Pierre Elliott Trudeau, *Federalism and the French Canadians* (Toronto: Macmillan, 1968).

207 Trudeau's speech is transcribed in Peter Cumming et al., eds., *Native Rights in Canada*, 2nd ed. (Toronto: Indian-Eskimo Association, 1972), 331.

208 Government of Canada, *Canada on Indian Policy, 1969* (Ottawa: Department of Indian Affairs and Northern Development, 1969), 11

209 See John Hutcheson, "Mr. Trudeau's Canada," *Canadian Forum* 64 (April 1984): 4.

210 Harold Cardinal, *The Unjust Society: The Tragedy of Canada's Indians* (Edmonton: Hurtig, 1969), 36, 30, 50

211 Harold Cardinal, "Treaties Six and Seven: The Next Century," in Ian A.L. Getty and Donald B. Smith, eds., *One Century Later: Western Canadian Indian Reserve Indians since Treaty 7* (Vancouver: UBC Press, 1978), 133

212 See Thomas R. Berger, "The Nishga Indians and Aboriginal Rights," in Berger, *Fragile Freedoms: Human Rights and Dissent in Canada* (Toronto: Clark, Irwin, 1982), 219–54. See also Daniel Raunet, *Without Surrender, Without Consent: A History of Nishga Land Claims* (Vancouver: Douglas and McIntyre, 1984).

213 See *Practically Millionaires: A Report on the James Bay Agreement* (Ottawa: National Indian Brotherhood, 1982); Sylvie Vincent and Garry Bowerseds, *Baie James et Nord Québécois. Dix ans après* (Montreal: Recherches amérindiennes au Québec, 1988). Scc also Kcn Coates, ed., *Aboriginal Land Claims in Canada: A Regional Perspective* (Toronto: Copp Clark Pitman, 1992); Boyce Richardson, ed; *Drum Beat: Anger and Renewal in Indian Country* (Toronto: Summerhill Press, 1989).

214 Manuel and Poslums, *The Fourth World*, 85

215 Cited in *Through Indian Eyes: The Untold Story of Native Peoples* (Montreal: Reader's Digest Association, 1996), 371

216 Jack D. Forbes, "The United States and Native America: The Colossus at the Crossroads," in Forbes, *Tribes and Masses: Explorations in Red, White and Black* (Davis, Cal.: D-Q University Press, 1978), 83

217 Section 141 of the Indian Act, 1927

218 Manuel and Posluns, *The Fourth World*, 221 (italics in original)

219 Cornel West, *Keeping Faith: Philosophy and Race in America* (New York: Routledge, 1993), 283

220 See Menno Boldt, *Surviving as Indians: The Challenge of Self-Government* (Toronto: University of Toronto Press, 1993), 117–166.

221 See Graeme Patterson, *History and Communications: Harold Innis, Marshall McLuhan, and the Interpretation of History* (Toronto: University of Toronto Press, 1990), 135–69; Chester Martin, *Empire and Commonwealth: Studies in Governance and Self-Government in Canada* (Oxford: Clarendon Press, 1929); John Manning Ward, *Colonial Self-Government: The British Experience, 1759–1856* (London: Macmillan, 1976).

222 See Arthur R.M. Lower, *Colony to Nation: A History of Canada* (Toronto: Longmans, Green, 1946).

223 See J. Rick Ponting, "Internationalization: Perspectives on an Emerging Direction in Aboriginal Affairs," *Canadian Ethnic Studies* 22, 3 (1990): 85–109; Pierre-Gerlier Forest et Thierry Rodon, "Les activités internationales des autochtones du Canada," *Études internationales* 26, 1 (1995):

35–57; Russell Lawrence Barsh, "Aboriginal Issues in Canadian Foreign Policy, 1984–1994," *International Journal of Canadian Studies* 12 (fall 1995): 107–33; Boyce Richardson, *People of Terra Nulius: Betrayal and Rebirth in Aboriginal Canada* (Vancouver: Douglas & McIntyre, 1993), 344–57.

224 For a caustic yet penetrating and disturbing commentary on the drift of Canada away from its anchor in the British constitutional heritage, see John Farthing, *Freedom Wears a Crown* (Toronto: Kingswood House, 1957). See also A. Jacomy-Milette, *Treaty Law in Canada* (Ottawa: University of Ottawa Press, 1975).

225 On Indian treaties as covenants with the British sovereign, see particularly the transcript of negotiations in the making of Treaty 4 in the Qu'Appelle Valley of Saskatchewan in 1874. Alexander Morris, *The Treaties of Canada with the Indians of Manitoba and the North-West Territories;* reprint, Saskatoon: Firth House, 1991), 111–23. See also Dorothy V. Jones, *License for Empire: Colonialism by Treaty in Early America* (Chicago: University of Chicago Press, 1982).

226 See, for instance, George R. Mellor, *British Imperial Trusteeship, 1783–1850* (London: Farber and Farber, 1951); Ian Brownlie, *Treaties with Indigenous Peoples: The Robb Lectures* (Oxford: Clarendon Press, 1992); Paul McHugh, *The Maori Magna Carta: New Zealand Law and the Treaty of Waitangi* (Auckland: Oxford University Press, 1991); Francis Jennings, *The Founders of America* (New York: W.W. Norton, 1993); R.W. Van Alstyne, *The Rising American Empire* (Oxford: Basil Blackwell, 1960); Tony Hall, "Native Limited Identities and Newcomer Metropolitanism in Upper Canada, 1814–1867," in David Keane and Colin Read, eds., *Old Ontario: Essays in Honour of J.M.S. Careless* (Toronto: Dundurn, 1990), 159–68.

227 Manuel and Posluns, *The Fourth World,* 218, 232

228 Ibid., xi–xii

CHAPTER FOUR

1 Richard Drinnon, *Facing West: The Metaphysics of Indian-Hating and Empire-Building* (New York: New American Library, 1980), 3, 368, 451

2 Fred L. Ragsdale Jr, "The Deception of Geography," in Vine Deloria Jr. ed., *American Indian Policy in the Twentieth Century* (Norman: University of Oklahoma Press, 1985), 68–9

3 Alistair Cooke, *Alistair Cooke's America* (New York: Alfred A. Knopf, 1973), 19

4 Harold A. Innis, *The Fur Trade in Canada: An Introduction to Canadian Economic History,* rev. ed. (1930; Toronto: University of Toronto Press, 1975), 392

5 Indian and Northern Affairs Canada, "Population Growth Rates" (Ottawa, 1996). The proportion of registered Indians under fourteen is 38 percent, about twice as high as the proportion among Canadians generally. The Indian baby boom is beginning to surge into the workforce, into postsecondary education, and, if present trends continue, into the jails and related criminal justice agencies of Canada.

6　See, for instance, Marshall McLuhan's introduction to Harold Innis, *The Bias of Communication* (Toronto: University of Toronto Press, 1973); Arthur Kroker, *Technology and the Canadian Mind: Innis/McLuhan/Grant* (Montreal: New World Perspectives, 1984); Graeme Patterson, *History and Communications: Harold Innis, Marshall McLuhan, and the Interpretation of History* (Toronto: University of Toronto Press, 1990).

7　Richard White, *The Middle Ground: Indians, Empires, and Republics in the Great Lakes, 1650–1815* (Cambridge: Cambridge University Press, 1991)

8　Fernand Braudel, *The Perspective of the World* (London: William Collins, 1985), 387–8

9　Frantz Fanon, *The Wretched of the Earth*, trans. Constance Farrington (New York: Grove Press, 1968), 313

10　Samuel Huntington, *The Clash of Civiliizations and the Making of World Order* (New York: Simon and Schuster, 1996), 311; Arthur M. Schlesinger Jr, *The Disuniting of America: Reflections on a Multicultural Society* (New York: W.W. Norton, 1993), 126–7

11　See Benedict Anderson, *Imagined Communities: Reflections on the Origin and Spread of Nationalism*, rev. ed. (London: Verso, 1991).

12　J. Lloyd Mecham, "The Church in Colonial Spanish America," in A. Curtis Wilgus, ed., *Colonial Hispanic America* (New York: Russell and Russell, 1963), 200–39

13　James (Sakej) Youngblood Henderson, *The Mikmaw Concordat* (Halifax: Fernwood, 1997), 43

14　Cited in L.C. Green and Olive Dickason, *The Law of Nations and the New World* (Edmonton: University of Alberta Press, 1989), 18

15　Cited in ibid., 40. See Franciso de Vitoria, *Political Writings*, eds. Anthony Pagden and Jeremy Lawrence (Cambridge: Cambridge University Press, 1991); also see S. James Anaya, *Indigenous Peoples in International Law* (New York: Oxford University Press, 2000); J.L. Brierly, *The Law of Nations: An Introduction to the International Law of Peace*, 6th ed. (Oxford: Clarendon Press, 1963); Robert A. Williams Jr, *The American Indian in Western Legal Discourse* (New York: Oxford University Press, 1990), 96–108; Jennings C. Wise, *The Red Man in the New World Drama: A Politico-Legal Study with a Pageantry of American Indian History* (New York: Macmillan, 1971), 33–8.

16　Lewis Hanke, *The Spanish Struggle for Justice in the Conquest of America* (Boston: Little, Brown, 1965); J. Friede and B. Keen, eds., *Bartolome de Las Casas in History: Toward an Understanding of His Life and Work* (DeKalb: Northern Illinois University Press, 1971); Greg C. Marks, "Indigenous Peoples in International Law: The Significance of Francisco de Vitoria and Bartolome de las Casas," *Australian Yearbook of International Law* 13 (1992): 1–51

17　See Anthony Pagden, *Spanish Imperialism and the Political Imagination* (New Haven: Yale University Press, 1990).

18　Frances Rose-Troup, *The Massachusetts Bay Company and Its Predecessors* (Bowie, Md.: Heritage Books, 1998); George Louis Beer, *The Origins of the British Colonial System, 1578–1660* (New York: P. Smith, 1933)

19 James Lang, *Conquest and Commerce: Spain and England in the Americas* (New York: Academic Press, 1975), 146–9

20 Anthony Pagden, *Lords of All the World: Ideologies of Empire in Spain, Britain and France, c. 1500–c. 1800* (New Haven: Yale University Press, 1995), 137–9; Salvador de Madariaga, *The Rise of the Spanish American Empire* (New York: The Free Press, 1965)

21 Maryland Charter, cited in Wise, *The Red Man in the New World Drama*, 74

22 John Winthrop, cited ibid., 78

23 Patricia Seed, *Ceremonies of Possession in Europe's Conquest of the New World, 1492–1640* (Cambridge: Cambridge University Press, 1995), 16–40

24 John Winthrop, cited in Wise, *The Red Man in the New World Drama*, 78–9

25 Charles M. Segal and David C. Stineback, *Puritans, Indians and Manifest Destiny* (New York: G. Putnam's Sons, 1977); Perry Miller, *The New England Mind, The Seventeenth Century* (Cambridge, Mass.: Harvard University Press, 1954); Miller, *The New England Mind from Colony to Province* (Cambridge, Mass.: Harvard University Press, 1962); Neal Salisbury, *Manitou and Providence: Indians, Europeans and the Making of New England, 1500–1643* (New York: Oxford University Press, 1982); Conrad Cherry, *God's New Israel: Religious Interpretations of American Destiny* (Englewood Cliffs, NJ: Prentice Hall, 1971); Anders Stephanson, *Manifest Destiny: American Expansionism and the Empire of Right* (New York: Hill and Wang, 1995)

26 C.B. Macpherson, *The Political Theory of Possessive Individualism: Hobbes to Locke* (Oxford: Oxford University Press, 1979), 3; see also James Tully, *An Approach to Political Philosophy: Locke in Contexts* (Cambridge: Cambridge University Press, 1993).

27 Thomas Pownall, *The Administration of Colonies*, 2nd ed. (London 1765), 157, cited in Pagden, *Lords of All the World*, 77

28 John Cotton, cited in Seed, *Ceremonies of Possession*, 30

29 Cotton Mather, cited in David Horowitz, *The First Frontier: The Indian Wars and America's Origins, 1607–1776* (New York: Simon and Schuster, 1978), 55–6

30 Mather, cited in Vandana Shiva, *Monocultures of the Mind: Perspectives on Biodiversity and Biotechnology* (London: Zed Books, 1993), 27

31 See William Kellaway, *The New England Company, 1649–1776: Missionary Society to the American Indians* (Westport, Conn.: Greenwood Press, 1975).

32 Robert Boyle, cited in Brian Easlea, *Science and Sexual Oppression: Patriarchy's Confrontation with Woman and Nature* (London: Weidenfeld and Nicholson, 1981), 64

33 Pagden, *Lords of All the World*, 153

34 See Barbara Arneil, *John Locke and America: The Defence of English Colonialism* (Oxford: Clarendon Press, 1996).

35 Locke, *Two Treatises of Government*, introduction and notes by Peter Laslett (New York: New American Library, 1965), 336

36 See Jack M. Sosin, *Whitehall and the Wilderness: The Middle West in British Colonial Policy, 1760–1775* (Lincoln: University of Nebraska Press, 1961).

37 See Thomas Jefferson, *A Summary View of the Rights of British America* (Williams-

burg: Printed by Clementina Rind, 1774); Williams Jr, *The American Indian in Western Legal Thought*, 265–71.

38 Ibid., 246; see also Gary Wills, *Inventing America: Jefferson's Declaration of Independence* (New York: Doubleday, 1978).

39 Locke, *Two Treatises*, 395

40 The accusation completes the list of eighteen allegations aimed at the British monarch in the Declaration of Independence. See in S.F. Wise, "The American Revolution in Indian History," in John S. Moir, *Character and Circumstance: Essays in Honour of Donald Grant Creighton* (Toronto: Macmillan, 1970), 182

41 Isabel Thompson Kelsay, *Joseph Brant, 1743–1807: Man of Two Worlds* (Syracuse: Syracuse University Press, 1984), 138–319; Barbara Graymont, *The Iroquois and the American Revolution* (Syracuse: Syracuse University Press, 1972)

42 Paul Brodeur, *Secrets: A Writer in the Cold War* (Boston and London: Faber & Faber, 1997); John Marks, *The Search for the "Manchurian Candidate"* (New York: Times Books, 1979). See also Angus MacKenzie, *Secrets: The CIA's War at Home* (Berkley: University of California Press, 1997).

43 Francis Jennings, *The Invasion of America: Indians, Colonialism, and the Cant of Conquest* (New York: W.W. Norton), 177–227

44 Stephen S. Webb, *1676: The End of American Independence* (New York: Alfred A. Knopf, 1984)

45 See Richard Slotkin, *Regeneration through Violence: The Mythology of the American Frontier* (Middletown: Wesleyan University Press, 1973).

46 Harry M. Ward, *The United Colonies of New England, 1643–1690* (New York: Vantage Press, 1961)

47 Timothy J. Shannon, *Indians and Colonists at the Crossroads of Empire: The Albany Conference of 1754* (Ithaca, NY: Cornell University Press, 2000)

48 W. Sitt Robinson Jr, *The Southern Colonial Frontier, 1607–1763* (Albuquerque: University of New Mexico Press, 1979), 107–20; Verner W. Crane, *The Southern Frontier, 1670–1732* (New York: W.W. Norton, 1981)

49 Douglas E. Leach, *Arms for Empire: A Military History of the British Colonies in North America, 1607–1763* (New York: Macmillan, 1973); David Horowitz, *The First Frontier: The Indian Wars and America's Origins, 1607–1776* (New York: Simon & Schuster, 1978)

50 Williams Jr, *The American Indian in Western Legal Thought*, 265

51 Cited in Wise, "The American Revolution and Indian History," 186–7

52 Wise, "The American Revolution and Indian History," 182–200

53 John K. Mahon, "Indian-United States Military Situation, 1775–1848," in Wilcomb E. Washburn, ed., *Handbook of North American Indians*, vol. 4: *History of Indian-White Relations* (Washington: Smithsonian Institution, 1988), 144

54 William Henry Drayton, cited in Edward Countryman, "Indians, the Colonial Order, and the Social Significance of the American Revolution," *The William and Mary Quarterly*, third series, 53, 2 (1996): 355–6

55 On the larger implications of the application of the doctrine of discovery, past and present, see Williams, *The American Indian in Western Legal Discourse*, 325–33

56 Cited in Wilcomb E. Washburn, *Red Man's Land/ White Man's Law: A Study of the Past and Present Status of the American Indian* (New York : Charles Scribner's Sons, 1971), 43

57 See Webb, *1676*.

58 Wilcomb E. Washburn, *The Governor and the Rebel: A History of Bacon's Rebellion in Virginia* (Chapel Hill: University of North Carolina Press, 1957)

59 Washburn, *Red Man's Land/ White Man's Law*, 43

60 Roger Williams, *A Key to the Language of America* (London: Gregory Dexter, 1643)

61 Roger Williams, *Christenings Make Not Christians* (London: Jane Coe, 1645)

62 Roger Williams, cited in Jennings, *The Invasion of America*, 142

63 Roger Williams, cited in D'Arcy McNickle, *Native American Tribalism: Indian Survivals and Renewals* (London: Oxford University Press, 1973), 32

64 John Cotton, Cited in Washburn, *Red Man's Land/White Man's Law*, 41

65 See Perry Miller, *Roger Williams: His Contributions to the American Tradition* (New York: Atheneum, 1965), 49–72. Edmund S. Morgan, *Roger Williams: The Church and the State* (New York: Harcourt, Brace and World, 1967)

66 See Samuel M. Janney, *The Life of William Penn* (1851; Freeport, NY: Books for Libraries Press, 1970), 164–70, 185–6; Edward C.O. Beatty, *William Penn as Social Philosopher* (New York: Columbia University Press, 1939), 266–73; Wise, *The Red Man in the New World Drama*, 88–95.

67 Wise, *The Red Man in the New World Drama*, 1; Paul Hazard, *The European Mind, 1680–1715*, trans. J. Lewis May (New York: Meridian, 1963), 275

68 Francis Jennings, "Dutch and Swedish Indian Policies," in Washburn, ed., *History of Indian-White Relations*, 13–19

69 See Jerry Martien, *Shell Game: A True Account of Beads and Money in North America* (San Francisco: Mercury House, 1996).

70 See Daniel K. Richter, *The Ordeal of the Longhouse: The People of the Iroquois League in the Era of European Colonization* (Chapel Hill: University of North Carolina Press, 1992).

71 Francis Jennings, *The Ambiguous Iroquois Empire: The Covenant Chain Confederation of Indian Tribes with English Colonies from Its Beginnings to the Lancaster Treaty of 1744* (New York: W.W. Norton, 1984)

72 See Bruce G. Trigger, *Natives and Newcomers: Canada's "Heroic Age" Reconsidered* (Montreal: McGill-Queen's University Press, 1986), 226–97.

73 Anka Muhlstein, *La Salle: Explorer of the North American Frontier*, trans. Willard Wood (New York: Arcade Publishing, 1994)

74 Cited in Jennings, *The Invasion of America*, 285–6

75 Cited ibid., 286

76 Francis Jennings, "The Constitutional Evolution of the Covenant Chain," *Proceedings of the American Philosophical Society* 115, 2 (1971): 88–96

77 Wilbur R. Jacobs, ed., *The Appalachain Indian Frontier: The Edmond Aitkin Report and Plan of 1755* (Lincoln: University of Nebraska Press, 1967), 7–8, 3–4

78 Hendrick, cited in Robert Allen, *His Majesty's Indian Allies: British Indian Policy in Defence of Canada, 1774–1815* (Toronto: Dundurn, 1993), 20

79 John R. Alden, "The Albany Congress and the Creation of the Indian Super-intendencies," *Mississippi Valley Historical Review* 27 (1940): 198–200

80 Duncan Campbell Scott, "Indian Affairs, 1763–1841," in Adam Shortt and Arthur G. Doughty, eds., *Canada and Its Provinces* (Toronto: Glasgow, Brook and Co., 1914), 4: 698

81 See Patricia U. Bonomi, *A Fractious People: Politics and Society in Colonial New York* (New York: Coumbia University Press, 1971).

82 Johnson, cited in Timothy J. Shannon, "Dressing for Success on the Mohawk Frontier: Hendrick, William Johnson and Indian Fashion," *William and Mary Quarterly*, third series, 53, 1 (1996): 40

83 See Allen, *His Majesty's Indian Allies*, 22–38.

84 Red Head, cited in Shannon, "Dressing for Success on the Mohawk Frontier," 36

85 Johnson, cited ibid., 40

86 Francis Jennings, *Empire of Fortune: Crowns, Colonies, and Tribes in the Seven Years' War in America* (New York: W.W. Norton, 1988), 369–404

87 See Anthony F.C. Wallace, *Teedyuscung: King of the Delawares, 1700–1763* (1949; Salem, NH: Ayer, 1984).

88 Cited in Jennings, *Empire of Fortune*, 388

89 Francis Jennings, *Benjamin Franklin: Politician* (New York: W.W. Norton, 1996)

90 Cited in Adam Shortt and Arthur G. Doughty, eds., *Documents Relating to the Constitutional History of Canada, 1759–1791*, 2 vols. (Ottawa: King's Printer, 1918), 1: 33

91 See George F.G. Stanley, "The First Indian 'Reserves' in Canada," *Revue d'Histoire de l'Amérique Française* 4 (1950): 178–210.

92 Robert Rogers, *Journals of Major Robert Rogers* (1765; reprinted: Readex Microprint, 1966), 15

93 Richard White, *The Middle Ground: Indians, Empires, and Republics in the Great Lakes Region, 1650–1815* (Cambridge: Cambridge University Press, 1991), 36

94 See W.J. Eccles, "The French Forces in North America during the Seven Years' War," *Dictionary of Canadian Biography*, vol. 3 (Toronto: University of Toronto Press, 1974), xv–xxiii.

95 White, *The Middle Ground*, 257

96 Ibid., 256–68

97 James Kenny, cited ibid., 279

98 Ibid., 278–85. See also Jane T. Merrit, "Dreaming of the Saviour's Blood: Moravians and the Indian Great Awakening in Pennsylvania," *The William and Mary Quarterly*, third series, 54, 4 (1997): 723–46.

99 White, *The Middle Ground*, 283

100 Louis Chevrette, "Pontiac," *Dictionary of Canadian Biography*, vol. 3 (Toronto: University of Toronto Press, 1974), 525–31; Howard H. Peckham, *Pontiac and the Indian Uprising* (Princeton, NJ: Princeton University Press, 1947)

101 The Royal Proclamation of 1763 is published in its original English and French entirety in Ian A.L. Getty and Antoine S. Lussier, eds., *As Long as the*

Sun Shines and the Water Flows: A Reader in Canadian Native Studies (Vancouver: UBC Press, 1983). The quoted passage is on page 31.

102 News of the Indian stand was influential in convincing the Board of Trade to adopt a more easterly boundary and to forbid private purchases directly from Indian groups and individuals. See Ray Allen Billington, *Westward Expansion: A History of the American Frontier* (New York: Macmillan, 1964), 139–40.

103 Amherst, cited in Chevrette, "Pontiac," 529

104 Bouquet, cited in White, *The Middle Ground,* 288

105 See W.J. Eccles, "Sovereignty-Association,1500–1783," *Canadian Historical Review* 65, 4 (1984): 475–510.

106 Alexander Henry, *Travels and Adventures in Canada and the Indian Territories Between 1760 and 1776* (Edmonton: Hurtig, 1969), 44–5

107 Charlot Kaske, cited in White, *The Middle Ground,* 307

108 Cited by Bruce Clark, *Justice in Paradise* (Montreal: McGill-Queen's University Press, 1999), 361

109 Johnson, cited in Dorothy V. Jones, *License for Empire: Colonialism by Treaty in Early America* (Chicago: University of Chicago Press, 1982), 70

110 Johnson, cited in White, *The Middle Ground,* 299

111 Johnson enumerated the different Indian groups of Canada in 1763. See Jones, *License for Empire,* 65–6; Bruce G. Trigger, ed., *Handbook of North American Indians,* vol. 15: *Northeast* (Washington: Smithsonian Institution, 1978).

112 See Arthur J. Ray, *Indians in the Fur Trade: Their Role as Trappers, Hunters and Middlemen in the Lands Southwest of Hudson's Bay, 1660–1670* (Toronto: University of Toronto Press, 1974).

113 White, *The Middle Ground,* 305–17

114 Tom Paine in *Public Good* (1781), cited in Williams, *The American Indian in Western Legal Discourse,* 298

115 See C.P. Stacey, "Robert Rogers," *Dictionary of Canadian Biography,* vol. 4 (Toronto: University of Toronto Press, 1979), 681.

116 Francis Parkman, *The Conspiracy of Pontiac and the Indian War after the Conquest of Canada* (Boston: Little, Brown, 1898)

117 The Royal Proclamation of 1763 is cited in Getty and Lussier, eds., *As Long as the Sun Shines,* 33.

118 *Campbell* v. *Hall* is published in *The English Reports,* vol. 98, King's Bench division 27 (Edinburgh: William Green and Sons, 1909), nos. 655–748.

119 Pagden, *Lords of All the World,* 85. See James Youngblood Henderson, "The Doctrine of Aboriginal Rights in Western Legal Tradition," in Menno Boldt and Anthony J. Long, eds., *The Quest for Justice: Aboriginal Peoples and Aboriginal Rights* (Toronto: University of Toronto Press, 1985), 185–229; Clark, *Justice in Paradise,* 89–92, 326–9; Bruce Clark, *Native Liberty, Crown Sovereignty: The Existing Aboriginal Right of Self-Government in Canada* (Montreal: McGill-Queeen's University Press, 1990), 38–47.

120 See J.H. Smith, *Appeals to the Privy Council from the American Plantations* (New York: Columbia University Press, 1950), 417–42.

121 Commissioner Horsmanden, cited ibid, 431

122 Eric Hinderaker, *Elusive Empires: Constructing Colonialism in the Ohio Valley, 1673–1800* (New York: Cambridge University Press, 1997), xi

123 Ronald Robinson and John Gallagher, *Africa and the Victorians: The Official Mind of Imperialism* (London: Macmillan, 1967), 470–1

124 The Royal Proclamation, Getty and Lussier, eds., *As Long as the Sun Shines,* 35

125 Jennings, *The Invasion of America,* 128–45

126 See Williams, *The American Indian in Western Legal Thought,* 227–89; Clarence Walworth Alvord, *The Mississippi Valley in British Politics: A Study of the Trade, Land Speculation and Experiments in Imperialism Culminating in the American Revolution,* 2 vols. (Cleveland: Arthur H. Clark Company, 1917).

127 The Royal Proclamation, Getty and Lussier, eds., *As Long as the Sun Shines,* 33

128 The connections between taxation of the Anglo-American colonies and western Indian policy are explored in Sosin, *Whitehall and the Wilderness.*

129 Lords of Trade to Sir William Johnson, Whitehall, 10 July 1764, in E.B. O'Callaghan, ed., *Documents Relative to the Colonial History of the State of New York* (Albany: Weed, Parsons and Company, 1856), 7: 635

130 Representation of the Lords of Trade on the State of Indian Affairs, 7 March 1768, to the King's Most Excellent Majesty, in Clarence W. Alvord and Clarence Edwin Carter, eds, *Trade and Politics, 1767–1769: Collections of the Illinois State Historical Library,* vol. 16: *British Series,* vol 3 (Springfield: Illinois State Historical Library, 1921), 190

131 See John Shy, *Toward Lexington: The Role of the British Army in the Coming of the American Revolution* (Princeton: Princeton University Press, 1965).

132 Henry Ellis, cited in Brian Slattery, "The Land Rights of Indigenous Peoples, as Affected by the Crown's Acquisition of Their Territories" (PhD thesis, Oxford University, 1979), 191

133 Ibid., 183–204

134 L.F.S. Upton, *Micmacs and Colonists: Indian-White Relations in the Maritimes, 1713–1867* (Vancouver: UBC Press, 1979), 42–4

135 Cited ibid., 58

136 Bob Beal, "Don't Blame the Mi'kmaq, Blame History," *Globe and Mail,* 10 November 1999, A17; Kenneth Coates, *The Marshall Decision and Native Rights* (Montreal: McGill-Queen's University Press, 2000)

137 See Benjamin Woods Larabee, *The Boston Tea Party* (London: Oxford University Press, 1975).

138 Fred Anderson, *Crucible of War: The Seven Years' War and the Fate of Empire in British North America, 1754–1766* (New York: Vintage Books, 2000), 412

139 See Sosin, *Whitehall and the Wilderness.*

140 John Jay, cited in Williams Jr, *The American Indian in Western Legal Thought,* 252

141 On the continuation of this centralized approach to Canadian governance, see Gordon T. Stewart, *The Origins of Canadian Politics: A Comparative Approach* (Vancouver: UBC Press, 1986).

142 Alvord, *The Mississippi Valley in British Politics;* Thomas Perkins Abernathy, *Western Lands and the American Revolution* (1937; New York: Russell and Russell, 1959); Williams Jr, *The American Indian in Western Legal Thought,* 271–323; Jones, *License for Empire;* Billington, *Westward Expansion,* 132–53, 199–220; Francis Jennings, *The Creation of America through Revolution to Empire* (Cambridge: Cambridge University Press, 2000); Sosin, *Whitehall and the Wilderness.* See also Shaw Livermore, *Early American Land Companies* (New York: The Commonwealth Fund, 1939).

143 The Royal Proclamation, Getty and Lussier, eds., *As Long as the Sun Shines,* 32–3

144 Ada Hope, "George Washington: Land Speculator," *Journal of the Illinois State Historical Society,* 11, 4 (1919): 566–75

145 Washington, cited in Billington, *Western Expansion,* 143

146 Williams Jr, *The American Indian in Western Legal Thought,* 288–99

147 Billington, *Western Expansion,* 168–73

148 See Leonard W. Larabee et al., eds., *The Papers of Benjamin Franklin* (New Haven, Conn.: Yale University Press, 1959), 12: 395–400, 403–6; 15: 264–5, 275–9; Jennings, *Benjamin Franklin.*

149 See Nicholas B. Wainwright, *George Croghan: Wilderness Diplomat* (Chapel Hill: University of North Carolina Press, 1959).

150 See George E. Lewis, *The Indiana Company, 1763–1798* (Glendale, Cal.: Arthur H. Clark Co., 1941).

151 Williams Jr, *The American Indian in Western Legal Thought,* 263

152 Peter Marshall, "Lord Hillsborough, Samuel Wharton, and the Ohio Grant, 1769–1775," *English Historical Review* 80 (1965): 717–39

153 The Camden-York opinion, cited in Billington, *Western Expansion,* 151–2

154 Edward Countryman, "Indians, the Colonial Order, and the Social Significance of the American Revolution," *William and Mary Quarterly,* third series, 53, 2 (1996): 342–62

155 Croghan and Johnson, cited in White, *The Middle Ground,* 345

156 See Luana Ross, *Inventing the Savage: The Social Construction of Native American Criminality* (Austin: University of Texas Press, 1996).

157 Croghan, cited in White, *The Middle Ground,* 348

158 Potawatomies of Saint Joseph, cited ibid., 284

159 Menno Boldt, *Surviving as Indians: The Challenge of Self-Government* (Toronto: University of Toronto Press, 1993), 3

160 G.R. Mellor, *British Imperial Trusteeship* (London: Faber & Faber, 1951)

161 See, for instance, Lawrence Henry Gibson, *The Coming Revolution, 1763–1775* (New York: Harper & Row, 1954); Bernard Bailyn, *The Ideological Origins of the American Revolution* (Cambridge, Mass.: Harvard University Press, 1967); Marc Egnal, *A Mighty Empire: The Origins of the American Revolution* (Ithaca: Cornell University Press, 1988); Gordon S. Wood, *The Radicalism of the American Revolution* (New York: Random House, 1991).

162 Countryman, "Indians, the Colonial Order, and the Social Significance of the American Revolution," 354–5

163 Williams Jr, *The American Indian in Western Legal Thought*, 298–300
164 Alvord, *The Mississippi Valley in British Politics*. On speculation on Indian lands in the era of the American Revolution, see also Abernathy, *Western Lands and the American Revolution*; Jones, *License for Empire*.
165 Frederick Jackson Turner, "The Significance of the Frontier in American History," in Walker D. Wyman and Clifton B. Kroeker, eds., *The Frontier in Perspective* (Madison: University of Wisconsin Press, 1965), 2. See David A. Nichols, "Civilization over Savage: Frederick Jackson Turner and the Indian," *South Dakota History* 2 (fall 1972): 385–405.
166 Clarence Alvord, *The Mississippi Valley in British Politics* 1: 103–4
167 See B.W. Poe, *A Canada of Light* (Toronto: Somerville House, 1997).
168 Alvord, *The Mississippi Valley in British Politics* 1: 348, 94
169 Clarence Alvord, "Lord Shelburne and the Founding of British-American Goodwill," Annual Raleigh Lecture in History, *Proceedings of the British Academy*, 1924–25, 384
170 Kevin Phillips, *The Cousins' Wars: Religion, Politics, and the Triumph of Anglo-America* (New York: Basic Books, 1999)
171 Jennings, *The Creation of America through Revolution to Empire*
172 Richard W. Van Alstyne, *The Rising American Empire* (1960; Chicago: Quadrangle, 1965), 1
173 See Samuel Flagg Bemis, *The Latin American Policy of the United States: An Historical Interpretation* (New York: Harcourt, Brace and World, 1943).
174 Noam Chomsky, *American Power and the New Mandarins* (New York: Pantheon Books, 1969)
175 Lester D. Langely, *The Banana Wars: An Inner History of the American Empire, 1900–1934* (Lexington: University of Kentucky Press, 1983); Noam Chomsky, *Turning the Tide: U.S. Intervention in Central America and the Struggle for Peace* (Boston: South End Press, 1985)
176 John F. Kennedy, cited in David Horowitz, *The Free World Colossus: A Critique of American Foreign Policy during the Cold War*, rev. ed. (New York: Hill and Wang, 1971), 14
177 J. Arnold Toynbee, *America and the World Revolution* (Oxford: Oxford University Press, 1961), cited in Horowitz, *The Free World Colossus*, 15
178 D.F. Fleming, *The Cold War and Its Origins, 1917–1960*, 2 vols. (New York: Doubleday, 1961)
179 Robert T. Holt and Robert W. van de Velde, *Strategic Psychological Operations and American Foreign Policy* (Chicago: University of Chicago Press, 1960)
180 Conor Cruise O'Brien, "The Congo: A Balance Sheet," *New Left Review* 31 (May–June 1965)
181 Stephen Schlesinger and Stephen Kinzer, *Bitter Fruit: The Story of the American Coup in Guatemala*, expanded ed. (Cambridge, Mass.: Harvard University Press, 1999); Nick Cullather, *Secret History: The CIA's Classified Account of Its Operation in Guatemala, 1952–1954* (Stanford, Cal.: Stanford University Press, 1999)
182 Piero Gleijes, Afterward, in Cullather, *Secret History*, xx

183 United States Government, Department of State White Paper, *Intervention of International Communism in Guatemala*, 1954, cited in Horowitz, *The Free World Colossus*, 162

184 Susanne Jonas, *The Battle for Guatemala: Rebels, Death Squads, and U.S. Power* (Boulder: Westview Press, 1991), 149

185 William Blum, *Rogue State: A Guide to the World's Only Superpower* (London: Zed Books, 2002), 60–7

186 Amnesty International, *Guatemala: A Government Program of Political Murder* (London 1981); US Embassy report, cited in Jonas, *The Battle for Guatemala*, 198

187 *New York Times*, 5 December 1982, 1

188 Jonas, *The Battle for Guatemala*, 149

189 John Bacher, *Petrotyranny* (Toronto: Dundurn Press, 2000), 210

190 David Maybury-Lewis, "Conclusion: Living in Leviathan, Ethnic Groups and the State," in Maybury-Lewis, ed., *The Prospect of Plural Societies: 1982 Proceedings of the American Ethnological Society* (Washington, DC: The American Ethnological Society, 1984), 224–5. For a discussion of the atrocities as genocide, see Ricardo Falla, "We Charge Genocide," in Susanne Jonas, ed., *Guatemala: Tyranny on Trial* (San Francisco: Synthesis, 1984), 112–17

191 Hector Gramajo, cited in Victor Perera, *Unfinished Conquest: The Guatemalan Tragedy* (Berkeley: University of California Press, 1993), 53

192 Reginald Horsman, *Race and Manifest Destiny: The Origins of American Racial Anglo-Saxonism* (Cambridge, Mass.: Harvard University Press, 1981), 100

193 See Gabriel Kolko, *Confronting the Third World: United States Foreign Policy, 1945–1980* (New York: Pantheon Books, 1988); V.G. Kiernan, *America, The New Imperialism: From White Settlement to World Hegemony* (London: Zed, 1978); Stephen E. Ambrose and Douglas G. Brinkley, *Rise to Globalism: American Foreign Policy since 1938*, eighth ed (New York: Penguin, 1997); Chalmers Johnson, *Blowback: The Costs and Consequences of American Empire* (New York: Henry Holt, 2000); William Blum, *Killing Hope: US Military and CIA Interventions since World War II* (Monroe, Me.: Common Courage Press, 1995); Noam Chomsky, *Year 501: The Conquest Continues* (Montreal: Black Rose Books, 1993).

194 John Collier, *Indians of the Americas* (New York: W.W. Norton, 1947); Collier, *From Every Zenith: A Memoir and Some Essays on Life and Thought* (Denver: Sage Books, 1963); Collier, *On the Gleaming Way* (Denver: Sage Books, 1962); Jay Brian Nash, *The New Deal for the Indians: A Survey of the Workings of the Indian Reorganization Act of 1934* (New York: Academy Press, 1938); Graham D. Taylor, *The New Deal and American Indian Tribalism: The Administration of the Indian Reorganization Act, 1934–45* (Lincoln: University of Nebraska Press, 1980); Lawrence M. Hauptman, *The Iroquois and the New Deal* (Syracuse: Syracuse University Press, 1981); Kenneth R. Philp, ed., *Indian Self-Rule: First Hand Accounts of Indian-White Relations from Roosevelt to Reagan* (Salt Lake City, Utah: Institute of the American West, 1986). See also Lawrence C. Kelly, *The Assault on Assimilation: John Collier and the Ori-*

gins of Indian Policy Reform (Albuquerque: University of New Mexico Press, 1983).

195 Edward W. Said, *Culture and Imperialism* (New York: Vintage Books, 1994), 295

196 See Giovanni Arrighi, *The Long Twentieth Century* (London: Verso, 1994).

197 Adlai Stevenson's address to the UN Security Council, 23 October 1962, cited in Horowitz, *The Free World Colossus*, 12

198 Richard Barnet, *The Roots of War* (New York: Atheneum, 1972), 21

199 Pagden, *Lords of all the World*, 200

CHAPTER FIVE

1 See Peter S. Onuf, *Statehood and Union: A History of the Northwest Ordinance* (Bloomington: Indiana University Press, 1987).

2 Goldwin Smith, *The United States: An Outline of Political History, 1492–1871* (New York: Macmillan, 1893), 129

3 Stephen A. Ambrose, *Undaunted Courage: Meriwether Lewis, Thomas Jefferson and the Opening of the American West* (New York: Touchstone, 1996), 56–7

4 See Clarence Walworth Alvord, *The Mississippi Valley in British Politics*, 2 vols. (Cleveland: Arthur H. Clark, 1917); Paul Wallace Gates, "The Role of the Land Speculator in Western Development," in Vernon Carstensen, *The Public Lands: Studies in the History of the Public Domain* (Madison: University of Wisconsin Press, 1963); Alfred D. Chandler Jr, *The Visible Hand: The Managerial Revolution in American Business* (Cambridge, Mass.: Harvard University Press, 1977), 81–187.

5 Miriam Beard, *A History of Business*, vol. 2: *From Monopolists to Organization Man* (Ann Arbor: University of Michigan Press, 1965), 161

6 Northwest Ordinance, 1787, from Albert L. Hurtado and Peter Iverson, eds., *Major Problems in American Indian History: Documents and Essays* (Lexington, Mass.: D.C. Heath, 1994), 168–9

7 Ramsay MacMullen, *Christianizing the Roman Empire: A.D. 100–400* (New Haven: Yale University Press, 1984)

8 Anthony Pagden, *Lords of All the World: Ideologies of Empire, c. 1500–c. 1800* (New Haven: Yale University Press, 1995), 31

9 Cited ibid., 34. See Marcel Trudel, *Histoire de la Nouvelle France: La seigneurie des Cents Associés, 1627–1663* (Montreal: Fides, 1979).

10 Cited in Pagden, *Lords of All the World*, 35

11 Francis Jennings, *The Invasion of America: Indians, Colonialism and the Cant of Conquest* (New York: W.W. Norton, 1975), 229

12 Olive Patricia Dickason, "From 'One Nation' in the Northeast to 'New Nation' in the Northwest: A Look at the Emergence of the Métis," in Jacqueline Peterson and Jennifer S.H. Brown, eds., *The New Peoples: Being and Becoming Métis in North America* (Winnipeg: University of Manitoba Press, 1985), 19–36

13 The Treaty of Fort Stanwix is in E.B. O'Callighan, ed., *Documents Relative to the*

Colonial History of the State of New York, 15 vols. (Albany: Weed, Parsons, 1853–87), 8: 135–7.

14 Frederick Haldimand to Lord North, 27 November 1783, cited in Colin G. Calloway, *Crown and Calumet: British-Indian Relations, 1783–1815* (Norman: University of Oklahoma Press, 1987), 9

15 See Charles M. Johnson, ed., *The Valley of the Six Nations: A Collection of Documents on the Indian Lands of the Grand River* (Toronto: University of Toronto Press, 1964); Sally M. Weaver, "The Six Nations of Grand River," in Bruce G. Trigger, ed., *Handbook of North American Indians,* vol. 15: *Northeast* (Washington, DC: Smithsonian Institution, 1978), 525–36; C.H. Torok, "The Tyendinaga Mohawks," *Ontario History* 58 (March 1956), 69–77

16 Elma E. Gray in collaboration with Leslie Robb Gray, *Wilderness Christians: The Moravian Mission to the Delaware Indians* (Toronto: Macmillan, 1956)

17 See Wiley Sword, *President Washington's Indian War: The Struggle for the Old Northwest, 1790–1795* (Norman: University of Oklahoma Press, 1985); Randolphe C. Downes, *Council Fires on the Upper Ohio: A Narrative of Indian Affairs in the Upper Ohio Valley until 1795* (Pittsburgh: University of Pittsburgh Press, 1940); Reginald Horsman, *Expansion and American Indian Policy, 1783–1812* (East Lansing: Michigan State University Press, 1967).

18 S.F. Wise, "The Indian Diplomacy of John Graves Simcoe," in Canadian Historical Association, *Report of the Annual Meeting with Historical Papers,* 1953, 39–44

19 See William Nelson, *The American Tory* (Oxford: The Clarendon Press, 1960).

20 A.L. Burt, *The United States, Great Britain and British North America* (New Haven: Yale University Press, 1940), 82–140; Robert S. Allen, *His Majesty's Indian Allies: British Indian Policy in Defence of Canada, 1774–1815* (Toronto: Dunford Press, 1992), 57–88

21 The Speech of the Commissioners of the United States to the Deputies of the Confederate Indian Nations Assembled at Rapids of the Miamis River, 31 July 1793, in E.A. Cruikshank, ed., *The Correspondence of Lieutenant Governor John Graves Simcoe* (Toronto: The Ontario Historical Society, 1923), 1: 405–9

22 Dave R. Palmer, *1794: America, Its Army, and the Birth of a Nation* (Novato, Cal.: Presido, 1994), xiii

23 See Samuel Flagg Bemis, *Jay's Treaty: A Study in Commerce and Diplomacy* (New Haven: Yale University Press, 1962).

24 Gregory Evans Dowd, *A Spirited Resistance: The North American Indian Struggle for Unity, 1745–1815* (Baltimore: Johns Hopkins University Press, 1992), 143

25 Richard White, *The Middle Ground: Indians, Empires, and Republics in the Great Lakes Region, 1650–1815* (Cambridge: Cambridge University Press, 1991)

26 For an ethnographic survey of Aboriginal cultural areas in Canada, see Alan D. MacMillan, *Native Peoples and Cultures of Canada: An Anthropological Overview* (Vancouver: Douglas & McIntyre, 1988).

27 Bruce G. Trigger, *The Children of Aataentsic: A History of Huron People to 1660,* 2 Vols. (Montreal: McGill-Queen's University Press, 1976), 2: 826

28 James Axtell, "The White Indians of Colonial America," in Axtell, *The European and the Indian: Essays in the Ethnohistory of Colonial North America* (Oxford: Oxford University Press, 1981), 168–206; A. Irving Hallowell, "American Indians, White and Black: The Phenomenon of Transculturation," *Current Anthropology* 4 (1963): 519–31; J. Norman Heard, *White into Red: A Study of the Assimilation of White Persons Captured by Indian* (Metuchen, NJ: The Scarecrow Press, 1973); Richard Drinnon, *White Savage: The Case of John Dunn Hunter* (New York: Schocken Press, 1972); James Axtell, *The Invasion Within: The Contest of Cultures in Colonial North America* (New York: Oxford University Press, 1985)

29 Hector St John de Crevecoeur, "Letter XII, Distresses of a Frontier Man," in Crevecoeur, *Letters from an American Farmer* (1782; London: J.M. Dent and Sons, 1962), 215

30 Captain George Turnbull, cited in White, *The Middle Ground*, 316

31 George Croghan, cited ibid. On Croghan, a close colleague of Sir William Johnson, see Nicholas B. Wainwright, *George Croghan: Wilderness Diplomat* (Chapel Hill: University of North Carolina Press, 1959).

32 W.J. Eccles, "Sovereignty-Association, 1500–1783," *Canadian Historical Review* 65, 4 (1984): 475–510

33 See William Loren Katz, *Black Indians: A Hidden Heritage* (New York: Atheneum, 1986); Jack D. Forbes, *Black Africans and Native Americans* (Oxford: Blackwell, 1988). See also Forbes, "The Manipulation of Race, Caste and Identity," *Journal of Ethnic Studies*, 17, 4 (1990), 1–51.

34 White, *The Middle Ground*, 186–222

35 Paul W. Wallace, *The White Roots of Peace* (Port Washington, NY: Ira J. Friedman, 1968). There is a large literature on the history and political organization of the League of the Iroquois. The seminal work is Lewis Henry Morgan, *League of the Ho-de-no-sau-nee or Iroquois* (New York: Sage Books, 1851). The dean of "Iroquoian Studies" in recent years has been William N. Fenton. A representative sample of the work of his students and colleagues is presented in Michael K. Foster, Jack Campsi, and Marianne Mithun, eds., *Extending the Rafters: Interdisciplinary Approaches to Iroquoian Studies* (Albany: State University of New York Press, 1984). A book which reflects some of the work being done by contemporary Six Nations scholars is Oren Lyons et al., *Exiled in the Land of the Free: Democracy, Indian Nations and the U.S. Constitution* (Santa Fe: Clear Light Publishers, 1992).

36 Isabel Thompson Kelsay, *Joseph Brant, 1743–1807: Man of Two Worlds* (Syracuse: Syracuse University Press, 1984)

37 See Francis Jennings, *The Ambiguous Iroquois Empire: The Covenant Chain Confederation of Indian Tribes with English Colonies from Its Beginning to the Lancaster Treaty of 1744* (New York: W.W. Norton, 1984). On the Covenant Chain, see also Jennings et al., eds., *The History and Culture of Iroquois Diplomacy: An Interdisciplinary Guide to the Treaties of the Six Nations and Their League* (Syracuse: Syracuse University Press, 1985); Daniel K. Richter and James H. Merrell, eds., *Beyond the Covenant Chain: The Iroquois and Their Neighbours in Indian*

North America, 1600–1800 (Syracuse: Syracuse University Press, 1987); Richard Aquila, *The Iroquois Restoration: Iroquois Diplomacy on the Colonial Frontier, 1701–1754* (Detroit: Wayne State University Press, 1983); Georgiana C. Nammack, *Fraud, Politics, and the Dispossession of the Indians: The Iroquois Land Frontier in the Colonial Period* (Norman: University of Oklahoma Press, 1969); Daniel K. Richter, *The Ordeal of the Longhouse: The Peoples of the Iroquois League in the Era of European Colonization* (Chapel Hill: University of North Carolina Press, 1992); Dean R. Snow, *The Iroquois* (Oxford: Blackwell, 1994).

38 See Allen, *His Majesty's Indian Allies*, 12–38; Milton W. Hamilton, *Sir William Johnson: Colonial American, 1715–1763* (Port Washington, NY: Kennikat Press, 1976); J.J. Sullivan, ed., *The Papers of Sir William Johnson*, 14 vols. (Albany: University of the State of New York, 1921–65); John Guzzardo, "Sir William Johnson's Official Family: Patrons and Clients in an Anglo-American Empire" (PhD dissertation, Syracuse University, 1975).

39 Jean Johnston, "Molly Brant: Mohawk Matron," *Ontario History* 56, 2 (1964): 105–24; H. Pearson Gundy, "Molly Brant – Loyalist." Ontario Historical Society, *Papers and Records* 45, 1 (1953): 97–108; Earle Thomas, *The Three Faces of Molly Brant: A Biography* (Kingston: Quarry Press, 1996); Gretchen Green, "Molly Brant, Catherine Brant and Their Daughters: A Story of Colonial Acculturation," *Ontario History* 81, 3 (1989): 235–50

40 Isabel Thompson Kelsay, *Joseph Brant, 1743–1807*, 70–3; James Axtell, "Dr. Wheelock's Little Red School," in Axtell, *The European and the Indian: Essays in the Ethnohistory of Colonial North America* (New York: Oxford, 1981), 87–109

41 Dorothy V. Jones, *License for Empire: Colonialism by Treaty in Early America* (Chicago: University of Chicago Press, 1982), 5–18

42 See Olive Patricia Dickason, *The Myth of the Savage and the Beginnings of French Colonialism in the Americas* (Edmonton: University of Alberta Press, 1984), 183–202

43 On wampum, see Tehanetorens, *Wampum Belts* (Onchiota, NY: Six Nations Indian Museum, nd); Michael K. Foster, "Another Look at the Function of Wampum in Iroquois White Councils," in Jennings et al., eds., *The History and Culture of Iroquois Diplomacy*, 99–114; Jerry Martien, *Shell Game: A True Account of Beads and Money in North America* (San Francisco: Mercury House, 1996).

44 Brant cited in White, *The Middle Ground*, 441

45 Longhouse sachems, cited ibid.

46 William W. Warren, *History of the Ojibway People* (1885; St Paul: Minnesota Historical Society Press, 1984), 82–3

47 Stephan Saunders Webb, *1676: The End of American Independence* (New York: Alfred A. Knopf, 1984), xvii

48 See Reginald Horsman, *Mathew Elliot: British Indian Agent* (Detroit: Wayne State University Press, 1964), 90

49 Gage to Stuart, New York, 19 September 1770, cited in Dowd, *A Spirited Resistance*, 66

50 See Charles M. Johnston, "Joseph Brant, The Grand River Lands and the

Northwest Crisis," *Ontario History* 55, 4 (1963): 267–82; Kelsay, *Joseph Brant*, 553–78

51 Kelsay, *Joseph Brant*, 483–520

52 See Johnson, "Joseph Brant."

53 Kelsay, *Joseph Brant*, 597–613

54 See Samuel F. Bemis, *Jay's Treaty: A Study in Commerce and Diplomacy* (New Haven: Yale University Press, 1962); John Leslie, *The Treaty of Amity, Commerce and Navigation, 1794–1796: The Jay Treaty* (Ottawa: Department of Indian and Northern Affairs Canada, 1979); A.L. Burt, *The United States Great Britain and British North America* (New Haven: Yale University Press, 1940), 141–65.

55 White, *The Middle Ground*, chaps. 8–10; James Wallace Hammack Jr, *Kentucky and the Second American Revolution* (Lexington: University of Kentucky Press, 1976)

56 Reuben G. Thwaites, *Daniel Boone* (New York: D. Appleton, 1902); John L. Bakeless, *Master of the Wilderness: Daniel Boone* (New York: W. Morrow, 1939)

57 See David R. Edmunds, *The Shawnee Prophet* (Lincoln: University of Nebraska Press, 1983).

58 The major primary sources on Tecumseh are Benjamin Drake, *Life of Tecumseh and of His Brother The Prophet; With a Historical Sketch of the Shawnee Indians* 1858; New York: Kraus Reprint Co., 1969) and Logan Esarey, ed., *Messages and Letters of William Henry Harrison*, 2 vols. (Indianapolis: ? 1922); Carl F. Klinck has gathered a representative sampling of a number of sources on Tecumseh and arranged them under topic headings in *Tecumseh: Fact and Fiction in Early Records* (Ottawa: The Tecumseh Press, 1978). I have depended heavily in this account on Herbert Charles Walter Goltz, "Tecumseh, The Prophet and the Rise of the Northwest Indian Confederation." (PhD thesis, University of Western Ontario, 1973). See also David R. Edmunds, *Tecumseh and the Quest for Indian Leadership* (Boston: Little, Brown, 1984); John Sugden, *Tecumseh: A Life* (New York: Henry Holt, 1998).

59 See Howard Peckham, *Pontiac and the Indian Uprising* (Chicago: University of Chicago Press, 1947); White, *The Middle Ground*, 269–314; Dorothy Jones, *License for Empire*, 68–75; C.-M. Boisonnault, "Les Canadiens et la revolte de Pontiac," *La Revue de l'université Laval* 2 (1947–48): 778–87.

60 Edmunds, *Tecumseh*, 22

61 Tenswatawa, cited in Allen, *His Majesty's Indian Allies*, 109, and in Goltz, "Tecumseh, The Prophet and the Rise of the Northwest Indian Confederation," 67

62 See Robert Allen, *The British Indian Department and the Frontier in North America. 1755–1830* (Ottawa: Department of Indian and Northern Affairs Canada; Canadian Historic Sites, *Occasional Papers in Archaeology and History*, no. 14, 1975).

63 See Horsman, *Mathew Elliot.*

64 Consul Willshire Butterfield, *History of the Girtys* (1890; Columbus Ohio: Long's College Book Co., 1950)

65 E.A. Cruikshank, "Robert Dickson, the Indian Trader," *Wisconsin Historical*

Collections 12 (1892): 133–53; L.A. Tohill, "Robert Dickson, British Fur Trade on the Upper Mississippi," *North Dakota Historical Quarterly* 2 (1928): 5–49; 3 (1928): 83–128, 182–203

66 Allen, *His Majesty's Indian Allies*, 109–22

67 Ibid., 83; White, *The Middle Ground*, 515; Goltz, "Tecumseh, The Prophet and the Rise of Northwest Indian Confederation," 45–8, 90–4

68 Drake, *Life of Tecumseh*, 124–30

69 Harrison to Eustis, 6 August 1810, in Esarey, ed., *Messages and Letters of William Henry Harrison*, 1: 457

70 See John Sugden, *Tecumseh's Last Stand* (Norman: University of Oklahoma Press, 1985).

71 Tecumseh's work among the Creeks, to whom he was related on his mother's side, is discussed at some length in Florette Henri, *The Southern Indians and Benjamin Hawkins, 1796–1816* (Norman: University of Oklahoma Press, 1985), 268–88; Joel W. Marten, *Sacred Revolt: The Mushkogees' Struggle for a New World* (Boston: Beacon Press, 1991), 114–32; H.B. Cushman, *History of the Choctaw, Chickasaw, and Natchez Indians* (Greenville, Tex., 1899), 303–10.

72 See Peter Douglas Elias, *The Dakota of the Canadian Northwest: Lessons for Survival* (Winnipeg: University of Manitoba Press, 1988), 6–15

73 Sir John Johnson's notes on a meeting of Sauks, Foxes, and northern Ottawas and Potawatomis held at Amherstburg, 8 June 1805, cited in White, *The Middle Ground*, 512

74 See Henry Lewis Carter, *The Life and Times of Little Turtle: First Sagamore of the Wabash* (Urbana: University of Illinois Press, 1987). See Wiley Sword, *President Washington's Indian War* (Norman: University of Oklahoma Press, 1985).

75 See Francis Jennings, *The Founders of America* (New York: W.W. Norton, 1993), 324–7.

76 See Bernard Sheehan, *Seeds of Extinction: Jeffersonian Philanthropy and the American Indian* (Chapel Hill: University of North Carolina Press, 1973).

77 Drake, *Life of Tecumseh and of His Brother The Prophet*, 126

78 Goltz, "Tecumseh, The Prophet and the Rise of the Northwest Indian Confederacy," 155–62

79 On Pokagan, see James A. Clifton, "Simon Pokagan," in Frederick E. Hoxie, ed., *Encyclopedia of North American Indians* (Boston: Houghton Mifflin, 1996), 493–5.

80 Simon Pokagon, "The Massacre of Fort Dearborn at Chicago," *Harper's Magazine* 98 (1899): 649–56

81 Ibid., 651

82 Harrison to Eustis, 7 August 1811, in Esarey ed., *Messages and Letters of William Henry Harrison*, 1: 548–51, cited in Goltz, "Tecumseh, The Prophet and the Rise of the Northwest Indian Confederation," 255–6

83 Edmunds, *The Shawnee Prophet*, 94–116

84 Hull, cited in George F.G. Stanley, "The Indians in the War of 1812," in Morris Zaslow, ed., *The Defended Border: Upper Canada and the War of 1812* (Toronto: Macmillan, 1964), 177

85 See Joel W. Martin, *Sacred Revolt: The Muskogees, Struggle for a New World* (Boston: Beacon Press, 1991).

86 John K. Mahon, "British Strategy and Southern Indians: War of 1812," *Florida Historical Quarterly* 44, 4 (1966): 285–302; Mahon, *The War of 1812* (Gainsville: University of Florida Press, 1972); Patricia R. Wickman, *Osceola's Legacy* (Tuscaloosa: University of Alabama Press, 1991)

87 Johnson, cited in Goltz, "Tecumseh, The Prophet and the Rise of the Northwest Indian Confederacy," 352

88 Pratt, cited in Patrick C.T. White, *A Nation on Trial: America and the War of 1812* (New York: John Wiley, 1967), 99

89 Jefferson and Adams, cited in Richard Drinnon, *Facing West: The Metaphysics of Indian-Hating and Empire-Building* (New York: New American Library, 1980), 93–8

90 Major John Richardson, *Richardson's War of 1812, with Notes and a Life of the Author by Alexander Clark Casselman* (1902; Toronto: Coles, 1974), 85, 87, 6

91 Allen, *His Majesty's Indian Allies*, 120–127; see also Alec R. Gilpin, *The War of 1912 in the Old Northwest* (East Lansing: Michigan State University Press, 1958).

92 Burt, *The United States, Great Britain and British North America*, 330

93 Sandy Antal, *A Wampum Denied: Procter's War of 1812* (Ottawa: Carleton University Press, 1998), 103–6

94 Burt, *The United States, Great Britain and British North America*, 350

95 Ibid., 360

96 National Archives of Canada, Colonial Office Records 42 (co 42), vol. 159, John Richardson, chairman, Committee of Trade at Montreal, and James Irvine, chairman, Commission of Trade at Quebec, to George Provost, Capt. General, and Governor in Chief over the Province of Lower and Upper Canada, 14 and 24 October 1812

97 Inglis Ellis Co. to the Right Honourable Earl Bathurst, Secretary of State for War and Colonies, 7 May 1814, in Gordon Charles Davidson, *The North West Company* (Berkeley: University of California Press, 1918), appendix N, 300

98 James McGill, cited in Stanley, "The Indians in the War of 1812," 178

99 Richardson and Irvine to Provost, 14 and 24 October 1812

100 Inglis Ellis Co. to Bathurst, 7 May, 1814, London England

101 Richardson and Irvine to Provost, 14 and 24 October, 1812. Emphasis in original

102 Michael Paul Rogin, *Fathers and Children: Andrew Jackson and the Subjugation of the American Indian* (New York: Alfred A. Knopf, 1975)

103 Ronald N. Satz, *American Indian Policy in the Jacksonian Era* (Lincoln: University of Nebraska Press, 1975)

104 See Thomas R. Hietala, *Manifest Design: Anxious Aggrandizement in Late Jacksonian America* (Ithaca: Cornell University Press, 1985).

105 See Angie Debo, *And Still the Waters Run: The Betrayal of the Five Civilized Tribes* (Princeton, NJ: Princeton University Press, 1940).

106 Charles Warren, *The Supreme Court in United States History* (Boston: Little, Brown, 1923), 189

107 *Worcester* v. *Georgia*, cited in Russel Lawrence Barsh and James Youngblood Henderson, *The Road: Indian Tribes and Political Liberty* (Berkeley: University of California Press, 1980), 56–7. On Marshall, see G. Edward White, *The Marshall Court and Cultural Change, 1815–35* (New York: Macmillan, 1988). On the Cherokee cases, see Charles Wilkinson, *American Indians, Time, and the Law* (New Haven: Yale University Press, 1987), 14–26; Sidney L. Harring, *Crow Dog's Case: American Indian Sovereignty, Tribal Law, and United States Law in the Nineteenth Century* (Cambridge: Cambridge University Press, 1994), 25–36; Chief Justice Marshall's Cherokee rulings are published in Joseph Cotton, Jr., ed., *The Constitutional Decisions of John Marshall*, 2 vols. (New York: Da Capo Press, 1969), 2: 2–37, 309–20, 334–77.

108 *Cherokee Nation* v. *Georgia*, cited in Francis Paul Prucha, *The Great Father: The United States and the American Indians*, abridged ed. (Lincoln: University of Nebraska Press, 1986), 75–7

109 See Robert A. Williams Jr, *The American Indian in Western Legal Thought: The Discourse of Conquest* (New York: Oxford University Press, 1990), 308–17.

110 *Johnson* v. *McIntosh*, cited ibid., 314–15; also 312.

111 Cited in William T. Hagan, *American Indians* (Chicago: University of Chicago Press, 1961), 75

112 The Indian Removal Act of 1830, cited in Prucha, *The Great Father*, abridged ed., 75

113 See J. Leith Wright, *The Only Land They Knew: The Tragic Story of American Indians in the Old South* (New York: The Free Press, 1981); James A. Clifton, *A Place of Refuge for All Time: Migration of American Potawatomi into Upper Canada, 1830–1850*, National Museum of Man Mercury Series, Canadian Ethnology Service Paper no. 26 (Ottawa, 1975); Robert M. Utley, "The Indian-United States Military Situation, 1848–1891," in Wilcomb E. Washburn, ed., *Handbook of North American Indians*, vol. 4: *History of Indian-White Relations* (Washington, DC: Smithsonian Institution, 1988), 176–77.

114 Chief Joseph, cited in Benjamin Capps, *The Great Chiefs* (Alexandria, Va: Time Life Books, 1975), 185

115 Benjamin Drake, *Life of Tecumseh and of His Brother The Prophet*, 231

116 Ibid., 231–2

117 Constance Backhouse, *Petticoats and Prejudice: Women and Law in Nineteenth-Century Canada* (Toronto: Published for the Osgoode Society by the Women's Press, 1991), 9–28; Sidney L. Harring, *White Man's Law: Native People in Nineteenth-Century Canadian Jurisprudence* (Toronto: Published for the Osgoode Society by the University of Toronto Press, 1998), 169–73

118 Cited in Backhouse, *Petticoats and Prejudice*, 18

119 Cited in Harring, *White Man's Law*, 171, 170

120 Dorchester, by His Excellency's Command, Additional Instructions, Indian Department, 26 December 1794, in Cruickshank, ed., *The Correspondence of Lieutenant Governor John Graves Simcoe* 3: 241–2 (my emphasis)

121 Harring, *Crow Dog's Case: American Indian Sovereignty, Tribal Law, and United States Law in the Nineteenth Century* (Cambridge: Cambridge University Press, 1995)

122 Harring, *White Man's Law*, 281

123 Alan C. Cairns, *Citizens Plus: Aboriginal Peoples and the Canadian State* (Vancouver: UBC Press, 2000)

124 Harry B. Hawthorne et al., *A Survey of the Contemporary Indians of Canada: A Report on the Economic, Political, Educational Needs and Policies*, 2 vols. (Ottawa: Indian Affairs Branch, 1966)

125 John Borrows, "Wampum at Niagara: The Royal Proclamation, Canadian Legal History, and Self-Government," in Michael Asch, ed., *Aboriginal and Treaty Rights in Canada: Essays on Law, Equity, and Respect for Difference* (Vancouver: UBC Press, 1997), 171

126 Antal, *A Wampum Denied*, 20

127 L.F.S. Upton, *Micmacs and Colonists: Indian-White Relations in the Maritimes, 1713–1867* (Vancouver: UBC Press, 1979), 82–7

128 C.L.R. James, *The Black Jacobins: Toussaint L'Ouverture and the San Domingo Revolution*, 2nd ed. revised (New York: Vintage Books, 1963); Aimé Césaire, *Toussaint Louverture: la révolution française et le problème colonial* (Paris: Présence Africaine, 1961)

129 Leon Poliakov, *The Aryan Myth: A History of Racist and Nationalist Ideas in Europe* (New York: Basic Books, 1974)

130 Adam Hochschild, *King Leopold's Ghost: A Story of Greed, Terror, and Heroism in Colonial Africa* (Boston: Houghton Mifflin, 1999)

131 See Anthony J. Hall, "*The St. Catherine's Milling and Lumber Company versus the Queen*: Indian Land Rights as a Factor in Federal-Provincial Relations in Nineteenth-Century Canada," in Kerry Abel and Jean Friesen, eds., *Aboriginal Resource Use in Canada: Historical and Legal Aspects* (Winnipeg: University of Manitoba Press, 1991), 267–86.

132 See Christopher Armstrong, *The Politics of Federalism: Ontario's Relations with the Federal Government, 1867–1942* (Toronto: University of Toronto Press, 1981); Paul Romney, *Mr. Attorney: The Attorney General for Ontario in Court, Cabinet and Legislature, 1791–1899* (Toronto: The Osgoode Society, 1986).

133 See Morris Zaslow, "The Ontario Boundary Question," in Ontario Historical Society, *Profiles of a Province: Studies in the History of Ontario* (Toronto, 1967), 107–17.

134 Canada, *Reports of the Supreme Court*, vol. 13 (Ottawa: Queen's Printer, 1887), pp. 596–7. On *Calvin's* case, see Geoffrey S. Lester, "The Territorial Rights of the Inuit of the Canadian Northwestern Territory: A Legal Argument," 2 vols. (PhD thesis, York University, 1981), 1: 342–55; Williams Jr, *The American Indian in Western Legal Thought*, 199–200, 269–70.

135 See C. Vann Woodward, *The Strange Career of Jim Crow*, 2nd ed. (London: Oxford University Press, 1966).

136 Robert Sheppard and Michael Valpy, *The National Deal: The Fight for a National Constitution* (Toronto: Fleet Books, 1982), 224–44

137 See Nell Jessup Newton, "Federal Power over Indians: Its Source, Scope and Limitations," *Pennsylavania Law Review* 132 (1984): 195–288.

138 Jennings, *The Founders of America,* 129

139 *The Ontario Reports* 10 (1885): 228

140 Great Britain, *Appeal Cases before the House of Lords and the Judicial Committee of the Privy Council,* vol. 14 (London: Council of Law Reporting, 1889), 54, 59

141 Canada, *Reports of the Supreme Court* 13: 609–10

142 See Edward Eggleston and Lillie Eggleston Seelye, *Tecumseh and the Shawnee Prophet, including Sketches of George Rogers Clark, Simon Kenton, William Henry Harrison, Cornstalk, Blackhoof, Blue Jacket, the Shawnee Logan, and Others Famous in the Frontier Wars of Tecumseh's Time* (New York: Dodd, Mead, 1878).

143 Drake, *Life of Tecumseh,* 234

144 Goldwin Smith, *The United States: An Outline of Political History, 1492–1871* (New York: Macmillan, 1893), 206–9

145 George Grant, "Canadian Fate and Imperialism," in Grant, *Technology and Empire* (Toronto: House of Anansi, 1969), 68

146 David Orchard, *The Fight for Canada: Four Centuries of Resistance to American Expansionism* (Toronto: Stoddart, 1993)

147 Eduardo Galeano, "The Blue Tiger and the Promised Land," *Report on the Americas* 24, 5 (1991): 15

148 Harrison, cited in Goltz, "Tecumseh, The Prophet and the Rising of the Northwest Indian Confederation," 253

149 See Stephan J. Randall and Herman W. Konrad, eds., NAFTA *in Transition* (Calgary: University of Calgary Press, 1995).

CHAPTER SIX

1 Nick and Helma Mika, *United Empire Loyalists: Pioneers of Upper Canada* (Belleville: Mika Publishing, 1976), 135

2 Earle Thomas, "Sir John Johnson," *Dictionary of Canadian Biography,* vol. 6 (Toronto: University of Toronto Press, 1987), 352–4

3 See George E. Reaman, *The Trail of the Iroquois Indians: How the Iroquois Nations Saved Canada for the British Empire* (London: Muller, 1967)

4 Sally M, Weaver, "Six Nations of the Grand River, Ontario," in Bruce G. Trigger, ed., *Handbook of North American Indians,* vol. 15: *Northeast* (Washington, DC: Smithsonian Institution, 1978), 526

5 See Daniel N. Paul, *We Were Not the Savages: A Micmac Perspective on the Collision of European and Aboriginal Civilizations* (Halifax: Nimbus Publishing, 1993); Jennifer Reid, *Myth, Symbol, and Colonial Encounter: British and Mi'kmaq in Acadia, 1700–1867* (Ottawa: University of Ottawa Press, 1995).

6 Marie Battiste, "Micmac Literacy and Cognative Assimilation," in Jean Barman, Yvonne Hebert, and Don McCaskill, eds., *Indian Education in Canada,* vol. 1: *The Legacy* (Vancouver: UBC Press, 1986), 34

7 See J.R. Miller "The Oka Controversy and the Federal Land-Claims Process,"

in Ken Coates, ed., *Aboriginal Land Claims in Canada: A Regional Perspective* (Toronto: Copp Clark Pitman, 1992), 215–41

8 Jack A. Frisch, "Iroquois of the West," in Trigger, ed., *Northeast*, 544–6; Theodore Binnema, *Common and Contested Ground: A Human and Environmental History of the Northwestern Plains* (Norman: University of Oklahoma Press, 2001), 172

9 See John C. Jackson, *Children of the Fur Trade: Forgotten Metis of the Pacific Northwest* (Missoula, Mont.: Mountain Press Publishing), 10–58.

10 V. Callihoo, "The Iroquois of Alberta," *Alberta Historical Review* 7, 2 (1959): 17–18

11 Roy MacLaren, *Canadians on the Nile, 1882–1898, Being the Adventures of the Voyageurs on the Khartoum Relief Expedition and Other Exploits* (Vancouver: UBC Press, 1978)

12 See Joseph Mitchell, "The Mohawks in High Steel," in Edmund Wilson, *Apologies to the Iroquois* (New York: Farrar, Strauss & Giroux, 1960), 3–36.

13 Henry Roxborough, *One Hundred – Not Out: The Story of Nineteenth-Century Canadian Sport* (Toronto: Ryerson Press, 1966), 39–47

14 Cleve Dheensaw, *Lacrosse 100: One Hundred Years of Lacrosse in B.C.* (Victoria: Orca Publishers, 1990), 17

15 Larry Villeneuve, revised and updated by Daniel Francis, *The Historical Background of Indian Reserves and Settlements in the Province of Quebec* (Ottawa: Indian and Northern Affairs Canada, 1984)

16 Wilbur R. Jacobs, *Wilderness Politics and Indian Gifts: The Northern Colonial Frontier, 1748–1763* (Lincoln: University of Nebraska Press, 1950); Anthony J. Hall, "The Red Man's Burden: Land, Law and the Lord in the Indian Affairs of Upper Canada" (PhD thesis, University of Toronto, 1984), chaps. 2 and 3; Catherine A. Sims, "Algonkian-British Relations in the Upper Great Lakes Region: Gathering to Give and Receive Presents, 1815–1843" (PhD thesis, University of Western Ontario, 1992)

17 Schedule of the Prices of Various Articles of which the Indian Presents Are Composed for the Year 1830 in Great Britain, House of Commons, *Parliamentary Paper*, vol. 617; *Aboriginal Tribes in North America, New South Wales, Van Dieman's Land and British Guiana: Return to Several Addresses to His Majesty, 17 March 1834* (London: King's Printer, 1834), 132

18 See L.F.S. Upton, "The Origins of Canadian Indian Policy," *Journal of Canadian Studies* 8, 4 (1973): 51–61; R.J. Surtees, "The Development of an Indian Reserve Policy in Upper Canada," *Ontario History* 61 (June 1969): 87–98.

19 John Sheridan Milloy, "The Era of Civilization – British Policy for the Indians of Canada, 1830–1830" (PhD thesis, Oxford University, 1978)

20 See James Douglas Leighton, "The Development of Federal Indian Policy, 1840–1890" (PhD thesis, University of Western Ontario, 1975); Marion Joan Boswell, "Civilizing the Indian: Government Administration of Indians, 1876–1899" (PhD thesis, University of Ottawa, 1978); E. Brian Titley, *A Narrow Vision: Duncan Campbell Scott and the Administration of Indian Affairs in Canada* (Vancouver: UBC Press, 1986).

21 See Hall, "The Red Man's Burden," 128–81.
22 Head to Glenelg, 20 November 1836, in Great Britain, *Parliamentary Papers* (Commons), vol. 323, *British North America. Return of an Address of the Honourable House of Commons, dated 11 June 1839; for, Copies of Extracts of Correspondence, since 1st April 1835 between the Secretary of State for the Colonies and the British North American Provinces, respecting Indians in the Provinces* (London: Queen's Printer, 1839), 124
23 Head to Glenelg, 20 August 1836, ibid., 121
24 See Lillian F. Gates, *Land Policies in Upper Canada* (Toronto: University of Toronto Press, 1968).
25 Head to Glenelg, 20 August 1836, in National Archives of Canada, Colonial Office Record (CO 42), vol. 431
26 Sir Francis Bond Head, *The Emigrant* (London: John Murray, 1846), 145
27 Ibid., 148
28 Treaty enclosed in Head to Glenelg, 20 August 1836, in Great Britain, *Parliamentary Papers*, vol. 323, "Indians," 123
29 John Locke, *Two Treatises of Government*, ed. Peter Laslett (New York: Mentor, 1965), 331
30 See Donald B. Smith, *Sacred Feathers: The Reverend Peter Jones (Kahkewaquonaby) and the Mississauga Indians* (Toronto: University of Toronto Press, 1987); Peter S. Schmalz, *The Ojibwa of Southern Ontario* (Toronto: University of Toronto Press, 1991); Elizabeth Graham, *Medicine Man to Missionary: Missionaries as Agents of Social Change among the Indians of Southern Ontario, 1784–1867* (Toronto: Peter Martin Associates, 1975).
31 Treaty enclosed in Head to Glenelg, 20 August 1836, in Great Britain, *Parliamentary Papers*, vol. 323, "Indians," 123
32 See Peter Schmaltz, *The History of the Saugeen Indians* (Ottawa: Ontario Historical Society, 1977).
33 Joseph Stinson, cited in Egerton Ryerson to Glenelg, nd, in Aborigines' Protection Society, *Report on the Indians of Upper Canada* (London: J. Haddon, 1839), 31–2
34 Schmalz, *The History of the Saugeen Indians*, 67–8
35 Treaty enclosed in Head to Glenelg, 20 August 1836 in Great Britain, *Parliamentary Papers*, vol. 323, "Indians," 124
36 Joseph Stinson, cited in Egerton Ryerson to Glenelg, nd, in Aborigines Protection Society, *Report*, 126
37 John Hill, cited in George Hodgins, ed., *Documentary History of Education in Upper Canada from the Passing of the Constitutional Act of 1791 to the Close of Dr. Ryerson's Administration of the Education Department of 1876* (Toronto: Warwick Brothers and Rutter, 1894), 5: 297
38 Head to Glenelg, 20 November 1836, in Great Britain, *Parliamentary Papers*, vol. 323, "Indians," 126
39 Head to Glenelg, 20 August 1836, CO42, vol. 431
40 G.R. Mellor, *British Imperial Trusteeship* (London: Faber and Faber, 1951); M.F.

Lindley, *The Acquisition and Government of Backward Territory in International Law* (New York: Longmans, Green, 1926)

41 Bond Head's reply to House of Assembly, nd, NA, Indian Department Records (RG10), vol. 60

42 Bond Head, *The Emigrant*, 148

43 Head to Glenelg, 20 November 1836, in Great Britain, *Parliamentary Papers*, vol. 323, 126

44 Glenelg to Head, 20 January 1837, in Aborigines' Protection Society, *Report on the Indians of Upper Canada*, 20–1

45 Noel Mostert, *Frontiers: The Epic of South Africa's Creation and the Tragedy of the Xhosa People* (New York: Alfrd A. Knopf, 1992), 775

46 Irving Hexham, *The Irony of Apartheid: The Struggle for National Independence of Africaner Calvinism against British Imperialism* (New York: The Edwin Mellen Press, 1981); Allister Sparks, *The Mind of South Africa* (London: Mandarin, 1990)

47 Glenelg to D'Urban, 26 December 1835, in Kenneth N. Bell and W.P. Mdorrell, eds., *Select Documents in British Colonial Policy, 1830–1860* (Oxford: Clarendon Press, 1928), 476

48 Eugene Stock, *History of the Church Missionary Society*, 2 vols. (London: CMS, 1899), 2: 250–69. See also Ernest Marshall House, *Saints in Politics: The "Clapham Sect" and the Growth of Freedom* (London: George Allen & Unwin, 1953).

49 Statement of Eighty Men, received at Colonial Office, 10 April 1837, attached to Robert Alder to Glenelg, 14 December 1837, in Great Britain, *Parliamentary Papers*, vol. 323, "Indians," 97–9; Aborigines' Protection Society, *Report on the Indians of Upper Canada* (London: J. Haddon, 1839)

50 William Higgins, August D'Este, and Samuel Blackburn, on behalf of the Aborigines' Protection Society, to Glenelg, nd, in Great Britain, *Parliamentary Papers*, vol. 323, "Indians," 101–2

51 Great Britain, *Sessional Papers* (Commons), vol. 7, "Report of the Select Committee on Aborigines in British Settlement, 26 June 1837" (London: King's Printer, 1837), 29–30

52 Cited in Bell and Morrell, eds., *Select Documents on British Colonial Policy*, 545–6

53 Great Britain, Sessional Papers (Commons), vol. 7, "Report," 30. Quoted in Canada, *Journal of the Legislative Assembly*, 11 Vic., 1847, appendix T, "General Recommendations," np

54 Noel Mostert, *Frontiers*, 802

55 Harrison, cited in Logan Esarey, ed., *Messages and Letters of William Henry Harrison*, 2 vols. (Indianapolis: Indiana Historical Commission, 1922), 1: 492–3

56 Cited in Bell and Morrell, eds. *Select Documents on British Colonial Policy*, 545–6

57 Anderson to Jarvis, 28 March 1838, Indian Department Records, vol. 68

58 J.M.S. Careless, *The Union of the Canadas: The Growth of Canadian Institutions* (Toronto: McClelland & Stewart, 1967)

59 See J.E. Hodgetts, *Pioneer Public Service: An Administrative History of the United Canadas, 1841–1867* (Toronto: University of Toronto Press, 1955).

60 See John S. Milloy, "The Early Indian Acts: Developmental Strategy and Constitutional Change," in Ian A.L. Getty and Antoine S. Lussier, eds., *As Long as the Sun Shines and Water Flows: A Reader in Canadian Native Studies* (Vancouver: UBC Press, 1983), 56–64; Anthony J. Hall, "Native Limited Identities and Newcomer Metropolitanism in Upper Canada, 1814–1867," in David Keane and Colin Read, eds., *Old Ontario: Essays in Honour of J.M.S. Careless* (Toronto: Dundurn, 1990), 157–68

61 Jean Morrison, introduction to *The North West Company in Rebellion: Simon McGillivray's Fort William Notebook, 1815* (Thunderbay: Thunder Bay Historical Museum Society, 1988), 6–15

62 See Margaret MacLeod and W.L. Morton, *Cuthbert Grant of Grantown* (Toronto: McClelland & Stewart, 1974).

63 See Donald Creighton, *The Commercial Empire of the St. Lawrence* (Toronto: Ryerson Press, 1937).

64 Ibid., 349–85

65 W.T. Easterbrook and Hugh G.T. Aitken, *Canadian Economic History* (Toronto: Macmillan, 1956), 361–5

66 Ibid., 274–7, 297

67 Allan McNab, cited in Oscar D. Skelton, *The Railway Builders: A Chronicle of Overland Highways* (Toronto: Glasgow, Brook, 1916), 53. See T.C. Keefer, *Philosophy of Railroads and Other Essays*, ed. H.V. Nelles (1849; Toronto: University of Toronto Press, 1972)

68 James Morrison, "The Robinson Treaties of 1850: A Case Study," Prepared for the Royal Commission on Aboriginal Peoples: Treaty and Land Research Section (Haileyburg, 1993), 36

69 Ibid., 37–84

70 Janet E. Chute, *The Legacy of Shingwaukonse: A Century of Native Leadership* (Toronto: University of Toronto Press, 1998)

71 Donald Swainson, "Allan Macdonell," in *Dictionary of Canadian Biography*, vol. 11: *1881–1890* (Toronto: University of Toronto Press, 1982), 552–4

72 Jesse Edgar Middleton and Fred Landon, *The Province of Ontario: A History, 1615–1927*, 2 vols. (Toronto: Dominion Publishing Company, 1927), 1: 30

73 Morrison, "The Robinson Treaties of 1850," 70. See J.M. Bumsted, "Alexander Macdonell," *Dictionary of Canadian Biography*, vol. 7: 1836–1850 (Toronto: University of Toronto Press, 1988), 554–6

74 Morrison, "The Robinson Treaties of 1850," 67–8

75 Macdonell, quoted in Report of Commissioner A. Vidal and T.G. Anderson on a Visit to the Indians on the North Shore, in Archives of Ontario, Aemelius Irving Papers, MU 1464. Also cited in Morrison, "The Robinson Treaties of 1850," 212

76 Cited in Chute, *The Legacy of Shingwaukonse*, 119–20

77 Report of Denis-Benjamin Papineau, Commissiner of Crown Lands, on Indian Claims, 1847, in Indian Department Records, vol. 163, 94982–5. Cited in Morrison, "The Robinson Treaties of 1850," 46

78 Ibid., 85–90

79 *The Patriot*, 19, 29 December, 1849

80 See J.M.S. Careless, *Brown of the Globe*, 2 vols. (Toronto: Macmillan, 1959, 1963).

81 *The Patriot*, 29 December 1849

82 W.B. Robinson to Hon. Col. Bruce, 24 September 1850, Toronto, in Alexander Morris, *The Treaties of Canada with the Indians of Manitoba and the North-West Territories* (1880; Toronto: Coles, 1979), 17–19

83 See Mgr L.-A. Pâquet, "A Sermon on the Vocation of the French Race in America, 1902," in Ramsay Cook, ed., *French-Canadian Nationalism: An Anthology* (Toronto: Macmillan, 1969), 160–2. See also John Webster Grant, *Moon of Wintertime: Missionaries and the Indians of Canada in Encounter since 1534* (Toronto: University of Toronto Press, 1984), 3–70

84 See George F.G. Stanley, "The First Indian Reserves in Canada," *Revue d'histoire de l'Amérique Française* 4 (September 1950).

85 Julien Paquin, "Modern Jesuit Missions in Ontario," in Jesuit Archives, Regis College, Toronto, Paquin Papers. See also Lorenzo Cadieux and Robert Toupin, *Les robes noire á l'isle du Manitou, 1853–1870*, Documents historic no. 75 (Sudbury: Société historique du Nouvel-Ontario, 1982).

86 Hall, "Native Limited Identities and Newcomer Metropolitanism in Upper Canada, 1814–1867," 165–7

87 Province of Canada, Legislative Assembly, "Report of the Special Commissioners Appointed 8th of September, 1856 to Investigate Indian Affairs in Canada," *Sessional Papers*, appendix 21. See John Leslie, "The Bagot Commission: Developing a Corporate Memory for the Indian Department," Canadian Historical Association. *Historical Papers*, 1982.

88 Indian Department Records, vol. 284, Speech of Wahkaikeghik, 19 January 1863

89 Ibid., Speech of Misheguong-pai, 19 January 1863

90 Transcript of the trial of Louis Riel, 1885, in Canada, *Sessional Papers* 19, 12 (1886), appendix 43, 213

91 Paul L.A.H. Chartrand, *Manitoba's Métis Settlement Scheme of 1870* (Saskatoon: Native Law Centre, University of Saskatchewan, 1991). See also D.N. Sprague, *Canada and the Métis, 1869–1885* (Waterloo, Ont.: Wilfrid Laurier University Press, 1988).

92 Rennard Strickland, *Fire and Spirits: Cherokee Law from Clan to Court* (Norman: University of Oklahoma Press, 1975), 49

93 R. David Edmunds, *American Indian Leaders: Studies in Diversity* (Lincoln: University of Nebraska Press, 1980), 41–63, 88–106

94 Grace Steele Woodward, *The Cherokee* (Norman: University of Oklahoma Press, 1963), 84–6

95 See Jean Delanglez, *Frontenac and the Jesuits* (Chicago: Institute of Jesuit History, 1939), 35–65; Cornelius J. Jaenen, *Friend and Foe: Aspects of French-Amerindien Cultural Contact in the Sixteenth and Seventeenth Centuries* (Toronto: McClelland & Stewart, 1976).

96 Marquis de Mirabeau, *L'ami des hommes, ou traite de la population*, 3 vols. (1758), 3: 226, cited in Anthony Pagden, *Lords of All the World: Ideologies of*

Empire in Spain, Britain and France,c. 1500–c. 1800 (New Haven: Yale University Press, 1995), 151

97 Elizabeth Arthur, "Simon J. Dawson," *Dictionary of Canadian Biography, Vol. 13* (Toronto: University of Toronto Press, 1994), 261–2

98 Elaine Allan Mitchell, "The Scots in the Fur Trade," in W. Stanford Reid, ed., *The Scottish Tradition in Canada* (Toronto: McClelland & Stewart, 1976), 27–48; John Nicks, Orkneymen in the HBC, 1780–1821," in Carol M. Judd and Arthur J. Ray, eds., *Old Trails and New Directions: Papers of the Third North American Fur-Trade Conference* (Toronto: University of Toronto Press, 1980), 102–26

99 Carl F. Klinck and James J. Talman, eds., *The Journal of Major John Norton, 1816* (Toronto: The Champlain Society, 1970); Charles M. Johnston, "William Claus and John Norton: A Struggle for Power in Old Ontario," *Ontario History* 57, 1 (.): 101–8

100 Reverend Jeremiah Evarts, *Cherokee Removal: The "William Penn" Essays and Other Writings*, ed. Francis Paul Prucha (Knoxville: University of Tennessee Press, 1981)

101 John Ridge, cited in Theodore W. Allen, *The Invention of the White Race*, vol. 1: *Racial Oppression and Social Control* (London: Verso, 1995), 137

102 Philip Drucker, *The Native Brotherhoods: Modern Intertribal Organizations on the Northwest Coast*, Smithsonian Institution. Bureau of American Ethnology Bulletin 168 (Washington, DC: Government Printing Office, 1958), 147–8

103 Douglas Cole and Ira Chaikan, *An Iron Hand upon the People: The Law against the Potlach on the Northwest Coast* (Vancouver: Douglas & McIntyre, 1990)

104 J. Lloyd Mecham, "The Church in Colonial Spanish America," in A. Curtis Wilgus, ed., *Colonial Hispanic America* (New York: Russell & Russell, 1963), 200

105 Charles R. Cutter, *The Protector de Indios in Colonial New Mexico, 1659–1821* (Albuquerque: University of New Mexico Press, 1986)

106 Demetrio Cojti Cuxil, cited in Victor Perera, *Unfinished Conquest: The Guatemalan Tragedy* (Berkeley: University of California Press, 1993), 317

107 Daniel H. Levine, *Popular Voices in Latin American Catholicism* (Princeton, NJ: Princeton University Press, 1992); Gregory Baum, "Liberal Capitalism: Has John Paul II Changed His Mind?" in Baum, *Essays in Critical Theology* (Kansas City: Sheed and Ward, 1994), 205–22; John Pilger, "Bishop Belo," in Pilger, *Hidden Agendas* (London: Vintage, 1999) 305–12

108 PBS Television Network in the United States, "Jean Paul II: The Millennial Pope," Front-line show 1801, air date: 28 September 1999

109 *Guardian*, 22 September 1996, cited in John Pilger, "The Terrorists," in Pilger, *Hidden Agendas*, 27

110 Archbishop Rivera y Damas, cited in John Pilger, "The Terrorists," 28

111 John Bacher, *Petrotyranny* (Toronto: Dundurn Press, 2000), 210–12

112 Julian Burger, *Report from the Frontier: The State of the World's Indigenous Peoples* (London: Zed Books, 1987), 235–45

113 Rigobertu Menchu, *I, Regobertu Menchu, an Indian Woman in Guatemala*, ed. Elisabeth Burgos-Debray, trans. Ann Wright (London: Verso, 1991)

114 Ibid., 102–4

115 Adrian Tanner, *Bringing Home Animals: Religious Ideology and Mode of Produc-tion of the Mistassini Cree Hunters* (St John's: Institute of Social and Economic Research, Memorial University of Newfoundland, 1979)

116 Grant, *Moon of Wintertime*, 262–3

117 Jean Usher, *William Duncan of Metlakalta: A Victorian Missionary in British Columbia*, National Museum of Man Publications in History no. 5 (Ottawa: National Museum of Man, 1974)

118 Paul Tennant, *Aboriginal Peoples and Politics: The Indian Land Question in British Columbia, 1849–1989* (Vancouver: UBC Press, 1990), 79

119 See Valerie Alia, *Un/covering the North: News, Media and Aboriginal People* (Vancouver: UBC Press, 1999); William Joel Neuheimer, *Indigenous Television in the Canadian North: Evolution, Operation and Impact on Cultural Preservation* (Ann Arbor: University Microfilms International, 1994).

120 See James B. Waldram, *As Long as the Rivers Run: Hydroelectric Development and Native Communities in Western Canada* (Winnipeg: University of Manitoba Press, 1988); Boyce Richardson, *Strangers Devour the Land: The Cree Hunters of the James Bay Area versus Premier Bourassa and the James Bay Development Corpo-ration* (Toronto: Macmillan, 1975).

121 Floyd W. Rudmin, *Bordering on Aggression: Evidence of US Military Preparations against Canada* (Hull, Que.: Voyageur, 1993), 142–3

122 Richard C. Bocking, *Canada's Water: For Sale?* (Toronto: James Lewis & Samuel Publishers, 1972), 58–59

123 Robert Bourassa, *Power from the North* (Scarborough, Ont.: Prentice Hall, 1985)

124 See Daniel Francis and Toby Morantz, *Partners in Fur: A History of the Fur Trade in Eastern James Bay, 1600–1870* (Montreal: McGill-Queen's University Press, 1983).

125 See Paul Barnsley, "National Chief's Religion Cause for Discussion," *Wind-speaker* 18, 5 (2000): 3; Roy MacGregor, *Chief: The Fearless Vision of Billy Dia-mond* (Markham, Ont.: Viking, 1989).

126 Pauline Comeau, *Elijah: No Ordinary Hero* (Vancouver: Douglas & McIntyre, 1993)

CHAPTER SEVEN

1 See Jonathan Friedman, "Indigenous Struggles and the Discreet Charm of the Bourgeoisie," in Roxann Prazniak and Arif Dirlik, eds., *Places and Politics in an Age of Globalization* (New York: Rowman & Littlefield, 2001), 15–52; Arif Dirlik, *The Postcolonial Aura: Third World Criticism in the Age of Global Capitalism* (Boulder, Col.: Westview Press, 1997)..

2 Román de la Campa, "Latin, Latino, American: Split States and Global Imagi-naries," *Comparative Literature* (Special Issue on Globalization and the Human-ities) 53, 4 (2001): 373

3 Edwin Black, *IBM and the Holocaust: The Strategic Alliance between Nazi Germany*

and America's Most Powerful Corporation (New York: Crown Publishers, 2001)

4 Joseph Borkin, *The Crime and Punishment of I.G. Farben* (New York: Free Press, 1978); Christopher Simpson, *The Splendid Blond Beast: Money, Law and Genocide in the Twentieth Century* (Monroe, Me.: Common Courage Press, 1995); Charles Higham, *Trading with the Enemy: An Exposé of the Nazi-American Money Plot, 1933–1949* (New York: Delacorte Press, 1983)

5 George W. Bush, cited in Paul Knox, "It's time to be a statesman, Mr. Bush," *Globe and Mail*, 11 September 2002, A13

6 George W. Bush, cited in Paul Koring, "U.S. President Plans Sept. 11 Pilgrimage," *Globe and Mail*, 11 September 2002, A8

7 Thucydides, cited in Eugen Weber, *The Western Tradition from the Ancient World to Louis XIV: A Book of Readings* (Boston: D.C. Heath, 1965), 56

8 See John Milloy, "The Early Indian Acts: Development Strategy and Constitutional Change," in Ian A.L. Getty and Antoine S. Lussier, eds., *As Long as the Sun Shines and the Water Flows: A Reader in Canadian Native Studies* (Vancouver: UBC Press, 1983), 39–56.

9 See Richard H. Bartlett, "Citizens Minus: Indians and the Right to Vote," *Saskatchewan Law Review* 44 (1979): 168.

10 Canada, House of Commons, *Debates*, 4 May 1885, cited ibid., 169

11 Mr Landry in House of Commons, *Debates*, 2 May 1885, cited ibid., 173–4

12 House of Commons, *Debates*, 2 May 1885, cited ibid., 173

13 See S. Barry Cottam, "Indian Title as a 'Celestial Institution': David Mills and the *St. Catherine's Milling* Case," in Kerry Abel and Jean Friesen, eds., *Aboriginal Resource Use in Canada: Historical and Legal Aspects* (Winnipeg: University of Manitoba Press, 1991), 247–65

14 House of Commons, *Debates*, 30 April, 1 May 1885, in Bartlett, "Citizens Minus," 171

15 See Edward Blake, *The Ontario Lands Case: Argument of Mr. Blake, Q.C., before the Privy Council* (Toronto: The Budget, 1888).

16 House of Commons, *Debates*, 30 April 1885, cited in Bartlett, "Citizens Minus," 171

17 See Blair Stonechild and Bill Waiser, *Loyal Till Death: Indians and the North-West Rebellion* (Saskatoon: Fifth House, 1997).

18 House of Commons, *Debates*, 30 April 1885, cited in Bartlett, "Citizens Minus," 169

19 Mr Fisher in House of Commons, *Debates*, 1 May 1885, cited ibid., 179–80

20 Theodore Roosevelt, *The Winning of the West*, 6 vols. (New York: G.P. Putnam's Sons, 1889–1906)

21 See Robert E. Beider, *Science Encounters the Indian, 1820–1880: The Early Years of American Ethnology* (Norman: University of Oklahoma Press, nnnn?), 146–93.

22 House of Commons, *Debates*, 1 May 1885, in Bartlett, "Citizens Minus," 174–5

23 Chief Jones to John A. Macdonald, 8 August 1886, cited ibid., 177

24 House of Commons, *Debates*, 26 May 1885, cited ibid., 177

25 See Brian A. Titley, *A Narrow Vision: Duncan Campbell Scott and the Administration of Indian Affairs in Canada* (Vancouver: UBC Press, 1986); Stan Dragland, *Floating Voice: Duncan Campbell Scott and the Literature of Treaty 9* (Toronto: Anansi, 1994).

26 Ella Cork, *"The Worst of the Bargain"* concerning the Dilemmas Inherited from Their Forefathers along with the Lands by the Iroquois Nation of the Canadian Grand River Reserve (San Jacinto, Cal.: Foundation for Social Research, 1962), 129

27 See John L. Tobias, "Protection, Civilization, Assimilation: An Outline of Canada's Indian Policy," *Western Canadian Journal of Anthropology* 6, 2 (1976): 13–20; Douglas Cole and Ira Chaikin, *An Iron Hand upon the People: The Law Against the Potlatch on the Northwest Coast* (Vancouver: Douglas & McIntyre, 1990); Katherine Pettipas, *Severing the Ties That Bind: Government Repression of Indigenous Religious Ceremonies on the Prairies* (Winnipeg: University of Manitoba Press, 1994).

28 F.L. Barron, "The Indian Pass System in the Canadian West, 1882–1935," *Prairie Forum* 13, 1 (1988): 25–42

29 J.R. Miller, "Owen Glendower, Hotspur, and Canadian Indian Policy," in Miller, ed., *Sweet Promises: A Reader on Indian-White Relations in Canada* (Toronto: University of Toronto Press, 1991), 323–52

30 Peter Kulchyski, "A Considerable Unrest: F.O. Loft and the League of Indians," *Native Studies Review* 4, 1 and 2 (1988): 95–117

31 National Archives of Canada (NA), Indian Department Records, RG 10, Vol. 245, D. Thornburn to R. Pennefather, 13 October 1858

32 "Report of the Special Commissioners Appointed on 8th of September, 1856, to Investigate Indian Affairs in Canada," The Province of Canada, *Sessional Papers* (Legislative Assembly), 1858, appendix 21, np

33 Enemikeese, *The Indian Chief: An Account of the Labours, Losses and Sufferings and Oppression of Ke-zig-ko-e-ne-ne (David Sawyer), a Chief of the Ojibbeway Indians of Canada West* (London: 1867), 114–59

34 *The Times*, 4 July 1860

35 Indian Department Records, RG 10, vol. 256, W.R. Bartlett to Richard Pennefather, 25 September 1860. See Anthony Hall, "Native Limited Identities and Newcomer Metropolitanism in Upper Canada, 1814–1867," in David Keane and Colin Read, eds., *Old Ontario: Essays in Honour of J.M.S. Careless* (Toronto: Dundurn, 1990), 163–4

36 See Reverend Edward F. Wilson, *Missionary Work among the Ojebway Indians* (London: Society for Promoting Christian Knowledge, 1886).

37 David A. Nock, *A Victorian Missionary and Canadian Indian Policy: Cultural Synthesis vs Cultural Replacement* (Waterloo: Wilfrid Laurier University Press, 1988)

38 These essays are published in their entirety, ibid, 163–76.

39 See John Webster Grant, *Moon of Wintertime: Missionaries and the Indians of Canada in Encounter since 1534* (Toronto: University of Toronto Press, 1992), 192–6

40 S.H. Blake, *The Call of the Red Man as Answered by the Commissioner of Indian Affairs in the United States of America: What Will Be the Answer of the Dominion of Canada?* (Toronto: Bryant Press, 1908), 17

41 R.V. Sinclair, *Canadian Indians* (Ottawa: Thorburn and Abbott Book Sellers and the Ottawa Evening Journal, 1911), 8

42 Roger L. Nichols, *Indians in the United States and Canada: A Comparative History* (Lincoln: University of Nebraska Press, 1999), 269–70; Malcolm Montgomery, "The Legal Status of the Six Nations in Canada," *Ontario History* 55 (June 1963): 93–105

41 Constance Backhouse, *Colour Coded: A Legal History of Racism in Canada, 1900–1950* (Toronto: Published for the Osgoode Society for Canadian Legal History by University of Toronto Press, 1999), 103–31

44 Richard Veatch, *Canadian Foreign Policy and the League of Nations* (Toronto: University of Toronto Press, 1975), 91–100

45 Nellie Ketchukian, "Chief Deskaheh, George Decker and the Six Nations vs The Government of Canada," *The Iroquoian* 11 (fall 1985): 12–18

46 See Warren F. Kuehl, *Seeking World Order: The United States and International Organization to 1920* (Nashville: Vanderbilt University Press, 1969); Warren F. Kuehl and Lynne K. Dunn, *Keeping the Covenant: American Internationalists and the League of Nations, 1920–1939* (Kent Ohio: Kent State University Press, 1997).

47 Woodrow Wilson to Congress, 1917, cited in Ellen Anderson, "The Indigenous People of Saskatchewan: Their Rights under International Law," *American Indian Journal* 7, 1 (1981): 8

48 Joelle Rostkowski, "The Redman's Appeal for Justice: Deskaheh and the League of Nations," in Christian F. Feest, *Indians and Europe: An Interdisciplinary Collection of Essays* (Aachen: Alano Edition Herodot, 1989), 446

49 Deskahe, *The Red Man's Appeal for Justice, August 6, 1923* (London: Kealeys, 1923)

50 Letter from the Canadian Government to the Secretary-General of the League of Nations, Ottawa, 7 February 1924, in *League of Nations: Official Journal*, C 154, M 31, 1924, 7: 834–5

51 See Annmarie Shimony, "Alexander General, 'Deskahe,' Cayuga-Oneida, 1889–1965," in Margot Liberty, ed., *American Indian Intellectuals, Proceedings of the American Ethnological Society, 1976* (St Paul: West Publishing, 1978), 158–75

52 Sally M. Weaver, "Six Nations of the Grand River, Ontario," in Bruce G. Trigger, ed., *Handbook of North American Indians*, vol. 15: *Northeast* (Washington, DC: Smithsonian Institute, 1978), 525–36; Titley, *A Narrow Vision*, 109–34

53 *Family Herald and Weekly Star*, 11 July 1928, cited ibid., 129

54 Donald Creighton, *Canada's First Century, 1867–1967* (Toronto: Macmillan, 1970), 183

55 See Fred Gaffen, *Forgotten Soldiers* (Penticton: Theytus Books, 1985).

56 The changes in the Indian Act in 1951 and the extension of the franchise to Indians in 1960 are covered in Hugh A. Dempsey, *The Gentle Persuader: A Biography of James Gladstone, Indian Senator* (Saskatoon: Western Producer Prairie Books, 1986). See also Bartlett, "Citizens Minus: Indians and the Right to Vote," 164–94

57 F. Laurie Barron, *Walking in Indian Moccasins: The Native Policies of Tommy Douglas and the CCF* (Vancouver: UBC Press, 1997)

58 Protest slogans referred to in *Ottawa Citizen*, 15 January 1960, cited in Dempsey, *The Gentle Persuader*, 175

59 See Sally Weaver, *Making Canadian Indian Policy: The Hidden Agenda, 1968–1970* (Toronto: University of Toronto Press, 1981).

60 Tim Naumetz, "PM rejects comparison of Canadian Indians to South African blacks," *Globe and Mail*, 27 January 1987, A1–A2

61 James Walsh, "Hitler: The Evil That Won't Die," *Time Magazine*, 8 May 1995, 42–7

62 See Frank Cassidy and Robert L. Bish, *Indian Government: Its Meaning in Practice* (Lantzville, BC: Oolichan Books, 1989).

63 Bernard Makhosezwe Magubane, *The Making of a Racist State: British Imperialism and the Union of South Africa, 1875–1910* (Trenton, NJ/Asmara, Eritrea: African World Press, 1996)

64 Leonard Thompson, *The Political Mythology of Apartheid* (New Haven: Yale University Press, 1985)

65 J. C. Smuts, cited in Mugabane, *The Making of a Racist State*, 279–80

66 Ibid., 289. See Carl Berger, *The Sense of Power: Studies in the Idea of Canadian Imperialism, 1867–1914* (Toronto: University of Toronto Press, 1973).

67 Lord Milner, cited in Mugabane, *The Making of a Racist State*, 289

68 Lord Balfour, cited ibid., 295

69 P. A. Silman, *The Governance of Empire* (1910; Port Washington, NY: Kennikat Press, 1971), 169–70

70 Ibid., 227

71 Many of these South African reports are in RG 10, vol. 6823, file 494–5–1, part 1; vol. 8588, file 1/1–10–3, part 0.

72 Linda Freeman, *Ambiguous Champion: Canada and South Africa in the Trudeau and Mulroney Years* (Toronto: University of Toronto Press, 1997), 308

73 See, for instance, I. Schapera, ed., *Western Civilization and the Natives of South Africa: Studies in Culture Contact* (London: Routledge & Kegan Paul, 1967).

74 Indian Department Records, RG 10, vol. 6823, file 494–5–1, part 1, C.J. Burchell, high commissioner for Canada in South Africa, to Secretary of State for External Affairs, 4 July 1945

75 Burchell to J.E.Read, 1 November 1944, cited in Brian Douglas Tennyson, *Canadian Relations with South Africa: A Diplomatic History* (Washington, DC: University Press of America, 1982), 116

76 Indian Department Records, RG 10, vol. 8588, file 1/10–4, part 5, J.S. Cross, deputy minister of citizenship and immigration, to Colonel H.M. Jones, Director of Indian Affairs, 20 December 1956; Frederick J. Van Wyk, care of the Carnegie Corporation of New York, to Mr McInnis, 23 November, 1956; Under-Secretary of State for External Affairs (no signature) to the Deputy Minister of Citizenship and Immigration, 13 December 1956

77 Ibid., Union of South Africa, *Report of the Department of Native Affairs for the Year 1953–54* (Pretoria: Government Printer, 1956), 5–12

78 Diefenbaker, cited in Tennyson, *Canadian Relations With South Africa*, 155–78
79 Indian Department Records, RG 10, vol. 8588, file 1/10–4, pt. 5, J.D. Minnis, assistant regional supervisor, Manitoba, Indian Affairs Branch, to Col. H.M. Jones, 9 July 1962
80 Ibid., W.F.B. Pugh to Col. H.M. Jones, 9 July 1962
81 Ibid., W. Dirkse-van-Schalwyk, Suid-Africaanse ambassade to Dr G.F. Davidson, deputy minister of citizenship and immigration, 26 July 1962
82 George W. Brown, J.M.S. Careless, Gerald M. Craig, and Eldon Ray, *Canada and the Commonwealth* (Toronto: J.M. Dent and Sons, 1953)
83 Angus M. Gunn, *South Africa: A World Challenged* (West Vancouver: Legacy Press, 1989), 31
84 President P.W. Botha, cited in Titus Alexander, *Unravelling Global Apartheid: An Overview of World Politics* (Cambridge: Polity Press, 1996), 178
85 Ovide Mercredi, quoted in James Cullingham, "How Far Will He Go? Phil Fontaine's New Regional Vision," *Now Magazine*, 7–13 August 1997, 21
86 See Allister Sparks, *Tomorrow Is Another Country* (London: Heinemann, 1995).
87 Andrew Armitage, *Comparing the Policy of Aboriginal Assimilation: Australia, Canada, and New Zealand* (Vancouver: UBC Press, 1995), 19–22
88 See Robert Sheppard and Michael Valpy, *The National Deal: The Fight for a Canadian Constitution* (Toronto: Fleet Books, 1982); Anthony Hall, "What Are We? Chopped Liver? Aboriginal Affairs in the Constitutional Politics of Canada in the 1980s," in Michael D. Behiels, ed., *The Meech Lake Primer: Conflicting Views of the 1987 Constitutional Accord* (Ottawa: University of Ottawa Press, 1989), 423–56.
89 See Terry L. Anderson, *Sovereign Nations or Reservations? An Economic History of American Indians* (San Francisco: Pacific Research Institute for Public Policy, 1995).
90 Ralph Nader, *The Ralph Nader Reader* (New York: Seven Stories Press, 2000), 55–206; Joshua Karliner, *The Corporate Planet: Ecology and Politics in the Age of Globalization* (San Francisco: Sierra Books, 1997); George Ritzer, *The McDonaldization of Society: An Investigation into the Changing Character of Contemporary Social Life* (Thousand Oaks: Pine Forge Press, 1996)
91 Bruce Clark, *Native Liberty, Crown Sovereignty: The Existing Aboriginal Right of Self-Government in Canada* (Montréal: McGill-Queen's University Press, 1990), 193
92 Will Kymlicka, *Liberalism, Community, and Culture* (Oxford: Clarendon Press, 1989), 154, 257–258
93 Arno J. Mayer, *Political Origins of the New Diplomacy, 1917–1918* (New York: Vintage Books, 1970); Victor S. Mamatey, *The United States and East Central Europe, 1914–1918* (Princeton: Princeton University Press, 1957)
94 Antonio Cassese, "The Self-Determination of Peoples," in Louis Henkin, ed., *The International Bill of Rights: The Covenant on Civil and Political Rights* (New York: Columbia University Press, 1981), 92–113; Rupert Emerson, *From Empire to Nation: The Rise to Self-Assertion of Asian and African Peoples* (Cambridge: Harvard University Press, 1967), 295–362

95 Derek Ferguson, "Indian Chief exploits Pretoria's envoy to show squalor of reserve to the world," *Toronto Star*, 11 March 1987, A1, A25

96 Freeman, *The Ambiguous Champion*, 179

97 See Palmer Patterson, "The Colonial Parallel: A View of Indian History," *Ethnohistory* 18, 1 (1971): 1–17.

98 George M. Frederickson, *White Supremacy: A Comparative Study in American and South African History* (Oxford: Oxford University Press, 1981)

99 R.F. Alfred Hoernlé, *South African Native Policy and the Liberal Spirit* (New York: Negro University Press, 1969). See G.R. Mellor, *British Imperial Trusteeship* (London: Faber and Faber, 1951); Walter L. Williams, "American Imperialism and the Indians," in Hoxie, ed., *Indians in American History*, 231–49; James E. Falkowski, *Indian Law/Race Law: A Five-Hundred-Year History* (New York: Praeger, 1992).

100 Samuel Huntington, *The Clash of Civilizations and the Remaking of World Order* (New York: Simon & Schuster, 1996), 51

101 J.A. Hobson, *Imperialism: A Study* (1902; Ann Arbour: The University of Michigan Press, 1965)

102 V.I. Lenin, *Imperialism, the Highest Stage of Capitalism: A Popular Outline* (1916; Moscow: Progress Publishers, 1966)

103 The scholarly controversies generated by Hobson's text are discussed in C.C. Eldridge, *Victorian Imperialism* (London: Hodder and Stoughton, 1978), 124–48

104 Alexander, *Unravelling Global Apartheid*, 9–10, 12

105 Prime Minister Jean Chrétien, cited in Shawn McCarthy, "PM says US attitude helped fuel Sept. 11," *Globe and Mail*, 12 September 2002, A1

106 Alan Freeman, "Schroeder calls for controls on capital flow," *Globe and Mail*, 2 February 1999, A10. For statistics and interpretations on growing disparities of wealth, see Bruce R. Scott, "The Great Divide in the Global Village," *Foreign Affairs*, January/February 2001; Nelson Mandela, "Globalizing Responsibility," *Boston Globe*, 4 January 2000; David Cay Johnson, "On a new map, the income gap grows," *New York Times*, 17 September 2000; David R. Francis, "Signs point to greater rich-poor wage gap," *Christian Science Monitor*, 3 September 2002; Steve Gatkin, Rich-poor gap as wide as ever in Latin America," *Times of India*, 5 September 2000; Gumisai Mutume, "Boon years see inequality," Interpress Service, 25 August 2000.

107 John R. MacArthur, "Mr. I-Feel-Your-Pain was better at inflicting It," *Globe and Mail*, 20 January 2001, A13

108 Human Rights Watch Prison Project, published on the Internet at www.hrw.org/advocacy/prisons/u-s.htm

109 Boyce Richardson, "Corporations: How Do We Curb Their Obscene Power," unpublished manuscript Ottawa, April 1997

110 Ibid.

111 David C. Korten, "Life After Capitalism," Presentation for Edmonton, Calgary, and Saskatoon, 6

112 AFLCIO Paywatch website at www.aflcio.org/paywatch/ceopax.htm

113 William Lerach and Al Myerhoff, "Why Insiders Get Rich and Little Guys Lose," The Enron Fraud Website, www.enronfraud.com/insidersvslittle.html

114 Naomi Klein, *No Logo: Taking Aim at the Brand Bullies* (Toronto: Vintage Canada, 2000)

115 See Eric N. Baklanoff, *Expropriation of U.S. Investments in Cuba, Mexico, and Chile* (New York: Praeger, 1975).

116 Text of speech delivered by Cuban president Fidel Castro at the Palace of Nations in Geneva on the occasion of the presentation to him of the Health for All Medal by the World Health Organization, 14 May 1998 (minor editing by author)

117 Mandella, cited in Richard Meares, "Mandela's parting words bitter toward rich whites," *Globe and Mail,* 17 December, 1997, A12

118 Oliver Hoedman et al., "MAIgalomania: The New Corporate Agenda," *The Ecologist* 28, 3 (1998): 154–60; Tony Clarke and Maude Barlow, *MAI: The Multilateral Agreement on Investment and the Threat to Canadian Sovereignty* (Toronto: Stoddart, 1997)

119 Carlos Fuentes, *Latin America: At War with the Past* (Toronto: CBC Enterprises, 1985), 39–43

120 Fred Anderson, *The Crucible of War: The Seven Years' War and the Fate of the Empire of British North America, 1754–1766* (New York: Vintage Books, 2000)

121 Benedict Anderson, *Imagined Communities: Reflections on the Origin and Spread of Nationalism. Revised Edition* (London: Verso, 1991), p.202, 191

122 Taisier M. Ali and Robert O. Matthews, eds., *Civil Wars in Africa: Roots and Resolution* (Montreal: McGill-Queen's University Press, 1999)

123 Jack David Eller, *From Culture to Ethnicity to Conflict: An Anthropological Perspective on International Ethnic Conflict* (Ann Arbor: University of Michigan Press, 1999)

124 Serious reckoning with this historical legacy is lacking in Michael Ignatieff's trilogy. See Ignatieff, *Blood and Belonging: Journies into the New Nationalism* (London: Chatto and Windus, 1993); *The Warrior's Honour: Ethnic War and the Modern Conscience* (London: Chatto and Windus, 1998); *Virtual War: Kosovo and Beyond* (Toronto: Viking, 2000).

125 See Francis Jennings, *The Creation of America through Revolution to Empire* (Cambridge: Cambridge University Press, 2000).

126 See Alexander Ewen, ed., *Voice of Indigenous Peoples: Native People Address the United Nations* (Sante Fe: Clear Light Publishers, 1994); Lydia van de Fliert, ed., *Indigenous Peoples and International Organizations* (Nottingham, Eng.: Spokesman, 1994).

127 United Nations Document E/CN.4/GR.1987/7/Add.1230, September 1987, 18–19, cited in Frank Wilmer, *The Indigenous Voice in World Politics: Since Time Immemorial* (Newbury Park: Sage Publications, 1993), 58

128 Francis Paul Prucha, *American Indian Treaties: The History of a Political Anomaly* (Berkeley: University of California Press, 1994); Charles J. Kappler, *Indian Affairs: Laws and Treaties,* 5 vols. (Washington, DC: Government Printing Office, 1903–41)

129 Hayden Ralston, *The Senate and Treaties, 1789–1817: The Development of the Treaty-Making Functions of the United States during Their Formative Period* (New York: Macmillan, 1920)

130 Jeremiah Evarts, *Cherokee Removal: The "William Penn" Essays and Other Writings*, ed. Francis Paul Prucha (Knoxville: University of Tennessee Press, 1981)

131 Cited in John R. Wunder, "No More Treaties: The Resolution of 1871 and the Alteration of Indian Rights to Their Homelands," in Wunder, ed., *Working The Range: Essays on the History of Western Land Management and the Environment* (Westport, Conn.: Greenwood Press, 1985), 39

132 Ibid., 53

133 United States Commission on National Security (USCNS), *New World Coming: American Security in the Twenty-First Century*, Phase I, September 1999; *Seeking a National Strategy: A Concert for Preserving Security and Preserving Freedom*, Phase II, April 2000; *Road Map for National Security; Imperative for Change*, Phase III (Report of the US Commission on National Security/ Twenty-First Century, January 2001, www.nssg.gov, 5 February 2001)

134 USCNS, *Road Map for National Security*, 7, 2

135 See Richard Slotkin, *Gunfighter Nation: The Myth of the Frontier in Twentieth-First Century America* (New York: Atheneum, 1992)

136 Rousseau, cited in Charles M. Andrews, ed., *Famous Utopias: Being the Complete Text of Rousseau's Social Contract, More's Utopia, Bacon's New Atlantis, and Campanella's City of the Sun* (New York: Tudor, 1901), 10

137 See Jeffrey Butler, Robert I. Rotberg, and John Adams, *The Black Homelands of South Africa: The Political Development of Bophuthatswana and KwaZulu* (Berkeley: University of California Press, 1977).

138 Sha Zukang, cited in Jeff Sallot, "China wants Ottawa's aid in stopping U.S. shield," *Globe and Mail*, 19 February 2001, A1

139 Jean Chrétien, cited in Marcus Gee, "Don't blame the victim, Mr Chretien," *Globe and Mail*, 14 September, 2002, A15

140 USCNS, *Road Map for National Security*, 5

141 Paul M. Wood, *Biodiversity and Democracy: Rethinking Society and Nature* (Vancouver: UBC Press, 2000)

142 On the genesis of thinking leading to the push to create a Free Trade Area of the Americas, see Gordon Mace et al., *The Americas in Transition: The Contours of Regionalism* (Boulder, Col.: Lynne Rienner Publishers, 1999).

143 Colonel Henry Proctor, cited in Sandy Antal, *A Wampum Denied: Proctor's War of 1812* (Ottawa: Carleton University Press, 1998), 72

Index

Abacha, Gen. Sami, 150

Abenaki people, 314, 329, 343

Abernathy, Thomas Perkins, 347

Aboriginal academics, 51, 247, 257

Aboriginal agenda: defined by George Manuel, 287

Aboriginal allodial title, 47–48, 411. *See also* Aboriginal and treaty rights, Aboriginal rights, Aboriginal title

Aboriginal Americans, 5, 177, 248

Aboriginal capitalism, 24

Aboriginal civilization of the Americas, 93–107; Bartolome de Las Casas as witness to assaults against, 178; and domestication of plants, 107–12; historical misrepresentation as means of negating, 164; Inca realm a stronghold of, 223; and New Spain, 305. *See also* Western civilization

Aboriginal civilization of the Mississippi Valley, 105

Aboriginal claims: Canada's prohibition on transfers of money to advance, 251. *See also* Aboriginal and treaty rights, Aboriginal rights, Aboriginal title

Aboriginal commons: breakup of through collaboration with Aboriginal comprador class, 360–1

Aboriginal constitutions: and unwritten constitutional law of Great Britain, 409

Aboriginal contributions to world civilization, as conceived of by George Manuel, 243

Aboriginal country, 465

Aboriginal creation stories, 100–3

Aboriginal dominion, 74; vision of Tecumseh, 388–97, 399

Aboriginal elites: and homeless urban poor, 285

Aboriginal fighting forces, 317, 398

Aboriginal gift exchanges, 318–19

Aboriginal hemisphere, 248

Aboriginal horticulture, 50, 107–12, 213, 469

Aboriginal hunters, 107, 183–4; John Locke's idealization of, 308–9

Aboriginal inmates, 286; genesis of the American Indian Movement, 261–2

Aboriginal irrigation, 105, 113

Aboriginal issues: domestication of by governments of nation-states, 302–3

Aboriginality and conservation, 35

Aboriginal jurisdiction, 302

Aboriginal knowledge, 64, 243

Aboriginal land claims, 159. *See also* Aboriginal and treaty rights, Aboriginal rights, Aboriginal title

Aboriginal lands, 64, 262, 284–5

Aboriginal languages: silencing of, 63–5, 218

Aboriginal law: Judge Monk on, 409; Louis Cameron on, 274; within larger framework of British Empire, 409

Aboriginal leadership, 55, 202–3, 196–200, 216, 249, 260, 280; in Canada in making representations to the United Nations, 288; colonial powers try to co-opt or compromise through gifts and bribes, 283–7

Aboriginal literature, 194–6

Aboriginal media societies, 465

Aboriginal medicine, 101, 248

Aboriginal organizations in Canada, 89, 202–3, 249–60. *See also* Assembly of First Nations, Coalition of First Nations, Federated

Saskatchewan Indian Nations, National Indian Brotherhood, North American Indian Brotherhood, Ojibway Warriors' Society
Aboriginal orthodoxy, 127
Aboriginal patriotism, 253
Aboriginal peoples. *See* First Nations, Indigenous peoples
Aboriginal poverty: bondage deriving from, 286; debate in Indian-Eskimo Associations over, 264–5
Aboriginal preachers, 331
Aboriginal renovation from within: work of George Manuel as example of, 244 ,247, 249
Aboriginal resistance movement, 367
Aboriginal rights: in Australia, 141; Bartolome de Las Casas as pioneer of, 78; and communism, 40; and courts, 42; exploitation of in defence of British Imperial Canada, 399–400; impact on by expanding colonial self-rule, 436; in New Spain, 305; rejection of by American Revolutionaries, 360
Aboriginal spirituality: in American Indian Movement, 261
Aboriginal title, 31, 41,43, 45, 47, 82; abuse of in British Imperial Canada, 399; allodial title, 48; attempts to purchase in pre-revolutionary British North America, 346–53; in Australia, 139; and British Columbia, 83, 158, 247, 249–253; British pressure on USA to recognize, 378; and concept of parliamentary supremacy, 142; and Edmund Burke, 75; evasion of by United States, xxiii, 264; expression other than through

ceding treaties, 356; George Manuel's conception of in context of Canadian, British, and world history, 287; in international law, 378; and land speculation companies in pre-revolutionary British North America, 346–53; and Pequot War, 317; Peter Julls on, 152; philosophy of in the Americas, 204–5; role of academics in Canada on reopening negotiations on in mid-1960s, 265; and Royal Proclamation, 314–26. *See also* Aboriginal and treaty rights, Aboriginal rights, Royal Proclamation of 1763
Aboriginal trade unionism, 251
Aboriginal and treaty rights, 16, 28–31, 34–36; Aboriginal representatives lack vote in constitutional process of defining, 202; abuse of, 438–9; in *Akwesasne Notes* and *America before Columbus*, 270; Allan Macdonell and Shingwaukonse recognize Indian rights in charter mining businesses, 450–1; and American Revolution, 81–3; arbitration of begins at Valladolid in 1550, 305; British Empire concept of after American Revolution, 320; Canadian constitutional process to define, 53, 196–200; and defence of British Imperial Canada, 399; different interpretations of, 416; in domestic courts, 47–9; and Enlightenment ideas, 132; French, Dutch, and British imperialist attitudes to, 322; in international law and politics, 45–6, 151, 302–3; legal arguments of Georgia and Ontario to extinguish,

417–18; liberalism and, 512; Lockean rationales for extinguishment of, 185; negotiations of at Niagara Falls in 1764, 155; and North American history, 152–60; and Pontiac's patriotic stand, 330–1; proposals for means of expressing, 356; Reform Party agenda to terminate, 509; Royal Proclamation and, 314–26, 336; and royalties, 451; and rule of law in the Americas, Australia, Southeast Asia, and Africa, 302; shopping cart of, 39–42; *Spirit of Haida Gwaii* as icon of, 206–7; and *St Catherine's Milling* case, 415–21; termination and, 46; and Treaty of Ghent, 400; Trudeau government tries to extinguish through White Paper, 278–80; and White Paper, 497; William Penn and Quakers on, 317–18; and withdrawal of British military from Great Lakes area, 388; as work in progress, 47–9; younger generation inpatient with tactics in defending, 263. *See also* Aboriginal rights, Aboriginal title, Indian Country of Canada, Royal Proclamation of 1763
Aboriginal visual arts and sculpture, 244–5
Aboriginal women: and constitutional politics in Canada, 203–4; and male-dominated Aboriginal elites, 285; and politics of Nah-nee-ba-we-quay as forerunner to those of Native Women's Association of Canada, 484–5; status of, 192; and work, 192
Aborigines in Australia, 137–42; comparison with treatment of Indigenous

peoples in Canada, 159; George Manuel visits, 239; new treaties with, 258; studied by Sally Weaver, 242

Aborigines in British settlements: British parliamentary inquiry on 1837, 443–5, 447, 457–8. *See also* Aborigines Protection Society, British House of Commons Select Committee on Aborigines in British Settlements

Aborigines Protection Society, 7, 13, 141, 499; Francis Bond Head's new Indian policy, 443–4. *See also* Aborigines in British settlements, British House of Commons Select Committee on Aborigines in British Settlements

Abraham, 121, 307

Abraham, Bernard, 17, 51

Abraham, Frances, 51

Acadia: expulsion of Acadians from, 343

Act for the Gradual Civilization of Indian Tribes in Canada, 1857, 483, 493; aims rejected by Indian groups at assembly, 173–4; consistency with White Paper and Sechelt Self-Government Act, 1988, 498; and gathering of Six Nations peoples, 483. *See also* Indian Act of Canada

Adams, Hank, 270

Adams, Howard, 195, 246

Adams, John Quincy, 77, 397; and conquest of Canada, 398

Adario (Kondiaronk),164–5, 186, 335, 359, 532

Adena culture, 104

adoption: by Cherokee and Creek of Euro-Americans, 456; of Euro-Americans by various Indian peoples, 382–3; Longhouse people build up numbers by, 319; refusal of adopted to

return to Euro-American families, 383

Afghanistan: US war in, 317

Africa: adoption of crops from the Americas, 105; Basil Davidson on alienation of Indigenous peoples from traditions, 237; convergence with Europe and America, 5; decolonization movement stimulates George Manuel's vision of the Fourth World, 238–40; dictatorships in, 237; imperial administration of, 338; partition after 1885, 225

African Americans, 89, 123; Edward Countryman on in American Revolution, 353; join Indigenous peoples in war against USA, 396; liberation struggles and class tensions among, 283; policies towards compared with those for North America Indians, 283–4; and slavery, 212; unrepresented in forging of US Constitution, 205

African Lakes Company, 23

African National Congress, 238, 513–14, 521

African slaves: cultivation of commercialized monocultures in the Americas, 469; revolt in San Domingo, 169–70. *See also* African Americans

Afrikaners: Calvinist theology of and move to interior to escape British rule, 442; as Dutch Creoles with same Calvinist roots as New England Puritans, 470; General J.C. Smuts on racial position of, 500. *See also* apartheid, South Africa

Agecouty, John Henry, 255

agribusiness, 25–6, 63; changes in Mexican constitution of land tenure in support of, 220–1

agriculture, 60, 80, 107–12, 313, 469; biblical sanctions for disqualification of Indian approaches to, 307; commercialized monocultures and Darwinian evolutionary theory, 226–7; and John Locke, 182–6, 308–9. *See also* Aboriginal horticulture, Andean farmers of Peru, monocultures

Ahenakew, Rev. Edward, 280

AIM. *See* American Indian Movement

Aitken, Edmond: 1755 report on the strategic role of Indian Affairs in North America, 445

Akwesasne reserve: members as fur traders, voyageurs, high steel workers, and lacrosse players, 430–1; protest extension of franchise to registered Indians, 496; protest violation of Jay's Treaty, 267–70; response of leaders to Indian Act of 1857, 483

Akwesasne Notes, 269–70

Alaska, 74, 425; Native Claims Settlement Act of 1971, 24; Protestant adaptation to Aboriginal societies, 460; status of mixed breeds under Russian rule, 212; Tsimshian people build village theocracy, 465

Albany Conference of 1754, 313

Alberta, 244, 279; elder Albert Lightning and Treaty 6, 496

Alcatraz Island, 88; occupation by Indians, 266–9

alcohol, 255–6, 496; abuse of by Indians discussed by Louis Hall, 277; American whiskey traders, 432; Canadian laws re purchase and consumption by registered Indians, 255–6, 496; reduced supply helped

Pontiac, 330; used to obtain Aboriginal land sessions, 392–3
Alert, 225–6
Alexander, Titus: theory of global apartheid as system to extract wealth from Majority World to West, 517–18
Alexis, Sherman, 89
Alfred, Gerald, 246
Algeria, 273; revolution, 236
Algonkian-speaking peoples, 192, 388; dictionary on languages, 316
Alliance Party of Canada, 142
All Indian Pueblo Council, 86
Allied Indian Tribes of British Columbia, 250
Alta hydroelectric dam, Norway, 242
Alvord, Clarence Walworth, 54, 347, 373; ideas opposing those of Tecumseh, George Manuel, and Fourth World, 361–2
Amaru, Tupac. See Tupac Amaru
Amazon: peoples, 92–3; rainforest, 93, 112
The Ambiguous Iroquois Empire, 385
America, 296; forests of, 108–9; intellectual construction of, 217; John F. Kennedy on role of in world freedom, 364; Old World of, 412; simultaneously a country, a continent, or a whole hemisphere, 300–1; US Army enforces racial integration in, 418. See also American Declaration of Independence, American empire, American empire of private property, American expansionism, United States of America
America before Columbus, 269–70
American Board of Commis-

sioners for Foreign Missions, 459
American Civil Rights Movement: colour-blind constitution distracts legal attention from status of Indigenous peoples, 512–13
American Civil War, xxv, 83, 157, 367; and possible secession of Quebec, 200; as result of conflicting constitutional interpretations of state and federal law, 418
American Declaration of Independence, 6, 76, 96, 122–3, 494; influence of Locke and Jefferson on reference to "merciless Indian savages," 310–12; prototype for UN Charter, 230; synthesis of urge towards empire building and decolonization, 357
American empire, xix–xx, 15, 22, 52, 54, 74, 81, 89, 90, 116–17; Aboriginal scholars as critics of, 246; Canada and Indian Country as obstacle to expansion of, 132; character revealed in Banana Wars in Central America and Caribbean, 364; and Coca-Cola Company, 145; dominant world force, 530; draws on culture and laws of England, 300; dynamics of, 346; and ethnic cleansing, 499; expansion of through extinguishment of Aboriginal rights and titles in Canada, 196; extension into Latin America, 209–17; and Free Trade Agreement of the Americas, 146; global dominance of, 529; ideological contention with Soviet empire, 189; incorporation of Mexico in through NAFTA, 118; justification for expansion of, 134–5; and legacy of

slavery and Aboriginal dispossession, 206; as major expression of globalization, 366–7; and President Jackson's scheme of partition and apartheid, 499; Richard Van Alstyne on, 364; role of Indian Affairs in rise of from British Empire, 300; role of land speculation companies and Royal Proclamation in stimulating inception of, 192, 346–70; role of Six Nations Iroquois in, 195; and sabotaging of decolonization struggles in Africa and Asia, 281; and tariffs with British North America, 448; and US Commission on National Security, 527. See also America, American Declaration of Independence, American empire of private property, American exceptionalism, American expansism, globalization, United States of America
American empire of private property: and appropriation of heavens, 527; Benjamin Franklin and Lord Shelburne as key architects of, 361; biblical rationales for the elimination of Indians in creating living space for, 307; and commodification of culture, 219; Darwinian ethos and consolidation of rule in, 526; as enemy of the Indian County of Canada; 299; ethnically cleansed land of, 499; expansion into upper Ohio Valley based on diplomacy with Indian groups, 328; extension of by infusing heightened materialism into Old Worlds of Indigenous peoples, 509; and George Manuel's vision of Fourth World, 291; land specula-

tors and Lord Dunmore's war on Shawnee people, 314; and possessive individualism, 532; Royal Proclamation reveals antagonism between Indian Country of Canada and, 336; Samuel Wharton anticipates, 352; Sir Francis Bond Head integrates Canada into, 435; slaves as founding capital of, 106. *See also* America, American Declaration of Independence, American empire, American Revolution, globalization, United States of America

American exceptionalism, 171–2; Richard Barnet on, 369

American expansionism, 532; American Indian resistance to, 391; dominant force of globalization, 298; Indian Confederacy saves Canada from, 398; and Louisiana Purchase, 392; Northwest Ordinance in genesis of, 372–5; and property law, 369; and removal of Aboriginal groups, 475

American Fur Company: John Jacob Astor, 447

American Holocaust, The, 205

American Indian Defense Association: founded by John Collier, 264

American Indian Federation: opposition to Indian Reorganization Act of 1934, 257

American Indian Movement: background and emergence of, 260–77; Frantz Fanon and Jack Forbes on, 281–2; infiltration by federal government secret agents, 271; and Leonard Peltier, 89; return to Wounded Knee, 33; shares positions with Black Panthers, 283; state terrorism against, 202. *See also* Dennis Banks, Vine Deloria Jr, Indians of All Tribes, Mohawk Warriors' Society, Ojibway Warriors' Society, Pine Ridge reservation, Splitting The Sky, Chief Richard Wilson

American Long Knives. *See* Long Knives

American Marine Corps: and Banana Wars, 364

American Revolution, 9, 14, 22, 25, 28–9, 35, 38, 53–4, 200, 385, 387, 415, 427–8, 450; Bacon's rebellion as prelude to, 316; begins as civil war, 75; British imperialists disagree over Aboriginal and treaty rights, 314–15; Canada joins Aboriginal and French Canadian peoples over, 423; Clarence Alvord's view of land speculators in, 361–3; conservatism of loyalist side, 156; distribution of presents during, 190; Edward Countyman's account of Indian and Black roles in, 353; Euro-American opposition to imperial regulations protecting lands reserved for Indigenous people, 445; Great Trek in South Africa in 1836–8 based on similar colonial tensions, 442; history of central to all peoples, xxiv–xxv, 358–9; impact on modern-day Mexico, 81; Indian adoption of Tory refugees in era of, 456; and Indian Country 313–14; Indian land finances revolutionary side in, 335; Indian opposition to, 78; interpretation of and support of laws and institutions, 121; and John Locke, 182–6; Kevin Phillips on, 83; land speculation companies and, 346–53; military course of, 525; model for Creole revolutions in Latin America, 209; Thomas Jefferson and, 310–12. *See also* American Declaration of Independence, American empire, American empire of private property, American expansionism, globalization, United States

American whiskey traders, 232

Americas: Indian history as common theme throughout, 95; transfer of constitutional powers from imperial capitals in Europe to national capitals in, 211. *See also* Western Hemisphere

Amerindian farmers, 105–7, 164, 213, 243; land tenure in Mexico, 220–1; role of John Locke in engineering ignorance of, 182–6. *See also* Aboriginal horticulture, agriculture, Andean farmers of Peru

Amherst, Jeffery: and Pontiac's patriotic stand, 330; spreads smallpox to Indians, 332

Amnesty International, 366

Anabaptists, 423

Anahareo (Gertrude Bernard), 166

Anasazi civilization: architecture of, 103–4

Ancient Society, 179–82

"Ancient Usages and Customs of the Indians": Lord Dorchester's instructions in 1794 concerning, 410

Andean countries: Maybury-Lewis on assault of Indians in, 366

Andean farmers of Peru, 25–6, 213

Anderson, Benedict, 524

Anderson, Fred, 344–5; view of Seven Years' War, 523

Anderson, Wallace (Mad Bear), 268

Andros, Edmond: founding
of Covenant Chain, 322
*Andy Paull: As I Knew Him
and Understood His Times,*
252–3
Anglican Church: influence
in Hudson Bay lowlands in
northern Ontario and
Quebec, 463–5; and Red
Tories, 423; Rev. Arthur
O'Meara and Indian title
in British Columbia, 132;
Rev. John Strachan in
Upper Canada, 175; Rev.
William Duncan and Met-
lakalta, syllabic script, and
Royal Proclamation, 465;
Rev. E.F. Wilson and
Samuel Blake in Ontario,
486–8
Anglo-America, 77–8, 363;
racism of in early twentieth century, 152–3; tri-
umph of, 83–4
Anglo-Americans, taken captive in childhood, 459
Angola, 273
Anicinabe Park, Kenora,
Ontario: 1974 confronta-
tion in, 272–4
animal husbandry: minor
role in the Americas in
pre-Columbian time, 106;
Puritan justification for
displacement of Indians,
308–10
Anishinabek peoples
(Anishinaabaig), 24, 88–9;
Francis Bond Head
obtains Saugeen territory
in Treaty of 1836, 436;
and laws concerning wild
rice, 111–12; response to
passage of Act for the
Gradual Civilization of the
Indian Tribes in Canada,
483
anthropology, 126–7; Abo-
riginal pioneers in, 194;
Creole invention of native
identities, 470; develop-
ments in Mexico, 221; and
Fourth World, 241–3; gen-
esis in representing

Indigenous peoples,
177–9; informants for,
195; John Collier and professionalization of applied,
224; Karl Polanyi on con-
nection between study of
economics and of, 187–9;
Kwakuitl of British Columbia as subject for, 195;
Scandinavian contribution
of to Fourth World,
241–2; William Duff and
colleagues reopen negotiations on Aboriginal title in
British Columbia and
Canada, 265. *See also*
applied anthropology,
ethnography, Social Dar-
winism, social sciences
Aoteara (New Zealand), 147
Apache helicopters, xvii, 245
apartheid: and Brian Mul-
roney, 514; Canadian Indian Act as model for South
African, 488; comparison
between Canada and
South Africa, 495–509;
Fourth World must not be
tainted with, 248; and
global theory of Titus
Alexander, 517–18; and
heritage of Western civi-
lization, 497; and H.J. Verwoerd, 505; MAI and,
515; Royal Proclamation
and history of, 499–500;
Thomas Jefferson's view of
Mississippi River as marker
for American version of,
334; Woodstock genera-
tion's rejection of American version of, 243
applied anthropology: John
Collier's role in development of, 224; relationship
to indirect rule in British
Nigeria, 224. *See also*
anthropology
Arab culture: Edward Said
on US attitudes towards,
368
Arab oil embargo, 1973, 244
Arbenz, Jacob, 365
archaeologists: AIM and

Toronto's protest against
disturbance of Indian
burials, 226; Manuel
Gamio's education in the
Mexican Revolution, 221
Arendt, Hannah, 219
Argentina, 217, 224, 225–6
Arguedas, Jose Maria, 223
Armstrong, Jeanette, 195
Articles of the Capitulation
of Montreal, 1760: article
40 on Indian rights, 328
Asia: Christian bearers of
European imperialism,
458–9
Asian financial downturn, 67
Asian origins of Native
Americans: theories of,
194
Asian-Pacific Economic Cooperation, 149
Askin, John, 170–2
Assembly of First Nations, 8,
92, 203–4; agreement with
National Congress of
American Indians, 252
Assiginack, Francis, 194
assimilation: Aborigines in
Australia, 140–1; as
advanced by Protestantism
and English language
throughout Canada, 253;
advanced by some Aborigi-
nal elites, 272; and Canadian Indian policy before
1969, 127; and empire of
possessive individualism,
367; First Nations' ability
to incorporate immi-
grants, 168–73, 382, 412,
453–8; and Fourth World,
148; and imperialism,
320; and Indian New
Deal, 368; Indigenous
peoples as teachers in
global struggle against,
149; John Ridge on extent
of Cherokee exercises in,
459; justified through evolutionary theory, 227; and
process of forging one
economic community
from pluralism of two continents, 160–1; as tenden-

cy of government-funded Aboriginal institutions and technocracies, 285; and Thomas Jefferson, 432

Astor, John Jacob: and American Fur Company, 447

Athabasca, 408, 412

Attenborough, Richard, 167

Atwood, Margaret, 168–74, 398, 458

Australia, 31, 33, 118, 135, 137–42, 147, 211, 220, 242, 287, 289, 355, 508; Australian Human Rights and Equal Opportunities Commission, 140–1; centennial, 138; citizenship of Aborigines, 508; comparison with Canada's constitutional approach to Aboriginal issues, 159–60; ethnic cleansing of Indigenous people, 501; little tension between competing imperial powers in colonial history of, 154; new treaties with Indigenous peoples, 258; reconciliation movement in, 137–42, 514; relationship of state wealth to Aboriginal dispossession, 521; as theatre of tensions between Fourth World and monoculture of possessive individualism, 206

Australian Reconciliation Movement, 137–42; and Henry Reynolds, 531

Aztec Empire, 103

Babb, Glen, 514

Bacher, John, 366

Bacon, Nathaniel, 313, 315–16; arguments for annihilation of Indian peoples copied from justifications for Christendom's attacks on the Muslim world, 417; murderous campaign in Virginia directed towards Indians, 417

Bacon's Rebellion: over status of Indians in Virginia, 315–16

Badger case, 30

balance of power: role of Indigenous peoples in North America in determining, 154

Bakker, Peter, 64–5

Balfour, Lord: reflections on Indigenous peoples in British parliamentary debate concerning governance of South Africans, 501

Balkans: and genocide, 524

Ballet Folkloric, 221

Baltimore, Lord: founding of Maryland, 306–7

Banana Wars, 364

Bandler, Faith, 141

Banks, Dennis, 272–3

Barbeau, Marius, 177–8

Barber, Benjamin, 59

Barnet, Richard, 369

Basuto peoples: system of land tenure, 516–17

Basutoland: J.A. Hobson on, 516; P.A. Silburn on treaty agreement between Great Britain and people of, 502–3

Battiste, Marie, 429

Battle of Fallen Timbers, 390, 409; and Jay's Treaty, 388

Battle of Gustafsen Lake, 18–20, 54, 207–8

Battle of La Belle Famille, 329

Battle of Lake George: and Sir William Johnson, 326

Battle of Little Bighorn, 19, 207, 261, 532

Battle of New Orleans: and Andrew Jackson, 403

Battle of Seattle, 80; and Millennial Round of the WTO, 118

Battle of the Thames: and killing of Tecumseh, 391

Battle of Tippecanoe, 422; and Harrison's removal of

Indians from, 395; as setback for Tecumseh, 395

Bay of Quinte, 377

Baynton, Wharton and Morgan Company: launching of Indiana Company, 350; Pontiac killed at post of, 335; role in negotiations of Treaty of Fort Stanwix, 1768, 350; transformation from fur-trade company to land speculation company, 350

Bear, Leon, 85

Beard, Miriam, 373

Becancour: Abenaki settlement at, 329

Behind the Trail of Broken Treaties: An Indian Declaration of Independence, 270

Beijing University, 89

Belaney, Archie (Grey Owl), 165–8, 477

Belcher, Jonathan, 343

Belgium: withdrawal of government from imperial role in Congo, 365

Bellecourt, Clyde, 262

Belo, Bishop Carlos Filipe: protector of Indigenous peoples in East Timor, 462

Bemis, Henry Flagg, 210

Benedict, Ernest, 51, 246

Benedict, Ruth, 127, 177–8

Benton Benai, Eddie, 262

Benton, Thomas Hart, 185

Beothuck Patrol, 275

Beothuk people: extinction of in Newfoundland, 275

Berger, Thomas, 30, 178, 265

Berkeley, Sir William: governor of Virginia during Bacon's Rebellion, 315–16

Berlin Wall, 60

Bernal, Martin, 126

Bernard, Gertrude (Anahareo): relationship with Grey Owl, 166

Berry, Wendell, 24–6

Big Bear, 391; incarceration of, 261; and Indian resistance to extension of

Canada's jurisdiction in prairies, 483
Big Trout Lake, 158
Billington, Ray Allen, 347
bin Laden, Osama: and us government, 528
Biodiversity and Democracy, 63
biological diversity, 5, 25–6, 45; and Aboriginal horticulturists , 107–12; American Revolution enlivens moving frontier in history dividing monocultures from, 81–2; application of fire to land, 107; British Columbia rich in cultural pluralism and, 257; defence of translates into opposition to standardized property law, 150; and ecological equilibrium, 69; and Enlightenment values, 133; equivalent of cultural pluralism, 60; extinguishment of and killing of Indians as vermin in Anglo-American colonies, 185; flourishes with diversity of ideas in areas where intercultural collaboration emphasized, 152; Grey Owl and globalization of consciousness linking cultural pluralism with, 168; impoverishment of, 69; and Indigenous peoples, 70; and onslaught of neo-liberalism, 120; and single system of property law and property relations, 269; and Sinkyone Wilderness project, 86; *Spirit of Haida Gwaii* as symbol of, 206; tools needed to embrace and stimulate, 358. *See also* cultural pluralism, monocultures
biological warfare: Jeffrey Amherst and distribution of blankets from smallpox hospital to Indians, 332
biotechnology, 63, 65, 103, 107; begins with enclosure movement and selective breeding of livestock, 458;

patents and ownership of title deeds to DNA blueprints, 72–3; property regime centred in United States, 160; ultimate expression of privatization, 136. *See also* enclosures, monocultures
Black Athena, 126
Black Hawk, xv–xvi, 249, 391
Black Hills, 112; sacredness of and violations of treaties covering, 271
Black Hoof: disappointment of as lesson for Tecumseh, 392
Black Legend, 305–6
Black Man's Burden: Africa and the Curse of the Nation State, The, 237
Black Panthers, 283–4
Black people in America, 512. *See also* African Americans, slavery
Black Power: rhetoric of and issues surrounding, 283. *See also* African Americans, slavery
Black South Africans: comparison of treatment of with that of Indians in Canada, 441–6, 503–9; and Nelson Mandela on racialized economy of, 521; role of in one of world's richest states, 517
Blackfoot people, 52, 86, 158; and Tom King, 89
Blake, Edward, 417; lawyer for Ontario government in *St Catherine's Milling* case, 415–21; in parliamentary debate on extension of federal franchise to registered Indians, 477–80
Blainey, Geoffrey: accusation that Henry Reynolds and others write black armband history, 141–2
Blair, Tony, xxii
Blood people, 238
Bloom, Allan, 61, 127, 129, 135

Blue Jackets, 495
Blue Quills School, 244
Boards of Trade of Montreal and Quebec City, 401
Boas, Franz, 126, 127, 133, 135, 177–8, 195; opposition to ban on West Coast potlatch, 241
Boer War: British conquest of Dutch Afrikaners in South Africa, 500
Boldt, Menno, 51, 359, 361; interpretation of the Royal Proclamation, 354–5
Bolivar, Simon, 93; effort to encourage Hispanic identity, 212; as George Washington of Spanish America, 210; as leader of Creole liberation movement, 215; and suspicion of the us, 211
Bolivia, 92, 224
Bolivian bloc, 210
Bond Head, Francis: Indian policies of as lieutenant-governor of Upper Canada, 431–46
Bonnin, Gertrude, 257
Book of the Fourth World, 244
Boone, Daniel: role in founding Kentucky, 349–50; as romanticized archetype, 388
Boots, Francis, 51, 246
Born-Again New World empire of the United States, 154
Borrows, John: opposition to domestication of existing Aboriginal and treaty rights, 411; treaty negotiation of principles of Royal Proclamation at Niagara Falls in 1764, 411
Boston, 9, 343, 373
Boston Tea Party: connections between Indian Affairs, taxation, and self-determination of Anglo-American colonists, 344
Botha, P.W., 507
Bourassa, Henri, 422
Boutros, Boutros Ghali, 59

bowl with one spoon, 54–5; and British Imperial Indian Department, 390; depiction of on wampum belts, 78–9; embodied in turtle shell, 101; Indian Confederacy controls land at end of War of 1812, 399; legacy of in recent times, 421–6; as metaphor for Indian Confederacy of Canada, 386; role of some Indian organizations in bringing ideas of forward, 285; symbol that land is held in common, 386; US officials divide land in defiance of principles of, 391; US replacement of with "the international security commons," 529

bowl of Indian unity: single eating vessel as metaphor, 454

Boyd, John, Judge, 419

branch plants: Canada as site of first US-based, 287

Brando, Marlin, 263–4

Brant, Beth, 195

Brant, Joseph (Thayendanegea), 11; animosity between Indian peoples, 386–7; comparison with Tecumseh's strategies in Indian Country, 384–7; continuity in transition between Covenant Chain and Indian Confederacy of Canada, 387; key role in renewal of Covenant Chain, 385; personal involvement in land speculation undermines credibility of, 387

Brant, Molly, 10–11, 170–1, 385, 532

Brant-Castellano, Marlene, 246

Braudel, Fernand, 299–300

Brazil, 26, 44, 92, 210, 224, 303–4

Brebeuf, Jean de, 163

Bretton Woods institutions, 369

Briggs, Geraldine, 141

British-American Land Company, 448

British and Foreign Anti-Slavery Society, 7, 73

British Columbia: and Aboriginal rights, 18; addition to Dominion of Canada, 474; AIM-inspired blockade at Cache Creek, 274; base of North American Indian Brotherhood, 260; Battle of Gustafsen Lake, 19–20; Bill Vander Zalm on Aboriginal rights in, 39–40; comparison with situation in Australia, 142; *Delgamuukw* case strengthens hand of Indigenous peoples in, 158–9; and George Manuel, 287; and Haida Gwaii, 206; Indian Country of, 55; Kwakiutl people as subjects of anthropological work, 195; and Nisga'a, 24, 55, 140, 142, 251–80; opposition to banning of potlatch in; 244; persistence of Indian resistance in, 93; Protestant adaptation to Aboriginal societies in, 460; referendum on treaty process, 142; and Sechelt peoples, 498; symbolic significance globally of dispute over land title in, 258; treaty making in relevant to Royal Proclamation, 287; treaty negotiations in, 117–18

British Commonwealth, 142, 147, 214, 220; George Manuel's politics and ideas reflect genesis of, 287–92

British conquest of Canada, 82, 200, 297

British Constitution: Mahatma Gandhi inspired by, 235–6

British Empire, 12–14, 20,116–17; alliances between Indigenous peoples and crown in Canada, 371–426, 533; annexation of New Netherlands sets stage for that of Canada, 322; Canada between commercial frontier of American empire and constitutional frontier of, 298; Canadian and South African Aboriginal politics converge in politics of, 441–6, 515; centralization of imperial authority in Anglo-American settlements during Seven Years' War, 523; colonization of Australia, 139; complexities of extension of into territories of Acadian Indians, 343; conception in of Aboriginal and treaty rights after American Revolution, 320; connection to American empire, 21, 54; decline of in North America, 363; devolution of constitution to Canada, 196; devolution of power in white dominions and negative effects for Indigenous peoples, 355; emergence of ethnic nationalism, 524; Indian Department of, 392, 410, 490; legacies of as check on monopolistic and monocultural propensities of United States, xxii, 74; land speculators generate tensions in before American Revolution, 346–53; most pluralistic polity world has seen, 288; need to define Canada's constitution outside structure of, 195, 205; negotiations with Indigenous peoples of Basutoland, 502–3; opposition by W.L.M. King to Longhouse government and treaty heritage of the Covenant Chain as attack on, 489–95; relationship to ideas and politics of George Manuel, 286–92; prospect of sovereign Indian Country in America as key to the reversal of Columbian conquests, 533; revolutionary emergence of USA, 72; role of Six Nations Iroquois in, 195; Royal Proclamation, 336–46; triumphalism of similar to American Manifest Destiny, 152–3; visits of Indians to metropolitan centres of, 166. *See also* American empire, American empire of private property, British Commonwealth, British imperial Canada, British imperialism, British North America, New England, Royal Proclamation of 1763, War of 1812

British House of Commons Select Committee on Aborigines in British Settlements (Select Committee), 443; advice of not followed, 447; and British imperial expansionism, 445; and P.A. Silburn's theories on Basutoland and imperial federation, 502; paternalism and potential for conflict of interest in dealing with Aborigines, 444

British imperial Canada, 11, 82, 435; conservative alliance joins in defence of, 154; and Lord Dorchester on integrity of Aboriginal jurisdictional sphere in, 410; and protection of by Indian allies during War of 1812, 397–402; and pressure on Indigenous peoples to give up more lands and resources after War of 1812, 428–9; and Tory governors of, 247; and Tory identification with

Aboriginal and treaty rights as integral to defence of, 453; and Tecumseh's work in, 390. *See also* British Empire, British imperialism, Indian Confederacy, Royal Proclamation of 1763, Tecumseh, War of 1812, William Johnson, Covenant Chain, Indian Confederacy of Canada

British imperialism: increased central authority in Anglo-American settlements, 523; schism leading to American Revolution due to conflict over rights and titles of Indigenous peoples, 336–63

British Navy, 343; as major factor in outcome of Seven Years' War, 326–7

British North America, 9, 11, 28, 30, 38, 75, 116–17, 399; 49th parallel as border between United States and, 413; affect of Royal Proclamation on, 336–46; American Revolution as conflict over place of Indian Country in, 211, 314–5; assimilation policy and railroads, 459; common legacies in Canada and USA, 160; competing schools of imperialism within, 154; constitutional genesis affected by Roger William's Treaty with Narragansett Indians, 316–17; counter-revolutionary polity, 156; empire building through absorption and privatization of western Indian Country, 524; expansion through British imperial success in Seven Years' War, 328–31; fur-trade community of New France renewed in and expanded, 376; George Manuel's vision of constitutional change in,

288–92; Indian policy of after 1763 and American Revolution, 311–12; land speculation in civil war that divided, 346–53, 367; missionaries to the Indians in colonization of, 192–4; monarchy as ally of Indigenous peoples in, 211; and North American conservatism, 423; patriation of Canadian Constitution stimulates move to go beyond, 195–6; privatization of lands and resources of, 448; Roman Catholic Church in, 430; transformation into federal dominion and independent country, 225–6; treaties with Indigenous peoples in, 304; uniting Canada, 446. *See also* British Empire, British imperialism, Royal Proclamation of 1763, Tecumseh, War of 1812, William Johnson

British North America Act, 416–17; dominion parliament's legislative responsibility for Indians and lands reserved for Indians, 415; exclusion of provincial governments from controlling natural resources subject to trusts, 419–20

British South African Company, 23

Brock, Isaac: interest in creation of Indian buffer state, 398–9; and Tecumseh, 396

Brody, Hugh, 178

bronze age, 125–6

Brotherston, Gordon, 244

Brown, Dee, 90

Brown, George W., 506

Bruised Head, Mike, 51

Buffalo, Marilyn, 88

buffalo, 218; destruction of, 190

Buhkwajjenene, 166–7

Bull, Edmund, 207
Bull, Oswin Boys: partnership of church and state in operation of Indian residential schools, 504
Bull Shields, Melinda, 51
Buller, Ed, 51
Bundjalurg people, 139
Burchell, C.J.: as Canadian representative in South Africa, 504
Bureau of Indian Affairs: AIM's occupation of headquarters of in 1972, 271; Chief Dick Wilson as puppet of, 272; crusade against by Carlos Montezuma, 256–7; and John Collier as head and chief architect of Indian New Deal, 223–4; and National Congress of American Indians, 259; and Samuel Blake, 488
Burgoyne, General John, 314
Burke, Edmund, 36–8, 46, 307; and British parliamentary debate on role of Indians in American Revolution, 314; and origins of Manifest Destiny, 75–6
Burnstick, Ed, 176
Burt, A.L.: and Indian buffer state in negotiation of Treaty of Ghent, 399
Bush, George, Jr, xxi–xxii, 129–30; controversy over 2000 presidential election, 518, 527; militarization of space, 527; military agenda, 528–9; and September 11 attack, 473–4
Bush, George, Sr, 69, 83
bush planes, 158
Buxton, Thomas Favel, 443

Cache Creek: AIM-inspired blockade at, 274
Caciques: Inca elites recognized by Spanish crown, 213–4
Cahokia, 103; Pontiac assassinated at, 334

Cairns, Alan: and idea of "citizens plus" as alternative to Indian treaties as nation-to-nation agreements, 411
Calder, Frank, 280
Calgary Stampede: and cowboy and Indians imagery of, 276
Calgary Urban Treaty Indian Alliance (CUTIA), 276, 285
California, 85–6, 266–8, 295
Call of the Red Man as Answered by the Commissioner of Indian Affairs of the United States of America: What Will Be the Answer of the Dominion of Canada, The, 488
Callihoo, John, 258, 280
Callihoo, Michel and Baptiste, 430
Calvinist Protestantism, 76, 83, 85, 306–10; Afrikaners and Americans have similar theological roots in, 442; Puritans organize United Colonies of New England as instrument for conquest of Indian Country, 321; split over Indian policy of Roger Williams, 316–17
Camden, Lord, 352–3
Camden-York Legal Opinion of 1772, 404; corporate purchase of land title directly from Indians, 353
Cameron, Louis, 272–5, 290
Campbell, Maria, 195
Campbell v. Hall: sovereign can act unilaterally in establishing new jurisdictions in British Empire, 336
Campo people, 85–6
Canada: Aboriginal jurisdiction in laws of fur trade, 408; Aboriginal and treaty rights affirmed in constitution yet fought by governments in courts, 356; alliance among Indians, French Canadians, and

British imperialists, 297; alliances with Indian peoples negated, 485; Anglo-American Manifest Destiny, 77–8; and apartheid regime in South Africa, 505; Assembly of First Nations as response to patriation, 260; assertion of authority to conduct relations with Indian people, 416; assertion of sovereign independence often tied to subjugation of Indian nations in, 493; assimilationist Indian policy, 450; attack on Longhouse government by W.L.M. King government, 489–95; and Australia, 138; and baron de Lahontan, 162–5; canoe as icon of, 381; charter granted to colonize and evangelize Indians in, 374; citizenship and federalism in, 496; citizenship of Indians, Inuit, and Métis unclear in, 508; collaboration with government of South Africa, 503; colonized mentality of as satellite of the United States, 159; confederation, 55, 297; conservatism and protection of rights of Indigenous peoples, 132; constitutional negotiations with First Nations in, 89,196–200, 202–6, 508; constitutional struggle between governments of Ontario and Canada in St Catherine's Milling case, 415–21; continuity between crown adaptation to colonists of New Netherlands and New France, 322; early transcultural mestizo character of, 161; ethnic cleansing of Indigenous peoples in, 501; free trade agreements, 425; frontier position between dwindling British empire and commercially expanding American empire, 298; fur trade and Royal Proclamation in genesis of, 154–5; fur-trade foundation gives way to commercial hinterland of American empire, 152; geopolitical need to recognize rather than extinguish distinct Indian societies, 402; and George Manuel's international perspective, 286–92; Grey Owl and, 165–8; Hudson's Bay Company lands transferred to, 474; Huronia in early history of, 106; Indian Act, 475; Indian Act and enfranchisement of registered Indians, 446–7; Indian policy, 478; 152; Indian politics in twentieth century, 249–60; Indian summer, 13; intercultural cooperation in, 82,455–8; international law and recognition of Indians, Inuit, and Métis as Aboriginal people, 231; Métis suppression as extension of American conquest of the Indians, 223; Jean Morisset on Métis, canadiens, and Canadians, 155; law of wardship, 475; legacy of Tecumseh and bowl with one spoon, 422; Longhouse mission to League of Nations to condemn for treatment of Six Nations Iroquois, 268; Meech Lake accord, 17–18; and Mexico, 168; missionaries to Indians promote immigration to, 192–4; nationalism of, 423; New France, 355; Oka, 17; parallels US system, 417–18; perceived as inhospitable and useful primarily for fur trading, 296; Peter Jull on negotia-

tions with Indigenous peoples in, 152; privatization of Aboriginal lands and resources in, 448; protection of Indian rights as essential to security of, 397–402, 409–10; provinces assert ownership over ancestral lands of Indigenous peoples, 419; provinces license international corporations to extract resources, 419; Reform/Alliance Party compared with Australia's One Nation Party, 142; registered Indians and the franchise, 474–80; Six Nations and international border, 93; St Lawrence–Great Lakes axis, 320; term from Iroquoian language, 13; territory where compromise between Natives and newcomers most fully developed, 247–8; Tom Flanagan on the Royal Commission on Aboriginal Peoples, 127; and Tom King, 89; toxic dumps, 85; transplanted populations form majority in, 147; treatment of Indigenous people, 502; Treaty of Paris of 1783 and Indian policy, 401; violation of Indian treaties in Cold War politics, 270; westward expansion of, 474–5. See also Aboriginal and treaty rights, Constitution of Canada, Indian Confederacy of Canada, Indian Country of Canada
Canada Act: passage of in Great Britain, 196
Canada and the Canadian Question, 78
Canada Company, 448
Canada West. See Ontario, Upper Canada
Canadian Association for Adult Education, 264

Canadian Association in Support of the Native People (CASNP), 266
Canadian Bill of Rights: extension of federal franchise to registered Indians in 1960, 505–6
Canadian Broadcasting Corporation, 20, 129, 197; extends concept of bowl with one spoon, 422–3
Canadian Constitution: Aboriginal and treaty rights as bridge between domestic law and law of United Nations, 530–1; academic literature on patriation of, 159; and Assembly of First Nations, 260; and Australian Constitution, 138; and Australia Native Title Act, 159; and Charlottetown accord, 7–8; compared with that of USA on Aboriginal issues, 89; courts extinguish and negate Aboriginal and treaty rights as recognized and affirmed in, 356; Elijah Harper and Meech Lake accord, 17–18; George Manuel and, 286–92, 298; and Indigenous peoples throughout Americas, 91; and international law of Indigenous peoples, 231; and lands reserved for Indians as hunting grounds, 154–5; and legacy of War of 1812, 172; and Native Peoples Caravan, 274; negotiations concerning patriation, Quebec, and Aboriginal and treaty rights, 196–206; as point of contestation between Indian Country of Canada and American empire of private property, 299; provincial jurisdiction, 173–4; Rev. E.F. Wilson on Indian government as one of three orders of Canadian

government, 132, 486–7;
rights of Ojibway people
to wild rice, 111–12; Royal
Proclamation as basis of,
314–36; section 35 of
Constitution Act, 1982,
30–57; and *St Catherine's
Milling* case, 414–21, 477.
See also Aboriginal and
treaty rights, courts of law,
Crown-Aboriginal treaties,
international law, Royal
Proclamation of 1763,
Section 35 of Constitution
Act 1982
Canadian Fur Trade Treaty
of 1701, 164–5
Canadian Indian, The, 486–7
Canadian Institute, 194
Canadian National Railway,
17
Canadian North-West Territories: conflict over border
with Ontario, 416
Cape Breton Island: as Isle
Royal under French, 326
Cape Colony, South Africa,
502
capitalism: American Declaration of Independence
and global expansion of,
311; Cold War and, 124,
232; global expansion of
modelled on treatment of
Indigenous peoples,
310–12; and global finan-
cial system, 510; Indige-
nous people as wards of
state under, 174; John
Locke and, 182–9; Louis
Cameron of Ojibway War-
rior's Society on, 274; and
moral relativism in expansion of, 134; nation-states
subordinate to, 149;
Native American attitudes
to, 125; and neo-liberal-
ism, 80; and plutocracy in
USA, 84–5; and postmod-
ernism, 126, 128; and privatization, 21; Reforma-
tion in England and the
Netherlands encourages
development of, 303; as

shield against commu-
nism, 228; Social Darwin-
ism as justification for,
226–7; United States at
core of single world eco-
nomic system, 369; United
States as leader of, 160;
universalism of, 60, 70,
369–70; values of in international system, 234; and
wars on Indian Country,
91; and *Wealth of Nations*,
6. *See also* commercial
trade treaties, commodification, corporations, global corporations, monocul-
tures
Cardensa, Lazaro, 221
Cardinal, Harold, 265;
response to 1969 White
Paper, 279
Careless, J.M.S., 506
Carghill Company, 149
Carib people, 95
Carlisle Indian Boarding
School, 256
Carnegie, Andrew, 84
Carnegie Corporation: F.J.
Van Wyk's visit to Canada,
504
Carson, Christopher, 192,
245
Castro, Fidel, 269, 520
Catawba people, 313, 324
Catholic Irish: conquest of
by Cromwell's Puritan
armies linked to anti-Indi-
an crusades in America,
223; as losers of the
Cousin's War, 83–4
Catlin, George: and per-
forming Indians, 194
Cayuga nation: Levi General
and clan title "Deskahu,"
489–90
Cayuga people, 12
Central Africa, 367
Central Intelligence Agency
(CIA): and Arbenz regime
in Guatemala, 1954, 365;
and coups in Chile and
Guatemala, 91
A Century of Dishonour,
264

Champlain, Samuel, 106,
422; governor of New
France allies with Huron,
319
Charles I, King, 306
Charles II, King, 320
Charlottetown accord,
198–9; significance of,
204–5
Charter of Rights and Freedoms, 38
Charlevoix, Pierre de,
163–5, 187
Chemehueri people, 295
Cherokee Nation v. Georgia,
404
Cherokee people, 88,170,
313, 324, 392; adoption
of Tory refugees, 456–7;
forced removal of, 459;
missionaries to, 404
Chevron Corporation, 86
Chiapas, Mexico, 34, 79, 97,
143, 178; Bishop Samuel
Ruiz, 462
Chickasaw people, 324, 392
Chile, 210, 224, 366, 463;
coup in, 91; FTAA Summit
in Santiago, 93; and New
Zealand, 148
China, 89, 369; Communist
overthrow of old regime,
179; as enemy of USA,
527; and Indian corn,
105; Tibetan peoples'
land and resources expro-
priated by, 521
Chisholm, Andrew G.: lawyer
for Longhouse League
sovereignists, 490
Chocktaw people, 113, 190,
324, 392
Choudry, Aziz, 148–9
Chrétien, Jean, 19; on disparities in world economy,
517–18; and Free Trade
Area of the Americas,
93–4; inequality as primary source of global instability, 529; as minister of
Indian and Northern
Affairs, 278; veto powers
extended to provincial
governments, 199

Christianity: Aboriginal
authors, 194; abuse of
power of, 439–40;
alliances with Indigenous
peoples, 132; and Aztecs,
104; and charity, 73;
Cherokee adoption of,
459; Christ and Trickster,
107; and civilizing mission
in Indian Country, 173;
and colonization of New
Spain, 302–6; and Darwin-
ian evolutionary theory,
226; denominational con-
flict among Indigenous
people in British Colum-
bia, 251–5; Enlightenment
and, 121–5; and global
transformation, 469–70;
and immigration, 192–4;
and imperialism,
xxviii–xxix, 227; Indian
missions, 174–5; and Indian title, 132; Indians
encouraged to accept,
432; Jesuit writings on
Canada and French
Enlightenment, 162–5;
and legal principles for
Crusades, 417; and Long-
house government, 490;
and Manifest Destiny,
306–10; missionaries as
bearers of European impe-
rialism, 458; missionaries
and British Empire,
339–46; Nah-nee-ba-we-
quay and Quakers, 484–5;
Neolin and, 331; New
England Company mis-
sionary work, 309; and
Northwest Ordinance,
1787, 373–5; and Norval
Morrisseau, 244; private
property as religious principle, 124; Protestant missionaries and Indian Policy, 440–1; Protestant
victory in English civil war,
182; Puritan ethos and
American business, 84–5;
residential schools, 438–9,
475, 486–8; and sover-
eignty, 47; struggle in

North America between
Roman Catholic and
Protestant empires, 154;
Rev. E.F. Wilson and
Samuel Blake and govern-
ment Indian policy,
486–8; Roger Williams on,
316; and state church in
Upper Canada, 174–6;
theocracies in northern
Indian communities
decline, 468; Tupac
Amaru takes Christian
name, 213; and United
Colonies of New England,
321. See also Anglican
Church, civilizing mission,
Manifest Destiny, New
England, New France,
New Spain, Reformation,
Roman Catholic Church
Churchill, Ward, 27–9, 90,
272
Chute, Janet, 51, 171–2
citizenship, 264; Aboriginal
people denied, 512–13;
First Nations people and,
255–6; corporations
acquire rights of, 512–13;
Indians as wards of state,
495; Nah-nee-ba-we-quay
and rights of registered
Indians to, 484–5; R.V.
Sinclair protests Indian
loss of rights of, 488–9
"citizens plus": as metaphor
for Indian status in Canada, 411
civilization and capitalism,
299
civilization and savagery: and
Darwinism, 125; and Declaration of Independence,
310–12; Fourth World pro-
ponents reject theories of,
240; and Francis Parkman,
355; historical misrepresentation of, 164; idea of, 95;
international laws premised
on idea of, 413; and US
conquest of Indian Coun-
try, 131; views of Engels,
Locke, Marx, Morgan, and
Rousseau on, 179–87

civilizing mission: and Aboriginal languages and traditions, 438; Christian
heritage in, 438; Jeffer-
son's abandonment of,
397; John Ridge and
Cherokee adoption of,
459; and Northwest Ordi-
nance, 373–5; and social
engineering, 173–6; as
vehicle for westward
expansion in Canada,
192–4
Claparede, Rene: ally of
Deskahe, 491
Clark, Bruce, 18–19, 30,
116, 178; criticism of US
liberal jurisprudence,
511–12
Clash of Civilizations and the
Remaking of World Order,
69, 96–9, 515
class exploitation: and American empire, 360; Frantz
Fanon's view of, 236; in
funding of Aboriginal
organizations, 277–86; in
Indian Country, 272; views
of Morgan, Engels, and
Marx on, 179–82
clergy reserves, Upper Canada, 174–5
Clinton, Bill, 89
Clinton, George: and New
York, 325
Closing of the American Mind,
The, 257
Cloud, Henry Roe, 257
Coalition of First Nations,
203: constitutional patriation in Canada, 508
Coalition of Indigenous
Organizations of the Ama-
zon (COICA), 92
Coke, Lord Edward: and
Calvin's case in 1608, 417
Cold War: Aboriginal resis-
tance movements out-
lawed, 312; cover for US
advancement of self-inter-
ested economics, 366; pol-
itics of decolonization dur-
ing, 189, 228–38; Six
Nations Iroquois passports

recognized by Cuba, 269; "terrorist" enemy replaces communist enemy, 527; and US global military expansion, 471–2; violation of Indian treaties, 270. *See also* American expansionism, Manifest Destiny, Soviet empire, Soviet Union, United States

Colden, Cadwallader, 10, 319

Coldwater and the Narrows Indian reserve, 175

Colebrook, Sir George: director of East Indian Company, 352

collateral damage, 83–5

Collier, John, 116, 178, 223–5, 242, 254, 257, 264, 368, 532

Colombia, 90–1, 93, 210, 224

colonialism: condemnation of at the United Nations, 232; co-opting leadership in oppressed countries, 281–6; repressiveness of, 494

Colony to Nation, 154, 287

Columbian conquests, 21, 23, 25, 31, 43, 64, 71, 95, 458; and Aboriginal title, 357; Anthony Pagden on universal applicability of capitalism, 369–70; and armistice in, 458; boundaries on Indian territories through, 218; constitutional orientation in Americas for, 204, 220; and Creole nationalism, 146–7; and cultures of dependency, 189–92; efforts to reverse in Australia and Mexico, 143; and global role of USA, 160; and Indian collaborators, 272; and Indian title in British Columbia, 250; justification for, 142–3, 184; and US militarization of space, 527; moral rela-

tivism of, 302; and neo-liberalism, 81, 131. *See also* American empire, American empire of private property, British Empire, British imperialism, global corporations, globalization, neo-liberalism, Spanish Empire, United States, Western civilization, Western Hemisphere

Columbian Exchange, The, 114

Columbian Exposition, Chicago, in 1893, 168

Columbian River basin: Iroquois economic activity in, 430

Columbus, Christopher, 4–7, 79, 95, 205; founder of New Spain, 217

Commanger, Henry Steele, 164

commercial trade treaties, 22, 30–1, 44, 49, 50–1, 79, 148; changing conditions within countries and between countries, 290; and Indian treaties, 161; and negotiation of Canada's constitution, 290; and US power disguised by, 369. *See also* Free Trade Area of the Americas, International Monetary Fund, Multilateral Agreement on Investment, North American Free Trade Agreement, World Trade Organization

Committee on Un-American Activities, 132

commodification: cooperation between nation-states and global corporations, 149; culture represents new frontier of, 218; of Indian lands, 355; Karl Polanyi on market fundamentalism, 187–9; and monocultures, 134; Puritans extinguish nature not useful for, 308–9; transformation of land into property, 123

communism, 40, 59; anti-imperialist doctrine, 232; Cold War and USA, 312, 365–6; and imagery of Noble Savage, 124–5; and Marx, Engels, Rousseau, and Morgan in genesis of, 60, 179–82; and private property in USA, 368–9; as Soviet conspiracy during Cold War, 365; Subcommandante Marcos's background of, 144; and terrorism, 130; USA leads global fight against, 228. *See also* capitalism, Frederick Engels, Karl Marx, Soviet Union

Company of One Hundred Associates, 374

comprador class, 360; Tecumseh and treaty negotiations, 393, 424; Confederation of the Fourth World, 248

Congo: decolonization movement, 365

Connolly, Amelia, 408, 413

Connolly, John: legitimacy in British Empire of Aboriginal law, 408–15

Connolly, William: fur-trade marriage to Susanne Pas-de-nom, 408–15

Connolly v. Woolich, 408–15; USA and Manifest Destiny, 525; USA preoccupation with, 156

conquest of Indigenous peoples: doctrine of and Indian treaties, 185, 525–6; and Manifest Destiny and militarization of space, 527–8; by Puritans, 76; Rousseau on, 528; Thomas Hart Benton's justification of, 185; US preoccupation with, 156, 527

conquest of Normans: and Thomas Jefferson, 311

conquistadors: agents in expansion of New Spain, 460; descendants of, 94; sexual violence of, 461

conscription: and Indians
and French Canadians of
Quebec, 253
conservatism: advocacy of
Aboriginal and treaty
rights, 132; and crown-
Aboriginal treaties, 156;
and Indian Department
officials, 171; Old World
proponents of versus New
World, 154, 195–6, 310;
and Rev. John Strachan,
174; Trudeau's hostility
towards, 278–9. *See also*
Toryism
Constantine: adoption of
Christianity in Roman
Empire, 374
Continental Congress: and
land speculation on eve of
American Revolution,
352; pressure on to recognize land titles purchased
directly from Indians, 360
constitutional monarchy:
Aboriginal issues and,
159; appeals of Indige-
nous peoples in British
Columbia to, 214; in Aus-
tralia, 138; in Brazil after
break with Portugal, 210;
origins of in English history, 182; Parti Québécois
and, 220; and Queen Eliz-
abeth II in Canada, 196;
and Royal Proclamation of
1763, 336. *See also* British
Commonwealth, British
Empire, British imperial-
ism, King George III,
Royal Proclamation of
1763
Convention of 1818: establishment of 49th parallel
as international border,
425
Cooke, Alistair, 296
Cook, Lynne Elizabeth, 246
Coon Come, Matthew, 467
Cooper, James Fenimore,
116, 194
Co-operative Commonwealth
Federation: forms of gov-
ernment of Saskatchewan

in 1944, 254; and League
for Social Reconstruction,
423
Copeway, George, 194
copper: mined in Ojibway
territory, 449–53
Cork, Ella, 481
corn, beans, and squash:
Huron staple crops,
105–6; as three sisters,
108
corn belt (USA), 107–8
Cornell, Stephen, 90
corporations: and Alaska
Claims Settlement Act,
1971, 23–4; and biotech-
nology, 65; created by
monarchs of Protestant
powers to advance colo-
nization, 306; environ-
mentalists and Indigenous
peoples at annual meet-
ings of, 91; extension to
of legal status of natural
persons, 513; as exten-
sions of government, 44;
frontiers of Indigenous
peoples connected to
expanding frontiers of,
149–50; globalization of
European and Creole peo-
ples as prelude to globalization of US-based,
471–2; IBM, I.G. Farben
Chemicals, and Standard
Oil as instruments and
supporters of Nazi Ger-
many, 471; as instrument
of Aboriginal self-government, 23–4; and land
speculation in genesis and
outcome of American Rev-
olution, 346–70; legal
expansion of in USA, 300;
logos in economics of,
218–9; and power, 67,
84–5; United Fruit Com-
pany in Latin America,
91; US government
extends same rights and
liberties to as adhere to
individuals, 123; and use
of language of civil rights,
50. *See also* commercial

trade treaties, commodification, global corpora-
tions, neo-liberalism
Corrigan, Sam, 51
Cortes, Hernan, 317
Cotton, John, 309; and
patent of the Massachu-
setts Bay Company, 316
Council at Niagara, 1764; as
memorialized in wampum,
434
Council of Aboriginal Reconciliation, 137, 140
counter-insurgency, 227, 366
Counter Reformation: Jesuits
as leaders of, 162–5; neo-
liberal economists repli-
cate zealotry of, 188
Countryman, Edward, 90,
354; and definition of
Indian lands as huge US
trove of free capital, 359
Courchene, Dave, 280
Court of Castile, 211, 217
courts of law: and 1882 case
that transforms Indian
Country in USA from geo-
graphical concept into
something else, 296; and
Aboriginal title in British
Columbia, 251, 280; and
arbitration of Aboriginal
and treaty rights con-
tained within domestic
courts, 303; and Aus-
tralian High Court, 31;
and biases of domestic
courts in arbitrating Aboriginal and treaty rights,
42–4; *Campbell v. Hall*,
1774, 336; and Canadian
Supreme Court, 30; clo-
sure of access to Indige-
nous peoples as wards of
state, 355; *Delgamuukw*,
30, 118, 142, 158–9; and
fiduciary responsibilities,
356; and globalization,
119; *Guerin, Sioui, Badger,
Degamuukw*, and *Marshall*
cases in determining con-
tent of Aboriginal and
treaty rights, 30; and
imperialism, 119; and

interpretation in 1999 of Maritime Indian Treaties in Canada, 38, 343; lawyers and Aboriginal peoples, 47; and legalization of politics, 41–2; and litigiousness of Indian groups in New Spain, 211; *Mabo* case in Australia, 31, 33, 118, 137–40; *Mohegan Indians v. Connecticut*, 211, 337–8; and oral traditions of Aboriginal peoples, 118; and poverty as barrier to, 510; and Quakers in Pennsylvania, 318; and *St Catherine's Milling* case, 414–1, 429, 476; and trial at Valladolid in 1550, 178, 305; and war on international communism or terrorism, 130; and wild rice cultivation, 111–12. *See also* Constitution of Canada, international law

Cousin's War, 83–5, 182

Couture, Joe, 51

Covenant Chain, 8–9, 13, 14, 16, 29, 41, 53, 117–18, 384, 410, 435; Edmond Andros and founding of, 322; failure to renew, 523; federal police crush, 530; and Imperial Indian policy of 1763, 341–2; and incorporation of Dutch-Indian relations into structure of British empire, 363; and Indian Confederacy of Canada, 387; Joseph Brant and, 11; as laboratory of human relations, 12; and Longhouse League, 319, 493; as model for Tecumseh, 530; and negotiation of Treaty of Fort Stanwix in 1768, 350; and Royal Proclamation, 155; rusty and almost broken, 324; and Sir William Johnson, 170–1, 324–6, 331; and W.L.M. King, 495. *See also* crown-Aboriginal treaties,

Joseph Brant, Longhouse League, Sir William Johnson, Six Nations Iroquois

Cowboys and Indians, 16–17, 99; imagery of at Calgary Stampede, 276

Craig, Gerald M., 506

Crazy Horse, 261

Crear, T.A., 254

Cree people, 47, 52, 64–5, 85, 102, 112, 145–6, 158, 238, 334; conditions of around Hudson Bay, 463–8; legality in British Empire of marriage laws of, 409; Quebec government's movement into territories of, 467; and sovereignty movement in Quebec, 465; and St James Anglican Church, 464–5

Creek peoples, 96, 216, 218, 313, 392, 459; and adoption of Tory refugees, 456; Red Sticks of, 405, and uprising against Americans, 396

Creighton, Donald, 154, 448

Creole (Criollo, Crioula): definition of, 209, 212; and globalization, 469–74

Creole nationalism, 21, 29, 36, 93, 469–74; Aboriginal reserves as monuments to ethnic cleansing and partition, 509; Afrikaner identity as, 470; assault on Louis Riel and Métis as expression of, 223; and Benedict Anderson, 524; Canada and, 153–4; and concept of Diaspora, 470; and cosmology of George W. Bush, 473; criticisms of by Aboriginal scholars, 246; as developed in Latin America, 209–17; emergence of US as first example of, 146; and expansion of commercialized monocultures through institution of slavery, 469; and

Fourth World, 240; and Ladino and Hispanic identities, 93, 473; as name of Russian-Aboriginals in Alaska, 212; and private property after Second World War, 233; and rights, titles, and interests of Indigenous peoples, 289

Creole revolts: and hostility between Indigenous peoples and monarchy, 214

Crevecoeur, Hector St John de, 206

crimes against humanity, 187; Louis Cameron on First Nations in North America and, 273–4; Mayan peasantry in Guatemala and, 365–7; in Rwanda and Burundi, 237

criminal justice system, 54, 72; and Indian peoples in pre-revolutionary British North America, 354; and Quaker founders of Pennsylvania, 317–18

criminalization of Aboriginal laws, ceremonies, and customs, 482, 494; and American Indian Movement, 260–77; and experience of author with RCMP, 54; Indian Act prohibits Indian claims in 1927, 251, 282, 495; and Indian use of alcohol, 495; and League of Nations of North American Indians, 260; and Longhouse government at Six Nations reserve, 490–5; Shuswap Defenders at Battle of Gustafsen Lake, 18–20, 207–8

Crocker, Mark, 26–7

Croghan, George, 350; and rates of murder of Indians, 354; and views of French adoption of Indian ways, 383

Crompton, Lyn, 51

Cromwell, Oliver: as negative

example for USA, 380;
Puritan conquests of Ireland as prelude to assault
on Métis in western Canada and Indians in western
USA, 223
Cronon, William, 109
Crook, General George, xvii,
192
Crosby, Alfred, 114
Cross, J.S., 504
Crow Dog's case, 411
crown-Aboriginal treaties:
and Bowl with One Spoon,
55; and British Imperial
Canada, 155; and Dutch-
Indian alliances in New
Netherlands, 318–20; and
fur trade, 159; and idea of
sovereign Aboriginal
dominion after American
Revolution, 320; interpretation of in courts, 43; as
instruments of conservative orientation, 156; and
Jules Sioui, 253; Longhouse League protests
Canada's violation of, 268,
490–5; and nation building through land theft, 47;
and negotiation of Fort
Stanwix Treaty in 1768,
350–1; *Nisga'a* case
reopened, 279–80; and
Quaker role in negotiation
of Easton Treaty, 327–8;
and Royal Proclamation,
154–5; and Six Nations
Iroquois, 268; and Treaty
of Waiting, 117, 147–9;
William Penn in genesis
of, 317–18; and world history, 157. *See also* British
Empire, Covenant Chain,
Royal Proclamation of
1763, Sir William Johnson
Crown of Castile, 303–4,
414, 419; and Islam, 374;
and Europe's Hoy, 417
Cuba: accepts passports of
Six Nations and Miccosukees, 269
cultural genocide, 28, 226,
496

cultural pluralism: Adlai
Stevenson on, 369; and
America Indian Defense
Association, 264; and biodiversity, 152; and biological
diversity, 5; British Columbia rich in biological diversity and, 251; and democracy, 67–8; destruction of
buffalo herds diminishes,
218; and ecological equilibrium, 69; and economic
regimes to support, 358;
and Enlightenment values,
133; of fur trade, 298;
George Manuel on, 286;
Grey Owl on, 168; as hallmark of Fourth World, 71;
and impoverishment of
with universalized regimes
of property law and property relations, 369; and liberalism, 509–10; and new
international agencies to
safeguard, 128; and NGOs,
73; and story telling, 115,
120, 124. *See also* biological
diversity, democracy, ecology, international law, monocultures
cultural relativity: Franz Boas
and students on, 126;
racism reduced by, 133;
Todd Gitlin and Bruce
Trigger on, 128; Tom
Flanagan on, 127; Vandana Shiva's denunciation
of, 134. *See also* moral relativism, post-colonialism,
post-modernism
Cultural Survival, 242, 366
culture: and Aboriginal languages, 218; and adaptive
innovations of Fourth
World, 109; Allan Bloom
on Enlightenment and,
127; and blending of, 456;
and blues, jazz, rock and
roll, 115; of dependency,
189, 192; definition of,
62; and economic relationships, 71; and evolutionary theory, 128–9; of
global corporations,

218–19; Herder and relativism of, 126; Indian New
Deal rejects melting pot
and supports multiculturalism, 368; and legal construction of aboriginality,
213; and pluralistic
regimes of property relations, 358; and political
agenda of Zapatistas in
Mexico, 144–5; and powers of Quebec government, 198; pre-eminence
of, 69; role of in story
telling, 113–21; and
treaties with Indigenous
people, 156; and variations of indigenismo, 244.
See also cultural pluralism,
ecology, monocultures,
multiculturalism
Culture and Imperialism,
115–16, 225
Cumberland House, 408
Cumming, Peter A., 265
Currie, Jon, 51
Cushing, Frank Hamilton,
177–8
Custer, General George, xvi,
207
Custo, Rupert, 246
Cuthand, Rev. Stanley,
280
Cuxil, Demietrio Cojte: and
sexual and cultural violence, 461

Dakota Territory, 375
Dakotas, North and South,
375; and Aboriginal incarceration, 262
Darwin, Charles, 125–6,
178–80, 226–7
Darwinism, 119, 125–6;
explanation of, 226–7;
and extinguishment of
Indian Country, 295; and
Fourth World, 240; and
Francis Parkman, 335; and
global geopolitics, 234;
and Jared Diamond, 135;
and Marx, Engels, and
Morgan, 179–82; and
Naziism, 228

D'Aubisson, Roberto: El Salvadorian death squads of, 462
David, Dan, 246
Davidson, Basil, 237
Davidson, Malcolm, 51
Dawes Act, 1887, 186
Dawson, Simon, Jr: supporter of Indian peoples in struggles with government, 457
Debassige, Ernie, 51
Debassige, Gus, 280
Debassige, Lewis, 51
Decker, George: lawyer for Longhouse League, 490
Declaration of Independence. *See* American Declaration of Independence
Declaratoin of Kinship and Cooperation among the Indigenous Peoples and Nations of North America, 1999, 259
Declaration of the Rights of Man and Citizen, 37, 181, 186, 414
decolonization, xxix, in Africa and Asia, 65–6; in Canada, 32–3; and class exploitation, 281–6; Frantz Fanon eschews European models of, 236; George Manuel's philosophy of, 238–49, 286–92; and Indigenous peoples as minority, 355; and Indigenous peoples in Latin America, 211; multiculturalism as domestic version of, 368; and neo-liberal economics, 219; and politics of Cold War, 228–38; and Royal Proclamation, 358; and successor states of European empires, 70; and United Nations, 231–8; and USA, 130–2, 364, 524; and wealth extraction, 72. *See also* American empire, American empire of private property, British Empire,

democracy, Fourth World, Indigenous peoples
deeds game: and unregulated land purchases from Indian groups, 339
Deer, Phillip, 246
deism, 162, 178
Delaware peoples (Lenni Lapi peoples), 377; and agriculture, 436; Francis Bond Head and land of, 439; and treaties with William Penn, 317–18
Delgamuukw case, 30, 118, 142, 158–9
Deloria, Vine J., 90, 195, 245, 270–1, 291–2
democracy: Aboriginal self-government in Canada and, 197–8; betrayal of by elites in decolonization, 236; and biodiversity, 63; Boston Tea Party and, 344; and crown-Aboriginal treaties, 155–6; and cultural relativism and postmodernism, 128; and equality, 39–40; erosion of, 88; George Manuel's vision of, 286–92; illusion of, 369; Indian Act as impediment to, 510; and international civil society, 73–4; and legal equivalence of corporate and human persons, 513; and legal remedies available within, 41–2, 510; and limitations of, 228–38; and monocultures, 50, 61; and power of capital, 149; and Royal Proclamation, 340–1; and rule of force, 130; sovereignty, property, and, 21; subcommandante Marcos influenced by Mayan system of decentralized, 144; theories of and Turner's frontier thesis, 168–9; transcultural, 32; and violations involving treaties, WTO, NAFTA, and FTAA, 119, 264. *See also* American empire,

American empire of private property, American Revolution, British Empire, cultural pluralism, decolonization, ecology, Fourth World
demography: of Canada, 297–8; and controversy over pre-Columbian population of North America, 27, 261; and environmental determinism of Jared Diamond, 134–5
Dene people, 158, 238, 241, 244
Department of Indian Affairs and Northern Development (Canada): and 1969 White Paper, 186, 278–81, 497; exchanges with South African Department of Native Affairs, 503–9; and Indian women's rights after marriage to non-Indian, 484; and Mulroney, 514; origins of, 11; pre-1969 Indian policy, 127. *See also* Indian Act of Canada, Indian Department of British Imperial Canada, Northern Division of the British Imperial Indian Department
deregulation, 67; corporate efforts in pre-revolutionary British North America to purchase land directly from Indians set pattern of, 348–52; and worldwide growth of US-based corporate power, 348–9
Descent of Man, The, 226
Deskahe (Levi General), 268; as international ambassador of Longhouse League at League of Nations, 489–95
despoiling of species, 120
Detroit, 331, 399; canadien settlement at, 383
Dewdney, Sewyn, 465
diabetes: in Aboriginal communities, 81

Dialogues between Kondi-
arankand and baron de
Lahonton, 165
Diamond, Jared, 134–6
Diashowa-Maruben Interna-
tional, 24, 149
Dickason, Olive, 51
Dickson, Lovat, 167
Dickson, Robert, 390
Diderot, Denis, 7, 124,
163
Diefenbaker, John, 255; and
enfranchisement of regis-
tered Indians, 505–6; and
Fourth World's ideals,
118;
Dion, Joe, 280
Dirkse-van-Schalwyk, W.: as
South Africa's ambassador
to Canada tours Indian
reserves, 506
discovery of America: 400th
anniversary of at Chicago's
Columbian Exposition,
168; dependence of Eng-
lish colonizers on legal
theories derived from,
306; Father Francisco de
Vitoria on legal theory
based on, 304; impact on
development of ethnogra-
phy, anthropology, and
social sciences, 177–9;
legitimacy of laws and
titles derived from, 315;
merchant class derives
commercial advantage
from, 303
disease: and Hurons, 319;
and smallpox-infected
blankets, 332
distinct peoples, 65, 68, 69,
71–2; *Mohegan Indians v.
Connecticut* defines Indians
as, 337
Divine, Heather, 14–15
DNA: patented as intellectual
private property, 50
domestic laws: refusal of Six
Nations Iroquois to be
contained within, 269
Dominican Order, 211, 305;
partnership with Spanish
crown, 460

Dominion Electoral Fran-
chise Act, 1885, 474–80
Dorchester, Lord, 378;
recognition of Aboriginal
jurisdictional sphere, 410
Dorris, Michael, 89
Douglas, James, 413
Douglas, Tommy: extension
of provincial franchise to
registered Indians, 254–5,
479, 496
Dow Jones, 466
downsizing of public govern-
ment, 67; economists as
high priests of, 189; in
New Zealand, 148
Drake, Benjamin: on Tecum-
seh, 406–7, 422
Drayton, William Henry: and
enslavement of Indians
and appropriation of Indi-
an lands in South Caroli-
na, 314
Dreaver, Joe, 280
Drinnon, Richard, 90, 185,
222
Drucker, Phillip, 460
Duff, Wilson, 265
Duke of Newcastle, 485
Duke of York: as future King
James II, 322
Dumont, Jim, 51
Duncan, Rev. William, 465
Dunlop, Father Francis,
252–3
Dunmore, Lord, 314
Dutch East India Company,
23
Dutch Empire: in America,
318–19
Dutch West India Company,
31

E Pluribus Unum, 368
East Florida, 336
East India Company.
See English East India
Company
East Timor: genocide of
Indigenous peoples of,
462, 514
Eastman, Charles A., 259
Easton Treaty of 1758: and
Covenant Chain, 384–5;

and Pennsylvania Quakers,
327–8
ecocide, 26, 28, 44, 45, 65;
Aboriginal responses to,
133; destroys indepen-
dence of Indigenous peo-
ples, 190; and genocide of
Indigenous peoples, 218;
legal protection against,
134; Puritan ideas in
advancing, 309
ecological egalitarianism of
Indigenous peoples: and
Robert Boyle, 309
ecological holocaust, 134
Ecological Indian, The,
112–13
ecology: and Aboriginal
languages, 318; adapta-
tion of Aboriginal soci-
eties to, 148–9; crisis of
and alternative models of
globalization, 299;
deconstruction of, 94;
and democracy, 136; and
diversity in human, plant,
and animal life, 136; and
economists, 188; and failure to heed Indigenous
voices, 120; and fire technology of Aboriginal peo-
ple, 108–10, 381; and
First Nations, 248–9; and
Fourth World 241, 291;
and genocide of Indige-
nous peoples, 218;
George Manuel's vision
of, 151; global disaster
of, 94; and Grey Owl,
167–8; and human and
biological diversity,
69–70; language of,
59–65; and Marx, Engels,
and Morgan, 179–82;
and monoculture, 358;
and neo-liberal globalization, 146; and reptiles,
101; and symbolism of
crown-Aboriginal treaties,
156–7; and *The Spirit of
Haida Gwaii,* 206; and
universal protection
codes, 133; and web of
life, 136. *See also* biologi-

cal pluralism, cultural pluralism
economics profession: Karl Polany's and Patricia Marchak's critiques of, 187–9
Ecuador, 92, 210
Eeyou Estchee: Cree term for Cree land, 200
Egan, Timothy, 87
Einstein, Albert, 126
El Salvador, 366; and Archbishop Oscar Romero, 462
Eletronorte Power Company, Brazil, 24
Elgin, Lord: and Aboriginal title, 449
Eliot, Rev. John, 162–3
Elliot, Mathew, 390
empire builders: in Europe and Creole America, 218–19
empire of communications: Harold Innis on, 298
Empire of Fortune, 11, 295
empire of man: Robert Boyle on, 309
empire of private property, 28, 73, 90, 360, 529; and breakup of Indian Confederacy, 527; and disparities of wealth, 368; and Fourth World in Australia, Canada, and Mexico, 206; and Indigenous peoples, 497; and Pontiac, 367; and privatization of remaining Aboriginal domains, 509. *See also* American empire, American empire of private property, United States of America
empire of proprietorship: United States as heartland of, 160
Empire of Reason: How Europe Imagined and America Realized the Enlightenment, 164
enclosures, 26, 85: and biotechnology through scientific breeding of livestock, 458; and containment of Indigenous peoples within domestic

law and courts, 43; in English civil war, 308; global corporatism's emphasis on privatized, 118; and industrialized agriculture, 110; opposition in Europe and America, 458; and schemes to privatize Indian lands. 360. *See also* capitalism, commodification
End of History, The, 60, 71, 96, 99, 144
enforced dependency: cultures of, 189–94
enfranchisement, 132; debate within First Nations on, 255–6; extension of to registered Indians, 474–80; and Indigenous peoples, 173–4; and John Diefenbaker, 255–6, 496, 505–6
Engels, Frederick, 124, 177, 179–82, 186
English Civil War, 83, 182, 308; and American Revolution, 359; and Royal Proclamation, 336
English East Indian Company, 23, 149, 352, 353
English: as linga franca of Indian Country in North America, 252
English-speaking nations: self-conception as pillars of liberal democracy, 498
English-speaking race: Goldwin Smith on, 78
Enlightenment, 6–7, 35–6, 38, 40–1, 49, 61; and Aboriginal rights, 498; in America, 121–6, 301, 368; and American Revolution, 358–9; and British Empire, 414; and Canadian Constitution's recognition of rights of Aboriginal peoples, 231; and centrality of human reason, 163–4; contrasted with Columbian conquests, 160; and economics profession, 187–9; and emphasis on reason in

USA, 76; and ethos and ideas of Fourth World, 134, 248–9, 531; failures of, 133; and global rule of law, 131; and identification of peoples as fundamental democratic unit, 230–1; and Indian Country of Canada, 162–5; and Locke and Rousseau, 179–89; and Michel Foucault, 132; and New Right, 128; renunciation of, 415; and Royal Proclamation, 356; and social sciences, 125; and Tecumseh, 413–14; and Tory Indian policy in American Revolution, 328; USA as bastion of, 122, 129, 183; USA betrays ideals of, 130. *See also* Western Civilization
Enron Company, 519
environmentalists: alliances with Indigenous peoples, 91–2; Coalition of Indigenous Organizations of the Amazon as, 93; Grey Owl as pioneering example of, 165–8
Eppler, Erhard, 3
equality before the law, 36; of nations, 65; Pierre Trudeau's vision of, 278–9; violation of with Darwinian rationales, 119
Erasmus, Georges, 88–9
Erdrick, Louis, 89
Erie Canal, 402
Erie people, 319
Estevan, Miro: Spanish governor of Louisiana, 216
ethnic bias: and Canadian reaction to Deskahe's mission, 491
ethnic cleansing, 27–8, 44, 61, 227; and Andrew Jackson, 403–7; and colonization of New Spain, 305; and decolonization, ethnic nationalism, and tribalism, 237, 524–5; and exceptions to policy of apartheid in USA, 499; and

geographic determinism,
135; John Bacher on in
Guatemala, 316; Lord Bal-
four on among Aboriginal
groups, 500; memory and,
164; Nathaniel Bacon's
assault on Indians in Virginia, 313, 315–16, 417;
and Pequot War of 1637,
317; rationales for, 106,
184
ethnic conflict: in early Indian wars and policies of
USA, 237, 301, 524; partition as primary interna-
tional response to, 233–4
ethnic enclaves: balkanization of Yugoslavia and of
Indian Country through
reserves, 233–4. See also
enclosures
ethnic fundamentalism:
George Manuel resists,
243
ethnic nationalism: Aboriginal realm and immigrants,
169, 453–8; of Creole
nationalities, 93, 215; and
linkages to decolonization,
237, 301, 524; and sover-
eignty, 301; and Tupac
Amaru, 213–15
ethnic relations: John Collier
on globalization and, 224;
and partition, 233–4
ethnic violence: along western frontiers of US expansion, 301
ethnicity: and Creole self-
understanding 93,
209–16, 469–74, 524; and
decolonization, 237, 301,
524; Kay B. Warren on,
61–2; and Social Darwin-
ism, 227
ethnocentrism, 126; and
Francis Jennings on
founding of USA, 295; and
liberties of Protestant
Anglo-Americans, 346;
and Social Darwinism,
226–7
ethnography, 125; Aboriginal authors participate in,

194; and adoption of Abo-
riginal transportation
technology, 381; and con-
tribution to Fourth World
movement, 241–2; Euro-
pean exploration in gene-
sis of, 177–9; European
ideas about the role of climate in configurations of,
296; and Jesuit writing on,
162–3; John Locke on,
183; and Lahonton's writ-
ing, 164; and political
economy, 184; Wilson
Duff and negotiations on
Aboriginal title, 265. See
also anthropology, social
sciences
Eurocentrism, 71, 126; and
globalization and rise of
capitalism after 1492,
302–3; and Royal Procla-
mation, 354; and theories
of civilizational hierarchy,
99–107, 413; and treaties
with Indigenous peoples,
304, 425
Europe: Canada as last country in Americas to sever
ties with, 290; continuing
influence of, 5, 235; and
depiction of Indians as
noble and ignoble savages,
113; diminution of laws of
in Indian Country of
Canada, 409; dismantling
of empires of, 225–8; divisions within drive imperialism and globalization,
227; Edward Said on
imperialism of, 115–16;
enclosure movement and
emigration from, 470; and
Enlightenment, 121–5,
176–89; and globalization
through emigration from,
469–70; imperialism of,
125–34; and imposition of
international borders, 66,
218, 225–6; land grabs of
begin 1492, 302; posses-
sive individualism in, 310;
property regimes of glob-
alized after Second World

War, 233; and role of in
imperialism and empire
building, 20–1; and Social
Darwinism, 226–7; succes-
sor states emanating from
imperialism of, 48, 70,
130, 174, 233, 301; and
theories of civilizational
hierarchy, 99–107, 413;
USA as a global instrument
of, 85, 310; USA continues
civilization mission of, 90,
97, 299–300, 373; and
war, 523
European imperialism: and
alliances and collabora-
tion with Indigenous peo-
ples, 320; and Christian
evangelization in Asia,
Africa, and the Americas,
458–9; and Creole nation-
alism, 211–15, 469–74;
decline of, 228; economic
inequities of, 131; and
empire building of USA,
152; enclosure movement
of and emigration, 470;
and genesis of Latin
America, 209–17, 460–4;
and ingestion by USA, 217;
and J.A. Hobson, 516–17;
and mercantilism and cap-
italism, 6; modified by
ideas of Vitoria, Las Casas,
and treaty making with
Indigenous people, 317;
and moral relativism, 135;
movement to dismantle,
235–6; and patents of discovery, 73; racist attributes
of edified by Darwinism,
226–7; and reserves, eth-
nic cleansing, and Creole
nationalism, 509; response
of Woodrow Wilson to,
357, 513; and social sci-
ences, 125; Soviet Union
as last example of, 228;
and successor states, 48,
70, 130, 174, 233, 301;
and treaties with Indige-
nous peoples, 425; and
Vladimir Illich Lenin, 232,
513, 516–17. See also

American empire of private property, British Empire, British imperialism, decolonisation, Spanish Empire
European Parliament, 93, 151
Evans, Rev. James, 193, 465
Evarts, Rev. Jeremiah, 178; and systematic violation of rule of law in USA, 459, 526
evolutionary theory: Bruce Trigger on, 128; Charles Darwin on, 125; development of by theorists in social sciences, 226–7. *See also* Darwinism, Social Darwinism, social sciences
Expo 67: Indian pavilion at Montreal, 265
extinguishment of Indian Country, 82, 161, 174; and bribery of Aboriginals, 360–1, 393; and decentralists in pre-revolutionary British North America, 345–6; and *E Pluribus Unum*, 206; and empire building in North America, 315; and English-speaking Protestants, 459; and expansion of USA through, 525–7; and founding of New Spain, 302–6; and Francis Bond Head, 431–42; and history since 1492, 531; and individual ownership, 360; John Locke on, 182–6, 310–12; and land speculation companies in British North America, 346–63; and machinery for implementing, 295; and New England Puritans, 306–10, 317; realized in USA through war, treaties, or relocation, 375; resistance to, 213; and role of state and provincial governments in North America, 246, 414–21; and Thomas Jefferson, 397–8; and

United Empire Loyalists, 427–9
Extradition Treaty between Canada and USA, 207–8

Fadden, Ray, 246
Fairfield: establishment of as Moravian mission in Upper Canada, 377
Family Herald, 493
Fanon, Frantz: on decolonization models that eschew European, 236–7, 531; Harvey McCue on, 245–6; on sabotaging of decolonization struggles through co-opting of leadership, 236–7, 281; and view of America, 299–300
fascism: and American finaciers and industrialists, 471; in Germany, 228, 498; in Indian politics of Jules Sioui and Alice Lee Jemison, 257–8
federal territories: constitutional character of in Canada and USA, 371–5
federalism: Aboriginal quest for inclusion of in Canada, 202; in Australia, 141–2; British Parliamentary Committee of 1837 on, 445; in Canada without incorporation of Aboriginal and treaty rights, 196; George Manuel on, 28; and Northwest Ordinance of 1787 in USA, 371–5; as overlapping sovereignties in international system, 234; and role of Indian Affairs in determining balance of power in North America, 246, 414–21
federalization of Aboriginal territories, 375
Federated Saskatchewan Indian Nations, 254
Fenton, William, 177–8
Ferguson, Niall, xxii, xxiv, xxvi, xxvii–xxviii
feudalism: decline of in Europe, 308; Thomas Jef-

ferson on alliance of Indians and British sovereign as return to, 311
fiduciary responsibilities: violation of by Canadian government, 356
Fiji, 160, 502
fire: as stimulant to biological diversity, 108–10
First Ministers Constitutional Conferences on Aboriginal Matters in Canada, 197, 202–3
First Nations: and absorption of immigrants, 168–73, 412, 453–8; and alliances with conservatives and Tory fur traders in North America, 132, 397–402, 410; as allies to Canada, 401, 453–8; and American Indian Movement, 33, 89, 260–77, 283; and Assembly of, 8, 92, 203–4, 260; and assimilationist Indian policy in Upper Canada, 432; of Australia, 137–42; as Burkean aristocracy in North America, 30; and citizenship, 474–80, 496–7, 507–9; and constitutional politics in Canada, 196–206; and continental and international frames of reference, 261; criteria for inclusion in, 49; and ecological approaches to human organization, 248; and economic self-determination, 193; and education and training, 438; and Enlightenment principles, 133; and environmentalists, 86–7; experience of as distillation of colonialism, 74; and Fourth World, 238–49, 283, 286–92, 458; and Indian Act, 480–2; and Indian education, 243; and Indian pavilion at Expo 67, 265; and intermarriage, 170–3, 408–10, 412–13, 456–8, 461, 484; and international treaty

making, 413; and laws of, 408–15; and legal determination of land title, 404–5; and litigation within, 42; minority rights within, 49; and patriation of Canadian Constitution, 196; perception of as lawless outsiders to Christendom, 309; property law in territory of, 423; protests in Canada to defend rights of, 483–95; and residential schools, 438; and retention by British of French Empire's Aboriginal policies, 430; and Royal Proclamation, 336–63, 410; and scholarship of in North America, 245–6; and section 35, 46–9; and Seven Years' War, 326–36; and sovereignty movement, 54; and suicide epidemics, 468; and treaties with US government, 157–8; and treaties with, 47, 55, 147–9, 155–9, 253, 268, 280, 317–20, 327–8, 350–1, 490–5, 526; wampum protocols and legal traditions of, 412. *See also* Indian Confederacy of Canada, Indian Country of Canada, Indians, Indigenous peoples

First World War: and founding of League of Nations, 253

First World: as dominated by USA, 240; prosperity of, 85

Fisher, Rayno, 51

fish-ins: in Washington state, 263, 270

fixed boundary: and Easton Treaty in Pennsylvania, 327

Flanagan, Tom, 39–40, 127

Florida, 185; under Spanish and British rule, 216–18

Floridian Spaniards, 313

Fontaine, Phil, 88

Fools Crow, 271

Forbes, Brig.-Gen. John, 327

Forbes, Jack, 90, 101, 246, 282

Forjando Patria, 221

Fort Benning, Georgia: School of the Americas in, 365; training of military and police agents at, 462

Fort Chippeweyan, 408

Fort Dusquesne: French withdrawal from, 326–8

Fort Nassau, 319

Fort Necessity, 326

Fort Orange, 319

Fort Pitt, 331; transformation into Fort Dusquesne, 326–7

Foucault, Michel, 132

Four Kings of Canada, 166, 324

Fourth World, 52, 55, 117; adaptive capacity of, 169; AIM sets stage for, 262; as alternative to neo-liberal globalization, 291, 530–4; assimilation of Europeans and Euro-Americans into, 173, 412, 168–73, 453–8; backlash against in Australia and British Columbia, 509; Battle of Seattle protestors as multicultural avant-guard of, 118; Clarence Alvord as spokesperson against, 361; class and economic tensions in, 282; conflict with neo-liberal models of globalization in Canada, 199–200; and Creole decolonization, 529–30; and cultural pluralism, 71, 99; and definitions of progress, 152; and Enlightenment thought, 133–4, 248–9, 531; and George Manuel, 195; and global transformation, 204; history and ideology of, 238–49, 283, 286–92, 458, 530–4; and ideas of Tupac Amaru, Kondiaronk, Pontiac, Tecumseh, and George Manuel, 291,

335; and Indian response to 1969 White Paper, 278; international civil society and, 502; Iroquois nationalism advances global awareness of, 269; and laws of British imperialism, 287; Ogoni activism in Nigeria as inspiration for, 150–1; reciprocal pluralism of, 358; and restructuring of nation states, 160; rise of in Australia, New Zealand, Mexico, and Canada, 149; and Royal Proclamation, 358–9; and self-determination of peoples, 237–8; songs of, 208; *Spirit of Haida Gwaii* as icon of, 206; and veneration of plant and animal spirits, 101; and vision of pluralistic global community, 291. *See also* biological diversity, cultural pluralism, ecology, George Manuel

Fourth World: An Indian Reality, The, 228, 250, 287; Louis Cameron at launching of, 227–8

Fox people, 334

Fox, Vincente, 145

Foxwood, Casino, 24, 87

France, 142, 217, 378; and American Revolution, 395; Clarence Alvord on, 361; and Enlightenment, 161; Frantz Fanon on imperialism of, 236; and sale of Louisiana, 291; and Seven Years' War, 219–20; and Thomas Guillaume Raynal, 6–7, 231; and Treaty of Paris in 1783, 362. *See also* French in America, French Revolution, New France

Franklin, William, 351

Free Trade Agreement of 1988, 79, 94–5, 369, 425; and Canadian election of 1988, 118

Free Trade Areas of the

Americas, 31, 49, 290, 425; activists at Quebec City meeting of, 94, 146, 531; and Aboriginal role in negotiation of, 205–6; and judicial arbitration, 119; Santiago Summit of, 93; as vehicle for extension of Monroe Doctrine and informal American empire, 146–7

free trade, 22, 30–1; and concentration of wealth and power, 150; economics profession on, 188–9; from fur trade to, 53; and politics of land speculators in British North America, 346–54; and property law, 50–1, 72. *See also* commercial trade treaties, private property, property law, property regimes, property relations

French and Indian War, 200, 313, 326–335, 363, 383, 467. *See also* Seven Years' War

French Declaration of Rights in 1795, 231

French in America, 10, 12, 20; and Acadian expulsion, 343; Claude Levi-Strauss on, 155; fall of empire of after 1758, 329; francophile elements in Indian Country attached to, 343; and fur trade, 383; hostility towards, 78; and Huronia, 106–7, 319; impact on Americas, 219–20; Indian Affairs in governance of, 322–35; Indian Country influence on France, 162–5; Indian influence in political economy of, 155; La Salle's plans for, 320; and Métis identity, 456; and New France, 12–13, 28–9; perceptions of in Anglo-American colonies, 296; and rebels opposing British imperialism, 378;

Samuel de Champlain and, 319; and withdrawal from North America, 219, 523. *See also* France, New France

French Revolution in 1789, 35–7, 75, 164, 186–7, 213, 216–17, 231

French-Aboriginal Canada, 200–6, 383; and James Bay Hydroelectric Project, 280, 431, 467; and Seven Years' War, 219–20, 326–35

French-Canadian nationalism: and impact on Jules Sioui, 253

Freud, Sigmund, 102

Friday, Verna, 51

Friedman, Milton, 80

Frontenac, Count de, 165

Frontiers: The Epics of South Africa's Creation and the Tragedy of the Xhosa People, 442

frontier school of American historiography, 168–9, 361

frontier thesis. *See* frontier school of American historiography

Frye, Northrop, 299

Fuentes, Carlos, 522

Fukuyama, Francis, 60, 71, 83, 129, 135, 144; and Indian as savage "other" in America, 99

full-bloods: as referred to in usa, 269

fundamentalism, xx, 126–34; and ethnicity, 243; Karl Polanyi on market, 187–9; Karl Popper on, 136; and moral relativism, 134–6; of Protestants, 127

fur trade, 12; and Aboriginal law, 409; and Archie Belaney, 165–6; and baron de Lahonton, 163; and Baynton, Wharton and Morgan, 350; Canada as domain of, 296; civilizing mission and, 173; collapse of Montreal base of, 447;

and conservative side of American Revolution, 82; continuity of in transition from New France to British imperial Canada, 337–8, 376; and crown-Aboriginal alliances and treaties, 159; and development of Canada as mestizo polity, 204; Euro-centric power in advancement of, 309; and excessive Indian hunting, 113; as glue of middle ground in Great Lakes region of Canada, 247; and infiltration of Hurons' trade network, 106–7; influence of on Canada, 93,155; and intellectual life in France, 162; and international boundaries in North America, 380; Jay's Treaty as legacy of, 269; Jeffrey Amherst's effort to make market ethos prevail over traditional culture of, 330; Louis Riel and Métis and, 223; and mercantilism, 342; Montreal as North American hub of, 345; pioneering of by Dutch-Iroquois alliance, 319; revival of cross-cultural dynamism of in Canada, 298; Sault Ste Marie area as hub of, 171; Sir William Johnson and, 324–6; transformation of through treaty of 1701, 164–5. *See also* Indian Country of Canada

Fur Trade in Canada, The, 298

Fussell, Betty, 105

G7 countries, 68

G8 countries: and legacy of racial hierarchy, 517

Gabriel, Ellen, 246

Gage, Gen. Thomas, 333; on plan to unite Indian nations in America, 387

Galeano, Eduardo, 424

Gallagher, John, 338
Gallatin, Albert, 104
Galloway, Joseph, 351
Gambler, The, 47, 49
gambling, 87; pacifying
  effect on Indians, 90
Gamio, Manuel, 146, 224–5,
  242; inspires Indigenismo
  movement in Mexico,
  221
Gandhi, Mahatma, 235–6,
  393
Ganienkeh, Mohawk land,
  277
gender relations, 65–6, 108,
  173; Aboriginal women
  and constitutional politics
  in Canada, 203–4; Aboriginal women's groups and
  federally funded Aboriginal organizations, 285;
  and Anna Jameson, 192;
  and expansion of fran-
  chise to women, 358;
  intermarriage, 170–3,
  408–10, 412–13, 456–8,
  461, 484; Marx, Engels,
  and Morgan on patriar-
  chal monogamy and
  exploitation of women,
  179–82; and politics of
  Nah-nee-ba-we-quay as
  forerunner to those of the
  Native Women's Associa-
  tion of Canada, 484–5
General Agreement on Tar-
  iffs and Trade, 80, 230,
  369
Genesis 1:28: importance of
  in justifying displacement
  of Indians in growth of
  New England, 307
genetic commons, 65
Geneva, 491
genocide, 26, 27, 28; Aboriginal responses to, 133; and
  Aboriginal title, 317; and
  baptism of America, 95;
  Cotton Mather and, 309;
  and criminalization of
  Aboriginal self-defence,
  494; ethnic cleansing and
  the Trail of Tears 406; and
  Fidel Castro, 520; law of,

27; governments implicat-
  ed in, 44; in Guatemala in
  1980s, 91, 365–6, 473;
  and law of self-determination, 45; and legal orders,
  72; and literature, 97–9;
  Nathaniel Bacon and, 316;
  in Rwanda and Burundi,
  237; and Samuel Huntington, 97–8; Thomas Jefferson and, 397–8; Ward
  Churchill on, 27–9, 98.
  See also ethnic cleansing,
  extinguishment of Indian
  Country
gentes: in evolutionary theory of Lewis Henry Morgan,
  180–2
geographical determinism,
  134–6
George III, King, 8, 11, 12;
  as alleged instigator of
  Indian hostility against
  Anglo-American colonies,
  310–12, 397; and collaboration with Lord Halifax
  after news of Pontiac's
  patriotic stand, 331; and
  ideas that lead towards
  Fourth World, 358; and
  Niagra Council in 1764,
  155; and Royal Proclamation, 336–46
Georgia: and appropriation
  of Cherokee territory, 459;
  imposition of jurisdiction
  of on Cherokee people,
  404; and Johnson v. McIn-
  tosh, 415–21; New York
  Treaty and, 216; Worcester
  v. Georgia, 404
Geronimo, xvii–xix
Gershwin, George, 96
Gibson, Gordon, 39–40
Gilbert, Kevin, 141
Girty, George, James and
  Simon, 390
Gitlin, Todd, 128
Glacier National Park, 86
Gladstone, Senator James,
  280; as yes-man for
  Ottawa, 496
Gleijes, Piero, 365
Glenelg, Lord: colonial poli-

cy of offends Protestant
  missionary societies,
  441–3
global apartheid, 189,
  515–22
global banking institutions:
  and terms of decolonization, 233
global biosphere: and Earth
  Summit in Rio de Janiero
  in 1992, 157
global commons: privatization of, 361; USA founded
  to privatize major portions
  of, 359
global corporate citizens:
  gain access to supernation-
  al courts not available to
  human citizens, 510
global corporations, 23, 44;
  and biotechnology, 72–3;
  and citizens' rights, 510;
  and concentration of
  wealth, 519–20; and corporatism, 66, 70, 118,
  128; and disparities arising from racialized economy, 515–22; expansion of,
  68–70; and George
  Manuel 151, 238; and
  global business culture,
  94; iconography of, 218;
  Indigenous peoples' experience of as forecast, 176;
  and J.D. Rockefeller, J.P.
  Morgan, and Andrew
  Carnegie, 84; and Ogoni
  people, 150–7; and power
  of executive branches of,
  84–5, 519; and scandals
  of, 519; and slavery, 521;
  and UN Charter, 230; and
  world governance by, 60.
  See also commercial trade
  treaties, corporations,
  monocultures, possessive
  individualism, private
  property, property law,
  property regimes, transnational corporations
globalization: and American
  Declaration of Indepen-
  dence, 310–12; begins in
  1492, 4–7; Bouttros

Boutros-Ghali and Michael Ignatieff on, 59; and Canada as Indian Country and Fourth World frontier, 298; and colonization of Australia, 139; and corporate capitalism, 144; and creation of cultures of dependency, 191–2; and Creole identity politics, 469–74; and cultural relativism, 134; definition of, 59–60; and democracy, 21; different visions of, 400; and disempowerment of distinct peoples, 120; ecological, 30; and end to history, 99; and English language, 84; and European heritage, 235; and George Manuel, 152, 291, 243–4; and global sameness, 59; and international agencies, 128; and John Collier, 224; and Jose Vasconcelos's view of mestizaje, 225; and language, 65; and laws of, 117–19; and legal interpretation, 114–21; and monocultures, 65; neo-liberal modes of, 68; and Native American ideas, 164; and photography of Earth from space, 228; and privatization, 21; and protection of capital, 521; and Social Darwinism, 226–7; and social sciences, 125–34; and the westward expansion of USA, 234; and transnational corporations, 33, 518; and Zapatistas, 80, 143–6, 513–14

global Manifest Destiny: Kevin Phillips on Anglo-America and, 363
global music business, 115
global property law, 72–3
global rule of commerce: enforcement of without global rule of law, 50, 120
global rule of law: and Royal

Proclamation, 357; USA and quest for, 131, 348–9, 529
Glorious Revolution, 182
Golden Gate, 267
Goldwater, Barry, 80
Goodstriker, Wilton, 51
GOON squad: paramilitary force on Pine Ridge reservation in 1970s, 272
Gorman, R.C., 244–5
Goshute people, 85
Gospel Outreach Church: conversion of Guatemalan president Rios Montt, 463
Gottlieb, Gideon, 235
Gramajo, Hector, 366
Gran Columbia, 210
Granatstein, J.L., 61
Grand Ohio Company, 352–3
Grand River Valley, 171, 387
Grand, Mogul: Camden-York legal opinion, 353
Grant, George, 60, 83, 298, 423
Grant, John Webster, 465
Great American Desert, 105
Great Britain: and commodification of Indian land in Canada, 448; and dependence on formal treaties in America, Africa, and India, 385; and failure to include Indigenous peoples in highest levels of international negotiations, 399–400, 413; and imperial expansion, 445; and role in Latin America, 211. See also British Empire, British imperial Canada, British imperialism, British North America, Royal Proclamation of 1763
Great Depression, 166, 223–4, 368
Great Lakes: and Aboriginal struggle in War of 1812, 396; and Indian Country, 388
Great Lakes–Mississippi Valley area: and War of 1812, 396

Great Law of the Longhouse League, 268
Great Spirit: and Janice Switlo on Aboriginal allodial title, 47–8; Shingwaukonse on gifts of, 451; Tenskwatawa on intentions of, 391
Great Transformation, The, 71–2, 187–9
Great Trek: exodus of Afrikaners from Cape Colony, 442
Great White Pine of Peace: as symbol of Longhouse League, 384
Greco-Roman heritage, 96, 98
Green Party, 88
Green Revolution, 108
Green, Jack, 217
Greenpeace, 86
Greider, William, 67
Grenada: as legally constituted by Royal Proclamation, 336
Grenville, George, 352
Grey Owl, 165–8, 178, 296, 359, 458, 532
Grey Owl syndrome: Margaret Atwood on, 168–73, 398, 412
Grinder, Donald, Jr, 90
gringo empire of the United States, 146
Grotius, Hugo, 318
Group of Seven, Canada, 153
Guardian Spirit: George Manuel on, 249
Guatemala, 61, 244; constitutional change in, 93; and Mayan people, 145, 462; and Rigoberta Menchu, 91–3; and role of USA in civil war in, 365–7
Guerin case, 30
Guilded Age, 373
"guilt industry": Australian prime minister John Howard on, 141
Gumbayyngirr people, 138
gunfighter nation: USA as, 527

Gunn, Angus M.: and pro-Apartheid stance of, 507
Guns, Germs and Steel, 134–6
Gurindji people, 139
Gustafsen Lake under Siege, 47
Gustafsen Lake, 18–20, 54, 207–8, 495

Hagan, William, 90
Haida Gwaii, 206
Haida people, 206
Haiti, 219, 290, 366–7; slave revolt in creation of, 470
Haldimand, Gov. Frederick, 376
Hall, Louis, 246, 265: as key figure in American Indian Movement and Mohawk Warriors, 276–7; on suicide of Nelson Small Legs Jr, 277
Hall-Onabigon, Riley, 17
Hall-Onabigon, Sampson, 3, 8, 16–17
Hallowell, Irving, 177–8
Hamar's Humiliation, 378
Hamilton, Ontario, 387
hang-around-the-fort-Indians, 272
Hanover, court of, 165
Hanson, Pauline, 141
Hare, Susan and Joe, 51
Harkin, James, 166
Harmar, Brig. General Joseph, 378
Harper, Elijah, 17, 88, 467; and constitutional negotiations, 290; and Meech Lake accord, 198, 205
Harpers Magazine: and Simon Pokagan's account of Tecumseh's oratory skills, 394
Harring, Sidney, 411
Harrison, William Henry, xvi, 77, 391, 395, 397, 422
Hart, Gary: as co-chair of United States Committee on National Security, 527
Harvard University, xxvii, 242, 245
Haudonosaunee. *See* Longhouse League
Hauptman, Laurence, 90

Havanna, 269
Hawke, Bob, 139
Hawthorne, H.B., 265, 411
Hayak, F.A., 80
Hayden, Tom, 144, 178, 245
Head, Sir Francis Bond, 431–46, 499
Head-Smashed-In Buffalo Jump Interpretive Centre, 53
Hegel, Friedrich, 60
Henderson, Judge Richard, 349–50, 360; and land speculation in America, 388
Hendrick (Theyanoguin), 324
Henry, Alexander, 332–3
Henry, E.L., 11
Henry, George, 194
Henry, Jeanette, 246
Herder, Johann Gottfried, 126
heredity and treaty rights: as asserted by Native Peoples' Caravan in 1974, 274
Hewitt, John Brinton, 194
Hidatsa people, 108
Hidden Cities, 104–5
High Court of Australia, 31, 118, 137–40
Highway, Tom, 52, 102, 195
Hill, John, 438
Hill, Tom, 246
Hillsborough, Lord, 352
Hinderaker, Eric, 338
Hinduism, 97
Hispanic identity, 93; as developed in USA, 212, 215
Histoire philosophique et politique des établissements et du commerce des Européens dans les deux Indes, 3, 6–7, 231
History of the Ojibway People, 194
Hitler, Adolf, 67; demonization of, 498
Hobbes, Thomas, 177
Hobson, J.A.: on Cecil Rhodes and the British South Africa Company, 516; on theories of imperialism, 517
Hodgins, Bruce, 51

Hohokam people, 113
Holland, 182
Hollywood westerns, 99, 168
Holy Roman Empire: designation of Spanish sovereign as emperor of, 374
home rule: George Manuel on, 287
Homeland Security: as term applied to Bantustans in South Africa, 528; of USA, 129–30, 528
Honduras, 224
Hoover Institute: and pro-Apartheid stance of Angus M. Gunn, 507
Hopewell culture, 104
Hopi people: and response of US government to before UN Human Rights Commission, 525
Horn, Kahn-Tineta, 246; questions two founding nations theory, 265
Horsman, Reginald, 90, 367
horticulture, 60, 164, 213, 243; Indian origins of in America, 105, 108
House Made of Dawn, 245
House of Burgesses of Virginia, 350
Houser, Allan, 244–5
Howard, John, 142–2
Hudson, Henry: and exploration for Dutch East India Company, 318
Hudson Bay–James Bay: as hydroelectric frontier of the American empire, 466
Hudson River: exploration of, 318–9
Hudson's Bay Company, 409, 425, 465, 467; as basis of British imperialism in North America, 375; and east-west transportation, 447; and Iroquois in fur trade of in Oregon area, 430; and James Bay watershed, 466; lands of become North-West Territory, 371; lands of excluded from Royal Proclamation, 340; legal

viability of Charter of, 409; and merger with North West Company in 1821, 297; territorial extent covered by Charter of, 297; transfer of titles of to Dominion of Canada, 23, 49, 223,149, 154–5; and violations of international law, 409

Hughs, Robert, 61, 128

Hull, Gen. William, 396

human reason: as cherished by Indians, 163–4

human rights, 130–1; Aboriginal and treaty rights as, 49–50; in Australia, 137–42; Canada's constitutional treatment of, 290; and criminalizing of Aboriginal law, customs, and self-determination, 495; and ecological understanding, 358; and Enlightenment, 121–3; and groups considered unsuitable for franchise, 475; and Indigenous peoples lives, lands, and culture, 301–2; and international, transnational, or supranational agencies, 44, 303; in international law, 355; language of appropriated by corporations, 50; and Marlon Brando, 263; protection for, 44–6, 130–1; and Royal Proclamation, 355; and slavery and property rights, 123; and United Nations Charter, 66. See also Aboriginal and treaty rights, Aboriginal rights, Aboriginal title, Royal Proclamation of 1763

Humphrey, John, 229–30

Hunt, George, 195

Hunter, John Dunn, 178

Huntington, Samuel P., 61, 69, 96–9, 300; and ascent of the West through superiority of organized violence, 515

Huron peoples, 100, 164, 334, 382; and activism of Jules Sioui, 253–4; as agriculturalists and in French-Aboriginal fur trade of Canada, 106–7, 319; and American Revolution, 314; and Five Nations Iroquois in 1649, 319; and settlement at Ancienne Lorette, 329

Huronia: as model Indian community, 432

Hussein, Saddam: hostility of US government to, 527; as seen by Edward Said, 368

hybridization, 212

Hydro-Québec, 24, 112, 149, 244, 430

I.G. Farben Chemical Company: as extension in Nazi Germany of Standard Oil, 471

Ignace, William, 51

Ignatieff, Michael, 59

Île-à-la-Crosse, 408

Illinois Country, 334

Illinois people, 334

Illinois-Wabash Company, 349, 353, 404

imperial mission: and Northwest Ordinance, 373

imperial trusteeship: and Royal Proclamation, 355

Imperialism: The Highest Stage of Capitalism, 232, 516–17

imperium: George Washington on USA as, 363

Inca Empire, 223

Inca people: as continuing power in Peru, 223; and irrigation 105; as road builders, 93, 103–4; Tupac Amaru and resistance of, 213–17

incarceration: bondage involved in, 288; and enfranchisement, 132, 173–4, 255–6, 474–80, 496, 505–6; as metaphor of treatment of Indigenous peoples in occupation of Alcatraz Island,

266–7; of Native Americans in the genesis of the American Indian Movement, 261; Neolin comments on destructiveness of to Native people, 354; representation of those who suffer from, 285

inclusiveness: and Fourth World, 243

India, 31, 287, 353; and Mahatma Gandhi, 235–6

Indian Act of Canada, 482; and Act for the Gradual Civilization of the Indian Tribes in Canada, 1857, 473–4; and alcohol, 256; and apartheid in South Africa, 498–9; as artifact to transform Indigenous peoples into wards of colonial authority, 174; assimilationist philosophy of, 127, 498; changes in after 1951, 495–6; and creation of reserves, 480–2; and criminalization of traditional spiritual observances, 482; and dispossession of Indigenous peoples, 510–11; Ella Cork on, 481; and enfranchisement, 132, 173–4, 255–6, 474–80, 496, 498, 505–6; and exclusion of registered Indians from rights and responsibilities of legal persons, 476; imposed by RCMP on Six Nations people near Brantford, 490–5; and prohibition of money transfer to advance Indian claims, 251, 282, 495; repeal of demanded in Manifesto of Native Peoples Caravan, 274; and representation in Canada's constitutional negotiations, 202–3; and Sechelt Self-Government Act, 498; as symbol of imperial treatment of Indigenous peoples globally, 174; and

treatment of Indians as
non-persons even as cor-
porations are treated in
law as persons, 510; and
wardship, 480; and White
Paper, 278–80, 497
Indian agent: modelled on
British colonial governors,
481; powers of, 482
Indian apples, 272
Indian Association of Alberta, 255–6; Harold Cardi-
nal as president of, 279
Indian band: as creature of
federal legislation vesting
power in hands of federal
Indian agent, 481
Indian buffer state: A.L. Burt
on role of in peace negotiations of 1814, 399; in
strategic thinking of some
British imperialists, 378;
and vision of Tecumseh,
388–97, 533. See also Aboriginal dominion, bowl
with one spoon, Indian
Confederacy of Canada
Indian burials: AIM's campaign against disturbance
of by archaeologists, 176
Indian Confederacy of Canada, xvi, 78, 117, 201, 207,
259, 261; and American
army, 380; and bowl with
one spoon, 386; and
British pressure on USA to
recognize Aboriginal title
of, 378; and control of
land, 399; and Covenant
Chain and Longhouse,
384–6, 530; defeat of US
army in Harmer's Humili-
ation and St. Clair's shame
in 1790–1, 377–80; gene-
sis and character of,
380–7; and international
controversy over status of,
363; and international law,
424; and New England's
Indian wars, 313; and
Tecumseh, 380–402, 407,
414, 422–3; and Tippeca-
noe, 422; and US recogni-
tion that "right of the soil"

invested in, 375–80; and
War of 1812, 396–402;
and withdrawal of France
from North America, 320.
See also Indian Country of
Canada
Indian consent: and status of
Aboriginal lands in Royal
Proclamation, 356
Indian Country of Canada,
11–13, 15; and Aborigi-
nal literature, 195; and
American empire of pri-
vate property, 299; and
Anglican missionaries,
465; as asylum for Indian
refugees from USA, 206;
British defence of, 400;
and British negotiations
with Indians in Ohio Val-
ley, 328; British use of in
written treaties, 385; and
Canadian constitutional
negotiations, 196–206;
canadien liberty in, 456;
canoe and satellite dish
as icons of, 465; capitalist
financial systems and
resources of, 509; class
conflicts in, 277–86; conservative branches of,
496; control of by Domin-
ion and Ontario govern-
ments, 415–21; defini-
tions of, 295–6;
demographic growth of,
297–8; as depicted in
prose, poetry, politics,
and painting, 153; and
enfranchisement, 132,
173–4, 255–6, 474–80,
496, 498, 505–6;
eographic scope of, 401;
extinguishment and pri-
vatization of, 427–9;
frauds perpetrated in,
339; as frontier for
expansion of American
empire, 530; genesis and
character of, 380–7; gen-
esis of twentieth-century
politics in, 249–60; and
George Manuel, 238;
global importance of in

contentions between con-
stitutionality of British
Empire and economics of
American empire, 287;
and Grey Owl, 530; as
home for African and
African American people,
383; and Indian Act,
480–482; and Indian
Affairs, 496; and Indian
buffer state in, 380–97;
Indian republics in, 384;
and Indigenous cultures,
466; intellectual influ-
ence of on France,
162–5; and Jay's Treaty,
388; Kondiaronk's impor-
tance in, 164; and legal
persons, 476, 510 ;
manipulation of for
British benefit, 390; and
Manitoulin Island, 433–7,
499; and multicultural
villages, 396–7; and Pon-
tiac, 330–6, 532; and
pressure on to relinquish
land and resources,
428–9; privatization and
enclosure of, 458;
Reform Party agenda to
terminate reserves of,
509; and relationship to
Fourth World and empire
of possessive individual-
ism, 530–4; and Royal
Proclamation, 336; and
Sir Francis Bond Head,
431–46, 499; and Sir
William Johnson, 334;
status of laws in as
defined in Connolly v.
Woolich, 408–13; and
Tecumseh and War of
1812, 380–402, 407, 414,
422–3; and transfer of
Louisiana to USA, 380,
392, 395–6; transfer of
territories of to USA in
1783, 362–3; United
Indian Nations council as
sovereign government of,
391; use of plants in,
381. See also Indian Con-
federacy of Canada

Indian Country of North America: and *canadien* assimilation into, 383

Indian Defense League of America: and annual marches across Peace Bridge, 268

Indian Department of British Imperial Canada: and civilizing mission in 1730, 173; and Christian missionaries, 174–6; founding of in 1755, 322–4; Métis staff of, 171; patronage available to staff of, 171

Indian Department of the Dominion of Canada, 482

Indian Federation of Saskatchewan, 254–5

Indian Gaming Regulation Act, 1988, 87

Indian give-a-ways, 495; criminalizing of, 482

Indian Hall of Fame: Art Solomon and, 276

Indian horticulture: in Mexico, 220–1; and global political economy, 105–12; and John Locke, 182–6; and Puritans, 307

Indian lobby in London, England, 196

Indian New Deal: and Alice Lee Jemison and American Indian Federation, 257; and John Collier, 223–4; and Indian tribal administration, 281; influence of in Saskatchewan after 1944, 254; and rejection of assimilation, 368; and US Indian policy, 261

Indian Reorganization Act, 1934, 22–4, 223–4, 257; and Constitution of the National Congress of American Indians, 259

Indian Rights Association: and Helen Hunt Jackson, 264

Indian scalps: payment for in North Carolina, 314

Indian schools: as designed and run by Indians, 244; discussion of during occupation of Alcatraz Island, 267. *See also* Christian residential schools

Indian Territory: definitions of, 77, 295–6, 375. *See also* Indian Country of Canada

Indian title. *See* Aboriginal title

Indian Treaties: and founding of Rhode Island in 1635, 361–7; Frederick Haldimand on, 376; and law of English colonization, 317; Louis Cameron on, 274; and name of British sovereign in, 385; and Six Nations Iroquois, 268; as permanent institution not to be cancelled by politicians, 289; symbolism of signifying status of Indian nations in international law, 270; violation of in USA, 526; in White Paper of 1969, 278–80. *See also* Covenant Chain, crown-Aboriginal Treaties, modern-day treaties, numbered treaties, Royal Proclamation of 1763, treaty making with Indigenous peoples, United States Indian Treaties

Indian War of Independence: War of 1812 as, 396–7

Indian wars: and American Declaration of Independence reference to "merciless Indian savages," 312; and American Indian Movement, 260–77; and American power, 156, 367, 373; in colonial North America, 76, 313–26; and Pontiac's patriotic stand, 330–6; and Tecumseh and War of 1812, 380–402, 407, 414, 422–3; Thomas Hart Benton on, 185; and US doctrine of conquest in 1987, 185; Vietnam conflict as extension of, 178, 245; within Seven Years' War, 326–35

Indiana grant: Indiana Company acquires through Treaty of Fort Stanwix in 1768, 351; and Samuel Wharton's lobby of Continental Congress, 360

Indiana Territory: Gov. William Henry Harrison opposes Indian Confederacy, 391–5

Indiana, 402

Indian-Eskimo Association: becomes Canadian Association in Support of the Native People, 266; emerges from Canadian Association for Adult Education, 264–6

Indians of All Tribes, 266–8

Indians: adoption of white captives into families of, 382; and agriculture, 105–12, 436; as allies of British North America, 156; as "animals and vermin" in Anglo-American colonies, 183; of Canada, 12; Christopher Columbus and semantic origin of, 95; David Maybury-Lewis on genocide in Guatemala directed at, 366; and enfranchisement, 132, 173–4, 255–6, 474–80, 496, 498, 505–6; imperial enclaves of never extinguished, 511; and Indian Country, 380–8; international significance of Canada's recognition of as "peoples," 231; Jean Morisset on, 155; and land of the bowl with one spoon, 391–2; and Manifest Destiny, 74–85; Nathaniel Bacon on "Robbers and Thieves," 315–16; nation-state economics based on expropriation of lands of, 521;

non-citizenship of in
Canada, 448; policies of
Tommy Douglas
(Saskatchewan) towards,
254–5; prohibition of
involvement in legisla-
tures, courts, and land
markets, 475; and recognition in Mexico, 145–6;
Red Coates and, 16–17;
restricted opportunity to
parent children, 475;
rights of in Northwest
Ordinance, 372; schooling
of, 243; Sir Francis Bond
Head and land tenure of,
436; subject to papal international law, 302–6;
Thomas Jefferson on, 392,
397–8; US government
derives centralized authority from power over, 419;
US government treats as
lower order of humanity,
393; as wards of state, 119,
475; women and forced
sterilization, 475. See also
First Nations, Indigenous
peoples
Indigenismo, 82–3; and Aboriginal scholars, 245; and
Fourth World movement,
241; Jose Maria Arguedas
and literary expression of,
223; Jose Vasconcelos
writes on, 225; and Mexi-
can Revolution, 221–33;
new forms of in North
America, 244; Zapatismo
and, 82–3
Indigenous peoples: and
Aboriginal civilization of
the Americas, 96–9; and
activism within Canada
and USA, 16–21, 53–4,
196–206, 238–86, 446–53,
483–5, 490–6; and agriculture, 105–12; and
alliances with monarchical
and conservative forces in
the Americas, 36–8, 75,
132, 154, 156, 171–4,
211, 214, 336–46,
359–60, 397–402, 413,

423, 465, 530–4; Ameri-
can Revolution as continuation of wars with,
313–26, 525; and Angli-
can Church, 132, 175,
463–5, 486–8; in Aus-
tralia, 137–42, 159, 258,
339; and civilizing mis-
sion, 173–6, 192–4,
372–5, 438; and cultures
of dependency, 113,
189–92; and emergence
of USA, 336–70, 469–74;
and international politics,
151, 225–38, 286–92,
299–310, 512–34; and
languages, 62–5, 98, 139,
145, 218, 439; in Mexico
and Latin America, 33–4,
92, 143–6, 209–25, 424–5,
460–3; as repositories of
cultural pluralism, 70;
social scientists on,
125–36, 160–89, 194,
221, 224, 241–3, 470,
495–509; and sovereignty,
41, 46–7, 67, 72, 124,
147–9, 156, 199–200,
269, 287–8, 300–2, 532;
and Tecumseh and War of
1812, 380–402, 407, 414,
422–3; treatment of in
Canada and South Africa,
431–46, 495–509. See also
cultural pluralism, First
Nations, Fourth World,
Indian Country of Cana-
da, Indians, names of individual groups, Native
Americans
indirect rule, 367
Indonesia, 367
infidels: in Lord Baltimore's
charter to colonize Mary-
land, 306–7
Innis, Harold, 154, 297–8
Innuit Broadcasting Corporation, 465
Institutional Revolutionary
Party: corruption of,
220
institutionalized theft: and
founding acts of by the
Americas, 315

intellectual property, 50, 60,
72–3
Inter-American Develop-
ment Bank, 93
Interamerican Indigenous
Institute, 224, 242
intercultural: collaboration,
152; democracy, 161; self-
determination, 234
intermarriage, 170–3,
408–10, 412–13, 456–8,
461, 484
internal colonization, 182
International Business
Machines Company: and
Nazi campaign, 471
International Convention on
the Elimination of All
Forms of Racial Hatred,
142
International Labour Organization, 93, 151
international law, 22, 29,
35–6, 43, 45, 47, 67, 271,
473–4, 530; and Canada's
changing constitution,
196–206; and collective
self-determination,
228–35; definitions of,
302; and demise of Euro-
pean empires in Latin
America, 211–12; and
Deskahe, 490–5; in divi-
sion of Americas and
Africa, 291; Eurocentric
application of, 413, 425;
Gideon Gottlieb on, 235;
and Hudson's Bay Charter,
408–9; and Hugo Grotius,
318; and human rights,
305; and law of nations,
302; making of, 228–36;
and New Spain, 211,
303–5; and overlapping
sovereignty, 234–5; and
Royal Proclamation,
353–8; Tecumseh and,
412–14; Toussaint L'Over-
ture on, 414; US position
outside of, 161; Vine Deloria Jr on, 270–1; Woodrow
Wilson on, 222, 357, 491,
513
International Monetary

Fund, 72, 131; and global apartheid, 517
International Nickel Corporation, 24
international security commons, United States as self-appointed keeper of, 529
international treaties, 49, 66, 82, 131–2, 156, 362–3, 375–80, 399, 400, 420, 425, 431; and concept of higher and lower orders of humanity, 413, 425; and preamble to UN Charter, 230. See commercial trade treaties
International Whaling Commission, 87
International Work Group on Indigenous Affairs, 241
Internet, 73: support on for Zapatistas, 79, 143
interregnum, 320–1
Introduction to a Science of Mythology, 155
Inuit Country, 465
Inuit Tapirisat of Canada, 8
Inuit, 24, 93, 152, 244; recognition of as "people," 231, 530
Inupiat People, 87
Ipperwash: confrontation at, 203
Iran, 367
Iraq: US attack as part of War on Terrorism, xi, 528; US-led attack on in 1991, 69, 368
Ireland: Cromwell's assault on as prelude to expansionism in North America, 223; and Inca potatoes, 104
iron age, 125, 226
Ironside, George, 85
Ironside, Melvina, 85
Iroquoia, 523
Iroquois empire, 328; and British-French competition, 523; Francis Jennings on, 319
Iroquois League. See Covenant Chain, Long-

house League, Six Nations Iroquois
Iroquois people: as voyageurs, high steel workers, lacrosse players, and fur traders, 430–1. See also Covenant Chain, Longhouse League, Six Nations Iroquois
Islam, 97, 419, 458; Christian Crusades against, 368, 374, 414, 417; Conor Cruise O'Brien on, 129; and jihad, 59
Isleta Pueblo people, 86
Israel, xxiii, 76, 161; as justification for conquest of Indians in Florida, 185; New England as a new, 3–8
Italy: US government attacks Communist Party of during Cold War, 365

Jackson, Andrew, 216, 459, 486; and conquest of Indian lands, xvi, 403; military actions of in Indian Country, 403–7; opposes Judge Marshall, 405; and partition of USA, 499; subordinates rule of law to political expediency, 418–19
Jackson, Helen Hunt, 178, 264
Jackson, Henry, 280, 483
Jackson, Richard: and Board of Trade, 352
"Jacksonian democracy": enforced removal and extermination of Indian peoples, 403
Jacob, Rev. Peter, 194
Jacobs, Jane, 70
Jacobs, Wilbur, 90
James II, King, 322
James Bay and Northern Quebec Agreement of 1975: as first modern-day treaty in Canada, 280, 431
James Bay Cree: exchanges with African National Congress, 514
James Bay hydroelectric project, 431, 467

James Bay watershed: conflict over, 200; and Cree peoples, 467
Jameson, Anna, 191–2, 412
Jamison, Roberta, 246
Japan, 48
Jay, John, 345
Jay's Treaty of 1794, 377; and Britain's agreement to withdraw troops from south of the Great Lakes after Battle of Fallen Timbers, 380, 388; as point of contention at Akwesasne, 209
Jefferson, Thomas: and abandonment of civilizing mission, 397–8; and capitalist plutocracy, 84; and condemnation of crown-Indian alliances in British North America 311; and Declaration of Independence, Louisiana Purchase, and Manifest Destiny, 76–7; and decolonization movement, 235; encourages Indians to become Christian and civilized, 432; and expansion of USA, 392; and expulsion of European influence from New World, 215; and Locke's ideas on Indians and property in American Revolution and Declaration of Independence, 311–12; and Louisiana as basis for American system of apartheid, 334; and the Norman Yolk, 311; as student of Mound Builders of Turtle Island, 104; and Tenskwatawa, 397–8
Jemison, Alice Lee, 195, 257–8, 282
Jennings, Francis, 116, 174, 295, 319, 339, 347, 385, 419; and Covenant Chain series, 11, 54; on Indian agriculture, 107; and invasion of America, 90, 95
Jerry Springer Show, 466

Jesuit Order, 455; and Indian missions among Mohawks at Sault-St Louis and St Regis, 328; literature of, 162–3; and missions in Huronia, 319; and resistance of Odawa people (Anisinabek) at Wikwemikong to ceding treaty on Manitoulin Island, 454

Jesuit Relations and Allied Documents, The, 162

Jihad vs McWorld, 59, 65

Jogginosh, 13

Johnson Hall, 8–17, 22, 28–9, 53, 117, 170, 334

Johnson v. McIntosh, 415–21; as vehicle for transplanting of Eurocentric legal theories into us law, 404

Johnson, Basil, 51, 246

Johnson, John Smoke: Indian opposition to new Indian Act of Province of Canada, 483–4

Johnson, Pauline, 195, 483

Johnson, Richard: claimed killer of Tecumseh, 397

Johnson, Sir John: and division of Quebec into Lower and Upper Canada, 427–8; as minister of loyalists and Indian affairs, 428

Johnson, Sir William (Warraghiyagey), 385, 412, 423, 450; and Anglo-American attitudes to murder of Indian people, 354; bridges Indian policy of New France and British imperial administration, 324; career of, 8–16, 324–6, 333–5; children of, 171; contrast with George Washington, 22; Duncan Campbell Scott on, 324; estate of, 8–16; and extension of Covenant Chain linking British crown with Longhouse Confederacy, 170–1, 532; as founding patriarch of British imperial Canada, 170; and George Crogan, 350; and

Indian Council in 1764 at Niagra, 155; as manor lord, 83; and Molly Brant, 10–11, 170–1, 385, 532; and Treaty of Fort Stanwix, 350–2

Joint Council of Indigenous Peoples and Organizations of Brazil, 92

Jonas, Susanne, 366

Jones, Col. H.M., 504

Jones, Dorothy, 31, 90, 117, 347, 385

Jones, Rev. Peter, 166–7, 193, 194; and testimony to British Parliamentary Committee on Aborigines in British Settlements, 444

Josephy, Alvin M., 90

Judeo-Christian heritage, 98

Judicial Committee of the Privy Council: ruling on use of Indian lands, 419; on *Mohegans v. Connecticut*, 337

judiciaries of globalization: lack of transparency in, 119–20; and recognition of founding stories of all peoples, 120–1; in war on communism and war on terror, 130

Jull, Peter, 152

Jung, Carl, 102

juries: William Penn on Indian representation in, 318

Kaffir, 500; atrocities against in South Africa, 443

Kagegamic, Joshim, 244–5

Kahkewaquonaby. *See* Jones, Rev. Peter

Kaminawash, Chief Roy, 513–14

Kanesatake: Mohawk community of Oka, 329

Kanewake, 430; boatmen of transport supplies up Nile River, 430; develops from Jesuit mission at Sault-Saint Louis, 329; extension of federal franchise to citizens of, 496

Kanhai, Nahun, 51

Kasabonika: structure of, 465

Kashtin: Innu-language musical performances of, 465

Kaskaskia: adoption of white captives into, 383

Kaske, Charlot, 333–4

Kaurua people, 139

Keating, Paul, 140–1

Kellogg bothers, 108

Kelly, James, 51

Kelly, Rev. Peter, 250, 252, 256

Kelman, Evelyn, 51

Kennedy, Dan, 280

Kennedy, John, F., 231, 364–5

Kennedy, Roger G., 104–5

Kenny, George, 195

Kenora, Ont.: and armed confrontation at Anicinabe, 272–4

Kentucky Country, 350; Richard Henderson and Daniel Boone as archetypes of American frontier spirit, 388

Kickapoo people, 334

Kidd, Kenneth, 51

King George's War, 326

King James' Bible, 466

King Phillip's War, 313, 317

King, Martin Luther, 143–4; social movement and White Paper, 497

King, Martin Luther, 283–4

King, Tom, 89

King, William Lyon Mackenzie: efforts to terminate Longhouse League and legacy of the Covenant Chain, 493, 530; efforts to undermine Deskahe's mission to the League of Nations, 490–5

King's Royal Regiment of New York: settlement of, 428

Kipling, Rudyard, 534; and imperialism as white man's burden, 478

Kirk, William: and Black

Hoof's agricultural community, 392;
Kirkness, Verna, 246
Kissinger, Henry, xxvii
Kiss of the Fur Queen, 52
Klamath people, 110
Klein, Naomi, 143–4, 219
Kleivan, Helge, 241
kleptocratic borderlands of juridical order: extraction of wealth from, 72
Knight, Allan, 221
Knowlton, Stanley, 51
Knox, Henry: secretary of war under George Washington, 216
Kojeve, Alexander, 60
Kondiaronk (Adario), 164–5, 186, 335, 359, 532
Koori Renaissance, 141
Korean War, 228
Kosovo, 27
Krech III, Shepard, 112–13
Kroeber, Alfred, 117–18
Kulchyski, Peter, 33, 51
Kuwait, 270
Kwakiutl people, 195
Kymlicka, Will: on liberalism and Aboriginal rights, 511–12

labour organizations: report of on wage differences between workers and management, 519
labour unions: as model for pan-Indian associations in Canada, 482
lacrosse (baggataway), 430–1; as source of funding for activities in Europe of Deskahe, 492
ladinos, 91, 212
La Duke, Winona, 88
Lafitau, Father Joseph François, 162, 177–8, 187
La Flesche, Francis, 194
Lahontan, baron de, 153, 177, 186–7, 319, 355, 421; and Aboriginal criticisms of French civilization, 532; role of in French Enlightenment, 163–5

laissez-faire: as basis for the expansion of us-based corporate power, 348–9
Lake Athabasca, 408
Lake of the Woods (Lac des Deux-Montagnes, Oka, Kanesatake), 329, 408, 413
Lake of Two Mountains: Roman Catholic mission at, 453
Lake Ontario, 402
Lament for a Nation, 83
"land and dignity": slogan of Aboriginal protests in Bolivia, 92
land grab: American Revolution as prelude to, 359
land reform: of Arbenz regime in Guatemala hurts United Fruit Company, 365
land speculation companies: in Clarence Alvord's interpretation of American Revolution, 361; and Continental Congress, 360; as pattern for railway companies and worldwide operations of us companies, 348; political intrigues of, 346–53; in province of Canada and Maritime provinces, 448; role of in civil war in British North America, 367; scholarship on, 347; and the United Fruit Company, 366–7. *See also* corporations, global corporations, railway companies
land speculation: America as Europe's primary, 301; as catalyst of civil war in British North America, 367; in genesis of American Revolution, 346; and genesis of Lord Dunmore's war on Shawnee people, 314; of George Washington, 349; Miriam Beard on, 373; politics of in pre-revolutionary British North America, 346–53; of Samuel Whar-

ton, 350, 360; and Sir Francis Bond Head, 435–436; and Thomas Pownall, 308–9; and William Johnson, 324
land-grant certificates: for British veterans of Seven Years' War, 349
lands reserved to Indians as hunting grounds. *See* Aboriginal and treaty rights, British North America Act, Constitution of Canada, Royal Proclamation of 1763, *St Catherine's Milling* case
languages, 45, 388, 390, 512; of Aboriginal Australia, 139; Bantu groups defined by, 505; broadcast of Aboriginal, 466; and buffalo herd loss, 218; civilizing mission and weakening of, 439; disappearance of, 218; emergence of Oji-Cree, 466; and English, 84, 252; global numbers, 62–5, 98, 218; importance for agents of imperialism, 320; Muskogean, 216; Nahuatl, 220; Oblate Order missionary outreach and French, 252; Quechua, 214; and Roger Williams, 316; Spanish in Latin America, 304; and species extinguishment, 98; Zapatista campaign for renewal of in Mexico, 145. *See also* cultural pluralism, ecology
La Roque, Emma, 246
La Salle, Robert Cavelier de, 320
Las Casas, Bartolome de, 116, 178, 211, 317; Francisco de Vitoria's theories adopted and extended by, 305; and opposition to Juan Gines de Sepulveda at Trail of Vallodia, 305
Latin America: At War with the Past, 522
Latin America: Jack Forbes

on, 282; making of,
205–17; as outgrowth of
Roman Empire through
Roman Catholic Church,
213; puppet regimes in
and governance of reser-
vations in USA, 87; reg-
istries of Indian status in,
225; repressiveness of
right-wing regimes in, 462;
subcommandante Marcos
on effect of globalization
on Indigenous peoples in,
146; US-backed Creole
regimes in, 91
law of nations, 302–3
Law Reform Commission,
Australia, 142
Lawrence, D.H., 224
Le Penn, Jean-Marie, 142
Leacock, Stephen, 152–3,
164, 500
League for Social Recon-
struction, 423
League of Indians of Canada, 253; Canadian govern-
ment and independent
funding for, 282
League of Nations of North
American Indians, 260
League of Nations: Long-
house League request for
recognition by, 268,
490–5; and Woodrow Wil-
son, 513
League of the Hau-de-no-
sau-nee. See Longhouse
League
Lee, Richard, 311
Left, the: Todd Gitlin on
balkanization of, 127
Legacy of Shingwaukonse: The,
171
legal personhood: denial of
to Indians, 476, 488–9,
510. See also enfranchisement
legalized theft of Aboriginal
lands and resources,
520–1
Leibnitz, Gottfried, 165
Lenin, Vladimir I., 232, 513,
516–17
Lenni Lape people

(Delawares) 318;
inequitable application of
criminal laws to, 354
Leopold II, King (Belgium):
claims sovereign jurisdiction over Congo River
Basin, 414
Les Damnes de la Terre, 236
Levant Company, 23
Levesque, René, 422
Levi General (Deskahe),
268; leader of Longhouse
traditionalists, 490–6
Levi-Strauss, Claude, 105,
110, 155, 177–8
Leyes de la Indias, 306
liberal democracies: and
Indigenous peoples, 119
liberal imperialist: Lord Milner as, 500–1
liberalism, 49; Bruce Clark
on, 511; and decoloniza-
tion movement, 287; and
Enlightenment ideals in
constitutional form, 532;
Francis Fukuyama on, 60;
and free trade orthodox-
ies, 79–80; George Grant
on melting-pot philosophy
of USA, 83, 298, 423; and
imposition of Euro-centric
models of nationalism on
Indigenous peoples, 235;
and Indigenous peoples,
509–15; and pluralism,
individualism, and minority rights within First
Nations, 49; and White
Paper of 1969, 278–9;
Will Kymlicka on,
511–12
Liberalism, Community and
Culture, 512
Liberation Day, Havanna,
269
Liberation Theology: stunted by Vatican role in Cold
War, 462
licence for empire, 117, 304;
and treaties with Indige-
nous peoples, 31
License for Empire: Colonization
by Treaty in Early North
America, 385

"life, liberty and the pursuit
of happiness": and John
Locke, 311–12; and prop-
erty regimes, 357–8
Lightning, Elder Albert,
496
Like a Hurricane: The Indian
Movement from Alcatraz to
Wounded Knee, 266
Limerick, Patricia, 90
Lincoln, Abraham, xxi–xxii,
opposition to Confederacy
of American States, 418
Lingiari, Vincent, 139, 151
Little Bear, Leroy, 51, 246
Little Chief, Roy, 276
Little Matter of Genocide: Holo-
caust and Denial in the
Americas, 1492 to Present,
A, 27–9
Little Moustache, Mike, 51
Little Red School House in
St Paul- Minneapolis, 244
Little Turtle, xxiii, 392
Locke, John, 107, 124, 125,
177, 179, 435; and decen-
tralist school of British
imperialism in prelude to
American Revolution,
346; influence on Declaration of Independence
through Thomas Jeffer-
son, 310–12; as theorist of
possessive individualism,
308–9; view of property
contrasted with that of
Jean-Jacques Rousseau,
182–5
Locust Grove serpent
mound, 104
Loft, Lt Fred, 253, 280, 282,
288, 482–3
London, 349–50, 408
Long Knives (Algonkian
term for Americans):
expansionism of republic
and empire of, 532; Indi-
an Confederacy opposi-
tion to preserves crown
title in Upper Canada and
Rupert's Land, 421
Long Lake reserve 17, 58
Longhouse Confederacy,
523, 532

Longhouse Government: Canadian government's attack on, 489–95

Longhouse League, 13, 55; adoption of Hurons after 1649, 382; and ambiguous Iroqois empire, 523; Canadian federal police crush, 530; clans of, 20; and Deskahe at League of Nations, 490–5, 530; Ely S. Parker as interpreter of for Lewis Henry Morgan, 195; global importance of Great Law as constitution of Aboriginal America, 268; Great White Pine of Peace as symbol of, 534; and history of sovereign alliances with imperial crown, 490; Lewis Henry Morgan on, 179–83; and Louis Hall, 276–7; as model for Tecumseh and Indian Confederacy of Canada, 385–7, 530; news of disseminated by baron de Lahontan, Lewis Henry Morgan, and Cadwallader Colden, 319; political power of split by American Revolution, 314, 386; power of in Easton Treaty in 1758 and Treaty of Fort Stanwix in 1768, 326–9, 350; and protest in 1858 against Act for the Gradual Civilization of the Indian Tribes in Canada, 483; relocation to Upper Canada, 207, 377; and Royal Proclamation, 337; Sir William Johnson and protocols of, 324–6; transition to international venues to fight for rights, 490; two-row wampum as symbol, 412. See also Covenant Chain, Six Nations Iroquois

Longone, J.B., 108

Lords of All the World, 369–70

Lords of Trade and Plantations, 322

Louisa Company, 353

Louis XIII, King: charter granted to Company of One Hundred Associates to colonize Canada, 374

Louisbourg: British capture of in 1758, 326; second British capture of, 343

Louisiana, 74: changes of jurisdiction in, 217; Edmond Aitkin on French Indian policy in, 322; La Salle's plan to link trade of with that of Canada, 322

Louisiana Purchase, 1803, 77, 217, 402, 425; consultations with Indigenous peoples, 291; and Napoleon, 395; Sioux respond to, 392

L'Overture, Toussaint, 414

Lower Canada: and British-American Land Company, 448; and Indigenous peoples, 430–1; and resistance to British imperialism, 446; and Superior Court of in Montreal, 408

Lower, Arthur, 153–4

Loyalism: and genesis of Upper Canada, 427–9; in era of American Revolution, 156; and Joseph Brant, 311–12, 429. See also conservatism, Toryism

Lubbock, John, 181

Luhan, Mabel Dodge, 224

Lussier, Antoine, 51

Luther, Martin, 185

Luxenbourg, 270

Lyons, Oren, 246

The Learneds (Learned Societies of Canada), 3–4

Mabo case, 1992, 31, 33, 118, 137–8, 139; wording of Australian High Court, 140

Macdonald, John A.: and Louis Riel and Manitoba Act, 455; and parliamentary debate on extending franchise to registered Indians, 474–80, 496; and

St. Catherine's Milling case, 415, 476

MacDonald, Peter, 88

Macdonell, Allan: and estate of Sir William Johnson, 449–50; and Sihingwaukonse press for crown recognition of Aboriginal title north of Great Lakes, 449–53, 530

Mackay, Chief Gerry, 513–14

Mackenzie, Alexander: and Indian Act of 1876, 476

Mackenzie, William Lyon: leader of revolt for annexation of Canada to USA, 493–4; seeks American help to "liberate" Upper Canada from British yolk, 446

Mackinac Island, 14

Mackinaw Island, 100

Macpherson, C.B., 308–9

Magubane, Bernard Makhosezwe, 499–501

Maine, Henry Sumner, 181

Mairosi, Chief: and Basuto resistance to Cape Colony in South Africa, 502

maize, 105–8

Majority World: Titus Alexander on extraction of wealth from, 517

Makaw people, 87

Making of a Racist State, 499–501

Malcolm X: as Black separatist, 284

Maliseet people, 38, 314, 343

Mandan people, 108

Mandela, Nelson, 282, 393; and majority rule for Black people in South Africa, 508, 521; and racialized economy inherited from colonialism, 521

Manette, Ottawa wife of John Askin, 170

Manifest Destiny: and American expansionism, xii–xiii, xxvi, xxviii, 74–85, 453; and British triumphalism, 152–3; exploitation of by corporate executives, 123; and global expansion of Columbian conquests, 523; and global property law, 123; incursions of into Mexico, 222–3; justification of through moral relativism, 135; and Puritans of New England, 307–8; as reflected in US history, 364; and Social Darwinism, 227; and War of 1812, 172; and Western Civilization, 374. *See also* American empire, American empire of private property, United States of America

Manifesto of the Native Peoples' Caravan of 1974, 270–4

Manitoba Legislature, 17–18, 198, 205

Manitoba: and Aboriginal incarceration, 262; and conflict over border with Ontario, 416; flooding of northern portion of, 44, 132, 247; and Meech Lake accord, 198

Manitoulin Island: and Indian removal policy of Sir Francis Bond Head, 436–7; present distribution ceremonies at, 191; Roman Catholic defence of Indian rights on, 132; as stronghold of Jesuits Order, 454; Wah-kai-keghik and Misheguong-pai debate fate of, 454–5; Wikwemikong Indians refuse to cede, 454

Manitowabi, Edna and Liza, 51

Manitowaning: present distribution ceremonies at, 191

Mankiller, Wilma, 88

manomin (wild rice), 111–12, 120

Manomin Law, 111–12

Manuel, George, 55, 99, 117, 195, 204, 359; analy-
sis of class and economic relations in Indian Canada, 283–6; anticipates larger role for Indian nations, 298; as bridge builder among Indigenous peoples, 258; and Clarence Alvord, 361; and federal funding, 282; honesty of, 283; and leadership at National Indian Brotherhood, 277; life and ideas of, 238–92; and place of First Nations, 286–9; as prophet of globalization, 151; and relationship to Tupac Amaru, Pontiac, and Tecumseh, 400, 533; and Robert Satiacum, 263; role of American Indian Movement in setting stage for, 262; and self-determination of peoples, 237–8. *See also* Fourth World

Maori peoples, 117, 147–9. *See also* Treaty of Waitangi

Mapuche peoples: murders of by Augusto Pinochet's regime, 463

Maracle, Brian, 246

Marchand, Senator Len, 280

Marcos, Subcommandante: on heritage of Indigenous peoples, 534; on neo-liberal globalization and Aboriginal rights in Mexico, 145–6. *See also* Zapatista Liberation Army, Zapatistas

Mariategui, Jose Carlos, 223

Marines: take control of Mexican port of Veracruz in 1914, 222

Maritime Indian Treaty of 1760–1, 38–9, 343–4

market fundamentalism: as basis of new totalitarianism, 136; Karl Polanyi on, 187–9

Marlboro Country, 296

Marquis de Mirabeau, 456

Marshall case, 30, 38–9, 344

Marshall Plan, 228

Marshall, Chief Justice John:
Supreme Court rulings of, 404–5, 414–16, 418–19, 526

Marshall, Donald, Jr, 38, 344

Marule, Jake, 238

Marule, Marie Smallface, 238

Marx, Karl, 124, 127, 177–82, 186, 235

Marxism: and Subcommandante Marcos, 144; and Columbian conquests, 336; and Lewis Henry Morgan, 179. *See also* communism

Maryland: founding charter of, 306–7

Mascouten people, 334

Mashanttucket Pequot people, 87

mass consumerism: North America as heartland of, 246; as stimulated by expansion and homogenization, 218

Massachusetts Bay Company, 149, 306; John Cotton on patent affording legitimacy to, 316; and mission to Christianize Indians, 374

Massachusetts, 162–3; and relations between Roger Williams, Narraganset Indians, and Rhode Island, 316–17

Mather, Cotton: and extremes of Puritan zealotry, 309

Matthiessen, Peter, 90, 178

Mauritius, 270

Mayan people, 61, 79; and Aboriginal civilization in the Americas, 96; and calendar and mathematics, 103; and genocide in Guatemala, 91, 365–6; and Indianness, 93; support Zapatista Liberation Army, 92; and Zapatistas, 143

Maybury-Lewis, David, 366

McCue, Harvey, 51, 245

McDougall, Revs. George and John, 193

McDougall, William: and Manitoulin Island, 454–5
McGill University, 152–3, 229
McGill, James, 156, 401
McGillvray, Alexander: as leader of Creek Confederacy, 216–18, 456, 530
McKee, Alexander and Thomas, 390
McLuhan, Marshall: extends Harold Innis's work on communications, 298
McNab, Allan: as Tory politician and railway promoter, 448
McNab, Dave, 51
McTavish, Simon, 14–15
Mead, Margaret, 127
Meadow Lake Tribal Council, 85
Means, Russell, 272–3
Mecham, J. Lloyd: on powers of Roman Catholic Church in New Spain, 460
Medicine, Beatrice, 246
Meech Lake accord, 17, 196, 199, 205
melting pot: Indian New Deal implies criticism of, 368
Melting Tallow, Dave, 51
Men of the Last Frontier, 166
Menchu, Rigoberta, 91–3, 463
Mennonites, 378
Menominee people, 111, 334
mercantilism, 182; and capitalism and Adam Smith's Wealth of Nations, 6, 182 ; and rise of Montreal, 345; Royal Proclamation and Quebec Act as British imperial instruments of, 342–3
"merciless Indian savages": in American Declaration of Independence, 311–12, 494
Mercredi, Ovide, 51, 88, 89
mercury poisoning, 273
Mescalero Apache people, 85

Mesoamerica, 103, 107, 143
mestizaje, 171; process in Mexico anticipates larger global patterns, 225
mestizo, 92, 211, 466; and blending of identities in Latin America, 461; and identity in Mexico, Latin America, and French-Aboriginal Canada, 217, 224; and Mexico's personality, 221–2; and middle ground, 247; role of churches in genesis of, 461. See also Intermarriage, Métis
Metacom (King Phillip): as Wampanoag sachem, 313
Methodist Indian Missions in Upper Canada, 174–6, 194
Methodist missionary work, 174–6, 192–3; Aboriginal ministry of Upper Canada, 194; and Haida aristocrat, Rev. Peter Kelly, 350
Métis: in Canada and throughout Western Hemisphere, 92; conflict at Seven Oaks between Hudson's Bay Company settlers and, 447; and constitutional politics in Canada, 203; legal implications of Canada's recognition of Indians, Inuit, and Métis as Aboriginal peoples, 231, 530–1; and movement of Scots Highlanders into Indian Country of Canada and Cherokee and Creek clans, 455–8; and Native Council of Canada, 266; numbers of in Sault Ste Marie area, 171–2; Orangemen's role in repressing Louis Riel and, 223; and Orkney Islanders, 457; prominence of mixed-ancestry families in early Upper Canada, 171; relationship with canadiens, 155, 456; Richard White on, 247;

Roman Catholic support of, 132, 455, 461; Saskatchewan government and, 254. See also intermarriage, mestizo
metissage: fur trade and culture of, 171
Metlakata: Rev. William Duncan's Anglican theocracy for Tsimshian people, 465
Mexican Constitution: section 27 of, 220–1
Mexican Revolution, 143, 220–2
Mexico City, 32, 81; Museum of Anthropology, 221; and Tenochtitlan, 103
Mi'kmaq (Micmac, Micmaw) people, 38–9, 48, 238, 343, 429, 496
Miami people, 334
Mica Bay, 451
Michif: language of Métis, 64–5
Michigan Territory, 375
Michigan, 375
Michilmackinac, 332, 399; adopted white captives settle in, 383
Middle East, 374
middle ground, 49, 171, 178, 213; Richard White on, 247, 298,
Middle Ground: Indians, Empires, and Republics in the Great Lakes Region, 1650–1895, The, 247, 298
Midewiwin Society, 194
Milando, Mbuto: as Tanzanian source of term "Fourth World," 238
militarization of space, 130, 527
Mill, John Stuart, 235
Milloy, John, 51
Mills, David: and enfranchisement of Indian peoples, 476–8; involvement in Ontario's border dispute and St Catherine's Milling case, 476–7
Milner, Lord: as Liberal Imperialist, 500–1
Milosevic, Slobodan, 44–5

Minavavana, 332–3

Mingo people, 334

mining industry: in Australia, 142; in Canada, 297, 446–53; rush after 1973 to exploit resources in North America, 244

Ministry of Aboriginal Affairs, Australia, 139

Ministry of Maori Development, New Zealand, and Mutilateral Agreement on Investment, 148

Minnesota: and Aboriginal incarceration, 262

Misheguong-pai: and reasons to accept Manitoulin Island Treaty, 455

Mississauga people: agricultural settlements of at Grape Island and Credit mission, 436

Mississippi Company, 349

Mississippi River: as boundary between Indian and non-Indian people, 403, 418, 434

Mississippi Valley in British Politics: A Study of Trade, Land Speculation, and Experiments in Imperialism Culminating in the American Revolution, The, 54, 361–2

Mississippi Valley: Indians from northern reaches of attend present distribution ceremonies, 191; northern reaches of integral to New France and to fur trade of British imperial Canada, 375

Missouri, 108

Mitchell, Mike, 51, 100, 246

modern-day treaties, 117–18; and Aboriginal title, 356; Bill Vander Zalm on, 40; and creation of corporations, 24; as instrument to extinguish or renew Indian Country, 159; and intercultural democracy, 157; international implications of Canadian, 159; with Inuvialuit of Beaufort

Sea, Inuit of Nunavut, and Nisga'a of British Columbia, 24; James Bay and Northern Quebec Agreement of 1975 as, 280, 431; negotiation of in Canada after 1973, 158–9. *See also* crown-Aboriginal treaties, Indian treaties, Nisga'a Treaty, numbered treaties, Nunavut

modernization theory: rejection of by proponents of Fourth World, 240

Modoc people, 110

Mohawk people, 10, 17–18, 145, 265, 267–8, 276–7, 319, 379, 382, 430, 438, 479; and Act for the Gradual Civilization of the Indian Tribes in Canada, 1857, 483; and adoption of Huron people after 1629, 382. *See also* Covenant Chain, Longhouse League, Six Nations Iroquois

Mohawk Valley, 8, 12, 15, 20, 55, 325, 377, 402, 450

Mohawk Warriors, 17–18, 199, 265

Mohawk Workers Club: RCMP undercover agent in, 492

Mohawk, John, 100, 246

Mohegan Indians v. Connecticut, 1704, 211, 339–40; and constitutional principles codified in Royal Proclamation, 337–8

Momaday, N. Scott, 88, 98–9, 245

monarchy: and absolutist claims of Vatican in colonies, 303; and acquisition of lands of Indigenous peoples, 301; and Anglo-American rejection of, 336–63; and British imperial Indian Department, 323–4; and colonization companies, 306; and conquests and discoveries of New World, 303;

and control over Indian policy in Anglo-American colonies after 1664, 320–1; George Manuel and Canada's shift away from, 288; and protection of Indigenous peoples in colonies, 211, 321; and recognition of Aboriginal and treaty rights, 288; and supremacy of parliament, 308; Thomas Jefferson on British, 311; Tupac Amaru on, 289. *See also* conservatism, sovereignty, Toryism

Monk, Judge Samuel Cornwallis: on legitimacy of Aboriginal customs and law in Indian Country of Canada, 408–14

Monocultures of the Mind, 60–1

monocultures: and agriculture, 63, 107–12; in American empire, 288; Andean farmers oppose, 25; and beneficiaries of imperialism, 520; and commodification of nature, 150, 218; Cotton Mathers and, 309; and demise of linguistic pluralism and biological diversity, 218; and democracy, 61; and economic theory, 70, 218; expansion of rooted in "weeding" out Indians, 185; expression of, 65; and extinguishment of Indigenous peoples, 110–11; Fourth World opposition to, 358, 530; and global corporations, 60, 70, 73, 207, 218; and Lockean ideals of property relations, 369; and neo-liberal fundamentalism, 134; and neo-liberalism, 115; NGO opposition to, 73; opponents of require new legal and political tools, 94, 358; in opposition to Royal Proclamation and Quebec

Act, 345–6; and possessive individualism, 509; Samuel P. Huntington on, 96–9; and story telling, 115; in Third World thinking, 241; and universal and homogenous state, 65; unsustainability of, 299; and US info-entertainment industry, 218; and US melting pot liberalism, 82–3, 298, 423; Vandana Shiva on, 60; WTO as symbol of, 80. *See also* American empire of private property, cultural pluralism, ecology, Fourth World, languages

monotheism: connection to universalist faith in applicability of capitalism, 369–70

Monroe Doctrine, xxv, 147, 215, 364

Monsanto Company, 24, 149

Montalban, Manuel Vasquez, 143

Montana Territory, 375

Montana, 86, 375

Montcalm, General, 328

Montezuma, Carlos, 195, 282; crusade against US Bureau of Indian Affairs, 256–7

Montmagny, Charles Huault de: and derivation of name Onontio, 329

Montour, Laurie, 51

Montreal, 14, 388; Board of Trade support Indians during War of 1812, 401–2; and burning of Province of Canada legislative building, 448; and *Connolly v. Woolich*, 408–9; and Scottish entrepreneurs in fur trade, 375–6; and vigilantism in 1990, 199

Montt, Gen. Efrain Rios: and crimes against humanity in Guatemala in 1980s, 366

moon of wampum: and bowl with one spoon, 385

Moon, Chief John, 51

Mooney, James, 101

moral relativism, 134–6

Moravian missionaries: and mission to Indians in Upper Canada led by David Zeisberger, 377; and teachings of Neolin, 331

More, Thomas, 177

Morgan, Col. C.E.: role in South Africa and in Six Nations reserve, 492

Morgan, J.P., 84

Morgan, Louis Henry, 127, 177–82, 186, 194, 195

Morisset, Jean, 51, 155, 199

Morita, Akio, 67, 69, 71–2, 80, 83

Morris, Alexander, 47, 49

Morrisseau, Norval, 244–5, 530

Morse, Brad, 51

Moses, 121

Mostert, Noel, 442, 445

Mother Maize and King Corn, 108

mound builders of North America, 104–5

Mountain Horse, Mike, 280

Mowat, Oliver: attack on Aboriginal and treaty rights through *St Catherine's Milling* case, 415–417, 477

Mulroney, Brian: and comparison of treatment of Indigenous peoples in Canada and South Africa, 497

multiculturalism, 61, 65; Canada's official recognition of, 206; and Enlightenment ideals, 132; within Hispanic identity, 121; and imperialists advocating central authority embodied in Royal Proclamation and Quebec Act, 345; and Indian New Deal, 368; and Jesuit missionary work in New

France, 162; and mosaic or melting pot, 157; New Right condemns, 128; opposition to official recognition of, 61, 97, 128; Samuel Huntington on, 97; of United Empire Loyalists, 378; White Paper of 1969 as introduction to Pierre Trudeau's policy of, 278. *See also* cultural pluralism, Fourth World

Multilateral Agreement Investment: failed effort to entrench, 73; as initiative to protect owners of capital, 521–2; language of appropriated from civil rights movement, 522; Maori resistance to, 148. *See also* commercial trade treaties

murder of Indian people: George Croghan and William Johnson on, 354

Murray, William, 360; and establishment of Illinois-Wabash Company, 349, 353

Muscovy Company, 23

Muskego Cree (Swampy Cree), 466

Muskogean-speaking peoples, 392; Alexander McGillvray leads Creek confederacy of, 216

Muskokman, Harry, 280

Musqueam people, 259

Myers, Mike, 100

Nabigon, Herb, 51

Nader, Ralph, 88

Nahdoways: Algonkian term for Six Nations Iroquois, 386

Nah-nee-ba-we-quay (Catherine Sutton), 484–5, 530

Nahuatl-speaking peoples: Emiliano Zapata as representative of, 221

Nanabozoo. *See* Nanabush

Nanabush, 52, 102

Napi, 52, 102

Napoleon, 186; role in transfer of European title to
Louisiana from France to
the United States, 395
Napoleonic Wars, 216–17,
395–6
Narranganselt people: extend
legitimacy to Rhode Island
through negotiation of
treaty with Roger
Williams, 317
Naticoke people, 377
National Aboriginal Conference, Australia, 139
National Congress of American Indians, 59, 259, 263,
283
National Indian Brother-
hood, 238, 242, 248,
265–6, 277, 280; and
Assembly of First Nations,
260; George Manuel and
federal funding of, 282–5;
and links to government
of Pierre Trudeau, 275;
and political legacy of
North American Indian
Brotherhood and National
Indian Council, 260; and
World Council of Indige-
nous Peoples, 248
National Indian Council,
Canada, 260
National Indian Youth Council, 262, 269–70, 285
nationalism, 61; in Australia,
137–42; Frantz Fanon on,
236–7; genesis of in Latin
America, 209–17; John
Collier and Manuel Gamio
on Aboriginal cultures
and, 224; Mahatma Gand-
hi on, 235; and peoples'
rights, 231. See also decolonization
National Lacrosse Association, USA, 431
national security: United
States Commission on,
527–9; US conceptions of
override international law,
130
National Tribal Chairmen's
Association: allegations of

manipulation of through
federal funding, 272
Native Alliance for Red
Power: in Vancouver, 275
Native American Construc-
tion Company, 88
Native American Embassy,
271
Native American Studies,
266; Vine Deloria as official dean of, 291
Native Americans, 83–4,
124–5; and American
jurisprudence, 415–21;
John Locke and Jean-
Jacques Rousseau on,
179–89; migration to
Canada from USA, 207;
and occupation of Alca-
traz Island, 266; political
activism of, 245–77; and
privatized systems of land
tenure, 186; reduction in
numbers of, 134; school-
ing of, 244; and tax-
exempt status in USA, 263;
as university professors,
245; Vine Deloria on, 245.
See also First Nations, Indians, Indigenous peoples
Native Brotherhood of
British Columbia, 251;
dominance of by Protes-
tant leaders, 254
Native Liberty, Crown Sovereignty, 511–12
Native Peoples' Caravan,
274–5
Native Peoples' Embassy:
established on Victoria
Island in Ottawa in 1974,
275
Native Rights in Canada:
effect of on Canadian
jurisprudence, 265
Native Studies: as distinct
academic field in Canada
and USA, 266
Native Titles Act, Australia,
1993, 140, 142; similarity
of with Canadian instru-
ments, 159
Native Women's Association
of Canada: and Canadian

Charter of Rights and
Freedoms in Indian Coun-
try, 485; politics of anticipated by those of Nah-nee-
ba-we-quay, 485. See also
Aboriginal women, gender
relations
nativist movements, 257–8
natural history: as survival of
the fittest, 227
natural law: abuses of by
moral relativists, 135; and
capitalism, 370; false conceptions of, 68; and genocide, 134; identification
of, 125; Jesuitical texts on,
163; and natural right,
122; and notions of Abo-
riginal inferiority, 133;
Polanyi on markets and,
71–2; and privatization,
134; Social Darwinists on,
226–7; and the social sciences, 125–34; Vandana
Shiva on, 60–1
natural right: and Enlightenment, 121–5; and land
speculation, 353; and
Manifest Destiny, 76; and
natural law, 122
natural selection: Charles
Darwin's theory of, 226–7
natural servitude: Juan Gines
de Sepulveda on, 305
naturales: alternative term
for indios, 211
Navajo people, 88, 113, 190
Navajo-Hopi Land Dispute,
88
Nazi Germany: and Adolf
Hitler, 167, 498; and Darwinian master-race fan-
tasies, 495; and develop-
ment of Aboriginal
organizations in Canada,
253; and Enlightenment's
egalitarian idealism, 414;
eugenic totalitarianism of,
478; and racist applica-
tions of Social Darwinism,
228; and Theodore Roo-
sevelt's Winning of the West,
478; and US financiers and
industrialists, 471

Ndobele people, 505
Nebennigoebing: role in negotiation of Robinson Treaties, 449–50
neo-colonialism: in governance of North America's Indian Country, 285
neo-liberalism, 40, 68; in Australia, 141; and ecological crisis, 120; Francis Fukuyama and, 99; as fundamentalist creed, 134; and GATT and NAFTA, 92; and global corporations, 509–10; globalization of, 219; Indigenous peoples as critics of, 80–1; in international treaties, 290–1; and New Right, 188–9; in New Zealand, 148; Pierre Trudeau's advocacy of, 278–9; and privilege, 144; and property law in Indian treaties, 118; and Zapatistas, 143–6. See also commodification, global corporations, monocultures, private property, property law, property regimes, property relations
Neolin: and Pontiac, 330–1; as model for relationship between Tenskwatawa and Tecumseh, 335, 389
Netherlands: Protestantism of and colonialism, 303; supports Deskahe at League of Nations, 491
Neutral people, 319
New Brunswick: Mi'kmaq and Maliseet peoples, 429, 473
New Deal, 258, 368; Indian New Deal in Saskatchewan, 254; and Native Americans, 223–4; United Nations as extension of, 229
New Democratic Party, 423
New England Company, 309
New England, 13–4, 116, 122, 162–3, 174, 211, 369; Puritan view of, 308; role of religion in settle-

ment of, 305–10; violence towards Indians, 185
New France, 12–13, 28–9, 174; conquest of, 297; Edmond Aitkin on French-Indian policy in, 322–3; French-Indian relations in, 322, 500; fur trade community of, 376; fur trade south of Great Lakes in, 375; and Huronia, 106–7; and incorporation into British Empire, 322; Indian alliance with, 313; and Indian resistance, 383; Jesuit authors and baron de Lahontan on, 162–5; La Salle's plan to link with Louisiana, 320; less violent than New England, 185; missionary work in, 162–3; posts in, 383; Roman Catholic Church and Aboriginal rights and title in, 453; and Royal Proclamation, 338; Samuel de Champlain and, 319; and Sir William Johnson, 325. See also France, French in America
New Granada: vice-royalty of in New Spain, 210
New Israel: New England conceived by Puritans as, 308
New Jersey, 51
New Mexico, 37, 85, 86, 211, 224
New Netherlands, 13, 28, 55, 117, 124; and Covenant Chain, 363; fur trade and treaty making with Indigenous peoples in, 318–20; and Huronia, 319; as model for French-Indian relations after conquest of Canada, 322, 363, 500; as model for South Africa, 500; and Royal Proclamation, 337; wampum in, 318–19
New Orleans, 9, 217
New Right, 80; and assump-

tions about its history, 132–3; and attack on relativism, 127–8; dogmatism and narrow materialism of, 188
New South Wales, 174
New Spain, 26, 28, 55, 117, 319; and Aboriginal civilization of the Americas, 178; and Black Legend, 305–6; clergy in, 460; and Creole rebels, 209–13, 215; crown-Indian alliances in, 305; as extension of heritage of Roman Empire, 374; Herman Cortes's divide-and-conquer techniques, 317; influence of in Upper Canada, 217; laws of colonization developed by, 303–6; legacy of in USA, 217; as neighbouring polity to USA, 216–18; protection of rights of Indigenous peoples in, 321; Tupac Amaru's revolt against, 213–15
New Sweden, 117, 319
new white nation, 207, 403; Sioux characterization of USA as, 392
New World Coming, 527
New World Order, 74, 83; Anthony Pagden on international monetary organizations in, 369–70; crown-Aboriginal treaties in, 156; George W. Bush and war on Iraq, 69, 368; and global corporations, 84–5; Indigenous peoples in, xxiv, 154; marginalizing of weakest members of society in, 119; and Old World Ecological Order, 101
New World: Akio Morita (Sony Corporation) on changing economic order, 68, 97; Alcatraz Island as reminder of maltreatment of Indigenous peoples in, 267; civilizing mission of, 174; distinction between

settlers of from both European mother countries and Indigenous peoples, 210, 469; and empire, 20, 66, 147, 152; fortune seekers in, 305; Frederick Jackson Turner on, 168–9; and high finance, 84; Indigenous peoples as obstacles to, 71; lack of soul in countries of, 153–4; meaning of encapsulated in American revolutionaries, 358–9; as place to extend old civilizations or invent new ones, 138; and proprietorships, 72; reports from in genesis of social sciences, 177–89; social engineering of Indigenous peoples in, 176; supposed discovery of, 4–5; term for the Americas after 1492, 144; Thomas Jefferson on, 215; and Tom Flanagan on retardation of Indigenous peoples in, 127; and treatment of Indigenous peoples, 302

New York, 129–30, 312–13, 350, 373, 384, 430, 445, 500,

New York Colony: establishment of and development of Covenant Chain, 322; and Indian treaties, 117

New York Indians, 268: Alice Lee Jemison on, 258; Richard Oakes and Mad Bear Anderson in occupation of Alcatraz Island, 268. See also Akwesasne, Six Nations Iroquois

New York Times, 85, 87

New Zealand, 31, 36, 117, 147–9, 160, 174, 214, 220, 239, 287, 289, 355, 502; Treaty of Waitangi, 258

Newberry, Ed, 51

Newfoundland: and Beothuck people, 275

Newton, Isaac, 182

Nez Perces people: and Chief Joseph's failed attempt to reach Canada, 207

Niagara, 20, 155, 329, 331

Niagra Council of 1764, 155

Nicauragua, 222, 224

Nigeria, 150–1, 160, 224, 521

Nisga'a case, 1973, 140, 142, 158, 251, 280

Nisga'a people, 40, 55, 158; and Aboriginal title, 251

Nisga'a Treaty, 24, 29, 40, 55, 117–18

Nishnawbe Institute: established at Toronto's Rochdale College, 275–6

noble savage: depiction of Indians as inhabitants of Garden of Eden, 114; Jean-Jaques Rousseau on, 124; in literary legacy of Jesuits and baron de Lahontan, 162–5; Richard White and Shepard Kreech III on, 112–13

non-government organizations (NGOs): and founding of United Nations, 229; and growth of transnational civil society, 90; and monocultural imperialism of global corporatism, 73

Norman Conquest, 1066: Thomas Jefferson on, 311

North American Free Trade Agreement, 30, 425; and constitutional politics in the Americas, 205–6, 290; and Free Trade of the Americas, 94; and unity of continent, 99; and Zapatista narratives of resistance, 118; and Zapatista opposition to, 78–9, 143

North American Free Trade Authority, 22, 44, 94, 119

North American Indian Brotherhood: as Andy Paull's personal vehicle, 260; founding of in

Ottawa in 1994, 254, 259

North American Indian Travelling College, 100

North Atlantic Community, 154; genesis of, 160–1

North Atlantic Treaty Organization, 27, 44–5; bombing campaign of, 131, 234; and genocidal heritage of North Atlantic community, 84; as symbol of transatlantic community, 160–1; US leadership of during Cold War, 228; US military power in Europe based in, 369

North Carolina: and Yamasee War, 313

North, Lord, 376

North Peigan, Glen, 51

North Shore Indians: Vancouver lacrosse team coached by Andy Paull, 431

North West Company, 14, 16, 47, 154–5; as basis of British imperialism in North America, 375; and decline of fur trade, 408; and merger with Hudson's Bay Company in 1821, 297

Northern Division of the British Imperial Indian Department, 12, 170; as seed of English-speaking Canada, 324; Sir William Johnson's role in, 322–6

Northern Sotho people, 505

Northern Territory, Australia, 139

Northwest Ordinance, 1787: as imperial mission, 372–4

North-West Territories: and War of 1812, 421

Northwest Territory, 416; and Canada, 380; and Northwest Ordinance of 1787, 372–4; perceptions of among Indian groups, US citizens, and some British imperialists, 371–80

Norton, John (Teyonin-
hokarawen), 170; and
Aborigines Protection
Society, 457–8
Norway House, 408
Norway, 160, 241–2, 521
Nova Scotia, 412: enclosures
of Micmac and Maliseet
peoples in, 474; as Loyalist
jurisdiction in American
Revolution, 312; Royal
Proclamation directs set-
tlement towards, 343;
treaties with Indigenous
peoples in, 38, 343–4
nuclear waste sites, 85
numbered treaties, 29, 158;
Canadian prairies as heart-
land of, 253
Nunavut, 24, 48, 117
Nuremberg Trial, 27
Nyerere, Julius, 239–40

Oakes, Richard, 267–8
Oblate Order: as missionar-
ies to Indians of Canada,
252; and relationship to
French language, 252
O'Brien, Conor Cruise, 76,
122, 129
Occidental Petroleum Com-
pany, 90–1
Occum, Samson, 166–7
O'Chiese, Peter, 51
Odawa people: and resis-
tance to ceding of Mani-
toulin Island, 454
Odenak: settlement of
Abenaki people, 329
Odjig, Daphne, 244–5
Ogoni people, 150–1
Ohio River, 423; direct purchase of lands from Indi-
ans at juncture with Mississippi River, 349; Indian
Country north of, 380–7;
Indian groups west of
viewed as subservient peoples, 386; Indian leaders
split over boundary of territory at Muskingum River
or at, 387; Tecumseh and
Indian Confederacy
defend lands north of,

388–402; Treaty of Fort
Stanwix as boundary of
reserved Indian territory,
350–1; visions of North
America's future in lands
north of, 371–80;
wampum belts describe
land north of as shared
domain of Indian Confed-
eracy, 385–6
Ohio Territory: transformation into Ohio state, 375
Ohio Valley: Seven Years'
War as struggle over con-
trol of, 326–35, 523; de
La Salle's views on, 320
Ojibway people, 52, 102,
111, 171–2, 334, 450; and
commercialized agricul-
ture, 436; Midewiwin Society of, 194; migration
from USA to Canada, 207;
and Quebec Mining Com-
pany, 451; Robinson-
Huron Treaty and Robin-
son-Superior Treaty and,
452–3
Ojibway Warriors' Society,
227–8, 273–5, 282, 285
Oji-Cree people, 198, 466
Oka, 17, 166; conflict at in
1990, 199–200, 203, 514;
and Roman Catholic mis-
sion, 453. See also Kanesatake, Lake of Two Moun-
tains
Old Northwest: transformation from land of the bowl
with one spoon to US
industrial heartland,
78–9
Old Testament: colonization
by God's Chosen People
and, 470; destruction of
Aztec culture and, 104;
Edmond Burke and, 76;
Thomas Hart Benton and,
185
Old World of Indigenous
Peoples, 84, 205, 243–4,
205; power to absorb and
assimilate immigrants
from Europe, 169
old-growth forests: destruc-

tion of, 218; in Temagami,
18
Oldman River Dam, 54
On the Indians Lately Discov-
ered, 304
Onabigon, Bertha, 51
one big market, 68, 72, 74;
entire planet as, 530
One Nation Party, Australia,
141–2, 509
One World, Ready or Not, 67
Oneida people, 12; and pur-
chase of land, 483; and
response to Act for the
Gradual Civilization of the
Indian Tribes in Canada,
483; Wisconsin and New
York state groups of, 88
Onondaga Council House,
173–4
Onondaga people, 12, 382,
523; and adoption of
Hurons after 1649, 382
Onontio: term for governor
of New France in Indian
Country, 329–30, 334
Ononwarogo (Red Head):
Sir William Johnson,
325
Ontario, 375, 430; position
between Old World impe-
rialism of the British
Empire and New World
commercialism of Ameri-
can empire, 428–9; and St
Catherine's Milling case,
414–21, 428–9. See also
Upper Canada
Ontario Provincial Police,
274, 474
Operation Condor, 91
oral tradition, 52, 102; and
silencing of Aboriginal
languages, 118
Orange Free State: Afrikaner
founding of, 442
Orange Order: and suppression of Roman Catholic
Métis in western Canada,
223
Oregon Territory, 74
Organization for Economic
Co-operation and Devel-
opment: legacy of racial

hierarchy in, 517; and
MAI, 522
Organization of American
States: and Inter-American
Indigenista Institute, 224
*Origin of the Family, Private
Property and the State,*
179–82
original sin of America: theft
of a hemisphere through
fraud inherent in the doc-
trine of discovery, 315
Origins of Inequality, The,
124–5
Orkney Islands, 457
Orkneymen, 457
Ortiz, Alfonso, 246
Ortiz, Roxanne Dunbar, 246
Orzozo, Clemente, 221
Osage people, 392
Osceola: Red Stick refugee
from the Creeks who led
Seminoles in guerrilla
resistance in Florida, 396
Osnaburgh reserve: Chiefs
Roy Kaminawash and
Gerry Mackay host
Desmond Tutu of the
African National Congress
on tour of, 514
O'Sullivan, John, 75, 79
Oswego: opening of road to
by Sir William Johnson,
325
Otomi people, 222
Ottawa Evening Herald: letters
of R.V. Sinclair criticizing
Canadian Indian policy,
488
Ottawa people (Odawa):
immigration from USA to
Canada, 207; resistance to
Manitoulin Treaty, 454–5;
and Sir Francis Bond
Head, 433–8
outside agitators: Chief
Richard Wilson's criticism
of American Indian Move-
ment as, 272
overlapping sovereignty: in
international system, 234

Pacific Coast Native Fishermen's Association, 251

pacification, 227
Pagden, Anthony, 337,
369–70
Paine, Robert, 241–2
Paine, Thomas, 37, 40, 362;
on land as natural fund of
America, 335
Pakeha: term for non-Maori
of New Zealand, 148–9
Palestine, xxiii, 161
Panama, 210, 224
pan-Indianism, 378; Aboriginal activism and, 238–92;
and Christian residential
schools, 252; George
Manuel as proponent of,
238, 289; and Indian Con-
federacy of Canada, 320,
376–87, 398–9; and New
England's Indian Wars,
313; and World Council of
Indigenous Peoples, 55,
155, 241, 248. *See also*
American Indian Move-
ment, Fourth World,
Indigenous Peoples
Papal Bull of Demarcation,
1493; and donation by
pope of the Americas to
Spain and Portugal, 303–4
Papen, Robert A., 64–5
Papineau, Denis-Benjamin:
and rejection of Ojibway
claims, 451
Papineau, Louis-Joseph: and
uprising of 1837 in Lower
Canada, 446
Paraguay, 224
Parker, Arthur C., 257
Parker, Ely S., 195
Parker, Quanah, xviii
Parkman, Francis, 194; on
Pontiac, 335
Parliamentary Committee on
Aborigines in British Set-
tlements, 499
partition, 33–4; Europeans
in Africa and, 225; limita-
tions of in international
law, 233–4; and possibility
of Quebec independence,
200
Pas-de-nom, Susanne:
William Connolly's mar-

riage to subject of *Connolly
v. Woolich,* 408
Passamaquody, 28, 343
passports: of Six Nations Iroquois accepted by Cuba,
269
patois, 212
patriarchal monogamy:
Lewis Henry Morgan on,
180
patriation: of Canadian Constitution, 196–206
Patriot, The: and Allan Macdonell on crown's recognition of Aboriginal title,
452
Paull, Andy: George Manuel
as protégé of, 256; as
hockey and lacrosse
coach, 431; and Indian
politics in British Columbia, 258; life and times of,
250–4; political activities
of, 280
Pawnee people, 190
Pearce, Roy Henry, 90, 222
Pearson, Lester, 97
Pearson, Noel, 141
Peguis reserve: visit of South
African ambassador Glenn
Babb to, 514
Peigan Lonefighters Society,
54
Peigan people, 54, 276
Peigan reserve: and Nelson
Small Legs Jr, 276
Peltier, Leonard, 19, 89,
207; conviction for mur-
der, 272
Pemberton, Israel, 327
Penn, William, 317–18, 324
Pennsylvania, 117; Indian
treaties on, 351
Pentagon: attack on,
129–30, 245
people's treaties: at Rio
Earth Summit, 157
peoples, 524; betrayal of
rights and titles of in
decolonization after the
Second World War,
228–38; coalitions of resist
New World imperialism,
117; configurations of, 52;

nationalism and sovereignty of, 231; death sentence on from one big market, 68; Derek Rasmussen on, 48; and dilemmas of liberalism, 509–10; division of into entitled minority and dispossessed majority, 520; George Manuel on, 291; global crisis in governance of, 21; international implications of constitutional identification in Canada of Indians, Inuit, and Métis as, 199, 231; international protection of, 131; Jean Morisset on Métis and *les peuples canadien*, 155; League of Nations' and United Nations' position on, 230–1, 513; as primary collective unit in legitimacy of United Nations, 66, 230, 513; require diversity of property regimes, 358; Thomas Guillaume Raynal on governance of all, 7, 231; Woodrow Wilson on right of self-determination of all, 222, 357, 491, 513. *See also* Decolonisation, distinct peoples, Fourth World, Indigenous peoples, self-determination

Peoria people, 334

Pequot people, 24, 313, 317; of Mashantucket, 87

Pequot War of 1637; role of Puritan-Narragansett alliance in, 317

person: Indians denied legal status as, 509–10

Peru, 93, 213–15, 223, 224

Peters, Omer, 280

Petrofina Corporation, 86

Petrotyranny, 366

Phear, John Budd, 181

Philadelphia, 350– 1

Philippines, 366

Phillip, King: leader of early Indian Confederacy in New England, 313

Phillips, Kevin, 83–5, 363

Piankeshaw people, 334

Pilger, John, 141

Pilgrims of the Wild, 166

Pine, Dan, 51

Pine Ridge Reservation, 33, 271–2; class exploitation in, 281; murders on, 271–2

Pinochet, General Augusto: and murder of Mapuche people, 463; and US-backed coup in Chile, 463

pipelines: move to construct in Dene and Inuit hunting territories, 244

Piper, Helen, 51

Pitawanakwat, James, 19, 207

Pitjantjatjari people, 139

Pittsburgh: founding of, 328

Pizarro, Francisco, 213

Plain Facts: Being an Examination into the Rights of Indian Nations in America, 360

Plain, Fred, 280

Plains of Abraham, 467; as site of British conquest of New France, 297, 328

Polanyi, Karl, 71–2, 187–9

Political Theory of Possessive Individualism, The, 308

Ponca people, 263

Ponteach, or The Savages of America: A Tragedy, 335

Pontiac, 201, 238, 249, 359; and Aboriginal and treaty rights in Canada, 331; assassination of, 334; Captain Rogers and Francis Parkman on, 335; influence on Royal Proclamation, 338, 532; as model for Tecumseh, 335, 389; and Neolin's message, 331; as premonition, 367; Sir William Johnson courts and, 333–4

Pope Alexander VI, 374

Pope John Paul II, 461–3

Pope Paul III: as source of Papal Bull *Sublimus deus sic dilexit*, 304

Popper, Karl, 136

Porter, Tommy, 51, 246

Portugal, 303; donation of Brazil to, 373

Portuguese Empire: revolt against in Brazil, 210; role of Vatican in creating, 302–3

Posluns, Michael, 243

possessive individualism: and American Revolution, 310–12; conquering army of, 418; constrained by feudalism in Europe and by Indigenous people in North America, 310; and Indian wars, 529; and international system after Second World War, 233; John Locke and C.B. Macpherson on, 308–9; and land speculation companies, 347, 360; and monoculturalism, 206; and neo-liberal fundamentalists, 134; and slavery, 123; totalitarian globalization of, 510–11. *See also* American empire of private property, empire of private property

post-colonialism: and influx of Native Americans into literature departments of North American universities, 245; literature of, 126–7

postmodernism, 126–34; relativism of, 135

post-structuralism, 126–7

potatoes, 25, 105–6; and Inca farmers, 107

Potawatomi people, 334; migration from USA to Canada, 207

potlatch: criminalizing of, 460, 482; Franz Boas on, 241; prohibition lifted in 1951, 495

Poundmaker: incarceration of, 261; and Indian resistance to extension of Canada's jurisdiction to prairies, 483

Powe, B.W., 69–70

power over Indians: US fed-

eral government derives authority from, 419
Pownall, Thomas, 308–9, 352; on support to Indians, 397
Pratt, Richard H.: and Carlisle Indian Boarding School, 256
"praying towns," Massachusetts, 162–3
Precambrian Shield: and Group of Seven, 153
pre-Columbian era, 79, 103–12; America as Garden of Eden, 114; controversy over population demography during, 27, 261; Garcilasco de la Vega on Inca, 231; Lewis Henry Morgan on, 179–82; of Mexico, 221–2; as pre-history, 118; symbolism of invoked by National Indian Youth Council in *America before Columbus*, 269–70; William Warren, Peter Jones, George Copway, and Francis Assiginack on Anishnabek, 194–5
presents: alliances with Indigenous peoples and, 190, 390; Anna Jameson attends ceremony to distribute, 191–2; blankets from smallpox hospital as, 332; bribery and coopting of Aboriginal leadership and, 281; as military pensions paid to Indians, 191, 431; patronage surrounding, 171; Sir Francis Bond Head and, 433–9; and Sir William Johnson, 325
Prince of Wales, 431; and audience for Indians, 485
private property: and atomizing of shared Indian domain, 391–3, 447; Indian Reorganization Act as shield against, 257; Jean-Jacques Rousseau on, 124–5; and John Locke on, 182–6; Joseph Brant and, 397; and local gov-

ernments in pre-revolutionary British North America, 355; Martin Luther on, 185; and patriarchal monogamy, 180; symbolism of in USA, 368. *See also* American empire of private property, capitalism, corporations, global corporations, property law, property regimes
privatization: American Revolution and, 361; attacks on public enterprises and, 423; Bill Vander Zalm on Aboriginal title and, 40; and bribery of Aboriginal leaders, 360; concept of, 21; elimination of pluralism and, 136; expressions of sovereignty and, 301–2, 347–8; formation of USA and, 529; imperialism and, 502–3, 516–17; Indian Reorganization Act of 1934 and, 257; new types of sovereignty and, 347–8; patronage power from wealth generated by, 372–3; and role of NAFTA in Mexico, 220–1; Royal Proclamation and, 156; and secularization, 65; and slavery, 123, 160, 212, 471; USA as instrument to transform global commons through, 347–8. *See also* American empire of private property, capitalism, corporations, global corporations, property law, property regimes
Privy Council of Great Britain, 419, 477
Progressive Movement, 368
Promotion of Bantu Self-Government Act of 1959, 505
property law: Aboriginal titles of Scots Highlanders and European peasants before enclosure movement, 456–7; and conditions of Indigenous peo-

ples and African Americans, 283–4; and corporate law in US westward expansion, 300; and Dawes Act of 1887, 186; and distinct Indian right of the soil, 337–8, 375–80; exclusion of Indians from framework of, 308–9; in international relations among governments, 234; land speculation companies and, 346–70; Mexican Constitution amendment changes land tenure, 221; and monocultures, 63, 65, 80, 134, 150, 280, 369; New England Puritans on biblical origins of, 307–8; papal articulation of, 304–5; role of Indian Affairs in genesis of in USA and Canada, 371; Royal Proclamation and, 155; and social sciences, 125–36, 187–9; standardization of in creation of dependencies, 190–2; US opposition to pluralistic types of, 369; USA founded to embody new regime of, 358–9. *See also* American empire of private property, capitalism, corporations, global corporations, property regimes
property or right of the soil: in *Mohegan Indians v. Connecticut*, 337–8; as vested in Confederate Indian Nations, 375–80, 402
property regimes: American Indian Defense Association on collective ownership of reservation lands, 264; Bible on, 307–8; and capitalism, 60–1, 70, 84, 91, 160, 226–7, 234, 303; and capitalist plutocracy in USA, 84; centrality of ownership in USA, 121–5; Columbian conquests and, 160; and communism, 40,

59, 130, 179–83, 228, 365–6; and corporations, 44, 50, 84–5, 91, 123–24, 149, 218–19, 346–70, 471–2, 513; and cultures of dependency, 189–92; dispute over after Conquest of New France, 330–3; DNA as intellectual property, 50, 63, 65, 72–3, 103, 107, 136; Edmond Burke on, 35; feudal character of in New York colony, 15; freehold land tenure in international system, 234; global standardization of, 21, 25, 67, 72, 80, 82, 118; Indigenous peoples as landed aristocracy, 37; international agencies as protectors of pluralism of, 134; John Jay on, 345; John Locke and Jean-Jacques Rousseau on, 179–89, 310–12; Karl Polyani on, 187–9; and land speculation companies in pre-revolutionary British North America, 346–53; in Latin America, 91; Louis Cameron on Ojibway Warriors' Society and, 273–4; and new forms of supranational authority, 66, 119, 149, 369; papacy dictates for the Americas, 304–5; and Royal Proclamation, 155; 336–346, 358; Samuel Wharton on, 360; and slavery, 106, 212, 214, 231, 283–4, 304, 314; as transformed by England by civil war, 308; as transformed in Mexico by NAFTA, 220–1. *See also* American empire of private property, capitalism, commercial trade treaties, communism, corporations, global corporations, private property, privatisation
property: as creation of law,

417; Lt-Gov. Jonathan Belcher promises crown land laws to protect Indians, 343
Prophetstown, 389, 421
Protestant civilization: Cherokees accept, 459; emergence and ethos of, 303; New England and frontier expansionism of, 306–10
provincial governments in Canada: and defence of monopoly control of natural resources, 197, 414–21
Prucha, Francis, 90
Psalms 115:16: New England Puritans use to justify acquisition of Indian land, 307; Puritans condemned for land policy based on, 321
psychological warfare, 54; and residential schools, 487; and suicide of Nelson Small Legs Jr, 277; as waged on Italian Communist Party by US government, 365
public relations, 175–6
Pueblo people: architecture of, 37, 103; litigiousness of in New Spain, Mexico, and USA, 211
Pugh, W.E.B.: Indian agent in Morley and Sarcee agencies in Alberta, 506
Puritan fundamentalism, 308
Puritan-Narragansett alliance, 317
Puritans: Calvinism of Dutch in South Africa, 442, 470; and conquest of Catholic Ireland by Oliver Cromwell, 223; Edmund Burke on Indian policies of, 76; and Enlightenment, 122–3; and executives as God's elect, 84–5; and Manifest Destiny, 75, 307–8; Pequot War and King Phillip's War confirm

hostility of towards Indians, 313; Rhode Island founded after rift among, 316–17; royal commissions in 1664 counter expansionary Indian policies of, 321; as shareholders and settlers of Massachusetts Bay Company, 306; view unconverted Indians as unredeemed sinners, 162. *See also* Christianity, New England

Quaker Treaties with Delaware, 317–18, 327–8
Quakers (Society of Friends): and missionary William Kirk, 392; and treaty making with Lenni Lappi people, 317–18; among United Empire Loyalists, 378
Quakers' Friendly Association: ideas codified in Royal Proclamation, 327; in negotiating Easton Treaty of 1758, 327–8
Qu'Appelle Valley, 37
Quebec: as British colony, 12; British policies to appease Roman Catholic Church in, 297; clash with Cree over natural resources, 467; colony and province of, 8; and complexities of independence movement, 200–6; as distinct society, 198; division into Lower and Upper Canada, 428; excluded from patriation of Canadian Constitution in 1982, 198, 508; failure of Parti Québécois to render as sovereign country, 220; flooding of northern portion of, 247; as French-speaking heartland of North America, 199; Jane Jacobs on independence of, 70; as major centre of Roman Catholicism, 132; and Royal Commission on

Biligualism and Biculturalism, 267; treaties being
negotiated in, 156; and
White Paper of 1969 as
prelude to Pierre
Trudeau's attack on
nationalists of, 278
Quebec Act, 1774: British
accommodation of Roman
Catholicism and civil code
derived from New France,
346; and British conquest
of Canada, 200; and
British restrictions on
westward expansion of
Anglo-American settlers,
427; and Edmund Burke
and genesis of American
Revolution, 75; and mer-
cantilism, 342
Quebec City: and Board of
Trade, 401; emergence of
Jules Sioui from Huron
reserve in, 253; as site of
Free Trade Area of the
Americas Summit in 2001,
94, 146, 531
Quebec Mining Company:
Shingwaukonse shuts
down, 451
Quechua-speaking peoples,
214
Queen Adelaide, new South
African province of: Lord
Glenelg orders imperial
withdrawal and orderly
return of land to Xhosa
people, 442
Queen Charlotte Islands
(Haida Gwaii), 206
Queen Elizabeth I, 220
Queen Elizabeth II, 196,
220
Queen Victoria, 226, 444,
485
Quincentennary, 4–8, 20

Race and Manifest Destiny,
367
racism, 125; Australia's quest
to transcend, 138–9;
Bernard Makhosezwe
Magubane on in South
Africa, 499–501; Charles

Darwin's justification of,
226–7; in Clarence
Alvord's interpretation,
361–2; continuing force
of, 133; and disproportion
of Blacks in US prisons,
518; effect of on property
law as related to African
Americans and Indige-
nous peoples, 284; and
Enlightenment's egalitarian idealism, 414; as issue
to be addressed by Indian-
Eskimo Association,
264–5; in Nazi Germany,
228, 495; Nelson Mandela
on economic dimension
of, 520–1; pervasiveness of
in English-speaking world
in early twentieth century,
152–3; and Social Darwin-
ism, 126; Theodore Roo-
sevelt on in The Winning of
the West, 478; Titus Alexander on South Africa as
microcosm of global
apartheid, 517–18; and
treatment of Indians and
Blacks in Canada and
South Africa, 504–9; and
Tupac Amaru in opposing
Spanish imperialists,
213–15; and UN Charter,
229
Radin, Paul, 177–8
Rae, Bob, 18
Ragsdale, Fred, 295–6
railway companies: connections to assimilationist
Indian policy, 459; and
land speculation compa-
nies, 373; as link to global
operations of US-based oil
and gas companies, 348;
Province of Canada char-
ters, 448
rain forests, 64, 93
Rainy Lake, 408
Raleigh, Sir Walter, 220
Rama Casino, 24
Ramonet, Ignacio, 145–6
Rasmussen, Derek, 48–9
Raven, 102
Ray, Carl, 244–5

Raynal, Thomas Guillaume,
6–7, 163, 231
Reagan, Ronald, xvii, 67, 80,
127, 129, 141, 189; role
in crimes against humani-
ty in Guatemala, 366, 473
Reconciliation Movement in
Australia, 137–42; and
prospect of new treaties
with Indigenous peoples,
258
Reconciliation, 152
Red Bull singers, 207
Red Coats and Blue Jackets,
495
Red Coats and Indians,
16–17; image of in genesis
of American Revolution,
311–12
Red Man's Appeal to Justice,
491
Red Power, 266
Red River (Assiniboia), 223
Red Squirrel Road, Tamaga-
mi, 18
Red Sticks: as pro-Tecumseh
and pro-British faction of
Creek people, 396, 405
Red Tory tradition, 132–3,
152–3; consistency with
tradition of the bowl with
one spoon, 422–4
Reed Pulp and Paper Com-
pany: and mercury poison-
ing of waters in northwestern Ontario, 273
referendum on treaty
process in British Colum-
bia, 2002, 142
Reformation: Jesuit Order as
avant-guard of Roman
Catholic response to, 162;
and notions of private
property, 184–5; strong
element of in philosophy
of John Locke, 182–3; USA
as mixture of Enlighten-
ment secularization and
religious zealotry of, 122,
183, 301
regime change, 227
registered Indians in Canada: form National Indian
Brotherhood, 260

Reid, Bill, 206, 244, 530
religious freedom: and us Constitution, 85
renovation from within, 244; role of Aboriginal scholars in, 246
representation: of baron de Lahontan's writings as fiction, 164; cowboy-and-Indian imagery of Calgary Stampede criticized by Calgary Urban Treaty Indian Alliance, 176; George Manuel and Scott Momaday on, 98–9; Group of Seven paintings as Canadian *terra nullius*, 153; of Indian Country in genesis of ethnography, anthropology, and social sciences, 177–89
residential schools: end of, 243; leaders of decolonization movement educated at, 176; Paul Tennant on importance of pan-Indian associations at, 252; and treaty negotiations on education, 438–9
responsible government: autonomy for New World nationalities means less for Indigenous peoples, 493; George Manuel's conception of, 258, 287; implementation of in Canada limits Indian access to imperial government, 485, 493
Reynolds, Henry: and Australian Reconciliation Movement, 137–8, 141; and Fourth World ideals, 531
Rhode Island Colony, 109; and Indian treaties, 117
Rhode Island Treaty of 1635, 316–17
Rhode Island: relationship among theocracy of Massachusetts, Roger Williams, Narragansett Indians, and, 316–17
Rice Lake, 483

Richardson, Maj. John, 170–2, 398
Richardson, Mr Justice, 148
Richelieu, Cardinal, 374
Rickard, Clinton, 268
Ridge, John: on success of Cherokee transformations to conform to American civilization, 459
Ridgeway, Senator Aden, 138
Riel, Louis, 18–19, 199, 422; as embodiment of Indian, French, and Roman Catholic mixture of fur trade, 223; hanging of, 261; and Jules Soui, 253; negotiation of Manitoba Act with John A. Macdonald, 455
Rights of Man, The, 37
rights talk, 41
Riley, Delbert: as founding national chief of Assembly of First Nations, 260
Riley, Rob, 141
Rio Earth Summit, 1992, 157
Rising of the American Empire, The, 364
Rivera, Diego, 221
Rivers of Blood, Rivers of Gold, 26–7
Riviere-aux-Rats, 408
Robinson Treaties, 452–3
Robinson, John: undersecretary of the treasury of Great Britain and land speculator, 352
Robinson, Ronald, 338
Robinson, William Benjamin: fur trader and treaty commissioner, 452–3
Rochdale College: blend of Indian and hippie culture, 275–6
Rockefeller family conglomerate: William Lyon Mackenzie King as adviser to, 493
Rockefeller, J.D., 84; and I.G. Farben and Standard Oil, 471

Rogers, Capt. Robert, 325, 329
Rogin, Michael Paul, 90
Roman Catholic Church: attachment of to Indians in Acadia, New France, and Quebec, 223, 297, 329, 343; and Brother Bartolome de Las Casas, 116, 178, 211, 305, 317; central role of in Mexico, 222; clergy support for poorest of poor, 462; and Company of One Hundred, 374; Dominican Order and protection of Indian rights in New Spain, 211, 304; and Indian activism of Andy Paull, Jules Sioui, and John Tootoosis, 352; and Indian Federation of Saskatchewan, 255; and Jesuit Order, 162–5; as legacy of Roman Empire in Latin America, 213; and legal theory of Father Francisco Vitoria, 304–5, 317, 328; and Louis Riel, 223, 296–7, 455; and mestizo identities, 223, 461; and murder of Archbishop Oscar Romero, 462; paternalistic and conservative support for rights and titles of Indigenous peoples, 453; and Quebec Act, 346; retains titles to Indian missions in Quebec and Lower Canada, 430; Scot Highlander adherents move into fur trade of Canada, 449, 456–7; settler intermarriage with Indigenous peoples in areas dominated by, 459; and Tory pro-Indian politics of Allan Macdonell; and transfer of titles to lands, 303–4, 460; and treaty making on Manitoulin Island, 455; and Vatican's betrayal of Liberation Theology in the

Americas, 461–2; William
Connolly and, 408. *See also*
Christianity
Roman Empire: Arnold
Toynbee compares to USA,
365; continuation of legacy in Spanish Empire and
global role of USA, 213,
374; as model for English
role in American empire,
300
Romero, Archbishop Oscar:
murder of, 462
Roosevelt, Eleanor, 229
Roosevelt, Franklin D., xviii,
223–4, 368. *See also* Indian
New Deal, New Deal
Roosevelt, Theodore, 94;
preoccupation with con-
cepts of race in *The Winning of the West*, 478; role
in Progressive Movement,
368
Roots of Dependence, 190–1
Ross, John, 456; and
removal of Cherokees
from Aboriginal territo-
ries, 405
Rough Rock Demonstration
School, Navajo reserva-
tion, 244
round dance, 207–8
Rousseau, Jean-Jacques,
124–5, 163, 177, 179,
182, 186, 235, 528
Royal Canadian Mounted
Police: American Indian
wars spread to Canada in
1990s, 495; confrontations
at Oka and Gustafsen
Lake, 495; harassment of
Chief Ed Thompson on
Peguis reserve, 260; Native
Peoples Caravan reception
by riot squad, 274; and
Peigan Lonefighters, 53–4;
on Six Nations reserve,
490–5; smear campaign at
Gustafsen Lake, 20, 55;
violation of Aboriginal and
treaty rights through political abuse of criminal justice system, 54
royal charters: legitimacy of

without land cessions from
Indigenous peoples, 315;
and overseas colonization,
306
*Royal Commentaries of the Incas
and a General History of
Peru*, 213
Royal Commission on Abo-
riginal Peoples, 127
Royal Commission on Bilingualism and Biculturalism,
265
royal commissioners: report
on Indian Affairs in New
England in 1664, 320–4
royal hunting preserves:
model for King George's
reservations in the Royal
Proclamation, 342
Royal Ontario Museum:
American Indian Move-
ment's occupation of vault
of, 276
Royal Proclamation of 1763:
agents of land speculation
companies question legal
authority of, 346–53; and
American Indian policy,
378–9; background of,
314–36; between New
World and Old World
empires of the Americas,
196; and British Colum-
bia, 158, 250–1, 287; and
Canada's constitutional
affirmation of Aboriginal
and treaty rights, 53,
287–9; central govern-
ment as shield for protection of Aboriginal and
treaty rights, 445; and
conservatism, 132, 155;
and Covenant Chain, 13,
29, 155; and crown-Abo-
riginal treaties in Canada,
154, 289; Dutch influence
on, 337; Edmund Burke
on, 75; and founding of
USA, 310–12, 359; and fur
trade, 14; James Bay and
Northern Quebec Agree-
ment as first modern-day
treaty negotiated accord-
ing to terms of, 280; John

Borrows on, 411; and
John Locke, 184. Joseph
Brant's violation of, 387;
and mathematical formula
for granting land-grant
certificates to British veterans, 349; Menno Boldt
interprets, 354–5, 359;
and *Mohegan Indians v.
Connecticut*, 337; North-
west Ordinance of 1787
and recognition that Con-
federate Indian Nations
possess property right in
the soil, 372–80; as out-
come of British conquests
of Canada, 200; and Pontiac's patriotic stand, 330–2;
Quaker influence on, 327,
337; and recognition of
treaties as means of negotiation with Indigenous
peoples, 258; role of in
genesis of American Dec-
laration of Independence,
310–12; significance of for
international law and
world history, 28, 54,
353–63, 511; and Sir
William Johnson, 8–9,
333; and *St. Catherine's
Milling* case, 415, 417,
421; Tecumseh and Great
Wampum signifying terms
of, 412; terms of, 155–6,
336–46; and treaty council
at Niagara in 1764, 155,
411; and Treaty of Fort
Stanwix, 350–1, 376; as
wedge between centraliza-
tion of imperial power
and local autonomy in
pre-revolutionary British
North America, 336–46,
355. *See also* Covent
Chain, crown-Aboriginal
treaties, Pontiac, Seven
Years' War
Rudman, Warren B.: and
United States Committee
on National Security,
527–9
Ruiz, Bishop Samuel: as
intermediary between Zap-

atista Liberation Army and Mexican government, 462

rule of conquest, 131

rule of force: subordination of rule of law to, 76, 130, 156–8, 161, 185, 310–12, 348–9, 523–9

rule of law: and enforcement of Aboriginal and treaty rights, 302; treatment of Indigenous peoples within USA holds key to global future of, 131; and violation of Indian treaties, 302; and Washington state fish-ins, 264

Russia, 179, 425: and expropriation of Aboriginal lands and resources, 521; and imperial rule of Alaska, 212; and Napoleonic Wars, 396

Rwanda, 61, 237, 524

Ryerson, Rev. Egerton, 174–6

Saami Action Group: hunger strike of in Oslo in 1979, 242

Saami people, 238, 241–2

Said, Edward, 115–16, 225, 368

Saint Clair, Gen. Arthur, 378

Sainte-Marie, Buffie, 207

Salinas, Carlos, 221

Sampson, Joe, 280

San Carlos University, 461

San Domingo: slave revolt in, 219

San Francisco, 9, 145, 229, 266–8

San Martin, Jose, 210, 215

Sante Fe, 37

Saramago, Jose, 143–4

Saro-Wiwa, Ken, 150

Saskatchewan, 47, 185, 263, 496; high rates of Aboriginal incarceration in, 262

Satiacum, Robert: prominence of in Washington state fish-in, 264; and reference in US Constitution to Indians not taxed, 263

Saudi Arabia, 367

Sauer, Carl O., 107–8

Saugeen Treaty, 1836, 437–9

Sauk people, 334; Sioux act through to resist confiscation of Aboriginal territory with Louisiana Purchase, 392

Sault Ste Marie, 171–2, 449

Saulteaux people, 47, 158

Saunders, Douglas E., 242, 265

savage hordes: and theory of law distinguishing higher from lower orders of humanity, 413

Saxons: Thomas Jefferson on freedom of, 311

Scandinavia: and activism of Saami people, 242; importance of some anthropologists in Fourth World movement, 241–2

Schlesinger, Arthur M., Jr, 61, 129; and rejection of Turnerian School of American historical historiography, 300

Scholder, Fritz, 244–5

School of the Americas: role of in assisting genocide in Guatemala, 365; Spanish language manuals of, 462

Schoolcraft, Henry Rowe, 127, 177–8

science: aura of given to imperialism and capitalism through elaboration of Social Darwinism, 60–1 266–7

Scots Highlander people: and immigration into Indian Country, 449–50, 456–8

Scots–First Nations marriages, 456

Scott, Duncan Campbell, 324, 480

Scout, Yvonne, 51

Scow, William, 280

Sea Shepard Conservation, 87

Seattle: and World Trade Organization meeting in 1999, 80, 118, 531

Seaway International Bridge: blockage of in 1968, 269

Sechelt peoples: and powers of self-administration, 498

Second World War, 27, 126, 228, 513

Second World, 240

secret payoffs: used frequently in USA to obtain Indian land cessions, 392

Section 35 of the Constitution Act, 1982, 30, 34–5, 38, 48–9, 53: as basis for future national treaties in Canada, 199; and continuing legacy of Royal Proclamation, 287–92; and international significance of mention of Aboriginal peoples, 231. See also Constitution of Canada, courts of law, Royal Proclamation of 1763

secularization: Enlightenment as force of, 121–2; USA as combination of religious zealotry and, 122, 183, 301

Seed, Patricia, 307

Seeds, Spades, Hearths, and Herds, 107–8

segregationist-integrationist dichotomy: in contrasting interpretation of Indian rights by Helen Hunt Jackson and Marlon Brando, 264; in decolonization movements, 255; in franchise in Indian Country, 255–6. See also enfranchisement

self-defence: Declaration of Independence negates law of for "merciless Indian savages," 310–12

self-determination, 22, 30, 33, 34, 45, 69; and African Americans, 283; and Australia, 138; and Australian Aborigines, 139; and corporate power, 91, 123, 149, 150, 346–53, 471–2, 509–10, 513; Creole nationalism and, 209–17,

469–74; and decoloniza-
tion, 228–38; and disparities in powers of, 234–5;
and economics, 71–2;
Frantz Fanon on betrayal
of, 236–7; George
Manuel's philosophy of,
238–9; and Indian-Eskimo
Association, 264; and
indigenous peoples in
domestic law, courts, and
policies, 302–3, 514; and
Indigenous peoples in
global struggle against
monocultures and stan-
dardized property law, 150;
international law on, 45,
234–5, 270–1, 291, 302–5,
412–14, 425, 490–5; legitimacy of requires that
power of government lies
with consent of the gov-
erned, 529; Mahatma
Gandhi on, 235–6; of peo-
ples, 21, 68, 131, 231, 358,
513; in Quebec–First
Nations relations in Canada, 199–206; and Royal
Proclamation and Ameri-
can Revolution, 336–46,
353–70; and transnational
democratic movement,
150; undermining of
through ecocide, standardization of technology and
property law, addictive
drugs, and credit, 189–91;
Woodrow Wilson on, 222,
357, 491, 513. See also
Fourth World, international law, nationalism, peoples
self-government. See Fourth
World, peoples, self-determination
Selkirk, Lord: and Scots
farming settlement in Red
River area, 447
Seminole people, 185, 216,
392, 396
Seneca people, 12, 195, 257,
334, 382; and adoption of
Hurons after 1649, 382
separate schools in Ontario,
176

September 11, 2001,
129–30, 312, 527
Sepulveda, Juan Gines de,
305
Sero, Eliza: and sovereign
alliance between British
crown and Mohawk peo-
ple, 490
Seton, Ernest Thompson,
170
Seven Nations of Canada,
329
Seven Oaks, 447–8
Seven Years' War, xxiv, xxv,
12, 313, 320, 467; course
of, 326–35; distribution of
presents to Indians dur-
ing, 190; and capitulation
of Montreal in 1760, 328;
and Easton Treaty of
1758, 326–8; and emer-
gence of USA from British
Empire, 523; and French
power in the Americas,
219–20; Indian land cer-
tificates granted to British
veterans of, 349; Neolin
and Pontiac assert not
conquest of Indian Coun-
try, 330–5
Seventh Cavalry: and
revenge at Wounded Knee
for defeat at Battle of Little Bighorn, 261
Shaftesbury, Earl of: Lord
Proprietor of Carolina
with John Locke as secre-
tary, 183
Shakespeare, William, 96,
177
Sharpville massacre: in
South Africa in 1960, 505
Shawnee people, 314, 334,
387
Shelburne, Lord: influence
on theories of Adam
Smith, 448; and Treaty of
Paris, 361–2
Shell Oil Company, 149–51
Sherman, Gen. George
William Tecumseh, 182
Shingwaukonse, 166–7,
171–2; and integrating
interests of Indian Coun-

try and Canada, 530; and
Robinson Treaties, 449–53
Shinnawap, Jeremiah, 465
Shirley, William, 329
Shiva, Vandana, 60–1, 110,
134, 532
Shuswap people, 151, 238,
198
Sidney Harbour Bridge, Aus-
tralia, 137–8, 143
Sierra Club, 88
Sierra Leone: and genocide,
524
Silburn, P.A.: and imperial
federation, 502–3; and
J.A. Hobson, 516
Silko, Leslie Marmon, 89
Simcoe, Sir John Graves,
378, 450
Sinclair, R.V., 488–9
Sinkyone Wilderness Project,
86
Sioui case, 30
Sioui, Georges, 51
Sioui, Jules, 252–4, 256,
282, 483; and Indian-Eskimo Association, 483
Sioux peoples, 112, 257;
join Indian Confederacy
of Canada, 392; migration
to Canada from USA, 207;
pushed by Cree and Ojib-
way from Eastern Wood-
lands into prairies, 334;
and Wounded Knee I,
261; and Wounded Knee
II on Pine Ridge reserva-
tion, 271–2
Siqueiros, David, 221
Sitting Bull, xvii, 19, 161,
207, 249, 391
Six Nations Iroquois: and
adopting groups and indi-
viduals, 173, 319, 382,
412, 457–8; and Akwesasne
Notes, 269–70; and Ameri-
can Indian Movement,
269; and Ashinabek, 13,
386; corn, beans, and
squash venerated as "the
three sisters," 108; cre-
ation story of, 100; and
Easton Treaty and Treaty
of Fort Stanwix, 326–9,

350; and Ely S. Parker, 195; and franchise offer, 479; intelligensia of, 246; at League of Nations against Canada's subordination of, 268, 490–5, 530; and Lewis Henry Morgan, 179–82, 195; migration to Canada after American Revolution, 207, 377; as Nahdoways, 386; and Pauline Johnson, 195, 483; and protest against Act for the Gradual Civilization of the Indian Tribes in Canada, 483; relationship between Longhouse League of and Covenant Chain, 319; and Royal Proclamation, 337; and Sir William Johnson, 324–6; and sovereign transcendance of division of Aboriginal lands between Canada and USA, 93; and sovereignty of Indigenous peoples in international community, 268–70, 490–5, 530; unity of, 314. *See also* Covenant Chain, Longhouse League

Six Nations reserve, 173, 483, 489–95

Slattery, Brian, 49

slavery: abolition of, 358; of Aborigines in Australia, 132; and Aborigines' Protection Society, 442–5, 457–8; Bartolome de Las Casas on, 305; Guillaume Raynal on movement to abolish, 6–7, 231; of Jews by I. G. Farben Company and Standard Oil, 471; and John Norton, 457–8; Kondiaronk on, 163; in Latin American economy, 212; legacy of among African Americans, 283–4; New Spain debates inclusion of Indians in, 178; papal prohibition on inducting Indians into, 304; and patriarchal

monogamy, 180; role of in American pre-eminence, 160; San Domingo slave revolt, 219; Tupac Amaru on, 214; victims of flee to Upper Canada, 378; William Drayton authorizes enslavement of Indians in South Carolina, 314

Slotkin, Richard, 90, 527

Small Legs, Nelson, Jr: suicide of, 276

Smith, Adam, 6, 182, 188, 231, 346, 448

Smith, Donald, 51

Smith, Goldwin, 77–9

Smith, Paul Chaat, 266, 271

Smithsonian Institution, 101, 194

smoke signals, 109

Smuts, Gen. Jan E., 469, 500

social contract: Jean-Jacques Rousseau's conception of influences founders of USA, 124

Social Darwinism: and Charles Darwin, 226–8; Clarence Alvord's interpretation of American Revolution based on, 361; and Fourth World, 240; Gertrude Himmelfarb on as justification for capitalism, imperialism, racism, and Manifest Destiny, 227; Herber Spencer and Edward Tylor as theorists of, 226; permeates thinking of Lewis Henry Morgan, Karl Marx, and Frederick Engels, 179–82; racist applications of discredited by Nazi Germany, 228, 495; racist tone of after late nineteenth century, 414; and reverse chauvinism, 126; as rationale for extinguishing titles, cultures, and lives of Indigenous peoples, 346

social engineering, 174–6

social sciences: anthropology and political economy in genesis of, 186; and

Enlightenment and Europe's explorations, 121–5; and Fourth World, 242; Frederick Engels and communist school of, 179; Indigenous peoples as subject of, 177–89; and Nazi Germany, 228, 495; and Social Darwinism, 226–7. *See also* anthropology, ethnography, Social Darwinism

social welfare state: Saskatchewan government of Premier Tommy Douglas, 254

Society of American Indians, 257

Society of Friends, 317–18

Society of Jesus. *See* Jesuit Order

Sociocultural Evolution, 128

Soloman, Arthur, 51, 262; and American Indian Movement and Indian Hall of Fame, 276

Soloman, Casper, 51

Sony Corporation: Akio Morita's ideas of world as one big market, 68, 400

Soop, Everett, 51

Sorry Books, Australia, 141

Sosin, Jack, 347

South Africa, 31, 55; Afrikaners in as Dutch Creoles, 470; apartheid system in, 499–501; Bernard Makhosezwe Magubane on origins of state racism in, 499–501; and Brian Mulroney, 497, 514; C.E. Morgan as colonial administrator in, 491–2; Calvinism of Boers, 442, 470; Glenn Babb visits Peguis reserve in Manitoba, 514; Great Trek of 1836–8, 442, 470; Indigenous peoples in and Indian policy of Sir Francis Bond Head in Upper Canada, 441–6, 499; J.A. Hobson and imperialism in, 516–17; John Diefen-

baker and, 496, 505–6;
Native Affair Ministry in
and Indian Affairs Department in Canada, 503–9;
Nelson Mandela on racial-
ized economy in, 521–2;
Noel Mostert on political
and cultural origins of,
442–5; P.A. Silburn on
Basutoland, 502–3, 516;
Rev. Desmond Tutu visits
Osnaburgh reserve in
northern Ontario,
514–15; and Sharpville
massacre, 505; Titus
Alexander on global
apartheid, 517–18
South Carolina: and authorization for Indian
enslavement in, 314
South Dakota, 271–2
Southern Christian Leadership Conference, 283
Southern Division of British
Imperial Indian Depart-
ment, 324
Southern Sotho people, 505
sovereignty, 532; acquisition
of Aboriginal lands tests
different theories and configurations of, 81, 301;
changing notions and con-
structions of, 41, 67, 532;
conflict of interest in
crown courts arbitrating
competing assertions of,
42–4; controversies over
nature and locus of in
genesis of decolonization
and United Nations sys-
tem, 228–38; and corpo-
rate power, 91, 123, 149,
150, 346–53, 471–2,
509–10, 513; crown-Abo-
riginal treaties as symbols
of overlapping regimes of,
156; global corporations
and changing construc-
tions of, 348; Hugo
Grotius on, 318; Indian
Affairs and competing
assertions of in federal systems of Canada and USA,
404–6, 414–21; Indige-

nous peoples and Quebe-
cers attitudes to, 200–6,
220; Jean-Jacques
Rousseau on people as
legitimate source of, 124;
land speculation compa-
nies as lobbyists to invest
corporations with attributes of, 346–70; of Long-
house League and Micco-
sukees of Florida
recognized by Cuba, 269;
and political activism of
Indigenous peoples in
North America, 238–92;
role of Vatican and Span-
ish clergy in shaping, 211,
302–5; Six Nations Iro-
quois claim that all Indigenous peoples hold inter-
national, 93, 268–70,
490–5, 530; Tecumseh
and Indian Confederacy
of Canada seek in Aboriginal dominion, 74,
380–402, 407, 421–6;
Tecumseh on internalizing
property law within self-
determination, 423; USA
as vehicle to expedite western expansion of and to
hasten privatization of
lands, 335, 347–8; viola-
tions of international principles of through covert
regime change, illegal military interventions, and
support of puppet
regimes, 312, 364–9,
461–4, 471–4, 525–9
Soviet Empire, 18, 83, 189,
234, 368
Soviet Union, 59–60; as centre of worldwide commu-
nist conspiracy, 365; and
decolonization, 232; emergence from theories of
Rousseau, Marx, Engels,
and Morgan, 176–86; offi-
cial atheism of, 124; and
superpower rivalry, 59–60,
80, 83, 96, 523; US hostility towards, 228–9; and
Vladimir I. Lenin, 232,

516–17; and Yugoslavia,
234
Spain: in America, 209–17,
303–6; empire of, 204;
and Manuel Vasquez Mon-
talban, 143; promotes
Quincentenary, 5, 20; and
Roman Catholic Church,
303–5, 373
Spanish conquest of Mexico,
317
Spanish Empire, 29: based
on papal donation in
1493, 303–4, 373; demise
of in the Americas
through Creole revolts,
209–17; monarch's power
of patronage extended to
Roman Catholic Church,
303; USA moves into vacu-
um created by, 364
Special Committee of the
Senate and House of
Commons, Canada, 1927:
investigates dispute over
Indian title in British
Columbia, 251
species extinction, 63, 65,
134
Spence, Rev. Ahab, 280
Spencer, Herbert, 181, 226
spinning wheel: as Gandhi's
symbol of self-determina-
tion for India, 236
Spirit of Haida Gwaii, The,
206–7
Splitting The Sky, 18–19, 51,
246
Squamish people, 250–3
Stamp Act: and Royal Proclamation, 341–2
Standard Oil Company: and
Third Reich, 471
standardization of property
law. *See* commercial trade
treaties, commodification,
monocultures, private
property, privatization,
property law, property
regimes
Stannard, David E., 205
Star Wars, 129–30, 527
state of nature: John Locke
on Native Americans and,

183; self-regulating markets as expressions of, 187
Statue of Liberty, 266
St Catherine's Milling case, 414, 476–7, 415–21, 429
St Clair's Shame, 378
Steinhauer, Augustine, 280
Steinhauer, Rev. Henry, 193
Stevenson, Adlai, 369
Stevenson, Chief Louis: as host to South African ambassador to Canada, Glenn Babbs
Stewart, Judge Janice, 19–20, 207
St Lawrence–Great Lakes Axis: early North American history as contest against Hudson River–Mohawk Valley corridor, 320
Stockenstrom Treaties: with Xhosa people of South Africa, 442
Stockenstrom, Andries, 442
Stolen Generation Aborigines, 140
Stolo people, 259
stone age, 125, 226, 240
Stone, Oliver, 143
Stoney Mountains, 403
story telling: importance of in forming culture, law, and institutions, 113–21
Strachan, Rev. John, 174–5
St Regis (Akwesasne): Jesuit mission at, 329
Strong, Samuel Henry: and *St Catherine's Milling* case, 420; and Tecumseh, 421
Student Nonviolent Coordinating Committee, 283
Subcommnadante Marcos, 34, 144–6
Subliminus deus sic dilexit: papal bull issued in 1537, 304–5
sub-Saharan Africa, 225
successor states: acquire powers exercised by European sovereigns, 233; competing assertions of sovereignty in acquisition of Aboriginal lands by

empires and, 301; and French support in gaining objectives, 388; Indian Act used to transform Indigenous peoples into wards of empires and, 174; as outcome of decolonization of European empires, 70; USA as first, 70, 130–64, 301
Sudan: and genocide, 524
Sugden, John, 90
Suggashie, Fred, 51
suicide: of Nelson Small Legs Jr, 276–7
Sulpician Order: as founders of Montreal and Lac des Deux-Montagnes mission at Oka, 329
Summary View of the Rights of British America: as expression of Thomas Jefferson's hostility to British monarchy, 311
sun dances: criminalization of, 482; prohibition of lifted, 495
Sunday, Rev. John, 193, 194, 444
supranational institutions: afford money and investment more protections than human rights, 44, 303; and denationalization of instruments of financial power, 66; and standardization of property law, 22, 44; and power to change economic relationships within and between countries, 290; opposition to Aboriginal and treaty rights moving into international, transnational, and, 302–3; World Trade Organization, 22, 44, 149
Supreme Court of Canada: and *Delgamuukw* and *Mabo* rulings, 142; and *Donald Marshall* case, 251; and ruling on Indian title in British Columbia, 1973 and 1997, 343; and *St*

Catherine's Milling case, 415. *See also* courts of law
Survival International, 241
survival of the fittest: and Charles Darwin's theory of natural selection, 226
Surviving as Indians: The Challenge of Self-Government, 254
Susanne Pas-de-nom, 409. *See also* Pas-de-nom, Susanne
Susquehannock people: as victims of genocidal assault in Bacon's Rebellion, 316
Sutton, Mrs Catherine (Nahnee-ba-we-quay), 484–5, 530
swaraj: Gandhi's characterization of home-rule through self-purification, 236
Swazi people, 505
Sweden, 93: wealth of derived in part from appropriation of Saami lands and resources, 521
Switlo, Janice G.A.E., 47–8, 411
Sydney Olympics, 2001, 138
Symons, Thomas H.B., 266

Tahontaenrat Huron people: adopted by Seneca people, 382
Taliban regime: and US-led war on, 317
Tamanend: as legendary Delaware leader, 318
Tanner, John, 172
Tanzania: George Manuel's friendship with Julius Nyerere, 238–40
Taos Pueblo, 37, 461
Tate, Henry, 195
taxation, 72, 81: Andy Paull's campaign to unify Aboriginal resistance to extension of to off-reserve Indians, 251; and locus of control over westward expansion of Euro-American settlements, 345–6;

Robert Satiacum on refer-
ence in US Constitution to
Indians and, 263; and
unextinguished Aboriginal
title, 356
technology, 69, 167; and
dependencies among
Indigenous peoples, 189;
role of railway companies
in developing and exploiting, 373
Tecumseh, xxv, 22, 55, 74,
152, 172, 207, 238, 249,
259, 282; on American
government bribing and
co-opting chiefs, 360–1,
392–3, 424; Benjamin
Drake on, 406–7, 422;
claimed killing of by
Richard Johnson, 412; and
Declaration of the Rights
of Man, 414; Enlighten-
ment legacy through
Tupac Amaru, Kondi-
aronk, Pontiac, Grey Owl,
George Manuel, and, 359;
fight to change interna-
tional law by breaking ethnocentric mould of Creole
decolonization, 410, 414,
529–30; and George
Manuel's vision of Fourth
World, 400; international
status of Indigenous peo-
ples compared with that of
US government, 406–7;
and legacy of bowl with
one spoon, 421–6; life,
times, and ideals of,
380–402, 407, 411; on
legacy of Pontiac, 335,
395; Longhouse League
and Covenant Chain as
models for, 530; Neolin
and Pontiac as models for
partnership with brother,
335, 389; and struggle to
reverse internalized colonization among his peo-
ples, 393; and Toussaint
L'Overture, 414; treat-
ment of in US historiography, 422; and Tupac
Amaru, 291; and wampum

from Niagara Council of
1764 in negotiation of
crown-Indian alliance during War of 1812, 412. See
also Aboriginal dominion,
Indian Confederacy of
Canada, War of 1812
Teedyuscung: as Delaware
leader involved in Easton
Treaty, 327–8
Temagami land dispute, 18
Temagami, Ontario: and
blockade of Red Squirrel
Road, 18; and Grey Owl,
165–6
Tennant, Paul, 252, 465
Tenochtitlan, 103, 143. See
also Mexico City
Tenskwatawa, 389, 397
termination and relocation
policies: Eisenhower
administration plan for
Native Americans, 266
terra nullius, 31, 118, 139,
140; Group of Seven's
artistic depiction of Precambrian Shield as, 153
territorial integrity: and Aboriginal and treaty rights,
43, 302–3
terrorism: implications of
war on in reference to
"merciless Indian savages"
in American Declaration
of Independence, 312;
patterns of continuity in
US role in Cold War and
more recent war on, 130;
of US government in
covert war on American
Indian Movement, 202
Texas, 225
Teyoninhokarawen (John
Norton), 457
Thatcher, Margaret, 80, 141
Thayendanegea. See Joseph
Brant
theory of relativity, 126
Theyanoguin (Hendrick),
324
Third World: and neo-colonialism, 285; poverty of,
85; and underdevelop-
ment, 189, 240

third-party arbitration: and
competing assertions of
sovereignty, 44; and inter-
vention by Queen Anne in
dispute between Connecti-
cut and Mohegan Indians
in 1704, 211
thirst dances: criminalization
of, 482
Thomas, Bob, 246
Thomas, Jake, 51, 246
Thompson, Albert Ed: and
League of Nations of
North American Indians,
260
Thompson, Joey, 19
Thoreau, Henry David, 209
Thornton, Russell, 27
Thorp, Jim: as Olympic
champion, 268
Thorpe, Grace, 268
Three Affiliated Tribes of
the Fort Berthold Reserva-
tion, 87
Three Fires Confederacy,
334
Thunderbird University, 267
Thurow, Lester, 518
Tippecanoe, 389; and mili-
tary victory of William
Henry Harrison, 422
Titley, Brian, 51
To Know Ourselves, 266
Todd, Anthony: as postmas-
ter of Great Britain and
land speculator, 352
Toderov, Tzvetan, 4, 6–7, 26
Tootootsis, John, 253, 255,
260
Torre, Haya de la, 223
Torres, Gerald, 212
Tory architects of British
imperial Canada, 155
Toryism: and Edmund
Burke, 37–8, 76; and
Enlightenment thought,
328, 532; Florida as
stronghold of, 216; in fur-
trade economy of British
imperial Canada, 155,
397–402; and genesis of
Canada in American Revo-
lution, 38; as ideology of
British Imperial Indian

Department, 171–2; and legacy of bowl with one spoon, 421–6; multiculturalism of, 14–15, 378; Royal Proclamation and Quebec Act as attempts to reassert imperatives of over Whig ascendance, 310–11; as source of protection for Indigenous peoples, 132. *See also* conservatism, monarchy, Red Toryism, Royal Proclamation of 1763

toxic waste, 85

Toynbee, Arnold, 363–5

traditional foods: and junk food in Aboriginal communities, 81

traditionalists: American Indian Movement as alliance of urban-based Native people and reserve-based, 269; characterize opponents as Vichy Indians, hang-around-the-fort Indians, and apples, 272

Trail of Broken Treaties: ends in occupation of Bureau of Indian Affairs, 270–1

Trail of Tears: blatant example of ethnic cleansing, 405

transcultural migration: Grey Owl as symbol of, 172

transcultural treaties, 206

transnational civil society, 92

transnational corporate rule: Fourth World as alternative to, 291

transnational corporations. *See* global corporations

transnational financial institutions, 233

Transvaal: Afrikaner founding of through Great Trek, 442

Transylvania Company, 1775–7: prelude to Kentucky County, 349–50

treaties among Indigenous peoples: between Assembly of First Nations and National Congress of American Indians, 259; as signified with wampum belts, 78

treaty making with Indigenous peoples, 24, 28–9, 31–2; by Andries Stockenstrom and Xhosa people in South Africa, 442; in Australia, 139; as basis of military defence of Canada before War of 1812, 380–402; British North America and Dominion of Canada as culmination of, 304; constitutional negotiations in Canada as a new kind of, 196–200; and Covenant Chain and Longhouse Confederacy, 385; Covenant Chain as prime example of, 12, 155, 322, 324–6, 350, 363, 387, 490–5, 530; development of in negotiations between William Penn and Delaware Indians, 317–18; Dutch-Aboriginal connection in genesis of British tradition of, 318–19; impact of Treaty of Paris on, 388; and intercultural collaboration in making of Canada, 82; litigation concerning, 404–5, 414–21; as medium for infusion of Enlightenment thought into changing conceptions of sovereignty, 532; Nahnee-ba-we-quay on abuses of, 484–5; name of British sovereign invoked in, 385; in New France, New England, and New Sweden, 117; and Odawa peoples' refusal to cede Manitoulin Island, 454–5; as process leading to larger coalitions of Indigenous peoples, 258; process reopened in 1973 in Canada after Supreme Court ruling, 280; and Quaker role at Easton, Penn., in 1758, 327–8; Roger Williams on need for, 316–17; and settlement of North America by non-Indians, 258; Six Nations Iroquois and complex heritage of, 268; in South Africa, New Zealand, India, and Southeast Asia, 31–2, 117; and Sovereignty of British crown in North America, 201; Treaty of Waitangi, 117, 147–9; William Lyon Mackenzie King opposes, 494–5. *See also* Aboriginal and treaty rights, Covenant Chain, crown-Aboriginal treaties, numbered treaties, Royal Proclamation of 1763, United States Indian treaties

Treaty Nine, 158

Treaty of Boston and Annapolis, 343

Treaty of Canandaigua, 258

Treaty of Fort Laramie, 271

Treaty of Fort Stanwix, 360, 384, 428; pushes boundaries of Indian reserve westward in applying principles of Royal Proclamation, 350–1; wrongful violation of in Treaty of Paris, 362, 376

Treaty of Fort Wayne: Tecumseh labels Indian signatories as traitors, 392

Treaty of Ghent, xxiv, 400; and Aboriginal and treaty rights in international law and diplomacy, 399; A.L. Burt on Indian buffer state in negotiation of, 399; entrenches aspects of Treaty of Paris, 399; and fur business of North West Company, 477; and geographic location of many of crown's Indian allies in usa, 431; Indian consent ignored, 413, 425

Treaty of Greenville, xxiii
Treaty of Guadalupe Hidal-
    go, 425
Treaty of Hard Labor, 351
Treaty of Lochaber, 351
Treaty of New York: between
    Creeks and US govern-
    ment, 216
Treaty of Paris, 1763, 331–2
Treaty of Paris, 1783, 82,
    156; axis of understanding
    between Benjamin
    Franklin and Lord Shel-
    burn essential to negotia-
    tion of, 362; and British
    government military posts
    south of Great Lakes, 377;
    Clarence Alvord on, 362;
    negotiated without Aborig-
    inal involvement or con-
    sent, 425; reversal of,
    375–80; and ruling of
    Chief Justice John Marshall
    on Great Britain as source
    of title to US lands, 404–5;
    and sovereign status of
    USA, 404–5, 471; and status
    of Indian Confederacy in
    international law and rela-
    tions, 237, 362, 377; and
    transfer of Canada from
    France to Britain, 332
Treaty of Pensacola: Creek-
    Spanish alliance, 216
Treaty of Sycamore Shoals:
    and direct purchase of
    title from Cherokee in
    founding of Transylvania,
    353
Treaty of Waitangi Act, 1975,
    147
Treaty of Waitangi, 117,
    147–9; international sig-
    nificance of, 258
Treaty Six: and Michel and
    Baptiste Callihoo, 430
Treaty Termination Resolu-
    tion of 1871: US govern-
    ment cancels adherence
    to principles of Northwest
    Ordinance and to interna-
    tional law of Aboriginal
    and treaty rights, 157–8,
    161, 526–7

Treaty Three: and Anisi-
    naabaig Manomin Man-
    agement Board, 111–12;
    and St Catherine's Milling
    case, 417
tree plantations: as represen-
    tative of monocultural
    conformity, 109
Trent University: and Harvey
    McCue, 245–6; Thomas
    H.B. Symons founds First
    Nations Studies depart-
    ment in Canada, 266
tribalism: African groups use
    to combat militarism of
    dictators, 237; Fourth
    World as basis of unifying
    alternative to, 240; virus
    of, 61–2
trickster figure, 52, 102–3,
    120
Trigger, Bruce, 57, 128, 154
Trinidad, 270
truck houses: term describ-
    ing complex of under-
    standings in Maritime
    Indian Treaty of 1760–1,
    343
Trudeau, Pierre, 37–8, 40,
    422; and 1969 White
    Paper on Indian policy,
    278–80, 496–7; on suicide
    of Nelson Small Legs Jr,
    276
Truman, Harry: and Cold
    War, 365
Truth and Reconciliation
    Commission: as chaired by
    Desmond Tutu in South
    Africa, 507
Ts'peten Defenders, 20
Tsimshian people, 465
Tsonga people, 505
Tswana people, 505
Tuktoyaktuk, 225–6
Tully, James, 206–7
Tupac Amaru, 55, 152,
    213–15, 223, 291, 286,
    533
Turner, Frederick Jackson,
    116, 168–73, 300, 361,
    457
Turtle Island: North America
    as, 99–101

turtle: religious symbolism
    of, 100–1
Tuscarora people, 268,
    313
Tutelo people, 377
Tutu, Bishop Desmond: as
    chair of Truth and Recon-
    ciliation Commission, 507;
    visits to Osnaburgh
    reserve in northern
    Ontario, 514
twenty-point plan: and
    American Indian Move-
    ment's Trail of Broken
    Treaties, 270
Twigg, Troy, 195
Twilight of Common Dreams,
    The, 128
Two Treatises of Government,
    182–86
Twoaxe, Lawrence: and
    League of Nations of
    North American Indians,
    260
Tyendinaga reserve: estab-
    lishment of in Bay of
    Quinte area, 377; rejec-
    tion at of John A. Macdon-
    ald's effort to extend fran-
    chise to Indians, 479
Tyler, Edward, 181, 226

Uncle Tomahawks, 263
Union of Ontario Indians,
    281
United Colonies of New
    England: central authority
    as shield against local vio-
    lations of Aboriginal and
    treaty rights, 445; creation
    of, 313; further conquest
    of Indian lands prohibited
    by English royal commis-
    sioners in 1664, 321
United Empire Loyalists: in
    Florida, 216; Mohawks of
    Tyendinaga move to
    Upper Canada along with
    wave of, 377; multicultur-
    alism of, 378
United Fruit Company, 24,
    91; as successor enterprise
    of pre-revolutionary
    British North American

land speculation companies, 366–7
United Indian Nations: confederacy of as sole authority capable of negotiating sovereign status of Indian lands, 391
United Nations: Aboriginal and treaty rights and, 151; Aboriginal leaders from Canada tend to be more active at than US counterparts, 288; as assembly of peoples, 66, 230, 513; Charter of, 66, 229–30, 270; and coalition of Indigenous Organizations of the Amazon, 93; creation of, 228–30; failure of to provide ways for distinct peoples without nation-states to achieve self-determination, 235; and international covenants on right of peoples to self-determination, 232; and power to charter existence of new states, 233; and resolution condemning atrocities in Guatemala, 366; and Security Council, 131; Six Nations Iroquois assertions of sovereignty at, 269; and US report citing conquest as basis of sovereign authority over lands and Indians, 185; and Working Group on Indigenous Population, 151
United Nations Declaration on the Granting of Independence to Colonial Countries and Peoples, 1960, 231–2
United Nations Permanent Forum on Indigenous Issues, 151
United Nations Security Council: and global apartheid, 517
United Nations sovereignty club, 133–4, 513
United Nations Working

Group on Indigenous Populations, 242
United States Commission on National Security, 527
United States Congress, 372
United States Indian Treaties: of Canandaigua, 258; Congress terminates further in 1871, 157–8, 161, 526–7; and doctrine of conquest, 525–6; of Fort Laramie, 271; of Fort Wayne, 392; of New York, 216; and Northwest Ordinance of 1787, 372–5; and Trail of Broken Treaties and twenty-point plan, 270–1; Vine Deloria on future of, 271; and Washington state fish-ins, 263–4
United States of America: absorbs colonial lands and techniques of empires of Spain, France, Holland, Russia, and Great Britain, 146, 217–18; accepts Confederate Indian Nations' right of the soil, 378–80; and aftermath of September 11, 2001, 129–30, 472–3; Alcatraz Island occupation by Indians of All Tribes, 266–8; and Alice Lee Jemison, 195, 257–82; Alistair Cook on environmental determinism and, 296; Allan Bloom on school curricula in, 127; and American Indian Movement, 33, 89, 202, 266–77, 281, 283; banana wars of, 364; Canada as satellite of, 159; Canadian desire for amalgamation with, 77–9, 448; Carlos Montezuma and American Indian Federation, 256–7; and Chief Justice John Marshall, 404–5, 414–16, 418–19, 526; and China, 527; citizenship of extended to Indians, 508; Coca-Cola Company as icon of

global role of, 145; conflicting philosophies of law and governance, 21–2; Constitution of, 85, 205, 263, 372–5, 405; corporate culture of, 23, 219, 228, 346–70, 473–4; and corn, 108; and Creole decolonization movements in Latin America, 209–17; and Creole identity politics, 471–4; Dave Palmer on roots of modern army in Indian wars, 380; and destruction of Earth Mounds, 104–5; and doctrine of conquest, 76, 156, 185, 525–6; early wars of on Indian Country also wars on Canada, 74; Enlightenment values in, 122, 129, 183; ethnic nationalism of, 93, 215, 237, 301, 524; expansion of into Indian Country, 90; as expression of Europe's characteristics, 299–300; and frontier thesis of Frederick Jackson Turner, 168–9; global role of, 21, 66, 146, 218–19, 244, 282, 311–12, 367–70, 462, 471, 525–9; government of promotes Quincentenary, 5; and Guatemala, 91, 365–6, 462–3; Indian Affairs and balance of power in, 404–5, 418–19; Indian fighters elected as president, 422, 525; Indian personality of southwest region of, 33, 461; and Indian removal, 313, 315–16, 392, 403–7, 417–19, 474, 499, 521, 524; and Indian treaties, 156–7, 161, 258, 263, 270, 272–5, 526–7; and Indianness, 90, 222; indigenismo movement in Mexico parallels work of John Collier, 224; info-entertainment industry in,

89; and international law, 29, 130–1, 161, 228–36, 270, 473–4; Jack Forbes on, 90, 282; and John Locke's view of property, 182–6; in Latin America supports ladino elites over native and mixed-blood masses, 282; Leonard Pelltier as political prisoner of, 89; and liberal preoccupation with a colour-blind constitution, 512; Little Turtle's acceptance of sovereignty of, 392; Louisiana incorporated into, 74, 77, 217, 291, 392, 395, 402; and Manifest Destiny, 74–85, 123, 135, 152–3, 172, 227, 307–8, 364, 374, 523; as melting pot, 15; and mestizo cultures of Mexico and French-Aboriginal Canada, 168; and militarization of space, 129–30, 527; Native American literature of, 89; Native Americans' legal and political status ignored, 88, 512; and Nazi Germany, 228, 471, 478; Progressive Movement of, 368; Puritans of New England influence, 76, 84–5, 163, 305–10, 313, 316–17, 321, 470; racism and inequality in, 90, 518; and Red Sicks, 396, 405; and Royal Proclamation, 155–6, 310–12, 336–46, 349, 352, 353–63, 372, 376, 378–9, 499; Seven Years' War as central event in emergence of, 326–35, 523; Six Nations Iroquois and international border of, 93, 209, 268; and slavery, 160, 283–4, 358, 378, 471, 515; and toxic dumps, 85; and treatment of Indians in era of War of 1812, 401–2; triumphalism of, 83–5; and United

Nations, xiv, 185, 228–36, 288, 366; universalized capitalism of, 21, 22, 67–8, 70, 72, 83–5, 121–5, 160, 226–7, 234, 311–12, 369–70, 510; vacuum of power after dismantling of European empires filled by, 218; and Vietnam, 168, 228, 243, 245, 284, 295; and War of 1812, 22, 380–402, 410; and Washington state fish-in, 263–4; western expansion of as prototype for international regimes of property relations, 234; and Woodrow Wilson, 222, 357, 491, 513; and Zapatistas, 80, 143–6, 513–14. *See also* American empire, American empire of private property, corporations, global corporations, land speculations companies, New World Order
United States of America v. James Pitawanakwat, 19, 207–8
universal and homogenous state, 60, 65; Fourth World alternative to tyranny of, 291
universalism: assumptions of in imperialism and monotheism permeate assumptions about of capitalism, 369–70; of Christian claims affect pan-Indian teachings of Neolin, 331; economists downgrade culture and anthropology in elaborating theories of commercial, 187–8; and Enlightenment, 121–5; Indigenous peoples outside schemes of scientific, 309; and relativism in social sciences, 125–34; science as Western civilization's pillar of, 128
University of British Columbia, 265

University of Chicago, 60; and formation of National Indian Youth Council, 262
University of Minnesota: as host of first Native American Studies department in USA, 266
University of Prince Edward Island, 7
University of Toronto, 51, 275, 276
Unjust Society, The, 279
Unsettling of America: Culture and Agriculture, 24–6
Upper Canada, 174–6, 191–2, 194, 217, 377–8, 380–402, 423, 427–9, 431–53, 457–8
Utley, Robert, 90
Utopia, 177
U'wa people, 90–1

Vallodolid: trial at, 1550, 178, 305
Van Wyk, F.J.: visits from South Africa to study integration of Indian peoples into Canadian social and economic structure, 504
Vancouver Province, 19
Vandalia, 352
Vander Zalm, Bill, 40
Vasconcelos, Jose: writings on future forces in globalization, 225
Vasquez, Grimaldo Rengifo, 213
Vatican, 462, 497; Andy Paull awarded Bene Merenti medal, 252; and colonization in New Spain, 302–6; Conor Cruise O'Brien on as enemy of Enlightenment, 129; donation of the Americas to Spain and Portugal, 117, 291
Vega, Garcilasco de la, 213
Venda people, 505
Venezuala, 210, 224
Verwoerd, Hendrik F.: and South African apartheid, 505
Lord Vestey, 139, 149

Vichy Indians, 272
victory culture of the United
   States, 168
Vietnam War, xvii, American
   army in equates enemy territory with Indian Country,
   295; anti-war movement
   converges with civil rights
   movement, 284; and Australia, 140; as extension of
   Indian Wars, 245; opposition of Woodstock Generation to, 243; Tom Hayden
   on US role in, 245; USA
   replaces imperialist France
   in, 168, 228
Vikings, 318
Village des Hurons, 453
Vincennes: adopted captives
   settle in, 383
Virginia Company, 374
Virginia: and Bacon's Rebellion, 313–16; and territorial push north, 388
Vitoria, Francisco de, 304–5,
   317, 328
Vizenor, Gerald, 102
Voltaire, Francois, 124, 163,
   177
volunteerism: as primary
   basis of Indian involvement in politics in Canada
   before 1969, 280

Wabash Country, 334
Wabash River, 378
Wabigoon Council, 111–12,
   120
Wacousta, 170–2; and John
   Norton, 457
Wadena, Darrell, 87–8
Wah-kai-keghik: and bowl of
   Indian unity, 454
Waitangi Treaty Tribunal,
   147–8
Wallace, Anthony F.C., 90
Wallerstein, Emmanuel, 190
Walpole Company, 352
Walpole Island, 483
Walpole, Thomas, 352
Wampanoag people, 313
Wampum Denied, 412
wampum shells: as currency
   in New England, New

Netherlands, and New
   Sweden, 319
wampun belts: bowl with one
   spoon depicted on, 78,
   285, 386, 422; and
   Covenant Chain, 324; of
   Indian Confederacy
   treaties, 386–7, 412; at
   Indian Council at Niagra
   in 1764 signifying terms of
   Royal Proclamation, 155;
   and Pontiac's patriotic
   stand, 330; and Sir William
   Johnson in diplomacy, 325;
   two-rows as metaphor of
   dual autonomy, 412
Wandering Spirit Survival
   School, Toronto, 244
wardship: debilitating outcomes of, 475–82; effects
   of, 355; of Indigenous
   peoples, 439
War of 1812, xxv, 19, 22, 53,
   74, 81, 261, 297, 320, 351,
   363, 364, 380–402, 406–7,
   409, 410, 432, 435, 445,
   448; as alliance between
   British imperial government and Indian Confederacy of Canada, 132, 154,
   449, 532; and distribution
   of presents to Indians, 190;
   influence of Pine family
   rooted in, 171–2; James
   McGill on, 156
War of American Indepen-
   dence. See American Revolution
War of Austrian Succession,
   313
War on Terrorism, xiii–xiv,
   xix, xx
War ... Peace in Canada: The
   Invaders Responsible for the
   Death of Louis Riel, 253
Warraghiyagey. See Sir
   William Johnson
Warren Admiral John Bar-
   lose: as proponent of Abo-
   riginal dominion, 399
Warren, Kay B., 61
Warren, Peter: as uncle of
   William Johnson, 324–5
Warren, William, 194

Warrior, Clyde, 263–4
Warrior, Robert, 89, 266,
   271
Washburn, Wilcomb E., 90;
   and Bacon's rebellion,
   316
Washington state, 93, 263–4
Washington, DC: as national
   capital, 372; Spirit of Haida
   Gwaii at Canadian
   Embassy in, 206; symbolic
   significance of relationship to District of Columbia, 217
Washington, George, 7; compared to Sir William Johnson, 210; defeat of at Fort
   Necessary, 326; as land
   speculator trading on certificates granted by Britain
   for service in Seven Years'
   War, 349; negotiates New
   York Treaty with Creek
   Indians, 216; personal
   wealth and patronage
   from Indian Country, 441;
   recognizes "right of the
   soil" (property) vested in
   Confederate Indian
   Nations, 378–80; as US
   president and commander
   of American Army, 380
Wassaja: Freedom's Signal for
   the Indian, 256–7
Watson, Paul, 87
Waubageshig (Harvey
   McCue), 245–6
Wawanosh, David, 485
Wawatay Communications
   Society: print and broad-
   cast media to Oji-Cree
   speakers in northwestern
   Ontario and northern
   Manitoba, 466
Wayne, Anthony, xxiii
Wealth of Nations, 6, 182,
   231, 346
Weas people, 334
Weaver, Sally, 177–8, 242
web of life, 101, 115, 136,
   309
Webb, Walter Prescott, 168
Weesageechak: as trickster
   figure, 102

Weinberg, Albert K., 76
Welch, James, 89
Wenjack: death of gives
    name to Toronto's Ameri-
    can Indian Movement,
    276
West Africa, 117, 287
West Florida, 336
West Indies, 502
West, Cornel, 283
Western civilization: Aborigi-
    nal authors on spread of
    into Indian Country,
    194–6; and Aboriginal civ-
    ilization of the Americas,
    93–107, 305; descriptions
    of Indigenous peoples
    used in intellectual con-
    struction of, 138–9,
    176–89; encounters on
    edges of shape develop-
    ments in metropolitan
    cores, 52; and Enlighten-
    ment, 121; and fear of
    multiculturalism, 129; and
    frontier thesis of Frederick
    Jackson Turner, 168–9;
    imagined distinctions
    between savagery and,
    478; reserves and reserva-
    tions as monuments to
    ethnic cleansing in, 509;
    and social engineering,
    173–6; USA as Europe's
    appointed agent in expan-
    sion of, 131; western
    expansion of USA as fastest
    growth spurt of, 300
Western Hemisphere: Abo-
    riginal and treaty rights in,
    31; Akwesasne Notes in,
    270; development of Cre-
    ole nationalisms in,
    207–17, 469–74; Free
    Trade Area of the Americ-
    as in as extension of Mon-
    roe Doctrine, 146–7; Indi-
    an ancestry dominant in,
    91; Inter-american Indi-
    genista Institute and study
    of Indigenous people in,
    225; Latin America as part
    of, 213; nationalisms in
    and Aboriginal heritage,

224. See also Free Trade
    Area of the Americas,
    Monroe Doctrine
Westmorland, Gen. William,
    245
Weyerhauser Company,
    149
Wharton, Samuel: and Ben-
    jamin Franklin, 350; and
    direct land purchase from
    Indians, 360; and Indiana
    Company, 351; as land
    speculator, 351–2
Wheatly, Fred, 51, 246
whiskey: use of to obtain
    Aboriginal land, 392
White Dominions: Canada,
    New Zealand, Australia,
    and South Africa
    described as, 355
White Man's Law, 411
White Paper on Canadian
    Indian Policy, 1969,
    278–80, 496–7; and infu-
    sion of funds into Indian
    band and Aboriginal orga-
    nizations, 281
White, Richard, 90, 112–13,
    154, 190–1, 247, 298,
    330–1
Wik case, 139–40
wild fisheries, destruction of,
    218
wild rice, 120; and Wabi-
    goon Council, 111–12
Wilkinson, Wilbur, 87
willed amnesia, 27, 40, 89,
    134; and blinkered recol-
    lection, 164; as essential
    feature in rise of USA to
    global power, 219
William IV, King, 441
William and Mary of
    Orange, 182; as celebrat-
    ed by Orangemen of
    Canada, 223
Williams, Guy, 280
Williams, Michael, 108–9
Williams, Robert A., Jr, 90,
    347, 405
Williams, Roger, 109, 324,
    328; and Rhode Island
    Treaty of 1635 with Narra-
    gansett people, 316–17

Wilson, Chief Richard, ·
    271–2
Wilson, E.O., 63
Wilson, Rev. E. F., 132, 178;
    and assimilationist thrust
    of Canadian Indian policy,
    486–7
Wilson, Woodrow, 222, 357,
    491, 513
Winnebago people, 257, 334
Winning of the West, The, 478
Winnipeg, 9, 223
Winnipegtonga, Simon, 51
Winter Studies and Summer
    Rambles in Canada, 191–2
Winthrop, John: and Bible
    as justification for dispos-
    session of Indians, 307
Witt, Shirley Hill, 246, 263
Wolfe, Gen. James, 328
Womack, Craig, 89
Women for Wik, 140
Wood, Paul, 63
Woodhenge, at Cahokia, 103
Woodstock Generation,
    243–4
Woodsworth, J.S., 422
Woolrich, Julia: and Connolly
    v. Woolich, 408
Worcester v. Georgia, 1832,
    404, 414, 526; and Geor-
    gia's effort to impose juris-
    diction on Cherokees,
    404, 414, 526
Working Group on Indige-
    nous Populations, 151
World Bank, 73, 93, 131,
    161, 369; and demonstra-
    tions during meeting of in
    Prague, 531; and global
    apartheid, 517
World Council of Indige-
    nous Peoples, 55, 151;
    founding of in Port
    Alberni, BC, 241; and
    National Indian Brother-
    hood in Canada, 248
World Trade Center, 321;
    attacks on, 129–30, 528
World Trade Organization,
    22, 44, 49, 73, 80, 119,
    149, 229–30, 290, 369;
    and global apartheid
    through, 517; and MAI,

522; and power of global corporate citizens, 510; Seattle meeting of, 531; and trickster, 102

World Wrestling Federation, 466

Worldwide Fund for Nature, 73

Wounded Knee I in 1890, 271; defeat of Seventh Cavalry at in Battle of Little Bighorn, 261

Wounded Knee II in 1973, 33, 88, 261, 271, 514

Wovoka, 249

Wretched of the Earth, The, 236, 299–300

Wright, Ronald, 178, 223

Wunder, John R.: on US violation of international law in Termination Resolution of 1871, 526–7

Wunniman Lake: and Cree community, 464

Wyandot people, 334, 339–40

Xhosa people, 441–2, 505

Yamasee War, 313

Yanomami people, 112

Yavapai people, 256

Yolngu people, 139

York Factory, 408

York, Charles, 353

Yugoslavia, 17, 44, 61–2, 83–4, 130–1, 233

Yukon, 375

Yunupingu, Galarrway, 141

Zambia, 238

Zambos: people of Indian and African ancestry, 211

Zapata, Emiliano, 137, 143; and Section 27 of Mexican Constitution, 220

Zapatismo, 81, 143, 146, 149–50, 221; and new treaties with Indians in Mexico, 258; Tom Hayden as interpreter of, 245; transition from indigenismo to, 90

Zapatista Liberation Army, 33–4, 92, 143, 221, 425–56

Zapatistas, 23, 97, 112, 143–6; and Internet support, 79; opponents to as neo-liberals, 513; and uprising in Chiapas, 514

Zapatour, 34, 81

Zapotec people, 222

Zeisberger, David, 377

Zocalo Square, 34, 14

Zukang, Sha: and relationship of China to Star Wars, 528